THE NEW ENCYCLOPEDIA OF

American Scandal

GEORGE CHILDS KOHN

EDITOR

Facts On File, Inc.

The New Encyclopedia of American Scandal

Copyright © 2001, 1989 by George Childs Kohn

Checkmark Books
An imprint of Facts On File, Inc.
11 Penn Plaza
New York NY 10001

Library of Congress Cataloging-in-Publication Data

The New Encyclopedia of American scandal / George Childs Kohn, editor.
    p. cm.
  Rev. ed. of: Encyclopedia of American scandal / George C. Kohn. c1989
  Includes bibliographical references and index.
  ISBN 0-8160-4225-X (hc : alk. paper)—ISBN 0-8160-4420-1 (pbk. : alk. paper)
  1. Scandals—United States—History—Dictionaries. 2. United States—History—Miscellanea—Dictionaries.
  I. Kohn, George C. II. Kohn, George C. Encyclopedia of American scandal.

E179 .N53 2001
973'03–dc21
00-034099

EDITOR

George Childs Kohn

CONTRIBUTORS

Mary L. Allison
Joan R. Bothell
Charles W. Carey, Jr.
Marlene A. Clark
Beverly R. Dorsey
Stephen J. Fox
Silvia E. Hines
George Childs Kohn
Jutta K. Kohn
Christina M. Palaia
Ashwinee Sadanand
Howard G. Zettler

CONTENTS

PREFACE

Every period in American history has had its own particular and sensational episodes of disgrace, shame, outrage, depravity, veniality, graft, and corruption. *The New Encyclopedia of American Scandal* records, plainly and unabashedly, these scandals, their perpetrators and victims—from Roger Williams and Anne Hutchinson in the 1630s to O. J. Simpson and Bill Clinton in the 1990s. It is not a book intending to shock readers, nor one of muckraking and scandalmongering (that is, one intending to repeat and spread gossip, rumors, and half-truths). Instead, it is an endeavor to detail and explain concisely and objectively the stories of numerous noteworthy men, women, and incidents considered scandalous at one time or another. There are cases in which, rightfully or wrongfully, successful careers and distinguished reputations have been altered negatively or ruined irreparably. There are cases where bubbles have been burst.

A scandal in this book has been regarded as a grave loss of or injury to reputation resulting from actual or apparent breach or violation of morality, ethics, propriety, or law. Unseemly, sleazy, and perverse behavior or conduct have often brought on the sudden and unexpected collapse or downfall of the reputations of "big people" and powerful organizations. This book is a chronicle of such dire happenings.

If there has been one guiding principle in the research and writing of this book, it has been that of fairness. Futhermore, the intention was not to include every actual and alleged, major and minor, so-called scandal recorded somewhere. This was beyond the desired scope of the book, which proffers only persons and episodes of outstanding and special historical notoriety. In addition, the aim was to produce an authoritative compendium that was generally tightly structured but also lively, readable, and clear.

Deceit, bribery, sex, power, and fame are the elements of most scandals. Murder and suicide are also found sometimes, although they do not per se make a scandal. There has to be some extra element as well—something untoward, shocking, or reprehensible to the public. A successful man or woman or group trying to get away with outrageous or improper conduct, such as espionage, treason, transvestism, wife-beating, criminality, or public obscenity, and then getting caught, makes an appropriate scandal because the public's image or perception is so drastically changed by the revelations. Sleaziness has upended or dislodged the famous and lionized from on high in numerous instances.

The media is often accused of seizing readily on scandalous circumstances and stories and pursuing them zealously to unnecessary extremes. And yet the public always seems fascinated, maybe because it sees scandal as a common denominator of humanity. The majority of people understand human failures and frailties, pecadilloes and sins. Indeed, the world has seen scandal ever since religion and history were first recorded. Interestingly, the Bible itself places scandal side by side with knowledge in the story of Adam and Eve in the garden of Eden. After Eve eats the forbidden fruit from "the tree of the knowledge of good and evil," the eyes of both Adam and Eve are opened to the fact that they are naked; they feel ashamed and are banished from the garden. Scandal has been around ever since. All are capable of falling into scandal, but some are more naturally predisposed or susceptible than others. Common to all is human weakness.

In compiling and writing the book, persons and incidents have been drawn from the worlds of politics, government, business, sports, religion, the arts, high society, show business, and the military. Included are such well-known figures as Benedict Arnold, Aaron Burr, Warren G. Harding, John F. Kennedy, Hedy Lamarr, William "Billy" Mitchell, Errol Flynn, Elvis Presley, Denny McLain, Pete Rose, Mike Tyson, Charles Keating, Michael Milken, Bob Packwood, and Robert Vesco. There are also infamous incidents with famous names, such as the Thomas-Hill Scandal, Tailhook, Salomon Brothers Trading Scandal, BCCI, Teapot Dome, Watergate, the Mississippi Bubble, Scopes Trial, Chappaquiddick, and the Kent State Shootings. But there are also lesser known personalities and events, such as William Aramony, Mike Boorda, Ted Kaczynski, Sol Wachtler, Fife Symington, Tonya Harding, Larry Lawrence, Vince Foster, Heidi Fleiss, Thomas Capano, Ninian Edwards, Otto Kerner, Charles Lee, Jake LaMotta, Harry Crosby, Donald Manes, George Parr, Bernard Bergman, Robert Schenck, Peg Entwistle, the Mulligan Letters, the Dirty Derby, the Yazoo Land Frauds, and the Great Salad Oil Swindle. From a myriad of source materials—newspapers, magazines, biographies, diaries, public records and history books, among others—the facts and information have been culled and pared down for inclusion in this reference work.

At all times I have tried to be evenhanded in my treatment and not to give offense. And yet, in order to show and explain a scandal fully, I have sometimes had to use explicit language, quoted directly from the speaker. Undoubtedly, there will be some readers who profess disdain for the scandalous words and information contained here. To them, recalling—let alone writing about—shameful and ignominious circumstances is not quite right or nice and is better left hidden or forgotten. I don't agree in most instances. The study of history requires, I think, that improper, unlawful, unethical, and gross activities be revealed if a true and accurate picture of life at any particular time is to be understood properly and correctly. In other words, uncensored accounts of people's lives are needed at times in an effort to penetrate the enigmas and secrets of remarkable individuals, both those who have "fallen" and those who haven't.

The book's purpose is to be informational as well as enlightening and entertaining. I hope a calm, dispassionate look at these scandals, which constantly show a sad and seamy side of life, will enable readers not to be sanctimonious or self-righteous in their assessment of those who have fallen, for it is dangerous indeed to make moralistic and ethical judgments, because society's standards keep changing, and what was once considered morally reprehensible may one day be acceptable, or vice versa.

The writing of this book has been a shared experience. Most important were the contributors, whose help was indispensable and who are listed separately on a preceding page; many thanks are extended to them. In the preparation of the revision, I would like to thank the Facts On File staff, especially my editor, James Chambers, without whom the book certainly would never have been completed. Finally, thanks also to the libraries, public and private, and photo archives and agencies, that have provided much information and appropriate illustrations with permission to reproduce them throughout the book.

—George Childs Kohn

"A. B. PLOT." See Ninian EDWARDS: rash politician.

ABSCAM

In the Washington, D.C., of 1978 and 1979, the word was out in certain political circles that an enterprising group of Arab sheiks were willing and eager to give cash payments in exchange for promises of legislative "favors." Avaricious bigwigs met with the wealthy Arabs and their associates in a number of secret, swank locations—a rented Washington townhouse, several New York City hotel rooms, a luxurious Florida home, and an elegant yacht off the Florida coast, to name a few. The sheiks and their representatives sought political and business help in making investments, constructing hotels, securing casino licenses, and obtaining immigration permission for other Arabs.

What the Washington politicians didn't know was that these Arabs and their company, Abdul Enterprises, were in reality completely bogus, agents in a "sting" operation set up by the Federal Bureau of Investigation (FBI), and that hidden in all of these posh meeting spots, videotape and recording devices were planted and secretly monitored the dealings.

The American public first learned of this clandestine FBI "sting" operation in early February 1980 when 31 public officials were named as subjects in the so-called Abscam (for Arab scam) investigation. The public was especially shocked when law-enforcement officers disclosed the involvement of United States congressmen, seven of whom were indicted in 1980 on charges of bribery and conspiracy by different federal grand juries in Washington, D.C., and Brooklyn, New York. The seven were U.S. Representatives Michael O. Myers (Dem., Pa.), Raymond F. Lederer (Dem., Pa.), John M. Murphy (Dem., N.Y.), Frank Thompson, Jr. (Dem., N.J.), John W. Jenrette, Jr. (Dem., S.Car.), and Richard Kelly (Rep., Fla.), and U.S. Senator Harrison A. Williams, Jr. (Dem., N.J.). Also indicted (and later convicted and sentenced to prison) was Mayor Angelo J. Errichetti of Camden, New Jersey, an important figure

at the start of the FBI investigation, who introduced the "Arabs" to other politicos and business friends. The ethics committees of both houses of Congress launched searching inquiries into the bribery charges, notwithstanding some objections by the attorney general of the United States, who thought the government's criminal prosecution in the cases might be jeopardized by the congressional probe. Some of the press was severely criticized for obtaining and then leaking secret Abscam information before federal grand jurors saw it. In addition, there was much heated public debate over the propriety of the "entrapment" by the FBI. Some contended that the government had gone too far and had stretched the federal statutes in gaining evidence against those accused; recordings and videotapes clearly showed the culprits accepting cash bribes for political influence, however. Despite the controversial nature of the situation, the U.S. Justice Department defended the Abscam "sting" throughout all of the trials and said that the politicians and others involved had entrapped themselves by their greed.

Representative Myers was shown taking $50,000 in return for promising to introduce private legislation to permit Arabs to enter and remain in the United States; his conviction came on August 30, 1980. Afterward the House, stunned, recommended his immediate expulsion and voted affirmatively for this on October 2, 1980; Myers became the first House member expelled since 1861. Next, Representative Jenrette was convicted, having taken a $50,000 bribe (half of the money was discovered by his wife, Rita, hidden in one of his shoes, and was passed on to authorities; see Rita JENRETTE). Grand jurors found both Thompson and Murphy guilty (December 3, 1980) but the latter was acquitted of the charge of bribery (a charge of which all his Washington colleagues were found guilty): Murphy had received "an unlawful gratuity." Representative Lederer, strongly pleading his case of illegal entrapment by the FBI, was also found guilty (again, a $50,000 bribe), and about two weeks later, on January 26, 1981, a

1

Washington federal court decided that former congressman Kelly (he and all the other Abscam indicted representatives, except Lederer, had lost their House seats in the 1980 elections) was guilty (a verdict overturned in 1982); Kelly was the only congressman to admit taking a bribe ($25,000) and claimed he took the money as part of his own investigation into congressional graft and corruption. The incriminating videotape recording showed Kelly agreeing to help two bogus sheiks emigrate to the United States, declaring as he pocketed the money, "If I told you how poor I am, you would cry."

New Jersey's Senator Williams stood trial like the others and was convicted of nine counts of bribery and conspiracy in federal court in Brooklyn, New York, on May 1, 1981. Damning videotaped and recorded evidence showed him agreeing to help obtain a federal contract for Abdul Enterprises to build a titanium mine in Virginia; in return the senator would receive more than $12.5 million and partial control of the mine. Although claiming innocence and unlawful entrapment, Williams was sentenced to prison (Murphy, Myers, and Lederer were, too) and fined $50,000. Knowing he faced almost certain expulsion from the Senate, where he had served for the last 23 years, he resigned his seat on March 11, 1982. New Jersey's "most popular politician" in 1981 became the first of that legislative body in more than half a century to do so in the face of allegations of misconduct.

Brock ADAMS: guilty of sexual misconduct?

Brock Adams spent much of his life in public service. Born in 1927, he enlisted in the U.S. Navy at age 17 to fight during World War II. In 1961 he gave up a successful law practice to accept an appointment from President John F. Kennedy as U.S. attorney for the Western District of Washington State. Three years later, at age 37, he was elected to the U.S. House of Representatives and served seven consecutive terms. From 1977 to 1979 he served as President Jimmy Carter's Secretary of Transportation, and in 1986 the lifelong Democrat was elected to represent Washington in the U.S. Senate.

As a congressman, Adams championed the cause of women's rights. He was an outspoken supporter of a woman's legal right to obtain an abortion. He also sponsored bills to fund research into the prevention of infertility and breast cancer and supported a number of other bills related to women's health care. As chairman of the Senate subcommittee on aging, he held the first congressional hearing on menopause.

In 1989 it became clear that Adam's interest in women went far beyond his duty as a public servant. Kari Tupper, the daughter of lifelong friends of Adams, publicly accused the senator of sexually molesting her two years earlier, shortly after his election to the Senate. According to Tupper, who was 24 years old at the time, she met the senator in his Washington, D.C., home for drinks. But something was wrong with her drink, and she blacked out. When she came to, she was completely nude and Adams was pawing her body. Tupper filed charges against Adams, but when the U.S. attorney's office hemmed and hawed for 18 months before finally refusing to prosecute him for lack of evidence, she contacted the Seattle Times.

Following publication of Tupper's story in 1989, the Times received anonymous calls from eight women who claimed to have been sexually mistreated by Adams. One woman, who had worked for Adams in the U.S. Department of Transportation, claimed that in 1978 he gave her a glass of wine with what appeared to be two crushed pills in the bottom of the glass. Although she did not drink from the glass, Adams fondled and kissed her anyway. Another woman claimed that Adam gave her a funny-looking glass of champagne which made her feel woozy. Adams took her home, where she blacked out; when she came to, Adams was removing her clothing.

The most serious charge came from a woman who accused Adams of raping her. She claimed that when she complained to Adams of having a cold, he offered her two vitamin C pills. But the pills made her feel funny, so he graciously took her home. Once inside, he made a pass at her, which she refused. Undaunted, Adams then forced the helpless woman onto the couch, removed her panties, and then penetrated her against her will. As he left, he gave her $200 in cash.

Although none of the women would allow the paper to print their names, in 1992 each of them signed an affidavit stating that she would testify in court in the event that Adams sued the Times for defamation of character. So the Times ran a second story, this time accusing Adams of two decades of sexual misconduct. Adams, who was running for reelection at the time, denied the charges. He claimed that his political enemies were orchestrating a smear campaign against him which he could not fight because of the women's anonymity. The Times countered that all of his accusers were active members of the Democratic Party who had nothing to gain by coming forward with their allegations. Shortly thereafter Adams withdrew from the race, and when his term expired he returned to private life.

John ADAMS: "The Duke of Braintree" canard

Politically inspired canards seem to be self-perpetuating, sometimes with the help of historians unwilling to dig out the facts. Consider the canard circulated in 1801 by the Democrat-Republican press (supportive of Thomas Jefferson) against the defeated Federalist incumbent John Adams. The press sneered that he had slyly packed 23 new circuit courts with friends who formed an honor roll of Federalism and, adding a charge of nepotism, with a nephew—all by burning the midnight oil on the night before Jefferson's presidential inauguration.

As president, Adams sought to reform the federal court system by increasing the number of district courts from three to six. The bill enabling the change proved to be ill-timed: it was passed after the national presidential election of 1800. Even though the Electoral College had not met, Adams, who had run for reelection, was certain that its choice would be between Democratic-Republicans Jefferson and Aaron Burr. Thus, even though the reform plan had been devised before the election, implementation of the act would inevitably bring charges of political expediency against Adams.

Nonetheless, he went ahead as quickly as possible to develop a nominations list for the 23 new judges, submitting them to the Senate on December 8, 1800. The appointees were Federalists, and included a relative, one William Cranch.

Apparently Adams's opponents, eager to score points with the less sophisticated readers of their papers, considered anything Adams did reprehensible and attackable. And the Senate, aware of Adams's intolerable position, delayed confirmation actions until February 1801 and was still at work on Adams's list when the Electoral College met and named Jefferson as Adams's successor. Some confirmations had been made in February, and Adams had signed their commissions; but the Senate did not complete its work until the last day of Adams's presidency. The confirmations reached Adams late in the day of March 3, 1801 (including one for William Cranch), and it is these for whom Adams signed commissions—for five-year terms—during the evening before his early morning exodus for New York—not exactly by burning the midnight oil.

These facts were less important to the press than the opportunity to harangue on Adams's dubious timing. Labeled "The Duke of Braintree's Midnight Judges" (implying that Adams ran his residence town of Braintree, Massachusetts, as a feudal fief), the appointees' installments were cited as examples of Adams's "harsh and implacable spirit," as Federalist wrenches in the gears of the new administration. And when Adams somewhat rudely refused to participate in Jefferson's inauguration, they reran for the second of three times the canard about the "midnight judges" and invented new ones. Adams, they claimed, to avoid his political funeral at Jefferson's swearing-in achieved the remarkable feat of riding on horseback in *one* day the muddy 250 miles from Washington to New York!

The two press attacks on Adams at Jefferson's accession were augmented by a third attack soon after the Congress was installed. At Jefferson's direction, the judicial reformation act was repealed and the Adams appointees were dumped unceremoniously out of office. The third publication of the attacks accusing Adams of "duplicity" in commissioning the "midnight judges" may have been instrumental in convincing earlier historians that the charges were true.

Adams and the out-of-office Federalists knew better; but they had, until the writing of Page Smith in the 20th century, been thoroughly discredited. Adams had at least one solace: his appointment of John Marshall, his secretary of state and Jefferson's bitterest enemy, as chief justice of the Supreme Court assured him that Federalist principles would not be totally ignored.

Sherman ADAMS: political liability

Sherman Adams, onetime governor of New Hampshire and President Eisenhower's closest and most trusted aide, had been an integral part of the White House for five years, presiding over the daily operations of the staff. Though some of his detractors found him stern, curt, and sometimes rude, his closeness to the president was later attested to by Eisenhower's praise of his aide's "tireless service" and "brilliant performance."

But in June of 1958, Adams' relationship with Bernard Goldfine, a wealthy Boston industrialist and textile manufacturer, became subject to an investigation which would end in Adams's reluctant resignation and contribute to a major decline in popularity for the entire Republican Party.

That summer, the House Subcommittee on Legislative Oversight, under the chairmanship of Oren Harris (Dem., Ark.), began investigating the relationship of Goldfine to the Federal Trade Commission (FTC) and the Securities and Exchange Commission (SEC). The subcommittee learned that Adams had intervened on several occasions with both the FTC and SEC to gain "preferred treatment" for Goldfine, a friend of Adams for more than 15 years, who had been accused by a government agency of violations of manufacturing law. Goldfine had sold coats with their fabric contents incorrectly stated as 90 percent wool and 10 percent vicuña, when actually they contained nylon.

During the subcommittee's hearings, the 59-year-old Adams was accused of receiving gifts of clothing (notably a $700 vicuña coat from the Goldfine factory) and accepting payment of hotel bills (some $2,000 worth) from Goldfine, who had also entertained Mr. and Mrs. Adams in his home. These disclosures caused a great public furor, and Adams's political enemies, Democrats and conservative Republicans, particularly of the Old Guard, delighted in them, seeing an opportunity to get rid of Adams and his "liberalism."

To counter his public chastisement, especially by the press, the assistant to the president voluntarily appeared before the House subcommittee on June 17, 1958. Although he admitted that he should have acted with "a little more prudence" in his dealings with Goldfine, he denied that he had influenced the FTC and the SEC in any way and stated that his intentions had always been upright (he later said he might have erred in judgment).

At a press conference the next day, President Eisenhower affirmed his belief in his besieged assistant, saying

"I believe that the presentation made by Governor Adams . . . truthfully represents the pertinent facts. I personally like Governor Adams. I admire his abilities. I respect him because of his personal and official integrity. I need him." The subcommittee then exonerated Adams of any guilt, but Goldfine was cited for contempt by the House of Representatives and later given a prison term following conviction for violations on tax returns.

The questionable ethics of Adams caused implacable distress in the Eisenhower administration and brought calls for his removal as a "political embarrassment" from wealthy, vocal members of the Republican Party, which began to see him as a liability in an election year (1958). Democrats kept the public continually debating Adams's "influence peddling" and his alleged acceptance of bribes (supposedly more than $1 million worth, including a tractor, a miniature golf course, horses, cattle, electric kitchen appliances, and an expensive carpet). The public was scandalized by these accusations against the presidential assistant, who was thought unquestioningly to be an unselfish official.

The political and public pressure grew until Adams, on September 22, 1958, finally handed his resignation to President Eisenhower, who sadly accepted it. Adams maintained that he had done no wrong, was a victim of a "campaign of villification," and wanted to save the Republican Party further embarrassment by resigning. In time, President Eisenhower, who attested to his loyal friend's "tireless service" and "brilliant performance," realized that the Adams crisis helped contribute to the Democratic sweep in the national elections in November of that year.

William AGEE. See Mary CUNNINGHAM: promoted for favors?

Spiro AGNEW: dishonest vice president resigns

When in the spring of 1973 President Richard Nixon was involved in the unfolding WATERGATE scandal, it seemed entirely possible at the time that Vice President Spiro T. Agnew might inherit the American presidency. Yet in the space of a few months, Agnew's public profile changed from presidential to criminal.

In early August 1973, Agnew revealed that he was under federal grand jury investigation for violation of criminal law. United States Attorney for Maryland George Beall alleged that Agnew had received kickbacks from contractors, architects, and engineers while he was Baltimore County Executive and then governor of Maryland.

In the charges, which included bribery, conspiracy, extortion, and tax fraud, he was alleged to have received $1,000 a week while county executive and governor and a lump-sum payment of $50,000 after becoming vice president. Government prosecutors said Agnew continued to receive payments after becoming vice

president, with the understanding that he could help in the awarding of federal work contracts. In all, the government believed Agnew accepted at least $100,000 in bribes.

At first Agnew denied any involvement, calling the reports "damned lies." He said they were "accusations . . . coming from those who have found themselves in very deep trouble and are looking to extricate themselves from this trouble and are flirting with the idea that they can obtain immunity or reduced charges, perhaps, by doing so."

President Nixon unequivocally expressed his support for Agnew; however, as time went on and evidence mounted, his support was reported to be "hedged" or "carefully calibrated," and eventually he was described as nonsupportive.

At the end of September 1973, the federal grand jury began to hear evidence in the case. On October 10, Agnew pleaded *nolo contendere* (no contest) to the income-tax-evasion charge and resigned from the vice presidency. It was part of a plea-bargaining deal in which he agreed to resign and plead guilty to a relatively minor charge to save the government the trouble and expense of proving the larger charges against him. The principal goal of Agnew's lawyers had been to keep him out of jail. The evidence for extortion was so strong that, according to U.S. Attorney James Thompson, "if [the case] had gone to trial, a conviction would have resulted. The man is a crook."

Although some of the prosecutors wanted very much to see Agnew in jail, the chief prosecutor, U.S. Attorney

At a news conference on August 8, 1973, Vice President Spiro Agnew labeled allegations that he was involved in a bribery and kickback scheme in his home state of Maryland "a damned lie." About two months later, under a federal investigation, Agnew quit the vice presidency, also pleaded no contest to tax evasion charges, and admitted that in 1969 he did not pay taxes on taxable income. (UPI/Bettmann Newsphotos)

General Elliot Richardson, was willing to let Agnew escape that fate as a key concession in the plea bargaining, saying conviction of a felony and resignation from office were punishment enough. Richardson also agreed that Agnew would not have to admit he received illegal payoffs, and Agnew's lawyers, in exchange, agreed to publication of all the evidence the prosecution had assembled. Richardson urged in court that Agnew be spared a jail sentence "out of compassion to the man, out of respect for the office he held, and out of appreciation for the fact that by his resignation he has spared the nation the prolonged agony that would have attended upon his trial." The settlement also prevented the need for facing two constitutional issues. First, Agnew had claimed that a sitting vice president of the United States could not be indicted. Second, there was some question as to whether newspersons could be subpoenaed to appear in court and forced to reveal their sources. This issue was constantly discussed with regard to continual news leaks in the case.

Presiding Judge Walter Hoffman acknowledged that the approved deal would not satisfy everyone and that it left open the question of Agnew's guilt or innocence on the graft charges. He said that ordinary business or professional persons convicted of the same crime would be jailed. He ordered a fine of $10,000 and a three-year probation.

Agnew had pointed out in court that in Maryland, payments to politicians were so commonplace they were simply budgeted for. Perhaps the greatest irony was that the man whom Richard Nixon chose as his running mate, at least in part because of his "law and order" stand, turned out to be a white-collar criminal.

On October 12, Nixon named House Republican Minority Leader Gerald R. Ford as the new vice president of the United States. In May 1974, Agnew was disbarred by a Maryland court of appeals.

Agnew's demise was greeted with various degrees of restraint and harshness by the press. He was never a favorite of the press because of his frequent verbal attacks on their methods. For example, he called the Watergate reporting techniques of the media "a very short jump from McCarthyism." Shortly before his conviction, he urged those with a "morbid preoccupation" with Watergate to stop thwarting the will of the American people. NBC news commentator David Brinkley, whom Agnew had often attacked, described Agnew as "a tragic and almost pathetic figure."

The magnitude of Agnew's misdeeds may have been muted by the timing of their disclosure. Said Eric Sevareid of CBS News, paraphrasing an English proverb: "Agnew was stealing the goose from the common, while the Watergate conspirators were trying to steal the common from the goose."

In 1982, while living in Rancho Mirage, California, Agnew repaid the state of Maryland $248,735 (restitu-

tion for past alleged kickbacks to him). He tried to deduct the amount from his California tax return as an expenditure but was not allowed to. In 1996 he died at age 77, in Maryland.

Marv ALBERT: NBC sportscaster assaults lover

During the 1980s and 1990s, Marv Albert was one of America's most popular sportscasters. A native of Brooklyn, New York, he began his broadcasting career in 1966 with the National Basketball Association's New York Knicks. He was later hired to provide commentary for the National Hockey League's New York Rangers as well, and he soon became a well-known figure to New York sports fans. Although he continued to work for the Madison Square Garden Network, which televised Knicks and Rangers games, in the 1980s he began broadcasting coast-to-coast for the National Broadcasting Corporation (NBC). His high-energy style contributed to the success of the network's coverage of the NBA, National Football League, and Olympic Games, and in 1991, the first year he worked the NBA Finals as the play-by-play announcer, NBC won an Emmy for its telecast of that event. His signature call was "Yesss!" which he shouted out after a particularly impressive play. Young Americans were so taken with this simple but enthusiastic expression that millions of them used it to celebrate just about every event in their lives that turned out surprisingly well. Albert's devotion to his career was total, as evidenced by the title of his 1993 autobiography, *I'd Love to but I Have a Game: Twenty-Seven Years Without a Life.*

In 1997 it turned out that Albert did have a life outside of sportscasting, albeit a seamy one. The divorced father of four was accused of forcible sodomy, a felony, by a woman with whom he had enjoyed a 10-year-long sexual relationship. She claimed that Albert met her in a hotel just outside Washington, D.C., where they watched pornographic movies. An argument apparently ensued over her refusal to engage in three-way sex with Albert and another man, and he bit her viciously and repeatedly on the neck and back, then forced her to perform oral sex on him. Albert emphatically denied the charges.

Not long after the accusation, Albert's name and phone number were found among the possessions of a New York City dominatrix who had been murdered. During his trial a surprise female witness for the prosecution testified that Albert had sexually assaulted her in 1994 in Dallas, Texas. The witness worked at the hotel in which Albert was staying, and when she went up to his room, supposedly to help him send a fax, he allegedly met her at the door clad only in women's panties and a garter belt. She testified that he grabbed her head, pulled it toward his fully erect penis, and bit her on the neck before she managed to escape.

The surprise witness's testimony led Albert to plead guilty to assault and battery, a misdemeanor, on the fourth day of his trial. That same day, NBC fired him, and shortly thereafter he resigned from the Madison Square Garden Network. Although his career as a nationally known television sports announcer was ruined, he was fortunate in that he received no jail time; instead, he was placed on probation for one year. He got counseling, remarried, and returned to sportscasting as the radio play-by-play announcer for the Knicks and as the host of a New York City radio sports talk show. In 1998, following the successful completion of his probation, the misdemeanor conviction was removed from his record.

Horatio ALGER: lover of boys

That imprudence can be disastrous was the lesson learned by Horatio Alger, Jr., on March 20, 1866. His carelessness had cost him his ecclesiastical reputation, his job, the cordiality of his father, and his clerical career. But because the news of his folly was almost totally suppressed until the 1970s, Alger was able to develop a new career and win lasting fame as the writer of more than 100 books illustrating the doctrine that poor but diligent boys could progress from poverty to pelf and honor.

The son of a highly regarded Unitarian clergyman, also named Horatio, Alger had been carefully trained by his father to become the family's second cleric. Despite poor health, he experienced a normal school life, matriculating at Harvard College at the age of 16. There he discovered a literary talent, through which he hoped to support himself; but, after he was graduated in 1852, only to find that publication of his poems and sketches brought him little money, he reluctantly matriculated in 1857 at Harvard Divinity School in the hope that he could become a minister-writer.

His career there was interrupted by unsuccessful attempts to make a living as a writer. Receiving his degree in 1860, he further delayed ordination by futilely combining writing, editorial work, part-time teaching, and occasional preaching. He gained some renown through inclusion in Evert Duyckinsk's *Cyclopedia of American Literature* and his appearance as part of a contemporary authors group, but he was barely able to support himself.

In the late fall of 1864, after a period as a supply clergyman to the nearly moribund First Unitarian Parish of Brewster, Massachusetts, Alger became its full-time clerical leader. At the time he was 32 years old, short (5 feet, 2 inches), and balding. In the pulpit, he was a vigorous and eloquent speaker. His tendency to become totally absorbed in and dedicated to groups and causes made him active in every department of the parish's life.

He was especially zealous about organizing and participating in boys' groups. He joined them in their sports, hiking, and study activities. Parishioners noted that he "was always with the boys," and some of the women of the parish were disappointed that their young parson, an eligible bachelor, had not squired the equally eligible young women in the congregation. In early 1866, they began to ask why, first to each other, then to their husbands, and finally through an investigating committee made up of the male lay officers of the church.

What they discovered, according to parish records made public in the 1970s, was that Alger and the boys were involved in acts "too revolting to relate." In Brewster, Alger had discovered a second talent: the ability to seduce young men. The records name two parish youngsters with whom Alger was so involved, and hints that others were also the recipients of his affection.

Called before the committee and confronted with their findings, Alger did not deny the charges; instead, with remarkable *sang-froid,* he stated that he had been "imprudent." He also stated that he considered his connection with the Brewster parish at an end. Alger left Brewster forever on the evening train. Letters followed him, in which the parish leaders alerted other Massachusetts parishes of his dismissal without disclosing particulars. The parishioners of Brewster ended their investigation after recording their incomplete disclosures and then squelched the record for more than a century. Informed, Alger's father began a permanent estrangement from his son. Some parents threatened court proceedings but were dissuaded by the officials of the statewide church, who noted that Alger had promised never to practice again as a clergyman, and withdrew their notice.

Alger fled to the anonymity of New York City, entered wholeheartedly into his alternative career of writing, and until the end of his life worked with highly applauded dedication for the prosperity of the city's Newsboys' Lodging House. Because no record of further imprudence has been unearthed, Alger was apparently able to sublimate his homosexual interests totally. His most recent biographer suggests that he began a permanent "literary ministry" as an expiation of his moral transgressions—a dedication to the writing of moral tracts celebrating a connection between hard work and success which led to his "canonization" in the 1940s as one of the most influential writers of America's 19th century.

Russell ALGER: the embarrassment of incompetence

When the author Dr. Laurence J. Peter made Americans smirk knowingly with his announcement of the Peter Principle ("In a hierarchy every employee tends to rise to his level of incompetence"), almost no one, including Peter himself, realized that American governmental history supported his findings through the person of Russell Alexander Alger.

Log-cabin born, Alger was—at first—a self-made man. He quit an unremunerative Ohio law practice to develop a large fortune in Michigan lumber. The latter (coupled with an extensive popularity) made him governor of Michigan, "favorite son" candidate during the Republican nominating convention of 1888, and in 1889 commander of the influential league of Union veterans of the Civil War called the Grand Army of the Republic.

In 1897, Alger was rewarded politically by U.S. President William McKinley by appointment to the post of secretary of war. It was here that he reached his level of incompetence. Both before and during the Spanish-American War, he functioned so ineptly that he was forced to resign under a cloud of humiliation and embarrassment.

When Alger became secretary of war, he found himself to be in charge of a department riddled with inefficiencies: command posts filled with elderly officers lying low until retirement, a bureaucracy of 25,000 persons in the War Department, and active jealousies between officers of the line and the War Department bureaus that governed them. A Civil War veteran with the rank of brevet major-general, Alger would in theory have been so immediately aware of these problems that he would have quickly corrected them. Instead he did nothing. Moreover, although relations between Spain and the United States had been deteriorating since the 1870s because of expansionist American interventions in Cuba, Alger saw nothing seriously amiss in the fact that his department lacked a general staff and had not prepared systematic studies of problems that could arise in the event of a war with Spain. Instead, Alger ran his department in a kindly, routine way, becoming the target of the antagonisms existing between it and the military post commanders. Illogic also played a part in his executive decisions: he blamed the condition of the War Department upon civilian indifference and failed to realize that as the civilian head of a military department, it was his job to lead the American citizenry toward demanding the needed improvements.

Even after March 9, 1898, when the United States battleship *Maine* was sunk in Havana harbor, Alger seemed petrified. Congress had voted an appropriation on February 15, 1898, of $50 million "for the national defense," but Alger did not act at all until after Congress had declared war against Spain on April 25.

As a result, even though the war was brief, Alger's department was unprepared for it. Hospital services were inadequate, winter clothing was sent for the fighting of a war in the Tropics, and guns and ammunition were procured on a hit-or-miss basis. Even the food provided to American troops was of a very poor quality: among the loud criticisms of Alger were angry cries about "embalmed beef" as the soldiers' main sustenance. Moreover, Alger himself may have been responsible for the early failure of the Santiago campaign in Cuba by having refused the Army's supreme commander permission to go to Cuba, instead sending a Michigan crony, the dangerously obese William R. Shafter, who was incapacitated for most of the expedition. (Only the actions of U.S. colonels Leonard Wood and Theodore Roosevelt, with the "Rough Riders" [a volunteer cavalry unit], forced the surrender of Santiago.)

After the war, Alger's commissary general was court martialed, and Alger was to be considered next. However, an investigation by a presidential commission failed to establish the extent of Alger's responsibility for the maladministration of the War Department, and President McKinley refused to fire Alger until political pressure forced him to request Alger's resignation in July 1899. Alger was humiliated enough to write in 1901 a self-serving defense of his conduct in office. President McKinley was assassinated before he had an opportunity to comment on Alger's careful rationalizations.

Despite the seeming totality of Alger's ineptitude in office, he decided to run for United States senator from Michigan in 1902. Even more surprising is that he was elected. Regardless of the scandal Alger had brought upon the War Department, Michigan was still enthralled with its past governor. As a senator, however, Alger kept such a low profile that nothing memorable was recorded about him in the Senate annals.

See also "EMBALMED BEEF" SCANDAL.

ALIEN PROPERTY CUSTODIAL SCANDAL. See Thomas MILLER: fraud as Harding's Alien Property Custodian.

Ira ALLEN: alleged treason in Vermont
Of the four Allen brothers, whose names are inextricably intertwined with that of Vermont, the most familiar is Ethan, who led the Green Mountain Boys in protecting Vermont from the militia of the New York colony, which from 1749 until 1777—at times with royal backing—considered the Vermont territory its own. But an Allen equally deserving of fame is Ira (1751–1814), the youngest of the brothers and theoretician of the Vermont settlers, who risked the charge of treason to protect Vermont during the American Revolutionary War.

Once a part of New Hampshire west of the Connecticut River, the Vermont territory developed from New Hampshire lands granted from 1749 through 1764. Ira Allen surveyed much of these grants, found them valuable, and with his brothers and a cousin formed the Onion River Land company, which occupied 77,000 acres between the Onion (now Winooski) River in Vermont and Lake Champlain. In 1764, a royal decision had assigned the Vermont territory to the New York colony; and in 1770 a self-seeking New York colonial court had declared all New Hampshire grants invalid; and the New York militia had marched in to take possession of them. The Vermonters resisted, with Ethan Allen directing the fighting of the Green Mountain Boys until the Revolution began, while Ira laid out a road and began constructing the city of Burlington, Vermont.

The Revolution stopped the New York militia, which was needed elsewhere from its incursion, while the Green Mountain Boys espoused the patriot cause. In 1777, at the Westminster Convention in Vermont, Ira and Ethan Allen, Thomas Chittenden, and Jonas Fay led the delegates to declare Vermont an independent republic, a decision confirmed later that year at Dorset, along with the first declaration of universal manhood suffrage in the New World.

The Continental Congress, influenced by New York's claims and prominence, refused to recognize these declarations, but the British did in 1779, offering Ethan Allen and Vermont self-government under the Crown. In 1780, the Vermonters replied when negotiations soon to be guided by Ira Allen began with the British general Frederick Haldimand. Ira's aim was to save Vermont whatever the outcome of the war.

Members of the Continental Congress and some Vermonters considered Ira's actions and the Haldimand negotiations treasonous and berated Ira in print. But most Vermonters regarded the Allens' opportunism as a sign of shrewdness and backed the maneuver. In the early years of the Revolutionary War, when British victory or at best a compromise with Britain seemed imminent, Ira's diplomatic cleverness kept the Vermonters from being pressed to agree to British control and absorption into Canada. But in 1781, the defeat of Cornwallis at Yorktown made the negotiations unnecessary.

In 1783, however, New York renewed its territorial claims on Vermont, and Ira again led the resistance until 1790 when a payment of $30,000 ended the controversy. By 1791, when Vermont was admitted to the Union, Ira had almost been ruined financially, but it later became clear that his shrewdness during the Haldimand negotiations had saved the Vermont territory and helped lead to its statehood.

Richard ALLEN: the "forgotten" money

In November 1981, the White House was extremely discomfited by a Japanese newspaper report that U.S. President Ronald Reagan's trusted assistant for national security affairs, Richard V. Allen, had taken an alleged $1,000 cash bribe from a Japanese women's magazine for helping arrange an interview with the president's wife, Nancy. The interview, between three Japanese journalists and Mrs. Reagan, had taken place the day after the president's inauguration in January 1981. The First Lady was reportedly vexed by the public disclosure of Allen's dealings and the subsequent governmental investigations into them.

The gifts that federal officeholders can legally accept are strictly limited in the United States, whereas in Japan, presents or payments given in return for a favor (such as an interview) are considered a traditional practice or custom.

Immediately after the Japanese newspaper revelation of the gifts, the White House reported that the Justice Department was looking into whether Allen had broken the law. Allen, known among associates for his jocose, waggish nature, acknowledged that he had received the Japanese request for the interview and also the money but said that he had not set up the interview himself and had not solicited the money. Instead, said Allen, the money had been put into his office safe by his secretary, where it had been "forgotten" when he switched offices soon afterward. According to Allen, he had planned to hand over the cash to federal authorities.

Concurrent with the Justice Department probe was an FBI inquiry into Allen's business conduct. This revealed alleged illegalities in the January 1978 sale of Allen's company—a consulting firm, showing that he had in fact sold the firm in January 1981. Moreover, unlisted on Allen's taxable income was some $5,000 that the company had paid him in fees, besides his having been on company payroll since the purported 1978 sale. The FBI also probed into a gift of two Seiko watches that Allen had received from the Japanese journalists following the interview with Mrs. Reagan. This contradicted Allen's statement that the watches had been presented to him before his swearing-in.

Although the FBI study initially cleared Allen of any wrongdoing, doubts persisted and, fueled by press reports, brought on another FBI search into Allen's affairs, on orders from the White House.

Serious questions were raised about whether the envelope in the safe contained $1,000 (the amount found in it) or $10,000 (the figure written on the outside of the envelope and on a receipt). Edwin Meese, Allen's boss and counselor to President Reagan, stood firmly by the beleaguered national security adviser, who faced much hostility from the American public as he tried desperately to calm the increasing storm. Secretary of the Navy John Lehman came forward on Allen's behalf, saying he had witnessed Allen receiving the $1,000 and seen Allen show "chagrin and amazement" at getting the money in cash.

But there was also conflicting evidence. One of the Japanese journalists who had interviewed the First Lady said that she had asked for but never received a receipt for the money. And a long-time Japanese friend of Allen revealed that he had handed Allen "a big present" to help his journalist wife win an interview with Mrs. Reagan.

On November 29, 1981, Allen announced that he was taking a leave of absence from his post (which he hoped to retake following the Justice Department inquiry). Appearing on the three major American television networks to defend and explain himself, he said that those who had started the "false" stories about him would be dealt with legally, and he reiterated that the envelope with the money had been inadvertently "forgotten" in his office safe. In December 1981, the Justice Department cleared Allen of all criminal misconduct charges—notably, bribery concerning the acceptance of a cash payment. Nonetheless, the White House seemed highly embarrassed by the scandal, and Allen apparently reluctantly tendered his resignation. On January 1, 1982, the White House announced this, and three days later, William P. Clark, Jr., a deputy secretary of state, was named the new presidential adviser for national security affairs.

Patently discredited, Allen continued in government employment as a consultant on the President's Foreign Intelligence Advisory Board. An executive branch review confirmed that he had met and dined with former clients of his company in the White House but had committed no misconduct or impropriety.

Woody ALLEN: accused of family abuse by Mia Farrow
Scandals are commonplace in the film industry; yet, the scandal that ruptured the fairy-tale romance of writer/director/actor Woody Allen and actress Mia Farrow was anything but that. It involved their seven-year-old adopted daughter Dylan and Farrow's 21-year-old adopted daughter (from her marriage to composer Andre Previn), Soon-Yi.

The scandal broke when Farrow found nude Polaroid pictures of Soon-Yi (taken at her suggestion) in Allen's New York apartment on January 13, 1992. Allen admitted having an affair with Soon-Yi since December 1991 and an irate Farrow ended their 11-year relationship. Then, in August 1992, Allen sued for custody of Dylan and 15-year-old Moses Farrow (both of whom he had formally adopted in December 1991) and five-year-old Satchel Farrow, his biological child. A week later, Farrow alleged that Allen had sexually molested Dylan at her Connecticut home. Allen denied the charges, saying that Farrow had concocted them in retaliation for his affair with Soon-Yi and to influence the outcome of the custody case.

A baby-sitter walking by the living room window in Farrow's Connecticut home reported seeing Allen with his head between Dylan's knees. Farrow questioned Dylan about the incident on videotape and shared it with a reporter and two producers from a New York television station. Then she made an appointment to meet the costume designer of Allen's next film. In April 1993, Allen's lawyer, Elkan Abramowitz, charged that law-enforcement officials were helping Farrow's cause by giving her lawyers exclusive access to important evidence (e.g., a videotape). Apparently, Abramowitz had asked to see the tape but received no response. After a six-month investigation, a team from the Yale–New Haven Hospital concluded

in March 1993 that no sexual abuse had taken place. However, the team noted that both Allen and Farrow had disturbed relations with Dylan. Farrow's lawyers termed the report "incomplete and inaccurate." Frank S. Maco, the Litchfield County state's attorney, asked for a copy of the report even as he discredited its findings. Maco said that he had enough evidence to take the case to trial and to have Allen arrested but had decided not to for Dylan's sake. These remarks were vehemently criticized by Allen's lawyers and legal experts. On April 7, 1993 a child psychiatrist testified that the Yale report's conclusions were based on bungled interviews and faulty methodology.

On the stand, Allen acknowledged that his affair with Soon-Yi was perhaps "wrong, not wise" but that he didn't think that it would cause such a furor. Farrow testified that Allen was so obsessively preoccupied with Dylan that he ignored the other children (she had 11). Still, she allowed him to adopt Dylan in 1991—a fact that she could not explain. Farrow charged Allen with pushing Dylan's face into some hot spaghetti and threatening to break Satchel's leg. Her lawyers read an angry letter from Moses to Allen who retorted that it seemed as if Farrow had dictated it. Allen countered with allegations of his own: Farrow had mistreated her adopted children and physically abused Soon-Yi and torn up her clothes when she found out about their affair. He claimed that Farrow had demanded a $7 million payoff to withdraw the abuse charges. And so the charges flew back and forth. Even their lawyers traded barbs and allegations.

Finally, on June 7, 1993, Judge Elliott Wilk granted custody of the three children to Farrow. Allen's access to them was limited; he could only visit Satchel. He appealed the ruling. Wilk described Allen's conduct with Dylan as "grossly inappropriate" and said he was upset that Dylan had to undergo two simultaneous and traumatic sex-abuse investigations in New York (the case was dropped in October 1993 because the charges were deemed baseless) and Connecticut. The New York authorities should have withdrawn in favor of Connecticut, Wilk felt. Allen reiterated his innocence and said that the Connecticut authorities had pursued him relentlessly because he was a celebrity and an outsider, whereas Farrow was a state resident. He proposed a truce for the sake of the children but was immediately turned down. Farrow instead appealed to the Surrogate's Court in Manhattan to overturn and nullify Allen's adoption of Dylan and Moses.

In October 1993, Allen filed complaints against Maco with two Connecticut state agencies. He said that Maco had violated legal ethics in statements made during his press conference. On November 3, 1993, a criminal justice panel voted unanimously to dismiss Allen's complaint.

Isaac ALLERTON: false accusations of dishonesty

Trader, Puritan settler, and one of the six most important leaders during the Pilgrims' residence in Leyden, Holland, before 1620, Isaac Allerton lost a high place in the history of the Plymouth Colony because, after 1630, William Bradford and other leaders opposed his solutions to the problems of the struggling settlement in America. The writings of the colonists show this opposition in the form of accusations of dishonesty against Allerton, but these are exaggerations that have incorrectly blemished Allerton's repute.

Allerton had been one of the four men to complete the arrangements for the Pilgrims' departure for America; in 1621, when Bradford became the colony's governor, Allerton was named his assistant, and the two men administered the colony without other officials through 1624. In 1625, when the original merchant-financiers of the venture refused further capital for it, Allerton began traveling to England to resolve the difficulty. He made arrangements to repay the original loans, borrowed funds for supplies to reduce the poverty of the first settlers, helped the remainder of the Leyden congregation to emigrate to Plymouth, found a new group of merchant-financiers, and induced others to try their fortunes in the New World. But Allerton angered the Bradford group in securing the Patent of 1630, which gave the settlers title to lands and property. Although this last achievement ensured the future of the colony, the Bradford party did not like the terms and began to view Allerton's activities negatively.

Convinced that trading ventures would enrich the colony, where infertile soil hampered farming, Allerton persuaded his new English associates, borrowed further sums of money, equipped a ship for trading, and returned to Plymouth with goods the Pilgrims had not ordered. He had exceeded his authority and more than doubled the colony's debt, but the Bradford group charged him with dishonesty rather than arrogance and dismissed him as the colony's agent. False rumors of knavery by Allerton spread throughout the colony, and the misrepresentations found permanence in the colony's records. Shunned, Allerton departed.

Allerton's conviction that trade would prove superior to agriculture was finally realized by the colony; it developed a well-managed fur trade and, for better land, expanded to Scituate and Duxbury, Massachusetts. But the Bradford group's resistance had cut them off from the guidance and vision of Allerton, who, after some initial difficulty, established himself in New Haven, Connecticut, and traded prosperously, as Plymouth might have, with New Amsterdam, Chesapeake Bay, Virginia, and the West Indies.

Aldrich AMES: Soviets' CIA Mole

Aldrich Hazen Ames dropped out of college after two years to work for the Central Intelligence Agency (CIA) as his father had done before him. During the mid-1980s when many of the CIA's Soviet operations went awry, he was the chief of the Soviet counterintelligence branch of the agency's Soviet/East Europe Division. Coincidentally, for much of that period, he was also spying for the Soviets and being paid well for his efforts. Ames had no qualms about flaunting his newfound wealth, but it took the CIA several years to uncover Ames and arrest him on espionage charges in what became one of the worst spy scandals since the end of World War II.

The year 1985 was notorious for its spy scandals. In fact, it was known as the "Year of the Spy" and, according to the Federal Bureau of Investigation (FBI), it was the year Ames put himself on the Soviet payroll; his bank account showed a deposit of $9,000 on May 18, 1985, the first of many deposits. Ames's first 20 years at the CIA were not particularly noteworthy. He developed a drinking problem and his marriage appeared to be in jeopardy. In 1981, the CIA deputed him to Mexico City to recruit spies. Although still married, Ames became sexually involved with his first new recruit (a foreign national) in the agency's safe haven, in clear violation of the agency's rules. However, there were no reprisals. Instead, Ames was rewarded with a plum assignment—managing the counterintelligence operations against the Soviets in Washington. The FBI later found that under the guise of recruiting Soviet officials as spies in 1984, Ames had offered his services to the Soviets.

Ames regularly passed on very sensitive, highly classified information (especially the names of the agents used by the CIA against the Soviets) to the KGB, the CIA's counterpart there. It is estimated that the KGB used this information to perhaps torture and then execute at least 10 agents and to thwart more than 20 CIA operations there. Also, he enabled Moscow to plant several double agents who passed on real and bogus information to their CIA handlers. Even after the CIA found out in 1991, it continued to passed on this classified information to the White House and the Pentagon with no mention made of the fact that some of it might be dubious. After the fall of communism, Ames continued to work for the Russian Foreign Intelligence Service, the SVR. Reports indicate that Ames was paid more than $1.5 million ($2.5 million, plus a promise of an additional $2 million, according to other estimates) between 1985 and 1994, and he was always pushing for more money to finance his worsening drinking habit and for his divorce proceedings. Also, he spent lavishly—paying cash for a $540,000 house, amassing $455,000 on his credit cards and $30,000 in phone bills, and driving to work in a Jaguar. Ames even made a $5,000 contribution to the

Democratic National Committee. Strangely, none of these sudden expenditures attracted the CIA's attention then.

Finally, in 1991, the CIA and the FBI joined forces to form a special interagency task force to try to discover the identity of the person who had sold out to the Russians. The task force prepared an initial list and began interviewing potential candidates. One of their interviewees suggested that they look instead at the spending habits of Aldrich Ames, whose name was at the bottom of the list. That's when the scandal began unraveling for Ames, even though the FBI let five more months pass before it opened its criminal case against him. They tapped Ames's phone line and his computer, trailed him everywhere, and even went through his trash to see what it might reveal. Twice before, in 1986 and 1991, Ames, had "beaten" the polygraph machine using techniques taught to him by the Russians. Also, he had failed to report his foreign travels as required—to Caracas in 1992 and to Bogotá a year later, where he met with his Russian contacts.

Ames was now remarried to Rosario Casas Dupuy, who had assisted in his spying since 1992. Taped phone conversations between the two show a picture of a henpecked husband. While the investigation was going on, Ames was transferred to a position in the counternarcotics division. However, for a while he continued to have access to classified top-secret documents which the FBI later found in his office. This access helped him to betray another Soviet agent working for the CIA, who may have been killed when the Russians found out. Finally, on February 21, 1994, Ames was arrested as he was getting ready to leave for Moscow on routine business.

There seemed no end to the damage Ames could cause if he revealed all he knew. Initially, his lawyer, Plato Cacheris, was not willing to cooperate. After spending a night in jail away from their five-year-old son, Rosario relented and agreed to talk in return for reduced prison time. Ames and Rosario pleaded guilty; he was sentenced on April 28, 1994, to life in prison without parole; Rosario received slightly more than five years in prison.

The Ames case caused an uproar within the CIA, which vowed to take steps to prevent a recurrence. However, barely two months after Ames's sentencing, another CIA agent, Harold J. Nicholson, was found on the Soviet payroll—receiving $12,000 as his first payment. This time, the sudden influx of deposits in his bank account attracted attention and he was arrested before he could inflict damage on the scale that Ames did. In August 1995, the CIA donated $500,000 from the sale of Ames's suburban home and his Jaguar to the Justice Department's Crime Victims Fund. In 1996, Ames filed a lawsuit against the last

two CIA directors and 20 others claiming that they had violated his constitutional rights as a federal prisoner.

Marian ANDERSON: the DAR fumbles

America's aficionados and celebrities of the music, stage, screen, and academic worlds were angered in February 1939 when news leaked out that the Daughters of the American Revolution (DAR) had declined to make available Constitution Hall in Washington, D.C., to Marian Anderson, one of America's best known and best loved contraltos. The DAR at first claimed that the hall had been previously engaged, but that explanation was soon shown to be an excuse for the real reason: Miss Anderson was black.

Her supporters acted quickly. They made public statements and sent vituperative messages to the DAR and its president, Mrs. Henry M. Robert, Jr. The DAR representatives told reporters "No comment," and Mrs. Robert remained "unavailable." Miss Anderson stayed silent, too, expressing the remarkable poise and quiet dignity that had endeared her to audiences for almost two decades.

The flood of protest from such organizations as the American Union for Democracy and from such individuals as Fiorello LaGuardia, mayor of New York, Sylvia Sidney, screen artist, and Harold Ickes, United States secretary of the interior, reached its zenith when the nation's first lady, Eleanor Roosevelt, resigned her DAR membership. Again, the DAR declined comment.

Fans of Miss Anderson tried to secure the auditorium of Washington's Central High School but were turned down twice, first because Miss Anderson's concert was a commercial venture and second because her appearance would break a tradition against allowing two engagements on a single calendar day. Eleanor Roosevelt again intervened, persuading Secretary Ickes to open the Lincoln Memorial area to Miss Anderson for a free outdoor concert.

Thousands attended on Easter Sunday, 1939, laughing when Mr. Ickes indirectly backhanded the DAR in his introduction of the famed black singer, saying that "In our time too many pay mere lip service to those twin planets [Jefferson and Lincoln] in our national heavens. In this great auditorium all of us are free." They reveled in Miss Anderson's singing.

This embarrassing event had three minor climaxes. Mrs. Roosevelt held a White House tea for the DAR, as scheduled, but she refused to lend the affair dignity by attending personally. The DAR publicly indicated its hurt. Next, Mrs. Robert spoke out on April 25, 1939, lamely arguing that the uproar made impossible the bending of the DAR's rule against black performers in Constitution Hall. And Miss Anderson, maintaining poise and dignified silence, went on to become the first

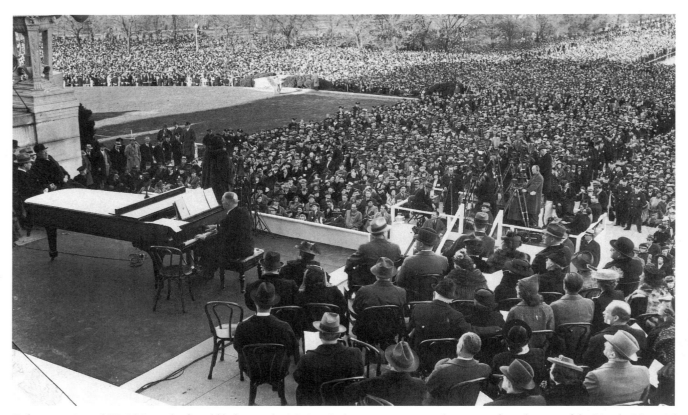

Before an estimated 75,000 people, famed black contralto Marian Anderson sang at an outdoor concert from the steps of the Lincoln Memorial in Washington, D.C., on Easter Sunday, 1939. Secretary of the Interior Harold Ickes, who introduced her, Secretary of the Treasury Henry Morgenthau and his wife, Supreme Court Justice Hugo Black, and others high in official life were on the stand listening to her (seen on stage in left foreground). The concert had been arranged after two auditoriums were closed to Anderson. (AP/Wide World Photos)

black to be a permanent member of the Metropolitan Opera (1955), to act as an alternate delegate to the United Nations (1958), and to receive the President's Medal of Freedom (1963).

She retired in 1965 after a long farewell tour, received other honors and awards, and died at age 96 in 1993.

ANDERSONVILLE PRISON. See Henry WIRZ: Andersonville's last victim.

Susan B. ANTHONY. See Ward HUNT: the farcical trial of Susan B. Anthony.

ANTI-MASONRY: reaction begets reform
Citizens of northwestern New York acted swiftly in 1826 when they heard the news that William Morgan had disappeared. Morgan, described by an historian of politics as "a somewhat down at heel citizen of Batavia," was a disgruntled Mason who had written a book alleged to be an exposé of Masonic secrets. Rumors contended that the Masons had murdered Morgan. The Order, for its part, maintained a stolid and uncooperative silence, and so local political organizations campaigned to keep support from office-seeking Masons. One new organization, the Anti-Masonry Party, at-

tracted those in the populace who distrusted the Masons and other secret societies. It grew almost overnight, and the party's power base soon stretched from western New York to Pennsylvania, Ohio, New Jersey, Massachusetts, and Vermont.

In the rush of growth of the anti-Masonic movement, the initiating impetus for it was submerged, and neither the fate of Morgan nor the culpability of the Masonic Order was ascertained. Instead, the new and liberal Anti-Masonry Party became the voice of the poorer citizen against the well-to-do (and most Masons were regarded as rich), the spokesman for the orthodox against Unitarianism and other liberal sects, a supporter of temperance and antislavery activities, and a cheerleader for some features of Jacksonian Democracy against the autocratic Federalists. It opposed not only secret societies and government-in-secret, but also imprisonment for debt and drafts for state militia service.

But as the party gathered strength it also began to move from the left to the right, supporting tariffs on imported goods to prevent the collapse of local industries, better canals for more efficient transport, and banks free from regulatory taxes. As such, it was vainly used by politicians for their own ends, chiefly anti-Jacksonian: Thurlow Weed and William H. Seward tried unsuccessfully through the Anti-Masonry Party to overthrow Martin van Buren's Albany Regency (informal group of Democratic leaders in New York), and politician Thad Stevens in Pennsylvania tried to use it to increase his power. Soon the new party was voting with the National Republican Party against the Jacksonians; by 1834 it had moved entirely to the right, for it helped found the reactionary Whig Party, which absorbed the Anti-Masonry Party in 1836.

Nevertheless, what had begun as a grass-roots reaction to secret societies achieved some positive and permanent ends. Some secret societies, including Phi Beta Kappa (but not the Masons), became more open. Moreover, the Anti-Masonry Party grew powerful enough to take part in the 1832 presidential campaign, in which its candidate, William Wirt, gained seven electoral votes. Most important, the short-lived party contributed two important "firsts" to American political life: in 1831 in Baltimore it held the first nominating convention in American history, and it established the practice of requiring a three-fourths majority for nomination on a presidential ticket. Additionally, the party issued the first written party platform in American history. The major parties were quick to imitate, and the practice of secret nominating caucuses was forced to assume a different form.

APPLETONS' CYCLOPAEDIA: famous scientists who never were

Appleton's Cyclopaedia of American Biography, published in 1887–89, was one of the first important American biographical dictionaries. Though it is now out of print, many libraries contain copies of the work, and for many years it was regarded as a reliable source of information. Even after it was largely superseded by the *Dictionary of American Biography,* it was still considered a useful reference work for areas not covered by the DAB.

But some 30 years after its publication, Dr. Joseph Hendley Barnhart, who was compiling a bibliography for the New York Botanical Garden, discovered that the work contained at least 14 fake biographies of botanists. In a 1919 article in the *Journal of the New York Botanical Garden,* Barnhart wrote:

> "It is difficult to believe that, in this day of enlightenment, standard works of reference should contain purely fictitious accounts of scientists who, if they ever existed, certainly never did nor wrote those deeds and writings with which they are credited. . . . At first these products of the vivid imagination of some gifted writer—for they bear internal evidence of no small degree of ingenuity—were ignored, and did no particular harm. But during the last few years they have been making an impression upon the literature of scientific biography and bibliography, and it has become very necessary to expose their true character."

The writer of the fictitious biographies had been clever in his choice of subjects. He had invented characters whose existence and accomplishments would be difficult for *Appletons'* editors, working in New York City and under severe time pressure, to verify, had they suspected any irregularities. Of the 14 spurious botanists scattered through the six volumes of the *Cyclopaedia,* all but one were said to be Europeans engaged in the study of Latin American botany; the one exception was described as a native of the West Indies who later settled in France. None of them spent much time in the United States, where records might be expected to be readily available, nor did their putative publications concern what was then United States territory; all of the individuals were said to have died in Europe or South America. They all flourished in the 17th, 18th, or early 19th centuries.

Barnhart, who suspected but could not say with certainty that several other botanists listed in the *Cyclopaedia* had never existed, was not the only one who was finding peculiarities in the reference book. The staff of Sabin's *Dictionary of Books Relating to America* began finding titles in the *Cyclopaedia* that could not be verified. Since the Sabin bibliography was nearing completion when significant irregularities were noticed, the staff kept a record of abnormalities only for the letter V and the first part of W. They found 17 men for whom no published titles could be verified (two of these were also in Barnhart's list).

In 1937, additional fake biographies were uncovered. Writing in the *American Historical Review,* Margaret Castle Schindler announced that, upon studying a sample consisting of selected articles in the letter H, she had found 18 more false sketches. Schindler looked closely at articles on people who had lived and died before 1850 and who were connected with the history of Latin America, as these were the suspicious areas.

The evidence in the false articles was largely bibliographic: though the subjects were said to have published important works, none of these works existed in three of the world's largest libraries (the British Museum, the French Bibliothèque nationale, and the U.S. Library of Congress) or in other reliable bibliographic sources. Other errors were also detected. For example, Charles Henry Huon de Penanster was said to have broken the Spanish monopoly on the valuable cochineal dye industry by smuggling the cochineal insect and the plant on which it feeds out of Mexico in 1755. This deed was actually accomplished more than 20 years later by Nicholas Joseph Thiery de Menonville, whose biography also appears in the *Cyclopaedia.* The fictitious Huon de Penanster is also credited with publications that bear a remarkable similarity to Thiery's genuine titles.

Could the articles have been honest mistakes, with erroneous information gleaned from earlier works? That solution seems unlikely, since none of the researchers found an earlier source with the same false information.

The author (or, less likely, authors) of the fake articles remains unknown. The articles themselves are unsigned, and the list of contributors at the beginning of each volume is not sufficiently detailed to establish authorship of the questionable items. The publishers, the editors James Grant Wilson and John Fiske, and the managing editor, Rossiter Johnson, were never suspected of involvement in or knowledge of the false entries. An unscrupulous contributor, however, would have found it possible and profitable to invent subjects because contributors not only were paid by the amount of space for each article they contributed, but also were invited to suggest names for inclusion in the *Cyclopaedia*. A contributor who could toss off some quick articles without doing any research (or using research already completed for genuine articles) could earn his money with little fear of detection. The editors of *Appletons' Cyclopaedia* did not attempt to verify every fact or every title and would have very likely been unfamiliar with the details of Latin American history.

That the articles escaped detection for so long suggests that the writer did have some knowledge of his subjects. Since most of the fictitious entries are for scientists, he presumably had some scientific training. And he knew a fair amount about the geography and history of Latin America. He also managed to invent or adapt titles in six languages.

Before the false entries became public knowledge, the information from them had crept into many other works, including bibliographies, biographical dictionaries, and scientific articles. Though the genuine *Cyclopaedia* articles are still considered valuable for certain types of information not contained in later reference books, the work must now be read with some caution.

William ARAMONY: charity paid for his diversions

Until 1992, William Aramony was known as the high-profile chief executive officer and president of the United Way of America (UWA), who transformed it into one of the nation's best known charities. Under his leadership, UWA raked in more than $3.5 billion a year, mainly through corporate fund drives. His 22-year career at UWA, however, ended abruptly on February 28, 1992, when he was forced to resign amid a scandal of his own making.

Flamboyant and self-promoting, Aramony's fund-raising skills had become legendary and were never in question. He was responsible for raising the charity's profile in the community and for drawing the more than 2,000 independent local United Way groups into a cohesive whole. However, his lavish lifestyle and womanizing had long provided fodder for gossip at UWA headquarters in Alexandria, Virginia. Late in 1991,

Charles E. Shepard, Pulitzer Prize–winning journalist with the *Washington Post*, began making enquiries about Aramony and his management of UWA's operations. Aramony promptly launched an internal investigation to look into company policies and operations that might attract scrutiny. Hardly had the UWA's executive committee expressed its confidence in his leadership when several newspapers ran articles about his handling of UWA funds. The first article, "Charity Begins at Home for United Way" by Jack Anderson and Michael Binstein, was syndicated nationally on February 12, 1992. Shepard's first article was a full-page cover story on February 16. The media blitz and public anger generated by the story forced Aramony into immediate retirement. The UWA board established a committee to oversee its new and stricter code of ethics. In May 1992, the U.S. Department of Justice seized the company's records.

Aramony's salary and perks (totaling $463,000) were too generous, many thought, for a nonprofit organization. Still, he continued to draw on UWA personnel, funds, and resources for private purposes. For instance, he evidently used funds from Partnership Umbrella, Inc. (PUI), one of UWA's many spin-off organizations, to support his teenage mistress, Lori Villasor, in lavish comfort. As described in his indictment on September 13, 1994, Aramony wooed her with flowers, limousine rides, vacations in New York City and Las Vegas, and even a monthly stipend ("consulting fees") of up to $1,833—all at UWA's expense! Rina Duncan, an aide and a former mistress, was given a job with Partnership Umbrella. Her husband was later hired by United Way International.

Aramony was also criticized for appointing friends and relatives to high-level positions at United Way. Thomas J. Merlo, a close friend who became UWA's chief financial officer, was given an annual salary of $211,000 and a rent-free apartment, plus the company also paid for his weekly commuting expenses to his home in Florida. Aramony's son Robert was hired (the post was apparently never advertised) as president and chief executive officer of Sales Service/America, another UWA spin-off started with a $1.5 million loan from the parent company. Robert had previously worked for three other spin-offs—as a consultant for Professional Travel Systems and as vice president of PUI, and for Charities Fund Transfer.

Every year Aramony traveled with his aides and closest friends to the Super Bowl at company expense, apparently to cultivate the National Football League (NFL). Often, those who traveled were members of the board of PUI—this was Aramony's way of thanking them for volunteering. UWA's argument was that since the NFL provided it with $45 million worth of free advertising, the tickets should be considered a legitimate business expense.

PUI was one of the more dubious spin-offs. It purchased for $430,000 a New York condominium for Aramony (he suggested that it was only used by PUI staff). PUI also purchased a condominium in Florida for $125,000 from another spin-off, only to sell it in April 1991. Also, PUI paid off a $200,000 loan to an already defunct (since 1987) spin-off—Professional Travel Systems.

During the four-week court trial, neither Aramony nor Merlo or Stephen Paulachak (president of PUI) called in any witnesses or discussed the charges. The prosecution argued that Aramony treated UWA as his "private play toy." Aramony was characterized as a womanizer (this was later acknowledged by his lawyer) who habitually wooed his female employees with the charity's funds. Rina Duncan, a former aide with whom he apparently had an affair, testified that Aramony had asked her to bill his personal expenses to UWA. Outside the court, Aramony's lawyer said that the scandal had been caused by employees who could not distinguish between personal and business expenses. He said that the 37-member UWA board was aware of Aramony's

spending habits but did not address the issue because of his fund-raising skills.

Assistant U.S. Attorney Randy I. Bellows advised the federal grand jury in Alexandria, Virginia, that this was a case of "three men who looted and plundered one of the country's most important institutions of charity." In April 1995, after deliberating for seven days, the jury found Aramony guilty of 25 counts of fraud, conspiracy, money laundering, and falsifying his income tax returns, each of which carried a maximum sentence of 10 years in prison. Merlo was convicted on 17 counts and Paulachak on eight. They were charged with siphoning $600,000 for their personal use from UWA and PUI.

Roscoe "Fatty" ARBUCKLE: comedian, carouser, and culprit

By 1921 the fun-loving, hard-drinking, 266-pound Roscoe "Fatty" Arbuckle had become one of Hollywood's most popular and highest paid film comedians, with Charlie Chaplin considered his only serious rival. After signing a new three-year, $3-million contract with Paramount studios, Arbuckle decided to celebrate by having one of his notorious wild parties. Followed by several carloads of his merrymaking film friends, he took

Looking grim on September 23, 1921, Roscoe "Fatty" Arbuckle (fourth from left, with hands folded), seated with attorneys, awaits a hearing from the grand jury following his indictment for manslaughter in the killing of Virginia Rappe. The comedian Arbuckle, worn from steady questioning by attorneys for the state, shows no sign of the smile that made his name famous throughout the world. (AP/Wide World Photos)

off in his new $25,000 custom-made Pierce Arrow automobile for San Francisco, some 400 miles away. One of those accompanying Arbuckle in his flashy car was a "loose," pretty starlet named Virginia Rappe, whom Arbuckle had taken a fancy to and planned to make his leading lady in one of his forthcoming comedies. The party began immediately after the group checked into San Francisco's St. Francis Hotel on Saturday evening of the 1921 Labor Day weekend.

Arbuckle, who had taken three luxurious adjoining suites on the 12th floor of the hotel, obtained several cases of bootleg liquor, turned on some radio music, and proceeded to hold a boisterous "open house" revelry. Local showgirls and movie businessmen were invited to join Arbuckle and his cronies, and the booze flowed freely for over two days. With the party still going strong on Labor Day afternoon, Monday, September 5, the carousing Arbuckle, clad in pajamas, herded the lovely Miss Rappe, amorously tipsy herself, into the bedroom of suite 1221. Before he locked the bedroom door, nearby revelers heard him say, "This is the chance I've waited for for a long time."

About 20 minutes later, frenzied screams were heard from the room, and Miss Rappe groaned out, in a strange voice, "I'm dying, I'm dying . . . He hurt me," when Arbuckle opened the door, walked out in ripped pajamas, and scoffed to the bewildered revelers, "Go in and get her dressed and take her to the Palace. She makes too much noise." Miss Rappe was found lying almost naked in blood among her torn clothes, crying out in agony, ". . . I'm dying. Roscoe did it." But Arbuckle jeered, "She's acting it up. She's always been a lousy actress," and shouted at her, "Shut up or I'll throw you out of the window," while Miss Rappe continued to moan hysterically. Placed in another hotel room, she was not brought to a hospital until three days later, and there fell into a coma, dying of a burst bladder on September 10, 1921.

San Francisco's deputy coroner, suspicious about the cause of death, examined Miss Rappe's private parts and concluded that her bladder had been ruptured through some kind of violence. Upon learning that there was an apparent cover-up going on about the severity of the victim's injuries, the district attorney made some inquiries. He finally charged Arbuckle with Miss Rappe's rape and murder, causing a nationwide sensation fueled by the press. Arbuckle became a symbol of what was wrong with the Hollywood lifestyle. The public, in general, damed him and his movies and a "lynch Fatty" mood began to pervade much of America. All kinds of rumors about what had happened floated about: that Arbuckle, impotent because he was drunk, had raped the young beauty with a bottle in a fit of rage or that Arbuckle, supposedly having a well-endowed sexual organ, had caused serious damage during intercourse.

In mid-November 1921, Arbuckle, pleading innocent, stood trial in San Francisco and won a mistrial after the jury voted acquittal, 10–2. Despite the shocking revelations about Arbuckle's conduct, witnesses for the prosecution vanished or gave seemingly perjured testimony, thus helping the defendant's case. The district attorney, disturbed by conflicting evidence, ordered another trial, and this time the jury voted 10–2 conviction on a charge of manslaughter. The hung jury once again kept Arbuckle free on bail (he was then having to sell his possessions to pay his attorneys' fees). A third trial, however, ended on April 12, 1922, with the comedian's full acquittal by the jury, which had deliberated for just six minutes before making its decision. The jury stated, "We feel a grave injustice has been done him and there was not the slightest proof to connect him in any way with the commission of any crime." The defense had denigrated Miss Rappe's reputation and shown that witnesses' conflicting testimony was the result of the lack of clear thinking, due to drinking, at the time of the 1921 incident. Charges of jury tampering and bribery, as well as interference with witnesses, were rampant for a brief while but came to naught.

The American public clearly did not agree with the verdict, for it soon criticized the once-loved "Fatty" to such an extent that the newly formed Hays Office, which was Hollywood's attempt to clean up its tarnished image, banned his movies. Paramount Pictures canceled his contract, and Arbuckle was then banned from acting, falling into despair, with few friends remaining faithful to him. Unable to act, Arbuckle had to assume a different name, that of William Goodrich, to find work as a gag writer or director, and he turned to drinking heavily to forget what the public would not. By 1933 many had forgiven him, and Warner Brothers then offered him his first movie acting role since the scandal erupted. In the early morning of June 29, 1933, just hours after finishing the filming of *In the Dough,* he died of a heart attack in his sleep in his New York hotel room. Two years earlier, Arbuckle had said he held "no resentment against anybody for what [had] happened."

Robert ARCHBALD: unworthy of public office

In 1913, at the age of 64 and after nearly 29 years on the bench, Robert W. Archbald, judge of the U.S. Commerce Court and former United States district court judge in Pennsylvania, was impeached and convicted by the U.S. Senate on charges of using his office and influence for his own financial benefit. While serving on a court that had judicial jurisdiction over railroad companies, Archbald had amassed stocks, leaseholds, and other interests in railroads, coal companies, and gold-mining operations.

Archbald, a native of Pennsylvania, had graduated from Yale University in 1871. After studying law in Scranton, he became a district judge in Pennsylvania and was later named presiding judge of his district, a post he resigned in 1901 to become a United States district court judge. In 1910 President William Howard Taft appointed Archbald a United States circuit judge and assigned him to the Commerce Court.

Archbald's problems with railroads and coal companies were a theme throughout his career. He had lost all the money he had inherited from his father, a railroad engineer; when a coal company in which Archbald held a great deal of stock collapsed, Archbald was criticized by the Supreme Court of Pennsylvania for his part in that company's transactions, which were described as "evasive of the law and a fraud upon the public."

In 1912 the U.S. Justice Department began probing conflict-of-interest charges against Archbald. Investigators learned that Archbald had used his position on the Commerce Court to induce railroads to sell cheaply or to lease coal companies to him. Among other improprieties, he had accepted a free trip to Europe for his family and himself from a railroad executive whose companies had matters pending before the Commerce Court. He had accepted substantial sums of money from a railroad in exchange for his support in its litigation with another railroad over the transfer of coal leases. And he himself had speculated in coal properties while on the bench. And although the Commerce Court on which he served had been created to review the orders and decisions of the U.S. Interstate Commerce Commission (which regulated railroads and other carriers in interstate commerce), Archbald had accepted money to intervene in cases before the ICC.

Archbald was also charged with a series of crimes while serving as district judge. He was accused of accepting "loans" from attorneys and their clients while presiding over their cases. Two court officers whom Archbald had appointed solicited money on his behalf. Archbald had also appointed the general counsel to the Lehigh Valley Railroad Company to act as a jury commissioner in the judge's district, a position that allowed the counsel to select prospective jurors for cases involving his own railroad company.

At his 1913 trial before the Senate, Archbald faced 13 articles of impeachment. The judge admitted many of the facts charged against him but denied any criminal intent. The Senate acquitted him of the charges dating from his years as district judge but found him guilty of actions while serving on the Commerce Court. He was convicted of four articles of impeachment involving cases with the Erie Railroad, the Lehigh Valley Railroad, the Louisville & Nashville Railroad, and the Philadelphia & Reading Railroad. The fifth article of which he was found guilty was a blanket charge summarizing the long list of specific complaints against him.

Upon conviction, Archbald was removed from office. The Senate also voted that he be "forever disqualified to hold and enjoy any office of honor, trust or profit under the United States." In an editorial following the decision, the *New York Times* stated, "The Judge was removed from his office because it was proved that his standard of judicial conduct was low, that he was hopelessly dull to the requirements of his position, and that he set an example that made corruption easier."

After his removal from office, Archbald practiced law in Scranton, Pennsylvania. In 1914, apparently little chagrined by his conviction, he sued the government to recover $588 for expenses he had incurred in his last few months on the bench, a period during which impeachment proceedings against him were already underway.

ARMY'S ABERDEEN SEX SCANDAL. See U.S. ARMY'S ABERDEEN SEX SCANDAL.

ARMY-McCARTHY HEARINGS. See Joseph McCARTHY: outgunned by the Army.

Benedict ARNOLD: hero turned traitor

At the outbreak of the American Revolution in 1775, Benedict Arnold, a prosperous merchant in New Haven, Connecticut, and captain of the local militia, immediately volunteered his services. As a commissioned colonel in America's revolutionary army, he gained battlefield glory against the British at Ticonderoga, New York, and again at Saint Johns, Quebec. His courageous, daring attempt to seize the well-fortified city of Quebec in late 1775 ended in failure, with the killing of General Richard Montgomery, whose American forces had combined with Arnold's in the attack. Arnold also was left with a severe leg wound. The Continental Congress later made Arnold a brigadier general, despite some protests against Arnold's apparent rashness.

Arnold held Montreal until forced to retreat in mid-1776. On Lake Champlain he constructed a flotilla that checked the larger British fleet until October of that year, after which Arnold was compelled to retreat to Ticonderoga. Although he viewed his actions in these events as remarkable military exploits against superior British forces, Congress was apparently less impressed. In February of 1777 it promoted five brigadier generals who were Arnold's juniors to major generals. Insulted, he threatened to resign his commission. General George Washington managed to persuade him to remain in the army, and later in 1777, after Arnold's gallant leadership in crushing the British in battle in western Connecticut, Congress was forced to make him a major general. It did not restore his seniority, however, which rankled him to the point of near resignation. Again, Washington coaxed him to remain.

Still feeling his honor slighted, Arnold nonetheless performed brilliantly, leading troops to halt British advances in upper New York, where he was seriously wounded in battle at Saratoga in October 1777. For his outstanding service in helping gain an American victory there, Congress sent him a commission as a major general and restored his seniority in rank.

In June 1778, General Washington appointed Arnold commander of the Philadelphia area, and there the latter led a highly social life, incurring large debts from his extravagances and becoming involved in quarrels with Pennsylvania authorities over the arbitrary use of his military authority and his supposed favoritism to Loyalists. Arnold's marriage in 1779 to Peggy Shippen, daughter of a wealthy Pennsylvania judge who had Tory connections, brought him in contact with Sir Henry Clinton, British commander-in-chief in North America, with whom he carried on a secret correspondence for a few months in 1779. Past injustices and increasing dissatisfaction with the American cause then led Arnold to offer secretly military information to the British in exchange for a considerable sum of money.

Meanwhile, Arnold's enemies in Congress managed to bring charges of both military and civil impropriety against him, and he sought to clear himself by requesting an immediate court-martial, which was held in Norris's Tavern in Morristown, New Jersey, on December 23, 1779. Arnold's main accusers were the president and secretary of the Pennsylvania State Council, Joseph Reed and Timothy Matlack, respectively, and the charges against him consisted of giving a military pass to an alleged Loyalist businessman in Philadelphia, of closing stores arbitrarily to the public, of forcing "free" persons to do menial tasks, and of using public (state) wagons to carry private property. After hearing Arnold personally and eloquently defend himself, the court acquitted him of intentional wrongdoing but recommended that he receive a reprimand from his commander in chief, Washington, who reluctantly did so. The rebuke apparently infuriated Arnold, who renewed his clandestine correspondence with Clinton and revealed an American proposal to invade Canada. Given command of West Point, New York, in August 1780, Arnold secretly offered to surrender the vital fort to Clinton for £20,000, but the deal fell through when Major John André, Clinton's messenger, was taken into custody by American troops and some papers about the surrender plan were found hidden in his stocking. Arnold managed to escape to New York City and board a British warship, leaving André to be hanged as a spy. Arnold secured a British brigadier general's commission and a sum of money, led marauding expeditions in Virginia (1780) and Connecticut (1781), and became increasingly despised by Americans. His burning of New London, Connecticut, and massacre of the nearby garrison of Fort Griswold in September 1781, were never forgiven by his one-time Connecticut neighbors.

In late 1781 Arnold sailed to England. The British, however, never gave him the recognition or praise that he had deeply longed for. Their dislike for Arnold was almost as strong as that of the Americans. To the British,

Arnold's "sacrifice" of André was heinous. Deeply embittered, Arnold and his wife lived on small government pensions in England. Having tried without success to begin life anew in trade in Canada and the West Indies, Arnold died meanly in London on June 14, 1801.

ASBESTOS SCANDAL. See JOHNS-MANVILLE ASBESTOS CASE: products hazardous to health.

Mary ASTOR: the "purple" diary

For a time in 1936 the American public was both shocked and enthralled by revelations from a leather, blue-bound, personal diary supposedly penned by one of Hollywood's most spotless beauties, 30-year-old Mary Astor. The diary, written between 1929 and 1934, contained some exceptionally uninhibited remarks about screen luminaries and their life, as well as the alleged sensational sexual liaison between Mary Astor and George S. Kaufman, noted New York critic, playwright, and director. The urbane Kaufman, not particularly attractive with his large nose and thick glasses, and the lovely, innocent-looking Astor seemed an unlikely pair to have a torrid affair that brought moments of "thrilling ecstasy," as stated in the diary.

Actress Mary Astor adjusts her hat in a Los Angeles courtroom in August 1936 when she sought full custody of her four-year-old daughter, Marilyn. The case caused a sensation across the country because of revelations about her earlier extramarital trysts with playwright George S. Kaufman and publication of details from her personal diary. (AP/Wide World Photos)

The tabloids and other newspapers obtained from a "reliable source" entries in the diary and published them. The public's imagination went wild on reading such passages as "remarkable staying power. I don't see how he does it!" and "we saw every show in town, had grand fun together and went frequently to 73rd Street where he fucked the living daylights out of me." and "Was any woman happier? It seems that George is just hard all the time. I don't see how he does it, he is perfect." Astor denied writing the most salacious entries or claimed the press had distorted them. Just the same, she was viewed differently with each titillating clause, such as "Ah, desert night—with George's body plunging into mine, naked under the stars."

The popular screen actress's three-year-long marriage to Dr. Franklyn Thorpe had been falling apart when she left Hollywood, where she had been working steadily under contract in various film roles, to take a break in New York City in the summer of 1933. There she soon met and fell in love with the talented Kaufman, with whom she attended the theater and many parties and purportedly began extramarital trysts that went on into 1935. Kaufman, who was also married, introduced her to many friends, such as Moss Hart, and made her life quite "wonderful" (one diary entry said, "Once George lays down his glasses, he is *quite* a different man.").

Dr. Thorpe found the diary in his wife's bedroom drawer by accident in 1935 and promptly confronted her about the affair, which she refused to end. In retaliation, he apparently took up with a number of blonde showgirls and then sued Mary for divorce and de-manded custody of their daughter Marilyn. She did not contest the divorce but filed a countersuit to retain custody of Marilyn, whom she adored immeasurably. Their legal battle for custody of the child went to court in 1936.

On the first day of the trial, Thorpe's attorneys attempted to introduce as evidence the diary, previously kept secret, which presiding judge Goodwin Knight (soon to be elected California governor) refused to accept but which the press somehow latched onto with all its lurid details. Americans saw both parties attempt to denigrate the character of each other to prove they were more fit to raise the child; published excerpts from the diary heightened public interest in Hollywood personalities, who feared for their careers because of nefarious innuendoes. The highly publicized trial was held at night to allow Astor to complete work on her latest film for Samuel Goldwyn. The case was finally decided (1936), with custody of Marilyn going to Astor for nine months each year and to Thorpe for three months. The diary was destroyed by the court.

Mary Astor's career did not suffer from these revelations. Filmgoers liked her acting, which won her an Academy Award for best supporting actress in *The Great Lie* in 1941. Her career flourished until 1949, when she entered a sanatorium for alcoholics. After recovering, she turned to writing (six novels and two memoirs), with occasional movie appearances. In 1987, at age 81, she died of respiratory failure due to pulmonary emphysema.

B

Benjamin Franklin BACHE: vengeance through journalism

During the early years of the American republic, political journalism was far removed from objective coverage and often crossed the border into slander. Against such Federalists as George Washington and John Adams, Republican journalists freely used lies, canards, and misrepresentations in their newspapers until 1798, when, to protect themselves, the Federalist incumbents passed the Sedition Act. One of the most vicious slanderers was Benjamin Franklin Bache, young grandson of Benjamin Franklin and publisher of Philadelphia's *General Advertiser* (later, *The Aurora*), who was determined by hook or by crook to destroy George Washington's reputation.

Often called "Benny," young Bache also had a second nickname, "Lightning Rod, Junior." He gained the moniker because of his habit of administering high-voltage verbal shocks to prominent Federalists like John Jay and presidents Washington and Adams. But he also had a personal grudge against George Washington which made him attack the first president with scurrilities whose falsity and personal nature remain unsurpassed.

Bache believed that political leaders are obliged to reward their friends, even to the third generation. Washington opposed this doctrine of patronage when Bache's father had asked to be named postmaster general in 1782; his rejection made Bache believe, without evidence, that Washington had personally blocked the appointment. Bache himself had been turned down for another government job. The cause, he felt, was Washington's ingratitude to the first Benjamin Franklin. Washington was therefore a scapegrace who had to be punished.

Unaware of the doctrine that one should not get angry but instead get even, Bache yielded to anger and then yielded to the temptation to get even.

To punish Washington, Bache descended from yellow journalism to flights of personal vituperation which should have been combatted by libel suits. Washington, however, was a gentleman (as Bache proved not to be); he did not believe in libel suits or duels, and certainly not between a man in his 50s and another in his 20s.

Washington suffered when the venom-tongued Bache accused him of putting on royal airs, of possessing "treacherous mazes of passion," of being a "despotic, anemic counterfeit of the English Georges." He remained publicly silent when Bache printed the attacks of others as an addendum to his own. Bache had become aware that Thomas Paine, whose *Rights of Man* had effusively praised Washington, was now the president's detractor. Like Bache, Paine believed that a man in power should help his friends; when Washington had refused to violate his own Neutrality Act to free the British-born author from a British jail, Paine exploded, attacking the president violently as apathetic and ungrateful. Bache gleefully printed the attack.

He also sank so low as to reprint a series of seven letters falsely attributed to Washington. Conceived in 1776 by a British ministry, they had been forgotten by the 1790s, and many now believed their insinuations that Washington had a busy extramarital life and longed for a return of British control. With these letters as background, Bache accused his enemy of having been a secret traitor during the American War of Independence.

Bache's attempt to be personally destructive did not stop when Washington returned to Mount Vernon as a private citizen. He asserted his joy upon Washington's retirement, moralistically stating that "If ever a nation has been debauched by a man, the American nation has been debauched by Washington."

Washington now broke his silence by writing to a sympathetic friend: "The man Bache has a celebrity in a certain way. His calumnies are exceeded only by his Impudence [sic], and both stand unrivalled."

Washington refused to respond to Bache's revilement or to seek legal redress. But John Adams did: relying on the newly passed Sedition Act of 1798 (soon to be proven unconstitutional), he had Bache charged and arrested. Bache's reputation fell; it was already low among the Federalists, who considered him an agent of the French Directory. Released on parole, Bache quieted his language. He died of yellow fever in 1798, before he could face legal punishment for his libelous vituperations.

Tony BAEKELAND: decadence and death among the elite

The great-grandson of Leo Baekeland, the "father of plastics," 26-year-old Antony or Tony Baekeland seemed to have everything going for him. Young, handsome, and wealthy, Tony was born into an elite and glamorous family. But in 1972 he created a scandal which shocked the entire nation. While living abroad in London he quarreled with his mother over a minor matter and in a rage grabbed a kitchen knife and fatally stabbed her in the heart. Sentenced to Broadmoor Special Hospital for the criminally insane, he was sent home to America seven years later to live with Nini, his 86-year-old bedridden maternal grandmother but within a week attacked her, too, and was again arrested. He took his own life eight months later in a jail cell on New York's Rikers Island.

Tony Baekeland had several strikes against him from the moment he was born, for there were genetic defects in the families of both parents. His great-grandfather, Leo, had amassed a fortune from his invention of Bakelite, the first plastic, but was a tyrannical, masochistic man. His grandson, Brooks, Tony's father, had a brilliant mind but never used it for any constructive purpose. On Tony's mother's side, the Dalys came from a long line of violent, aberrant, and suicidal men.

As an only child, Tony was alternately smothered by his mother's excessive attentions or neglected while his parents gallivanted to parties and reveled in long weekends. Acquaintances reported that his upbringing was "appalling." His beautiful redheaded mother, Barbara, was flamboyant, charming, artistic, and tempestuous, while his philandering father largely ignored him. His parents fought constantly, and Barbara slashed her wrists once when Brooks threatened divorce. Four times she attempted suicide.

After exhausting the pleasure of New York society, the Baekelands set out to conquer Europe in 1954 and thereafter resided in a succession of rented villas and apartments in Paris, Mallorca, London, and elsewhere, while living like a latter-day Caresse and Harry CROSBY. It soon became apparent that young Tony was a homosexual, admitting to one of his many psychiatrists that he had his first sexual experience when he was eight. At 14, when his parents were absent, he went out at night, picked up older boys, and brought them home. When she found this out, his mother became hysterical, trying everything she could think of to "cure" him. When Tony became a young man (he attended numerous prep schools), his mother tried unsuccessfully to

set him up with older girls. One such girl, Sylvie, turned out to be a good friend whom Tony's father then seduced, after which the two of them ran off to Brittany together. In desperation, and after a suicide attempt, Barbara herself seduced her son. Both confessed to friends that they were sleeping incestuously together.

It also became apparent that Tony was suffering from mental illness. He had hallucinations, delusions, and periods of mania. In March 1971, a doctor diagnosed him as having paranoid schizophrenia and recommended hospitalization and psychotherapy, but his father was unwilling to pay for his treatment, claiming it as more of the "fun and games" that Tony and his mother were playing. With his illness and a drug habit that included cocaine, marijuana, hashish, or LSD, the younger Baekeland's behavior grew increasingly outlandish. At a dinner party given by his mother, he stalked from the table, reappeared stark naked, and streaked across the room.

Those who knew Tony and his mother intimately were not surprised at the matricide. On a weekend at East Hampton, New York, the two accused each other of sexual misconduct and threw things at each other. While his mother taunted him, Tony seized a knife, which a guest wrestled from his hand. The guest then pulled him off his mother, whom he was trying to choke. On another occasion, in London, Tony chased his mother from the house, grabbed her by the hair, and tried to throw her in front of passing cars. Eighteen days before the murder, a psychoanalyst warned Barbara that her son would kill her. She didn't believe him.

On the fatal afternoon of November 11, 1972, Tony and Barbara began to quarrel. He hit her with his fist and she ran into the kitchen. He raced after her, snatched a knife, and plunged it into her heart. He then called an ambulance. The police followed, and Tony was driven off to prison.

Seven months later he was brought to trial in London and found "guilty of manslaughter under diminished responsibility." For the next seven years he was confined to Broadmoor, where he gradually began to function normally. His beloved grandmother, Nini Daly, and friends sought his repatriation, but his father objected, saying "The tiger still rages within." The Home Office eventually authorized the younger Baekeland's release, and on Monday, July 17, 1980, he flew to the United States "to look after Nini and cook for her and do marvelous things for her."

But it didn't work out that way. Nini's tiny apartment was hot and confining, and the pictures of his mother and her ashes in an urn on the mantle upset Tony. He began to hallucinate again. By Sunday he decided to leave and began telephoning airlines to find a flight to Mallorca. When his grandmother begged him to stop, he yelled at her to "shut up" and threw the telephone at the frail old lady, knocking her down. He rushed to the kitchen, returned with a knife, and began stabbing her in the chest and arms. At that moment the elderly woman's day nurse arrived, heard the screaming, and ran to call the police and an ambulance. Miraculously Nini survived this savage attack.

Tony was sent to the New York City penitentiary on Rikers Island to await trial for attempted murder. On March 30, 1981, after returning from a court session at which he had been denied bail, he asked to be locked in his cell. About an hour later, a correction officer found his lifeless body stretched out on the bed under a blanket. He had suffocated himself by tying a plastic bag over his head.

The horrific story of Tony and the prominent Baekelands, whose psychic tensions grew over a span of four generations and erupted in matricide, is presented in a long, indirect chronicle called *Savage Grace* (1985) by Natalie Robins and Steven M. L. Aronson. It is an unforgettable true story.

Bobby BAKER: wheeler-dealer with high-level machinations

In 1955, Robert Gene "Bobby" Baker, a former Senate page boy from South Carolina who had become an effective legislative strategist on Capitol Hill, was hired by Senate Majority Leader Lyndon B. Johnson to be his secretary at a yearly salary of $9,000 (at the time, Baker's net worth was estimated to be $11,000). Eight years later, in 1963, Baker's annual salary had risen to $19,600 and his personal fortune was put at about $2,250,000. Baker's extensive business dealings, which supposedly involved numerous important Washington, D.C., politicians, then became the subject of a long, tangled Senate investigation following public disclosure that Baker allegedly improperly used his influence in the Senate to obtain defense plant contracts for his vending machine firm, the Serv-U Corporation. Political backroom maneuvers failed to stop the investigation, which sought to unravel Baker's connections to high-level public officials and his reported receipt of illegal payments, as well as his payoffs. The scandal involving Baker frightened a number of powerful persons in the Washington establishment in 1963–64.

The American public first learned of Baker's business shenanigans when the *Washington Post* revealed on September 12, 1963, that a federal court suit had been filed against him by a disgruntled fellow vending-machine-company owner, who objected to paying a $5,600 fee to Baker in order to get his machines into a company that was working for the government. Baker was charged with using political influence to gain contracts for his vending machine company; his name was closely linked with Johnson, who had become vice president of the United States in 1961 and who had treated him like "a son" for many years in the past.

Baker was immediately suspected of having used his high contacts for personal gain; some of his business ventures had received tax breaks through specially passed House legislation. At the urging of Republicans hoping to tarnish the image of the Democratic Kennedy-Johnson administration, the Senate decided to investigate Baker and his financial affairs. But to escape interrogation by Senate leaders in executive session, Baker resigned on October 7, 1963. Johnson continued to try to curtail any inquiry, especially that of Republican Senator John J. Williams of Delaware. He also estranged himself completely and his former protégé. But even after Kennedy's assassination had elevated Johnson to the presidency, he still could not stop the probe by the Senate Rules Committee into Baker's activities.

At hearings held by the Senate committee in 1964, witnesses gave some damning testimony against Baker, who was accused of helping a friend sell Johnson expensive life-insurance policies (more than $200,000 worth) in the 1950s, in return for the friend's agreement to buy advertising time on Mrs. Johnson's Texas radio station. Baker was also accused of giving an alleged $100,000 payoff to Johnson for pushing through a $7-billion TFX plane contract for the Texas-based General Dynamics Corporation. Besides this, Baker was also accused of receiving an illegal $25,000 payment, allegedly from Democratic National Committee Treasurer Matthew H. McCloskey, to be channeled into the 1960 Kennedy-Johnson campaign fund. Members of the committee were unable to get much out of Baker when he appeared before them in February 1964; he said nothing to hurt his friends in high places and invoked the Fifth Amendment to the Constitution against self-incrimination. The hearings ended on March 25, 1964, and in July the committee said Baker had been "guilty of many gross improprieties" in his business dealings, which included oil, land, and bank operations, having used his Washington connections and inside information to buy properties, float companies, and help business friends.

In the months afterward, the Bobby Baker scandal became a hot political issue, with Republican presidential candidate Barry M. Goldwater charging that "Baker's affairs lead right straight into the White House." The public was not especially scandalized, but it did gloat over charges that Baker had allegedly supplied his male political friends with young female beauties on numerous occasions in the past. Congressmen, lobbyists, and aides were known to frequent Washington's Quorum Club, which Baker had helped found and partly owned and where scantily clad lovelies served customers in erotically decorated surroundings. To many, Baker was just a shrewd, middle-aged playboy.

After President Johnson won reelection in 1964, the U.S. Justice Department and Treasury Department uncovered new evidence of wrongdoing by the fun-loving

South Carolinian, who was finally brought to trial in January 1967. Baker was charged with seven counts of tax evasion, one count of theft, and one count of conspiracy to defraud the government. He was found guilty, made a series of vain appeals, and eventually went to the federal penitentiary in Lewisburg, Pennsylvania, in January 1971 to serve a one-to-three year sentence. In 1972, after serving 17 months, he was paroled.

Jim BAKKER: adulterous Christian evangelist

On March 19, 1987, the Reverend Jim Bakker, a popular Pentecostal evangelist, suddenly and unexpectedly announced his resignation as head of the PTL (for Praise the Lord or People That Love) Network, carried by cable television to 13.5 million American households. Legal action was pending against him because of a one-time-only sexual encounter he had had with a comely church secretary seven years earlier. The subsequent revelations about the boyish-looking, 47-year-old Bakker, who gave up control of a vast Christian entertainment operation that he had built up over the past 13 years, tainted every gospel ministry in America. To many critics and viewers alike, the gospel telecasting

Jim and Tammy Bakker confront newsmen outside their Palm Springs, California, home on May 28, 1987. Earlier that evening, the couple had defended themselves on the ABC-TV show Nightline, *hosted by Ted Koppel, while they discussed the scandal surrounding their role at the head of the PTL ministry. (AP/Wide World Photos)*

preachers seemed to be more concerned with the God of Mammon than with the spirit of Christ.

Almost simultaneously with Bakker's announcement that he was quitting came the shocking news of his fateful sexual dalliance, which first broke in the Charlotte, North Carolina, *Observer.* The PTL Network was headquartered nearby. Immediately the story was picked up and spread nationwide by the media. According to various reports, the Reverend Bakker had met Jessica Hahn, a 21-year-old brunette, during a visit to Clearwater Beach, Florida, in December 1980. At the time, Bakker's 19-year marriage to his wife Tammy Faye, who was co-host on his religious TV show, was foundering, and the preacher engaged in sex for an hour at a hotel with Hahn, who was then a secretary for the Full Gospel Tabernacle, a Pentecostal church in Massapequa, New York. Hahn reportedly suffered emotional distress after the brief illicit liaison with Bakker, and in 1985 she and her representatives struck a deal with his representatives from the PTL. The Reverend Richard Dortch, Bakker's top aide, helped negotiate the deal and was reportedly involved in buying Hahn's silence, arranging "hush money" of $265,000 to be paid to her and her representatives or advisers. The PTL people agreed to pay the Hahn people $115,000 and established a $150,000 trust fund, with interest paid out monthly to the latter. In return, Hahn was to keep quiet about her liaison with Bakker and was not to file a lawsuit for the next 20 years. By so doing, she would eventually get the $150,000 in the covert trust fund.

However, the Reverend Jimmy SWAGGART, a fiery evangelist and rival of Bakker's, heard rumors about Bakker's tryst with Hahn and shortly alerted the officials of the Assemblies of God, the Pentecostal denomination in which both he and Bakker were clergymen. Swaggart, whose ministries earned in 1986 an estimated $140 million and were based in Baton Rouge, Louisiana, was a crusading revivalist with a television audience of 8 million people. Church leaders began an investigation into Bakker's apparent "moral failure" and cover-up.

Just before the scandalous public disclosures about himself, Bakker quit the PTL, admitted his adultery and payment of "blackmail," and handed control of the PTL to fellow TV preacher Jerry Falwell. The Reverend Falwell, a well-known Baptist fundamentalist based in Lynchburg, Virginia, aired his sermons on a program called the *Old Time Gospel Hour* over 350 television stations.

Bakker said that he had quit to stop a "diabolical plot" by a rival evangelist (later said to be Swaggart) to take over his multimillion-dollar ministry and affiliated enterprises. The PTL empire encompassed the cable television network, the daily television talk show hosted by Jim and Tammy Bakker, and a 2,300-acre Christian amusement park and resort complex (called "Heritage

USA") in Fort Mill, South Carolina. These enterprises had taken in $129 million in revenues in 1986.

Only days before Bakker quit, his 45-year-old wife Tammy created a minor scandal by admitting publicly on their TV show that she was drug dependent. By the end of March 1987, she and her husband were under treatment at a California center for addicts, and various "televangelists," including Swaggart and Oral Roberts (another Pentecostal preacher, headquartered in Tulsa, Oklahoma), were feuding about the Bakker scandal and charges of greed, sex, and un-Christian ministerial rivalries. The Reverend Falwell helped to reconstitute the PTL board of directors and promised that the ministry's house would be put in order and its policies would be laid bare; he hoped to check and patch up the damage done by the exposés.

The Bakkers' overturn was painful to both of them. "Jim and I are both very sad," said Tammy at a lavish hideaway in Palm Springs, California, in April 1987. "We're hurting." About four weeks later, however, Jim Bakker was supposedly threatening a "holy war" to regain control of the PTL empire. At the same time, new allegations were made that he had had relations with prostitutes, had engaged in homosexuality, and had allowed wife-swapping among his assistants.

On May 6, 1987, Bakker and Dortch were dismissed as ministers of the Assemblies of God church, whose board, in Bakker's case, cited "alleged misconduct involving bisexual activity." A Southern Baptist televangelist from Tennessee, the Reverend John Ankerberg, had claimed shortly before this that he had evidence that Bakker had engaged in homosexual acts and used prostitutes and that PTL leaders engaged in wife-swapping. Bakker denied Ankerberg's allegations.

While the PTL ministry was going bankrupt and its control was being fought over, Hahn appeared on the cover of the November issue of *Playboy* magazine, which supposedly paid three-quarters of a million dollars for a topless photo display of her and a lengthy interview in which Hahn said, "I'm not a bimbo." When the former owner of a house of prostitution claimed that Hahn had worked for her as a prostitute in the late 1970s, Hahn vehemently claimed that she was a virgin before her 1980 encounter with Bakker. By 1988, the entire scandal had become a seeming caricature of an age of people obsessed with money, power, and status to the point of fanaticism.

In a federal trial in Charlotte, North Carolina, in October 1989, Bakker was found guilty as charged on all 24 counts of defrauding the public of $3.7 million via TV, telephone, and mail. Dortch, who testified for the prosecution, had earlier received eight years in prison and a $200,000 fine; other staff members who provided evidence received prison terms for tax evasion. Bakker was sentenced to 45 years in prison and fined $500,000. He was released from prison in 1994 after serving about

five years, during which time his wife Tammy divorced him and married his best friend from his PTL days. Both Bakker and Tammy Faye Messner published books in 1996: *I Was Wrong: The Untold Story of the Shocking Journey from PTL Power to Prison and Beyond* and *Tammy: Telling It My Way*, respectively.

BALLINGER-PINCHOT CONTROVERSY

Recipe for an effective conflict: mix a large portion of disagreement over policy, one change in administration, a well-aged interdepartmental rivalry, at least three inflexible personalities, a suppressed report alleging fraud, and several ineffectual attempts to bring about peace and order. Simmer at a moderate temperature for three years. Raise the temperature to high during the next year by adding two dismissals and a muckraking congressional investigation. The result will be a delicious tidbit to delight historians, cause indigestion among the public, and split the Republican party. Antidote: the election of a Democratic president.

The formula above describes the highly complex Ballinger-Pinchot controversy over conservation policies. It helped cause the failure of the reelection bid of U.S. President William Howard Taft and the ascendancy of Woodrow Wilson.

At bottom, the controversy revolved around whether public Alaskan coal lands would be leased or sold. Conservationists then argued that sale of the lands through 160-acre claims opened the possibility of their development by robber-baron financiers; the policies of Theodore Roosevelt emphasized the leasing procedure. But in 1906 Richard Achilles Ballinger, then head of the U.S. General Land Office, had, despite the Roosevelt policies, approved the claims of one Clarence Cunningham to 5,280 acres of Alaskan coalfields. The approval was questioned as illegal by Land Office special agents, including one Louis Russell Glavis, was referred to Roosevelt's secretary of the interior, James Richard Garfield, and was promptly rescinded.

The 1908 election of Taft briefly made Ballinger a private citizen and, in defiance of existing regulations, he became Cunningham's legal advisor. When he was appointed Taft's interior secretary in 1909, one of Ballinger's first acts was another violation of regulations: he reapproved the Cunningham claims.

Reenter Glavis, who presented evidence that Cunningham had a connection with financial interests of the huge J. P. Morgan-Guggenheim empire. Because the Cunningham claims lay adjacent to a national forest, Glavis also alerted Gifford Pinchot, head of the Forest Service of the U.S. Department of Agriculture, whose forest policy had been opposed by western anticonservationists, including Ballinger. Pinchot saw an opportunity to oust Ballinger if the Glavis evidence were rejected.

DAVID BALTIMORE 25

It was. Ballinger sent it to a supporter in the Justice Department, who decided that the evidence was too weak for consideration. Then, angry at Glavis for alerting Pinchot and thereby revealing that he was not a team player, Ballinger went to Taft, who saw in the controversy a plot by Garfield (now a private and powerful conservationist) and Pinchot to embarrass him. But Taft, anxious to prevent the ancient rivalry between Agriculture and Interior departments from being made public, and annoyed by Glavis and Pinchot, played by the rules and tried to act as mediator. Glavis sent him a 50-page argument; Ballinger sent a 1,000-page memorandum. Taft decided the important matter by its weight rather than his promise to maintain the Roosevelt policies. He also accepted Ballinger's recommendation that Glavis be fired "for disloyalty to his superior officers in making a false charge against them." His judgment satisfied all contemporary civil-service rules.

Glavis's reaction was, by civil service proprieties, a colossal insubordination: late in 1909, he sold his version of the controversy to the muckraking *Collier's Weekly.* Other media picked it up, and the conflict gained international coverage.

Taft again tried to mediate but failed because Pinchot went public. To support Ballinger, Taft fired Pinchot and found himself the subject of a congressional investigation from January 26 through May 20, 1910.

Labeled by many a "whitewash," the investigation decided in favor of Ballinger, but the publicity destroyed both Ballinger and Taft. During the hearing, Louis D. Brandeis, then an attorney retained as counsel for Glavis by *Collier's,* had, through careful questioning, caused astute journalists (but not a majority of the investigators) to become aware of weaknesses in the administration's case.

Brandeis isolated and emphasized Ballinger's violations concerning Cunningham's claims, Ballinger's ineptness in concentrating on his defense of his reputation (which caused him to attack Roosevelt's policies), and Taft's errors. He was able to show that Ballinger had not been Taft's choice but that of his patronage broker, Postmaster General Frank H. Hitchcock. He disclosed that Taft had not studied the Glavis and Ballinger memoranda but had relied on the judgment of a Ballinger supporter in the Justice Department. And he disclosed that Taft had lied about the dismissal of Glavis.

Taft—famed for his procrastination—delayed the obvious cover-up for the lie; he announced that he had "misremembered" after the press had convicted him and Ballinger and vindicated Glavis and Pinchot.

Taft had lost politically by dismissing Glavis and Pinchot in order to support Ballinger. His maneuvering had cost him Roosevelt's support, and it had split the Republican Party into an "Old Guard" of traditionalists and a new group of "Bull Moose" progressives. By 1912, the split enabled the Democrats to elect Woodrow Wilson.

David BALTIMORE: data falsification at MIT?

Lying. Cheating. Stealing. Pretenses aside, this is what Nobel Laureate David Baltimore found himself accused of for his involvement with a published report suspected of containing fabricated experimental results.

In 1985, Margot O'Toole, a postdoctoral fellow at the Massachusetts Institute of Technology (MIT), was assigned to conduct experiments which would further the research findings of noted Brazilian immunologist Thereza Imanishi-Kari. The results had been published in a collaborative report with Baltimore as the senior author. When O'Toole could not reproduce Imanishi-Kari's results, she surmised that the data was fudged. She complained to a friend, who alerted authorities at the National Institutes of Health (NIH), which then launched a full-scale investigation of the matter. It became known as the "Baltimore Case," named after the experiment's lead scientist, and spanned the length of a decade. The case pitted the government against the scientific community and tossed the public's perception of the fallibility of modern science into the tangle.

John Dingell led the investigation by the House Subcommittee on Oversight and Investigation and the NIH's Office of Scientific Integrity. According to an NIH draft report, the committee found a pattern of data falsification for Imanishi-Kari's contribution to the paper. In an age when federal funding for basic research had begun to dwindle, the public and media wondered whether the apparent fudging was a ruse to secure financial support by assuring astounding experimental results.

In 1975, Baltimore was awarded the Nobel Prize in Physiology or Medicine for his work with Renato Dulbecco and Howard M. Temin when they experimentally verified Temin's hypothesis that cancer cells may affect genetic material. For a time, he conducted virology research at the Salk Institute and later took a professorship at MIT. He became a big name, with a big lab, and a big budget.

The questionable experiment was a complicated one that continued his research in the field of immunology and genetics. Baltimore stood behind his Brazilian colleague and vouched for her integrity. Though others were involved, Baltimore's name was listed first on the report, and so his standing within the scientific community took a beating. At first, scientists around the country sided with him as they took exception to the investigation, calling it a "witch hunt." Soon, though, the tide turned, and as the campaign dragged on, even Baltimore tried to distance himself from the paper in question, asking in 1991 that it be retracted. He left Imanishi-Kari alone to defend her findings and face the chance of having her funding cut off. After nearly a decade of investigation, Imanishi-Kari was eventually cleared of charges.

Though Baltimore went on to become the president of the California Institute of Technology in Pasadena, California, the effects of the investigation had dire consequences for Baltimore's career at the time. He was forced to resign from his post as president of Rockefeller University in the early 1990s, and his reputation as a scientist was jeopardized.

Though the field of science is self-regulatory for the most part, the Baltimore case not only hinted at the threat of deeper government involvement and regulation of the scientific domain, but it also illustrated how easy it may be to violate the strict ethical code of science and nearly get away with it.

Sydney Biddle BARROWS: the "Mayflower Madam"

"I had no moral problems, because escort services fill an age old, human need."

These may sound like the words of some street-smart pimp, but the author was, in fact a young, attractive college graduate with a nearly impeccable family background. Sydney Biddle Barrows, descendant of two *Mayflower* Pilgrims whose name was listed in the social register, was as strong-willed and unrepentant about her occupation as her ancestors must have been about leaving England two centuries earlier.

Barrows was indicted in December 1984 in New York City on charges of promoting prostitution in the third degree. Under the guise of a temporary-employment agency, she operated three escort services as covers for an expensive call-girl operation. Using the name Sheila Devin, she hired and trained call girls who earned as much as $2,000 a night. At the time of her arrest, she employed 20 girls in a $1-million-a-year business.

Barrows' nickname, the "Mayflower Madam," was bestowed on her by the tabloid press when it was discovered that her socially prominent family was directly connected with *Mayflower* ancestors, including the Elder William Brewster, the minister who led the group that landed at Plymouth Rock in 1620. The press jumped on the story of this 32-year-old woman who was in the Social Register yet had chosen as her calling the oldest profession.

In July 1985, Barrows pleaded guilty in New York State Superior Court to the misdemeanor of fourth-degree promotion of prostitution, as part of a deal offered by the district attorney. She paid a fine of $5,000 and received an unconditional discharge as well as a certificate of relief from civil penalties, which included the stipulation that no employment opportunities be denied her because of her criminal record.

Additionally, the district attorney returned documents seized at the time of her arrest containing the information about her clients, which meant that no names of clients would be released. She had claimed that her clientele included scores of prominent businessmen.

Barrows blamed getting caught on a vindictive landlord who happened to get together with a sergeant in the New York City Police Department who wanted a promotion. She claimed, on the *Donahue* show on television, that nobody had gone to jail in New York State in the last hundred years for what she did.

Barrows's popularity with the press was only partly based on the irony of her *Mayflower* ancestors; she also made forthright comments about sexuality. She said all women were prostitutes, basically, because they withheld favors from their husbands when they were angry.

"As I saw it," she wrote about her prostitution business, "this was a sector of the economy that was crying out for the application of good management skills—not to mention a little common sense and decency."

She also said she felt women needed to be more realistic about the desires of men for new sexual experiences. "But when it comes to my own life," she wrote, "I am monogamous and rather old-fashioned."

Barrows differed from the stereotyped madam in her insistence on hiring only intelligent, articulate women and in her institution of humane policies, such as letting the girls choose the nights they worked and allowing clients to pay after the services were rendered.

Barrows had a background in fashion, having graduated from the Fashion Institute of Technology in New York, where she studied merchandising and business management. She quit her job as a fashion buyer when she suspected her supervisor was taking kickbacks and got a job through a friend answering the phone for an escort service. Thinking she could run a better escort service, she started her own.

"I sometimes wonder what my *Mayflower* ancestors would have made of my situation," wrote Barrows in her book. "(G)ranted they were not exactly famous for their enlightened sexual attitudes. On the other hand, having escaped from religious persecution, they were genuinely passionate on the subject of freedom. Had they lived in a more enlightened era, they would have understood that the private behavior of consenting adults is not the business of the state."

When TV host Phil Donahue asked her what her grandmother, who died shortly before Barrows's appearance on the show in 1986, thought about the whole thing, she didn't have to think long. "She was not amused," Barrows answered without hesitation.

Thoroughly convinced that she was in the right, Barrows went on to capitalize on the scandal. She wrote a best-selling book detailing her experiences up to and including her arrest. The book was later condensed in one of America's slickest women's magazines. Her frequent television appearances were equally rewarding. In the end, Barrows lost none of her self-respect and reaped the financial benefit of her situation. See also Heidi FLEISS: the "Hollywood Madam."

Marion BARRY: D.C. mayor convicted

The war on drugs in the United States was in full swing during the 1980s when Marion Barry, mayor of Washington, D.C., was arrested late in his third term as a result of a complicated FBI sting operation which charged him with buying drugs from a federal agent. Barry was caught on videotape attempting to caress his former lover, model Rasheeda Moore, and, after her rebuffs, puffing twice on a crack cocaine pipe. At that point, FBI agents rushed into the downtown hotel room and arrested the mayor. This operation followed several previous investigations into corruption within the Barry administration. Barry supporters decried the bust as entrapment and a Republican plot to try to roust a successful black Democrat from office.

During the trial, Moore and other female witness testified against Barry while his then wife Effi looked on coldly. Barry was charged with 11 misdemeanor counts of possessing or conspiring to possess cocaine and three felony counts of lying to a federal grand jury in 1989 about drugs. In testimony, Moore claimed that begin-

District of Columbia mayor Marion Barry leaves U.S. District Court in Washington after being found guilty of one cocaine possession charge in August 1990. A mistrial was declared on 12 other charges. An FBI videotape had caught Barry allegedly lighting a crack cocaine pipe in a Washington hotel on January 18, 1990. (AP/Wide World Photos)

ning in 1986 she shared cocaine with Barry more than 100 times in hotel rooms, friends' homes, and various other locations. She told how she would buy crack and deliver it to him at his district building office. Moore stated that the affair ended in 1988 after Barry treated her roughly.

Barry dismissed his former lover's tale. The defense tried to discredit her, and the prosecution tried to subdue the fact that she had previously admitted that Barry came to her hotel room that night more interested in having sex than in drugs. After six weeks of trial, Barry was convicted of one misdemeanor count of possessing cocaine and acquitted on one other misdemeanor, but no verdict was found for the other 12 counts, including the felony charges. If the mayor had been found guilty of a felony, he would no longer have been able to hold an elected public office.

After the trial, Barry checked in to the Hanley-Hazelden Center in West Palm Beach, Florida, for drug and alcohol rehabilitation. In public statements, Barry refused to utter a word about a drug problem, and his aides' press releases emphasized alcoholism as the central issue. The U.S. Conference of mayors' midwinter meeting in Washington, of which Barry was to be host, went on without him; ironically, drugs had been planned as the main topic of discussion.

Meanwhile, as Barry served his six months in prison, the city was in turmoil. Drug-related murders were at an unprecedented high, the widespread use of crack was killing young people and leaving growing numbers of babies orphaned in hospitals, the middle-class tax base was dwindling, and the city was becoming further divided along racial and economic lines. But overall, informal public opinion polls showed respondents' attitudes toward Barry to be hopeful of his return to health and eager to welcome him back to run the city.

Upon Barry's return to politics in fall 1990, he switched his party affiliation and ran an unsuccessful campaign for a district council seat as an independent. Better luck in 1992 allowed him to secure a seat for two years, all the while planning his comeback as mayor. He focused his campaign on "the least, the lost, and the last." For this fourth campaign, Barry had lost the support of his minority white voters, which had (with the lower-income black base) helped him into office in his first election in 1978. In fact, most of the white constituency had jumped ship. Barry began registering new voters, mostly lower-income blacks, at a furious pace to make up the difference.

In 1994, Barry was victorious in the primary and then elected into an unprecedented fourth term as mayor of Washington, D.C. Though he ran his campaign counting on his voters' forgiveness and redemption, more likely he was counting on their short political memories and the weakness of the competition.

Robert BAUMAN: out of the closet in Congress

A strong tide of conservatism in American politics in 1980 helped usher many conservative Republicans, including presidential candidate Ronald Reagan, into political office. However, one of the leading congressional conservatives in the Republican Party would lose his bid for a fourth term in the U.S. House of Representatives. Right-wing Congressman Robert E. Bauman of Maryland, espouser of limited homosexual rights, was arrested on charges of soliciting sex from a teenage male prostitute and then admitted to having "homosexual tendencies."

A Roman Catholic with a wife and family, Bauman was president of the country's largest conservative organization—the American Conservative Union. He was acknowledged by many Republicans as the party's floor leader in the House of Representatives. He voiced the rhetoric of traditional values and national pride at almost every opportunity, and the Republicans considered him an easy win at the polls before the news of his homosexuality became public in 1980.

With a month to go in the 1980 election campaign, Maryland voters and other Americans learned that the 43-year-old Bauman had been charged with a sex misdemeanor, based on allegations that he had solicited sex from a 16-year-old boy in March of that year. A week after this shocking public revelation, James A. Regina was charged with attempting to extort $2,000 from Bauman in exchange for keeping quiet about an alleged homosexual relationship with the congressman. These revelations, along with that of Bauman's alcoholism, would soon end his political career in Congress and break up his marriage.

Regarded as a powerful politician with an acid tongue when debating on the House floor, Bauman espoused the spectrum of right-wing views, including speaking against abortions and (ironically) consistently backing legislation that limited homosexual rights. He also was the leading sponsor of the Family Protection Act, which provided that employers may discriminate against "individuals who are homosexuals or proclaim homosexual tendencies." Further, he was a sponsor of legislation to deny certain veterans' benefits to those discharged from the military for homosexuality. Neither of the latter bills reached the House floor, but the impressions left on the voting public would come back to judge him.

The shift in the election against Bauman happened almost overnight, following his revelations. The campaign to win Maryland's First Congressional District, considered a "safe" district by Republicans and a loss by Democrats, suddenly turned into a real political race between Bauman and his Democratic opponent, Roy Dyson. (The once popular Bauman had won the 1976 election against Dyson with 54 percent of the vote, and had taken the 1978 election against Joseph Quinn with 63 percent of the vote.) Almost immediately, Dyson received additional publicity and more campaign contributions, as his party realized that he was one of their best shots at unseating an established, incumbent Republican.

Bauman originally tried to use his alcoholism as a defense for his homosexuality. There were calls for his resignation from top conservative leaders and withdrawals of financial support for his campaign. The Republican National Committee and several conservative groups "disowned" him politically and financially after the revelations. "Bauman was one of the leading spokesmen on conservative and pro-family causes. We asked him to resign [from Congress and the American Conservative Union] because he can no longer be a credible spokesman for these causes," declared Paul Weyrich of the Committee for the Survival of a Free Congress. However, Bauman's perceived self-righteousness kept him in the race, even though the inescapable writing was on the wall. "I have something to offer the district and the Congress," he maintained.

But the damage was done and the voters' response was swift. What appeared to most upset his constituents in his conservative, rural Maryland district wasn't the evidence of Bauman's gayness, but rather his apparent preaching about one thing and doing quite the opposite while on Capitol Hill. Dyson defeated him, taking 52 percent of the vote.

The U.S. Justice Department subsequently dropped its charges against Bauman in 1981 after he underwent six months of counseling and publicly professed his alcoholic and homosexual behavior. In 1986 he published a poignant autobiography, *The Gentleman from Maryland: The Conscience of a Gay Conservative,* in which he candidly revealed the closet gay life and alcoholism that led to the destruction of his political career and marriage. He stated that the little-known gay world of top-echelon Washington, D.C., comprises a number of congressmen, presidential aides, and corporate and professional leaders, among others (all nameless). Financial demands, Bauman claimed, forced him to write his memoirs, which seem like a "near-perfect Greek tragedy" of a gentleman "flawed by a great weakness." There are those who might disagree.

BCCI: not just a bank

In 1972 Agha Hasan Abedi, a Pakistani banker and financial supporter of a succession of prime ministers in his country, founded the Bank of Credit and Commerce International (BCCI), a Third-World consortium bank based in London, England. By 1990 BCCI controlled assets worth about $23 billion and did business in over 70 countries.

From the beginning, BCCI tried to establish a major presence in the United States. One reason was that many wealthy Third World citizens living in the United States would almost certainly be eager to deal with a global bank like BCCI. Another reason was the fact that American banks were the world's most secure depositories because the U.S. government guaranteed savings deposits to a substantial degree via the Federal Deposit Insurance Corporation (FDIC). By controlling one or more FDIC-member banks, BCCI could offer valuable protection to its customers around the world. However, U.S. banking laws and regulations prevented a foreign bank from acquiring a domestic bank if the foreign bank did not come under the purview of a primary regulator. Such was the case with BCCI; although it was based in London, the Bank of England made no pretense of regulating it and, in fact, restricted its operations in Great Britain. After several failed attempts to buy an American bank, BCCI set out to acquire one secretly and illegally.

In 1978 Ghaith Pharaon, a BCCI front man, purchased the National Bank of Georgia (NBG) from Bert Lance, a major financial supporter of President Jimmy Carter who had recently resigned under pressure as director of the U.S. Office of Management and Budget. Lance's loose management of NBG had gotten him and his bank in deep financial trouble, and he was eager to sell. Lance was represented legally by Clark Clifford, former U.S. Secretary of Defense and a major figure in the Democratic Party, and his law partner Robert Altman. BCCI purchased NBG despite its shaky status, in large part because it would give BCCI access to Lance's and Clifford's influence. In 1980 Clifford and Altman helped Credit and Commerce American Holidays (CCAH), a Dutch corporation owned by several BCCI front men, acquire First American Bank, the largest bank in Washington, D.C. BCCI immediately put key employees in charge of both banks and in 1981 made Clifford and Altman chairman of the board and president, respectively, of First American.

In 1981 BCCI opened branches under its own name in several U.S. cities, despite the fact that as a foreign bank it could not legally accept deposits from American citizens. The plan was to attract deposits from noncitizen import-export businessmen and then funnel this money through its FDIC-member banks. In fact BCCI's best customers were arms smugglers and drug dealers attempting to launder their profits. A 1986 U.S. Customs sting operation involving drug money laundering in Tampa, Florida, focused on BCCI, and two years later a number of BCCI employees and customers were arrested. The sting operation also uncovered evidence related to other criminal behavior by BCCI, including its illegal ownership of NBG and First American. However, Clifford and Altman, who headed BCCI's defense team, were able to work out a plea arrangement with the U.S. Justice Department whereby only five BCCI employees, none of them upper-level executives, were jailed and BCCI was allowed to continue operating its U.S. branches outside Florida. Not

until after July 5, 1991, when the Bank of England shut down BCCI, thus prompting banking officials in other countries to do likewise, did the U.S. Justice Department realize that BCCI was not just a bank but an international criminal organization.

Later that year the Justice Department forced Clifford and Altman to resign from First American and charged BCCI with racketeering, fraud, and money laundering. BCCI pleaded guilty in order to avoid further criminal prosecution and surrendered its entire U.S. assets of about $550 million, the largest criminal forfeiture in U.S. history. Further investigations revealed that BCCI had been a major player in illegal international arms deals, serving as broker and financier of dozens of major sales, including the transfer of nuclear weapons technology to Libya, Iraq, and Pakistan. In 1992 a U.S. Senate subcommittee discovered that BCCI and the Central Intelligence Agency (CIA) had enjoyed a clandestine relationship since 1982, that the CIA had known about BCCI's illegal U.S. operations almost from the beginning, that two of the CCAH front men were high-ranking Saudi Arabian intelligence officials, that a third CCAH front man had been involved in illegal Saudi arms purchases from U.S. aircraft manufacturers Boeing and Lockheed, and that Adnan Khashoggi, one of the principal brokers in the Iran/Contra arms deal, was both a CIA contact and a BCCI customer (see IRAN-CONTRA SCANDAL).

In 1992 the federal government charged Clifford and Altman, who allegedly made about $40 million from their involvement with BCCI, with seven counts of fraud related to that involvement. Both men insisted that they had been completely and totally deceived about BCCI's secret ownership of First American and its other U.S. operations. Clifford, who was 84, was not tried because of his advanced age and poor health, while Altman was eventually found not guilty on all seven counts. However, BCCI-related civil lawsuits against the two men remained active until 1998 when Clifford and Altman paid a total of $5 million to settle them out of court.

Dave BECK: unethical labor leader

In 1952 David D. Beck, having established himself as an aggressive labor leader and effective bargainer, was elected president of the nation's largest single union: the 1.4-million-member International Brotherhood of Teamsters. He was rich, powerful, influential and respected. But before the decade ended, Beck would be stripped of his power and influence and held up as a shameful example of corruption and greed within the labor-union movement.

Beck met his downfall in 1957 when he faced the Senate Select Committee on Improper Activities in Labor or Management. Chaired by Arkansas Senator John McClellan, with future U.S. Attorney General Robert

F. Kennedy as chief counsel, the "rackets committee" exposed the greed of a number of union officials, many of whom had allied themselves with underworld figures and who had ransacked their union treasuries for personal profit.

The committee presented evidence that Beck had used union funds to become a millionaire and to maintain that standard of living. The committee charged that between 1949 and 1953, Beck had taken more than $320,000 from the Teamsters Union funds in Seattle, Washington. Included in this was more than $196,500 for home and property improvements and an additional $85,000 to pay off personal loans. Beck's home had been built with union funds and featured an artificial waterfall, a swimming pool, gardens, and a basement movie theater. The committee also charged that Beck had used union money to buy two lots for $39,000 and had sold them back to the union for $135,000. To account for money he took from the union, Beck had to borrow $200,000 in 1954, stated Kennedy. He also arranged to sell his home back to the union for $163,215 to extricate himself from his tax problems.

At the start of the investigation, Beck said that he had nothing to fear and called the committee "antilabor." However, he invoked the Fifth Amendment to the Constitution 7,200 times before the committee. As a result of these actions, the AFL-CIO, of which Beck was a vice president and council member, expelled him under its then newly adopted policy of ousting officials who refused to answer questions during an investigation. It directed AFL-CIO President George Meany to file charges against Beck for "bringing the labor movement into disrepute and for failure to explain the charges against him." Beck said he hoped to clear himself, as well as others, and approached the Teamsters for $1 million to launch a publicity campaign to help his cause. The union rejected the scheme, and the McClellan Committee issued a scathing indictment against the fallen labor leader. In assessing his actions, the committee declared that Beck had shown "utter contempt for" the committee, for Congress, and for the federal government and had shown "flagrant disregard and disrespect for honest and reputable unionism."

Beck was convicted in 1957 for embezzling $1,900 he had received for the sale of a union-owned Cadillac. He said he had lost track of the money in involved union bookkeeping. He also was indicted for violating the Taft-Hartley Act for borrowing $200,000 from the trucking industry, for income tax evasion, and for filing false tax returns from the Teamsters. In 1959 he was convicted on the last of these charges, despite his having returned approximately $370,000 to the union treasury in an attempt to stave off punishment. The conviction was based on the contention that Beck had greatly overstated figures in listing what the Teamsters made as tax payments in 1950 and 1952.

Beck entered prison in 1962 and was paroled in 1964. His $50,000 annual pension from the Teamsters was intact, but he owed the United States government $1.3 million in back taxes.

Beck maintained his innocence throughout. "I haven't done a single solitary thing wrong," he proclaimed when the tax evasion charges were dropped and later stated, "I never took a nickel from anyone in my life." His only regret, he said, was that he did not keep better records.

Beck was pardoned by President Gerald Ford in 1975. In 1979 John B. Connolly, secretary of the treasury under President Richard M. Nixon, approved a plan for a moratorium on the debt. The Teamsters Union became Nixon's strongest supporters in the labor movement.

One result of the McClellan Committee investigation was a recommendation for labor reform legislation. Such legislation became law in 1959 with the Labor-Management Reporting and Disclosure Act, commonly known as the Labor Anti-Corruption Act.

Beck remained unrepentant, saying in a 1983 interview, "Beck gave his best to the American labor movement. If I had it to do all over again, I'd do it exactly the same way." He died in a hospital near his home in Seattle, Washington, on December 26, 1993; he was 99.

Henry Ward BEECHER: sermons and sensuality

Controversy seems always to have shadowed Henry Ward Beecher. His dramatic and eloquent speaking style, his emotionalism, and his tendency toward the impulsive won him admirers when he occupied the pulpit of Brooklyn's fashionable Plymouth Congregational Church. It attracted both adherents and detractors when he used it to support the abolitionist cause, the growing campaign for women's rights, and the theory of natural selection. But none of the controversies associated with him exceeded in scope and energy the one prompted by the charge of his former friend and parishioner Theodore Tilton that Beecher had seduced Tilton's wife.

Although Beecher's acts of specialized pastoral care for Mrs. Tilton had begun in October 1868, his adultery remained a secret until 1870 when a conscience-stricken Mrs. Tilton confessed her turpitude to her lecturer-journalist husband. Enter controversy, intensified and expanded in latitude and audience until a sensational six-month trial in 1875 gained extensive nationwide (and some international) press coverage for as long as it continued to furnish Brooklyn's chief entertainment of the year.

Beecher's extraclerical ministrations were but the kernel of the controversy, which remained only briefly a matter of triangular concern. Each member of the triangle talked and wrote too much about the matter to too many others; confidants wrote and talked until Tilton was finally forced, in 1874, to legal action. Then Victoria Woodhull, Tilton's confidant and an outspo-

In 1874 the beloved Reverend Henry Ward Beecher was accused by his friend Theodore Tilton, a member of his Brooklyn Plymouth Church congregation, of having seduced Tilton's wife, Elizabeth. Beecher was brought to trial, which ended in a hung jury, and afterward returned to his church with a slightly tarnished image. (Yale University Archives/Yale University Library)

ken feminist, publisher, and candidate for public office on a "free-love" ticket, dared Beecher in print to have the courage of his adulterous predilections and "fess up." (Her letter caused Anthony Comstock to have her jailed for six months for using immoral language.)

Evidence both outside and inside the trial suggests that four years of frenzied activity among Beecher, Tilton, and their partisans involved efforts to reach an accommodation. One mutual friend, Frank Moulton, tried to protect and advise both men. He wisely made a record of oral negotiations and kept a file of written materials in the matter. His archive reveals Beecher's maneuvers to save his face and his alternation of confessions and denials, culminating in his caddish assertion that Mrs. Tilton was "unbalanced"; it preserves Mrs. Tilton's wavering, her assertions that Beecher's actions were only "unhandsome advances," and her posttrial statement (1878) that she was guilty of adultery. Moulton's record also includes an extraordinary "letter of

contrition" from Beecher to Tilton, a report of Beecher's sister's berating him for repeating hanky-panky that spiced his earlier pastoral career in Ohio, and an even more fascinating agreement to a "conspiracy of silence" among Beecher, Tilton, and Moulton, which only Moulton adhered to.

The trial, which was inconclusive because the jury was too confused to reach a verdict, drew packed houses daily. Free tickets were scalped at five dollars each, but as many as 3,000 persons were turned away daily. Vendors sold sandwiches and soft drinks before and after the court sessions and also rented binoculars. Flowers arrived from fans of both sides, mostly for Beecher, but frequently for Mrs. Tilton, who was not permitted to testify. The audience reacted audibly to the 12 witnesses for Tilton's side. Tilton himself was an ineffective witness: he foolishly dramatized himself and did nothing to hide or explain a brief residence with Victoria Woodhull which looked strongly like adultery.

Beecher was an even poorer witness because of his tendency to contradict the testimony of the 95 witnesses who appeared for the defense. He also claimed to be "unable to remember" 900 times. The *New York Times* editorialized unhappily that "every theory which he put forward to account for his conduct before the trial was expressly contradicted by himself or his counsel during the trial."

But the controversy and the exposure did little to destroy Beecher's influence, even when, after the trial, he avenged himself on Moulton and others as he had on Tilton before the trial, by having them drummed out of Plymouth Church.

David BEGELMAN: do box-office successes excuse forgery?

In February 1977, actor Cliff Robertson found a document from the accounts department of Columbia Pictures informing him that he had received $10,000 for services rendered. Because he had not worked for Columbia Pictures recently and therefore was not owed any money, he investigated further and uncovered a check, made out to him for $10,000 but cashed by David Begelman, president of Columbia Pictures' film and television divisions. Robertson, breaking a Hollywood tradition of keeping quiet for fear of jeopardizing one's career, informed the Beverly Hills and Burbank, California, police and the Federal Bureau of Investigation about the check, with no apparent results. When Robertson finally went public with his charge that Begelman had forged his endorsement on the check, a Pandora's box of troubles was opened about questionable accounting methods and financial practices in the film industry. Begelman eventually confessed to having forged his signature on the check, but Robertson was apparently blacklisted in the film industry for four years as a result of breaking the Hollywood code of silence.

In 1973 Begelman had been recruited by Columbia Pictures to take the important position of studio president. He was largely credited with having revived the studio and rescued it from the brink of bankruptcy with box-office successes, including the movies *Shampoo* and *The Deep.* His annual salary was about $250,000, with "perks" worth another $150,000. Yet by late 1976, his huge financial obligations, including heavy gambling losses, supposedly exceeded his income.

Under suspicion, Begelman finally had to confront the Columbia Pictures' board of directors in October 1977. He admitted to them (and to their parent company, Columbia Pictures Industries) that he had embezzled more than $84,000 from Columbia Pictures by forging $61,000 in checks and padding his expense account by $23,000. He was ordered to pay back the $84,000 and to take a six-week leave of absence. Claiming that emotional and psychological difficulties had caused him to embezzle the money, Begelman began seeing a top Hollywood psychiatrist, who reported to the board after six weeks that Begelman's actions had been done during a "temporary period of self-destructive behavior" and that his client was "completely cured." All of this happened before Robertson went public.

Evidently, Herbert Allen, president of the Wall Street investment banking firm of Allen & Company, which dominated the Columbia Pictures board of directors, had intended to reinstate Begelman as president. Begelman's leadership had been instrumental in the company's recent $100 million profit for its stockholders. In addition, the just-released movie *Close Encounters of the Third Kind,* which Begelman had put together, was fast becoming one of the biggest moneymakers in film history. Now Columbia could be a very profitable company in contrast to its position in 1973 when Allen (assisted by Ray Stark, one of Hollywood's most powerful producers) engineered the takeover of Columbia Pictures for $2 a share by Allen & Company. Allen and Columbia's board of directors, responsible to about 12,000 owners of stock, undoubtedly wanted to hush up the Begelman scandal in an effort to keep up the stock's price. At first, Begelman's reinstatement was protested by Alan Hirschfield, the president and chief executive officer of Columbia Pictures Industries, who finally relented under pressure by mid-December 1977. (There was speculation that Hirschfield, connected with Allen & Company since 1959, wanted to take over ownership of Columbia.) After a few weeks of suspension, Begelman was reinstated and was back at work at Columbia Pictures. But a week later, Robertson's story appeared in the *Washington Post,* tending to leave Herbert Allen stuck with his claims about Begelman's "rehabilitation" and reparations to Columbia and his possible hope of seeing Columbia stock split or selling out at a handsome profit.

Begelman resigned as president of the motion-picture firm on February 9, 1978, following a probe into "certain unauthorized transactions." Immediately the board of Columbia Pictures offered him a three-year, $1.5 million contract as an independent producer, seemingly more lucrative than the post he had just resigned. Begelman, soon confronted with embezzlement charges, saw his past controversy about his alleged fleecing of singer-actress Judy Garland resurface in the press (Garland had accused Begelman, who was her agent in the 1960s, of withholding much money owed to her; she sued but later dropped the case). Begelman pleaded no contest to charges of grand theft and received three-years probation and a $5,000 fine; the judge ordered him to continue psychiatric treatment and to do some community service work. Aside from his court costs, Begelman spent about $35,000 in 1978 producing a documentary film called *Angel Death,* showing the dangers of PCP (a powerful psychedelic drug), and went on to produce *Electric Horseman* for Columbia Pictures, the presidency of which he was again offered and accepted in late 1978.

Begelman's felonious crime was reduced to a misdemeanor when he went before the Burbank Municipal Court again in June 1979; the charges against him were dropped, along with the remaining two years of his probation. In December 1979, Begelman accepted the presidency of Metro-Goldwyn-Mayer (MGM), a rival movie studio, and subsequently produced other box-office successes there.

An ongoing investigation of Columbia Pictures by the Securities and Exchange Commission dwindled and died, finding no evidence that federal laws had been violated by anyone at Columbia. In 1982, Allen & Company sold its interest in Columbia Pictures to the Coca-Cola Company, making a profit of approximately $30 million. In the next year, the Begelman scandal became a best-selling book, *Indecent Exposure: A True Story of Hollywood and Wall Street,* written by David McClintick.

BELKNAP SCANDAL: he followed in his wife's path
William W. Belknap, a lawyer, served as a Union officer in the American Civil War, rising to the rank of major general in 1865. In 1869, shortly following the election of his friend, Ulysses S. Grant, to president, Belknap received an appointment to be Secretary of War, a post he would hold for the next seven years (Grant was re-elected in 1872). Although Grant's administration would become known for its excessive graft and corruption, none was as glaring as Belknap's. Fueled by the greedy machinations of his socially ambitious wife, Belknap acquired a predilection for graft and bribery which would nearly land him in prison.

Belknap's annual salary of $8,000 as Secretary of War was evidently not enough for him and his wife, who desired to live and entertain in a grand style. She communicated with a wealthy friend of hers, a New York contractor named Caleb P. Marsh, to whom she proposed a deal: she would secure for him the lucrative Indian trading post at Fort Sill, Oklahoma, if he agreed to pass on to her some of the profits. At the time the post was held by one John S. Evans, who refused to relinquish it because of its large investment profitability to him, but he agreed to pay Marsh $12,000 annually if he could keep the tradership. The agreement was made, and Marsh gave half of his yearly payments to the acquisitive Mrs. Belknap. After her death, the monies were sent to Belknap himself, who subsequently received nearly $25,000 in "kickbacks" from the Fort Sill trader.

In early 1875 Belknap was suspected of malfeasance in office by a congressional investigating committee, which continued to probe, soon finding that the Secretary of War had been connected with the widespread sale of Indian post traderships and that the president's brother, Orville, had admittedly benefited from the same selfish practice. The American press, especially the *New York Herald,* exposed the sordid details of the Belknap scandal in February 1876, greatly upsetting the public and helping propel Congress to action.

The special investigating committee of the House of Representatives discovered that Belknap had accepted bribes from employees of the United States government's Indian Service and had been caught spending the money. Despite Belknap's hastily submitted resignation on March 2, 1876 (which President Grant accepted "with great regret"), the committee recommended impeachment. On that same day, the House unanimously passed it.

Despite his seemingly impending doom, Belknap managed to avoid his comeuppance. Although the Senate Court of Impeachment heard the case all through the summer, on August 1, 1876, it finally voted 35 to 25 to acquit Belknap, failing to obtain the necessary two-thirds vote for conviction. Of the 25 senators who voted "not guilty," 23 declared that Belknap's innocence was not the deciding factor in their vote; instead, the Senate's lack of jurisdiction over a resigned government official had determined their vote of acquittal. Thus, Belknap escaped a disgraceful conviction through his quick resignation and Grant's quick acceptance of it. The former Secretary of War later became a private lawyer in Washington, D.C., dying at the age of 61 in 1890.

"BELMONT STING"

During the ninth horse race at Belmont Park, New York, on September 23, 1977, a 57-1 longshot named Lebon won by four lengths and paid out $116 for each $2 bet. Hardly anyone had bet on him. Hardly anyone, that is, except for a race track veterinarian named Mark (Mike) Gerard, who had bet $1,300 for Lebon to win

and $300 for him to show. Such a high bet on a longshot would seem strange in any event. Under investigation, Gerard's luck started to look stranger and stranger. The doctor eventually emerged as the engineer of a wily horse-swapping "sting."

Dr. Mike Gerard, well-known at tracks in New York State and elsewhere as a veterinarian of thoroughbreds, supplemented his sizable income by importing race horses from South America. In June 1977, he brought three racers from Uruguay—Lebon, Cinzano, and Boots Colonero—to his farm on Long Island. Lebon was sold to Jack Morgan, a former associate of Gerard, for $10,000; Cinzano was sold to Joseph Taub, a computer-firm executive, for $150,000, and Taub immediately insured his new horse for that amount. Several weeks later, Gerard telephoned Taub and told him that Cinzano had fractured his skull in a barn accident and had died. Taub filed a claim with his insurance company and was promptly paid his $150,000.

Early in September, Jack Morgan entered Lebon in a race at Belmont. Although a 7-1 favorite, the horse finished in 11th place. Hardly anyone except Gerard backed him in the September 23 race. Gerard bet $1,300 for Lebon to win and $300 for him to show. Almost from the start, Lebon took the lead by four lengths and maintained that pace to the finish line. Gerard collected $80,440.

The event would probably have been remembered largely as a bit of extraordinary luck if sharp-eyed journalists in Uruguay had not seen photographs in their newspapers of Lebon in the winner's circle. They recognized the horse as Cinzano, Uruguay's 1976 Horse of the Year. Both Lebon and Cinzano were bays (reddish brown horses), and both had a white star on their foreheads, but Cinzano's star was more elongated, like that of the horse in the photographs. Further, Cinzano had a scar on his shoulder while Lebon did not. The Uruguayans conveyed their doubts to a countryman in New York, who in turn notified the authorities at Belmont.

Gerard was immediately questioned. He denied having any knowledge of wrongdoing and said that someone else must have switched the two look-alike bay horses. When asked what had happened to the carcass of the dead Cinzano, Gerard declared that it had been sold to a renderer to be made into dog food. The renderer, however, had no record of the sale or pickup of the dead horse. Gerard was charged with grand larceny but was acquitted on the basis of insufficient evidence. In 1978, however, he was convicted of a misdemeanor (entering a horse in a contest of speed under a false name) and sentenced to a year in jail and a fine of $1,000. But the sentence was successfully appealed and Gerard's actual punishment was less severe.

Several years later, a jockey from Uruguay who had formerly ridden Cinzano was in the United States and positively identified Lebon as the former Cinzano. In 1981, another bogus race horse was discovered when it was revealed that de Pique, which Gerard had imported from Argentina in 1975, was in fact the horse Enchumao. Gerard has been suspect ever since.

John BELUSHI: lunacy and self-destruction

Moon-faced superstar John Belushi, famed for his irreverent and gross comic acting on television and in the movies, was found dead in Hollywood, California, on March 5, 1982. His hectic life had gotten out of control during a five-day binge with friend Cathy Evelyn Smith, a drug addict and aspiring rock-and-roll singer, who had injected him with a lethal "speedball" of cocaine and heroin and was charged with his murder. Four years later Smith received a three-year prison sentence after pleading no contest to involuntary manslaughter.

Born in Chicago in 1949, the always high-spirited Belushi, who made a brief attempt at college before becoming a stage comedian, rose to national fame when he was cast in NBC-TVs *Saturday Night Live*, an outrageous and controversial comedy show in which he acted from 1975 to 1979. He created a series of unique, lunatic characters for the show, which both thrilled and repulsed audiences. No one before had built his popularity on being disgusting. Belushi achieved phenomenal success. The short, stout, and insecure Belushi formed a deep friendship with actor Dan Aykroyd, who also starred in *Saturday Night Live*. About his relationship with Aykroyd, Belushi said, "He's Mr. Careful and I'm Mr. Fuck it." In 1977 Belushi married Judith Jacklin, whom he had known since high school and lived with for several years.

The filmmaking industry soon grabbed hold of Belushi, and in 1978 he starred in two wild and nutty movies, *The Blues Brothers* and National Lampoon's *Animal House*. He cut a very successful record album with his band (called The Blues Brothers on *Saturday Night Live*). The more fame and success came to Belushi, the more frenzied and furious became his lifestyle. He spent little time with his wife, a writer and book designer who was devoted to him, and moved constantly from coast to coast doing his TV show and making movies, including *Goin' South* (with Jack Nicholson), *Old Boyfriends, Neighbors* (with Aykroyd), and *Continental Divide* (in which Belushi showed some fine dramatic acting).

But all the while the comedian lived in the "fast lane," indulging himself in partying, carousing, drinking and eating to excess, chain-smoking, and drug-taking. In early March 1982, while staying in a $200-a-day bungalow at a Hollywood hotel, the Chateau Marmont, the 33-year-old Belushi plunged into a five-day-long nightmare of dissipation, drinking with fellow celebrities and friends in clubs all over Los Angeles. Cathy Smith, a known drug user and dealer whom Belushi had known

for five years, stayed with him in his bungalow where she helped inject cocaine (or coke) and heroin into him. "I kept the sucker alive for five days," she later said. Belushi sank into a coma and, within hours, died on March 5.

The Los Angeles police first stated that he had died of natural causes; there was much speculation that Belushi had fatally choked on food or succumbed to a heart attack. But Belushi's arms had many red splotches from needle injections, and after Smith was taken in and questioned by the police, she became suspect and was accused of murdering him. Later she claimed that she had acted on Belushi's directions by intravenously giving him a combination of cocaine and heroin.

Brought to trial in Los Angeles Superior Court in September 1986, Smith and her lawyers contended that she had merely done what Belushi wanted and that he had been responsible for his own death. The judge concurred but told Smith: "That fact does not, however, absolve you of responsibility for your own action. You provided drugs for several people and you injected those drugs into several people. You did so on a continuing basis and for a substantial period of time. . . . As a result of your actions, John Belushi is dead. That behavior to me is totally unacceptable." The 39-year-old, attractive former rock back-up singer coldly accepted the judge's sentence of three years behind bars.

In mid-March 1988, Smith was paroled after serving a year and a half in a California prison; she then returned to Toronto, Canada, her hometown.

John BENNETT: America's biggest charity scammer

It was called the biggest charity scam in the history of the United States, and it challenged the bankruptcy laws then on the books. In March 1997, John G. Bennett, Jr., the 59-year-old head of the Foundation for New Era Philanthropy, was brought up on 82 counts of money laundering, fraud, and tax violations. He faced a possible sentence of 907 years in prison and $28 million in fines for swindling hundreds of charities, universities, and nonprofit organizations out of $135 million.

Since 1989, when the suburban Philadelphia foundation was established in order to fund a check-kiting scheme, Bennett lured hundreds of nonprofit organizations to donate money to New Era by promising to double their investments within six months with matching funds from anonymous donors. In reality, there were no anonymous donors. Nevertheless, the scheme at first succeeded as funds from the newest donors were shuffled to the earlier investors, increasing investment monies as promised; all appeared to be on the up-and-up. However, when New Era went bankrupt in May 1985, hundreds of donors including the Philadelphia Orchestra, the United Way, the American Red Cross, the Salvation Army, the University of Pennsylvania, Harvard and Princeton Universities, the World Harvest

Mission, and two child-welfare-oriented charities from Minnesota, among others, collectively stood to lose more than $354 million in projected revenue.

The Securities and Exchange Commission sued the foundation. Bennett was known to be a religious man; at one point in the investigation, he claimed to have had hallucinations and said he was driven to change the world in order to proclaim God's glory. After the collapse of his organization, he became suicidal but still pleaded not guilty when brought to trial. His defense planned to argue that he was brain damaged from two recent car accidents and that he suffered from a personality disorder, but the judge restricted the use of these arguments. In sentencing, Bennett was required to forfeit $1.2 million in personal assets, though he had diverted over $4.2 million of donated money into personal accounts and businesses. He was also required to serve 12 years in prison.

The victim organizations were compensated for their losses at approximately 65 cents on the dollar. Organizations that had gained from the New Era investment scheme were required to return the profits in order to reimburse the losers. Although the tangled web of claims against the defendant threatened to get out of control, a huge effort was made to minimize litigation in order to keep legal fees from swallowing the assets and to prevent distant and obscure claims from appearing.

BENSON FAMILY MURDERS

Many families have a "problem child," and to Mrs. Margaret Benson, a wealthy 63-year old widow and heiress to the $10 million fortune of the Lancaster Leaf Tobacco Company, the "problem child" of her family seemed to be her violent, drug-dependent adopted son, Scott. Her older son, Steven, on the other hand, appeared to be the ideal son. But when a pipe bomb went off in the car parked outside the Benson's home on July 9, 1985, it became clear that appearances can be deceiving. Mrs. Benson and the 21-year-old Scott were killed outright in the explosion, and Carol Lynn Benson Kendall, Mrs. Benson's married daughter, was severely injured. Oddly enough, Steven emerged without a scratch. The "ideal" son's true colors were soon to be shown.

After the death of her wealthy husband in 1980, Mrs. Benson and her grown children moved to a $400,000 home in the fashionable part of Naples, Florida, and proceeded to live a life of ease and self-indulgence; the children were generously supported by their mother. Mrs. Benson had adopted Scott when he was an infant and fondly raised him as her son. As a young man, he professed to want a career as a professional tennis player, but he was evidently too addicted to drugs to maintain the routine and physical fitness required of a top athlete. Instead, Scott became a playboy who raced around in expensive sports cars, snorted cocaine and inhaled nitrous oxide (laughing gas), and had trouble making ends meet with a $7,000 monthly allowance. He could also be violent, flying into a tantrum on one occasion when his mother asked him to remove a vicious guard dog that he kept in the house. On another occasion he beat his mother and sister so fiercely that the police had to intervene, dragging him forcibly to a drug-treatment center.

In strong contrast to Scott was Steven, who had taken over the management of the family's affairs after his father's death. He was the peacemaker when there were family quarrels and apparently lost his temper only when Scott became abusive. Steven truly appeared to be the ideal loving son. After he purchased a $215,000 home, complete with a swimming pool and tennis court, however, his mother, wondering how he could afford it, suspected that he had been skimming money from a company which she had helped him establish. Afterward, she threatened to cut Steven out of her will. On the day of the bombing, she had sent for the family lawyer to inspect the company's books. Steven was aware of this approaching audit.

On that fateful summer day in 1985, Mrs. Benson, Scott, Steven, and Carol were about to drive off together in the family's Chevrolet Suburban van when Steven excused himself, saying he had forgotten something in the house. Moments after he left, the van was demolished by the explosion of the two pipe bombs. After she recovered, Carol testified that Steven had made no effort to help her and had demonstrated no emotion at the scene of the tragedy.

A year later, at Steven's well-publicized Florida trial, Carol Benson Kendall was the prosecution's star witness and stunned the court with even more shocking testimony when she disclosed that Scott had been her illegitimate son and that her mother—his own grandmother—had adopted him. The defense sought to show that the drug-crazed Scott could have made and installed the pipe bombs as an act of spite against the family. Fifty-two witnesses testified for the prosecution. One declared that Steven had once told him that he had learned how to make pipe bombs years ago. Other evidence against Steven included a purchase order for materials that could be used to make pipe bombs. The purchase order bore Steven's finger and palm prints. No one had actually seen Steven plant the two bombs in the car, but the circumstantial evidence seemed so overwhelming that the jury, after 11 hours of deliberation, returned a guilty verdict.

Steven was convicted on two counts of first-degree murder and one count of attempted murder, as well as six counts of buying and making explosive materials. The 35-year-old avaricious heir and killer could have been sentenced to death in the electric chair, but instead the judge sentenced him to two consecutive terms of life imprisonment without a chance of parole for 50 years (the jury had made a nonbinding recommendation against the death penalty).

Richard BERENDZEN: university president's obscene calls

Until 1990, Richard Berendzen was known as the Harvard-trained astronomer and physicist who took over as president of American University in Washington, D.C., and transformed it into a nationally recognized school. Early that year, he was felicitated for his outstanding contributions and service to the university during his 10 years at the helm. In particular, his fund-raising skills (for instance, he secured a $5 million donation for a sports center and convocation hall from Saudi billionaire Adnan Khashoggi in 1984) were lauded. So, when he suddenly and unexpectedly resigned as president on April 8, 1990, just weeks before the semester was to end, everyone was stunned. The official statement cited sheer exhaustion, a highly plausible reason, given that Berendzen was a workaholic who worked more than 100 hours a week and had not taken a vacation during his 16 years at the university. However, as it turned out later, it wasn't the real reason.

On May 11, Berendzen was charged with making a series of obscene phone calls to a woman in Fairfax County, Virginia, an offense punishable by a maximum fine of $1,000 and a one-year prison sentence. The 33-year-old woman had placed ads in the local newspaper offering child care. Posing as a prospective parent, Berendzen first called her in March 1990 from his private office at American University. Following the pattern of his previous calls to other women, he soon turned the conversation to the issue of children and sexuality. Most of the women he called did not respond to this trend in the conversation and there the calls ended. But this woman did not hang up when he talked of sexual involvement between children and parents. Rather, she allowed the conversation to continue and persuaded him to call again. Meanwhile, however, she had the police attach a taping device to her phone so that Berendzen's calls could be recorded and traced. Over the next few weeks, he called 30 to 40 times and each time fabricated stories about the weird sexual activities his family engaged in and questioned her about the sexual activities in her family. She wanted to keep the calls coming, she later told the *Washington Post*, so her answers were deliberate. And he kept calling her because she was the first person he had encountered who was willing to discuss openly child sexual abuse with a total stranger. In his final call, Berendzen reportedly told the woman that his entire life had been destroyed and that she was the guilty party.

It was later revealed that Berendzen was sexually abused by his own mother from the time he was eight years old until his teenage years. He had told no one of this abuse and never received counseling or any other treatment. These repressed feelings were apparently awakened when he visited his childhood home in Dallas for his father's funeral in 1987. From then on till 1990, he admitted to having made several such calls, usually months apart. But since January 1990, the compulsion to call had become overwhelming and, over the next three months, he called 10 to 15 child care providers from newspaper ads. Berendzen said that most of the calls were made in the afternoon when he was most depressed, and all were made from his study in the university. He later claimed that he was merely trying to get information about childhood sexual abuse. Even the prosecutor who studied these recordings agreed that these weren't average obscene calls—because they were not littered with obscene words.

In a statement read by his lawyer, Berendzen said, "I cannot begin to convey my embarrassment, or my torment." The day after his resignation Berendzen admitted himself into the Sexual Disorders Clinic at Johns Hopkins University Hospital in Baltimore, where he remained for nearly one month, until May 4. He said that he would fully cooperate with the Fairfax County police in their investigation. On May 23, he pled guilty to two misdemeanor charges. Later, the hospital released the story of his abusive childhood, saying that he had made the calls as a way of resolving these issues. He was sentenced to 30 days in jail on each charge, but the jail time was suspended provided Berendzen avoided any more trouble, continued treatment, and reported regularly to the court. After a one-year sabbatical, Berendzen resumed teaching physics and astronomy at American University.

Bernard BERGMAN: crooked millionaire rabbi

New York's largest nursing home business belonged to 65-year-old Rabbi Bernard Bergman when, in 1976, he was imprisoned for the theft of close to $3 million in public funds intended for the aged, sick, and poor. Many were shocked not only that the benevolent rabbi had grown rich as a "trafficker in human misery," but also that this influential Jewish leader got off with such a light prison sentence—four months at the federal minimum security penitentiary at Allenwood in northern Pennsylvania. His punishment was decried by some as a travesty of justice, and yet this once powerful and proud man felt the pain of a public humiliation that would not be forgotten, let alone ignored.

Bergman, who had been born in Hungary, had rabbis on both sides of his family for generations. After studying religion in the late 1930s in Palestine, where he was ordained a rabbi, he settled permanently in the United States with his wife and family after World War II, soon gaining stature in the New York Jewish community because of his extreme friendliness, compassion, and generosity. A persuasive public speaker, Bergman successfully raised much money for the cause of Zionism and Israel and for Soviet Jews, as well as for the United Jewish Appeal. For some 25 years he was a prominent figure at fund-raising dinners while at the same time buying up at cheap prices old buildings with many rooms in New York, New Jersey, and Connecticut and then renovating them into nursing homes for the old, chronically ill, and senile. Elderly persons of means found accommodations in his homes, where their special individual needs were supposedly met. In the 1960s Bergman established a big nursing-home syndicate with the help of many friends, including politicians to whom he had given funds and public support.

After the mid-1960s, when the United States Congress enacted the Medicaid law, the nursing home business became one of the fastest growing industries in America. Medicaid permitted millions of elderly citizens to enter a nursing facility, either private or public, and have their care underwritten by the government. Under Medicaid laws, elderly persons who had used up all their "nest egg" funds on nursing-home care were automatically drawn into the Medicaid program, participating in it until death. Bergman, like other nursing-home owners, found an influx of new patients, often elderly women seeking safety from rampant crime on the city streets.

By 1973, Rabbi Bergman was estimated to be worth some $25 million; he had a home in Jerusalem and real estate all over New York, New Jersey, and Connecticut. By then, however, flagrant abuse and neglect of patients in many nursing homes had been revealed; the quality of care was substandard; doctors' visits to ailing patients were unconscionably infrequent; and Medicaid funds seemed to have been wasted through fraud. Living conditions at Bergman's Towers Nursing Home in New York City had been labeled appalling as early as 1971. State investigators had said that many of his homes were firetraps, had roach-infested food-storage rooms, and had patients with communicable illnesses who were not properly isolated from others. Billing and bookkeeping errors were discovered in the ledgers; Bergman had billed Medicaid for nurses who never existed; and losses were listed on income-tax statements when actually there had been profits that were sometimes as great as 40 percent on Bergman's investments. Probably the worst discovery was of elderly patients living in filth or shock, often dehydrated, sometimes ulcerated or infected, and suffering from general medical inattention.

New York Assemblyman Andrew Stein, who had been looking into the "unfit" Towers Nursing Home, headed a state commission that joined with the U.S. Senate Commission on Aging and Long Term Care to investigate the deception, administrative mismanagement, and fraud apparent in the Medicaid system, its providers, and the recipients of its benefits. Charges against Bergman had cropped up again and again in past years, but nothing had been done to correct the millionaire rabbi's violations and alleged fraud. Stein's unrelenting probe into the nursing-home industry angered several of Bergman's supporters, particularly two New York assemblymen, Albert Howard Blumenthal and Stanley Steingut. Blumenthal had vouched for Bergman's good management of the Towers Nursing Home, calling it "spotless." The reason for Blumenthal's support soon became apparent. The seemingly exemplary politician was indicted in late 1975, charged with taking a bribe from Bergman to help gain a license to open the Park Crescent Nursing Home in New York City, which city and state inspectors claimed was not properly renovated and thus would endanger patients. Unexpectedly, in April 1976, the charge against Blumenthal was dropped on grounds that the special prosecutor had exceeded his jurisdiction and had unduly coerced the investigating grand jury. The nursing home probe continued full force, however, as the state legislature granted more funds to the investigation.

As for Bergman, it was discovered that he had carefully kept his name from the legal ownership of almost all the nursing homes in his syndicate; many were owned by his wife Anna or son Stanley; others were nominally operated by relatives or trusted friends. Also found out was that the Towers Nursing Home had not lost, as it had claimed to the New York City Health Department, well over a million dollars from 1966 through 1973 but instead had made a profit of almost a million dollars. The probe led to charges against other nursing-home magnates, such as Eugene Hollander, who pleaded guilty to defrauding Medicaid of hundreds of thousands of dollars. Finally, Bergman himself pleaded guilty to fraud and theft charges under a plea-bargaining agreement that granted immunity from prosecution to his wife and son. He testified that he had indeed bribed Blumenthal, who was stunned and called Bergman "a liar," and who eventually resigned from the legislature. Federal Judge Marvin Frankel's "stern" four-month prison sentence to Bergman was strongly denounced by the public as "injustice" and "a slap on the wrist." The judge twice stayed the rabbi's incarceration but, in late September, 1976, forced him to begin serving his time at the Allenwood penitentiary in Pennsylvania. Pale and worn, Bergman returned to free society in January 1977. Though his sentence had been far lighter than he deserved, his punishment was never truly over. This once proud and powerful man would be branded forever as an ex-con.

BERGMAN-ROSSELLINI AFFAIR

Beautiful, talented Ingrid Bergman was probably America's most idolized actress of the 1940s. After starring in such films as *The Bells of St. Mary's* (1945) and *Joan of Arc* (1948), she became associated with the virtuous image of the "girl-next-door." This image was perma-

Actress Ingrid Bergman (right), bride of Italian film director Roberto Rossellini (center), pictured in Venice, Italy, when they attended the International Film Festival in August 1950. Rossellini's films Stromboli *and* Saint Francis *were shown during the festival, two officials of which are seen talking with the famed director. (AP/Wide World Photos)*

nently shattered and the public thoroughly alienated, however, when in 1949 she left her husband and child for the flamboyant Italian film director and playboy Roberto Rossellini. An even greater furor was created the following year, when she bore an illegitimate child by him. The actress was severely censured in the United States, to which she did not return until 1957.

Swedish-born Bergman, who won an Academy Award for best actress for her work in the movie *Gaslight,* in 1944, was married to Dr. Peter Lindstrom and had a young daughter, Pia, when she first met Rossellini in 1949. She had asked to work with the Italian director after viewing his neorealist movies, having become unhappy with the less than challenging roles offered to her in Hollywood. Rossellini was delighted with the prospect of making a film with her, and while filming *Stromboli* (1949) together in Rome, Italy, they fell in love. Bergman's marriage to Lindstrom had been faltering for some time, perhaps because their divergent careers had often kept them apart (he was a successful dentist-turned-neurosurgeon). In August 1949, Bergman sought a divorce, but her husband refused to consent. She nevertheless moved in with Rossellini and declared that she would marry him. The film director was also married but had obtained an annulment that was held valid by an Italian court.

Bergman's divorce, however, was not quite so simple. She filed suit in Mexico for a divorce in January 1950. Following the birth of her son (little Robertino) in Italy on February 2, 1950, she received the divorce and then officially named Rossellini as the boy's father. Bergman and Rossellini were wed by proxy in Juárez, Mexico, in May 1950. Prior to the marriage, the actress sued for custody of her daughter, Pia. Lindstrom, however, was also suing for divorce then, as well as for custody of Pia. In November 1950, he obtained a divorce from Bergman, then had Pia naturalized as an American, and changed her name to Jenny Ann. A year later Lindstrom received a final divorce decree in California and gained custody of Jenny Ann.

Meanwhile, the American public's self-righteous anger over Bergman's all too human fall from a Hollywood-created saintliness was seen and heard in many places: ministers denounced her in churches; priggish ladies fleered at her; and filmgoers frequently picketed her films. Newspapers created a huge scandal because she had committed adultery at a time when people were less accepting of a strong female spirit of independence.

In 1952 Bergman and Rossellini had a set of twins. She attempted to bring Pia (Jenny Ann) to Italy for a visit but was barred from doing so by Lindstrom and the courts. An insanely jealous husband, Rossellini would not permit Bergman to star in films unless he directed them; she disobeyed him after starring in seven unsuccessful Rossellini movies, announcing later to him that "artistically we are no good for each other." She also found life increasingly difficult because of Rossellini's manic-depressive swings of temperament and his womanizing.

The Swedish press repeatedly published stories that Bergman felt attacked her and her family unreasonably. In 1959, dissatisfied with her work and marriage, she angrily lashed out at the press and declared she would never return to her homeland, Sweden. Although she had announced in 1953 that she would retire from filmmaking, she did not and returned to the United States in January 1957, receiving the New York Film Critics' Award for best actress (she had won a second Academy Award as best actress for her role in *Anastasia* in 1956, which she had had to film in Britain). In 1957, she also separated from Rossellini, whom she later divorced. The American public forgave her completely, and Bergman, who had a third marriage, gleaned another Oscar as best supporting actress for her work in *Murder on the Orient Express* (1974). She died of cancer on August 29, 1982, on her 67th birthday. Rossellini had died of a heart attack in Rome in 1977, at the age of 71.

BERRIGAN BROTHERS: priests, peace activists, lawbreakers

The two Berrigan brothers, Daniel and Philip, were the first Roman Catholic priests to receive federal prison sentences for peace agitation in the United States. They were part of a group of several hundred priests, nuns, former clerics, and lay people known as the Catholic Resistance, which actively protested against America's involvement in the Vietnam War in the 1960s and early 1970s. Daniel and Philip Berrigan were viewed as disruptive subversives by the United States government, which prosecuted them for their law-breaking activities. Nonetheless, they became symbols of the struggle to reform "the system" and government policy.

Daniel once explained part of his radical antiwar involvement in this way: "Although I was too old to carry a draft card, there were other ways of getting in trouble with a state that seemed determined upon multiplying the dead, totally intent upon a war, the meaning of which no sane man could tell."

Daniel and Philip, born in 1921 and 1923, respectively, grew up in a poor, working-class, Catholic family in a home near Syracuse, New York. Their father was politically inclined to the left. Because of their own plight, they tended to empathize with others in privation and, as young men, became devoted priests in the Catholic Church as a way to serve humanity and God. Daniel, a Jesuit, did priestly work in France, where his radical Christianity was nourished among the common people. Philip, a priest in the Josephite order, worked with the poor and with black people in Baltimore, Maryland.

The radicalization of the Berrigans occurred slowly, over a number of years. Both attempted to bring about reforms—redressing poverty and discrimination within America—inside and outside their orders, initially by working within the system. However, they consistently met disfavor from the Catholic hierarchy and were thus compelled to direct their efforts toward reform outside the establishment.

In 1965, when U.S. President Lyndon B. Johnson escalated the involvement of American forces in Vietnam, the Berrigans became the only clerics to promote total "noncooperation" with the country's Vietnam policies by signing a "declaration of conscience." Other signers included Dr. Martin Luther King, Jr., Dr. Benjamin Spock, and civil rights activist Bayard Rustin. The Berrigans turned to civil disobedience to protest the war. Daniel's public speeches and actions so angered Francis Cardinal Spellman of New York that the latter had him sent on a sabbatical to Mexico for four months. His order was forced to recall him after many Catholic priests, nuns, seminarians, and lay persons protested against his forced exile.

The Berrigans are probably best known for two incidents involving the destruction of federal draft records. In October 1967, Philip Berrigan led three other persons in a raid on the Baltimore, Maryland, Customs House, in which the group (later called the Baltimore Four) prayed while pouring animal blood on the city's draft board files. Philip then joined his brother in jail, the latter having been arrested a week earlier in a massive antiwar demonstration at the Pentagon. In May 1968, the Berrigans led seven others into the draft board offices in Catonsville, Maryland, and prayed while burning records with homemade napalm. Photographers and reporters were present, and the "Catonsville Nine" made headlines all over the United States. Tried and convicted, Philip and Daniel were sent to prison for the Catonsville destruction.

While in prison in 1971, Philip was indicted with six other persons for conspiring to kidnap Henry A. Kissinger, President Richard Nixon's foreign policy adviser, and for plotting to blow up the heating systems of federal buildings to protest the war. In Harrisburg, Pennsylvania, the government prosecuted the seven activists. The 12-member jury convicted Philip Berrigan and Elizabeth McAlister, a New York nun who later married Philip (which resulted in his dismissal from his order), of smuggling letters into and out of a federal prison, but the jury became deadlocked 10 to 2 in favor of acquittal of the conspiracy charges against the so-called Harrisburg Seven. Afterward, United States attorneys decided to drop all conspiracy charges against the group. Daniel was paroled while the Harrisburg trial was going on, and in late 1972 Philip was also set free from prison. Six of the seven counts of smuggling against Father Berrigan and Sister McAlister were overturned on a legality by a federal appeals court in Philadelphia in 1973.

Years later, on September 8, 1980, rallying with the biblical words "beating swords into plowshares," the Berrigan brothers and six friends broke into a General Electric Company plant outside Philadelphia. The group, which became known as the Plowshares Eight, damaged missile nose cones and poured blood on documents at the plant which produced missile guidance systems. The Berrigans and the others were tried, convicted, and sentenced to prison in 1981. Nevertheless, the Plowshares movement, which grew to have scores of peace activists, had begun, and anti-nuclear advocates trespassed on government and private properties, symbolically disarming and damaging nuclear weapons systems. On Thanksgiving Day, 1983, Elizabeth McAlister, who had been dismissed from the Sacred Heart order after marrying Philip, and others vandalized a B-52 bomber converted to carry cruise missiles, and the former nun subsequently received a three-year prison sentence.

Bruno BETTELHEIM: a life of lies?

A world-renowned psychotherapist, Bruno Bettelheim was considered an expert on the treatment of emotionally disturbed children, especially autistic children. As the director of the Sonia Shankman Orthogenic School at the University of Chicago from 1944 to 1973, Bettelheim claimed to have created a therapeutic setting in which children with severe emotional problems would heal in a gentle and permissive atmosphere. But soon after his suicide in 1990 (the 86-year-old Bettelheim had been suffering from heart, circulatory, and other medical problems), Bettelheim's former students went public with statements that treatment at the Orthogenic School had included physical abuse. Investigators then learned that Bettelheim had lied about or exaggerated almost every aspect of his life, including his training, his early work with autistic children, his concentration camp experiences during the Holocaust, his methods of treatment, and his successes. He had also appropriated the works of other scholars and claimed them as his own. A 1997 biography by Richard Pollak, entitled *The Cre-*

ation of Dr. B, documented the extent of Bettelheim's falsehoods. The psychotherapist, according to Pollak, had been a pathological liar.

Bettelheim was born into a middle-class Jewish family in Vienna in 1903 and earned his Ph.D from the University of Vienna in 1938. Although he later claimed to have trained as a psychoanalyst and to have studied with Sigmund Freud, he actually studied art history and there is no evidence that he ever met Freud. He also later claimed to have done pioneering work with an autistic child in Vienna, although the child was actually treated by Bettelheim's first wife, Gina Alstadt, while Bettelheim ran a family lumber business. With the Nazi takeover of Austria, Bettelheim was sent first to Dachau and then to Buchenwald.

Released in 1939, Bettelheim emigrated to the United States, where he first worked as a research associate with the Progressive Education Association at the University of Chicago. In 1943 he wrote an article entitled "Individual and Mass Behavior in Extreme Situations," an essay on the psychology of concentration camp prisoners based on his own experiences. In the article Bettelheim argued that the extraordinary stress of camp life transformed inmates into childlike adults who grew to admire their captors. This paper attracted considerable attention, and soon after its publication Bettelheim was appointed assistant professor of psychology at the University of Chicago and director of the Orthogenic School, a residential laboratory school for emotionally disturbed children between the ages of six and 14.

At the Orthogenic School Bettelheim explored the idea that, just as concentration camp prisoners became childlike, so children were like prisoners. He therefore tried to create a setting that was the complete opposite of a concentration camp. Considered an expert in the treatment of autism, Bettelheim argued that unresponsive or bad parenting (especially by mothers) during early childhood was the underlying cause of the condition. Bettelheim held to his theories even after evidence mounted that autism has an organic, rather than psychological, cause.

During his tenure in Chicago, Bettelheim became a widely respected authority on child psychology and child rearing. Over the course of his career he wrote some 18 books, including *Love Is Not Enough* (1950), *Truants from Life* (1954), *The Informed Heart* (1960), and *The Empty Fortress* (1967). In *Children of the Dream* (1967) he praised the communal child-rearing practices of the Israeli kibbutzim.

After retiring from the Orthogenic School in 1973, Bettelheim moved to California, where he wrote *The Uses of Enchantment* (1976), a psychoanalytic interpretation of fairy tales. In that influential book, which won the 1977 National Book Award for contemporary thought, he argued that frightening fairy tales serve as important outlets for childhood fears. Yet according to his biographer, Pollak, this work was largely plagiarized from Julius Heuscher's *Psychiatric Study of Fairy Tales* (1963). Nonetheless, when Bettelheim died in 1990, his reputation was still intact.

Bettelheim was apparently influenced early on by a philosophical belief that people can act in meaningful ways even if their actions are based on fictions, because their illusions help them see the world objectively. He wrote, "We must live by fictions—not just to find meaning in life but to make it bearable." Bettelheim seems to have led his life by fictions; perhaps they made life bearable for him.

Mario BIAGGI: a senior congressman's sudden comedown

United States Representative Mario Biaggi of New York descended into grief on November 5, 1987, after being sentenced to two and a half years in jail and fined $500,000 for illegally accepting gratuities from a Brooklyn political leader, Meade Esposito. "The only thing wrong that I did, as it developed, was I accepted personal hospitality from an old and dear friend," lamented the 70-year-old Biaggi, a highly decorated former police officer who had become a popular 10-term congressman. But on September 22, 1987, at the U.S. District Court in Brooklyn, New York, a jury that had cleared Biaggi of charges of bribery and conspiracy found him guilty of obstruction of justice and of taking illegal gratuities and illegally crossing state lines to do so.

"If ever there was a Greek tragedy, it is this one," said federal Judge Jack B. Weinstein, who presided at both Biaggi's and Esposito's jury trials. "The hero (Biaggi) is today struck low and grief descends." Weinstein also said that the two men's crimes "were bred in greed and arrogance."

In March of 1987, Biaggi, a long-time Democratic power broker from the Bronx, who was first elected to Congress in 1969, was charged in a federal indictment with accepting two Florida vacations (all-expense paid trips) from Esposito, a former Democratic Party boss in Brooklyn. Biaggi received the vacations in exchange for using his influence to help a failing Brooklyn ship-repair company (the troubled Coastal Dry Dock and Ship Repair Company) in which Esposito had a financial stake. There had been an 18-month federal probe into allegations of wrongdoing by Brooklyn's Democratic machine, run by the cigar-smoking Esposito until his retirement in 1983. Federal prosecutors claimed that Esposito wanted to protect his insurance company's interest in Coastal Dry Dock and Ship Repair by having Biaggi influence the United States government to speed payments on contracts held by the company. Biaggi and Esposito were accused of conspiracy, bribery, and offering and receiving gratuities and travel in the aid of racketeering. Biaggi also was accused of obstructing jus-

tice by supposedly having encouraged Esposito to lie to an investigating grand jury.

The federal case against the two men centered on two vacations which Biaggi (whose wife was then gravely ill with Hodgkin's disease) took with his lady-friend, Barbara Barlow, to a resort in Fort Lauderdale, Florida, and another vacation he took to the Caribbean island of St. Maarten. Esposito was said to have paid for the St. Maarten trip (1984) and for resort expenses for Biaggi and Barlow in a Florida hotel-spa, where the congressman and his lady-friend shared a room (1984 and 1985).

Although he claimed to be innocent of wrongdoing, Biaggi's career seemed to be unraveling fast. As a police officer for 23 years before being elected repeatedly by overwhelming majorities to Congress, he had received 28 citations for bravery before retiring in 1965 as the most decorated officer in the history of the New York City police force; he had been wounded 10 times in the line of duty. His friend Esposito, about 10 years older than Biaggi, was known as a politician of the old school who had delivered the Brooklyn vote to the Democrats for 16 years as boss of one of the nation's largest county organizations. When he was indicted, Biaggi also faced federal and state charges for influence peddling involving the Wedtech Corporation, a Bronx defense contractor accused of theft and bribery.

"Both men have been corrupt public figures for some period of time and the citizens of New York will be well served by their removal from public life," said the chief prosecutor after Biaggi and Esposito were convicted. (The latter was found guilty of giving Biaggi gratuities [the Florida vacations] and of charges of unlawful interstate travel and received a two-year suspended prison term, $500,000 in fines, and 500 hours of community service as a sentence). "I'm angry. I'm not sad. I'm not bitter. I'm just—damned angry," said Esposito before he was sentenced on October 23, 1987. "If this is corruption, I'm sorry. I didn't know," he added.

Biaggi, who faced possible expulsion from the House of Representatives for his influence-peddling conviction, went on trial again—this time in 1988 on federal racketeering charges in connection with a scheme that helped transform the Wedtech Corporation from a small machine shop into a $100-million-a-year manufacturing company. On August 4, 1988, after nearly a five-month jury trial, he was convicted of 15 felony counts, notably extorting $1.8 million in Wedtech stock and $50,000 in cash in exchange for using his influence to gain federal defense/military contracts for Wedtech. Also found guilty on various charges in the Wedtech scandal were Biaggi's son Richard, Wedtech founder and chairman John Mariotta, former Bronx Borough President Stanley Simon, Biaggi's former law partner Bernard Ehrlich, and former head of the federal Small Business Administration Peter Neglia. The next day Mario Biaggi, called "a thug in a congressman's suit" by a federal prosecutor, plaintively resigned his seat in Congress.

Also involved in the Wedtech scandal was U.S. Representative Robert Garcia, who represented the South Bronx in Congress for 12 years. Found guilty of extorting payoffs from Wedtech, he and his wife Jane were sentenced to three years in jail in January 1990 (he resigned his seat in Congress and apologized to his constituents); both were eligible for parole after serving six months.

The U.S. Supreme Court rejected Mario Biaggi's appeal of his 1987 illegal gratuities conviction (it upheld Esposito's conviction, too). After serving more than two years in prison, Biaggi was released, still maintaining his innocence and still suffering from a long-time heart condition. In 1992 he unsuccessfully tried to regain the Bronx congressional seat he had surrendered in disgrace four years earlier.

BLACK FRIDAY. See Jay GOULD and James FISK: Black Friday 1869.

BLACK SOX SCANDAL: "Say it ain't so, Joe"
The integrity of baseball, America's favorite pastime was tarnished by the "fixing" of the 1919 World Series, when the American League-pennant-champion Chicago White Sox lost the series to the underdog National League-champion Cincinnati Reds. Although influencing the outcome of sporting events was known to happen, most Americans were galled to learn how greed had infected eight talented White Sox players, causing the Reds to take the series five games to three (a new best-of-nine game basis was being tried out that year). The scandalous "fix" would result in the barring of seven players from the sport and would earn the team the disdainful nickname of the "Black Sox."

Chicago's star first baseman, Charles Arnold "Chick" Gandil, who was earning $4,000 a year in 1919, apparently conceived the idea of "throwing" the series and approached his casual friend Joseph "Sport" Sullivan, a bookmaker in Boston, with whom he made a lucrative deal promising the cooperation of other fellow players. Afterward, Sullivan told of his plan to William "Sleepy Bill" Burns of New York, an ex-pitcher turned oilman-gambler. Together the two sought additional money to pull off a colossal "killing" at the betting parlors and went to Arnold Rothstein, New York's "Mr. Big" in gambling and fixes. Rothstein's personal involvement was unclear. Probably, knowing about the fix, he shrewdly paid out no bribe money and supposedly later collected some $270,000 on a $60,000 bet on the Reds. However, Rothstein's friend Abe Attell, a former featherweight boxing champion, became involved with Burns and Sullivan, and, before the opening of the series on October 1, Gandil had secretly lined up seven of his White Sox teammates: Eddie Cicotte and Claude "Lefty" Williams, two outstanding pitchers with 52 wins combined; shortstop Charles A. "Swede" Risberg; center fielder Oscar Emil "Happy" Felsch; left fielder Joseph Jefferson "Shoeless Joe" Jackson, one of the greatest hitters ever; third baseman George Davis "Buck" Weaver, who joined reluctantly and later dropped out; and Fred McMullin, a utility infielder who overheard the others talking about the fix and was taken in.

In the opening game at Cincinnati, Cicotte's pitching fell apart in the fourth inning, and the Reds won 9–1. In the second game, Williams's uncharacteristic wild pitching resulted in another Reds' victory, 4–2. Somehow, rumors spread that there was a fix and that the Reds would win; betting increased heavily in their favor (they had been definite underdogs at the start, with odds as great as 5–1 against them in some gambling spots). Game three, however, was a 3–0 White Sox victory because of the good pitching of Dickie Kerr of Chicago. Game four went to the Reds, 2–0, largely due to Cicotte's errors and Gandil's failure to drive in runs. Bad playing by Williams, Felsch, and Risberg helped Cincinnati win the next game, 5–0. Games six and seven were Chicago victories. Now trailing 4–3 in the series, the White Sox seemed as if they might win but instead lost when poor pitching by Williams in game eight helped the Reds take the series.

Gandil's payoff was $35,000, and his conspiring teammates received, in most instances, $5,000 each (Weaver was not a recipient, having bowed out and having had 11 hits in the series). The tight-fisted owner of the White Sox, Charles A. Comiskey, attempted to cover-up anything suggesting a fix, but suspicions grew to the point at which a grand jury investigated, examined evidence, and finally, almost a year later (1920), brought fraud indictments against the eight conspirators. Comiskey had to suspend and later fire all eight; Gandil had earlier "retired" in California.

The culprits testified before the same grand jury, and when "Shoeless Joe" Jackson was leaving after his testimony, he was confronted by a group of children in the Chicago courthouse corridor. A young boy asked, "It ain't true, is it, Joe?" Jackson replied, "I'm afraid it is." The boy's question was later slightly altered to the noted lament, "Say it ain't so, Joe."

The accused players stood trial in the summer of 1921 and were given legal help by baseball bigwigs to contest the charges. Though the jury acquitted them, Illinois federal Judge Kenesaw Mountain Landis, who was the newly appointed baseball commissioner, barred them from ever playing professional baseball again. Sullivan, Burns, Attell, and Rothstein were never punished as part of the scandal.

James G. BLAINE: "rum, Romanism, and rebellion"
In politics, a sin of omission can be as destructive as one of commission. James G. Blaine, Republican candidate for president in 1884, learned this essential lesson painfully, losing the race to Grover Cleveland.

Blaine, former representative and senator from Maine and once Secretary of State for President Garfield, had a wealth of political experience; he had also been a presidential aspirant in the 1876 and 1880 elections. He had applied all his learned skills in the race for the 1884 nomination, which had not been easy: Blaine was opposed on one hand by a faction of Republicans known as the "Stalwarts" and led by Roscoe Conkling, and on the other hand by a group of reform Republicans known as the "Mugwumps," controlled by Carl Schurz. Both factions and the Democrats had attacked Blaine for exceeding his authority in Arkansas railroad matters (see MULLIGAN LETTERS). The election campaign offered no surcease: although both Blaine and Cleveland had vowed to run "clean" operations, their followers disobeyed them. Cleveland was attacked for the immorality of his mistress and his illegitimate son, almost a capital crime for a former clergyman; Blaine, in response, was bombarded by innuendos about his double marriage to his wife, with snide comments about virginity and "shotgun marriage" drawing guffaws in smoke-filled saloons. Blaine had been maligned by Tammany Hall (New York City's Democratic bosses), and newspaper publisher Joseph Pulitzer had labeled him "the greatest public menace since Catiline."

And so Blaine may have been exhausted on October 29, 1884, when he failed to act. On that date, in order to woo Mugwumps away from Cleveland, a delegation of clergy had waited on Blaine at his headquarters in New York's Fifth Avenue Hotel. A public attestation to their belief in Blaine's moral viewpoints would reinforce the Irish Catholic vote that Blaine then controlled. Their spokesman had been delayed, and a substitute, the Reverend Dr. Samuel D. Burchard, a Presbyterian, filled in. It was a substitution that Blaine would rue forever.

At one point in his speech, the Reverend Burchard condemned the Democrats as "the party whose antecedents have been rum, Romanism, and rebellion." Fatigue, momentary deafness, inattention, or misunderstanding kept Blaine from contradicting Burchard's malicious charge.

A partisan reporter noted Blaine's lapse, dashed to Democratic headquarters, and related the anecdote to ears eager for destructive information. On the following Sunday, handbills were distributed to thousands of Catholics after Masses. Some pointed up Blaine's omission; others, overwhelmed by political fervor, attributed the remark to Blaine himself. A day later Blaine would pillory Burchard as "a Silurian or early Paleozoic bigot." But his response came a day too late.

The result: the Democrats took New York by a plurality of 1149 votes—enough to gain the electoral majority (then 201 out of 401) by 18 votes.

Blaine, always a gentleman in public, cordially extended his best wishes to Cleveland. No one has found a record of his private chagrin at being tight-lipped when he should have been quick to reply.

James G. BLAINE: the Delmonico's blunder
A man of wide and varied political experience, James Gillespie Blaine should have been a constant winner. A founder of the Republican Party in Maine, a three-term state legislator, a United States representative in Congress from 1863 to 1876 (and House speaker from 1869 to 1875), a United States senator, and briefly President Garfield's Secretary of State, he should have known *all* the political answers. But Blaine's career reveals that he had a remarkable and disastrous tendency to be politically accident-prone.

This tendency had cost him the 1876 presidential nomination (see MULLIGAN LETTERS) and the 1880 nomination for president of the United States (he had failed to gain the support of New York's political boss Roscoe Conkling); it would lose him the 1884 election.

By 1884, Blaine had gained the nomination for president despite a two-way split in the Republican Party. His opposition had been a new enemy, a reforming faction led by Carl Schurz called the "Mugwumps," who backed his Democratic rival, New York Governor Grover CLEVELAND, a man with problems of his own.

Blaine should have been careful and astute. He lost because he made two politically stupid blunders which denied him election in the State of New York.

In early October, 1884, New York was almost surely in Blaine's hands. Despite Conkling, Blaine had an apparent majority. He was considered the candidate of the common man and, because he had carefully avoided any sign of religious bias, he had the backing of Catholic immigrant workers, especially the Irish.

Then he erred, apparently unwittingly, and perhaps because of fatigue from the rigors of the campaign, regarded as one of the most bitter in history. Both mistakes occurred on the same day, October 29, 1884. In the morning, inattention, momentary deafness, or misunderstanding cost him New York's Catholic vote, and especially the Irish vote; in the evening, attendance at an extravagant dinner party deprived him of many votes from the common man.

The first error lay in Blaine's failure to respond until it was too late to the intolerant alliteration of an unthinking clergyman that the Democrats were the party of "rum, Romanism, and rebellion."

The second error had two parts: accepting the invitation to dine at Delmonico's and then actually attending. No one among Blaine's supporters seemed to have questioned the wisdom of allowing the candidate of the common man to join the commercially wealthy as the "businessman's candidate." These wealthy, apparently presided over at the dinner at Delmonico's by the notorious Jay GOULD, were symbols of oppression and corruption to the common man; Delmonico's velvet and crystal made it the favorite watering place of the carriage trade, the very financiers and entrepeneurs who kept the laborers poor and jammed into crowded tenements in New York.

As a support-gaining device, the Delmonico's dinner was a failure, despite Blaine's portrayal of the Republicans as the party of prosperity; as a device to introduce Blaine as a friend of business, it was tantamount to destroying his image as the protector of the common man.

Blaine's enemies expressed their fury that he had attended a sybaritic, conspicuously extravagant affair while the national economy was painfully depressed. The *New York World,* a mouthpiece for the Democrats, gave the Delmonico's party front-page coverage on October 30; they labeled the gathering "Belshazzar's Feast." The newspapers saw the handwriting on the wall and spread the word.

Their prophecy was accurate: on November 4, 1884, Blaine was defeated in the State of New York by 1149 votes; with the state's electoral votes going to Grover Cleveland to gain him an Electoral College majority of 219 out of 401, Blaine once again, within the same day, became the victim of his own political blundering. See also James G. BLAINE: "rum, Romanism, and rebellion."

BLOOMINGDALE-MORGAN AFFAIR

In 1982 beautiful, playgirl-model Vicki Morgan instituted a shocking $10 million palimony suit against the estate of multimillionaire Alfred Bloomingdale, scion of the Bloomingdale department store family and longtime "pal" of President Ronald Reagan. As Bloomingdale's 30-year-old mistress, Morgan alleged publicly that he had derived sexual pleasure by regularly inflicting physical pain on her and numerous prostitutes. She said she possessed videotapes of herself and high United States government officials at sex parties. The White House was acutely embarrassed by Morgan's alleged sordid relationship with Bloomingdale, whose wife Betsy was a good friend of the president's wife, Nancy. There was a deafening silence about the affair.

Alfred Bloomingdale, whose grandfather co-founded with his brother the well-known department store chain, had gained fame and fortune for developing the Diners Club credit card, which spurred on the growth of "plastic money" in the United States, and had been chairman of the board of Diners Club International from 1964 to 1970. For a while he became a Hollywood agent and producer and strongly supported the rise to prominence in national politics of his close friend, Ronald Reagan, who served as California's governor from 1967 to 1975 and won the United States presidency in 1980. Bloomingdale was a member of Reagan's so-called "kitchen cabinet"—a group of old political advisers and supporters of the president. After the 1980 election, Bloomingdale spoke of becoming American ambassador to France, undoubtedly seeing the prominent post as a "payoff" for his loyal political patronage. However, for about a year, he received no appointment from the public-image-conscious Reagan, who was undoubtedly aware of his friend's earlier swinging lifestyle. Bloomingdale was then appointed to the President's Foreign Intelligence Advisory Board, which was made up of "trustworthy and distinguished citizens outside the government" and whose job was to review the operations of American intelligence and counterintelligence agencies.

Bloomingdale began suffering from throat cancer and was hospitalized in 1982. His wife, Betsy, soon discovered that he had been secretly giving Miss Morgan a monthly "allowance" of $18,000. During the 1970s the sexy, young woman, who fancied becoming a magazine cover girl and movie star, had been "kept" by the rich and famous. Picked up by Bloomingdale, who became obsessed by her, she had allegedly indulged in sexual perversions and sadomasochistic orgies with him and had received large sums of money that kept her bound to him. Shocked and infuriated, Betsy Bloomingdale summarily cut off Morgan's monthly payment. Morgan responded by promptly naming Bloomingdale in a $5 million palimony suit on July 8, 1982; she claimed she had been his "confidante," traveling companion, and business partner. Three weeks later, Morgan amended her suit to ask for an additional $5 million from Betsy, whom she accused of unfairly terminating her promised $18,000 periodic allowances from Bloomingdale. Before Morgan's case went to court, the 66-year-old Bloomingdale died of cancer in Santa Monica, California, on August 20, 1982. Five weeks later, a judge dismissed most of her $10 million palimony suit, ruling that the relationship between her and Bloomingdale had been "no more than that of a wealthy, older paramour and a young, well-paid mistress." However, Morgan's claims of a written contract assuring her a $10,000 monthly payment and a part of Bloomingdale's business interests were not struck down by the judge.

Miss Morgan's story was not to be a happy one. In 1983, depressed and bitter, she moved into a North Hollywood condominium, where she was joined by a former friend, Marvin Pancoast. Her constant complaints about money soon maddened Pancoast, a homosexual, who used a baseball bat to bludgeon her to

Model and aspiring actress Vicki Morgan (left) was picked up by Alfred Bloomingdale, scion of the famous department-store family (seen here in 1958), who allegedly bound her to him with large amounts of money. In 1982, after Bloomingdale's wife cut this money off, Morgan instituted a palimony suit, but he died and then she was slain in 1983. (AP/Wide World Photos)

death on July 7, 1983. Pancoast then promptly turned himself in to the police, to whom he gave a confession to the murder. Later, he recanted his confession.

But the Reagan administration was later to be still further embarrassed when Robert K. Steinberg, a well-known criminal lawyer who said he had been asked to represent Pancoast at his murder trial, claimed that he had videotapes showing the late Bloomingdale and Miss Morgan engaging in group and sadomasochistic sex with top government officials. Steinberg said the persons involved "would definitely embarrass the president, just like Mr. Bloomingdale did." But shortly afterward, the lawyer announced that the tapes had been stolen. He was later charged with a misdemeanor for having filed a false report that the videotapes had been stolen, and most observers agreed that the tapes had probably never existed.

Pancoast pleaded innocent by reason of insanity at his trial in Van Nuys, California, in 1984. His defense attorney, Arthur Barens, showed Pancoast's psychiatric records, revealing that at various times in the past 13 years his client had been diagnosed as manic depressive, masochistic, and psychotic depressive. It was also pointed out that Pancoast had once even "confessed" to the TATE-LABIANCA murders committed by the Charles Manson family. Besides this, the defense tried to show that others had a motive to kill Miss Morgan because of her claims to having had wild sex with high United States government officials. The jury was not swayed, however, finding the 34-year-old Pancoast guilty of murdering Morgan. He was sentenced to 26 years to life in prison.

Meantime, the Morgan estate continued litigation in Los Angeles against the Bloomingdale estate, which, on December 21, 1984, was finally ordered by a jury to pay $200,000 (money which would pass to Miss Morgan's 15-year-old son, Todd, according to California law). The jurors decided that Alfred Bloomingdale, before he died, had made an enforceable contract with his mistress, Miss Morgan, by promising, in a letter of February 12, 1982, to pay her the sum of $240,000 in return for her agreeing to spend time with him in the hospital, of which Morgan had received $40,000 before the Bloomingdale family had cut off payments.

William BLOUNT: impeachment through conspiracy

Tradition holds, and history illustrates, that even the most honorable of men have elements of weakness in their make-up that at the very least test their integrity and honor. For some, the test leaves them inoperative, as was so in the case of William Blount. The exercise of self-interest made Blount the holder of a dubious fame as the first legislator to be expelled from the U.S. Senate and the first American to be a candidate for the impeachment process.

North Carolina born, Blount had earned a good if unremarkable reputation as paymaster for various units of North Carolina's troops during the American Revolution, as a six-term member of the state's legislature, and as a representative from his state to the Congress created by the Articles of Confederation. A delegate to the 1787 Constitutional Convention in Philadelphia, he took no part in the debates but signed the document and voted for its ratification in the 1789 North Carolina convention. Neither a speaker nor debater, he was regarded by a colleague as "plain, honest, and sincere."

But William Blount was politically ambitious. Defeated in a 1789 bid for the U.S. Senate, he went into territories west of the Allegheny Mountains ceded to the United States by North Carolina; in 1790, when Congress voted a government for the territory, Blount applied for the territorial governorship and received the appointment from President George Washington.

At first, because his political goals had been achieved, he was a politically adroit and effective governor. He had early discovered a hostility on the part of the Indians toward the increasing number of settlers entering the territory and an anger among the settlers toward the pacific Indian policies of the national government. He made and kept the peace, but, finding time on his hands and discovering in himself a desire for riches, he began to speculate illegally in the real estate of this part of the early West, a practice denied to territorial governors. Sensing that his speculations might prosper more quickly if the territory were a state, Blount began to agitate for statehood for the territory (as the state of Tennessee), presided over the 1796 convention which developed its successful application, and became one of the first two United States senators from Tennessee.

After he became Senator Blount, his now legal land speculations continued but did not flourish. In financial difficulties, he began to compromise his integrity as a federal official because of his need to avoid fiscal demise. Ignoring the legal prohibition against state and individual interference in the conduct of foreign policy by the federal administration, Blount schemed with the Indians he had befriended and with his followers among the settlers to help the British force the Spanish out of Florida and Louisiana. As a British agent, he planned a land attack by his friends and followers in combination with actions by a British fleet.

The scheme failed to be implemented, for President John Adams acquired by accident a letter Blount had meant to send to his Indian friends, describing his plans. Adams sent the letter to the Congress on July 3, 1797. Blount acknowledged that the revelation had made "a damnable fuss" in Congress, but he expected the Congress to see the good in his plan, rationalizing that he had intended it to benefit the young country. The Congress did not view his scheme as quite so benign, seeing instead only that he had intended to benefit himself through his arrogant assumption of administrative functions. The Senate acted accordingly and expelled him on July 8, 1797, by a vote of 25 to 1. The House of Representatives began impeachment proceedings on the same day.

Delays in the House made them deliver their case in January 1799, but the impeachment was dismissed, probably as no longer necessary, since the official explanation cited a lack of jurisdiction over the case. In Philadelphia, however, Blount's name remained a target of scorn.

Foiled in his attempt to add fiscal soundness to his achievement of high political office, Blount had escaped to Tennessee in 1797, a profoundly dismayed man. Discovering that he was still exceptionally popular there, he stood for the state's senate in 1798 and was elected and elevated to its speakership. Soon he had recovered financial health but at the cost of physical soundness. Had he not died in 1800, it is probable that he would have begun a new campaign for political advancement.

John and Lorena BOBBITT: marital assault in extremis

On the night of June 23, 1993, John Wayne Bobbitt, 26, of Manassas, Virginia, went drinking with a friend. After stumbling home in the wee hours of the morning, he crawled into bed with his wife, Lorena Gallo Bobbitt, 24. What happened next is not clear: did she cuddle up against him as he drifted off to sleep, as he claimed, or did he wake her up and have sexual intercourse with her against her will, as she claimed? But what happened after that is perfectly clear. While John slept, Lorena tiptoed into the kitchen, picked up a knife in one hand, crept back to the bedroom, grabbed his penis in the other hand, and hacked it in two. Then, while he writhed in agony, she ran to the car and sped away, still clutching his severed member in her hand.

Lorena told investigators that she had mutilated her husband because he raped her that night, as he had done many nights before. On the strength of her statement, John was charged with marital sexual assault. To some, Lorena became an accidental heroine for battered and abused women. Some of her supporters flashed the V-for-victory sign, but with a twist; they snapped the two fingers together to simulate the cutting motion of a pair of scissors.

Although John's trial was a classic case of "he said, she said," the weight of evidence seemed to be in his favor. On the night of the alleged rape, Lorena told investigators that John climaxed before she did, but instead of bringing her to orgasm he selfishly fell asleep. She also indicated that this had happened many times before, thus making her sound more like a victim of sexual frustration than of spousal abuse. And the prosecution was unable to provide medical evidence that Lorena had been forcibly penetrated or that she had even had sex on the night in question. After a two-day trial, the jury deliberated for four hours before finding John not guilty.

Within months of John's acquittal, Lorena was tried for malicious wounding. Although she was clearly guilty of attacking John, the jury felt that she had been abused in a way that partially justified her actions. Not able to acquit her and not willing to convict her, the jury found her not guilty on the grounds of temporary insanity. She spent 45 days under observation in a mental health facility and was then released.

The Bobbitts were divorced in 1995. Lorena moved in with her parents, who lived in nearby Woodbridge, Virginia, and in 1997 she was charged with assaulting her mother. While the older woman sat watching television, Lorena began punching her with her fist; the mother received only minor cuts and scratches, and the charges were eventually dropped. John (whose penis, found on the side of the road where Lorena had flung it, was later reattached surgically) moved to Las Vegas, Nevada. He was briefly engaged to a former topless dancer until she charged him with slamming her into a wall during an argument. He went on to become a popular guest on talk shows and even starred in a pornographic movie, *John Wayne Bobbitt . . . Uncut*. In 1997 he moved to the small town of Fallon, Nevada, where four of his brothers lived, to write a book about his life and find a job.

Ivan BOESKY: fraudulent Wall Street superstar

"There are no easy ways to make money in the securities market . . . there are no esoteric tricks that enable arbitragers to outwit the system," wrote opportunistic multimillionaire Ivan F. Boesky in 1985 in his book *Merger Mania* (subtitled *Arbitrage: Wall Street's Best Kept Money-Making Secret*). He was trying to dignify his controversial career as a high-rolling stock speculator and notorious risk arbitrager (one of the Wall Street professional traders who risk huge sums of money trying to profit by buying and selling stocks in companies that seem on the verge of merging or being taken over by other companies). However, the tall, lanky, and impeccably tailored Boesky scandalized Americans when the Securities and Exchange Commission (SEC) snared him in 1986 in the biggest insider-trading case ever exposed.

In Washington, D.C., on November 14, 1986, SEC Chairman John Shad made a startling announcement: Manhattan-based, 49-year-old Ivan F. Boesky had agreed to pay a $100 million penalty for violating United States government securities laws by purchasing stocks while in possession of legally confidential ("inside") financial information. Under the SEC's consent judgment, Boesky agreed to give up $50 million in illegal profits and to pay an equal sum in civil indemnities for his actions. Insider-trading, a crime in the United States, may be roughly defined as illicit profiting from information about company dealings before that knowledge has reached the public.

Boesky faced a single, unspecified, federal criminal charge, which had a possible five-year prison term upon conviction. He also accepted eventual expulsion from professional stock trading for life (he was given a 16½-month transition period in which to dispose of his enormous holdings) and agreed to tell investigators about the stock trades he had made using his insider information. The savvy wheeler-dealer was far from ruined financially, still having an estimated worth of $200 million, and probably more. He had gone very far, very fast, before his spectacular downfall.

Son of a Russian immigrant, Boesky was born and reared in Detroit, Michigan, where his parents eventually owned a chain of restaurants. He attended three different colleges before earning a degree from the Detroit College of Law in 1964. In law school in 1962, Boesky married the daughter of a wealthy real-estate developer. Intensely ambitious and energetic, he had worked briefly as a law clerk, then as an accountant, before moving with his family to Manhattan in 1966. Risk arbitrage fascinated him after stints working first at the investment firm of L. F. Rothschild and then at the brokerage house of Edwards & Hanly. In 1975, Boesky started his own arbitrage firm with $700,000 in capital and quickly earned a reputation on Wall Street as an audacious risk taker. He worked zealously and relentlessly, putting in 18-hour days at his lavish mid-Manhattan offices, behind a 300-line telephone bank. His arbitrage fund, Ivan F. Boesky & Company, was a limited partnership into which prominent individuals and companies put millions of dollars in capital on Boesky's speculative ventures, which usually succeeded. "Ivan the Terrible," as he was called, often gambled tens of millions of dollars on single corporate takeover bids and rode to staggering success. By 1986 his diverse business empire held some $2 billion worth of securities.

Boesky, seemingly a driven man seeking recognition and control, lived with his wife and four children in a

10-bedroom, Georgian-style mansion on a 200-acre estate in New York's suburban Westchester County. He also maintained an expensive apartment overlooking Manhattan's East River. Social recognition came to Boesky, who sat on various boards and donated generously to charities as he frenetically carried on his stock-trading deals.

Boesky's illegal dealings were disclosed when, in May 1986, the SEC filed a complaint against 33-year-old Dennis Levine, a hotshot managing director of the Drexel Burnham Lambert investment banking firm. Levine was charged with illicit trading in 54 stocks and with amassing $12.6 million in profits in five years from illegal trading on inside information (he had operated through a secret bank account in the Bahamas). A merger and acquisition specialist, Levine subsequently pleaded guilty to four criminal charges and gave up $11.6 million in illegal profits. His testimony to the SEC revealed that Boesky had evidently received secret tips from Levine and others about impending corporate mergers or takeovers. The SEC said that Boesky had agreed to pay Levine, by the spring of 1985, a lump sum of $2.4 million for his illegal tips.

Through Levine's "singing," federal investigators built a big case against Boesky, who later, after his unmasking by the SEC, agreed to cooperate with authorities in the ongoing probe into other Wall Street principals, notably some at Drexel Burnham Lambert. Boesky reportedly permitted investigators to listen into and tape his phone conversations while he carried out his stock-trading activities. This sent profound jitters through many brokers who might be implicated in the scandal.

Legitimate arbitragers and ordinary stock traders worried that the public would cynically lose confidence in them and in the stock market generally because of the Boesky scandal, which seemed to symbolize the boundless avarice existing on Wall Street. To prevent this, pressure was put on Congress, which promised to hold hearings on the insider-trading issue and make reforms.

On December 18, 1987, a U.S. district court judge in Manhattan sentenced Boesky to three years in prison for his role in the insider-trading scandal. As part of a plea bargain, Boesky cooperated with prosecutors and admitted to one count of lying to the SEC; he revealed involvement in far more widespread illegal operations, including stock-price manipulation, unlawful takeover activity, and false record keeping. Boesky provided prosecutors with information leading to jury convictions and guilty pleas in cases involving stockbroker Boyd Jeffries, investment banker Martin Siegel, take-over strategist Paul Bilzerian, Princeton-Newport Partners, GAF Corporation, stock speculators Salim Lewis and John Mulheren, and others. The biggest cases in which Boesky "squealed" involved Drexel Burnham Lambert Inc. and junk bond financier Michael MILKEN,

who tearfully pleaded guilty in federal court in April 1990. The then 53-year-old Boesky, who had said he was "deeply ashamed," was released early from a halfway house, having served two years in federal prison custody (1988–90).

BONUS MARCH. See Herbert HOOVER: exaggerated response in Bonus March.

Jeremy BOORDA: suicide from fear of disgrace?

In 1996 Admiral Jeremy M. (Mike) Boorda, chief of naval operations (CNO), the top man in the U.S. Navy, fatally shot himself in the heart. The reason for this drastic action seems to have been Boorda's desire to avoid disgracing himself and the navy over a matter of honor that most civilians found trivial.

In 1956, the 17-year-old Boorda lied about his age to enlist as a seaman, thereby escaping an unhappy home life. Over the next 38 years he rose gradually through the ranks until, in 1994, President Bill Clinton appointed him chief of naval operations. Boorda was the first enlisted man to become CNO, a matter of great pride to sailors throughout the service. His many assignments included two tours of duty in Vietnam, both times abroad combat vessels stationed in the South China Sea, which was technically part of the combat zone.

Boorda's predecessor as CNO had been forced to retire early because of the navy's TAILHOOK scandal, which involved widespread sexual harassment of female aviators by male pilots. Boorda immediately set out to clean up the service's image by boosting its sense of honor and pride. His task was not an easy one. Public outrage concerning the continuing fallout from Tailhook, coupled with disclosures that a number of midshipmen at the U.S. Naval Academy had cheated on exams and that other midshipmen had engaged in criminal activities before entering the academy, led him to shake up the upper echelon of the navy's officer corps. Meanwhile, old-school navy men, among then James Webb, former secretary of the navy, criticized Boorda for overreacting to political pressure instead of defending navy traditions and called for his resignation.

Boorda seemed to be taking the pressures of the job in stride. However, a media investigation involving two combat awards which he wore without authorization from 1985 to 1995 seemed to be his undoing. The awards in question were the combat "V" (for "valor") pins which he wore on his Vietnam tour-of-duty badges. Apparently Boorda thought he was entitled to wear the pins because he was twice commended for serving in the Vietnam combat zone. However, naval regulations stipulate that "V"s may only be worn by "individuals who are exposed to personal hazard due to direct hostile action," and neither commendation stated specifically that he was entitled to wear a "V." In fact, the matter is unclear; Elmo Zumwalt, a retired admiral and former CNO, stated that he believed Boorda's wearing of the pins was appropriate, and a navy awards manual published in 1965, the year of Boorda's first tour of duty in Vietnam, can be interpreted as okaying his wearing of a ''V,'' at least for that tour.

Civilians have trouble understanding the flap over something as seemingly trivial as wearing two tiny pins. However, career military people take such things very seriously. To them, wearing an award one did not earn is like taking credit for something one did not do and is one of the most dishonorable deeds a leader of soldiers can commit. As the man entrusted with restoring the honor of the navy, Boorda (who stopped wearing the pins as soon as they became an issue) felt that he had only brought further disgrace to it. In a suicide note addressed to ''the sailors,'' he apologized for embarrassing the military branch which had become his life. He committed suicide just hours before two civilian reporters were scheduled to interview him in detail about the awards.

John Wilkes BOOTH: a dramatic ending

Although he was widely acclaimed in the South as an actor, John Wilkes Booth is remembered today not for his earlier dramatic success, but for the major histrionic performance of his life: his assassination of U.S. President Abraham Lincoln on April 14, 1865.

Booth had at least two reasons for his fatal attack upon Lincoln. The first, often considered too obvious to be described in accounts of his somewhat melodramatic assassination, was his intellectual rationale: he was convinced of the rightness of the Confederate position in the Civil War and was a truly ardent hater of Lincoln. This stance had prompted his joining a Richmond, Virginia, militia that hanged the abolitionist John Brown in 1859 and his serving as a Confederate secret service agent during the Civil War. This stance also prompted him to abortive attempts to abduct Lincoln and convey him to Richmond, Virginia, for what probably would have been a show trial followed by a spectacularly dramatic execution.

Booth's second motivation, seldom found in accounts of his felony, is his emotional reason; it derives from the fact that he was the ninth of 10 children fathered by the famous actor Junius Brutus Booth. As a child, John Wilkes Booth had revealed a tendency to emotional instability and abnormal egocentricity; as an adult, he retained these tendencies and augmented them with a powerful jealousy of his older brother Edwin's success (he was the most celebrated *Hamlet* actor before John Barrymore). Sibling rivalry, perhaps, made John Wilkes Booth want to surpass his brother Edwin. By 1865, John Wilkes had gained fame in the South equivalent to Edwin's in the North; an exceptionally dramatic action might enable him finally to outshine his fraternal rival.

The deranged actor John Wilkes Booth (above) assassinated President Abraham Lincoln, causing a scandal that made Booth's famous brother, Edwin Thomas Booth, retire as an actor from the stage. However, audiences rallied to Edwin's support, and he soon returned to perform to critical acclaim. Yet today, more people remember John. (Picture Group 500, Archives, History and Genealogy Unit, Connecticut State Library)

His assassination action was indeed dramatic, and it succeeded not because John Wilkes was somehow superior to his brother, but because of the stupidities and negligences of others. Booth had learned that President Lincoln was to attend a performance of *Our American Cousin* on Good Friday, April 14, 1865, in Ford's Theatre in Washington, D.C. With others, he planned three assassinations: the vice president of the United States, Andrew Johnson, was to be killed elsewhere, as was the secretary of state, William H. Seward. Booth, as star of the performance, would handle the assassination of the president alone.

The actor entered the unguarded theatre at about six o'clock in the evening, where he tampered with the door of the presidential box so that it could be jammed from the inside. Despite earlier threats against Lincoln's life, no representative of the Union's secret service kept the box under surveillance; when Booth returned during the third act of the play, the guard assigned to the president was having a beer in a nearby tavern. No evidence suggests that these derelictions were deliberate;

they were merely accidents that luckily coincided with Booth's plan.

Booth entered the box, jammed the door, and assaulted the president behind the ear with a one-shot derringer pistol, shouting, in a calculated theatrical style, *Sic semper tyrannis* ("thus ever to tyrants"), and then leaped to the stage yelling "The South is avenged." The action, in thespian terms, was truly bravura. Unfortunately, he broke a bone in his left leg, but was able to make his escape to an alleyway and a waiting horse.

Twelve days later, a body removed from a burning barn near Bowling Green, Virginia, was identified as Booth's. Many persons denied the identification, and some still do today. Yet the acceptance of Booth's second motive makes the assignment of identity plausible.

The two persons held up in the tobacco barn had been told that they had to surrender or burn. From inside, someone called out, "Let us have a little time to consider it." One man (David Herold), a fellow conspirator, eventually ran from the barn and surrendered. The other, in the manner of a defiant dramatic hero, had moments before offered to fight the commander of the encircling Union troops despite his crippled leg. The offer was rejected; the barn was set afire. Next, a shot—from Booth? from a Union soldier?—ended the debate. From inside the barn came the request "Tell Mother I die for my country." As a son, Booth might have been expected to say farewell to his parents, but only as an actor would he remember Horace's *Dulce et decorum est, pro patria mori.*

Both the exit speech from Ford's Theatre and that from the burning barn suggest that, emotionally, Booth was implying, "Tell Edwin that I've beaten him."

Booth was 27 when he died; he had, momentarily, capped his brother's fame.

Lizzie BORDEN: alleged parricide

Most Americans know the late 19th-century children's jingle, "Lizzie Borden took an axe/And gave her mother forty whacks;/When she saw what she had done/She gave her father forty-one!" Most, however, are not aware that, as a summary of late 19th-century America's most sensational murder, it is in error.

The facts are these: On the morning of August 4, 1892—one of the hottest days of that summer—at 92 Second Street, Fall River, Massachusetts, Abby Durfee Borden, aged 65, stepmother of Lizzie and Emma Borden, died from 21 blows of an axe to the back of her head and neck; later that morning, their father Andrew Jackson Borden, a wealthy bank president aged 70, died from 10 axe blows to one side of his head and face.

Labeled variously an "inside job" or "the action of a maniac intruder" by some 40 newspapers that covered the 1893 trial in the county seat of New Bedford, Massachusetts, the crime very quickly gained national notice; it was deemed important enough to attract reporters from the *New York Times* and the *Baltimore Sun.* An investigation by local police and state authorities failed to bring an arrest; a private inquest lasting one week alarmed those who felt that the rich had special privileges (Mr. Borden had been a bank president), but it also produced no arrest. The inquest testimony resulted in the comment by a judge presiding at a preliminary grand jury meeting that Lizzie Borden was probably guilty. Lizzie was promptly arrested, and a grand jury, after hearing her inquest testimony, voted, 21–1, a true bill (bill of indictment, warranting prosecution) against her. The Borden's maid, Bridget Sullivan, and a visiting uncle, John Morse, were also arrested as possible accessories. But the testimony so convincing to the grand jury was, through maneuvers of the defense, successfully excluded from the 1893 New Bedford trial. As a result of this exclusion and other errors noted in critiques printed in the *American Law Review* and, under the byline of a senior Massachusetts judge, in the Boston *Daily Advertiser,* Lizzie Borden was found not guilty.

One reason for the errors in the trial may lie in the fact that the case took on the dimensions of a class war. The laboring Irish and Lancashire mill workers of Fall River saw Lizzie as guilty; the rich, Yankee-descended dwellers in better districts saw the solitary Lizzie as one of their own who needed protection, support, and assistance. So did the judges who ruled for the defense on almost every disputed legal point. And so did the newspapers, who backed Lizzie as a person maltreated by the police and hounded by the prosecution. Many attacked the "experts" from Harvard University's medical school who identified the fatal axehead. And when Lizzie was acquitted, a *New York Times* editorial not only condemned the authorities who allowed her to suffer the ordeal of the trial, but also praised the verdict. (Jurors in those days were still permitted to see newspapers.)

Within a few years, however, Lizzie Borden was totally cut off by her peers and by her sister Emma, who seemed in their afterthoughts to agree with the opinion of the judge presiding at the preliminary hearing.

Reconsideration of the testimony in the trial had led many investigators to feel that Lizzie Borden was probably guilty. She had cause to hate her stepmother, and they lived together hostilely—a point weakly handled at the trial. Her stepmother feared Lizzie would poison her; according to evidence excluded from the trial and never followed up by the prosecution, Lizzie had tried several times to buy the volatile poison prussic acid. In addition, although Lizzie could be assigned no clear motive for the murder, she had the opportunity. Moreover, her testimony contained many contradictions, especially about the burning of an axe handle (the murder weapon was found handleless, its handle freshly broken off) and about her movements on the morning of August 4 (she claimed to be simultaneously in the barn and in the pear orchard), as well as about her burning of a dress splashed with brown paint (or possibly dried blood?). Most important of all, the trial excluded evidence that Lizzie had since puberty suffered attacks of temporal (psychomotor) epilepsy at least three or four times a year (usually during her menses), which caused rages and, more essentially, periods of partial amnesia; August 3 had been one of her "bad" days.

Lizzie Andrew Borden, born in 1860, lived an empty life in Fall River after 1893, a kind of Ishmael until her death *(as Lisbeth Andrews Borden)* and her secret burial in 1927. She had frequently avowed her innocence to the few believers she had remaining, but to many who study the record of her life, the children's jingle seems to come very close to the truth.

Clara BOW: boyfriends and breakdowns

The 1921 "Fame and Fortune" contest sponsored by *Motion Picture* magazine was won by 16-year-old Clara Bow, a Brooklyn-born redheaded beauty, who was then awarded a part in a silent motion picture, the first of many during the next 10 years. Her ebullience and energy fit the times, the jazz-crazed "Roaring Twenties," gaining her the nicknames "The Brooklyn Bonfire" and "The Hottest Jazz Baby in Films." After starring in a film called *It* (1927), Bow was forever labeled the "It Girl," for she epitomized, according to writer Elinor Glyn, that special "It," an extraordinary sexual magnetism.

America was enthralled with Hollywood's hottest redhead, whose looks and habits were copied by millions of women: scarlet, bow-shaped lips, bobbed hair, and going without underwear became fashionable. Paramount studios kept the star busy making movies because of her great box-office success, and movie magazines wrote about her continually to the delight of her many fans. Bow was the personification of a free spirit, one who was full of life and fun; she liked to drive around in her red Kissel convertible with seven Chow dogs and occasionally a monkey, all dyed red to match the color of her hair. Everyone seemed to love her, especially members of film crews who looked upon this young star from New York as a pal. Her roles on screen—waitresses, manicurists, salesgirls, dance-hall entertainers, and working girls in general—seemed to suit her, but Hollywood stardom evidently helped to make her into someone else, a girl gone wrong, a scamp, and a "scarlet woman." In 1927, probably at the peak of her career, Bow undoubtedly revealed something about herself with these words, "I think wildly gay people are usually hiding from something in themselves. . . . The best life has taught them is to snatch at every moment of fun and excitement, because they feel sure fate is going to hit them over the head with a club at the first opportunity." But a glamorous life of wild parties and love affairs had caught hold of "Little Miss Bow,"

one-time New York slum girl, who didn't appear to have a care in the world between 1926 and 1930.

The love life of this carefree redhead was notorious and nonstop; she slept with many actors she worked with, including Eddie Cantor, who co-starred with her in *Kid Boots* (1926), and Gary Cooper, who played with her in *Wings* (1927). Other Hollywood males she entertained in the Chinese Den of her Beverly Hills home included Richard Arlen, Buddy Rogers, John Gilbert, Gilbert Roland, Victor Fleming, Frederic March, and Bela Lugosi. Bow's quest for carnal pleasure seemed insatiable and, with her insomnia, compelled her to sometimes have two, three, or more men a night. Her wantonness became legendary, and she was alleged to have entertained the entire 1927 University of Southern California football team, the so-called "Thundering Herd," during roaring weekend beer parties (she supplied bootleg booze to fraternities at the university). But constantly jangled "nerves" made her also seek "therapy" from Dr. William Earl Pearson, Hollywood's society physician, whom she apparently accommodated sexually and who was consequently divorced by his wife. Mrs. Pearson named Bow in the divorce case and sued her for alienation of affections; the actress ended up paying $30,000 to the doctor's wife, but by then, bad publicity was beginning to hurt her. Disclosure of her spectacular gambling debts in Reno, Nevada, later contributed to increasing public disenchantment with the "It Girl," whose dissolute lifestyle was completely exposed in 1930 when Daisy DeVoe, her blonde friend and secretary for the past four years, sold, to a sleazy New York tabloid and for a high price, her memoirs about those hectic years with Bow. The paper gladly published the lurid details about the actress's suitors and lusts.

DeVoe had been fired after Bow's cowboy lover, Rex Bell, accidentally discovered that she had been stealing much money from Bow's bank account. Some clothes, furs, jewels, love letters, and other items of Bow's had also been missing. DeVoe's vengeful attempt to blackmail her former employer had failed at a time when Bow refused to be victimized any longer, and so the American public was treated to a red-hot scandal in 1930. Enraged by the DeVoe exposé, Bow took her to court in Los Angeles on charges of theft and won a kind of Pyrrhic victory: DeVoe received an 18-month jail sentence for pilfering money, but Bow received a fatal blow to her career. It was 1931, during the Great Depression, when few could feel sorry for a sick, immoral actress's personal problems. Bow soon collapsed, having a nervous breakdown that sent her to a sanitarium, and Paramount decided not to renew her contract, which was due to expire. All the while, Rex Bell stood by her. He married her in 1931 and consoled her during her forced "early retirement" from filmmaking.

Bow recovered to attempt a comeback, but her first talking film was a flop because the public was not prepared for her Brooklyn accent. She had another stint in the sanitarium and in 1932 made a successful talkie for Twentieth Century-Fox, *Call Her Savage*. But plagued by breakdowns and upset by growing public indifference to her, Bow retired forever from movie-making in 1933. For the remainder of her life she suffered fits of nerves that periodically landed her in private mental hospitals. She eventually became very reclusive and died of a heart attack at the age of 60 in 1965.

Christopher BOYCE: traitorous, counterculture falconer

"When I was 21," convicted American spy Christopher John Boyce wrote in 1977 as he petitioned the judge for a lesser prison sentence, "and not so very wise, I considered American society and government degenerate and, being disillusioned, I committed a nonconstructive act. . . ." But his attempt to justify his treason—selling top secrets to Soviet agents in Mexico City—on the basis of his country's evil degeneracy was in vain. Forty years' imprisonment (and later more) became his plight.

A college dropout with a genius IQ, Boyce was hired by TRW Systems Group, a major military-defense contractor in southern California that was working on secret American satellite surveillance systems under contract with the U.S. Central Intelligence Agency (CIA). Boyce's father and uncle were former agents of the Federal Bureau of Investigation (FBI), and his father, at the time a security executive, had helped him land a job as a security communications clerk at TRW in mid-1974 when Boyce was 21. Handsome and cleancut, there was nothing to arouse suspicion in Boyce's appearance. He did have one unusual skill: Boyce was an experienced falconer with an intimate knowledge of the wild and traveled to Africa, Alaska, and Mexico. He worked at the TRW plant in Redondo Beach (near Los Angeles), California, until 1976 and then became a University of California student.

As a TRW security clerk, Boyce was evidently investigated before he gained top security clearance and subsequently unusual access to very sensitive data in the secret communications room called the "black vault," where U.S. National Security Agency codes were stored with other material. His unexpected access to highly classified information prompted him in 1975 to enter into a scheme with a boyhood friend, Andrew Daulton Lee, a cabinetmaker and dope peddler in southern California. The two decided to begin a commercial enterprise by selling top secrets to contacts at the Soviet embassy in Mexico City. After Lee made the first contact at the embassy, he and Boyce delivered to Soviet agents the contents of thousands of documents containing classified information about CIA crytographic ci-

phers and data about American spy satellites, including the "Pyramider," then in development. Over an 18-month period, Boyce collected about $15,000 and Lee about $60,000 for passing along highly secret material to the Russians.

Mexico City police caught Lee trying to deliver a message through the gate of the Soviet embassy on January 6, 1977. Lee was arrested, and in his pockets were found microfilms of highly secret American documents. The FBI soon linked Lee to Boyce and the latter was arrested 10 days later in Riverside, California. The federal government prosecuted the two; Boyce was found guilty of eight counts of espionage and conspiracy to commit espionage and received a 40-year prison sentence. The friendship between the two traitors had apparently disintegrated by this time: Boyce later claimed that after disclosing secret information regarding the CIA's misrepresentation of U.S. Spy Satellite information to Australia to Lee, Lee had tried to blackmail him. Lee was convicted separately in 1977 and sentenced to life in prison.

Boyce's knowledge of the wild was not to go untapped. At the federal prison in Lompoc, California, Boyce scaled a 10-foot fence and disappeared into the rugged back country on January 21, 1980. He immediately became America's most wanted spy, the focus of a nationwide manhunt by United States marshals and FBI agents for the next 19 months. Investigators conducted 800 interviews and checked out 100 reported sightings of Boyce, who had assumed another identity, calling himself Anthony Lester. Through various tips and leads, the lawmen narrowed their search to the rugged Olympic Peninsula in the State of Washington and, on August 21, 1981, caught Boyce in Port Angeles. Bank security photographs also identified him as the disguised robber in 16 holdups during the period in which he had been a fugitive. Boyce was given another 28 years in prison and became the real-life Falcon of a book and film called *The Falcon and the Snowman,* written by *New York Times* reporter Robert Lindsey, to whom Boyce had granted an interview in prison.

The selling of industrial secrets about microelectronics, computers, signal-processing techniques, and other issues was investigated by the U.S. Senate Permanent Subcommittee on Investigations in April 1985. Called to testify at the subcommittee's hearing, Boyce made some startling accusations. After easily obtaining top-secret clearance and seeing how weak security procedures were, he said he "decided the intelligence community was a great, bumbling, bluffing deception." His 1974 security check "was a joke," he declared, adding that if investigators had checked his friends, they would have found a "room full of disillusioned longhairs, counterculture falconers, druggie surfers, several wounded, paranoid vets, pot-smoking, anti-establishment types." Yet Boyce was hired and monitored a secret global communications network between TRW and the CIA. He said he easily photographed code books after breaking their seals. He also disclosed the embarrassing information that in TRW's "black vault," some clerks "used the code-destruction blender for making banana daiquiris and mai tais."

Afterward, the government demanded tighter security controls by its defense contractors, especially by the mollified TRW company. It sought to deter the growing number of Americans with few or no political convictions who were willing to commit espionage for sheer monetary gain.

Tony BOYLE: powerful labor leader, embezzler, and murderer

On January 5, 1970, the dead bodies of 59-year-old Joseph A. (Jock) Yablonski, his 57-year-old wife Margaret, and their 25-year-old daughter Charlotte were found in their farmhouse in Clarksville, Pennsylvania; they had been shot six days earlier while asleep in their beds. About three weeks before, in a bitter and sometimes violent battle for the presidency of the United Mine Workers (UMW) union, Jock Yablonski had lost his bid to unseat William Anthony (Tony) Boyle, who had ruled the UMW as president since 1963, often with an iron fist. "Tough Tony" Boyle was eventually brought to trial for ordering the murders, having used

W. A. "Tony" Boyle, former United Mine Workers president, is guarded and escorted by two FBI agents after he was charged (1973) with arranging the 1969 slayings of Joseph Yablonski, a union rival, and Yablonski's wife and daughter. Boyle pleaded innocent, but in 1974, a jury convicted him. (AP/Wide World Photos)

money from the UMW coffers to pay off the triggermen. He was found guilty in 1974.

Boyle was a coal miner before becoming UMW District 27 vice-president in 1960 under Thomas Kennedy. In 1963, he was voted president. Boyle's ascendancy to the presidency of the union remained secure through the years until 1969, when Jock Yablonski, a member of the union's executive board, broke ranks and challenged Boyle for the top office. After Boyle won the election by a 2–1 voting margin, his rebellious rival contended that it had been rigged. During the fierce campaign, Yablonski had been beaten up and often kept from speaking. Boyle's henchmen had apparently refused to reveal the locations of many voting places or to announce voting hours. Along with these charges, Yablonski also claimed that Boyle was ignoring the miners' health and safety. The UMW president had committed fraud and embezzlement and had used the miners' bimonthly publication as a prime tool for distorting key campaign issues, according to Yablonski. The latter pledged to expose union corruption to a federal grand jury and instituted a lawsuit against the UMW hierarchy, including Boyle, charging misappropriation of millions of union dollars. All of this had been told to the United States secretary of labor with no results until after Yablonski's murder.

Boyle had reportedly considered having Yablonski slain before the 1969 election, but the conspirators had decided it might appear too suspicious. The decision to have him killed was evidently made between Boyle, William J. Turnblazer (a lawyer and former UMW District 19 president), and Albert E. Pass (a member of UMW's international executive board) outside the union's national headquarters in June 1969. Boyle was reported to have said "Yablonski ought to be killed or done away with." Pass, who seemed to be in charge of the operation, contacted Silous Huddleston, a minor UMW official, who recruited his son-in-law, Paul E. Gilly, a Cleveland house-painter, to do the job. Gilly's wife Annette, who was also an accomplice, eventually fingered her father in order to escape a possible death penalty at her trial in 1972.

Gilly hired two other accomplices from Appalachia, Claude E. Vealey (a convicted felon and drifter) and Aubran W. Martin (another drifter). A special "research and information fund" of $20,000 was set up to pay the hired killers. Vealey and Martin apparently thought the murder contract was for $5,200, of which they would each receive one-third. Gilly, who didn't reveal the larger amount, received the lion's share of the $20,000, from which sums were also taken by various union officials. After at least two bungled attempts to carry out the crime, Vealey, Martin, and Gilly cut the wires to the Yablonski home and flattened the family car's tires before entering the Clarksville home in their stockinged feet on December 31, 1969; they first shot Charlotte and then Jock and Margaret.

By January 20, 1970, agents of the Federal Bureau of Investigation had Vealey, Martin, and Gilly in custody. In 1971, Vealey pleaded guilty to the slayings, which he said were paid for by a man known as "Tony." Later in 1971, a jury found Martin guilty on three counts of first-degree murder, and in 1972 another jury found Gilly similarly guilty. Huddleston and Pass, both of whom were implicated in the slayings, were also found guilty in 1972–73. Federal prosecuting attorney Richard A. Sprague was relentless in his drive to follow the case to the top echelon of the UMW, namely Boyle.

By 1971 Boyle had been indicted by a federal grand jury on charges of conspiring to embezzle $49,250 in union funds for illegal use as political campaign contributions (direct political contributions by labor unions are banned by the Federal Corrupt Practices Act). Members of the UMW had also filed a $25-million damage suit against the hot-tempered Boyle, charging that millions of dollars in union welfare and retirement funds were kept without interest in the UMW-owned National Bank of Washington, thus allowing the bank to reap huge profits on loans from the money. In addition, Yablonski's surviving sons, Joseph and Kenneth, brought a suit against the 1969 election of Boyle. As a result, on May 1, 1972, a federal judge overturned Boyle's election, ruling that the union leader had illegally used UMW funds and facilities to defeat Yablonski. At a cost of $4 million and under the supervision of the U.S. Labor Department, a new UMW election was held in December 1972, in which Boyle lost to Arnold R. Miller, a supporter of Yablonski. Boyle was convicted of embezzlement.

Although Pass had refused to implicate Boyle in the Yablonski killings, Turnblazer finally did in September 1973, confessing that Boyle had masterminded the plan. The deposed union leader, who suffered from anemia and heart disease, was then serving a three-year prison sentence for embezzling and making illegal campaign contributions (for which he had also been fined $130,000). On September 24, just before he was to appear in court on the charge of instigating the plan to murder Yablonski, the 71-year-old Boyle tried unsuccessfully to kill himself with an overdose of barbiturates.

In Media, Pennsylvania, in April 1974, Boyle was tried and found guilty of first-degree murder for ordering the murders of Yablonski, his wife, and his daughter. Claiming innocence, Boyle said he had put up a $50,000 reward for the apprehension of the Yablonski killers. But this was refuted by Boyle's executive assistant, who said she had proposed a $100,000 reward, which he had rejected before agreeing to the $50,000 sum. The cantankerous Boyle was sentenced in 1975 to three consecutive terms of life imprisonment. Turnblazer pleaded guilty to a federal charge of conspiring to kill Yablonski.

The ex-president of the UMW appealed and won a new trial when the Pennsylvania Supreme Court ruled, in 1977, that certain testimony had been wrongly excluded from his first trial. Boyle was again found guilty, given the same sentence, and returned to prison in 1978. He still proclaimed his innocence, and on May 31, 1985, he died of a heart attack in prison in Wilkes-Barre, Pennsylvania, at the age of 83.

Joseph P. BRADLEY: the stolen election of 1876

That rigid adherence to principle can be the cause of major scandal seems paradoxical, but Joseph P. Bradley, an associate justice of the U.S. Supreme Court, once held so firmly to a legal prescript that he can be justly held responsible for the stealing of a presidential election. He had followed his convictions as the "swing" member of a congressional commission charged with settling the highly contested presidential election of 1876 pitting Republican candidate Rutherford B. Hayes against Democratic candidate Samuel Jones Tilden.

The 1876 contest was especially crucial to the Democrats, as they had not had an incumbent in the White House since James Buchanan had left office in 1861. It was also important to the Republicans, who had held power since Abraham Lincoln's accession as Buchanan's successor but who were in trouble. The Democrats had gained control of the House in 1874; the Republicans barely held the Senate. The election of a Republican would give the Senate strength; if a Democrat were elected the Senate would lose dominance as a fighter for the rights of former slaves and, frequently, the chief beneficiary of the corruptions perpetrated under President Ulysses S. Grant's nose.

The vote on November 7, 1876, was heavy as the nation chose its new president. The 38 states divided 18 for Hayes and 17 for Tilden, but Tilden carried the most heavily populated states, and, by November 10, held the greatest number of electoral votes, 184 to 166. On that day, returns from Florida, Louisiana, and South Carolina totaling 19 electoral votes were declared in doubt. And that doubt, according to the Constitution, was to be resolved by both houses of Congress acting through a special electoral commission.

The commission, as set up by the legislators, reflected the partisan majorities of the separate Houses. Each chose seven agents: the House, four Democrats and three Republicans; the Senate, four Republicans and three Democrats. Because this framework almost guaranteed a partisan split, the U.S. Supreme Court was asked to designate a 15th delegate with the hope that this would provide a neutral "swing" vote. Offered first to Justice David Davis, who declined because he was to become a senator in 1877, the swing vote was then offered to Justice Bradley, a Republican whose decisions had previously inclined toward the Democrats and gained him praise for fairness and objectivity.

By the time the commission met, the electoral vote of a fourth state, Oregon, was in doubt. Had Oregon's three votes gone for Tilden, he would have become president. And had the commission adopted a truly investigatory procedure, they almost surely would have.

Two procedures were possible. The first was to examine only the electoral votes in question and to choose between multiple and contradictory returns. The single return thus validated would have its figure added to the national tally. The second procedure was to "go behind the vote," that is, to examine the popular vote which underlay the electoral return and then to decide the correct electoral figure. The second procedure, which would involve a long, tedious, and surely acrimonious investigation, was favored by the Democrats despite obvious frauds in the voting wards of the southern states, which all made returns in Tilden's favor, and the political infighting in Oregon, which finally returned to Hayes's advantage.

Bradley resolved the problem. Long a believer in the separation of state and federal powers, he argued that the legality of a popular vote was a state problem and that problems involving the electoral vote were a federal concern. To him, the job of the commission was restricted to deciding the legality of specific electoral-vote returns, a matter of the legality of a specific Returning Board. In pushing for adherence to the letter of the law, Bradley avoided concern with the fairness and honesty of the four states' popular votes.

With this view, he thus joined the Republicans, who rejected the procedure of going behind the vote; his adherence to the separation principle also forced him to ignore the evidence behind Louisiana's two reports, both signed by persons ineligible to attest to the figures given.

It was soon obvious that partisan splits were guaranteed by this procedural decision and that Bradley would break the tie in only one way: by voting with the Republicans.

He did, and Hayes gained the 19 votes of the three southern states and retained Oregon's three, to win the election by a vote of 185 to 184.

Democratic historians have attacked Bradley's actions as inconsistent, for the details underlying the legality of a specific return varied. But Bradley ignored these details with stolid consistency. Republican commentators applaud his loyalty to principle and argue that an examination of the popular vote for Tilden would show that the citizenry in the southern states had really voted for Hayes. Both are wrong. Bradley, who never fully explained his decisions, had consistently followed three paths: that of expediency and efficiency, that of adherence to the state-versus-federal principle, and that of partisan loyalty.

The result was double: a single term for a president whose administration, because of the continuation of partisan hostility within the nation, was rated as "conservative and efficient no more," and a lingering shadow of doubt about the intellectual integrity of an otherwise unremarkable Supreme Court justice.

George BRENNER: forgery and larceny by a former judge

On January 12, 1959, George A. Brenner, a successful New York attorney, a former judge, and a Democratic party leader and twice candidate for Congress, crashed a borrowed car into an expressway abutment in New York City. The bizarre accident, which left Brenner alive but seriously injured, was a public puzzle for only a short period. Within a week, headlines announced that Brenner had been indicted on charges of forgery and larceny, accused of cheating creditors—including banks, corporations, friends, and business associates—out of more than $1.3 million.

Until the indictment was handed down, Brenner had seemed to personify the American success story. Born in New York City, he had graduated first in his class from Fordham University and had worked his way through law school. He became particularly interested in labor law and, as a pioneer in efforts to educate rank-and-file union members, had taught at the respected Xavier Labor School in New York City. He gradually developed a lucrative practice specializing in labor law, counting among his clients the International Longshoremens Association and the Teamsters Union. He was active in civic and lay religious groups.

Brenner also became involved in local politics. He twice ran for Congress on the Democratic ticket in Westchester County, New York, where he lived; he lost in the largely Republican area but achieved a substantial number of votes for a Democrat. He was appointed a county judge in Yonkers in 1955 and a county surrogate in 1957, though he failed to win later elections to these offices. He was on the track for eventual nomination to state office.

Apparently money problems arose during Brenner's unsuccessful but expensive congressional campaigns, problems that were exacerbated by his equally unsuccessful judgeship campaigns. Brenner began to borrow heavily, sometimes from less than reputable individuals. Nonetheless, the attorney continued to live well: he bought a new house in a better neighborhood, another car, and a boat, and he moved his law offices.

By 1958 Brenner's creditors were pressing him. An acquaintance of Brenner's, a convicted swindler named William Singer, suggested that the attorney purchase and resell at a profit a midtown Manhattan hotel, the Shelton Towers, as a means of paying off his debts. Brenner had to borrow more money for a partial down payment on the property, and to do so he used as collateral 7,500 shares of stock in the First National Bank of Yonkers, New York, of which he was a director. Singer and some other colleagues then forged duplicate stock certificates, using exactly the same numbers as the genuine certificates, in case the new creditor checked to see whether those numbers had been issued to Brenner. These forgeries were used as collateral for an additional $190,000 personal loan from an investment firm to Brenner to complete the down payment on the hotel purchase. That technique proved so successful that when Brenner failed to find a buyer for the hotel and needed money to repay other notes, he and his associates forged additional copies of the First National shares to use as collateral for new loans. Brenner used the same shares 11 times as collateral for loans from various banks and individuals.

Brenner also possessed some promissory notes for a fee of several hundred thousand dollars that the International Longshoremens Association owed him for his legal services. Some of these notes he had discounted for cash; others had served as security for loans. When all the legitimate promissory notes were gone, Brenner forged more. Brenner also mortgaged property that he no longer owned and engaged in other financial shenanigans. All the while he continued to live high on the hog, buying an even more expensive new home and a cabin cruiser.

Brenner's downfall came when a creditor learned accidentally that the collateral he was holding on a loan was also securing another loan elsewhere. As Brenner's financial dealings were gradually unraveled, it was discovered that he had mortgaged his law firm's offices in New York City and had taken large amounts of the profits for his personal use.

In January 1960, just before his case came to trial, Brenner pleaded guilty to seven charges of grand larceny, forgery, and conspiracy as outlined in an indictment resulting from $718,425 gained in the stock fraud. Singer and Brenner's secretary also admitted their part in the fraud. The 56-year-old Brenner was sentenced to four to seven years in prison. Judge Samuel R. Pierce, Jr., who sentenced Brenner, described him as a "man with an insatiable appetite for worldly goods; with an abnormal thirst for power; with a foolhardy desire to maintain a public image which required ostentatious and extravagant living far beyond his means." A month later Brenner's name was stricken from the roll of attorneys admitted to practice before the U.S. Supreme Court.

BRIEFINGATE: 1980 Reagan Campaign Committee
Many citizens who were still sanguine about the moral state of American politics were shocked in 1983 by the revelation of two incidents involving the 1980 Reagan Campaign Committee: somehow, a copy of the confidential presidential-debate briefing book prepared for Jimmy Carter had found its way into the hands of the Reagan forces and, in a brazen manner, the members of the campaign committee had both kept and used what did not belong to them. These incidents, wittily labeled "Briefingate" and "Debategate" in allusion to earlier political chicanery, represented, to those who were disturbed by it, the moral tone of the Republican campaign and the first Reagan administration.

Two questions troubled those who were morally shocked by the incident: How was the briefing book acquired, and who had received and transmitted it? They are still unsatisfactorily answered. A third and far more profound question has, since then, been partially answered through the Reagan Campaign Committee's later actions: How should America's leaders react to receiving stolen political goods?

Despite the thesis by Laurence I. Barrett, in his 1983 book *Gambling with History,* that a Carter mole gratuitously supplied the book—a thesis supported by memos written by a low-level Reagan volunteer, Daniel Jones—no evidence points to the Carter White House. On the other hand, evidence from the Campaign Committee (and, later, the White House staff) is confused and contradictory. Jones's memos were addressed to Reagan staffers Robert Gray, William V. Casey (later director of the U.S. Central Intelligence Agency), and Edwin H. Meese (later attorney general of the United States). These staffers, however, told inconsistent stories, as did those who later became the first White House chief of staff (James Baker) and the then director of communications (David R. Gergen). The briefing book was seen, among others, by President Reagan; David Stockman, later director of the budget; Wayne Valis, a Reagan aide; and, in a surprising revelation also made in 1983, George WILL, theoretically an independent political commentator of conservative outlook.

A Justice Department inquiry into the matter suffered the fate of most in-house investigations: no final answers were found, and thus no prosecutions were followed. The Carter camp persisted in their claim that the Reagan group, in the fashion of Watergate, had mounted an effort to penetrate the Carter White House; the Reagan aides, like frightened culprits, fumed at all the furor created by journalists and labeled the mess a brouhaha promoted by the Democrats, worthy only of the label "Pseudogate." To them, the matter was sheer piffle, a mere foible.

In the midst of media publicity, the third question went almost completely ignored. A few pundits and editorial writers (inwardly commenting, "Oh, what fun!") agreed with Carter's Attorney General Griffin Bell that "morals in Washington, D.C., are different from morals in the rest of the country"; then they fell silent. A few who had remained silent found inspiration in the Watergate-inspired cynicism of columnist William Safire that "Everybody's doing it." But a few, unwilling to be satisfied by attitudes that regarded the event as trivial, questioned earlier participants in political battle and found that most would have returned the book unread. Some agreed with Carter's Press Secretary Jody Powell, who said he hoped that he'd have enough moral courage to return it.

The Reagan staff apparently lacked that much moral courage. Moreover, they used the book to prepare Reagan for his debate victory over Carter.

Because many concerned with political ethics still believed that a gentleman who was also a politician would, above all, have nothing to do with stolen political goods, a new question arose: Are political ethics outmoded?

Reagan wisely declined comment on the media's remarks. His spokesman, Larry Speakes, did not refrain, remarking, "It's the way politics works."

And those who recalled the words of an 18th-century British poet, Thomas, Lord Denman, that "We may our ends by our beginnings know," felt that they had become aware of the level of moral attitudes in the Reagan White House.

Nan BRITTON. See HARDING-BRITTON AFFAIR: passion, paternity, and pelf.

Preston BROOKS: the bitter fruits of wrath

On May 22, 1856, concern for family honor and regional loyalty stimulated South Carolina Congressman Preston Smith Brooks to an act of violence he ultimately came to regret as he brutally whipped Massachusetts Senator Charles Sumner so severely that his victim was still incompletely recovered when he returned in 1859 to retake his Senate seat.

Brooks's colleagues in the House of Representatives considered him gentle and gracious in manner when he appeared in 1852 as a member of the Thirty-third Congress. They also remembered that he spoke rarely in the House, but that on the few occasions when he had made formal declamations, he had revealed remarkable oratorical skills. Only a few recalled that Brooks possessed an extremely savage temper that overwhelmed his rational faculties when it erupted.

Sumner, on the other hand, was an arrogant, outspoken abolitionist whose frequent, aggressive speeches were so violent and coarse that many opponents forced themselves vigorously to suppress their temptations to maim, if not to murder, him.

In 1856, tempers in both houses of Congress were on edge over the slavery question. The abolitionists were angry that pressure politics had upset the 1850 Missouri Compromise and its provision that slavery would not be introduced into the territories of Kansas and Nebraska; when pro-slavery legislators maneuvered through the Kansas-Nebraska Act of 1854, under which Kansas would by law become a slave territory, northern ire reached a new peak. Sumner, whose thinking on the slavery question would brook no opposition, busied himself by attempting to destroy verbally those involved in what he considered to be treachery against the United States.

Sumner unleashed some of his heaviest verbal artillery in a long Senate speech delivered on May 19 and 20, 1856, under the title "The Crime against Kansas." Among those he tried to annihilate politically was the absent South Carolina Senator Andrew Pickens Butler, Brooks's revered uncle. In his vituperative speech about the South, Sumner suggested that the elderly (and moderate) Butler had chosen "the harlot, Slavery" to be his "mistress."

Brooks allowed two days to pass so that Sumner would have time to make amends by apologizing. He did not act, and on May 22 Brooks found Sumner at his desk in the Senate Room and struck him over the head repeatedly with a gutta-percha cane, using such force that the cane broke. Then Brooks left, allowing Sumner to remain unconscious on the Senate Room floor.

Brooks's action had moved North-South tension from the verbal level to the physical, and both support for and attacks against Brooks revealed extreme partisan excitement. A House committee reported in favor of Brooks's expulsion, but the motion failed. Instead, Brooks resigned and returned to South Carolina to have southern states and communities pass approving resolutions and present gold-headed canes as tokens of their esteem for him and his stance. A proud constituency unanimously reelected him a United States representative and returned him to Washington.

Brooks's new stay in the capital was very brief, for he died in January 1857, at the age of 38. His friends reported that he had brooded constantly about the damage he had caused by yielding to his temper. His concern, however, was not for Sumner; instead, Brooks was full of regret that the scandal had injured the constituency he had been trying to defend.

B. Gratz BROWN: otherwise known as Boozy Gratz

For the fiery and abrasive Benjamin Gratz Brown, the Missouri gubernatorial election of 1870 proved to be the peak of his career. His campaign for the presidency was reduced to one for the vice presidency and in the end was completely washed down the drain by his embarrassing drunken *faux pas*. In the complicated realignments of political parties following the Civil War, Brown, who had represented Missouri in the U.S. Senate from 1863 to 1867, was nominated for governor by Missouri's newly formed Liberal Republican Party. Brown had become a prominent member of that state's liberal movement, which opposed the drastic test-oaths that were instituted after the war and were intended to disenfranchise supporters of the Confederacy. Favoring reconciliation between North and South, in opposition to the radical Republican reconstruction policies,

Brown campaigned on the issues of universal suffrage and universal amnesty for former rebels.

With support from both liberal Republicans and Democrats, Brown won a smashing victory, gaining the governorship by more than 40,000 votes. The success of the liberals in Missouri encouraged reformers in other states and led in 1872 to the establishment of the national Liberal Republican Party, which opposed the renomination of President Ulysses S. Grant. Brown became a serious contender for the liberal party's presidential nomination.

But as the campaign intensified, long-standing rumors about Brown's drinking problem resurfaced. His political opponents had often labeled him a heavy drinker, extreme even in an era when serious drinking was more tolerated in politicians. It was said that his move from his native Kentucky to Missouri in 1849 was in part an attempt to escape his growing reputation as a problem drinker. Numerous reports circulated about Brown being drunk at various public events, including commencement exercises at the University of Missouri, the emancipation convention of 1863, and even the 1870 convention that nominated him for the governorship. Though Brown denied the charges, there was evidently more than a grain of truth in them. Drinking was not, however, Brown's only political problem. Opponents could with equal justification charge that he was a political chameleon, changing his views (and party— from Kentucky Whig to Missouri Democrat to radical Republican to Liberal Republican and eventually to Southern Democrat) to suit the shifting tides of public opinion, concerned only with advancing his career.

At the May 1872 convention of the Liberal Republican Party in Cincinnati, Ohio, Brown placed fourth on the first ballot for the presidential nomination. But suspecting that his delegates were being lured into another camp, he surprised the convention by throwing his support to controversial newspaper editor Horace Greeley, who was nominated on the sixth ballot. Brown was nominated as the vice-presidential candidate.

Though Brown campaigned actively, his efforts can have had little benefit for his party. By this time, expecting defeat at the polls, he was tired and sick. He even visited a phrenologist "to have his head examined." Greeley himself was so viciously attacked during the course of the campaign that he maintained that he scarcely knew whether he was running for the presidency or the penitentiary.

In one of the low points of the campaign and of Brown's career, the vice-presidential candidate, while attending a class banquet at Yale University (from which he had been graduated in 1847), became thoroughly intoxicated and delivered an embarrassing, incomprehensible speech criticizing easterners and their effete institutions. In a ludicrous attempt to praise his running mate, he claimed that Greeley had "the largest head in America." His collapse the following day was officially blamed on cholera morbus from eating soft-shell crab, but his political opponents blamed drink and promoted his nickname of "Boozy Gratz."

The 1872 campaign marked the end of Brown's political career. He and Greeley garnered a respectable number of popular votes but lost the election. For the remainder of his life Brown devoted himself to the practice of law, specializing in railway cases. By 1874 he had gone over to the Democratic Party but never again ran for office. He died in 1885.

"Peaches" and "Daddy" BROWNING: a mismatched marriage

The 1926 marriage of 51-year-old Edward ("Daddy") Browning and 15-year-old Frances ("Peaches") Heenan made the front pages of newspapers across the United States. The couple made news wherever they went, and they both reveled in the publicity, which increased tremendously after Peaches left her husband in October 1926, after seven months of marriage. She made sensational accusations against him when she sued for divorce, but the presiding judge dismissed her charges; Browning then sued for and won a separation from her.

Edward West Browning made millions of dollars in New York real estate and was very generous with his money, especially giving it to projects that helped poor children. His bigheartedness earned him the sobriquets of "Daddy" and "Cinderella man." Browning and his first wife, who was 15 years his junior, adopted two girls, and when they were divorced in 1923, each took one of the children. Dorothy ("Sunshine") Browning was 11 years old at the time and missed her sister, so her father advertised for a girl of about 14 who wanted to be adopted. He received 12,000 replies and selected Mary Louise Spas of Astoria, Queens, who was supposedly 16 years old. After the adoption, Browning discovered that she was really 21, and the adoption was annulled. Mary Spas later tried unsuccessfully to sue him, alleging that he had attacked her and threatened her with a gun.

Shortly after this thwarted adoption, Browning became interested in the Phi Lambda Tau sorority of the Textile High School in New York City and attended the students' dances. At one such dance, a rather chubby girl with short, curly hair caught his eye, and he was introduced to Frances Heenan. Thereafter he frequently took her for rides in his blue Rolls-Royce and visited her and her mother at their modest New York apartment. "Peaches" expressed the desire to go on the stage as a dancer, and Browning helped arrange for her to appear in Earl Carroll's *Vanities*. Browning sat in a front-row seat, with his car waiting at the stage door. However, the stage manager complained that Peaches did not measure up to the standards required of chorus girls, and the young girl appeared only once.

This episode and all the publicity in the tabloid newspapers about Browning's gallantry brought Peaches to the attention of the Society of Prevention of Cruelty to Children. It investigated her past and found out that for several years she had been allowed to attend parties, movies, and dances late at night without any chaperones and that a girlfriend had died suddenly of a heart attack after a party and car ride with Peaches and Daddy. The society brought legal action in children's court to remove Peaches from the guardianship of her mother. The day before Mrs. Heenan and her daughter were due to appear in court, their lawyer presented a certificate signed by a doctor, stating that the girl could not be moved because of burns from acid that some unknown person had thrown on her face and arms. When Browning learned of the acid attack, he rushed to Peaches's side and summoned physicians. He also proposed marriage, and Peaches replied ''yes.''

Three days later, on April 10, 1926, Peaches and Daddy Browning were married by a justice of the peace in the village of Cold Spring on New York's Hudson River. Both of the girl's parents, who were themselves separated, attended the simple ceremony and approved the union of their teenage daughter with a man 36 years her senior. Witnesses of the event reported there were no signs of any burns on Peaches's face, and detectives who had investigated the alleged attack would not disclose their findings.

Peaches's mother moved into the 15-room mansion that Browning had rented for his young bride in Cold Spring and lived with the couple throughout their marriage. She and Peaches lived lives of luxury they had never enjoyed before. Peaches had breakfast in bed every morning, learned to play golf and tennis, was introduced to society, was entertained every evening, and gained 20 pounds. But she was dissatisfied, and in early October she and her mother packed up and left Browning's home. She instituted a divorce suit that became one of the nastiest and most publicized of the decade.

Peaches accused Browning of penuriousness because he would not rent a 15-room apartment for her and her mother, would not buy her a fancy car, and would not purchase all the clothes and jewelry she wanted. She asked for $25,000 for counsel fees and $4,000 per month alimony, but a judge reduced the alimony to $300 a week and counsel fees to $8,500.

After Peaches lost her divorce case, Browning sued for separation, and his young wife countersued. The trial became increasingly lurid. Peaches charged her husband with cruelty and abnormal and unnatural acts and practices. She tearfully told of how Browning had locked her in her room and returned drunk and threatened to shoot her. She also insinuated that his behavior with his adopted daughter was improper. She introduced her diary and letters written during her marriage to corroborate her allegations, but these were proved to be heavily edited, false copies and were not permitted as evidence.

The trial ended on February 2, 1927. Justice Seeger dismissed Peaches's suit on March 22, saying she had ''tired of her aged husband and preferred alimony to his society.'' However, by losing her suit she lost her alimony and fees. ''In short,'' ruled the judge, ''the defendant and her mother have falsified, exaggerated, and magnified to such an extent as to render their testimony entirely unbelieveable.'' Browning won the separation action and was a free man again.

Lenny BRUCE: "sick comic"

In the late 1950s and early 1960s, American comedian Lenny Bruce shocked audiences with his pungent social satire and obscene words and gestures. He poked fun at religion, sex, marriage, politics, prejudices, and the law; he was continually harassed and arrested on obscenity and narcotics charges. Apparently desiring to startle people into a realization of the many absurdities of life, Bruce was nonetheless called ''crude and coarse'' and ''foul-mouthed'' and, according to *Time* magazine, ''the sickest comic of them all.''

Comedian Lenny Bruce, making a V-sign while stepping from a plane at London's airport, was barred from entering Britain on April 8, 1963, on the ground that it was ''in the public interest.'' He then returned to the United States, where he faced charges involving narcotics and alleged obscenity in his nightclub act. (AP/Wide World Photos)

Bruce was born Leonard Alfred Schneider in Mineola, New York, in 1926. He completed only the eighth grade in school before being influenced by his mother, Sally Marr (the first female comic-satirist), to somehow make a career in show business. Following his discharge from the U.S. Navy in 1946, he studied acting in Hollywood under the G.I. Bill of Rights and gained some national attention in 1948 when he appeared as a comic on the radio version of *Arthur Godfrey's Talent Scouts.* By then he had chosen the name Bruce and began to get some good bookings in burlesque houses, jazz joints, and nightclubs. In 1951 Bruce met red-haired stripteaser and singer Honey Harlowe, who soon married him and later bore him a daughter, Kitty. Although they divorced in 1957, they maintained a continuing relationship, with Bruce taking custody of Kitty while Harlowe was imprisoned for two years for drug possession.

Now on the nightclub circuit, Bruce began offending some audiences and delighting others with sacrilegious jokes and a naked honesty that upset the conventions of the 1950s. He used the shock technique of language and behavior, seemingly to slice through apathy, evasion, and tradition; expressions like *cocksucker, bullshit, motherfucker, asshole, cunt, prick,* and *tits and ass* seemed to be a routine part of his talk. He asked people why certain words were labeled obscene and who had made them so and why. Many Catholics were riled by his joking about priests longing for good "horny" confessions instead of the usual boring ones, such as a parishioner confessing again and again that he smelled bloomers. In another joke, Bruce said, "Eleanor Roosevelt had nice tits. She really did. A friend of mine saw them and said they were terrific. He walked into the bedroom and—." In New York's Carnegie Hall and in London, large audiences heard his vulgarisms and laughed and cheered.

Arrested in 1963 in California for possession of heroin, Bruce was legally declared a drug addict and committed to a narcotics rehabilitation center. This was the beginning of his legal battles and trials (five of which he won) that consumed him obsessively and devoured his money for the rest of his life. Because of Bruce's controversial reputation, many nightclub owners hesitated or refused to book him, and his career began to collapse.

In 1964 Bruce's most publicized arrest on obscenity charges occurred at New York City's Café Au Go Go in Greenwich Village. He had previously been arrested on similar charges in San Francisco and Chicago, where he was found guilty of obscenity (later, the Illinois Supreme Court reversed the ruling). His trial in New York set precedents on questions of freedom of speech; more than 100 persons prominent in the arts protested his arrest and trial. The Committee on Poetry, headed by the Beat Generation poet Allen Ginsberg, later stated that Bruce's words in his comedy act were used "within the context of his satirical intent and not to arouse the prurient interests of his listeners." The committee's statement called him a social satirist "in the tradition of Swift, Rabelais, and Twain," and its signers included theologian Reinhold Niebuhr and authors Lionel Trilling, Norman Mailer, John Updike, and Robert Lowell. The trial itself developed into an arena for discussing broad, clouded social issues, the basic one being the definition of the limits of language and conduct of a comic entertainer who was a social critic. Bruce eventually fired his attorney and acted as his own defense. In the end (December 1964), he was found guilty—his performances were judged "patently offensive to the average person in the community as judged by present day standards." Bruce's sentence—four months in jail—was stayed pending appeal.

In March 1965, the U.S. Supreme Court denied a hearing on Bruce's request to bar New York authorities from interfering with his nightclub acts. Continual police harassment, he claimed, had cost him his livelihood, while he spent his considerable savings on court battles. He declared bankruptcy, an action that was supported by the United States district court in San Francisco in October 1965. Bruce now sought to enjoin the police from arresting him without first obtaining a court ruling that his nightclub act was obscene. Day after day he fought to clear his name of charges against him—notably of possession of heroin, of which he was finally convicted in Los Angeles in 1966.

Four months later, on August 3, 1966, Bruce was found dead with a needle in his arm, lying on the bathroom floor of his home in Hollywood, California. Though some considered his death a suicide, it was ruled accidental, the result of acute morphine poisoning. His autobiography, *How to Talk Dirty and Influence People,* was published in 1965 and was read by many alienated American youths and others who considered Bruce a cult hero.

Anita BRYANT: singer shaken as anti-gay crusader

In January 1977, despite protests, the Dade County Commission for the Miami, Florida, area passed a controversial ordinance prohibiting discrimination against homosexuals in employment, housing, and public accommodations. By early spring, popular singer Anita Jane Bryant, the wholesome spokeswoman for the Florida Citrus Commission since 1968 and former Miss America runner-up in 1959, had begun leading a crusade to repeal the ordinance, claiming that she had been tapped by God to become "His vessel" in His war against homosexuals. Gays and gay defenders, however, were not going to take the word of God, as relayed through his self-appointed vessel, lying down. The opposition of viewpoints soon escalated into a major nationwide showdown over civil rights for gays. In the end, though it may be said that Bryant won the battle, she certainly lost the war.

Anita Bryant, who had recorded popular and religious music albums, was earning an estimated $350,000 a year (including $100,000 from the Florida Citrus Commission) when her crusading group, called "Save Our Children," produced petitions with 64,000 signatures to force the Dade County Commission to repeal the ordinance or call a special election vote. At the time, in March 1977, Bryant stated that she did not hate homosexuals, but only the sin of homosexuality, although at one gathering she was less tactful, evidently referring to homosexuals as "human garbage." She based her objections on biblical and religious grounds, frequently quoting scripture. The ordinance, she said, was an attempt to "legitimize homosexuals and their recruitment of our children." Her strongest objection seemed to be the effect of the law on children, especially the inability of private schools to discriminate against homosexuals in their hiring practices.

The attractive singer-crusader, who in advertisements touted the benefits of drinking Florida fresh orange juice, received substantial support in her campaign from the Miami community and from across the country. Among those who endorsed her were Governor Reubin Askew of Florida, U.S. Senator Jesse Helms of North Carolina, prominent members of the Catholic clergy, fundamentalist Protestant ministers, and orthodox Jews. Local television stations and newspapers favored her, too. Bryant claimed that housing and job discrimination were not problems for "closet" homosexuals, that gay-rights activists were "really asking to be blessed in their abnormal lifestyle," and that gays evidently sought "the legal right to propose to our children" that there was an acceptable alternative to heterosexuality.

In Miami, gay activists led by Jack Campbell rallied and began a movement in strong opposition to Bryant. They received $350,000 in contributions and support from feminist leader Gloria Steinem, poet Rod McKuen, former U.S. Attorney General Ramsey Clark, the National Council of Churches, and the Dade County Democratic party, among others. Numerous conservative, closet gays in Miami openly backed the ordinance; a hostile backlash against the gay community was felt, including the beating death of a homosexual. Gay activists proclaimed the Miami showdown as their "Selma" in their struggle for equal rights. The name was borrowed from the great march led by Dr. Martin Luther King in 1968 from Selma to Montgomery, Alabama, to protest discrimination against blacks.

In June 1977, Dade County voters repealed the homosexual rights ordinance by a 2–1 majority. The 37-year-old, Oklahoma-born Bryant heralded: "We will prevail in our fight to repeal similar laws throughout the nation which attempt to legitimize a lifestyle that is both perverse and dangerous." Gay activists had seemingly overdramatized their case; some had worn a pink triangle on their clothes, reminiscent of the yellow star that Jews had been forced to wear in Hitler's Nazi Germany. The issue was seen by many as a vote on moral decline and permissiveness, not human rights. Despite the defeat, gay leaders claimed that Bryant had united them and vowed to press for civil rights.

By the fall of 1977, Bryant's crusade had fizzled, along with her singing career. Her contract with the Florida Citrus Commission was renewed until 1979, but financial difficulties prevailed.

In May 1980, she again shocked the country by announcing that she was divorcing Bob Green, her husband of 20 years. Divorce was considered an unforgivable sin by the fundamentalists who had been among her supporters, and they now derided and condemned her. Having lost her Florida orange juice contract and most television and concert singing engagements, as well as ministry fees from two nonprofit organizations set up by her and Green, Bryant was unhappily forced to sell her mansion in Miami Beach. She alleged that her husband had been emotionally cruel, and that as the major breadwinner of the two she had been unable to "submit" to him as the Bible instructs. Feeling apparently discriminated against by the fundamentalist churches, she asserted that "the church needs to wake up and find some way to cope with divorce and women's problems." And she added: "What has happened to me makes me understand why there are angry women who want to pass the Equal Rights Amendment."

In 1981 Bryant and three other women opened a dress shop. Plainly she showed none of her past antagonism while involving herself in the fashion world, a heavily gay field. "Anyway, I can't tell who's gay and who isn't," she announced.

In 1990 Bryant married former NASA test crewman Charlie Dry, a childhood friend from Tishomingo, Oklahoma; together in 1995 they bought the Anita Bryant Theater in Branson, Missouri, where Bryant sings country favorites and gospel songs to large crowds. She refrains from public talk about homosexual issues, but in 1996 she stated to the *Washington Post*, "What I did, I feel today still was right."

Claus von BÜLOW. See Claus VÖN BULOW.

Anne BURFORD. See ENVIRONMENTAL PROTECTION AGENCY (EPA): "sweetheart deals" with industry?

BURR-HAMILTON DUEL

The longstanding political antagonism between Alexander Hamilton, a Federalist, and Aaron Burr, a Jeffersonian Democrat elected vice president of the United States (1801–05), came to a head following the New York gubernatorial campaign of April 1804. Nominated for the governorship by his friends in the New York legislature, Burr was attacked verbally by Hamilton at the state capital, Albany. During the election campaign, Hamilton was reported to have called Burr "a dangerous man and one who ought not be trusted with the reins of government." In addition, Hamilton allegedly referred to Burr as "despicable," implying furthermore that Burr was disloyal to the Union and that a victory by him could bring secession from the United States by New York and the New England States. After Burr's defeat, he learned about Hamilton's serious defamation of his character (the Albany *Register* had published letters written by one Dr. Charles D. Cooper that stated Hamilton's invective against Burr), and he wrote to Hamilton for an explanation and also challenged him to a duel.

In a punctilious correspondence with his riled adversary, whom he had denounced in years past for lack of integrity, private misconduct, and almost treasonous activity, Hamilton made no denials and did not back down from dueling to settle the matter, although he had recently experienced the death of his son, Philip, in a tragic duel with one George Eacker. Hamilton undoubtedly felt that his honor was at stake and, knowing that his leadership in the Federalist party was precarious at the time, believed that he would be contemptible if he didn't take up the gauntlet. Burr, who had engaged in other duels without harm to himself or his opponents, believed that Hamilton had indulged himself too freely in defaming him in the past. The duel seemed almost planned by fate as a way for the two to settle their long animosity.

On the morning of July 11, 1804, both gentlemen, elegantly dressed, and in separate boats, crossed the Hudson River from New York City to Weehawken, New Jersey, the site agreed upon for the 7 A.M. duel. Burr arrived first, and his second (attendant), Van Ness, soon went over the exact arrangements for the duel with Hamilton's second, Nathaniel Pendleton. Then the two opponents took their places, 10 full paces apart, affirmed they were ready, heard the signal to shoot, then fired their pistols. Precisely what happened then is not definite, but eyewitnesses all agreed that Hamilton fell almost immediately afterward. Burr later claimed that he fired after Hamilton did, but some evidence shows that Burr's gun went off first and Hamilton, hit by Burr's bullet, may have accidentally fired his gun. Burr hurriedly left the dueling site after briefly advancing toward his fallen victim in what was seemingly a gesture of concern. Mortally wounded in the liver and surrounding area, Hamilton died the next afternoon at his home in New York City; he was 49, a year older than Burr. As Hamilton lay dying, Burr had sent a formal, short mis-

sive to Dr. Hosack, the former's physician, inquiring about him and the prospect of his recovery.

Soon afterward, malicious stories began to circulate about Burr, accusing him of being a murderous "wretch." Such stories helped to whip up indictments against him for murder in both New York and New Jersey. Burr had to flee incognito to Philadelphia, where he found refuge with his friend Charles Biddle. Despite his attempts to justify his duel and its cause, his political career was ruined.

Hamilton's words in his will, saying that he had decided to "receive and throw away" his first shot and maybe his second, contributed to the general condemnation of Burr. His dying words made Hamilton seem all the more heroic, and Burr the more villainous. "I have no ill will against Colonel Burr. I met him with a fixed resolution to do him no harm. I forgive all that happened." (See also BURR'S CONSPIRACY.)

BURR'S CONSPIRACY

After U.S. Vice President Aaron Burr mortally wounded Alexander Hamilton in 1804 (see BURR-HAMILTON DUEL), Burr's political career was finished. His career in scandal, however, was just beginning. Seeking to free himself of large debts and to gain new power, Burr made contact with his old friend General James WILKINSON, a U.S. Army officer clandestinely working for Spanish officials in New Orleans. Wilkinson had helped in the negotiated transfer of the Louisiana Territory from France to the United States in late 1803, and he saw personal gain in playing both the American and Spanish sides in the exploitation of the territory. At the time there were various Spanish con-

Vice President Aaron Burr (left) mortally wounded Alexander Hamilton in a pistol duel in Weehawken, New Jersey, on July 11, 1804. Angered by Hamilton's reported insults against him, Burr had challenged him. Afterward he was indicted for murder in New Jersey and New York and fled, first to Philadelphia and then to the South. (Edward Everett Hale, ed., Giants of the Republic, *1897)*

spiracies to secure control of the lower Mississippi Valley because of its strategic importance.

War seemed imminent then between the United States and Spain over boundary disputes. Burr, who knew nothing about Wilkinson's Spanish involvement, made secret plans with Wilkinson to invade and colonize Spanish territory in the West. In addition, they apparently schemed to stir up a secessionist movement in the West or to seize Spanish territory there and in Mexico and, ultimately, to establish an independent "Empire of the West" on a Napoleonic model. The conspirators also proposed an invasion of Mexico to take control of that nation. New Orleans, where Wilkinson was military commandant, was to be the capital of their planned empire.

In April 1805, Colonel Burr, who was no longer vice president, having been dumped by the Jeffersonians, began traveling west to put his plans into motion. He failed to secure British aid in an endeavor to detach western states from the United States. Burr crossed through Pennsylvania to Pittsburgh, where he obtained a river-boat on which he continued on down the Ohio River. Along the way, he visited a wealthy gentleman scholar named Harman Blennerhassett, an Irish emigrant who lived with his pretty wife Margaret on an island in the middle of the river (Margaret's baby, born in 1806, was alleged to have been fathered by Burr, who apparently fascinated her during his visit). Blennerhassett, eager to join Burr in his schemes, advanced money to him which enabled Burr to later purchase the Bastrop lands on the Ouachita River in present-day northern Louisiana, to serve as a base for his operations across the border into the Southwest. Burr recruited frontiersmen, filibusters, adventurers, and others during his journey down-river to New Orleans, where he was heartily welcomed in 1806. His intentions of colonization, conquest, or secession appealed to many, who gave him added support and money. However, he came under increasing suspicion until his supposed friend Wilkinson, who had been stationed on the Sabine River on the Spanish border with the United States, turned against him in order not to be charged with treason himself (Burr's talkativeness had spread rumors of treason). President Thomas Jefferson, notified by Wilkinson about the sinister plot, ordered the arrest of Burr, who was then seized in late 1806 near Natchez, Mississippi, while attempting to flee into Spanish territory.

Brought back east to stand trial on an indictment for treason, Burr faced U.S. Chief Justice John Marshall in the circuit court at Richmond, Virginia, in May 1807. On behalf of the accused during his trial, Marshall requested the court appearance of Jefferson, who had earlier readied a statement of Burr's crimes for Congress, but the president refused to appear (thus setting a precedent for future presidents). Because Burr had committed no overt act of treason, he was found not guilty, though there was deep distrust by many concerning his evident plot. He lived out his life generally upbraided by Americans, dying at the age of 80 in New York City in 1836.

Jake BUTCHER: greedy banker

The onetime Democratic candidate for governor of Tennessee and organizer of the 1982 World's Fair in Knoxville, Jacob "Jake" Franklin Butcher was once one of the most powerful figures in Tennessee banking circles. A popular, respected financier and member of the Tennessee elite, Jake often hobnobbed with the likes of Jimmy Carter and Bert LANCE. But in 1983, Jake's popularity and success began to teeter on the peak of a long, hard fall. Jake's crime, defrauding his own banks, was not to be viewed sympathetically. He single-handedly destroyed the deep-held faith that people put in their banks. He ended up receiving one of the stiffest sentences ever for a white-collar crime—one comparable to the sentence one might get for armed robbery.

Butcher earned himself millions of dollars in the 1970s with his aggressive style, grabbing up banks with borrowed money. Before the decline of his financial empire in early 1985, he owned and controlled 26 banks in Tennessee and Kentucky. Eleven of these banks would end up failing and going bankrupt because of his illicit dealings. The bank closings would wind up costing the Federal Deposit Insurance Corporation (FDIC) more than $700 million.

Butcher's downfall began in early 1983 when United States government regulators declared his United American Bank (UAB) in Knoxville—the flagship of his UAB chain—insolvent. It was discovered that the Knoxville bank had distributed more than $40 million in bad loans, primarily to friends and relatives of bank employees.

An obvious crack had developed in the fortress of the Butcher banking empire, and it showed that Butcher and his wife had debts totaling more than $200 million—the result of an extravagant lifestyle gone amuck. Federal prosecutors determined that Butcher had diverted money from his banks—sometimes by forging names—to pay for his personal expenses and high-priced "toys." Included in his playthings was a 60-foot yacht worth about $400,000. In all, prosecutors determined that Butcher had taken $40.8 million from banks that were once part of a $1.5-billion business.

"I am innocent," Butcher maintained at first but by June 1986 pleaded guilty to some of the multiple federal charges facing him in the hope of winning a lesser sentence through a plea bargain. In a Knoxville court, while wiping away tears, the 49-year-old financier told federal Judge William K. Thomas: "I want to apologize for what I've done. . . . I pray for the opportunity to try to restore or right some of the wrongs. . . . My little boy there, nine years old, thinks I'm going to be gone 20 years." Unmoved, Judge Thomas sentenced Butcher to two concurrent 20-year prison terms for defrauding his banks of $30 million. This was the maximum sentence he could receive. Said Judge Thomas, "The fact that you used multiple frauds to obtain millions from your own banks warrants a sentence comparable to one that would be imposed on a person who uses violence to obtain a far smaller amount of money from one of your banks."

During sentencing, Thomas said that faith needed to be restored in the state's banks, a faith that had been badly undermined by Butcher's illegal activities. The judge had apparently decided to make an example of Butcher by sending the message to other white-collar criminals in financial and political circles that this type of behavior was not acceptable and would be dealt with harshly by the courts. Before the Butcher case came to trial, financial criminals had not usually been looked upon by the judicial community as serious offenders. In fact, most people were not jailed for financial crimes before 1970.

Butcher's gross indiscretions did not end with fraud, either. He also failed to report nearly $38.5 million in income between 1978 and 1982 and was sentenced to an additional 14 years in prison for this. In addition, he received another 20-year prison sentence for defrauding two Kentucky banks of $4.2 million. The two-year investigations carried on by the U.S. Justice Department, the Internal Revenue Service, and the FDIC resulted in 100 different charges against Butcher.

Earl BUTZ: racist jokester and tax evader

During the 1976 presidential election campaign, President Gerald Ford's secretary of agriculture, Earl L. Butz, found himself on an airplane flight to Los Angeles with John Dean, a WATERGATE veteran who was currently working as a journalist for *Rolling Stone* magazine. In

Earl Butz, U.S. Secretary of Agriculture from 1971 to 1976, gestures during a speaking engagement in Anaheim, California, in October 1976. He had resigned as secretary a week before (October 4) because of a national furor over his racially insensitive remarks. He said he would have left office anyway in three to four months. (AP/Wide World Photos)

Dean's presence, Butz, well known for his lowbrow—even crude—sense of humor, started talking with singer Pat Boone, a conservative Republican. When Boone asked Butz why the party of Lincoln did not attract more black people, Butz replied with an obscene and insulting joke about black preferences in sex, shoes, and bathroom arrangements.

Dean decided to report the remark in *Rolling Stone,* though he attributed it only to an anonymous Cabinet official. But the *New Times* magazine ferreted out Butz's identity, and word of his "racism" was soon everywhere.

Republicans and Democrats alike condemned the joke as tasteless and disgraceful. Black and white officials were outraged and began calling for Butz's resignation. President Ford, in the midst of a heated campaign, was faced with a disturbing political problem, for Butz was popular among farmers, and his dismissal might mean a loss of Republican support in key farm states. Ford called Butz into his office and issued a "stern reprimand" but did not immediately fire the secretary of agriculture.

But Butz's public apology did not calm the furor over his remark, and it became clear that he was now a political liability rather than an asset. Though he resigned from office on October 4, 1976, Butz still seemed puzzled by the strong reaction to his joke. He said to a *Time* magazine reporter, "I've paid a tremendous price. . . . I don't know how many times I told that joke, and everywhere—political groups, church groups—nobody took offense, and nobody should. I like humor. I'm human."

This incident was scarcely the first time Butz's tongue had caused trouble. In 1974, for example, when reporters asked him to comment on Pope Paul VI's birth-control stand, Butz replied, "He no play-a da game, he no make-a da rules." Many Catholics and Italians were enraged, and after Ford chastised him, Butz apologized publicly. Other Butz targets were Senator Sam Ervin (whom he called "senile") and consumer advocate Ralph Nader (whom Butz described as not knowing the difference "between a hayfork and a manure fork").

Butz's policies as well as his words had been controversial. While Butz was popular among big producers and agribusinesses for helping to increase the net income of farmers by encouraging production and fostering the export of farm surpluses, many smaller farmers felt that he ignored their problems. And Butz's belief that American consumers did not pay enough for their food angered many people. (He described supporters of a 1973 meat boycott as "stupid women and crazed housewives.") In 1972 he oversaw a highly controversial grain deal with the Soviet Union, in which the Soviets bought up 25 percent of the American wheat crop as well as huge quantities of corn and soybeans at bargain rates, resulting in a domestic food shortage and increased domestic food prices. A Senate subcommittee charged the agriculture department with "inept management" and "total lack of planning."

After his resignation Butz returned to Purdue University, where he had served on the faculty for more than 30 years before joining the Nixon Cabinet in 1971. He lectured widely, supplementing his salary as dean emeritus at Purdue's School of Agriculture with substantial lecture fees, and he remained popular with farmers, whom he called his "clientele." His lectures and conversations continued to be laced with his brand of barnyard humor and racial slurs.

But Butz ran into serious trouble again in 1981, not for his remarks but for failing to report to the Internal Revenue Service a considerable income, largely derived from his lecture fees. In May of that year Butz pleaded guilty to one count of income-tax evasion, admitting that he had deliberately understated his 1978 income by more than $148,000. He owed more than $74,000 in taxes. Waving his right to be indicted by a grand jury and to have a jury trial, the then 71-year-old former agriculture secretary told the United States district court judge presiding at the trial that "I have no justification for what I've done," although he explained that he had had cash-flow problems. In return for the guilty plea, the United States attorney agreed not to make a recommendation on sentencing and not to file charges on possible 1977 tax violations.

Butz was fined $10,000 and sentenced to 30 days in jail (he was released after 25 days). He made complete restitution of the tax money he owed.

Erskine CALDWELL: "the South's literary bad boy"

In the 1930s Erskine Caldwell's earthy, sexually explicit novels about the seamier side of life among poor Southern whites scandalized American readers. Although scarcely shocking by today's standards, Caldwell's *Tobacco Road* (published in 1932 and adapted for the stage in 1934) and *God's Little Acre* (1934) aroused efforts at censorship across the nation. The ensuing controversy generated more curiosity about Caldwell's writing, and sales of these and other of his works soared, making Caldwell both one of America's most banned and censored writers and one of its most financially successful. A prolific writer, Caldwell had more than 64 million copies of his books published in 34 countries in languages ranging from Chinese to Turkish.

Tobacco Road, which did not become a best-seller until after its dramatization by Jack Kirkland, presents the story of a poor and illiterate backcountry Georgia family living in squalor and degradation, surviving through sheer animal will. Their bleak day-to-day existence offers no prospects of a brighter future. Jeeter Lester, a cotton farmer who is too poor to buy necessary seed or fertilizer, lives in a ramshackle cabin with his wife, his starving mother (with whom he refuses to share any food), and two children. In a series of telling episodes, the young son, who is interested only in automobiles, marries an older, self-ordained woman evangelist so that he can drive her new car. When a black is hit and killed by the new car, the Lesters are indifferent to the death. They are equally indifferent when Jeeter's own mother is knocked down and killed by the same automobile. They are people whom life has reduced to a subhuman level. Finally, Jeeter and his wife are killed in their sleep when their cabin catches fire in the early morning hours. A comic grotesqueness, punctuated by bawdy sexual adventures, lightens the otherwise grim story.

Though some critics at the time found literary merit in the book, others were disgusted or merely amused by its bawdy humor. The play based on the novel also opened in New York to mixed reviews but eventually ran for more than seven years and 3,000 performances, becoming a staple of the American theater. But when the play moved to Chicago in 1935, Mayor Edward Kelly denounced it as "just a mess of filth and degeneracy, without any plot, rhyme or reason." Kelly effectively banned the drama by withdrawing the license of the theater where it was to play. The producers of *Tobacco Road* obtained a temporary injunction in federal court. In the ensuing litigation a parade of witnesses, including the mayor and other political and legal personages, testified that the play was too obscene for Chicago's community standards. Other witnesses argued that, to the contrary, the play was actually unobjectionable, even inspiring. Nonetheless, the U.S. Circuit Court of Appeals upheld the mayor.

Detroit authorities acted similarly, and police closed the production there after a four-week run. The judge of the circuit court for Detroit characterized the play as "devoid of merit, stupid, profane, obscene, and degrading." In Washington, D.C., a Georgia congressman asked local authorities to stop a production of the play at the National Theater on the grounds that its portrayal of southerners was an "infamous wicked untruth." In the long run, however, the censors failed. *Tobacco Road* was made into a motion picture in 1941.

God's Little Acre engendered a like storm of protest across the nation when it was published because of its portrayal of sexuality. In this now-famous novel, Ty Ty Walden, a Georgia farmer, and his two sons have for 15 years been digging enormous holes in his farmland in search of gold. When Walden becomes convinced that an albino man can divine the lode, he kidnaps him in a comic episode. But later, jealousy over the favors of Griselda, Walden's beautiful daughter-in-law, creates a rift between her husband and the other men in the family. Her husband ultimately kills his own brother, while a brother-in-law dies in a mill strike.

In 1933 John S. Sumner, secretary of the New York Society for the Suppression of Vice, brought criminal proceedings against Viking Press for publishing *God's*

Little Acre. Sumner claimed that the book was a violation of the pornography law because it was "obscene, lewd, lascivious, filthy, indecent or disgusting." The publisher presented reviews and letters from a large and prestigious group of writers and critics on behalf of the book, arguing its literary merit. Despite Sumner's objections to the testimony of the literati, the New York City magistrate who heard the case ruled in favor of *God's Little Acre,* stating that "the author has chosen to write what he believes to be the truth about a certain group in American life. To my way of thinking, truth should always be accepted as a justification for literature."

Nonetheless some libraries, including the library of Teachers College of Columbia University, banned *God's Little Acre* and *Tobacco Road.* And 16 years after the New York ruling, the Supreme Judicial Court of Massachusetts found *God's Little Acre* to be obscene. The book, which sold more than 8 million paperback copies in the United States alone, was made into a film in 1959.

Caldwell, a Georgia native and the son of a minister, continued to write novels and stories about the rural poor, mixing sex, violence, and grotesque comedy with concerns with social justice. None of his later works, however, achieved the notoriety of *Tobacco Road* and *God's Little Acre.* Critics have dismissed most of the works, especially the later ones, as minor.

Divorced from his first wife in 1938, Caldwell in 1939 married the noted photographer Margaret Bourke-White, with whom he collaborated on several photojournalistic books, including *You Have Seen Their Faces* (1937), a poignant study of impoverished sharecroppers. The two parted in a much-publicized divorce in 1942. Caldwell subsequently married two more times before dying of lung cancer in 1987.

William CALLEY. See MY LAI massacre.

Joseph CANNON: the "revolution of 1910"

As speaker of the U.S. House of Representatives from 1903 to 1911, Joseph Gurney Cannon of Illinois wielded autocratic control through his sole right to appoint members of the all-powerful House Committee on Rules. Angry Progressive Republicans, joined by the Democratic minority, finally forced changes in the House's rules in the spring of 1910 and effectively squashed Cannon's authority.

During U.S. President Theodore Roosevelt's second administration (1905–09), Progressive Republicans were gaining in strength and numbers to press for congressional and other reforms. Ably led by Congressman George W. Norris of Nebraska, they particularly wanted to curb the power of the Speaker of the House—the blustering and tobacco-chewing Joseph Cannon. Under the traditional authority of his office, Cannon appointed like-minded Republican conservatives as members of the legislative committees, especially

the Committee on Rules, which determined what proposed legislation would go to the floor of the House for discussion. Cannon arbitrarily controlled the House's actions. He appointed reactionary Republicans like himself to the committees, which then developed legislation reflecting their views. Such issues as tariff reform, railroad regulation, and child-labor laws received little or no attention under Cannon's stand-pat, tight, and overweening rule. Thus, resentment of the speaker and his high-handed tactics grew both within and outside of the House of Representatives.

When Roosevelt's personally chosen Republican successor, William Howard Taft, was elected president in 1908, he openly supported George Norris and his followers. However, the portly and popular Taft wanted a tariff revision more than reform in the House. Cannon and his cronies, many of whom were part of the "Old Guard" (conservative Republicans who stood for the status quo), told President Taft they would back the tariff only if he would "call off the dogs" harassing Cannon; Taft agreed. Clever "Uncle Joe" Cannon was reelected Speaker of the House and could be removed only when the Republican Party caucus so decided or when a faction of the majority party joined with the minority party, an unlikely action at the time.

But the victory of the Old Guard Republicans was short-lived. In March 1910, a revolt against "Cannonism" occurred in which 40 insurgent Republicans, annoyed by the speaker's attempts to chastise them for their opposition, joined with the Democratic minority to break the dictatorial rule under which they smarted. Together the two groups were able to overrule a decision of Speaker Cannon, and a four-day parliamentary battle ensued on the House floor. When it was over, the Committee on Rules had been reorganized and enlarged from five to 10 members; thereafter the committee was to be chosen by the House, not by the speaker, who was barred from serving on it. In defeat, Cannon entertained a motion to vacate his chair, but the motion was defeated. His great power was broken, however. A mere majority, by changing the rules when necessary, could now pass the legislation it wanted. The November elections of that year (1910) swept the Democrats into the majority, and they completed the biting "revolution of 1910" by depriving the speaker of the right to appoint any committees. Afterward the speaker's principal function was to preside over the House's proceedings.

Thomas CAPANO: cold-blooded lawyer and murderer

Late in 1998, residents of the Wilmington, Delaware, area hardly noticed President Clinton's impeachment proceedings taking place 100 miles to the south; their attention was riveted on a hometown drama in which the lurid private lives of many prominent local people were exposed. Former state prosecutor and high-profile attorney Thomas Capano, 48, was on trial for slaying his former lover, Anne Marie Fahey, 30, who had been missing since June 27, 1996. But with no body, no weapon, and no eyewitnesses, the prosecution had only a stained Styrofoam cooler and the questionable testimonies of Capano's two brothers with which to work toward his conviction. During the course of the trial, it became known that Capano had had a very active extramarital sex life, fraught with risqué love letters, voyeurism, and threesomes involving other high-profile people.

Capano and Fahey met through Delaware governor Thomas Carper's office, in which Fahey was the scheduling secretary. Though Capano was married at the time, he and the vivacious Fahey began to date secretly. After her disappearance, letters from Capano and a diary in which she wrote of the relationship's ups and downs were found in her apartment, leading investigators to Capano. After three years, Fahey wrote in her diary that she wanted to end the affair. She had met a beau her own age and planned to disengage from her older lover. Witnesses attested to stories Fahey related of Capano's aggression toward her when she attempted to break up with him previously.

Capano was the last to see Fahey on the night of her disappearance when they dined together at an upscale Philadelphia restaurant. The following morning, Capano turned up at his younger brother Gerald's house asking for help. Gerald Capano, 34, squeezed by the prosecution with a possible charge for possession of illegal drugs and weapons hanging over his head, testified that he had used his boat to help Capano dispose of a body at sea. A few weeks earlier, Gerald said, Thomas had told him that a couple of people were trying to extort him and that he might have to kill them and borrow the boat to dump the bodies. Gerald thought Thomas was calling in that favor. They voyaged about 60 miles off the New Jersey coast and pushed a large cooler weighted with an anchor overboard. When it wouldn't sink right away, they shot a hole in it. Gerald said he saw a human foot and part of a lower leg disappear into the water. A few weeks later, fishermen found the empty pinkish-stained cooler.

Louis Capano, Jr., millionaire owner of a local construction business, also turned on his younger brother Thomas during the trial, testifying to seeing a stained sofa deposited in one of his company dumpsters. Other bits of circumstantial evidence accumulated: Thomas's purchase of a cheap oriental rug to replace perfectly good wall-to-wall carpeting, his purchase of Carbona blood and milk remover a few days after Fahey's disappearance, and his purchase of the cooler—all traceable to his credit cards. Also, bloodstains, which were eventually linked to Fahey, were found in Capano's house.

In a surprising twist in the trial, Capano admitted on the witness stand that he had indeed stuffed Fahey's body into the three-foot ice chest and dumped it with

his brother's help. But, in a calculated attempt to save his own skin, Capano implicated another lover in the homicide. According to Capano, Deborah MacIntyre, his steady mistress for the past 17 years, showed up at Capano's rented house that evening in a jealous rage, threatening to kill herself. As he tried to wrest the gun from her, he said, she accidentally shot Fahey. Panicking, he disposed of Fahey's body in order to protect MacIntyre.

Unfortunately for Capano, MacIntyre had a solid alibi for that evening, and worse, she admitted that, by his request, she had purchased a gun for Capano about six weeks before the incident. In prison, when Capano found out about MacIntyre's testimony, he tried to use a fellow inmate to plan a burglary of her house in order to intimidate her. His would-be accomplice turned over to the prosecution six pages of handwritten instructions and sketches for the job. The relentless Capano then attempted to hire a hitman to kill two key witnesses: MacIntyre and his own brother, Gerald.

After a 12-week trial, the jury voted 10–2 for the death penalty. In March 1999, the judge sentenced Capano to death by lethal injection, citing the fact that he was a "ruthless murderer who feels compassion for no one. . . . He is a malignant force from whom no one he deems disloyal or adversarial can be secure, even if he is incarcerated for the rest of his life." His execution date, set for June 28, 1999, was delayed through court appeal.

CARDIFF GIANT HOAX: made-to-order antiquity

During the 19th century, news from Europe of buried archaeological and art objects, both authentic and fake, prompted the plotting of deceptions in America. Among the most interesting frauds was that of George Hull of Fort Dodge, Iowa, a former Binghamton, New York, tobacconist, perpetrated during the late 1860s: he commissioned Edward Salle, a Chicago stonecutter, to direct the sculpting of a block of Fort Dodge gypsum into an oversize supine statue of a man with his knees drawn up in pain. The result, 10 feet 4 inches tall and weighing about 300 pounds, was pierced by needles to suggest pores, washed with sand and water to simulate wear, and bathed in sulfuric acid to effect antiquity. Boxed and shipped East, it was surreptitiously buried on the land of William Newell, a Hull relative and Cardiff, New York, farmer. After it rested for a year in the earth, laborers for Newell, at work on a well, were said to have discovered it accidentally on October 16, 1869.

Reactions to the news of its finding proved the correctness of P. T. Barnum's saying that "The American people like to be humbugged": the object was declared a petrified giant, identified as a statue made by Jesuit missionaries, labeled a Phoenician idol by a graduate of the Yale Divinity School, and recognized by an Onondaga squaw as the body of a gigantic Indian prophet who promised to reappear to give his tribes members one last look at him. Although the statue baffled the director of the New York State Museum, an eminent Yale professor and paleontologist named Othniel C. Marsh recognized its fraudulence; he considered it neither a human body nor a good work of art. Instead, he said, it was "a most decided humbug."

Newell capitalized on the find and its attendant publicity by erecting a tent and charging admission for viewings of the statue. Later, a consortium of local businessmen bought the majority of Newell's interest for $30,000 and began to exhibit it at summer fairs. Even Barnum was interested. When he could not buy it for $60,000, he had a replica carved in wood and exhibited in New York City to larger crowds than those attracted to the original statue, located since 1948 in the Farmers' Museum at Cooperstown, New York.

Barnum had the last word about this ambitious deception: sued by Newell for fraudulent imitation, he won his case. He testified that the Cardiff Giant was a hoax, and then pointed out that his giant was therefore only a hoax of a hoax.

Wendy CARLOS: sex change for a modern musician
"Switched-on Bach" won a Grammy Award in 1969. The musical composition was arranged and played on the Moog electronic synthesizer by a 29-year-old musician named Walter Carlos, who had also co-designed the innovative synthesizer. He was well on his way to a promising career when he dropped out of public life and seemed to disappear. Almost a decade later, another electronic musician made news with a nine-movement *Digital Moonscapes* suite. It was composed by Wendy Carlos, formerly Walter, who had undergone a sex-change operation in 1972.

Since early childhood, Walter Carlos had suffered from a chronic psychological condition called gender dysphoria; he felt as if he were a girl trapped within a boy's body. His unhappiness continued into adolescence and youth and became more severe as he grew older. He sought help from Dr. Harry Benjamin, who was an expert on transsexual problems and who prescribed a special estrogen treatment for Carlos several years prior to the latter's sex-change operation.

But Walter's problems were not over after he became Wendy. Her friends feared her musical career would be ruined if she revealed her new identity, so she continued to compose and produce records under Walter's name. She also composed the scores for *A Clockwork Orange* (working with filmmaker Stanley Kubrick), *The Shining,* and *Tron,* all while using Walter's name. Ironically, she frequently disguised herself as a man when it was necessary to conduct business face to face. The "Switched-on Bach" music continued to be a best-seller and sold well over a million copies through the years.

To escape publicity, Wendy Carlos traveled extensively and went to many exotic places to observe eclipses of the sun and moon. She even gained a reputation as a professional photographer of eclipses. While living mainly in seclusion, she gradually confided to a few new friends that she used to be Walter Carlos. In time she granted an interview to *Playboy* magazine and officially publicly disclosed her new identity as Wendy in the magazine's issue of May 1979.

Later, Wendy Carlos commented: "The public turned out to be amazingly tolerant or, if you wish, indifferent. There had never been any need of this secrecy. It has proven a monstrous waste of years of my life."

Andrew CARNEGIE: architect of monopoly
To history-minded Americans, Andrew Carnegie was a person of three reputations. He was first an immigrant's son whose intelligence and perseverance enabled him to rise from bobbin boy to director of a mammoth steel company. He was last a great philanthropist, a paragon of generosity whose benefactions totaling almost $350 million include New York's Carnegie Hall and almost 3,000 community libraries.

In between, Carnegie belonged to a class of conscienceless entrepeneurs whom historian Charles Francis Adams styled in 1878 as "robber barons"—industrialists and financiers who, in their pursuit of power and prosperity, broke laws and took the coin of their fellow Americans without scruple or remorse. It is this view of Carnegie that partly dominates today.

Although Carnegie was less ruthless than many of his confreres, he believed he was to play a major role in the monopoly capitalism of America's late 19th century, and he was not above using unscrupulous methods as he achieved his favorite sobriquet, "King of the Vulcans."

During the Civil War, Carnegie foresaw that metals industries in America, especially iron and steel, promised a lucrative future. He invested in an iron-manufacturing factory and, in 1864, stopped being a railroad executive to pursue his destiny. He first bought into an iron-bridge plant and then into a company making railroad car axles in Pittsburgh, Pennsylvania. Through a ruse, he bought out one partner and combined the bridge and axle plants as the Union Iron Mills of Pittsburgh. By the mid-1870s, several manipulations, mostly honest, made him sole owner of the facility.

Carnegie saw early the necessity for control of both supplies and finishing plants, and to avoid paying profits to local pig-iron producers, he built his own blast furnace. To make sure he had enough fuel to run his furnaces, he invested heavily in the coal and coke monopoly of the far more ruthless Henry Clay FRICK, himself busily acquiring shares of Carnegie's enterprises. By 1889, Frick, Carnegie, and another industrialist genius, Charles Schwab, were working together, acquiring competitors' facilities and eventually forming, in 1892, a new entity called the Carnegie Steel Company.

The new complex was, by federal law (the Sherman Antitrust Act of 1890), an illegal organization of a type called a vertical combination. Its aim was to control, if not own, sources of supply, fabrication, and distribution so as to be able to set prices without fear of competition. Carnegie apparently saw no wrong in creating a monopoly and violating the federal law. Although far-sighted, the Sherman Act was ineffective before the 20th century because the U.S. Congress had neglected to designate methods or provide funds for its implementation. When Frick in 1893 proposed leasing and then acquiring the world's largest iron-ore beds in Mesabi, Minnesota, Carnegie finally concurred. In that year, the Carnegie Steel Company became almost a perfect vertical combination; it lacked only its own long-line railroad, a shortcoming to which Carnegie applied himself to overcome. Because of Frick's dominance of the Homestead strike at the Carnegie steel mills in 1892, the Carnegie Steel Company also controlled labor costs. And because of its size, Carnegie's monopolistic organization could offer painful competition to all smaller metals companies.

The Carnegie-Frick-Schwab combination became a model for other American trusts: in 1898 the Federal Steel Company, headed by John Warne "Bet-a-Million" GATES, and in 1901 the United States Steel Corporation, the world's largest vertical combination, created by Gates, J. P. Morgan, and Elbert Gary (see GATES/MORGAN/GARY). They also were illegal and remained so until the early 20th century, when federal legal artillery gave the Sherman Act facilities for control of those who use the economy and the public to their own ends.

But by this time, Andrew Carnegie was only mildly interested in the metals industry. He had received more than $300 million when his vertical combination became the foundation for the United States Steel Corporation, and so he retired and, until his death in 1919, cultivated his new image as one of the world's most magnanimous philanthropists.

Billy CARTER: a paid agent for Libya

In July 1980, with the Democratic National Convention only a month away, incumbent President Jimmy Carter encountered a political shock and infamy involving his younger, outspoken, beer-swilling and fun-loving brother, Billy Carter. Billy registered as an agent of the government of Libya and publicly revealed that he had privily received $220,000 in payments he called "loans" from the African country. The president's hopes for reelection appeared to sink in the ensuing investigations by the Justice Department and a Senate subcommittee to determine if Billy's relationship with Libya had or might influence United States foreign policy.

The Justice Department forced the president's brother to register as a paid Libyan agent after agreeing not to file criminal charges against him for his neglect in reporting his assistance to the Libyan government beginning in September 1978. Like many Americans,

President Carter was stunned on hearing Billy's public disclosure that he had gotten $20,000 in December 1979 and $200,000 in April 1980 from Libya. Billy had, however, failed to disclose the sums when questioned earlier by the Justice Department, an official of which announced that Billy could be prosecuted if his statements about his connections to Libya were proven false. No admission or denial was made by Billy that he had violated the U.S. Foreign Agents Registration Act, and the president said that he was unaware of his brother's close ties with and monetary receipts from the Libyans. The president's popularity, already hurt because of his failure to win the release of American hostages being held in Iran, fell sharply following Billy's controversial news in mid-July 1980.

Quickly the Justice Department stepped up its inquiry, while Billy's activities began to be probed by a special Senate subcommittee that gathered evidence and heard testimony for nine weeks. It was revealed by the White House that the hostage situation had been discussed during a 1979 meeting among National Security Adviser Zbigniew Brzezinski, Billy Carter, and Libya's chief representative to the United States Ali el-Houderi. Afterward Iran's leader, the Ayatollah Ruhollah Khomeini, received a Libyan request to free the American hostages. There were further revelations about Billy, whom Rosalynn Carter, the president's wife, had suggested use his friendship with Libya to help try to win the hostages' freedom. Billy had made two trips to Libya, the first in September 1978, prior to which he had evidently been briefed on American-Libyan relations by a foreign-policy staff member of the National Security Council. A five-week visit by Libyans to the United States had been hosted by Billy, who also became involved with obtaining Libyan oil for an American firm, the Charter Oil Company, which apparently would pay Billy a commission of up to 50 cents a barrel. President Carter was clearly embarrassed by the continual disclosures about his alcoholic brother, who once had to "dry out" in an alcoholics' clinic in Georgia and who now seemed his high-spirited self when he saw newspaper photos of his fraternization with the Libyans; one picture showed him sitting in seats reserved for the Palestine Liberation Organization (PLO), right next to an arms supplier to the PLO. Responding to critics who questioned whether his close ties with the Libyans might jeopardize President Carter's support from Jewish voters, Billy replied, "Jewish critics can kiss my ass."

Meanwhile, President Carter made known low-level classified State Department cables from the United States embassy in Libya. They concerned Billy's first Libyan visit in 1978 and showed that he had agreed not to comment politically during the visit. One of the cables had a note saying "You did a good job under the 'dry' circumstances—Jimmy." Jody Powell, the president's press secretary, claimed the cables were no more

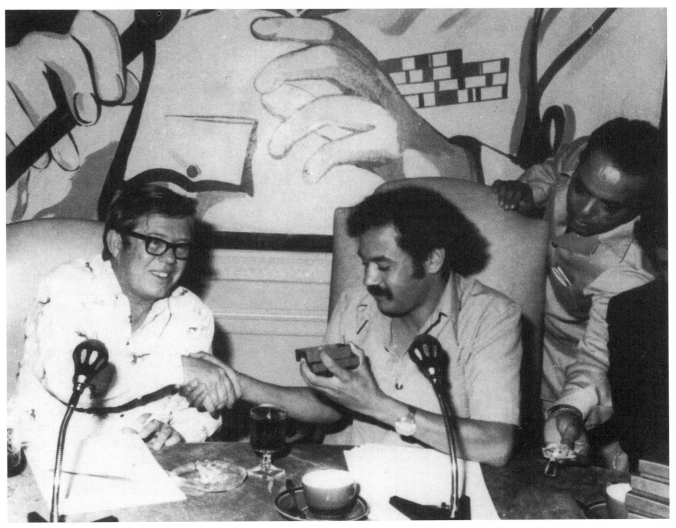

Billy Carter (left), President Jimmy Carter's brother, is seen shaking hands with the mayor of Tripoli, who gave him a key to the city, a gold medallion, a key chain, and other gifts during a ceremony honoring him in the mayor's office in Tripoli's government center. He was honored during a 1978 trip to Libya. (AP/Wide World Photos)

than a "hill of beans." In a televised news conference on August 4, 1980, the president declared "categorically" that Billy had in no way influenced foreign policy. He said that he himself might have used "bad judgment" in having Billy set up a meeting with a Libyan official to help win freedom for the hostages in Iran. "I did what I thought was best for our country and best for the hostages," the president declared; he felt he had committed no impropriety in his dealings with Billy, whose actions he said he could not control. He had opposed Billy's second Libyan trip, as well as often attempted to curtail his brother's contacts with Libya. President Carter gave a long report on the matter to the investigating Senate subcommittee, which heard testimony under oath from Billy on August 21, 1980.

"Billy Carter is not a buffoon, a boob, or a whacko," said Billy in testimony before the subcommittee. "I am a common citizen with uncommon financial and family problems. . . . I would never do anything to hurt America because I love my country." Billy went on to say he had never been asked by Libya to influence American policy. His $220,000 loan, he said, was an advance on $500,000 he reckoned on getting to solve his "problems." He planned to repay the sum from future monies gleaned from the Charter Oil Company—Libya deal.

The Senate subcommittee eventually concluded that Billy had not violated any law but criticized his conduct. The president and high officials in his administration displayed poor judgment in their handling of Billy's relationship with Libya, the committee said. There was no evidence of illegal governmental conduct but perhaps only some unprofessionalism by Brzezinski, Attorney General Benjamin Civiletti, and CIA Director Stansfield Turner in how they handled information available to them about the case. President Carter, who may have misjudged the public's tremendous interest in the scandal, was the Democratic standard bearer in the 1980 presidental election but was badly trounced by his Republican opponent, Ronald W. Reagan.

In 1981 the Justice Department said that no American official had broken the law in the Billy Carter case, but it reported that the former president's brother had "lied to government agents" probing into his duty to register as an agent for Libya.

Billy died of cancer in 1988.

CATHOLIC CHURCH: some priestly, sexual misconduct

For most of the last two decades, the Roman Catholic Church in the United States has been mired in a sea of scandals from which it has been struggling to extricate itself. Starting in the mid-1980s, allegations of sexual abuse of minors by priests began to be reported from dioceses across the country. Initially, there was much covering-up on the part of the church, but as the allegations and the lawsuits snowballed, it became impossible to continue doing that.

One of the earliest scandals to surface (in 1984) was in Louisiana where seven Roman Catholic priests were accused of sexually molesting young boys. (See Gilbert GAUTHE: pederast priest.) In February 1990, Father Bruce Ritter, founder and president of Covenant House, a shelter for homeless teenagers in New York City, was charged with having sexual relationships with four of his former charges. In December 1989, 26-year-old Kevin Kite, a former prostitute and drug dealer, had reported an eight-month-long sexual affair with Ritter, who apparently funneled $25,000 from the Covenant House account to pay for it. In January 1990, three other young men came forth with similar allegations. Ritter, the man behind Covenant House's tremendous success, was suspended pending an investigation into these charges.

In Atlanta, in July 1990, Eugene Marino (the first black archbishop in the United States Roman Catholic Church) resigned. The church's version was that he was stressed out and exhausted. In reality, it was his two-year romance with Vicki Long, 27, that caused his downfall. Marino paid $1,500 (his monthly salary) to Long for living expenses, and he also helped her buy a house. Also, it was later revealed, unspecified church funds were used to pay for her medical treatment (its nature or duration not disclosed). In mid-1993, Robert Sanchez, the archbishop of Santa Fe, New Mexico, resigned over similar charges from three young women. In a 12-month period, this diocese alone settled 48 cases of abuse against its priests.

In 1993, an investigation by the Capuchins concluded that nine friars at their St. Lawrence Seminary in Mount Calvary, Wisconsin, were guilty of sexually abusing at least 21 students between 1968 and 1992. A civil suit was filed against the Capuchins. In 1993, the court case

against 58-year-old James R. Porter, a former Catholic priest, drew much national attention. Many adults claimed they had been molested by Porter as children in the 1960s when he was a priest at Massachusetts parishes in North Attleboro, Fall River, and New Bedford; they accused the dioceses of covering up their complaints. Porter admitted he was a pedophile and pleaded guilty on October 5, 1993, to 27 charges of indecent assault and battery of a child under 14, as well as related charges stemming from the 1960s. Before sentencing Porter to at least 18 years in prison for child molesting, the judge stated that the former priest had become "an effigy representing all the other named and unnamed child abusers."

These cases and hundreds like them led many to ask for reforms within the Catholic Church; many suggested making the 870-year-old tradition of celibacy optional. In 1990, a Baltimore psychotherapist and former Benedictine monk named A. W. Richard Sipe estimated (and published in *A Secret World: Sexuality and the Search for Celibacy*), on the basis of extensive interviews conducted over 25 years with 1,000 priests and 500 others (mainly the sexual partners of priests), that half of the 53,000 priests in the Roman Catholic Church were not adhering to their oath of celibacy. Sipe found that 28 percent of priests had been in relationships with women, another 10 to 13 percent had engaged in homosexual affairs, and 6 percent had had inappropriate contact with adolescents, primarily male. These figures were misleading, said the church, given that most of the priests Sipe had interviewed were already in therapy. Another survey, by Father Andrew Greeley, found that most American priests want celibacy to be optional.

With lawsuits against errant clergy running into the hundreds of millions of dollars, the church was finally forced to confront the prevalence of deviant sexual behavior among its clergy. The issue was hotly debated by advocates for the church and for the victims at the first-ever national conference on clerical sexual abuse held in Minneapolis in October 1992. Whereas formerly, the accused priests would have been moved from parish to parish, they are now encouraged to undergo therapy, including individual and group psychotherapy, spiritual counseling, drug treatment to reduce the sex drive, and physical exercise. The therapy and the damages awarded to victims was estimated to cost the church $50 million annually in the 1990s. The Servants of the Paraclete center in New Mexico and the St. Luke Institute in Suitland, Maryland, are among the best known treatment centers for clergy. Statistics indicate that most of the priests who complete these programs return to active ministry, with the help of support groups and under strict supervision.

The Catholic Church has agreed to include a sexual education course in its seminaries and to screen would-be priests more thoroughly than in the past when, because of thinning ranks, the standards were somewhat lax. The Chicago Archdiocese has established a telephone hot line to help victims report such cases and an independent body to investigate their claims. Other dioceses have set up new criteria for handling these allegations, including timely reporting to the civil authorities. All the 188 dioceses in the United States are independent and report directly to the Vatican. Each diocese settles its own cases, so a nationwide policy is hard to draft or implement. For instance, in July 1998, the Diocese of Dallas agreed to pay $23.4 million to nine former altar boys who said they had been molested by a priest, 52-year-old Rudolph "Rudy" Kors, who earlier was convicted and sentenced to life imprisonment. The church was accused of ignoring the allegations against him.

In June 1993, in a letter to American Catholic bishops, Pope John Paul II finally admitted the full extent of the problem. However, he blamed the media for exacerbating it with their often sensationalist coverage. He reiterated the church's commitment to celibacy its commitment to the punishment of aberrant clergy behavior under Article 1395 of the Code of Canon Law. Such behavior, the Vatican felt, also reflected the permissive culture of American society.

T. Lamar CAUDLE: fraud within the Justice Department

In November 1951, T. Lamar Caudle, head of the Tax Division of the U.S. Department of Justice, was asked to resign by President Harry S. Truman, on the grounds that "he had been engaged in outside activities which the President feels are incompatible with the duties of his office." Those "outside activities" were in the process of being uncovered by the House Ways and Means subcommittee, chaired by Representative Cecil R. King (Dem., Calif.), then investigating irregularities in tax collection and in the prosecution of tax fraud.

Until this scandal erupted, Caudle's legal career had progressed steadily from the time he received a law degree from Wake Forest College in 1926 and joined his father's law firm in Wadesboro, North Carolina. Within a few years he was appointed prosecuting attorney for Anson County, and in 1940 President Franklin D. Roosevelt appointed him United States attorney for the western district of North Carolina.

Five years later President Truman named Caudle assistant attorney general in charge of the Criminal Division of the Justice Department, responsible for directing all criminal prosecution in the federal courts. In 1947 he became head of the department's tax division.

In 1951, however, King's subcommittee called Caudle to testify. A long series of questionable or illegal activities emerged. Caudle admitted that two wine merchants had underwritten his expenses on a 1950 trip to

Italy in return for various favors. He told the subcommittee that his wife had purchased a $4,000 mink coat for $1,500 through the intervention of a New York City tax attorney; the wives of other government officials had also benefited from discount prices. Caudle also admitted to receiving a $5,000 commission on the sale of an airplane to a representative of a defendant in a tax case and to accepting a television set from a tax lawyer.

The House subcommittee also began investigating why the Justice Department had dropped certain tax-fraud cases that tax agents from the Bureau of Internal Revenue had requested be prosecuted. Columnist Drew Pearson later claimed that about half of all tax-fraud cases investigated and recommended for prosecution had been quashed by Caudle or other government officials. Assistant Attorney General John Mitchell testified that Caudle had pressured him to stop tax-fraud prosecution of officials of an Alabama tobacco company, though Caudle denied that charge. He did admit to accepting gifts from individuals under investigation, including a free airplane ride from a North Carolina executive for whom he later interceded to have two substantial tax liens removed from the executive's property.

The inquiry dredged up allegations of bribes and shakedowns as well. The names of Caudle and several Bureau of Internal Revenue officials had been used to attempt to extort money from a Chicago lawyer in a tax-fraud case, although Caudle denied involvement in this scheme.

In his defense, the florid and theatrical Caudle told another investigatory subcommittee, chaired by Representative Frank Chelf (Dem., Ky.), that some government officials had applied "more than normal" pressure on him in tax cases. He claimed that Attorney General Tom C. Clark had forced him to drop several important cases. By the end of these hearings, Chelf concluded that Caudle was a "scapegoat" for higher officials in the Justice Department, honest but "indiscreet in his associations and a pliant conformer to the peculiar moral climate of Washington." Chelf blamed the Justice Department itself, calling it a "sick public agency" and Caudle merely a "reflection of decay within the department."

Others blamed Caudle more directly. Truman, worried about the political implications of the scandalous revelations, fired Caudle on November 16, 1951. Soon after this, King accused Caudle of betraying the public trust: "The damage you have done your Government will be hard to repair."

In early 1952 Caudle paid the government some $1,000 to settle his income taxes for 1950. But his troubles were not over. In 1955 Caudle and Matthew J. CONNELLY were indicted on charges of conspiring to defraud the government, bribery, and perjury. According to the indictment, the two men had conspired to sidetrack the prosecuting of a St. Louis shoe manufacturer named Irving Sachs, who had been charged with tax evasion. The following year they were convicted of accepting oil royalties in exhange for using their influence in that case, and were sentenced to two years in prison.

Unsuccessful appeals delayed execution of the sentence, but Caudle did eventually serve six months in federal prison in Tallahassee, Florida. He was paroled in 1961 and pardoned by President Lyndon B. Johnson in 1965. He died in 1969.

Cassie CHADWICK: queen of con women

Cassie Chadwick may have been born the daughter of a Canadian section hand, but by her 37th birthday she had finagled her way into the upper echelons of Cleveland society on the premise that she was Andrew Carnegie's illegitimate daughter. Born Elizabeth Bigley in about 1860, Chadwick was a lush auburn-haired beauty with a great talent for impersonation and an even greater affinity for money and high living. Her life was a roller coaster ride that took her from rags to riches and back down again. The cagey Chadwick accumulated in her lifetime some $20 million from the men she charmed and duped.

Cassie earned her first wealth by bringing satisfaction to a lovesick Canadian adolescent and realized her thespian skills after a spree of check-kiting, when she charmed a judge into letting her go. She then invaded the United States, embarking on a whirlwind courtship and three-day marriage; her husband apparently fainted upon receiving her trousseau bill. As soon as he had sufficiently revived, he divorced her. Cassie then mortgaged her Cleveland sister's furniture for travel money and toured under various guises: in Buffalo as an absent millionaire's wife; in Erie, Pennsylvania, as General William "Tecumseh" Sherman's niece; and in Toledo, Ohio, as a clairvoyant (meanwhile fronting a blackmail racket). But her lust for money caught up with her in 1887: tried and imprisoned for forging $20,000 in notes, she languished nine years in a Columbus, Ohio, prison and vowed never to fail again.

By 1897 she had married a socialite Cleveland doctor, Leroy Chadwick, who let her handle, then provide, and finally destroy his fortune. It was during this period that Cassie Chadwick pulled her most famous ploy, bamboozling a Cleveland lawyer into believing that she was Andrew Carnegie's bastard and promiscuous daughter. Both smitten and bemused enough to believe that she was backed by $11 million of Carnegie's money, he provided her with an entré into Cleveland banking circles. Equally charmed and easily cozened, the bankers provided her with generous lines of credit, asking only her "curves" as collateral.

Thereafter, she and Dr. Chadwick briefly lived high both socially and financially: overseas tours smoothed by letters of introduction, lavish parties, expensive gifts, friendships with senators who smuggled her taxable purchases into the diplomatic pouch, and extensive borrowings at high interest.

By 1904, a mortgage on the Chadwick mansion was about to be foreclosed, rumors spread that Cleveland's leading socialite was an ex-convict, banks experienced runs, and some of Cassie Chadwick's favorite financial sources failed. Tried on 16 fraud indictments in 1905, she was found guilty of six and sentenced to 10 years' imprisonment.

Cassie Chadwick then remembered her vow of almost two decades before and, wearied by the pace of her life, nearly 50 and looking it, she turned her face to the wall, sickened, and died in early 1907.

Robert CHAMBERS: the preppy murder case

A crowded New York bar. The swirl of youthful vigor. A smoky gaze from across the way. The stage is set: two people meet and decide to leave together. Though this is a common occurrence, the outcome of such an attraction is usually more benign than the meeting of Jennifer Levin, 18, and Robert Chambers, 19, one fateful evening in August 1986. These two, from New York City's Upper East Side prep school set, retreated together to Central Park. But only Robert emerged alive later that night, for he had killed Jennifer and left her partially nude body where they had lain together.

Chambers claimed the girl's death was accidental, that she had hurt him so badly during sex that he struck her, inadvertently crushing her windpipe. This case became known as the Preppy Murder and served to focus the nation's attention on underage drinking and sex among high school students.

Throughout the 11-week trail, the prosecution had trouble finding a motive for the murder. Did Chambers accidentally kill the girl during rough sex, as he said, or did he beat her and choke her afterward as she taunted him about inadequacy? They showed pictures of Levin's facial bruises, which showed she had suffered before she died, and they called attention to the fact that, at five feet seven inches tall and weighing 120 pounds, Levin could hardly have been a threat to the six feet four inches, 220-pound Chambers.

On the other hand, the defense claimed that Levin was the aggressor and that she made repeated advances, which Chambers rejected. In the park, Chambers said, she became playful and tied his hands with her panties, then straddled him, and stroked him. When she began squeezing his testicles, he freed his hands and, in pain, delivered the blow that killed the girl.

If the prosecution demonstrated that he purposely killed Levin, Chambers faced second-degree murder charges. If they established that he purposely meant to cause serious injury, he would be charged with first-degree manslaughter. If he had acted recklessly, he faced second-degree manslaughter charges. If he chose to ignore that his actions might have lead to the girl's death, he could have been charged with criminally negligent homicide.

As it turned out, on the ninth day of the trial, Chambers surprised the court by striking a plea bargain with the prosecution that reduced the murder charges to first-degree manslaughter. He showed little remorse while on trial. When the judge asked him whether he had intended serious injury to Levin, Chambers said yes but that in his heart he hadn't meant to kill her.

He was sentenced to five to 15 years in prison. After five years, he was turned down for parole; he had been caught with marijuana and had assaulted a prison guard prior to the parole hearing.

Levin's mother, Ellen Levin, petitioned to keep Chambers in jail, saying that five years was not enough time to pay for her daughter's life. She started an advocacy group called Justice for All which lobbies for victims rights and against the early release of violent felons. Ellen Levin was also part of the legal experiment of having a representative of the victim on the defendant's parole board.

Chambers's lawyer claimed that the parole board was improperly influenced by Ellen Levin and the media attention that her petitioning caused. In all, Chambers was denied parole three times. His original sentence will reach its maximum in 2003.

Whittaker CHAMBERS. See Alger HISS: traitor or scapegoat?

CHAPLIN-BARRY AFFAIR
In the spring of 1941 in Hollywood, California, Charles ("Charlie") Spencer Chaplin, 52-year-old, internationally famous, British-born actor and comedian, and veteran of three failed marriages, took a fancy to a young, red-haired, aspiring actress named Joan Barry. He added her to his long list of Hollywood protégées and paid for acting and singing lessons for her, hoping to make her the leading lady in a movie he was planning. For a time Chaplin and Barry had a quiet affair that lasted into the autumn of 1942 when the latter went to New York, supposedly followed by Chaplin. The pair, however, shortly became estranged. Later Barry alleged that she had forced her way into Chaplin's California house at Christmastime, 1942, brandishing a gun and consequently exciting them both erotically to the point at which they went to bed together. A few months afterward she was arrested for unlawful entry into Chaplin's house and received a 30-day jail sentence.

Upon her release in 1943, Barry, who was then very much pregnant, went in a fury to one of Hollywood's most notorious gossip columnists, Hedda Hopper, and told her that she had been impregnated by none other than the renowned Chaplin. Immediately Hopper,

whose writing was often punctuated with innuendoes and moralizing, announced the news in her column; for many years she had loathed Chaplin because of his personal conduct (his contempt for her and his sordid relationships with teenage girls, among other things) and politics (his left-wing sympathies and his not taking out American citizenship). Hopper stirred up public opinion against Chaplin, who denied he was the father of Barry's unborn child. For a while Chaplin postponed his marriage to Oona O'Neill, his new love, and attempted to quell the rumors without success. In June 1943, Barry filed a paternity suit against Chaplin, claiming he was the father of her child.

Before the paternity case reached court, the Federal Bureau of Investigation (FBI) accused Chaplin of violating the Mann Act, a federal law prohibiting the interstate transportation of females for immoral purposes. Barry alleged that she had traveled to New York in the fall of 1942 at Chaplin's expense and had had relations with him there in his hotel room. Accordingly, he could be prosecuted under the act, and in April 1944, he was. Chaplin hired a well-known, crafty lawyer named Jerry Giesler to defend him at his trial in New York. Although Chaplin tearfully admitted to having had an affair with Barry, his lawyer convincingly argued that it had been a private romance between them and that Chaplin had not had to take his young paramour to New York to have sex with her. The defendant was acquitted, but the highly publicized case intensified a growing anti-Chaplin atmosphere.

When the paternity case went to court in December 1944, Chaplin used his regular lawyer instead of Giesler; a fact he may have later regretted. He disclaimed fathering Barry's infant girl, who had been born on October 2, 1943.

Each day the child was brought to court by her mother. This contributed to the bad publicity which Barry's lawyers seemed able to whip up against Chaplin, whose past philandering reputation was magnified by Barry's juicy court testimony about their affair. Blood tests showed that Chaplin, who had been paying Barry's medical and other expenses for more than a year, could not have been the girl's father, and his lawyer stated that the plaintiff had definitely had another lover during the Chaplin period and that some of her travel costs had seemed to have been paid by the oil tycoon J. Paul Getty, although this point was not pursued. Although a mistrial was finally declared, the court ordered the defendant Chaplin to pay child support of a substantial sum. By now, public opinion had convicted Chaplin of gross indiscretions.

Many American filmgoers boycotted Chaplin's next movie, *Monsieur Verdoux* (1947), which was thus a financial failure despite being an artistic tour de force. The press attacked him for his behavior and supposed support of subversive causes, and the U.S. government claimed that he owed back taxes. Silently and bitterly suffering public humiliation, Chaplin left the United States with his wife, Oona, and children in 1952, settling permanently in Switzerland. However, before his death in 1977, he returned once (1972) to America to be honored for his lasting, brilliant, motion-picture work. As for Barry, she was committed to a California state hospital with mental problems in 1953. Her child, Carol Ann Chaplin, disappeared from public view.

CHAPPAQUIDDICK: Kennedy-Kopechne accident

The Kennedy clan has long been one of the most glamorous and respected families in American politics. But in the summer of 1969, Edward M. Kennedy, U.S. senator from Massachusetts, plunged himself and his family into a scandal which lingers on more than 30 years later. The exact circumstances on the night of July 18 are still open to speculation, but these basic facts are clear: The senator offered a ride home to a beautiful young secretary. When the car was accidentally driven off a bridge, the young woman was drowned. Kennedy, however, survived—and failed to report the accident until nearly 10 hours later. Pretty, 28-year-old secretary Mary Jo Kopechne had been a political campaign worker for the late Senator Robert F. Kennedy, Edward Kennedy's older brother, who had been assassinated in 1968. She went to the island of Martha's Vineyard, Massachusetts, for a barbecue party during that July regatta weekend, which was also a reunion for former staff members of Robert Kennedy. The party took place on Chappaquiddick Island, off Martha's Vineyard, and was attended by Senator Edward Kennedy, who offered Miss Kopechne a ride home near midnight. With Kopechne as his passenger, the senator left the party in a black 1967 Oldsmobile sedan, mistook some turns on a country road on the island, and accidentally drove the car off unmarked Dike Bridge into Poucha Pond (a tidal pool) on Chappaquiddick. The car plunged into water about eight feet deep, where the fatal drowning occurred. Kennedy, who claimed he had attempted to save the young woman from the immersed Oldsmobile without success, unaccountably did not report the fatal accident to the police until the next morning. Local police on Martha's Vineyard retrieved Kopechne's body from the water on July 19, but serious questions were immediately raised by the press and others about the 37-year-old senator's judgment and conduct.

Following public disclosure of the accident, Senator Kennedy went into seclusion at his home at Hyannis Port, Massachussetts and received considerable advice from friends and others, including several important advisors of the late President John F. Kennedy (the senator's and Robert's older brother, who had been assassinated in 1963). Many persons began to think the senator's silence about what had occurred that fatal night indicated he had something to hide that would damage his political career; some speculated that he and Miss Kopechne had had an affair or were lovers at the time. On July 25, 1969, Kennedy pleaded guilty in the Edgartown district court to a charge of leaving the scene of an accident, and he explained what had happened on national television and radio. He said he had come back to the scene of the accident later that night with two other persons who had been at the party, and the three had attempted unsuccessfully to extricate Miss Kopechne from the car. Not reporting the accident immediately to the local authorities was, in Kennedy's own words, "indefensible," and he appealed for understanding, saying that if his constituents thought he should not continue in office he would remove himself. The senator's office announced strong favor for Kennedy shortly afterward, and he resumed his work in the Senate. Kennedy's driver's license was revoked, and he received a two-month suspended jail sentence and was placed on probation for one year.

Although the Edgartown authorities closed the case, the federal district attorney for southern Massachusetts initiated an inquest on July 31, 1969, that lasted through the summer and into the fall. Court hearings took place in Massachusetts and Pennsylvania, where Kopechne's parents lived in the city of Wilkes-Barre. The Kopechnes stopped the exhumation of their daughter's body for an autopsy (the body had been buried in Larksville near Wilkes-Barre). An investigating grand jury decided to indict no one. The press, sometimes a hound for any incriminating or sordid details pertaining to a scandal, was barred from a closed inquest hearing granted to Senator Kennedy by the Massachusetts supreme Court in late October 1969. The senator suffered no further legally and won reelection to the Senate in 1970; he had, however, announced that he would not seek the presidency in 1972 and remained faithful to his word.

The incident at Chappaquiddick became a lasting liability for Senator Kennedy, who never won the Democratic nomination for president but was reelected to his Senate seat in 1976, 1982, 1988, and 1994.

Samuel CHASE. See JEFFERSONIAN REPUBLICANS: the attempted impeachment of Samuel Chase.

Benjamin CHURCH: illustrious doctor's treason

At the start of the American Revolution in 1775, Samuel Adams, John Hancock, James Otis, and other leading patriots in Massachusetts were unaware that in their midst was a clever traitor, Dr. Benjamin Church. Named director and chief physician of the Continental Army, Church was subsequently unmasked through the discovery of a correspondence with the enemy, the British.

Church was born in Newport, Rhode Island, in 1734 and at the age of 20 graduated from Harvard College.

Afterward he earned a medical degree in England, married a young English woman, and later (1768) settled down in an impressive home he had built in Raynham, Massachusetts. The construction of the house put him in extreme debt and just may have made him more predisposed to treasonable dealings to win needed funds.

In the pre-Revolutionary period, Church wrote poetry, notably *The Choice* in 1757—a poem modeled on one by the same name by the English poet John Pomfret. As tensions mounted between the Americans and the British, Church wrote slick pamphlets that appeared to support the colonists' desire and struggle for independence. He supposedly also secretly wrote articles for a Tory (pro-British American) paper, poking fun at his Whig brethren who felt their rights were being violated and infringed upon by the British.

By the time of the Boston Massacre (1770), when some British soldiers fired on a heckling mob of Americans, killing five and wounding six others, Church was in the confidence of Samuel Adams and his rebel cohorts. In 1722, the "good" doctor was made a member of Boston's 21-member standing committee of correspondence, organized at the suggestion of Adams for the purpose of exchanging information with other towns and promoting the patriots' cause. Church spoke and wrote some liberal words while being privy to the scheming of Adams and other agitators in Boston. In 1774 Paul Revere, the famous patriot, was said to have suspected Church of some nefariousness. Revere's suspicion was raised when the rebellious colonist's actions at a private meeting became almost immediately known to the British.

Church and other important Whigs hastened from Boston the day before the battles of Lexington and Concord (April 19, 1775). He quickly returned to the city after the fighting had ended, saying he needed to get medicine for the wounded. Church proclaimed that he had been seized while going for the medicine and had been brought before British General Thomas Gage, the colonial governor of Massachusetts. But a patriot spy had a different story to tell. Church had gone to Gage voluntarily, he announced. Yet nothing happened to Church after this disclosure. In fact, he attended the Continental Congress in Philadelphia in May 1775 and was unanimously elected head physician and director of the newly formed Continental Army, the colonies' military forces. Paid four dollars a day, Church was stationed at Cambridge, Massachussetts, where the first American army hospital was set up.

In time, a letter in cipher written by Church to the commander of a British ship at Newport was intercepted and handed over to General George Washington, commander-in-chief of the Continental Army. The doctor was promptly arrested and court-martialed, with Washington presiding over the trial in October 1775. Church was found guilty of "holding criminal correspondence with the enemy." His ill health at the time induced the authorities not to imprison him at Norwich, Connecticut, but to remove him to Massachusetts, where he was paroled and told not to flee the colony. In due course permission was given him to leave for the West Indies, and in 1778, Church apparently sailed from Boston but was lost at sea with the ship during the trip. Significantly, his family was granted a pension by the British Crown.

Incriminating evidence that Church had been a Loyalist and British informer during at least the six weeks before the battles of Lexington and Concord was not discovered until the 20th century; there seems little doubt that he had passed confidential American plans to General Gage, who had ordered the arrest of Adams, John Hancock, and other rebels in the colonists cause.

Henry CISNEROS: cabinet officer's mistress and lies

At the height of his career, Henry Cisneros was the most prominent Hispanic politician in the United States. Born in 1947 in San Antonio, Texas, he entered public life as an administrative assistant to the city manager. He won a seat on the city council in 1978, and three years later the 34-year-old Democrat was elected mayor of San Antonio, thus becoming the first Hispanic to serve as mayor of a major U.S. city. He was reelected to three more two-year terms, and in 1985 he became president of the National League of Cities. His good looks, charm, ethnic background, and political acumen made him a rising star in the Democratic Party and convinced many that he stood an excellent chance of becoming the U.S.'s first Hispanic president.

However, Cisneros was forced to retire temporarily from public life in 1989 following the public airing of his adulterous relationship with Linda Medlar, his former campaign fund-raiser. The brief affair began in 1987 and ended the following year after the affair became common knowledge, Medlar was divorced from her husband while Cisneros eventually reconciled with his wife. For the next four years Cisneros ran his own asset management company and from its proceeds gave $4,000 a month to the unemployed Medlar, who resumed the use of her maiden name, Jones.

Cisneros returned to public life in 1993 to serve as President Bill Clinton's Secretary of Housing and Urban Development, thus becoming the first Hispanic to serve in the Cabinet. Once again, the talk about a future run for the presidency began to circulate, only to be derailed a second time by his affair with Jones. Citing his greatly reduced income as a public servant, Cisneros stopped making support payments to his former mistress. In turn, she sued him for $250,000 for breach of contract and sold tapes and transcriptions of telephone conversations between herself and Cisneros to a tabloid television show. In May 1995 Cisneros and Jones settled the case for $49,000.

Meanwhile, the publicity surrounding Jones's lawsuit attracted the attention of U.S. Attorney General Janet Reno. She was concerned because the payments disclosed by Jones in her case against Cisneros were almost five times higher than what he had told FBI investigators during his confirmation proceedings as a cabinet officer. Part of those proceedings included the granting of a top secret security clearance to Cisneros, and his unwillingness to tell the full truth about his financial dealings with Jones suggested that he could be blackmailed by a foreign power to disclose government secrets.

In March 1995 Reno appointed an independent counsel to investigate the matter. Eighteen months later Jones was charged with 26 counts of conspiracy, bank fraud, money laundering, and obstruction of justice. In 1999 she was sentenced to three and a half years in federal prison, mostly because she lied repeatedly under oath during her civil suit against Cisneros. Also indicted were Jones's sister and brother-in-law and two of Cisneros's former partners in the asset management company. In January 1997 Cisneros resigned his cabinet position and moved to Los Angeles to become president and chief operating officer of Univision, the nation's largest Spanish-language television network. In December 1997 he was charged with 18 counts of conspiracy, obstructing justice, and making false statements to the FBI. In 1999 he pleaded guilty to reduced charges; he was fined $10,000 but received no jail time.

Despite his marital and legal problems, Cisneros remains a popular figure among Hispanics. Although his political future is not as bright as it once was, the possibility still exists that he will one day make a spirited run for the White House.

Harry CLAIBORNE: felonious federal judge

The disgrace of being the first sitting federal judge in American history to be sent to prison belongs to Harry E. Claiborne, who was convicted in 1984 of tax evasion and sentenced to two years' imprisonment. He then brought even more ignominy on himself by adamantly refusing to quit the bench and suffering removal through impeachment and conviction by Congress in 1986.

For many years Claiborne had been a successful private lawyer in Las Vegas, Nevada, often handling criminal cases and being active in politics. At one time his clients included celebrities such as Judy Garland and Frank Sinatra, and he liked to say to juries: "I stand here until the blood runs in my socks fighting for the rights of my clients." In 1978 President Jimmy Carter successfully nominated him to be chief judge of the United States district court in Nevada, at the urging of Claiborne's former political foe, then U.S. Senator Howard Cannon. Years earlier, in 1964, Cannon had won a Senate primary fight against Claiborne, who had afterward

Federal judge Harry Claiborne (sitting) is guarded by two United States marshals during 1986 Senate impeachment hearings that would determine Claiborne's future on the bench. The Nevada judge, who had been convicted of tax evasion and was then serving a two-year jail sentence, was found guilty and removed from the bench. (UPI/Bettmann Newsphotos)

backed Cannon in his narrow defeat of Republican Paul Laxalt.

While on the federal bench, Claiborne got into serious financial straits because of the collapse of a house sale and his former wife's stiff monetary demands on him. In 1979 he received $41,000 in residuary fees from his former law firm but told his accountant he'd gotten only $22,000. The next year Claiborne hired a new accountant to prepare his income-tax returns: Jerry Watson, head of Creative Tax Planning, Incorporated of Las Vegas. The $88,000 in residuary legal fees received by Claiborne in 1980 were not reported as income.

Suspicion about Claiborne's dealings led to a grand-jury investigation and his indictment in 1982 on charges of taking bribes and evading taxes. His case went to trial but ended with a hung jury. In 1984 Claiborne was tried again, strictly for income-tax evasion, and found guilty of failing to report a total of $106,651 in legal fees on his 1979 and 1980 federal tax returns. The judge appealed, but the U.S. Court of Appeals for the Ninth Circuit unanimously upheld his conviction in July 1985. The U.S. Supreme Court refused to review the case, and Claiborne was packed off to the minimum security federal prison camp at Maxwell Air Force Base in Montgomery, Alabama, to begin serving his two-year sentence.

Unabashed, Claiborne stubbornly refused to resign his lifetime federal judgeship, feeling that he had been the victim of an unfair Justice Department "sting" operation coordinated with the Federal Bureau of Investigation (FBI). He continued to draw his full annual salary of $78,700 while in prison. Many thought this an outrage, but the Constitution does not permit a federal official's salary to be cut off while he or she is still in office. Some congressmen then began calling for the impeachment process to remove Claiborne. United States Representative Hamilton Fish of New York said that Congress had to eject him, or else he would sit again on the bench after serving his jail term, and then retire at full pay in 1988. Representative Bruce Morrison of Connecticut declared: "We must send a message to the American people. We will not tolerate felons on the federal bench."

The House of Representatives initiated the abstruse process to impeach (bring charges against) Claiborne, who defiantly said he was free from wrongdoing. On July 22, 1986, the House voted 406 to 0 for four articles of impeachment against the 69-year-old judge and then sent them to the Senate, where, two months later, Claiborne became the first impeached United States judge to stand trial in half a century. Testimony was given by Claiborne's Las Vegas accountant Jerry Watson, who insisted that any of the judge's tax-preparation mistakes had not been his because "I just own the company—I don't do the work." Asked by Claiborne's lawyer if he knew anything about his client's tax returns, the cowboy-booted Watson replied, "Not very much." He also wasn't certain what "capital gains" meant. Watson's remarks evoked guffaws, laughter, and shock from the senators. Finally, Claiborne, in impassioned words, said: "I have been stripped of my freedom, stripped of my reputation, stripped of my good name and my honor. Maybe the best heritage I could leave my grandchildren is a heritage of courage and guts."

After a 10-day trial, the senators, on October 9, 1986, overwhelmingly pronounced Claiborne guilty under three of the four impeachment articles against him. He was convicted of "high crimes and misdemeanors" by willfully cheating on his income-tax returns of 1979 and 1980 (two of the impeachment articles). He had also "betrayed the trust of the people of the United States . . . and thereby brought disrepute on the federal courts and the administration of justice" (the third article).

The next day Claiborne was back in prison, stripped of both his judicial robes and his salary.

CLEVELAND-HALPIN AFFAIR

The presidential campaign of 1884—usually ranked as the dirtiest in American political history—was enlivened by charges of immorality from both sides. The Democratic candidate, Grover Cleveland, met the accusation with a surprise: he told the truth, acknowledging his adultery with Maria Crofts Halpin and his fathering of a son by her. And despite his confession, he won the election.

Famed after 1882 for his actions as a reformer while mayor of Buffalo and governor of New York, Stephen Grover Cleveland in his earlier days had a lighter side shared only with his intimates. In 1871, while the forceful sheriff of Erie County, New York, and known as "Big Steve," he and his friends had formed a fishing club called the "Jolly Reefers," which partied in a clubhouse on Niagara Island. The parties were stag gatherings; the only women admitted were those whom the club members found accommodating. Among them was Maria Crofts Halpin, a comely, well-educated widow whose two children stayed with relatives in New Rochelle, New York, while she worked as a department-store clerk.

Maria moved in with "Big Steve" in 1874 after she had borne a son, Oscar Folsom, named for Cleveland's closest friend and law partner, whose daughter the son married in 1886. The boy's last name appears in documents as both Halpin and Cleveland, for the paternity was acknowledged and Cleveland supported both Maria and her son. But despite her nagging, he refused to marry Maria and acquire a ready-made family.

Her badgering forced him to move out, and she complicated their relationship by drinking too much. Cleveland was obliged to act on the child's behalf in 1875. He moved, without court order, to have the boy admitted to an orphanage and Maria committed to an institution, where she was forced to stop drinking. He supported the boy until his adoption and aided Maria by setting her up in business. At the same time, Cleveland supported Oscar Folsom's widow and made her young daughter his ward.

But Maria would not quit. She kidnapped the boy for three months and, when he was adopted, tried through an attorney to get custody of him. Cleveland offered her $500 to drop the case and leave the area. She did so in 1876 and remained silent, refusing to comment to reporters during Cleveland's campaign for the presidency. In 1895, she (or someone purporting to be Maria Halpin) wrote a blackmail letter to Cleveland, demanding money on the threat of disclosing details of their relationship. Cleveland did not reply.

In July 1884, however, after news of the affair appeared in the Republican-oriented Buffalo *Evening Telegraph* and spread throughout the country, Cleveland was forced to reply. His campaign committee and Democratic editors tried to deny the charge or to blame the paternity upon Oscar Folsom, but Cleveland wired them from Albany, giving instructions and ordering them to "Above all, tell the truth." They were forced to, for all sorts of publicity-seeking clergymen were demanding, often on false information, that Cleveland be defeated as immoral. Some gave strong but disastrous support to his Republican rival (see James G. BLAINE: "rum, Romanism, and rebellion"). Only one well-known clergyman defended Cleveland, Henry Ward BEECHER—who, ironically, was having his own troubles with charges of adultery.

Both the attacking clergyman and Republican newspaper editors were at first completely unconcerned with the facts of the affair, and they invented horror stories depicting Cleveland as thoroughly immoral in every way. Charles Dana of the Republican New York *Sun* indulged in yellow journalism and libelously called Cleveland "a coarse debauchee who would bring his harlots with him to Washington and hire lodgings for them convenient to the White House."

However, Cleveland's acknowledgment of the truth, plus the help of adequate time before the election in which to disseminate that truth, destroyed the Republican attacks, which nevertheless persisted until election eve. In the torchlight parades that made colorful 19th-century campaigns, Republicans would taunt, "Ma! Ma!/ Where's my Pa?" The Democrats would retort, "Gone to the White House! / Ha! Ha! Ha!"

The retort proved to be correct.

Bill CLINTON: impeached U.S. president

William Jefferson Clinton became in 1998 the second president in U.S. history to be impeached. The entire affair was the result of several scandals: Clinton's sexual misconduct which led to his impeachment on charges of perjury and obstruction of justice, independent counsel Kenneth Starr's relentless investigation into Clinton's financial dealings and personal life, and the Republican Party's apparent obsession with pinning a major political scandal on the Democrats.

In 1995 Bill Clinton (then 49) began having an affair with Monica S. Lewinsky, a 21-year-old White House intern. Clinton knew that he was being investigated by Starr, who was looking into alleged financial wrongdoing by Clinton and his wife, Hillary. He also knew that Paula Corbin Jones, a former Arkansas state employee, was suing him for an act of sexual misconduct which occurred when he was governor of Arkansas and that her attorneys were investigating several rumors regarding his extramarital affairs. Despite these very real dangers to his presidency, Clinton recklessly and repeatedly received oral sex from Lewinsky in the Oval Office of the White House until her internship ended in 1997. Clinton was indisputably guilty of felonious stupidity, secret trysts, recklessness, and deception.

Starr's investigation began shortly after Clinton's inauguration in early 1993. At first it focused on Whitewater, a real estate development company which Bill and Hillary Clinton owned jointly from 1978 to 1992 with Jim and Susan McDougal, co-owners of Madison Guaranty Savings and Loan. Starr contended that the S & L, which had folded, loaned the Clintons $300,000

that they never repaid. In 1996 Starr obtained the McDougals' convictions on multiple charges of bank fraud. He also got Jim McDougal to state for the record that Bill Clinton had indeed received a loan under circumstances which Clinton knew to be fraudulent. However, Starr was never able to get Susan McDougal to verify her husband's claim and was therefore unable to pin anything substantive on the president.

Having failed to "get" Clinton over the incidents of Whitewater, Starr began looking for other misconduct or wrongdoing possibly committed by the president. He turned his attention to Jones's suit, which contended that Clinton had violated her civil rights by sexually harassing her while both worked for the state of Arkansas and then caused her to be discriminated against at work until she quit her state job. Jones's attorneys heard rumors of Clinton's affair with Lewinsky and questioned him about it under oath. After Clinton denied any sexual involvement with Lewinsky, Starr obtained from Linda R. Tripp, one of Lewinsky's friends, taped recordings of Lewinsky telling Tripp in detail about the sexual affair with Clinton. Starr also got Tripp to claim that Lewinsky told her that Clinton had urged Lewinsky to lie about the affair and that he had taken steps to cover it up. Having spent six years and over $40 million pursuing the president, Starr finally had some sort of case against him. In his report to Congress, Starr contended that "substantial and credible information" supported impeaching Clinton for perjury, obstruction of justice, witness tampering, and abuse of power.

Ever since the WATERGATE scandal of 1972–74, when U.S. President Richard M. Nixon resigned from office rather than be impeached for tampering with a federal election, numerous Republicans had been hoping for a scandal of similar scale to pin on the Democrats. Starr's report gave the Republicans, who controlled both houses of Congress, exactly what they wanted. On December 19, 1998 the House of Representatives narrowly impeached Clinton for perjury and obstruction of justice; by a vote of 228-206, it accused him of lying under oath to Starr's grand jury about his affair with Lewinsky; by a vote of 221-212, it accused him of obstructing justice by coaching his secretary, Betty Currie, to lie about his relationship with Lewinsky.

For almost four months the nation's business was put on hold while the Senate conducted impeachment hearings. Democratic senators insisted that lying about a sexual indiscretion and then trying to hide it from one's wife did not constitute "Treason, Bribery, or other high Crimes and Misdemeanors," the only grounds for impeachment allowed by the U.S. Constitution. Meanwhile Republican senators insisted that President Clinton had lied under oath, doing irreparable harm to the nation's judicial system. (Clinton had never had sex with Lewinsky, as he defined it "in his own mind," according to his lawyers. But many saw Clinton's problem to be using wordplay to mask the truth, such as his unforgettable remark in sworn testimony to prosecutors: "It depends on what the meaning of the word 'is' is.") Finally, on February 12, 1999, the Senate acquitted Clinton of both charges.

Clinton's impeachment was an embarrassment for Democrats and Republicans. Despite some accomplishments as president, Clinton will be remembered primarily for his sexual hijinks. Rather than being considered a hero who courageously exposed wrongdoing in high places, Starr will be remembered as Clinton's failed inquisitor and adversary.

Bill CLINTON: "slick Willie" womanizing and lying

During the 1990s, President Bill Clinton was plagued by a number of sex scandals. These scandals involved just about everything from consensual extramarital affairs to rape. Some of his sexual shenanigans took place while he was attorney general and governor of Arkansas, and others took place in the White House. The scandals ultimately led to his impeachment in 1998.

Rumors of Clinton's womanizing began circulating while he was serving five terms as governor of Arkansas (where he was born in Hope in 1946). These rumors became national news when Clinton first ran for U.S. president. In 1992 Gennifer Flowers, an Arkansas state employee, disclosed to the press that from 1977 to 1989 she had been Clinton's girlfriend. As proof, she provided eight taped conversations between her and Clinton; however, the tapes were not found to confirm her allegations. Although Clinton admitted publicly that his 16-year marriage to Hillary Rodham Clinton had not always gone smoothly and that he and Flowers had once been friendly, he emphatically denied Flowers's charges.

In 1993 Roger Perry and Larry Patterson, Arkansas state troopers who had been Governor Clinton's bodyguards, told the press that part of their job had been to arrange Clinton's sexual liaisons. They claimed that they delivered Clinton's pick-up messages to attractive women, then rented hotel rooms where those women who were willing could have sex with the governor. Clinton emphatically denied the charges.

In 1994 Paula Corbin Jones, a former Arkansas state employee, sued Clinton for sexually harassing her while he was governor. It was the first time a sitting president had been sued for something he had done before he became president. Jones alleged that in 1991 Clinton sent Danny Ferguson, one of his state trooper bodyguards, to invite her to Clinton's hotel room on the pretense of offering her a promotion, but instead Clinton exposed himself and asked her for oral sex. As proof, she claimed she could describe "distinguishing characteristics in Clinton's genital area." She also alleged that her refusal to gratify Clinton resulted in her being discriminated against as long as she worked for the state.

Clinton emphatically denied the charges and denied that he had ever met Jones.

To make Jones's charges more credible, her lawyers set out to prove that Clinton had a long history of using his several elected positions to pressure women into having sex with him. In 1997 Jones's lawyers subpoenaed Monica S. Lewinsky, a former White House intern, who they claimed had a sexual relationship with President Clinton while she was working in the White House. Clinton emphatically denied the charges, this time under oath as part of his testimony during the Jones trial. Then Linda Tripp, a friend of Lewinsky, produced tapes of Lewinsky talking about her affair with Clinton in vivid detail. Shortly thereafter Clinton confessed to the Lewinsky affair. He also admitted to having sex with Gennifer Flowers on one occasion. And although he continued to deny Jones's charges, in 1999 he settled out of court with her to the tune of $850,000.

The hefty cash settlement was not the only punishment Clinton suffered as a result of the Jones trial. He was already under investigation for financial wrongdoing during his term as governor, and his perjury involving his relationship with Lewinsky opened the door for charges that he had attempted to subvert the legal process, charges which in 1998 led to his impeachment. On July 29, 1999, in Little Rock, Arkansas, U.S. District Judge Susan Webber Wright ordered Clinton to pay about $89,000 to Jones's lawyers for giving "deliberately" false testimony when he denied a sexual relationship with Lewinsky. Clinton didn't contest the penalty, which was also aimed at deterring others "who might consider emulating the president's misconduct."

During Clinton's impeachment ordeal, other women came forward with more sordid tales regarding his sexual appetite. Kathleen E. Willey, a former White House volunteer, claimed on national television that one day in the White House near the Oval Office, Clinton groped her and asked for sex. And in 1999, shortly before the end of the impeachment trial, Juanita Broaddrick, a nursing home operator in Arkansas, alleged that in 1978 Clinton raped her. At the time he was Arkansas's attorney general and she was a volunteer in his gubernatorial campaign. According to Broaddrick, they met to talk in the coffee shop of her hotel in Little Rock. Clinton suggested they go to her room to avoid reporters, and when they did he attacked her, bruising her lip in the process. Rumors of the rape had circulated for years, and Broaddrick had denied them in 1992 during Clinton's first presidential campaign. She said that she was recanting her denial only because Jones's lawyers brought up the rumors during the Jones trial and contended that Clinton had paid Broaddrick to keep her quiet. Clinton emphatically denied Willey's and Broaddrick's charges.

Still other women, including Elizabeth Ward Gracen (a TV actress and former Miss America), Sally Perdue (a former Miss Arkansas), and Dolly Kyle Browning (a Texas real estate lawyer who had known Clinton since childhood), also went public with claims of brief or longtime affairs or intimacies with Clinton in the 1970s, 1980s, and 1990s. When asked about them, Clinton remained his charming self, using his golden gift of gab, denying, hoping things would go away, and pleasing the audience at hand. See also Bill CLINTON: impeached U.S. president.

Cardinal CODY: ". . . accusations against the shepherd . . ."

John Patrick Cardinal Cody, leader of the largest Roman Catholic archdiocese in the United States, became the first prelate in the history of American Catholicism to come under an acknowledged federal tax investigation. In 1981 a series of front-page stories in the *Chicago Sun-Times* revealed a federal grand-jury probe into allegations that the cardinal had improperly diverted up to $1 million in tax-exempt church funds to benefit his step-cousin, Helen Dolan Wilson. Cody fought back, refused to hand over documents subpoenaed by the U.S. government, and gained much sympathy from the Chicago Catholic community as well as others.

Born and raised in St. Louis, Missouri, Cody was considered a bright, young priest of the Roman Catholic Church following his ordination in 1931. He earned doctorate degrees in philosophy, theology, and canon law, and the Vatican secretariat engaged him in staff work in Rome, where he became the protégé of two important churchmen who would both rise to be pope, Pius XII and Paul VI. Cody returned to Missouri to serve the church in bishoprics in St. Louis, St. Joseph, and Kansas City. In 1964 he was made archbishop of New Orleans, Louisiana, where he commanded national attention by effecting desegregation of the Catholic archdiocesan schools despite aggressive opposition. In 1965 Pope Paul VI named Cody archbishop of Chicago. Referred to as "Louisiana Fats" by many of his Catholic flock when he first came to the city, the corpulent Cody soon proved less amusing than his Irish heritage might suggest and showed himself to be a stern boss of Chicago's 2.3 million Catholics. In 1967 he was named a cardinal, becoming for certain the nation's most powerful Catholic prelate.

During his 16-year rule of Chicago's two-county archdiocese, the autocratic Cody was a skillful administrator, unwavering in his old conservative stance and his keen management of an estimated $1 billion in archdiocesan properties. With his extensive church powers and strong support from the Vatican, he beat down any dissension from priests, nuns, and lay people who might oppose him. Cardinal Cody largely disregarded the Second Vatican Council's decentralizing policy that called for including wider opinions in decision making. Prominent clergy and laity rankled quietly under Cody's

dominance; some felt there was a need for a new archbishop—one younger, more alert to Chicago's modern-day needs and problems.

Reporters of the *Chicago Sun-Times* probed into Cody's affairs for 18 months, finally breaking the news that the federal government was trying to find out whether the cardinal had misused as much as $1 million in church money to help his lifelong friend, Helen Dolan Wilson. Her father had married the sister of Cody's mother after the death of his first wife, Wilson's mother. Cody called Helen "sis" and considered her a family member. According to the copyrighted *Sun-Times* stories, Cody had allegedly gotten Helen modest-paying jobs in St. Louis and Chicago archdioceses, paid for a $100,000 home for her in Boca Raton, Florida, and made her the apparent beneficiary of a $100,000 life-insurance policy, on which he had paid annual premiums of $3,528 since taking it out in 1954 (when Cody was making only $4,000 yearly as a bishop). Cody's annual church salary had never been more than $12,000. The *Sun Times* reported that Helen's net worth had risen to almost $1 million through the years, but she flatly denied this and claimed her assets amounted to only about $350,000. The government's investigation apparently centered on two bank accounts of supposed church funds under Cody's personal control and not subject to audit; church monies are tax-exempt unless they are diverted to personal use.

Replying to the public allegations, Cardinal Cody put on a good face against his critics, stating, "Any accusations against the shepherd are also against the church." He implied that the government investigation was the result of newspaper sensationalism and anti-Catholicism. Many Chicago Catholics, including some of his most severe past critics, and others sympathized with the beleaguered cardinal, who was ailing from congestive heart disease and diabetes. They felt that he should be able to finish out his term in peace and dignity (the church's retirement age for cardinals was 75, and Cody turned 74 on December 24, 1981, having celebrated 50 years as a priest at a special mass about two weeks earlier).

In February 1982, an announcement came that Cody would retire as prelate on his 75th birthday, Christmas Eve, 1982. By that time he was rarely seen and conducted business from his Chicago mansion residence. Perhaps there was relief when he died of congestive heart failure on April 25. Federal investigators brought no indictments in his case, which was closed on July 6, 1982.

Roy COHN: a lifetime without scruple

The familiar comment by Lord Acton that "power tends to corrupt" may have been deliberately kept ambiguous because its originator, in a letter, did not wish to spell out the dozens of ways in which authority, or the hope of it, can undermine a person's soul. When Acton died in 1902, he was too early for the phenomenon of Roy Marcus Cohn, to whom power and integrity were semantic antitheses.

To Cohn, who died at age 59 on August 2, 1986, of problems related to the AIDS virus, the Acton observation applies, as may another equally famous dictum, Persius's *De nihilo nihilum* ("nothing can come out of nothing"). For when Cohn was disbarred a month before his death, he had been guilty of breaches of ethics for nearly 40 years.

To prove his unethical and unprofessional conduct, the New York State Supreme Court's Appellate Division (which disbarred him because he had been found guilty of deceit, fraud, and misrepresentation) had many instances of Cohn's unscrupulous actions to choose among. It selected only four. Two might have been construed as minor incidents, almost peccadilloes, had they not illustrated so clearly Cohn's modus operandi, slyness, and mendacity.

In one case, Cohn had made devious maneuvers, including court hearings, for 17 years to avoid the repayment of a $100,000 loan. A client served in a divorce matter had made the loan, and Cohn alleged in letters that integrity would prompt his repayment of the money. Publicly, however, Cohn cynically told the press that the money was an advance on "future services." The debt was erased only after a May 1984 court order was handed down. (Cohn tended to be forgetful about his debts. He died almost $5.25 million in arrears, $3.25 million of it in back taxes.)

The second case involved a 1982 application for admission to the District of Columbia bar, made while his creditor was suing him for repayment. Cohn had lied in stating that he had no client complaints pending against him.

The others were offenses serious enough to keep Cohn, who had planned to appeal his disbarment, from obtaining bar-association membership in any of the 50 states.

One offense, labeled "particularly reprehensible" by the court, involved guiding the hand of a wealthy but comatose man to gain an illegible "signature" on a codicil to a will involving millions of dollars. The will protected the estate for a daughter; the codicil named two relatives and one Roy M. Cohn executors and trustees, endangering the claim of the original legatee. A Florida court decided that Cohn had "misrepresented . . . the nature, content, and purpose of the document." He should have been, but was not, immediately barred from practicing in Florida.

The fourth instance was described as "failing to protect a client's escrow account." In this matter Cohn's client, a yacht-chartering corporation and seven of its officers, had been indicted for securities fraud, and the escrow was to have been a protection against future stockholder claims. Cohn's law firm took custody of two yachts and sold one but failed to put the money in an interest-earning account; instead, the money went into the checking account of a Cohn partner. The second yacht, under Cohn's signed order, was remortgaged. Its insurance was doubled with Lloyd's of London, and it was then scuttled, accidentally causing the death of the first mate. A lawsuit had forced Cohn's law firm to repay $219,000 or face disbarment.

The firm paid.

These facts stood out clearly to the appellate division's five-judge panel. In an effort to establish a counterweight, persons acting as "character references" testified to Cohn's "high personal integrity." They included prominent journalists, professional men of religion, federal and state judges, academics, establishment lawyers, politicians, millionaires, White House officials, an ambassador, and a former high official of the Federal Bureau of Investigation. Cohn clearly had built up a lot of connections during his years of unscrupulous actions. The testimonial markers seemed ready to forget Cohn's past actions in order to ensure their own futures.

However, those past actions included two deeds that should have crippled Cohn's future years earlier. In 1951, Cohn—freshly out of law school—had engaged in improper *ex parte* communications with Judge Irving R. Kaufman concerning the sentencing of Julius and Ethel ROSENBERG. Both lawmen should have been disbarred had the meeting not been kept secret until 1972, for Judge Kaufman, in an unprecedented peacetime decision, had ordered the death penalty for the Rosenbergs.

The five-judge panel may have remembered Cohn's unscrupulous behavior in 1951, as well as Cohn's Iago-like promptings of Senator Joseph MCCARTHY during the senator's opportunistic congressional investigations that wrecked countless lives and careers. As McCarthy gained almost dictatorial power in Washington, D.C., Cohn was determined to share in it. Complacently, Cohn actually threatened the U.S. Army if his current favorite, David Schine, was not given special privileges. The Army accepted Cohn's challenge, and the resulting Army-McCarthy hearings (1954) cost McCarthy his power base. They did no harm to Cohn, however, perhaps because the system that had protected Kaufman and Cohn in 1951 needed him as he needed it. Cohn thereafter went undeterred into his subsequent career as a shark lawyer.

Cohn's death ended his nefarious influence and his unscrupulous actions, little troubling the system of which he was a part. He deserves no valedictions.

Schuyler COLFAX: under a cloud of suspicion

During his incumbency of the vice presidency of the United States from 1869 to 1873, the honorable Schuyler Colfax, at age 49, was charged with complicity in the infamous CRÉDIT MOBILIER scandal and in postal frauds. The scandal, which came to light in 1872, rocked the administration of President Ulysses S. Grant, who dropped Colfax and chose Senator Henry Wilson of Massachusetts as his vice-presidential running mate when he ran for reelection that same year. Although Colfax was never prosecuted for any crime, his political career was hopelessly wrecked, and he left office under a cloud of suspicion that never really dissipated.

The Crédit Mobilier scandal was completely opened to the American public after the *New York Sun* ran a sensational exposé on September 4, 1872. Along with other prominent politicians in Washington, D.C., the 49-year-old Colfax was accused of having had corrupt transactions with Crédit Mobilier of America, which acted as the construction company for the Union Pacific Railroad (the railroad promoters received heavy government financing and secretly diverted the profits they gained from building the railway line to themselves).

Crédit Mobilier had apparently "sold" stock in the company to Washington legislators in return for favorable political influence; the stock had been sold at half its market value to persons who "would do the most good" to secure legislation for railroad rights-of-way and land grants. The large blocks of stock had also been sold to help head off a congressional inquiry into the company.

The principal "bagman" in the Crédit Mobilier payoff operation was Representative Oakes Ames of Massachusetts, a major officer in the company and a member of the Pacific Railroad Committee in the U.S. House of Representatives. He had evidently managed to buy the goodwill, among other politicians, of Colfax when the latter served as Speaker of the House from 1863 to 1869; Colfax, a Radical Republican from Indiana, was a United States representative from 1855 until 1869, when he became vice president under Grant.

Public disclosure by the press of high-level involvement in the railroad company by members of the U.S. government, together with the huge rights and profits connected with the company, soon brought on congressional investigations. A congressional committee accused Colfax of having once accepted a bribe of 20 shares of stock in Crédit Mobilier. In testimony, Colfax flatly denied this charge and also denied having ever received any dividends from the company. In challenge to this statement, the committee showed him a $1,200 canceled check made out to him by Oakes Ames. After Colfax tried to save face by saying he hadn't received and cashed the check, the committee uncovered and displayed his bank records to show that he had deposited $1,200 to his account on the same day that the Ames check was paid. Colfax was a bit flabbergasted and, afterward, was increasingly at a loss for meaningful explanations for the deposit.

President Grant was supportive, on one occasion even personally writing a letter to his vice president,

saying that he sympathized with him and was "satisfied now (as I have ever been) of your integrity, patriotism, and freedom from the charges imputed, as if I know of my own knowledge your innocence." But despite Grant's faith, Colfax was on the way out. The congressional probe continued and discovered that Colfax had taken an 1868 political campaign contribution of $4,000 from a contractor who had sold envelopes to the federal government at a time when Colfax was chairman of the House Committee on Post Offices and Post Roads.

At one point, the House Judiciary Committee, deeply disturbed by the unfolding scandal, even wondered whether the House of Representatives should impeach the vice president. In the end, however, the committee reasoned that Colfax's impeachment couldn't stand up because his alleged criminal transgressions had occurred years earlier when he was serving as House Speaker. Colfax, discredited, went into political retirement when his vice-presidential term ended. He died at the age of 61 in Mankato, Minnesota.

Anthony COMSTOCK: malicious moralist

Comstockery today is a term which refers to the prudish pursuit and censorship of alleged immorality, particularly in literature and in pictures. The term, invented in 1905 by playwright and critic George Bernard Shaw and originally defined as "the world's standing joke at the expense of the United States," was based on an overly zealous moral crusader named Anthony Comstock. This supposedly upright Christian was honored in 1892 and 1897 for his achievements. It was not until the early 20th century that Comstock, a man who had once boasted of causing the imprisonment of enough persons to fill a 60-car train of 60 persons each and that he had reveled in the fact that his actions had caused 15 suicides, would be reevaluated with ridicule and disdain.

Comstock was a 19th-century "born again" moral crusader who devoted most of his life to defeating the forces of those he considered propagandists for immorality and heterodoxy. Today, however, he is less complacently viewed as one of a noble army of fanatics whose zeal for the Lord rendered them more sinning than sinned against.

A Connecticut-born "New Puritan" whose sense of his own sinfulness led him to see the Devil everywhere, Comstock had led a narrow and unsophisticated life. An 1868 YMCA campaign against obscene literature influenced him enough to secure the arrest of two publishers. The YMCA, impressed by Comstock's private crusades, accepted his services in 1871 as its moral agent and, in 1873, as secretary of the then YMCA-supported New York Society for the Suppression of Vice. Freed by these appointments to give up his job as a dry-goods salesman, Comstock adopted the profession of full-time reformer.

Comstock evidently regarded anything that aroused the Devil in him as condemnable. Since he regarded passion as a disease, sexual arousal (outside the marital state) as a sign of the Devil and the modern world as strongly under the control of the demonic, he felt it incumbent upon himself to attack publishers, booksellers, quacks, abortionists, birth-control advocates, gamblers, lotteries, dishonest advertisers, patent-medicine vendors, and all art in the nude.

To his credit, Comstock's attacks upon gamblers, patent-medicine vendors, and quacks are still highly regarded, but his whirlwind actions against all the others in his array of infamy are still the subject of ridicule. Many consider him an enemy of liberty of thought as well as the values of literature and art.

Though he prided himself on his moralistic ends, his means were sneaky at best, dishonest and unchristian at worst. His chief means of stopping an adversary was entrapment, then still a legal action; he also used Joseph A. Britton as an *agent provocateur*. Throughout his career he penned thousands of decoy letters under aliases, luring various products to his New Jersey post office box. And when the products were received, he brought suit against their vendors under federal laws. In short, in his zeal for the Lord, Comstock became *particeps criminis*—an accomplice in crime—for the sake of what he saw as good.

Britton wasn't Comstock's only accomplice; he found an equally illiberal jurist in Judge Charles L. Benedict of the U.S. District Court. Comstock often boasted that he never lost a case argued before Benedict, and for good reason: Benedict often rejected any evidence not submitted by Comstock, allowed no defense or cross-examination, and failed to demand that evidence be corroborated. Moreover, Benedict believed with Comstock that sinners should suffer both deeply and extendedly. His ignorance seemed to be as great as Comstock's. He once fined a publisher $500 and sent him to jail for a year because a title on his list was "obscene." The book—Ovid's *Art of Love*.

The formidable power afforded Comstock, who remained secretary of the Society for the Suppression of Vice until his death at age 71 in 1915, made him crusade far and wide. Because he grew irrational in matters in which sex was concerned, he attacked the supporters of birth control (which he confused with abortion), punishing Margaret Sanger by arresting her husband, achieving the fining of Havelock Ellis, banning Emmeline Pankhurst's pioneer study of the evils of prostitution, and arresting the enlightened gynecologist Dr. Sara B. Chase for selling two vaginal syringes. In fact, all "arousing" manifestations of the sexual were confronted by Comstock's wrath and might: he banned the mailing of medical textbooks and the sale or posting of classical statuary (then all carefully fig-leaved), attacked the concept of models posing in the nude at the Arts Students League, tried to stop belly-dancing at the 1895 World's Fair, and acted against physical education in tight exercise outfits. Without even reading it, he forbade the production of Shaw's *Mrs. Warren's Profession*.

Matthew CONNELLY: bribery and perjury in the executive branch

Matthew J. Connelly, a 1930 graduate of Fordham College whose hope of studying the law was thwarted by the Great Depression, moved to Washington, D.C., in 1935 and joined President Franklin D. Roosevelt's Works Progress Administration as an investigator. After he began working in 1939 as an investigator for various congressional committees checking into unemployment, campaign spending, and relief racketeering, he became friendly with Harry S. Truman, then Democratic senator from Missouri.

In 1941 Truman became head of the Senate's War Investigating Committee and hired Connelly as chief investigator. When Truman was elected vice president in 1944, Connelly became his executive secretary, and when Truman acceded to the presidency, Connelly was quickly named his appointments secretary, a post that allowed him to control access to the president. Connelly became Truman's confidant, a crony with whom the chief executive liked to spend his off-hours. Connelly was described as a likeable, easygoing man; one journalist called him a "cool, behind-the-scenes operator," a man with a knack for politics who knew the inner workings of the White House.

As a member of the White House staff, Connelly helped plan Truman's 1948 whistle-stop campaign. After Truman's election, Connelly was put in charge of a two-man congressional relations team. While continuing his job as appointments secretary until the end of the Truman administration, Connelly also expanded his sphere of influence to include such high-level political matters as job appointments.

A minor scandal erupted in 1949 when the Senate Permanent Investigations Subcommittee identified Connelly as one of several government officials who had accepted the gift of a freezer from a manufacturer seeking scarce wartime goods in 1945. Connelly was not, however, accused of wrongdoing.

When Truman left office in 1953, Connelly began a public-relations business in New York. He largely dropped from public view until 1955 when a federal grand jury indicted Connelly, Truman's former assistant attorney general T. Lamar CAUDLE, and an attorney named H. J. Schwimmer for conspiring to defraud the government. Connelly was also charged with bribery and perjury.

The charges stemmed from a 1951 tax case in which a St. Louis shoe manufacturer, Irving Sachs, had pleaded guilty to charges of evading payment of more than $118,000 in federal income taxes. Sachs was fined $40,000 but was spared a prison term on the grounds of poor health. The grand jury in 1955 argued that Sachs's lawyer, Schwimmer, had bribed Connelly and Caudle, first to stop the prosecution (which they had been unable to achieve) and then to prevent Sachs's imprisonment. Connelly was accused of accepting a $7,500 oil royalty (for which he had paid Schwimmer only $750), a topcoat, and two suits for his part in the arrangement.

Connelly maintained his innocence, countering with a charge that the Republican administration had timed his indictment to coincide with the 1956 election and so embarrass the Democratic Party. "There is a little group of willful men now in power in Washington," he said. "They have called Harry S. Truman a traitor. Now, because of my association with him, they are calling me a crook." At his trial Connelly claimed that he had paid Schwimmer for the oil royalty without knowing its true cost. His White House associates believed in his innocence and thought the former Truman aide had been framed by the Republicans. Nonetheless, in 1956 a federal court in St. Louis found Connelly, along with Caudle and Schwimmer, guilty of tax-fraud conspiracy. He was sentenced to two years in prison.

Unsuccessful appeals delayed his incarceration until 1960 when Connelly served six months at the federal prison in Danbury, Connecticut, before being paroled. He returned to his public relations business in New York. In 1962 President John F. Kennedy, reportedly at Truman's request, granted Connelly a full and unconditional pardon. Connelly died in 1976.

CONWAY CABAL: botched conspiracy

When the Continental Congress named Virginia's George Washington commander-in-chief of the Continental Army, causing New England leaders to lose power and control of the American Revolution and the army, some never-identified members of the Congress plotted in 1777 and 1778 to reverse the result. These angry New England members then conspired to regain dominance by replacing General Washington with one of their own. The complotters' scheme failed, and two generals on the fringe of the cabal suffered for the offenses of the entire group. One of these generals, Thomas Conway, experienced the additional ignominy of having historians name the intrigue after him.

The cabal's candidate as replacement for Washington was General Horatio Gates, commander of the American forces in the Saratoga campaign, which had defeated Britain's General John Burgoyne in 1777. Gates was already popular with the Continental Congress; his victory had been rewarded by his appointment as president of the Revolutionary Board of War.

On the fringe of the plot was Thomas Conway, an Irish-born general in the French armies that had come to America with the marquis de Lafayette and whom the Congress had later made a brigadier general. Conway performed well in battles at Brandywine and Germantown, Pennsylvania. But when Conway was refused promotion to major general by Washington (who preferred to recognize equally deserving American officers), he agreed to help unseat the commander-in-chief. He was not mollified when, after a fit of pique that

caused him to resign, Congress rejected the resignation, promoted him to his desired rank, and named him inspector-general of the Continental Army.

A hothead and a loudmouth who had nearly died from a dueling wound, Conway then wrote an ill-advised letter to Gates strongly criticizing Washington. His action caused exposure of the plot, for a disgruntled aide to Gates passed along a garbled, supplemented, and sensationalized version of the letter to others, which finally reached Washington. Alerted, Washington acted resourcefully; he informed Conway of what had been reported and sent (through the Congress) a long reply to Gates. This public exposure made Washington's supporters in Congress and many public-spirited citizens rally to his defense and defeat both the unknown plotters in the Congress and their military conspirators.

Conway was forced to resign from the army, for the Congress planned to replace him with General Friedrich von Steuben; in addition, Lafayette, angered by Conway's underhandedness, refused to allow him to be his second in command for a proposed Canadian military campaign. Conway then made Washington a complete apology and returned to France.

Greater punishment awaited Gates, despite the fact that he had merely supported the cabal's goal and not participated in its machinations. Congress stripped him of his northern command, sent him south to the Carolinas and his defeat at Camden, South Carolina (1780), and ultimately replaced him with Nathanael Greene.

After the 1781 American victory over the British at Yorktown, Virginia, the real leaders of the cabal, whose earlier actions had suggested the dominance of regaining control over independence, must have, in hindsight, been relieved that their intrigue had failed.

Frederick COOK: controversial explorer

Every child learns in grade school that Robert Edwin Peary was the first person to reach the North Pole. But for a few brief days the honor and glory of that distinction were held by Frederick Albert Cook, a physician from Brooklyn, New York. In 1909 Cook claimed he had reached the North Pole a year ago, on April 21. Though his sham would surely have been uncovered sooner or later, Peary's fortuitous discovery on April 6, 1909, caused a huge uproar against the deception, forcing Cook to disappear from public view. He remained, however, a persistent con artist.

Peary knew Cook, who had been a surgeon on Peary's exploratory Arctic expedition of 1891–92 and who had also been on a Belgian Antarctic expedition in 1897–99. Additionally, Cook had claimed to have climbed Mt. McKinley in Alaska, North America's highest mountain, in 1906. After learning from the two Eskimos who accompanied Cook on the expedition to the pole that they had never been out of sight of land the whole time (the North Pole is encircled by a vast sea), Peary was convinced that Cook had duped the world and challenged him to produce scientific and astronomical observations to prove his accomplishment. Cook gloried in his worldwide fame, delaying the release of any substantial evidence supporting his claim and receiving numerous plaudits as he toured about, earning large fees for his lectures.

According to Cook, he had kept secret his plan to reach the pole, had sailed (1907) north to a spot the Eskimos called Annooktok in northern Greenland, and had been put ashore there with enough supplies to last him three years. After months of planning and preparation, he had set out on February 19, 1908, with 11 Eskimos and 103 huskies pulling sledges, traveling first to Ellesmere Island, crossing the Nansen Strait, and then reaching Axel Heiberg Island. Cook said that he had decided to make his run for the pole in the winter when the ice was more firmly packed and drifting ice floes were less dangerous.

To make a dash to the pole and back in the unendurable cold, Cook had chosen two Eskimos and 26 dogs and, after sending the rest of the expedition south, had set out over the polar sea. One by one the dogs had dropped in their tracks, frozen to death, said Cook. Calculating by means of a sextant, Cook determined that his group had reached the pole, where they remained for two days before heading homeward. According to the explorer, the journey back had been harrowing, with the expedition struggling through cracking ice packs and only barely surviving starvation. Cook said he had rested nearly a year at Etah, Greenland, before going south and boarding a Danish ship bound for Copenhagen, Denmark, where he was feted as a hero before sailing to America.

In 1909 Cook published *My Attainment of the Pole,* a book vividly describing his feat. His supporters discounted the growing suspicion that he was a liar, but he had provided no scientific proof that he had discovered the pole, whereas Peary had made known his records about his courageous journey (1908–9) with Matthew Henson and four Eskimos, and was supported by the National Geographic Society, the U.S. Navy, and the U.S. government.

Cook's downfall came when two men signed an affidavit that they had been paid by him to write false astronomical observations to substantiate his claim. In addition, Cook's guide during his expedition on Mt. McKinley publicly declared that Cook had not scaled the peak and had deceived the public into honoring him. Soon afterward Cook disappeared from public view, and in 1911, after his and Peary's records had been studied and compared, the U.S. Congress officially recognized Peary as the first to reach the North Pole.

Cook resurfaced in 1923 when he got into trouble with the law while working for some Texas oil companies as a publicist urging people to invest in them. He was found guilty of using the mails with intent to defraud and received a 14-year prison sentence. A pardon from President Franklin Roosevelt freed him in 1933. Cook continued to put forward his polar and Mt. McKinley claims until his death in 1940. A few scientists, explorers, and admirers have contended that Cook honestly deceived himself during his Arctic trip; others have rejected his polar claim on the grounds that he submitted insufficient scientific evidence to verify it.

The Cook-Peary controversy was reawakened in 1988 by findings by the National Geographic Society that Peary may have missed the North Pole by 30 to 60 miles. Recent support for Cook's 1908 discovery prompted the Peary family to release old documents— Peary's expedition diary, private notes, and astronomical observations—which the National Geographic then asked a British polar expert to study thoroughly. Some modern scholars now conclude that both Cook and Peary were charlatans, and neither one reached the pole.

Ellen COOKE: embezzling church treasurer

Over the course of five years, Ellen Cooke, national treasurer for the Episcopal Church, secretly funneled $2.2 million of church funds into her personal bank accounts. A month after her resignation in 1995, outside auditors discovered her crimes. Cooke was ordered by a federal district court judge to serve five years in prison and to make restitution to the church.

In her own defense, Cooke claimed she was a victim of a bipolar psychiatric disorder that prevented her from remembering her actions. She also said she suffered from a mental breakdown caused by the "pain, abuse, and powerlessness" she endured as a woman occupying one of the Episcopal Church's highest-ranking offices for lay persons.

Cooke was the national treasurer for nine years. During this time, her annual salary was approximately $125,000 and her husband (Reverend Nicholas Cooke) was paid $70,000 a year as an Episcopal priest. Cooke's salary was second only to the presiding bishop. Despite the comfortable wages, from 1990 to 1995, Ellen Cooke "systematically diverted," according to outside auditors, church funds into her own accounts. All this happened at a time when the church was struggling with waning financial support from members, eventually resulting in severe cuts to the church staff and budget. Cooke seemed to have no problem slashing program funding and firing fellow church administrators while she pilfered funds from the foundering institution.

Cooke used her newfound money to live a lavish life. She and her husband paid a total of nearly $1 million for an 18th-century house in Montclair, New Jersey, and a 23-acre vacation farm in Virginia. They refurbished the historic New Jersey home, adding tennis courts, and they had a 140-foot dock constructed for the Virginia property. Cooke enrolled her two children in private schools and splurged on lavish gifts of crystal and jewelry from Christie's for herself and friends. She ran up huge restaurant bills and began paying for airfare for flights between New Jersey and Virginia—not only for herself and her family, but for northern friends who came to visit the farm in Virginia. Observers and friends thought the grand lifestyle came from old family money and shrewd investments, plus the comfortable Episcopal salaries.

Many religious institutions face the danger of embezzlement because they do not have an effective set of checks and balances in place to catch potential thieves. Also, much of the funds donated by supporters leave no paper trail and are therefore easy money for embezzlers. After cooperating with federal officials in the prosecution of Ellen Cooke, the Episcopal Church finally implemented a system which they hope will protect it in the future.

The church was able to recover $1.6 million from insurance settlements and the sale of the Cookes' properties and other assets. Although its net loss was $422,094 after court costs, the church suffered a loss of integrity due to the scandal as some members and supporters wondered about the trust of their church donations.

Janet COOKE: fabricated prize-winning story

The story of "Jimmy," an eight-year-old heroin addict living in the slums of Washington, D.C., stirred reactions of pity and anger when it was published in the *Washington Post.* The story of the child-junkie was reported in vivid detail by a talented black staff reporter, Janet Cooke, who claimed to have written an eyewitness account. On April 13, 1981, Cooke received a Pulitzer Prize for featured writing at the 65th annual Pulitzer awards in New York City. Two days later in an unprecedented scandal, the *Post* announced that the award-winning article published in the newspaper the year before was a fabrication.

It was a major embarrassment for one of the nation's most prestigious daily papers. Immediately, the *Post,* which declined the Pulitzer Prize, apologized to its readers in an editorial, while Cooke, who was forced to resign, issued a statement printed in the paper at the same time. Her story was a "serious misrepresentation, which I deeply regret," she said. She further stated: "I apologize to my newspaper, my profession, the Pulitzer board, and all seekers of the truth."

This was the first time in the 64-year history of these illustrious awards that a written entry had been falsified and a prize relinquished. The Pulitzer's 17-member board then gave the feature-writing prize to Teresa Carpenter, a freelance writer for the *Village Voice;* the board had originally decided against its jury's preference for Carpenter, granting the award instead to Cooke.

When Cooke's powerful and sensational story of eight-year-old "Jimmy" appeared in print in the *Post* on September 28, 1980, questions were raised straightway about its truthfulness. Both Washington's Mayor Marion Barry, Jr., and Police Chief Burtell M. Jefferson were doubtful about its veracity and attempted to uncover "Jimmy's World," the title of Cooke's article. They and others wondered how real was Cooke's eyewitness account of Jimmy (an otherwise unnamed, street-smart boy), who was changed into a heroin addict by "Ron," a 27-year-old boyfriend of his mother, a former prostitute. It was a grim look into the dark slum life of Jimmy, with "needle marks freckling the baby-smooth skin of his thin brown arms." Cooke vividly described, in an eyewitness account, Ron injecting heroin into Jimmy's arm, while the latter said his life's desire was to be a good drug dealer. The police, searching for the elusive Jimmy, doubted some of Cooke's writing about the drug culture, drug users, and drug dealers. They even challenged the *Post,* threatening to subpoena it, to reveal its sources, which the paper declined to do, citing First Amendment rights. The *Post's* executive editor, Benjamin C. Bradlee, and his editors accepted Cooke's story, though some questions had been raised at first about its veracity. The anonymity of Cooke's sources was assured her; she claimed her life was in peril by drug dealers if she disclosed the names of the boy Jimmy and the others involved in the story, and the editors did not pressure her to reveal her sources.

Cooke's sudden downfall, prompting the discovery of the hoax, began when her academic credentials, listed in the Pulitzer Prize announcements, were called into question and found to be untrue. She claimed to have spent a year at the Sorbonne in Paris, being a magna cum laude graduate of Vassar College in 1976 and receiving a master's degree from the University of Toledo in 1977. She had falsified the job résumé she had submitted to the *Post,* which had hired her in 1979. It was discovered that she had gone to Vassar for only her freshman year (1972–73), leaving for some unknown reason, and had earned a bachelor's degree in English literature (without honors) from the University of Toledo in 1976. She had then worked as a reporter for WGTE-TV in Toledo and then for the *Toledo Blade* before going to the *Post.*

On April 15, 1981, after undergoing thorough questioning by her editors and maintaining at first that her story was accurate, Cooke finally confessed that it had been an invention. According to Bradlee, she said her account was a "composite" and "that the quotes attributed to the child were fabricated and that certain events described as eyewitnessed did not in fact happen."

Not until late January 1982 did Cooke make her first public statements about the scandal, which she said she knew would "come out" when she heard she had won the Pulitzer Prize. Appearing on a broadcast television interview, she explained that she "felt terrible about it," adding that "in my case, the temptation didn't derive from ambition. I simply wanted to write a story I had been working on so that I would not have to go back and say, 'I cannot do it.' I did not want to fail." About her bogus academic claims, she explained: "I felt that on the strength of my own accurate credentials, I would never have been hired at the *Washington Post,* regardless of what sort of experience I had had or what type of writer I was."

Lord CORNBURY: public transvestism

Royal governors in the American colonial period were expected to be faithful representatives of the English Crown, but none took the matter of representation so literally as Edward Hyde, viscount of Cornbury and, after 1709, third earl of Clarendon. Upon opening the New York assembly in 1702, Lord Cornbury, who was dressed as his cousin Queen Anne, declared: "In this place and on this occasion, I represent a woman and in all respects I ought to represent her as faithfully as I can."

A notorious transvestite within his gubernatorial domains, Cornbury's displays in hoopskirts were not restricted to state functions. He often appeared at night on the docks in New York City in the raiments of a high-class tart. To say that his feminine accoutrement was poorly received by the public would be an understatement; on some outings, Lord Cornbury barely escaped arrest. He managed to avoid it only because his close relationship to the queen made such a strong impression on the lesser colonial authorities, who treated him with almost absolute deference, at least at first.

A man of royal lineage, Edward Hyde, Lord Cornbury was related to queens Mary II and Anne through their common grandfather, the first earl of Clarendon. The former had aided Cornbury when he deserted the Stuart cause to support William of Orange; the latter appointed him governor-general, first in New York (1702) and a few months later, when it became a royal colony, in New Jersey. His appointment, which lasted through 1708, was the result of his personal request to the Crown; his aim was to overcome private financial difficulties, and no evidence exists that he gained his powerful position on the basis of any proven administrative talent. It is therefore not surprising that, as a royal governor, Lord Cornbury was a colossal failure.

Unconventional not only in dress, Lord Cornbury also flouted most of the legislative conventions of the time, even attempting to rule without the input of the colonies' assemblies. He forced from the New York assembly a "gift" of £2,000, and theoretically to support the second intercolonial war, obtained grants from both assemblies, only to embezzle the funds for his own use. The assemblies fought back, forcing him to accept a treasurer elected by and responsible to them for the handling of future public funds; the first moneys were never recovered. Cornbury also illegally seized properties and prosecuted individuals. His actions severely undermined English rule in the two colonies.

Besides this, Cornbury took no heed of assembly votes, illegally made gifts of large tracts of land to his friends, and, insensitive to the religious variety of his constituents, established taxes for the sole support of the Church of England. He lived far beyond his means with little evident concern for his family; his wife resorted to theft to supply her personal needs. In redress, the colonies' assemblies complained repeatedly to the Privy Council of Queen Anne.

In May 1707, the Assembly of the Jerseys adopted a serious remonstrance read publicly to Lord Cornbury and then conveyed to England for redress. It condemned Cornbury's administrative faults and excesses, but it more strongly accused him of forfeiting respect by publicly appearing in woman's attire. It is not clear which charges most convinced the Crown that Cornbury was a hopeless governor, but in 1708 he was recalled. His return to England was delayed by his immediate incarceration in debtor's prison, a condition relieved by the death of his father, which made Cornbury both a rich heir and the third earl of Clarendon. His departure left his former colonial subjects suffering from substantial trade losses to Boston and Philadelphia because of his irresponsible acts. Although his recall to England seemed a punitive action, Cornbury never actually suffered: upon his return his cousin, Her Majesty Queen Anne, inexplicably made him a member of her Privy Council.

Bernie CORNFELD: fast financier

The international financial manipulations of supersalesman Bernie or Bernard Cornfeld, the so-called Midas of Mutual Funds, enabled him to amass a fortune worth about $150 million on paper before his business bubble burst in 1970 when he lost control of his enormous mutual fund company, Investors Overseas Services (IOS). Despite losing his financial empire and narrowly escaping conviction for fraud in Switzerland, Cornfeld continued to lead a life of hedonism and debauchery. His indiscreet sexual activity brought him nearly as much notoriety as his financial dealings.

Born in Istanbul and raised in Brooklyn, New York, Cornfeld became a colorful American promoter for the Dreyfus Fund, created by New York stockbroker Jack J. Dreyfus, Jr., in 1955. Operating in Europe, he sold financial advice to small investors, many of whom were on American military bases. In 1956 in Paris he solely founded IOS, an offshore mutual funds syndicate, and then registered it in Panama. Promising a high return on investment in IOS, Cornfeld began successfully sell-

Millionaire financier Bernie Cornfeld, surrounded by girlfriends, gave a news conference at his luxury home in London, England, on April 6, 1974. Cornfeld, charged with fraud, had been released from prison in Switzerland the day before, after he had paid a huge bail. (UPI/ Bettmann Newsphotos)

ing shares in the fund to unsuspecting American servicemen, French investors, and others who gave him small amounts of money. Cornfeld's idea was to take in thousands of "little" investors, pool their money, and buy securities they wouldn't normally acquire as "little people" in the financial world. Since his worldwide mutual fund was designed to get around strict regulations and laws about currency and taxes by operating outside the United States and Great Britain, many invested with the bearded, thickset Cornfeld, who claimed he was a socialist working for the common people but apparently preyed on the wishes of many gullibles who wanted to become rich.

Cornfeld made certain he kept control of IOS, although he hired numerous "associates" who bought into his company. He paid these salesmen higher commissions than were permitted by American law to bring new clients and their money into IOS, which became headquartered in Geneva, Switzerland, after the autumn of 1958. A list of Cornfeld's many investors was locked in a Swiss bank, and it allegedly contained some well-off American expatriates who sought to avoid paying taxes, as well as some organized-crime bosses who sought profits through the "laundering" of illegally obtained money. Small investors were sometimes confused by the literature published by IOS and supposedly were misled into thinking their money would triple in a few years, when in fact it wouldn't. The suspicious movement of the company's funds aroused Swiss authorities to investigate in 1966, without much success, but Cornfeld's dealings became questionable and undoubtedly helped bring about the formation of his own banks in

the latter 1960s. Investors Overseas Services had more than $2 billion in funds at its peak, before it ran into dire trouble in 1970 after many persons cashed in their IOS holdings and caused a big cash-flow squeeze. The company's profits then slumped badly in the declining New York stock market of 1970, and some IOS employees accused the company of illegal business practices, as well as mismanagement.

In financial desperation, Cornfeld put an interim board in control of IOS, which was approached by financial entrepreneur Robert L. VESCO and offered a large "rescue" loan by him. Cornfeld reluctantly relinquished control of IOS to the 34-year-old Vesco, nine years his junior, who assumed the IOS chairmanship early in 1971. Though Cornfeld sold his shares in IOS to Vesco, he reportedly was worth an estimated $25 million afterward. But IOS continued to decline under Vesco, who eventually was accused of draining $224 million from the company and had to flee to Costa Rica in 1972 to escape prosecution.

Abroad again, Cornfeld received more bad publicity when convicted of sexually attacking a young woman at his residence in London in 1973. "Twenty years of sex and this is the first time it's happened," he bantered to reporters. "I expected to have sexual intercourse with her." He then went back to Geneva, where Swiss authorities took him into custody on charges of fraud related to IOS. Many former company employees indicted him with illicit practices. For 11 months Cornfeld awaited trial, eventually gaining release when some 100 friends, including *Playboy* publisher Hugh Hefner and several Hollywood actors, raised his necessary bail money of $1.5 million. Continuing his lavish and promiscuous living, Cornfeld then purchased Pickfair, Mary Pickford's mansion in Beverly Hills. Despite the enormous size of Pickfair, Cornfeld probably never suffered from loneliness. Over the course of the year 1975, he reportedly lived with over a dozen different women, sometimes bringing to bed two or three at a time. At age 49 he married a former model named Lorraine Armbruster, who was pregnant with his child at the time. In Swiss courts, Cornfeld was happily relieved to hear all IOS-linked charges against him were successively dropped in 1977 and 1979.

Bill COSBY: shattered image as TV father figure

In 1997 popular comedian and actor Bill Cosby (born in 1937) suffered many weeks of embarrassing and damaging publicity when he was accused of fathering a daughter, Autumn Jackson, out of wedlock more than 20 years before. As the longtime star of his own TV show, Cosby had a reputation as "America's Dearest Dad" (as Dr. Huxtable in the show) that was seriously tarnished when he admitted to having had an affair with Autumn's mother, Shawn Upshaw, and that paternity of Autumn was "a possibility."

On January 16, 1997, the very day that Ennis Cosby, the 27-year-old son of Bill and his wife Camille, was murdered in Los Angeles, 22-year-old Autumn Jackson and some cohorts were attempting to extort $40 million from Bill Cosby in exchange for not selling her "story of desperation" to the tabloids for publication. Two days later, Autumn was arrested in New York City after signing a $24 million payoff agreement with Cosby's attorneys, who had negotiated a "sting" with the Federal Bureau of Investigation (FBI). Autumn had threatened to go public with her claim of being Cosby's illegitimate daughter.

In an interview on CBS-TV with Dan Rather in January 1997, Cosby admitted that he had had a "rendezvous" with Autumn's mother long ago and said "there is a possibility" he was the father. Cosby said: "If you said, 'Did you make love to the woman?' the answer is yes. 'Are you the father? No.' " Nonetheless, his image as America's most devoted family man was hurt, and Cosby then seemed to make his case against Autumn and her colleagues a moral crusade.

The disputants—Bill Cosby and Autumn Jackson—eventually battled in a federal courthouse in New York City in July 1997. Charged with trying to extort $40 million from Cosby, Autumn insisted that he was her father. Cosby denied it but admitted to having sex with her mother, Shawn, many years ago and to providing more than $100,000 in financial support to both of them over the years. During the trial, Cosby testified that he told Autumn: "I will be for you a father figure, but I am not your father." The issue of paternity, however, was ruled irrelevant to the charges against Autumn, who was finally found guilty by a 12-member jury and sentenced to 26 months behind bars for extortion, conspiracy, and crossing state lines to commit a crime (December 1997).

Listed on Autumn's birth certificate as her father was the name Jerald Jackson, apparently Shawn Upshaw's former boyfriend. He claimed he was Autumn's real father and had had a relationship with her mother while she was a prostitute (although Shawn denied ever working as a prostitute). A third man emerged who could have been Autumn's father: a Mexican immigrant and former busboy named Jesus Vasquez, whom Shawn had apparently married in 1973, a year before Autumn's birth. But Shawn said she never lived or had sex with Vasquez.

Bill and Camille Cosby, married more than 33 years, found some needed solace when the murderer of their son Ennis was caught and convicted. The 19-year-old Mikail Markhasev had fatally shot Ennis during an apparent holdup on a dark Los Angeles highway, where Ennis had stopped to change a flat tire. Markhasev was sentenced to life in prison without parole on August 11, 1998.

F. Donald COSTER. See Philip MUSICA: dignified duplicities.

Father COUGHLIN: once America's No. 1 fascist
In May 1942, authorities of the U.S. government, acting with the archbishop of Detroit, moved against the pastor of the Shrine of the Little Flower in Royal Oak, Michigan, depriving him of his avocation. From his archbishop, he received a choice: cease writing and other nonreligious activities or be defrocked. The government gave no choice; acting under provisions of the Espionage Act of 1917, it stripped his magazine *Social Justice* of its mailing privileges. In both cases, the grievance against the Reverend Charles Edward Coughlin was the same: sedition.

Had the federal authorities been so inclined, a second charge could have been leveled: treason. Both before and during World War II, Father Coughlin had been America's most vocal backer of Europe's fascistic governments, our wartime foes.

Coughlin had not always been seditious and unpatriotic. Ordained in 1916, the Ontario-born priest had only one enemy: marxism. He had been imbued with theories of Social Catholicism during his seminary training, and he believed that Catholic principles in economics could save the common man. But he went beyond these precepts; impressed by the Vatican's signing of concordats with Adolf Hitler, Benito Mussolini, and Francisco Franco, he mistakenly believed that these dictators had the approval of the church. They therefore deserved his support, for all were in conflict with Marxist-Leninist principles.

Augmented by his tendency to regard himself as a consummate politician and an infallible historian as well as his egocentrism, Coughlin's misconception grew into the making of a full-blown scandal.

Good looking, with a rich, melodious voice, Coughlin was soon well on his way to popularity and success.

The first "radio priest" in America, Coughlin opened the purses of his listeners so effectively that between 1926 and 1929 he had been able to pay for the building of the million-dollar Shrine at Royal Oak; at their 1935 peak, his broadcasts were heard from Maine to California. More than a hundred clerks were paid to process his mail.

Impressed by the response to his Sunday sermons, Coughlin's bishops indulgently permitted him to dedicate his programs to the defeat of socialism and bolshevism. His audience grew. He attracted many with his populist concepts but failed to understand that many of his listeners were the disgruntled and underprivileged from the lower and middle classes, who agreed only emotionally with his harangues against big business, big government, bankers, and internationalism. They liked him for his decisive style and his choice of targets but were unconcerned with his intellectual rationales. Inspired by the approval, Father Coughlin began to act as if he knew all the answers and as if all the answers were his. With the approval and imprimatur of his bishop, he began to offer ill-digested history and economics; he blamed the Depression on the Versailles Treaty, accepted the theory that an "international banking conspiracy" continued the economic slump, and saw Prohibition as a capitalist plot. With no well-informed individuals to destroy his illusions, and with constantly growing approval from his listeners, he began to go farther awry.

He berated President Herbert Hoover for his ineffectuality and at first backed Franklin Delano Roosevelt under the motto "Roosevelt or ruin." But when President Roosevelt rejected his plan for a monetary program based on silver, and when his speculations in silver with Shrine funds were discovered, Coughlin felt himself double-crossed. After 1934, when he began his National Union for Social Justice and attracted a new audience with its magazine, he consistently attacked President Roosevelt. He even began a third political party, the National Union, to oppose Roosevelt in 1936. Its failure to elect its candidates did not affect his exposition and promulgation of his own ideas.

These ideas gradually became outspokenly fascistic. Coughlin suggested a corporate state like Mussolini's, crudely attacked Roosevelt as communist-influenced, openly promoted American fascists, and accused the Congress of Industrial Organizations, a major labor union, of being "Red." Even the Vatican expressed its embarrassment with him.

Father Couglin, however, is remembered more for his attempt to keep America neutral after 1939, his opposition to the Lend-Lease program, his attacks on the British as effete, his defense of fascism as a valid opposition to Marxism, his glorification of the fascist dictators, his literal translations of German propaganda, his unremitting attacks on Jews as the creators and backers of communism, and his advice to Americans after 1941 that they should be prepared to surrender. He is recalled for applauding, if not creating, the Christian Front or "Christian Klan," which terrorized New York Jews with the approval of the Brooklyn archdiocesan newspaper *The Tablet* and the noninterference of any church prelates. New York had become a laboratory of carefully developed fascistic experimentation.

Coughlin approved of all this. Evidence of disapproval and criticism made him compare his personal suffering from opponents to that of Jesus Christ on the Cross. Even after the FBI seized his papers, he continued to speak and write hate literature.

The actions of 1942 stopped him cold. Further legal action would make him a marytr; further resistance would make him a fool. Accepting the inevitable, Father Coughlin devoted himself quietly to his pastoral duties until his retirement in 1966, 13 years before his death.

Daniel B. CRANE. See PAGE SCANDAL IN CONGRESS.

Joseph CRATER: vanished judge

On the night of August 6, 1930, New York State Supreme Court Judge Joseph Force Crater disappeared and was never heard of again. A well-respected Democratic jurist who had recently been appointed to the bench, he was to testify soon in hearings concerning charges of office-buying by his friend Magistrate George F. Ewald. At the time, Samuel Seabury was heading investigations into New York City Mayor Jimmy Walker's powerful Tammany Hall Democratic political machine, uncovering graft and corruption among politicians, officials, and judges. Had Crater been corrupted before his mysterious disappearance? Many thought so.

An ambitious and knowledgable lawyer in Manhattan, Crater was hired in 1920 as personal secretary of New York State Supreme Court Judge Robert Ferdinand Wagner, who became his mentor and later supposedly helped him gain a judgeship. Crater was always properly and fashionably attired and lived well with his attractive wife, Stella, in a Fifth Avenue apartment. Although he was a highly admired law-school lecturer on the side, he turned his main legal talent toward specializing in receiverships, earning as much as $75,000 to $100,000 a year. It was later said that he was involved in several shady receivership deals in New York City, including one involving Libby's Hotel, which was sold in 1929 to a mortgage loan company for $75,000 and then, only two months later, resold to New York City for $2,850,000. Apparently without his wife knowing, Crater also had numerous extramarital affairs with beautiful models and Broadway chorus girls, who found him willing to spend quite extravagantly for his passionate trystings.

When a vacancy opened on the New York State Supreme Court in 1930, Crater lobbied his old Tammany friends to prod Governor Franklin D. Roosevelt to appoint him to the bench. He especially sought help from Martin J. Healy, who controlled the city's 19th assembly district, in which Crater was president of the prestigious Cayuga Democratic Club. Magistrate Ewald supported him for the vacated judgeship, which Crater was appointed to fill on April 8, 1930. Crater was expected to be elected to the 14-year post in November and perhaps, some day, to gain appointment to the U.S. Supreme Court, his wish. His ambition led him to give up a lucrative law practice for the judgeship's relatively meager yearly salary of $22,500. Later it was alleged that he had paid that amount for the eminent appointment (in those days, a person was expected to pay a year's salary for the post or office he was buying). City Magistrate Ewald was indicted with his wife on a charge of purchasing his post for $10,000 from Tammany district leader Healy; the case was later dropped because of the jury's failure to agree, but Ewald resigned under pressure, discredited.

Three days before his disappearance, Judge Crater returned to Manhattan from his summer vacation home in Belgrade Lakes, Maine, where he left his wife, telling her he would be back by August 9 to celebrate her birthday. On August 6, in his New York office, the judge busily collected and stacked together numerous papers and documents and sent his court attendant, Joseph L. Mara, to cash two checks totaling $5,150 in large bills (it was thought that the money might have been to pay off a showgirl who had threatened to expose a sex affair with the judge or to pay a woman to drop a breach-of-promise suit against him). That evening Crater dined with friends at Billy Haa's Chophouse on West 45th Street, then stepped alone into a taxi to go to the Belasco Theater, and was never seen again, although in the months following the announcement of his disappearance newspapers across the country ran endless stories of reported "sightings" of the missing judge—in the Adirondacks, in Nova Scotia, in Atlantic City, and in Chicago. The stacked papers and cash that the 41-year-old Crater took from his office were never found. Slowly, investigators directed by New York District Attorney Thomas C. T. Crain, helped by curious news reporters, made public Judge Crater's connections to the freewheeling Walker administration, attempting to link him to routine bribery in the city judiciary. In an unprecedented move, Mayor Walker posted a $5,000 reward for information about the judge, even while he maneuvered to keep the investigation confined to secret grand-jury testimony. Although the grand jury took testimony from more than 300 persons acquainted with the judge, including many showgirls, no evidence ever came to light to clarify his disappearance.

Mrs. Crater recovered from a nervous collapse and stayed in her Maine home until January 1931, when she returned to Manhattan. Miraculously, she discovered in her apartment a manila envelope hidden in a drawer which contained $6,619 in cash, some securities and checks, life-insurance policies on Crater valued at $30,000, and a 16-line will written five years earlier by the judge, leaving everything to her. When the judge was legally declared dead in 1939, Mrs. Crater—remarried then as Mrs. Kunz—collected $20,500 from the insurance companies.

What happened to Judge Crater? Some claim that he voluntarily or premeditatedly vanished to avoid the impending scandal; others say he committed suicide; and others say he was murdered by either fearful Tammany associates or underworld elements. Today, *to pull a Crater* is entered in the dictionary as meaning to disappear completely.

Joan CRAWFORD: marble-hearted mother

The image of Joan Crawford, glamorous and sophisticated American movie star for more than 50 years, was sullied forever when her 39-year-old daughter Christina published *Mommie Dearest* (1978), a shocking biographical exposé showing her mother's hidden tyrannical nature. Christina, who was cut out of her mother's will like her younger brother Christopher (Joan Crawford died in New York City on May 10, 1977), denied that she was seeking vengeance and claimed only that she wished to tell the grievous truth and to call national attention to child abuse. To some people, the daughter was considered mean, condemnable, thankless, and self-serving for writing the book (the sale of the book and film rights to it made her a millionaire); to others, she was just trying to rid herself of childhood pain inflicted by her famous mother, whom the public had admired for so long without knowing the complete story of her personal life.

The Hollywood-fashioned actress was apparently not the affectionate, warm-hearted, caring mother the movie-studio publicists depicted her to be. Although known as brassy and self-confident, she had a terrible cruel streak, according to Christina, and was quick to punish her four adopted children (Christina, the oldest, had been the first adopted, in 1940). Their mother, who began to drink heavily after 1945, whimsically punished the kids for misbehaving, wrote Christina; refusal to eat a meal meant that the child would be served the same meal until it was eaten; thumbsucking sometimes meant that the child was tied to the bed at night; unpredictable fits of drunken rage by Joan ended in her smashing things to pieces in the children's rooms on numerous nights. Evidently, the actress was "a woman with no heart," as she was described in an article in *Viva* magazine, and didn't really care for her children. Christina said that continually washing floors, wearing dirty clothes for days without changing, and having their mouths washed out with soap for swearing were other punishments mercilessly served out by their mother. The children grew to loathe her, according to Christina, who was herself sent away to a lonely convent and robbed of seeing her mother for over a year. And four times Christopher ran away from home. During these goings on, the beautiful actress's main concern was her personal career; "she learned to be a dancer . . . an actress . . . a star. She just never had any time left over to learn how to be a human being," was the way her unhappy daughter put it. Christina also speculated that her mother may have suffered sexual abuse as a child and was in need of psychiatric help. There is no doubt that Joan's life was quite unusual.

Born to unwed parents in San Antonio, Texas, in 1908, Lucille LeSueur (Joan Crawford's original name) grew up poor and suffered whippings as punishment during her strict upbringing. As a waitress she worked her way through boarding school and college in Missouri (a college sorority refused her because it didn't take "girls who work"). After dancing in nightclubs under the name Billie Cassin, she became a Broadway chorus dancer in 1924 and began appearing in Hollywood movies in 1926. This vivacious Jazz Age flapper achieved stardom in films such as *Our Dancing Daughters* (1928), *Grand Hotel* (1932), and *Dancing Lady* (1933). During the Depression she lived luxuriously, feeling that her adoring public expected it from a star and rationalizing it by saying, "I believe in the dollar. Everything I earn, I spend." She had rich furs, jewels, and gowns, magnificent motorcars and mansions, and well-publicized love affairs with actors Clark Gable, Spencer Tracy, and others. She also had four marriages: to Douglas Fairbanks, Jr. (1929–33), Franchot Tone (1935–39), Philip Terry (1942–46), and Alfred N. Steele (1955–59), the only one of the four not an actor, who was instead chairman of the Pepsi-Cola Company.

A great determination to succeed and a shrewd use of publicity were what made Joan a top box-office attraction for many years. To have and hold a glamorous job and appearance was of the utmost importance to her, propelling her to take the euphonious, stately name Joan Crawford, to change her birth date to be older at the start of her career, and to later regularly undergo cosmetic surgery in order to hide wrinkles. Serious dramatic film roles won her much acclaim, particularly for *The Women* (1939), *A Woman's Face* (1941), and *Mildred Pierce* (1945), which gained her an Academy Award for best actress. Undoubtedly the problems of raising children were a burden that she didn't want, especially as her beauty aged. Her sadistic streak showed as her children aged and endured more punishments, such as being locked in a cupboard (Christopher) and having their hair cut off (Christina). Yet their mother, whose gambling put her in deep debt in the early 1950s, still was loved by her many fans, made more successful films, including *Whatever Happened to Baby Jane* in 1962, and kept up a resplendent appearance in public until the end of her life.

CRÉDIT MOBILIER SCANDAL

In 1878, when historian Charles Francis Adams published his revealing book *Railroads: Their Origin and Problems* and coined for perpetuity the fitting phrase *robber barons,* Americans became aware of the almost infinite depth of the sink of corruption that surrounded the history of U.S. railroads after the Civil War. Outstanding in this corruption was the cause célèbre surrounding Crédit Mobilier of America, which indirectly led to the 1873 bankruptcy of Jay Cooke, one of the late 19th

century's few basically honest financiers (see DREXEL, MORGAN, & COMPANY: the panic of 1873). It also pointed out how policy makers as well as railroad men had been caught up in the corruption.

Crédit Mobilier, organized in 1864, was a holding company, then legal, established to oversee the construction of the Union Pacific Railroad westward from the Missouri River until it met the tracks of the Central Pacific Railroad. Its founders were Oakes Ames, a United States representative from Massachusetts; Thomas C. Durant, a professional railroad builder; and seven others, including Ames's brother. Another job of Crédit Mobilier, which also functioned as an ephemeral construction company, was to complete the remaining 667 miles of track-laying for the Union Pacific to Promontory Point, near Ogden, Utah, a task ended on May 10, 1869.

The holding company, at its earliest controlled by Durant and the Ames brothers, manipulated the capitalization of the Union Pacific—supported by Congress with a first mortgage of $27 million in bonds—to $111 million. Durant fired the original engineer-estimator for the task, Peter A. Dey, and hired a second, Hoxie, who used Dey's specifications but tripled the estimated cost per mile. The nine-man cabal in Crédit Mobilier then contracted among themselves for the actual construction, gradually raising the cost per mile from $66,000 to $80,000, then to $96,000, and finally to $114,000 so that the final cost of the linkage was not the $44 million originally figured but $94 million. Crédit Mobilier had enriched the cabal by $50 million.

To safeguard the conspirators, Oakes Ames sold congressional leaders, Cabinet officers, and legislators shares in Crédit Mobilier at par value (half of their New York Stock Exchange value) and distributed other shares to "railroad congressmen." Ames was motivated by the thesis that ownership of Crédit Mobilier should be placed "where it will do the most good for us." And good it did: the company's first dividend (1867) was for 100 percent of value. Thus, through 1869, all involved in the scandal had a free ride.

Congressional insight into the state of affairs surrounding Crédit Mobilier did not surface until a fight between an Ames faction and a Durant faction became public; a congressional investigation in 1873 revealed how much public servants in high places had become corrupted. Ames had sold shares to such eminent politicians as Representative James G. Blaine of Maine (House Speaker from 1869 to 1875), Vice President Schuyler COLFAX (House Speaker from 1863 to 1869), Representative James Brooks of New York, Senator Henry Wilson of Massachusetts, and Representative James A. Garfield of Ohio (later to be elected president in 1880). Most of the legislators were exonerated during the investigations. Ames and Brooks were censured on

February 27, 1873. No prosecutions followed, despite the fact that federal monies were involved. Many, like Garfield and Wilson (who was Colfax's successor as vice president during Grant's second presidential term), escaped unscathed. Colfax lost political favor, and Blaine suffered because of the MULLIGAN LETTERS, which contributed to the failure of his presidential try in 1884 (see James G. BLAINE: "rum, Romanism, and rebellion").

The Crédit Mobilier scandal, with its almost incredible waste, crime, and corruption of basic principles, shook the country, set many weak organizations to toppling, and made cynical the average American affected by it. The weak congressional discipline in the affair hardly frightened financier Jay GOULD who had fronted a similar holding-construction company while he controlled the building of the Northern Pacific Railroad (1870–73). In the Panic of 1873, that construction stopped, and the wily Gould escaped with his gains untouched by even minor congressional concern.

Harry CROSBY: obsessed with sun and death
Harry Crosby was one of the most flamboyant expatriate American poets in Paris during the 1920s. He and his wife, Caresse, who also wrote poetry, traveled extensively, lived luxuriously, and had many sexual partners. Harry particularly loved young women and often carried on affairs with two, three, or even four at the same time. On the evening of December 10, 1929, after his wife and mother became worried when he failed to meet them for tea, dinner, and the theater, they called a painter friend to seek his whereabouts. The friend had let Harry Crosby and Josephine Bigelow use a bedroom in his studio and had hurried home upon hearing from Crosby's wife. The door was locked from the inside and had to be smashed down with an ax. Josephine's and Harry's bodies were lying on a bed, each with a small bullet hole in the temple, but Josephine had been dead two hours longer than Harry.

Harry Crosby was the only son of an old and wealthy Back Bay family of Boston and attended the exclusive St. Mark's School in Southborough, Massachusetts. The United States entered World War I shortly after he graduated, and Harry rushed to volunteer in the American Field Service Ambulance Corps in France. He then enlisted in the army and was assigned to the ambulance section, which saw heavy action at Verdun and the Battle of the Orme. Once, when Harry was rescuing an injured soldier, a shell hit his ambulance and completely destroyed it. He felt God had made a point of saving his life. After the war, the French government awarded him the Croix de Guerre for his bravery on the battlefields.

Harry returned to Boston and went to Harvard as his forefathers had done. At a Fourth of July party in 1920, he met Polly Peabody, about seven years older than he and the married mother of two small children; immediately he fell madly in love with her, and the two were soon sleeping together. Crosby threatened to commit suicide if Polly wouldn't marry him. The Peabodys did divorce early in 1922, but Polly refused to commit herself to another marriage until six months later. Meanwhile, Harry had quit his job at the Shawmut National Bank in Boston and had taken a new one at a J. P. Morgan bank in Paris. He hated the job, quit, and never again worked for wages. He didn't need to, since he was independently wealthy and in 1928 inherited more money from a cousin.

Once in Paris, Harry completely repudiated the values of Boston society, although he remained on close terms with his mother. He began to buy racehorses, gamble, smoke opium, experiment with other drugs, and study the symbols and rituals of sun worship. While in Egypt, he paid a Hindu to tattoo a six-inch-diameter sun on his back, and on another occasion he had the soles of his feet tattooed with a Christian cross and a pagan sun symbol. In 1927, Harry and Polly Crosby founded the Black Sun Press, and the titles of many of Harry's books contained the word *sun* (e.g., *Shadows of the Sun* and *Chariot of the Sun*). Harry also became immersed in mystic poets such as Rimbaud, Blake, and Baudelaire, all of whom influenced his poetry, and he constantly pondered the meaning of death.

Before the publication of her first book of verse, Polly and Harry decided she should change her name to something more distinctive, and she chose Caresse. The Crosby's friends, mainly writers and artists, thought the couple charming, witty, and sometimes quite mad. Women found Harry irresistible. Caresse rarely displayed any jealousy, for she knew that although her husband was a libertine, he would return to her. Harry was a law unto himself.

In July 1928, Harry met Josephine Rotch on the beach at the Lido outside Venice, and she became his "Fire Princess" for eight days. Josephine married Albert Bigelow of Boston the following June but continued to correspond with Harry. The Crosbys returned to the United States in time for the 1929 Harvard-Yale football game after a stormy ocean crossing, during which Harry resumed an affair with Constance Coolidge, the Comtesse de Jumilhac. The trio traveled together to Boston, where Harry slipped away for a rendezvous with Josephine before the game. They saw a good bit of each other during the next two weeks and even went to Detroit for three days, where they registered at a hotel as Mr. and Mrs. Harry Crane.

When Harry returned to Caresse at the Savoy Plaza Hotel in New York City, he suggested to her one morning that they jump together from the window of their 27th floor hotel room. She refused. Harry usually told Caresse of his plans for the day, even if in vague terms, and she was therefore concerned when on the fateful day he did not show up for the scheduled dinner and theater with poet Hart Crane. It was then that she called painter Stanley Mortimer, whose studio Harry used for liaisons with women and who rushed to investigate. Mortimer found the bodies of Harry and Josephine lying under a silk coverlet, fully clad except for their bare feet. His toenails were painted a brilliant red. The couple's left hands were clasped and in Harry's right hand was a small Belgian automatic pistol with a sun engraved on its handle. No suicide note could be found, but in the bedroom the police discovered Harry's yellow sun ring, which he had sworn to Caresse he would never take off. It had been stamped flat.

At first the police assumed there had been a suicide pact, but the medical examiner declared that Josephine had been dead for two hours before Harry shot himself. The deaths were a case of homicide and suicide. Friends felt that Harry had decided it was time to die and wanted one of his "princesses" to accompany him on his last journey. This was borne out by a note Caresse found that Josephine had written to Harry on the evening of December 9, reading "Death is *our* marriage."

Harry CROSWELL: truth led to libel conviction
The fights in post-Revolutionary America between government and publishers over freedom of the press yielded their first victim in 1803. Harry Croswell, a Connecticut-born journalist, was convicted of committing an indiscretion that a court called libel: he had told the truth about an improper action by Thomas Jefferson, then third president of the United States. Croswell's imprudent courage soon cost him his publishing career, but the court trials quickly resulted in legislation that reduced the power of politicians to use libel as a means for censoring the press, a law that eventually guided two nations.

Harry Croswell owned two newspapers in Hudson, New York: an independent weekly called the *Balance* and, beginning in 1802, a Federalist-supporting, letter-size sheet called the *Wasp,* whose choice of name was well suited to its caustic opinions. The *Wasp* particularly offended its rival, the *Bee,* an avid press supporter of the Republicans and Thomas Jefferson.

In 1803, Croswell editorialized on James Callender, a conscienceless Republican journalist who, as historians have since discovered, attacked keenly at Jefferson's behest the opponents of Jefferson's policies. He did so in a scurrilous, shabby manner, as in his 1797 attack on Alexander Hamilton in a pamphlet grandiosely entitled "A History of the United States for 1796." It had especially delighted Jefferson and James Monroe, a fellow Virginia statesman (see HAMILTON–REYNOLDS AFFAIR).

Croswell's assertion that Callender was a paid journalistic assassin infuriated Jefferson, the *Bee,* and a newly appointed federal judge in Hudson, who by chance was also a Republican. Croswell next found himself in a court that did not follow the precedent established in the Peter ZENGER CASE of 1734–35; instead, it followed an English precedent verbalized as "the greater the truth, the greater the libel." Because only the fact of Croswell's publication of his comment was considered, the truth of the comment was not examined, and Croswell found himself judged guilty in the end. His right to publish the *Wasp* was withdrawn.

Then came a surprise. Alexander Hamilton, himself hurt by Callender, undertook the guidance of Croswell's appeal before a four-judge court. In the most effective presentation of his legal career, Hamilton reminded the court of the Zenger precedent and argued that freedom of the press in the First Amendment to the Constitution consisted of the right to print the truth even if that truth reflected upon "the government, magistracy or individuals." Two judges disagreed, and the appeal was lost.

Croswell learned that the *Balance* would no longer support his family and, impressed with a Federalist offer to support a new paper, moved to Albany, New York. But the support failed to materialize, and Croswell fell into debt and was jailed, ironically, by a Federalist creditor. Eschewing journalism, he then became an Episcopal minister and confined his editorializing to religious matters.

Hamilton's argument, however, had impressed a New York legislator, who instituted passage of a model libel law in 1805 which embodied Hamilton's ideas. That law impressed both British and American courts, for in 1868 it became the national libel rule in both countries; in 1964 it was superseded by an even more liberal law in the United States.

Andrew CUNANAN: gay serial killer of Gianni Versace
Andrew Phillip Cunanan was one of the most unusual serial killers of the 20th century. Born in 1970, Cunanan grew up in La Jolla, California, a well-to-do suburb of San Diego. In 1988 he graduated from a prestigious private school, where his classmates voted him "Least Likely To Be Forgotten." This honor came about largely because Cunanan made no attempt to hide his homosexuality; he made passes at the members of the boys' water polo team and dated older men, one of whom he brought to a school dance. Cunanan's father was a stockbroker who misappropriated his clients' funds, and the year Cunanan graduated, his father fled either to the Philippines or to a new life with a new identity on the West Coast. Cunanan's mother eventually moved to Eureka, Illinois, where she lived in a public housing project. Cunanan remained in the San Diego area, where in local gay hangouts he gained a reputation as an eccentric big spender with a penchant for violence. Although he claimed to have gotten his money from his rich Jewish parents, he actually made a living illegally dealing prescription drugs and as a pros-

WANTED BY THE FBI

Andrew Phillip Cunanan

Unlawful Flight to Avoid Prosecution · Murder

Race: White; Sex: Male; Height: 5'9" - 5'11"; Weight: 160-185 lbs.
Date of Birth: 8/31/69; Hair: Brown (short); Eyes: Brown; Wears glasses and/or contact lenses
CAUTION: CONSIDER ARMED AND DANGEROUS
Please contact the nearest FBI office if you have any information
on Andrew Phillip Cunanan.

The FBI distributed this handout about 27-year-old Andrew Phillip Cunanan, who was sought for the shooting death of Italian fashion designer Gianni Versace at his Miami Beach mansion on July 15, 1997. Cunanan, who had eluded authorities since May, after killing three men, committed suicide about a week later. (AP/Wide World Photos)

titute for Gamma Mu, a discreet social club for wealthy gay men.

In April 1997 Cunanan threw a lavish going-away party for himself and told his guests that he was moving to San Francisco. Instead, he caught a plane to Minneapolis, Minnesota, where David Madson, a former lover, lived. On April 27 Cunanan lured Jeffrey Trail, another former lover living in Minneapolis, to Madson's apartment. After a loud and violent struggle he bludgeoned Trail to death with a claw hammer and left the corpse in the apartment. Four days later Cunanan and Madson drove to a lake north of Minneapolis, where Cunanan shot Madson three times with a .40-caliber pistol.

After the two murders, Cunanan drove Madson's Jeep Cherokee to Chicago's fashionable North Side. On May 4 he broke into the home of Lee Miglin, a wealthy real estate developer. Cunanan surprised Miglin, tied him up, forced him into the garage, and wrapped his head with masking tape, leaving only a narrow breathing slit under the nose. Then, in an apparent attempt to force Miglin to give him cash or valuables, Cunanan tortured him by stabbing him repeatedly with a pair of gardening shears. He finally murdered Miglin by cutting his throat with a gardener's bow saw.

Cunanan stole Miglin's Lexus and took off for the East Coast. On May 9 he shot William Reese, the caretaker for Finn's Point National Cemetery in southern New Jersey, in his basement office at the cemetery and stole his Chevy pickup truck. Then Cunanan disappeared.

Having murdered three people, Cunanan made the Federal Bureau of Investigation's Most Wanted List. Agents from 10 FBI field offices looked for Cunanan and went so far as to contact gay and lesbian organizations on the East Coast in an effort to identify places where a gay man on the run might be able to hide. But the agents were unable to locate Cunanan until he struck again on July 15, 1997, this time in Miami Beach, Florida.

Cunanan's last victim was Gianni Versace, an internationally known fashion designer, whom he shot at the gates of his beachfront mansion. Cunanan took refuge on a sailboat docked nearby but later moved to an unoccupied houseboat that was moored just two miles away. On July 23, 1997, he was discovered by a caretaker who summoned law enforcement officials, but before they could make their way onto the houseboat, Cunanan committed suicide by shooting himself in the head.

Why Cunanan killed the five men remains a mystery. One possibility is that Cunanan was a jealous jilted lover seeking revenge for having been dumped by Trail and Madson, and that having killed twice he could not stop himself from killing again. Another possibility is that Cunanan had become addicted to methamphetamines, which can send some people into uncontrollably violent rages, particularly people like Cunanan who already have a violent temper. Yet another is that Cunanan had AIDS, and he blamed Trail and Madson for giving it to him. According to one source, Versace may have been murdered because he had once turned down Cunanan's application as a model. More likely, Cunanan simply decided to target a celebrity—various sources indicate that he had an obsession with actors Tom Cruise and Nicole Kidman and had made inquiries while in Miami Beach regarding the whereabouts and habits of Sylvester Stallone and Madonna—and Versace happened to be the first celebrity he could find. But in the absence of a suicide note or any other evidence from Cunanan, the real reasons for his bizarre actions will never be known.

Mary CUNNINGHAM: promoted for favors?

In the 1970s, as women began to rise in executive positions in the United States, sexual harassment in the workplace became a serious feminist issue. Women did not want to trade sexual favors for success, nor did they want to be wrongly accused of doing so. Thus feminists watched closely in the fall of 1980 when rumors emerged about Mary Cunningham's rapid promotion at the Bendix Corporation: Her rise in 15 months from executive assistant to vice president for strategic planning was linked to a romantic relationship with her boss, William Agee, the chairman and president of Bendix.

When the gossip started, Agee, then recently divorced from his wife, denied the allegations at a meeting of 600 top-level employees of Bendix, saying Cunningham was a close friend and that her appointment as his top advisor was totally justified. Cunningham claimed the gossip was sexist: "Unfortunately," she said, "we're culturally bound by norms that preclude in many minds the existence of someone like myself," implying that people didn't believe it possible to be both exceptionally attractive and intelligent.

Rather than quelling the rumors, the announcements put the two in the spotlight, and the national press became involved in the story. Cunningham asked for a leave of absence until the controversy abated, but a committee of the board of directors of the Bendix Corporation turned her down, saying it would be unjust for the corporation to respond to speculation, and requested that she stay in her job. The full board, however, decided soon afterward to ask her to resign, which she did, stating that the rumors impaired her ability to carry out her responsibilities as a corporate officer of Bendix.

Public reaction to her 1980 resignation was mixed. A male corporation attorney in Detroit claimed there was "not a 29-year-old in the country who is qualified to have risen as she did in only 15 months." On the other hand, supporters pointed out that Cunningham was a Phi Beta Kappa graduate of Wellesley College and held a master's degree in business administration from the Harvard Business School, qualifications that couldn't be overlooked.

Some young women executives were angry that Cunningham took most of the responsibility for what had happened, saying that Agee had erred by allowing the romance to become a topic of public speculation. They feared attractive women would now be handicapped in the business world. Other women felt Cunningham was insensitive to the necessity for extreme discretion as a female executive.

Besides coverage in almost every major newspaper and magazine in America, the story was publicized in a five-part newspaper series written by Gail Sheehy, author of the popular book *Passages*. Sheehy depicted Cunningham as a gifted, scrupulously moral woman who wanted to "improve the world through human capitalism" but who had an unfortunate desire for off-limits men that had begun in her childhood when she observed her divorced mother's platonic love for a priest. (Agee vehemently denied Sheehy's allegation that he was taking Catholic instruction from that priest.) Sheehy's "true-confessions" style narrative, called "slobbering" by rival newspapers that didn't run the se-

ries, probably didn't do much for Cunningham's cause at Bendix; however, Cunningham subsequently received over 60 offers of top executive positions, including the directorship of a Harvard Business School study of women in the executive suite, as well as offers of television and movie deals for her story. By age 30, she was an executive vice president at Seagram & Sons. Cunningham earned her revenge with a best-selling book called *Powerplay: What Really Happened at Bendix* and later married Agee.

The reaction of the press was sharp witted, if not unified. The *New York Times* pointed out that had Cunningham been a man, "no newspaper would dream of publishing the tale. . . . In the upper ranks of the FOR-TUNE 500, unfortunately, women are more visible as receptionists, secretaries, and charwomen than as makers of policy." The *Boston Globe* claimed that envious colleagues of a successful woman often found excuses for her success, such as sexual favoritism, affirmative action, or "window dressing." *Globe* columnist Ellen Goodman called the reaction "absolutely ripe with hostility toward uppity women. If women can sleep their way to the top," she asked, "why aren't they there?"

Lex CUSACK: phony Kennedy papers?

The documents that Lawrence (Lex) X. Cusack III was peddling in the early 1990s were provocative and very valuable. More than 100 investors had paid some $7 million for hundreds of papers—from index cards to White House stationery—said to be in the handwriting of John F. KENNEDY. They included letters and other documents purportedly written by Kennedy concerning his alleged sexual affair with Marilyn MONROE and his reputed connections with Mafia boss Sam Giancana. The most dramatic were secret agreements dating from the early 1960s in which Kennedy apparently promised hush money (in the form of a $600,000 trust fund for Monroe's institutionalized mother, Gladys Baker) if the actress agreed to keep quiet about her relationship with the president.

It was not just investors who were interested in these "Kennedy papers": Pulitzer Prize-winning investigative reporter Seymour Hersh was using them as a source for his forthcoming book entitled *The Darker Side of Camelot* (1997), an exposé of the Kennedy years, and ABC was planning a television documentary based in part on those papers.

Cusack, a former paralegal from Connecticut, claimed that he had found the 324 documents in 1985 in files belonging to his deceased father, Lawrence X. Cusack, Jr. The elder Cusack had been a respected New York City lawyer whose clients had included the Archdiocese of New York. The younger Cusack maintained that his father had been a close confidant and adviser of Kennedy from 1959 until the president's death in 1963. The documents were said to consist of 740 pages of correspondence between Kennedy and the elder Cusack. The younger Cusack also claimed that he had had the papers authenticated by handwriting experts.

But people working on the documentary materials began to notice historic inconsistencies. For example, one letter purported to have been written in 1961 contained a ZIP code, although ZIP codes were yet not in use in 1961. ABC and Hersh decided to hire forensic consultants. Although handwriting analysis was inconclusive and no Kennedy fingerprints were found, analysis of the typewriting led experts to conclude that the documents were forgeries. The typewriters used to create the documents had self-correcting tape, which was not available during Kennedy's lifetime. In October 1997 ABC announced on the program *20/20* that the papers were most likely fakes. Hersh removed from his book those parts based on the Cusack materials, and ABC eliminated mention of the materials from its documentary.

On March 16, 1998, federal prosecutors arrested Cusack and charged him with mail fraud, claiming he had forged the papers and sold them to unsuspecting investors. They argued that there was no evidence of a relationship between the elder Cusack and the president and maintained that many of the documents were created long after Kennedy's death. Prosecutors also claimed that notebooks in Cusack's handwriting contained drafts of the "Kennedy" documents and practice signatures of various historical figures.

Cusack and his supporters continued to claim that the papers were genuine, that news reports about the forgeries were disinformation, and that the charges were trumped up to discredit the documents and to protect the reputation of JFK.

During his three-week trial, prosecutors argued that Cusack was motivated by money. They pointed to Cusack's luxurious lifestyle. Although his salary as a law clerk for his father's firm had never exceeded $40,000, Cusack and his wife had recently purchased a $1.3 million home in Southport, Connecticut, a $540,000 weekend home in Southampton, New York, and expensive cars and clothing. Prosecutors estimated that Cusack made about $5 million in profit from the sales of the documents, while another $2 million went to his partners, who were not implicated in the forgeries. Cusack's defense lawyers argued that even if not all of the documents were genuine, Cusack and his partners believed they were. Like his documents, his claims of innocence were not convincing, and in April 1999 a jury in Manhattan's federal district court found the 48-year-old Cusack guilty of 13 counts of wire and mail fraud.

CUSTER'S LAST STAND

The checkered military career of George Armstrong Custer culminated, perhaps fittingly, in the most enduringly controversial battle of the American Indian wars: the Battle of the Little Bighorn, better known as "Custer's Last Stand" (June 25, 1876). The battle resulted in the tragic loss of an entire unit, the main reason for the fiasco is still unclear. Blame rests perhaps on the slowness of one general and perhaps on the impetuous stupidity of another.

Custer was graduated last in his class from West Point in 1861 and, despite a minor court-martial on his record, was quickly assigned to the Union Army as a second lieutenant in the Civil War. His bold, heroic actions in various battles eventually won him the rank of brevet major general in April 1865. After the war, with the reduction of the army, Custer was forced to accept a reduction in rank and was assigned to the Seventh Cavalry as a lieutenant colonel to fight the hostile Plains Indians, but a year later (1867) he was suspended from service for a year after another (second) court-martial for absence from duty. Reinstated, he then became a fierce, dashing, and successful fighter-commander against the Cheyenne and Sioux Indians, especially in the Dakota Territory.

With the discovery of gold on sacred Indian lands in the Black Hills of western South Dakota and the influx of settlers in the area, the U.S. government directed the various Indian tribes to move onto reservations by the end of January 1876. When the Cheyenne and Sioux disregarded the directive, which many of them probably did not receive because they were scattered about in the wintertime, an army expedition set out under the command of General Alfred H. Terry in May 1876, intending to crush the rebel Indians, who had now gathered together at Chief Sitting Bull's encampment along the Little Bighorn River in present-day southern Montana.

Colonel Custer, participating in Terry's plan to envelop the Indians, was ordered by him to lead the Seventh Cavalry regiment up the Rosebud River and have his 700 troops encircle Sitting Bull's encampment from the rear, while Terry and Colonel John Gibbon came in from the north with their Gatling gun division (which slowed them down). Custer, known as "Long Hair" by the Indians, advanced too directly and rapidly, making forced marches late into the night, tiring his men and horses, and arriving near the Indians' Little Bighorn encampment on the evening of June 24 (Terry and Custer had planned to meet there on June 26).

Custer, however, did not wait for Terry, and the next morning he divided his troops into three separate units and, despite his scouts' warnings that the Sioux and Cheyenne vastly outnumbered him, launched a surprise attack. He deployed Captain Frederick W. Benteen with one unit to the left to push back any Indians he found and then sent Major Marcus A. Reno with his soldiers into the encampment to drive the Indians to the rear, where Custer and the main unit, made up of 266 men, planned to attack and destroy them. Warriors led by chiefs Crazy Horse, Gall, Crow King, and Sitting Bull (the latter did not fight but gave orders) forced the retreat of Reno's men, who were soon after joined by Benteen. Unable to circle the Indians (some 2,500 braves strong), Custer and his soldiers took a stand on a hill and were all surrounded and killed in less than an hour. The Indians then turned and attacked Reno and Benteen, who had secured defensive positions within gunshot sounds of Custer, and the battle lasted until nightfall and was resumed in the morning. The Indians withdrew when Terry arrived.

Who was to blame for the Little Bighorn massacre—the army's worst defeat in its western Indian campaigns? Some say Custer was impetuous and vainglorious, acted on his own, and sought national stature as a hero; others say he acted within orders; and still others blame Reno and Benteen for their slowness and failure to relieve Custer. There is much conflicting evidence that will never settle why Custer was defeated.

D

Harry DAUGHERTY: the appearance of evil

To Washington, D.C. Democrats during the early 1920s, the name Harry Daugherty was a dirty word. Attorney general during the brief Harding period and, until 1924, during the Coolidge administration, Daugherty was assailed by Democrats in speeches and the press as if he were Beelzebub himself. Nonetheless, despite his commission of some serious errors, his political enemies were never able to prove him guilty of a crime greater than that of operating on the narrow boundary between the legal and the illegal, and some historians view his questionable reputation as attorney general as based on misleading appearances.

Part of the rationale behind the abuse of Harry Micajah Daugherty involved political jealousy and fear. A highly successful corporation lawyer in Ohio, Daugherty made himself the leader of that state's Republican Party. His leadership had gained Senator Warren G. Harding the 29th presidency of the United States, and the Democrats feared that Daugherty's appointment as attorney general would erode their already diminished foundation of power.

As a result, Harding's appointment of Daugherty was the most controversial of his short presidential career. Though he always remained within the boundaries of the law, Daugherty had played many sly tricks in Ohio, and his reputation for wiliness was well known in Washington. He had many enemies on the national level, especially among the controllers of the Democratic press, but Harding was determined to reward his chief benefactor and, despite powerful opposition, raised him to attorney general, the nation's most prominent legal post in 1921.

Once in office, Daugherty made two eventually disastrous appointments, disastrous because the actions of the appointees caused Daugherty's reputation to be even more severely battered. His nominee to the Justice Department's Bureau of Investigation, created in 1908, was William J. Burns, who assumed office with his young and eager assistant, J. Edgar Hoover, then only 26. Founder of the Burns Detective Agency, Burns was

Daugherty's controversial appointment, for the Democrats and the American Federation of Labor (AFL) despised his antilabor activities. They attacked Daugherty by attacking him. Burns's assistant, Hoover, already controversial because of his role in the so-called Palmer raids to arrest and deport aliens who were communists, was also subject to the acrimonious commentary, which continued through 1924, but he was able to exclude himself from the pressures that forced Burns to resign in 1924, becoming head of the equally controversial Federal Bureau of Investigation (FBI).

Daugherty's second error was not an appointment, for the individual involved in it was not a federal employee; nonetheless, Jesse SMITH proved to be a source of criticism for the rest of Daugherty's life.

As attorney general, Daugherty continued to be the target of political and journalistic attacks, in part because of his shady-dealing effectiveness and in part because of his administrative errors. His Ohio experience had made known to him the dishonest among those approaching Harding for patronage positions, and Daugherty made as many astute appointments as possible. [Although he was blamed for them, the appointments of those most responsible for the discrediting of the Harding Administration—Albert Fall (see TEAPOT DOME), Charles R. FORBES, and Thomas MILLER—were solely Harding's errors.]

Administratively, however, Daugherty was careless, and the misdoings of his underlings redounded to his discredit. He mishandled war fraud cases until forced by a 1922 congressional campaign to collect several million dollars he would otherwise have abandoned. He failed to oversee the Alien Property office, failed to note that Jesse Smith and others were collecting bribes to restrict prosecution in Prohibition law violations, and had no insight into the Forbes frauds involving the Veterans' Bureau until the press threw a blinding light on those frauds.

The 1922 attacks almost led to a congressional investigation: the AFL's hatred of Burns led it to demand impeachment proceedings against Daugherty. The *New York World* called Daugherty "the moral test of the Harding administration," and Herbert Hoover (then secretary of commerce) denigrated him because he supported the Federal Trade Commission created in 1915 by Woodrow Wilson, a Democrat. Daugherty had become the whipping boy for the entire Harding Administration.

The Teapot Dome scandal allowed congressional enemies of the administration to get their way in 1923. Republicans fearful for the party joined the Democrats, and Democratic Senator Burton Wheeler of Montana chaired a highly sensational public investigation predominantly featuring Daugherty's enemies. Jesse Smith's widow, who hated Daugherty, testified that Daugherty knew of, directed, and benefited from Smith's misdoings; investigator Gaston Means, angry because he had been fired from the FBI, accused Daugherty of direct connections with the "Ohio Gang." In retaliation, Daugherty had Burns threaten, harass, and vilify Wheeler, an error that cost Burns his job and led the investigation to yield firm charges only against Miller, Smith, and some minor persons.

The congressional investigation yielded two other important results. Daugherty lost his job in 1924 when he refused, by virtue of executive privilege, to yield Justice Department files to the investigators, and President Coolidge refused to support him. His name was introduced, without indictment, into the 1926 trial of Miller and the long-dead Smith. Daugherty testified but continued to claim executive privilege and the possession of information which, for security reasons, he could not divulge.

Two juries believed him, but most of the press did not. Although no guilt was proved, Daugherty's name was now so blackened that his 1932 vindication was pilloried as "an unabashed justification of his every move."

One fact about Harry Daugherty suggests that he had not benefited as his enemies had wanted to believe: in 1941 he left an even smaller estate than Jesse Smith, only $175,000.

DAUGHTERS OF THE AMERICAN REVOLUTION (DAR). See Marian ANDERSON: the DAR fumbles.

DEEP THROAT: the sexual brutalization of Linda Lovelace

In 1972 the pornographic film *Deep Throat* starring 23-year-old Linda Lovelace (whose real name was Linda Boreman) was released and quickly became a fashionable film to see. Lovelace played the part of a young woman whose clitoris was located in her throat and thus had a wild passion for fellatio. The film was quite graphic in its depiction of Lovelace's passion. She be-

Actress Linda Lovelace, star of the controversial porno film Deep Throat, *views herself in a mirror before making her first stage appearance in the revival of the comedy* Pajama Tops *in late December 1973. She appeared in a see-through blouse in the first act. (AP/Wide World Photos)*

came a celebrity, but when in 1980 she published her autobiography, *Ordeal,* she shocked the public even more by declaring that she had been held hostage by her former mentor and husband Chuck Traynor and brutally forced into perverse sexual servitude, including the making of *Deep Throat.*

Apparently, the idea of making *Deep Throat* came from porno-film director and writer Gerry Damiano, who "discovered" Linda during a party in which she served as a prostitute performing fellatio—an act she evidently had been expertly taught by her husband Traynor. Learning to loosen her throat muscles like a sword swallower does, she had perfected the trick of "deep throating." Although Lovelace was chosen to star in the film because of her seeming look of innocence, Damiano's financial backer, Lou Peraino, resisted at first because she was not blonde and big bosomed. Lovelace claimed later that Traynor had forced her to give Peraino a demonstration of her erotic specialty. Afterward, he gave her the part.

Deep Throat took six days to shoot and three months to edit and complete for release. Its cost was about $40,000 and it was 62 minutes long. Traynor received $1,200 for Linda's part (money she allegedly never saw). By early 1973 the movie had grossed an estimated $3.2

million, and by 1980 it had earned more than $600 million. Damiano evidently sold his interest in the movie to partners Peraino and Phil Parisi before it began to draw well at the box office; he was reportedly forced to do this by unnamed persons. In 1980 Peraino was arrested by FBI agents for criminal activities in the pornographic-film industry.

At the height of *Deep Throat*'s phenomenal popularity, Lovelace seemed less than unhappy. She stated during an interview: "I totally enjoyed making the movie. I don't have any inhibitions about sex. I just hope that everybody who goes to see the film . . . loses some of their inhibitions." At the time, the porno star was said to be earning $250 a week.

The notorious movie was quickly brought to court in New York City and elsewhere on obscenity charges hinging on whether or not it was socially redeeming and in conformity with then-current standards of public display. Some came to its defense. In a trial in New York, a professor of medical psychology from Johns Hopkins University stated in testimony that "*Deep Throat,* with explicit sex acts, convinced viewers there was nothing shameful about sex and therefore produced saner, healthier attitudes about it." Detractors, however, stated that despite the movie's occasional comic moments, bouncy music, and good color, it was overwhelmingly "male chauvinistic," pandering, like most pornographic films, to male sexual fantasies, with women being submissive.

According to Lovelace (now Marchiano) in her book *Ordeal,* she had made three unsuccessful attempts to escape from Traynor, who had totally dominated her. He had subjected her to gang rapes and harsh beatings. During the third attempt to flee from her gun-toting husband (who collected hand grenades and had a machine gun), she was sheltered by friends after they learned he had forced her to star in a porno movie with a German shepherd dog, ostensibly in acts of bestiality. Traynor, who she said had married her to keep her from being able to testify against him on drug charges, once allegedly put a garden hose up her rectum, threatening to turn on the water if she didn't strip and perform publicly. Their marriage finally ended in divorce after he met porno star Marilyn Chambers in 1974. Chambers, who had once modeled as Proctor and Gamble's Ivory Snow Girl, was the star of another chic and profitable porno film called *Behind the Green Door.* Traynor and Chambers eventually married. Marchiano also remarried and later, in 1978, got reporter Mike McGrady to assist her in writing *Ordeal,* an undertaking which included an 11-hour lie detector test taken by her and administered by a former chief polygraphist of the New York City district attorney's office. Marchiano claimed she had suffered permanent damage to blood vessels in her legs and internal damage from repeated beatings and rapings. When she tried to do legitimate acting, she was only offered roles requiring nudity; she said she had rejected offers of up to $3 million to make another porno movie. "I wouldn't do any of that again even if I could get $50 million," she declared. She allegedly lost jobs because of her disreputable past.

Subsequently, Linda Marchiano gave birth to two children and appeared on various talk shows, including Phil Donahue's, to speak out against pornography and sexual violence against women. She underwent extensive breast surgery to remove the silicone injected into her breasts to enlarge them in 1971.

When the Minneapolis, Minnesota, City Council began considering a legal amendment defining pornography as a form of discrimination against women, Marchiano testified before it in 1983, stating that she had been a prisoner under threat of death for the two-year period in which *Deep Throat* was conceived and produced. She said that "Every time someone watches that movie, they are watching me being raped."

Out of Bondage, published in 1986, was Linda's follow-up book to *Ordeal.* Written with Mike McGrady and with an introduction by feminist leader Gloria Steinem, it tells about her painful degradation and plight, including the stress of living in debt and on welfare, and with continued attacks on her credibility.

Albert DEKKER: kinky finis
To many who knew him, veteran character actor Albert Dekker seemed most unlikely to commit suicide; yet that was what investigating police first supposed had happened in the actor's Hollywood apartment on May 3, 1968. The utter kinkiness of his death, however, puzzled the police and the coroner, who eventually listed it as an accident, not a suicide. The case is closed, but Dekker's grotesque "finale" at the age of 62 remains a shock and a matter of speculation.

Dekker, a large man, was found naked with some women's silk lingerie in his Hollywood bathroom, the door of which had been chainlocked from the inside. His wrists were handcuffed, and leather ropes were tied around his ankles, waist, chest, and neck. His arms and right buttock showed punctures from a hypodermic needle, which lay beside him. Written in bright red lipstick on various parts of his body were the words "slave," "cocksucker," "whip," and "make me suck." Below his stomach was drawn a vagina. The horrendous scene caused fashion model Geraldine Saunders, Dekker's long-time fiancée whom he was shortly going to marry, to faint when she and the apartment manager forced open the bathroom door on Sunday morning, May 5 (Saunders had grown concerned after failing to contact Dekker by phone on Friday and Saturday). An investigation determined that Dekker had been dead since that Friday. Police found no indications of a struggle in the bathroom.

Born in New York City, Dekker was cultured and intellectual. He was a graduate of Bowdoin College (1927), where he had shown talent as an actor in several college productions. He was introduced to famous stage actor Alfred Lunt, who convinced him to give up any plans of going into the field of psychology or psychiatry and helped him begin a successful career in the theater. His first Broadway appearance was in Ibsen's *An Enemy of the People* in 1927. During a long stage life, he performed memorably and impressively in *Grand Hotel* (1931), *Death of a Salesman* (1950), *The Andersonville Trial* (1959), and *A Man for All Seasons* (1961), among others. The Hollywood movie industry lured him to take parts in various films, including *Dr. Cyclops* (1941), in which he played the title role of mad Dr. Thorkel, a scientist who reduces people to doll size. Naturally spooky-looking, Dekker also excelled in playing spooky character roles and appeared in more than 100 films during his life, including *The Killers* (1946), *Gentleman's Agreement* (1947), *East of Eden* (1955), and *The Wild Bunch* (1968). By his marriage to New York actress Ester T. Guerini (1929), the actor had two sons and a daughter. In the mid-1950s, although he had served as an elected member of the California legislature from Hollywood in 1945–46, his Democratic liberal politics became suspect when he publicly denounced U.S. Senator Joseph McCarthy's witch hunt for Communists; he was consequently blacklisted as an actor and, for a long while, had difficulty finding work. He earned a livelihood giving lectures on American drama and poetry until the political climate became more favorable, allowing him fresh stage and film work. Dekker was distraught when his 16-year-old son, Jan, accidentally fatally shot himself at their home in Hastings-on-Hudson, New York, in 1967.

The actor's death was much theorized about. A drug had definitely been injected into him, according to police, but it was unidentifiable. To have been bound and choked the way he had been, with a leather rope, seemed to indicate that he had not been alone and was unconscious at the time of his death. Furthermore, $70,000 in cash that Dekker was known to have had in his Hollywood apartment (money from his film and TV work) was missing, along with an expensive camera. Someone he knew must have been involved, according to his friends, because he was supposedly not the type to act, let alone kill himself, in so kinky and autoerotic a fashion.

John DeLOREAN: corporate swashbuckler

Flamboyant, 57-year-old multimillionaire and automobile manufacturer John Zachary DeLorean, who had founded a company that produced expensive sports cars bearing his name, was arrested by U.S. government agents in Los Angeles, California, on October 19, 1982. Charged with possession of 59 pounds of cocaine and with conspiracy to distribute it, the prominent, silver-haired automaker was also accused of masterminding a scheme to smuggle some 220 pounds of Colombian cocaine into the United States for sale. He would allegedly have netted $24 million in the drug deal. Before he went to trial on charges of drug trafficking and racketeering in 1984, DeLorean declared "I'm a fighter" and "I'm absolutely an innocent man," adding that his case was "a pure frame-up and FBI cheap shot."

DeLorean came from America's auto capital, Detroit, Michigan, and had graduated from the nearby Lawrence Institute of Technology. He was an enterprising research engineer at Chrysler and then at the Packard Motor Company before joining General Motors (GM) in 1956. At age 44, he had risen to general manager of the Chevrolet division of GM and was known for his innovative design and marketing ideas. Promoted in 1972 to vice president of GM's North American car and truck division, DeLorean was widely expected to one day win the company presidency. But his frequent disagreements with company policies and his high-flown lifestyle in the "fast lane" soon made his future with the company dubious.

DeLorean had divorced his first wife and proceeded to live the life of a playboy. In 1969 he married 20-year-old fashion model Kelly Harmon, and later 22-year-old model Cristina Ferrare (1973). The brash auto executive was receiving $650,000 annually in salary and bonuses when he resigned from GM in 1973. (Later, DeLorean would say he "fired" GM when he left it.)

DeLorean intended to develop a modern, state-of-the-art sports car—his dream car—that would have style, fuel efficiency, and a reasonable price tag. In 1978 the British government agreed to invest at least $110 million into his plan to build a new, showcase automobile factory in strife-torn Belfast, Northern Ireland. DeLorean's stainless-steel, gull-winged, two-seat, DMC-12 sports car would be manufactured at the Northern Ireland plant, which would provide thousands of jobs for unemployed workers. DeLorean's venture was seen as a boon to the British government, which offered fistfuls of grants and low-interest loans to the DeLorean Motor Company, headquartered in New York. There were also many wealthy American investors in the venture. The long-awaited first DeLorean sports coupe, priced at $25,000 to be exported to the United States, rolled off the Belfast assembly line in 1981. In this time of worldwide recession, however, the car's reception was less than enthusiastic.

In 1982, after more than 7,000 DeLoreans had been built, production was halted and the company was placed in receivership by the British government, which later announced that the Belfast plant would be shut down permanently. Ironically, the announcement came only hours before DeLorean was arrested in Los Angeles on charges of dealing in drugs. His role in an alleged

$50-million cocaine deal captured news headlines everywhere, and in 1984 a sensational 22-week trial was held in a United States district court in Los Angeles to determine whether DeLorean had been guilty of drug conspiracy, possession, and distribution.

Accused of eight counts connected with an alleged conspiracy to sell $24 million worth of cocaine in an attempt to bail out his bankrupt car company, DeLorean contended that he was the victim of an FBI sting operation and he had been entrapped improperly by overzealous law-enforcement officials. DeLorean's attorneys claimed that he had been set up by federal agents who knew he was desperately in need of funds. The government prosecutors based their case on evidence drawn from a complicated undercover operation in which federal agents had posed as drug dealers. They repeatedly showed videotapes that supposedly revealed DeLorean's drug-dealing negotiations. But because undercover operations of this kind had just recently been severely criticized by a subcommittee of the U.S. House of Representatives, it was not especially surprising that the jury's decision, voiced on August 16, 1984, was acquittal. Some jurors felt the automaker had been entrapped, and others said the government charges against him had not been proved.

DeLorean's victory, however, was bittersweet. His wife Cristina said she was leaving him just before the trial ended. In 1985 she divorced him, remarrying two weeks later. Soon after she went into court to fight successfully for a share of DeLorean's estimated $10-million estate, which included a large, $5-million apartment in Manhattan and a $3.5-million mansion in Bedminster, New Jersey. Additionally, federal investigators made new charges against DeLorean, of mail and wire fraud, interstate transportation of stolen money, and income-tax evasion. (In 1978 the DeLorean Motor Company had funneled $17.6 million in corporate funds to a secret Panamanian company, GPD Services, Incorporated, set up by two of DeLorean's business associates, which in turn had deposited funds for him in a bank in Amsterdam. About $8.5 million in cash from his backers had then been diverted to a New York bank escrow account controlled by DeLorean, according to inverstigators.)

In addition to the federal tax and racketeering charges against DeLorean, at least three lawsuits were lodged in 1986 by investors and creditors against Arthur Andersen & Company, the nation's largest accounting firm, which was denounced for having given the DeLorean Motor company unqualified audit approval despite indications of improper activity.

On December 17, 1986, DeLorean was found innocent of embezzling $8.5 million from his failed auto company; in Detroit, a federal jury cleared him of all 15 charges of fraud and racketeering connected with his company, which owed more than $100 million to creditors. Eight months later, in 1987, a federal bankruptcy judge in Detroit approved a settlement under which DeLorean was told to pay creditors only $9.36 million of his company's debt.

In March 1998, a New York state jury found that Arthur Andersen had committed negligence and breach of contract for giving clean audits of the DeLorean Motor Company in 1978 and 1979. In an out-of-court settlement in May 1999, Arthur Andersen agreed, without admitting guilt, to pay about $27.2 million to compensate creditors and shareholders of the defunct DeLorean Motor Company (then under a bankruptcy trustee).

DEMPSEY-WILLARD FIGHT: foul play?
Jack Dempsey, considered one of history's greatest boxers, wrested the world heavyweight boxing crown away from champion Jess Willard in a brutal and bloody fight that went three rounds in Toledo, Ohio, on July 4, 1919. In a horrifying display of power that night, in 115-degree heat, the 24-year-old Dempsey, nicknamed "the Manassa Mauler," knocked Willard down seven times in the first round. Hovering over his dazed opponent each time he felled him, Dempsey thought he had won when Willard could not get up after the seventh knockdown, which came near the end of the round. The official timekeeper, however, said that Willard had been down only seven seconds when the bell sounded ending the first round.

During the next two rounds, Dempsey relentlessly pounded the bigger Willard, who stood six feet five inches tall. At the start of the fourth round Willard had been so badly beaten he was unable to answer the bell; he could barely see with cuts above and below both his eyes, accompanied by huge swellings all over his face. Bleeding from inside his mouth, he had had six teeth knocked out and a broken jaw. Dempsey then reigned as heavyweight boxing champion until 1926, when he was defeated by Gene Tunney.

"Jack the Giant Killer" (another of Dempsey's nicknames) "took it on the chin" many years later when, in 1964, his ex-trainer and manager, Jack "Doc" Kearns, published his memoirs in *Sports Illustrated* magazine. The relationship between the great fighter and his manager had never been very good and, at times, had been stormy. According to Kearns, he had secretly "loaded" Dempsey's boxing gloves for the Willard fight, applying plaster of Paris and water to the boxer's bandaged hands before he put his gloves on; Dempsey was told it had been done "to keep his hands comfortable" in the heat. Kearns also supposedly told Dempsey, who was being paid $27,000 for the fight, that he had placed a $10,000 bet for him at 10-1 odds that Dempsey would knock out the champ in the first round.

In his memoirs, Kearns said that the young Dempsey was totally innocent of any knowledge that his gloves had been fixed because he was so awed by the fact that he had won the fight (Willard had been a 5-4 favorite).

Heavyweight boxing champion Jess Willard (sitting on the canvas) takes one of his many counts in his title fight against Jack Dempsey (right) in Toledo, Ohio, on July 4, 1919. "Doc" Kearns, Dempsey's manager at the time, claimed in his 1964 memoirs that Dempsey fought the 1919 match with "loaded" gloves. (AP/Wide World Photos)

Said Kearns: "Afterward, when I cracked the bandages and ditched them, he was so dumb at being the heavyweight champion of the world that you could have hit him with a hammer and he wouldn't have blinked an eye."

After the scandalous memoirs were published, Willard said the 1919 fixed fight was a story he had been trying to make public for years. "I've been trying for almost 45 years to get the story printed, but nobody believed me. They thought it was just a loser complaining. I'm glad Kearns has finally admitted it. My jaw is still caved in from the beating that fellow gave me with cement on his hands." The then 82-year-old Willard, who died three years later in 1968, said that "the first time Dempsey hit me, I knew the gloves were loaded."

About the controversial fight, Kearns wrote that he had "had to smile as the call came to enter the ring. Every punch landing with the hollow sound of a mallet crunching into a watermelon raised knots on him or tore him open."

These revelations of Kearns shocked boxing fans worldwide and Americans in particular, for Dempsey had become an American hero as a former great champion. Many people were incensed by Kearns's apparent character assassination of Dempsey and charged that the ex-manager was a liar.

Dempsey steadfastly denied Kearns's allegations, saying he had always taped his own hands before a fight. "If any plaster of Paris was used, I certainly was not aware of it. In the first place, the plaster of Paris would not have had time to set. I certainly wasn't that stupid that Kearns could have pulled that type of trick on me," Dempsey said. Numerous boxing pundits and sportswriters who were at ringside that night in 1919 discounted Kearns's claims, and experiments were even conducted to see if the wet plaster of Paris could dry in time, following the procedure Kearns had allegedly used. These experiments failed, with the plaster of Paris crumbling as soon as it hit another object.

Even if the plaster had been able to harden, some critics say that Willard could not have survived. "If Dempsey's hands had been taped with plaster of Paris, the gloves . . . would have been broken and every bone in Willard's face would have been broken too," claimed former bantamweight champion Peter Herman, who owned the gloves Dempsey had used in the Willard fight. Herman said they were definitely not loaded for the bout.

Dempsey ended up suing *Sports Illustrated* and its parent company, Time, Incorporated, for publishing Kearns's memoirs. He eventually reached an out-of-court agreement with the two companies, which included a printed apology. Dempsey also claimed that "the people at Time Inc. knew that Kearns was a self-admitted rogue and rascal and therefore should have investigated further before suggesting that I had acquired my title under fraudulent circumstances." Dempsey died in 1983.

DIAMOND HOAX. See William RALSTON: the Great Diamond Hoax.

Charles DIGGS: censured congressman

Voting unanimously 414 to 0 on July 31, 1979, the U.S. House of Representatives censured Charles C. Diggs, Jr., the senior black member of the House and founder of the Congressional Black Caucus. A 13-term Democratic congressman from Michigan, Diggs had admitted to using public funds to pay personal bills and became the first member of the House to be censured since 1921.

Diggs was a respected, powerful politician who came under a federal grand-jury investigation for improper congressional payments. On March 23, 1978, the federal jury charged the Michigan Democrat with allegedly taking kickbacks from staff employees and having on his congressional payroll employees who did not work for Congress. When the charges were announced, Diggs was touring Africa as chairman of the Subcommittee of the House International Relations Committee, and he promptly denied them, grumbling about his "mission to Africa" being possibly blunted by the "unfortunate insensitivity" of the charges.

Later in 1978 Diggs stood trial on the charges and heard testimony from congressional employees who stated how he had padded and inflated their salaries so that he would have extra money to pay his bills. Diggs apparently used his position as chairman of the House District of Columbia Committee to increase the salaries of certain staff members. During the trial, he admitted to raising the salaries of staffers Ofield Dukes and Felix

R. Matlock so that they could be reimbursed for paying his official expenses. Using this rationalization, Diggs said he never had any intention of defrauding the government. "I would not have jeopardized my congressional career on that basis," he declared.

Dukes had originally been hired as a consultant at $12,000 a year, a salary that later rose to $37,000 a year. Dukes said the procedure of paying bills and then sending them to the congressman's office for reimbursement was "normal practice." Not normal, though, was the fact that Dukes, who wasn't working for the House in any capacity, had been put on the congressional payroll by Diggs.

The manager of Diggs's congressional office, Jean G. Stultz, said she had also been put on the payroll of the House District of Columbia Committee. First approached about the scheme when Diggs became the committee's chairman in 1973, Stultz claimed that at one time, her $800-per-month congressional paycheck was used for her personal expenses while a second, $1,200 a month check from the committee's payroll was used for Diggs's personal affairs. She testified that she had used cashier's checks, money orders, and her personal checks to pay Diggs's mortgage payments, personal loans, car payments, insurance premiums, and a five-dollar subscription to a financial-advice magazine. She objected, Stultz said, to being used by Diggs, but said she feared for her job and went along with the scheme before quitting her position in 1976. In response, Diggs testified that Stultz had voluntarily used part of her salary to pay his bills. Paying his bills was not a condition of employment for Stultz, he maintained. "I said, 'Can you help me out?' She said, 'Yes, I'm prepared to help you.' She could have cut it off any time she wanted to."

At the trial, character witnesses who appeared for Diggs included Detroit's Mayor Coleman Young, U.S. Ambassador to the United Nations Andrew Young, the Reverend Jesse Jackson, and Coretta Scott King. There were some complaints after the trial about the brevity of the jury's deliberations (less than nine hours), as well as claims of racial bias by the jurors. Diggs was convicted on October 7, 1978, of 11 counts of mail fraud and 18 counts of filing false congressional payroll forms amounting to more than $66,000. He maintained during his trial and afterward that he had done nothing wrong. And many of his constituents felt that he was just one of many doing the same thing and was unfortunate enough to get caught.

Maintaining his innocence after his conviction, Diggs ran for reelection in 1978 and won his 13th term in the House, getting 79 percent of his district's vote. His easy win turned a few heads in Michigan and elsewhere.

On November 20, 1978, Diggs was sentenced to three years in jail for the payroll kickback scheme. Afterward he made appeals, had his imprisonment deferred, and took his seat in Congress while his appeals went through the courts to the U.S. Supreme Court, which refused to hear his case.

Meanwhile there were outcries to expel Diggs from the House of Representatives. The House rejected such an attempt to do so on March 1, 1979. Five months later came the censure resolution, accepted by Diggs, who stood silently in the well of the House chamber while it was read. The next day he resigned and began serving his three-year jail term.

"I leave Congress with a clear conscience and with deep appreciation of the historic role I have been privileged to play for the past 26 years on behalf of the disadvantaged both here and abroad," said the 57-year-old Diggs after his resignation. He agreed to repay some $40,000 to the U.S. Treasury to cover his misdeeds. After 14 months behind bars, he was freed on parole because of good behavior.

DIOXIN. See ENVIRONMENTAL PROTECTION AGENCY (EPA): "sweetheart deals" with industry?

"DIRTY DERBY"

The annual Kentucky Derby, one of the classic American horse races, was marred in 1933 by disgraceful misconduct on the part of two jockeys riding competing horses down the final stretch. Although one of the most exciting horse races in history, it later became known as the Dirty Derby.

On May 6, 1933, the horse Head Play, ridden by jockey Herb Fisher, was a favorite to win the Kentucky Derby, held at Churchill Downs track in Louisville, Kentucky. Favored also was Ladysman, another of the 12 horses competing in the mile-and-a-quarter race. At the last minute before the race began, Head Play, a frisky thoroughbred, was shifted to the outside of the track, an unfavorable starting position. After the starting gun fired to begin the race, Head Play worked his way toward the rail and had the lead at the half-mile mark. Rounding the corner into the final stretch, Head Play maintained the lead with Ladysman close behind. Then suddenly Brokers Tip, an underdog ridden by Donald Meade, a talented, tough, loudmouthed jockey, broke out of ninth place from the trailing horses at the rear of the closely knit pack and surged forward along the rail. Within seconds he was alongside Head Play, and the two horses now sprinted neck and neck, stride for stride, toward the finish, while their jockeys flailed them forward. As the thundering horses crossed the finish line, Brokers Tip was ahead by a nose and was declared the winner. Fisher immediately protested.

Close observers saw the two horses bumping each other, and some thought Meade's whip had struck Fisher in the face, which could have happened acciden-

tally. Fisher claimed that Meade had grabbed Head Play's saddle blanket. In response, Meade claimed that Fisher had crowded and bumped him against the rail. A photograph taken from the ground at the finish showed Meade's right hand clutching Fisher's shoulder and Fisher's left hand grabbing at Brokers Tip's saddle. Both jockeys were leaning sideways toward each other. As soon as they dismounted, Fisher attacked Meade with his whip and lashed him in the face in full view of the crowd.

Fisher then stormed over to the judges' stand and hotly complained that he had been fouled. If Head Play had won, Meade would have had an equally valid claim of foul play. However, the judges rejected Fisher's protest and declared Brokers Tip, who was owned by the respected Colonel E. R. Bradley, the winner. In those days there were no official films of horse races. Fisher was so enraged that he slumped onto a bench and burst into angry tears. The Churchill Downs stewards suspended both jockeys for 30 days. Still, in the jockeys' dressing room, the two rivals fought each other with their fists after Fisher lunged at Meade with a bootjack. For this, Fisher received an additional five days' suspension.

The Churchill Downs stewards announced that, according to race observers and photographs, both young men—Meade and Fisher—had been guilty of rough riding and of grasping the equipment of the other. Such "unhorseman-like" behavior was contrary to all rules of horse racing and could not be tolerated. The two jockeys didn't speak to each for the next 32 years.

Father DIVINE: clerical miscegenation

From the inception of his ministry, secrecy, vagueness, and the creation of an air of mystery were features of the mode of operation of Father Divine, the celebrated black American religious leader. He began to call himself Father Divine in the 1930s, and speculation about his real name has been constant since that time; he is variously referred to as Major J. Divine, M. J. Divine, and F. Divine. Even the name under which he was born and which was never registered is a subject of controversy that its holder refused to clarify; most authorities state that he was born George Baker about 1882, but the *New York Times* stubbornly asserts that his original first name was Joe.

Moreover, his policies and positions, even if published, were subject to constant revision; except for doctrines relating to membership in his Peace Mission, outsiders found the phenomenon finally named Father Divine to be obscured by a murky cloud of inexactitude.

Of all the actions of this religious figure, none better illustrated his manner of operation than his marriage at about the age of 64 on April 29, 1946, to Edna Rose Hitchings, a 21-year-old white Canadian woman who had been part of his cadre of private secretaries under the religious name Sweet Angel.

When the wedding was revealed on August 8, 1946, the role of secrecy was immediately made clear. Father Divine and Mother Divine-to-be had motored secretly from Philadelphia to Washington, D.C., where they had applied for a marriage license under her name and that of Major F. Divine, aged 41 years. They were married privately in the home of the Reverend Albert L. Shadd, a Baptist clergyman. Father Divine had registered himself as a widower—significant because, after the August revelation, he had had to announce that the first Mother Divine had died earlier in the year, an occurrence that Father Divine had hinted at in an early August sermon given in Philadelphia's Circle Mission Church. He had stated then that the first Mother Divine, who had years earlier been declared "immortal," would approve his marrying again were she to depart.

The leak on August 8 may have been engineered by Divine himself; the record is unclear. Whatever its history, Father Divine immediately moved to blunt the wave of public criticism that appeared in the black press. He announced the marriage on the evening of the leak, transforming the dinner at the Circle Mission into a wedding banquet. When his religious competitors attacked the marriage in their newspapers, he vigorously defended it. They had recalled his fulminations against marriage for the Divinities (his followers) and his threats of anathema to mixed marriages; the cruder newspapers attacked Mother Divine, questioning both her motives and her virginity.

From August 9, 1946, Father Diviner obscurely defended the spiritual nature of the pairing of himself and his second wife, declaring that "God is not married," and stating as a doctrine of belief that the Divinities have "One Father and One Mother—God—personified by Father Divine and His Spotless Virgin Bride—Mother Divine." When the ferocity of the attacks—prompted in part by powerful black fears of miscegenation—increased, Father Divine bluntly noted that Sweet Angel slept apart from him, under the protection of his other secretaries.

The American religious leader was facing the strongest blows that he had ever endured to his reputation. They continued for months despite his pronouncements and then gradually dwindled. Among the Divinities there was no doubt about Father Divine's declarations regarding the spirituality of his marriage, but when he died in 1965 and Mother Divine was declared his successor, opposition papers still expressed their disbelief in the morality and sanctity of his interracial union.

Father DIVINE: flirtations with the Communist Party

Americans were shocked in 1933 when black religious leader Father Divine (whose real name was George Baker) and 7,000 faithful from his Peace Mission in New York City's Harlem marched in that year's May Day parade alongside 33,000 other people, many of them members of the Communist Party. Newspapers reported their presence, often in accusatory language; but few noted that the banners of the "Divinites" stressed religion while the other marchers carried signs reading "Fight War and Fascism." Only a few observed that upon the marchers' arrival at Madison Square Park, the Divinites surrounded Father Divine, led him to the platform, and kept other paraders to the rear. Almost none reported that Father Divine's gentle remarks gained greater responses than those of the more politically doctrinary speakers. But thus began the rumor, attacked in recent studies, that Father Divine was a Communist.

Father Divine asserted in 1933 that "Communism seemed to offer equality and a sense of dignity no other fighting group had ever offered before" to the blacks of Harlem. Candidates for municipal offices had often requested the votes of Harlem's black population but once elected had seemed to forget that Harlem existed. The Communist Party's newspaper, the *Daily Worker,* had regarded Father Divine in 1933 as "absolutely honest, sincere, and of constructive benefit to the people"; the Peace Mission viewed the parade and the apparent liaison of religion and politics as a recognition of brotherhood and of God's working in the affairs of men. At that time Father Divine saw some positive value in the connection, as did many Harlem clergy clutching at straws that might offer relief to the plight of their suffering congregations. And because Father Divine's work was known from coast to coast—in short, because he was news—his action and that of his followers was nationally reported and nationally regarded as a sign of radicalism.

Examined closely, the apparent liaison was really a flirtation, carried on with caution from both sides. At first, Father Divine was frequently invited to speak from Communist Party platforms, but as his followers came in large numbers and dominated the meetings through their excitability and responsiveness, the party leaders realized that they had gained less than they had lost, and invitations to him became less frequent.

The flirtation, dimming year by year, lasted until 1941 when Father Divine rejected the Communist Party as "ungodly and cruel and un-American." Attacks upon him resumed in the party press, especially against his antiunion positions. By early 1952, Father Divine declared himself "a righteous fighter against the forces of communism." The break had been inevitable: in 1936 he had begun to create a program of his own in the Righteous Government platform, almost all of which ran counter to Marxist tenets.

Thomas DODD: censured senator

One of the most dramatic moments in U.S. Senate history occurred on June 23, 1967, when 60-year-old Senator Thomas J. Dodd of Connecticut was censured by his colleagues for improprieties in his financial affairs. He had diverted to his own use over $116,000 received from testimonial dinners and campaign contributions. This distinguished, white-haired gentleman, who *Newsweek* magazine once said looked "the perfect picture of a Roman senator," became the sixth United States senator to suffer censure. He took his fate gracefully, but shame haunted him afterward.

Dodd had an outstanding career as a lawyer and politician. A graduate of Yale Law School (1933), he served for a time as a special assistant in the Justice Department (1938–54). He was highly honored for his work as executive trial counsel at the Nuremberg War Crimes Trial in 1945–46. Keenly interested in Connecticut Democratic Party politics, he was elected a United States representative in 1952 and won reelection two years later but failed as the Democratic senatorial candidate in 1956 to defeat incumbent Connecticut Republican Senator Prescott S. Bush. As the Democratic candidate again in 1958, Dodd won against incumbent Senator William A. Purtell and was elected to two six-year terms in the Senate.

In Congress, Dodd was a close friend of Lyndon B. Johnson, who wielded great power as Senate majority leader, then as vice president, and finally as president. Dodd supported public-school integration, sponsored civil rights and welfare legislation, and consistently promoted stricter gun-control legislation. Labeled a Democratic conservative, he was also known for his zealous anti-Communist stance, particularly for his emotional tirades against congressional colleagues whom he thought weak-kneed against communism. Arkansas Senator James W. Fulbright, chairman of the Foreign Relations Committee, of which Dodd was a member, sometimes received fervent tongue-lashings from the Connecticut senator, who at times impugned his and others' motives.

In 1966 Dodd came under fire when syndicated newspaper columnists Drew Pearson and Jack Anderson published articles alleging that he had been guilty of financial misconduct. He had evidently diverted campaign and testimonial funds to his personal use. Pearson and Anderson had gotten hold of some 4,000 documents given to them by four former Dodd employees, who had taken the papers from the senator's office files. An intensive year-long investigation, encouraged publicly by Dodd, resulted in hearings conducted by the six-member Senate Select Committee on Standards and Conduct on March 13–17, 1967. The white-haired senator, noted for his resonant voice and sculptured features, firmly announced "I have not enriched myself from public office." During the hearings, Dodd acknowledged that he had received several hundred thousand dollars in political campaign funds and testimonial funds between 1961 and 1965 and that he had indeed defrayed some private expenses from these two sources of funds, he said. Buyers of tickets to his testimonial dinners, according to the senator, knew that they weren't making a campaign contribution but a tax-free money gift for him to use as he saw fit; they knew he had large debts to pay. However, the committee learned that Dodd's personal expenditures included about $81,000 to repay some private debts, $8,000 to have a book written, $3,900 to be given to one of his sons, and about $150,000 to be deposited into joint banking accounts belonging to him and his wife. Other outlays went for private club dues and family travel.

On April 27, 1967, the Senate committee unanimously recommended that Senator Dodd be censured for using campaign and testimonial funds "for his personal benefit." He steadfastly denied the charges of wrongdoing, but on June 23, before the crowded, hushed galleries of the U.S. Senate, a resolution was read aloud. Dodd was to be "so censured for his conduct, which is contrary to accepted morals, derogates from the public trust expected of a senator, and tends to bring the Senate into dishonor and disrepute." He had diverted to his own use "at least $116,083" of $450,273 received from seven testimonial dinners and from campaign contributions. Dodd once again defended himself—this time in a quavering voice—after the resolution was passed by a vote of 92 to 5. From the Senate floor, he pronounced the colleagues who had voted against him to be "all honorable men, decent

Senator Thomas Dodd of Connecticut talks to news reporters on Capitol Hill as his Senate censure trial neared its end in June 1967. Dodd, who expressed confidence his colleagues would clear his name, was censured for financial misconduct the next day, June 23. (UPI/ Bettmann Newsphotos)

men, and I do not think they intended to visit an injustice on me," and added that "in my heart I do not have any feeling of wrongdoing. If I did, I do not think I would show up here again." Then the Senate voted 51 to 45 to exonerate Dodd of a second charge of intentional double billing for air travel (he had already been reimbursed for $1,700 by groups that had asked him to speak before them, but had apparently charged the government for this).

Dodd was hospitalized soon afterward for nervous exhaustion. He later vainly pursued a $1-million damage suit against the columnists Pearson and Anderson; in 1969 the Supreme Court denied him a review of his case, thus allowing to stand a lower court's decision that his suit wasn't valid. In 1971, at the age of 64, Dodd died of a heart attack in Old Lyme, Connecticut; his wife and six children received condolences from President Richard Nixon, former President Johnson, and the U.S. Senate. The year before, running as an independent because Democratic state party leaders had dropped him in favor of the Reverend Joseph Duffey as their senatorial candidate, Dodd had gamely gone down in defeat as Lowell P. Weicker, Jr., the Republican candidate, won his Senate seat. Some say Dodd's long, seemingly "holier-than-thou" air had helped do him in.

John DOERFER: FCC chairman as a freeloader

Sponging off friends may be common practice for some, but when the sponger is the respected chairman of the U.S. Federal Communications Commission (FCC) and the spongee is the owner of five television and seven radio stations, the situation is less than commendable. In March 1960, John Charles Doerfer, the FCC chairman, after indulging in numerous free plane trips and vacations, was forced to resign his post because of his freeloading ways.

Throughout the 1950s the FCC was constantly criticized for its lack of backbone and failure to enforce its own regulations. There were revelations that radio disc jockeys were secretly paid to play and promote certain phonograph records on the air (see "PAYOLA" SCANDAL) and that quiz-show contestants were surreptitiously coached and given correct answers ahead of time (see TELEVISION QUIZ SHOW SCANDAL). Richard A. Mack, a member of the FCC, was indicted in 1958 on charges of conspiring to influence the award of a television channel in Miami to Public Service TV, Incorporated, a subsidiary of National Airlines. Before he could be sentenced, Mack was hospitalized for alcoholism in Fort Lauderdale, Florida. His friend and co-conspirator Thurman Whiteside, a Miami attorney and lobbyist, who had a record of giving gifts to regulatory officials, told the press that he had paid Mack's medical bills when the latter had been in a mental institution several years earlier; Mack, marked by public disgrace, did not recover this time. He remained in a mental hos-

pital, too broken a figure to be prosecuted further. Whiteside committed suicide.

Also in 1958, the FCC chairman, John Doerfer, had been rebuked for accepting a free airplane trip to the Bahama Islands with his friend George B. Storer, the wealthy owner of television and radio stations in the Miami area. The Storer Broadcasting Company, according to newspapers, had also evidently treated Doerfer and his good wife to a free vacation on the Bahamian island of Bimini.

President Dwight D. Eisenhower, uneasy, directed U.S. Attorney General William P. Rogers to investigate what the government could do to clean up the television and radio abuses and improprieties. Rogers reported that the FCC and the Federal Trade Commission already had "adequate authority under existing law" to stop the corruption and deception. However, Doerfer did not want to use the FCC powers of enforcement; he believed the nation's broadcasting industry should police itself.

Early in 1960 the U.S. House of Representatives propelled its Legislative Oversight Subcommittee to probe more deeply into what was being done to prevent further payola scandals and into Doerfer's actions. Doerfer admitted that the FCC had not yet analyzed the replies to a questionnaire it had mailed out to radio stations on this sensitive subject. The subcommittee also learned that Doerfer and his wife had again accepted George Storer's hospitality; they had spent six nights on Storer's yacht, *Lazy Girl,* and had flown free to Miami on Storer's private plane. One of Storer's stations' license to broadcast was coming up for renewal in several months. Doerfer denied he had done anything wrong, improper, or unethical. "I don't think a commissioner should be a second class citizen," he asserted. Yet Doerfer's apparent grabbings for industry gratuities and billings to the government for reimbursement of travel expenses that had been paid by private businesses had brought him into disgrace in the Eisenhower Administration.

Clearly made uncomfortable by the revelations, President Eisenhower called Doerfer to the White House for a 20-minute conference; the usual easygoing, affable FCC chairman had a downcast expression when he left. The next day he offered his resignation in a letter in which he defended his conduct but stated that he would leave in order "to avoid possible embarrassment to the President and the Administration." Eisenhower quickly appointed Frederick W. Ford, a tough, ethical three-year member of the FCC, to take Doerfer's position.

DONNER PARTY: driven to cannibalism

One of the most tragic and controversial episodes in American history involved a California-bound group of pioneer emigrants, the Donner Party, headed by George and Jacob Donner and James F. Reed. This ill-fated expedition, stranded in the high Sierra Nevada during

The Pioneer Monument, dedicated in 1918, stands in Donner Memorial State Park on the east end of Donner Lake, near Truckee, California. It rests where the Donner Party, snowbound in 1846, built one of its cabins; some of the travelers survived by eating the flesh of those who died. The monument's stone portion rises 22½ feet—the depth of the snow there in the winter of 1846–47. (Courtesy of Robert D. Bodington)

the winter of 1846–47, suffered through bitter cold and starvation before finally being rescued. About half the party's 82 members survived, some of whom were forced to resort to cannibalism. Since then, the morality of those who have eaten human flesh has frequently been debated and questioned, but one thing seems certain: everyone in the Donner Party would have perished if cannibalism had not been resorted to, providentially or otherwise.

The westward-moving Donner wagon caravan, which had started in Sangamon County, Illinois, and consisted of families mainly from Illinois and Iowa, passed through Independence, Missouri, and generally followed the Oregon Trail as far as Fort Bridger in what is now southwestern Wyoming. There the expedition divided into two. George and Jacob Donner and James Reed led one group on a southern route reported to be shorter and thus quicker than the northern route taken by the remainder of the expedition, which encountered little trouble during the rest of the journey to California. The Donner Party, however, encountered time-consuming difficulties traveling to the present-day site of Salt Lake City, Utah, sometimes losing their way

crossing the Wasatch Mountains. Their westward trip across the arid Great Basin (Nevada desert) enervated them in the summer and fall of 1846, and by the time the 82 people reached what is now Donner Lake in the Sierra Nevada, they were grumbling among themselves. Early blizzards forced them to stop by October 28 and to hastily build three log cabins and several huts near Donner Lake; winter had set in early and was to be the cruelest in 30 years. Heavy snows and bitter cold trapped the two Donner families and the others in their encampments on Alder Creek and Donner Lake. Their animals soon became buried and lost in the snow. When food supplies, including available oxen meat which lasted some six weeks, were almost depleted, they all knew that death by starvation now faced them, and in December 1846, a group of 15 set out bravely to cross the Sierra Nevada for help.

After three days of trudging, they had consumed their meager provisions and, when more foodless days went by, saw colleagues collapse and die. Snowstorms hindered their progress, and eventually, to survive the grim trek, those who did not die turned to the only solution: use the dead for food. Of the 15, seven (two men and five women) reached safety alive, recounted what had happened, and put in motion four successive relief expeditions from California's Sacramento Valley which carried food to and rescued the remaining members, some of whom also had resorted to cannibalism.

The survivors' ordeal was mercifully understood by most Americans already in California, but one of the last rescued, Lewis Keseberg, became the subject of harsh criticism (evidently unjustified) for his conduct. Keseberg, who had a badly injured foot, was accused of staying behind on purpose to rob and kill wealthy Mr. and Mrs. George Donner; rescuers in the last relief party found him alone in a cabin in March 1847 with horribly dismembered bodies strewn about and forced him to disclose where he had hidden money; Keseberg was accused of living off the dead bodies without any repugnance (he was later even said to have found human flesh tastier than California beef). Though Keseberg won a court fight in May 1847 against those who had slandered him, he suffered minor persecution until his death in Sacramento in 1895.

Frederick DOUGLASS: marriage to a white woman

Frederick Douglass was a former slave who fled north to freedom and became the leading black abolitionist on both sides of the Atlantic Ocean. After his first wife died, Douglass married a white woman who worked in the office where he served as recorder of deeds in Washington, D.C. There was a hue and cry of dismay from the white press and much of the black press too. Many whites viewed the marriage as offensive and unnatural, while blacks found it insulting that Douglass hadn't chosen a black wife. Even Douglass's own children shunned their stepmother.

Frederick Douglass was born into slavery in Maryland in 1817; he never knew who his white father was. His childhood in Baltimore was relatively carefree. He secretly taught himself to read and write, skills forbidden a slave, and began dreaming of freedom. At 16 he was sent into the fields to work, and there he experienced the brutality of slavery with repeated whippings and beatings. His master later sent him to labor in the shipyards, where he became a skilled worker. At a self-help association, he met and became close friends with Anna Murray, a freeborn black. She gave him all her savings, and in September 1838 he boarded a train disguised as a sailor and escaped to New York. Two weeks later Anna joined him, and they were married. Since her husband was a fugitive in the eyes of the law and could be sent back to the South if captured, the newly married couple moved to New Bedford, Massachusetts, and changed their last name from Bailey to Douglass for greater safety. Frederick Douglass then began to attend abolitionist meetings and in August 1841 addressed an antislavery convention in Nantucket at which he described his personal experiences as a slave. The audience was deeply moved, and Douglass's career as a lecturer and journalist was launched.

For the next four years, Douglass worked for the Massachusetts Anti-Slavery Society as a lecturer and agent and traveled throughout New England and the mid-Atlantic states advocating the abolitionist cause. He spent 20 months touring Ireland, Scotland, and England and earned enough money to purchase his freedom. In 1847 the Douglasses settled in Rochester, New York, where Frederick Douglass began publishing an abolitionist paper, *The North Star,* while continuing to lecture. The following year, Douglass became involved in the women's rights movement—a cause which he was to support actively all his life. He attended the meeting at Seneca Falls, New York, at which the women's rights movement was started. In his newspaper and on the lecture circuit, he spoke for universal suffrage. Many of the suffragist leaders in the United States and Great Britain became his good personal friends. During the Civil War, Douglass helped organize black troops, and two of his sons served in the Union forces.

Anna Douglass took no part in these activities. She stayed home and took care of the household. Illiterate, she showed no interest in her husband's ideas, opinions, or friends, who favored sweeping social reforms. She felt uncomfortable in the presence of whites, although many of them stayed at the Douglass home many times for long periods. Though Douglass had remained a faithful husband and father, he and Anna had little in common. She died in 1882 after 44 years of marriage.

It came as no surprise to Douglass's friends when, in 1884, he remarried, this time to a white, college-educated, suffragist named Helen Pitts. She shared his love of music as well as his dedication to reform and equality. But most of the world was shocked. The Pitts family renounced her for marrying a black, while the Douglass children ignored their white stepmother. The white press declared that the marriage proved that the black man's highest aspiration was to have a white wife, while the black press questioned why no black woman was good enough for Douglass. Since Helen was 20 years younger than Frederick, some accused her of being a schemer who had married to inherit his money. Douglass countered all these accusations by pointing out that his first wife "was the color of my mother, and the second the color of my father." Further, he declared, he had always believed that racial distinctions were irrational, prejudicial, and unnatural.

The storm of criticism did not affect the Douglasses much. They continued to be invited to social and political receptions, to literary societies, and to reform meetings in Washington, D.C., and in Europe. They were proud of each other's accomplishments and enjoyed one another's intellectual and artistic companionship. Until Douglass's sudden death of a heart attack on February 20, 1895, he and Helen never regretted their marriage. (See also Walter WHITE: intermarriage equals ostracism.)

Theodore DREISER. See *SISTER CARRIE:* Theodore Dreiser's legend of "suppression."

DREXEL, MORGAN & COMPANY: the panic of 1873
In 1870, Anthony Drexel, owner of Philadelphia's second largest bank, began a series of moves against his competitor, Jay Cooke, a famed patriot whose invention of bond drives had financed the Union side in the Civil War. As owner of Philadelphia's largest bank, Cooke was considered the greatest banker in the country. In 1871 Drexel united with J. P. Morgan to form Morgan, Drexel & Company. He thus gained the backing of Dabney, Morgan & Company in New York and J. S. Morgan in London. Thus shored up, Drexel began his moves against Cooke. Though he was ultimately successful in his petty goal, he accomplished it at the expense of millions of people, who suffered in unemployment during the winter of 1873–74. The resulting rash of unemployment is now referred to as the panic of 1873.

Drexel had long envied Cooke's virtual monopoly of government financing and was determined either to reduce Cooke's share or to gain that prominence himself, even if attainment of his goal meant destroying Cooke. He was especially unhappy because Cooke, after 1865, had conducted bond drives for a variety of governmental purposes and had succeeded because thousands of persons who had never bought federal bonds before did so because they believed in Cooke's integrity. When in 1869 Cooke agreed to conduct a bond drive on behalf of the Northern Pacific Railroad (whose congressional grants gave it land but not money for construction), Drexel decided that his method of attack would be to destroy Cooke's integrity. He waited until 1887, and with Morgan's strength behind him, he began his first foray.

His instrument of destruction was his newspaper, the Philadelphia *Ledger*. It began to attack Cooke, who had asked Congress to pass a bill permitting the issuance of $300 million in bonds for the Northern Pacific's construction. The *Ledger* variously charged that passage of the bill would bring Cooke's bank to insolvency, that the bill was really a screen to obscure Cooke's losses, and that the drive was to be conducted to enrich Cooke and his cohorts.

The allegations were Drexel's second weapon. They were only half truths, but they were believed. Cooke, optimistic as always about bond drives, had pledged $5.5 million of his bank's money to the effort, but the bank was not seriously in trouble. Cooke had also proposed what today would be considered extraordinary fees for the selling of the bonds: a 20 percent commission for each thousand dollars in sales and a 12 percent commission for each bond. His fees were normal for the period and not a sign that he was in trouble or promoting a fortune for himself. The *Ledger*'s timing, however, was fortunate: Philadelphia was astounded by the embezzlement of the city's funds by a city official, and upset by the CRÉDIT MOBILIER SCANDAL. The Franco-Prussian war stopped Cooke's European bond sales. The financing bill failed to pass because no legislator would risk another railroad scandal and because the nation's mood had suddenly turned anti-railroad.

Almost immediately, Cooke's credit began to fail. He remained calm when bank runs began to occur and two brokerages involved in railroad construction failed. Then Cooke's New York bank failed and, on September 18, 1873, his Philadelphia bank closed its doors.

Cooke wept, but on that day, 37 other banks and brokerages also closed their doors. Trading on the New York Stock Exchange stopped. Railroad construction across the nation ceased. Within two days, holders of government bonds were demanding their money; more bank runs occurred and more banks failed; over 5,000 industries ultimately closed their doors. Because the panic, which had begun in New York and Philadelphia, had become national, President Ulysses S. Grant and the secretary of the treasury tried to intervene, but financial leaders, including Morgan, refused to help. Shipping and railroad magnate Cornelius "Commodore" Vanderbilt perhaps best summed up their attitude, saying: "Building railroads from nowhere to nowhere is not a legitimate business."

But reorganizing stricken railroads is legitimate, and soon Vanderbilt, Rockefeller, and Morgan were heavily involved in it.

Cooke had been successfuly deposed, the Drexel bank now ruled Philadelphia, and millions of Americans whose lives had hardly been more than a passing concern suffered.

John DU PONT: millionaire, sick murderer

On January 26, 1996, John Eleuthere du Pont, an heir to the Du Pont chemical company fortune, shot Olympic gold medalist freestyle wrestler David Schultz three times at point-blank range, killing the athlete in the driveway of his residence on du Pont's suburban Philadelphia estate, Foxcatcher Farm. Why du Pont would kill a man who may have been considered one of his only friends, his ardent defender, and most loyal supporter is not apparent, but it was stickingly evident that du Pont's behavior, unchecked, had become more erratic, beyond his usual eccentricities, within the past few years.

After a 48-hour standoff with more than 75 police officers and SWAT team members, du Pont finally emerged and was taken into police custody without further violence. There was no doubt that he had killed the well-liked Schultz—there were eyewitnesses—but whether du Pont was mentally stable at the time of the killing was one issue, and whether his considerable wealth would allow him to escape due justice was the even larger issue.

John du Pont was the great-great-grandson of Eleuthère Irénée du Pont and an heir to the chemical company fortune. His inherited wealth allowed him to lead a privileged life and indulge his whims to whatever extremes his nature dictated. And from a very young age, du Pont's nature ran to extremes—from his especially close relationship with his mother to his immense collection of seashells and stuffed birds, which totaled in the millions. While at university, du Pont developed interests in swimming and the pentathlon. When his dreams of Olympic-level competition were dashed, he used his fortune to become a major supporter of amateur athletics and the Olympics. Soon his interest in wrestling grew to obsessive proportions. Du Pont began to make large donations to USA Wrestling, the governing body of the sport, which gave him great influence in the wrestling world.

Du Pont renovated his estate, Foxcatcher Farm, turning it into a private, state-of-the-art training facility for wrestlers. Early in the program, du Pont hired wrestler Dave Schultz as the Team Foxcatcher coach. Schultz also began to train for the 1996 Olympics in which he hoped to win a medal again.

Around this time, du Pont's behavior deviated from normal. Also at this time, his mother died, and a brief marriage ended in divorce after only six months. A cou-

Chemical-company heir and sports enthusiast John E. Du Pont, shown at age 29 in this 1967 photo, befriended Olympic wrestler and gold medalist David Schultz in the 1990s. Du Pont shot and killed the 36-year-old Schultz at Du Pont's sprawling Philadelphia estate on January 26, 1996. He surrendered to the police two days later. (AP/Wide World Photos)

ple of lawsuits were brought against du Pont for several assaults and threats he made. He took to carrying a loaded assault rifle with him around the estate and began to shoot at bushes rustling in the breeze and to complain of ghosts in his walls and ticks covering the wrestling mats. He believed that the clocks on the treadmills were sending him backward in time. He cruised around his property in an army personnel carrier; bouts of paranoia transformed his normally subdued personality into one of suspicion and rage.

Dave Schultz believed he might be able to help du Pont. He went for walks with him and tried moderate the mood swings. If anyone said anything negative about du Pont, Schultz would defend him. He became the mediator between the wrestlers and their benefactor. Friends and family tried to warn Schultz to move with his wife and two children away from the deepening madness, but he was steadfast in his resolve to stay. In fact he had only a smile and a wave for du Pont the day the millionaire pulled into Schultz's driveway and sud-

denly shot him in the arm. When Schultz fell in the snow, du Pont pumped two more bullets into his friend's back. Schultz died in the driveway as du Pont drove back to his estate house.

The trial was delayed for nearly a year on account of du Pont's mental incompetence. Then in February 1997, du Pont was found guilty of murder in the third degree but declared mentally ill. While awaiting his sentence, du Pont spent months in an isolated jail cell far from the luxurious he was accustomed to. His appearance grew steadily more unkempt until the day of his sentencing, when he washed and trimmed his hair and beard and donned a new warm-up suit stitched with the Team Foxcatcher name.

After a courtroom apology to Schultz's widow and children, du Pont was sentenced to 13 to 30 years in prison or a mental health facility, with the possibility of parole after 13 years. He was ordered to pay court costs of $700,000. Although the Delaware County district attorney was pleased with the verdict, emphasizing the fact that du Pont's wealth and privilege had not allowed him to escape justice, Schultz's mother, Jeanne St. Germain, denounced her son's killer, saying all his charitable acts had been wiped away by this final act: "You have slaughtered a great man," she said, "That will be your legacy."

David DURENBERGER: "dishonor and disrepute" to the Senate

When former vice president and presidential candidate Hubert Humphrey died in 1978, David Durenberger was appointed to finish out Humphrey's term as a U.S. senator from Minnesota. Durenberger quickly established his reputation as a senator who refused to play by the standard political rules. A member of his state's Independent-Republican Party, Durenberger pursued an independent role in Washington D.C., by voting with opposition Democrats almost as often as he voted with his follow Republicans. In 1981 he became one of the few Republicans to receive the American Academy of Pediatrics Excellence in Public Service Award. The voters back home showed their approval of his statesmanlike approach to the nation's business by electing him to a term of his own in 1982 and then reelecting him in 1988.

Shortly after his reelection it became increasingly clear that Durenberger's disdain for the rules was not confined to politics, and in 1990 the Senate Select Committee on Ethics began investigating allegations that he had broken several Senate rules regulating its members' outside income. The most damning charge was that he had evaded the Senate's limit on speaking fees by laundering approximately $100,000 to make it look like book royalties. In 1985 and 1986 Piranha Press, publisher of Durenberger's two books, collected speaking fees from 113 groups addressed by the senator. These fees were then paid to Durenberger for promoting the books, even though they were rarely mentioned or even sold in conjunction with his talks. (A similar deal involving half as much money resulted in congressman Jim Wright's resignation as Speaker of the House in 1989.)

Durenberger was accused of a number of lesser infractions as well. According to the committee's investigators, he accepted the free use of a limousine for personal travel without reporting it as taxable income as required by the tax code. He committed a criminal offense by charging admission to speeches he gave in the Senate office building. He spent a $5,000 campaign contribution on personal expenses. On several occasions in 1987 he stayed in a Minneapolis condominium which he owned and then requested a $29,000 reimbursement from the Senate as he would have if it were a hotel room. He spent five weeks rent-free in a friend's Florida condominium without disclosing it and then recommended the friend for a government position. He failed to report a bank loan of almost $500,000, which he had taken out to buy a house in Washington's Virginia suburbs.

For "knowingly and willfully" violating its rules, the full Senate voted 96–0 to denounce Durenberger for bringing "dishonor and disrepute" to the Senate. He was also ordered to give back the speaking fees he had collected from Piranha Press and to reimburse the Senate for the $29,000 "hotel room." Short of expulsion, it was the most serious punishment Durenberger could receive from the Senate. The denunciation was only the 24th time in U.S. history that the Senate had publicly reprimanded one of its members.

Following the Senate's decision in late July 1990, Durenberger had his license to practice law revoked. Faced with an almost certain rejection at the polls in 1994, he declined to run for reelection. He also drew the attention of federal prosecutors, and in August 1995 he pleaded guilty to five misdemeanor counts of stealing public funds by abusing his congressional expense account.

Budd DWYER: a state official's public suicide

Convicted for his involvement in a government bribery-conspiracy scandal, second term state treasurer of Pennsylvania Budd Dwyer called a news conference on the day before his sentencing, January 22, 1987. At the close of the conference, after proclaiming his innocence and recounting his past good works, he removed a large manila envelope from his briefcase. Clearly anxious, he wiped the perspiration from his forehead. In front of a dazed crowd of news reporters, state treasury aides, and others, the 47-year-old former state representative and senator drew out a .357 caliber Magnum pistol. As people cried "Don't! Don't!" in seeming desperation,

Dwyer checked them with a motion from his left hand, placed the gun barrel in his mouth, and pulled the trigger. The television cameras were rolling throughout.

In December 1986, Treasurer Dwyer, married and the father of two college-age children, was found guilty after a five-week trial in federal court in Williamsport, Pennsylvania, of agreeing to accept a $300,000 bribe in return for steering a state contract to a California computer company. No money, however, changed hands, and the state computer contract was canceled when the crooked dealings were publicly exposed. Dwyer was also convicted of five counts of mail fraud, four counts of interstate transportation in aid of racketeering, one count of perjury, and one count of conspiracy to commit perjury. Facing up to 55 years behind bars, he seemed certain to receive a lengthy prison sentence.

The likable, thick-set state treasurer called a news conference on the morning of the day before his sentencing. His treasury department assistants and family members had no idea that he was planning to kill himself. They and the host of television and press reporters who attended the conference in Dwyer's state office in Harrisburg, Pennsylvania, expected him only to announce his resignation. Standing behind an old lectern which he said had been given him 25 years earlier by some high-school students, Dwyer talked about his political career of more than 20 years and what he had accomplished. In regard to his past good works, he declared, "Needless to say, this is what I'd like to be remembered for, but I know, you know, my obituary and everything else will have CTA [the name given to the bribery-conspiracy scandal], and that's all I will be remembered for." In addition, he criticized the media, said he had been wrongly convicted, and mentioned changes needed in the judiciary.

During the half-hour news conference, Dwyer read from part of a 21-page statement that he handed out to reporters, who also received a press release whose last page was missing (a note stated that the page could be picked up afterward). Three of Dwyer's aides were each presented with sealed envelopes, which, when opened later, revealed an organ-donor card, requests concerning Dwyer's funeral, and a letter to newly elected Pennsylvania Governor Robert P. Casey suggesting that Dwyer's wife succeed him as treasurer.

Two days later, at a memorial service for Dwyer, his wife calmly said that he had "felt ashamed and a failure," and betrayed by the system. "But Budd was not a failure; he was a hero," she declared. At his funeral near Meadville, Pennsylvania, where he had grown up and taught public school before involving himself in politics, a rueful minister eulogized the late state treasurer as "one who loved the system so much that he would even take desperate action to promote its healing."

Thomas EAGLETON: haunted by his depression

George S. McGovern undoubtedly chose Thomas F. Eagleton as his running mate in the American presidential race of 1972 because the two were closely matched on the issues. Both of these Democrats were in favor of withdrawal of American forces from Vietnam, cutting unnecessary military spending, expanding social-welfare programs, and tax reform. However, Senator Eagleton's private history of a mental health problem unknown to his senatorial colleagues turned out to be more significant than the candidates' agreement on the issues and ultimately resulted in Eagleton's replacement on the ticket.

When it was disclosed after Eagleton's nomination in July 1972 that he had been hospitalized three times in the 1960s for treatment of mental depression and had on two of those occasions received electroconvulsive therapy—commonly called shock treatment—McGovern at first pledged his full support and intent to keep Eagleton as his running mate. Many Democratic leaders, however, were eager for Eagleton to withdraw his candidacy, fearing the disclosure would seriously hurt the ticket.

To complicate matters, there were charges that Eagleton had been arrested several times for drunken driving and speeding, which Eagleton denounced angrily. Syndicated columnist Jack Anderson reported that Eagleton had received 11 such citations and attributed his information to a "former high official whose reliability is beyond question," adding that Eagleton hadn't actually been arrested because he was a high state official. Anderson later retracted his charges and apologized, explaining that he hadn't properly documented his information in an attempt to "score a scoop." He had discovered that the charges were part of a political smear campaign waged in 1968, as Eagleton had contended.

Eagleton described himself as an "intense and hardfighting person," who in the past had pushed himself beyond his limits and who had received the "prescribed treatment" for manifestations of emotional depression.

He insisted that his ability to make rational judgments had at no time been affected by his depression and that he was fully able to fulfill the vice presidency. He said he had learned as a result of illness to pace himself and knew the limits of his endurance. A recent physical examination, he said, showed that he was two pounds overweight and had half a hemorrhoid.

In the furor that followed the disclosure, it is most likely that the American public reacted less to the fact that Eagleton had been depressed—a stigma, but a common one—than to the fact that his condition had been considered serious enough to twice warrant electroshock treatments. Not only was the public ignorant about shock therapy, but doctors themselves did not know its mode of action. Authorities variously claimed that it caused a metabolic shift, stopped the patient from thinking about his preoccupations, frightened patients into normalcy (rather than submit to another treatment), or affected memory molecules by shunting them or actually destroying brain tissue.

The American Psychiatric Association (APA) and the National Association for Mental Health issued statements in an attempt to dissuade the public from allowing their fears of mental illness to affect their evaluation of Eagleton's competency. "In general," the APA stated, "the assumption of normal activities by countless thousands of people who have been successfully treated for depression is compelling evidence that the existence of an episode of depression in a person's medical history should be considered in the same manner as a wide range of successfully treated illnesses."

McGovern held that Eagleton was fully qualified "in mind, body and spirit to be the vice president of the United States and, if necessary, to take on the presidency of the United States on a moment's notice." He admitted that he hadn't known anything about Eagleton's mental health history when he had chosen him as running mate but claimed he would have chosen him even if he had known.

"I know enough about American history," McGovern said, "to know that some of our most honored presidents have survived illnesses far more serious than anything Senator Eagleton has touched on today." The *Washington Post* reported that McGovern rejected an offer by Eagleton to withdraw from the race.

Actually, rumors of Eagleton's hospitalization and that he had a drinking problem had reached the McGovern staff before the nomination was made, but only a cursory investigation had been carried out, and Eagleton had not been contacted. When it was revealed that Frank Mankiewicz, McGovern's campaign coordinator, had at that time asked Eagleton if he had any skeletons rattling around in his closet and Eagleton had answered no, Eagleton defended himself by saying he didn't consider the hospitalizations as skeletons. Skeletons were sinister, corrupt, evil, or filthy deeds, he said.

Nevertheless, Eagleton said he had made a mistake in not revealing his medical history to McGovern before accepting the nomination. He vowed to watch the polls for two weeks after the disclosure and withdraw if the response of the American public was unfavorable.

On July 31, 1972, two weeks after the disclosure, Eagleton announced his withdrawal from the ticket. Most key Democrats were in agreement that the events had obscured the political issues of the campaign and would hurt the Democrats' chances of election in the fall. Although many Americans criticized Eagleton, many others sympathized with him and criticized McGovern for failing to foresee the problem.

McGovern stated that Eagleton's health history was not a factor in the withdrawal but that continued debate about it would divide the party and the nation. On August 8, the Democratic National Committee named Sargent Shriver as the new vice-presidential candidate.

The New Republic magazine, in bemoaning the power of Eagleton's hospitalizations to override his impressive record as a senator from Missouri, pointed out that Winston Churchill had been troubled throughout his life by bouts of melancholy and depression. "But in the Victorian England of Churchill's young days, one didn't go to psychiatrists, one withdrew to an upper room and pulled down the blinds. Tom Eagleton is of another age and had the sense to get help when he needed it."

EATON AFFAIR

On New Year's Day, 1829, Tennessee Senator John Henry Eaton married an attractive widow named Margaret ("Peggy") O'Neale. Eaton had met Peggy at her father's Washington, D.C., tavern, where he had been a frequent boarder. Rumor had it that they had been intimate before their marriage. When newly elected President Andrew Jackson appointed his long-time friend Eaton the new secretary of war and thus made him a member of his cabinet, Washington high society was highly disturbed and the Eatons were swiftly ostracized. Jackson's new democratic political order frightened many in the permanent Washington aristocracy, which now looked upon Peggy Eaton, an ex-barmaid, as the epitome of what the Jackson administration stood for. Besides, the president himself had approved of the scandalous marriage.

For more than two years (1829–31) the Eaton affair split the Jackson Administration into opposing camps. The social status of Peggy Eaton became a political issue. Mrs. John C. Calhoun, wife of the vice president and a leading socialite, snubbed and excluded Mrs. Eaton, whose "unsavory" reputation and virtue were attacked through vicious innuendoes and accusations about her past, allegedly licentious conduct. Wives of other cabinet members also intrigued against her, refusing to invite her to social functions. Peggy's "morals" were publicly discussed, and her fortuitous marriage into Washington's fashionable society was considered an outrage and unacceptable. However, the president strongly supported the Eatons (Jackson's trust and affection for his war secretary dated back to his unsuccessful 1824 presidential campaign, during which Eaton had demonstrated a great deal of loyalty). Secretary of State Martin Van Buren, a widower, was the only cabinet member to join Jackson in his defense of the Eatons and consequently locked horns with John C. Calhoun, a political rival. Because politics and society are closely linked in Washington, Calhoun's rejection of Peggy Eaton was linked to his inability to make John Eaton his political tool (Calhoun wished to reduce the power of tariff protectionists, such as Eaton and Van Buren, in the Jackson administration). The social persecution of the Eatons persisted while the political rivalry between Calhoun and Van Buren to succeed Jackson increased in 1830–31. Attempts by Jackson to solve the dissension in his "kitchen cabinet" (his political advisers) were unsuccessful, as were his efforts to gain social recognition for Peggy, and a definitive break occurred between Jackson and Calhoun in 1830.

The fight between Peggy Eaton and Washington society finally came to a head in April 1831 when John Eaton and Van Buren resigned to permit a cabinet reorganization; when three pro-Calhoun cabinet members—Secretary of the Treasury Samuel D. Ingham, Secretary of the Navy John Branch, and Attorney General John M. Berrien—were then forced to resign, the American public learned in detail about Peggy Eaton's disruption of Washington's societal order and seemed to side with her. Peggy Eaton, smart and attractive, dared to upset the moral standards of her time without gaining a lasting reputation for any indecency. In the end, the character of Washington was besmirched far more than she was.

Ninian EDWARDS: rash politician

In 1823, William H. Crawford, who had been treasury secretary since his appointment by President Madison in 1816, decided to run for president. Crawford and his followers soon became locked in a political contest for power against Secretary of War John C. Calhoun and his supporters. During this time a Washington, D.C., journal, the *Republican,* which was a mouthpiece of the Calhoun forces, published a series of articles attacking Crawford for malfeasance in office, for allegedly using his banking connections to gain political advantage, and for supposedly concealing letters from the House looking into banking, currency, and revenue-collection practices. The articles were signed only with the mysterious signature "A. B."

The author, it was later discovered, was Ninian Edwards, a noted Kentucky politician and supporter of Calhoun. Edwards seemed bent on ruining Crawford as a presidential candidate for 1824. It was a reckless scheme he was later to regret.

The well-educated, cultured Edwards, who was born in 1775, became a successful practicing lawyer in Kentucky, where he entered politics and, at the age of 32, was made chief justice of the Kentucky Court of Appeals. He was the nephew and protégé of John Edwards, one of Kentucky's first two United States senators. Politically ambitious but apparently without strong convictions (many later said that he was also lacking in judgment), Ninian Edwards was appointed in 1809 by President James Madison to be governor of the Illinois Territory, a position he held until 1818 when the territory became a state. He was then elected a United States senator from Illinois and kept the post as an undistinguished congressman until 1824.

The battle for political power between the Calhoun and Crawford factions began in the early 1820s. Crawford had been accused of trying to set up a new political party in opposition to the administration of President James Monroe but denied it and assured the president of his loyalty; Monroe was satisfied, but the fight for political supremacy persisted among his Democratic-Republican Party colleagues.

Edwards resigned from the Senate to accept President Monroe's appointment of him as the new American minister to Mexico on March 4, 1824. While traveling west to take up the post, he was recalled to testify before a seven-man House investigating committee about formal and open charges of wrongdoing he had recently made against Crawford. Unable to support his charges, now labeled reckless and irresponsible, Edwards was obliged to resign his ministership. The treasury secretary, who had suffered an impairing paralytic stroke in 1823, was exonerated on May 25, 1824. In the 1824 presidential election, Crawford was a leading candidate but finished third in the voting. Because none of the four candidates (Crawford, Henry Clay, Andrew Jackson, and John Quincy Adams) got a majority of the electoral vote, the House decided the election, choosing Adams and Calhoun (who had been on both the Adams and Jackson tickets as the vice-presidential candidate, having earlier withdrawn as a presidential contender).

Although his political prestige had sharply declined because of the A. B. Plot, Edwards managed to reestablish himself in Illinois politics, winning the governorship there by a narrow margin in 1826. But his popularity and power continued to wane. He did not seek reelection in 1830, and his attempt to win a seat in Congress in 1832 was in vain. In 1833, he died of cholera.

Ira EINHORN: convicted counterculture fugitive

Helen "Holly" Maddux of Tyler, Texas, was bludgeoned to death in 1977. Her body was then stuffed into a trunk in an apartment closet, where it lay for 18 months until the neighbors found the stench unbearable and called the police in March 1979. Who killed Helen Maddux and why? It would have been just another unsolved mystery except that Helen was the girlfriend of

American ex-hippie and fugitive Ira Einhorn and his companion Annika Flodin arrive at the courthouse in Bordeaux, France, on February 18, 1999. The French court accepted a U.S. request for the extradition of Einhorn (convicted in absentia in Pennsylvania for the 1977 murder of his girlfriend Holly Maddux) but only on the condition that he not face the death penalty in Pennsylvania. Einhorn said he would appeal the decision. (AP/Wide World Photos)

the hippie guru Ira Einhorn, an antiwar activist leader who also ran for mayor of Philadelphia. Because Helen had wanted to terminate their five-year relationship and Einhorn had invited her to town, he became a prime suspect. He insisted that Helen had gone to the food co-op and never returned, but her family got suspicious and hired a private detective. When Einhorn callously fled the country in January 1981 just before the murder trial got underway, it created a scandal and a manhunt that lasted for 16 years.

Einhorn was an eccentric figure who attracted a large following of the rich and powerful with his New Age philosophy during the 1970s. Many of these followers, led by Einhorn's attorney, Arlen Specter (now a U.S. senator), testified to his peaceful and gentle nature and declared that he could never be a murderer. Einhorn was released on $40,000 bail, only 10 percent of which had to be put up in cash. He promptly fled to Europe (visiting Ireland, Wales, England, Sweden, and France) where he remained a fugitive from justice for 16 years. Meanwhile, in 1993, a Philadelphia court tried and convicted him in absentia for the murder of Helen Maddux. He was sentenced to life in prison.

Finally, on June 13, 1997, Einhorn's life on the run came to an end. He was arrested by French police in a rural area of Bordeaux where he had been living (under the assumed name of Eugene Mallon) in a converted windmill with his Swedish girlfriend, Annika Flodin, since 1992. A viewer watching a feature on Einhorn on the TV show *Unsolved Mysteries* had tipped police as to his whereabouts. Annika's application for a French driver's license had led police directly to Einhorn's residence in the village of Champagne-Mouton in southwestern Bordeaux. There the story should have ended, but it didn't.

On December 4, 1997, a French appeals court refused the U.S. request to extradite Einhorn so that he could finally receive his punishment. Trying him in absentia violated the European Convention on Human Rights, his lawyers argued. However, he was required to report to the local police station every week. The Pennsylvania officials continued to press for his extradition and even changed a state law to grant him a new trial, as required under the French system for extradition. On September 22, 1998, Einhorn was rearrested as he made his weekly check-in at the local police station. Again, Einhorn maintained, "I am innocent of the crime as charged, and I will declare that until my dying breath," as his lawyer appealed for his release. Pending the results of the second extradition hearing, Einhorn was not allowed to remain free; he was held in a prison in Gradignan. In May 1999, the French supreme court denied Einhorn's appeal against his deportation.

In July 1999, a jury in the civil case against Ira Einhorn returned a wrongful-death verdict. In Philadelphia

Judge Sandra Moser Moss said that since Einhorn had not responded to legal summons sent to his house, it did in fact signify an admission of guilt. She instructed the jury to decide on the amount that Einhorn should pay. The jury awarded the Maddux family $752 million in punitive damages and $155 million in compensatory damages. The family said that money wasn't the motive. Rather, they hoped to prevent Einhorn from profiting from his crime—for instance, by signing lucrative book or movie deals. Einhorn apparently did not profit from the NBC miniseries *The Hunt for the Unicorn Killer*, which had aired earlier in 1999.

EISENHOWER-SUMMERSBY AFFAIR: ambition versus romance

Personal ambition, a move to keep his reputation unsullied, and orders from the top combined to cut short General of the Army Dwight David Eisenhower's wartime dalliance with Kay Summersby, an extramarital affair that had become a true romance threatening his military and political career.

Their relationship began innocently enough in 1942 when Major General Eisenhower, nicknamed "Ike," made a visit to wartime London with other American top brass; he was assigned Summersby as a civilian driver. She was somewhat displeased by the assignment, for at that time Ike had only two stars. Others had been delegated to chauffeur those of highest rank.

Summersby's private reaction fit her status. She was no London-typist-turned-volunteer, but an Irish woman of upper-class background, rendered socially more sophisticated than Ike through her family estate of Inish Beg in County Cork. Ike, who had come from lower-class stock living on the wrong side of the tracks in Abilene, Kansas, was fascinated by her, as he had always been by those superior to him in social, educational, and financial status. Although not pretty, Summersby was attractive and full of good humor and exuberance. Divorced, she was engaged to be married in 1944 to an officer later killed in Oran.

She hid her initial reaction and charmed Ike; he charmed her, too, for shortly thereafter Clare Booth Luce nominated him as "what the fair sex looks for—a combination of father, brother, and son."

When Ike later returned to London on assignment, Summersby had become a member of the Women's Army Corps (WAC) and, as Captain Summersby, became his personal secretary and military aide. She accompanied him on tours in Europe, North Africa, and the Middle East. In London she was his riding companion, his hostess at dinners and card parties, and his frequent guest at Telegraph Cottage, Ike's 10-acre hideaway near London. Their relationship grew closer.

Their growing closeness was not disclosed by Ike, but by Summersby, whose 1948 book *Eisenhower Was My*

Boss implied that they had become intimate but never stated explicitly the degree of closeness. That impropriety was assumed by others and can be concluded from two sets of details. The first, from Summersby, concerns a 1944 visit to Washington, D.C., which, besides involving a cordial Mamie (Ike's wife), Summersby found uncomfortable because the Washington "ladies" made her aware that they considered her a camp follower. The second, deduced from Ike's letters to Mamie, concerns his constant assurances to her that Kay Summersby was only his driver or his secretary.

The affair ended abruptly and coldly. Ike flew to Washington in 1944 and returned as commander of the Supreme Headquarters of the Allied Expeditionary Force (SHAEF), while Summersby was transferred elsewhere. When she tried to contact him, he was embarrassed. "It won't work," he told her. But he apparently lacked the courage to give her a full explanation of his change of heart. His official biographers and Army historians refuse to recognize that an explanation was necessary.

But truth has a way of expressing itself. By accident, a biography of President Harry S. Truman reinforces the impression that the dalliance had turned serious. In this book, Truman reported a conversation with General George C. Marshall about an Eisenhower letter asking to be relieved of his command so that he could obtain a divorce and marry Summersby. Marshall rebuked Ike in very direct terms and shortly thereafter had Ike return to Washington and the promotion to SHAEF. (Truman said that he had ordered Ike's personal letter file burned, for which reason the army can truthfully assert that no such letter exists.)

Summersby's second book, *Past Forgetting,* told all. Officially denied, her story stands up under investigation. Moreover, unofficial biographers suggest that in 1944 Ike was convincingly informed that his political career was more important than his romantic satisfaction; he realized that further dalliance would be disastrous. By gradual steps, he was being groomed for high office: he gained five stars (1944), became the Army's chief of staff (1945), and was subsequently appointed (1948) president of Columbia University (where rebellious students thumbed their noses at authority by naughtily retitling Summersby's 1948 book *My Years Under Eisenhower*). He was wooed by both the Republican and Democratic parties as a presidential candidate. During this time he scrupulously avoided contact with Summersby. Invited with Mamie to a Summersby dinner party in a public restaurant, he did not respond, but sent his son with the terse explanation, "It won't work."

Rumors asserted that, during Ike's presidential campaign, his rich friends paid Summersby to stay in London. Actually, she was in New York, employed in a fashionable dress shop. But the rumor persisted, for the rich and powerful are thought to be forced to protect their own.

A reviewer of Summersby's second book considered the relationship of Ike and "the Cleopatra from County Cork" one of the great love stories of World War II, but another commentator, hostile to Ike because he was too cowardly to be forthright and honest to Summersby, cynically notes that Eisenhower was the winner of two prizes: Kay Summersby and promotion to America's highest office.

ELECTION OF 1876. See Joseph P. BRADLEY: the stolen election of 1876.

"EMBALMED BEEF" SCANDAL

During the Spanish-American War (1898), extreme public indignation arose against the U.S. War Department and American capitalistic "beef barons" or meat-packers, particularly the Chicago-based giant Armour & Company. The secretary of war, Russell A. ALGER, was accused of mismanaging his department and sending large amounts of "diseased" meat and "embalmed beef" to American soldiers fighting abroad. Much of the meat came from Armour & Company, which had been organized in 1870 by the multimillionaire Philip Danforth Armour, and, although guilt was never proven, was said to be knowingly bad and tainted.

When the American press widely publicized allegations by American soldiers and officers that they were being fed bad and diseased meat, causing the deaths of numerous soldiers, U.S. President William McKinley was forced to name a special commission to look into the matter. After the war ended, some shocking revelations were made especially concerning Armour & Company. Yet despite suffering brief disgrace, and despite American author and muckraker Upton Sinclair's exposé of the allegedly flagrant abuses in Chicago's slaughterhouses and meat-packing plants in his sensational and successful novel *The Jungle* (1906), Armour & Company prospered enormously during the 20th century.

At the close of the war, the McKinley-appointed commission held a court of inquiry and took testimony from various witnesses, chief among them being U.S. Major General Nelson A. Miles, who had led the troops that invaded and occupied Puerto Rico in 1898. Miles claimed that Alger and other War Department officials had deliberately connived with American meat packers to buy and send impure meat, injected with harmful chemicals or preservatives, to the country's fighting men overseas. Miles's charges could not be substantiated, but they helped bring on the resignation of Alger. During the inquiry, some light was shed upon the meat-packing industry and its methods and led to U.S. government inspection to guarantee pork, lamb, beef, and other meat products against forms of unwholesomeness and adulteration.

The enormity of the "condemned meat industry" was strikingly and scandalously made clear through one man's action. He was Thomas F. Dolan, who had previously worked as one of the superintendents at Armour & Company. After reading about the tragic death rate in the Army during the Spanish-American War, Dolan made an affidavit about what he had experienced at Armour and handed it to the *New York Journal*, which published it on March 4, 1899. It created an uproar. Philip D. Armour branded Dolan's definite and explicit charges as "absolutely false" but curiously didn't have his accuser arrested for criminal libel, nor did he bring a libel suit against the *Journal*, a Hearst newspaper. However, Armour did allegedly attempt, although apparently in vain, to bribe Dolan with $5,000 to declare publicly in another affidavit that his former declarations were untrue and that the *Journal* had paid him considerable money to make them. The following is part of what Dolan's affidavit said:

"Whenever a beef got past the yard inspectors with a case of lumpy jaw and came into the slaughter-house or the 'killing-bed,' I was authorized . . . to take his head off, thus removing the evidence of lumpy jaw, and after casting the smitten portion into the tank where refuse goes, to send the rest of the carcass on its way to market.

"In cases where tuberculosis became evident to the men who were skinning the cattle it was their duty, on instructions . . . through me, at once to remove the tubercles and cast them into a trapdoor provided for that purpose.

"I have seen as much as forty pounds of flesh afflicted with gangrene cut from the carcass of a beef, in order that the rest of the animal might be utilized in trade."

Dolan also swore that he saw cattle condemned by government inspectors secretly hauled back again to the cutting-room to be prepared for the market. And he further attested that: "Of all the evils of the stock-yards, the canning department is perhaps the worst. It is there that the cattle . . . no matter how scrawny or debilitated . . . are steamed. . . . Bundles of gristle and bone melt into pulpy masses and are stirred up for the canning department." And near the end of his sworn statement, Dolan had a shocker: "In other words, the Armour establishment was selling carrion."

Later, Jonathan Ogden Armour, son of Philip and successor as head of his father's company, readily answered the attacks by muckrakers such as Sinclair, in his book *The Packers, The Private Car Lines, and The People* (1906). At Jonathan Armour's retirement in 1923, Armour & Company was the largest meat-packing firm in the world, and the "embalmed beef" scandal was well forgotten.

Peg ENTWISTLE: death leap

On the evening of September 24, 1932, a young Broadway actress named Peg Entwistle had dinner with her uncle, whom she was staying with in Hollywood, California. Though she had recently received another disappointment in a long line of career failures, Peg seemed quite composed when, after the meal, she set out to buy a book and visit a friend. She walked up the steep slopes of Mount Lee, where the great white "HOLLYWOODLAND" sign stood. At the 50-foot-high letter "H" was a workman's ladder, up which she climbed after leaving her jacket and purse on the ground below. A shoe fell off as she struggled upward, feeling hopeless in the face of Hollywood's apparent indifference. From the top, she jumped to her death in the rocks and bushes below.

Born Lillian Millicent Entwistle in London, England, the fine-featured, blue-eyed blonde began her public stage appearances with the Boston Repertory Company and afterward, at the age of 17, was offered work by New York's famed Theater Guild. As a budding young actress she appeared in several good Broadway productions, including the hit show *Tommy* in 1929, and received some excellent reviews by critics. She married actor Robert Lee Keith, but after two years their marriage broke up in 1929. Her promising career went downhill because of a series of unfortunate Broadway flops in which she appeared in 1931–32. Losing faith in her ability, she decided to go to glamorous, faraway Hollywood to begin anew as an actress.

Entwistle's only living relative, her Uncle Harold, lived in Hollywood and gladly took his niece in when she arrived there in April 1932. Within a short time she got a good part in a play relevantly named *The Mad Hopes,* which starred actress Billie Burke. But while Entwistle got good press notices, the play itself attracted small audiences and had to close after a two-week run in Los Angeles. Downhearted and dejected, she felt like a failure once again but undoubtedly found some solace taking almost daily horseback rides along the trails surrounding the great "HOLLYWOODLAND" sign on Mount Lee. Spelling out the name of film producer Mack Sennett's abortive 1923 real-estate development, the sign was later abbreviated to "Hollywood."

After several weeks of trudging around looking for work, the young actress was hired by RKO Studios and given a small role in a murder mystery film called *Thirteen Women,* starring Myrna Loy. Because she had done well in her performance, she was extremely hopeful of good reviews for the film. But it received unfavorable notice in August 1932, and RKO informed her that there wasn't any more work at the time. Nor did other studios have anything for her. Trying not to show her deep, bitter disappointment, Entwistle attempted in vain to raise enough money to go back to New York and Broadway. Shortly afterward, she made her fatal jump.

Her body was discovered several days later by a passing hitchhiker. Found in her purse was a note saying, "I am afraid I am a coward. I am sorry for everything. If I had done this a long time ago, it would have saved a lot of pain. P.E." She would never know that on the night of her suicide, the Beverly Hills Community Players were sending her an offer in the mail for an exciting part in their next drama—the role, ironically, of a girl who eventually kills herself.

Though fame eluded her in life, she gained swift notoriety after her death. Her leap initiated a trend to be followed by other disillusioned starlets, who used the same spot to say their final farewells.

ENVIRONMENTAL PROTECTION AGENCY
(EPA): "sweetheart deals" with industry?

While campaigning for the American presidency in 1980, Ronald W. Reagan, a conservative Republican, promised to lessen government interference in American businesses, big and small, if they would contribute to his campaign fund and vote for him. Elected, President Reagan saw his administration, especially the Environmental Protection Agency (EPA), come under increased scrutiny because of the federal government's

Anne Gorsuch (later Burford), head of the Environmental Protection Agency, talks to reporters at EPA headquarters in Washington, D.C., about the 418 most dangerous hazardous waste sites in the country. Five days earlier, on December 16, 1982, she had been cited for contempt of Congress after her refusal, on presidential orders, to turn over documents to the House. Burford later quit her post amid congressional probes into charges of unethical conduct, political manipulation, and "sweetheart deals" between the EPA and some corporations it was regulating. (AP/Wide World Photos)

seeming disregard for the environment, brought on by steady reductions in the EPA's budget and an apparent attitude of allowing private industry to follow its own path, with little government regulation.

The EPA had been told by Congress, through the Resources Conservation and Recovery Act passed in 1976, to establish a way to follow hazardous industrial wastes from start to burial; it had also been told to set up safety regulations for landfills and to establish penalties for those who broke the rules. But businesses received exemptions from the rules if they produced less than a ton of toxic waste a month, or if they recycled the waste, or if they mixed the waste with other substances. The U.S. Senate attempted to eliminate some of these exemptions, or "loopholes" but was hampered by the EPA, which earlier had balked at issuing Congress's mandated regulations for the agency. In 1982 the EPA, arguing that the United States had 60,000 large "hazardous waste generators" and 15,000 waste haulers, discontinued the regulation that waste generators and haulers file yearly reports about the dissolution and burial of their toxic wastes; the regulation was too hard to enforce, said the EPA.

In late 1982 the citizens of Times Beach, Missouri, were exposed to excessive levels of dioxin, a highly toxic chemical contaminant used in herbicides. Dioxin had been proven carcinogenic in rats and was possibly linked to miscarriages. Times Beach had become contaminated and subsequently unfit for human habitation. In the 1970s a waste hauler had mixed dioxin with used oil and had spread the product on dirt and gravel roads to help control the dust. In 1983 the federal government bought the entire town of Times Beach (800 homes and 50 businesses) for $33 million to compensate the 2,500 inhabitants because of the terrible dioxin pollution. In July 1990, after seven years of study and negotiations, federal and state environmental officials announced an agreement for the cleanup of the dioxin-contaminated ghost town of Times Beach, which would then be safe again for habitation.

Also in 1983, the Reagan administration and the EPA became engulfed in controversy over charges of mismanagement, conflicts of interest, and "sweetheart deals" with corporate and industrial polluters of the environment. At the center of the controversy was a tug-of-war between the executive branch and Congress as to what information House and Senate subcommittees were allowed to see pertaining to the internal operations of the EPA. The EPA administrators attempted to block congressional investigations into several conflict-of-interest charges by refusing to give the congressional subcommittees critical documents relating to the EPA's program of cleaning up toxic-waste dumps throughout the country.

In the fall of 1982 the subcommittees had begun looking into the operations of the EPA's $1.6-billion

Rita Lavelle, fired a few days earlier as assistant administrator of the Environmental Protection Agency and accused of collaborating too closely with polluting industries, frowns in her lawyer's office in Washington, D.C., in mid-February, 1983. She was tried for contempt of Congress in July and was acquitted; later she was found guilty of perjury and obstructing a congressional probe. (AP/Wide World Photos)

"superfund" to clean up toxic-waste dumps. In charge of the superfund was Rita Lavelle, who before joining the EPA had been employed by the Aerojet General Corporation, a California firm labeled as one of the state's chief polluters (it was listed as having dumped wastes at one of the clean-up sites). Pursuing allegations of political manipulation by the EPA, special favors to business, and conflict of interest, the congressional subcommittees subpoenaed documents about the superfund's operation.

President Reagan, threatening Congress with invoking the doctrine of "executive privilege," prevented the EPA's chief administrator, Anne Gorsuch Burford, from handing over the documents; the president and officials in the Justice Department reasoned that the documents the subcommittees had asked for were "enforcement sensitive," would jeopardize ongoing investigations of the agency, and could therefore be protected by executive privilege. Burford, a conservative Republican legislator in Colorado before being asked to head the EPA in 1981, refused to hand over the requested documents, resulting in the House holding her in contempt of Congress by a 259 to 105 vote.

The heated dispute between the two branches of government prompted U.S. Representative James M. Shannon (Dem., Mass.) to remark: "In a sense this is the ultimate issue in which the Reagan administration reveals its true self. We have been saying all along that they are the servants of the large corporations, but when we made that argument in terms of taxes and the budget, the middle class didn't get worked up. When we make it about health and the environment, they do get worked up." Tensions between Congress and the Reagan administration continued to mount for nearly six months, with neither the Democratic-controlled House nor the Republican president budging from their opposing positions.

The issue seemed to come to a head on March 9, 1983, when Burford succumbed to pressure and resigned from her post. Even though she had the full support of Reagan (who would later say she had been forced out by a "lynch mob") and at one time had said that she would go to jail before turning over the requested documents, Burford explained that she had to quit because "it is clear that my resignation is essential to termination of the controversy and confusion generated by the outstanding dispute over access to certain EPA materials."

President Reagan dismissed Lavelle after she refused to resign at Burford's request. Lavelle, whom Burford later described as "overweight, an unnatural blonde," and "blowzy," ended up being accused of perjury in testimony before two House subcommittees investigating her conflicts of interest; she was sentenced to six months' imprisonment and served more than four months in a California prison before her release in September 1985.

Besides Lavelle, two other high-ranking EPA officials were ousted in 1983. In addition, the controversial and conservative James G. Watt, who had been United States secretary of the interior since 1981, resigned on October 9, 1983, after creating a nationwide uproar by saying that his appointees to a federal advisory commission on coal leasing were "balanced" because they included "a black . . . a woman, two Jews and a cripple." His attempt at humor was seen as mere bigotry. Watt was also once quoted as having said that his environmental critics were "pursuing a greater objective of central control in society, as the Nazis and Bolsheviks did."

The president eventually released the documents requested by Congress, hoping to ward off growing criticism of his administration's actions. He said that he didn't wish to prolong "fostering suspicion in the public mind that, somehow, the important doctrine of executive privilege is being used to shield possible wrongdoing." Nonetheless, public-opinion polls concluded that Reagan was more favorable to polluters than to the public. And Burford, out of office, later professed that the president "doesn't care about the environment."

EQUITY FUNDING CORPORATION: phantom insurance

In March 1973, rumors began to fly through the financial community that Equity Funding Corporation of America, one of the world's largest conglomerates of financial services, was in trouble. When the U.S. Securities and Exchange Commission (SEC) and a number of state regulatory agencies investigated, they found thousands of bogus insurance policies, false accounting entries, counterfeit bonds, and the extensive dumping of company stock by Equity officials and investors with insider information. On April 3, Equity President Stanley Goldblum and Executive Vice-President Fred Leven resigned; on April 5, Equity filed for bankruptcy. Its story is one of the biggest business scandals in American history.

In 1969, when sales of mutual funds had fallen off, Equity's officers decided to raise cash by entering false insurance policies on their books. They then sold the policies to reinsurance companies that paid $1.80 for each dollar Equity received in premium payments during the first year the policies were in effect. To maintain this fiction, Equity had to generate more false policies each year. Among other findings, SEC investigators discovered one Equity office with 10 employees whose sole job was to manufacture false documents. Of the 93,000 insurance policies on Equity's books, about two-thirds were fictitious and one-third authentic. The reinsuring companies, including Connecticut General of Hartford and Ranger National Life Insurance of Houston, were among the principal losers of about $1.757 billion. There were sufficient assets to cover the genuine insurance policies.

Additionally, more than $60 million in counterfeit corporate bonds were discovered in various Equity safe-deposit boxes; moreover, some other bonds had disappeared, although their existence had been certified at the end of 1972.

Stockholders and banks that had lent Equity about $55 million also took a beating in the scandal. Stocks that had once sold for $80 a share plummeted to zero when the news of the scandal broke. Experienced money managers for such organizations as the Loews Corporation, Dreyfus Fund, Fidelity Corporation, Ford Foundation, Ohio State Teachers' Retirement System, and a host of foreign banks found themselves with large blocks of worthless stock that had once been worth billions. Others, among them the Chemical Bank, Bankers Trust, and the Sears Pension Fund, were more fortunate, having sold their large holdings before the New York Stock Exchange stopped trading in Equity shares on March 27, 1973.

The fraudulent manipulations came to light when Ronald H. Secrist blew the whistle on his former employer. Secrist, who had been an officer of the conglomerate's key subsidiary, the Equity Funding Life Insurance Company, divulged the scam to an insurance specialist on Wall Street, who in turn informed the SEC. It later came out that the fraud, carried out on computers, had caused several systems analysts at Equity to be suspicious. They had complained to management about not being adequately informed about the meaning of certain terms such as *Dept. 99,* which turned out to be the listing of phony policyholders. Further, the data-processing division of Equity was forbidden to have contact with the actuarial division, which had its own computer system.

It took state and federal investigators months to unravel the mess at Equity. Many institutions were hurt by its fraudulent practices. An attorney at the Dreyfus Fund remarked ruefully, "When we bought, the company looked good—and nobody suspected its executives were anything but honest."

ERIE RAILROAD "WAR"

Hyperbolically labeled "wars" by journalists, rivalries for control of railroads plagued 19-century America. All were costly to minority stockholders and the general public. One of the most extreme of these was waged by a wily trio of men who dared to outsmart the multimillionaire capitalist Cornelius "Commodore" Vanderbilt.

The war began because Vanderbilt, then assembling his New York Central Railroad system, wanted an outlet to Chicago and the rapidly developing West. He saw as his best possibility a small railroad then reaching as far as Michigan, the New York and Erie Railroad Company. He acquired enough stock in it to gain a seat on its board of directors and then tried amicably to gain control of the company through a merger.

A powerful trio ran the Erie: Daniel Drew, Jay GOULD, and James Fisk. They saw in Vanderbilt's merger offer an opportunity to make fortunes. Already infamous for plundering railroad treasuries, the three developed a plan to bilk Vanderbilt. They declined Vanderbilt's offer and then proceeded against him cunningly.

Drew, the Erie's treasurer, who had already made one fortune by selling Erie stock short, feigned interest in the Vanderbilt scheme and suggested that Vanderbilt acquire majority control of the Erie by purchasing more shares of its stock. Drew then cooperated with Gould and Fisk to prevent Vanderbilt's success. Vanderbilt quietly bought Erie's common shares, and the trio, who had invested heavily in Erie's convertible bonds, pressured the railroad's board to allow conversion. Vanderbilt purchased and the trio secretly converted, dumping

100,000 new shares anonymously on the market. The scheme prevented Vanderbilt from reaching 51 percent ownership. The cost to Vanderbilt was $7 million and the profits made by the trio were $6 million.

In early 1868, when Vanderbilt discovered he had been tricked, he turned to the courts. He had a judge under his control issue an injunction against the bond conversions. The trio answered by having their own bribed judge issue a countermanding order. Vanderbilt's judge then issued an order for their arrest, and the war escalated to increasingly bizarre proportions.

Drew, Gould, and Fisk decamped to Jersey City, taking the Erie's books, stocks, and $6 million in cash with them. They took space in a hotel, Taylor's Castle, which the trio renamed "Fort Taylor." When Vanderbilt ordered their kidnapping, they hired thugs to protect them, gained the protection of the Jersey City police, and started a "navy" of rowboats commanded by "Admiral" Fisk. Fisk had taken his mistress, the notorious Josie Mansfield, along. Always a showman, he offered her along with champagne at frequent press conferences. Some of the public found their antics laughable; the Erie stockholders fumed with anger.

In the meantime the abstemious and humorless Gould implemented two ploys: he began a rate war between the Erie and the New York Central to keep Vanderbilt occupied, and he went with bundles of cash to Albany, New York, where, with the help of state Senator William "Boss" Tweed, he bribed the legislators into declaring, ex post facto, that the conversion of the Erie bonds had been legal. However, Vanderbilt freed himself from this work long enough to bribe other legislators and to have Gould placed under house arrest. Nevertheless, the trio maintained control of the Erie.

Vanderbilt did not give up. To regain some of his lost fortune, he watered down his New York Central stock, declared a dividend, and issued himself another $26 million saleable bonds. He then returned to Albany to attempt, vainly, the repeal of the bond conversion law and a Gould-inspired statute forbidding the interlocking of the Erie board and that of another railroad—a move making the acquisition of the Erie of no further interest to Vanderbilt.

Now desiring to end the war, Vanderbilt tempted Drew (who was fearful of losing his own fortune) and earned him the enmity of his former partner. The trio settled, paying Vanderbilt $4.75 million; Vanderbilt sold his Erie stock without further loss and devoted himself in other ways to the enhancement of the New York Central.

Because of dealings with Vanderbilt, Drew lost his place on the Erie board of directors. Gould next used a Vanderbilt trick, recapitalizing the Erie to $54 million, declaring a dividend, and making an instant $20 million, some of which he shared with Fisk and Tweed. Then he and Fisk began a bear raid, driving down Erie stock prices from $70 to $35 to avenge themselves on Drew, who was forced into bankruptcy. In 1872, when Fisk was murdered by a rival for Josie Mansfield's charms, Gould was forced out of the Erie railroad by a coalition of long-angry minority stockholders. He left it a debt of $64 million, rendering it unable to declare a dividend until 1942.

ESM GOVERNMENT SECURITIES SCANDAL

"It's probably one of the most colossal, stupendous frauds I've ever seen." This remark was made by one of the investigators of ESM Government Securities, a Florida-based securities dealer. When it collapsed suddenly in 1985, ESM owed creditors more than $315 million and caused a run on savings and loan institutions in Ohio.

ESM Government Securities, Incorporated, specialized in offering investors high returns on short-term loans backed by government securities. Many savings and loans associations in southern Ohio, which were privately insured, invested in the U.S. Treasury bills and bonds offered by ESM and were pleased to see their assets soar. But then, in the spring of 1985, ESM suddenly folded. The banks that were not insured by the Federal Savings and Loan Insurance Corporation found themselves facing huge losses. The Home State Savings Bank of Cincinnati was the hardest hit, standing to lose $150 million. When the news leaked to the bank's depositors, they began withdrawing their savings so fast that banking regulators ordered the bank closed. The panic spread from Cincinnati to other, smaller thrift institutions across the state as hundreds of people lined up to withdraw their funds. Ohio's Governor Richard F. Celeste issued an emergency decree ordering the 70 privately insured thrift institutions to close down for a week while the legislature devised strategies for restoring them to business. The chairperson of the U.S. League of Savings Institutions commented: "Home State really made bad investments, and, basically, they were dealing with crooks. This is not the usual way S and L's operate."

Meanwhile, back in Florida, the court had appointed an attorney to act as receiver for ESM and was investigating the failure of the Fort Lauderdale firm. Many of the government securities listed in its inventories could not be found, and numerous individuals were implicated in the scandal. The Securities and Exchange Commission discovered that ESM's accounting firm in Chicago, Alexander Grant & Company, had also been involved in the scandal. One of its auditors, Jose L. Gomez, had been bribed for five years to prepare false financial reports showing that ESM was in fine shape when, in fact, it was losing increasing sums of money. Later in the investigation, Alexander Grant was also cited for arranging out-of-court settlements with a few banks.

Many officers of ESM were prime suspects in the fraud, and they reluctantly admitted their guilt. ESM President Nicholas Wallace and Vice President Stanley Wolfe pleaded innocence, but the jury found only Wolfe innocent. On July 2, 1986, Wallace was convicted on 16 counts of conspiracy and mail and wire fraud and received 30 years in the penitentiary. The former controller, who had pleaded guilty, committed suicide before he was sentenced. Jose Gomez was given 12 years. Four others, including ESM co-founder and Chairman Ron R. Ewton and co-founder George Mead, were also sent to prison in 1987.

Alexander Grant, which had changed its name to Grant Thornton by the fall of 1986, was ordered by a federal judge to pay a $50-million settlement to 17 municipalities that had lost money when ESM failed. They claimed they had relied on Grant's audited financial statements, which had shown ESM to be a healthy and sound company.

Meade ESPOSITO. See Mario BIAGGI: a senior congressman's sudden comedown.

Billie Sol ESTES: flamboyant con man

At the time of his arrest by the FBI on March 29, 1962, Billie Sol Estes seemed to personify the poor boy who had "made good." The son of a religious and hard-working but impoverished farmer in West Texas, Estes had built a $150 million empire before he reached the age of 40. He was a pillar of his small community of Pecos, Texas, a Bible-quoting elder and lay preacher in the fundamentalist Church of Christ, an abstainer from alcohol and tobacco, and a substantial contributor to local charities and to the state and national Democratic Party. In 1953 the National Junior Chamber of Commerce had named Estes one of the 10 outstanding young men in the country. In 1951 he was appointed to the U.S. Agriculture Department's National Cotton Advisory Committee. But behind his impressive credentials as it turned out, he was a gigantic swindler who had milked the federal government's farm-subsidy program and whose fortune was based on the fraudulent sale of nonexistent fertilizer tanks to West Texas farmers.

According to Estes, he got his start in farming and business when his parents gave him a ewe lamb for his 13th birthday in 1938. From that sheep he built a flock and boasted of amassing $38,000 by the time he was 18. After settling in Pecos, Texas, in 1951, he began raising cotton; within a few years he was selling anhydrous ammonia, a chemical fertilizer that greatly increased yields for cotton and grain sorghums, another important crop in West Texas. By late 1958 the fertilizer business was growing and Estes admitted that by underselling his competitors, he was trying to drive them out of business so that he could monopolize the

West Texas financier Billie Sol Estes, accused of perpetrating elaborate frauds mainly concerning cotton-price supports and grain-storage fees paid for by taxpayers, leaves the federal court in El Paso, Texas, on May 23, 1962, following his indictment. (AP/Wide World Photos)

regional fertilizer market. At the same time he was developing a grain storage business, again by undercutting his competition. Generous federal subsidies for the storage of surplus crops made this an extremely lucrative endeavor.

His business techniques brought on large debts, and by 1959 Estes began to sell, then lease back, nonexistent fertilizer tanks. He used the mortgages on the fictitious tanks to borrow between $22 and $30 million from commercial finance companies. The following year he started to expand his cotton acreage by circumventing the federal government's allotment program, which limited the number of acres a farmer could use for cotton. Estes sold land to farmers who had unused allotments, then leased it back, in effect illegally purchasing cotton allotments.

In 1962, the *Pecos Independent and Enterprise,* a rival to a Pecos newspaper owned by Estes, published an exposé of the fertilizer-tank loan scheme, and soon the entire Estes empire came under scrutiny. In what proved to be the first major scandal of the Kennedy Administration, Republicans charged serious improprieties within the Agriculture Department in regard to Estes. In 1961 the department had accepted, without trying to verify, a false financial statement from Estes designed to reduce the bond required for his participation in the federal grain-storage program. The department had also failed to rule promptly on the legality of Estes's acquisition of cotton allotments. Moreover, Estes had bragged of his connections with Democrats Lyndon B. Johnson, then vice president, and Orville L. Freeman, secretary of agriculture.

After an investigation of the Estes scandal, Senator John L. McClellan's Permanent Investigations Subcommittee of the Government Operations Committee concluded that the Agriculture Department had not been in collusion with Estes but that tighter control of farm programs was needed. Estes was fined more than half a million dollars by the department for his cotton-allotment schemes. His fertilizer-tank operations yielded a federal conviction for mail fraud and conspiracy. Estes served nearly six and a half years of his 15-year federal sentence.

He was released in 1971, claiming that he planned to lead a simple life. But within a few years, federal prosecutors later charged, he was involved in a scheme similar to his earlier fertilizer-tank operation. In 1979, while still on parole, he was indicted by a federal grand jury on charges of income-tax evasion, mail fraud, interstate transportation of stolen property, and concealing assets from the Internal Revenue Service. He was charged with bilking investors by borrowing money and using as collateral nonexistent steam cleaners used to wash oil-field equipment. One of his victims, a Texas used-car dealer named J. H. Burkett who lent Estes his life savings of $50,000 in 1975, called Estes "the world's best salesman." Though Estes claimed that the Justice Department was persecuting him, he was convicted in 1979 of conspiracy to defraud investors and concealing assets. Sentenced to 10 years in prison, he was paroled in 1983.

Judith Campbell EXNER. See KENNEDY-CAMPBELL AFFAIR.

Albert FALL. See TEAPOT DOME.

FANNY HILL: over two centuries on trial

John Cleland's *Memoirs of a Woman of Pleasure,* popularly known as *Fanny Hill,* was fresh from the press in 1749 when its author and his bookseller-publisher were called before England's Privy Council on charges of obscenity. Because Cleland pleaded poverty and a noble relative promised him a pension if he would refrain from immortalizing future Fanny Hills, he and his partner were set free without a fine. But a judicial habit of punishing booksellers was established in 1761 when a man named Drybutter was pilloried for peddling the novel. This custom of suppression by the courts became the norm in the United States, where it lasted until 1966, when the U.S. Supreme Court ruled the book not obscene.

Court actions, however, had prompted clandestine editions on a regular basis, and in 1821 what had been solely an English scandal also became an American problem. In that year the Massachusetts Circuit Court of Common Pleas judged one Peter Holmes guilty of a misdemeanor for publishing an illustrated edition of the Cleland novel. Clandestine editions, however, continued to appear, and court suits followed. They usually ended with the fining or imprisonment of the offenders, or both; more often than not, most of the editions were destroyed. Some copies found their way into judicial or law-officers' libraries, perhaps on the basis of the dictum that one must know what one is fighting.

This pattern continued in the United States until June 24, 1957, when the U.S. Supreme Court, in the *Roth* decision (which concerned a periodical alleged to be pornographic), established a new definition of obscenity. It required courts to examine thoroughly offensive materials and allowed their condemnation only if they were "without any redeeming social importance whatever." This decision became the key to the eventual freeing of *Fanny Hill* from its bad name.

After *Roth,* a New York publisher, G. P. Putnam's Sons, felt free to publish *Fanny Hill.* It almost immediately found itself in court in the states of New York, New Jersey, and Massachusetts. In New York, the book was first cleared by a trial court, held obscene in an appellate judgment, and then cleared by a court of appeals. In New Jersey, a Hackensack decision against the book was not appealed, for in Boston an adverse judgment had been appealed to the U.S. Supreme Court, which on March 21, 1966, ruled that the novel was not obscene, by extending the *Roth* definition so that "a book cannot be proscribed unless it is found to be *utterly* without redeeming social value." So measured, *Fanny Hill* was found fit to deserve the protection of the First Amendment.

And Fanny was free to describe, in very ladylike language, the various sexual experiences of her busy career. Her letters make up a novel that many still regard as pornographic, but now legally so.

Frances FARMER: "liquor in my milk"

"Listen, I put liquor in my milk. I put liquor in my coffee and in my orange juice. What do you want me to do, starve to death? I drink everything I can get, including benzedrine." These words were hurled in 1943 by Frances ("Fran") Farmer, one of Hollywood's rising stars. But they were not lines in a movie. Farmer's defiant words were spoken at a court trial in front of a police judge, in response to questions about her excessive drinking. Her hysterical courtroom behavior marked the beginning of her startling and public emotional breakdown, one that would render her mentally unsound for nearly 30 years.

A graduate of the University of Washington, Farmer broke into the movies after winning a magazine popularity contest in 1935 in Seattle, her hometown. The Paramount movie studio then signed this attractive young woman to a seven-year contract and began touting her as a "new Garbo." She was lent to other studios to make more money (little of which she saw) and gained considerable success in the Goldwyn film *Come and Get It* (1936). But Farmer wanted to play serious

The disheveled Frances Farmer (left), appearing at the Los Angeles County Jail on January 14, 1943, to begin serving 180 days behind bars for violating parole on a drunk driving conviction, looked much different from the glamorous movie actress she once was (right). (AP/ Wide World Photos)

theatrical roles, not light Hollywood parts, and performed on the New York stage, notably in *Golden Boy* (1937). The public, however, recognized her more for starring roles in various films with actors Tyrone Power, Cary Grant, and Ray Milland. Farmer openly declared her loathing for everything "Hollywood" (except the money), which greatly infuriated her studio bosses, who were continually upset because of her individualistic, nonconforming, impertinent behavior, which they felt did not befit a star. In the early 1940s Farmer's left-wing political activities in Hollywood, New York, and Philadelphia helped to brand her a communist in some minds. Hollywood was exploiting her, she claimed, and the place just didn't seem to fit her.

On the evening of October 19, 1942, the high-strung actress was arrested in Santa Monica, California, for a small traffic violation on the Pacific Coast Highway. She was charged with being drunk and without a license and with driving with her car headlights on in a dim-out area (which was against wartime regulations). After a violent argument with the police, she was hauled off to jail, convicted of driving while intoxicated, given a

180-day jail sentence, and put on probation. Afterward, the distraught Farmer was said to be hearing "voices" both night and day.

A few months later, in January 1943, when she failed to report to her parole officer, police went to the Knickerbocker Hotel in Hollywood, where she was staying, and had to break down the door of her bathroom to get to her inside. They had to carry her off—nude, screaming, and kicking through the hotel lobby—to the Hollywood police headquarters. There, to the shock of many, she signed her occupation as "cocksucker." The day before, she had gone on a wild, 24-hour drunken rampage, none of which she seemed to remember, participating in a nightclub brawl, losing her sweater, hitting and dislocating the jaw of a lady hairdresser, and running topless through traffic on Sunset Boulevard. Farmer's studio bosses were deeply vexed; shortly thereafter the Monogram studio announced that Mary Brian had replaced her in the leading role in *No Escape*.

After the judge gave her a 180-day jail sentence, she yelled, "Fine! Have you ever had a broken heart?" (apparently referring to being divorced by actor Leif Ericson in the fall of 1942 and being ignored by dramatist Clifford Odets, with whom she had recently fallen in love). While being taken from the court and denied permission to make a phone call, Farmer kicked and hit a police matron, knocked down a policeman, and finally had to be dragged off in a straightjacket to a jail cell. In Seattle, Farmer's mother callously told reporters that her daughter's antics were probably a publicity stunt, all designed to give her real experience as a jailbird. Realizing later that her daughter's nervous breakdown was no stunt, Farmer's mother signed papers committing her daughter as a mental incompetent. Although the court-imposed jail sentence was revoked, Fanny's future remained grim. Insulin shock treatments were administered to the "mad" actress in a private sanitarium. In 1944 she was adjudged insane after vain attempts to cope with life outside the institution. Confined at that time to another institution in Steilacoom, Washington, she endured cruel treatment for many years at the hands of brutal nurses and matrons.

Finally released, Farmer attempted a film comeback in *The Party Crashers* (1958). It was her final screen appearance, and a listless one. She remarried and a dozen years later died of cancer at the age of 55 in 1970. Her posthumous autobiography, *Will There Really Be a Morning?* (1972), tells about her long struggle with mental illness and alcoholism, and her gruesome experiences as a patient.

Orval FAUBUS: foe of school integration

As a progressive governor of Arkansas after 1955, Orval Eugene Faubus scrupulously obeyed the directives developed from the U.S. Supreme Court's 1954 *Brown* v. *Board of Education* decision by integrating seven state-supported colleges and permitting three major Arkansas communities to integrate their public schools. In 1957, however, he reversed a campaign promise of non-interference in the integration process by defying a federal court order to integrate Little Rock's Central High School and in so acting gained contempt from those who had believed that he was leading Arkansas out of a post-Civil War twilight.

Two factors influenced Faubus's reversal of attitude: the 1956 report by a gubernatorial commission studying Virginia's "interposition plan," and a poll of Arkansas citizens' attitudes toward public-school integration. The first, suggesting that Arkansas delay full compliance with federal regulations and achieve only partial integration by having school officials assign blacks to specific schools, was adopted. The second, revealing that 85 percent of Arkansans opposed integration, made Faubus state that he could not "be a party to any attempt to force acceptance of a change . . . so overwhelmingly opposed." Further desegregation then stopped.

Late in 1956, a plan for the gradual integration of Central High School was approved by a federal district court and ordered implemented in 1957. Faubus, acting

to preserve order and to prevent the integration, called up the Arkansas National Guard.

The result was exactly the reverse of Faubus's intentions. The mobilization of the National Guard incited disorder: it alerted die-hard segregationists to come to Little Rock and agitate. A federal court then ordered Faubus to stop his "defiance," and he withdrew the troops. As a result, on September 23, 1957, when nine black students went nervously into Central High School by its front door, riots outside and disturbances inside caused the nine to be ejected through a side door of the school.

Central High School was again white, but only for one day. Faubus had not assisted, but instead resisted the original court order through his ultimate inaction. Forced to act to save the integrity of the federal district court, U.S. President Dwight Eisenhower, who had publicly expressed reservations about the 1954 decision, sent in the Army.

Soldiers surrounded the school on September 24, and the nine black students were again able to enter. Outside, demonstrators chanted and waved placards beyond a human fence of paratroopers commanded by then Brigadier General Edwin A. Walker. Inside, other soldiers, including members of the Arkansan National Guard, federalized to help the paratroopers, kept peace. None of the nine very frightened black students was ejected a second time.

But tossed out for good was Arkansas's plan to thwart the Supreme and district courts. And as one historian of school desegregation noted, tossed out also were Faubus's hopes to be regarded as one of the South's leaders in the fight against integration. That role had to await the actions of George C. WALLACE. Faubus remained in office until 1967, then worked as a bank clerk, and made unsuccessful bids for the governorship in 1970, 1974, and 1986. He died in 1994 at age 84.

John FEDDERS: SEC official with "black moods"

"The glare of publicity on my private life threatens to undermine the effectiveness of the division of enforcement and of the commission," declared 43-year-old John M. Fedders, the chief enforcement officer of the U.S. Securities and Exchange Commission (SEC) on February 26, 1985. Fedders had just submitted his resignation following shocking revelations in the press that he had violently beaten his 41-year-old wife, Charlotte, on several occasions in the past. An SEC spokeswoman refused to say whether his leaving was encouraged by a clearly embarrassed Reagan administration, which decried "family violence" and extolled "family values" as a national virtue during the presidential campaign of 1984.

The American public first learned about Fedders's marital and financial "private difficulties" in a lengthy and vivid front-page story in the *Wall Street Journal*, which was accused by some of being overzealous in its attack on him. The dramatic exposé, which appeared on February 25, 1985, revealed that Fedders had admitted during divorce proceedings earlier that month that he had once beaten his wife so severely that he had ruptured her eardrum. Seven "regrettable episodes" of wife abuse were acknowledged by Fedders, a church-going Catholic, who publicly expressed remorse for his behavior. To many, the SEC enforcement chief seemed the pillar of rectitude, known for his scrupulousness, integrity, and hard work. The picture that now emerged was sad and shameful: a seemingly overbearing man with a history of "black moods" who was living beyond his means, beset by money worries.

A former basketball center at Marquette University, the 6-foot, 10-inch Fedders rose to be a successful securities lawyer working for a Washington, D.C., law firm. When he joined the SEC in 1981, he took a salary cut from $161,000 to $59,900. Nonetheless, he kept up his rich lifestyle while becoming highly respected for vigorous probes into insider trading as the SEC's chief enforcement officer, supervising a staff of 200 persons. He had a 70-acre farm in Virginia, sent his five sons to private schools, belonged to the classy Congressional Country Club, and borrowed heavily to pay his state and federal taxes. A 1982–83 federal grand jury investigation of the Southland Corporation, accused of bribing state officials and convicted of criminal conspiracy, resulted in Fedders (of whom Southland had been a former client) being "questioned" about his part in the corporation's own internal probe, which concluded that there had been no wrongdoing. In 1983 Fedders's wife Charlotte separated from him and, about 18 months later, began divorce proceedings; she had earlier told about her husband's violent abuse of her in a letter, which was forwarded by her sister to presidential counsel Fred Fielding. In the letter, Charlotte Fedders wrote, "I do not understand how a man can enforce one set of laws and abuse another." President Reagan avoided talking about the case, apparently hoping that the couple might reconcile.

Charlotte Fedders eventually sued for divorce after 18 years of marriage, and her court testimony in Maryland became known in late February 1985. Calling herself "a classic abused wife," she had had to demand that her husband vacate their $250,000 house in Potomac, Maryland, and she recounted how, after two years of marriage, he had once hit her on the side of the head and broken one of her eardrums. She also claimed that while she had been pregnant with her first son, Fedders had beaten her on the abdomen. "I remember," she said, "he was yelling he didn't care if he killed me or killed the baby." On yet another occasion she had suffered a neck injury when her husband had held her by the hair and attempted to throw her over a five-foot banister in their home. All the while, she said, she had devotedly waited on her fastidious husband, who didn't let anyone wear shoes on the carpets and did a thor-

oughly "outstanding" job at the SEC for three and a half years, according to SEC Chairman John S. R. Shad, who accepted Fedders's resignation "with regret" and praised him for his effectiveness. The Fedders broke apart completely in mid-1983 when John discontinued psychotherapy after about six sessions.

Feeling "great remorse over the violent incidents," Fedders was forced, following his resignation from the SEC, to go to divorce court to resolve differences with his wife on alimony and child support. Said she, "I just think the whole situation is very sad." And a top-drawer attorney in Washington said of Fedders that "he may be a damned good securities lawyer, but he's going to find it tough to land a job in this town."

After the divorce, Charlotte Fedders wrote a book entitled *Shattered Dreams* (1987), telling her shocking story of her violent abuse by her husband. But publication of the book triggered a legal battle instigated by John, who took her to court for a share of the profits from the sale of the book (he claimed she could not have written the book without him). In 1987 a Maryland state divorce arbiter ruled in his favor, awarding him 25 percent of his former wife's earnings on the book. She promptly appealed the decision. In February 1988 a circuit court judge in Maryland reversed the arbiter's action, ruling that John could not share in the profits from his wife's book. The judge, however, reduced John's alimony payments to $400 a month (previously the divorce arbiter had lowered them from $750 to $500 a month in 1987).

FIRESTONE "500" SCANDAL

In 1977, the U.S. National Highway Traffic Safety Administration (NHTSA) revealed that, according to a survey it mailed to 87,000 buyers of new cars, serious tire problems were reported by 46 percent of those who responded who owned Firestone "500" steel-belted radial tires. The Firestone Tire & Rubber Company, America's second largest tire manufacturer, protested immediately and claimed the survey was unscientific. It attempted to keep the survey hushed but, within a year, was compelled to recall 13.5-million "500" radial tires—the largest recall in automobile history. Afterward, Firestone officials continued to insist that the tires were safe.

Earlier, between 1975 and 1977, the Firestone company had voluntarily called back 410,000 of its "500" radials because of various defects, including improper vulcanizing and rubber compounding, as well as possible vibrations at high speeds when the tires were under- or overinflated. The company had been unable to reduce the radials' 8 percent "adjustment rate" (the percentage of tires returned to dealers because of customer dissatisfaction); the tire-industry average was 3 to 4 percent.

Admitting that its survey had been unscientific, the NHTSA continued to compile evidence against the "500" radials, claiming the tires were prone to blowouts, blistering, and cracking. The tires, it claimed, were suspect in auto accidents causing 41 deaths and 65 injuries. The U.S. House Subcommittee on Oversight and Investigation reported that, since 1973, there had been 15 highway deaths in which Firestone "500" blowouts had been the major contributing factor. Firestone officials countered by claiming that there had been more "500s" involved in accidents because the tire company had sold more radials than its competitors. The radial tires, which had rigid steel-reinforced belts circling them beneath the tread, seemed to blow out from heat building up within them, causing the tread to separate from the steel-belted inner layer.

In August 1978, the NHTSA released to the public a letter written by Montgomery Ward & Company to the Firestone Company. In it, Montgomery Ward complained that the "500s" Firestone had manufactured for it were a bad product. At hearings before the NHTSA, Firestone officials reportedly maintained that many of the problems with the "500s" could be traced to other causes, such as improper inflation. Nevertheless, by October 1978, the scandal of the "500s" had become nationwide, and Firestone conceded that the NHTSA might have a case against the "500s." The company agreed to recall millions of tires and replace them with Firestone "721" radials. Contending that the tires were indeed safe, Firestone's chairman, Richard A. Riley, said that the adverse, widespread publicity about them had forced the company to capitulate. In addition to class-action lawsuits filed against Firestone, there were approximately 150 consumer lawsuits concerning the "500" radials, seeking damages of up to $2 billion. Because of the enormous recall, Firestone claimed a $148.3-million loss in 1978.

Fourteen of 21 senior executives left the Firestone company by July 1979, yet the company insisted this "attrition" was not because of the "500s" scandal; the departing officials were close-mouthed about their reasons for leaving. It was suspected that Firestone was skidding toward bankruptcy; from 1977 to 1979 the company had a negative cash flow of about $400 million. Its losses for fiscal 1980 were about $106 million, and its share of the American tire market had dropped from 22 percent in 1978 to 15 percent in 1981.

In December 1979, Firestone's president, Mario DiFederico, took early retirement and was replaced by John Nevin, who was soon credited with bringing the company back to financial health. Seven company plants were closed; the number of employees was reduced from 107,000 to 83,000; and a $121-million profit resulted in the first nine months of fiscal 1981. Firestone had finally overcome the "500s" radial problem, but it never officially admitted the apparent deficiencies in the "500s."

FISHER-BUTTAFUOCO AFFAIR

A precocious teenager with long chestnut tresses; a beefy 36-year-old auto mechanic; an unsuspecting wife; a handgun; a surprise visit—they are the ingredients of a Hollywood movie, except this particular combination of factors occurred in real life. In the spring of 1992, on Long Island, New York, Amy Fisher, 17, shot Mary Jo Buttafuoco, her alleged lover's wife, in the head in the front doorway of the Buttafuoco's residence—and Hollywood did not miss the opportunity to cash in on the ensuing drama.

Fisher pleaded guilty to assault and was sentenced to 5 to 15 years in prison. Mary Jo Buttafuoco survived the shooting but was left partially paralyzed on one side and still has a bullet lodged near the base of her brain. Joey Buttafuoco, the owner of an auto body repair shop, denied he was having an affair with the teenager, but nevertheless pleaded guilty to statutory rape and served a sentence of six months in prison with five years' probation, and paid a $5,000 fine.

At first people assumed it was the story of a lovelorn teenager being manipulated by a calculating older lover to commit a heinous crime. But then it became known that Fisher was working after school for a local escort service as a prostitute. Fisher claimed Buttafuoco knew of her plans to kill his wife, and that he encouraged her to do it. Buttafuoco, however, amidst his patent denial of the whole affair, said the shooting came after he tried to distance himself from Fisher, since she was obsessed with him.

This crime drew international attention. The media dubbed Fisher the "Long Island Lolita." Photographs of her pale face, screened from direct view by her flowing hair, punctuated news broadcasts and newspaper pages across the United States. The affair also drew the attention of Hollywood movie producers, who relentlessly pursued the players in this drama, offering large sums for the rights to their stories. Three made-for-TV movies were produced and the Fisher-Buttafuoco affair was the topic of numerous talk shows for months afterward. Fisher's bail was paid with money garnered from one of these deals.

Fisher, who had allegedly been sexually abused at age three by her father, blamed Joey Buttafuoco for the affair, which she said started when she was a 16-year-old with braces; he took her to expensive restaurants and cheap motels. She claimed the shooting was an accident, and that she meant only to hit Mary Jo on the head with the gun. The judge and jury disagreed. Fisher was found to have stalked Mary Jo for months; the shooting was thus declared to be neither spontaneous nor impulsive. However, Fisher agreed to a plea bargain that reduced the charges from attempted murder to assault.

Fisher was denied parole after five years' imprisonment. She spent a total of seven years in jail, during which time she was disciplined for more than 20 minor infractions, including wearing unauthorized jewelry, refusing to obey direct orders, not having her identification, and one sexual offense. Fisher wanted an appeal; she said her original lawyer tricked her into believing she would be eligible for work release after only three and one-half years in prison if she pleaded guilty to the assault charges. Also, in 1996, Fisher filed suit against several prison guards at Albion prison, claiming she had been raped by them. Later, she dropped the charges.

While in prison, Fisher began corresponding with Mary Jo Buttafuoco, who eventually wrote to the district attorney's office asking for Fisher's release. Mrs. Buttafuoco felt the young woman had done her penance. Upon recommendation to the judge, the 1992 sentence was thrown out and Fisher was resentenced to three-and-a-half to 10 and one-half years. Fisher was granted parole in May 1999. In court one month before her release, she issued an apology to Mary Jo Buttafuoco in which she took full responsibility for the shooting.

The Buttafuocos moved (1996) to the Los Angeles area; Joey's dreams of a movie career failed and he runs an auto shop today. In mid-2000 the couple separated after 23 years of marriage.

JAMES FISK. See Jay GOULD and James FISK: Black Friday 1869.

Zelda and F. Scott FITZGERALD: victims of the Jazz Age

Creator of the phrase "Jazz Age," F. Scott Fitzgerald not only wrote brilliantly about the zany and madcap Roaring Twenties; with his wife Zelda, he also epitomized the era. Dashing, glamorous, and daring, the two became the golden couple of American letters, as famous for their wild antics and frenzied social life as for Scott's novels. Their heyday, however, was short-lived. In the end they fell victims to the era they had helped create.

Son of a commercially failed father descended from a prestigious Maryland family, and darling of an eccentric mother whom he described as "straight 1850 potato-famine Irish," Fitzgerald was from childhood a divided personality. He admired the beautiful manners and elegant dress of his father and condemned the vulgarity of his mother, even as she spoiled him. Because the family always lived frugally in or near better neighborhoods, Fitzgerald was perpetually avid for riches; because the family was Catholic in a Protestant milieu, he felt himself an outsider; shy and sensitive, he always craved acceptance and adulation; determined to succeed, he worked very hard when he worked, a pattern begun when he devoted his too-small, too-light body to the injurious rigors of football.

Accepted by a hair at Princeton, Fitzgerald was a poor scholar and a constant mixer, devoting his spare time to football and his remarkable verbal skills to stories, poetry, and lyrics for highly praised skits. At Princeton, he met what was to prove his nemesis, alcohol. He had a low tolerance for liquor but wanted acceptance by hard-drinking groups, and so he set out to emulate if not outdo them. Seeking admiration, he often pretended to be drunker than he was; his antics won him the popularity he sought. His partying, however, ultimately made his degree unachievable.

Departure from Princeton led him to the army as a noncombatant officer and enabled him to meet and fall in love with Zelda Sayre, a free-spirited girl belonging to a distinguished Alabama family. She too wanted to be important, to be noticed, and to have fun by participating in high jinks. And like Fitzgerald, she had a poor head for alcohol but echoed him by becoming a toper.

To win her hand, Fitzgerald needed money, and so he wrote a novel, *This Side of Paradise,* published in 1920, which was so successful that Zelda agreed to marry him and join him in his quest for notice, notoriety, and fun. An extraordinary first novel, *This Side of Paradise* helped create the Jazz Age. Semi-autobiographical, it concerns an egotistical young Princetonian who turns to literature and high life when he cannot become a football hero. He marries a young, madcap girl from an old Southern family, who prompts him into wild escapades until he decides he must develop into something more than a playboy. The novel's final tone of Byronic despair, cultivated by an excess of success, develops against a hedonistic background of reckless high jinks, frenzied partying, and Prohibition-engendered defiant drinking.

The book's success allowed the Fitzgeralds to find room at the top for almost a decade. They lived the American dream of success, love, and riches as the golden couple of American letters. In the early years they had money, and so they glamorized the lost generation and its mystique by living it; they were irreformable undergraduates whose blend of dignified flippancy and refined glamor caught the mood of the moment. They were never vulgar, but their antics lost them admission to Fitzgerald's Princeton club and caused Zelda to be ejected from the Waldorf Hotel for dancing on tabletops.

Gradually, the Fitzgeralds' marriage became unstable. Zelda wanted fun and attention from Scott, who needed domestic quiet to be able to write. She had no concept of artistic achievement, considering publication in the high-paying *Saturday Evening Post* the acme of success. And Fitzgerald was soon forced to write what he considered "potboilers" in order to keep afloat financially.

His second novel, *The Beautiful and the Damned* (1922), pictures some of their dilemma. Concerning an artist whose abilities are lost through dissipation, it contains a warning neither Scott nor Zelda took. Fitzgerald went on long binges which were not helped by trips to Europe and Hollywood. Travel merely changed the locale of the couple's capers. The critically acclaimed but poor selling novel *The Great Gatsby* (1925) established a time of a thousand parties and no work, during which the Fitzgeralds' glamor declined. Fitzgerald threw or broke things to get attention; Zelda once boiled her female guests' handbags and compacts in tomato sauce.

In 1930 Zelda revealed the first clear symptoms of schizophrenia that led her to alternate hospital commitments and home visits until her death in a hospital fire in 1947.

Caught among Zelda's mental illness, his own desire to write well, his constant need for money, and his full-scale alcoholism, Fitzgerald was either deeply despairing and self-deprecating or, because he said he could "be almost human when sober," zealously industrious when "dry." During the last 10 years of his life, he wrote under both conditions, producing works so bad that neither his agent nor the *Saturday Evening Post* would touch them, but also creating his remarkable novel *Tender Is the Night* (1934), his revealing "Crack-up" essay (1933), and the unfinished masterpiece *The Last Tycoon* (published in 1941). Scriptwriting for Hollywood and a love affair with the Hollywood columnist Sheilah Graham gave his life some purpose and meaning.

Fitzgerald died prematurely in 1940, at the age of 44. His books, especially *The Great Gatsby,* are still considered classics today.

Heidi FLEISS: the "Hollywood Madam"

A tremor ran through Hollywood—and not from any geologic causes—the day the world learned that Heidi Fleiss, 27, the self-proclaimed madam to the stars, was arrested. All of her business-related possessions had been confiscated by the authorities, including her notebooks, audio- and videotapes, and her infamous "little black book." It was rumored that Fleiss might reveal the names of some of her clientele, which supposedly consisted of many famous married celebrities as well as top executives at movie houses who were reported to have paid for services with money written off as production expenses. Statements soon came flooding in from the stars' and executives' press agents denying any connection to Fleiss.

Fleiss was a high school dropout from an upper-middle-class family, the third daughter to a local pediatrician and a former schoolteacher. Her parents were permissive and she grew up rarely having to face the consequences of her thrillseeking misadventures. In junior high she shoplifted. In high school she cut class to make bets at the racetrack. Sharp with money, she would pay her classmates to let her cheat off them and nurtured a small business growing and selling marijuana. She was convinced from a young age that she would be a legend someday.

At the age of 19, she became involved with Bernie CORNFELD, a much older international financier, who introduced her to the good life. In 1988, when their relationship ended after four years, Fleiss became involved with another older man, Ivan Nagy, a Hungarian-born director. Nagy introduced young Fleiss to

Charged with five counts of felony pandering and a drug violation, 27-year-old Heidi Fleiss, the "Hollywood Madam," pleaded not guilty during her arraignment in a Los Angeles court on August 9, 1993. Police said she operated a high-priced prostitution ring catering to the entertainment-industry elite. (AP/Wide World Photos)

Elizabeth ("Madam Alex") Adams, then the eminent leader of a ring of call girls. Supposedly, Nagy forced Fleiss to work for Madam Alex to pay off a gambling debt. Soon, though, the ambitious Fleiss, having learned the tricks of the trade from the best in the business, struck off on her own.

She was young, slim, and attractive, and she hung out in all the cool Hollywood rock clubs and bistros. She bragged she knew at least half a percent of the world's richest people. She had no problem finding willing beautiful young women to work for her. Fleiss set up the "dates" and charged clients a minimum of $1,500 for a visit with one of her girls; she skimmed 40 percent off the top.

Catering to the high end of the call-girl market, she was soon able to move into a $1.6 million Benedict Canyon residence formerly owned by actor Michael Douglas. For three years she ran a lucrative business. She loved the business and she loved her notoriety, but that was to be her downfall. She conducted her affairs in a conspicuous way that attracted more than the passing attention of the Los Angeles Police Department, which set up a bust in which an undercover officer posed as a Hawaiian businessman looking for entertainment for international clients. Fleiss sent over a girl, who was taken into custody, and the police and FBI subsequently raided Fleiss's Benedict Canyon home, arresting her.

In December 1994, she was convicted in the state court of pandering, but this conviction was overturned on account of jury misconduct. This did not, however, affect her federal convictions, which came a year later and included conspiracy, tax evasion (she reported an income of $33,000 on her 1992 tax return even though she had made hundreds of thousands of dollars that year), and money laundering. She was sentenced to 37 months in a minimum-security facility, three years' probation, and 300 hours of community service. She was also required to forfeit $375,000 from the proceeds of the sale of her mansion and to repay $175,000 of the money she had laundered through bank accounts held in others' names (one account was under the name of her father, Paul Fleiss). Normally flip by nature, Fleiss tearfully apologized to the judge, her family, the world at large for "the trouble I've caused."

To help pay for her defense, Fleiss started a mail-order clothing business and then later opened a small retail shop selling bras, boxer shorts, and sweatshirts emblazoned with her name: "HeidiWear." She worked day and night selling T-shirts, she said, and hardly made any money; things had changed.

Fleiss served 20 months of the 37-month sentence behind bars. She was then released to a halfway house, but after a couple of days, she chose to go back to prison to serve out her sentence. Through it all, Fleiss refused to divulge the secrets contained in her "trick book," despite numerous million-dollar offers.

Kelly FLINN: duty, passion, and lies

For a short time, First Lieutenant Kelly Flinn, 26, the first woman to fly the B-52 bomber, was a star shining bright for the United States Air Force. A model student, a responsible officer, she was the perfect poster girl for the service—that is, until she fell in love with the wrong man and her high regard took a nose dive. After promising to keep their relationship secret, that man betrayed Flinn, voluntarily offering military police explicit details of their affair. Flinn was brought up on charges of adultery, fraternization with an enlisted man, failure to obey lawful orders, conduct unbecoming an officer, and making false statements. She faced up to nine and a half years in prison if found guilty of all charges.

Flinn was stationed in Minot, North Dakota, a small northern town with a windswept air base. She played soccer in a recreational league during her free time. That's where she met Marc Zigo, 24, a civilian hired to be the youth soccer coach for the base. Zigo convinced Flinn that he was legally separated from his wife Gayla (an enlisted airman) and the two began to date. Flinn fell in love.

However, Zigo was not estranged from his wife; he had not played professional soccer as he claimed on his job application; he had lied about his birthplace and his parents' occupations; the ring he gave Flinn as an engagement promise had been a present to him from his wife; and Zigo was on probation for wife beating. Flinn learned these details only after she became embroiled in the humiliating investigation.

When Gayla Zigo happened to find a love letter from Flinn to her husband, she discreetly brought it to her commanding officer. Flinn was issued a friendly warning from a colleague to stay away from the married man. Though the matter could have subsided here—Flinn did break off relations with Zigo—another officer under investigation for an adulterous affair, apparently determined to take others down with him, began pointing fingers. Besides tattling about Flinn's affair with Zigo, the informant even mentioned an aberrant one-night stand Flinn had had with an enlisted man.

In the military, officers are forbidden to fraternize with enlisted persons because of the implicit potential for abuse of power. Also, under the Uniform Code of Military Justice, adultery is considered a felony. Everyone is assumed to be aware of these rules. Flinn was called in by base police and questioned for hours about her private life and sexual preferences. When asked about Zigo, desperate to put an end to this seeming inquisition, she lied and said she had not had sex with him. Unbeknownst to her, Zigo voluntarily issued his own statement detailing the nature of the affair; he went so far as to sketch a drawing of Flinn's house and point out places in the bedroom where they "did it."

When later asked why she continued to be involved with Zigo, Flinn could only comment on his overwhelming charisma and say that she loved him very much. Meanwhile, she went quickly to her commanding officer, since she had lied and wanted to rectify the situation. The officer brushed her aside and refused to help.

As the investigation wore on, Flinn was stripped of her security clearance, forbidden to fly, and ordered to stay more than 100 feet away from Zigo at all times. She disobeyed this last order when it was issued, for the couple had begun living together in Flinn's house after Zigo's wife finally kicked him out.

At this point, Flinn could have resigned to avoid a court-martial, but she wanted to stay and fight the air force. Only after hours of persuasion did her family finally convince her to put in a plea for an honorable discharge. Secretary of the Air Force Sheila Widnall reviewed Flinn's case and offered a general discharge—no military flying or benefits in the future. The military viewed the lying and disobedience to a direct order to be Flinn's most critical mistakes. She was an officer in charge of nuclear weapons on board an attack vessel; lying and inability to follow orders were potentially detrimental. She reluctantly accepted the general discharge.

Errol FLYNN: errant movie Lothario

Handsome, charming, easygoing Errol Flynn, born in Tasmania in 1909, was a highly paid American movie actor and a matinée idol adored by women of all ages. The Hollywood movie studios usually cast him as a swashbuckler, perpetuating a public image of him as virile and heroic. Films such as *Captain Blood* (1935), *The Adventures of Robin Hood* (1938), and *The Sea Hawk* (1940) made Flynn a top star at the box office despite the public's awareness that he was a carouser and womanizer, one who particularly had a penchant for young girls. For a time in 1942–43 Flynn's movie career seemed in jeopardy because of serious charges that he had raped two underage girls on different occasions, but the magnetic Lothario was found innocent and went on to make more successful films. However, about two decades after his death in 1959, the book *Errol Flynn: The Untold Story,* by Charles Higham, accused Flynn of being bisexual and a Nazi agent. Though many derided the book, it tarnished Flynn's once adored image and likeability.

Flynn's troubles with teenage girls became public when he was accused of having had sexual intercourse with 17-year-old Betty Hansen, a curvaceous, blue-eyed blonde, and 15-year-old Peggy La Rue Satterlee, a buxom dancer. Hansen, whom the Los Angeles police had picked up for vagrancy, insisted that she had been raped by Flynn in an upstairs bedroom at a Bel Air house party. California law prohibited sex with a minor (anyone under 18), even with her (or his) consent, and such relations constituted statutory rape. In October 1942, a Los Angeles grand jury heard Hansen's complaint, decided it to be unfounded, and did not indict Flynn. Shortly afterward, however, the district attorney's office inexplicably dug up an earlier complaint made by the mother of Peggy Satterlee, who claimed that her daughter had been raped twice by Flynn in 1941 while a guest aboard his yacht, *Sirocco.* Flynn, whose fiery marriage to sensual Lili Damita (his first wife) came to an end in 1942, was brought to trial on three counts of statutory rape, two involving Satterlee and one involving Hansen (her original charge), but his shrewd Hollywood lawyer, Jerry Giesler, saved him from conviction and the ignominy of going to prison.

During the famed actor's well-publicized trial before a 12-member jury (including nine women) in Los Angeles County Superior Court in January 1943, the prosecution was unable to match the courtroom skill of Giesler, who worked to impugn the credibility of the testimony of Hansen and Satterlee. He made the jurors see that the two girls were perhaps not sexually innocent before the alleged "act of intercourse" each had with Flynn "against her will." Hansen testified that the gallant Flynn had kept his socks on after undressing her and himself (she first told police she had undressed herself), and she affirmed that he had "inserted his private parts

in [her] private parts." Giesler's cross-examination indicated that the two could have "victimized" the handsome actor, rather than his raping them. Ultimately, Flynn was acquitted on all counts, which was hardly surprising considering his enormous popularity. The public and critics hailed his next film, *Gentleman Jim,* but his career remained controversial, with numerous teenaged mistresses and continual problems with creditors and government tax agents.

Following his 1943 acquittal, he married Nora Eddington, a teenage redhead, whom he soon jilted for other beauties just as he had his first wife. Patrice Wymore replaced Eddington in 1950, but this third wife fared no better and was jilted too. Eventually, Flynn's dissipation in sex, alcohol, and drugs helped bring on his early death from heart failure on October 14, 1959, in a hotel room in Vancouver, British Columbia; his "companion" at the time was pretty Beverly Aadland, a 16-year-old, whom he had "rewarded" earlier with a co-starring role in his 49th and last film, *Cuba Rebel Girls,* which was a fizzle.

The 1980 publication of Charles Higham's scandalous book about Flynn was met with hostility by the actor's many supporters, but Higham's ugly allegations certainly changed some perceptions of Flynn. He had supposedly been an active Nazi agent in Hollywood during World War II and had had close ties with a known German agent named Dr. Hermann Friedrich Erben, whom he helped smuggle across the American border into Mexico to escape arrest. Information from Flynn about American harbors and naval facilities, photographed by him, was alleged to have been passed to Dr. Erben. In addition to these revelations, Higham accused Flynn of being bisexual and of having had a secret liaison with actor Tyrone Power in 1939. Public opinion of Flynn, the seducer and cradle snatcher, received a clear jolt from the new disclosures, which church groups and moralists cited as further proof that he was "no good." But many continued to hold Flynn in high regard for daring to enjoy a life "far richer than any of the wildest movies he ever made." They agreed with and loved him as a man who had "seen everything twice," which was how he described himself shortly before he died. Even today the expression "in like Flynn" carries the connotation of winning the day.

Larry FLYNT: self-defaming scandalizer

Larry Flynt is a born-again Christian. He is also the owner of Hustler, Inc., a Los Angeles based publishing company that specializes in pornographic materials, including the infamous *Hustler* magazine. In 1978 Flynt went to Lawrenceville, Georgia, to face an obscenity charge. There, he argued on the street with another born-again Christian. The man was also a white supremacist and was a convicted murderer. Flynt had picked the wrong man to argue with. He wound up being shot so severely that he was permanently paralyzed from the waist down. This trauma failed to put a dent in Flynt's pursuits of obscenity. If anything, it seems to have augmented them, leaving Flynt with a host of enemies.

If Flynt was despised by some before 1976, the appearance of another men's magazine, *Chic,* widened the circle of his detractors.

In 1977, Flynt was brought to trial and put in front of an Ohio jury which ignored U.S. Supreme Court rulings supporting the First Amendment right to freedom of the press by convicting him of pandering obscenity and engaging in criminal activity. Released on a $50,000 bond pending appeal, he went to face charges in Lawrenceville, where he was crippled.

Yet despite the declaration of a mistrial in the Lawrenceville case, the hatred and contempt for Flynt continued and 1979 brought a second obscenity trial in Atlanta, the capital of Georgia. Here Flynt was found guilty of obscenity, but his sentence was suspended on the proviso that he never again break Georgia's obscenity laws.

Some of the contempt for Flynt became sardonic in 1980 when Robert Guccione, publisher of a rival men's magazine, *Penthouse,* won a libel suit because Flynt had published in *Hustler* a photograph suggesting that Guccione was homosexual. The plaintiff won an award of almost $40 million, an award later reduced by 90 percent through appeal.

Because of the 1980 case, a fourth attitude toward Flynt began to develop; it attributed his bizarre behavior to his paralysis claiming that this had affected him psychologically.

The new theory may explain Flynt's actions from 1983 to the present. In that year he moved in four different directions, announcing plans to run for president of the United States on the Republican ticket; disrupting and being ejected from a Supreme Court hearing into a libel suit brought by an assistant publisher of *Penthouse;* trying to purchase videotapes of orgies involving government officials and Vicki Morgan, murdered mistress of the late Alfred Bloomingdale (see BLOOMINGDALE-MORGAN AFFAIR); and selling to the Columbia Broadcasting System (CBS) and the television program "60 Minutes" fake tapes of John Z. DELOREAN, then under indictment on a drug-trafficking charge. The last action again drew Flynt into court, where he admitted the fakery and faced both a jail sentence and a $42,000 fine for contempt of court for wearing a diaper made from an American flag when he appeared and refused to reveal the source of the tape.

In 1984 Flynt's behavior became even more bizarre. Released from federal prison for medical reasons, he sued the federal government, complaining that the prison authorities had allowed him no medical care. He also lost a libel suit brought by the Reverend Jerry Falwell, whom Flynt had accused of alcoholism and incest with his mother.

Flynt's descent in reputation gained momentum, and the extent of the disdain felt toward Flynt was revealed when the Falwell-case jury, finding no evidence of libel, nonetheless awarded Falwell $200,000 to compensate for "emotional distress." Flynt's appeal was dismissed in 1985.

In 1984 Flynt also lost control of his estate to two conservators, and many people began to regard him as no longer in a condition to achieve any redemption of his reputation.

In 1988 the U.S. Supreme Court heard Flynt's appeal concerning the 1984 Falwell case, and it ruled against the jury's $200,000 award to Falwell. According to the court, the parody depicting Falwell as an incestuous drunk (published three times in *Hustler* as a bogus advertisement) had not purported to be factual and thus had not involved reckless disregard of the truth. Flynt was buoyant.

Later, in 1997, Flynt's daughter Tonya Flynt-Vega publicly claimed that she and her two sisters had been periodically molested as teenagers by their father, who denied her allegations. She said the popular movie based on his life, *The People vs. Larry Flynt,* was full of "distortions, omissions, and fabrications." She also said that *Hustler* "eroticizes violence against women." In a plea bargain agreement in 1999, Flynt and his younger brother Jimmy agreed to stop selling hard-core pornography videos at their Cincinnati bookstore; prosecutors then dropped obscenity charges against them.

Jim FOLSOM: governor defeated by racists and alcohol
"Big Jim" Folsom, hard-drinking, wisecracking, an enormous six-feet-eight-inches tall and weighing 270 pounds, appeared to be almost a caricature of a "good ol' " Southern boy during his two terms as governor of Alabama. But the popular politician, once known as "Kissin' Jim" because of his predilection for embracing attractive female voters, lost the election of 1962 and never got back on his feet again. His liberal segregationist policies were not taken kindly to in the Alabama of the early '60s, and Folsom's penchant for the bottle finished off any hopes he had for reelection.

Folsom, the son of a farmer and grandson of a Confederate soldier, was born in 1908 near Elbe, Alabama. He briefly attended the University of Alabama and Howard College in Birmingham but had to leave school when his family could no longer afford the tuition. After service in the merchant marine, he worked in the Alabama Relief Administration until 1936 when he entered his first of several unsuccessful campaigns for public office: for U.S. Congress in 1936 and 1938 and for governor of Alabama in 1942.

After World War II Folsom's luck changed. Upon winning the 1946 Democratic nomination for governor of Alabama, the "little man's big friend" undertook a flamboyant and lively campaign. He toured the state, accompanied by a hillbilly band called the "Strawberry Pickers" and waving a mop with which to "clean out" the state legislature. A supporter of the New Deal, Folsom advocated a reasonable minimum wage for teachers, old-age pensions, improved roads, repeal of the poll tax, and aid to farmers and small businessmen. During his administration as governor, he pressed the legislature for the establishment of a black state university and law school, an increase in appropriations to black colleges, and a new building program. And in a move directed against the Ku Klux Klan, the legislature, at Folsom's urging, outlawed the wearing of masks. Folsom stated that "hooded thugs" would not be tolerated while he was governor. He also ended the practice of flogging as a means of punishment in Alabama prisons. Constitutionally prohibited from succeeding himself, Folsom left office in 1951, trailed by a prison scandal and a paternity suit (which was later dropped).

However, Folsom was again elected governor in 1954, winning more votes than all of his six opponents combined. Soon after his election the U.S. Supreme Court issued its momentous school desegregation decision in *Brown* v. *Board of Education*. When a few months later the Alabama state legislature passed a resolution trying to nullify that decision, Folsom refused to sign the resolution, which he called "hogwash." He also teased the segregationists, saying: "No Negro child will be forced to go to school with white children as long as I am Governor in Alabama." At the time of the Montgomery bus boycott the governor told a young Martin Luther King, Jr., not to ask for crumbs but to seek the whole loaf and hope to get at least half.

In an incident that stirred up Alabama racists, Folsom invited black Democratic Congressman Adam Clayton POWELL to the Executive Mansion for a drink while Powell was visiting the state. When Folsom was taunted that he and Powell had drunk Scotch and soda, the governor answered, "Shucks, you folks know old Big Jim don't drink nothing fancy like that. I drink hard likker just like you."

Again constitutionally barred from succeeding himself, Folsom left office in 1959. But he ran again in the election in 1962, with a campaign that employed the same flamboyant tactics that had proved successful in the past. Promising to "grind up the ham [state funds] and save the gravy [the good life]," Folsom nonetheless campaigned seriously on a platform of racial peace. But racial violence had already erupted in Alabama, and Folsom's belief in the inevitability of integration no longer suited the mood of the voters.

Even more damage to his campaign was an embarrassing incident just before the May Democratic primary, when Folsom appeared on a television program, apparently drunk. Viewers gasped when he failed to remember his children's names and imitated a cuckoo clock, among other things. He came in third in a field of seven; the winner was segregationist George C. WALLACE.

Folsom ran for state office several times after his 1962 defeat but made poor showings in the races. As late as 1974 the 65-year-old politician was still trying to stage a comeback in another gubernatorial race. He supported the Equal Rights Amendment and the preservation of the Bill of Rights. "They was sayin' 20 years ago, 30 years ago, that ol' Jim would drink himself to death. Well, I'm still here, and I'm walkin'." But he wasn't reelected, and at age 79 in 1987, he died of a heart attack at his Alabama home.

Charles R. FORBES: mismanager of the Veterans' Bureau

Superficially, Charles R. Forbes was outgoing, magnetic, and well spoken. Warren G. Harding met the man who was to become manager of his Veterans' Bureau on a 1915 senatorial junket and was immediately charmed by him. Forbes became an election worker in the Northwest during Harding's 1920 presidential campaign, changing parties to do so. He had been a hero in World War I, emerging a lieutenant colonel with a Distinguished Service Medal and a Croix de Guerre.

Charlie Forbes's other and real face was not disclosed until the U.S. Senate investigated in 1923 his handling of the Veterans' Bureau. Then what had been seen as affability was regarded as self-promotion, and what had been regarded as alacrity was seen to be opportunism. The investigation discovered that Forbes had deserted the army before 1914, had served a prison term, and had a history of wife-beating.

For Forbes, being appointed to manage the Veterans' Bureau was the equivalent of finding buried treasure. The bureau then had $450 million to distribute annually and had received an additional $36 million for hospital construction. The latter sum was solely under Forbes's control after 1922 when the Treasury Department, despite the efforts of its secretary, found out that Harding had given Forbes sole authority over both government-hospital construction and the handling of medical supplies.

Once in office, Forbes's opportunism and venality quickly came to rule his every action. Guided by a crony and by Elias H. Mortimer, an agent for a contractor, Forbes set up a contract-splitting scheme among the three and the company. Not satisfied, he speculated in land sites for the hospitals to be built by his bureau, using the assistance of another crony, Charles F. Cramer, legal counsel for the Veterans' Bureau. Still not satisfied, he sold, without public bid, $3 million worth of medical supplies for only $600,000, claiming (with the help of bribes) that most of the supplies were spoiled.

These details became public knowledge during the Senate investigation, as did one especially damning revelation: the whistleblower against Forbes had been Mrs. Harding's personal physician, Dr. (and Brigadier General) Charles Sawyer, with whom Forbes had clashed over bureau policy. Sawyer told Attorney General Harry M. DAUGHERTY, who told President Harding.

But Harding vacillated. He twice saw Forbes privately and on the second visit advised Forbes to go abroad and resign from his post from overseas.

No one knows for sure how much money Forbes had acquired fraudulently and perhaps deposited in Switzerland, but Forbes followed Harding's advice. The resignation arrived on February 15, 1923.

Just before the Senate investigation began on March 2 (delayed because Forbes had to be granted time to return), Cramer committed suicide, and Forbes looked guilty even before the facts were made public.

His trial at the end of the year gained him only two years' imprisonment and a $10,000 fine—something analogous to a two-mill (one-thousandth of a dollar) fine on a $15 parking ticket. He was released from the federal penitentiary at Leavenworth, Kansas, after 18 months and made instant publicity by falsely declaring Daugherty and Sawyer the architects of the Harding administration's chicanery.

Forbes's opportunism had not been eliminated by his imprisonment. He gained a small fame by promoting his cellmate, Dr. Frederick A. COOK (jailed for mail fraud), as the winner of the Cook-Peary race for the North Pole.

Written documents suggest that the 74-year-old Forbes died in obscurity on April 10, 1952, but many believe that his last breath was self-promoting.

Henry FORD: father of an illegitimate son?

In 1978 a man named John Coté Dahlinger wrote a scandalous book entitled *The Secret Life of Henry Ford*, in which he claimed that Ford, a pioneer in the automobile industry and the founder of the Ford Motor Company, was his real father. He wrote that his bold-spirited mother, born Evangeline Côté, had captivated the famed auto tycoon, who was 30 years older than she, after she began working for him as a teenager. Supposedly, Ford had arranged her marriage to Ray Dahlinger, a test driver whom he had hired and was very fond of. Next to Ford's secluded and grand Dearborn estate, known as Fairlane, the industrialist erected a splendid home for the Dahlingers. According to John Dahlinger, there was a hidden staircase leading to his mother's bedroom. After John's birth, Ford lavished much affection as well as many gifts on the baby boy, who grew up in the Detroit area romping with Ford's grandchildren. The author wrote that his parents (Evangeline and Ray) had top jobs in the Ford Motor Company until the

Henry Ford, the famous automobile industrialist, appeared on the cover of the book The Secret Life of Henry Ford, *published in 1977. The author, John Coté Dahlinger of Dearborn, Michigan, also appeared on the cover as a small boy (sitting on the step) and claimed he was the illegitimate son of Ford. (AP/Wide World Photos)*

death of Ford's wife in 1950; old man Ford had died three years earlier at the age of 83.

Dahlinger's story came as no surprise to many. Ford's relationship to Evangeline had been the subject of much gossip for many years.

Ford founded the Ford Motor Company in 1903 and became an extremely wealthy man by the end of World War I. In addition to his many manufacturing plants in Michigan, Great Britain, and Europe, he owned large estates and farms. The manager of the farms, who supervised the work of 700 men, was Ray Dahlinger. Dahlinger's pretty wife Evangeline had worked for Ford even longer than her husband. She had started out as a stenographer, was promoted to head of the department, and later became the personal secretary of C. Harold Wills, a high Ford executive and close friend of the company's president. Ford was very fond of the Dahlingers and spent much time with them. Besides the large house in Dearborn, he gave them a summer home on a lake, which included a docking ramp for Evangeline's personal seaplane.

The attention and gifts that Ford, who was usually frugal and even penny-pinching, showered upon the

Dahlingers created gossip, and when the young couple's only son John was born in 1923, it became widely rumored that Ford was the child's real father. When in 1933 Ford embarked upon his pet project of building Greenfield Village and its museum outside Dearborn, Ray Dahlinger was put in charge, and Evangeline helped find and buy old buildings and antiques for the recreation of the early American rural village. As Ford spent increasing time with the Dahlinger family, the gossip continued.

Some found the notion that Ford would have had an affair with Evangeline ridiculous. The automobile pioneer was at various times an opinionated, anti-intellectual, anti-Semitic, anti-Catholic, and puritanical man who was happily married to a devoted wife. On the other hand, Evangeline's attractive and fun-loving nature and her liking for adventure, dancing, horseback riding, and driving fast speedboats and cars may have appealed to the older man. In later years, Ford's grandson, Henry Ford II, succeeded in squelching the rumors once and for all. Only Evangeline Dahlinger and Henry Ford knew whether the claims about them had ever been true.

FORD PINTO CASE

In the 1970s the Ford Motor Company suffered much unfavorable publicity because of the deaths and injuries of persons in crashes of its subcompact Pinto automobile, which the company began manufacturing in 1971. The gas tanks of the early Pintos, situated only seven inches from the rear bumper, were said to explode in rear-end collisions and to be the cause of unnecessary fatalities. While Ford's share of the domestic auto market was declining, its reputation was badly stained by two well-publicized trials in which the company, unsuccessfully in one case and successfully in the other, contended that the Pintos' fuel tanks were not the main cause of fatal fires when the cars were hit from behind by other vehicles in accidents. Ford became the first American corporation to stand trial on criminal charges in a product-defects case.

By 1978 the company had sold about two million Pintos allegedly having a serious design flaw in the fuel tank. The company estimated that to change the Pinto would entail about $137 million in costs, whereas they would probably only have to shell out about $49.5 million for cases involving accidents with the car. Apparently, the company calculated that some 2,100 cars would burst into flames upon collision from the rear, about 180 persons would burn to death, and another 180 would have burn injuries.

These bloodless calculations were proven wrong. In a monumental personal-injury case against it, Ford received a devastating bombshell when Richard Grimshaw, the victim of a 1972 Pinto accident, won a multimillion-dollar suit against the company on February 6, 1978, in Santa Ana, California.

Young Grimshaw had been 13 years old when in 1972 he and Lily Gray, the driver of a brand-new Pinto, stalled on a highway near Pasadena, California, and were struck from behind by another car. The Pinto's fuel tank had ruptured and ignited, severely burning both occupants; Gray died in the hospital and Grimshaw later underwent 52 operations for burns covering 90 percent of his body. Five years later, when his case went to superior court, his face was a mass of scar tissue.

The jury found the Ford company liable for punitive damages of $128.5 million, at the time the largest personal-injury award ever made. Grimshaw was awarded $125 million, and the jury also gave him and the relatives of Gray a total of $3.5 million in compensatory damages. Grimshaw's attorneys had argued that Ford had deliberately neglected the safety of its customers by failing to correct the alleged design flaw in the Pinto gas tank. Countering, the company claimed that the 1972 Pinto had "met all applicable federal safety standards." On March 31, 1978, a California superior court judge reduced the record award, saying the jury's judgment had been "excessive as a matter of law" and slashing its award to Grimshaw to $3.5 million.

The conclusions reached by federal safety investigators were that the Pintos' fuel tanks were dangerous and that the cars were susceptible to exploding in relatively minor rear-end collisions. Ford, however, vigorously defended the fuel system. The barrage of bad reports in the press fueled the national controversy over the safety of the Pinto's gas tank, eventually forcing the company to voluntarily recall 1.5 million of the cars in June 1978 in order to modify the fuel system by increasing its resistance to leakage and the risk of fire.

But in the winter of 1980, worldwide attention again focused on the Pinto in an unprecedented criminal trial in Winamac, Indiana, in which Ford stood accused of reckless homicide in the 1978 deaths of three young women in a 1973 model Pinto. This was a product-defect case, and only monetary penalties were involved, but the company was again gravely concerned about the outcome, since it could be exposed to punitive, multimillion-dollar damages in nearly 40 Pinto cases still pending. In August 1978, Judy and Lyn Ulrich, two sisters aged 18 and 16, respectively, and their cousin Donna Ulrich, 18, had been killed when their Pinto erupted in flame after being hit from behind by a van in Goshen, Indiana. They were the 57th, 58th, and 59th victims of fatal crashes involving the subcompact. The state prosecution, headed by Michael Cosentino, charged that Ford officials knew the early Pintos' tanks were unsafe but had done nothing to correct this; instead, they had apparently decided against installing a $6.65 part that would have helped safeguard the tank, though they did an improvement later. Ford's defense team, reportedly paid more than $1 million for arguing the case, was led by James F. Neal, who had prosecuted the major cases resulting from the WATERGATE SCANDAL. It denied the charges against the company, saying that the Pinto was as safe as its competitors and calling upon important automobile-industry consultants and executives to testify about safety and "closing speed" (the difference in the speed of two vehicles at the time of crash impact).

During the trial, Pulaski County Circuit Judge Harold Staffeldt tightly restricted the evidence given by the state prosecution, which had planned to use much internal Ford company material to prove that the automaker knew there were critical safety problems with the Pinto fuel system. As a result, the prosecution was allowed to show the jury only about 24 of the more than 200 documents it wanted to. The 10-week trial ended on March 13, 1980. The jury, after deliberating for 25 hours over a four-day period, voted to acquit Ford on the three charges of reckless homicide in connection with the three deaths. Prosecutor Cosentino nevertheless saw the trial as valuable in that it taught corporations that "they can be brought to trial and have 12 citizens judge their actions." The relieved Neal said that the verdict had vindicated Ford and that the Pinto auto had been "maligned by one-sided articles in the national media." Ford's retiring chairman, Henry Ford II, and his successor Philip Caldwell, cheered and, in the words of the latter, were "elated" because "we stood for a principle and that principle has been exonerated by 12 of our peers." Added Chairman Caldwell, "the principle that came out of this was that there must be responsibility on the part of those who use products as well as those who design and build them."

James FORRESTAL: suicide of a public servant

For almost nine years, James Vincent Forrestal was among the most powerful figures in the administrations of President Franklin D. Roosevelt and President Harry S Truman. He served as secretary of the navy and later as secretary of defense. Under extreme pressure from the separate divisions of the newly joined army, navy, and air force, Forrestal's behavior changed radically. His descent into paranoia ended on May 22, 1949, when he jumped from the window of a 16th floor tower in the Bethesda Naval Hospital.

Forrestal was born in Beacon, New York, in 1892 and attended Princeton University until the United States entered World War I, when he became a flyer for the Navy. In 1923 he began a career as an investment banker with Dillon, Read and Company in New York City and later became involved with Democratic Party politics. He accepted the post of administrative assistant to President Roosevelt in June 1940 and two years later was named undersecretary of the navy. At that time the

army and the navy were separate, rival departments, and there was no overall unified command. In 1944 Forrestal was appointed secretary of the navy, and after the conclusion of World War II he vigorously opposed the merger of the navy, the army, and the newly formed air force into one unified body called the armed forces. In 1947, however, Congress passed the National Security Act, which set up a rather nebulous National Military Establishment that later became the Department of Defense. Forrestal was named its first secretary.

Shortly after this appointment, his troubles began in earnest. The infighting between the three services was ferocious and bitter. Air Force Secretary W. Stuart Symington felt that the new B-36 bomber, which was designed to carry atomic bombs, should be the focal point of military strategy, while the navy argued that its proposed supercarrier, the *United States,* was better equipped to deliver air power throughout the world. The army resented the emergence of the air force as a separate entity, and all three branches of the armed forces were unhappy about their curtailed budgets.

During this same period the cold war was intensifying, especially after the Soviet invasion of Czechoslovakia in 1948. Yet demobilization was continuing to reduce the size of the armed forces, and the Joint Chiefs of Staff were unable to agree on plans for the future. Forrestal tried in vain to stop the feuding among his subordinates, who often went so far as to criticize him in public as well as to attempt blatantly to undermine each other with members of Congress and the press.

When the budget for 1950 was being drawn up in late 1948, the Pentagon asked for $30 billion, but President Truman, fearful of inflation and desperately wanting to reduce the war-imposed national debt, firmly set a ceiling of $14.4 billion for the military. It was Forrestal's job to allot this sum among the services, and the pressures from all quarters increased. Forrestal also antagonized many persons by opposing the recognition of Israel and by not actively participating in Truman's reelection campaign of 1948. Nevertheless, Truman reappointed him secretary of defense in January 1949.

Soon after this, people began to notice strange changes in Forrestal's behavior. He became depressed, forgetful, and paranoid, saying that his phone was being tapped and that the FBI, Zionists, and communists were spying on him. He must have realized his deteriorating condition, for he resigned on March 28, 1949, and went into the Bethesda Naval Hospital for psychiatric treatment. About two months later, on May 22, he jumped from a window of the hospital's tower and plunged to an instant death. Forrestal must have felt misused and misunderstood, for he wrote in his diary, "I am a victim of the Washington scene."

Abe FORTAS: quit Supreme Court under public pressure

Since his appointment in 1965, Abe Fortas served with distinction as an Assistant Justice of the U.S. Supreme Court. But on May 14, 1969, the liberal Fortas's illustrious career was ruined by an exposé in *Life* magazine, in which he was accused of accepting thousands of dollars in bribery. Fortas maintained that "there has been no wrongdoing on my part." Some in Congress thought otherwise, even threatening possible impeachment. Fortas's resignation became the first ever made under public pressure in the history of the nation's highest court.

Fortas, born in Memphis, Tennessee, in 1910, was a brilliant lawyer and jurist. He was graduated first in his class from Yale Law School in 1933 and taught there for the next four years. But his interest seemed to lie in public service. He became a significant contributor to President Franklin D. Roosevelt's "Brain Trust," a small group of professors and other experts who assisted the administration in its early policy making and reformist social and economic programs. The young Fortas held positions in numerous New Deal agencies before serv-

The 1969 resignation of U.S. Supreme Court Justice Abe Fortas was the first made under public pressure in the high court's long history. (Yale University Archives/Historical Picture Collection/Yale University Library)

ing as undersecretary of the interior (1942–46). Afterward he went into private law practice and co-founded the law firm of Arnold, Fortas & Porter in Washington, D.C., which became a prominent firm dispensing smart legal advice to many influential people.

Before winning the U.S. Senate seat from Texas in 1948, Lyndon B. Johnson, who became president in 1963, faced an arch-conservative opponent named Coke Stevenson in the Democratic primary. By the incredibly narrow margin of 87 votes of a total of 900,000 votes cast, Johnson, who had softened his liberal appeal with some old-fashioned Southern views about the race issue, won the primary. Later, however, there were accusations of fraud in the election, coupled with threatened court challenges to his slim victory. Johnson's close friend Fortas then carried out some legal maneuvers to preserve Johnson's election, an investigation of which was halted by Supreme Court Justice Hugo Black.

Fortas's political history was, in general, impressive. He argued the celebrated case of *Gideon v. Wainwright* before the Supreme Court, which in 1963 unanimously ruled that states must provide free legal counsel to poor defendants in criminal trials. In 1963 Fortas briefly represented Bobby BAKER, who was under investigation for shady business dealings but withdrew when the Baker case started to get troublesome. In 1965 Fortas was nominated to be a Supreme Court justice by then President Johnson, who once presented his long-time friend and adviser with a photograph of himself with the inscription "To Abe, who makes the most of the horsepower God gave him." After his appointment to the high bench, Fortas continued to work for the expansion of civil and criminal rights. He wrote a number of majority opinions and generally voted with other liberal justices. In 1966 he voted with Justices Hugo Black, William Douglas, William Brennan, and Earl Warren, the chief justice of the United States, in ruling in *Miranda v. Arizona* that the police must warn all persons taken into custody that they have the right to legal counsel and to remain silent. In a 1969 court ruling written by Fortas, high-school students won the right to wear black armbands as a protest against the Vietnam War.

In 1968, however, Fortas's political view and continued closeness to President Johnson caused a controversy when the president nominated him to succeed the retiring Earl Warren as chief justice of the Supreme Court. In the Senate, Republicans and Southern Democrats held a filibuster against Fortas's nomination, blocking his confirmation and eventually forcing the president to withdraw the nomination.

Then in 1969, Fortas's right to sit as an associate justice came under fierce public attack after *Life* magazine published an article revealing that Fortas, while on the bench, had accepted $20,000 from a private charitable foundation established by the family of convicted stock manipulator Louis WOLFSON, who was serving a year in prison. Attorney General John Mitchell disclosed that in 1966 Fortas had taken the $20,000 from Wolfson, a Wall Street financier who had been under investigation for breaking security regulations. The money was for law lectures and had been the first annual payment of a lifetime arrangement by the foundation to Fortas, who had since given back the $20,000. But many congressmen called for a thorough probe into the justice's conduct, and some of them wanted impeachment proceedings to begin. Ten days after the *Life* exposé appeared, Fortas stepped down from the court, feeling public insistence demanded it. In his explanatory letter to Chief Justice Warren, Fortas said his departure would allow the tribunal to "proceed with its vital work free from extraneous stress." President Richard M. Nixon accepted his resignation, and Fortas returned to private life and law practice in Washington, D.C., where he died in 1982 at the age of 71.

Vince FOSTER: mysterious death of the Clintons' friend
Vincent Foster, Jr., was President Bill Clinton's deputy White House counsel and boyhood friend. He also had been Bill and Hillary Clinton's personal attorney. In July 1993, the 48-year-old Foster's body was found under a tree in Fort Marcy Park in suburban Virginia. He had been shot in the head, and he was clutching his father's antique .38-caliber Colt revolver. His death came on the heels of embarrassments involving Senate confirmation of Clinton nominees and a bungled investigation into irregularities in the White House travel office for which Foster, among others, had been criticized in the press. Several colleagues recalled recent comments by Foster as to the extreme difficulty of his job at the White House. He had recently begun taking an antidepressant, and his wife reported that he had lately seemed distracted, if not depressed. His death was ruled a suicide.

Foster died during the Whitewater investigation into Clinton's past financial dealings. Because Foster had served as the Clintons' legal adviser when those dealings took place, some suspected that he may have been murdered as part of a Watergate-type coverup. These suspicions were nurtured by what seemed to be a bungled investigation on the part of the U.S. Park Police, in whose jurisdiction the body was found, and by significant discrepancies in the testimony of witnesses at the death scene and investigative experts.

The biggest source of suspicion was Foster's suicide note. It was discovered, torn into little bits, inside his briefcase shortly after his death, but it was not made known to the public until after Justice Department officials determined that it did not contain any information that might be covered by executive privilege. Meanwhile, Bernard Nussbaum, the White House counsel and Foster's immediate supervisor, denied the

note's existence. Later, a handwriting analyst pronounced the note an obvious forgery. This situation with the note led many to wonder if Clinton had something to hide and, if so, was Foster's possible murder being made to look like suicide.

Other aspects of Foster's death aroused suspicion as well. While Nussbaum delayed the park police from entering and searching Foster's office, a file concerning Clinton's connection to the Whitewater investigation was removed and given to David Kendall, the president's personal attorney. The few photographs which the police took were improperly developed by the FBI crime laboratory. At one point the Justice Department took control of the investigation, only to return it later to the park police. Although Foster died from a head wound, no X ray of his skull was taken during the autopsy.

Witness testimony concerning the scene of Foster's death was surprisingly contradictory. The person who found the body later complained that an FBI report substantially altered his testimony. Two of the first medics to arrive at the scene could not agree as to the exact location of Foster's body. A medical examiner remarked that there was not much blood under Foster's head, while Special Counsel Robert Fiske reported that there was. One investigator remarked that Foster's grip on the death weapon, which was found under Foster's leg, struck him as odd. Other witnesses remembered seeing an automatic, not an antique revolver, while one witness said that Foster had no weapon at all. Perhaps most strangely, Foster's glasses were found 19 feet from his dead body. The police suggested that Foster had thrown them away before shooting himself, and yet they showed traces of gunpowder. To many people, these discrepancies suggested that Foster was murdered somewhere else and his body was dumped in the park.

In all likelihood, a despondent Foster shot himself at Fort Marcy Park. However, the manner in which the investigation was conducted and the contradictory nature of some of the witnesses' testimony left ample room for doubt and for lingering questions about where, why, and how Foster died.

Fanny FOXE. See Wilbur MILLS: the Tidal Basin incident.

Barney FRANK: reprimanded gay representatives
Among the recent riot of scandals in the United States Congress, the one concerning Representative Barney Frank (Dem., Mass.) may perhaps rank toward the lower end of the spectrum given the stiff competition in the field. He did not use his office or public funds for private gain, nor did he sexually exploit minors.

In August 1989, a Washington, D.C., newspaper reported that the five-term Massachusetts congressman had hired a male prostitute, Stephen L. Gobie, for sex.

Frank then retained Gobie as his personal assistant and sometimes allowed him the use of his city apartment and his car. He paid for Gobie's psychiatric treatment and wrote letters on his behalf to his probation officer. A year and a half later, Frank apparently found that Gobie was using his apartment as a prostitution den and dismissed him from service. Gobie insisted that Frank was aware that his apartment was being used for this purpose, but Frank disclaimed any prior knowledge. Realizing that he could profit from this affair, Gobie tried to interest the *Washington Post* in his story for a fee. They turned him down, so he offered it gratis to the *Washington Times*. He expected to sign a lucrative deal to write a tell-all book along the lines of *The Mayflower Madam* by Sidney Biddle BARROWS and appeared on the TV show *Geraldo* to talk about the proposed television miniseries.

Frank, who is single, had publicly disclosed his homosexuality in 1987. He first met Gobie, 32, in 1985 through an ad in a gay magazine and paid him $80 for his services. Later, when he hired Gobie to do his errands and chores (apparently in the hope of drawing him away from a life of prostitution and drugs), he paid him from his own pocket. After Gobie was dismissed in 1987, he charged Frank with using his congressional privileges to avoid paying for Gobie's parking tickets. Also, he said that he had been procuring sex partners for Frank at his behest. Frank denied both charges.

Frank apologized for his lack of judgment and asked the House Ethics Committee to investigate his conduct so that the record could be cleared. The case was investigated by a 12-member panel of the House Committee on Standards of Official Conduct, chaired by Julian C. Dixon, a California Democrat. In July 1990, the committee recommended that Barney Frank be reprimanded before the full House for his actions on behalf of a male prostitute that "reflected discredit upon the House." Specifically, the panel found that Frank had used his office to settle 33 parking tickets, some of them accumulated by Gobie when he was driving Frank's car for personal use. Also, Frank's letter to Gobie's probation officer, which ended up in the hands of a Virginia prosecutor and could have influenced Gobie's probation, was found to have contained misleading information about Gobie. The panel concluded that Frank did not know that Gobie ran a prostitution ring out of his house. It also rejected Gobie's statement that the two had had sex in the House gymnasium and found many of Gobie's statements to be false.

House Republicans, unhappy with the recommendation to reprimand, said that they would push for a vote to expel or, at the very least, to censure Frank (this would have cost him his subcommittee chairmanship). Frank's actions, they argued, called for more than a mere slap on the wrist. They were disappointed the following week, when the House rejected the move to expel

Frank by a 390-38 vote. Congressman Newt GINGRICH's move to censure Frank also suffered defeat, 287-141. Later, the House voted 408-18 (244 Democrats and 164 Republicans voted for the reprimand; seven Democrats and 11 Republicans voted against it) to reprimand Frank. He was ordered to pay the District of Columbia for the improperly dismissed parking tickets. Shortly before the vote, Frank admitted that the memo he wrote to Gobie's probation officer was "the most serious" of his mistakes and that he had misrepresented the facts to "conceal my homosexuality." A contrite Frank said, "I should have known better."

Leo FRANK: victim of injustice

On Saturday, April 26, 1913, the body of 14-year-old Mary Phagan was found in the basement of the National Pencil Company factory in Atlanta, Georgia. The young white girl, who had been discovered by the nightwatchman, had been beaten, raped, and then strangled to death. Near the girl's body were found two hastily penciled notes supposedly scrawled by the victim; the words on one saying "that long tall black negro" seemed to point to the murderer. The night watchman himself fit the description but was let go after undergoing a thorough police interrogation that concluded he was being framed. Their subsequent suspicions fell on 29-year-old Leo Frank, a Jewish New Yorker who was the factory's superintendent and part-owner. His eventual sentencing and lynching called up the old issue of southern anti-Semitism, creating anger and discomfort for all involved.

To many Georgians, especially Protestant fundamentalists, Frank seemed a likely object of suspicion. To these essentially agricultural people, the 29-year-old Frank, who had been born in Brooklyn, New York, was an "outsider" and a capitalistic businessman. Furthermore, a number of Frank's female employees informed the police that he had made indecent "passes" at them. Taken into police custody, Frank was found to have seen Mary Phagan on the day of the murder when she had come to his office to collect her weekly pay. Many southerners, caught up in an atmosphere of frenzy and anti-Semitism, declared him guilty long before the start of his month-long trial in the summer of 1913. Some talked outright of lynching him.

During Frank's trial, the prosecution's main witness was Jim Conley, a hard-drinking black man and a janitor at the pencil factory. He testified under oath that he had seen Mary Phagan go to the second floor of the factory on the day of the murder, had heard her scream, and had shortly afterward been called upstairs by Frank, who showed him the dead body of the girl. The two men had then taken the body on the elevator to the basement, where Frank had Conley scrawl the two notes to incriminate the night watchman. Frank's defense lawyers attempted to impugn Conley's testimony through rigorous, detailed cross-examination but were unable to find major discrepancies in his story. Frank insisted he was innocent and that Conley was a liar. The unruly crowd that followed the trial from day to day grew increasingly hysterical and blood thirsty as they shouted slurs against the "filthy perverted Jew from New York." The trial's proceedings were widely covered by America's newsmen, and many Americans considered Frank a victim of irrational bigotry when the jury pronounced him guilty on August 25, 1913. The presiding judge then sentenced him to be hanged for murder, and during the next two years the defendant's lawyers made appeals that went as far as the U.S. Supreme Court, but that court, as all the others had, turned Frank down.

Petitions signed by many Americans protesting the verdict were sent to Governor John M. Slaton of Georgia, who studied new evidence submitted by Frank's lawyers, hearing that there was an alleged police frame-up and that Conley had told a black female, a former lover, that he had slain Mary Phagan (the woman even signed a statement that this was true). Finally, on June 21, 1915, Slaton commuted Frank's hanging sentence to life in prison. The governor's political future was immediately ruined (he was to leave office within a week when he signed the commutation order); the National Guard had to be called out to protect him from a rabid, torch-carrying throng of Georgians. At the time, Frank was incarcerated at the state prison farm at Milledgeville, Georgia, and Conley was free after serving a year on a Georgia chain gang as an accessory after the fact in the murder.

On the morning of August 17, 1915, a group of about 25 men calling themselves the Knights of Mary Phagan entered the Milledgeville prison, forced aside the warden and his guards, and seized Frank. The "vigilantes" drove him about 150 miles north to Marietta, Georgia, the hometown of Mary Phagan, where they called on him to confess his guilt and, when he refused, blindfolded and hanged him from an oak tree. The perpetrators were never punished. A resurgence of the Ku Klux Klan had occurred across the South, to be met by new civil rights groups, particularly the Anti-Defamation League of B'nai B'rith, devoted to combating anti-Semitism. The Mary Phagan killing and Leo Frank lynching kindled strong emotions that have never since been extinguished. What happened shows a judicial system can be corrupted by prejudice, and the injustice that can be done by an angry mob.

Henry Clay FRICK: the "battle of Homestead"

Henry Clay Frick was the brilliant organizer of a coal and coke-oven empire in western Pennsylvania and the principal architect of the illegal vertical combination or trust known as the Carnegie Steel Company. But Frick is best known to Americans as the instigator of one of the bitterest, bloodiest strikes in American history, the Homestead strike of 1892. Frick's machinations may have saved the company a great deal of money, but in the end he sacrificed many lives, as well as almost losing his own.

Neither Frick nor Andrew CARNEGIE had respect for labor organizations, viewing them as a risk to production and profits, but Frick, frequently over Carnegie's objections, usually dealt harshly with workers. His handling of the Homestead clash instituted a tradition of antiunionism in the steel industry that lasted for 45 years.

In 1892, a three-year contract won through an earlier strike by the Amalgamated Association of Iron and Steel Workers was slated for renewal. Frick wanted to break the union's "industrial control," and he carefully prepared for a strike. He made plans to shift Homestead orders to other Carnegie plants, brought in officials from the Pinkerton detective agency to study the plant, erected a high wooden fence around it with peepholes large enough for rifle barrels, and ordered 300 armed Pinkerton bullies to remain on standby orders. He then prepared a new contract proposal calling for a decrease in wages, despite the fact that the Homestead plant had earned a profit of $4 million the previous year. The workers, as expected, rejected the contract and announced a strike to begin on July 1, 1892.

Frick then followed a standard Carnegie procedure: he locked out all of the workers and announced that the plant would operate, with new workers, beginning on July 6. But in employing the Pinkerton toughs, Frick followed his own tradition; he did not request assistance from the police or state militia. Instead, on the night of July 5, he ordered two armored scows, which contained the Pinkerton strike-breakers, to be pushed up the Monongahela River to Homestead.

A steam whistle sounded to warn the strikers of the scows, and they ran for the docks. One laborer fired a rifle, and the leader of the Pinkerton men lay dead. The battle raged for almost 24 hours, during which the hired thugs, outnumbered 10 to 1, exchanged shots with the strikers. The latter fired a cannon across the river and sent a petrol-doused raft toward the scows between shots and barrages of dynamite sticks.

On the night of the July 6, the Pinkerton men were promised safe passage to an old skating rink, but the strikers and their wives charged them, using stones, fists, and umbrellas. One Pinkerton man lost an eye. More than 40 of the Pinkerton agents had to be dragged or carried to the rink, which became a kind of fort. Before a state militia was able to take control on July 12, 14 people had died and 63 had suffered serious wounds.

Most laborers in America hated Frick, and although most newspapers did not support the strikers wholeheartedly, they condemned Frick's methods editorially.

Pulpit oratory also condemned him, and he briefly became one of the most loathed men in America.

The strike's less violent phase lasted until November 20, 1892; it would have lasted longer had not an adolescent New York anarchist tried to assassinate Frick a few days earlier. Frick wrestled with his attacker and lived, and his reputation rose dramatically because his struggle with the assassin was considered "glorious." His comment that "we had to teach the workers a lesson" was applauded by all steel magnates, and Carnegie, on vacation in Scotland, was rebuked for forcing Frick to face "the enemy" alone.

The Homestead plant reopened with a totally new work force, hired at the proffered lower rate, and because all of their labor costs dropped 20 percent, Carnegie's plants prospered. The strike had cost $2 million, but Homestead declared a 16 percent profit ($4 million) in its declared capital for 1892.

The only permanent losers were the dead on both sides and the fired workers, their families, and the Pinkerton agency, still detested by organized labor almost a century later.

Stanley FRIEDMAN: pugnacious politician

"I'm not giving up," declared Stanley M. Friedman, the 50-year-old Bronx Democratic Party chairman and a powerful figure in New York politics, after his conviction on federal charges of racketeering, conspiracy, and mail fraud on November 25, 1986. "I've never quit a fight in my life." Friedman had been found guilty, along with three co-defendants in a bribe scheme that was called a gross "enterprise for illegal plunder," according to U.S. Attorney Rudolph W. Giuliani in Manhattan.

During the winter of 1986, the Democratic administration of New York City Mayor Edward I. Koch was thrown almost completely off balance by allegations of corruption, favoritism, and conflicts of interest on the part of public officials. At that time more than 20 city officials resigned; some simply decided to move on, but others, such as Koch's taxi, transportation, and investigations commissioners, left under a cloud. Stanley Friedman was accused of transforming the city's Parking Violations Bureau (PVB) into a "cesspool of corruption," a fountain of bribes and kickbacks. Government prosecutors charged that the PVB had since 1980 handed out valuable contracts to debt-collection companies in exchange for bribes. Flagrant charges of contract-fixing and bribe-taking were leveled at Friedman, who was alleged to have brokered an enormous bribe in connection with the awarding of a lucrative PVB contract to a computer company.

Because of sensational pretrial publicity, Friedman and his three fellow defendants requested that the trial be transferred from New York City to the United States district court in New Haven, Connecticut. Accused with Friedman were 58-year-old Michael Lazar, New York City's former transportation administrator; 44-year-old Lester Shafran, former director of the PVB; and 55-year-old Marvin Kaplan, a New York City computer-company owner who was accused of paying a $1.5-million bribe to receive a PVB contract, worth some $22 million, to make hand-held computers that printed out traffic summonses. Friedman vehemently pleaded innocent.

During the court proceedings, which began in New Haven on September 22, 1986, the prosecution presented 26 witnesses, half of whom testified after gaining immunity or plea-bargain agreements. The star witness was 53-year-old Geoffrey G. Lindenauer, former PVB deputy director and confidant of the late Donald R. MANES. Manes, the powerful Democratic president of the borough of Queens, New York, had committed suicide on March 13, 1986, after the scandal broke. The 250-pound Lindenauer, a convicted extortionist and one-time psychotherapist who admitted to having slept with four women patients, had pleaded guilty to a number of charges and had agreed to testify for the prosecution. He said he had collected bribes and had split some $500,000 with Manes.

The defense presented only seven witnesses, and none seemed particularly effective. Later, Friedman's noted attorney, Thomas P. Puccio, claimed that the defense had been crippled by U.S. District Judge Whitman Knapp, who presided at the trial. "He rejected our attempts to put on witnesses we thought were important," Puccio told reporters.

After a nine-week trial, the 12-member jury deliberated for four days before reaching guilty verdicts against Friedman, Lazar, Shafran, and Kaplan. Friedman was convicted of receiving $1.5-million worth of stock from Kaplan's computer company as a bribe from Kaplan (the stock was to have been split among Friedman, Manes, and Lindenauer, according to the prosecution). The Bronx Democratic leader was also found guilty of accepting a $30,000 bribe and of committing perjury.

Just hours after his conviction, Friedman and his wife got into a fracas with a part-time female photographer for the *New York Daily News*. She claimed that the Friedmans assaulted her when she tried to take their pictures while they were eating lunch at a New Haven restaurant. Although the third-degree criminal assault charges filed mutually by both sides were dismissed, the photographer said she would file a civil suit seeking damages for minor injuries she suffered.

By the year's end, Friedman had given up his Bronx Democratic chairmanship. He appealed his case without success, and on March 11, 1987, Judge Knapp sentenced him to 12 years in prison and ordered him to serve five years' probation and to stay completely out of politics during that period. Kaplan received four years' imprisonment and a $250,000 fine; Lazar got three years and a $200,000 fine; and Shafran received six months in prison and five years' probation. Knapp ordered Friedman to begin serving his jail time within three weeks of the sentencing, but he allowed the others to remain free on bail pending their appeals. On the same day that Friedman was sentenced, his protégé Stanley Simon resigned as Bronx borough president, a post he had held for almost two decades; the 56-year-old Simon faced imminent indictment on bribery charges but maintained that he was innocent of wrongdoing. On June 3, 1987, Simon was named with six other men, including U.S. Representative Mario BIAGGI of New York, in an indictment of violating federal antiracketeering laws in taking bribes and extorting payments from Wedtech Corporation, a New York firm in the South Bronx accused of making illegal payments to public officials in exchange for government business.

FRUITS OF PHILOSOPHY, THE. See KNEELAND and KNOWLTON: early advocacy of birth control.

GABOR-RUBIROSA AFFAIR

In 1953–54, Hungarian-born American actress Zsa Zsa Gabor and playboy Porfirio Rubirosa conducted a notorious on-again, off-again romance that was widely publicized and shocked the sensibilities of many. Although both had earlier garnered press headlines for their various affairs and marriages, their passionate and turbulent relationship seemed clearly to overstep proper marital behavior but was apparently "acceptable" to them. Their amorous careers validated this.

The beautiful Zsa Zsa Gabor gained fame as Miss Hungary in 1936, when she was about 16 years old. She then had several failed marriages, including one to multimillionaire hotel-owner Conrad Hilton and another to suave British actor George Sanders in 1949. Rich jewels and clothing usually adorned her curvaceous body to excess, but Gabor loved to be glamorous and the center of attention.

The short, dark-complexioned, and shrewd Rubirosa, who spoke English with a French accent, was born in the Dominican Republic and became a flamboyant diplomatic representative for his country, serving abroad in Germany, Austria, France, Belgium, and Cuba. At the time that he and Gabor began seriously cavorting around in public together in the spring of 1953, Rubirosa had had three failed marriages, the last to multimillionaire tobacco heiress Doris Duke, from whom he had won an "extremely generous" settlement of their divorce in 1948 after a 13-month wedlock. Gabor and Sanders had become almost completely estranged and had openly made numerous biting remarks about each other. In 1951 Sanders had said that Gabor had discarded him "like a squeezed lemon" and later publicly announced that he hadn't "spoken a word to Zsa Zsa since she said yes," in response to which Gabor angrily told the press, "My marriage to George won't end in divorce; it'll end in murder. We fight all the time." Sanders, who wanted out of what he called "a ridiculous marriage," became increasingly upset by Gabor's extramarital philandering with Rubirosa, who seemed as nonchalant as Gabor about the press coverage of their romance and public quarrels.

At Christmastime, 1953, Sanders threw a gift-wrapped brick through the bedroom window of the house in which Gabor and Rubirosa were apparently making love at the time. With two detectives, he

Glamorous Zsa Zsa Gabor and her beau Porfirio Rubirosa, Dominican Republic diplomat and international playboy, arrive at New York's Idlewild International Airport on June 29, 1954. The pair had flown from Paris, and she was en route to Hollywood to begin work on a film. (UPI/Bettmann Newsphotos)

stormed into the bedroom, having climbed through the balcony outside, and shortly announced that he was through with Gabor for good. Later, in April 1954, Gabor and Sanders were divorced but remained "friends" afterward. Sanders once commented that "Zsa Zsa was like champagne, and I as her husband was hard put to it to keep up with her standard of effervescence."

Meanwhile, in late 1953, the amorous "Toujours Prêt" ("Always Ready"), the nickname given to Rubirosa, went ahead and married the wealthy Barbara Hutton, heiress to the Woolworth fortune, who had had four previous marriages. ("The Poor Little Rich Girl," as Hutton was called, eventually married seven times.) Gabor told the press she was elated by the marriage and that she had rejected Rubirosa's marriage proposal to her, which had resulted in another fight; wearing a black patch over her right eye, she claimed it had been a "gift" from Rubirosa a few days before he wedded the 41-year-old Hutton, who looked exceedingly troubled during the ceremony on December 31, 1953. The marriage was a debacle; during their honeymoon Rubirosa took off for a time to see Gabor. About 11 weeks later the marriage ended, and the Dominican playboy obtained a settlement of between $1 million and $5 million and took up with Gabor until their relationship completely collapsed within a year.

Rubirosa later married his fifth wife, a young French starlet, with whom he lived happily for about nine years until his death in an auto crash in Paris in 1965 at the age of 56. After Gabor, Sanders married a third and fourth time, the last to Magda Gabor, sister of Zsa Zsa, in 1971; he killed himself in Spain in 1972, at age 65. After her many marriages, Hutton became reclusive, suffering from ill health and dying at age 66 in 1979.

Saucy and seductive, Zsa Zsa made eight trips down the marriage aisle, the last in August 1986 to West Germany's Duke of Saxony, Frederick von Anhalt (reportedly married seven times and really Robert Hans Lichtenberg, a convicted con man who bought his title, according to West German newspapers; von Anhalt denied these accusations). Actress Elke Sommer later brought a libel suit against Zsa Zsa and her husband for remarking to the German press that Sommer was impoverished, balding, and a patron of sleazy bars; in December 1993 a Santa Monica, California, jury awarded Sommer a total of $3.3 million in compensatory and punitive damages as a result.

Zsa Zsa earlier won notoriety for slapping a Beverly Hills police officer who stopped her Rolls-Royce automobile in June 1989 for having an expired license; she later spent three days in jail in July 1990 as part of her municipal court sentence by Judge Charles Rubin, who said that she had "milked this trial" for publicity reasons.

Cornelius GALLAGHER: tied to organized crime and tax evasion

In the 1960s, Cornelius ("Neil") Gallagher seemed to be the fair-haired boy of New Jersey Democratic Party politics. Representing the state's 13th congressional district in Washington, D.C., he served on the House Committee on Foreign Affairs and the House Government Operations Committee. In 1964 Lyndon B. Johnson had seriously considered Gallagher as a possible running mate. Gallagher was particularly active as chairman of a special subcommittee on the invasion of privacy, noted for his opposition to electronic eavesdropping and computer data banks. Ironically, it was with the aid of one such electronic eavesdropping device that Gallagher's gleaming reputation was first tarnished. Though it didn't directly cause his downfall, the electronic surveillance device revealed the congressman's shady dealings with a Mafia capo and started the ball rolling on his descent into infamy.

Gallagher, a native of Bayonne, New Jersey, and a graduate of the John Marshall Law School, had many appealing qualities as a candidate: a reputation as a hardworking liberal who had served in the House of Representatives since 1959, an impressive set of military decorations from World War II and Korea, personal charm, and silver-haired good looks.

Major scandal first touched Gallagher in 1968 when *Life* magazine linked the congressman to New Jersey Cosa Nostra capo Joseph Zicarelli. According to *Life*, electronic surveillance of Zicarelli by the Department of Justice had revealed that the congressman had helped the mobster in 1960 by arranging a "fix" when New Jersey police threatened Zicarelli's profitable gambling operations. This all took place during the time that Gallagher was becoming a leading opponent of electronic eavesdropping and computer data banks as invasions of privacy. At a congressional hearing on the federal effort against organized crime, Gallagher maintained that the power of the Mafia was overestimated and that governmental snooping was a cure worse than the disease it aimed to correct.

Life also linked Gallagher to a series of other illegal or questionable activities, from trying to help Zicarelli buy the Dominican Republic's faltering airline in 1966 for both legitimate business and Cosa Nostra purposes, to promoting secret traffic in the controversial and illegal anticancer drug laetrile, to disposing of the corpse of a minor crook named Bernard O'Brien (the corpse was said to have made its way mysteriously and embarrassingly into Gallagher's basement). Gallagher denied all the charges, which were never proved.

Though his political career survived these spectacular accusations, more mundane charges of income-tax evasion proved Gallagher's downfall. In 1972, after a two-year investigation, a federal grand jury in Newark indicted the 51-year-old congressman on seven counts of conspiracy, perjury, and the evasion of more than $102,000 in income tax. The indictment charged that Gallagher had received $327,000 from two former Jersey City politicians for his assistance in a $3 million dollar kickback scheme with contractors doing business with Hudson County, New Jersey. Gallagher was said to have laundered the dirty money by buying tax-free municipal bonds through a Bayonne bank of which he had once been a director; the local politicians then hid the laundered funds in a secret, numbered bank account in Miami Beach.

Gallagher was also charged with lying to the grand jury about $350,000 worth of other bonds he claimed to have bought from 1960 to 1967, using Democratic Party funds, in trust for the Hudson County Democratic organization. Gallagher had told the grand jury that he had received permission from party leaders to clip $27,000 in coupons from the bonds to use toward his campaign debts. The indictment stated that Gallagher had lied about the amount of coupons he had clipped (actually $61,000) and that he had really bought the bonds for his personal profit, not as a party trustee.

Though Gallagher denied that he was acting for his own benefit, he failed to satisfy the grand jury about why he had carried the bonds around in a suitcase for five years without documentation that they belonged to the Democratic Party and without ever turning them over to party officials.

Finally, Gallagher was accused of reporting only $52,000 in income in 1966 and 1967—rather than the $237,000 the federal government calculated—to avoid paying more than $100,000 in federal income tax.

This scandal erupted just as Gallagher was facing a tough political battle because state redistricting had put him in direct competition with another Democratic congressman for his House seat. Gallagher, a seven-term veteran, lost the 1972 primary after the indictment. The following year he pleaded guilty to some of the charges and was sentenced to two years in prison and a $10,000 fine for "willfully and knowingly" failing to pay $75,000 in taxes in 1966.

Robert GARCIA. See Mario BIAGGI: a senior congresman's sudden comedown.

GARLAND-HERRIN CASE

Yale University has long been one of the most respected institutions of higher learning in the country, attracting the best and brightest of America's youth. When Yale graduate Richard Herrin brutally murdered his ex-girlfriend, Bonnie Garland (also a Yale student) in the early morning hours of July 7, 1977, an ardent "crusade of passion" for Herrin sprang up in the Catholic community at the university, where Richard and Bonnie

had met as fellow students and fallen in love. Bonnie's life had been taken, but Richard's could be saved, contended many persons, who also felt that Richard's mental problems freed him from criminal culpability in Bonnie's death. Bonnie's parents, however, felt differently, believing that Richard's Yale connection got him undeservedly off the hook.

"He got away with murder," decried Paul Garland, Bonnie's father, who was a successful international attorney living in Scarsdale, New York. Joan Garland, Bonnie's mother, tearfully declared: "If you have . . . a defense fund, a Yale connection, and a clergy connection, you're entitled to one free hammer murder. . . . Because you can buy fancy psychiatric testimony shouldn't let you get away with murder."

In 1974 Bonnie Jean Garland, an attractive, red-haired freshman at Yale, met Richard James Herrin, a tall, handsome senior with a full scholarship at the university. Bonnie had graduated as valedictorian of her class from a private school in Virginia; she came from a privileged and wealthy background and was a talented singer. Richard came from an impoverished Mexican-American background in Los Angeles; his father, who had never married his mother, abandoned the family when Richard was three. As high-school valedictorian, Richard went on to Yale, where his interests centered on sports, Catholicism, guitar-playing, and the Chicano group on campus. He had to attend summer school after his senior year in order to receive his Yale degree in 1975.

The two began dating steadily and entered into an intense relationship that lasted for more than two years. Apparently Bonnie suffered emotionally and academically because of her accelerated study program. She was to graduate in three years instead of the typical four. This step had been prompted by Richard to hasten their reunion following his graduation and enrollment in graduate school at Texas Christian University. He frequently wrote to tell Bonnie how much he missed her. Under pressure in 1977, she began seeing a psychiatrist, began dating other Yale boys, and finally wrote to Richard to say she was ending their relationship.

Richard was devastated. He put off moving to Washington, D.C., where he was supposed to enter a Ph.D. program there at George Washington University. Instead, he focused on reclaiming his "Bonnie Beautiful," without whom he couldn't imagine life. Bonnie knew her decision was very upsetting to Richard but was resolute in breaking up with him. When he telephoned her, she invited him to spend a few days at her parents' Scarsdale home to assuage his pain. Her rejection of him supposedly reminded Richard of his traumatic childhood and recent discovery of his own illegitimacy, and while staying at the Garlands, he supposedly considered suicide or a murder-suicide. On the fatal night, while the Garlands were all sleeping, Richard took a claw hammer from the basement, stole to Bonnie's room, and repeatedly clubbed her on the head, throat, and chest. He would later say that her skull "broke open like a watermelon." Barefoot and shirtless, he fled, taking one of the Garlands' cars and driving aimlessly around for several hours before stopping at a Catholic church in Coxsackie, New York. There he told a priest that he had just killed his 20-year-old girlfriend. The priest assisted him in contacting the police, who went to the Garlands' home. Joan Garland found her daughter unconscious and struggling for breath, her hair caked with blood. Bonnie died in the hospital that evening.

After his arrest, Richard's many friends mounted a huge show of support for him. Clergymen, nuns, lawyers, bankers, and Yale officials, among others, wrote letters attesting to his good character and attributes. More than $11,000 were raised by his family and friends for his bail, and 24-year-old Richard was released to the Christian Brothers Community, a Roman Catholic monastery in Albany, New York, which had offered to take him in. The Catholic community at Yale helped provide Richard with an able attorney, Jack Litman, who, during Richard's 1978 trial, called in four psychiatrists in an effort to prove his client's plea of innocence by reason of temporary insanity. Litman contended that Richard, burdened by his long-time psychological and sexual insecurities, had been driven momentarily psychotic by fear of losing Bonnie. His defenders claimed he was the victim of an impoverished and traumatic childhood and of the permissive and affluent climate at Yale in the 1970s. Richard's positive behavior before and after the murder, as well as his great potential, were cited and emphasized by religious leaders and others testifying in his behalf. In the end, the jury found him guilty of first-degree manslaughter (June 18, 1978), and the judge sentenced him to the maximum allowable prison term—eight-and-a-third to 25 years. Because the murder had been committed under the influence of extreme emotional disturbance, the original charge of first-degree murder against Richard had been reduced to manslaughter.

Richard was bitter about his punishment, calling it unjust and too severe because his imprisonment would not "help" Bonnie. The Garlands appeared even more bitter, feeling that justice had not been done.

John Warne "Bet-a-Million" GATES: industrialist as robber baron

Among the most flamboyant robber barons of America's post-Civil War era was John Warne Gates, a florid, portly backslapper who was willing to gamble on anything: horses, faro, roulette, the stock market, or big industrial schemes. A barbed-wire salesman turned manufacturer, he won his glamorous nickname during a Pullman car poker game in which he bet (and lost) a million dollars in a single hand.

His wagering excesses themselves would enliven a biography, but Gates is better remembered for his imitation of John D. ROCKEFELLER's South Improvement Company. His application of a horizontal combination theory to the creation of industrial monopolies gained him negative repute.

Like his fellow industrial barons, Gates had no regard for the law. When his sales experiences made him establish his own wire factory in St. Louis, Missouri, he infringed on basic patents. Forced to relocate in several states, he quickly learned the value of nearby sources of raw materials and convenient transportation in reducing costs and increasing profits. By 1880 he had begun to put together a sort of "barbed-wire trust" of wire companies, and by 1882 it had become the horizontal or cooperative combination known as American Steel and Wire of New Jersey, under Gates's control. The buying power of this cooperative enabled Gates to bully suppliers, force railroad rebates, and drive his smaller competitors out of business. He personally sold its stock and made $15 million doing so. Capitalized at $80 million (much of it, sniffed J. P. Morgan, "is 'water' "), he was able to raise wire prices 200 to 300 percent and make an enormous profit.

Even though he was now a major industrialist, Gates continued gambling on the stock market; and he illegally used American Steel and Wire assets to help himself. To make money, he disregarded responsibilities (if he felt he had any) to his workers, shareholders, and customers. Once, when he had sold his American Steel and Wire stock short, he closed a Chicago plant during good times, caused the stock price to fall, bought cheaply the stocks he had sold short, recouped his money, and then reopened his plant. During that year many of his workers earned under $500, but Gates had plenty to bet with.

His activities began to attract the positive interest of the previously skeptical Morgan. Gates had become president of Illinois Steel and made it American Steel and Wire's chief supplier. With help from Morgan, whose goal was to defeat Andrew Carnegie's steel company, founded in 1892, Gates also acquired two smaller steel companies, the Minnesota Iron Company, and a railroad, naming the 1898 complex Federal Steel. This was a vertical trust, taking as its model the Carnegie Steel Company and owning sources of supply, fabrication, and distribution, but it was somewhat larger than Carnegie's combination, having $56 million in assets and over $200 million in capitalization—as usual, much of it "water." (See Andrew CARNEGIE: architect of monopoly.)

After the Carnegie and Gates successes, trusts became the rage. The National Biscuit Trust, a tin-plate trust, and a steel-hoop trust earned the farsighted entrepreneurs the honor of many imitators.

When the Spanish-American War ended in 1898, steel moguls were angry as Carnegie refused to continue noncompetitive, high prices. Carnegie undersold Federal; and Morgan, using a plan to destroy Carnegie devised by Elbert Gary, a rapacious Chicago lawyer who looked like a clergyman, purchased Federal Steel from Gates for $500 million. It became the foundation for the GATES/MORGAN/GARY creation of United States Steel, the world's first billion-dollar corporation, and because its various units formed a supply-distribution continuum, the world's largest vertical combination.

After 1901, Gates was no longer useful to Morgan and Gary. He was eased out of U.S. Steel for a large sum and went south to Texas, gambling as he went and gaining prominence without undue scandal in the development of Port Arthur.

GATES/MORGAN/GARY: the creation of U.S. Steel
Industrialists and financiers have often dreamed of a perfect monopoly, a complex in which one person or group of persons owned everything: all sources of supply, all fabricating plants, and all structures of distribution. Without competition, the individual or persons controlling this monopoly would have no worry about labor interference or prices; the only concerns would be production efficiency and profits. John D. ROCKEFELLER had been among the first to attempt such a monopoly in his Southern Improvement Company scheme, and even after restrictive but ineffective federal laws were passed against such monopolies, others continued to try to establish them. The trio of John Warne "Bet-a-Million" Gates, J. P. Morgan, and Elbert Gary almost succeeded: in 1901 they created the first billion-dollar corporation in the world, a nearly perfect vertical trust, the United States Steel Corporation.

Gates had shown the way industrially in the 1880s with his American Steel and Wire complex (see John Warne "Bet-a-Million" GATES: industrialist as robber baron). With the help of Morgan and Gary, he had bettered his first attempt during the 1890s by establishing Federal Steel. But even though it was the largest in the world, it was not a perfect monopoly. Andrew Carnegie's company still offered strong competition. As part of Morgan's plan to crush Carnegie, Gates turned Federal Steel over to Morgan and Gary in 1898, with Gary as its president.

Their next move was delayed by the Spanish-American War, during which all steel companies made money by colluding on a single price schedule. In 1899, however, Carnegie, tired of fighting with Henry Clay FRICK over making Carnegie Steel a part of the larger Morgan consolidation, forced a crisis: he broke the pact by lowering the price of steel rails. A small steel "war" ensued.

Morgan, whose involvements included National Tube and National Steel as well as Federal Steel, protected himself by forcing a counter crisis: he ordered his metal interests to stop buying raw steel from Carnegie. Carnegie responded by deciding to make finished goods himself, which he could sell below the Morgan interests' price because his plants were more cost-efficient. Morgan retaliated by raising rates on his Pennsylvania and Baltimore and Ohio railroads, a move Carnegie countered by enlarging his Bessemer line to work with the Western Maryland in order to gain the eastern seaboard.

By 1900, Morgan was amenable to buying Carnegie out; the scheme to crush him was proving too complicated. When Carnegie's lieutenant Charles Schwab reported that Carnegie was asking a price of $425 million, Morgan accepted it without haggling. He next took over Gates's American Steel and Wire, American Tin Plate, American Steel Hoop, and American Bridge, adding them to Federal Steel, National Steel, and National Tube. Morgan also purchased Rockefeller's Mesabi (Minnesota) iron ore deposits, then the largest in the world. With Carnegie Steel, his holdings would become the largest major metals complex in the world.

On April 1, 1901, the huge industrial creation was announced. Believers in monopolistic structures applauded; opponents, aware that attempts to enforce the Sherman Antitrust Act of 1890 had failed in courts presided over by judges who supported big-business, ground their teeth. Once again, big business had proved itself more powerful than the federal government.

All parties made money. Carnegie, who never met Morgan, made a profit of $300 million. Morgan, who had recapitalized the business behemoth for $1.4 billion had gained $11.5 million for the House of Morgan. In order to make still more, he immediately ordered an across-the-board increase in steel prices.

Morgan, who was soon to say "I owe the public nothing," gave little thought to the fact that he had broken an ineffective federal law. He was pleased with himself and, as a reward, left for an all-too-brief European vacation. See also NORTHERN PACIFIC "BUBBLE."

Gilbert GAUTHE: pederast priest
America's Roman Catholic Church was painfully embarrassed in 1985 when a number of its priests were publicly charged with pedophilia (sexual improprieties with children) or pederasty (sex relations between males, especially between men and boys). The nation's attention was riveted to court cases in Idaho, Wisconsin, Rhode Island, and Louisiana, four states in which church fathers were tried and sent to prison on various convictions of sexual abuse and molestation of minors. The most severely punished of the convicted priests was the defrocked Gilbert Gauthe, Jr., who received 20

years' imprisonment at hard labor by a court in Lafayette, Louisiana. Over an 11-year period the priest had committed sexual acts with at least 36 children, most of them altar boys.

Father Gauthe admitted to sexually abusing children—mainly young boys—in every parish he had served in from his ordination as a priest in the Roman Catholic Church in 1971 until his dismissal from his priestly duties for misconduct in 1983. At that time his secret sexual perversions became publicly known in Louisiana's Vermilion Parish, where he had served for six years as pastor of St. John's Church in the small rural town of Henry. Gauthe had been a winsome priest, respected by the community for his wondrous funeral sermons and good deeds (he had once freed a man caught under an overturned tractor). He played games with the children, took them on trips, and asked favorite boys to spend weekends in the rectory.

In 1984, several families in the parish filed civil lawsuits and depositions against Gauthe, charging him with sexual abuse of their youngsters. The discharged priest was put under treatment at a mental hospital run by the Catholic Church. At first he pleaded not guilty by reason of insanity, but eventually he confessed to his numerous transgressions. Church officials were deeply perplexed and chagrined by this and other cases involving sodomy between priests and children. In June 1985 a U.S. Catholic bishops' conference set up a special committee to study the problem, and many dioceses took action to correct alleged incidents of child molesting.

To spare Gauthe's young victims the trauma of testifying in court, a plea-bargaining agreement was reached between the lawyers representing the parents and Gauthe, who pleaded guilty to criminal charges (October 14, 1985) that he had sexually molested 11 boys in his Henry, Louisiana, parish. The 40-year-old ex-priest was told by Judge Hugh Brunson that "God in his infinite mercy may find forgiveness for your crimes" but that society needed "to protect its most defenseless and vulnerable members, the children." Gauthe was then sentenced to 20 years in prison.

The Roman Catholic Church obviously preferred out-of-court settlements of the suits against Gauthe, whose sordid activities had supposedly been brought to the attention of church officials as early as 1973 and who had promised to reform when confronted with them. When lawsuits were later brought against Gauthe, the Catholic diocese of Lafayette, Louisiana, and its insurance companies paid out $5.5 million in 13 out-of-court agreements.

Most of the parents whose children had been molested shied away form going to court against Gauthe, but Faye and Glenn Gastal did not, filing a $12 million suit against him and officials of the diocese of Lafayette,

blaming them for not removing Gauthe when they first learned about his doings. At the February 1986 trial in Abbeville, Louisiana, the defense conceded that Gauthe's sexual abuse of the Gastals' son (by then 11 years old) had occurred but attempted to limit the monetary damage award. The boy testified that Gauthe had coerced him and other lads to perform sex acts in a group: the priest had also taken photographs during the sex performances, the boy claimed, and added that he had hidden the molestation from his father, a farmer and crawfish grower, because Gauthe said "he would hurt my daddy or kill him" if he found out. A testifying clinical psychologist, who had treated the Gastals' son since 1984, predicted that the boy would need therapy for his entire life. In the end, the jury awarded $1 million to the boy and $250,000 to his parents. The Catholic Church was glad the case was over and sought to prevent others from going public with their complaints of alleged pederasty.

However, the church was sued again by the family of another victim of Gauthe, and in late 1987 the Catholic diocese of Lafayette, Louisiana, was ordered to pay $1.8 million to the family of Calvin John Mire, a former altar boy who had been abused by Gauthe at St. John's Church in Henry. In both the Mire and Gastal cases, the church admitted liability, leaving the jury to determine only the amount of the award. See also CATHOLIC CHURCH: some priestly, sexual misconduct.

Kitty GENOVESE: a symbol of public apathy
"We thought it was a lovers' quarrel"; "I didn't want my husband to get involved"; "I don't know"; "I was tired."

These are some of the answers witnesses gave when questioned about why they didn't do anything when 28-year-old Catherine "Kitty" Genovese was stabbed to death before their eyes. The brutal death of this young tavern-manager was witnessed by 38 persons; none of who did anything to prevent it. Today the name of Kitty Genovese remains a tragic symbol of public apathy; many still consider her slaying a national disgrace.

Coming home from work shortly after 3:00 A.M. on March 13, 1964, Genovese parked her car in a lot not far from her apartment in Kew Gardens, a quiet, middle-class neighborhood in the borough of Queens, New York City. In the darkness, a strange man (later identified as 29-year-old Winston Moseley) began stalking her. She quickened her steps but, before reaching a police call box to summon help, was grabbed by the man near a street light on Austin Street.

Her screams were piercing. "Oh, my God, he stabbed me! Please help me! Please help me!" Apartment lights in a building across the street went on; windows opened; and a man called out, "Let that girl alone." The stabber ran off but, after the apartment lights went out, returned in his car to again stalk Genovese, who had staggered toward the doorway of an apartment building. Her assailant found her and stabbed her again. "I'm dying! I'm dying!" she screamed, causing lights to go on and windows to be opened again. No one helped her, and the killer, who had fled in his car, returned a few minutes later to find Genovese slumped in a building's entranceway, where she had crawled for safety. There he inflicted the fatal wounds, and then drove off.

From apartment windows, 38 persons watched or heard all or part of the murderous attacks, which lasted about 35 minutes, but no one called the police during the whole time. A couple who saw it all later said that they had put out their lights to have a better look. After the final attack, the first call to the police was made at 3:50 A.M., from a fearful man who first phoned a friend to find out what to do and then decided to phone the police. He said he "didn't want to get involved."

Moseley was taken into police custody in another section of Queens about a week after Genovese's death, when a person reported him apparently stealing a television set from a fellow tenant's apartment. He openly admitted to killing the woman, and four of the 38 witnesses to the killing testified against him at his weeklong trial, during which Moseley's lawyer vainly claimed that he had been deranged at the time of the murder and not responsible for his actions. Found guilty, Moseley was sentenced on June 16, 1964, to death in the electric chair, but because New York's death penalty had been abolished, his sentence was commuted to life in prison. In 1995 Mosely told parole officials that the suffering of his victims was "a one-minute affair, but for the person who's caught, it's forever." He felt he was the real victim and sought a new trial in vain.

The Genovese tragedy has had a lasting impact on American society. Social scientists have launched studies to find out why so many people failed to act and how to prevent a future "wrong." Citizens in small towns attributed the witnesses' failure to act to living in big cities—a depersonalized environment in which people easily feel anonymous and lose touch with one another in the enormously crowded conditions. The experts concurred, adding that people's inability to feel in control of their environment was primary in their refusal to take responsibility for one another.

Frank GIFFORD: famed football broadcaster-turned-cheater

On May 1, 1997, Frank Gifford, former football Hall of Famer and longtime announcer for Monday Night Football, had lunch with his famous wife, Kathie Lee, then cohost of the popular morning TV show *Live with Regis and Kathie Lee,* then took a cab across New York City to the Regency Hotel. He met Suzen Johnson, a former flight attendant, in her room, which, unbeknownst to Gifford, had previously been wired for sound and video. They had a quick glass of wine, skipped the foreplay, and transformed Gifford into an unfaithful husband.

The world was informed of this illicit affair when the *Globe,* a supermarket tabloid, published transcripts of the encounter. Kathie Lee Gifford publicly called the *Globe's* report an outright lie and fabrication; the fidelity of her 10-year marriage was impenetrable, she maintained. Such a statement fueled the *Globe's* fires, and soon racy pictures of Gifford groping Johnson were plastered across the tabloid's pages. Although Frank and Kathie Lee continued to make the public appearances work required, they retreated to the harbor of their family and close friends and asked the public for privacy to heal.

Frank Gifford had met Johnson four years earlier when he was seated next to her on a return flight from Fort Lauderdale. They started chatting and soon Gifford was complaining about his indefatigable wife, Kathie Lee. Frank and Suzen kept up a four-year phone friendship, which eventually evolved into phone sex. Perhaps Johnson thought that Gifford would leave his wife for her. Perhaps she just wanted a payoff. In any event, she reportedly was paid approximately $75,000 by the *Globe* to lure Gifford into the affair in the camera-ready hotel room. (Apparently, the *Globe* did not distinguish between reporting the news and creating it.)

Meanwhile, though Frank was a victim of entrapment by the tabloids, and though this was the second media nightmare that year for Kathie Lee (earlier, she had come under fire for endorsing a clothing line that was reportedly produced in Honduran sweatshops), the Giffords were determined to work out the problems in their marriage. Kathie Lee maintained that the infidelity was an aberration in her husband's life and that Frank was a good man who had done a bad thing. Around this time, Kathie Lee would routinely spend the first 15 minutes of her morning television show talking cheerfully about Frank and their two children; she painted the picture of the perfect life and perfect marriage.

Her irrepressible chirpy, energetic personality had helped her earlier to put a positive spin on the Honduran sweatshop scandal when she became an activist working for code of conduct laws on wages and working conditions for American companies doing business internationally. That same pluck stood her in good stead after her husband's affair. After nine months, the couple again began making public appearances together.

Having an extramarital affair was the stupidest thing he ever got involved in, Gifford maintained. Though he was knocked from his premier Monday Night Football spot to cohost a pregame show on television, he was happy to be able to spend more time at home with his family.

Newt GINGRICH: speaker's ethics violations

Newt Gingrich was one of the most controversial politicians of the late 20th century. Born in 1943 in Harrisburg, Pennsylvania, Gingrich relocated to Georgia where he was elected to the U.S. House of Representatives in 1978. He quickly became one of the most combative Republicans in Congress. He earned the enmity of Democratic congressmen by accusing a number of them of ethics violations, and in 1987 he led the campaign to force Speaker of the House Jim Wright, a Democrat, to resign his position on the grounds that his fundraising efforts had violated the House's code of ethics. In the 1990s Gingrich became the driving force behind the Republican Party's resurgence in Congress, and he was largely responsible for the development and adoption of its "Contract with America" in 1994. This document presented the party's promise to reform American government if the electorate would give the Republicans control of both houses of Congress.

Following the party's overwhelming victory at the polls that November, Gingrich was elected Speaker of the House, and for the next two years he exerted an astounding influence over the American political process. (Some believed he had more influence than President Bill CLINTON.) As Speaker, Gingrich persisted

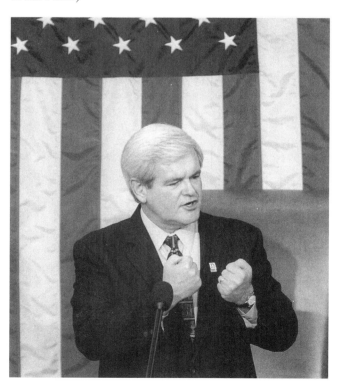

House Speaker Newt Gingrich, congressman from Georgia, gestures while speaking at the opening session of the 105th Congress on Capitol Hill on January 7, 1997. Gingrich became the first Republican in 68 years to be reelected as Speaker. However, he was later reprimanded by the House for ethics violations. (AP/Wide World Photos)

with his confrontational style of politics; he twice brought the federal government to a standstill because he could not engineer a compromise with the president concerning the federal budget, and political cartoonist Garry Trudeau often portrayed him as a bomb with a lit fuse.

Ironically, just months before Gingrich became Speaker, he also became the target of an ethics investigation. The charges centered around the activities of GOPAC, a political action committee whose stated purpose was to help the Republicans gain control of the House. In 1993 and 1994 Gingrich, who was GOPAC's general chairman, taught a course at Kennesaw State College and Reinhardt College in Georgia called Renewing American Civilization; it was later broadcast as a lecture series on national cable television. The course presented 14 steps by which, Gingrich claimed, the United States could make the transition from a "welfare state" to an "opportunity society." This message was a major theme of GOPAC and the Republicans, and GOPAC personnel developed and produced the course in such a way that it clearly promoted the prevailing Republican ideology. However, the course was funded in large part by the Progress and Freedom Foundation, a tax-exempt organization, and GOPAC fundraisers solicited donations to the foundation by touting the course as a means of educating thousands of Republican activists. Although it was not entirely clear whether or not this arrangement was illegal, federal tax laws generally prohibit tax-exempt organizations from engaging in partisan politics, so it certainly appeared as if Gingrich had acted improperly if not illegally.

Surprisingly, Gingrich twice submitted documents to the ethics subcommittee of the House Committee on Standards of Official Conduct claiming that the course was educational, not political, and that GOPAC had not been involved in any way with the course. This claim failed to jibe with the facts as gathered by a special investigator, who uncovered other evidence that suggested Gingrich and GOPAC had misused at least one other tax-exempt organization. In 1990 GOPAC undertook the American Opportunity Workshop, a project similar to Renewing American Civilization. A television program designed to influence voters to support Republican congressional candidates was produced and then transferred to the Abraham Lincoln Opportunity Foundation (ALOF), a tax-exempt organization that was supposedly raising money for needy inner-city children. ALOF then funded broadcasting of the program.

Although it remained for the Internal Revenue Service to determine whether or not Gingrich had violated any federal tax laws, the ethics subcommittee concluded that Gingrich had provided it with statements that were "inaccurate, incomplete and unreliable." Gingrich responded by blaming his lawyer for the false statements and claimed to be "naive" about the tax codes.

Gingrich was reelected Speaker of the House in 1997, but he was also reprimanded by the House for ethics violations and fined $300,000. The scandal greatly diminished his popularity with the American public and his effectiveness as a leader of his party. Following a major setback for the Republicans at the polls in 1998, which many political analysts perceived to be a backlash against Gingrich, he stepped down as Speaker and resigned from Congress.

Ralph GINZBERG: testing the limits of obscenity

Critics of the U.S. Supreme Court often focus upon its inconsistency in interpreting laws, especially in its decisions concerning obscenity. They note that trials involving *ULYSSES, FANNY HILL, LADY CHATTERLEY'S LOVER,* and the *TROPICS OF CANCER* and *CAPRICORN* had, in 30 years, yielded decisions that liberalized and expanded the standards used to judge a book alleged to be pornographic; some commentators had predicted a future "anything-goes" position. Ralph Ginzberg, a publisher of soft-core erotica, apparently believed their prophecy and overlooked the evolutionary pattern in the court's opinions, for in 1966 he discovered that he had exceeded a limit unconsidered in previous litigation: he was found guilty of "pandering."

To increase subscriptions to his publications *Eros, Liaison Newsletter,* and *Documentary Books,* Ginzberg had planned a massive mail-solicitation campaign. He rented an extensive mailing list and, to evoke interest, obtained mailing permits from locales with such suggestive names as Blue Ball and Intercourse, Pennsylvania. His mailing pieces contained artwork and words designed to titillate and arouse; however, they also labeled the publication as pornographic. Yet despite his care to see that the publications were, even by the standards of the 1960s, well within the boundaries earlier established by the Supreme Court, Ginzberg erred in not taking equal precautions with his advertising methods. His biggest mistake was made by not screening his mailing list for those persons who might take offense to his publications. This oversight caused his mailing pieces to reach and anger Roman Catholic clergy and other custodians of public morals, and they almost immediately filed suit against him.

Ginzberg's attorneys expected the suit to be dismissed on the basis of earlier precedents, but the Supreme Court did not examine the contents of Ginzberg's publications; instead, it examined his promotional pieces and advertising methods. The examination caused the justices, in March 1966, to reach a 5-4 decision that Ginzberg had been guilty of misconduct that merited five-years of imprisonment.

Chief Justice Earl Warren declared "that the conduct of the defendant is the central issue, not the obscenity of a book or picture." Justice William Brennan, who wrote the majority opinion, introduced into the judging of obscenity cases a new criterion: "the circumstances of presentation and dissemination of material are equally relevant to determining whether social importance claimed for material in the courtroom, was, in the circumstances, pretense or reality." The majority had found the social importance to be pretense, and Ginzberg was found guilty of having failed the so-called pandering test, which dissenting Justice William O. Douglas condemned as "an ex post facto law."

Ginzberg's attorneys tried vainly to obtain a rehearing and then tried three times, with equivalent failure, to get an appeals court to quash, suspend, or shorten the five-year sentence. In another attempt, a Philadelphia federal court shortened the sentence to three years in May 1970. Ginzberg was still not satisfied; he appealed in vain to the Supreme Court and, with help from supporters, published a full-page exculpatory advertisement in the *New York Times.* But in February, 1972, he was finally incarcerated, only to make appeals for parole in April and July. On October 10, after serving eight months behind bars, he was released on parole. He then vowed to reopen the case but did not. His experience, which had cost him his small publishing empire, had taught him not to tempt the nation's highest court.

GOD'S LITTLE ACRE. See Erskine CALDWELL: "the South's literary bad boy."

Bernard GOLDFINE. See Sherman ADAMS: political liability.

Emma GOLDMAN: anarchist queen

On the morning of December 21, 1919, at Ellis Island in New York City, Emma Goldman and 248 other immigrant radicals were marched aboard an old army transport ship and deported from the United States. For her beliefs and actions as an anarchist and a radical feminist, Goldman was stripped of her acquired American citizenship and sent back to Russia, the land from which she had emigrated in 1885. The young J. Edgar Hoover, who considered Goldman one of the most dangerous women in America, took a personal interest in her deportation and showed up to witness her departure on the "Red Ark."

Goldman had arrived in the United States at the age of 17. Like many other immigrants, she had expected freedom and opportunity; instead she had found poverty and vile working conditions in a Rochester, New York, clothing factory. In 1887, after the hanging of four anarchists for their alleged participation in Chicago's bloody Haymarket Riot, Goldman found a purpose and a passion to her life: she became a revolutionary, dedicating herself to achieving a society based on complete freedom, voluntary cooperation, and mutual aid rather than on authority and institutions.

Goldman soon moved to New York City, where she met her lifelong friend and lover Alexander Berkman, a Russian-born anarchist. She made one effort at organizing a strike—for a newly formed dress- and cloak-makers' union in 1890—but found even union membership too confining and too tame for her anarchist spirit. She was searching for a dramatic event that might spark the working masses into revolution.

In 1892 Goldman and Berkman found what they thought was the right psychological moment for an individual act of terrorism that would call attention to the anarchists' struggle against social iniquities and arouse the workers against their capitalist oppressors. A steelworkers strike against the Carnegie Steel Corporation in Homestead, Pennsylvania, had been brutally suppressed by Pinkerton guards. Some strikers and Pinkerton agents had been killed and hundreds had been injured. Berkman and Goldman decided to assassinate Carnegie's chairman of the board, Henry Clay FRICK. Berkman was to shoot Frick and then commit suicide; Goldman was to explain his action to the people.

On July 23, 1892, Berkman forced his way into Frick's office and fired several bullets before being subdued. Frick received serious but nonfatal wounds, and Berkman's suicide plan miscarried. He eventually served 14 years in prison for the deed, which, instead of drawing support for revolutionary change, brought repudiations from the labor movement, including the Homestead strikers, and other anarchists. Berkman's action served only to increase the nation's fear of anarchism. Goldman, who almost alone defended Berkman, was never convicted for her complicity.

With Berkman in prison, Goldman continued her anarchist activities. In 1903 she was arrested for inciting unemployed New York workers to riot when she urged them to "ask for work. If [the capitalists] do not give you work, ask for bread. If they do not give you work or bread, then take bread." Though no riot occurred, Goldman was convicted and sentenced to a year in prison. By the time of her release she had become a celebrity, "Red Emma." She traveled around the United States and to Europe, lectured brilliantly against the state, electoral politics, capitalism, religion, and marriage, and promoted communist anarchism, free love, and the independence of women.

After the 1901 assassination of U.S. President William McKinley by an anarchist named Leon Czolgosz, Goldman was arrested as an accomplice, though by that time she had reversed her earlier position and opposed such methods. She was released for lack of evidence, but during the repression of anarchists that followed McKinley's death, Goldman went underground for several years, living and working quietly as E. G. Smith.

In 1906 Goldman began publishing *Mother Earth,* a radical monthly. When Berkman was released from prison he joined her as coeditor of the magazine. She also published a book of essays and resumed her lecture tours, generating controversy wherever she traveled. She was arrested frequently.

Before and even after the United States entered World War I, she and Berkman worked against conscription and held antiwar rallies. Finally, they had gone too far. In 1917 the two anarchists were arrested for conspiracy to obstruct the draft. They were convicted, fined, and imprisoned for two years. Then, after an immigration hearing before J. Edgar Hoover and other officials, in which Goldman's citizenship through an early marriage was revoked, they were deported to the Soviet Union.

Within two years, Goldman and Berkman, disillusioned with postrevolutionary Russia, left the Soviet Union, "desolate and denuded of dreams," for England and France. Goldman's criticisms of Bolshevik tyranny now made her an outcast even among radicals. By 1934 American hostility had diminished enough for Goldman to enter the United States for a short lecture tour. With the outbreak of the Spanish Civil War, the now 67-year-old anarchist found another cause that evoked her passionate dreams of a new society. While in Canada raising funds for Spain in 1940, she suffered a stroke and died. She was buried in Chicago among the Haymarket victims whose execution had first led her into anarchism decades earlier.

GORDON-GORDON RAILROAD HOAX

Passing himself off as a pseudonymous lord, a Scotsman who came to Minneapolis in 1871 managed to swindle the Northern Pacific Railroad and financier Jay GOULD of the Erie Railroad out of thousands of dollars in hard cash and negotiable securities. The clever con man almost got away with his crime. He escaped to Canada and nearly instigated an international conflict. In the end, it was the broad exposure he received for his crimes that brought him his comeuppance.

In 1868, a con man who called himself Lord Glencairn contrived to defraud a jeweler in Edinburgh of £40,000, a considerable sum in those days. Three years later, the same man showed up in Minneapolis as Lord Gordon-Gordon and opened a bank account of $40,000. At that time the Northern Pacific Railroad was struggling to extend its line from Duluth, Minnesota, to Seattle, Washington, and like most western railroads of that era, was experiencing severe financial problems. Gordon-Gordon let it be known that he was anxious to purchase thousands of acres of prime land on which to resettle Scotch tenant farmers. Land the railroad had, for the federal government had granted to the railroad companies a six-mile wide strip along the proposed routes. The officials of the Northern Railroad did all they could to oblige Gordon-Gordon to buy their land by offering him bribes and expensive gifts. After three months, when he had picked the land he would buy, Gordon-Gordon returned to New York City, presumably to arrange for funds to be transferred from Scotland to the Minneapolis bank. He left with a letter of introduction to Jay Gould, and nobody knows how much cash.

At the time, Gould was engaged in an internal struggle for control of the Erie Railroad, the longest rail line in the world, and he welcomed Gordon-Gordon, who presented himself as a large stockholder as well as the holder of proxies for many European friends. With this number of stockholders on his side, Gould was sure he could retain control of the Erie, but there was a price to pay. Gordon-Gordon wanted an active part in managing the railroad. To cement their deal, Gould gave his new partner $1 million in cash and negotiable securities, which Gordon-Gordon soon started selling in large quantities. Gould, realizing he had been conned, brought legal action against Gordon-Gordon, but the latter had already departed for Canada, which had no extradition treaty with the United States.

Gordon-Gordon told Canadian officials that the Americans were jealous and angry because he had decided to invest his funds in Canadian land. Seeing that legal means to stop him had failed, a group of Minnesota railroaders, who may have been paid by Gould, crossed the border and kidnapped Gordon-Gordon in July 1873. They were soon stopped by Canada's Northwest Mounted Police and flung into jail without bail. The governor of Minnesota then ordered up the state militia, and hundreds volunteered to serve in an expeditionary force to rescue the kidnappers. Before the two countries came to blows, U.S. President Ulysses S. Grant and Prime Minister Sir John MacDonald of Canada worked out an agreement in which the kidnappers were allowed to go free on bail.

The affair received worldwide attention, and the owners of Marshall and Son Jewelers of Edinburgh recognized the description of Gordon-Gordon as being very much like that of Lord Glencairn. They dispatched a clerk to investigate, and he reported that the two "lords" were indeed the same man. Facing trial, Gordon-Gordon tried to develop a legal defense without success. When he was ordered back to Edinburgh to stand trial, he realized his ploys had failed and fatally shot himself in the head in 1873.

Jay GOULD: the deception of Western Union

In 1881 the stockholders of the Western Union Telegraph Company were shocked and not a little angered to discover that the company had a new majority stockholder: Jay Gould, who from 1877 had been Western Union's worst enemy. Gould's maneuvers had caused the value of the stockholders' shares to fall 12 points below their stated value of $100. For three years after

The Western Union Telegraph Company, formed by Jay Gould and William Henry Vanderbilt, was a telegraph monopoly. In this political cartoon from Puck *magazine, 1881, Uncle Sam removes the two powerful operators, Gould and Vanderbilt, to break their exclusive control of the service. (The Bettmann Archive)*

this, however, the stockholders were happy: Gould had recapitalized the company to $80 million (from $41 million) and declared a remarkable dividend of 38½ percent ($15 million). They did not realize that he had made millions himself because he had seen to it that at least 25 percent of the new capitalization was "water."

The motives behind this singular occurrence were two: money and revenge. In 1877 Gould had seen the advantages to himself of a monopoly over telegraph lines; he had also wanted to punish William Vanderbilt and William Astor, controlling shareholders in Western Union, for refusing to allow him to join the New York Yacht Club. He planned his maneuvers and then began to war on Western Union through his newspaper, the *New York World*. Western Union was the largest among several competing telegraph companies, but the *World* condemned it as monopolistic, labeled it un-American, accused it of ruining businesses by overcharging them for its service, and promoted a rival line, the Atlantic and Pacific Telegraph Company.

During the 1870s, Atlantic and Pacific just happened to be erecting lines along railroad tracks that just happened to be owned by Jay Gould. The company's rates soon undercut Western Union's, and the latter's stock fell in value. To counter this Western Union had, at the end of 1877, acquired Atlantic and Pacific at an inflated price of $10 million. Western Union had also reacquired the services of Thomas Alva Edison, who had been lured to Atlantic and Pacific along with his newly invented high-speed transmission device. But Western Union would not grant Gould a seat on its board.

Gould avenged himself by starting yet another rival company, American Union. He forced the Union Pacific Railroad, in which he was the majority stockholder, to replace its Western Union lines with those of American Union. Again Western Union's stock fell to $88 a share. Because Gould made money whether he acted as a bear (expecting prices to fall) or as a bull (expecting prices to rise) he made $840,000 on this move alone. He also forced Western Union to buy American Union at an inflated price.

Vanquished by 1881, Vanderbilt had Gould visit his home to discuss the merger with American Union. Gould achieved the social recognition he desired, but he was not through financially. He made money on Western Union's sudden rise from $88 to $103 and, on a second day, to $114. Gould had made money on his sale of American Union, on the increase in value of his Western Union shares, and—after he and three of his employees formed the majority on the Western Union board—on the recapitalization of the company. Within a few months, his new stock of capital enabled him to own the company, and he moved his office from his Erie Railroad quarters to Western Union's building. He had fulfilled both of his 1877 motives.

In 1884, however, Gould almost lost Western Union when organized attacks brought him close to bankruptcy. His wit as "a malefactor of great wealth" saved him: he transferred his estate, his yacht, and unencumbered property to his family (roughly one-third of his wealth), gained a loan using Western Union shares as collateral, bailed out the Missouri Pacific (another Gould railroad), and brought Western Union once again into the high $80s per share.

Gould's methods for acquiring Western Union were then, as now, illegal. They were a form of financial thievery behind which lay a heartlessness that made those who suffered in the ERIE RAILROAD "WAR," the BLACK FRIDAY OF 1869, and the Western Union ploy regard him as a destroyer rather than a builder in the tradition of robber barons like Carnegie, Morgan, and Rockefeller.

Jay GOULD and James FISK: Black Friday, 1869

The foundations of business ethics quaked and half of Wall Street was involved in ruin on September 24, 1869—a day history has labeled Black Friday—when Jay Gould, the captain of 19th-century financial pirates, and his partner James Fisk tried to put a corner on the nation's gold supply. His reputation already blackened by his decimation of the Erie Railroad's treasury, Gould was so zealous to make a fortune that he was heedless of the harm he would cause to others by limiting gold. He disregarded the effects of his actions on even those who were close to him. His partner, Fisk, and his broker were two who suffered because of him.

Before the full gold standard backing American currency was established in 1900, the federal government did not set the price of gold, and its value was therefore subject to manipulation in the Gold Room of the New York Stock Exchange. Release by the federal government of some of its gold holdings could lower prices, and hoarding could raise them. Believing that the government could be manipulated into retaining its gold supply, Gould developed an ingenious scheme to drive up the price of gold, force down the value of paper money, increase the value of grain the Erie would haul, and make more valuable the $6 million to $10 million Gould and Fisk handled through New York banks for the Erie and its 10th National Bank of New York. He envisioned interest charges of as high as 100 percent on loans he would make.

Gould already controlled $7 million of the $15 million in gold then in circulation; he need buy only an additional $8 million to hold it all, and could then work upward both its price and the value of the federal gold. But he had one problem: he could not be sure that the U.S. Treasury would not offer some of its holdings to the market.

Gould used a common ploy of financial pirates: bribery. Hearing that President Ulysses Grant's brother-in-law, Abel R. Corbin, had the president's ear, Gould convinced him that his higher-price-for-gold theory had merit. He then bought $1.5 million in gold at $133 per ounce in Corbin's name and offered him the proceeds, which were about $100,000. Gould and Fisk also wined and dined both Grant and Secretary of the Treasury George S. Boutwell as they explained their monetary theory. Grant was noncommittal; Boutwell seemed convinced, for he encouraged the gold speculators.

Meanwhile, Gould and Fisk secretly purchased gold, often through and in the name of their brokers, Belden & Speyer (who also bought on their own), and made investments in the names of Mrs. Grant, Mrs. Corbin, the assistant secretary of the treasury, and others. Gold rose to $137 and then to $144, and Gould held $50 million in contracts and gold futures.

Journalists took sides on the "Gold Bugs" theory. The farm press, eager for profits and unaware that it too was being manipulated, backed Gould and Fisk. Horace Greeley, on the other hand, thunderously appealed for federal release of gold.

On September 22, 1869, a distressed Corbin appeared before Gould, demanding his $100,000 and advising that Grant was displeased with the speculators and pondering release of some gold by the Treasury Department. Gould swore Corbin to secrecy and began, covertly, to sell. For an unexplained motive, the cold-blooded Gould did not tell his partner Fisk about this.

Despite Gould's selling, gold advanced to $150 per ounce by 10 A.M. on September 24. Firms were forced into bankruptcy because the value of paper money had declined. By 11:30, gold had risen to $160 and then went to $164 per ounce. A ruined broker committed suicide.

At noon, New York received from Washington the Treasury Department's announcement that it would release $5 million in gold, and the price of the metal fell rapidly to $133. Most speculators had lost more than they had made, and the losers wanted violent revenge on Gould and Fisk, who had escaped, Gould to the well-guarded Erie offices, Fisk to berate Corbin.

Both partners refused to honor contracts that had been made for gold at prices above $160 per ounce, and their bribed judges issued injunctions to prevent collection of such money. A Mr. Speyer, of Gould's brokerage firm, went briefly insane. Gould was the only person who didn't suffer in this financial fiasco. He made almost $11 million.

A congressional investigation, run by legislators already tainted by connections to Oakes Ames and CRÉDIT MOBILIER, decided that no law could punish Gould for using his right to speculate. The public condemned him and tried to develop ways to restrain him. But Gould apparently had no more regard for the public than he had shown for Fisk: he finagled with railroads until he designed his last great ploy, and his deception of Western Union (see Jay GOULD: the deception of Western Union).

Uysses S. GRANT. See WHISKEY RING: "Let no guilty man escape."

GREAT SALAD OIL SWINDLE

One of the biggest scandals in Wall Street history involved a complicated corporate swindle, now referred to as the "Great Salad Oil Swindle," which was engineered by little Anthony "Tino" DeAngelis. As a shrewd buyer of commodity-futures contracts, DeAngelis easily duped sophisticated bankers and brokers with his scheme, taking them for almost $150 million during the last two years before his exposure in 1963. Afterward, in lawsuits to collect damage claims, various individuals and companies maintained that DeAngelis had cheated them out of a total of $219 million. The scandal pointed up the careless laxity in the operations of America's commodity exchanges, resulting in reforms for investment safety.

DeAngelis, who had left high school in his third year for "economic reasons," was a foreman in a New York hog-processing plant by the time he was 20. Later he ran a butchering company and a meat-packing company, which went bankrupt in 1953 after the Securities and Exchange Commission accused him of understating his financial losses. In time, he put together the so-called Allied Crude Oil Refining Corporation, which was the hub of a complex of 12 closely held companies. In the late 1950s DeAngelis was deeply involved in buying and selling huge quantities of edible vegetable oils, mainly cottonseed and soybean oils, which are the two key ingredients in salad dressings and margarine. His corporation leased many huge storage tanks in Bayonne,

New Jersey, and stored millions of pounds of "salad" oils in them. From the Bayonne waterfront, the oils were easily shipped to European customers such as Spain and Russia.

The Allied Corporation eventually subleased most of its storage tanks to American Express (Amex) Warehousing, Limited and to the Harbor Tank Storage Company. These two warehousing concerns assumed incorrectly that they were storing far more oil for Allied than they actually were. When DeAngelis sold oil, he furnished "warehouse receipts" for the amount that was given to the purchaser, who could then use the receipts as collateral for loans. Numerous customers of Allied assumed, like Amex Warehousing and Harbor Tank Storage, that the receipts were valid and thus used them to get million-dollar loans from top banks in Britain, Germany, the Netherlands, and the United States (including the Bank of America, the Chase Manhattan Bank, and the First National City Bank). The receipts were also used unwittingly by some customers as down payments to purchase other commodities through brokers. Many of the warehouse receipts were false and worthless, although accepted and certified as genuine by both Amex Warehousing and Harbor Tank Storage.

After Allied went bankrupt in 1963, its employees testified in hearings that they had falsified inventory records without the knowledge of the storage companies. Through faulty measuring of the oil levels in storage tanks, they had made it appear that there was much more oil than there really was. Amex Warehousing thought, according to receipts supplied by Allied, that it was storing about 425 million pounds of oil more than its tanks could hold. It had issued certified receipts for this and was therefore forced into bankruptcy because of its enormous liability to the holders of its false receipts. Harbor Tank Storage had, unknowingly, stored nonexistent oil in nonexistent tanks, according to Allied's fake inventories and receipts. It was also discovered that DeAngelis had forged receipts indicating that Allied itself owned much more oil and had staked the receipts as collateral for loans to Allied. At the time of Allied's bankruptcy, it held about 100 million pounds of oil at Bayonne. An investigating grand jury charged DeAngelis with transporting more than $39 million in forged receipts from Bayonne to New York City; supposedly they certified the storage of nearly 400 million pounds of soybean oil. DeAngelis claimed he was innocent.

Before his 1963 downfall, DeAngelis had, in fact, almost cornered the market in both cottonseed-oil futures (traded mainly on the New York Produce Exchange) and soybean-oil futures (traded mainly on Chicago's Board of Trade). He owned contracts to purchase some 600 million pounds of cottonseed oil and about 700 million pounds of soybean oil in future months—a far greater share of both commodities than anyone else at the time. Like most other traders, DeAngelis had bought on margin, or down-payment; the money he had put up was only 10 percent of the contracts' value; sometimes he had paid nothing at all. As a result, his brokers paid his margin or became responsible for any losses that were incurred as prices fell, which they did. Two old, respected stock and commodity brokerage firms, Ira Haupt & Company and J. R. Williston & Beane, Incorporated, were badly hurt having to pay their client Allied's margin. Haupt's capital was fatally drained when it paid out $18 million, and the firm went under. Williston's payout was about $610,000, and it afterward merged with another firm. Low, irresponsible margin requirements for buying and smug, profit-hungry brokers and bankers had allowed DeAngelis and people like him to get away with "fraud."

Eventually, in 1965, the 50-year-old DeAngelis pleaded guilty to four federal counts of fraud and conspiracy and served seven years of a 20-year prison sentence, coming out of the federal penitentiary at Lewisburg, Pennsylvania, in 1972. He then wrote his memoirs and devoted himself to exposing other con artists like himself.

Hetty GREEN: richest female miser in America

If you had been a patron of New York's Chemical National Bank at 270 Broadway in the early years of the 20th century, this strange scene may have seemed commonplace: a woman in her 60s sits at a lone desk, directly across from the tellers' windows. She is shabbily clothed in black, wearing a dress so out of fashion as to seem a hand-me-down and so old and dirty that its blackness is almost green. Well-dressed men approach the desk, speak to her, and frequently exchange cash or papers with her. Nothing is recorded; the transaction is safe in her mental file. Neither the cash nor the papers involve the drawers of the desk; instead, sheltered by the desk top, she burrows into a strange petticoat covered with narrow, deep pockets, each capable of holding the contents of a safe-deposit box. They contain her cash (once as much as $500,000), her certificates, an unwrapped sandwich, and (after 1902) a pistol. At noon, she leaves the bank, goes into a nearby brokerage house, returns with a tin of hot water, and makes a bowl of oatmeal. Why does a prominent bank allow such unusual and indecorous behavior? Because the woman, Hetty (Henrietta) Howland Robinson Green, is the bank's largest depositor, one so stingy as to demand desk space as well as the paltry interest the bank pays. In her time, Hetty Green was known as the world's greatest female financier, the Western world's richest woman, and to her detractors as "the Witch of Wall Street."

Born in 1835 to a New Bedford, Massachusetts, Quaker family, Hetty was a daughter of wealth. Her mother, a withdrawn semi-invalid, came from a family that had founded an old and wealthy whaling and trading company; her father was a partner in the firm. Because she had no brothers, Hetty was trained in the translation of financial reports. She was also taught the Quaker value of frugality. These two factors attributed to her development into a miserly and extremely wealthy woman, worth an estimated $100 million at the time of her death in 1916.

Her financial ability caused her approvers to label her "the Queen of Wall Street," but her miserliness, long exaggerated by the press, is the characteristic by which she is remembered today. Hetty Green, who recognized herself as "Madame Ishmael, set against every man," almost made miserliness into a science.

Her parsimoniousness reached into almost every corner of her life. Bequeathed almost $1 million in 1865 and lifetime income from an aunt's estate, she parlayed the money (with help from her husband's fortune) into $26 million by 1885. Her methods were almost entirely honest: she never charged excessive interest, even during a financial crisis. Green outmaneuvered many of the greatest financial entrepreneurs of the age. Once she was implicated in what may have been a forgery in an attempt to get control of her aunt's fortune. But she made profits chiefly by practicing an excessive personal frugality, often making herself and her family suffer in order to avoid spending money.

Hetty always bought day-old bread. In winter she wore male underwear, adding newspaper as insulation on the coldest days. She moved constantly from cheap rent to cheaper rent to avoid, for tax purposes, establishing a permanent residence in New York. She cornered lawyers (including the famous Joseph Choate) for advice, feigning uncertainty about decisions, and then prepared her own cases on the basis of their knowledge. (Choate soon learned to avoid her and used her as a butt for jokes about her parsimony, her avarice, and her cunning.) She treated doctors similarly. When her son Ted injured a kneecap while sledding, she dressed him and herself in even more ragged clothing than her usual wear, visited a clinic several times, and when recognized refused to pay and never returned. (Ted's lower leg was amputated three years later.) At the time, Hetty Green was earning $5 million a year.

In 1885, she broke with her husband because his failure in a speculative venture had cost her money, an unforgiveable sin to a woman who learned by experience to hate male competitors. Her most vocal and tormented enemy was the railroad wizard (some say crook) Collis P. HUNTINGTON, whose dream of the Southern Pacific Railroad she confounded for years by acquiring the tiny Texas Midland Railroad and running it under her husband's and then her son's control. Huntington died during one of his many unsuccessful suits against her.

She hated lawyers instinctively: she carried a gun presented by opponents of Huntington "to protect myself against lawyers. I'm not so much afraid of burglars or highwaymen." Yet Hetty Green could be a person of sentimental emotion: she had nursed Ted, dressed up for her daughter's betrothal to a millionaire, and became ill when her pet mongrel Dewey died in 1910.

Was this person, most of whose behavior was eccentric and who was cited by William Jennings Bryan as the reason for a national income tax, a Wall Street queen or a witch?

Pincus GREEN. See Marc RICH: colossal tax cheat.

GROSS-ROSTAND CONTROVERSY

Edmond Rostand was one of France's most outstanding dramatists. His most celebrated play was *Cyrano de Bergerac* (1897), a tragic love story set in the 17th century about a man with a huge nose who expressed his feelings for the woman he loved by speaking to her in the guise of her handsome but inarticulate lover. A wealthy real estate operator in Chicago, Samuel Elbely Gross, claimed that Rostand had stolen *Cyrano*'s plot and characters from Gross's own romantic comedy, *The Merchant Prince of Cornville* (1896), and he sued in American, British, and French courts. Although Gross won his case in American courts, the French and other Europeans, as well as Rostand himself, did not initially take Gross's charges seriously.

When *Cyrano de Bergerac* opened at the Garden Theater in Chicago in October 1898, the 44-year-old Gross was in the audience watching. Before the play was over, he had asserted to friends that it had been copied from his *The Merchant Prince of Cornville.* He claimed that he had written his play in the mid–1870s, and that the play's manuscript had lain in a safe deposit box for 20 years. It had been protected by both American and British copyrights. In 1895, Gross submitted his work to the publisher Stone & Kimball, which brought out a handsome edition of the play that was circulated privately to Gross's friends. In the following year Gross's play was performed at the Novelty Theater in London, England, but had a short and uneventful run.

Rostand's *Cyrano* was first produced in 1897 at the Porte Saint-Martin Theater in Paris, with the famous French actor Coquelin Aîné in the title role. It was an immediate hit and was quickly translated into English, German, Russian, and several other languages and produced in the leading cities of Europe and America.

Gross first sued the American producers of *Cyrano de Bergerac*, especially the noted leading actor, Richard Mansfield, for copyright infringement. (In 1898 in New York City, Mansfield had scored a tremendous success in the role of Cyrano.) In 1902 a United States district court judge in Chicago issued a perpetual injunction against the production in the United States of Rostand's *Cyrano* and ordered that part of the profits of Mansfield's tour of the play be paid to Gross. But Mansfield paid no attention to the injunction and continued to act in *Cyrano* around the country with great critical and financial success.

Gross followed up his legal victory in the United States by suing Rostand for plagiarism in the British and French courts. In doing so he hired literary experts to testify to the similarities in the characters, dialogue, and plot in *Cyrano de Bergerac* and *The Merchant Prince of Cornville.* Although the case attracted international attention as a scandal, nothing much came of it abroad nor, eventually, at home. In 1912 Gross's contentions were sustained for a second time by a United States court, and while a reversal of this verdict occurred in 1915, all performances of *Cyrano* were stopped in America until 1923.

A colleague of Rostand, Victorien Sardou, once said in an interview, "the claims of Gross in the present case have not a leg to stand on. The method adopted in the judgment in Chicago of enumerating resemblances without alluding to dissimilarities is a most useless and misleading game. The idea of Rostand finding *Cyrano*, already prepared, perhaps in canned form, on the shore of Lake Michigan, is very funny." Rostand also scoffed at Gross's contentions and, on one occasion, declared sarcastically, "I have just purloined from the house of a Louisiana shipowner a great piece on 'Joan of Arc, the Maid of New Orleans.'"

Henry GRUNEWALD: notorious influence peddler

In 1951, public clamor over a series of federal tax scandals induced Congress to begin an investigation into the operation of the internal revenue laws. A subcommittee of the House Ways and Means Committee, chaired by Representative Cecil R. King (Dem., Calif.), began uncovering widespread misconduct at high levels of the Truman administration. The greatest perpetrator to be revealed was Henry W. Grunewald, a well-known Washington, D.C., influence peddler known as "The Dutchman."

Appearing before the King subcommittee, a Chicago real estate lawyer and property owner named Abraham Teitelbaum (whose claim to fame was that he had formerly represented gangster Al Capone) described a shakedown scheme in which a group of high-level tax fixers tried to extort $500,000 from him to prevent his prosecution for income-tax fraud. Teitelbaum implicated Grunewald; Charles A. Oliphant, the chief counsel of the Bureau of Internal Revenue (BIR); and George Schoeneman, a former BIR commissioner. J. Lamar CAUDLE, head of the Tax Division of the Department of Justice, was also named in the course of the investigation into Teitelbaum's claims. All of the officials denied involvement in the case.

Grunewald was little known to the public at the time of the subcommittee hearings, and newspaper reporters referred to him as a "man of mystery." Born in South Africa, "the Dutchman" had come to the United States in 1906. He briefly served as a Prohibition enforcement agent but was dismissed after being indicted for conspiracy to defraud the United States by falsely issuing

Henry ''The Dutchman'' Grunewald sits in silence before the House Ways and Means Committee in Washington, D.C., on January 29, 1952. His refusal to answer resulted in committee members beginning contempt of Congress proceedings against him; they wanted to know what Grunewald knew, if anything, about the purported $500,000 tax shakedown attempt against Abraham Teitelbaum, a Chicago lawyer. (AP/Wide World Photos)

customs permits and by fraudulently removing cases of champagne from the customs warehouse. He was later acquitted.

In 1919 Grunewald became a confidential secretary and investigator for insurance magnate Henry Marsh, through whom Grunewald met many powerful and important public and business leaders. In this role Grunewald gained access to vital information collected by banks, insurance companies, and federal agencies, all of which proved valuable in his later work. After Marsh's death, he began a career as a private investigator and public-relations man who specialized in collecting unsavory information on his subjects. For example, one such job was done for John L. Lewis, who hired Grunewald to investigate the personal life of a federal judge

who was considering a contempt case against the United Mine Workers Union, which Lewis led. Corporations hired Grunewald to dig up derogatory information about people who were suing them.

Grunewald's work was highly lucrative. He had an apartment in Washington, a $100,000 winter home in Florida, and a summer home in Spring Lake, New Jersey. He also owned three corporations. But with his numerous powerful connections, Grunewald took up influence peddling and eventually tax fixing and in 1950 was a witness in two inquiries into federal wiretapping. From then on he became a prominent figure in tax-evasion investigations, not as an evader himself, but as a ''tax-fix artist.''

At the King subcommittee hearings, Oliphant admitted to having accepted loans from Grunewald but denied involvement in the Teitelbaum case. Grunewald, who tried to avoid testifying before the subcommittee, appeared in December but refused to answer questions about the alleged extortion. Instead, he accused the subcommittee of ''violating the fundamental rights of our country.'' But when, in January 1952, he again refused to testify, he was cited in the House for contempt of Congress by a 332-0 vote. Eventually, Grunewald did testify before another House subcommittee, headed by Representative Robert W. Kean (Rep. N.J.), which continued the investigations during the Eisenhower administration.

Grunewald informed the subcommittee that he had collected fees from such clients as the American Broadcasting Company, Pan American Airways, and the United Mine Workers but refused to detail the kinds of investigations he had undertaken for these clients. He did admit that businessmen who were being investigated for tax fraud had paid him for ''investigative work and introductions,'' but he denied various charges of tax fixing, such as the accusation that he had received $60,000 in 1948 for fixing a criminal tax-fraud case brought against a New York meat company. The Kean subcommittee concluded that ''Henry W. Grunewald personifies the decay of the tax system during the period following World War II.''

In 1953, Grunewald pleaded guilty to one count of a 31-count indictment; he was fined $1,000, given a suspended 90-day jail sentence, and instructed to live a ''clean, temperate life'' during one year of probation. Within a few months of this, however, Grunewald was imprisoned for serious violations of his parole. In 1954 he was twice indicted for perjury by federal grand juries, and the following year he and two accomplices were convicted of having accepted $160,000 in 1949 to quash federal tax prosecutions against two companies. The three defendants won a retrial on a technicality, which resulted in a hung jury in 1958. ''The Dutchman'' died a few months later, at the age of 65, shortly before another scheduled trial.

HALL-MILLS MURDERS

On September 16, 1922, the bodies of 41-year-old Reverend Edward Wheeler Hall and 34-year-old Eleanor Mills, a choir singer in Hall's Episcopal Church, were discovered in a lover's lane in New Brunswick, New Jersey. The married pastor and the pretty, blond singer, who was married to the church's sexton, had been having an affair for some time. Reverend Hall had been shot in the head, while Mrs. Mills had three bullet holes in her forehead. Her throat had been slashed and her tongue cut out. Passionate love letters were strewn around the corpses. No suspects were arrested, and the case was closed for four years until the *New York Daily Mirror* began running front-page stories purporting to reveal evidence that Mrs. Frances Hall, the Reverend's wife, along with her brothers and a cousin, were responsible for the grisly crime.

The police investigating the double murder had initially claimed they could find no clues or leads. Interest in the case subsided until the *New York Daily Mirror* began publishing the articles that pointed a finger at Mrs. Hall and her three male relatives. In July 1926, the paper carried a story about Louise Geist, who had been a maid at the Hall's house at the time of the murder. Miss Geist had reportedly told Mrs. Hall that she had overheard Reverend Hall and Mrs. Mills planning to run away together. According to the *Mirror* story, Mrs. Hall and her brother Willie were driven to the trysting place by the chauffeur, and Miss Geist was given $5,000 to keep her mouth shut. Miss Geist and the chauffeur later completely denied that these events had ever taken place. The *Daily Mirror* also reported that Mrs. Hall and her cohorts had bribed the police and eyewitnesses at the time of the 1922 investigation. Finally the paper discovered a secret witness whose damaging testimony brought about the indictment of Mrs. Hall, her brothers Willie and Henry Stevens, and their cousin, Henry Carpender, a broker on the New York Stock Exchange, who was to be tried separately.

Three hundred reporters from around the world converged on the New Jersey village of Somerville to cover the 1926 trial in the county courthouse. Charlotte Mills identified her dead mother's love letters, and the prosecutor had no trouble establishing the fact that there had been an amorous relationship between the clergyman and his choir singer. Then the star witness appeared, Mrs. Jane Gibson. The press immediately nicknamed her the Pig Woman because she raised and sold pigs on a nearby farm. Suffering from stomach cancer, she had to testify from a hospital bed, attended by a doctor and a nurse.

Mrs. Gibson recalled that she had been passing De Russey's Lane in New Brunswick when she heard several people arguing. A woman said "Explain these letters." There were sounds of fighting, and somebody said "Ugh." Then a shot rang out, and Mrs. Gibson heard two women's voices. "One said, 'Oh Henry,' easy, very easy; and the other began to scream, scream, scream so loud, 'Oh my, oh my, oh my.' So terrible loud . . . that woman was screaming, screaming, trying to run away or something." As she turned to ride away on her mule, Mrs. Gibson said she heard three rapid shots. She then identified Mrs. Hall, her brothers, and Mr. Carpender as the four people she had seen in the moonlight, huddled under the crabapple tree where the bodies were found.

Mrs. Hall's so-called "million-dollar" defense team immediately pointed out discrepancies between the Pig Woman's trial testimony and the testimony she had given before a grand jury in 1922. Forcing her to admit that she couldn't remember when she had been married, if she had been divorced, or if she had remarried, they easily discredited her memory. Most damaging to Hall's testimony was her elderly mother, who sat in a front row seat mumbling, "She's a liar, a liar, a liar! That's what she is and what she's always been." As her bed was being rolled out of the courtroom, the Pig Woman rose up and yelled at the defendants, "I told the truth, so help me God. And you know it, you know it, you know it!''

Mrs. Hall, who was seven years older than her late husband and the daughter of a wealthy and socially prominent family, testified in such an icy, calm manner that the press dubbed her the "Iron Widow." She denied any knowledge of the murders and declared that the minister had always been "a loving, affectionate husband." Willie Stevens corroborated his sister's testimony about what they had been doing on the fatal night. Henry Stevens proved that he had been miles away fishing in Barnegat Bay.

The case went to the jury, which deliberated for only five hours before finding the three defendants not guilty. The indictment against Henry Carpender was dropped. Mrs. Hall and her brothers brought a $3-million libel suit against the *Daily Mirror*, which was settled out of court. The murderer or murderers were never found, and the mystery of the clergyman and the choir singer remains unsolved.

HAMILTON-REYNOLDS AFFAIR

The first United States secretary of the treasury and the creator of many of the *Federalist Papers*, Alexander Hamilton is remembered as a brilliant statesman and eloquent lawyer. Despite his savvy in the financial and political arenas, Hamilton was completely gullible where women were concerned. In 1791 the 36-year-old Hamilton was married and the father of four children. That summer he entered into an affair with an attractive and seemingly distressed young woman, never thinking the repercussions would involve blackmail and false accusations.

Hamilton first met Maria Reynolds when she visited him in the Philadelphia treasury office in a state of great distress. Claiming that she had broken with her odious husband she appealed to his chivalry as a fellow New Yorker, saying that she needed money to return to her family. Flattered, Hamilton promised to send the money to her residence.

That evening, he delivered the money himself to Mrs. Reynolds in her bedroom and stayed several hours to console her. Hamilton's consolation increased in both frequency and intimacy during the remainder of 1791. He saw Maria often, sometimes at his own home when his wife Betsey, once again pregnant, vacationed with her father. Late in the year, however, Maria's husband, James, returned. He demanded and quickly gained a reconciliation.

He soon demanded more, however, chiefly satisfaction from Hamilton, preferably in the form of money. Rather than risk his public efforts by allowing Reynolds to blacken his reputation, Hamilton yielded to a blackmail demand of $1,000.

But Reynolds demanded still more—at first a job. For allowing the affair to continue, Reynolds requested mi-

nor gifts of $30, $40, and $50. Blinded by his lust, Hamilton continued this liaison until late in 1792.

Reynolds then proved to be more than a blackmailer and a pimp; he was arrested with an accomplice for attempting a fraud against the U.S. Treasury Department. Expecting assistance from Hamilton and receiving none, the Reynoldses vowed revenge. Reynolds and his accomplice turned states' evidence against a Treasury Department employee and were released. Reynolds decamped, but the accomplice approached the Speaker of the U.S. House of Representatives and falsely accused Hamilton of secret speculations based on official information.

The House Speaker, with a fellow representative and James Monroe, collared Hamilton and learned that the speculation charge was false. But Hamilton was so unnerved that he told the embarrassed trio all about the Reynolds affair. Monroe, a careful man, made a private visit to Maria and her new lover (her husband's accomplice) and was told a lie: they claimed that Hamilton had fabricated the tale of the affair to cover his own speculations. Already Hamilton's political opponent, Monroe made and preserved a detailed memo of both investigations.

In 1797, when Monroe and Hamilton became fierce political enemies, Monroe was tempted to destroy Hamilton by publishing the memo. But President Thomas Jefferson, using other sources, beat him to it. He had his journalistic henchman, James Callender, publish his pamphlet "The History of the United States for 1796." An exaggerated and libelous piece, it charged Hamilton with political and fiscal chicanery, as well as with extended adultery.

Hamilton was faced with a dilemma: silence would ruin his political career for certain; protest and a disclaimer would ruin his reputation.

He told all, in a carefully crafted confession that disproved the charge of pecuniary speculation but affirmed the charge of adultery. "I can never cease to condemn myself . . ." he wrote.

Sensational and ribald commentary appeared in the press and almost destroyed Hamilton anyhow. But George Washington, for whom Hamilton had once been aide-de-camp, publicly offered his friendship and support. Washington's condoning of Hamilton left no room for mere mortals to condemn him, and when Betsey began to defend her husband and berate the villains who had forced him to face such severe emotional pain, Hamilton's political career was revived. Because of his great courage in risking his moral reputation, Hamilton's integrity as a public servant was saved.

Tonya HARDING: conspired against rival skater

On January 8, 1994, Tonya Harding stood atop the American figure skating world, having been crowned champion at the national competition in Detroit. Her euphoria was short-lived, however. Just two days later, she and ex-husband Jeff Gillooly were questioned by the Detroit police and the Federal Bureau of Investigations (FBI) for their alleged role in the attack on rival skater Nancy Kerrigan during a practice session on January 6, 1994. The attack shocked the sports world and the scandal became one of the biggest news events of the year, evidently beginning and ending in the following way.

Even before the nationals, headlines in the United States Figure Skating Association's (USFSA) official magazine all but proclaimed Tonya's archrival, Nancy Kerrigan, as the ultimate winner. Gillooly felt that this was unfair to Tonya. So he began plotting (with Tonya's full participation, according to him) to bring down Kerrigan and ease Tonya's path to the championship. On December 17, he called his friend Shawn Eckhardt to ask if he knew of someone who could hurt Kerrigan and put her out of contention. If Tonya won, Gillooly promised to give Eckhardt 10 percent of her endorsement contracts and hire him as her bodyguard. Then Eckhardt called his friend Derrick Smith in Phoenix and told him that he had a contract on Kerrigan from Gillooly. He offered Smith approximately $1,000 per week once the job was done. Next day, Smith called his wife's nephew, Shane Stant, and enlisted his help.

Smith and Stant met with Gillooly at Eckhardt's house on December 26. They secretly recorded the meeting so that they could use it against him later. Gillooly offered up to $6,500 and asked how they proposed to carry out the attack. He suggested breaking Kerrigan's landing leg. Smith asked for more information on the skater and a $2,000 advance. Tonya, meanwhile, waited outside in the pickup truck—apparently she had been against the meeting.

Tonya had found out from a librarian friend where Kerrigan trained. Next evening, while Tonya chatted with Eckhardt's mother downstairs, Gillooly gave him a full-page photo of Kerrigan, the address of the Massachusetts arena where she practiced, and 20 $100 bills. Stant flew to Boston immediately but didn't find the arena until New Year's Eve (when they had hoped to attack her, preferably partying outside a bar) and then watched the main entrance for two whole days without ever seeing Kerrigan. On January 3, he learned that Kerrigan was in Detroit. He left for Detroit where Smith met him. Tonya was getting impatient because nothing had happened yet, according to Eckhardt.

Tonya and Gillooly thought Kerrigan could be attacked in her room (Tonya got the number under a false pretext) at the Westin Hotel. Smith and Stant scouted the conditions at the Cobo Arena and decided to attack her as she left practice. On January 6, Stant hit Kerrigan with a baton three times, just an inch above the right kneecap, twice on the side of her leg and once on her head before she hit the ground. When Gillooly heard the news from Tonya, he withdrew $3,000 from the bank and took it to Eckhardt. Kerrigan was out of the reckoning at last.

After her win, Tonya said, "It won't be a complete title without having competed against Nancy." Her role in the vicious attack might have remained secret. However, Patty May Cook called the Detroit police from Oregon to report that she believed that Harding, Gillooly, Eckhardt, and several hit men were involved in the crime. Cook had heard this from Eckhardt's father, Ron, whom she knew. Before returning to Portland on January 10, Tonya underwent a grueling four-hour interview and was asked to sign a statement saying she did not know about the planned attack.

Both skaters competed in the Winter Olympics in Lillehammer, Norway, in February 1994, where Kerrigan won a silver medal and Harding's performance was disappointing. On March 21, 1994, Tonya pleaded guilty to the charge of hindering the prosecution. She was stripped of her coveted national title, permanently banned from the USFSA and from participating in international competitions. Tonya also received a three-year probation which restricted her to Oregon, Washington, and California. She was ordered to do 500 hours of community service and pay a $100,000 fine, plus $10,000 to the district attorney's office for "special costs" and another $50,000 to the Special Olympics. In August 1995, a judge denied her petition to direct $25,000 of this amount to "Loaves and Fishes," a soup kitchen for the elderly where she volunteered, and to be released from the remaining 100 hours of community service. On May 16, Eckhardt, Smith, and Stant pleaded guilty to charges of racketeering and conspiracy to commit second-degree assault. They all named Harding as a coconspirator. Each was sentenced to 18 months in prison. Gillooly pleaded guilty to racketeering and was given a two-year prison sentence and a $100,000 fine. He was released after six months, changed his name to Jeff Stone, and has since remarried.

Estranged from her mother and divorced (since 1997) from second husband Michael Rae Smith, Tonya tried acting in a C-grade movie, managed pro wrestler Al Barr, and even sang at a pop concert, where she was loudly booed. All five coconspirators made money by selling their exclusive stories to various tabloids and TV programs. In the end, however, Tonya admitted having paid too high a price: "I lost my life, my career, and everything else." She continued to practice skating and teach young skaters. Finally, in October 1999, she skated as a professional before a national television audience and received a standing ovation.

Warren G. HARDING: was he poisoned?

In August 1923, Warren Gamaliel Harding, the 29th president of the United States, died mysteriously in a San Francisco hotel just after he had seemingly recovered from a bout of food poisoning. Though physicians pointed out that the president suffered from hypertension, had an enlarged heart, and had had nervous breakdowns in his youth, they could not squash the rumors that had begun to circulate. The affable president with the movie-star looks and meandering ways had been poisoned by his jealous wife, said many. Others thought she had murdered him to save him from disgrace. Harding apparently was on the brink of impeachment because of the impending public disclosure of corruption in his administration.

Harding grew up in and around Marion, Ohio, and was graduated in 1882 from Ohio Central College, where he was editor of the college newspaper. Later he became a reporter and writer on the Marion *Star*, a weekly paper that he, with the aid of his father, purchased in 1884 after it fell into a moribund state. After Harding's marriage in 1891 to Florence Kling DeWolfe, the newspaper, now a daily, became very prosperous and influential, largely through the managerial skill of his wife. Five years older than Harding, Florence was domineering and plain looking. She was fitly known to her husband and his friends as "The Duchess" because of her cold and imperious nature.

Naturally interested in community life, the good-looking Harding gradually entered public service and was elected an Ohio state senator (1899–1902) and lieutenant governor (1903–04). An active Republican, he was elected to the U.S. Senate in 1914 but, though he had a statesmanlike appearance and was a gifted speaker, he served without distinction.

Harding had passionate extramarital affairs, notably with Carrie Phillips and Nan Britton, over a period of about 20 years; his strong-willed, homely wife seemed to do little to stop them, undoubtedly for political reasons. In 1920 Harding received the presidential nomination at the Republican Party national convention, as a compromise candidate; the three leading candidates had become deadlocked, forcing the party bosses to select him. Harding, a conservative who was noncommittal about domestic reforms and international involvement, won the general election overwhelmingly. As a president, however, he was generally too politically trusting of his friends, a number of whom he appointed to high government office and who secretly enriched themselves through graft and corruption.

In June 1923, when rumors of corruption were circulating in Washington, D.C., Harding set out on a cross-country goodwill tour that took him as far as Alaska, where he reportedly received definite word of gross misconduct by his friends in office. "My God, this is a hell of a job! I can take care of my enemies all right. But my friends, my God-damn friends, they're the ones that keep me walking the floor nights!" he said to one newsman.

On his return trip from Alaska, Harding became seriously ill, supposedly from food poisoning (the diagnosis of his physician, Charles Sawyer). He canceled some scheduled appearances and was taken to San Francisco, where he was put to bed in the Palace Hotel in a state of utter exhaustion. After several days, Harding's health had improved, and by August 2 he seemed out of danger. He spent that evening alone with Mrs. Harding, who read a magazine article to him. Minutes after she retired to her room across the hall, a nurse entered the president's room and saw his head suddenly quiver and drop. Harding, at the age of 57, was soon declared dead by Dr. Joel Boone, who later signed a statement with Sawyer and three other doctors that the cause of death was "probably apoplexy." The cause was never firmly established because Mrs. Harding never allowed an autopsy, and the body was embalmed before it left the hotel.

Rumors later began that Mrs. Harding had poisoned her husband, either to protect him from disgrace or to take revenge for his marital infidelities. Physicians, however, cited Harding's physical ailments. They also emphasized that he had grown extremely weary during the strenuous transcontinental trip. The medical evidence seemed to contradict the poison rumor, but it persisted anyway and eventually was put into a scandalous best-selling book, *The Strange Death of President Harding* (1930). The book was written by Gaston Bullock Means, an old friend of Harding's and a notorious con artist. Means alleged that Mrs. Harding had hired him as her personal detective to investigate her husband's love affairs; furthermore, he implied that she had poisoned her husband. Mrs. Harding herself had died in November 1924, months after the unexpected death of Dr. Sawyer, who was rumored to have helped her or to have known about the poisoning.

HARDING-BRITTON AFFAIR: passion, paternity, and pelf

In 1927, an attractive blond woman named Nan Britton published a book called *The President's Daughter*. Although it eventually became a best-seller, it almost wasn't published because of an attempt by government agents to seize the printing plates in New York. The book was a detailed autobiographical account of Britton's secret affair with President Warren Harding, to whom she bore an illegitimate child.

In 1910, while handsome, 45-year-old Warren G. Harding was running unsuccessfully for governor of Ohio, the pretty, 14-year-old Britton became infatuated with him. The infatuation continued throughout her high school years. Britton, who had pasted Harding's campaign pictures all over the walls of her bedroom, annoyed Harding's unattractive and domineering wife, Florence, because of her persistent girlish adoration of him; Nan wrote compositions about Harding for her high-school English teacher, who was Harding's sister Daisy, and apparently visited her "idol" while he worked as editor-publisher at the Marion, Ohio, *Star*.

After the death of Nan's father, who was a doctor and a friend of Harding's, the Brittons fell into financial difficulties, and her mother returned to public-school teaching. Later the family split up. By then, in 1915, Harding had been elected a U.S. senator and was serving in Washington, D.C. In 1916, after short-lived jobs in Cleveland and then Chicago, Nan went to New York for secretarial training and to find work. She wrote to Harding in 1917, asking if he remembered her and if he could help her in finding a job. Senator Harding responded immediately and came to New York from Washington to visit with her, taking a room at the Manhattan Hotel. Talk of job opportunities soon faded into desirous kisses. Harding tucked $30 into one of Britton's brand-new silk stockings just before they left for a taxi ride downtown, where he used his influence to obtain employment for her at the U.S. Steel Corporation office.

In the weeks and months ahead Harding and Britton had several trysts in Indianapolis, Chicago, and other places where the senator had speaking engagements. They exchanged passionate love letters frequently. The secret affair flourished during the following years, and Harding generously gave Britton gifts and money. The two traveled to and from New York and Washington, where in 1919 they conceived a child, either on the old couch or the carpeted floor of his Senate office. Harding, who thought he was sterile and never had children by his wife Florence, secretly took responsibility after Nan gave birth to a baby girl named Elizabeth Ann and continued to send money for her and the child's support.

At the Republican national convention in Chicago in 1920, where Harding was chosen as the party's presidential candidate, he carried on his covert meetings with Nan, urging her to have their child adopted by her married sister in Chicago. However, Nan kept the child; Harding was elected president; their trysts and correspondence went on with the latter using U.S. Secret Service agents to send notes and to hustle Nan in and out of the White House without detection. Their favorite trysting spot was an oversize coat closet off the presidential office. Mrs. Harding undoubtedly knew of the liaison, keeping quiet for political reasons and so as not to feed the increasing gossip. Harding's sudden death on August 2, 1923, caught his mistress by surprise, and in time, no longer receiving his generous sums, she was desperately in need of money. She supposedly attempted in vain to secure $50,000 for her young daughter's share of the Harding estate, following the death of Mrs. Harding in November, 1924.

Finally, in 1927, Nan Britton wrote *The President's Daughter*, in collaboration with an unscrupulous detective named Gaston Bullock Means, who later claimed that Mrs. Harding had hired him to investigate her husband's affair. At first, book reviewers looked askance at Britton's memoirs about the hidden affair and Harding's fathering of an illegitimate child, but when the fiery journalist H. L. Mencken reviewed it in the *Baltimore Sun*, the book took off and made a lot of money for her. Most people have since accepted her story as essentially true.

HARDING-PHILLIPS AFFAIR

A cynical student of American history might describe the "normalcy" promised the country during Warren G. Harding's presidential campaign and practiced during his incomplete term of office as a return to the corruption of President Ulysses S. Grant's administration, for both presidents are considered to have been basically honest men surrounded by scoundrels. But Harding's fiscal blamelessness is severely marred by his compulsive sensuality: he was guilty of two extended and partly simultaneous adulteries, the first with Carrie Phillips and the second with Nan BRITTON.

The Harding-Phillips affair began in 1905 and for several years was the best-kept secret in Marion, Ohio, where Carrie's husband owned a department store and Harding's wife Florence (Flossie) tried to rule her husband's life. The townsfolk knew of the affair very quickly: Harding's frequent daytime visits to the Phillips house and the rapid appearance of freshly laundered sheets on the clothesline were ostensibly carefully catalogued. But the Marionites apparently gossiped only among themselves; Flossie did not begin to catch on to her husband's infidelity until after 1914, and Carrie's husband found out (or was told by his wife) only after the 1920 termination of the liaison. In consequence, the Hardings and Phillipses traveled to Europe and Bermuda together, and the Harding-Phillips affair developed an international locale under the nonseeing eyes of the couple's partners.

The affair is still in part a secret because of court actions by Harding descendants in the 1960s over letters from Harding to Carrie, which she carefully preserved. In 1963, 250 letters were found, some over 40 pages long. (Carrie's part of the correspondence was presumably burned, either by Harding or by Flossie, who kept a fireplace going at white heat while she destroyed "papers" at the time of Harding's mysteriously sudden death in 1923.) All of Harding's letters have been read by Francis Russell, one of Harding's most thorough biographers, but under the terms of a court decision, their wording cannot be revealed until A.D. 2014.

The letters' factual content, however, has been extracted by Russell. Since we cannot judge the emotional content of the letters, we must take Russell's word that the affair was "the love of Harding's life."

The factual content of the letters is easily described. Harding and Jim Phillips had been friends for years before the latter's 1901 marriage to Carrie Fulton, a tall, strawberry blonde who had wed him not for love, but to escape the drudgery of painfully underpaid schoolmarming. The Phillipses had become a family of five by 1905, when Harding began to practice his highly developed method of ministration to a grief-stricken Carrie, whose son had died in 1904. Both Flossie Harding and Jim Phillips were then in hospitals; and Harding, who had promised to comfort Carrie, began to discover, according to Russell, depths of sensuality he had not known he possessed.

The affair continued at a strenuous pace until 1911, when Carrie, angry that Harding would not divorce Flossie (who had continued to ail) to marry her, took her daughter to Germany. Harding continued to write her what Russell calls "tumescent" letters, even after he had become a U.S. senator and was beginning his equally athletic affair with Nan Britton. Carrie continued to hector Harding about divorce without success; with equal failure, she tried to keep him from allowing an anti-German sentiment to affect his votes in the Senate.

She returned to America in 1914 and, because of Flossie's awareness (which made life hell for Harding), the competition of Nan Britton, and the difficulty the lovers had in finding privacy, the affair began to disintegrate. Carrie still pressed Harding for divorce and for a pro-German (or neutral) vote in the Senate, but she got neither. Instead, she gained the antagonism of Flossie, who would appear on the famous Harding front porch to shake a menacing feather duster (and on one occasion a piano stool) at a waving and retreating Carrie. Flossie would also mysteriously shake a fist from the speaker's platform at somebody in the audience listening to Harding's campaign speeches.

By 1920, when Harding received the Republican presidential nomination, the affair was physically close to moribund, but the party's National Committee sent Albert Lasker, the advertising mogul, to Marion to offer Carrie and Jim $20,000 and monthly expenses to travel outside the country for as long as Harding held public office. They went, to return after Harding's death in 1923.

The affair was over. Harding's feelings will be known in 2014. Carrie's will never be precisely known, not even those in response to attacks on her as a "common prostitute" in 1922 by the same man who had questioned Harding's racial ancestry, for she died penniless and senile in 1960. (The 1922 attack was the first time Carrie Phillips's name had been linked in print with Harding's.) Nor can Jim Phillips comment: he died of tuberculosis in 1939, speechless and without leaving memoirs.

Billy James HARGIS: bisexual evangelist

Anthropologists and other analysts of human behavior have often cited relationships between various religious doctrines and sexual excess; novelists, among them Sinclair Lewis and John Steinbeck, have dramatized the close connection between evangelical fervor and erotic ardency. But neither academic exposition nor literary art is as convincing to the American public as the direct discovery that a moral idol, like most of us, has clay feet.

The feet of Billy James Hargis (1925–), who became one of America's most formidable conservative evangelists, were discovered to be composed of the coarsest clay in 1974, but the exact composition of the argil was not revealed until 1976, when Hargis denounced the exposure of his delinquency as a libelous part of a "liberal plot."

Those who view the world ironically gave credence to the 1976 reports of Hargis's delinquency published by the *New York Times* and *Time* magazine. Those convinced of the reality of "liberal subversion" of American values took refuge in the belief, as one clerical commentator put it, that the media were being used "by the forces of Satan to silence the voice of anti-Communism."

After attending a public high school, Hargis studied at an unaccredited Bible college and gained degrees from a "degree mill." Then, by force of his powerful personality and remarkable rhetorical skill, he became one of the Southwest's most vocal opponents of sexual sin and what he regarded as the growing laxness of American society. Married and the father of four, he gained fame in the pulpit and through radio and television. He established the Christian Crusade, a bible-based onslaught on modernity, centered in Tulsa, Oklahoma. When Hargis's crusade became a political force, the Internal Revenue Service revoked, in 1964, its tax-exempt status. In response, Hargis formed the Church of the Christian Crusade and American Christian College and continued his Biblical-political campaigns with a new tax-exempt status, receiving millions of dollars in support of his policies.

In 1974, however, Hargis suddenly resigned from his college's presidency, claiming that two small strokes and a heart problem had forced him to reduce his activities. He had told only a partial truth: in that year, the college's trustees had learned, through a confession to its vice president, the Reverend David Noebel, that a male student had been entertained sexually by Hargis. Confronted, Hargis had confessed his misdeeds to Noebel and blamed "genes and chromosomes." Hargis then resigned his presidency on October 25, 1974.

In less than a year, however, Hargis was back demanding reinstatement to the college presidency. The trustees had meanwhile learned of a heterosexual encounter and, through three other male students, of Hargis's homosexual procedures: he seduced by citing Old Testament stories of David and Jonathan and protected himself by threatening to blacklist the students to whom he had made overtures if they talked. The trustees fought back and gained title to the college from Hargis, who punished them by reducing contributions to the college from the Church of the Christian Crusade and his media offerings. He also withdrew his confession and promulgated the "liberal plot" story to preserve his generous following.

The revelations of the sin of Billy James Hargis did little to diminish his loyal sectaries, but his remodeling of the ancient clay feet as an image for human weakness into "genes and chromosomes" provoked a letter-writer to *Time* to comment that it was "refreshing to learn that Marx and Satan aren't responsible for everything that goes wrong."

HARLOW-BERN SCANDAL

On the night of September 4, 1932, prominent MGM movie executive Paul Bern fatally shot himself through the head with a .38-caliber pistol in the bedroom of his famous actress wife of two months, Jean Harlow. Bern's nude body was found lying in front of his wife's full-length bathroom mirror. Beside it was a handwritten note that read, "Dearest Dear, Unfortunately this is the only way to make good the frightful wrong I have done you and to wipe out my abject humiliation. I love you. Paul. You understand that last night was only a comedy." MGM had to play down the note's implications. Harlow remained silent, and the couple's story was not known until after her tragic death five years later. Her agent, Arthur Landau, then gave out the details.

A prominent Hollywood sex symbol, Harlow was loved by moviegoers for her resplendent, platinum blonde hair and her wisecracking brand of comedy. In 1932, the 21-year-old star could probably have married any of Hollywood's great leading men. Oddly, she became interested in Paul Bern, a physically unprepossessing intellectual who was twice her age. Bern had worked his way up from scriptwriter to producer and director in the film industry, eventually becoming MGM chief Irving Thalberg's top assistant. Because he often listened compassionately to other people's problems, Bern had gotten the moniker "Father Confessor." He must have seemed an attractive, fatherlike figure to Harlow, whom Bern listened to thoughtfully and treated without condescension. The two fell in love and married quietly on July 2, 1932. Hollywood said the match was a good business arrangement that would undoubtedly help Harlow's rise in stardom.

Years later, it was revealed that their wedding night had been a total disaster. The happy couple had gone to their Beverly Hills home and proceeded to get merrily drunk together. Later that night, Arthur Landau had received a phone call from the new bride, who tearfully asked him to come over and take her away. Landau brought Harlow back to his house, where she confided the details of her experience with Bern to Landau and his wife.

Bern, apparently had become very elusive at one point, finally confiding to Harlow that he could not consummate their marriage and begging pathetically for understanding. Humiliated, he then began to rail at his young bride, furiously throwing her to the floor and beating her over and over with a cane, inflicting long bruises from her hips to her shoulders. He also bit her inner thighs and legs, drawing blood in the process. Harlow spent the rest of the night at the Landaus. The following morning, Landau had gone to Bern and found him nude and crying about his inability to get an erection and his impotency (his penis and testicles were apparently decidedly underdeveloped). Bern agonized over his uselessness and shattered self-worth. MGM executives were aghast when they learned about the incident; they maintained that the couple must keep up a good public appearance for the sake of Harlow's career in order to avoid any scandal. Perhaps after six months a quiet divorce could be arranged.

For the next two months Bern and Harlow lived together, with Harlow usually locked in her bedroom. One night, however, Bern strode into the room, wearing a huge leather dildo strapped to his body. Wild laughter burst from both of them as he pranced about, but the utter hopelessness of their love soon came back after Bern's alleged attempt to effect intercourse with the phony phallus. Bern then tore it from his body, cut it up into pieces, and flushed it down the toilet.

Two days afterward, the butler discovered Bern's naked dead body, drenched in Harlow's favorite perfume, facing down before the bathroom mirror. The actress was away at the time at her mother's, having left after a fight with her disturbed husband. MGM protected the grief-stricken Harlow, while the press had a field day speculating about the cryptic suicide note.

Three days after Bern's death, Dorothy Millette, an aspiring blonde actress, was found dead in the Sacramento River. Bern's secret common-law wife for over a decade, she had recently recovered from a long bout of "incurable amnesia" at a Connecticut sanitarium and had planned to take up life again with Bern before drowning herself in the river.

During the next five years, America's reigning sex symbol lost herself first in drunken sexual escapades (which MGM managed to keep out of the newspapers) and then in a grueling film-making schedule. The public and critics loved her and flocked to her movies. *Dinner At Eight* (1933) and *China Seas* (1935) were both huge successes. In 1937 Harlow, then engaged to actor William Powell, suddenly collapsed in exhaustion from overwork. She was already sickly from a recent gall bladder attack that had weakened her kidneys, which had been damaged during Bern's wedding-night beating of her. Resting under her mother's care, she quickly grew weaker and more pain-ridden. Her mother, a Christian Scientist, didn't allow her medical treatment until it was too late. On June 7, 1937, Harlow, at the age of 26, died an untimely death from uremic poisoning.

HARRIS-TARNOWER AFFAIR

On March 10, 1980, Dr. Herman Tarnower, the prominent, wealthy, 69-year-old cardiologist and originator of the popular "Scarsdale Diet," was shot and killed in the bedroom of his lavish home in Purchase, New York. About to drive away from the house was 56-year-old Jean S. Harris, whom local police picked up after they were called by Tarnower's maid, who heard the loud disturbance. The story of the long Harris-Tarnower love affair was soon unfolded by the press to a public that was held spellbound by revelations of the aging doctor's sexual promiscuity and long intimacy with Harris.

Jean Harris, charged with fatally shooting "Scarsdale Diet" doctor Herman Tarnower, carries materials from Westchester County Courthouse in White Plains, New York, in mid-February 1981. Intimate sexual details of her long liaison with Tarnower were revealed at her trial, which at times resembled a soap opera. (AP/Wide World Photos)

A cultured woman, Harris was the highly respected headmistress of the Madeira School, a prestigious private girls' school in Virginia. She had been Tarnower's companion and lover for 14 years before the fatal shooting and had assisted the bespectacled doctor in the writing of his best-selling book, *The Complete Scarsale Medical Diet,* whose sales had soon earned him millions of dollars and made him famous (Tarnower maintained that one could lose from 14 to 20 pounds in weight in two weeks). "Integrity Harris," as she was called by her students, spent many weekends and vacations with the doctor. Despite the fact that he had carried on affairs with some 30 other women since their relationship began, Harris fell deeply in love with the doctor. At one point he had proposed marriage to her, raising her hopes high, but later he called off the wedding.

Tarnower had hired Mrs. Lynne Tryforos to be his new administrative assistant. This attractive, younger woman also carried on a sex relationship with him, causing Harris to become increasingly fearful of her imagined impending rejection. She even thought of making herself young again through plastic surgery to win back the affection of the doctor. Only days before Tarnower's death, the matronly headmistress had written a long letter to him, bitterly calling Tryforos a "dishonest adultress . . . a slut and a psychotic whore," and saying that his life should be free of anything second-rate. The letter, however, never got to Tarnower. Harris, hoping to spend the weekend with him, had driven from Virginia to Tarnower's New York home and had gotten into a violent argument with him in the bedroom after finding a nightgown and hair curlers belonging to someone else. A struggle had ensued, during which she pulled out a .32-caliber revolver, while he began to shove her, saying, "Get out of here, you're crazy." Shots were fired, and Tarnower lay unconscious on the floor, bleeding profusely from three bullet wounds. About an hour later, he was declared dead in a nearby hospital. Meanwhile, Harris was taken into police custody where she handed over the gun. Charged with the slaying, she was released on bail and, about two weeks later, pleaded not guilty to a three-count indictment against her for intended murder. She claimed that she had gone to the doctor with the intention of having him kill her, for she had grown very distraught by his affair with Tryforos, whom he had planned to take to a dinner in his honor.

In a widely publicized, three-month-long trial in White Plains, New York, a 12-member jury (eight women and four men) heard much about the rich lifestyle and various girlfriends of Tarnower, whose female lovers seemed to leave their dresses, underwear, and cosmetics habitually in his house. At one point in the proceedings, Harris's own underwear was shown to the court, to her obvious embarrassment. Harris's defense claimed that the slaying had been strictly an accident, and she attempted to show this during her testimony.

Many women sympathized with Harris's plight, feeling she had been used and wronged by the doctor. They felt he had gotten what he deserved for "victimizing" her. The prosecution firmly asserted that jealousy over Tryforos had motivated Harris to deliberately kill Tarnower and debunked her assertion that she had only wanted to kill herself and that the doctor had been mortally wounded trying to save her. Finally, on February 24, 1981, after eight days of deliberation, the jury declared Harris guilty of second-degree murder. Harris was irate. "I can't sit in jail," she told her lawyer. And once behind bars, she exclaimed that she would not be kept like an animal in a cage and began a partial hunger strike. On March 20, 1981, a Westchester county judge sentenced her to 15 years in prison, the minimum period allowed under New York State law, stating that he wished "the events of March 10 had never taken place and that you'd never left Virginia."

Harris was incarcerated in New York's Bedford Hills Correctional Facility, where she became known for her educational efforts on behalf of the other inmates. She also suffered from medical problems while being a grade-A prisoner. New York's Governor Mario Cuomo eventually accepted her fourth appeal for clemency (December 29, 1992), just hours before she successfully underwent quadruple bypass heart surgery. In January 1993, a state Board of Parole panel unanimously granted her parole, and the 69-year-old Harris was then released after serving 12 years.

Gary HART: politics, power, passion, and the press

At a press conference at Dartmouth College on May 6, 1987, Gary W. Hart confronted what was undoubtedly the most hostile questioning of his noted political career. "Do you think adultery is immoral?" someone asked. "Yes," Hart replied. "Have you ever committed adultery?" was next asked. "I don't have to answer that question," Hart said. Just a few days earlier, he had been the leading Democratic contender for the 1988 presidential nomination. Despite his reputation as a womanizer, Hart's future looked bright. But when the *Miami Herald* published a story about how he had entertained an attractive, 29-year-old actress and model overnight at his townhouse in Washington, D.C., people were scandalized. Although both Hart and the woman, Donna Rice, vehemently denied the story, it was quickly picked up and spread nationwide by other news organizations.

After the story broke, serious questions were raised about Hart's judgment and fitness to occupy the nation's highest office. His relationships with women other than his wife became the overshadowing issue of his presidential campaign. Ever since his announced candidacy for the Democratic nomination on April 13, 1987, the 50-year-old Hart, a lawyer and former U.S. senator from Colorado, had been battling various rumors about

his personal life and questions about his $1.3-million political campaign debt left over from 1984. But it was this final scandal that ruined his attempt to gain the party nomination.

Hart wasn't the only one to come under fierce attack. As a result of its apparent snooping and scandalmongering, the press was reprimanded. Journalists and executives at the *Miami Herald* vigorously supported and defended the information they had reported regarding Hart and Rice. Still, some top news experts around the country sharply criticized the *Herald* and other newspapers for indulging in sensationalism and yellow journalism. Especially criticized was the secret stakeout of Hart's Washington townhouse by some *Herald* reporters, who reported the visit of Miss Rice (who had flown up from Miami, Florida). Critics pointed out an admitted gap in the *Herald*'s surveillance of the comings and goings of the two during May 1 and 2. Knowledge of Hart's troubled 28-year marriage to his wife Lee, coupled with persistent rumors of his infidelity and womanizing, fueled some of the press's beliefs that adultery had taken place. Whether it actually took place or not, the appearance of infidelity probably cost Hart his chance to be president

Adding fuel to Hart's supposed affair with Rice was the fact that they had sailed together aboard the yacht *Monkey Business* in March with another married man and a single woman to inspect another yacht that was being repaired in Bimini, in the Bahamas. Hart and Rice had stayed in Bimini overnight, although on separate boats, according to Hart. All said there had been no wrongdoing of any kind.

After the Dartmouth news conference, Hart received a second jolt when the *Washington Post* presented evidence that he had had another extramarital relationship. Crippled by continuous questioning about his private life, he left the campaign trail in New Hampshire to return to his home in Kittredge, Colorado. About a day later, on May 8, he announced his withdrawal from the presidential race, stunning both supporters and detractors. With his wife by his side, Hart announced his decision at a press conference in Denver. He explained that the political system and the press had forced a sudden end to his White House hopes. He admitted that he had made "big mistakes, but not bad mistakes," and said that the news organizations had run amok. "We are all going to have to seriously question the system for selecting our national leaders that reduces the press of this nation to hunters and presidential candidates to being hunted, that has reporters in bushes, false and inaccurate stories printed, photographers peeking in our windows, swarms of helicopters hovering over our roof, and my very strong wife close to tears because she can't even get in her own house at night without being harassed." Hart made no mention of any philanderings or of any of the numerous public discussions that centered on his personal behavior and suitability for the duties of the presidency.

Many Democratic politicians upbraided Hart following the incident. Said U.S. Representative Barbara B. Kennelly of Connecticut, "He really thought he was above the general rules of the game." And amid much heated criticism of the *Herald,* its publisher, Richard G. Capen, defended the "essential correctness of our story" and declared that "clearly, at a minimum, there was an appearance of impropriety." Americans had to admit there was a possible link between an individual's potential for handling the responsibilities of the nation's top office and his private conduct. Said James David Barber of Duke University, author of books on presidential character, "We have got to look at the personalities of these people. Think of the past presidents. It turned out after the fact that what we . . . should have been looking at was their characters."

On December 15, 1987, Hart made the startling announcement that he was back in the race for the Democratic presidential nomination. He returned to the race with his wife, Lee, at his side. There was no mention of Rice but only of the fact that Hart and his family understood clearly the difficulties that lay ahead. Many said his reconstituted candidacy would bog down over questions about his relationship with Rice. In an emotional interview on January 10, 1988, Hart said that if he was elected, he wouldn't "be the first adulterer in the White House."

Questions about Rice and his character and judgment dogged Hart, who received fewer and fewer votes in the 1988 state caucuses and primaries, until finally he decided to end his frustrated presidential campaign. His eyes teared slightly as he told news reporters in Denver on March 11, 1988: "I got a fair hearing. And the people have decided. And now, I clearly should not go forward."

About a year later, Rice, who said, "Everybody's got some old bones in their closet, and now mine are out," became a TV news reporter and an antipornography activist in the 1990s (as well as a married woman—Donna Rice Hughes). Hart became a lawyer specializing in international law and traveled several times to Cuba. He also wrote two novels, *Sins of the Fathers* and *I, Che,* under the pseudonym John Blackthorn in the late 1990s.

Alcee HASTINGS. See WALTER NIXON: perjury on the federal bench.

Rutherford B. HAYES. See Joseph P. BRADLEY: the stolen election of 1876.

Wayne HAYS: a grievous dalliance
The unexpected marriage of U.S. Representative Wayne L. Hays (Dem., Ohio), a veteran and influential member of the House for nearly 28 years, to the faithful director of his Ohio office, Pat Peak, undoubtedly infuriated beautiful, blonde Elizabeth Ray, a staff aide for the House Administration Committee, of which Hays was the chairman. About five weeks later, in mid-May 1976, Ray, a former stewardess and starlet, decided to reveal her alleged affair with Hays to the *Washington Post,* which had been publishing a series of exclusive reports about the sexual practices of certain members of Congress since the beginning of that year. Two *Post* reporters snooped into private talks between Hays and Ray. Her scandalous tale of being the congressman's secret mistress at government expense was first published in the *Post* on May 23, 1976.

According to Ray, after being hired by Hays, she had done very little actual office work for her $14,000-a-year salary. She said that she could not type or file or adequately answer the telephone and that she seldom went to her private office. However, about twice weekly, Hays had allegedly invited her out for dinner dates, picking her up around 7:00 P.M., enjoying a light meal with her, and afterward making love to her in her Arlington, Virginia, apartment. Hays would leave home by 9:30 P.M. His new wife was apparently unaware of the dalliances.

These revelations caused considerable commotion in Washington, D.C., where abuses of congressional staffing and payroll were known but generally kept quiet. The U.S. Justice Department began an investigation into the charges by Ray against Hays, who denied that he had maintained the "blonde bombshell" as his mistress and said, "I'm a happily married man." However, on May 25, 1976, the scandal-beleaguered congressman made an emotional speech before the House of Representatives, acknowledging that he had had a "personal relationship" with Ray and "had committed a grievous error in not presenting the facts." Standing by his denial that she had been hired to be his mistress, Hays exclaimed, "Only time will tell whether Miss Ray has been successful in destroying my career. I pray to God she will not have destroyed my marriage." The following day, Hays alleged that Ray had extorted more than $1,000 from him in the preceding five weeks under the threat of revealing the details of their relationship.

Hays was now viewed by much of the public as an old scoundrel with a roving eye, and by the end of May several fellow colleagues in the House had initiated a drive to strip him of his four House committee chairmanships. The widely publicized allegations of his improper and illegal conduct began to wear on him, causing him to agree to give up the chairmanship of the Democratic National Congressional Committee. After suffering a coma from taking an overdose of sleeping pills on June 10, 1976, Hays gave up the chairmanship of the House Administrative Committee. In August he announced that he would not seek reelection to the House that year. When the House Ethics Committee voted unanimously to hold public hearings into the Hays-Ray affair, the Ohio congressman resigned on September 1, 1976. Ray managed to make some money from the notoriety she had enjoyed but soon became forgotten among the numerous playgirls who scandalized Capitol Hill. She had, however, cost Hays his career and power in Congress.

The House Ethics Committee ended its investigation on grounds that Hays was no longer a congressman; the Justice Department decided not to prosecute on grounds it lacked evidence corroborating the account of Ray and her relationship with Hays. Returning to Ohio, Hays later died of an apparent heart attack at his home in Belmont, at age 77, in 1989.

"Big Bill" HAYWOOD: roughneck labor leader

In the summer of 1905, William ("Big Bill") Haywood, a massive, one-eyed labor organizer, took part in the creation of a revolutionary organization that was to become a legend in American labor history: the Industrial Workers of the World (IWW) (or Wobblies, as they came to be known). Haywood, a former metal miner, cowboy, and homesteader and at the time secretary-treasurer of the Western Federation of Miners (WFM), had long dreamed of one giant union that would encompass all industries, a militant alternative to the American Federation of Labor, which he considered too conservative. Addressing his fellow workers, Haywood declared that the IWW would have as its purpose "the emancipation of the working class from the slave bondage of capitalism." Many felt, however, that Haywood went too far in his efforts to free the working class from oppression. Americans were scandalized first by his implication in a union-related assassination and then by his conviction for attempting to sabotage the war effort.

On December 30, 1905, Frank Steunenberg, a former governor of Idaho who had helped brutally crush a miners union in 1899, was murdered by a man named Harry Orchard, who had some connections with the Western Federation of Miners. Idaho officials were convinced that the union was behind the assassination. Investigators extracted a confession from Orchard, claiming that he had been hired by Haywood and three other WFM members to kill Steunenberg. Because Haywood was then in Colorado and could not legally be extradited to Idaho, Idaho officials had him abducted in order to arrest him on a charge of conspiracy to murder. The U.S. Supreme Court, while acknowledging that Haywood's arrest had been illegal, allowed the state to continue its prosecution of him.

Haywood maintained his innocence at the time of the trial and throughout his life. But while he gained support from such labor leaders as Samuel Gompers and Eugene Debs, President Theodore Roosevelt proclaimed him an "undesirable citizen." In the murder trial, Haywood's defense attorney, the well-known Clarence Darrow, argued persuasively that the state's case rested solely on the testimony of Orchard, an admitted murderer and liar who hoped to gain leniency for implicating the others in the murder plot. After only one day of deliberation, the jury found Haywood not guilty. But Orchard continued to maintain that his confession was true. Historians are still divided on Haywood's guilt or innocence.

The trial brought Haywood national notoriety, which his subsequent activities only enhanced. He led major strikes among textile-mill workers in Lawrence, Massachusetts, in 1912 and among silk-mill workers in Paterson, New Jersey, in 1913. He was arrested many times, on charges ranging from disorderly conduct to inciting assault on a police force. Yet it was his opposition to war—which he considered to be capitalists' battles fought by workingmen—that proved to be his downfall. After the United States entered World War I, the IWW became a vulnerable target for its enemies. In 1917, the government raided the union's offices throughout the country and arrested hundreds of IWW members, including Bill Haywood, charging them with conspiracy to sabotage the war effort through strikes and other means and conspiracy to hinder registration for the draft.

In his opening statement at the conspiracy trial, the government's chief prosecutor characterized Haywood as the IWW's "evil genius," its "uncrowned king in a swivel chair . . . [who] gives his orders with unlimited power to the dupes and members of the organization."

Haywood testified that although the IWW had printed and circulated antiwar materials before the United States had entered the war, it had ceased to do so after war was declared. He claimed that the IWW was conspiring not against America's war efforts, but against exploitation. This time, however, his arguments were not persuasive. In August 1918, he was convicted and sentenced to serve 20 years in the federal penitentiary at Leavenworth, Kansas, and to pay a fine of $20,000.

Released on bail while his case was under appeal, Haywood was arrested again during the postwar period of impassioned anticommunism on charges of "criminal syndicalism" (the advocating of violent methods of achieving industrial or political reform) and conspiracy to overthrow the government.

Again free on bail but dispirited, Haywood began to decline in health from ulcers and diabetes. Facing the prospect of spending the rest of his life in prison, he accepted a Russian offer of asylum and, using a false passport, fled to the Soviet Union in 1921. His escape was a blow to the already weakened IWW, which never recovered its earlier strength, and to the friends who had posted Haywood's bond.

Haywood was welcomed as a hero in the Soviet Union, where he met privately with Lenin himself, but he soon became disillusioned with the realities of the "workers' paradise." He died in Moscow on March 16, 1928.

Patty HEARST: kidnap victim or terrorist?

On the evening of February 4, 1974, Patricia ("Patty") Campbell Hearst, the granddaughter of newspaper publishing tycoon William Randolph Hearst, was dragged screaming from her Berkeley, California, apartment by members of a radical revolutionary group calling itself the Symbionese Liberation Army (SLA). Seven weeks after her widely publicized kidnapping, Patty announced that she had joined the SLA's ranks. Following her identification as a gun-toting participant in a San Francisco bank robbery on April 15, 1974, she became the object of one of the largest FBI manhunts in American history; 19 months later, she was captured. Whether she had willingly joined her abductors or was brainwashed into their philosophy became the major issue at her trial.

At the time of the kidnapping, Patty Hearst had indicated no particular interest in politics. The SLA proclaimed that it had abducted the 19-year-old heiress to part of the Hearst fortune because the powerful Hearst family was a "corporate enemy of the people." In a series of tape recordings sent by the SLA, the group demanded that free food be distributed to the poor people in California and that legal aid be provided for two SLA members in prison for murder; Patty's release would then take place. Her multimillionaire father, Randolph A. Hearst, publisher of the *San Francisco Examiner* and owner of the rest of the Hearst Corporation, acquiesced to the SLA demands to raise some $6 million for free food for the poor. Nonetheless, the SLA accused Mr. Hearst of "deceit and dishonesty" in negotiating for his daughter's release. Patty herself accused her parents of not doing enough to bring it about.

Following this, public opinion began to turn against the Hearst family, moreso following Patty's announcement in a taped message to a Berkeley radio station (April 3, 1974) that she had joined the SLA. Two weeks later she was shown in photos taken by automatic bank-surveillance cameras taking part in the holdup of the San Francisco bank. Authorities speculated that she might have been held at gunpoint during the robbery. However Patty later sent a message to the San Francisco police department declaring that the weapon she had held in the bank robbery was loaded and that she was prepared to fire it. She called herself "Tania" now. Throughout 1974, the SLA was able to play with public opinion to its advantage by releasing a number of highly publicized tape recordings of Patty speaking. Because of these messages and her acts, many persons, including her former fiancé Steven Weed (with whom she had shared her Berkeley apartment), believed that Patty had indeed turned terrorist willingly.

While a federal grand jury was investigating Patty's participation in the robbery, SLA members William and Emily Harris, accompanied by Patty, were involved in a shootout with police after a shoplifting incident at a sporting-goods store. The Federal Bureau of Investigation (FBI) then classified Patty as an "armed and dangerous fugitive," filed felony charges against her in Los Angeles County Court, and charged her with bank robbery.

The FBI trail to Patty grew cold until mid-1975, when fingerprints of her underground associates were discovered in a Pennsylvania farmhouse. Following this lead, authorities were able to locate and arrest Patty, the two Harrises, and Wendy Misako Yoshimura (who had been sought by the FBI for three years after being indicted as part of a bombing conspiracy) in a San Francisco hideout. Patty had changed greatly. Her once long blonde hair was now short and reddish, and she looked gaunt and pale. Photographed after her capture with a clenched-fist salute, she listed her occupation on the booking sheet as "urban guerrilla." By September 23, 1975, however, an affidavit reported to have been signed by Patty told a different story: physical mistreatment, confinement, terror, and the possible use of the drug LSD had caused her to take part in the 1974 bank robbery. She also changed her occupational status to "not employed."

During Patty Hearst's 39-day trial, which opened on February 4, 1976, her defense team, headed by famed lawyer F. Lee Bailey, argued that she had been a victim of "coercive persuasion." The defendant testified that she had been kept for 57 days in a closet, tied, blindfolded, and brainwashed to reject her parents' and society's values. She also claimed that she had been forced to have sex with SLA leader Donald DeFreeze and SLA member William Wolfe (both slain in a 1974 gun battle with Los Angeles police). She said she had been compelled at gunpoint to participate in the bank robbery. Furthermore, she claimed that she had become a fugitive out of fear that the SLA would kill her if she left them and later that the FBI would also shoot her.

The jury, her own defense counsel, and the public wrestled with many contradictions, including those between her affidavit and her incriminatory tape recordings. Her own testimony was damaging: using the Fifth Amendment, she refused 42 times to answer questions in front of the jury about her activities for one year following the robbery. In the end, the jury did not believe she had been an innocent victim who had been forced to commit crimes. On March 20, 1976, in federal court in San Francisco, the jury found Patty Hearst guilty of armed robbery and the use of firearms to commit a felony. She was sentenced to seven years in prison. Also charged with 11 counts of kidnapping, robbery, and assault (arising from the shoplifting incident), she pleaded no contest to the armed robbery and assault charges and cooperated with federal authorities in building a strong case against the Harrises in exchange for leniency in her case. She was given five years on probation and the other nine charges were dropped. She entered prison on May 15, 1976, no longer considered a threat to society. Meanwhile, her wealthy and celebrated parents had begun a campaign to free her. Their legal efforts failed to overturn her conviction but succeeded in gaining a commuted sentence. She was released from prison on February 1, 1979, five months before her eligibility for parole.

The entire scandalous ordeal took its toll on the Hearst family, emotionally and financially. Patty's parents divorced, and after her release from prison, she lived in fear of possible retaliation by terrorists. On April 1, 1979, she married Bernard Shaw, her bodyguard during the time she had been free on bond. Her sensational abduction became the subject of a television film, *The Ordeal of Patty Hearst,* and her autobiographical book, *Every Secret Thing,* explained what she had gone through. She said she was "not proud" of her past activities with the SLA and that she had overcome adversity. Speaking of her SLA history, Patty Hearst said that "That girl was someone else."

HEARST-INCE SCANDAL

The mysterious death of noted pioneer filmmaker Thomas Harper Ince in 1924 remains one of Hollywood's most enduring and intriguing scandals. Many still believe there was a concerted cover-up of the facts or a skillful manipulation of them, supposedly to protect the powerful multimillionaire newspaper magnate William Randolph Hearst.

In the early 1920s, Hearst had established Cosmopolitan Productions to promote the acting career of his pretty mistress Marion Davies, a former New York chorus girl. Though married and a father, Hearst was captivated by Davies. He put her through acting classes, gave her major roles in films, and set her up in style in a house in Santa Monica, California, where she frequently entertained Hollywood celebrities. The Hearst-Davies affair produced some scandalous gossip.

In November 1924, Hearst and Davies decided to use the former's luxurious 280-foot yacht *Oneida* as the site of a party to celebrate the 43rd birthday of their friend Ince, with whom Hearst was then trying to negotiate a deal to merge their separate movie studios. Fifteen distinguished guests, including Charlie CHAPLIN, Aileen Pringle, Margaret Livingston, Elinor Glyn, Louella Parsons, and Dr. Daniel Carson Goodman were invited aboard the *Oneida,* which set sail on November 15 on a three-day cruise from San Pedro south to San Diego and Baja, California. Ince, who had to attend the premier of his latest film, was delayed in joining the party until the yacht docked in San Diego. Once on board, Ince entered into the frolic but was unexpectedly removed from the boat on a stretcher the next morning with an apparently acute attack of indigestion. His sudden death brought conflicting newspaper headlines, including: MOVIE PRODUCER SHOT ON HEARST YACHT,

and SPECIAL CAR RUSHES STRICKEN MAN HOME FROM RANCH (the latter appeared in the Hearst papers, with a preposterous story about Ince falling ill while visiting Hearst at his ranch). Rumors of foul play quickly began to circulate, while Hearst and all the others aboard the *Oneida* remained reticent to discuss the matter. Their silence gave rise to much speculation. Was a rich man covering up a murder or even getting away with one? Ince had reportedly been seen with a bullet hole in his head when carried off the yacht. One news story alleged that Hearst had accidentally shot Ince in a jealous rage. The press lord supposedly found Chaplin and Davies together, and believing they were having an affair, went momentarily berserk after grabbing his diamond-studded revolver (with which he sometimes showed his skill as an expert marksman) and fired wildly among the guests who had come running upon hearing the commotion in the galley. According to the story, Ince had been fatally wounded.

San Diego's district attorney conducted an investigation after Ince's funeral (November 21), which Hearst did not attend, having slipped away to New York to let the rumors die down. Only one of the persons who had been aboard the *Oneida* testified during the investigation; Dr. Goodman, production chief of Cosmopolitan, evidently confirmed the finding of an unofficial inquest that acute indigestion had caused Ince to suffer fatal heart failure. The case was then closed by the district attorney but not to the satisfaction of many people.

When the scandal had died down, Hearst and Davies resumed their personal and business relations as closely as before. He soon discreetly provided Ince's widow with a trust fund, which was wiped out in the Great Depression. After Hearst's death in 1951, Davies tried to gain control of the Hearst empire, and even though she lost, received a large monetary settlement as compensation.

Leona HELMSLEY: convicted "Queen of Mean"

The 1980s was a decade of lavishness and unapologetic excess in America, and no one personified this excess better than Leona Helmsley. Born in 1920, she grew up amid modest surroundings in Brooklyn, New York, where her father owned a hat shop. In 1972 Leona, a divorced 52-year-old secretary, married her boss, New York billionaire Harry Brakmann Helmsley, whose real estate holdings included the Empire State Building. Leona was Harry's second wife.

In 1980 Harry appointed Leona president of Helmsley Hotels, his chain of 27 hotels. She immediately embarked upon a multimillion-dollar advertising campaign promoting the lavishness of the chain's properties, particularly the Helmsley Palace Hotel in New York City. Bedecked in finery and jewels, Leona appeared in nearly every ad, which proclaimed that the Helmsley Palace was "the only palace in the world where the Queen stands guard." To complement the ad campaign, the

Leona Helmsley, 70-year-old billionaire hotelier, who once sneered that only "little people pay taxes," leaves New York State Supreme Court in Manhattan on February 8, 1990, following a brief court appearance concerning charges of tax evasion. Later found guilty of tax fraud, the "Queen of Mean," as she was dubbed, was sentenced to four years in prison in March 1992. (AP/Wide World Photos)

Helmsleys became a highly visible part of the New York social scene by attending numerous charity events and throwing fancy parties. Throughout the decade, Leona shamelessly promoted herself as the queen of extravagant living.

But in 1989, the queen came under siege when the federal government charged her with 41 counts of tax evasion, extortion, and mail fraud. The government's case revolved around $3 million in renovations which the Helmsleys made to Dunnellen Hall, their $11 million mansion in Greenwich, Connecticut. These renovations included such things as a $1.1 million swimming pool enclosure, a $130,000 indoor-outdoor stereo system, and a $13,000 barbecue pit. To pay for the renovations, the Helmsleys charged them to their hotels in such a way that made them appear to be legitimate tax deductions. In addition, Leona charged her hotels almost $1 million to cover the purchases of personal items such as lingerie, leg waxing, and membership in a crossword club. In so doing, Harry and Leona—who in 1983 told her housekeeper "We don't pay taxes. The little people pay taxes"—avoided paying $1.7 million to the Internal Revenue Service.

During her trail the prosecution portrayed Leona not only as a tax cheat but also as "the queen of mean" for the imperious manner in which she treated employees and suppliers alike. Her financial adviser testified that she had fired a whole department of employees just before Christmas in 1985 because she thought they were stealing from her. Several of the contractors who had renovated Dunnellen Hall testified that she had refused to pay them; when told that the man who built the barbecue pit needed his money desperately because he had six children to feed, she replied, "He should have kept his pants on." Suppliers to the hotel chain testified that she had demanded cash, liquor, and televisions from them before placing an order, and she once refused to pay the Helmsley Palace's meat bill because a late-night corned beef sandwich had not been to her liking. When her only son died in 1982, she sued and won most of his estate, leaving his widow and four children with practically nothing.

Found guilty on 33 counts of tax fraud (she was acquitted of extortion and mail fraud), Leona was sentenced to four years in prison, fined $7.1 million, and ordered to pay her back taxes (nearly $2 million). After unsuccessfully appealing the verdict, she served 18 months in federal prison, a month in a halfway house, and two months under house arrest in her posh New York City hotel (April 15, 1992, to January 26, 1994), after which she completed 250 hours of community service in each of the next three years. In 1996 Leona and Harry (who had been declared mentally unfit to stand trial and died in 1997 at age 87) were sued for $100 million by Alvin Schwartz and Irving Schneider, Harry's lifetime partners in Helmsley-Spear, a property management company. The suit alleged that since 1993, when Leona took her ailing husband's place in the company, she had removed $40 million from the company's bank accounts in an effort to bankrupt the company, thus avoiding paying Schwartz and Schneider what they were owed.

Pee-Wee HERMAN: indecent public exposure

One of the most popular figures in children's entertainment during the 1980s was Pee-Wee Herman. In essence, Pee-Wee was a live caricature of a little boy trapped in a man's body. He stood over five feet tall and always wore a gray business suit and white dress shirt, but his red clip-on bow-tie, white patent leather shoes, and black crew cut made him look more like an eight-year-old than an adult. And his nasal whine, prancing antics, smart-aleck smirk, and goofy comebacks like "I know you are but what am I?" and "I meant to do that!" marked him as the quintessential snot-nosed brat. Although many adults did not know what to make of Pee-Wee, children of all ages loved him.

Pee-Wee Herman was the alter ego of Paul Reubens. Born Paul Reubenfeld in 1952 in Peekskill, New York, he grew up in Sarasota, Florida, the winter home of the Ringling Brothers and Barnum & Bailey Circus. In 1971 he changed his name to Reubens and moved to Hollywood to become an actor. After seven years of small parts in regional theater productions and several appearances as a stand-up comic, he created Pee-Wee

Herman, who quickly became a local comedic sensation. In 1981 Pee-Wee did his own Home Box Office TV special, and in 1984 he sold out Carnegie Hall. In 1985 he made his first hit movie, *Pee-Wee's Big Adventure*, during which he travels the United States from New York to Texas in search of his stolen bicycle. His other hit movie was *Big Top Pee-Wee* (1988), in which a big windstorm drops a circus into his yard.

But Pee-Wee's major claim to fame was as the host of *Pee-Wee's Playhouse*, a kids' television show that aired every Saturday morning on CBS from 1986 to 1991. In addition to Pee-Wee's own shenanigans, the show featured the silly antics of such characters as Chairy the talking chair, Globey the talking globe, and Pterry the talking pterodactyl. The show won a number of Emmy Awards for excellence in children's programming, and Pee-Wee won three Emmys for his acting.

Pee-Wee's career hit a snag in April 1991 when CBS canceled *Pee-Wee's Playhouse''* at the end of the regular season, although the network planned to show reruns until the new season began. It ended abruptly in July while Reubens was in Sarasota visiting his parents. On July 26, 1991, while watching a pornographic movie, *Nancy Nurse*, in a local adult theater, he unzipped his pants and began to masturbate. Unfortunately for Reubens, the Sarasota County vice squad had staked out the theater and arrested him for indecent exposure. He was fined $50 plus $85 in court costs, and the incident was stricken from his record after he produced a 30-second antidrug commercial for the county.

The reaction to Reubens's arrest was as frenzied as an episode of *Pee-Wee's Playhouse*. CBS immediately canceled the five remaining reruns, Disney World stopped showing a short clip featuring Pee-Wee, Pee-Wee's star was removed from Hollywood Boulevard, Pee-Wee dolls and merchandise were taken off the shelves of toy stores across the country, and late-night talk show hosts made Pee-Wee the butt of countless masturbation jokes. Reubens's career almost came to an end as well. For several years he could obtain no roles other than bit parts in movies that appealed mostly to teenagers. He eventually landed a supporting role on the popular television series *Murphy Brown,* and between 1996 and 1999 he had major roles in four movies. And although the character of Pee-Wee did not survive the scandal, in the late 1990s the Fox Family Network began showing reruns of *Pee-Wee's Playhouse*.

Marvin HEWITT: imposter academic

While a doctoral degree certainly stands as testimony to proficiency in a particular field, it is not necessarily a prerequisite. No one illustrates this truth more clearly than Marvin Hewitt, a high school dropout who not only posed as a Ph.D. in physics, but who also received praise for his work from brilliant scholars. Detected in 1954 after almost a decade of successful teaching under

his own name and four aliases, he was not dropped from his last post because he was unqualified but because he had misrepresented himself.

Born in 1922 to a Philadelphia police sergeant's family, Hewitt left high school at the age of 17 because he was bored. Apparently none of his teachers had glimpsed his potential, for none had attempted to engage his mind on a level higher than that of the average mind, to which public education seems chiefly to minister. Yet the potential was there. However, in the public library, Hewitt discovered the beauties of mathematics. He had the extraordinary self-discipline to master its processes to so high a degree of specialization that he was also able to master physics.

Hewitt wanted very much to teach but found that his lack of credentials prevented the use of his abilities. Creatively, though illegally, he forged certificates denoting himself a Temple University graduate and effectively taught eighth-grade arithmetic, history, and geography at a military school. He next posed as an aerodynamicist, gaining a job in an aircraft factory under the name of an academically trained man but quitting because he feared detection.

This fraudulent pattern continued when loose security methods enabled him to secure the transcript of Julius Ashkin, a Columbia University Ph.D. in physics. Hewitt then pursued brief teaching jobs at the Philadelphia College of Pharmacy and Science, at Bemidji (Minnesota) State Teachers' College, and at St. Louis University—brief because he feared discovery of his fraud. At the University of Utah, Ashkin requested that Hewitt stop the imposture but offered to help him, and the university's president proposed a job as a research assistant (and opportunities for Hewitt to earn his own credentials) or support in entering another institution for study. Despite these offers, Hewitt felt defeated and disconsolate and returned to Philadelphia shortly afterwards.

Later interviewed by Harlow Shapley, the world-renowned astronomer, and brilliant physicist J. Robert Oppenheimer, Hewitt was offered a place at Princeton's famous Institute of Advanced Studies. Haunted by fears of public exposure, he declined but then taught under his own name (but with forged credentials) in Arkansas. Subsequently, he taught under an alias at the New York State Maritime College and finally passed himself off as Kenneth P. Yates, Ph.D., at the University of New Hampshire, where his imposture was discovered in 1954 and made public. A brief notoriety finally gained Hewitt recognition, job offers, and inquiries about his publications from such eminent research organizations as the U.S. Atomic Energy Commission, the California Institute of Technology, and Britain's Admiralty Office.

Thoughtful Americans offered Hewitt commiseration and suggested reforms of both the school system which had let Hewitt slip so easily through its fingers and the security provisions of the academic credentials system, but these were not implemented. They may be dusted off when the next Marvin Hewitt again shows the weaknesses of our academic structures.

HICKEY PLOT

In June 1776, a secret committee of the Provincial Congress of New York learned from several sources that a conspiracy was developing among members of General George Washington's guard and the army. The conspiracy planned to commit treason and assassinate the general when the British fleet reached New York. Mayor David Matthews of New York was said to be supplying funds and provisions. Sargeant Thomas Hickey of the guard, who was at the time in jail, appeared to be the ring leader. If it had not been for the keen ears and patriotism of his fellow inmates, Hickey's plot might well have succeeded.

Thomas Hickey and a companion, Michael Lynch, both soldiers in the Continental Army, had been jailed for trafficking in counterfeit money. Fellow prisoners overheard them denouncing the Americans and boasting that many army units would defect as soon as the British fleet reached New York Harbor. Their plan was to destroy Kings Bridge at the northern tip of Manhattan Island, in order to prevent reinforcements from coming to the aid of the Americans, and to turn a battery manned by secret Tories against their former companions. A member of the guard would stab General Washington, and the British would soon triumph. The other prisoners also reported that Hickey and Lynch were trying to recruit inmates to join their perfidious plot.

This testimony before a special committee of the Provincial Congress was borne out by further reports by two witnesses, William Leary and James Mason, that the British were covertly enlisting men to serve on British fighting ships as soon as they sailed into the harbor. Until then, their wages were being paid by Mayor David Matthews and perhaps by colonial Governor William Tryon of New York as well. Several days later, an arrested suspect confessed to the existence of the plot and gave further details.

Mayor Matthews was taken into custody at his home and put in prison. The guards at Washington's headquarters were surrounded in a surprise move by the police and directed to lay down their arms. Eight guards had been implicated by Hickey, but only one, Drummer William Greene, who was to have been the assassin, confessed and threw himself on the mercy of the court. Such treasonous conduct by those close to the high command called for swift and drastic action.

On June 26, 1776, Thomas Hickey was brought before a military court. Leary, Greene, and other witnesses repeated their damaging testimony, to which Hickey could produce no rebuttal. The court unanimously agreed that Hickey be sentenced to death by hanging.

General Washington concurred, and on the morning of June 28, Hickey was hanged in front of a large crowd.

In regarding the outcome of the plot, Washington proclaimed, "I am hopeful this example will produce many salutary consequences and deter others from entering into like traitorous practices."

Alger HISS: traitor or scapegoat?

Before November 1948, Alger Hiss could have boasted of a long and distinctive career. He had served as temporary secretary-general of the United Nations, an adviser to President Franklin Roosevelt, and for the past year had been president of the Carnegie Endowment for International Peace. But in that month, Whittaker Chambers, a senior editor at *Time* magazine who styled himself a repentant communist spy and courier, testified before the HOUSE COMMITTEE ON UN-AMERICAN ACTIVITIES (HUAC) that the former top-ranking State Department adviser had held Communist Party membership from at least 1934 to 1938. Chambers also accused Hiss of having helped him pass secret government documents to the Soviets in 1937. Chambers offered no

Whittaker Chambers (lower right foreground) testifies before the House Un-American Activities Committee (HUAC) in Washington, D.C., on August 25, 1948. Alger Hiss (third from left in second row behind Chambers, smiling) preceded him on the stand to deny Chambers's assertion that Hiss had been a member of a Communist underground group in the 1930s. (AP/Wide World Photos)

proof of his assertions, and his allegations were allowed to stand untested. His accusations eventually landed Hiss in prison. But the truth of Chambers's claims, as well as the purity of motives of all involved, remain questionable.

When Chambers's remarks were publicly reported, Hiss learned of the accusations through the press. He immediately petitioned the HUAC for an opportunity to assert his innocence. Permission was granted, and Hiss, a trained lawyer, appeared early at an HUAC executive session hoping to confront his accuser, Chambers. The latter did not appear, but he and the HUAC later conferred, for a press release revealed that Chambers had repeated his charges.

Hiss then requested that Chambers restate the charges without the protection of immunity that had been granted him by the HUAC. When Chambers did so, Hiss sued Chambers for libel. Chambers, who now believed himself to be "the chosen instrument to save the common man," began to make available to the HUAC and to a federal grand jury in New York City quantities of evidence, including what he claimed to be copies of State Department papers he alleged had been typed on Hiss's personal typewriter. He also gave the investigators microfilm he said had been retrieved from a hollowed-out pumpkin on his farm, which contained photographs of other classified government papers allegedly delivered by Hiss to Chambers for the Russians.

Hiss's libel suit failed; instead, the federal grand jury indicted Hiss in 1948 on two counts of perjury, charging that he had lied in denying that he had given Chambers secret papers and in denying that he had seen Chambers after January 1, 1937. The grand-jury foreman asserted that Hiss would have been charged with espionage had not the statute of limitations prevented such a charge.

Two trials ensued, both given verbatim coverage in major American newspapers. The first ended in 1949 with a 12-member hung jury (eight for conviction against four for acquittal); the second trial ended in 1950 with a conviction. Hiss then served three years of a five-year prison sentence before his release in 1954. His fortune gone, he had insufficient funds to request an appeal so that new evidence might be heard in court to vindicate his alleged innocence.

To both sides in this controversy, victory was crucial for reasons having little to do with the guilt or innocence of Hiss or with the truthfulness or mendacity of Chambers. National and personal issues not directly involving the two combatants made both into symbols that gave (and still give) some credence to the opinion that the trial was deficient in fairness. In the eyes of some, Hiss had been made into a scapegoat on the order of France's Alfred Dreyfus, a French army captain and wealthy Alsatian Jew who at the turn of the century was wrongly convicted of treason and imprisoned but was finally exonerated.

Over 20 books have been devoted to the Chambers-Hiss controversy, which still remains unresolved. It is clear from all commentaries on the matter that a variety of motivations superseded whatever may have been Whittaker Chambers's original impulses for confessing to the HUAC and the Federal Bureau of Investigation (FBI). In 1948, the HUAC was in trouble: it had achieved little during its entire existence, its term of office was due for hostile reconsideration, and its chairman, Representative J. Parnell THOMAS, was himself under criminal indictment. The Republican-dominated Congress was also in trouble because it could not control inflation. At the time, the mood of the nation had turned apprehensively anticommunist. Moreover, isolationists and conservatives, convinced that President Harry Truman was a weak leader, were trying as they had in the past to reverse the effects of the New Deal. The American common man (symbolized by Chambers) was up in arms against the Establishment (symbolized by Hiss), and was seeking a militant leader. And a relative newcomer to the U.S. House of Representatives, Richard M. Nixon, was ready to play that role, fully expectant to benefit personally; as a member of the HUAC, Nixon won national attention for his vehement questioning of Hiss and his rejection of Hiss's calm claims of innocence.

Against this background of mixed and often extraneous motives, it is not difficult to understand why both sides in the Chambers-Hiss matter have charged that mistakes and incorrect emphases were made between 1948 and 1950. The list of charges in support of Hiss is long, but it definitely deserves partial expression here.

Chambers's testimony is suspect for many reasons. Some people imply that Chambers's long history of unreliability, his incipient dottiness (he died a well-guarded hermit in 1961), and his long list of aliases bear investigation. Others recommend that an investigation of Chambers's private papers, including his poetry, be made to test a psychiatric assertion that Chambers had a psychopathic personality. Still others wish an investigation to test whether Chambers was punishing Hiss for rejection of a sexual overture. Also, some people detail a contradiction between Chambers's evidence during the two trials and that found in his book *Witness*.

Chambers's deficiencies and contradictions are not the only charges made. Some assert that Richard Nixon's omissions of evidence from his book *Six Crises* indicate that his prejudgments skewed his handling of the HUAC testimony in the Chambers-Hiss case. Research has suggested that the alleged Hiss typewriter (on which the classified papers were supposedly copied) that was introduced as evidence in the case was a fake, and a group of researchers have created their own machine to prove that a fraudulent machine was a possibility. Additionally, some people have focused on the copies of photos and documents used in the case to prove that

Hiss never had access to them and to assert that Chambers had other sources.

In 1975, because of Hiss's "moral and intellectual fitness," the Massachusetts Supreme Court recommended unanimously that he be reinstated as a lawyer (the then-70-year-old Hiss, whose disbarment occurred in 1952, was at the time a printing salesman in New York City). With this, Hiss became the first disbarred lawyer in Massachusetts ever to be readmitted to the state's bar.

Hiss worked for his vindication until his death in 1996. He thought it had finally come in 1992 when a Russian general in charge of the Soviet intelligence archives announced that Hiss had never been a spy but rather a victim of communist-hunting under Senator Joseph MCCARTHY and cold war hysteria. However, Hiss defenders were discomfited when the general recanted and when the U.S. National Security Agency began releasing (in 1995) the so-called Venona coded cables that Soviet spies in the United States had used to report to Moscow. The decrypted Venona messages clearly indicate that Soviet espionage penetrated deeply into American life, government, industry, and science in the 1930s and 1940s. Hiss is apparently the Soviet agent known as "Ales" in the coded cables, though some of his liberal defenders disagree. Conservative supporters of Chambers still think justice was served by Hiss's 1950 conviction and subsequent incarceration at the federal prison in Lewisburg, Pennsylvania. The U.S. government's release of further information may eventually decide whether Hiss was a spy or was framed.

Jimmy HOFFA: ex-Teamsters boss disappeared

One of the most corrupt leaders of the American labor union movement, the powerful president of the International Brotherhood of Teamsters, Chauffeurs, Warehousemen and Helpers of America from 1957 to 1971, James ("Jimmy") Riddle Hoffa, was a close associate of many mobsters and underworld figures. Hoffa had many enemies, both within and outside the union, and for years during the 1950s and 1960s, law enforcement agencies tried to convict him on various charges. In the summer of 1975, Hoffa drove to meet some business colleagues for lunch at a suburban Detroit restaurant and was seen getting into a car with them in a parking lot. The 62-year-old Hoffa then vanished and has not been seen nor heard from since.

Jimmy Hoffa was a tough, street-wise young man in Detroit, Michigan, when he led—and won—his first workers' strike at the age of 18. After that, the labor union became his life, and he gradually worked his way up the union ladder until he was elected president of the Teamsters by an overwhelming majority in 1957. During the following decade he proved himself to be a master negotiator at the bargaining table, where he won wage increases and fringe benefits for his union's members. He also proved to be violent, vicious, and unscrupulous. He invested union pension funds in shaky real estate and gambling operations and bought insurance policies for the Teamsters from underworld friends. Racketeers controlled numerous unions, and Hoffa personally both lent from and borrowed from union funds for himself and his cronies.

This activity did not go unnoticed by the authorities. In 1957, the Senate Select Committee on Improper Activities in the Labor or Management Field, commonly known as the McClellan Committee for its chairman, Senator John L. McClellan (Dem. Ark.), began an intensive three-year investigation into union corruption. The Teamsters and Hoffa were its principal targets. Although the committee's counsel, Robert F. Kennedy, cross-examined Hoffa 18 times on the witness stand during the hearings, the Teamsters president usually claimed that he could not remember incidents or events about which he was questioned. Despite his bad memory, it soon became obvious to the committee members that Hoffa and his union chiefs were manipulating funds and Teamsters members for their own purposes and gains. Said one committee member: "In the history of this country it would be hard to find a labor leader who has so shamelessly abused his trust."

In addition to the misuse of union monies, the investigators uncovered strong evidence that Hoffa had close connections with the Detroit underworld, through which he was linked to mobsters in New York, Chicago, Ohio, Indiana, Nevada, and other places. It was also uncovered that certain labor unions had deliberately hired ex-felons and rehired those who had been convicted of crimes, and that Hoffa had knowingly tolerated criminal activities among his underlings and the mistreatment of those union members who complained of misdeeds. In its final report, the Senate committee stated that it was "convinced that if Hoffa is unchecked he will successfully destroy the decent labor movement in the United States. Further, because of the tremendous economic power of the Teamsters, it will place the underworld in a position to dominate American economic life."

But Hoffa was difficult to convict. A 1957 trial for wiretapping and illegal possession of documents belonging to the McClellan Committee ended with a hung jury. Another case, charging Hoffa with using the mails to defraud union members, was dropped. And when in 1964 Hoffa and several associates were found guilty of obtaining loans from the Teamsters' pension funds and of funneling about $1.7 million into their own pockets, the case was appealed. In 1964, however, Hoffa was again brought to trial for "demanding and receiving improper payments" from a company employing Teamsters. Again the jury was hung, but evidence later came to light that Hoffa had bribed one of the jurors, and this brought about his downfall. After all appeals had been exhausted, concluding with the U.S. Supreme Court's rejection of his appeal in 1967, Hoffa was sentenced to eight years in a federal penitentiary. While behind bars, he retained his Teamsters' Union presidency until 1971. After serving 58 months, he finally relinquished it and received a presidential commutation from Richard Nixon, with a parole proviso that he not participate in Teamster affairs for 10 years.

Hoffa soon ignored this stipulation and was embroiled in union politics once again. Although thousands of union members considered him a hero, Hoffa had many enemies, especially among union officials who were running their own secret rackets and had their own ties to the underworld. When on July 30, 1975, Hoffa drove to the Machus Red Fox restaurant near Detroit, where he had an appointment to meet several union leaders and a Detroit underworld figure, he was trying to regain control of the Teamsters. The meeting had been set for 2 P.M. At 2:30 P.M. Hoffa telephoned his wife to tell her that the men had not shown up. That was the last time Mrs. Hoffa talked to her husband. What happened after 2:45 P.M., when witnesses reported that they had seen Hoffa and several others climb into an automobile in the restaurant's parking lot, remains a mystery.

Hundreds of police and FBI agents investigated Hoffa's disappearance for years but without success. They speculated that he had been murdered and his corpse disposed of. One particularly gruesome theory is that Hoffa's dead body was passed through a fat-rendering machine in a plant owned by the Mafia. Gradually the FBI narrowed the list of prime suspects in Hoffa's disappearance, all of whom had been arrested and convicted on other charges such as income-tax evasion, hijacking, and loansharking. Despite great police pressure, however, all of the suspects denied any knowledge of Hoffa's death. (See also Dave BECK: unethical labor leader.)

Harold HOFFMAN: embezzling public official

The crookedness of Harold Giles Hoffman, once governor of New Jersey, was not exposed until June 4, 1954, the day of his death. It was then revealed that he had deviously covered up a scheme of embezzlement of public funds for approximately 25 years, living well, spending freely, and appearing the upright citizen. Incredibly, the dissembling Hoffman had even been considered presidential timber at one point in his career.

A banker with a wife and children, Hoffman lived and worked in the New Jersey shoreline town of South Amboy, where he had been born and raised. He had served in World War I, gaining promotion through the ranks from private to captain in the U.S. Army and participating in the Meuse-Argonne campaign. In South Amboy, his friendliness and outgoing nature helped get him elected mayor (1925–26) and then United States representative from New Jersey's third district (1927–

31). However, in the late 1920s, Hoffman began secretly preying upon inactive accounts in his bank, moving funds around from one account to another and taking out sums that didn't belong to him. Apparently, the money Hoffman stole from the bank was used to advance his political career; he deftly manipulated these accounts without arousing any suspicion.

In 1929, the voters reelected Hoffman for a second congressional term, but he unexpectedly gave up the post in Washington, D.C., to accept the job of New Jersey's commissioner of motor vehicles in 1930. He seemed, to many people, to have stepped backward politically. But unbeknownst to everyone was Hoffman's need to keep a watchful eye on his bank in South Amboy, where shortages of funds just might be spotted by auditors and examiners. He also gained access to some public funds at the motor-vehicle department and quietly shifted them to his bank and then to his personal use.

In 1935 Hoffman was the Republican gubernatorial candidate in New Jersey, and the electorate took a fancy to his sociable, blustery manner. He won the governorship, and some Republican leaders soon began thinking of him as a possible contender for the presidency of the United States in 1936. He clearly seemed to desire higher governmental office.

Shortly after his election, however, his popularity began to decline because of his outspokenness concerning the Lindbergh case. Some claimed that he had purposely involved himself in it, not realizing the strong public criticism he would receive for stating his uncertainty about Bruno Richard Hauptmann's guilt. (The kidnapping and killing of the Lindbergh baby was pinned on Hauptmann, who was convicted in 1935 and sentenced to death.) Governor Hoffman stayed Hauptmann's execution for several months in order to hear more evidence in the case, which would possibly clear the condemned man. Nothing was uncovered, and Hoffman was widely denounced. The governor further aroused public ire when he called the Lindbergh case "the most bungled police job in history" and fired New Jersey's state police superintendent. The governor had lost favor and ruined his political aspirations, both for reelection and for the presidency.

When his gubernatorial term ended in 1937, it became evident that Hoffman had pilfered some $300,000. Later appointed to head New Jersey's unemployment compensation department, he carried on his sly manipulations until 1954, when the newly elected governor, Robert B. Meyner, ordered an investigation into financial irregularities in the department. Hoffman was suspended while the probe investigated doubtful supply purchases, outrageously high rentals for some department offices, and eventually favoritism on the part of Hoffman to some friends likely to make almost $2 million from a business investment that had amounted to only about $87,000. All the while, Hoffman appeared unperturbed. Then, on the morning of June 4, 1954, he died of a heart attack in a Manhattan hotel room rented for his use by the Circus Saints and Sinners (an association of which he had once been president, and which indulged in merrymaking and helping former circus people). In a written confession to one of his daughters, Hoffman explained that he had hoped to rectify his past embezzling but that his efforts had been in vain. New Jersey officials later discovered that several hundred thousand dollars of public funds, which were never found, had been deposited in Hoffman's own bank in an account, bearing no interest.

"HOLLYWOOD MADAM." See Heidi FLEISS: the "Hollywood Madam."

"HOLLYWOOD TEN." See HOUSE COMMITTEE ON UN-AMERICAN ACTIVITIES (HUAC): America's inquisition and the "Hollywood Ten."

Libby HOLMAN: sensational successes and suicides
During the 1920s and 1930s, Libby Holman was one of the glittering stars of the musical theater. She sang in a deep, husky voice and was famous for her torch songs. She was also notorious for her numerous love affairs with both men and women, her foul language, and her often outrageous behavior. Her life, however, was to be a tragic one. Her first husband died only six months after their marriage of a bullet wound that may have been self-inflicted. Her second husband also died mysteriously. Her beloved son was killed while climbing a mountain. Other close friends and family members perished violently, and Libby Holman herself ended her own life while in a state of deep depression at the age of 67.

At age 20, Holman had left her native Cincinnati determined to win fame and fortune as a great actress on Broadway. After much looking, she won a bit part in *The Sapphire Ring,* sang in the chorus of *The Garrick Gaieties,* and toured with the road company of *The Greenwich Village Follies.* She received her first big break in *Merry-Go-Round* in which her torrid rendering of the song "Hogan's Alley" received high praise. Her roles in *Rainbow* and *Gambols* were also applauded, although the shows were flops. During these years she began drinking, carousing at parties that lasted until dawn, and traveling with a fast set of friends to night clubs in Harlem and Manhattan.

In the spring of 1929, she appeared in a revue called *The Little Show* and introduced the hit songs "Moanin' Low" and "Can't We Be Friends?" The show was an immediate success, and Holman was the toast of Broadway. That summer she had her first serious love affair with a young writer. The affair was shortlived, however, and in the fall she met Louisa Carpenter, a wealthy member of the DuPont family, and the two fell in love. Another hit in 1930, *Three's Company,* starred Holman, Clifton Webb, and Fred Allen and contained the songs "Body and Soul," "Yaller," and many other now well-known tunes. By this time Holman was a celebrity and at the height of her career.

Smith Reynolds, a playboy heir to the R. J. Reynolds tobacco fortune, became infatuated with her and begged her to marry him. Although she ignored him for a long time, she eventually succumbed, and the two were secretly married in November 1931. After a honeymoon in Hong Kong, the couple moved to the Reynolds estate outside Winston-Salem, North Carolina. Smith became increasingly possessive and neurotic, Libby increasingly bored.

During the Fourth of July holiday, 1932, Smith threw a party at which moonshine and home brew flowed freely. Everyone, Libby included, was drunk. Exactly what happened after the guests departed will probably never be known, but a shot rang out from Libby's and Smith's bedroom. Ab Walker, Smith's best friend and personal secretary, rushed in, found Smith, blood oozing from his temple, his Mauser automatic pistol lying on the floor. Libby was sobbing hysterically. Smith was rushed to the nearest hospital but never regained consciousness.

Libby and Ab Walker were held as material witnesses to the crime. The jurors at the coroner's inquest concluded that they did "not know how Smith Reynolds met his death." Reporters from all over the country flocked to Winston-Salem, and the mysterious death became the sensation of the year. Excitement mounted when it was learned that Libby was two months pregnant, had disappeared from public view, and that a formal trial was scheduled for November. The powerful Reynolds family intervened, however, and the case was dropped. Christopher Smith Reynolds, later known as "Topper," was born prematurely in January 1933, and a two-year legal battle over his inheritance ensued. The boy finally inherited $6.25 million, and Libby Holman received a $750,000 settlement.

She returned to Broadway in *Revenge with Music* (1934) and resumed her flamboyant lifestyle in café society. She also had an affair with handsome actor Phillip Holmes and became pregnant again, but since she did not want to marry Holmes, she decided to get an abortion. She then took up with Holmes's younger brother Ralph, 11 years her junior, and married him in 1939. When World War II broke out, the brothers enlisted in the Royal Canadian Air Force. Phillip was killed in a collision of two military planes, and Ralph was sent to England.

Libby then became even more promiscuous than she had been, entertaining a series of men for brief periods at her luxurious home, Treetops, in Connecticut. She also had long affairs with a female journalist and a young woman she had hired as her secretary. When Libby and Josh White, a black singer and guitarist, toured night clubs and servicemen's clubs during the war years, it was widely rumored that they were lovers.

Ralph Holmes was discharged in August 1945 and started to drink heavily. Libby ordered him out of her house, and a month later, his body was found in an East Side apartment in New York City. The medical examiner said that Holmes had died of barbiturate poisoning, but no one knew whether his death had been an accidental or a deliberate act.

Another great tragedy occurred only five years later. Before entering Dartmouth College in the fall of 1950, Topper Holmes and a friend began driving across the country to California. They started off in high spirits to climb Mt. Whitney in California but did not return. Several days later, their frozen bodies were found high on the mountain. Libby, then touring Europe with her latest lover, flew back immediately, utterly shattered by her son's death.

In 1952, Libby Holman began what she called her "grand passion," a seven-year liaison with handsome actor Montgomery Clift. But the two gradually drifted apart after Clift was almost killed in a drunken car accident.

Soon after this, Libby met Louis Schanker, an abstract painter. She admired him and his art a great deal, and the two were married in December 1960. Schanker, however, turned out to be jealous, often intoxicated, and mean. Libby's numerous friends faded away and she became despondent. On a hot day in June 1971, clad only in a bikini bottom, she entered the garage at Treetops, closed the door, climbed into her Rolls-Royce, and turned on the engine, dying of carbon monoxide poisoning within a short time.

HOMESTEAD STRIKE. See Henry Clay FRICK: the "battle of Homestead."

J. Edgar HOOVER. See A. Mitchell PALMER: opportunism masked as idealism.

Herbert HOOVER: exaggerated response to the Bonus March

In 1921, Congress voted World War I veterans a bonus redeemable in 1945. The advent of the Depression in 1929, however, caused many of them to request a lump-sum payment, and Wright Patman, then a United States representative, had introduced into the Democratic House a bill to that effect. In 1932, to influence its passage, Walter W. Waters collected some veterans and marched them to Washington D.C. Thousands of others followed from all over the country. The majority of them set up a shantytown on some vacant land in Anacostia Flats. They were called the Bonus Expeditionary Force.

What initially looked to be a relatively peaceful march ended up as violent and bloody mayhem. The Patman bill failed on June 17, 1932. Many marchers went home. But some 5,000 remained, refusing to leave even when the police came. The ensuing riot resulted in two deaths, and the situation went from bad to worse. President Herbert Clark Hoover, convinced that this was a "Communist conspiracy," called in the armed forces. The marchers soon had to face tanks, bayonets, and tear gas. Their shantytown was burned to the ground.

The marchers fared badly, but Hoover suffered also. Few believed his accusations of communism and he was criticized for his lack of concern for the brutality that had taken place. Hoover's exaggerated response to the Bonus March was largely responsible for his failed bid for reelection that year.

Many of the details of the Bonus March are still unclear. The total number of marchers has not been determined, for apparently no precise count was ever taken. Democratic sources cite a figure of 22,000 to 25,000; Hoover's memoirs use the figure 11,000; most other authorities say there were from 12,000 to 20,000. What is clear is that until July 28, 1932, the marchers were orderly; some accounts compliment Waters on his success in maintaining discipline in the large group and ousting agitators from it. A few marchers squatted in empty Treasury Department office buildings on Pennsylvania Avenue; most set up the shantytown headquarters on vacant land made available by the District of Columbia police superintendent, Pelham D. Glassford. That they planned to stay is certain from the vegetable gardens they established in Anacostia.

The composition of the marchers is still a matter of controversy. A Veterans Administration survey made before July 28 found 94 percent of the men to have served in the army or navy, 67 percent of them overseas. The disabled among them totaled 20 percent. Hoover ignored this survey; his memoirs cite a survey, made after the military action, of some 2,000 marchers still remaining in Washington. Made by an undisclosed agency, it revealed that less than one-third were veterans and over 45 percent were ex-convicts and communists. From these figures come his "communist conspiracy" theory.

The marchers' presence did not assist passage of the Patman bill that June. Offers of train fare home reduced the marchers' numbers. On July 28, the Treasury Department asked the District of Columbia police to recover its buildings from the 5,000 remaining marchers, but a riot broke out when the police tried to act. Two policemen, beaten to the ground, fired their handguns and killed two marchers. Then, without the assent of Glassford, the District of Columbia police commissioners asked for federal troops to help them.

President Hoover gave orders to the secretary of war, Patrick J. Hurley, who sent Chief of Staff General

Douglas MacArthur, his aide Major Dwight D. Eisenhower (in his first experience of armed combat), and Major George Patton. Backing them up were a machine-gun detachment, men from the Twelfth and Thirteenth Infantry Divisions, a platoon of the Third Cavalry (Patton's men, many in tanks), some military police, and more than 3,000 tear-gas grenades. MacArthur's view of the whole situation was exaggerated. He later described the "bad looking mob" as one "animated by the essence of revolution." Motivated by his own inflated rhetoric and fearful "that the institutions of our Government would have been severely threatened," MacArthur went beyond his orders. He acted speedily and efficiently and far too forcefully.

The Anacostia Flats shantytown was set afire (Hoover claimed he had not ordered this), and hand-to-hand combat took place there and in the city, where marchers met the armed forces. No fatal shots were fired, but many marchers suffered wounds of various kinds, including bayonet stabs, before they were pushed out of Washington. Fortunatedly, despite claims by the Democrats, no one was killed.

Spread nationally, the news engendered a strong negative reaction. It was directed at Hoover as commander-in-chief, rather than at MacArthur (who was never disciplined for disobeying orders). Most labeled the brutal action as "excruciatingly bad politics" or saw it as "a somewhat less than realistic approach to the growing canker of depression."

As his memoirs show, President Hoover was never able to see beyond the "Communist conspiracy" explanation. To him, the march did not suggest broad implications of nationwide distress.

In 1933, when President Franklin D. Roosevelt was in the White House, many of the marchers returned, eventually, in 1936, causing Congress to disburse $2.5 billion in veterans' benefits. But in 1933 Roosevelt did not send troops; instead, he sent gallons of coffee and Eleanor, his wife.

HOUSE COMMITTEE ON UN-AMERICAN ACTIVITIES (HUAC): America's inquisition and the "Hollywood Ten"

Legislative disregard of United States constitutional provisions on civil rights began in 1798 with the Alien and Sedition Acts, but further attempts to limit civil liberties during times of peace occurred into the 20th century. In 1947 the House Committee on Un-American Activities (HUAC) tried to outlaw the Communist Party. Seventy-nine witnesses were called and 19 were subpoenaed. Eleven witnesses were actually heard and, in the course of the hearings, all were denied their First Amendment rights. Despite the undemocratic nature of the hearings, the careers of all involved were ruined.

An investigative body whose ostensible task was gathering information toward proposed legislation, the

HUAC had, since its inception in the 1930s, steadily worsened in reputation. Dedicated by its chairman and membership to quashing dissent, liberty of thought, and other symptoms of liberal or New Deal opinions, the committee had a history of intimidating, harassing, and vilifying hostile witnesses. Its third chairman, J. Parnell THOMAS, brought it to a new low. In all the years of its existence, it spent three-quarters of a million dollars without initiating any successful legislation.

In 1947, the HUAC decided to cure the media of un-American attitudes, starting with Hollywood. Because critics again carped that its mission was legislative rather than investigative, Parnell Thomas invented a proposal: a bill outlawing the Communist Party.

His announcement was a cover-up. Hollywood, through the Motion Picture Association for the Preservation of American Ideals (a producer-established, ultraconservative organization), had approached HUAC for its own purposes: to safeguard its income ($2 billion in 1946), to alleviate Hearst newspaper pressures for federal film censorship, and to defeat labor unions that threatened its profits, especially the very militant Screen Writers' Guild. Thomas's avowed purpose effectively obscured the fact that the Un-American Activities Committee had become the producers' tool.

Announcing that the HUAC would call 79 witnesses from a total of 300 who had been fingered by 30 "alert Americans," Parnell Thomas subpoenaed 19 of these witnesses for hearings beginning in Washington, D.C., on October 20, 1947. The hearings, broadcast and filmed on newsreel cameras, were to boost the HUAC's credibility. After the pandemonium of only 11 hearings, however, the committee decided, without announcement, to go out of business. No legislation resulted and the Hearst effort was stopped, but 10 livelihoods had been brutally damaged; and, after the vote of the House, the First Amendment lay under a cloud of endangerment from investigative bodies (chiefly by Senator Joseph MCCARTHY, until the mid-1950s saw a restructuring and liberalizing of the entire investigative committee process. The Communist Party in America remained legal until 1949, despite the efforts of the HUAC.

The 1949 HUAC hearings reveal that the committee made three major methodological errors. First, it relied upon "friendly" witnesses for its definition of communist subversion. Radio listeners heard actor Adolph Menjou denote as "Reds" those who had applauded Paul Robeson's singing of Soviet songs, actor Gary Cooper condemn all attacks on anything American, and Lela Rogers (mother of dancer-actress Ginger Rogers) claim that sad background music was subversive. A film executive, Jack L. Warner, declared the pro-Semitism of *Gentleman's Agreement* propagandistic and blamed the Screen Writers' Guild.

The so-called Hollywood Ten (shown here with two attorneys) on the steps of the U.S. District Court in Washington, D.C., in early 1948: left to right, first and second rows, inclusive, director-producer Herbert Biberman; writer Dalton Trumbo; attorney Martin Popper; writer John Lawson; attorney Robert W. Kenny; and writers Alvah Bessie, Albert Maltz, Samuel Ornitz, and Lester Cole. Rear, left to right, are: writer Ring Lardner, Jr.; director Edward Dmytryk; and producer Robert Adrian Scott. The "ten" were later found guilty of contempt of Congress for refusing to testify about their political beliefs before the House Committee on Un-American Activities (HUAC) and fined and sent to jail. (UPI/Bettmann Newsphotos)

The HUAC's second mistake was a failure to conceal its real purposes. Its inquisition consisted of two questions: Are you a member of the Screen Writers' Guild? (to please the Motion Picture Association) and "Are you now or have you ever been a member of the Communist Party of the United States?" (to satisfy increasingly vocal spokesmen for anti-Soviet views).

Because it wanted all of America to perceive the heroism of the committee and the shame of the witnesses, the HUAC designed a rigid format for its hearings. This rigidity was its third error: Parnell Thomas quickly lost control of the hearings; the inquiries turned into a travesty of justice. The examples of the committee's ridiculousness are many. It rejected a petition from defense lawyers concerning the First Amendment problems inherent in the investigation. It refused to allow nine of the 11 witnesses it heard the right to make a prefatory statement on their civil rights privileges (one intended comment was examined by Thomas and declared "offensive" to the committee). When 10 of the 11 witnesses refused to give yes or no answers to the two questions, Thomas commenced with incessant shouts and gavel-bangings. Extensive charges were listed on the order of "failed to support the candidacy of Thomas E. Dewey" and "favored the Fair Employment Practices Act," and 10 witnesses were cited for contempt of Congress. One witness, playwright Bertolt Brecht, was exonerated; the others, labeled by the press the Hollywood Ten, were Ring Lardner, Jr., Dalton Trumbo, Alvah Bessie, Albert Maltz, Samuel Ornitz, Herbert Biberman, Robert Adrian Scott, John Howard Lawson, Lester Cole, and Edward Dmytryk.

Reaction to the HUAC's behavior was strong, and much of it was condemnatory. As a result, when the

HUAC, which was required to get full House approval of its contempt citations, appeared before the House with an hour's time to argue the committee's case, Parnell Thomas granted most of the time to committee members. They argued rhetorically about a crisis in the nation that rendered inappropriate the unconstitutionality thesis of the few non-HUAC House members who gained the floor. One HUAC member, the racist Representative John Rankin of Mississippi, condemned a petition from the Committee for the First Amendment as "signed by Jews." The House of Representatives then supported the HUAC's behavior by a vote of 346 to 17.

The HUAC's face had been saved. But the Hollywood Ten, who were talented writers, directors, and producers, gained no relief from two hearings they had before politicized courts; they were found guilty of contempt, fined, jailed for a year, and afterward blacklisted (illegally, according to many) by a victorious Hollywood movie industry. And as had always been true of its behavior, the HUAC had proposed no legislation to rectify the "wrongs" it had uncovered.

The blacklist, in which friends betrayed friends, remains one of Hollywood's most shameful episodes. In 1997, the Writers Guild of America, which had not supported its blacklisted union members, restored the credits on almost 50 movies written by former blacklisted screenwriters, who had used pseudonyms or names of relatives or friends as covers in the 1950s. Hollywood's apologies are being given for its "wrongs."

HOUSE COMMITTEE ON UN-AMERICAN ACTIVITIES (HUAC): the destruction of Harry Dexter White

In the summer of 1948 two former Communist sympathizers appeared before the House Committee on Un-American Activities (HUAC). Both accused Harry Dexter White, former assistant secretary of the treasury and coauthor of the Bretton Woods monetary plan, of being a communist. Intent on defending his honor, White asked to appear before the committee himself. The resultant hearing did little to redeem his reputation and may well have cost him his life. White had been named as a "fellow traveler" (communist sympathizer) by both Elizabeth Bentley, who had fingered a long list of Communist Party members before a New York grand jury, and Whittaker Chambers (see Alger HISS: traitor or scapegoat?). White, like many of those named, was a perfect victim for a committee bent on finding juicy scandals to denigrate the era of President Franklin D. Roosevelt's administrations.

Angered and convinced that appearance before the HUAC on his own volition would erase what he considered to be canards, White requested that he be heard. He was advised to appear on August 13, 1948.

Critics of the HUAC assert that White was a victim of guilt by association and of the pernicious inventions of reformed ex-communists eager in their repentant humility to have a moment of glamour. White died on August 16 of that year, and many still place the blame on the canard. Many also suggest that the deportment of the committee on August 13 earned it the dubious historical honor of being White's destroyer.

Between the time of his petition and his appearance before the HUAC, White had suffered a serious heart attack, but because he felt his personal honor was at stake, he did not ask for a postponement of the hearing. He mentioned his recuperative condition to the committee on August 13, asking for and gaining moments for rest during his testimony. Otherwise, the hearing reflected the committee's usual hostility toward an accused person; reporters present described the hearing as "rough" and "gruelling."

One example of the rough manner in which the hearing was conducted is evident in an exchange between White and California Congressman Richard M. Nixon. To safeguard himself, White had reminded the committee that the Bill of Rights was added to the U.S. Constitution as a protection against "star chamber proceedings." He also reminded them of constitutional guarantees for witnesses, of the right of witnesses to cross-examine complainants against them, and other regulated protections. In making this memorandum, White illustrated his confusion regarding the boundary between an investigative body and a grand-jury proceeding, a confusion held by the public and perhaps also by the committee, which frequently had operated as if it were a judicial rather than a research body.

This confusion was sharply addressed in Nixon's response to White's memorandum: he asserted that Star Chamber hearings did not allow an accused person to defend himself (as White had in denying that he was a fellow traveler). Nixon then characterized White's denial of being a communist as a prevarication and announced his decision that White was guilty.

As the only trained lawyer on the committee at the time, Nixon would have known that hearsay (the testimony of Bentley and Chambers) was not the equivalent of firm evidence and that until such tested information were so produced, no judgment, either logical or legal, could be made. (It is important to note that neither Bentley nor Chambers gave detailed evidence. White, therefore, had no opportunity to make detailed rebuttal; no basis existed for any position except bias on Nixon's part.) Nonetheless, Nixon announced his opinion, inadvertently revealing to the public that the HUAC was willing to accept hearsay as proof—a denial of the legal right to be considered innocent until proven guilty that was to poison future HUAC hearings and infect the proceedings of the Senate investigative committee on communist infiltration of the army chaired in the early 1950s by Joseph MCCARTHY.

White left the hearing room knowing that he had no chance of being believed. Three days later, he was dead.

Not until 1995, when the U.S. National Security Agency began releasing decrypted cables that Soviet agents in the United States had used to report back to Moscow, had some clear evidence been found to prove that Bentley and Chambers testified honestly or knowledgeably about White. In the decryptions, the supposed martyr White is identified as an agent.

HOUSE OVERDRAFT SCANDAL: bad check writers identified

When the average American writes a bad check (one that is not covered by available funds), it bounces and he or she has to pay the bank overdraft charges (up to $25 per check, in some cases). If this happens regularly, his or her reputation and credit rating are definitely tarnished. Yet, many members of the United States House of Representatives routinely wrote bad checks on the House bank (for members only) during their tenure without facing these or any other consequences. All that changed when the numbers and the extent of the overdrafts were made public in a report released by the General Accounting Office (GAO) in October 1991.

The report said that hundreds of members regularly wrote bad checks on their accounts at the House bank. None had faced penalties before. The Democratic leadership of the House termed the overdrafts as a minor administrative snag and closed the bank. However, a cover-up proved embarrassing once the numbers were released. Apparently, a staggering 20,000 checks totaling $10.8 million had been written over a three-year period between July 1988 and October 3, 1991. As the details emerged, House members found themselves on the defensive, having to explain the burgeoning scandal to their constituents. The sense of embarrassment became acute when the House Ethics Committee voted 10-4 (March 5, 1992) to release the names of the worst offenders. According to the committee, 24 members (19 current and five former) qualified under this category. They wrote checks worth more than their monthly net pay at least eight times during the period under review. The committee proposed to disclose the identity of these people. Some members with over 800 checks to their (dis)credit did not qualify for inclusion in this list. One member had overdrawn on his monthly net pay for 35 of the 39 months. The legislator with the most overdrafts was former member Tommy Robinson (a Democrat turned Republican) of Arkansas who wrote 996 bad checks worth $251,000—one bad check a day! Democrat Robert Mrazek was not far behind with 920 overdrafts. Overall, 296 current and 59 former members overdrew their accounts at least once during this period.

The four Republicans who voted against the proposal said they supported disclosure of "all" the names on the list, including those who had written bad checks for smaller amounts. In a preemptive move, many legislators who knew they had overdrawn on their accounts confessed and apologized to their constituents. House

Democrats were overwhelmingly represented in the preliminary list, prompting Republicans to argue that this epidemic of overdrafts was caused by years of mismanagement by the Democratic Party. In mid-March, it was revealed that three of President George Bush's cabinet members were also implicated in the scandal. Defense Secretary Dick Cheney (25 checks), Agriculture Secretary Edward Madigan (49 checks), and Labor Secretary Lynn Martin (16 checks)—former House Republicans—had overdrawn their accounts by a total of $45,000. The Republican leader in the House, Newt GINGRICH, had written three bad checks, and Democratic Speaker Tom Foley had written a $540 check for stereo equipment.

Public outcry over this state of affairs forced the resignation of House sergeant-at-arms Jack Russ, who had managed the bank for nine years and was himself guilty of overdrafts at the bank. Apparently, Russ had been repeatedly cautioned by the GAO about reforming this check-writing privilege. Some of the offenders pointed out that the bank was really a disbursement center where their accounts did not earn interest. Also, they said that no public funds were involved because the bad checks were covered by deposits from congressional colleagues. Others blamed the bank's careless record-keeping for failing to keep them informed about the status of their accounts.

Finally, on April 1, 1992, the House Ethics Committee punished 22 current and former members of the House (in the interim, two members had successfully appealed their inclusion in the list) by identifying them as the worst offenders. The fallout of this scandal was felt most dramatically by the Democratic Party during the congressional elections later in the year.

HUD SCANDALS: Sam Pierce, Marilyn Harrell, Deborah Gore Dean, and others

Analysts agree that the scandals involving the federal Department of Housing and Urban Development (HUD) during the Reagan administration in the 1980s was the largest "looting" of federal funds to date. Numerous administrators, former employees, Republican supporters, and well-connected real estate developers scammed millions of dollars from building contracts and subsidies intended for low-income housing. As with most political imprudence, the HUD scandals eroded public confidence in the government's ability to appropriate federal funds.

There were three major areas of wrongdoing. In the area of rent subsidies, HUD official Deborah Gore Dean showed favoritism in awarding subsidies, tax credits, and consulting fees to well-connected contractors and consultants. Former attorney general John Mitchell and former secretary of the interior James Watt were recipients of such political favors. In the area of embezzlement, escrow agents stole funds from the sales of foreclosure properties. Agent Marilyn Harrell claimed she took the money in order to donate it to the poor. The federal area of Section 8 moderate-housing rehabilitation contracts received the most attention. At least 11 former HUD officials and well-known Republicans helped themselves to HUD funds by posing as consultants on housing issues. Former senator Edward Brooke of Massachusetts and former governor Louie Nunn of Kentucky, among others, received huge consultant's fees in exchange, apparently, for very little work.

Former secretary of housing and urban development Samuel Pierce, dubbed "Silent Sam" throughout this ordeal, denied accusations that he created an atmosphere of favoritism in HUD. However, evidence shows, for instance, that he authorized an $11 million, 151-unit, low-income housing project in Durham, North Carolina, which sat over a former hazardous waste storage site, because a former law associate lobbied for the project. Pierce also allegedly pulled what strings he could to save DRG Funding Corporation, a co-insurance company, after it was accused of inflating its appraisals and pocketing or distributing the profits made from federal funds. DRG later went on to issue $538 million in bad loans that HUD, and ultimately the U.S. taxpayers, would have to repay.

Pierce contends that he was betrayed by his staff. In fact, he mostly blames his executive assistant Deborah Gore Dean, cousin of Vice President Al Gore. She was found to be involved in unfairly awarding contracts to favored Republican consultants and political allies. Former HUD officials who went on to form their own businesses profited from Dean's disbursement of Section 8 monies. Dean, in turn, blamed Pierce for the transgressions because she was directed and authorized to make such decisions by him. Dean was indicted by a federal grand jury on 13 criminal charges of fraud, perjury, and conspiracy and was sentenced in 1994 to 21 months in prison and fined $5,000.

Marilyn Louise Harrell confessed in 1988 to embezzling $5.5 million from HUD. She says she took the funds from the sale of 99 properties for her own personal use and donated over $1.1 million to charities. She apparently had expected to get caught much sooner than she did, and so she decided to help as many poor people as she could before she was found out. Harrell was sentenced to 46 months in prison and fined $600,000. Nicknamed "Robin HUD," she became a symbol of the department's massive mismanagement.

About 20 consultants made more than $5.7 million over a five-year period by lobbying for Section 8 funds, and different states received disproportionate funds based on favoritism. However, in all fairness, abuse of HUD since its inception in 1965 under President Lyndon Johnson has been bipartisan and tied closely to political influence peddling and campaign support. Since then, politicians and officials have been so busy "lining their pockets" that HUD's real constituency—the needy—has been largely disregarded.

Rock HUDSON: Hollywood studios' superstar's public disclosure

A creation of the old Hollywood studio system, 59-year-old actor Rock Hudson shocked the public on July 25, 1985, by revealing he was suffering from AIDS (acquired immune deficiency syndrome), most of whose victims in the United States at that point had mostly been homosexual or bisexual men. Abroad in Paris at the time, where he had been hospitalized on July 21 after collapsing at the Ritz Hotel, his spokeswoman and personal friend Yannou Collart publicly disclosed the nature of his illness, which Hudson had decided to do—the first such disclosure by a celebrity of his stature.

Born in Winnetka, Illinois, in 1925, as Roy Scherer, Jr., he grew up in hard circumstances during the Great Depression. His father left the family after losing his job as an auto mechanic. In 1933 his mother married Wallace Fitzgerald (whose surname Hudson took) but the marriage failed after nine years. At New Trier High

The emaciated face of 59-year-old movie idol Rock Hudson, photographed at a news conference in Pebble Beach, California, in July 1985. Days later, he publicly revealed that he was suffering from AIDS, from which he died on October 2, 1985. With his disclosure, AIDS was no longer a faceless disease that struck nameless victims. (AP/Wide World Photos)

School, Roy failed to get parts in school plays because he couldn't remember his lines. After graduation, in 1944 he joined the U.S. Navy, served in the Philippines, and then returned to Winnetka to work as a piano mover and mail carrier. Ruggedly handsome and masculine (six feet, four inches tall, weighing about 200 pounds), but rather shy and introverted, he harbored a wish to act, went to Hollywood, failed to get into the University of Southern California to study dramatics because of low grades, and then began sending his photo and resume to various producers and directors.

In 1947 Henry Willson, talent scout for the Selznick studio, became his agent (Willson changed his name to Rock Hudson—Rock for the Rock of Gibraltar and Hudson for the Hudson River). Hudson's screen tests were poor overall, but Raoul Walsh, a director at Warner Brothers, helped him get acting lessons and small parts. In 1949 Universal-International Pictures signed up Hudson for work. Within six years, he had 28 movies to his credit, playing many different roles—detective, soldier, prizefighter, football player, sea captain, soda jerk, Indian chief's son, cowboy, and fur trapper, among others.

Universal paired Hudson with actress Jane Wyman in *The Magnificent Obsession* (1954), a movie that earned the studio about $5 million and made Hudson a top star. Other studios borrowed him to make money. He starred with beautiful actress Elizabeth Taylor in Warner Brothers' epic film *Giant* (1956), which earned him an Academy Award nomination for best actor for his portrayal of a Texas rancher. He played opposite Jennifer Jones in *A Farewell to Arms* (1957), produced by David O. Selznick and Twentieth Century Fox. Later Hudson costarred with Doris Day in *Pillow Talk* (1959), *Lover Come Back* (1962), and *Send Me No Flowers* (1964), three fluffy romantic comedies in which Hudson's performances are probably best remembered. In 1958, *Look* magazine explained Hudson's stardom this way: "The public got tired of decay. So now here's Rock Hudson. He's wholesome. He doesn't perspire. He has no pimples. He smells of milk. His whole appeal is cleanliness and respectability—this boy is pure."

Hudson's studio-encouraged marriage to Phyllis Gates (Willson's former secretary) in 1955 ended in divorce in 1958. Afterward he lived a bachelor life in California, making money for the studios as a top box-office draw into the late 1960s. His detective series on television, *McMillan and Wife,* ran for six successful seasons until 1977.

Before Hudson made public his illness, he had appeared in six episodes of the television series *Dynasty,* in which he had had love scenes with actress Linda Evans (this later caused a furor after Hudson's illness was disclosed). He went twice to Paris to visit the Institut Pasteur, a medical research institute then using experimental drugs to treat AIDS patients. Early reports, however, had indicated that Hudson was being treated for inoperable liver cancer. Finally, on October 2, 1985, some 15 months after being diagnosed as suffering from the disease, the once great screen idol, now emaciated, died in Beverly Hills, California. His death stimulated wide public support to fight AIDS, which many believed had been allowed to spread unchecked because of little news coverage, medical complacency, little funding for research, and government negligence and delay. Nonetheless, there continued to be controversy, earlier helped by an editorial in the *Journal of the American Medical Association* (June 20, 1985) that blamed AIDS on an "age of overindulgence" in which homosexuality had become "almost acceptable." The disease later killed Dack Rambo, Liberace, Anthony Perkins, Robert Reed, Howard Rollins, and other Hollywood people, in addition to millions of victims worldwide. Some criticized Hudson's long secrecy about AIDS for sustaining the stigma against it; others felt his death itself brought awareness into the mainstream.

HUGHES HOAX. See Clifford IRVING: author of fake Howard Hughes "autobiography."

Nelson Bunker HUNT: silver baron

To control the world's supply of silver might seem an idle fancy, but perhaps not if one happens to be a big, portly Texas billionaire named Nelson Bunker Hunt. In the summer of 1979 he already had vast holdings (including ownership of a large independent oil company, immense oil reserves, more than a million acres of land in Texas, Oklahoma, and Montana, and some 650 valuable racehorses) when he and his brother, W. Herbert Hunt, began purchasing a great deal of silver in the commodities markets. At about the same time, investors in gold started to see gold bullion prices climb and, by about mid-January 1980, soar to more than $800 an ounce on both the European and American markets.

In January 1980, the Hunt brothers (Nelson, Herbert, and Lamar) seemed to have possession of half the world's silver bullion, and they made enormous profits gambling that the price of silver would continue to rise. It did, to an incredible $52 an ounce. The Hunts had made a risky financial killing in an alleged attempt to control the supply of silver worldwide and to dictate its price (they later denied that they had attempted to corner the silver market, when they appeared before a subcommittee of the U.S. House of Representatives to answer questions about the disastrous collapse of their $2-billion silver empire, a stock market crash that took place on March 26–27, 1980).

When the price of silver futures fell sharply in wild trading on March 26, 1980, a number of American brokerage firms made margin calls to protect themselves against losses in trading, requesting additional cash from investors in order to preserve their equity in commodities bought on credit. The failure of the Hunt brothers to fulfill margin calls of $100 million, either because they were financially squeezed at the time or simply indisposed to do so, caused a panic in the silver market on March 27. Wall Street was in turmoil as the price of silver tumbled down to $10.50 an ounce (a fifth what it had been in January of that year). As the Hunt brothers' multimillion dollar losses (eventually around $235 million) became known, panicky traders began selling off their share holdings at any price. Many people suffered severe losses. The brokerage firm of Bache, Halsey, Stuart, Shields, Incorporated, which was about 5.5 percent owned by the Hunts and had attempted to sell off its holdings of the Hunts' silver futures and stock positions, reportedly contended with potential losses of some $50 million in connection with the Hunts, who were forced to raise many millions in cash to cover these and other (at least $400 million) losses that had resulted from their silver trading activities. By the end of March 1980, silver prices had completely stabilized, and investment houses had met their financial obligations, but with tarnished reputations. The Engelhard Minerals and Chemicals Corporation, agreeing to release the Hunt brothers from a contractual obligation to purchase 19-million ounces of silver at $35 an ounce (silver at the time was selling at slightly above $14 an ounce on the New York market), received in return from the Hunts extensive Canadian oil and gas properties worth an estimated $500 million and additional Hunt silver holdings (8.5 million ounces); thus the Hunts were able to cover their silver losses but at an enormous price. Nelson Bunker Hunt was even forced to mortgage his large Texas ranch, a personal casualty of his great silver caper that undoubtedly shamed him privately.

In November 1987, after nearly five years of investigation by the U.S. Commodity Futures Trading Commission, a regulatory hearing to determine whether the rich Hunt brothers had illegally manipulated the world silver market in 1980 began in Washington, D.C. The Hunts had successfully kept secret much of the information in the case; now they had to face proceedings open to the public.

No criminal charges were filed against the Hunts, who, however, faced civil cases against them now. One such case ended in August 1988, after a six-month trial, with a federal jury fining them more than $130 million in damages for conspiring to corner the silver market in 1979. The jury said that, because of the silver-price increases the Hunts had engineered to artificial heights, the Peruvian government's mineral marketing company, Minpeco S.A., had lost about $100 million in investments and interest. The jury's verdict seemed to mean that Nelson, age 62, Herbert, 59, and Lamar, 56, would think more frugally than prosperously in future actions.

Ward HUNT: the farcical trial of Susan B. Anthony

In 1873, Ward Hunt, a newly appointed associate justice of the U.S. Supreme Court, presided over a trial filled with procedural errors and found the defendant guilty of breaking federal criminal law. The defendant was Susan B. Anthony. Her crime: committing the felony of voting.

Widely remembered as a pioneer suffragist, Anthony was distressed when the Fifteenth Amendment to the Constitution, in 1870, allowed suffrage to black persons but did not extend it to women. "Wait your turn," she was told.

The polite but outspoken Anthony refused to wait. Armed with advice from lawyers and judges that the definition of *citizen* in the Fourteenth Amendment included women and that the Fifteenth Amendment, in failing to mention it, did not exclude woman suffrage, she and 14 other women successfully registered to vote in Rochester, New York, on November 1, 1872. Their action persuaded 36 more women to register. By Election Day, November 5, however, threats in Democratic newspapers to prosecute the voting officials and the female voters frightened away most of the registrants. Only Anthony and her 14 colleagues voted.

Their action gained them national press coverage of a mixed variety. Some papers applauded it, others were flippant or abusive. The New York *Graphic* printed mocking cartoons.

On November 18, Anthony and her colleagues were arrested, she by a blushing deputy United States marshal who charged her with the crime of voting illegally and refused, when she demanded it, to put her in handcuffs. At her first hearing, when she acknowledged that she was making a test of the law, Anthony was found guilty and offered a bail of $500. She refused, underwent two additional hearings, and had her bail—still unpaid—raised to $1,000 (equivalent to that demanded of a dangerous criminal). Her attorney paid the fee so that she could be free.

Anthony used her freedom to communicate her interpretation of federal law so effectively that the district court changed the venue of the trial so that a jury might not be prejudiced by what a Democratic and chauvinistic paper had called "a corruptionist." Her three-day trial therefore began in Canandaigua, New York, on June 17, 1893. By current standards, the trial was a farce but one that engendered no laughter. Ward Hunt was trying his first criminal case since his appointment to the Supreme Court; he was determined to please Roscoe Conkling, the suffragist-baiting boss of New York's Republican Party and Hunt's sponsor, and to convince Conkling that he was not above violating judicial procedure. His errors turned the trial into a misuse of the federal courts for political ends.

On the first day of the trial, Hunt ruled that Anthony was not competent to speak on her own behalf, admitted to the hearings testimony that her lawyers had objected as being incomplete and slanted, refused to have Anthony's motive considered, and at the moment the oral testimony on both sides ended, read his own written opinion, which had been prepared before the oral testimony had been given. At future sessions, Hunt turned to the jury and directed a verdict of guilty—a direction then forbidden in a criminal trial. When the jury balked and was refused permission to be polled, he dismissed it without consultation. (A reporter later learned that the jury would have voted acquittal.) In dismissing the jury, Hunt had deprived Anthony of the constitutional right to be heard by an impartial jury of her peers.

On the final day of the trial, Hunt refused to let Anthony give the traditional pre-sentencing speech and refused a motion for a new trial. He sentenced Anthony to a $100 fine and costs. When she announced that she would pay the costs but not the fine, he declined to remand her. This last action was shrewd, for had Anthony been jailed, a writ of habeas corpus would have automatically made possible appeal to the full Supreme Court of that era, where emphasis on Hunt's errors would have effected a reversal of the guilty verdict. Hunt's action stripped Anthony of appeal privileges in any federal court.

Anthony, being who she was, then appealed her case to the legal world, sending transcripts and arguments to law schools, law journals, judges, and newspapers. They responded, often in print, by questioning the propriety of Hunt's proceedings, especially his dismissal of the jury. Some considered him a tyrannical violator of the Constitution. He found few defenders, even among the opponents of woman suffrage. Hunt must have been frightened by the violence of the attacks upon him, for he did not try the other 14 females who had voted with Anthony.

Time seems to have softened the force of the criticisms hurled at Hunt. The *Dictionary of American Biography,* which often omits unfavorable information about its entries, does not mention the Anthony case under the Hunt entry but does conclude that Hunt was not a "conspicuous" member of the Supreme Court.

Collis P. HUNTINGTON: from hardware to highballing

When the U.S. Congress passed the Pacific Railroad Bill of 1862 and awarded a charter to the Central Pacific Railroad Company, Theodore D. Judah telegraphed to California, sending a cryptic message to two of his four bosses: "We have drawn the elephant." The charter was "pure gold" to the four recipients. They were to make their fortunes from it. In construction profits alone, they gained $36 million for their unscrupulous labors. The federal bill authorized the building of a railroad eastward from the Pacific Ocean until it met the Union Pacific

Railroad, building westward under separate legislation from Nebraska. The bill also authorized the winner of the charter to receive 9 million acres of land and a first mortgage of $27 million backed by bonds. The award was "pure gold," and it made the fortunes of four men.

The "we" in Judah's telegram were Collis Potter Huntington, his former hardware-store partner Mark Hopkins, Leland Stanford, and Charles Crocker, whose Central Pacific Railroad was capitalized (but only on paper) at $8.5 million. Their input had been only $200,000. They were also executives of Pacific Associates, a general business venture.

The land alone that the Central Pacific Railroad bill had granted had an amazing potential: in a time of rising profits, it furnished acreage for farms, towns, forests, mineral searches, harbor rights, and franchises worth millions. The railroad's construction offered similar fortunes. Through Pacific Associates, Judah, Hopkins, Stanford, and Crocker established a model for Oakes Ames and CRÉDIT MOBILIER to imitate: they set up a holding and ephemeral construction company, the Credit and Finance Corporation, and issued contracts to themselves. They then recapitalized the federal mortgage for the railroad through bonds of their own to an initial $51 million and forced the state of California to cough up $3 million. Stanford, as president of the Central Pacific, became the governor of California (1861–63) and managed to funnel an additional $825,000 into CP coffers. Next the quartet pressed towns and cities to turn over rights of way, terminal and harbor sites, and stock and bond subscriptions, threatening to refuse to provide rail service to them if they did not. And through Huntington's lobbying, the quartet gained an additional federal subsidy for each short section of construction.

Using cheap labor—some 3,000 Irish workers and 10,000 Chinese coolies at $1 a day each—they began construction eastward toward Promontory Point, Utah, on January 8, 1863. They built badly, however, and much of the winter work had to be redone in the spring. In constructing only 800 miles of track they managed to spend $79 million.

When threatening news appeared of a pending investigation into the high cost of constructing the railroad, the building that housed the Credit and Finance Corporation "accidentally" burned down, and the financial records of the company were destroyed. But U.S. government experts have given clues to the amount of graft involved; they estimate that 70 to 75 percent of the construction money for the railroad was wasted and that $36 million of the $79 million that was spent was "pure gravy." The fire prevented a congressional inquiry like that accorded Crédit Mobilier, and thus little national public indignation developed over the matter.

In California, however, Judah and his three associates were hated. Their initial profit apparently was not enough. They gouged and bribed, controlled state legislators and judges, influenced legislation protecting them from regulation, became "czars" of all types of public transportation, and charged the highest freight rates in the United States. Shrewdness enabled them to gain control of the Southern Pacific in 1884; united with Central Pacific, it gave the four railroad barons monopoly control in all of the West, much to the chagrin of oppressed farmers, who found already high freight rates doubled at harvest time.

Today Huntington, Hopkins, Stanford, and Crocker are memorialized in California as pioneers and philanthropists, and they are so regarded by the uninformed. But to the knowledgeable, they are outstanding practitioners of the policy "plunder, then philanthropize."

Anne HUTCHINSON: colonial feminist

Dissent in the Puritan theocracy of the Massachusetts Bay Colony, whether civil or religious, was swiftly and vigorously punished, at times with death. Nonconformists among the lower classes suffered physically: ears were lopped off, backs whipped, legs confined in stocks. Upper-class rebels were, if possible, publicly shamed or banished to restore order and equanimity. The rebel who most sorely tried the peace, order, and tranquility of the colony was, like her predecessors, banished. But she was a woman so well informed, so dynamic, and so filled with the courage of her convictions that she managed to gain, briefly, support from the majority of her fellow residents against the theocracy's magistrates and clergy.

Anne Marbury Hutchinson was the English-born daughter of a puritanistic Anglican clergyman. She had been raised in so intense an atmosphere of theological argument, scriptural study, and concern for ecclesiastical polity that she could, and did, hold her own in the almost constant disputations that characterized gatherings of Puritan intellectuals. She was convinced by study and coeval events that pressures for religious conformity from Anglican bishops and King James I of England were to be countered by nonconformity rather than by separatism. Taught by John Cotton, nonconformist vicar of St. Botolph's Church in Boston, England, Hutchinson believed that the purification of contemporary Anglicanism had to come from within and persuaded totally that a Christian lived and worshiped because of the internalized grace of God and not, in her words, through "ordinances, forms, and ceremonies imposed by man." Hutchinson, with her family, followed Cotton to Massachusetts in 1634.

Her outspokenness during the voyage to America won her both friends and enemies, not only because of the unconventionality of a woman's acting as a spiritual and doctrinal spokesman, but also because her pronouncements often contradicted established Puritan precepts and ventured onto doctrinal thin ice. She ar-

gued for Christian intuition (which brought her close to Puritan-detested Enthusiasm), for a Covenant of Grace rather than a Covenant of Laws (which smacked strongly of Puritan-dreaded Antinomianism and Lutheran faith-versus-works doctrines), and for the direct communication of God to His redeemed ones through Scripture. Because of these beliefs, her shipboard enemies delayed her reception into the Boston church for one week, and later spoke adversely of her during her trials.

Soon after landing, Hutchinson established the first ladies' club in the New World. For the colony's women, who in the 17th century were mere household drudges, it provided a source of entertainment. Its purpose was to discuss the Sunday sermons of the Boston church. In addition to this, it served as a means of educating the women doctrinally. But to the horror of the Boston magistrates, the club also acted as a vehicle for Hutchinson's ideas, made more dangerous to the theocracy when the meetings started to take place twice weekly and to attract men, including clergy and the colony's elected governor, Henry Vane. John Winthrop, a founder of the colony, became alarmed at Hutchinson's influence. He was especially fearful for the existence of the theocracy, but he also felt that valuable female time was being wasted because of the kind of intellectual woman he detested. Still bruised from his struggles in 1635 with Roger WILLIAMS, another nonconformist, Winthrop was determined to stop Hutchinson at any cost.

Winthrop began to act against Hutchinson with vigor in 1637. Enlisting John Wilson, pastor of the Boston, Massachusetts, church, and other anti-Hutchinsonians, he began what historians label the Antinomian controversy, so-called because Hutchinson was seen as rejecting a literal interpretation of Old Testament law in favor of the spiritual gospel of the New Testament. Hutchinson had angered Winthrop and many of the clergy by dividing the clergy into those supporting the concept of a Covenant of Grace and Faith (among them, Cotton) and those who advocated a Covenant of Law (Wilson and most of the others). The controversy almost tore Boston apart. Cotton was questioned and deemed basically sound, Hutchinson was interviewed hostilely by church authorities, Vane was defeated in his re-election bid by Winthrop, women's clubs were condemned as "disorderly" by a church synod, and most of Hutchinson's supporters, fearing that they might also be persecuted, dropped away. Even Cotton began to turn against her.

In a bitter trial before the colony's General Court, during which Winthrop as president of the colony spent much of his time baiting her, Hutchinson was found guilty of "traducing the ministers and their ministry." The punishment was banishment, but she was to be held under house arrest by an enemy so that she could have an opportunity to recant. She was next brought to the Boston church, questioned on some 30 "errors," allowed to go through a form of recantation, questioned again, and—when antagonism overrode her temper—was formally excommunicated. Orthodoxy had triumphed.

Forced out of the colony in 1638, Hutchinson founded a democratic Christian settlement at Aquidneck (now Portsmouth), Rhode Island, for which she acted as sometime preacher. She died in an Indian raid in Long Island in 1643.

E. F. HUTTON: a far-reaching cash management fraud

In May 1985, in one of the most widely publicized corporate crimes in American history, the investment firm of E. F. Hutton & Company pleaded guilty to 2,000 separate criminal charges of mail and wire fraud. Never before had a prestigious Wall Street investment house (at the time, E. F. Hutton was the nation's fifth largest investment firm) admitted such a major felony or fraud. The firm had used elaborate and sophisticated methods of "check kiting" that had provided it with interest-free loans of as much as $250 million a day. Check kiting allows checking accounts to be played off against each other in order to not bounce checks and to obtain interest-free, short-term loans. At the time of the verdict, Hutton's top executives denied any knowledge of wrongdoing while agreeing to pay $2 million in criminal fines and $750,000 in court costs and restitution to banks that had suffered losses as a result of the scheme.

The company's fraudulent cash-management practices took place for 20 months, beginning in July 1980 and ending in February 1982. During that time, state and federal banking authorities were alerted by two small banks on which E. F. Hutton had practiced so-called "chaining"—the artificial creation of delays in check clearing by transferring funds through networks of regional banks and thus holding on to the money value of the checks for as long as possible, therefore earning maximum interest. Government investigators then began checking millions of documents—customer checks, cash receipts, disbursement forms, and cash wire listings, among other information involving banks and E. F. Hutton—in a process that took three years.

It was not until 1985 that the U.S. Justice Department took direct control of the investigation. Until then E. F. Hutton had been claiming that check-kiting practices involving the company were merely isolated departures from company policy by low-level employees. Hutton branch officials deposited money in local bank accounts and afterward wrote out checks for amounts larger than what was in the accounts. The overdrafts were then covered a few days later by check deposits from other Hutton branches. In addition to "chaining," Hutton had engaged in two other check-kiting techniques to maximize the interest earned by individual or corporate

bank accounts. It had evidently "churned" checks written on its own accounts through various branch offices, creating the illusion of larger overnight balances than really existed, and had also apparently "crisscrossed" multimillion-dollar checks of equal amounts between company accounts at Manufacturers Hanover Trust and the Chemical Bank in New York.

At least 23 branch offices of E. F. Hutton were found to be involved in check-kiting operations between 1980 and 1982, bilking some 400 commercial banks out of approximately $10 billion. Because no individuals were named in the federal charges against Hutton, the Justice Department and U.S. Attorney General Edwin Meese III were criticized for prosecuting only companies and not specific employees, in cases involving white-collar crime. Charges of favoritism toward big business were lodged against the Justice Department. Hutton branch managers surely benefited from the check-kiting schemes because they were reportedly awarded bonuses equal to 10 percent of their branch profits. Attorney General Meese claimed that his decision to give immunity to rather than to go after and prosecute any Hutton employees was made "to push the investigation along." Robert Fomon, chairman and chief executive of the E. F. Hutton Group, Incorporated, which was the parent company to the investment firm, claimed that he had "no reason to believe that any members of top management were involved" and that no client or customer lost any money as a result of the illegal transactions.

E. F. Hutton hired former U.S. attorney general Griffin Bell to conduct an independent, internal investigation of the fraud case and to make a report of its findings. For four months, Bell and his team of 14 lawyers interviewed more than 370 current and former Hutton employees and executives, attempting to uncover who was responsible for the check-kiting scheme. In September 1985, an exhaustive report was released criticizing 15 Hutton executives in particular for managerial "shortcomings" but finding no one guilty of criminal acts. Fomon was fully exonerated, but three senior officials of Hutton were cited for failure to adequately oversee cash and management operations (the three promptly left the company). Cited also were two midlevel executives who were officially reprimanded, three regional managers who were suspended for 30 days without pay, and six branch managers who were fined between $25,000 and $50,000 each (all of the six earned more than $100,000 a year). Bell's investigators looked suspiciously at George L. Ball, the former president of Hutton, who was by then the head of Prudential-Bache Securities; he was thought to have contributed to the overdraft operation because he "constantly exhorted" Hutton branch managers to increase their earnings. In the end, however, Ball was not held accountable for the fraud. Bell's report was attacked for being too soft on E. F. Hutton & Company, which promised, however, to restructure its management and add controls to prevent any recurrences of fraud.

In October 1985, the Securities and Exchange Commission (SEC) charged Hutton with violating securities laws in its handling of customers' investments in its mutual funds. Without admitting any guilt, Hutton entered a consent decree, accepting a broad range of federal sanctions against it and agreeing to reimburse customers for more than $1 million. The firm had apparently not begun crediting dividends to investors in certain funds until six days after it got their purchase orders—one day longer than the prospectus for the funds promised. (After the firm's conviction in May 1985, it had won a temporary waiver of an SEC rule forbidding convicted felons from managing or underwriting mutual funds.)

The scandal clearly damaged E. F. Hutton, which depended on its good name and top-notch reputation as a securities firm to stay in business; by April 1986, when other brokerage houses saw their cash funds increase, Hutton's cash reserves had declined by more than $1 billion. Yet it continued to deny that the scandal had affected its retail brokerage business.

Following the recommendations of Griffin Bell, Hutton announced, in January 1986, a huge company reorganization that centralized policy making and recast Hutton's board of directors to include a majority of outsiders in place of corporate officers. However, controversy still lingered about the Justice Department's handling of the Hutton case, particularly its past decision not to indict individual employees of the company. Along with the SEC, the House Subcommittee on Crime, chaired by Representative William J. Hughes of New Jersey, further scrutinized Hutton's culpability in order to expose all the facts in the case, some of which seemed to have fallen through the cracks in the Justice Department's investigation. By 1987, the one-time "impeccable" investment house was still plagued by poor employee morale and loss of business. Many felt that in its check-kiting scandal, Hutton had betrayed the public trust.

Then, on December 3, 1987, rival brokerage Shearson Lehman Brothers announced a definitive agreement to buy E. F. Hutton for $960 million in cash and debt securities. Hutton's 83 years of feisty independence came to an end in 1988 with the formation of a giant Wall Street brokerage and investment house, Shearson Lehman Hutton Inc.

Samuel INSULL: a model of greed

A pew end in Blythburg, Suffolk, England, depicts Greed, one of the seven deadly sins, as a bearded, middle-aged man sitting on his cash box, hands extended and open to receive more money. If the sculpture were to be recreated in the 20th century, Samuel Insull could act as its model.

Born in London in 1859, Samuel Insull was to gain dubious fame as one of the "Pied Pipers of the bull market era." Insatiably greedy, he unscrupulously pursued his passion for wealth until 1932, extending his open hands to receive money as president of the Commonwealth Edison Company of Chicago and as the leading executive and "pocket liner" of a pyramid of other midwestern utility companies. He acquired so many millions of dollars that, with Ivar KREUGER, he gained notoriety as one of the most avaricious swindlers in history.

Protégé of and secretary to inventor Thomas Alva Edison, Insull held prominence in the industrial holdings of his mentor until 1892 when he was forced out of the Edison General Electric Company by eastern financiers. He then became president of Chicago's Commonwealth Edison, honestly earning his salary until, in middle age, he was caught up in the nationwide trend to combine small civic lighting enterprises under large holding companies. The covetous Insull did not cease his campaign for greater riches until 1932, when he fled the country to escape various criminal charges.

His method was simple. He first bought smaller, usually town-owned utility companies, using very little of his own money. Instead, he employed bank credit and sales of securities to small investors to finance his acquisitions. He linked five of these acquisitions to form, as a bargaining chip, the Public Service Company of Northern Illinois. In 1912, Insull hit a record high in terms of corruption. He formed a holding organization called Middle West Utilities Company and made two to three times his investment by buying stocks cheap and selling dear. Insull next developed a "pyramid"—an association of interlocking holding companies under his leadership which bought and sold among themselves. He issued masses of paper securities, gained even more money by charging huge management and engineering fees to the subsidiary utility companies in the pyramid, and pocketed millions in "change" for himself. To protect himself, Insull led the fight against the plans of seven cities to operate civic generators; he also bribed legislators and the Illinois Power Commission, whose chairman, Frank L. Smith, attained the U.S. Senate, only to be unseated as unfit in 1926. Furthermore, Insull took over all of Chicago's elevated transit systems and next pushed for "customer ownership" of his various holdings. By 1929, some 250,000 customers owned stock in his Insull Utilities Investments, founded in 1928 to be the top of his pyramid. The person whom President Franklin D. Roosevelt's staff labeled "Chicago's gold-plated anarchist" was worth over $150 million by the time of the 1929 stock market crash.

Insull's machinations enabled him to weather the crash. But when utility stocks began to decline in 1931, he tried to "peg" (support) his stocks in the market and used up all of the available cash of his pyramid in doing so. In 1932, his bubble burst. Banks in New York and Chicago took over his affairs, and both state and federal charges were lodged against him. Aged and sick, Insull fled to Europe to preserve his liberty. His customer investors, however, had lost more than a billion dollars.

Extradited from Istanbul in 1934, Insull stood trial three times on charges ranging from embezzlement to misuse of the mails to defraud and violations of federal bankruptcy laws. In each instance he was acquitted. Despite his misuse of so much of the public's money, the laws of that era allowed no basis for finding him guilty. Insull died in Paris in 1938, a man somewhat broken but by no means "broke." His chief monument is the Chicago Civic (now Lyric) Opera building, constructed in 1928 to house both the opera company and Insull's burgeoning headquarters. Its architectural massings caused Chicagoans to refer to it as "Insull's throne."

INTERNATIONAL NEWS SERVICE: news
agency piracy

Business competition in America has not been restricted to financiers and industrialists; it began to include news-gathering services as early as 1820 and reached a major crisis stage in 1914 when the Associated Press (AP) of New York hauled the Hearst papers' International News Service (INS) into federal court on a charge that some newspapers exaggeratedly labeled "piracy."

American newsgathering associations began as co-operative ventures among newspapers for a double purpose: to develop news items for the member papers and to keep those items from their rivals. The concern of such ventures in their earlier years was the collection and organization of news from Europe, and the success of some papers and associations in "scooping" others through exclusive stories caused several rival associations to be established. Regulating the exclusivity of these organizations' services was difficult at best, and it became even harder in 1906, when the Hearst papers founded the INS and offered its news copy to all customers, regardless of their associations with other news services. The chief enemy of the INS was the AP of New York City, a traditionally conservative cooperative, scrupulously concerned with restricting its news items to its member papers.

The AP action, fought both in court and, to the delight of readers, in rival newspapers, made clear the differing philosophies of the AP and INS. Among other charges, the AP alleged that the INS bribed employees of its member papers to furnish it with AP items received via telephone and telegraph before the AP's member papers could print them; the AP also complained that items printed in early—usually morning—newspapers were copied out by the INS and resold to non-AP papers.

The INS's lawyers argued ingeniously that the transmission of a news item constituted its "abandonment" to the public domain and that the INS's actions were therefore safeguarded by common law and could not be labeled piracy. The AP's lawyers argued the reverse: that copyright privileges protected their news articles and that membership in their association protected their exclusivity.

The two news organizations' legal battle eventually reached the U.S. Supreme Court, where a divided decision in 1915 found in the AP's favor and branded the INS guilty of unfair competition because it appropriated to itself "values created by the Associated Press." The AP's member newspapers were exultant. But papers that used the INS found solace in a dissenting opinion by Justices Oliver Wendell Holmes, Joseph McKenna, and Louis Brandeis. They opposed the unfair competition judgment, opening the way for further court tests of news exclusivity. They also suggested a solution to the dilemma of news ownership: papers would designate the source of an item and the designation would be the basis of a charge for service. This practice is still continued today.

No further blatant piracy occurred after the ruling. However, a separate 1915 decision concerning AP's rule that its member papers use only AP items favored the INS by opening up all newspapers to the services of all news agencies. This ruling increased rivalry among the agencies for both news items and customers and compelled the competing agencies to make their policies and products so similar that AP and the United Press (UP), after 1958 the owner of INS, became suppliers of news to all papers that hired their services.

IRAN-CONTRA SCANDAL

The credibility and competence of U.S. President Ronald W. Reagan were seriously questioned after November 1986 when the American public learned that millions of dollars had been paid for secret shipments of American weapons and spare parts to Iran in a murky effort to obtain the release of Americans held hostage in Lebanon by Iran-influenced Muslim zealots. Profits from the arms sales, which were shipped through Israel, were channeled (possibly illegally) to the contra rebels fighting against the Sandinista government in Nicaragua. There were strong indications that American laws had been broken, and the widespread prestige and popularity of the president diminished as investigators uncovered the details of the American arms sales to Iran. The scandal first came to light in an obscure Lebanese magazine, *Al Shiraa,* on November 4, 1986.

Grave damage was also done to American prestige and trust abroad. Some European allies of America felt betrayed by what they perceived as hypocrisy. The U.S. government had violated the same principles that they had urged on Europe, namely no negotiations or dealings with terrorists and so-called evil nations such as Iran and Libya. President Reagan had fervently advocated a strong stand against terrorism.

After the scandal broke, Reagan earnestly denied that he had been trading arms for hostages, but that was the public's general perception of the affair. At first the president refused to admit that he had made any mistakes and contended that the arms sent by the United States to Iran were purely defensive (though the antitank missiles that were sent could be used in an offensive military campaign). In trying to explain the matter to the public, the president said there had been secret diplomatic contacts with some Iranian officials. He assumed responsibility for the decision and operation to ship weapons to moderate Iranians, whom he felt could possibly wean Iran away from its violent anti-Americanism under its Islamic leader, the Ayatollah Ruhollah Khomeini. Reagan told reporters that "To eliminate the widespread but mistaken perception that we have been exchanging arms for hostages, I have directed that no further sales of arms of any kind be sent to Iran."

Perplexed and burdened, the president had earlier authorized U.S. Attorney General Edwin Meese III to conduct a probe into the brewing scandal. The report Meese made public revealed that the U.S. government had supplied $12 million in weapons and spare parts to Israeli representatives, who then sold them to Iran for a profit. The money paid for the arms (said to be from $10 million to $30 million) was then put into Swiss bank accounts, where it was under the control of agents of the Nicaraguan contras. The money was presumed to have been used to purchase arms for the contras to wage their guerilla war against the Marxist Sandinista government of Nicaragua. The Reagan administration fully backed the rebels. Later, it was disclosed that retired U.S. Air Force Major General Richard V. Secord had apparently helped in getting military supplies to the contras.

Curiously, the person who was behind the affair was supposedly a 43-year-old U.S. Marine lieutenant colonel named Oliver ("Ollie") L. North, a gung-ho, brassy patriot and ardent Reagan supporter. North, a deputy on the National Security Council (NSC) staff since 1981, had been the principal adviser behind an elaborate and private network designed to finance and support the contras. On November 25, 1986, he was fired from his NSC post when Meese disclosed the clandestine arms-sales profits' diversion. At the same time, President Reagan accepted the resignation of his national security adviser, Vice Admiral John M. Poindexter, who was North's boss. Just before North was fired, the destruction of some official documents took place in his office, located across the street from the White House.

Reagan's leadership was severely weakened by the revelation of these covert operations, which it turned out had been going on since early 1984. The national security adviser at that time, Robert ("Bud") C. McFarlane, had begun secret diplomatic contacts with Iran's government. He claimed that he had pursued the contacts on the president's behalf, even after his resignation on December 4, 1985, and replacement by Poindexter. Later, White House Chief of Staff Donald T. Regan criticized McFarlane for giving "lousy advice" about American policy toward Iran. McFarlane called the arms transfer a "mistake" and, in 1987, tried to commit suicide, blaming himself for not handling the matter properly.

In December 1986, various committees of the Senate and House began hearing testimony behind closed doors to try to get to the bottom of the scandal. There was concern about whether Reagan had broken Section 501 of the National Security Act. Amendments made to the section in 1980 required the president to keep Con-

gress's intelligence committees "fully and currently" informed of all American intelligence operations. The law allowed a delay in informing the committees about covert operations "if the President determines it is essential . . . to meet extraordinary circumstances affecting vital interests of the U.S." Yet the president was required to give "prior notice" when he invoked this clause, informing all committee members "in a timely fashion."

There was concern that a number of laws might have been broken by the arms shipments to Iran. The use of federal monies to aid the contras was strictly forbidden by the so-called Boland Amendments from October 1984 until October 1986 when the amendment expired. In the amendments was a prohibition against American solicitation of third-country financing, and Iranian money had supposedly passed to the contras when that prohibition was in force. American arms-export laws may also have been violated. This is difficult to determine, though, since there are waivers that permit the president to skirt such laws in times of crisis.

Both North and Poindexter, when called to testify before the Senate Intelligence Committee, invoked the Fifth Amendment to the Constitution, citing their right to avoid self-incrimination. Deeply troubled by the crisis, President Reagan appointed a three-member "Special Review Board" to study the NSC's function in the conduct of American foreign policy. About three months later, on February 26, 1987, the board (commonly called the Tower Commission for its chairman, John Tower, a former United States senator from Texas) issued its report, which criticized the president for his lack of oversight and knowledge of what was going on. The report also blamed North, who was seen as a "fanciful" freewheeler in his efforts to sell arms to Iran and keep funds and weapons flowing to the contras.

Reagan's past six years of presidential political initiative were undermined, and most of the American public felt deceived by the affair. Many perceived the president as very divorced from the daily operations of government and often unaware of the nuances of his policies. He had undoubtedly been deceived by members of his own staff and had blundered in his judgment.

In the summer of 1987, combined House and Senate investigating committees held 41 days of televised public hearings into the Iran-Contra scandal. They received testimony from many witnesses, among them Poindexter and Secretary of State George Shultz, who asserted that Poindexter and North had deliberately not informed him about what was going on. North admitted that he had misled Congress on the morality of his actions; his loyal secretary, Fawn Hall, who had helped North shred documents, told the House and Senate committees that there were times when one had to "go above the written law" but then retracted this statement. In their final report on the scandal, the two congressional committees said that President Reagan had failed in his constitutional obligation to faithfully execute the law. At the end of 1987, grand juries were probing the Iran-Contra affair and criminal indictments were possible.

A federal grand jury in March 1988 charged Poindexter, North, Secord, and Albert Hakim (an Iranian-born U.S. citizen and arms dealer) with conspiring to illegally divert profits from the U.S.-Iran arms sales to the Nicaraguan contras. In 1989 North was convicted of obstructing Congress, destroying NSC documents, and accepting an illegal gratuity; he received a suspended prison term, was put on two years' probation, was fined $150,000, and ordered to perform 1,200 hours of community service. Hakim pleaded guilty in 1989 to giving an illegal gratuity to North. He got two years' probation and was fined $5,000; he called the scandal a "soap opera."

Poindexter, who was judged the head of the Iran-Contra plan, was convicted on all five of the criminal counts against him (the most important victory by the office of independent counsel Lawrence E. Walsh); he then appealed but received a six-month prison term. Sentenced to two years' probation were Secord (who pleaded guilty to lying to congressional investigators), McFarlane (who pleaded guilty to four misdemeanor charges of withholding information from Congress), and Carl Channell and Richard Miller (two Contra fund-raisers who worked for North and pleaded guilty to conspiracy to defraud the government). Others were involved, including William J. Casey, CIA director, who died in May 1987 and may have put the grand scheme together.

Perhaps no one will ever know the full story, thanks to a partly successful coverup and a shield of official secrecy. Walsh's inconclusive investigation was frustrated by appeals court decisions (including the overturning of North and Poindexter's convictions) and presidential pardons for former defense secretary Caspar Weinberger and five others in 1992. In August 1993, Walsh filed a final report, which pointed to Meese's "false account" of a 1985 Iranian arms-for-hostages deal to protect President Reagan. Meese could not be indicted because the statute of limitations had expired; North, McFarlane, and Poindexter were supposedly "scapegoats," and Reagan reportedly was involved, but key officials scrambled to deflect blame from him and his cabinet.

Clifford IRVING: author of fake Howard Hughes "autobiography"

In the late fall of 1971, the McGraw-Hill Publishing Company and Time, Incorporated discovered to their chagrin that the $765,000 they thought they had paid to the eccentric billionaire recluse, Howard R. Hughes, for his autobiograhy had actually gone to a minor Amer-

Clifford Irving, author, and his wife, Edith, pleaded guilty on March 13, 1972, in Manhattan federal court to a charge of conspiring to defraud an American publisher with a fake autobiography of billionaire Howard Hughes. (AP/Wide World Photos)

ican novelist named Clifford Irving, who had written a bogus manuscript. Irving, his wife Edith, and his co-author Richard Suskind, were indicted by federal and New York State grand juries for grand larceny, mail fraud, perjury, plagiarism, and possession of forged documents. They had almost pulled off one of the greatest literary hoaxes of the century.

Clifford Irving, an expatriate American writer living on the Spanish island of Ibiza, came across the December 21, 1970, issue of *Newsweek,* which contained an article entitled "The Case of the Invisible Billionaire." This article, which included a photograph of a sample of Hughes' handwriting, sparked in Irving the idea of producing a fake autobiography of Hughes. He discussed his idea with his friend writer Richard Suskind, who agreed to cooperate with the research and writing. Edith, Irving's Swiss wife, consented to open a secret Swiss bank account in which to deposit the funds, intended for Hughes, that would come from the book.

Irving then approached McGraw-Hill, publisher of three of his novels, and told his editor that he had received several letters from Howard Hughes asking him to write his authorized biography. The McGraw-Hill editors never questioned the authenticity of the handwritten letters and, sensing a best-seller in the making, authorized Irving to proceed. In February 1971, Irving reported that he had met Hughes in Oaxaca, Mexico, for the first of many fictitious taping and discussion sessions, and in March he brought a forged letter of agreement from Hughes to his editor. A formal contract was signed, and a large advance was paid for the book, most of which was intended for Hughes but ended up in Switzerland.

Edith Irving then contacted the Swiss Consulate in Spain, saying she had lost her passport and wanted a new one. When it arrived, Irving doctored it by changing the serial number and the name to Helga R. Hughes. He also substituted the photograph of his blonde wife with another of her wearing glasses and a black wig. Thus disguised, Edith Irving went to Zurich and opened a bank account under the name of H. R. Hughes. Some time later, using the identification card of her first husband's wife, Hanne Rosenkranz, she opened a second account at another Swiss bank, into which funds from the first account were transferred. It seemed at the time an ideal method for laundering the McGraw-Hill advances.

Meanwhile, Irving was flying about to Puerto Rico, Florida, California, the Bahamas, and the Virgin Islands. Although he was purportedly conferring with Hughes, Irving was busy with other activities. He had a much publicized affair with the Danish singer Nina Van Pallandt and another with a scuba diver.

Much had been written about Howard Hughes over the years, and Irving and Suskind sought out this material in the New York and Houston Public Libraries and the Library of Congress. Their chief source of inside information, however, came from the draft of a manuscript written by an investigative reporter named James Phelan. Noah Dietrich, who for 32 years had served as Hughes's right-hand man and trouble-shooter, had hired Phelan to ghost-write Dietrich's autobiography, but he subsequently became frustrated at Phelan's slowness and hired another writer. The Phelan manuscript had been mailed out to several publishers before it was completed, and somewhere along the line it and 150 pages of transcripts of conversations with Dietrich about Hughes fell into Irving's hands. Irving made good use of them. Believing that the transcripts were those of Irving's conversations with Hughes, *Life*, a Time, In-corporated magazine, bought worldwide syndication rights for the most tantalizing excerpts from them. Irving also used the Phelan manuscript, sometimes embellished and sometimes verbatim, in his own "autobiography."

After the *Life* contract was signed, Irving received permission to use *Time*'s extensive reference library and files "to check his facts" and in the process picked up much more information about Hughes. He and Suskind also had access to the files of *Aviation Week*, a journal published by McGraw-Hill. It is ironic that the two publishing giants involved in the Hughes hoax paid for Irving's substantial use of their own material.

In September 1971, after they had written most of their manuscript, Irving and Suskind flew to Florida for another phony meeting with Hughes. Irving then informed McGraw-Hill that Hughes had advised him to take the book to another publisher. This news prompted McGraw-Hill to pay yet another large advance. On December 21, 1971, Irving turned over his 950-page manuscript, complete with notations in Hughes's "own" handwriting. (By that time, Irving had become an expert forger, so expert in fact that he fooled Osborn Associates, a firm specializing in handwriting analysis, for some weeks.)

About this time, the real Hanne Rosenkranz arrived in Zurich and opened an account in the same bank in which Edith Irving had opened her second account under a false name. Edith was then exposed as an impostor and accused of fraud, and the entire scheme for the spurious autobiography began to fall apart. James Phelan contacted *Time* reporter Frank McCulloch and told him of his suspicions that Irving had plagiarized his manuscript about Hughes. When the two documents were compared, there was no doubt about their similarity. Osborn Associates had second thoughts about its appraisal of the authenticity of the Hughes's handwriting. Suskind recanted his earlier assertion that he had met Hughes in Florida and admitted that he had never seen the man. Finally, Irving also confessed, after reveling in the notoriety of numerous press interviews and television appearances. He was given two and one-half years in prison, while Edith Irving and Suskind received lighter sentences. The Hughes "autobiography" was never published.

Andrew JACKSON: alleged adulterer and bigamist

While serving his first term as president of the United States, Andrew Jackson and his wife, Rachel, were accused of being adulterers and bigamists. The vicious rumors were widely circulated in newspapers and pamphlets by the followers of Jackson's political opponents, John Quincy Adams and Henry Clay, during the 1828 presidential campaign. Though the exaggerated allegations were hardly strong enough to stop Jackson from being reelected, they may have had a deleterious effect on Rachel's weak heart. She suffered a fatal heart attack in December of that year, just three months before Jackson's inauguration.

Had the hotheaded Jackson been a more reflective man, he might have realized that behind the exaggerated claims declaring the Jacksons adulterers and bigamists were facts traceable to errors that Jackson as a lawyer and judge should have been wise enough to avoid. Although the virulence of the attacks was inexcusable and may have had a fatal effect on Rachel Jackson's heart, the seeds of the scandal lay in Jackson's misjudgment.

Jackson had met Rachel Donelson Robards in 1788, when, as an itinerant federal attorney general in the Tennessee Territory, he boarded at the Donelson home in Nashville. Rachel was then married to the spitefully jealous Lewis Robards who, guilty of numerous adulteries, suspected his wife of his own sins. He tried to have Jackson arrested for alleged liberties with his wife, but the impulsive and aggressive—and innocent—Jackson scared him off. Robards left, alone and angry, for the Kentucky Territory.

In 1790, Robards threatened to return and take Rachel back by force. She fled to Natchez, Mississippi, in January 1791 under the protection of two gentlemen, one of them Jackson. Contemporary evidence indicates that her personal conduct was irreproachable, but her flight further inflamed Robards's jealousy. In retaliation, he sued for divorce in Kentucky, charging that she had "eloped with another man." This claim of adultery was libelously false, and failure to prove the allegation made the Virginia legislature (which then controlled the Kentucky Territory) dismiss the suit.

A confused account of the suit and its outcome reached Tennessee, and Rachel, again resident in Nashville, was regarded as a free agent. At this point Jackson made the greatest mistake of his life: a combination of passion and impulsiveness made him fail to check with the Virginia legislature about Rachel's marital status. Instead, he and Rachel returned to Natchez, where Jackson made a second mistake: he married Rachel. In a Roman Catholic area (Mississippi was then Spanish), Protestants had to have civil permission to marry, a regulation Jackson knew about but failed to consider when he and Rachel went through a Protestant ceremony in 1791 and returned to Nashville to live respectably as husband and wife.

On two levels, they were technically adulterers and bigamists. She was not divorced, and their Protestant marriage in Natchez had been illegal. But nothing in documents written or authorized by Jackson suggests that he was then aware of his legal mistakes.

Robards, now enraged, sued for divorce again, on the charge that Rachel was openly cohabiting with Jackson; he won his suit on September 27, 1793. Word of the divorce reached Nashville in late December. Convinced now that they were technically bigamists and adulterers, the Jacksons were hastily remarried on January 18, 1794.

Once discovered by his political enemies, these facts were grossly exaggerated into violent vocal and printed attacks on Jackson and his wife during 1827 and 1828. Jackson tried to protect her by keeping the slanders from her and by engaging in quarrels, fistfights, and two duels with persons who made such attacks. He allowed his supporters to publish the "true facts" of the couple's history, but they were disregarded by the rabid, often libelous opposition press of the period. Rachel was made aware of the violent criticisms after Jackson's successful 1828 reelection; her shock may have caused her fatal heart attack.

Jackson, until his death in 1845, continued to blame his political opponents (especially the once-cooperative Henry Clay) for the murder of his beloved Rachel.

JACKSON-DICKINSON DUEL

On May 30, 1806, Andrew Jackson met Charles Dickinson in Logan County, Kentucky, for a duel of honor. Dickinson a 27-year old lawyer and dandy, renowned for his excellent marksmanship, was in high spirits. The apprehensive Jackson, on the other hand, was solemn. He was certain that Dickinson, as the better shot, would shoot first. Dickinson did indeed shoot first. He put a bullet in Jackson's chest, narrowly missing his heart. Still standing, Jackson fired at Dickinson. He inflicted a wound that caused Dickinson to bleed to death. For this action, Jackson gained a reputation for vengefulness and violence which would follow him for the next six years.

The duel took place because of a horse race that was never held. Jackson's Truxton was to race a stallion called Plowboy, owned by a Captain Joseph Ervin; the stake was $2,000, and arrangements were made for a forfeit penalty of $800 in third-party promissory notes. Plowboy became lame, and Jackson gained the forfeit notes from Charles Dickinson, Ervin's son-in-law. Jackson's relationship with Dickinson then became strained when he learned that a drunken Dickinson had bad-mouthed Jackson's beloved wife, Rachel. Dickinson had a reputation for a facetious and not always careful tongue: approached by an angry Jackson, he quickly made an apology.

But Dickinson in turn became angry when reports circulated that Jackson considered the promissory notes faulty or not immediately collectible. Dickinson's friends became upset about this essentially trivial problem and tried to resolve it. One friend, however, Thomas Swann, confronted Jackson pompously. The hotheaded Jackson responded to the angry words of Swann, calling him a liar and further alleging that Dickinson was one, too. Swann then became insulting and later, in a public tavern, almost provoked Jackson to shoot him. Instead, Jackson caned and berated him, calling him a "stupid meddler" in front of everyone.

Following this, Swann went to Dickinson, who quickly wrote to Jackson, calling him a coward and an equivocator and offering him a duel of honor. Jackson did not immediately reply. Next, the hotheaded Swann decided to defend himself. In March 1806, he sent a letter to Nashville's only newspaper, calling General Jackson a boastful, falsifying coward. Jackson responded in print, calling Swann a "puppet and lying valet for a worthless, drunken, blackguard scoundrel." He also attacked friends of Dickinson and Swann, who retorted with their own invective and forced Jackson's friend John Coffee into an injurious duel.

Dickinson also used the Nashville paper to berate Jackson in May 1806, and Jackson, in a letter to Dickinson, challenged him to the fatal duel. By the time it took place, all of Nashville knew it was to occur. Bets were made, chiefly in Dickinson's favor, since he was famed as so accurate a gunman that he could cut a stretched string at 24 feet.

When Dickinson's bullet did not knock Jackson down, however, he realized that he had missed and was now at Jackson's mercy. Jackson could have aimed high or fired over Dickinson's head. Instead, he raised his pistol, took careful aim, stopped at half cock, and paused. He then drew back the hammer and fired the fatal bullet.

Again their friends wrangled. Seventy-three citizens of Nashville petitioned the newspaper to dress in mourning for Dickinson's loss. When Jackson asked for a list of the names of the petitioners, 26 immediately withdrew their signatures. Dickinson's friends called the duel a brutal, cold-blooded killing. Jackson's supporters argued that the severity of his wound (which was inoperable) kept Jackson from magnanimity. But some remembered that Dickinson had wagered $300 that he would kill Jackson, making it hard to place the blame on Jackson. Although Jackson was an outcast for some time after the duel, his social status instantly changed during the War of 1812 when he was lauded for successfully defending New Orleans against the British in early 1815.

Howard "Buddy" JACOBSON: horse trainer, womanizer, and murderer

A celebrated race-track figure and one of the country's leading horse trainers, Howard "Buddy" Jacobson had become a prosperous New York real-estate entrepreneur and owner of a model agency when, in August 1978, he committed a murder. At that time, 23-year-old Melanie Cain, Jacobson's top model and girlfriend, sought to end a long relationship with him and moved in with a divorced restaurauteur named Jack Tupper. All three lived in the same apartment building on Manhattan's Upper East Side, which was owned by Jacobson. Melanie, returning home one day after hunting for a new apartment, was unable to locate Tupper. She went down the hall to Jacobson's apartment to ask if he had seen him. Jacobson refused to let her in, but she was able to see that his apartment was in disarray and that there were blood stains on the carpet. Returning to her apartment, she telephoned the police, who shortly afterward arrested the 49-year-old Jacobson, charging him with beating, stabbing, and shooting Tupper and then attempting to dispose of his dead body by burning it in a crate in a vacant lot in the Bronx.

Ruggedly handsome, outgoing, and sometimes hot tempered, Jacobson had won more horse races than any other trainer by the late 1960s. After taking part in a racing strike in 1969, he lost his trainer's license while being suspended by the New York State Racing Commission for fraud, misrepresentation, and mishandling of funds. Although he had a comfortable home in Queens with a wife and two sons, Jacobson decided to pursue a more glamorous lifestyle involving real-estate investment in Manhattan. At his East Side building on 84th Street, he rented apartments to would-be fashion models, one of whom was Melanie Cain. In 1973, at the age of 17, Cain had moved to the city from the Midwest to be a model and soon found work through the prestigious Ford Agency. She met Jacobson, who pursued her ardently, and the two began an affair in late 1973. All the while she became more and more successful as a model, until finally she broke away from the Ford Agency at Jacobson's urging and formed an agency called My Fair Lady with him. During the next couple of years, her career flourished. The affair, however, faltered. Jacobson sometimes bedded other young women whom he recruited for the agency. Six times Cain vainly tried to end her relationship with Jacobson. She discovered that he had seduced other young women whom he recruited for the agency and that he had lied about his age, telling her that he was in his early 30s when, in fact, he was 15 years older. He had even tried to pass off his two sons as his brothers.

Then, in 1978, Cain told him that she had fallen in love with Jack Tupper, whom she had met with Jacobson a few years earlier. Tupper's disappearance and murder occurred shortly thereafter. The police investigation revealed that the My Fair Lady Agency had evidently been a cover for a high-class call-girl operation run by Jacobson.

At his long, sensational trial in the Bronx, New York, Jacobson pleaded innocent. The murder weapons were never found. At the trial a tape was played on which Jackson apparently offered Tupper $100,000 to give up Cain. Scores of witnesses testified, including Cain. The jury, which was at one point deadlocked, was finally convinced of Jacobson's guilt, chiefly because of Cain's testimony and police evidence.

On May 31, 1980, while in jail awaiting sentencing for second-degree murder, Jacobson and a man who identified himself as Jacobson's attorney (later identified as Anthony DeRosa—a man who owed Jacobson a favor) switched clothes while the guards changed shifts, and Jacobson strolled out of jail. He drove away with 22-year-old Audrey Barrett, his new girlfriend, and fled to California. Although Barrett surrendered to the police after a few weeks, Jacobson continued to flee. He used names found on tombstones as aliases, kept contact from public phone booths with friends, reportedly got money from friends, and attempted to reach journalists in the hope of selling his story proclaiming his innocence. After 40 days, he was apprehended while talking in a phone booth in Manhattan Beach, California, to his son, whose phone had been voluntarily tapped. Placed in maximum security, Jacobson faced new charges of escape, forgery, and tampering with public documents, adding time to his earlier 25-year sentence for murder. He claimed to have gone to California to find Tupper's real killer—a man he once named as Donald Brown.

In prison Jacobson contacted the notorious attorney Roy COHN and then former U.S. Attorney General Ramsey Clark to represent his appeal. He also attempted another jailbreak in 1981, in vain, and planned to write a book to show that he had been framed for Tupper's murder.

In 1989, while serving a life prison term at Attica, New York, Jacobson died of cancer at age 58. At the time, Cain said she still believed that Jacobson was guilty.

JAPANESE INTERNMENT CAMPS

Shortly after the United States entered World War II, approximately 120,000 Japanese-Americans and resident aliens on the West Cost were rounded up and sent to internment camps in desolate parts of the West. They were held there like prisoners for two or three years, their only crime being of Japanese descent. Their incarceration was not only racist, but illegal and unethical.

After the Japanese air force's surprise attack on Pearl Harbor on December 7, 1941, hysteria swept over much of the western United States. Rumors flew that the Japanese were planning a land invasion or were going to bomb San Francisco, Los Angeles, and Seattle. Lieutenant General John L. DeWitt, who was in charge of the security of the western United States, did nothing to calm the situation; in fact he inflamed it by recommending to the U.S. War Department that "alien subjects of enemy nations" be moved to the interior of America. This euphemism for the Japanese found a friendly ear in Assistant Secretary of War John J. McCloy, who strongly backed DeWitt and shared his belief that American citizens with Japanese ancestry would always be loyal to Japan.

DeWitt reported that ethnic Japanese were signaling to ships in the Pacific Ocean, but when the Federal Communications Commission investigated, it found that no signals had occurred. DeWitt also charged that the Japanese-Americans were committing espionage and sabotage, but the Federal Bureau of Investigation (FBI) could find no evidence of any subversion, and no documented evidence for it has been found to this day. However, by the end of December 1941, as the hysteria mounted, the ethnic Japanese were ordered to surrender their cameras, binoculars, short-wave radios, and any weapons they owned. The State Personnel Board of California decreed that no person whose ethnicity was that of a country at war with the United States could be hired for the state's civil service. The army designated 12 restricted areas in which "enemy aliens" had to observe a curfew and remain within five miles of their homes, except when traveling to or from work. Congressmen from the western states wrote President Franklin D. Roosevelt advising that the Japanese be removed, and DeWitt testified before a congressional committee that the need for this was urgent.

Although the War Department, U.S. Naval Intelligence, and the FBI were unable to verify the allegations that the ethnic Japanese were a threat, Roosevelt gave in to the political pressure and on February 19, 1942, signed Executive Order 9066, which permitted the U.S. Army to relocate and intern whomever it considered dangerous. DeWitt established a military area in the western half of Washington, Oregon, and California and ordered, "in the interest of military necessity," that all persons of Japanese ancestry be removed from it.

Japanese-American families were given only a few days' notice in which to sell their homes, businesses, farms, fishing boats, and cars. Many suffered severe financial losses. They were herded into fairgrounds and racetracks where they were held for months while barracks were hastily constructed in 10 camps scattered from the swamps of Arkansas to the mountains of Wyoming and the deserts of California. The camps were surrounded with high barbed-wire fences, and in the watchtowers at the corners, army guards stood day and night with machine guns aimed inward. More than 60 percent of the prisoners were American citizens, and of the 40,000 who were under the age of 19, 99.3 percent were native-born.

There was a second scandal within this scandalous episode. In 1942, three young Japanese-American men were arrested and clapped in jail for violating the curfew or being in a "military area." They appealed their convictions all the way to the U.S. Supreme Court and lost. More than 40 years later, the men were still trying to clear their names, and their cases were reopened. Much research revealed that in 1943 and 1944, U.S. government lawyers had fraudulently concealed from the Supreme Court documents that contradicted their contention that the order to intern Japanese-Americans had been required for military necessity and the threat of disloyalty. One of the lawyers for the plaintiffs, Peter Irons, declared this was "a legal scandal without precedent in the history of American law. Never before has evidence emerged that shows a deliberate campaign to present tainted records to the Supreme Court."

During the war, few Americans were aware that thousands of their fellow citizens had been imprisoned without trials and were languishing in bleak camps. It was a well-kept secret, but over time the truth began to surface. In 1976, President Gerald R. Ford publicly proclaimed that the wartime detention of the Japanese-Americans had been wrong. In 1980, Congress appointed a prestigious panel to investigate the entire matter. The report of the Commission on Wartime Relocation and Internment of Civilians, *Personal Justice*

Denied, assailed the action as a "grave injustice, which was unwarrented by anything remotely resembling military necessity. The broad historical causes which shaped these decisions," the commission found, "were race prejudice, war hysteria, and a failure of political leadership."

Afterward Congress debated legislation providing for restitution and apologies for the Japanese-American internment survivors. In 1988 a bill cleared both the U.S. Senate and House of Representatives calling for apologies and $20,000 tax-free payments to each of the approximately 60,000 survivors of the World War II internment camps. On August 10, 1988, President Ronald Reagan signed the bill, saying that "no payment can make up for those lost years, so what is most important in this bill has less to do with property than with honor, for here we admit wrong." The blot on American history will remain, nonetheless.

Thomas JEFFERSON: secret miscegenist

After more than 180 years of attempts to ignore, suppress, or explain it away, evidence continues to mount concerning a 38-year-long relationship between Thomas Jefferson and a lovely quadroon slave named Sally Hemings. It was an alliance that afforded them years of private happiness, apparently fostered seven children, and brought suffering and shame to Jefferson, who, to protect the relationship, was forced to remain silent within a society that savagely punished perpetrators of mixed marriage.

Sally Hemings came into Jefferson's life as a child, part of an inheritance of property gained by his wife, Martha Wayles Skelton Jefferson. Sally's arrival introduced miscegenation into the Jefferson household, for her mother, Elizabeth Hemings (a half-breed Negro) had become the mistress of Martha Jefferson's father, John Wayles, after the death of Martha's mother and had borne him six children. As a result, Sally was the quadroon and slave half-sister of Martha Jefferson.

In 1782, when Sally was nine, Martha Jefferson died, leaving the 39-year-old Jefferson an almost inconsolably grief-stricken leader of a family containing two daughters. Time and public service somewhat eased his pain; travel to France enabled his return to emotional equilibrium. In France, he returned so thoroughly to normality that, in order to keep his vow to his deceased wife never to remarry, he entered a passionate, intermittent affair with Maria Cosway, the unhappy and demanding wife of the English miniaturist Richard Cosway.

News in 1787 of a whooping-cough epidemic in Virginia caused Jefferson to order that his younger daughter Maria (christened Mary and called Polly) and a suitable slave escort travel to Paris. The child arrived with Sally, at almost 16 a lovely, intelligent woman easily mistaken for a Caucasian. Abigail Adams, who knew of Jefferson's dalliance with Maria Cosway, sensed an immediate danger and suggested that Sally be sent back to Virginia. She remained, however, and Adams's apprehension became a fact. Sally Hemings became Jefferson's mistress.

Jefferson returned home, but Sally and Polly stayed in Paris for several additional months. According to Sally's son Madison, Sally balked at returning until Jefferson promised that her children would be manumitted at the age of 21. Late in 1789, she reached Monticello with Polly, radiant, well-dressed, and visibly pregnant. Jefferson's oldest daughter Martha was shocked, but— loyal to her father—remained silent, at least at that time.

Between 1789 and 1805, Sally evidently bore four sons and three daughters to Jefferson, two of the latter dying in infancy. He kept his promise about freeing them from slavery, and one by one they disappeared from the records he kept at Monticello. Two were listed as "runaways" whom he made no effort to recover; one (Tom) was no longer listed on clothing distribution ledgers after his 21 birthday; two were freed before Jefferson's death.

Jefferson protected Sally by pretending that she did not exist. Her name does not appear in any of his records after 1789, nor is she named in his will. But after Jefferson's death in 1826, she lived with her sons Elston and Madison near Monticello, with the family carried on U.S. Census rolls for Albemarle County, Virginia, as being white. Sally died in 1835.

The pain Jefferson endured over their clandestine relationship, described by a recent biographer as both a kind of atonement for one opposed philosophically to slavery and a kind of self-crucifixion, began in 1802. At the time, James Callender, a neurotic and alcoholic scandalmonger and libeler of national leaders who had once been Jefferson's journalistic hatchetman (see HAMILTON-REYNOLDS AFFAIR), turned against Jefferson. He told the world all the details of the miscegenation. America's third president appeared to be in trouble.

Federalist newspapers hooted in derision, and some Republican publications concurred. Soon, Jefferson's first administration was endangered. Sally also suffered: John Quincy Adams, among others, wrote scurrilous doggerel behind a veil of anonymity about "Monticellian Sally" as handy "To breed a block of slaves for stock."

In the face of this clamor, President Jefferson vowed to prevent pain to Sally and remained silent even at the low point in which he faced a sadly threatened administration and his daughter Polly suddenly died. When he read of a nearby acquittal of a white man who had murdered his great uncle (Jefferson's law tutor) because he had taken a mulatto for a mistress and sired a "yellow," Jefferson dared not speak lest he endanger his secret family, one blessed richly by his integrity.

His public family, however, was not silent. His daughter Martha invented dodges, since disproved, claiming that Jefferson could not have sired Sally's children. Early biographers, unwilling to believe that their hero could stoop to miscegenation, adopted her legends as truths.

The formalizing of the great Louisiana Purchase in 1805 drew public attention away from President Jefferson's despised peccadillos and enabled his election to another term as the nation's leader.

Historians note that, by conventional standards, Jefferson was not a great president. But facing the truth about his relationship with Sally Hemings should enable them to conclude that his devotion, protectiveness, and integrity made him a great man, along with his outstanding talent as a writer, philosopher, scientist, and architect.

An article in *Nature* magazine (November 1998) pointed out the strong evidence (notably genetic material involved in DNA analysis) that the Jefferson-Hemings relationship produced at least one child, Eston, who was Hemings's last son. But critics contend that the DNA shows that any one of eight Jefferson males (for example, Field Jefferson, Thomas's uncle, or Randolph, Thomas's brother, could have sired Eston). Hemings's descendants claimed otherwise, pointing to Eston's Jeffersonlike red hair and freckles, as well as other factors.

JEFFERSONIAN REPUBLICANS: the attempted impeachment of Samuel Chase

Despite the profound idealism he revealed as a philosopher of democracy, Thomas Jefferson, as the third president of the Untied States, was not above indulging in practical politics, using his power in underhanded ways to protect or advance his programs. Jefferson advocated honor and openness, yet paid the unscrupulous journalist James Callender to compose and publish mixtures of truth, exaggeration, and lies to turn public opinion against such Federalists as John Adams and Alexander Hamilton. He believed in a free press; yet he did nothing to stop unjust libel proceedings against an editor who questioned his unethical use of Callender (see Harry CROSWELL: truth led to libel conviction). One of the most glaring examples of his hypocrisy may be seen in his treatment of Samuel Chase, a highly influential Federalist justice. Although Jefferson promoted an independent judiciary, his desire to have the U.S. Supreme Court advance his plans caused him to strive secretly for Chase's impeachment.

Samuel Chase was a notably brilliant Supreme Court justice before John Marshall was made the court's chief justice in 1801. His wide legal knowledge and exceptional mind made possible opinions still operative in American law today. However, Chase was also an extremely outspoken, impulsive, and profoundly conservative individual. Given to sudden and abusive comments, he was often the center of controversy. Chase had been appointed to the Supreme Court by George Washington in 1796. At the time, the justices announced their opinions in a certain series, the order of which was determined by their chronological appointment. As the latest appointment to that honored bench, Chase spoke first. His comments frequently led the other justices to follow his leads.

His opinions, nonetheless, often offended. Three of them especially riled Jefferson and the Republican party; in each, Chase had given encouragement to Federalist positions, and the Republicans had begun to believe that Chase was being unfair in his apparent discrimination against Jeffersonian ideas. When in 1803 Chase rashly expressed his deep pessimism about the recent adoption of manhood suffrage in Maryland, President Jefferson suggested to a Maryland member of the U.S. House of Representatives that Chase be impeached.

The obedient Republicans in the House complied in 1804 by a vote of 73 to 32. The Senate postponed its action in the matter until 1805. Hot debates had occurred about the definition of "high crimes and misdemeanors" stipulated as necessary for impeachment by the U.S. Constitution, with some parties calling for indictable offenses, others for conduct falling short of vaguely defined "good behavior." Eight articles of impeachment for Chase were finally agreed upon. But despite secret heavy pressure from Jefferson and the presence of 34 Republican senators, the impeachment effort failed. Only one of the articles received a majority vote, and one gained no votes at all. This outcome dealt a serious blow to Jefferson's prestige and to his manipulative strategies.

Chase's acquittal saved the Supreme Court. Had he been impeached, the Jeffersonians (Jefferson and his Republicans) would probably have next attempted to remove the only slightly less abrasive Marshall from the high court. Reactions to their efforts against Chase were negative. To avoid the development of increased political opposition and to prevent further public condemnation of Jefferson's unethical ploy, the Jefferson Administration and all those that followed it refrained from further efforts to impeach Supreme Court justices for purely political reasons.

Walter JENKINS: acute embarrassment to LBJ

Walter W. Jenkins was the chief White House aide and longtime close friend of President Lyndon B. Johnson and his family when, on October 7, 1964, he was arrested for "disorderly conduct" two blocks from the White House, in a pay toilet at the Young Men's Christian Association (YMCA). Public disclosure of the charge, which involved homosexuality, caused many to wrongly perceive Jenkins as a threat to the nation's se-

curity. Afraid of jeopardizing his reelection campaign for that year, Johnson was forced on October 15 to ask for the resignation of his friend and special assistant. Ironically, Jenkins himself had earlier requested that all heads of federal departments make careful security checks of all "appointees to the federal service."

As the chief White House aide, Jenkins gave advice to the president on his speeches, attended National Security Council and Cabinet meetings, and was one of the few at the White House trusted enough to have the authorization to sign Johnson's name to letters. His top-secret security clearance also enabled him to see atomic weapons information. It was this fact that caused Republicans to cry that Jenkins was a possible threat to the nation's security because of his compromised position.

Democrats generally agreed that an official within the Republican presidential campaign had leaked the information about Jenkins to the press. His conduct in the YMCA incident was said to have involved "indecent gestures." This wasn't the first time that Jenkins had been nabbed; the police had arrested him in the same place in January 1959 on a similar morals charge involving homosexuality. At that time Jenkins had escaped trial and also publicity through his forfeiture of collateral. Still, his 1959 episode must have been known by the Federal Bureau of Investigation (FBI) and its director, J. Edgar Hoover, who surely would have told Johnson. The president, however, later claimed complete ignorance of Jenkins's behavior.

After his arrest in 1964, Jenkins telephoned attorney Abe FORTAS, a close friend and adviser to President Johnson, to tell him of his predicament. Fortas, accompanied by lawyer Clark Clifford, hastened to the offices of the three major daily newspapers in Washington, D.C. (the *Star,* the *Post,* and the *Daily News*), convincing them not to publish the Jenkins story. However, when United Press International shortly ran the story, the Washington dailies reported it too. By then, Jenkins had checked into a hospital, on Fortas's advice, to avoid news reporters.

The Johnson Administration was visibly shaken by Republican allegations that it was attempting to cover up Jenkins's two arrests on morals charges. Quickly the president issued a statement about his special assistant's resignation. It read in part: "Until late yesterday no information or report of any kind to me had ever raised a question with respect to his personal conduct. Mr. Jenkins is now in the care of his physician. . . . For myself and Mrs. Johnson I want to say that our hearts go out with the deepest compassion for him and his wife and six children. . . . Within moments after being notified last night, I ordered Director J. Edgar Hoover of the FBI to make an immediate and comprehensive inquiry and report promptly to me and the American people."

The Republicans tried to capitalize on the scandal in several ways. They said that Jenkins might have been forced to leak vital national secrets to a Communist country. Republican vice-presidential candidate William E. Miller frequently brought up the moral issue on the campaign trail and declared: "Police records show that the president's close friend and chief White House aide has been involved for five years in a pitiful, sordid situation which made him a ready subject for blackmail and compromise to the highest secrets of government." Jenkins was unworthy of the voters' trust, cried Miller. Former vice-president Richard M. Nixon said that Johnson's ability to choose men as advisers was poor and that Americans "would not stand for immorality in the White House."

Senator Barry M. Goldwater, the Republican's staunchly conservative presidential candidate in 1964, at first said that he wouldn't make the Jenkins scandal a campaign issue, but he subsequently made allegations about a cover-up and charged the White House with moral indecency right up to Election Day. Some of the press jumped on the moralizing bandwagon too. "There can be no place on the White House staff or in the upper echelons in government for a person of markedly deviant behavior," said one *New York Times* editorial. Amidst all the uproar, the American Mental Health Foundation issued a statement saying "the fact that an individual is homosexual, as has been strongly implied in the case of Mr. Jenkins, does not *per se* make him more unstable and more a security risk than any other heterosexual person." Very few, however, listened.

Johnson, who generally managed to remain above the controversy, gradually increased his lead over Goldwater and won the 1964 election with 61 percent of the popular vote. Coming at a time when Nikita Krushchev had recently been deposed and the Chinese Communists had just exploded their first nuclear weapon, Johnson's victory does not totally dismiss the concern stimulated by the Jenkins expose. As national pollster Louis Harris had concluded days earlier: "It is not so much that the American people are unmoved by the Jenkins episode. Rather, the question of which candidate shall be in charge of foreign policy during the next four years has superseded every other issue in the campaign."

Another factor in Johnson's victory may have been an FBI report released two weeks before the election, which claimed that "a favorable appraisal of Mr. Jenkins' loyalty and dedication to the United States was given the FBI by more than three hundred of his associates, both business and social." There was also no information, said the FBI, that Jenkins had at any time "compromised the security or interests of the United States in any manner." In the report, however, Jenkins admitted to engaging in the two "indecent" acts but claimed that during his most recent arrest his mind had

been "befuddled by fatigue, alcohol, physical illness and lack of food." He declared he would "lay down his life before he would disclose any information that would damage the best interests of the United States." The FBI report also confirmed that Johnson did not know anything about the arrests until the day before Jenkins resigned.

Rita JENRETTE: opened Pandora's box of congressional sex

The cover story of the *Washington Post Magazine* on December 7, 1980, was entitled "Diary of a Mad Congresswife," written by Rita Jenrette, the 31-year-old wife of a prominent Democratic congressman. The article gained national attention immediately, for it mercilessly detailed the unfaithfulness and extramarital indiscretions of Rita's husband, John W. Jenrette, Jr., who represented the sixth congressional district in South Carolina. Rita appeared on television and radio talk shows, providing innumerable details about her husband's infidelities and Washington's seamy side. Soon afterward, *Playboy* magazine got interested, approached Rita, and ran an elaborated version of the "Diary of a Mad Congresswife" in two issues, along with some pic-

Standing outside the Capitol in 1976, attractive Rita Jenrette holds a glass donkey with her husband-congressman John W. Jenrette, Jr. Five years later she would tell of Washington, D.C., orgies in an article and a book, while her husband would be imprisoned on a conviction of conspiracy and accepting a $50,000 bribe during the FBI's ABSCAM operation. (AP/Wide World Photos)

tures of her semi-nude. Although Rita was accused of being an opportunist by some news reporters and columnists, she had started a definite trend. Similar confessions by a beautiful lobbyist and an aging madam made headlines shortly afterwards, further illuminating the scandalous behavior in the nation's capitol.

In 1975, Rita Carpenter had met and fallen in love with John Jenrette, a brash divorcé with a southern drawl. Jenrette, elected a Democratic United States representative from South Carolina during the WATER-GATE backlash in 1974, married the Texas-born Rita in 1976. According to her book, *My Capitol Secrets* (1981), she reluctantly became aware of John's sexual betrayals and of the larger hypocrisy of Washington in general, where, she alleged, "women gain status according to how powerful a man they're sleeping with." And she explained that "because many of these men are married, the liaisons often occur in borrowed apartments—and less predictable places. I know of three or four senators who rent a house near the Senate office building for 'nooners.' Quickies also take place in certain rooms in the bowels of the Capitol, rooms that are supposed to be for meetings." Rita also claimed that she and her husband, who had left her alone on their wedding night, had made love standing together on the steps of the Capitol while a major debate went on inside and some congressmen passed by them. Rita discovered the truth about her husband's philandering when she found him in bed with a woman about twice her age. John's heavy drinking and secret adultery, said Rita, drove her to finally divorce him and leave Washington to live in New York. The public heard her speak of frequent illegal use of drugs such as cocaine by leading congressmen, many of whom thought nothing of cheating on their wives. Her own husband, said Rita, had been caught with 15 different women by the time she left him in early 1981.

Attractive 30-year-old Paula Parkinson worked as a professional lobbyist on Capitol Hill, influencing congressmen to support and vote for legislation that helped the various organizations that hired her. She was apparently very effective. In March 1981, the press told about alleged videotapes owned by Paula, showing some respected politicians, both Democrats and Republicans, in compromising poses with her. Paula's "lovers' list" supposedly sent shudders down the spines of some Washington bigwigs, who must have sighed in relief when she denied charges by the Justice Department that she had traded sex for votes.

Some newspapers reported that Paula had enjoyed a "golfing" weekend in January 1980 in Florida with three Republican congressmen, who quickly said that no sexual activity had occurred. Later, she said she had an affair with U.S. Representative Thomas B. Evans, Jr., of Delaware, one of those on the Florida weekend, and had been propositioned then (1980) by Represen-

tative J. Danforth Quayle of Indiana (later a U.S. senator and vice president under U.S. President George Bush). She said she had rebuffed Quayle, who denounced what she claimed as "outrageous" and "outright lies."

Paula's attempt to sell her memoirs to top pornography magazines and book publishers failed, perhaps because of the apparent threat of lawsuits against her if she revealed certain politicians' names. In April 1981 she claimed that she didn't own videotapes of 17 different sexual occasions but had only one tape and a small list of lovers. She also declared that she had never had any idea of blackmailing congressmen.

While Paula and "Tell-All-Rita" made headlines, the retired, elderly former madam of a house of prostitution, Brandy Baldwin, finished writing her memoirs, in which she disclosed goings-on at the exclusive, male-only Bohemian Club outside San Francisco. For ten years, said Baldwin, she had operated that city's most elite bordello and each summer had taken some of her select prostitutes to a rented cottage near the Bohemian Club's 3,000-acre country estate, where about 2,000 club members and guests gathered annually. At "the greatest men's party on earth," as former President Herbert Hoover called the Bohemian summer camp, there was much sportive merrymaking and carousing. The "campers" included many celebrities and top businessmen and politicians; Baldwin named President Ronald Reagan, Vice-President George Bush, and former presidents Gerald Ford and Richard Nixon as among the club's 900 members. Baldwin's girls staged shows for the Bohemians at the camp and entered into the festivities with them. Many disillusioned Americans concluded that some of their elected public officials were not the most highly principled men. In 1981, the impression was that too many of them were "lushes" and "skirt-chasers."

JOHNS-MANVILLE ASBESTOS CASE: products hazardous to health

In the 1970s, the Johns-Manville Corporation, once the world's largest producer of asbestos products, began to come under lawsuit from workers who had developed cancer or asbestosis during their employment with the company and from the survivors of those employees who had died of these diseases. Because the thousands of lawsuits threatened to destroy the company, it filed for bankrupcy under Chapter 11 (a federal statute) which permits a company to continue its business while a settlement of its debts is being negotiated. The victims' lawyers accused the company of acting in bad faith and abusing the bankruptcy process. Fifteen months later, Johns-Manville announced its reorganization plans. It would split the company in two. One part would assume the asbestos liability and have a few assets, while the second would manage the other aspects of the business and give all profits after expenses to the first part to pay the asbestos claims. It also proposed setting up a computer program that would analyze each claimant's medical history and determine a payment. The victims, however, found this solution unacceptable.

Asbestos is a mineral obtained from open-pit mines by blasting and then separating the rocks and dirt from the asbestos. It is characterized by long, soft fibers that can be used to make fire-retarding, chemical-resistant, and nonconducting materials such as fiberboard, floor coverings, textured ceiling paint, commercial spackle, heat and frost covers, and many other products. For years asbestos was widely used for fireproofing and insulation in public buildings such as offices, schools, and theaters.

Workers who mine asbestos, who manufacture it into a wide variety of products, and who use these products in construction or textile manufacture inevitably breathe asbestos dust into their lungs. Their clothes carry the fibers, and their wives and children inhale them too. Twenty to 40 years later, there is a strong possibility that these people will develop asbestosis, a painful lung disease that causes a dry cough and makes breathing increasingly difficult. Often, the extremities of persons with the disease turn blue from lack of oxygen in the blood. There is no known cure. Asbestos fibers are also carcinogenic and can cause lung, stomach, colon, and rectal cancer.

Dr. Irving J. Selikoff of the Mount Sinai Medical School in New York City began warning the medical profession and any others who would listen about the dangers of asbestos in the early 1960s, but it was not until 1973 that Johns-Manville began to be seriously concerned. In 1976, employees at one of the company's asbestos plants in California staged a public memorial service for 12 coworkers who had died during the previous 14 months, and along with their union they began a highly visible campaign against Johns-Manville. They demanded physical examinations and care when needed, as well as safer working conditions. Some charged that the company had been aware of the hazards of asbestos since the 1930s but had issued no warnings nor taken any steps to develop safety measures.

The lawsuits against Johns-Manville and other companies working with asbestos and its products began to increase as older workers became disabled. In 1978, a federal jury in Norfolk, Virginia, awarded $750,000 in damages to the widow of a former Johns-Manville factory worker. Two years later, another jury found Johns-Manville guilty of causing physical harm to a worker and ordered it to pay him $1.2 million. In a later suit, Johns-Manville and the Metropolitan Life Insurance Company paid $15.5 million to 683 former workers of the company in Passaic, New Jersey, to compensate them for their disabilities stemming from their work.

During this period the federal and many state governments became involved by drawing up new regula-

tions to ensure worker safety in asbestos-related industries. The U.S. Consumer Product Safety Commission investigated 150 asbestos products, and the Environmental Protection Agency set up a program to remove asbestos from schools. A bill was introduced in the U.S. Senate to pay the injured employees workers' compensation. Suits and countersuits multiplied. Johns-Manville sued 24 insurance companies that had provided coverage for injuries to its workers, and the victims organized to press their cases against the company. Former Naval shipyard workers, especially those who had worked with boilers and insulation, also became ill and sued the government, but the United States attorney general asserted that the government had no responsibility for the shipyards.

By August 26, 1982, approximately 20,000 people had filed suits against Johns-Manville.

In August 1986, Johns-Manville came up with a new reorganization plan that would establish two separate trust funds to provide compensation to claimants. One would compensate people with asbestos-related diseases; the other would compensate creditors, security holders, and property-damage claimants. Present and future claimants could initiate suits only against these trusts, which would be financed by about 80 percent of Manville shares. The plan was widely publicized, and claimants were urged to obtain ballots to vote for or against it in the fall. Thousands approved. Johns-Manville had by this time completely divested itself of all asbestos mines and products and had developed new profitable items for the construction industry. On December 18, 1986, a federal bankruptcy court announced that the company's reorganization plan met statutory requirements and the firm could emerge from its bankruptcy in the coming year. A representative of Asbestos Victims of America, an advocacy organization, estimated that the average settlement would be around $26,000.

The Manville Personal Injury Settlement Trust was formed in 1988 as the company emerged from bankruptcy reorganization. By mid-1990, the trust was running out of money, having handled over 24,000 claims (each averaging $43,500) with more than 125,000 claims pending. Manville's stock (dependent on profits) was also used to supply the trust's income in order to settle claims over the next seven years. Thousands of asbestos lawsuits were filed against dozens of other U.S. companies, many of which were likely to become insolvent because of them.

Andrew JOHNSON: "Let them impeach and be damned!"

Immediately following the assassination of President Abraham Lincoln on April 15, 1865, his vice president, Andrew Johnson, was elevated to the presidency. Because of his extreme sympathy toward the South, the Tennessee president aroused a great deal of anger and became the first president to go on trial for impeachment (see Bill CLINTON: impeached U.S. president).

When his home state of Tennessee seceded from the Union in 1861 at the beginning of the American Civil War, U.S. Senator Andrew Johnson supported President Abraham Lincoln and remained at his post in the Senate, becoming the only southerner there. Denounced by the Confederacy for his loyalty to the Union, he felt the South's secession was invalid and, in 1862, was named military governor of Tennessee by Lincoln. In 1864 the president made Johnson, a war Democrat, his running mate in his successful bid for reelection. After Lincoln's death, numerous congressmen had reservations about the suitability of President Johnson, who was largely self-educated and sometimes coarsely indiscreet (he had appeared intoxicated at Lincoln's 1865 inauguration ceremony, a *faux pas* his enemies and critics never forgot).

After the South's defeat and surrender, Johnson was confronted with the large, grievous problem of the reconstruction of the Confederate states. The majority of Congress, which was controlled by the Republicans (Lincoln's party), clashed with the president's Reconstruction program, which he insisted was an executive, not a legislative, matter. The many "radical" Republicans favored strong military control of the South before the seceded states were readmitted to the Union; they opposed Johnson's lenient policy, which returned civil government to traditional, white southern hands (he did not disqualify from office Confederate leaders) and which did not give equal civil rights to the blacks. Congressional opposition increased and was led by Representative Thaddeus Stevens of Pennsylvania, who proposed that the southern states, being conquered provinces, be put under military rule as the basis for readmission to the Union. Johnson, however, failed to check the southern state legislatures, which enacted restrictive "Black Codes" against the newly emancipated blacks. On April 9, 1866, Congress passed the Civil Rights Act, declaring that blacks were citizens and as such had the same rights as whites; Johnson's unsuccessful veto of it condemned it as an unjustified infringement on states' rights. Johnson's uncompromising stubbornness had created a powerful, cohesive coalition of radical and conservative Republicans who opposed him.

On March 2, 1867, Congress passed the first Reconstruction Act, which divided the South into five military-governed districts, and the Tenure of Office Act, which declared that the president could not dismiss certain federal officials without the Senate's consent; the latter act was to protect Republicans in office from reprisal by the president when they did not support him. Johnson, who had tried to veto both acts, wanted very much to get rid of his secretary of war, Edwin M. Stan-

ton, who was an ardent ally of the radical Republicans and consequently untrustworthy as a cabinet adviser. Johnson's suspension of Stanton on December 12, 1867, was abrogated by the Senate a month later, furthering the animosity between the executive and legislative offices.

Citing his constitutional power and the unconstitutionality of the Tenure of Office Act, Johnson dismissed Stanton on February 21, 1868; this action enraged Congress, and immediately Stevens introduced a resolution of impeachment against Johnson in the House, which voted in favor of it and then drew up 11 articles of impeachment. The president brazenly stated, "Let them impeach and be damned!" He was seen as a tyrant by Congress, individual members of which he had often flagrantly attacked in public speeches in the preceding two years during the battle over Reconstruction policy. Although his violation of the Tenure of Office Act was the chief impeachment charge against him, Johnson was also accused of attempting "to bring into disgrace, ridicule, hatred, and reproach the Congress."

The impeachment trial of the president—the first such occurrence in American history—was held in the Senate chamber from March 5 to May 26, 1868. Wisely, Johnson, who had a short temper and might have alienated even more senators, stayed away and was represented by his counsel, who denied the criminal charges against the president in connection with the dismissal of Stanton and other alleged violations, criminal and civil. The president's enemies thought he would be found guilty on at least one of the charges, but an executive session of the Senate revealed that not enough of the 54 members would vote guilty on at least eight of the articles of impeachment. Supposedly the strongest article, the 11th, which summarized many of the charges in the other articles, was put forth first for balloting on May 16; the vote was 35 to 19 against the president, one vote short of the constitutionally required two-thirds necessary for conviction (all of the senators had voted as expected except for one, Edmund G. Ross of Kansas, a Republican, whose "not guilty" vote surely decided the outcome). The radicals then delayed the trial, which was presided over by Chief Justice Salmon P. Chase of the Supreme Court, until May 26, when the balloting on the second and third articles occurred with exactly the same results as on the 11th. The court of impeachment then adjourned *sine die*. Johnson, although exonerated, lost political power because of the trial and, in 1868, was not nominated for the presidency. Seven years later he was reelected to the Senate from Tennessee but died of a stroke in 1875, at the age of 67, soon after taking office.

Jack JOHNSON: the "big black menace"

The first black to hold the world's heavyweight boxing title, John Arthur "Jack" Johnson, defied convention by his interracial love affairs and marriages and his refusal to "keep his place" in American society. His preferences for white women and his "uppity nigger" behavior scandalized many whites and blacks alike, resulting in bitter, prejudicial, and shameful denunciations and persecutions of him during his celebrated boxing career. In their attempts to pillory this black hero who acted as if his skin were white, these moralistic people displayed the ignominious racism that Johnson battled in his flamboyant and indomitable spirit until the end.

Born into a large, poor, black family in Galveston, Texas, in 1878, Jack Johnson ran away from home at the age of 12 and worked at a variety of mundane jobs while learning how to defend himself through boxing. Blessed with natural athletic ability, the muscular, six-foot-tall Johnson gravitated to boxing for a livelihood and, by the turn of the century, had gained confidence and money in successful bouts as a pugilist. Cocky and combative, he beat the best fighters, flashing his shaven head and big smile showing his seven gold-plated teeth. As his quick fists brought in more money, he acquired a lavish lifestyle, buying and enjoying fine clothes, good food and drink, and attractive young women and "ladies of the evening." This black man refused to play Uncle Tom in segregated America, to the disdain of many.

Johnson's triumphant boxing finally got him a crack at fighting tough Tommy Burns, the world heavyweight champion, whom he licked fairly in a match in Sydney, Australia, on December 26, 1908. White America was stunned to have a black for the first time holding the illustrious world heavyweight title, and a search began for a "great white hope" to dethrone the so-called "Galveston Giant," who arrogantly cavorted about with both black and white women. Johnson turned back all contenders while boxing promoters looked for someone to defend the alleged athletic superiority of the white race. The promoters coaxed former champion Jim Jeffries, who had retired undefeated in 1905, to return to the ring to take on the "big black menace," as Johnson was called. Writers like Jack London and Rex Beach turned out much copy in favor of Jeffries because he was white—a so-called "legendary Teutonic warrior" (in London's words) and certain victor because of his "breeding and education" (in Beach's words). But in the "battle of the century" in Reno, Nevada, on July 4, 1910, Jeffries, the "great white hope," was soundly defeated.

White America, extremely angered by Johnson's victory and his arrogant, unconventional conduct, found that numerous "respectable" blacks dislike the champion too; his well-publicized involvements with pretty white women, whom he seemed to prefer over blacks, were attacked by the black press as well as the white. Johnson especially generated racial prejudice by his love affairs with three whites: alcoholic Hattie McLay, prostitute Belle Schreiber, and Etta Terry Duryea, a blonde

divorcée whom he married in 1909. His loose living made many think he thumbed his nose at society's morals. In 1912, Etta ended their marriage by committing suicide; according to the press, the cause of her death was not public pressure on her, but rather Johnson, because of his ways; irrational anger welled up against him in both whites and blacks. During the previous year, 1911, the internationally known fighter had opened a Chicago nightclub called the Cafe de Champion, where, he said unashamedly, whites and blacks could mix in fine surroundings.

Chicago reformers and federal authorities then set out to prove that Johnson had violated the 1910 Mann Act, which prohibited the interstate transportation of women for immoral purposes. They managed in 1912 to shut down Johnson's cafe. Trumped up abduction charges against him involving another white blonde, Lucille Cameron, whom Johnson married in 1912 soon after Etta's death, were eventually dismissed in Chicago's municipal court. Federal prosecutors, however, got Belle Schreiber, who wanted revenge on Johnson for discarding her, to testify in a jury trial, during which he steadfastly denied doing anything immoral, while Belle claimed he had taken her across state lines for prostitution and other immoral purposes. On May 13, 1913, the champion was convicted of violating the Mann Act and of trafficking in white slavery and was sentenced to a year in Illinois's Joliet Penitentiary. Out of jail on bail, Johnson and his wife Lucille skipped the country.

A fugitive from a federal warrant, Johnson lived and worked, boxing and touring in theatrical shows, in self-exile in Europe. In need of money in 1915, he agreed to fight the new "great white hope," big Jess Willard, in Havana, Cuba, for the heavyweight championship. The crowd screamed for blood as it watched Willard punish and knock out Johnson in the 26th round of the scheduled 45-round match. Johnson's enemies called it a "sweet victory." Later, the ex-champion claimed that the fight had been fixed, a charge that has never been proved; in return for letting Willard win, Johnson was supposedly offered $50,000 (he received $30,000 as the loser) and was promised help in having the charges against him dropped and in getting back into the United States. But he stayed abroad until 1920, when he returned and surrendered voluntarily to federal officials. Taken directly to Joliet and then to the federal penitentiary at Leavenworth, Kansas, Johnson served eight months of his one-year sentence (he was discharged early for good behavior) and returned to Chicago in July 1921. Lucille divorced him in 1924, and when he married his third blonde, white wife, Irene Marie Pineau in 1925, there was no public outcry whatsoever. Irene was devoted to him until his tragic death in a car accident near Franklinton, North Carolina, in 1946.

In a speech one night in Chicago in October 1912, when he was being viciously attacked for his ostensibly militant and shameless ways, the now idolized champion probably best described the long-standing controversy about him, as well as part of his philosophy of life:

> First I want to say that nothing ever is said of the white man who waylays the little colored girl when she goes to market. Nobody has anything to say about that. But when the Negro does something that is not nearly so serious there is a great hue and cry.
>
> I want to say that I never made the statement attributed to me to the effect that I could get any white woman I wanted. I can lay my hand upon the Bible and swear that I never made such a statement. . . .
>
> But I do want to say that I am not a slave and that I have the right to choose who my mate shall be without the dictation of any man. . . .
>
> So long as I do not interfere with any other man's wife, I shall claim the right to select the woman of my choice. Nobody else can do that for me. That is where the trouble lies.

Lyndon JOHNSON. See George PARR: the despotic "duke of Duval."

JOHNSON FAMILY SCANDAL

The six Johnson children had never been particularly fond of their stepmother, Barbara (Basia) Piasecka Johnson. She was their father's third wife, a Polish émigrée 42 years his junior and a former chambermaid in his house, who had married him a week after his divorce from his second wife. When their father, the late J. Seward Johnson (scion of the famous Johnson & Johnson group of companies), died in May 1983 and left nearly all of his estimated $500 million fortune to his third wife (only the eldest son received a summer house on Cape Cod and one million dollars), they resolved to fight her in court. The result was a bitter three-year-long family dispute played out in Manhattan surrogate court in the glare of the national and tabloid press, with no skeletons left in the closet.

Not that any of them was in dire circumstances. In 1944, their father had set up trust funds (worth about $110 million) for each of his six children from his first two marriages and even though they had dipped into the capital, none apparently was worth less than $23 million. The bequest would make Barbara Johnson, who had come to this country in 1968 armed with a degree in art history, a smattering of English, and $100 in her pocket, one of the richest women in the world. Since her assets were frozen during the trial, she was living on the proceeds of a $9 million trust in her $30 million, 140-acre home in New Jersey.

Since their marriage in 1971, J. Seward Johnson had altered his will 22 times—each modification giving his third wife a greater share of his estate. The contested will—the fourth in eight weeks—was drafted and signed (April 14, 1983) when he was of sound mind, according to Nina Zagat, attorney-executor. A Yale graduate and a Wall Street attorney, Zagat was a close friend of Barbara's and stood to gain almost $10 million in fees and commissions as coexecutor and trustee of the estate. The Johnson children charged that their stepmother was a shrewish woman who had been scheming with Zagat to divert their father's wealth solely for herself and that his last will—drafted when he was weakened and senile—was dictated by her. Barbara countered that J. Seward Johnson had already provided munificently for all his children (a $70 million trust was set up for his grandchildren) and had indicated in a series of previous wills that they would not get anything more. He had been offended by their scandalous behavior, she said. Her lawyer described her as a devoted and loving wife who had made her husband's last 12 years "a dream."

According to their lawyer, Edward Reily, the children's moral reason for contesting the will was that it did not provide for or mention Harbor Branch, the oceanographic institute their father founded in 1971 and was devoted to. Reilly also charged that Mrs. Johnson physically and verbally abused her ailing husband and had forced the terms of the last will by threatening to abandon him.

The protracted three-year case climaxed in a trial which lasted 17 weeks. However, as the jury waited and wondered if they would be asked to determine the validity of the will, Mrs. Johnson capitulated—remarking that "peace is better than prolonged litigation"—and reached a settlement with her stepchildren. She said she was saddened that the children "ridiculed their father in this way." According to the settlement, the six children would get approximately $5.9 million each, with the eldest son (J. Seward Johnson, Jr.) getting an extra $7 million as an executor of his father's will. Also, their legal group at Milbank, Tweed, Hadley & McCloy received about $10 million. Mrs. Johnson got to keep a mere $300 million. Lawyer Nina Zagat was among the "losers"—netting only $1.8 million against an expected almost $10 million.

William George JORDAN: the Larrovitch literary hoax
In 1917, William George Jordan, a member of the Author's Club of New York, invented a fictitious Russian author and an equally fictitious written work. Intending originally only to embarrass an unpopular fellow member of the club, Jordan soon found himself further and further involved in the establishment of this nonexistent writer. His white lie grew into a full-fledged literary hoax, which remained unexposed until 1932.

The fellow member Jordan was trying to fool was Gustave Simonson, a bibliophile who was reputed to have a photographic memory. Accounts of the hoax do not describe Simonson's personality, but apparently he was pedantic, totally unimpressionable, and outspoken, for when Jordan mentioned the fictitous work called *Vyvodne,* supposedly written in 1868 by an equally non-existent author named Feodor Larrovitch, Simonson is reported to have replied bluntly, "Never heard of them" and then to have changed the subject.

Jordan and another club member, Richardson Wright, then spent several weeks convincing Simonson that such a writer did exist. Wright began by inspiring interest among the club's members. He lectured on the neglected author and, on April 26, 1917, hosted a dinner in Larrovitch's honor. The dining room of the club was decorated for the event with memorabilia: a page from a manuscript of *Crasny Baba*; fake portraits of Larrovitch; pressed flowers from the supposed Yalta grave of the fictitious author; his embroidered shirt; and pictures of his death bed, his icon, his pen, and his ink pot. Readings from Larrovitch's poems and eulogies followed the dinner. The press gave a touching report on the event. Simonson was impressed but not convinced.

Next the conspirators involved other club members in the hoax and gained the aid of some literary journalists, who mentioned the works of Larrovitch favorably but vaguely. The journalists, however, made one grave mistake: They misspelled Larrovitch's name, leaving out the *t*. The change in spelling led to the exposure of the hoax 25 years later.

In 1919, Jordan, Wright, and several others published a book on Larrovitch, which was reviewed seriously by their journalist co-conspirators. A learned work, it contained translations, a biographical introduction, a critical commentary, reproductions of Larrovitch's letters, and a remarkable essay reporting conversations with the Russian writer.

Simonson and the conspirators must have been satisfied, for Feodor Larrovitch became an entry in the historical records of the Authors' Club, along with the names of members, scholars, and literary gentlemen too proud to acknowledge that they had never before heard of this neglected master of the Russian tongue and too timid to question his reality.

The unmasking of the hoax was an accident; it occurred an ocean away from the scene of the plot. A Swedish sportswriter for the newspaper *Stockholms-Tidningen* had perused the 1919 volume about Larrovitch, found a letter signed Alexis Larrovich, then questioned the first name and the spelling (why the double *r*? why *-ich* rather than *-itch*?), and finally published his reactions. When word reached the Authors' Club of New York, Simonson was gone, but those members who had been duped must have wondered whether he had realized that he had been taken in. The remaining members of the club were now wary of Jordan and Wright, who received no formal reproaches for their scandalous hoax.

Christine JORGENSEN: he-turned-she

Transsexualism is a controversial issue today, but not nearly as much as it was 50 years ago. It was at this time that George Jorgensen, a young man who had always felt himself to be a woman, astounded the nation by being the first American to undergo a sex-change operation. As a child in the Bronx, New York, George Jorgensen liked to play with the girls rather than the boys, preferring dolls and hopscotch over toy trains, football, and baseball, to the chagrin of his father. Generally unhappy with himself, he grew up feeling different and isolated, rejecting rough boys' clothing, and secretly wanting to be a girl in his teenage school years.

In an effort to renew himself and overcome his feelings of being different from everyone else, George Jorgensen immersed himself in the study of photography and landed a job as a professional photographer with Pathé News in New York. At the time, he fell in love with a young man, became apprehensive about the relationship, and never revealed he was a secret transvestite. Jorgensen was then summoned into the U.S. Army and served as a soldier, still harboring his latent female feelings. Following an honorable discharge from the army, he traveled to Los Angeles, California, to find work, having failed to regain his old job at Pathé. Demeaning work as a supermarket stock clerk eventually drove him east again to New York City, where his desire to become a woman led to his attending a medical-technical school to study human hormones. He confided his wish to become a woman to a doctor, who said that it could not be realized. Nevertheless, Jorgensen privately obtained some female hormones, which he began administering to himself and which changed his

Christine Jorgensen, speaking to news reporters in 1953 about published stories that she was merely a "mutilated male," said she would welcome an inquiry by the American Medical Association into her change of sex. She had undergone a series of operations in Denmark in the early 1950s. (Ap/Wide World Photos)

body to some extent. After discovering that Scandinavian doctors in Denmark might possibly help him, he went to Copenhagen to present his case in 1950.

The singularity of Jorgensen interested Copenhagen physicians, who agreed to his request to change his sex and also not to charge him anything for doing so because he would be the subject of a pioneering scientific experiment, the first known sex-change procedure in history. Under special care in a hospital for about two years, Jorgensen underwent numerous operations and supposedly received almost 2,000 hormone injections. In 1952, attractive Christine Jorgensen emerged as a medically and legally certified woman. The public was scandalized. An international sensation at the age of 26, Jorgensen became a curiosity often subjected to disdain and mockery, especially by some of the American press. Her career as a photographer was interrupted by her increasing notoriety. To remove human sex glands was

then illegal in the United States, where transsexualism was not usually openly discussed. Many American physicians denounced Jorgensen's operations as "multilative surgery."

Nevertheless, Christine Jorgensen went on to become a well-paid cabaret and nightclub singer, to have several minor stage roles, to write her autobiography, and to have a movie made about her life. Twice she was engaged to different men, though she never married. Her planned marriage to Howard Knox in 1959 fell apart, apparently after she was refused a marriage license because she was listed as a male on her birth certificate. Today, mores have changed, and American society has accepted Jorgensen and numerous other transsexual men who undergo surgery to become, in Jorgensen's words, "the woman I always wanted to be." Jorgensen died of cancer at age 62 in May 1989 in San Clemente, California.

Ted KACZYNSKI: the "Unabomber"

Between 1978 and 1995, the United States was plagued by a wave of mail bombings. Most of the bombs, which consisted of hundreds of nails, cut-up razor blades, and metal fragments, were made to look like ordinary parcels, and they exploded when their victims opened them. Because the earliest bombs targeted professors of computer science and engineering as well as executives of major airlines, the Federal Bureau of Investigation (FBI) dubbed the mysterious person behind the attacks the "Unabomber"; "Una" stands for "universities 'n' airlines." By 1995, the circle of potential targets had widened: the Unabomber's last two bombs killed an advertising executive and a lobbyist for the timber industry, and another bomb went off behind a computer store. The Unabomber struck 16 times, and his attacks killed three people, injured 23, and caused millions more to live in fear of their mail.

The Unabomber was motivated by an intense hatred for modern industry and technology. As he wrote in a 35,000-word document that the media dubbed the Unabomber Manifesto, the industrial and technological developments of the 20th century "have destabilized society, have made life unfulfilling, have subjected human beings to indignities, have led to widespread suffering, . . . [and] have inflicted severe damage on the natural world." He believed that the only way to restore humankind's self-esteem and individuality was to destroy those institutions that fostered industrial and technological innovation. To him, that meant killing those people whom he saw as primarily responsible for developing and implementing such innovation as well as those who he believed used technology to upset the tranquility and balance of nature.

The FBI spent 17 years and $50 million tracking down the Unabomber, the longest and most expensive manhunt in U.S. history. He was hard to catch because he covered his tracks so well. Although fingerprints were found on several bomb fragments, they were all missing the central whorls that make fingerprints identification conclusive. Agents were unable to collect enough DNA from the dried saliva on the backs of the stamps to do DNA testing on suspects and were unsure whether the hair and fiber bits found among the fragments belonged to the bomber or someone else.

Ironically, what eventually led to the Unabomber's capture was his insistence on gaining national exposure for his views. In 1995 he promised that, if the *Washington Post* and the *New York Times* would print his manifesto in its entirety, then he would stop killing people. At the request of the FBI director and the U.S. attorney general, both newspapers agreed to do so. David Kaczynski, a youth counselor in Albany, New York, read the "Unabomber Manifesto" and thought it sounded a lot like the work of his 52-year-old brother Ted. As an infant, Ted had suffered an allergic reaction to a drug and been hospitalized for six weeks, during which time no one, including his parents, had been allowed to hold him. For the rest of his life, he seemed to avoid social interaction. Although he was a genius who once taught mathematics at the University of California at Berkeley, Ted now lived in the mountains near Lincoln, Montana, in a rustic cabin without electricity or plumbing. David also knew that the FBI believed the Unabomber had grown up in the Chicago area and had spent time in Salt Lake City, Utah, and Berkeley, California, all of which Ted had done.

Reluctantly, David contacted the FBI through an intermediary, and in 1996 he gave federal agents other manuscripts authored by Ted so that they could compare them to the manifesto. When experts declared that there was a 90 percent probability that the manifesto's author had also written the manuscripts, the FBI arrested Ted on April 3, 1996. A search of his cabin turned up a finished bomb that had all the characteristics of a "Unabomb," as well as a hit list with the names of airline executives, computer scientists, and geneticists.

Ted Kaczynski pleaded guilty to the bombings and showed absolutely no remorse for his actions at his sentencing. He seemed to be unfazed by the testimony of his victims and their survivors, who described in graphic detail the pain and suffering he had inflicted on them and their loved ones. He denied that he was a random murderer and insisted that he was a revolutionary engaged in a noble struggle against the system. In 1998 he was sentenced to four consecutive life terms and incarcerated in the maximum-security federal penitentiary in Florence, Colorado.

Charles KEATING: convicted of S & L fraud

In the early 1980s, a rash of unscrupulous real-estate developers ventured into the savings and loan (S & L) business across the western United States. By the decade's end, most of these S & L's or "thrifts," were in desperate financial straits. Many collapsed while their owners amassed millions, and the taxpayers were left to finance the bailout at an estimated cost of $500 million to $1 trillion. The man who probably epitomized the worst excesses of this debacle was Charles H. Keating, Jr., an Arizona-based developer with a tarnished reputation, who was born in 1923 in Cincinnati, Ohio.

Keating bought Lincoln Savings and Loan (based in Irvine, California) in 1984 for $51 million (junk bond racketeer Michael MILKEN mediated this sale), twice Lincoln's net worth and three times its stock value. Using federally insured deposits, he increased Lincoln's holdings sixfold over five years to a record $5.5 billion. Most of Lincoln's lending had traditionally been to homebuyers. Under Keating's leadership, these loans shrank to less than 2 percent of its business. Instead, Lincoln invested in Milken's highly speculative junk bonds. Keating also put money into land development (often, these loans were made without appraising the properties) and stocks and about $280 million into the luxurious Phoenician resort in Scottsdale, Arizona. Lincoln loaned the Rancho Vistoso real-estate project in Tucson $115 million and incurred losses of $75 million.

Keating also had a way with bookkeeping. For instance, between 1986 and 1988, he transferred $94.8 million from Lincoln to its parent company, Phoenix-based American Continental Corporation (ACC) under a tax-sharing plan intended to cover the parent's tax liabilities. However, ACC did not owe any taxes on behalf of the thrift. During the same period, Keating and his family drew about $34 million from ACC in salaries, bonuses, and stock sales. Lincoln became a cash cow for Keating and ACC. Keating gave liberally from its coffers, including a $100 million check to Ivan BOESKY and millions to charities, such as that run by Mother Teresa in Calcutta and Covenant House in New York City.

In 1985, Crescent Hotel Group (one of Lincoln's many subsidiaries) purchased Detroit's Pontchartrain Hotel. A partnership formed by Keating and his cronies then bought the hotel from Crescent using $38 million advanced by Lincoln through a series of transactions. The partnership paid $490,000 in cash and a loan origination fee of $600,000 which resulted in a book income of $9.5 million for Crescent. More than $10 million of another indirect loan ($20 million) to Crescent in 1986 was gradually funneled to Keating's partnership. The loans were justified by artificially raising the hotel's appraised value to $44.4 million. The partnership also reaped $9 million in tax benefits. This was only the beginning of a vast and complicated accounting trail of just one nutty deal made by Keating.

By 1987, U.S. government regulators became suspicious of Keating's activities at Lincoln. However, Keating had contributed substantially to the campaigns and political committees of 24 members of Congress, including five senators (John McCain, Alan Cranston, Dennis DeConcini, John Glenn, and Don Riegle). The so-called Keating Five had accepted $1.3 million in campaign contributions and actively lobbied against Lincoln's closure in 1987 when the losses might have been more easily contained. The Senate Ethics Committee later investigated their role in this scandal. In 1989, Lincoln was already $948 million in the red.

Even Keating's bookkeeping maneuvers couldn't avert the inevitable demise of ACC (which filed for bankruptcy) and the $3.4 billion collapse of Lincoln Savings & Loan, the country's costliest S & L fiasco, in 1989. Thousands of older Californians lost more than $210 million on America's worthless junk bonds. The state of California and the federal government filed at least 90 charges of fraud, racketeering, and conspiracy. Keating and his associates were accused of defrauding Lincoln and of reversing $82 million in real-estate deals to falsify profits. The bailout was estimated to cost taxpayers $2.6 billion.

In 1991, California convicted Keating on 17 counts of securities fraud. He was given a 10-year prison term. In 1993, a federal court found him guilty of 73 charges and handed down a 12½-year prison sentence. After serving less than five years, Keating was released in October 1996 when both convictions were overturned. In the federal case, a judge ruled that the jury had been prejudiced by prior knowledge of the state's conviction. The state's verdict was overturned because Judge Lance Ito had illegally allowed Keating to be tried for aiding and abetting fraud even though the bond dealers had no such intentions. Both decisions were appealed.

On January 15, 1998, the federal court restored the previous convictions. The state's conviction was thrown out again because Judge Ito gave faulty instructions to the jury. Finally, in April 1999, in a deal with prosecutors, Keating pleaded guilty to four counts of fraud. Although this settled the government's case against Keating, the taxpayers will be paying for Keating's follies for several decades.

KEELY MOTOR COMPANY FRAUD

In 1874, John E. W. Keely gave a sensational public demonstration of water being converted into energy that would power motors for very little cost. Viewers were so impressed that they invested large sums of money in Keely's supposedly revolutionary machine, thus establishing the Keely Motor Company. Only after Keely's death in 1898 did investigators discover that the "motors" and "generators" in his workshop were driven by tremendously compressed air from a huge storage assembly hidden in the basement of his house.

While still a young boy in Philadelphia, Pennsylvania, John Keely saw both his parents die and thereafter had to fend for himself. At various times he worked as a carpenter, carnival and circus pitchman, and orchestra leader before finding his "true" calling as an "inventor." During the 1870s, there was considerable popular interest in perpetual motion, and the crafty Keely capitalized on this interest, announcing that he had discovered an endless source of energy "from intermolecular vibrations of ether." He claimed that he had invented a "hydro-pneumatic-pulsating vacue" machine that could transform a quart of water into a fuel that could drive a 30-car railroad train at one mile per minute for 75 minutes. Keely frequently demonstrated his machine, which was surrounded by nozzles, valves, metal globes, gauges, and tubing, in a workshop on the second floor of his house in Philadelphia.

His energy-producing machine was first shown in 1872. Two years later, four prominent businessmen—John J. Cisco, a noted banker, Charles B. Collier, a top lawyer, Charles B. Franklyn, an official of the well-known Cunard steamship company, and Henry S. Sergeant, president of the Ingersoll Rock Drill Company—were swayed to help finance and organize the Keely Motor Company at a cost of more than $1 million. Stock in the company was sold and traded on the New York Stock Exchange to more than 3,000 investors in the United States and Europe. Both the investors and the public were deceived by Keely's facile tongue. His eloquent use of scientific terms fooled many. For example, here are some of his words on his contraption: "With these three agents alone—air, water, and machine—unaided by any and every compound, heat, electricity, or galvanic action, I have produced in an unappreciable time by a simple manipulation of the machine, a vaporic substance at one expulsion of a volume of ten gallons having an elastic energy of ten thousand pounds to the square inch. . . ." Keely succeeded in fooling and swindling his gullible supporters for 24 years. At one time, even wealthy New York financier John Jacob Astor II thought about investing $2 million in Keely's firm, although he later changed his mind.

Soon after Keely's death in November 1898, the suspicious son of one of his financial backers rented the Keely house in Philadelphia and searched it with some witnesses. They discovered a giant, heavy, metal tank full of highly compressed air buried under the kitchen floor in the basement. Through a series of strong steel tubes and pipes, the compressed air traveled upward to a 16-inch ceiling space between the kitchen and Keely's second-floor workshop. In this space were tubes necessary for carrying the compressed air to the different motors Keely had shown off. *The Scientific American,* a respected journal that had often criticized Keely's notions about perpetual motion and had called his claims ludicrous, published an exposé of the scandalous fraud in its issue of February 4, 1899. "For a quarter of a century the prince of humbugs played his part," the journal announced in reaffirming the inviolability of the laws of nature.

Alex KELLY: star wrestler, playboy, and rapist

Alex Kelly, champion high school wrestler and convicted rapist, may have sealed his own fate by fleeing the country days before his first trial was set to begin in 1987. Many felt his action confirmed his guilt (or else why did he flee?) and it may have been pivotal in swaying jury opinion in his second trail.

The scandal that stunned the wealthy and preppy suburb of Darien, Connecticut, began on February 10, 1986, when handsome, 18-year-old Alex Kelly offered a 16-year-old Catholic school student a ride home from a party in a Jeep Wagoneer he had borrowed from girlfriend Amy Molitor's family. Instead of driving the 16-year-old home, he drove past her house into a cul-de-sac where he sexually assaulted her—a fact confirmed by her doctor the next day. After she arrived home, distressed and almost hysterical, her father called Alex Kelly's father to report the assault. Alex's response to his father was, "We had sex. Go to bed."

Four days later, another girl (this one 17 years old) charged Kelly with raping her. The circumstances surrounding this case were eerily similar to the previous one. Later that day, Darien police arrested Kelly on charges of kidnaping and raping the two women.

Alex Kelly spent 17 days in prison and was released on a $200,000 bond. He was suspended from school and received permission to move and work in Colorado until the trial began. His parents and then lawyer Michael Sherman visited him there days before the trial started. Sherman later admitted having cautioned Kelly that he doubted whether Kelly could get a "fair shake from the criminal justice system" because of the "horrendous pretrial publicity" and the fact that he was to be tried for both crimes simultaneously. The odds, Sherman felt, were against Kelly. Mysteriously, Alex was not heard from again for eight years (he had apparently fled) and even his parents claimed (falsely, as it turned out later) that they didn't know his whereabouts.

Meanwhile, playboy Kelly traveled and skied in Europe's finest resorts, a new Swedish girlfriend in tow.

His name was on the FBI's most-wanted list. Unfortunately for Kelly, his passport was soon to expire, so in January 1995, he surrendered to authorities in Zurich. His lawyer claimed that Kelly was finally ready to come home and prove his innocence.

Back in Connecticut, Assistant District Attorney Bruce Hudock and Kelly's two victims were ready and waiting for their chance to prove otherwise in Stamford Superior Court. The first victim, now 26 and married, said that Kelly had threatened to kill her if she told anyone and that she had lived in mortal dread since 1986. Meanwhile, Thomas Puccio (Kelly's new lawyer) tried to convince the jury that she had been drunk and had consented to the sex. An expert added that her hysteria may have been caused by guilt and worry over her first sexual experience. Several witnesses were questioned about how much beer the girl had drunk. According to eyewitnesses, she had had one glass and was sober when she left with Kelly. Puccio convinced the judge to try the two rape cases separately and not admit evidence pertaining to Kelly's flight. Records indicated that Kelly's sojourn in Europe had been financed by his parents. They had even visited him there. However, Hudock decided not to prosecute them for aiding and abetting Alex's escape because he realized that jurors might react sympathetically to the concept of parents helping their child in an emergency. The first trial ended in a mistrial less than a month after it had begun because the jury was deadlocked 4-2 in favor of a conviction.

Months before the second trial was to begin, the defense team asked that the testimony of the second rape victim be barred from this trial. This motion was denied. They even petitioned to have the charges against Kelly dismissed because they felt it would be impossible for him to get a fair trial. The second trial began on May 15, 1997. Two weeks later, Judge Kevin Tierney threw out the kidnaping charges against Kelly. On June 12, 1997 Alex Kelly was convicted of first-degree sexual assault (an offense which carries a maximum 20 year prison sentence) and allowed to remain free on the original $1 million bond. As he left court that day, Kelly maintained that he was not guilty as charged. Shortly before the sentencing on July 24, Kelly apologized to the victim but did not admit to the rape, saying that "my perception may be different from hers" and begging for a chance to be a "contributing member of society." Puccio said that Kelly had matured and read glowing testimonials from people who knew him here and abroad. He urged a shorter prison sentence. The victim, Adrienne Bak Ortolano, who had finally shed her anonymity a week after the conviction, said she hoped that the judge's decision would send a message to other rape victims. The judge sentenced Kelly to 16 years in prison (his plea to remain free on bond while he appealed his conviction was rejected) and gave him a $10,000 fine and 10 years' probation.

In September 1998, Kelly appealed the June 1997 conviction and the 16-year sentence imposed on him. In a 13-point appeal, Kelly's lawyers asked for a new trial because, among other issues, the judge had permitted the prosecution to present evidence of Kelly's flight. This evidence should not have been allowed, according to the defense, since Kelly fled before the trial but not immediately after the alleged crime. The prosecution argued in a detailed response (July 1999) that the jury needed to know the truth about the delay between the occurrence of the crime and its resolution. The case is now in the hands of the state's supreme court, which, by fall 1999, had twice heard arguments regarding Kelly's appeal of his conviction. A decision is still awaited.

Meanwhile, on December 23, 1998, Kelly had pleaded "no contest" to one count of sexual assault in the second case and guilty to a charge of failure to appear in court. Judge Martin Nigro of the State Superior Court in Stamford sentenced him to 10 years in prison for raping then 17-year-old Hillary Buchanan (her identity was not disclosed until September 1999 when a television channel aired an episode on Alex Kelly) of Stamford.

KENNEDY-CAMPBELL AFFAIR

President of the United States John F. Kennedy was idolized by many Americans, especially after his tragic death. Twelve years after the 1963 assassination, various women began appearing to tell about their alleged love affairs with him. White House secretaries, starlets, film actresses, stewardesses, journalists, socialites, and others all claimed to have had intimate involvements with the tall, good-looking president, who had come to embody for many the image of the trusted all-American family man. Despite these ongoing claims, the public was severely jolted in late 1975 when word leaked out about the secret, two-year romance the married president had had with a black-haired, blue-eyed beauty named Judith Campbell.

While probing into the secret activities of the nation's intelligence agencies in 1975, the Senate Select Committee on Intelligence Operations, under the chairmanship of Senator Frank Church (Dem., Id.), called on and interviewed Judith Campbell Exner, who had had close relationships with Chicago Mafia boss Sam "Momo" Giancana and his mobster friend Johnny Roselli, both of whom had been in some way connected with clandestine plots by the Central Intelligence Agency (CIA) to assassinate Cuban leader Fidel Castro. The committee wanted to find out what Judith Exner knew about the former CIA plots, and it apparently learned more than it wanted to when, in secret testimony, she claimed to have had a very close relationship with President Kennedy. At the same time that she had been romantically involved with him, said Exner, she had also been seeing

Giancana, who was mysteriously murdered two days before he was to testify, having been subpoenaed by Senator Church's committee.

When the committee made public its report in November 1975, it didn't even mention Judith Campbell Exner by name, referring to her instead as a "close friend" of Kennedy's. The *Washington Post* soon identified Exner as the "close friend." Other newspapers ran the story and gave more explicit details about the relationship. The lurid publicity propelled Exner to hold a press conference in San Diego, California, on December 17, 1975. "I can at this time emphatically state that my relationship with Jack Kennedy was of a close, personal nature and did not involve conspiratorial shenanigans of any kind," she stated at the conference, adding, "My relationship with Sam Giancana and my friendship with Johnny Roselli were of a personal nature and in no way related to or affected my relationship with Jack Kennedy, nor did I discuss either of them with the other." She also said she had no knowledge of underworld activities whatsoever.

In the ensuing months, the full story came out, while the public gasped in astonishment and sometimes horror. Judith Exner later wrote and published an autobiography, *My Story* (1977), revealing even more details about her life and illicit affair with the former president. In February 1960, according to Exner, singer Frank Sinatra, a sometimes lover, introduced her to John Kennedy, who was then a United States senator from Massachusetts, at a party in Las Vegas, Nevada. Exner said that Ted Kennedy, John's younger brother, also took a fancy to her but that she turned him down when he, too, tried to date her. Judith and John almost immediately began their trystings in many places across the United States, including Washington, D.C., Palm Beach, Los Angeles, and Chicago.

The dark-haired beauty, who bore a striking resemblance to Kennedy's wife, Jackie, claimed that the young senator told her his marriage was very shaky but that he and Jackie wouldn't get a divorce because it would probably ruin his political career. His driving ambition kept him married, he told her. Exner evidently met Kennedy at the White House at least 20 times, having lunch with him and carrying on their liaison. She said that Jackie was never present at the time and that the two of them had never met. The peak of their passionate affair apparently occurred in the middle of 1961, and it ended in the spring of 1962; they had parted without bitterness, said Exner, feeling that their love had waned and that outside pressures had grown too strong, making the affair too risky.

Although she described President Kennedy as a warm, energetic, and inquisitive man, Exner also spoke negatively about him and alleged that she had once angrily turned down a proposal by Kennedy for a ménage à trois with another woman. Because of his bad back, the president was increasingly forced to make love lying on his back reported Exner, which made it seem to her that she was there merely to service and satisfy him. She also reported that Kennedy was fascinated by Hollywood gossip and loved to hear from her about who was sleeping with whom, since she had grown up in Los Angeles where her parents' close ties to the entertainment industry had helped her to know numerous celebrities. Kennedy never discussed politics and government with her, but he apparently wanted her to attend important state affairs, which she declined to do because of the risk involved.

Exner also revealed that there had been many telephone calls between her and the president. J. Edgar Hoover, the director of the Federal Bureau of Investigation (FBI), who was waging a vigorous anti-Mafia crusade along with U.S. Attorney General Robert Kennedy, informed President Kennedy about Exner's connections with Giancana and Roselli. Hoover privately warned the president that continuation of his secret affair with her would probably eventually destroy his career. The FBI director claimed that in a 54-week period (1961–62), the two had talked to each other on the phone 70 times, and that some of Exner's calls to the White House had been made from Giancana's home (which she denied). Allegedly, Hoover used this information to pressure the president into allowing him to investigate, harass, and wiretap the phone of Martin Luther King, Jr., the civil rights leader who was assassinated in 1968. Hoover's disclosures and warnings supposedly caused the president to end the affair with Exner, despite her claims to the contrary.

In an October 1991 article in the *Sunday Times of London*, Exner claimed that "on at least 20 occasions" she carried both money and messages between Kennedy and Giancana, including details of a plot to assassinate Castro. She also said that "Jack fully participated in the CIA involvement with the underworld." Later, in a 1996 issue of *Vanity Fair*, Exner said she ended her two-year affair with Kennedy because she hated being "the other woman"; she also claimed she was both Kennedy's and Giancana's mistress at the same time and aborted Kennedy's child 10 months before he was assassinated. On September 24, 1999, Exner died of breast cancer at the age of 65.

KENNEDY-KOPECHNE ACCIDENT. See CHAPPAQUIDDICK: Kennedy-Kopechne accident.

KENNEDY-MEYER AFFAIR

President John F. Kennedy was notorious for his extramarital dalliances. Of his long-term love affairs, the last was with Mrs. Mary Pinchot Meyer, a Washington, D.C. socialite and artist. The two were still involved at the time of the president's assassination. News of the secret affair might never have leaked if it hadn't been for a bizarre and tragic sequence of circumstances only 11 month's after Kennedy's assassination. Mary Meyer herself was murdered. Shortly after her death, her best friend's husband decided to tell all, and the affair was made public.

Among his friends, Jack Kennedy had long been known as a womanizer and unfaithful husband. After breaking up with Judith Campbell (see KENNEDY-CAMPBELL AFFAIR), he turned his attention to Mrs. Mary Pinchot Meyer, the divorced wife of Cord Meyer, Jr., a founder of the United World Federalists and later head of the covert action staff of the U.S. Central Intelligence Agency (CIA). Besides being the sister-in-law of Benjamin C. Bradlee, a close Kennedy intimate, who in the early 1960s was chief of the Washington, D.C., bureau of *Newsweek* magazine, Mary Meyer was a friend of Jack Kennedy's wife, Jacqueline Bouvier Kennedy, whom the president had married in 1953. Together, Mary and Jacqueline Kennedy used to take long strolls along the towpath of the Old Chesapeake and Ohio Canal, a favorite hiking and biking trail paralleling the Potomac River outside Washington, where they talked with one another.

Mary Pinchot Meyer and Jack Kennedy had known each other since their days in college and renewed their acquaintance when she moved into a studio behind the Bradlees' house in Georgetown after her divorce from Cord Meyer in 1956. Kennedy was then 39 and a United States senator from Massachusetts. Mary, three years his junior, was frequently present at the small dinner parties the Kennedys and Bradlees gave for each other and their close friends, but Ben Bradlee swore that he was not aware of the love affair at the time it was going on. Mary's closest friends then were Ann Truitt, a sculptor, and her husband James Truitt, a vice president of the *Washington Post*. Evidently Mary communicated her secret affair with Jack to the Truitts, and many years after Jack Kennedy's assassination, Jim Truitt made the affair public, causing a sensation.

Apparently, Jack and Mary first went to bed together in December 1961, a year after he was elected president. By the spring of 1962, their affair had become a steady relationship. Whenever Jackie Kennedy was out of town, which was fairly often, Mary visited the White House. She recorded their visits in her personal diary, writing that she had once brought six "joints" of marijuana with her, of which she and the president smoked three before he stopped and reputedly said, "No more. Suppose the Russians did something now."

Mary was as stunned and grieved at the president's assassination on November 22, 1963, as were the rest of Kennedy's friends and admirers. Little did she realize that she herself would meet a violent end almost a year later, on October 13, 1964, as she was taking a noontime walk along the old canal towpath. She was shot twice, once in the head and once in the chest, with no apparent motive. The police arrested a 25-year-old laborer named Raymond Crump, Jr., whom a witness said he had seen struggling with Mrs. Meyer. There was, however, no hard evidence against Crump, who was tried, acquitted, and released. The murder weapon was never found.

To compound the mystery, a family member called up Ben Bradlee and told him Mary had kept a diary that she wanted burned in the event of her death. Ben and his wife Tony (Mary's sister) searched her studio but could not find any personal records. Months later, Tony found the diary, which allegedly contained so many references to Jack Kennedy that there could be no doubt that the two had had a passionate romance. The Bradlees gave the incriminating diary to a friend, James Angleton, who was then chief of CIA counterintelligence and an old friend of Mary's. Angleton either disposed of it discreetly, or, as James Truitt claimed, it was destroyed at CIA headquarters.

KENNEDY-SWANSON AFFAIR

Joseph P. Kennedy, Sr., founder of the Fitzgerald-Kennedy dynasty of Boston, Massachusetts, and father of John F., Robert F. and Edward M. Kennedy, was a brilliant financier and businessman. He wanted to be wealthy and powerful, and he achieved both through hard work and know-how. Although well-known as a family man with nine children Joe Kennedy, as he was popularly called, also loved beautiful women and maintained a string of mistresses over the years. His most notorious liaison was with Gloria Swanson, one of Hollywood's stars of the silver screen in the 1920s.

The son of a poor Irish saloon keeper in Boston, Joe Kennedy was determined at an early age to become an American success. He attended Harvard University and went on to a career in banking. After World War I, he had his first taste of the movie business when he acquired a chain of small theaters in New England that had a franchise for distributing the silent pictures produced by Universal Pictures. He soon became knowledgeable about the financial features of the film industry and, in 1926, acquired for next to nothing the lucrative Film Booking Office of America (FBO), a production and distribution company. The year 1928 found Kennedy, at age 39, in Hollywood overseeing the merger of three troubled show-business organizations; it was at this time that he became acquainted with the glamorous 29-year-old Swanson.

Actually it was Swanson who made the first advances in what was to be a two-year, largely clandestine relationship. She had left Paramount Pictures to join United Artists, an independent distributing company organized by actors Charlie Chaplin, Douglas Fairbanks, Sr., and other renowned stars who produced their own films with their own or others' money. Gloria Productions, Incorporated, had overspent its budget on the recently completed *Sadie Thompson* (1928), and Swanson was heavily in debt for the film as well as for maintaining her expensive, lavish lifestyle. A friend suggested that she seek financial advice from Joe Kennedy. She invited him to lunch, and he was immediately smitten by his petite, sophisticated hostess. He agreed to straighten out her business affairs at once and proceeded to do so. Within months, a new company was incorporated, and Kennedy had agreed to help finance and become involved in the production of a new motion picture to be directed by Erich von Stroheim.

At this time, Gloria Swanson was married to her third husband, a handsome and impoverished French nobleman, the Marquis Henri de la Falaise de la Coudraye, known as "Hank" around the movie studios. Kennedy invited the couple to visit him in Palm Beach, Florida, and there, while Hank was out deep-sea fishing, Joe and Gloria apparently made love for the first time. During this same visit, Joe offered Hank the job of manager of the Paris office of Pathé and FBO, an offer he could not refuse. Thereafter Gloria Swanson's life was divided between her own home in Beverly Hills, California, when Hank was on the West Coast, and Joe Kennedy's rented quarters on Rodeo Drive in Hollywood. At Joe's insistence, Gloria's adopted French orphan son, Joseph, was baptized into the Catholic Church.

Late in 1928, von Stroheim, after much delay, began shooting *Queen Kelly*. The first part, set in a European principality, went well, but the second part, set in East Africa, turned into a disaster. Von Stroheim began improvising and completely changed the movie script and the characters. Swanson walked off the set in disgust and telephoned Kennedy, saying "There's a madman in charge here. The scenes he's shooting will never get past Will Hays" (Hays, as president of the Motion Picture Producers and Distributors Association of America, was enforcing moral standards for films and actors). Kennedy rushed west on the next train, saw the rushes (first film prints), and agreed with Swanson that the work was unacceptable. Von Stroheim was fired. No other director was ever able to rescue the excessive footage that had already been shot for the film. More than $800,000 had been spent on a colossal flop. Kennedy, crushed, bemoaned loudly and often "my first failure."

Kennedy then backed Swanson in her first talking movie, *The Trespasser* (1929). Fortunately, unlike many silent-film stars, Swanson had a fine speaking voice and could also sing, so the the advent of "talkies" did not put her out of business. Kennedy arranged elaborate premières in Paris and London before the movie opened in New York, Chicago, and other American cities. He, his wife Rose, and his sister planned to travel together to Paris for the opening of the film, and he pleaded with Gloria to join them. At first she resisted but finally consented, provided she could share a stateroom of the ship with her old friend Virginia Bowker. When the group reached Paris after the Atlantic crossing, Hank was waiting to escort them around. The film was an enormous success at all its premières.

One afternoon in the fall of 1929, a Kennedy staff man called to tell Gloria that he would pick her up for an appointment with a person named O'Connell. Baffled, she went along, and in a hotel suite was introduced to William Cardinal O'Connell, the archbishop of Boston, who was a long-time Kennedy family friend. When they were alone, he said to her: "I am here to ask you to stop seeing Joseph Kennedy. Each time you see him, you become an occasion of sin for him." The cardinal then went on to report that Kennedy had sought official permission to maintain a second household with Swanson, since the church would not permit him to divorce his wife. O'Connell explained that such an arrangement was impossible and that Kennedy was exposing himself to scandal every time he appeared in public with Swanson. She was furious and retorted, "It's Mr. Kennedy you should be talking to. Tell him." No one knows to this day who or what instigated this private exchange.

Kennedy's third movie venture with Swanson was *What a Widow!* (1930), a wildly costumed musical comedy that was mildly successful. At the time it was being produced, Hank wrote to inform Gloria that he was beginning divorce proceedings (he had clearly perceived what was going on and eventually got his divorce). Despite the prospect of being single once again, Gloria, while having dinner with Kennedy at his Rodeo Drive home in November 1930, questioned one of his decisions about her personal bank account: Kennedy almost choked and left the room in anger. Several days later, he departed from Hollywood without calling to say goodbye to her. Shortly thereafter he liquidated most of his movie holdings for a profit of $5 million. In her memoirs, published in 1981, Gloria Swanson wrote with genuine affection about Joe Kennedy. She confessed at one point, however, that she was uncertain if his wife ever knew their relationship was more than a platonic one.

KENT STATE SHOOTINGS

On May 4, 1970, on the campus of Kent State University in Kent, Ohio, four students were killed and nine others wounded by the indiscriminate firing of their rifles by several Ohio National Guardsmen. The traumatic event instigated a tremendous controversy. Some claimed that the shooting was unjustifiable, while others said that demonstrating students provoked the fatal confrontation and were thus to blame. Eight and a half years of investigation and litigation ensued, at the end of which no one was found culpable for the shootings. A miscarriage of justice, claimed some; a proper verdict, said others.

In April 1970, the Ohio National Guard was called out to help civil authorities quell unruly student dem-

Ohio National Guardsmen line the center of Kent State University campus during disorders on Monday, May 4, 1970. In the foreground is the burned-out ROTC building. Behind the building (at upper left) is where four students were later fatally shot that day. (AP/Wide World Photos)

onstrations and disturbances in Cleveland, Oxford, Sandusky, and Columbus, Ohio. Throughout the United States, college campuses were being disrupted by Students for a Democratic Society (SDS) and other organizations and persons who advocated the overthrow of America's social and political systems. This anti-establishment movement opposed the Vietnam War, the military draft, the concept of military power, and any denial of civil rights. The SDS wanted to tear down the entire structure of American culture and rebuild it on a better pattern. Political liberals frequently joined with radicals and revolutionaries in their defiant public protests against traditional American values.

President Richard M. Nixon's order for an American "incursion" into Cambodia on May 1, 1970, immediately ignited a strong student protest at Kent State University in Kent, Ohio. Campus dissenters painted and put up signs all over the university, saying "U.S. Out of Cambodia" and "ROTC Off Campus," as well as less diplomatic statements, such as "Fuck the Pigs." A symbolic burial of the U.S. Constitution took place in the Kent State commons on May 1, and there were rallies on campus and disturbances in downtown Kent. On May 2, the mayor declared a state of civil emergency and requested the National Guard to keep order. More than 1,100 guardsmen arrived after Kent State's ROTC building was burned to the ground on the night of Saturday, May 2. Tension between the students and the authorities mounted on Sunday when Ohio's Governor John A. Rhodes arrived, denounced the disruptive students, and vowed to use all necessary force to keep the campus open. All demonstrations and rallies were then prohibited.

Late in the morning on Monday, May 4, increasing numbers of students assembled near a parking lot before Taylor Hall in the center of the Kent State campus. Using a bullhorn, National Guard leaders ordered the students to disperse and, when the students, numbering as many as 1,000, refused, ordered tear gas canisters to be thrown to break up the crowd. In retaliation, the students hurled stones and other objects at the advancing guardsmen, taunting them with phrases such as "shit heels," "half-ass pigs," "fascists," and "motherfuckers." At 12:25 P.M., some guardsmen opened fire for a period lasting 13 seconds, and their bullets hit 13 students, wounding nine and killing four (Jeffrey G. Miller, Allison B. Krause, William K. Schroeder, and Sandra Lee Scheuer). Both sides now seemed ready to attack each other, but three Kent State professors defused the situation through appeals and discussions. The Federal Bureau of Investigation (FBI) moved into Kent State immediately afterward and began a thorough probe. Later, the FBI and Justice Department declared that the shootings had not been necessary and were not in order. These findings provoked hot debate by those who felt the students were responsible for the tragedy.

Probably the most impressive of the various groups that investigated the Kent State tragedy was the Commission on Campus Unrest, which was appointed by President Nixon and headed by former Pennsylvania Governor William W. Scranton. After its full inquiry, the commission concluded that the students and guardsmen shared the blame for the tragedy; it called the guards' gunfire "unwarranted and inexcusable" and also condemned the student violence at Kent State. The commission appealed to President Nixon to exert moral leadership to reduce the perilous divisiveness among government, universities, and students. An end to the war in Indochina was recommended to help heal the nation, but the commission's report was rejected in Ohio and Washington, D.C. (where Vice President Spiro Agnew called it "pablum for permissiveness").

The Kent State tragedy was investigated by a special grand jury in Portage County, Ohio, which totally exonerated the National Guardsmen who had fired their weapons, saying that they had done so "in the honest and sincere belief that they would suffer serious bodily injury had they not done so." The jury criticized the Kent State administration, including university President Robert I. White, for fostering "an attitude of laxity, overindulgence, and permissiveness in its students and faculty." Citizens who harbored vindictive attitudes against the students endorsed the Portage County jury's findings.

The parents of the slain and wounded students filed civil and criminal suits against Governor Rhodes, President White of Kent State, and 27 National Guardsmen and their leaders for a total of $46 million in 13 separate cases. But although the cases stirred up fierce opposition, the plaintiffs persisted in their arguments and managed to overcome much hostility and many legal setbacks. In 1974 a federal judge in Cleveland, Frank J. Battisti, dismissed government charges against eight of the indicted guardsmen, declaring that they had willfully deprived the students of their civil rights, and in 1975 a Cleveland federal-court jury acquitted all of the guardsmen of responsibility in the shootings. The decision was an outrage to the plaintiffs, who concurred with Joseph Kelner, their chief counsel, who called it "a sad day in American justice."

An appeal was then made by the plaintiffs, procedural errors were discovered in the first trial, and a civil liability case was brought to court against Rhodes and the 27 guardsmen in December 1978, again in Cleveland. But before testimony was heard, an out-of-court agreement was reached in which the 13 plaintiffs received a total of $675,000 among them. Some observers called the payment a "payoff" for a "cover-up." Rhodes and the guardsmen also signed a statement of regret sought by the plaintiffs, which concluded with the words: "We hope that the agreement to end this litigation will help to assuage the tragic memories regarding that sad day."

Otto KERNER: convicted judge

In 1973 former Governor Otto Kerner of Illinois achieved the dubious distinction of becoming the first sitting federal appellate judge to be convicted of a felony. At the age of 64, he was convicted on 17 counts of conspiracy, fraud, perjury, bribery, and income-tax evasion in connection with the purchase and sale of racetrack stock during his term as governor of Illinois from 1961 to 1968. At the time of his conviction, Kerner was a judge of the U.S. Circuit Court of Appeals for the seventh circuit.

The prosecution contended, and the jury concurred, that Kerner and Theodore J. Isaacs, the state revenue director of Illinois during Kerner's governorship, had agreed to a lucrative stock offer that netted them more than $400,000 for an investment of $70,000. They bought the stock at a bargain rate in exchange for such favors as helping the racetrack owner to obtain a longer season and giving him permission to expand into harness racing. The two former state officials had declared their profits from sale of the stock as long-term capital gains when in fact the money should have been taxed as ordinary income.

The details of the deal were so complicated that the chief prosecutor in the case, U.S. attorney James R. Thompson, claimed he didn't understand it all himself. Kerner didn't deny having made the profits but only denied that they represented a bribe.

Newsweek magazine described Kerner as a "picture of public probity—a stiff patrician who rose from private to general in the National Guard, served a term as governor, chaired a celebrated presidential inquiry into ghetto riots, and finally achieved a seat on the U.S. Court of Appeals." *Time* magazine recollected that Kerner was "once known as the Mr. Clean of Illinois."

After his indictment, at which he perjured himself to the grand jury, Kerner took a leave of absence from the bench with pay. Because judges are appointed for life, he could not be removed from the bench unless impeachment proceedings were brought against him. Not only did he face up to 83 years in prison and $93,000 in fines, but the U.S. Internal Revenue Service (IRS) was seeking to recover from Kerner and Isaacs more than $80,000 in back taxes and penalties.

Because Kerner was a judge in the state of Illinois, and had friendships with other judges in the area, a judge was brought in from Tennessee to preside at the trial. Character witnesses who spoke in his behalf included Roy Wilkins of the National Association for the Advancement of Colored People (NAACP), who called Kerner a man of "impeccable character," and General William Westmoreland. Their statements, however, were not able to turn the tide of the trial.

In April 1973, Kerner was sentenced to three years in prison and fined $50,000. Under the terms of his sentence, he was to be immediately eligible for parole. He was deprived of his office space in Chicago after sentencing, a decision approved by Chief Justice of the U.S. Supreme Court Warren E. Burger. However, Paul Connolly, Kerner's lawyer, announced that Kerner did not intend to resign until his appeals were exhausted.

In June 1974, without comment or recorded dissent, the Supreme Court refused to hear Kerner's appeal. Kerner had argued that he could not be convicted of any crime until he was removed from the bench by Congress. He resigned from the U.S. Court of Appeals on July 24, 1974, and began serving his prison term on July 29.

Though many were infuriated by Kerner's actions, some of his fellow politicians were sympathetic. "The judgment of the court is a tragedy to Judge Kerner and his family," said Illinois Senator Adlai Stevenson III. "It is also another verdict of guilt against our politics." Said Daniel Walker, a successor of Kerner's as governor of Illinois, "Kerner's unblemished record was broken by his inability to withstand the enormous pressures of evil that descend upon the person who sits in the Governor's chair."

Billie Jean KING: stained tennis star

Conservative Americans were shocked when an unknown 32-year-old woman named Marilyn Barnett publicly alleged that she had had a lesbian relationship for seven years with 37-year-old Billie Jean King, one of the country's best-known female athletes and winner of numerous national and international singles, doubles, and mixed-doubles tennis championships. Barnett's revelation was made on April 29, 1981, when she filed a court suit in Los Angeles, California, against Mrs. King. Under California's modern "palimony laws," which permit unmarried couples to make agreements to share property if their relationship ends, Barnett contended that she was legally entitled to financial means and a

Tennis champion Billie Jean King, speaking at a news conference in Los Angeles in early May 1981, explains her love affair with a woman who was then suing her for support. (AP/Wide World Photos)

house in Malibu (worth an estimated $750,000) from King, who immediately expressed shock and disappointment at the woman's actions and then stated that the allegations against her were "untrue and unfounded." This unique palimony case between members of the same sex aroused the curiosity of numerous scandal-seeking news reporters and others. King, who had gained success as an aggressive competitor on the tennis court, especially in her highly publicized 1973 win against Bobby Riggs in the Houston Astrodome in the so-called battle of the sexes, had since become a nationally recognized, staunch "women's libber." Her strong participation in the women's rights movement seemed only to fuel the gossip about this scandalous circumstance.

The two women's relationship had apparently begun about six months after they first met each other in 1972 when Ms. Barnett was working as a hairdresser and was hired to be Mrs. King's personal secretary. Married to Larry King since 1965, Billie Jean (née Moffitt) had taken Barnett as a lover, living with her in the Malibu house where they shared the mortgage payments. The two females also spent time together in Billie Jean's apartment in New York City and elsewhere. In 1979 their affair ended, and the Kings demanded that Barnett vacate the valuable Malibu house so that they could sell it. The former hairdresser was deeply hurt by the turn of events and later threatened to take court action against the Kings for compensation.

On May 1, 1981, Mrs. King made a startling confession before the press, saying, "I've decided to talk with you as I've always talked—from the heart." With her parents and husband Larry at her side, she conceded that she and Barnett had been lovers and called the finished affair a "mistake" for which she accepted responsibility. More details then came out concerning the affair, which Mrs. King said had long been over. Ms. Barnett had apparently attempted to commit suicide twice since the end of the affair. She was now confined to a wheelchair because of a broken back suffered during a plunge from the Malibu house's balcony. This first suicide attempt had been followed by a second attempt, with a drug overdose.

The tennis star's public acknowledgment that she had tarnished her sport by her conduct drew sympathy from much of the press, which nonetheless ran news stories about purported rampant lesbianism on the women's tennis circuit. Half a dozen top players, notably Czech-born American champion Martina Navratilova, were said to have had lesbian affairs at some time. Meanwhile, Mrs. King appeared on television in an interview and said she had offered her husband a divorce. He was "understanding," said their marriage was sound, and blamed himself in part for what had happened because his many business interests had made him carelessly inattentive to his wife. When he first learned of her affair, said Larry King, he had felt "a twinge of jealousy" but evidently much less of one than if his wife's secret lover had been a man. A newspaper offered Barnett some $25,000 to publish Mrs. King's letters to her, but the Kings got an injunction preventing their publication. The scandal gradually faded out, and a settlement was reached between the two parties.

KNEELAND and KNOWLTON: early advocacy of birth control

The first American publication on birth control, entitled *The Fruits of Philosophy* (or *The Private Companion of Young Married People*), was authored by Dr. Charles Knowlton, a physician, and published by his friend Abner Kneeland of Boston in 1832 under the latter's own imprint. This pamphlet immediately caused a sensation and scandal; both Kneeland and Knowlton were hostilely accused of attacking the bedrock moral attitudes of all Christian people.

In 1831, the Massachusetts-born Kneeland had founded the rationalist, free-thinking newspaper named the *Boston Investigator*. He had been a Universalist minister from 1804 to 1829, when his belief in "the rule of reason" over divine authority compelled him to leave the church. He soon became an avowed free-thinker (one who forms his religious views independently, without regard to church authority) and began publishing his paper.

Curiously, the radical Kneeland was not indicted for publishing Knowlton's pamphlet. Instead, he was charged with publishing in his paper "a certain scandalous, impious . . . profane libel of and concerning God," and had to stand trial several times during the next five years. The fact that in Knowlton's published work Kneeland had disseminated information about the right to control conception seemed to be emphasized by the prosecution much more than the actual charges against Kneeland. Through appeals and the disagreements of the juries in the trials, Kneeland stayed out of jail until 1838 when he was finally convicted at the end of his third trial and jailed for three months. At this time, Boston's learned citizenry signed petitions for his release, while behind bars Kneeland wrote articles about his freedom of speech being denied in the supposed land of liberty, America.

Knowlton was also prosecuted after the appearance of *The Fruits of Philosophy*, in which he claimed to have found an important method for birth control. He advocated using a mixture of alum and some vegetative, astringent substance like raspberry or green tea leaves in a postcoital douche. For trying to sell his pamphlet, he was fined at Taunton and sent to jail for three months in a workhouse at Cambridge, Massachusetts, in 1833. All the publicity about the two men's trials resulted in a demand for Knowlton's work, and new editions had to be printed.

Upon his release from jail, Kneeland openly and vigorously supported *The Fruits of Philosophy*, of which about 250,000 copies subsequently went into circulation and also found readers in Great Britain. Growing tired of Boston, Kneeland and a group called the First Society of Free Enquirers journeyed to Iowa in 1839. There they set up an experimental colony known as Salubria, where Kneeland carried on his work and taught his free-thinking philosophy. He died there at the age of 71 in 1844.

He and his friend Knowlton, who died in 1850, would have enjoyed seeing *The Fruits of Philosophy* become the subject of a famous and controversial test case in England in 1877. For republishing Knowlton's pioneering work on birth control, Charles Bradlaugh and Annie Besant stood trial at London's Old Bailey Court. The case, *The Queen v. Charles Bradlaugh & Annie Besant*, began in court with the prosecution saying "this is a dirty, filthy book, and the test of it is that no human being would allow that book to lie on his table; no decently educated English husband would allow even his wife to have it." The defendants were accused of having "corrupt motives," but in the end the jury exonerated them, nonetheless stating that Knowlton's work was "calculated to deprave public morals." Bradlaugh and Besant appealed and gained the right to publish *The Fruits of Philosophy*—a milestone in the history of birth-control literature.

David KOPAY: gay football player

Homosexuality in football? Football is thought of as the last real bastion of masculinity by many Americans, who were scandalized in late 1975 when 33-year old David Kopay, a 10-year veteran player in the National Football League (NFL), publicly "came out of the closet" and revealed that he was a homosexual. Many felt that Kopay's masculine, athletic image could only be a sham or a joke. Kopay's rebuttal shocked his accusers. "Masculinity?" "Male homosexuality is pure masculinity," he said during a 1976 interview in Seattle, Washington. His dramatic revelation helped terminate his pro football career.

When a series of articles on the subject of homosexuality in sports appeared in the Washington, D.C., newspaper *The Washington Star* in December 1975, Kopay became certain that he had to "come out" and offered to be interviewed by the newspaper. He had remained unhappily silent about his true sexual preference out of fear, he said, and didn't want to hide any more. After the *Star* interviewed Kopay and ran his shocking story, other publications immediately picked it up and also talked with him; he soon appeared on numerous TV talk shows, receiving both strong negative and positive responses to his open homosexuality. He endured insults from strangers and stony silence from old friends. Kopay's parents were utterly appalled by his disclosure; his father threatened to kill him and his mother said she never wanted to see him again. Neither, however, held to their threats.

David Marquette Kopay came from a strict, authoritarian Roman Catholic background in Chicago, Illinois. His working-class family was very religious, often attending mass. He was the second of four children, having an older brother and younger sister and brother. In 1949 Kopay's family moved from Chicago to Los Angeles, where he went to a junior seminary (a boarding school that prepared its students for the Catholic priesthood) for a while before leaving to attend Notre Dame High School. Good-looking and with an outgoing personality, Kopay was a star football player and athlete in high school. In 1961 he matriculated at the University of Washington and proceeded to gain praise as a punter and halfback on the varsity football team. In his senior year he was chosen co-captain of Washington's Rose Bowl team (1964). Later in 1964 he signed with the San Francisco Forty-Niners professional football team as a running back, earning the nickname "Psyche" because he got so "psyched up" at football practices and games.

In 1968 Kopay was traded to the Detroit Lions. He was now plagued with knee injuries, and just before the start of the 1969 season, he was traded to the Washington Redskins, whose coach was the legendary Vince Lombardi. In 1969, 1970, and part of 1971 Kopay played for the Redskins. At the same time he secretly visited gay bars and discotheques. Though he occasionally had sex with women and even was married for a brief time, his main attraction was for men.

The Redskins cut Kopay from their roster in 1971, but soon after this the New Orleans Saints signed him on. About a year later he was traded to the Oakland Raiders and then to the Green Bay Packers in time for the 1972 season. Kopay played at different times for the Raiders and Packers as a veteran back or reserve player until his sudden pronouncement in late 1975.

When he spoke out publicly, many could not accept this "virile jock-as-faggot" who played a "man's game." Kopay's admission of gayness has since been debated as either an act of courage or one of stupidity; his case remains controversial, and homosexuality in football and other sports is still a taboo as a subject for open discussion. The full story of Kopay, the first NFL athlete to openly reveal his homosexuality, is told in his autobiography published in 1977, *The David Kopay Story*.

"KOREAGATE"

The Republicans were rocked by WATERGATE in 1973–74, at a time when some Democrats were evidently participating in "Koreagate," a political scandal exposed in 1977–78 involving illegal, covert South Korean influence peddling and bribery on Capitol Hill. Although several United States congressmen were indicted in the scandal, only one was found guilty in the end. Nonetheless, the American public was again disgusted by the venality of congressmen who could be "bought" or corrupted.

The seed of the Koreagate scandal was sown in 1970, when the Nixon administration prepared to remove 20,000 American troops from South Korea. The plan was opposed by South Korean President Park Chung Hee, who then contrived to manipulate United States congressmen through the covert use of the South Korean Central Intelligence Agency (KCIA). The U.S. State Department was reportedly aware of South Korean lobbying efforts to influence Congress in the early 1970s. American officials, mainly representatives and senators, were to be offered campaign contributions, free trips, women, and honorary degrees from Korean universities as incentives to favor Seoul's wishes. The largesse-dispensing scheme was directed by a South Korean businessman named Park Tong Sun (no relation to President Park), who was called Tongsun Park in the United States. Tongsun Park became sole agent of American rice sales to Korea in return for his "buying" of American congressmen, according to later testimony by the director of the KCIA to an investigating congressional committee. There are claims that Tongsun Park meted out between one half million and one million dollars annually to American officials. One State

Department official declared: "It was common knowledge in the United States embassy in Seoul that any senator could pick up $50,000 and any representative $30,000 for his campaign just by asking the South Koreans for it." This was during the 1974 American elections.

Rice trader and influence peddler Park threw lavish parties for influential Washington personages and handed out political contributions freely while Congress turned back every attempt to withdraw American troops from South Korea or to reduce aid to that country. Allegations of bribery of members of Congress led to investigations by the Justice Department and the House and Senate ethics committees. By mid-1977 there was talk of a deliberate cover-up by those involved, said to number at least 115 congressmen and former congressmen according to a reported survey of House members authorized by the House Ethics Committee. In July 1977, Philip A. Lacovara, the special counsel earlier engaged by the committee to direct the "Koreagate" investigation, resigned because of what he called conflicts and lack of trust between himself and committee chairman Representative John J. Flynt, Jr. (Dem., Ga.). Former Watergate prosecutor Leon A. Jaworski accepted the unpaid job and vowed to pursue the inquiry into alleged wrongdoing by Democratic congressmen as vigorously as he had looked into Watergate cover-ups by White House Republicans.

Tongsun Park had cooperated with the Justice Department until 1976 when he took a business trip to London and never returned to Washington. The South Korean government failed to cooperate in the investigation, refusing at first to extradite Tongsun Park to the United States to face charges of influence-buying there. Finally, in late December, 1977, the South Korean government said Tongsun Park could return to testify, with immunity, at the conspiracy and bribery hearings occurring in Congress.

Meanwhile a former member of the House of Representatives, Richard T. Hanna (Dem., Calif.), had been indicted on charges of conspiring with Tongsun Park and KCIA agents to influence Congress. Investigators had discovered secret, sophisticated, wide-ranging plans by the KCIA to manipulate Congress, the White House, the American press, and the clergy to South Korea's advantage. Hanna eventually pleaded guilty, becoming the first person ever to admit wrongdoing while a member of Congress. He was then sentenced to serve six to 30 months in prison for conspiring to defraud the U.S. government. He served little more than a year behind bars.

Another 1978 indictment that caused headlines in the scandal went to former U.S. Representative Otto E. Passman (Dem., La.), once a power in United States foreign-aid appropriations, who was charged with conspiring with Tongsun Park to defraud the government and with taking bribes. The 77-year-old ex-congressman, suffering from depression and senility in a New Orleans clinic, successfully maintained his innocence.

Among the others who were investigated, three Democratic congressmen from California received reprimands by a vote of the House on October 13, 1978. Earlier, the House Ethics Committee, chaired by John J. Flynt, Jr., had recommended that one of these congressmen, Representative Edward R. Roybal, be censured, after considering a proposal for his expulsion. Roybal had been charged with taking $1,000 for his personal use from Tongsun Park in 1974 and lying about it continually to the ethics committee. But the congressman was only reprimanded, along with Charles H. Wilson and John J. McFall, the two others involved in the scandalous activities.

The Justice Department dropped its charges against Tongsun Park in 1979, bringing an end to the Koreagate ordeal. In testimony to members of Congress, Park had said: "I thought I was taking part in the American political process. So far as I was concerned, I was helping congressional friends who were loyal to me." He also admitted giving about $850,000 to friendly congressmen.

Ivar KREUGER: history's greatest swindler

Many in the financial world have dreamed of the riches to be gained through sole control of the manufacture and distribution of a product, but few have achieved the near-perfect monopoly gained by the Swedish financier Ivar Kreuger, once known universally as "The Match King." In the end, however, his dishonest means caught up with him, and he took his own life.

Trained and practicing as a civil engineer in Sweden, Kreuger founded a match company in 1907. From that time on, he worked to create a personal monopoly. World War I assisted his attempt: his facility as a persuader enabled him to become managing director of Svenska Tändsticks AB (the Swedish Match Company) and concentrate the entire Swedish match industry under his control. When the war ended, Kreuger (heading the Swedish financial agency Kreuger and Toll) began moves to enlarge his scope. He gained the support of American financiers and worked secretly, behind the mask assigned to him by his supporters as a financial genius, to achieve world control of match production. By 1928, it is estimated that Kreuger held, through his holding company, power over more than 50 percent of the world's match production.

His methods included fraud and bribery, but superficially his transactions appeared to be long-term loans in dollars to the kings and ministers of countries short of money; all they had to do was to grant him monopoly rights on the manufacture and distribution of matches.

This technique engendered sales of Kreuger and Toll stocks and bonds totaling over 250 million dollars.

After 1929, as the American depression became universal, Kreuger's position became extremely strained; consequently, in 1932, he committed suicide in Paris. His chief American backer, Lee, Higginson and Company (one of America's three leading investment banking firms) had never questioned his methods or examined his records and was therefore shocked when Kreuger's Paris vault was opened, revealing that his cupboard was bare. Kreuger had speculated and gambled away all his cash assets but reported fictitious riches and amazing profits until he had worked not matches, but himself, into a corner. As a result, most of the component companies in his match trust went bankrupt; investors large and small lost millions.

Kreuger took advantage of a climate of gullibility during a time when, as J. B. M. Hoxsey, a New York Stock Exchange historian, noted, holding companies were a "temptation to defraud the public." The climate of gullibility still exists, for many regard the conglomerates of our own age as the natural children of the holding companies once headed by Samuel INSULL and Ivar Kreuger. But in the view of author Matthew Josephson, Kreuger remains "the most artful and, quantitatively, the greatest swindler in all history."

LADY CHATTERLEY'S LOVER: the power of four-letter words

Today, D. H. (for David Herbert) Lawrence is regarded as one of the greatest British writers of the 20th century. His book *Lady Chatterley's Lover* is considered a classic. Up until 1960, however, both the novel and the author were far more controversial. Before that year, *Lady Chatterley's Lover* was banned as immoral in both England and the United States.

Lawrence believed that sexual maturity was the foundation of psychic and social health, and he used his writings as a vehicle for this belief. In an England still caught in the rigors of Victorian morality, Lawrence confronted its moral leaders head on.

This clash began in 1915 when his novel *The Rainbow,* which concerned itself with the mating of three pairs of lovers, ran into police interference. The suppression of the book both humiliated and angered Lawrence, for he felt that the book had a high moral purpose. He had failed, however, to understand that his audience would not be ready for either his explicitness or his choice of subject.

Lawrence exiled himself from his homeland for long periods but neither gave up his theories nor refined his insight into his audience. He worked on three drafts of a novel first called *Tenderness* and finally called *Lady Chatterley's Lover,* which concerned a crippled and physically cold man, his frustrated and somewhat promiscuous wife, and her association with the willing and capable groundskeeper of the couple's estate. Not only did the novel violate silent rules against considering such a triangle, especially with its breach of England's class system, but it also offended through its explicit use of four-letter words. Its 1928 publication in Florence, Italy, thus encountered many of the objections made to Lawrence's 1915 novel but strongly increased in force, leading to its being banned as immoral in both England and the United States until 1960.

The court case in England that finally reversed the ban against publication of *Lady Chatterley's Lover* (*Regina v. Penguin Books Limited*) turned largely on the rightness of Lawrence's use of tabooed sex words. In the United States, the cases involving the book before 1959–60 turned upon both sex scenes and language, each without considering the novel's theme and purpose.

Unlike the contemporary rash of cases concerning the work of Henry Miller (See TROPICS OF CANCER AND CAPRICORN), those concerning Lawrence's *Lady* were only three in number, and they involved two versions of the book. The first case was brought by a vice-seeking group, the Watch and Ward Society of Boston, in 1929. Its agent entrapped a Cambridge, Massachusetts, bookseller into supplying a copy of the 1928 book and then charged him with selling obscene literature. He was found guilty, forced to pay a fine, and served a term in prison. An appeal to the Supreme Judicial Court of Massachusetts upheld the original verdict.

Next, in 1944, the Dial Press published the novel's first draft as *The First Lady Chatterley,* with a foreword by Lawrence's widow, Frieda Von Richtofen Lawrence. It was less explicit than the 1928 version and disguised the taboo words with dashes. Nevertheless, the New York Society for the Suppression of Vice complained, a magistrate ruled out literary merit as a criterion for publication of the book, and the case was heard in the New York Court of Special Sessions. Two of the three judges who heard the case ruled the novel obscene, and the verdict was not appealed. Following up the apparent liberalization of obscenity codes effected by the U.S. Supreme Court's 1957 *Roth* decision (see *FANNY HILL*), Grove Press published the 1928 version of Lawrence's novel, with its spelled-out taboo words, in 1959. The U.S. Post Office Department, acting under the 1873 Comstock Act forbidding the mailing of various obscene materials, seized 24 cartons of the edition, and the postmaster general declared *Lady Chatterley's Lover* obscene. Grove brought suit to restrain the postmaster.

On July 21, 1959, Judge Frederick Van Pelt Bryan of the U.S. District Court for Southern New York ruled

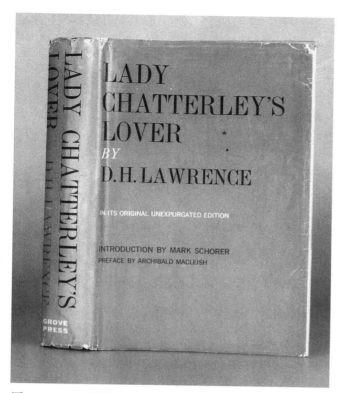

The timeworn 1959 dust jacket of D. H. Lawrence's controversial novel Lady Chatterley's Lover, *which was considered obscene and banned in the United States until 1959–60. U.S. Postmaster Arthur E. Summerfield, who challenged the distribution of this unexpurgated version of the novel published by New York's Grove Press, was overruled by federal Judge Frederick Van Pelt Bryan, who cited* Roth v. United States *(1957). Afterward Bryan received many letters calling him a dirty old man. The poet Archibald MacLeish said the book was "one of the most important works of fiction in the century." (Photografix/George Childs Kohn)*

that the book was not obscene. His explanation for his decision was very precise. He used as precedents the decisions in the *Ulysses* and *Roth* trials, made use of a literary-value criterion, noted that the explicit descriptions and taboo words did not submerge Lawrence's theme (he found them "relevant to the plot"), and argued for Lawrence's honesty, sincerity of purpose, artistic integrity, and lack of intent to attract prurient interest. The government appealed, but on March 25, 1960, the U.S. Court of Appeals upheld Judge Bryan's verdict.

Already weakened by the verdicts in earlier cases, and still to be further weakened by the *Tropic of Cancer* case of 1963, the power of the government to proscribe and prescribe the reading matter of mature persons had been drastically lessened by the decisions freeing Lawrence's much maltreated *Lady*.

Hedy LAMARR: beauty in the buff

The notorious film *Ecstasy* shocked audiences in the 1930s because of some scenes of a young woman frol-

icking *au naturel* in the wild. The role was played by beautiful Hedy Lamarr. At the age of 16, she had made the film, perhaps in pure naïveté or in daring desire of stardom. Her performance almost ruined her Hollywood career before it had begun.

Hedy Lamarr's original name was Hedwig Kiesler; she was born in 1915 in Vienna, Austria, where her father was a wealthy banker. In the early 1930s the girl's beauty attracted moviemakers, who gave her a starring role in *Ecstasy,* an arty Czech film directed by Gustav Machatý. She signed a contract, supposedly without reading all of its fine print, which compelled her to appear stark naked in the film. The movie producers would have made her repay them the film's cost if she had backed out. Stripped to the buff, Hedy Kiesler (she hadn't yet changed her name) gamboled seductively while the cameras recorded from a discreet distance, swimming and floating on her back in a pond and running merrily through the woods. Her parents walked out of the theater during the film's première in 1932. In general, moviegoers criticized the young actress's bad taste.

In 1933 Hedy met and soon married Fritz Mandl, a rich Austrian munitions maker, who became madly jealous after seeing *Ecstasy* and attempted to purchase every copy of the film to prevent the public from ogling his young bride. But while he spent much money to stifle the picture, he was unable to obtain its negative and to stop new versions from being made. Meanwhile, he isolated his new wife, keeping her hostage in his Austrian home and ordering his servants to guard her carefully.

A few years later, in London, Hedy met Louis B. Mayer, the powerful film producer and head of Metro-Goldwyn-Mayer (MGM) studios, who at first backed away from offering her a contract because of her scandalous image. Eventually, however, he succumbed to her charm, and a contract was signed. In 1937 she fled from Mandl to come to the United States and begin work there as Hedy Lamarr.

The film *Algiers* (1938) introduced Americans to Lamarr, who starred with Charles Boyer and emerged from the movie to become a great sex symbol. Success came to her not through good Hollywood scripts (she rejected those for *Casablanca* and *Gaslight,* movies that won high esteem for actress Ingrid Bergman), but through mediocre work. *Ziegfeld Girl* (1941), *White Cargo* (1942), and *Samson and Delilah* (1949) were among her big box-office attractions. Public interest in her waned in the 1950s; the press seemingly taking more notice of her divorces and marriages (six eventually) than her screen appearances.

In January 1966, Lamarr was arrested in the parking lot of a Los Angeles department store and was charged with shoplifting; some items for which she allegedly hadn't paid were found in her shopping bag. Although she claimed that she was innocent and had plenty of

Lovely young Hedy Lamarr, seen in the famous nude swimming scene in the movie Ecstasy *(1932), made scandalous history by taking off her clothes while making some scenes in the film. (Springer/Bettmann Film Archive)*

money to buy whatever she wanted, newsmen reported that her Beverly Hills home seemed shabby and in need of repairs for broken windows and other things; she also drove a 10-year-old Lincoln automobile. However, Lamarr maintained a stylish appearance before the press and later won an acquittal by a jury. Shortly afterward she moved east to New York. In 1966, the publication of her autobiography, *Ecstasy and Me: My Life as a Woman*, which seemed mainly a recounting of her love affairs, received some attention.

In her later years, Lamarr lived quietly in her modest home in Orlando, Florida, where she died at age 86 on January 19, 2000.

Jake LaMOTTA: lost fixed fight

Boxing fans were surprised—and suspicious—when an unknown light heavyweight named "Blackjack" Billy Fox defeated tough Jake LaMotta, a seasoned middle weight nicknamed the "Bronx Bull," in four rounds in a match at a sold-out Madison Square Garden on November 14, 1947. Thirteen years later, when the Senate Subcommittee on Antitrust and Monopoly was investigating the links between boxing and underworld criminal figures, LaMotta testified that he had intentionally faked and lost the 1947 Fox fight.

When the Lamotta-Fox match was announced, the Bronx Bull was the clear favorite to win, but by the time the fight rolled around, the odds had changed to 3 to 1 in favor of Fox. The betting was heavy. Fox, a Philadelphia fighter, was almost a novice with what was later discovered to be a phony record of knockouts, while LaMotta was an experienced, burly-chested boxer who had never been knocked off his feet. Those who

were familiar with LaMotta's usual aggressive, bullish tactics in the ring were stunned by his behavior on the night of the controversial 1947 fight in New York. Instead of continuing to punch strongly and dodge quickly, he retreated before Fox in the second round. LaMotta became more stationary in the ring and, in the fourth round, received a hard blow to the head from Fox. The Bronx Bull then staggered to the ropes and then to the center of the ring, his eyes glazed. The referee stepped in, stopped the fight, and declared Fox the winner by technical knockout; LaMotta was still standing.

This startling turn of events prompted New York District Attorney Frank Hogan to order a grand jury investigation of the bout. LaMotta testified that he had ruptured his spleen while training for the Fox fight but had not reported the injury to the authorities. He said that Fox had hit him in the vulnerable spot and that he was overcome with pain. He further reported that Fox's manager, Frank or "Blinky" Palermo, had offered him $100,000 to throw the fight but that he had flatly refused. The New York State Athletic Commission suspended LaMotta for seven months and fined him $1,000.

Years later LaMotta admitted he had lost the fight in return for a promise to have a crack at the middleweight boxing championship. His chance came in 1949 when he fought Marcel Cerdan, a Frenchman, and won to become world middleweight champion. LaMotta claimed he had had to pay Cerdan's agents $20,000 for the opportunity to fight. He held the title for only 13 months, during which time he was jeered and booed whenever he fought an opponent. Sugar Ray Robinson, the welterweight champion, took him on in February 1951 and decisively beat him in 13 rounds. LaMotta's boxing career ended thereafter; he had fought 106 matches over a 13-year period, and had earned about $1 million.

Blinky Palermo, also called The Numbers King of Philadelphia, was long associated with boxing's underworld. At the time of the U.S. Senate subcommittee's hearings in 1960, he was under indictment for extortion and conspiracy as the result of a boxing probe in California, and he refused to testify in Washington, D.C. Palermo was reputedly the chief henchman for the gangster Frankie Carbo, who, even when he was in prison, controlled all matters related to boxing in the United States. In 1960 Carbo was serving a two-year sentence at New York's Rikers Island prison for illegal boxing activities. Frank Marrone, a detective who had been investigating boxing for more than a decade, testified that Carbo had "controlled the boxing racket by himself for the past 30 years. There was not a prominent fighter . . . he did not control or have a piece of." Furthermore, declared Marrone, the situation was becoming worse as the mobsters moved into big-time money and the promotion of boxing on television. Others who were called to testify took the Fifth Amendment and refused to talk, some from fear of retaliation from gangsters who even penetrated prisons. The underworld's code of silence made it difficult to obtain hard evidence of the role of organized crime in boxing.

James D. Norris, the former president of the International Boxing Club, which had been disbanded by an antitrust decree issued by the U.S. Supreme Court, was closely associated with Carbo and Palermo but was not a hoodlum. Norris's club had monopolized the promotion of title fights, and Norris testified that cordial relations with Carbo were necessary in order "to get along in the boxing business." For three years Norris had kept Carbo's wife on his payroll for $40,000, although he could not describe what she did. Some said Norris, not Carbo, was the real "brains" and money in the shadowy world of boxing, but the Senate subcommittee unearthed no evidence of this.

LaMotta was one of the few witnesses who seemed to tell the whole truth at the 1960 Senate hearings. He confessed that he had perjured himself in 1947 and that, since the statute of limitations had run out, he wanted to "come clean" about fixing his fight with Fox. Fox did not appear to tell his version of the bout; at the time, he was a mental patient in a hospital on Long Island, New York.

Bert LANCE: controversial banker

In 1977, after only nine months as President Jimmy Carter's director of the U.S. Office of Management and Budget (OMB), 46-year-old Thomas Bertram (Bert) Lance was forced to resign the post because of alarming accusations of illegal banking practices against him. Before becoming budget director, he had been president and then chairman of the Calhoun First National Bank in Georgia. A native Georgian, Lance strongly denied that he had done anything improper and later fought federal lawsuits charging him with civil fraud, conspiracy, and violations of banking and securities laws.

The Senate Governmental Affairs Committee had confirmed the appointment of Lance as OMB director in January 1977 when it held hearings and received favorable reports about him. However, six months later, the Senate committee heard about a $3.4 million loan Lance had received from the First National City Bank of Chicago shortly after his Calhoun bank had established a correspondent relationship with the Chicago bank. After Lance's firm explanation for his financial actions, in which he said that nothing he had done was improper, the committee ended its inquiry.

Soon afterward, however, the office of U.S. Comptroller of the Currency John Heimann began an investigation into Lance's business and personal affairs after discovering that Lance had once received a large personal loan from the Manufacturers Hanover Trust Company of New York. He had apparently been connected with a $2.6-million personal loan from the New York bank in regard to the bank's opening of a correspondent relationship with the National Bank of Georgia, of which Lance was an official. Though there seemed to be possible banking violations in the matter, the comptroller's office concluded after an investigation that there were no grounds for criminal prosecution against the budget director. Comptroller Heimann, however, looked askance at Lance's financial dealings and borrowings as a Georgia banker. Lance family overdrafts were sometimes enormous and questionable. Although President Carter publicly reaffirmed his faith in the "character and competence" of his budget director, nagging questions persisted about apparent violations of conflict-of-interest rules that President Carter had established for his administration's officials. Then investigators found out that Lance's net-worth statement, given earlier to the Senate Governmental Affairs Committee, did not show all his holdings and debts. The investigators also claimed that Lance might have illegally used, for political purposes, an airplane belonging to his Georgia bank.

A full-scale inquiry into the former Georgia banker's financial ventures was launched by the Senate Governmental Affairs Committee and the office of the comptroller and revealed that some $3.5 million had been borrowed by Lance and his wife, LaBelle, over a 13-year period from Atlanta's Fulton National Bank, in which the Calhoun First National Bank kept large sums under a correspondent relationship. Before the Senate committee, Heimann stated that the Lance family had clearly misused its influential position to overdraft its bank accounts. Robert Bloom, the former acting United States comptroller of the currency, admitted, under intensive questioning from the senators, that he had unintentionally misinformed them about Lance in January 1977 when he had written a letter calling the Georgia banker "well-qualified" to be OMB director; he also said that he had left out unfavorable information about Lance.

Several days later, on September 15, 1977, the beleaguered budget director defended himself aggressively in hearings before the Senate committee. He gave details of his various personal financial affairs and charged the senators with slighting the "basic American principle of justice and fair play." Their acceptance of "destructive interpretations" of his affairs had damaged his good reputation, casting him in an unethical light that he said was unwarranted.

The Lancegate scandal (so-called because of the apparent cover-up resembling that in the Watergate scandal) remained prominent in the news, and finally, on September 21, 1977, Lance handed in his letter of resignation to President Carter. In it, he wrote that his conscience was clear but that the continuing, overblown controversy about his disputed financial activities had made him resign. Carter, who had stood by his close friend throughout the controversy, accepted the resignation with "regret and sorrow," adding that he believed Lance had "exonerated himself completely" and that he had not made a bad judgment in naming him to be budget director. Afterward the OMB was headed by Acting Director James T. McIntyre whom Carter later promoted to director at the end of 1977.

Despite Carter's convictions, the Securities and Exchange Commission and the comptroller's office continued to examine Lance's financial irregularities. They filed charges of fraud against him and in 1978 got him to agree to a court order forbidding him from banking practices considered underhanded by the two accusing federal agencies. A further investigation led to an Atlanta, Georgia, grand jury indicting Lance and three of his business friends on charges of conspiring to file false statements, to deceive government regulatory agencies, and to obtain $20 million in personal loans from more than 40 banks between 1970 and 1978 through misapplication of various bank funds. Two years later, in 1981, Lance was acquitted on all but three charges of bank fraud. When the jury deadlocked on those three, the federal government also decided to end its case against him.

After returning to the Calhoun bank in 1981, the former budget director began a personal and political comeback that eventually won him the chairmanship of the Georgia Democratic Party. In 1984, on the eve of the Democratic National Convention in San Francisco, Walter F. Mondale, the likely Democratic presidential candidate, decided to drop Democratic National Chairman Charles T. Manatt and replace him with Lance, who was at the time general chairman of Mondale's presidential campaign. Immediately there was a storm of protest, compelling Mondale to back down on his decision. New allegations of "suspected check-kiting and other suspicious transactions," brought by the comptroller's office against Lance in 1985, forced him to resign as chairman of the Georgia Democratic Party and, about six months later, in January 1986, to get out altogether from the Calhoun bank, in which he sold his interest. In the following month, the long battle between Lance and the comptroller's office was settled when Lance agreed, without admitting any guilt, to pay a $50,000 fine to federal bank regulators and consented to stay out of the banking business without the government's prior written sanction.

Carole LANDIS: "a hurt in the heart"

Americans were shaken by the sudden suicide of 29-year-old, popular movie actress Carole Landis on July 5, 1948, at her Pacific Palisades home in Hollywood, California. She had taken an overdose of sleeping pills. The name of the film star, who had been married four times, had recently been romantically linked to noted British actor Rex Harrison. His wife, actress Lilli Palmer, was the first to find Landis's dead body, sprawled on the bathroom floor with one hand holding a wrinkled envelope that still contained a sleeping pill.

Immediately many surmised that Landis had killed herself because of a "broken heart" over Harrison, whom she apparently had wanted to marry at the time. But significantly, Harrison was not mentioned in the suicide note he found on her bedroom vanity table. Addressed to her mother, the note said: "Dearest Mommie, I'm sorry, really sorry, to put you through this. But there is no way to avoid it. I love you darling. You have been the most wonderful mom ever. And that applies to all our family. I love each and every one of them dearly. Everything goes to you. Look in the files and there is a will which decrees everything. Goodbye, my angel. Pray for me. Your baby."

Nevertheless there was still reason to believe Harrison was part of the cause. Shortly before her death, Landis told *Photoplay* magazine, in an interview, that "every girl in the world wants to find the right man, someone who is sympathetic and understanding and helpful and strong, someone she can love madly. Actresses are no exceptions; glamour girls are certainly no exceptions. The glamour and the tinsel, the fame and the money mean very little if there is a hurt in the heart."

Other pressures may have contributed to her tragic act. The blonde beauty was rumored at the time of her suicide to be worried about her fading movie career, weary of her own leggy sex appeal, and burdened with debt. She was planning to divorce her fourth husband, W. Horace Schmidlapp, a Broadway producer. There was some talk that she was suffering from incurable cancer, and another rumor that she was distraught over a recent, hapless romance with a young army man.

Carole Landis was born Francis Lillian Mary Ridste in Fairchild, Wisconsin, in 1919. She competed in beauty contests as a young teenager, her pretty face and figure increasingly catching the public eye. At age 15 she eloped with a writer, but their marriage broke up after three weeks. The next year, after traveling west, she became a singer-dancer at a ritzy San Francisco nightclub. By the time she was 18, Landis was in Hollywood, where she was soon famous for having the "best legs in town." She began gallivanting about with bigwig movie directors and producers, such as Busby Berkeley (who helped her get a film contract) and Darryl Zanuck (whose constant backstage companion she was at Fox pictures, where she acquired the moniker "the studio hooker").

Stardom came to Landis in producer Hal Roach's movie *One Million B.C.* (1940), in which she played a primitive cavewoman. Afterward she generally got star billing, but her films, of which she made more than two dozen, were mediocre. They included *Road Show* (1941), *My Gal Sal* (1942), and *Four Jills in a Jeep* (1944), a movie based on Landis's real adventures as an entertainer of troops in World War II. While filming *The Noose* (1948) in England, she met Rex Harrison—long before he became known as "Sexy Rexy"—and the two became close friends. Harrison, who denied any love affair with Landis, attacked Hollywood for the scandal, in which it was implied that he was the cause of the celebrated sex symbol's death.

Mario LANZA: self-indulgent singer

The meteoric career of American tenor Mario Lanza, who died at the age of 38 in 1959, has stimulated much speculation, especially about the rapid decline that led ultimately (and perhaps inevitably) to his death. Lanza originally gained fame for his magical voice, which many likened to that of the great singer Enrico Caruso. During a 10-year Hollywood whirl however, Lanza abused his gift by reckless overindulgence in food, alcohol, drugs, and women. In time his volatile temperament and sybaritic lifestyle got so out of hand that it landed him in the obituary pages, perhaps courtesy of the Mafia.

Lanza was born in Philadelphia, Pennsylvania, with the name of Alfredo Arnold Cocozza. He showed little interest in school, eventually dropping out of high school to work for his grandfather, a wholesale grocer. Muscular and hefty, this curly-haired young man also lifted weights and worked as a piano-mover. Although he had taken some singing lessons as a young boy, he received no serious voice training until the age of 20. Spectacular national and international success as a tenor singer and sometime film actor came to him after his military service in World War II because of his "golden-throated" voice, which was powerful but not truly disciplined. In the late 1940s, MGM movie studios put him under contract and starred him in a number of tailor-made musicals, including *The Toast of New Orleans* (1950), *The Great Caruso* (1951), and *Because You're Mine* (1952). Mario Lanza, the name he had adopted (it was the masculine form of his mother's maiden name) because he felt it better suited a celebrated singer like himself, aspired to be a second Enrico Caruso, the great Italian operatic tenor, and grew to believe that Caruso's ghost talked to him periodically.

The "larger than life" romantic image that gave Lanza phenomenal popularity for a while in the 1950s seemed to swallow him up and made his volatile personality even more difficult for film executives, concert arrangers, and others to deal with. He lacked self-control, indulging often in eating bouts that made his weight fluctuate between about 180 and 280 pounds. This brought on violent fights with movie producers when he showed up on sets too fat to photograph. His unreliability and obesity upset MGM's filming of *The Student Prince* (1954), in which he was replaced by Edmund Purdom, and Lanza's voice was dubbed in afterward for the songs. MGM then sued Lanza for $5 million for his refusal to appear.

Lanza's recorded songs, notably *Be My Love* and *The Loveliest Night of the Year,* which sold more than a million copies each, added to his growing fortune. Unfortunately, however, the talented singer could not learn self-discipline, and gradually too much drinking, eating, pill-taking, and general hedonism took their toll. At times he was unable to go on stage for some physical reason or other and afterward was angrily threatened with lawsuits. His ego swelled along with his success, and he continued to act irresponsibly and miraculously get away with childish fits of temper and constant, reckless high-living. His performances suffered, and he sought solace in more alcohol, drugs, food, and women. The advent of competition from the new rock-and-roll music industry may also have contributed to his downfall.

On October 7, 1959, Lanza died, reportedly of a heart attack, in a medical clinic in Rome, Italy, where he had been under treatment for about a week for pneumonia and phlebitis. One report said that "He died singing one of his songs," a romantic end, but most likely fictitious. His grieving wife died of a drug overdose several months later.

Although Lanza's obesity was blamed for helping bring on his early demise, this premise was seriously questioned in 1976 when Raymond Strait's book *Star Babies* was published. Strait, a friend of Lanza, claimed that the tenor had been ordered by Mafia bosses to perform at a big underworld charity concert in Italy. A number of Americans were to attend with their Italian hosts, but Lanza supposedly balked, saying he was ill and going to the Rome clinic instead. There, according to Strait, someone secretly fooled with the intravenous tube feeding Lanza, and as a result, lethal air was injected into his veins. Lanza's daughter, age 14 at the time of his death, had been told this by the singer's chauffeur, who was keeping an eye on him at the clinic and who discovered the murderous act. Strait learned this from the daughter and also believed that the Sicilian-born American Mafia chieftain Charles "Lucky" Luciano was instrumental in having the singer killed. At the time of his death, Lanza had been reduced to making minor films, such as his last, *For the First Time* (1959).

LARROVITCH LITERARY HOAX. See William George JORDAN: the Larrovitch literary hoax.

Rita LAVELLE. See ENVIRONMENTAL PROTECTION AGENCY (EPA): "sweetheart deals" with industry?

Larry LAWRENCE: self-aggrandizing lies

U.S. envoy Larry Lawrence wished to be interred in Arlington Cemetery. Traditionally, this cemetery has been reserved for the nation's heroes: those who died

Multimillionaire Larry Lawrence testified before the Senate Foreign Relations Committee on November 10, 1993, during hearings on his nomination to become ambassador to Switzerland. He invented pieces of his past which went virtually undetected in his lifetime. (AP/ Wide World Photos).

during active duty, are retired from the military, or were highly decorated officers. Occasionally, those who performed extraordinary acts of public service were waivered in. When Maurice Larry Lawrence, multi-millionaire, philanthropist, Democratic Party contributor, and ambassador to Switzerland, died in 1996, President Bill Clinton delivered his eulogy, recounting Lawrence's World War II heroics and patriotism, as the former ambassador's body was lowered into the hallowed ground at Arlington. It wasn't until nearly two years later that questions were raised as to whether that was Lawrence's rightful resting place, for no records of his military service could be found and his ambassadorship alone would not have qualified him for burial there. Investigators were hard pressed to find a reason why Lawrence would have fabricated his past accomplishments other than for personal aggrandizement and a strong desire to secure a diplomatic job with the Clinton administration.

The irony is that to observers, Lawrence's life was remarkable enough not to need embellishment. He grew up poor and made his fortune as a real estate developer; he was worth nearly $300 million at his death in 1996, a feat in itself. But, as owner of the Hotel del Coronado near San Diego, Lawrence felt it necessary to claim that L. Frank Baum wrote part of *The Wizard of Oz* there and that Thomas Edison had personally supervised the electrical wiring during the construction of the hotel. Neither of these tales was true—but they sounded impressive.

About his wartime experiences, Lawrence stated he was 18 years old and serving as a merchant marine onboard the S.S. *Horace Bushnell* en route to Murmansk when it was torpedoed by the Germans during World War II. Suffering with grave head injuries—and it is at this point in his retelling that Lawrence's voice would become choked with emotion—he said he was jolted overboard into the icy arctic waters; he could remember nothing after that except waking up in a hospital bed in Chicago. He told everybody of his merchant marine exploits, including his children. He even showed one of his four wives his battle scar. (Though she would not reveal its location, she said it was not on his head.) For his bravery, he won the Russian Federation's Medal of Honor in 1993 and on his official application for the State Department he claimed to have been given the designation of SIC, an abbreviation for "seaman first class."

When congressional Republicans began an investigation into whether the Clinton administration had sold burial plots to generous campaign contributors, they came upon Lawrence's waiver into Arlington. Though they hunted, they could find no records confirming Lawrence's alleged involvement with the U.S. Merchant Marine, no records confirming his presence onboard the *Horace Bushnell* or of his name on the ship's injury list. In fact, it was proved that Lawrence had been a student at Wilbur Wright College in Chicago at the time of the torpedo hit on the merchant vessel.

A former assistant to Lawrence, Norma Nicolls, testified that in the early 1980s Lawrence had asked her to discreetly research the functions and activities of the merchant marines during World War II. Later, at the time of his nomination for ambassadorship, she said she alerted a State Department official to carefully check Lawrence's references and war record during his background check.

In December 1997, Lawrence's body was quietly disinterred from Arlington Cemetery, and his headstone removed. Most tale tellers are wily enough not to leave written traces; unfortunately for Lawrence, his lies were carved in stone.

Andrew Daulton LEE. See Christopher BOYCE: traitorous, counterculture falconer.

Bruce LEE: more famous after his death?

Known as "the Little Dragon," Bruce Lee was a celebrated Chinese-American movie actor and martial arts expert. His sudden death in 1973, at the age of only 32, gave rise to various wild speculations that he had been murdered by rivals or enemies. There was also the scandalous suggestion that his early demise was used to launch a Bruce Lee cult, for astonishingly, his movies won him the superstardom after his death that he had so craved in life.

Bruce Lee was born in San Francisco and raised in Hong Kong, where he worked in films as a boy and learned the martial arts of kung fu and karate. At age 18, Lee returned to the United States in order to retain his American citizenship. He studied philosophy at the University of Washington and developed his own special kung fu method, in which he became a master at using his hands, fists, legs, feet, and other parts of the body as lethal weapons. He gave lessons in the martial arts and, in 1964, married one of his students, Linda Emery. The glamor of a Hollywood film career beckoned the ambitious young Chinese American, and he managed to get parts in the television shows *Batman* and *The Green Hornet*, in which he played the chauffeur Kato. After Warner Brothers producers showed no interest in making him a star in its *Kung Fu* television series, the angry Lee returned to Hong Kong, where he soon hooked up with movie producer Raymond Chow and started making the action-packed, violent kung fu films that would become his hallmark. Audiences loved to watch him singlehandedly fight off hostile mobs with his martial-arts techniques. His films, made in Hong Kong, gained him great popularity and were big commercial successes.

Most American critics, however, continually panned Lee's films, such as *The Big Boss* (also called *Fist of Fury*) (1972), and *The Chinese Connection* (1972). Vincent Canby, the *New York Times* film critic, claimed that Lee's movies made "the worst Italian western look like the most solemn and noble achievements of the early Soviet cinema." Yet Lee became a legendary phenomenon. With his success, Warner Brothers offered to finance his new film *Enter the Dragon* (1973), during the making of which he evidently suffered a grand mal epileptic seizure. Lee quickly recovered, but about two months later, on July 20, 1973, he died in the Hong Kong apartment of his co-star Betty Ting-pei. The two had been working on a movie script when Lee had complained of a headache. Ting-pei, with whom Lee had been romantically linked, gave him Equagesic, a painkiller prescribed for her by her physician. Lee then decided to take a nap. He never woke up.

An official coroner's inquest took place when no discernible cause for his death could be found. Nothing could be ascertained, except perhaps that Lee had a hypersensitivity to Equagesic or some other drug (it was known that he had been taking pills for a long-lasting convulsive disorder). Traces of cannabis were found in his stomach, but that narcotic isn't lethal. Ting-pei and other friends were all adjudged to be blameless in the star's death, though they were very protective of Lee. His death was finally ruled the result of a "misadventure."

Rumors immediately began to circulate, however, and many of Lee's fans presumed that his death was a hoax and a publicity stunt, on the assumption that a vigorous man like Lee couldn't possibly die so early. There was some talk of possible overindulgence in sex and drugs, chiefly cocaine. One popular rumor was that the world's "fittest man" was the victim of an ancient and secret herbal poison known only in the Far East, used by enemy Hong Kong filmmakers or Chinese traditionalists who vehemently opposed Lee's arrogant public display of the Kung-fu sect's mysteries. Lee's exploitation of the historic Chinese-Japanese rivalry in his films undoubtedly angered some people in those two countries, possibly resulting in contracts being issued to do away with him. Suspicion still lingers about his death and helps keep alive the Bruce Lee cult. Without doubt, Hollywood moneymen exploited his death, reaping many more profits than they ever did while Lee was alive.

Charles LEE: disobedience and treachery

Though his name is not as well known as that of Benedict Arnold, General Charles Lee certainly rivals the infamous ARNOLD in terms of treason. His traitorous nature was revealed by letters found in 1858 in papers of British General Sir William Howe. Cashiered from the Continental Army for his shameful disobedience at the Battle of Monmouth in 1778, Lee had undoubtedly engaged in treasonable negotiations with the British while being held captive by them for nearly a year and a half beforehand.

Born in England in 1731, Lee became a British army officer and served in America in the French and Indian War. He later fought in Portugal and Poland, where he took part in revolutionary uprisings. In 1773 Lee immigrated from England to America, where he acquired land in Virginia to settle on, and soon became a supporter of colonial independence. When the American Revolution broke out in 1775, he fancifully and artfully touted and glorified his past military experiences before the Continental Congress, which was impressed by this ambitious tall-talker and consequently appointed him the second major general in the Continental Army, under General George Washington. Although Lee had become the ranking major general by March 1776, his actions on the field were without distinction and were frequently controversial. The ambitious Lee, who bore no love for Washington anyway, was eager to nudge Washington out of his position.

Lee's dislike of Washington showed itself at various times. Clashes between the two occurred over Lee's belief that American soldiers were no match for the disciplined British regulars in head-to-head combat. Lee, who believed his superior was "not fit to command a sergeant's guard," was also slow in obeying orders from Washington.

While Washington was with the main part of the Continental Army retreating through New Jersey in the fall of 1776, Lee was repeatedly ordered to join him but repeatedly hesitated, along with his division. Perhaps by winning a personal military success Lee hoped to supplant his commander-in-chief. His procrastination may have helped bring on his sudden capture by a small raiding party of British on December 13, 1776. Seized at his headquarters in Basking Ridge, New Jersey, Lee was taken away and imprisoned in New York City, where he involved himself in treasonable activities that did not come to light until 1858.

In captivity, Lee wrote out a plan for a campaign to end colonial resistance and to bring an early surrender of the Americans. The plan, dated "29th March 1777," concerned certain British troop movements and was based on Lee's awareness of the size and equipment of American forces. Sure that his plan would defeat the colonies, Lee wrote to General Howe, then British commander-in-chief in America, saying, "I am so confident of the event that I will venture to assert with the penalty of my life, if the plan is fully carried out and no accidents (such as a rupture betwixt the powers of Europe) intervene, that in less than two months from the date of the proclamation not a spark of this desolating war remains unextinguished in any part of the continent." Howe paid no heed to Lee's plan. While most historians assert that the plan was treasonous, some say that it was an intention by Lee to deceive the British. A few others claim that it was the rambling of an unbalanced mind.

In April 1778, Lee was exchanged as a prisoner of war. Far from being suspected of treason, he soon rejoined the American army at Valley Forge, Pennsylvania, as a heroic patriot. However, as papers have since revealed, Lee corresponded covertly with both Howe and Sir Henry Clinton, who succeeded Howe as the British supreme commander in North America in May 1778. At the same time, Lee grumbled to Congress about its promotion of other generals while he was a British captive.

In mid-June 1778, British troops 13,000 strong, led by General Clinton, evacuated Philadelphia and began crossing New Jersey toward New York City. American forces pursued, with General Lafayette leading the vanguard and receiving orders from General Washington to attack the British at Monmouth, New Jersey. Lee, who had turned down the command of the vanguard, learned that the battle was to be major and thus asserted his seniority to command the attack. Lafayette politely yielded, and the Americans attacked on June 28, 1778. At a critical moment in the fighting, without any warning, Lee suddenly, either by design or cowardice, fell back with the main American forces and left General Anthony Wayne's division unsupported and forced to retreat. With the Americans in confusion, the British turned to begin a rout of the enemy. Washington then rode up with his troops, ordered Lee off the field in harsh language, and proceeded to reform the leaderless and fleeing American columns. The Americans, some 13,000 in number, rallied under Washington's personal leadership, halted the British advance, and fought the British to a bloody draw by nightfall. By the next morning the British had decamped and shortly reached New York safely.

Lee afterward wrote an impertinent letter to Washington, demanding an apology from him for his rude remarks on the battlefield. Lee also demanded a court of inquiry. He received a court-martial instead, in 1778. In the trial he was found guilty of disobedience of orders, misbehavior in front of the enemy, and disrespect to the commander-in-chief. As punishment, he was suspended from the army for a year. In his idleness, Lee penned letters to Congress, abusing Washington and others with disrespectful words. One insulting letter to Congress brought on Lee's dismissal from the service in January 1780. Lee vainly attempted to vindicate himself in his final years, dying in Philadelphia on October 2, 1782.

Joseph LEITER: greedy young speculator

Joseph Leiter was not yet 30 years old when he engineered a financial fiasco that is estimated to have cost his wealthy father some 10 to 20 million dollars. In the late 1890s, Chicago was booming, with an enormous and profitable slaughtering industry largely controlled by a few companies, among them one led by Philip D. Armour (see "EMBALMED BEEF" SCANDAL). Armour also had a large share of the wheat market, and it was in this arena that Leiter chose, fatefully, to challenge his hegemony. Though his father bailed him out, Leiter soon became the subject of scandal again, this time because of his coal-mining speculations.

The ambitious young Leiter was the son of Levi Zeigler Leiter, a partner of Illinois financial greats Marshall Field and Potter Palmer. Levi Leiter had exchanged his mercantile interests for lucrative real-estate dealings. The young Joseph, a Harvard graduate (1891), became a clerk in his father's office and in 1893 assumed general charge of his father's business interests. As a result of Joseph's initial successes, his father gave him a million dollars so that his son could engage in his own business. Joseph began investing in public utilities, mining stocks, and traction companies.

In 1897 Joseph Leiter undertook to corner the wheat market on the Chicago board of trade. Rumors later circulated in the Windy City that Philip Armour had purposely "laid for" Leiter, but others argued that the meat packer was innocent and Leiter had simply underestimated the available wheat supply. In any event, Leiter began buying wheat in April 1897 at 72 ⅝ cents per bushel. He had soon purchased 40-million bushels (18 million of cash wheat and 21 million of futures). Thinking that he could force the price of wheat ever higher, Leiter refused an offer that would have brought him a tidy $4 million profit. Armour, however, was not sitting idly by. In midwinter he had the usually ice-blocked Straits of Mackinaw dynamited open so that millions of bushels of wheat could be transported to Chicago (the wheat was stored in special warehouses that had been quickly built on Goose Island). Armour then proceeded to dump 9 million bushels of wheat on the Chicago market, causing Leiter's corner to collapse. Leiter was forced to make voluntary assignment. With the help of his father and some banks, he arranged to market his wheat gradually, and by September 1898, all of his creditors and bank obligations had been paid.

Though the affair may have cost Leiter's father 10 million dollars or more, neither father nor son was left impoverished. The two men became particularly interested in coal mining through a new process of making coke from local coal and again became embroiled in scandal. They opened a mine in Zeigler, Illinois, in 1904. As soon as the mine began operation, the United Mine Workers Union initiated a strike that was marred by bloodshed. After the strike ended, other disasters followed. In April 1905, a gas explosion killed 50 men in Leiter's mine. While investigating the explosion a state mine inspector was killed. In November 1908, the mine caught on fire, luckily with no fatalities. At the urging of state fire inspectors, the company agreed to seal the mine for 90 days in the hope that lack of oxygen would extinguish the fire. But Leiter failed to keep the mine sealed, and the following January an explosion killed 26 men. Although inspectors then decided to seal the mine permanently or until the fire was out, the owners reopened the mine in less than a month. Following this, another explosion killed three additional men. Joseph Leiter finally sold his interest in the mine.

In 1913 Leiter inherited a large estate from his mother and maintained business interests in coal and railroads until his death in Chicago in 1932.

LEOPOLD and LOEB: murder as experiment

Richard A. Loeb, 18, and Nathan F. Leopold, Jr., 19, belonged to two of Chicago's richest, most influential, and most respected families. Loeb's father was vice president of Sears, Roebuck and Company, and Leopold's father was president of the Fibre Can Company. The combined wealth of the two families was estimated at $15 million. Despite such advantaged upbringings, the two young men committed one of the most sensational and controversial crimes of the century. On May 21, 1924, Leopold and Loeb kidnapped and murdered 14-year-old Bobby Franks, the son of retired businessman Jacob Franks, who was also a multimillionaire.

Leopold and Loeb considered themselves "supermen," above the reach of the law. Loeb, one of the youngest graduates of the University of Michigan, was a proud, brilliant graduate student at the University of Chicago, where Leopold was taking law courses. Having collaborated in several crimes including robbing homes, arson, and car theft, the two friends decided to carry out the "perfect murder," one worthy of their superior mental abilities. They scouted the Harvard School for Boys in nearby Kenwood, Illinois, for a likely victim. It was by sheer chance that they selected Franks, who turned out to be a distant cousin to Loeb; their intended victim was not in the schoolyard when they drove up in their rented car. They found Franks a short time afterwards and decided to carry out their plan with him.

After they lured Franks into the car, Loeb stuffed a gag in his mouth and smashed his skull four times with a tape covered chisel. Leopold and Loeb then drove to a swampy area on the outskirts of Chicago and carried the body along the tracks of the Pennsylvania Railroad. They held Franks's head under water to make sure he was dead, poured hydrochloric acid on his face to render identification difficult, and stuffed his body in a drainpipe. The youths had concocted an elaborate scheme to collect ransom from the victim's family and at midnight phoned Bobby's home, telling the family it would receive instructions on how to reclaim the boy. However, by the time the family received the typewritten ransom note demanding $10,000, a workman had discovered Bobby's body.

Despite their claims to possessing superior mental abilities, Leopold and Loeb were no geniuses when it came to murder. From the time they rented the car used in the crime, the careless young men scattered a trail of evidence against themselves that helped to establish their guilt. Leopold had dropped his eyeglasses near where the body was found, and the prescription was easily traced to him. The chisel was found near his home, and the typewriter used in typing the ransom note was also identified as his. When police questioned Leopold, he held to his story of innocence. However, after Loeb confessed, Leopold followed. Each then tried to throw guilt on the other.

The public was outraged. Interviews with the two depicted them as cool, arrogant, and conceited. Leopold was especially despicable. He likened the murder to a scientific experiment, comparing it to impaling a beetle on a pin. They did it to "experience" what a murderer experiences, he said. The public fully expected and demanded that the two be hanged.

Defending the pair was Clarence Darrow, the greatest defense lawyer of his day, a passionate opponent of the death penalty and a firm believer in the emerging science of psychiatry as it pertained to crime. Darrow had his clients plead guilty and throw themselves on the mercy of the court. For $100,000 Darrow promised to save the two from the gallows. Darrow's plea against the death penalty in the trial has become a classic denunciation of capital punishment, and his argument, which lasted three days, was one of the most grandiloquent pieces of courtroom drama to date.

Darrow contended that insanity was not his defense but that his clients' state of mind was a mitigating factor in the crime: the two were mentally ill but not insane. Darrow also argued that hanging the pair would not cure the "maladjustments of the world." It would "only add fuel to the flames with cruelty and hating." He invited the prosecution to perform the execution, which he described in ghastly detail.

Darrow won. Judge John R. Caverly, chief justice of the Criminal Court of Cook County, who was hearing the case without a jury, sentenced both Leopold and Loeb to life imprisonment for the murder of Bobby Franks, plus 99 years for kidnapping him. He warned Illinois officials to never parole them.

The public was affronted with the sentencing and continued to be outraged with reports that the two were receiving preferential treatment at the Illinois State Prison at Stateville, which they entered on September 11, 1924. The two were given private cells and were allowed to visit one another freely. They ate in the officers' lounge, separate from other prisoners, and had their meals cooked to order. They resumed studies while in prison and were provided with desks and filing cabinets.

Once they entered prison, however, their lives took different courses. Loeb became an aggressive homosexual and was slashed to death in 1936 in a shower-room brawl. Leopold, on the other hand, earned the reputation of being a model prisoner. By volunteering to become a guinea pig in an Army malaria research project, his term was decreased to 85 years, and the door to his parole was opened.

Leopold was paroled in 1958, after five appeals and with the support of poet Carl Sandburg. In his final plea he stated that, although he was guilty, he had reached the "ultimate point of contrition." He begged for a chance to be useful. After he left prison, he published *Life Plus 99 Years* and went to Puerto Rico to work among the poor as a medical missionary for $10 a month. He married in 1961 and died of a heart ailment in 1971.

Dennis LEVINE. See Ivan BOESKY: fraudulent Wall Street superstar.

Jerry Lee LEWIS: a taboo marriage
Cries of "cradle snatching" and incest were heard following the marriage in mid-1958 of 22-year-old Jerry Lee Lewis, famed rock-and-roll singer and songwriter, and 13-year-old Myra Brown, who was Lewis's second cousin. The union nearly ruined Lewis's successful musical career. He was censured in both America and England. Not until the mid-1960s, when national mores were changing, did Lewis begin to regain some of the fame and fortune he had earlier known.

Lewis was born in the town of Ferriday, Louisiana, where early marriages frequently occurred. Lewis himself was first married at the age of 14. Talented musically, he was playing the piano professionally in Memphis, Tennessee, by the early 1950s. While emulating rock-and-roll star Elvis PRESLEY, Lewis created his own original piano-boogie style of singing and recorded two sensational hit songs, "Great Balls of Fire" (1957) and "Whole Lotta Shakin' Goin' On" (1958). After he got married to Myra, his third wife, public condemnation descended on him at home and abroad. American radio stations declined to play his records, and television shows refused to line him up for performances.

In 1958, when Lewis arrived in England to give rock performances on tour, he encountered heated disapproval and personal abuse. At the Granada theater in Tooting, South London, spectators made catcalls and screamed "Go home, you crumb" and "Go home, baby snatcher" at Lewis.

Rock-and-roll singer Jerry Lee Lewis and his 13-year-old bride, Myra, are a cheerful twosome at New York's Idlewild International Airport after their return from England on board a Pan American Airways clipper on May 28, 1958. Lewis denied that public hostility to his marriage to the young girl from Tennessee had forced a British theater chain to cancel the remainder of a scheduled rock-and-roll tour. The couple had left after only four days of a 37-day trip. (AP/Wide World Photos)

Myra had arrived in Britain with him and was reputed to have become his wife prior to the close of his divorce from his previous wife. The United States embassy in London was contacted by Lewis's manager, who sought help in vain to find an official to remarry the young couple. The embassy said Myra was below the legal British age for marriage. Because of the condemnation, especially by the British press, the Rank Organization, a London theater chain, canceled a scheduled tour of 27 appearances by Lewis. His hotel even requested him to leave. Lewis and his wife returned to America, where he reportedly denied that they had been driven from England by attacks on what the British considered his illicit marriage.

His celebrity stature in the United States also plummeted, and for at least the next six years, he struggled to keep his musical career going. In time, changing American moral attitudes helped the public forgive Lewis's marriage to Myra, to whom he remained married for 13 years. By 1965 his career was reviving, and by the 1970s he had regained much popularity, having added by then more country flavor to his rock music.

Lewis's lifestyle remained quite extravagant. By the 1980s he had had a brush with death due to a stomach ailment and "related complications" and had entered into a sixth marriage with Trina Jones, a woman half his age. In 1986, when he was 51, his fourth child was born; he also had a daughter and two sons (who were both killed in accidents) from his previous marriages.

Meriwether LEWIS: murder or suicide?
Greatly honored as co-leader of the Lewis and Clark expedition, which explored much of the vast Louisiana Territory (1804–6), Captain Meriwether Lewis was appointed governor of the territory by his close friend President Thomas Jefferson in 1807. Lewis, who had earlier in 1806 resigned from the army after his return from the overland expedition, assumed his duties as governor at St. Louis in March 1808. The young governor, who apparently suffered from bouts of depression, died the following year of a bullet wound while en route to Washington, D.C., to defend himself against charges of fiscal mismanagement in the territory. The circumstances of his violent death remain shrouded in mystery.

Before his famous expedition to the Pacific Ocean, Lewis served as President Jefferson's private secretary (1801–03) and displayed energy and ability in administrative work. A protégé of Jefferson, he began courting the daughter of Vice President Aaron Burr. Burr disapproved of Lewis and supposedly encouraged the president to choose him to lead the expedition so as to break up the budding affair. Lewis's love for Miss Burr endured during his trip into the wilderness, but when he next saw her at her father's trial for treason in May 1807 (see BURR'S CONSPIRACY), she coldly rebuffed him. He became disheartened. This deep hurt and later his anxiety over his financial problems (some because of precarious investments in territorial lands) contributed to his fits of depression, according to some historians. In addition, Lewis's public expenditures as governor of the Louisiana Territory were disputed by some officials in Washington, although his records clearly indicate that no wrongdoing occurred in his use of government funds.

Weakened by a recent malarial illness and disturbed by the political calumny against him, Lewis set out for Washington to attempt to justify himself there before his enemies. He left St. Louis accompanied by a Major John Neely of the U.S. Army, traveling east until near Nashville, Tennessee, the northern end of the Natchez Trace (the overland route for traders and farmers from Natchez, Mississippi). There Neely went off alone to catch several pack mules which had broken loose in panic during a thunderstorm, and Lewis took lodging for the night in a humble inn run by John Griner and his wife. According to reports, the Griners had no idea of their visitor's identity; asking no questions of the strangers traveling through the area seemed a wise precaution. Lewis himself remained silent and retired to his room after supper. Indistinct utterances were heard by the Griners coming from Lewis's room later that night, and a gunshot was heard in or near the house shortly before daybreak on October 11, 1809. The innkeepers then found Lewis lying in blood on the floor of his room, groaning in pain; he murmured, "I am no coward . . . but it is hard to die . . . so young . . . so hard to die," and afterward died. He was only 35 years old. The Griners learned the identity of their distinguished guest upon opening the ledger he had with him and seeing his name on the flyleaf. They notified the local authorities, who later said the cause of death was suicide.

The idea that Lewis had committed suicide while in a fit of depression contradicted, however, some of the evidence at the time of his death. The Griners had smelled no pungent gunpowder which left an odor in those days when a weapon was fired; they also found Lewis's rifle, which had not been recently fired, in the corner of the room. No other weapon was found. Major Neely didn't arrive on the scene until the following day and presumably he didn't know whether Lewis had found lodging or not during the storm. The possibility that the governor's political foes, worried about charges he might establish against them for graft or fraud, secretly murdered him in order to look at his ledger seems as strong as the claim that he killed himself.

LIBRARY OF CONGRESS. See Tobia NICOTRA: autograph faker fooled Library of Congress.

Mary Todd LINCOLN: abused, eccentric, or insane?
No First Lady has been misunderstood so thoroughly nor slandered so viciously as was Mary Todd Lincoln, the wife and widow of President Abraham Lincoln. The practice of baiting her had become so habitual after 1861 that, in 1875, first the press and then an ill-constituted Illinois court adjudged her insane.

In the 1930s, however, historians began to examine closely the facts and fictions surrounding her life and found much of the opprobrium to be untrue. Since her childhood in Lexington, Kentucky, as one of 14 children in the well-to-do Todd family, she had exhibited symptoms of personality disorder, migraine affliction, and the unidentified cerebral disturbance which took her life in 1882. The thesis of numerous biographers concerning Mary Lincoln's sad insanity trial of 1875 is that she was simply driven to the brink of insanity by public ill-treatment, domestic calamities, and emotional upheavals after 1861.

The Mary Todd Lincoln who came from Springfield, Illinois, to Washington, D.C., in 1861 was a 43-year-old mother of four, the vivacious and rather outspoken wife of a man who had been a prominent Illinois lawyer, a state representative, a congressman, and the 1856 Republican vice-presidential candidate before being elected president. Yet she was unprepared for what she met in the nation's capital.

In both the North and South, the press vented its particular hostilities by often attacking President Lincoln's compromising attitudes and ways at the start of his administration. The *New York Herald,* which had insulted Lincoln by calling him "the Illinois gorilla," also began to malign his politically aware wife, once saying that she comported herself as "an American queen." Southern newspapers labeled her a traitor to her people, while Northern papers pilloried her as a Southerner who kept her husband from working to destroy slavery.

In addition to the bad press, the First Lady suffered from being shunned socially by Washington's high society, a group controlled in 1861 by Democrats and females sympathetic to the South. They refused to attend the Inaugural Ball, and they saw to it that she was excluded from the welcoming parties then current Washington practice. They stayed away from her receptions or came only to be distant and cliquish. Through the press, they criticized her refurbishing of the White House; her taste was repudiated as ostentatious and overexpensive. They also found fault with her flower-decorated gowns and her perpetual shopping tours and purchases. To this public damnation, Mary Lincoln gave high-strung credence, but she continued to overspend, keeping the amounts secret from her husband and, above all, from the press, lest public knowledge upset his 1864 reelection.

It seemed that society and the press had decided that Mary Lincoln's every move was wrong. When she hosted White House parties, the gatherings were rated too extravagant to exemplify a proper wartime spirit. When Willie, the first of the Lincolns' sons, died in 1862, Mary canceled a scheduled party and was censured for adding gloom to an already depressed national morale. The malicious gossip and censure must have preyed on her, for she once bewailed, "I seem to be scapegoat for both North and South!"

Willie's death profoundly disturbed her, and she tried to reach him through three spiritualists. Consequently, she was publicly scorned by anti-Spiritualists. The eventual death of three sons and her husband of 23 years exacted a severe toll on her, mentally and physically.

While President Lincoln was alive, he relieved the sting of press attacks on her with his wry humor; he discovered and settled her debts; he soothed her during migraine attacks. He even defended her against a Senate committee. Alarmed by Northern accusations that Mary was a Southern spy, the Senate Committee on the Conduct of the War began an investigation. The president appeared, uninvited, to state that no member of his family held treasonable communication with the enemy. The investigation was abandoned. In helping her husband carry his burden of the Civil War, Mary Lincoln took over many of his trips to military hospitals, bringing gifts she had bought herself. But these unselfish acts of hers were largely ignored by the press.

The death of her beloved, tubercular son Tad in 1871 precipitated a period of aberrant behavior and ill health that culminated in Mary Lincoln's insanity trial in 1875. She grieved constantly, acquired an edema, and traveled about in search of a cure. She worried about money constantly, although she had a small fortune and nervously carried $57,000 in securities in her petticoat pockets. Most of her time was spent in a darkened room, in which she consulted spiritualists who supposedly put her in touch with her sons and husband. She feared being poisoned, suffered from insomnia and headaches, and often prowled her house at night because she was afraid of fire and smoke.

Concerned about her vagaries, her son Robert Todd Lincoln hired inept Pinkerton detectives to shadow her. As a result, she acquired a new fear: strange men were pursuing her. She often hid behind clothing racks in department stores to escape them. Most of these actions gained her press coverage which titillated readers throughout the country.

Robert now petitioned for a sanity hearing for his mother. He argued that his mother was not a responsible person, but his concern seemed to center on her money's safety more than her personal safety.

During her insanity trial, Mary Lincoln's composure was remarkable. She listened quietly as old canards from the White House days were revived, failed to blanch when many witnesses, including her chambermaid, recited lurid tales of her supposedly crackbrained behavior, and did not react as Robert described her as "not wholly responsible." She and a jury heard many doctors (not one of them a specialist in mental problems) testify against her. She accepted the court's verdict of insanity with proud unconcern. That night, however, she attempted suicide.

Four months of care in a nursing home in Batavia, Illinois, and the attendance of a specialist in mental illnesses cured her, giving rise to the conclusion that her problem was physical weakness and neurosis, not psychosis. Removed to her sister's home in Springfield, she sent letters calling for help in all directions, resulting in sympathetic press assertions that she was only eccentric. When a second insanity hearing began in 1876, the public that had once abused her began to believe she had been a victim of a grave injustice. The 1875 verdict was reversed. Mary Lincoln then lived quietly and frugally in Springfield until 1879 when she went alone to France and Italy. A fall caused an uncorrectable spinal injury and her return to the United States. She went first to doctors in New York City and then, as a recluse, back to Springfield, where she died in 1882, senile at the age of 64, of a stroke.

This portrait of Mary Lincoln is very different from the traditional legendary one created in the 1889 bi-ography of Abraham Lincoln by W. H. Herndon and J. W. Weid, writers who implied that she was a psychotic demon who married Lincoln out of revenge for the spurious Ann Rutledge affair and an alleged jilting. Contemporary research suggests that the distorted conventional view of Mary Lincoln, like the insanity verdict, may be reversed.

Bob LIVINGSTON: "running for speaker, not sainthood"
On November 18, 1988, Robert L. Livingston (Republican from Louisiana) was unanimously nominated to succeed the flamboyant Newt GINGRICH as the next Speaker of the United States House of Representatives. Certainly, it seemed to be the culmination of Livingston's distinguished political career.

But on December 17, Livingston confessed (in a closed-door session with fellow Republicans) that he had occasionally "strayed" from his 33-year marriage and that "doing so nearly cost me my marriage and my family." He thus became the fourth Republican House member to admit to marital infidelities in the recent past. The timing of this startling admission—on the eve of the impeachment debate over President Bill CLINTON—couldn't have been more fortuitous. The stunned Republicans gave Livingston a standing ovation and closed ranks around him. The party line was that he would still be their next Speaker and that there was no question of resignation. Immediately, parallels were drawn between Livingston's indiscretions and those of President Clinton, a connection which the Republicans vehemently denied. Livingston said that, unlike President Clinton, his indiscretions did not involve his staff members nor was he ever asked to testify under oath about them. Other Republicans argued that while Livingston's infidelities were a personal issue between Livingston and his wife, Clinton's infidelities involved felonies and they were not. Besides, they said, Livingston had shown strong character by accepting responsibility for his indiscretions.

Roll Call (a Capitol Hill newspaper) had preempted Livingston's official announcement by displaying the news on its web site and adding that he might offer to step down. His confession was also not entirely voluntary, apparently being prompted by an article commissioned by Larry FLYNT of *Hustler* magazine on Livingston's personal life. Some leaders had advised him not to reveal the news but his wife, Bonnie, strongly encouraged him to tell his colleagues immediately. In a news conference in Los Angeles the next day, Flynt said that four women had admitted to having sexual liaisons with Livingston over the last 10 years. Livingston charged that the media and certain "individuals" were trying to exploit his past during the impeachment hearings and added that he would "not be intimated by these efforts." However, Livingston himself may have provided ammunition for this investigation by telling a reporter early in his candidacy that he "was running for Speaker, not sainthood." The White House and key House Democrats declined to comment on the issue.

The following day, Republican friends of Livingston polled members to ascertain the general reaction to his disclosure. While most expressed their disappointment at his conduct, they reiterated their support for his candidacy. However, the spokesperson for a small and vociferous minority informed Livingston on December 19, minutes before he was to open the impeachment debate on the House floor, that they were thinking of voting against him.

What happened next stunned the House and the entire nation. Livingston discussed why President Clinton should be impeached and urged him to resign from the presidency, wherepon the Democratic opposition heckled him and asked him to step down instead. He shocked everyone by doing just that. First he asked for forgiveness from his wife, family, friends, and colleagues and then he said that he would set an example "that I hope President Clinton will follow" by withdrawing his candidacy for the Speaker's position and resigning from his seat in the House in six months. The entire House erupted with an extended and emotional ovation. Many members—including some leading Democrats and even the White House—urged him to reconsider. Representative Tom DeLay, Republican from Texas, majority leader in the House, praised Livingston's courage and integrity. Everyone hoped that this unexpected turn in the proceedings would be the wake-up call to end the poisoned politics on Capitol Hill.

Frank K. LLOYD. See MARLBOROUGH GALLERY: the exploited estate of Mark Rothko.

LOCKHEED SCANDAL: bribes, kickbacks, coverups
In June 1975 the chief executive of the Northrop Corporation admitted to a Senate subcommittee investigating multinational corporations that his company had secret agreements with overseas consultants. When he told them that the agreements were patterned after the system used by the Lockheed Aircraft Corporation, a hornets' nest broke open. The subcommittee chairman, Senator Frank Church of Idaho, and the Securities and Exchange Commission immediately subpoenaed Lockheed's documents dealing with its overseas sales and commissions for the past five years. It soon became evident that Lockheed had paid millions of dollars to influential secret agents, businessmen, politicians, government officials, and military brass in many countries to obtain lucrative contracts for its military and commercial planes.

As the investigation progressed, it was revealed that prominent people were involved and that payments were obscured by using Swiss bank accounts, dummy companies, and fake charities and foundations. Further, all of this was done with the full knowledge and participation of Lockheed's chairman, Daniel Haughton, its president, Carl Kotchian, and their predecessors, who justified their actions by claiming that this was the way business was conducted abroad. The scandal did not stop in the Senate hearing room but spread to foreign courts, where many of the bribe-takers were put on trial and punished.

In 1958 a senior sales executive of Lockheed had been dispatched to Tokyo, where he set up an office and recruited a band of shadowy wheelers and dealers. He also recruited a secret agent, Yoshio Kodama, a political ultrarightist who was one of the most powerful men in Japan. Kodama engineered the reelection (1958) of his friend Nobusuke Kishi as prime minister and, the following year, the appointment of General Genda—the man who had planned and directed the attack on Pearl Harbor—as chief of the Japanese air-force staff. Genda visited Lockheed's headquarters in Burbank, California, where he flew a Starfighter and proclaimed it the best fighter plane in the world. That clinched the deal, and in 1960 the Japanese contracted for the purchase of 230 Starfighters. For his efforts, Kodama received more than $1.7 million in cash in yen through a devious procedure.

Twelve years later, in 1972, another expensive transaction occurred when Kotchian arrived to sell Lockheed's TriStar jumbo jets to Japan Airlines (JAL) and All Nippon (ANA) airways. The head of the Marubeni Corporation, Lockheed's official agent in Japan, told him that it would be wise to offer 500 million yen to Prime Minister Kakuei Tanaka, and Kodama, still on the Lockheed secret payroll, informed Kotchian that another 500 million yen should be offered to Kenji Osano, a crony of Tanaka. Kotchian agreed to both payments. The initial decision went against Lockheed, but the wily Kodama telephoned the minister of international trade and industry and urged him to reverse it. After Kotchian delivered another 120 million yen in cash to Marubeni, the president of ANA announced that Lockheed had won its contract. Over $12 million in commissions, fees, and payoffs were distributed to government officials, businessmen, and Kodama and his associates. As many as 14 men were brought to trial in 1977 after the findings of the Church subcommittee were published in Tokyo.

Lockheed also tried to sell Starfighters to West Germany in 1958 and convinced the minister of defense, Franz Joseph Strauss, to buy 96 planes in 1959. In return, the then chief executive of Lockheed made a secret "gentleman's agreement" to pay a percentage of all Lockheed sales to the West German air force to Strauss's political party, the Christian Socialist Union, as a "commission." When the German weekly *Der Spiegel* learned of this arrangement in mid-1962 and published articles denouncing Strauss, the latter was forced to resign. His

Lockheed liaison later told the Church subcommittee that he had distributed ''Christmas gratutities'' and outright bribes to others in the West German government and military establishment during this period.

The Dutch, too, were seriously considering purchasing Starfighters in 1958–59 and did so after the U.S. Department of Defense donated 25 planes from its military aid budget. Just how influential Prince Bernhard, Queen Juliana's husband, was in this decision is not clear, but Lockheed saw fit to pay him $1 million during 1960–62 through a conduit to a numbered Swiss bank account. In 1968, the Dutch considered a Lockheed naval patrol plane, which Bernhard pushed, but chose a French one instead. Lockheed, however, paid a fictitious ''Baarn Victor'' $100,000 for his help. When the Commissie van Drie investigated these matters in 1976, it concluded that Bernhard, who denied ever receiving a penny from Lockheed, had taken ''initiatives which were completely unacceptable.'' In disgrace, the Prince resigned all his public offices.

Lockheed's scandalous activities extended to Italy too. Ovidio Lefebye, a lawyer, and Camillo Crociani, a rich industrialist, were selected to be Lockheed's secret agents to sell the Hercules transport planes to the Italian government in 1969. Both were well connected with political, business, and military leaders, and both were experienced in ''laundering'' illegal funds through ghost companies and foundations. During the next two years, they spent more than $2 million greasing the palms of an Italian air force general, two ministers of defense, and numerous party and government officials, as well as receiving their own commissions. Lockheed willingly paid, for it received the desired order. After the disclosures of the Church subcommittee, most of the Italians who accepted bribes from the agents, and the agents themselves, were brought to trial.

Lockheed also had done business through an agent in Indonesia since the mid-1950s. However, when General Suharto assumed the presidency of Indonesia in 1966, he declared that no commissions could be paid to individuals but only to government-sponsored agencies. The generals of the Indonesian air force, AURI, suggested that the Widows' and Orphans' Fund, which AURI operated, be the recipient of 5 percent of all Lockheed sales in Indonesia. Lockheed Aircraft (Asia), Limited, was set up in Hong Kong as a buffer company, which forwarded payments to the fund in Singapore. In 1971, AURI insisted that the kickbacks increase to 10 percent, and Lockheed acquiesced.

The Church committee discovered that Lockheed's practice of hiring middlemen to bribe decision-makers was repeated in Saudi Arabia, Turkey, Spain, Brazil, and the Philippines. Many at Lockheed were shocked at the revelations. A special review committee undertook an internal investigation, publicly denounced the undercover methods of the past, and published a new code of business conduct to be followed by all Lockheed employees. Haughton and Kotchian, the principal perpetrators of the corruption, were forced to retire early.

Ann Trow LOHMAN. See Madame RESTELL: wicked abortionist's forced suicide.

Huey LONG: Southern dictator or radical?
Those who have studied the political career of Huey Pierce Long, former United States senator and governor of Louisiana, agree that it was colorful, exciting, and unusual. Others, however, view his career less favorably. Many of the books written about the tumultuous Long era judge him to have been a dictator or a fascist and thus a danger to the security of the United States. Long was an idealist who believed that the ends justify the means. In his relentless quest for political progressivism, he paid little heed to the rules of government, both implied and stated.

Born the eighth of 10 children in a lower-middle-class farming family living near Winnfield, Louisiana, Long was thoroughly inculcated in his parents' Populist political philosophy and trained in both the Bible and the family's evangelical Baptist theology. A glib high-school graduate, he gained enough information during one year's attendance at law schools to pass the state bar examination and hang up his shingle in Winnfield, Louisiana, in 1915 at the age of 22. His law practice introduced him to the political machinations of the period.

At the age of 25, this confident farmboy lawyer was elected to be a member (and later chairman) of Louisiana's Public Service Commission. The state was then one of the poorest in the country, retarded by both a high level of illiteracy and an almost moribund state government. The governing elite seemed to do as little as possible for the state's people. Moreover, under a clique of seldom-changing officials, New Orleans operated as if it were a state within the state. The governor had little real power.

Determined to bring Louisiana into the modern era by passing progressive and Populist legislation, Long ran unsuccessfully for governor in 1924. Because of his unconventional, boisterous, and crowd-pleasing campaigning methods, he came in second in a 1928 Democratic primary; the front runner refused a run-off, and Long became governor by default because no other party had run a candidate.

Sworn in, he lacked the legislative majority necessary to put his progressive program into the form of new laws. To overcome his foes, he lobbied personally on the legislative floor, acquired control of several state boards and their patronage, and made unauthorized expenditures. All of these actions were then legal in Louisiana. He also acted illegally by awarding state jobs to legislators in such high number that he gained the majority necessary to pass his modest initial program.

His program for 1928 established a free textbook system for all schools, public and parochial. His legislators pushed through $30 million in bonds for highway and bridge construction. However, he provoked the politically powerful in Louisiana into enmity by sponsoring a severance tax on oil refineries. Long's program was unique in that it taxed not the average citizen, but only the rich.

His opposition organized to fight him, annoyed that the Kingfish, as Long was nicknamed, had taken advantage of then-current legislative rules to speed up the passage of laws from three days to one. Patronage allowed him to buy loyalty to his programs by packing committees and boards with his own men (appointees were forced to write undated letters of resignation and were summarily removed if they proved disloyal). Patronage also enabled Long to gain power over parish (county) officials. Furthermore, his power extended into the underworld.

Through opposition legislators, the political powers of the state achieved a call for Long's impeachment in 1929. The attempt was defeated by only a legal fluke: 15 of the charges of official misconduct and bribery against him had been composed after the close of the legislative session. In a strange kind of poetic justice, 15 state senators loyal to Long argued that the impeachment proposal was therefore illegal. The proposal failed.

Long then continued his legislative program in 1929, with results. A hated poll tax was repealed; more bonds for road and bridge building were issued; and the legislature also gave Governor Long wider and more control. The state populace was generally pleased and elected him a United States senator in 1930.

Not wanting to allow his programs to be reversed, Long shrewdly remained in Baton Rouge, Louisiana's capital, until 1932 and continued to expand the highway program and other construction projects, including a new capitol building. Only after he had seen the election of his own men as governor and lieutenant governor did he report to the U.S. Senate in Washington for his swearing in.

Long's audacity made him the object of national and international press coverage, for in 1932 he was both a part of national legislation and the de facto governor of Louisiana. He spent long periods in Baton Rouge, outwitting the opposition by extending his Populist program, harassing the opposition machine in New Orleans, forcing the Standard Oil Company to willingly obey his legislation, and altering the structure of the state's government so as to give the governor almost absolute power. In Washington, D.C., he fought the Hoover administration's fumbling remedies for the Great Depression, campaigned for Franklin Delano Roosevelt (whom he mistakenly regarded as a progressive), and then gained Roosevelt's enmity by exposing the inadequacy of the president's national legislative programs.

President Roosevelt tried to punish Long by funneling federal patronage for Louisiana through the opposition's leaders and by harassing the state's attempt to control New Orleans. Long responded in 1934 by staging filibusters, announcing the formation of his "Share-the-Wealth" program, and indicating that he would be a presidential candidate in 1936. He was now Roosevelt's most formidable political opponent.

A large segment of the American public responded favorably to the Share-the-Wealth idea, a radical and socialist plan offered for the cure of the Depression. Essentially Populist in nature, it attempted to decentralize the enormous wealth of the United States by offering homestead grants to all families; it promised guaranteed annual incomes, pensions for the elderly, free higher education to all persons capable of it, and generous bonuses to veterans. Impractical as originally conceived, the plan offered benefits which made the Social Security Act of 1935 only a pale imitation. If enacted, it would have taxed only the rich.

Early in 1935, Long learned of two plots to assassinate him. He did little but inform the gangsterlike bodyguards who had ringed him since 1928. The assassin who fatally shot him on September 8, 1935, was 29-year-old Carl Weiss, a gun-collecting physician, who may have been a member of a group that considered Long a dictator. Fired on as he walked along the Capitol corridor in Baton Rouge, the Kingfish died two days later. Weiss was shot dead by Long's bodyguards, who, according to one story, had started firing wildly when the gun-toting Weiss had punched Long in the mouth; one of their stray bullets had supposedly killed Long. The Kingfish's men had put the blame on Weiss to protect themselves, according to their report. Like his life, Long's sudden death brought controversy about how and why it happened.

LONGET-SABICH AFFAIR

The 1976 shooting death of 31-year-old champion skier Vladimir "Spider" Sabich shook up the chic Rocky Mountain winter resort of Aspen, Colorado, where he was a well-liked resident. Many townsfolk there put the blame completely on 34-year-old Claudine Longet, a former show girl and actress, who had been Sabich's lover for the preceding two years. America's popular press took a keen, brief interest in the town's vilification and court case against her during the following year.

Born and raised in Paris, France, the lovely Longet had come to the United States in 1960 and performed as a leading dancer with the Folies-Bergère in Las Vegas, Nevada, when she met and later (1961) married singer Andy Williams, who was almost 12 years her senior. While living in Beverly Hills, California, her theatrical training won her some television and movie roles. In 1970 she separated from Williams. Six years later he granted her a divorce. Meanwhile, the dark-haired beauty began a close relationship with Sabich, whose former Olympic fame and professional success as an expert skier helped land him lucrative product-endorsement contracts that enabled him to live very well. In Aspen, he and Longet lived together, along with her three children from her marriage to Williams, in an expensive home put up by Sabich's brother Steve, a local builder. At the time, the town of Aspen, whose superb facilities for skiing and other winter sports made it an internationally known resort, was smarting from its growing reputation as a center for the rich, famous, powerful, and decadent. It had gained the nickname of the "cocaine capital." Heavy drinking, drug-taking, sex-frolicking, and wild partying in general were apparently a way of life in numerous lavish chalets and other places in the valley where the town was located. Many residents looked askance at these goings-on.

According to some, the relationship between Longet and Sabich seemed to be falling apart in the winter of 1976; they had heated arguments in public and in front of friends. On March 21, Sabich died in his Aspen home from a gunshot wound in his abdomen. Longet later claimed that he had been showing her how to operate his .22-caliber pistol, which she had found in the closet and wanted for protection when alone. She said that the gun had fired accidentally, killing Sabich. Longet had attempted to resuscitate him, without success, while her three children waited outside for the police and ambulance to arrive. Soon afterward Williams, her ex-husband, came to help her weather the public outrage that had arisen against her after the shooting. Longet had never been accepted in the community in the open-hearted way that her lover had, and although expressing deep sorrow for the tragic "accident," she was angrily told by Sabich's brother and parents to get out of the house. She remained, however, in Aspen, and bought herself an old Victorian home there later that year. Williams constantly stood by her side in the ensuing legal proceedings by the district attorney against her, while many of the local citizenry outrightly accused her of murder.

After being charged with reckless manslaughter (April 8, 1976), a felony carrying a maximum 10-year prison sentence and a $30,000 fine, Longet went into semi-seclusion to escape hounding news reporters and others. All kinds of rumors floated around concerning the slaying; it didn't seem likely that Longet could have a fair trial. She pleaded not guilty at a preliminary hearing in June 1976 (the press and the public were banned), and the trial, set for August, was postponed until January 1977. The prosecuting district attorney claimed that Longet's diary (which the Colorado Supreme Court later ruled as inadmissible evidence because it had been taken illegally by police from the house) would incriminate her because it indicated how unstable the lovers' relationship had become (later the diary was also said to contain details about affairs with other men). The supreme court also ruled inadmissible the findings from urine and blood tests performed on the actress on the day of the shooting, saying that they had been done unlawfully. Traces of cocaine were alleged to have been found in her blood.

It took about a week to put together a jury of unbiased Aspen citizens, who listened to testimony from a number of witnesses during the trial. Longet tearfully contended that she loved Sabich, that she had been uncertain about the loading of the gun and had thought its safety catch was on when it went off, and that she had never used the words *bang bang* when earlier recounting the shooting to a detective. A ballistics expert testified that the gun could have fired without the trigger being pulled. Williams denied that he had ever described the defendant as "a crazy gal who liked to take chances," words he allegedly used to people right after Sabich's death. On January 14, 1977, the jury found Longet guilty of criminally negligent homicide, a misdemeanor charge carrying a maximum sentence of two years' imprisonment and a $5,000 fine. On January 31, she was sentenced to 30 days in jail "at a time of her choosing" and placed on two years' probation and fined $25. Local opinion said justice had not been served. Longet made no appeal, served her sentence (in April and May of 1977) in an Aspen jail cell with a woman serving 30 days for drunken driving, and then fought a $1.3-million damage suit filed against her by Sabich's parents. Some dirty tricks were played on her thereafter in Aspen (manure and paint were dumped on her car) but soon the once bright entertainer faded from public view.

LOVE CANAL: dump site of Hooker Chemicals & Plastics Corporation

Today, the Love Canal in Niagara Falls, New York, has become synonymous with "toxic wastes," for it was here that residents began to have health problems in 1978 as chemicals dumped years earlier began percolating to the surface. Although one study conducted by the U.S. Environmental Protection Agency (EPA) seemed to negate the damage done, it soon became clear that chemicals had been improperly buried and the Hooker Chemicals & Plastics Corporation was to blame. By 1981, most of the homeowners in the immediate contaminated area sold their houses to the state and moved elsewhere.

When unpleasant smells, withered shrubbery, and unexplained respiratory ailments became prevalent around the ditch called Love Canal, residents began to realize that something was wrong with their environment. Led by Mrs. Lois Gibbs, they organized the Love Canal Homeowners' Association and began to fight for restitution of their property and health. They discovered an abnormally high rate of miscarriages among women in the neighborhood, as well as an abnormally high number of birth defects in the children of the area. The association filed a suit in 1978 against the Hooker

A bulldozer begins demolition work on a street in the chemically contaminated Love Canal area near Niagara Falls, New York, A worker hoses down a building to prevent toxic pollutants from escaping into the atmosphere. (UPI/Bettnmann Newsphotos)

Chemicals & Plastics Corporation in which it claimed that exposure to toxic wastes from improperly buried chemicals had damaged residents' health and made their homes worthless. The local newspaper supported this effort, and stories about the plight of Love Canal residents began appearing in newspapers across the country.

The EPA conducted a study in 1980 that found that residents of the area were suffering from chromosome damage, which can cause cancer and birth defects. President Jimmy Carter declared a state of emergency in the neighborhood and arranged for the relocation of some 2,500 residents. Some experts disputed the EPA report, and the federal government asked the Centers for Disease Control (CDC) to carry out another investigation. This study, released in 1983, found that people who lived near Love Canal were "no more likely to have chromosomal damage than other residents of Niagara Falls." Critics quickly pointed out that the CDC study's use of a control group from Niagara Falls skewed the results because chemical contamination was widespread throughout the city. There are a number of chemical plants in Niagara Falls, and they are the city's principal employers and the backbone of the local economy. Because of the concentration of chemical plants, the air in Niagara Falls contains many of the same chemicals found around Love Canal. Further, critics argued, the CDC study was suspect in that it seemed to satisfy a goal of former EPA toxic-waste chief Rita Lavelle to "change the perception of Love Canal from dangerous to benign."

A later study by researchers at the State University of New York (SUNY) at Binghamton involved the effects of the Canal area on voles—rodents resembling rats. Voles living near the canal lived only 54 days into adult-hood, while those living a mile away lived 100 days. Also, the voles in the contaminated area suffered liver damage. "The voles act as a warning against resettling Love Canal before all the evidence is in" concluded the SUNY report.

In the late 1970s the federal government sued Hooker for $124 million for dumping tons of chemical wastes from 1942 to 1953. The company acknowledged that the wastes might eventually leach into the Niagara River and admitted that there was contaminated soil on the grounds of a local water-treatment plant. Traces of chemicals had been found in the drinking water of Niagara Falls, but city officials insisted that the water was safe. A local attorney contested this "fact" and claimed that "all residents of Niagara Falls who drink the water are at high risk."

The lawsuits against Hooker dragged on, but in October 1983, the Occidental Petroleum Corporation, which had purchased Hooker in 1968, agreed to an out-of-court settlement of $25 million with 1,345 residents of the Love Canal area. The State of New York set up a Love Canal Revitalization Agency and bought the homes in the canal neighborhood. With the passage of time, they have been destroyed, and in the fall of 1986, 180 more abandoned houses in the area were leveled by bulldozers.

In 1990, after some $275 million had been spent for relocation and cleanup, the EPA said the Love Canal area was again safe; families began returning and buying homes at bargain prices.

Linda LOVELACE. See DEEP THROAT: the sexual brutalization of Linda Lovelace.

M

Joseph McCARTHY: an enemy from within

Egotism, ambition, and hypocrisy made Joseph Raymond McCarthy one of the most malevolent public figures in American history. A United States senator from Wisconsin from 1947 until his death in 1957, McCarthy had known poverty and isolation as a child; as an adult, he revealed a willingness to use any means, even the illegal, to achieve what he regarded as success, even if his pursuit of fame and power meant the injuring or destruction of others.

McCarthy graduated from law school with little distinction. A mediocre student, his lowest grade, not surprisingly, had been in legal ethics. One of his professors commented that "he knew little when he got here and very little more when he left." He ran an unsuccessful law practice on bluff, making it the foundation of the procedures he would use to achieve success.

The "big lie" was the next procedure he adopted. He defeated his opponent for office as a state circuit court judge through misrepresentation. He was so notoriously hasty in his decisions and so unethical that he was on the verge of impeachment when World War II saved him.

McCarthy, who felt that normal rules did not apply to him, broke Wisconsin law by applying for a commission in the U.S. Marines as an intelligence officer. He saw no combat but managed to convince people that he was "Tail Gunner Joe" and that an injured leg (actually hurt in a drunken fall during an equator-crossing party) came from 10 pounds of shrapnel.

He again ignored rules when he broke both Wisconsin and federal laws by campaigning for the seat of U.S. Senator Robert La Follette, Jr. Bluff, vigorous campaigning and the promulgation of his false war record enabled McCarthy to win.

In Washington, D.C., McCarthy's first three years saw his early refusal to observe Senate ethics. He served special interests, adding—on the Senate floor—to his technique two propaganda procedures that became his trademarks after 1950: shifty statistics rattled off so fast that they were incomprehensible, and the artful dodge, or introduction of arguable irrelevancies to distract others in Senate proceedings. He made money by serving the Pepsi-Cola Company and a real-estate lobby opposed to public housing for veterans. As chairman of hearings on a public housing bill, he developed other propaganda methods: abuse of witnesses, vilification, intimidation through confrontations involving lies, and refusing time to opposition witnesses or cropping their comments from official reports. His abuses were so flagrant and his graft so undisguised that fellow senators attempted to initiate an investigation of his procedures. Again, however, outside events saved his skin.

Assigned the task of delivering a 1950 Lincoln's Birthday speech in Wheeling, West Virginia, and uncertain of a sure-fire topic, McCarthy chose communist subversion, a potent public issue because of the Cold War, the Red takeover in China, the Alger Hiss trial, Russian achievement of an atomic bomb, and domestic problems that made America ripe for another ritual attack on minorities, aliens, and dissidents as scapegoats (see A. Mitchell PALMER: opportunism masked as idealism).

Although McCarthy himself never had more than an elementary knowledge of communist theories or subversion techniques, he posed as an expert. He announced that America was at the mercy of "enemies from within" and that he had a list of 205 such enemies at work in the State Department. He made his remarks without proof. As a trained lawyer and former judge, he should have used evidence to form the basis of his public remarks. The speech was pure bluff, a means to his ends, and it was the cause of catastrophe.

The public reacted enthusiastically; they had a scapegoat in communism. Top Republican leaders saw in McCarthy a means to their goal of ravaging the Democrats; they applauded his "astounding revelations."

However, many thinking persons did not applaud them, and when they demanded McCarthy's evidence for his claims, he used his shifty statistics technique, changing his figures several times and never producing for scrutiny any of the documents he claimed proved his charges. When he was assailed, he bluffed and attacked.

And he used a variation on the artful dodge, that of abandoning a failing ploy and trying a new one before he had been effectively embarrassed. He smeared in order to avoid having his purported evidence scrutinized: he assailed highly respected opponents such as President Harry Truman, Secretary of State Dean Acheson, and General George Marshall; he attacked the innocent, such as Owen Lattimore (vulnerable because he was an "old China hand"); and he impugned State Department employees in groups and as individuals. In fact, he attacked anyone upon whom he might successfully pin a "Red" label. And when a Senate committee under Millard Tydings investigated 10 persons named by McCarthy as State Department subversives and revealed that only four worked for the department as "cleared" personnel, McCarthy attacked Tydings and used illegal methods to defeat Tydings's reelection.

Using these techniques, McCarthy had by 1952 gained one of his goals: power. He intimidated his enemies and controlled his Republican supporters, interfering in Republican Dwight Eisenhower's presidential campaign and, after the Republican win in 1952, demanding and gaining direct influence in the appointment of ambassadors. His own reelection gained him control of the permanent Senate Subcommittee on Investigations, enabling him—with the help of reporters who knew he was a fraud but liked him anyhow—to keep up the tradition of a daily article on America's front pages.

To most of those who opposed him, McCarthy became the cause of helpless fear. But not to all: the well-known syndicated American cartoonist Herblock (Herbert Block) pondered the miasma McCarthy was spreading and labeled it McCarthyism in a series of bitter cartoons.

During his Senate subcommittee's public hearings on supposed communist infiltration of the U.S. Army in 1953, McCarthy revealed that he lacked all decorum: he intimidated witnesses, named innocent persons and challenged them to prove their innocence, harassed liberals under the guise of seeking out communists, constantly introduced unreliable evidence, attacked the Voice of America with false charges, and began a public war with the army, ignoring as he did so the dictates of the Constitution's Bill of Rights. Many commentators began to compare him with Hitler's propaganda minister, Joseph Goebbels.

McCarthy then began to be reckless. He attacked former British Prime Minister Clement Atlee as a communist, and European newspapers began to inquire who ran the United States, Eisenhower or McCarthy. Eisenhower also began to ask. When the Army-McCarthy

rancor grew intense, supporters of McCarthy among the Republican leadership began to slip away and then to oppose him. Former journalist advocates such as H. V. Kaltenborn and opponents such as Edward R. Murrow began to proclaim that power had corrupted him.

Now that he was seen as dangerous, McCarthy's fame began to tarnish. But he continued to bluff even after two incidents revealed to most Americans his utter shamelessness: televised public hearings of the Army-McCarthy dispute exposed both his total unfairness and his extreme subservience to the subcommittee's chief counsel, Roy COHN. It was after this that the Senate censured him by a vote of 67 to 22, on December 2, 1954.

For five years McCarthy had made headlines with his traveling circus on communism. Although he had made many people miserable and had imperiled the spirit of the nation, he had caught no Communist subversives.

When he died in 1957 at the age of 49 from a liver infection complicated by alcoholism, it was clear that McCarthy had been an enemy from within. He had been less an adversary of communism than a foe of America's basic institutions.

Joseph McCARTHY: outgunned by the Army

Joseph Raymond McCarthy's 1952 reelection as United States senator from Wisconsin on the Republican ticket, as well as the momentous national success of his flamboyant, reckless, and underhanded methods (see Joseph

Roy Cohn, chief counsel of the Senate permanent Subcommittee on Investigations, deposits some documents in front of Senator Joseph R. McCarthy, who continues his interrogation of Army Secretary Robert Stevens during the controversial Army-McCarthy hearings in 1954. (UPI/Bettmann Newsphotos)

MCCARTHY: an enemy from within), undoubtedly made him overconfident. He began to make mistakes, two of which now seem especially grievous: his attempt to gain influence over the U.S. Department of the Army and his hiring in 1953 of Roy COHN, first as an aide and later as chief counsel to the Senate Permanent Subcommittee on Investigations. The Army refused to become his subordinate, and losing the battle for control, McCarthy as chairman of the Senate subcommittee also lost his eminence.

McCarthy's initial attack on the U.S. Army had only one goal: power. By publicly expressing his doubts about the thoroughness of its investigation of alleged subversives at Fort Monmouth, New Jersey, he expected to humiliate the army and thereby gain influence in the army department's decision making. But Cohn's authority over McCarthy had begun to amount almost to co-direction, and the former expressed his wish that the Senate subcommittee's targets also include Camp Kilmer, New Jersey. Cohn's reasons for this were personal rather than political: his current favorite, G. David Schine, was, in Cohn's opinion, being tortured in basic training there, and Cohn wanted to pressure the army to release him. McCarthy already knew of Schine as having been Cohn's partner in a totally irresponsible investigation of subversive books in U.S. State Department libraries overseas and, regarding Schine as a former aide, concluded that Cohn's request offered the subcommittee a wider scope for opportunistic congressional investigations.

The subcommittee began to work on two levels: McCarthy proceeded in public and private hearings to lambast the army for its methods in the Fort Monmouth investigation, and to humiliate General Ralph Zwicker, Camp Kilmer's presiding officer, for his performance there. Privately, Cohn endeavored, usually by telephone, to gain weekend and weekday leaves, a special commission, and other unusual favors for Schine (whose work, Cohn alleged, was necessary to the subcommittee).

McCarthy and Cohn, for their separate ends, put pressure on the secretary of the army, Robert Stevens, who, in a 1954 "memorandum of understanding," at first promised such full cooperation with the subcommittee that the London *Times* called his servility "the surrender of the American army." Stevens, however, was a quick learner; he tightened up, refusing to give the subcommittee the army files it demanded, as well as ordering Schine's superiors to assert that he was no longer permitted special leaves.

That McCarthy knew of Cohn's pressures in Schine's favor is evident from a memo in which he advised Stevens that his only interest was in getting to the bottom of the Fort Monmouth problem. Apparently, however, McCarthy did not convince Cohn of the need to relax his private harassment, for transcripts of taped calls made later reveal that Cohn swore hysterically at Secretary Stevens and threatened to "get the army." (A resumé of Cohn's pressures was leaked to the press by an army staffer and gained the desired reaction: popular and legislative criticism of the subcommittee.)

Stevens next publicly stated that the McCarthy-led subcommittee was upsetting the army's morale, and U.S. President Dwight D. Eisenhower, in a speech at Dartmouth College in Hanover, New Hampshire, called for "fair play." Ever stubborn, McCarthy rejected the hint to tone down; he responded harshly to Eisenhower's mild speech, praised Cohn, and accused the army of trying to blackmail him into stopping the Fort Monmouth investigation and of holding Schine hostage as further compulsion to that end.

With discreet guidance from the White House, the angry army maneuvered to gain Senate arbitration of the power struggle; it developed a 26-charge bill of particulars. Publicly bellicose, McCarthy responded by issuing his own list of 46 countercharges. At the army's request, he agreed to step down temporarily as his subcommittee's chairman but refused other concessions. He retained the right of cross-examination; as a result, his usual antics colored the investigation, the first congressional investigation to be reported via television.

From the first day of the Army-McCarthy hearings on April 22, 1954, until their end during the 36th day of testimony on June 17, some 10 million people watched the Wisconsin senator perform. They heard his "point of order" shouts, often for negligible purposes. They observed his interruptions of testimony, his berating of witnesses, and his attempts to divert questioning by introducing extraneous topics. He was almost never silent. The viewers also observed the pale, slick-haired Cohn snaking his way to the wrought-up McCarthy's side, whispering to him, and then standing aside as McCarthy once again exploded.

As the hearings continued, the audience began to sour on the McCarthy-Cohn team and to admire the army's counsel, Joseph N. Welch. They appreciated Welch's persistent and sometimes folksy manner of questioning, quietly and courteously delivered despite the maddening uproar of the hearing room. They compared Welch to his opponents and found the latter lacking. Welch also impressed them by his sincere compassion. When McCarthy repeatedly insinuated that the army's counsel was subversive in even considering for his staff a young lawyer who had belonged to a group labeled disloyal by the Justice Department, Welch quietly responded by asking his inquisitor whether he had any honor at all. Welch earned from the viewers a highly deserved measure of fame.

The two months of testimony not only exposed the shallowness and insincerity of McCarthy; they also proved factually enlightening, despite the circuslike atmosphere. They revealed the fact that McCarthy was willing to suborn federal employees (including, briefly, Federal Bureau of Investigation director J. Edgar Hoover) into supplying classified documents to him, which he had used without authorization. For these subversive acts, the ostensible combatant against subversion deserved censure, if not trial.

The Wisconsin senator was never to undergo juridical examination, however, for the lengthy Army-McCarthy hearings proved inconclusive. The reason for this was that it led to the issuing of four very different reports. Republicans denied that McCarthy was guilty as charged by the army; they asserted that only Cohn and Schine could be so judged. Democrats accused both sides of having behaved badly and assigned no specific blame to McCarthy.

The report of the public was adverse, and McCarthy realized that he had opened his own jugular vein. His public approval rating of 50 percent in early 1954 dropped to 34 percent at the end of June.

His rating was to go lower. Democrats on the Senate subcommittee demanded that McCarthy purge his staff. Cohn departed on July 19—not to ignominy but instead to a partnership in a prestigious multimillion dollar law firm. (His later misdoings did little to enhance his future public reputation.)

Some members of the Senate voted to entertain a censure resolution against McCarthy. Originally, the resolution had contained five charges: contempt of the Senate and its committees, encouragement of federal employees to violate laws concerning restricted materials, receipt and use of classified information without authorization, abuse of other senators, and abuse of General Zwicker. Although refused permission to interrupt the censure proceedings, McCarthy artfully used his still faithful press outlets to quash four of the charges against him, leaving only contempt of the Senate and abuse of the censure investigation committee.

On December 2, 1954, the Senate voted 67 to 22 to censure McCarthy. He was no longer chairman of the subcommittee.

The "show" was not completely over, however. Aware that a mistake had been made, McCarthy blamed not himself but the army, the "Reds," the Senate, and all other groups opposed to him as responsible for his loss of power. He seems not to have realized that the essential good sense of Americans—voters and legislators alike—had not succumbed to his antics. (See also HOUSE COMMITTEE ON UN-AMERICAN ACTIVITIES (HUAC): America's Inquisition and the "Hollywood Ten.")

Jeffrey MacDONALD: fatally flawed

In the early morning hours of February 17, 1970, military police were summoned to the Fort Bragg, North Carolina, residence of Dr. Jeffrey Robert MacDonald, a Princeton-educated physician and captain in the Green Berets. They found there a bloody and horrible scene. MacDonald's wife, Collette, 26 years old and pregnant with the couple's third child, lay dead in the master bedroom. She had been stabbed nine times in the neck and seven times in the chest with a knife. She had also been stabbed 21 times in the chest with an icepick and hit at least six times in the head with a club. Both her arms had been broken, probably as she tried to defend herself. Her husband, motionless but alive, lay next to her. The word *PIG* had been written in blood across their headboard.

In another bedroom lay their daughter Kimberly, age five. She had died from at least two club blows to the right side of her head. She had also been clubbed on the left side of her face and stabbed with a knife some eight or 10 times. Across the hallway lay their second daughter, Kristen, two years old, also dead. She had been stabbed 17 times with a knife and about 15 times with an icepick.

When he arrived at Fort Bragg's Womack Hospital, MacDonald was found to have suffered only slight injuries, the most serious being a small stab wound on the chest, which caused a partial collapse of the right lung. He also had a bruise on his forehead and other superficial stab wounds, none of which even required stitches.

MacDonald told investigators that he had been sleeping on the living room sofa and awakened to the sound of screams from his wife and older daughter. He found four intruders—a black man in Army clothing, two white men, and a blond woman wearing "hippie style" clothing and carrying a candle—attacking him. The woman was chanting "Acid is groovy" and "Kill the pigs." MacDonald claimed that he had struggled with the intruders and then passed out.

When he awakened, he said, he went from room to room, trying to revive his family with mouth-to-mouth resuscitation. After checking his own injuries in the bathroom, he telephoned for help.

Besides the enormous difference in the severity of the injuries to MacDonald and those to the rest of his family, many aspects of the physical evidence, particularly the pattern of bloodstains and the location of fibers from MacDonald's pajama top, struck members of the army's Criminal Investigation Division as inconsistent with the physician's story. In 1970, MacDonald was accused of the murders. At a pre-court-martial hearing, MacDonald's attorney, Bernard L. Segal, attacked numerous sloppy features of the army investigation, including disturbance of the evidence by military police, loss of evidence, failure to establish roadblocks to search for the intruders, and failure to fully investigate another suspect. Against this incompetence was arrayed the testimony of character witnesses, among them Colette MacDonald's stepfather Freddy Kassab and psychiatrists who argued on MacDonald's behalf. After the charges, found by the investigating officer to be "not true," were dropped, MacDonald was honorably discharged from the army.

He soon moved to California, where he was named director of emergency services at St. Mary's Hospital in Long Beach. Active in community affairs, he became a nationally known expert on the recognition and treatment of child abuse.

But after close study of the hearing transcript, Colette's stepfather, initially one of MacDonald's strongest supporters, came to believe that his son-in-law was in fact guilty of the brutal slayings. He waged a one-man campaign that finally led to a federal grand jury indictment of MacDonald in 1975. At his 1979 trial, the physician was found guilty of second-degree murder of Colette and Kimberly and first-degree murder of Kristen; he was sentenced to three consecutive life terms and to become eligible for parole in 1991.

Before the trial MacDonald had asked Joe McGinniss, a writer, to tell his story. But McGinniss's best-selling book, entitled *Fatal Vision* (1983), concluded that the physician was guilty, perhaps committing the atrocities as a result of a psychological disorder, exhaustion, and amphetamine use. In 1984 MacDonald sought unsuccessfully to block the NBC broadcast of a miniseries based on the book and continued to maintain his innocence.

MacDonald brought a $15 million lawsuit against McGinness for breach of contract and fraud because his book had concluded that MacDonald was guilty of the 1970 murders. The case went to court in Los Angeles and ended in a mistrial in August 1987 because the six-member jury became deadlocked. Later, in December 1987, MacDonald settled out of court, accepting $325,000.

MacDonald's appeals filed in 1984 and 1990 were rejected up to the U.S. Supreme Court. In 1997 his lawyers vainly tried again to reopen the case, arguing that an FBI forensic expert gave misleading information about fiber evidence; MacDonald, then confined at a federal prison in Sheridan, Oregon, still maintained that drug-crazed intruders had killed his family.

Alexander Slidell MACKENZIE: mutiny or overreaction?

While rising through American naval ranks from midshipman (1815) to lieutenant (1825) to commander (1841) while serving aboard a number of vessels, Alexander Slidell (his original name until, at the request of a maternal uncle, he added his name Mackenzie in 1838) took time off for personal travels and to write, producing several books of note, including *A Year in Spain* (1829), *Popular Essays on Naval Subjects* (1833), and *Spain Revisited* (1836). In 1842 he was put in command of the small United States brigantine *Somers,* which was then being used as a naval training ship for apprentice officers and which set sail for Africa in September of that year.

No one could have guessed, especially Mackenzie, that a few months later, three men would die because of the commander's rash orders.

Mutinies on the high seas were quite common in those years because of large crews on ships, commanded by few officers, and long stays at sea and bad living conditions (including crowdedness, poor food, and illness). During Mackenzie's trip, which he disliked, the crew became uneasy and appeared on the verge of mutiny. In fact, Mackenzie learned from John W. Wales, a purser's steward, that midshipman Philip Spencer, the incorrigible 18-year-old son of U.S. Secretary of War John C. Spencer, had approached Wales with an alleged conspiracy to take control of the *Somers* and kill Mackenzie and his officers.

An investigation took place aboard ship and uncovered the three supposed ringleaders of the mutiny: Spencer, Samuel Cromwell (boatswain's mate on the ship), and Elisha Small (a seaman). Perhaps because he was afraid, Mackenzie rashly ordered the three executed, securing the approval of other officers beforehand, and on December 1, 1842, Spencer, Cromwell, and Small were hanged on the ship's yardarm.

When the *Somers* anchored in New York Harbor two weeks later, the executions were immediately disclosed and Mackenzie received some severe criticism. A court of inquiry began to look into the case, the last such to arise in the American navy, and Mackenzie requested a court-martial to clear himself of charges (three counts of murder, two counts of cruelty, illegal punishment, and conduct unbecoming an officer of the U.S. Navy). At his court-martial in Brooklyn on January 28, 1843, Mackenzie justified his actions at sea, saying that the circumstances had demanded, by duty and necessity, the hanging of the three crewmen; he pleaded innocent to all charges and was acquitted by the judges, who felt that as a commander trying to maintain discipline, he was blameless in the matter. Attempts by Spencer's illustrious father and certain friends to initiate civil action against Mackenzie were unsuccessful.

There was much public discussion about the court testimony of Mackenzie, Wales, and other officers of the *Somers,* and controversy over the case persisted, despite the court of inquiry and court-martial exonerating Mackenzie completely, because Spencer's, Cromwell's, and Small's side of the story remained unheard. The case, however, did bring about some changes in naval justice, for executions and floggings as punishments aboard ships at sea were abolished thereafter. In addition, the U.S. Naval Academy was opened in 1845 at Annapolis, Maryland, to mitigate the naval custom of training officers only on vessels such as the *Somers.*

Although Mackenzie left active duty for a period at the conclusion of his trial, he continued to write and eventually, in 1846, returned to the navy to take part in the Mexican War. He died on September 13, 1848, at his home in Tarrytown, New York. The famous no-vella *Billy Budd* by Herman Melville relates the hanging of an innocent seaman during a threatened mutiny like that on the *Somers,* aboard which Melville's cousin, a Lieutenant Gansevoort, sailed in 1842.

Gene McKINNEY: Army's top enlisted man court-martialed

As sergeant major of the army since 1995, Gene C. Mc-Kinney was the highest ranking enlisted man in the U.S. Army. The highly decorated, 28-year veteran occupied an office in the Pentagon across the hall from the army chief of staff whom he advised on all matters related to enlisted personnel, and he was known to the troops as a proponent of improved enlisted housing and health care. When a major sex scandal was uncovered at Ab-erdeen Proving Ground in 1996, McKinney was ap-pointed to a panel whose task was to find ways to prevent sexual harassment in the military. To that end McKinney made a video, which was shown to sol-diers everywhere, in which he told his audience force-fully that there was no room in the army for sexual harassment. On a fact-finding trip to Aberdeen, he urged female soldiers who had been sexually harassed or abused to step forward so that the perpetrators could be punished.

In 1997, McKinney was himself charged with sexual harassment. His first accuser was retired Sergeant Major Brenda Hoster, a 22-year veteran, former drill sergeant, winner of the Bronze Star, and McKinney's former public affairs specialist. Hoster claimed that in 1996, while the two were attending a military conference in Hawaii, McKinney came to her room late one night and propositioned her. When she refused and urged him to return to his wife who was just down the hall, he hinted that he would rape her if she did not cooperate. She continued to refuse his advances and, after about 20 minutes, he left the room but only after grabbing and kissing her. Several weeks later, the distraught Hoster told two of her superior officers about the incident and asked to be reassigned. But after two months it became evident that nothing would be done, and so Hoster re-tired. She only came forward when she did because Mc-Kinney's appointment to the sexual harassment panel had outraged her.

Hoster was backed up by five other women who also claimed to have been sexually harassed by McKinney. U.S. Navy Petty Officer First Class Johnna Vinson claimed that he had propositioned her in a hotel lobby in Denver, Colorado, while they were attending a con-ference on military health benefits. Major Michelle Gunzelman and Sergeant Rita Jeczala accused him of similar advances in similar situations. Sergeant Christine Fetrow claimed that he had hounded her in person and by telephone for two years and on several occasions attempted to kiss and fondle her. Sergeant Christina Roy claimed that he had successfully pressured her into having sexual intercourse with him while she was seven months pregnant. Altogether, McKinney was charged with 18 counts of sexual misconduct and suspended from his duties pending a trial.

McKinney declared himself innocent on all counts and claimed that, because he was black and all of his accusers were white, he was the victim of a racially mo-tivated witch hunt. His lead attorney claimed that Mc-Kinney was being treated unfairly because of his rank and threatened to publicize the names of at least four senior army officers accused of sexual misconduct, who were allowed to retire quietly rather than be court-martialed. During his court-martial the defense paraded a number of character witnesses on McKinney's behalf and succeeded in poking holes in the testimony of all six accusers. After deliberating for 20 hours, the six-man, two-woman military jury acquitted McKinney on all 18 counts of sexual misconduct. However, it did find him guilty of obstructing justice when Fetrow produced a tape recording in which McKinney urged her to lie to investigators about the nature of their telephone con-versations. He was reduced two grades in rank to master sergeant and officially reprimanded, but he did not re-ceive any jail time. Shortly after his court-martial, Mc-Kinney retired from the army. See also U.S. ARMY'S ABERDEEN SEX SCANDAL.

Denny McLAIN: champion pitcher's downfall in crime

As an outstanding pitcher for the Detroit Tigers profes-sional baseball team, Dennis "Denny" McLain won the American League's Most Valuable Player (MVP) Award in 1968 and the Cy Young Award (for best league pitcher) in 1968 and 1969. At the close of the 1968 season, the 24-year-old McLain had won 31 baseball games, becoming the first pitcher in 34 years to win 30 or more games in a season. But by 1970 his career had taken a scandalous nosedive because of his involvement in mobster-related bookmaking activities.

In early 1967, McLain, an accomplished musician, apparently became involved in an illegal bookmaking operation centered at Detroit's Shorthorn Steak House, where he had been hired to play the organ. A local bookie named George ("Jigs") Gazell, who was said to be a member of a Syrian mob loosely tied to Detroit's Mafia, reportedly offered get-rich-quick promises to McLain if he would back the bookmaking operation with a few thousand dollars. McLain, who liked to gam-ble, fell for the scheme, whose other partners included at least one Syrian mob boss. Previously, McLain had been betting with the Syrians on basketball and hockey games, apparently using the Detroit Tigers clubhouse telephone to place bets, and he had been losing.

Denny McLain, former ace pitcher of the Detroit Tigers, leaves the courthouse in handcuffs in Tampa, Florida, on April 19, 1985, after being sentenced to 23 years in federal prison for racketeering, extortion, and drug charges. In 1987 he was set free when an appeals court ruled he had had an unfair trial. (AP/Wide World Photos)

In the scheme with Gazell, the money that the bettors lost was pocketed by the Syrians, and the payouts on winning bets came partly from the money McLain invested. When a heavy gambler named Ed Voshen "hit" Gazell's bookmaking operation for a $46,000 score (win) on a racehorse, Gazell didn't have the cash to pay Voshen and evidently sent him to McLain and another member of the operation to collect. Failing to get his money, Voshen reportedly approached various mobsters for help, including Tony Giacalone, a Detroit Mafia enforcer. According to an exposé later published in *Sports Illustrated* magazine, Giacalone stomped on McLain's toes, dislocating two of them, in an effort to persuade him to straighten out his gambling debts. Voshen apparently never received the money he had won. He died soon afterwards in a suspicious car accident.

At the time, in September of 1967, when McLain's injury became public, he first claimed that he had stubbed his toes while chasing raccoons. He and his baseball teammates came up with a succession of explanations for his injury, including kicking clubhouse lockers, slipping in a bathtub, and twisting on the pitcher's mound. He did not pitch again until October 1, the final day of the 1967 season. The Detroit Tigers lost that game to the California Angels, thus giving the 1967 American League pennant to the Boston Red Sox by one game. With his injured toes, McLain had trouble pitching. After allowing three runs, he was removed in the third inning. A gangland source later revealed that Giacalone's brother Billy had bet heavily on Boston to win the 1967 pennant and heavily against Detroit in this final, pennant-deciding game with California.

Before *Sports Illustrated* publicized McLain's bookmaking activities, in early 1970, the celebrated Detroit ballplayer had pitched 55 winning games. However, his personality off the field had earned him the ignominious nicknames of "mighty mouth" and "super flake." McLain's $5,700 investment in the bookmaking ring resulted in baseball commissioner Bowie Kuhn suspending him from playing baseball from February 19 to July 1, 1970. McLain, whose annual income was estimated to be $200,000, was hounded by creditors and declared bankruptcy in 1970 after posting a dismal 3–5 record as a pitcher for the season. The next year he was traded to the Washington Senators, for whom he lost 22 games in 1971. He was then kicked down to the minor leagues. He never again regained his former skill.

McLain, who once said, "Me, I like to travel fast—and always first class," declared bankruptcy again in 1977. Afterwards, he seemed to grasp for any fast-money scheme that was offered and to think that he could get away with almost anything. Undoubtedly, these traits helped lead to his indictment in 1984 on multiple racketeering charges. After a 14-week trial ending in March 1985, McLain was convicted of loan sharking, extortion, bookmaking, and drug trafficking. At the time, he weighed 300 pounds (some 115 more than when he was a potential Hall of Famer in the late 1960s). His obesity was attributed to his heavy consumption of Pepsi-Cola. He was sentenced to 23 years at a federal penitentiary, with no eligibility for parole until 1992.

A federal court ruled in August 1987 that McLain had been denied a fair trial; he was subsequently released on a $200,000 bond, having served two and a half years at the federal prison in Talladega, Alabama.

Aimee Semple McPHERSON: vice versus veracity

From May 18, 1926, until January 10, 1927, Aimee Semple McPherson, already famed as a spellbinding female evangelist, was almost constantly front-page news. Americans were aware that she was described in many and contradictory ways: as a drowning casualty, kidnap victim, brave escapee, adored heroine, maligned prevaricator, suspected inamorata, accused hoaxer, public defender of her veracity, and vindicated spokesperson for both faith and femininity.

She gained all these labels in a series of ballyhooed controversies made public property by competing newspapers, radio exposés, rival pulpit commentators, and the ultimately clumsy legal machinery of both the county of Los Angeles and the state of California. Few of the statements, charges, and countercharges made during this period were ever completely investigated; because her status was never finally clarified, Sister Aimee emerged as both the object of insinuating titters and the subject of credulous adoration.

On May 18, 1926, Aimee Semple McPherson, 36-year-old founder of the International Church of the Foursquare Gospel and part-owner of the 5,000-seat Angelus Temple, disappeared during a swim in the Pacific Ocean. Her followers believed that she had been drowned. They mourned her spectacularly, dropping roses from airplanes on the waters and searching for her day and night, at a cost to the searchers of three lives.

Within three days, an undocumented telegram declared her alive and safe. After another four days, a ransom note mailed in San Francisco arrived. Temple members prayed publicly for her deliverance.

As is always the case when a celebrity is missing, false information poured in from several directions. Sister Aimee had been supposedly sighted in Denver, Colorado, El Paso, Texas, and Tucson, Arizona. Someone reported that she had been seen in Santa Barbara, California, in a car driven by the Temple's former radio engineer, Kenneth G. Ormiston.

A second ransom note arrived on June 18. It had been mailed on a train between El Paso and Tucson. At the same time, a Long Beach, California attorney claimed that kidnappers of Aimee had contacted him. The police were forced to double their search.

But on June 23, the problem was solved: Sister Aimee staggered across the border from Agua Prieta (Sonora), Mexico, into Douglas, Arizona, and collapsed. Hospitalized, she told a tale of a dramatic escape from her kidnappers and of a sun-scorched trek across desertlands near Agua Prieta. The Temple followers rejoiced and gave her a tumultuous welcome in Los Angeles, making her momentarily a local heroine.

Sympathy for Sister Aimee turned chilly, however, when most of the details of her story proved unverifiable. A rival in the evangelism business accused her of being a liar. Defending herself publicly in the Angelus Temple and over the temple radio (the third radio station to be established in Los Angeles), Sister Aimee maintained her story and made two much-photographed desert visits to help in its verification.

Even in broad outline, the subsequent events seem somewhat farcical.

Ambitious police and a district attorney anxious both to uphold the law and to gain publicity subpoenaed her into an irregular grand-jury hearing without making a charge. She felt obligated to attack innuendoes against her veracity, calling them part of the devil's plan to destroy the temple. Then the Santa Barbara sighting of her grew into the "Carmel Caper." Ambitious news reporters discovered that Ormiston and a lady friend had rented a cottage in Carmel-by-the-Sea from May 19

through May 29. Newspapers found witnesses who turned the lady friend into Sister Aimee. Papers printed headlines about a "honeymoon cottage" and a "love nest": Sister Aimee protested angrily before the Temple audience.

Through September 1926, more clues poured in, which led to more denials and defenses and more attempts to prove and disprove the "desert trek" story. A self-introduced helper to the temple turned against Sister Aimee and told the police that the kidnapping story was part of a hoax to cover up the Carmel activities. The district attorney, Asa Keyes, then arrested Sister Aimee, her mother (Minnie Kennedy), the disloyal helper (Lorraine Wiseman), and two absent persons (Ormiston and John Doe [sic] Martin) on charges including "conspiracy to commit acts injurious to public morals."

The result was a spectacular preliminary hearing-for-trial beginning on September 27. It established judicial history in California, proved almost nothing, and proceeded theatrically until November 3, accumulating a transcript of 3,600 pages. On good days, Sister Aimee preached on her pending triumph and vindication; on bad days, she wittily demolished the evidence of her detractors. The long-suffering judge found a basis for trial and gave Keyes until January 10, 1927, to file for trial.

Soon afterward, some of the testimony against Sister Aimee was discredited. The district attorney's chief witness on the hoax conspiracy, Lorraine Wiseman, was arrested on a bad-check charge and turned out to have previously been committed as insane because she was prone to elaborate prevarications. Keyes announced on December 29 that he would probably drop the case. Ormiston, however, who had kept in touch by mail, telegram, and affidavit, returned to Los Angeles (courtesy of the Hearst newspapers) and turned himself in. He admitted to sending the May 21 telegram among other things. On December 31, Keyes announced that he would request trial. Sister Aimee was furious.

All Los Angeles was on edge. H. L. Mencken, the famous satirical writer, saw the conflict as one between the newspapers and the radio. He voted for the radio (Sister Aimee's) and commented "Unless I err grievously, our Heavenly Father is on her side."

He was right. On January 10, 1927, Keyes announced that he was dropping all charges against Sister Aimee. He gave no explanation. Alerted, Sister Aimee fainted; on the next day, she left for the East Coast on a "Vindication Tour."

Keyes had noted in his dismissal announcement that decisions on whether Sister Aimee actually took the "desert trek" or was actually in Carmel would be made in the court of public opinion. Despite several books published since 1927 on this inglorious fiasco, the decisions about it have yet to be rendered.

Marvin MANDEL: governor convicted in office

On August 23, 1977, Governor Marvin Mandel of Maryland and five associates were found guilty on 18 charges of mail fraud and racketeering. A federal jury in Baltimore had deliberated the matter for 113 hours—the longest jury deliberation on record in a federal criminal case—before reaching the verdict. The conviction of the 57-year-old Mandel was the first of a sitting governor in more than 50 years, and it came after a lengthy trial that cost him his health, personal holdings, and reputation.

In 1976 the two-term Maryland governor had been brought to trial on the same charges of mail fraud and racketeering. He claimed that he was innocent, and after more than three months of testimony, a mistrial was declared after one of the jurors was reportedly offered a $10,000 bribe to acquit Mandel of all charges. Two men, Walter Weikers and Charles Neiswender, said to have Mafia connections, were found guilty of jury tampering in what was becoming a shady saga concerning the past and present dealings of Marvin Mandel.

At the beginning of his second trial, Governor Mandel's health problems became an important factor; he suffered a stroke and had to be hospitalized, thus forcing the first of several postponements in the court proceedings against him. He was a frail and pitiful figure when he finally went on trial; his own lawyer described him as "a broken man." Mandel continually claimed his innocence, protesting ignorance of the business activities of his five co-defendants—W. Dale Hess, Harry and William Rodgers, Ernest Cory, and Irvin Kovens. The five had illegally bought the Marlboro, Maryland, Race Track in 1972 and had illegally concealed their secret ownership of the track from state officials regulating the industry. Mandel claimed that he hadn't known that his five friends owned the race track when he had used his gubernatorial powers to obtain legislation granting 18 more days to the racing season at Marlboro.

The governor was convicted of accepting $357,000 in cash, loans, investments, goods, and services from the five friends, who were rich, powerful businessmen and politicians. He maintained that the money he received was either for legal fees or represented friendly gifts. One of the "loans" that had come to Mandel through one of his friends was for $42,000 from a Roman Catholic missionary order. It was to help in the governor's alimony payments during his 1974 reelection campaign. Also included in the bribery charges against Mandel were monetary aid in the divorce settlement with his first wife, Barbara (to whom he was married for 32 years), secret inclusion in a land deal and business venture, and thousands of dollars worth of clothing and jewelry that had been lavished on Mandel and his family over the years.

For a time, Barbara Mandel would not move out of the governor's mansion until the terms of the divorce agreement with her husband were guaranteed by Mandel's moneyed businessman friend Kovens. The terms of the agreement came out during the trial and included $120,000 in cash, a new Buick automobile, health insurance, a $100,000 life-insurance policy on the governor, and $135,000 worth of tax-exempt bonds. During the trial, prosecutors accused the governor of having a "corrupt relationship" with the five co-defendants; they charged that he not only condoned the corrupt dealings and subsequent cover-ups, but also joined in "orchestrating" all of the deals in which he and they had participated.

The widespread political influence of Governor Mandel in Maryland necessitated that Judge Robert L. Taylor be sent from Tennessee to hear the federal case. He described it as one of the most troubling in his history on the bench. For his crimes, Mandel could have received up to 105 years in prison and a $42,000 fine, but the judge was lenient and sentenced him, on October 7, 1977, to only four years in prison. By state law, Mandel was automatically suspended as governor of Maryland and from practicing law in the state. Financially insolvent after the trial, he saw his case overturned and then reinstated on appeal in 1979. It went all the way to the U.S. Supreme Court, which declined to hear the case in 1980. Mandel served two years in prison and was released on parole in 1982.

In mid-November, 1987, a federal district judge in Baltimore overturned Mandel's 1977 conviction; the judge cited a recent U.S. Supreme Court ruling that the federal mail-fraud statute could not be used in cases of government corruption. The federal government, however, said it would appeal because the decision could ruin the federal authorities' ability to prosecute local corruption cases.

Donald MANES: a political power's fast downfall

"I would have staked my life on the honesty of Donald Manes. But . . . I am convinced now that he engaged in being a crook," declared New York City's Mayor Edward I. Koch in early February 1986. Koch had just called for his long-time friend Manes to resign as Queens borough president and Queens Democratic party chairman. In a short while, Manes, who was implicated in an extensive extortion-bribery scheme in the city's Parking Violations Bureau (PVB) but was not charged with any crimes, resigned his two posts and, about one month later, committed suicide, tragically ending a once impressive and influential career in New York politics.

A native of New York City, Donald R. Manes was elected to the city council in 1965 at the age of 31. An amiable, burly man, he became, in 1971, the youngest ever to be elected president of the borough of Queens, New York City's largest and most populous administrative unit. With nearly 2 million people, Queens

County by itself would be the nation's fourth biggest city. Named chairman of the Queens County Democratic Organization in 1974, Manes held tight rein over a smooth, efficient, political machine in a borough that almost became his private fiefdom. He voted on the city Board of Estimate, selected the Democrats he wanted to run for local office in Queens, dispensed patronage jobs, and was courted by candidates for the American presidency. He even visited the White House when the Democrats were in power. In short, Manes wielded much political and financial influence for about 20 years.

The downfall of the Queens borough president began early on the morning of January 10, 1986, when police stopped him as he was driving his zigzagging car on a highway in Queens. He was found to be near death, bleeding profusely from knife cuts on his left wrist and ankle. At first he told investigating police that he had been kidnapped and attacked but later on January 21 admitted that the wounds had been self-inflicted.

Soon after Manes's apparent suicide attempt, his close associate and friend Geoffrey G. Lindenauer, who was the PVB's deputy director, was accused of taking a $5,000 payoff from a private company hired by the city to collect overdue and unpaid parking-ticket fines. More bribes from other contracted bill-collection companies had allegedly been paid to Lindenauer, who was suspended without pay from his city job. Apparent misconduct and fraud in the PVB and other New York City agencies led to the resignation of Transportation Commissioner Anthony Ameruso, who oversaw the PVB and was Lindenauer's supervisor. At the same time, the city's anticorruption chief, Investigations Commissioner Patrick McGinley, resigned over an unrelated matter (a city worker's installation of an air conditioner in McGinley's apartment and later application for disability benefits); McGinley denied any wrongdoing. The unfolding bribery scheme grew to implicate Bronx Democratic party leader Stanley FRIEDMAN, who was a Koch supporter. Manes, too, was implicated, for supposedly authorizing payments from a collection company to Lindenauer. He temporarily stepped aside as Queens borough president.

Mayor Koch was admittedly embarrassed and chagrined by the revelations, and city, state, and federal investigators began looking into allegations of graft and corruption within the various city agencies. The mayor said he felt betrayed by Manes, whom he had known for 20 years. Manes, who suffered a heart attack, was pressured to resign his $80,000-a-year borough presidency and nonpaying Democratic party chairmanship. He finally quit on February 11, 1986, citing ill health and accusations of wrongdoing against him as the reasons for his resignation.

There were many probes into city contracts made with companies hired to find parking-ticket scofflaws. These exposed that kickbacks to various city officials had supposedly been required in order to gain contracts for lucrative jobs. For weeks Lindenauer suffered under an intense investigation by federal prosecutors. He finally admitted in federal court on March 10, 1986, that he had extorted $410,000 in bribes from three contractors at the PVB and had shared the money with others.

Three days later, on the evening of March 13, the 52 year-old Manes, who was then under the care of a psychiatrist, ended his life in the kitchen of his home by plunging a 12-inch knife into his heart.

The Manes scandal rocked the Koch administration and spurred numerous investigations reaching into areas of New York City government beyond the purview and the dead Queens borough leader. Mayor Koch, fully aware of the city's often byzantine politics, said he would forbid officers of political parties to do business with the city and instituted other reforms to root out corruption.

Tommy MANVILLE: much money and matrimony

Thomas Franklyn Manville, Jr., the heir to the Johns-Manville asbestos fortune, rivaled Zsa Zsa Gabor and Elizabeth Taylor for trips to the altar. Over a period of 56 years, the perennial bridegroom was wed 13 times to 11 women; all blondes. Divorced nine times and widowed once, the celebrated playboy was married to a woman nearly 40 years his junior at the time of his death.

In 1911 when he was 17 years old, Tommy Manville met Florence Huber, a chorus girl, outside a Broadway theater and married her five days later. His father was furious and had the marriage annulled, but Tommy took Florence to New Jersey and remarried her there. He swore he would remarry her in each of the then 46 states if necessary. To punish his wayward son, Manville senior cut off his allowance and forced him to take a $15-a-week job in the family's factory in Pittsburgh, Pennsylvania, in order to survive. Tommy's marriage to Florence lasted 11 years, a record for him, although they had separated after six years before divorcing in 1922.

Tommy's second wife was none other than his father's 22-year-old stenographer, Lois Arline McCoin. A month after their marriage in 1925, his father died, and Tommy inherited about $10 million. Thereafter he defined his occupation as "looking after my estate." But money did not make a happy marriage, and after a year, Lois charged Tommy with desertion and received a $19,000-a-year settlement. Over the years to come, Tommy would pay out approximately $1.25 million in marriage settlements, all accompanied with much publicity and fanfare.

A series of short lived marriages followed. Number three was to a Ziegfeld Follies girl who had been married twice before herself. Avonne Taylor and Tommy separated in 1931 after 34 days of matrimony and were divorced within six months. In 1933, Tommy married another showgirl, Marcelle Edwards, and this union lasted four years. A fourth showgirl, Bonita Edwards, was next in 1941, but she and Tommy were divorced after three months. Subsequently, in 1942, Tommy married a young actress, Wilhemlina (Billy) Boze. They divorced five months later. Billy was unique among Tommy's wives in that she refused to accept any of his money as a settlement. Macie Marie "Sunny" Ainsworth was almost as fickle as Tommy, for she had been married four times before her marriage to him in 1943. They split after only eight hours.

During these years, Tommy and his wives lived in a 27 room mansion, Bon Repose, at Premium Point in New Rochelle, New York, on Long Island Sound. Between wives, he proudly entertained a vast array of women there. In 1944, he decided to auction off all his household goods. Thousands of people paid 50 cents apiece to walk through the house to inspect the items prior to the auction. When the sale began, even the auctioneer was amazed at the prices individuals were willing to pay for something that had belonged to the flamboyant Tommy Manville—$60 for a pair of chrome-plated trash cans, for example. The U.S. Office of Price Administration learned that radios and some photographic equipment were selling at the auction for more than their fixed wartime ceiling prices and obtained a court order to check the extravagant bidding. When Tommy heard about this, he exclaimed, "They should put a ceiling on blondes. That would have saved me a lot of money years ago."

Tommy's eighth wife, in 1945, was English-born Georgina Campbell, who was killed in an automobile crash in 1952. They had been separated at the time. Tommy did not remain a widower for long, however. He soon married songwriter Anita Frances Roddy-Eden, but within a month she went to Mexico to obtain a divorce which became effective in August 1952. Instead of alimony, she accepted a $100,000 settlement. When he was 63 years old in 1957, Tommy married 26-year-old Pat Gaston, yet another showgirl, but they were divorced six months later. Each marriage and divorce created a spate of publicity, which Tommy seemed to adore.

By this time Tommy had moved to a new estate in Chappaqua, New York. He called it his fortress, for it was protected by armed guards and an elaborate alarm system. He frequently strode around his grounds with pistols on his belt. Despite these precautions, burglers did break into the mansion while Tommy was away and stole an undetermined amount of furs, jewelry, cash, and men's clothes.

Tommy's last wife was Christina Erdlin. The 20-year-old blonde was married and working as a waitress when he met her while having dinner with his attorney. He fell for her and she for him in 1960. The "Marrying Manville," as he once called himself, wedded her, and they stayed together until Tommy's death on October 8, 1967, at the age of 73, in Chappaqua. He willed Christina and her daughter by her former husband the bulk of his fortune.

Edward MARKOWITZ: seller of spurious tax shelters
Government officials labeled the enormous financial sham engineered by Edward A. Markowitz "the largest tax-fraud case ever prosecuted." In a federal district court in New York City on April 25, 1985, the 35-year-old Markowitz pleaded guilty to charges of promoting fraudulent and illegal income-tax deductions amounting to at least $445 million. Some 200 investors, including a number of big-name celebrities, had been lured unwittingly into Markowitz's operation and subsequently lost most of their investments.

In 1983 the Internal Revenue Service (IRS) became suspicious of Markowitz's transactions. The successful financier, who was a graduate of the Massachusetts Institute of Technology and a former commodities trader for Merrill Lynch, Incorporated, had supposedly created and marketed nearly a half a billion dollars in bogus federal income-tax deductions through shelters involving the fictitious buying and selling of U.S. government securities and precious-metals, forward contracts (agreements for future delivery of specified amounts of gold and silver at a given date and price; such securities and contracts are not regulated by the U.S. government). From 1979 to 1983, Markowitz and some partners had reportedly carried on this colossal sham through offices he had set up in Washington, D.C. (where he usually lived and worked), New York, and Chicago. Investors in Markowitz's daring enterprise believed they were taking legitimate tax deductions, varying from $4 to $10 for every dollar they laid out. The deductions, they were told, were the result of the business's whopping losses in its securities activities, an acceptable tax write-off.

Government attorneys claimed that Markowitz faked his securities transactions, using phony documents to record phony trades. Evidently, $60 million of the tax deductions had gone to his colleagues in the five limited partnerships that he had formed to trade securities and stock. Additionally, over $385 million more in false deductions had been "sold" to individuals; the IRS believed that this amount might be recoverable from these investors, who faced monstrous bills for back taxes, interest, and penalties.

Among the scores of persons who had been taken in by Markowitz's tax shelter deals were filmmaker-comedian Woody Allen, entertainer Dick Cavett, comedian Bill Murray, author Erica Jong, actors Frank Langella and Christopher Walken, and other luminaries. On the supposedly sound advice of their financial experts, accountants, or lawyers, they had invested much money (sometimes hundreds of thousands of dollars) with Markowitz. However, as U.S. Attorney for New

York Rudolph Giuliani pointed out, these celebrities "didn't know Markowitz directly and thought the transactions were legal" and therefore were not prosecuted. In the federal probe of the bogus tax shelters, Markowitz's accountant, Peter Stefanou, pleaded guilty in New York City to tax evasion in June 1986. Other accountants and financial advisers who steered their well-to-do and wealthy clients to Markowitz were expected to be similarly charged.

Markowitz, whom associates once described as "a short, overweight young man who liked to wear jeans and deck shoes to the office and who didn't always pay attention to business details," agreed to plead guilty, to cooperate in the complex investigation, and to pay what he owed the government (possibly as much as $4.5 million); in addition, he faced long imprisonment and a stiff fine. The government seemed likely to confiscate his $500,000 home in Washington, D.C., his Park Avenue apartment in New York City, his several racehorses, and his 2.5 percent interest in the Washington Capitals ice-hockey team. The bearded Markowitz pleaded guilty to four federal charges: conspiracy to defraud the government, evading more than $1 million in taxes on his 1981 personal return, and two charges of helping to file false tax returns of limited partnerships.

MARLBOROUGH GALLERY: the exploited estate of Mark Rothko

A grandfather of Abstract Expressionism and one of the world's most renowned living artists, Mark Rothko, run down from excessive drinking and suffering from depression, took his own life on February 25, 1970. The 66-year-old artist had stipulated in his will that all of his unsold work—798 paintings—were to be left to the charitable foundation he had established earlier to safeguard his "artistic remains" after his death. A year later Frank K. Lloyd, multimillionaire owner of the Marlborough Gallery, the prestigious gallery where Rothko exhibited his work, was accused of conspiracy and conflict of interest in selling and consigning a large number of Rothko paintings. Accused along with him were the three executors of the Rothko estate.

The Russian-born Mark Rothko was a founder of New York's Abstract Expressionist School, the first world art movement to originate in the United States. Essentially a self-taught artist who first worked in a realistic style (his *Subway* series of the late 1930s is probably the most famous of these works), he was influenced by the surrealists, experimented with abstraction, and, after World War II, spent the remainder of his life refining an abstract style of arrangements of color and design, often painting immense canvases. *Black on Grey* (1970) was his last series of paintings. Sensitive, introspective, and independent, Rothko got caught up in the glamour of the modern art world after signing an exclusive contract with Frank Lloyd, who had been a co-founder of Marlborough Fine Arts in London, England.

The Austrian-born Lloyd, who had changed his name from Franz Kurt Levai after settling in England in 1940 when fleeing the Nazis, successfully set up associated art galleries around the world, such as New York's Marlborough Gallery, and masterfully merchandised art work of the Old Masters as well as contemporary artists. Lloyd's rich international Marlborough art cartel, which eventually ran some 21 legal entities (mostly in trusts from Switzerland), was expert at controlling the flow of art for public sale; the market value of art was manipulated by keeping a small supply to create a big demand. Lloyd's personal American assets were valued at about $30 million by 1975.

At first the value of Rothko's estate was set at $5 million; later, however, his canvases alone were set at $32 million. The executors of Rothko's will were painter Theodoros Stamos, Professor Morton Levine, and accountant Bernard J. Reis, who was director of the Rothko Foundation and a director and secretary of the New York Marlborough Gallery. Rothko's widow was furious when the gallery seized 13 paintings from his studio "for safekeeping." Though she demanded they be returned, the gallery took 13 more. She died several months later, and her daughter, Kate Rothko, became embroiled in the fight against the gallery and the executors of her father's estate.

Reis had told the two other executors that hundreds of thousands of dollars were needed by the foundation to care for the Rothko pictures, to pay large bills, and to cover legal expenses. Thus, 100 Rothkos were sold by the executors to the Marlborough Gallery for $1,800,000 (or $18,000 each), payable over 12 years without interest. The gallery, however, had already been contracted to purchase four Rothkos a year at the then-current market price however, of $50,000 each.

Stamos was granted a one-man art show for accommodating Lloyd and the Marlborough Gallery in the matter of the Rothko estate. Levine illegally borrowed $5,000 from Rothko's estate and later received another $5,000. Eventually, he paid back the $10,000 loan with interest when he discovered that borrowing money from an estate was illegal for an executor. Through the Lloyd/Marlborough cartel, Reis was eventually able to sell his personal art collection for more than $1 million, while Lloyd was able to sell in public some Rothko paintings for six to 10 times their cost.

Under New York State law, Kate Rothko went to court to claim about 150 paintings due her (after taxes) from her late father's estate. She charged that the three executors of the estate had "entered into a conspiracy with Marlborough Gallery . . . to defraud the estate of Mark Rothko." She also alleged that her father's charitable foundation had been defrauded. The public had been, too, she said. A court-ordered injunction to stop selling Rothko's paintings was given to Lloyd, who ignored it. In 1974 the trial between Kate Rothko and the executors of her father's estate and Frank Lloyd began and went on for eight months, during which the defendants seemed to be obstructing justice. Lloyd finally offered to return 658 paintings and $1 million. Yet there were 104 pictures unaccounted for, which he claimed were "gone" or "sold in bulk." Another 36 had been marketed for $2,474,250, said Lloyd. In time Lloyd turned over 43 of the "sold" 104 Rothko paintings. Kate Rothko was victorious, and the court awarded her damages of $9,252,000, including a fine of $3,875,000 against Lloyd himself for breaking the court's injunction against selling Rothko's paintings. Although Lloyd was accused of perjury and collusion in the case, no one was adjudged guilty, for the court said it was "unnecessary to this decision." Yet during the trial the Marlborough Gallery's record books seemed to have been tampered with: dates had been changed, pages were missing, and transactions concerning Rothko's paintings were incomplete.

The smooth Lloyd was indicted in 1977 for tampering with evidence. Living well in the Bahamas and elsewhere, he was considered "a fugitive from American justice" after a warrant was issued for his arrest. In the meantime, the Art Dealers Association of America expelled the Marlborough Gallery, which continued to prosper after the scandal had died down despite the departure of some of its major art estates, including those of Jackson Pollock and Adolph Gottlieb, two pioneer abstract expressionists. In 1981 Lloyd returned to the United States to face trial, which ended in his conviction for tampering with evidence (a criminal offense) on December 4, 1982. Rather than imprisonment for the 71-year-old offender, he was ordered to set up a scholarship fund and a series of art lectures and private showings for New York City high-school students.

"I collect money, not art," Lloyd once remarked. He also said, "There is only one measure of success in running a gallery: making money." Stricken by strokes in the 1990s, the speech-impaired, wheelchair-bound Lloyd died at his home in the Bahamas on April 7, 1998, at the age of 86.

MARTIAN INVASION: great radio scare of 1938
On the evening of October 30, 1938, the day before Halloween, millions of Americans sat, riveted to their radios as a newscaster on CBS radio announced that 10 spaceships from Mars had landed in Grovers Mills, New Jersey. Word of the invasion spread rapidly, causing mass hysteria throughout the nation. Many believed that the future of civilization was gravely imperiled. The hysteria soon turned to outrage when Americans learned that the radio show was pure science fiction. Although the Columbia Broadcasting System apologized to the public, saying it had not intended to mislead anyone, it

and the show's producers and actors were loudly castigated by various personages and regretted having caused such immediate terror to so many listeners.

The radio program, *The Men from Mars*, was the creation of Orson Welles, actor, director, and co-producer (with John Houseman) of CBS's *Mercury Theatre Of The Air*, which had put on a series of hour-long dramas since opening on July 11, 1938. Welles prevailed upon Howard Koch to write an original radio play based on the short novel *The War of the Worlds*, written by H. G. Wells. Koch was much under pressure to produce a script in six days before its broadcast on October 30. He changed Wells' fantastic Martian attack on Earth into a series of mock radio news bulletins, focusing on Grovers Mills as the supposed invasion point. His ingenious script had numerous authentic details, such as an excited newscaster interrupting "big band" music coming from New York hotels, and a "Professor Pierson" (played by Joseph Cotton) rushing to get to Grovers Mills to see the unidentified flying objects and their occupants. Many at CBS though that the show would be foolish and dull, but Orson Welles went on the air just the same, speaking as a newscaster while reading Koch's script. Although the radio audience heard the announcement that the Mercury Theatre was presenting a radio version of H. G. Wells's novel (it was announced several times during the program), the dramatic broadcast, helped by the authoritative, credible voice of Welles and the other actors, was not doubted. Listeners seemed to ignore CBS messages that the show was only a drama, actually thinking that earthlings were in peril from invading, superior Martians.

Panicky listeners in New Jersey and New York told family members, friends, and neighbors that 10 spaceships from Mars had landed; the "crisis" spread from coast to coast as persons tuned in to CBS radio stations. They believed the phony interviews with terrified government officials and scientists, as well as the killing of a reporter by a Martian ray gun. The panic was intense; telephone lines were tied up by many persons demanding information and advice. In Newark, New Jersey, there was a rumor of a gas bomb attack, and 15 people were hospitalized for shock; in Pittsburgh, Pennsylvania, a husband prevented his wife from fatally poisoning herself; in Kansas City, Missouri, two people suffered heart attacks; in San Francisco, California, a man telephoned saying, "My God, where can I volunteer my services? We've got to stop this awful thing!" It is estimated that as many as a third of the 4 to 6 million listeners (some say the audience totaled 12 million) to the program thought they were hearing the truth. Later, columnist Dorothy Thompson and other news interpreters fulminated against human gullibility as well as radio's inanity and waste.

The day after the unfortunate broadcast, CBS executives publicly apologized for causing the nationwide mass hysteria, which psychologists and other social scientists have studied since to try to understand why Americans reacted so strongly (perhaps the recessionary times and Hitler's dire threats and advances in Europe made people more credulous, and thus the possibility of Martians coming to Earth was considered more readily). The power of the radio was evident in making the drama so immediate. To escape harassment by enraged listeners and hounding journalists, Orson Welles retreated from public view until the furor had died down; "I don't think we will choose anything like this again," he stated to the press upon reappearing. The Federal Communications Commission called the radio show "regrettable" but made no official inquiry and seemed adequately placated when CBS vowed never again to employ "the technique of simulated news broadcast within a dramatization when the circumstances of the broadcast would cause immediate alarm to numbers of listeners."

Despite the widespread notoriety of the 1938 Martian panic, similar scares took place in Chile in 1944 and in Ecuador in 1949, when the radio script (translated into Spanish) was broadcast, with the Martian invasion occurring in those countries. Media responsibility has become a major concern since *The War of the Worlds* caused such consternation more than 50 years ago.

MARTIN and MITCHELL: defectors to the Soviet Union

In 1960, an American U-2 espionage plane was shot down over the Soviet Union and its pilot, Francis Gary Powers, was arrested as a spy. Shortly afterwards, in September of that year, two cryptologists in the National Security Agency (NSA), William H. Martin and his friend Bernon E. Mitchell, intentionally disappeared behind the Iron Curtain. Whether or not Martin and Mitchell, who were familiar with the U-2 spy program, alerted their Russian contacts to Powers's planned flight has never been proven but is strongly suspected. This suspicion is supported by the information released by the Pentagon that Powers's plane had been tracked by Russian radar even before it crossed the Soviet border.

Martin and Mitchell had led nearly parallel lives. Both grew up in typical small American towns on the West Coast, and both exhibited a strong interest and ability in mathematics and science at an early age. As young men, both rebelled against their families' religious beliefs and declared themselves agnostics. When they enlisted in the U.S. Navy, both were assigned to the Yokosuka Naval Base in Japan to do cryptographic work and inevitably became fast friends. After their two-year naval stint, they attended separate universities but kept in touch. Both Martin and Mitchell received bachelor of science degrees in June 1957 and were sworn in the following month as code clerks at the National Security Agency, where their job was to decode and evaluate messages picked up by the American satellite-based receiving stations that circled the Soviet Union. The pair also worked with the recorded messages the U-2s picked up over Russia.

The Federal Bureau of Investigation (FBI) had checked out Martin and Mitchell before they were hired by the NSA and had uncovered nothing suggesting they might someday be disloyal. Later, the FBI received an unconfirmed report that the men were homosexuals, but the charge was not investigated. Martin and Mitchell received top security clearances and had access to information in the NSA's most secret files. They knew the location of every American listening post on the ground and in the air throughout the world. They also knew the mathematical programs of the computers used to devise and break secret codes. This data would enable the Soviets to break the most secret American codes and to undermine the entire American radio intelligence network.

Neither Martin nor Mitchell had shown any interest in politics while in the navy or at college, but in the spring of 1959, they did feel so strongly against the U-2 espionage program that they visited a congressman from Ohio to warn him against its great dangers. How and for what length of time they had then been in contact with Russian agents is uncertain. Martin had studied the Russian language and knew it well enough to translate technical articles, while Mitchell was an avid and expert chess player who probably played with Russian chessplayers in Washington, D.C. Either of these interests could have put the men in touch with subversive agents. When Martin and Mitchell departed on their one-way trip to the Soviet Union in 1960, they took with them invaluable intelligence information. A Pentagon official declared that their defection was "one of the worst security breaches in the nation's history."

Lee MARVIN: pal + alimony

To many Americans, the new word *palimony* immediately brings to mind the name of Lee Marvin, well-heeled Hollywood movie star, who won an Academy Award as best actor of the year for his performance in *Cat Ballou* (1965). Marvin was often typecast as a macho tough guy. His starring roles in *The Man Who Shot Liberty Valance* (1962) and *The Dirty Dozen* (1967) epitomized the stereotype. In 1979 his off-screen personality proved to echo that of his roles. He became notorious for his callous and chauvinistic actions. In 1979, however, he was sued for over $1 million in alimony or, as it soon was called, palimony, by a former girlfriend, singer and actress Michelle Triola, with whom he had lived out of wedlock for six years. The case became the first significant test of the 1976 California Supreme Court decision allowing unmarried couples to sue for property settlements when their relationship ends or if one of them dies.

Actor Lee Marvin (left) ignores his former lover, Michelle Triola (holding a single rose), as they return to superior court in Los Angeles in mid-February 1979. The trial judge rejected an attempt by Triola to seek $1 million in punitive damages for fraud over and above her original demand for half of Marvin's earnings during the six years the two lived together out of wedlock. (UPI/Bettmann Newsphotos)

Michelle Triola claimed that her six-year love affair with Marvin had ended in May 1970 when the once divorced actor unexpectedly married his childhood sweetheart, Pamela. Four days before her relationship with the actor came to an end, Triola had legally changed her surname to Marvin, a strictly personal wish and not done to favor her financially, she asserted. Triola's cold brush-off by Mr. and Mrs. Marvin, as well as her financial cut-off from the prosperous actor, incited her to take legal action and to hire the well-known show-business lawyer Marvin Mitchelson who in 1979 pleaded her case for almost 12 weeks in Los Angeles Superior Court before Judge Arthur K. Marshall.

According to Triola, she had given up her career to take care of Marvin, who apparently fully and willingly supported her as his live-in lady love for six years. The court was shown her letters from the actor indicating his commitment to her and was told that she had had two abortions and a miscarriage because of Marvin's wish not to have any more children and couldn't have children because of this. Marvin's reputed, recurrent hell-raising and heavy boozing were also brought up before the court, which learned that Marvin, during a binge, had allegedly once held a young woman by her ankles out the window of a Las Vegas hotel room. Furthermore, Triola claimed that Marvin's drunken appearances at a nightclub where she had once worked as a singer had finally resulted in her being canned. Marvin casually dismissed his past declarations of true love for Triola as only "idle male promises," thus infuriating Triola and causing her to lash out even more at his alleged lies. In vain, she attempted to double her suit against him, but Judge Marshall rejected her claim to half of the $3.6 million Marvin had earned while the

two were living together and instead, on April 18, 1979, ordered the actor to pay her $104,000 for "rehabilitation purposes." The money was not alimony, according to the court, but for Triola to use to retrain or educate herself for future gainful employment. Undoubtedly the award was much smaller than she expected, but Triola proclaimed it an important feminist victory that would help other women who found themselves in similar circumstances. Marvin also saw the final outcome of the case as a victory, since the court-ordered payment was not considered to be alimony. Perhaps the greatest victor was attorney Mitchelson. He profited substantially, especially from the nationwide publicity about the case, subsequently handling the notable cases of the common-law wives of actor Nick Nolte and rock singer Alice Cooper. In 1980, Lee Marvin said that he was "a changed man," and the public accepted "palimony" as recompense claimed by or awarded to one member of a couple who were unwedded by law and who split up after having lived together for a considerable time. It was even thought to be applicable in cases regarding the breakup of homosexual relationships.

In 1987, at the age of 63, Marvin died of a heart attack in Tucson, Arizona, with his wife Pamela at his side.

MASONRY. See ANTI-MASONRY: reaction begets reform.

MASSIE CASE: rape and racial revenge
Two of the most explosive trials of the 1930s took place in Honolulu, Hawaii. The first involved five Japanese Hawaiians accused of gang-raping the wife of an American naval officer, Lieutenant Thomas H. Massie. The second involved Massie and three accomplices, who

were charged with the murder of one of the accused rapists. Race riots broke out in the islands, and feelings against what the press called "subject races" ran high on the mainland.

Thalia Massie, the attractive, young wife of Lieutenant Massie, left their shore cottage for a stroll by herself along the beach one evening in September 1931. She decided to wade in the ocean, and while splashing in the warm water, she was found by five Hawaiian beach boys who allegedly proceeded to rape her. She was hospitalized, and her mother, Mrs. Granville R. Fortescue, a prominent Washington, D.C., and Long Island, New York, socialite, flew to her side.

News of the event caused American sailors to riot in the streets of Honolulu. Five Hawaiian beach boys were arrested, charged with the rape, and then released on bond. One, Horace Ida, was reportedly captured by American sailors and beaten with a whip. The five were brought to trial, but Mrs. Massie did not testify, and the case against the five of them was not convincing. The jury became deadlocked, and a mistrial was declared. More rioting broke out as Americans and Hawaiians angrily fought each other in a racially tense atmosphere.

Lieutenant Massie then decided to take matters into his own hands. He directed two enlisted seamen, Albert O. Jones and Edward J. Lord, to find one of the boys and bring him to his house. Jones and Lord spotted Joseph Kahawawai on a street, grabbed him, and forced him into a car. A witness to his abduction wrote down the license plate number of the car and gave it to the police. Back at the Massie house, the lieutenant confronted the abducted young Hawaiian, who supposedly confessed to the rape. Enraged, Massie then drew his service revolver and shot Kahawawai in the chest, killing him instantly. Later, Massie testified that "Everyone was in a daze."

Massie and his cohorts decided to fling the body into the sea from a desolate cliff near Koko Head. Kahawawai's corpse was wrapped in a sheet and put in the trunk of the car. Mrs. Fortescue and the two seamen, who had all witnessed the murder, went along. The police, however, stopped the car before it reached its destination, and the four were arrested for murder.

Mrs. Fortescue hired the famous trial lawyer, Clarence Darrow, to represent her and the three other defendants in the case (Massie, Jones, and Lord). Darrow claimed that Massie had suffered from "temporary insanity" but did not admit that Massie had fired the revolver that killed Kahawawai. The trial, held in April 1932 in Honolulu, attracted such attention and unrest that the Marines were soon sent in to maintain order. A polyglot jury of Americans, Chinese, and Hawaiians was finally swayed by Darrow's arguments and found the four guilty of manslaughter instead of first

degree murder. The judge sentenced them to 10 years in prison each.

However, the verdict touched off another wave of race rioting in Hawaii and throughout the United States. Hearst newspapers carried headlines about "the honor slaying," and Congress expressed concern over the fact that as convicted criminals, the four would forfeit their civil rights. A United States senator from Connecticut went so far as to declare that the defendants were "illegally indicted, improperly tried, and never should have been convicted." Other congressmen sought a presidential pardon. Concerned over the matter, President Herbert Hoover called Governor Lawrence M. Judd of Hawaii, who was negotiating with the 75-year-old Darrow over the sentences. Subsequently, the governor ordered that the four defendants be brought to the courtroom dock where, after they were held for one hour, the governor commuted their sentences. As part of the sentencing arrangement, Massie, his wife, and his mother-in-law then immediately boarded a ship and sailed for San Francisco.

Lieutenant Massie remained in the navy, but in 1934, two years after the murder trial, the Massies were divorced. Both ultimately remarried, but Thalia's later life was marred by hospital confinements and suicide attempts, and in 1963, she committed suicide. The four remaining Hawaiian beach boys were never retried because the ex-Mrs. Massie would not testify against them. Her scandalous rape was eventually doubted. Her own gynecologist once stated that "If I had . . . to tell everything I knew . . . it would have made monkeys out of everybody."

"MAYFLOWER MADAM." See Sydney Biddle BARROWS: the "Mayflower Madam."

MAZZEI LETTER
During U.S. President George Washington's last year in office (1796), the friction between the two major American political parties—the Federalists and Republicans (Anti-Federalists)—became intense and virulent. A national scandal was set off when, because of these differing policies, a letter originally penned by Thomas Jefferson appeared in various newspapers across the nation. The letter denounced the Federalists in scathing terms, provoking ire from both Federalists and Republicans.

The Republicans (not to be confused with the Republican party of today, which was founded in 1854), whose principal leaders were Thomas JEFFERSON and Aaron Burr (see BURR-HAMILTON DUEL and BURR'S CONSPIRACY), were pro-French and in favor of strong state governments and an agrarian society. The Federalists, on the other hand, who were led by Alexander Hamilton (the first U.S. Secretary of the Treasury, 1789–95), Vice President John Adams, and President

Washington, were pro-British and conservative and favored a strong national (central) government and encouragement of commerce and manufacturing rather than agriculture. They also advocated a loose interpretation of the Constitution as opposed to the strict interpretation favored by the Jeffersonian Republicans, who defended self-government against the aristocratic and rather authoritarian tendencies of the Federalist party.

In his letter, written on April 24, 1796, Jefferson venomously expressed his sentiments about his Federalist opponents to a radical Italian friend, Filippo (Philip) Mazzei, who had once lived near Monticello (Jefferson's magnificent home near Charlottesville, Virginia). Mazzei, a physician and merchant, had brought from Italy men and materials to undertake silkworm and grape-growing culture in Virginia between 1773 and 1778; afterward he had maintained his friendship with Jefferson in letters from Europe. In his infamous 1796 letter, Jefferson described the Federalists as "an anglican, monarchical, and aristocratic party," and complained that "against us are the executive, the judiciary, and two out of three branches of the legislature." He then bitterly declaimed: "It would give you a fever were I to name to you the apostates who have gone over to these heresies, men who were Samsons in the field and Solomons in the council, but who have had their heads shorn by the harlot England."

The Mazzei letter was published in a newspaper in Florence, Italy, and later appeared in the *New York Minerva* in May 1797. Other newspapers across America picked up the story of Jefferson's criticism and reprinted the scurrilous letter. It was widely believed that the "Samsons" and "Solomons" referred to were Washington, Adams, and Hamilton, although Jefferson privately claimed that he had been alluding to the Society of the Cincinnati, an association of American officers of the Revolutionary War. In any case, personal relations between Washington and Jefferson broke because of the Mazzei letter, which also provoked much animosity and rage against Jefferson from other Federalists. Nonetheless, in the presidential election of 1796, Jefferson received the second largest number of electoral votes and the vice presidency, losing the presidency to Adams by only three electoral votes (68 to 71). (At that time it was possible for men of opposing parties, such as Jefferson and Adams, to win the number one and two positions in the national government because the Twelfth Amendment to the Constitution—clarifying which electoral votes are for the presidency and which for the vice presidency—was not adopted until 1804.) After this, many Federalists continued to distrust and dislike Jefferson, whose Republican party they smeared by giving it the then opprobrious label of "Democratic-Republican party." At this time, the term *democratic* denoted the common citizenry.

Evan MECHAM: governor booted out of office

On April 4, 1988, the Arizona State Senate convicted 63-year-old Governor Evan Mecham of two counts of wrongdoing: that he obstructed justice by discouraging a state official from cooperating in a grand jury investigation of an alleged death threat against one of his former top aides and that he misused $80,000 in public money from a protocol fund by loaning it to his automobile dealership, Mecham Pontiac. He became the first U.S. governor to be impeached and removed from office in nearly 60 years.

Ever since his election as Arizona's governor in 1986, the conservative Mecham had been a controversial figure; he had won the office in his fifth attempt, with 40 percent of the vote in a three-way race that had split the Democratic vote. In his first significant act as governor in early 1987, he rescinded the state's observation of the Martin Luther King, Jr., holiday and, in the following months, made comments, jokes, and slurs that alienated blacks, homosexuals, women, Jews, Japanese, and eventually his fellow Republicans. He defended the use of the word *pickaninnies* for blacks, asked for a listing of state employees who were gay, and later labeled a movement for a recall vote on him the work of a "few homosexuals and dissident Democrats." Embarassed Arizonans cringed in early 1988 when their governor publicly told how a group of Japanese "got round eyes" when talking about golf.

All the while, charges of incompetence, corruption, and impropriety swirled about his administration. He had made some doubtful appointments: his pick for a state investigator's office was a former, twice-court-martialed Marine; his own special assistant was accused of extortion. A special investigator told the Arizona House of Representatives in January 1988 that Mecham had deliberately concealed a $350,000 loan to his 1986 election campaign from a Tempe, Arizona, real estate developer and that the governor had used public funds for personal gain; a grand jury indicted him on two counts of fraud and one count of filing a false report about the large campaign loan. About two weeks later Mecham was officially told that he must resign by January 30 or run in a recall election (the successful result of a voter petition by the Mecham Recall Committee, which had gathered more than 300,000 signatures). The beleaguered governor denied any wrongdoing and refused to quit. All the while, the Arizona house debated over his impeachment.

Finally, the 60-member, Republican-controlled House voted 46–14 to impeach him on February 5, 1988, forcing him to step down from office pending a trial by the Arizona Senate. Mecham became the first governor to be impeached since Arizona was granted statehood in 1912. The House said he had committed high crimes, misdemeanors, and malfeasance in office.

"I remain convinced that if I receive a fair trial, the truth will prevail and I will be acquitted," said Mecham at the start of his trial on February 29. His lawyers insisted that the prosecution had insufficient evidence to convict Mecham of obstructing justice on the alleged death threat; they failed to get a dismissal of the charges against him—23 articles of impeachment (the Senate had, however, dismissed an impeachment charge dealing with the $350,000 loan). Mecham's lawyers urged the senators to acquit him and let him defend his office in a May 17 recall election. The two prosecutors called the governor a liar, citing repeated conflicts in his testimony during his trial.

Then came the verdict on April 4; Mecham showed no emotion and smiled when he walked out of the Senate chamber in Phoenix. "Well, they don't like my politics. So we've finished a political trial," he said. A motion to bar him from ever holding state office again in Arizona fell three votes short of the required two-thirds majority (17 voted in favor, 13 against). Acting governor Rose Mofford, a Democrat, became the new governor upon his conviction. Many felt the buffoonish Mecham had gotten a fair trial, but others said he had been politically assassinated by those who would gain by his ouster.

Earlier in the year, when he had begun collecting $2.5 million as a war chest for his recall campaign, Mecham had uttered these words: "I'm going to make sure the people of this state understand what they did when they elected me, and what they got and what we've done with this, and what the potential is, and what their choices are with somebody else." Arizonans understood and decided.

Mecham still faced a trial in criminal court on six felony counts of concealing the $350,000 campaign loan. On June 16, 1988, an eight-member jury in Phoenix acquitted him of scheming with his brother Willard (who had been treasurer of his 1986 gubernatorial campaign) to hide the loan. See also Fife SYMINGTON: lying over bank loans.

Erik and Lyle MENENDEZ: brothers who killed their parents

José Menendez was the personification of the American dream come true. Born in Cuba in 1948, he immigrated to the United States to escape the Castro regime and settled in southern California. He became involved in the entertainment business and eventually started his own music and video distribution company. The business was so successful that by age 45 he had amassed an estate worth $14 million and entertained the ambition of becoming the first Cuban-born U.S. senator.

The Menendez brothers, Erik (right) and Lyle, leave the courtroom in Santa Monica, California, on August 6, 1990; they were charged with gunning down their parents on August 20, 1989, in their Beverly Hills mansion. A California jury later convicted them (March 10, 1996) of first-degree murder and conspiracy in their second trial. (AP/Wide World Photos)

José's dream came to an abrupt end in August 1989, when he and his wife Kitty were found dead in the gore-splattered TV room of their Beverly Hills mansion. The cause of death was 15 shotgun blasts, two of which had been fired at point-blank range. The murdered couple was discovered by their sons Lyle, 21, and Erik, 18, who speculated that the perpetrators were Mafia hit men.

However, the search for the murderers pointed increasingly in the direction of the two brothers. The savagery of the murders argued against a Mafia hit, which is typically much cleaner and more efficient than the Menendez murders. Instead of grieving for their murdered parents, Lyle and Erik went on a $700,000 shopping spree. A search of the Menendez home turned up a computer disk which supposedly held Jose's revised will; however, investigators discovered that the disk had been erased. A shotgun shell was found in the pocket of Lyle's jacket. Finally, a woman told police that she overheard the brothers confess the murders to their psychoanalyst and that the confessions had been taped. Seven months after the murders, the brothers were behind bars for allegedly killing their parents.

In their defense, Lyle and Erik claimed that they were driven to murder José and Kitty by years of physical and sexual abuse which they had suffered at the hands of their parents. Both brothers testified that they had been beaten and punched by their father. Lyle claimed that José had sodomized him with a toothbrush when he was little and that Kitty had forced him to touch her intimately on a number of occasions until he was 13. Erik claimed that José had abused him sexually for years and had done so shortly before his death. When Erik told Lyle about the abusive relationship, Lyle confronted his father in an effort to protect Erik. But rather than agree to leave Erik alone, José made what Lyle claimed was a veiled threat against Lyle's life. Fearing that their parents were plotting to kill them in order to keep them from going to the police and ruining José's political future by charging him with incest, the brothers apparently murdered their parents in self-defense.

The brothers' legal strategy tested the limits of the "battered child syndrome" defense. According to this argument, a person who has been beaten for years can feel threatened by an action or look that would not be threatening in the slightest to a person who has not suffered such abuse. Consequently, the manner in which José and Kitty retired to the TV room on the night they were murdered may have been perceived by Erik and Lyle as a threat against the brothers' lives. In court, a parade of psychiatrists and child-abuse experts testified that the brothers had been so traumatized by parental abuse that they were driven to commit the murders as an act of self-defense and that the shame and humiliation they felt as a result of the abuse prevented them from reporting their parents to the police. The expert testimony was convincing enough that the juries (the brothers were tried simultaneously but before two different sets of jurors) deadlocked concerning their fate, resulting in two mistrials.

The brothers were retried together in 1996, and this time the jury rejected their claim of self-defense. Instead, the jury decided that the brothers had worked out the details of their "battered child syndrome" defense while in jail, and they convicted Lyle and Erik of premeditated (first-degree) murder. The judge sentenced the brothers to life in prison without parole.

METROPOLITAN MUSEUM OF ART. See RICCARDIS' ETRUSCAN FORGERIES: fakes in the Metropolitan Museum of Art.

General Bennett MEYERS: dereliction results in disgrace

In less than five years, revelation of the past delinquencies of former U.S. Major General Bennett ("Benny") E. Meyers permanently shattered his reputation. In 1945, Meyers had had the world by the tail, having been retired as a major general following distinguished service during World War II as the number two purchasing agent for the U.S. Air Force. Awarded the Distinguished Service Medal, he had been enrolled in the Legion of Merit for his Air Technical Service Command activity and had been granted a pension of $550 a month. Two years later, Meyers had been stripped of his honors, was deprived of his pension, and was about to face a federal court trial, a personal income-tax investigation, a corporate tax investigation, and a possible court-martial. By 1952 he was a ruined man.

Meyers's decline began late in 1947 when a U.S. Senate subcommittee investigating wartime contract irregularities heard his name in connection with the misdeeds of the Hughes Aircraft Corporation. Called to testify, Meyers lied, fabricating ingenious explanations for his involvement in contracts awarded to Hughes, falsehoods contradicted by Hughes and other witnesses. Their further testimony implicated Meyers in illegal purchases of government bonds on margin, in attempts to influence New York state officials into raising a ban on Hughes's film *The Outlaw,* in the unreported ownership of aviation stocks, and in falsely representing the Aviation Electric Corporation of Dayton, Ohio, by setting up a dummy president of the corporation, one Bleriot H. Lamarre, to camouflage Meyers's personal ownership of the firm. After his dissembling, this misrepresentation was Meyers's greatest abuse: Aviation Electric had received, through Meyers's finagling, a wartime contract of $470,000, from which Meyers had taken an undeclared profit of almost one-third.

After the Senate subcommittee hearings ended in December 1947, the false structure that Meyers had erected slowly collapsed. The air force not only took back his honors and his retirement pay, but also dismissed him dishonorably. The District of Columbia federal court found him guilty of perjuring himself before the Senate subcommittee, dictating a prison sentence of up to five years (appeals failing, Meyers requested release but achieved parole only in 1951). In April 1948, tax officials began to attach liens to his estate; when they grew to more than half a million dollars, Meyers had to sell his Long Island, New York, mansion. Dayton, Ohio, indicted him for tax evasion in May 1948, and he was slapped in June of that year with a defamation suit for falsely claiming that Lamarre's wife had been his mistress. In 1949, now without an estate, Meyers's offer to settle the federal tax-evasion case against him for $50,000 was refused and, adding insult to injury, his high-living wife sued for and gained a divorce from him.

Meyers's downfall continued through 1952, when his descent from war hero to convict reached its nadir. His parole in 1951 was almost immediately followed by a federal tax indictment, trial, and conviction; sentenced in April 1952, he appealed the verdict, but his appeal was turned down the following year.

MIDNIGHT JUDGES. See John ADAMS: "The Duke of Braintree" canard.

Michael MILKEN: fallen "junk bond king"

During the 1980s, American business was inundated by a wave of takeovers and buyouts. Many profitable companies were acquired by corporate raiders who then sold off the most lucrative divisions, while many more were bought by their executives and managers in an attempt to thwart a raid. Most of these takeovers and buyouts were financed by junk bonds, a type of security made popular by Michael R. Milken (1946–), the decade's most influential and powerful financier.

Junk bonds derived their name from the fact that they were usually offered by ailing and risky companies whose low credit ratings forced them to offer significantly higher interest rates than healthy companies. Milken became interested in junk bonds as an undergraduate business student at the University of California at Berkeley. He continued to study them at the University of Pennsylvania's Wharton School of Business and, after 1970, as a trader with the Philadelphia investment firm of Drexel Firestone (later known as Drexel Burnham Lambert). He discovered that junk bonds rarely defaulted; thus their high interest rates offered yields higher even than blue chip securities. He concluded that junk bonds presented small and medium companies, whose credit ratings were not as high as Fortune 500 corporations, with an excellent way to raise capital.

By 1978, when he moved Drexel's junk bond division from New York to California, Milken was selling millions of dollars of junk bonds issued by small and medium companies to institutional money managers, who were constantly looking for ways to obtain higher returns on their investments. But junk bonds did not take off until 1983 when Milken began touting them as a means by which corporate executives who were long on managerial expertise but short on capital could purchase their companies. He also began promoting junk bonds to major investors who wanted to acquire large corporations such as Gulf Oil, Revlon, and Safeway Stores. Four years later, as a result of Milken's pioneering role, investors held $150 billion in junk bonds. Milken, the "junk bond king" and the new darling of Wall Street, had pocketed $1.5 billion in salary, commissions, and fees.

In 1988 Milken's world began to unravel. A $220 million suit brought against Drexel by Staley Continental, which was settled out of court, charged that Drexel approached Staley's top executives in an effort to get them to buy their company, first by assuring them of making huge profits and then by suggesting that a raider could be found who would take over Staley and fire them. Then the Securities and Exchange Commission (SEC) charged Milken, Drexel, and several Drexel employees with insider trading, defrauding their own customers, disguising their ownership of certain stocks, and attempting to cover their tracks by destroying records. According to the government, between 1984 and 1986 Milken arranged for Ivan BOESKY, a Wall Street speculator, to use Boesky's and Drexel's money to buy and hold in Boesky's name large blocks of stock in companies that Milken's clients were trying to take over. This maneuver drove up the price of the stock, thus increasing the amount of the issues Milken was arranging for his clients as well as his fees and Drexel's profits.

Although it initially denied the charges, by year's end Drexel had agreed to plead guilty and pay a $650 million fine. In 1989 Milken was forced to resign from Drexel when the SEC charged him with 98 counts of criminal racketeering, securities fraud, and other crimes. Although he vowed to fight the charges against him, in April 1990 he pleaded guilty to six counts of securities fraud and later agreed to pay a $600 million fine, the largest fine ever levied against an individual in U.S. history. He was also sentenced to 10 years in federal prison, although he only served two (being released on March 2, 1993).

While Milken unsuccessfully sought a way out of his legal predicament, the junk bond industry that he worked so hard to build was collapsing. By 1990 the default rate on junk bonds had risen to 10 percent, a figure that many investors regarded as unacceptable. This development, combined with a slumping economy and a federal law prohibiting savings and loans from owning junk bonds, eroded the value of virtually all junk bonds, some by as much as half.

Milken was considered the chief architect of Wall Street's Roaring Eighties, a decade devoted to manic deal-making fueled by excessive greed. His fall marked the end of that era. In a jailhouse interview in early 1992, Milken said he "wasn't basically focused on making money," he regretted dealing with Boesky (whose "squealing" to authorities led to his prosecution), and he had sounded an early warning about high corporate debt and hostile takeovers and had never traded on insider information, as was alleged in the *Wall Street Journal* reporter James Stewart's best-selling book *Den of Thieves* (1991). In the end, after completing 1,800 hours of community service work to fulfill his 1990 sentence, Milken was left with several hundred million dollars still remaining from his 1980s fortune. See also Ivan BOESKY: fraudulent Wall Street superstar.

Thomas MILLER: fraud as Harding's Alien Property Custodian

Successful, respected, and well connected socially, Thomas Miller seemed the least likely person in the administration of Warren G. Harding to be involved in fraud. But his criminality, though not nearly as major as that of other Harding appointees (see TEAPOT DOME, Charles R. FORBES, and Jesse W. SMITH), was serious enough to land him in jail for over a year.

A war hero, a former Delaware congressman, and a highly regarded lawyer, Miller had commendable connections. He was one of the original incorporators of the American Legion and held membership in the Union League Club, the Yale Club, the National Press Club, and the prestigious Wilmington (Delaware) Country Club. His social connections have made some historians wonder why he yielded to temptation. Perhaps he was behind in his dues.

Miller's legal experience in handling cases of international importance made logical his appointment as alien property custodian, an office concerned with the American assets of companies owned by countries against whom World War I had been fought. Except for the error that put him in prison, Miller did the job well.

He was pressed into fraud by two of Harding's cronies, Jesse W. Smith and John T. King (a campaign manager for Harding's rival in Ohio's 1920 presidential primary). They got Miller to agree in 1921 to transfer the previously German-owned American Metal Company to a German syndicate headed by Richard Merton. Sold during World War I, with its purchase price turned into Liberty Bonds, the company, in the settlement engineered by Miller, cost American citizens $6.5 million.

To gain control of this plum, the German banking syndicate fronted by Merton was willing to pay substantial bribes. King acted as the broker in the deal, receiving cash and Liberty Bonds worth $441,300. He then gave Smith $224,000 of this and presented Miller with $50,000. And even though he and Smith were, administratively speaking, outsiders, King took the remainder, $267,300.

In the end, however, Miller got his comeuppance. A 1923 Senate investigation of the handling of foreign matters by the alien property custodian's office detected the crime, and in 1926 King and Miller were indicted for defrauding the government. Both were found guilty.

Miller received a fine of $5,000 and a prison term of 18 months, of which he served 13 months (for which, on the basis of his remaining illegal profit, he gained a "wage" of $3,461.54 per month). Released, he retreated into obscurity but not at the Wilmington County Club, which had revoked his membership at the time of his trial.

Wilbur MILLS: the Tidal Basin incident

As the long-time chairman of the House Ways and Means Committee, U.S. Representative Wilbur Daigh Mills (Dem., Ark.) wielded extraordinary legislative power and influence, frequently dictating what the federal government's fiscal policy would be. His boldness, independence, and tough-mindedness earned him at times the begrudging respect of Presidents Kennedy, Johnson, and Nixon. In 1974, however, Mills suffered an unexpected downfall. It was at this time that the public learned of his extramarital affair with Fanne Foxe, a striptease artist. Soon afterwards the Ways and Means Committee removed him from its chairmanship. Mills himself blamed alcoholism for his erratic and scandalous behavior.

The Tidal Basin in Washington, D.C., was the scene of a strange, loud disturbance at about 2 A.M. on the night of October 7, 1974. According to reports, 38-year-old Fanne Foxe (born as Annabel Battistella) had jumped out of Mills's car and somehow fallen into the waters of the Basin (she later denied the report that she had thrown herself in, in a suicide attempt). The police had followed the fast-moving car with its lights out and had come upon the car's three high-spirited passengers—Foxe, Mills, and a masseuse—who were then taken into custody (at first, Mills claimed that he had not been in the car, but his identity was later ascertained, and the noctural doings gained newspaper headlines).

The Arkansas Hunkerer, as Mills was nicknamed, first met The Argentine Firecracker, as Foxe was billed, in 1973 at a nightclub called the Silver Slipper, where the latter appeared on stage to do a striptease dance. Immediately Mills became enamored of Foxe's charms. He apparently even considered buying the club until he learned that at one time it had been shut down for prostitution. Mills was a big spender on the club's liquor, dropping hundreds of dollars for drinks. His reckless spending eventually aroused the attentions of congressional colleagues.

After the incident, which made her a minor celebrity, Foxe began billing herself as The Tidal Basin Bombshell. She received offers to appear in other clubs, and her weekly earnings went from some $600 to $3,000. Mills, who was surprisingly reelected to his House seat in November 1974, openly acknowledged the stripper as a good friend and appeared with her on the stage of a Boston, Massachusetts, burlesque house (to the shock of many), where he called her his "G-string hillbilly." The subject of derision, Mills seemed rather out of control at the time and, on December 3, 1974, was rushed to Bethesda Naval Medical Center pleading utter "physical exhaustion." Meanwhile, the House Democratic caucus secretly voted to take away the longstanding authority of the Ways and Means Committee (a major source of Mills's power) and to assign its members to other committees. The chairmanship was temporarily placed in the hands of U.S. Representative Al Ullman of Oregon, the committee's second-ranking Democrat. On December 10, Mills resigned his leadership.

Foxe was given a $13,000-a-week stage appearance, at the start of which she removed her G-string and was arrested for indecent exposure. After being set free on bail, she resumed her dancing but tearfully announced there would be no more stripping, since it was an embarassment to Mills. On December 30, 1974, the public heard the former Ways and Means Committee Chairman announce that his bizarre behavior was due to alcoholism and that he would be a teetotaler thereafter, committing himself to a medical clinic for help for about a month. At the time he also said he would keep his seat in the House. Later, he gave Foxe a Cadillac and attempted to take up with her again, but their relationship fell apart. The scandal petered out but not before Foxe's autobiography, *The Congressman and the Stripper,* was published, alleging that she had been impregnated by Mills but had had an abortion for fear that the baby would be malformed because of the congressman's alcoholism. All of this was denied by the 66-year-old Mills, who bowed out of politics in 1975 and subsequently turned much attention to combating alcoholism. He said that before recognizing that he was an alcoholic, he had thought he had a fatal brain tumor and added, "I guess I was trying to kill myself with liquor."

Mills headed the House Ways and Means Committee for nearly half of the 38 years he served in Congress; he wrote much of the tax code before leaving office. Later, as a recovered alcoholic, he spoke to civic clubs, state legislatures, and congressional committees about "curing" alcoholism. On May 2, 1992, he collapsed at his home in Kensett, Arkansas (his birthplace), and died at age 82.

MISSISSIPPI BUBBLE

Scottish financier John Law is remembered for founding the city of New Orleans, Louisiana, and for instigating the "Mississippi Bubble," which burst in 1720 and brought financial ruin to hundreds of thousands. To many, Law was a monetary genius, but his extraordinary ability was quickly discredited by the sudden bankruptcy of his stock company and the consequent collapse of his banking system.

At the death of King Louis XIV in 1715, France lacked financial stability, and its government wanted to establish some kind of central banking system, similar to those of its rivals Britain and Holland. The country had an enormous national debt that Law, who had earlier made a fortune through gambling and had settled in 1714 in Paris, claimed he could reduce while stimulating French trade and industry (in 1700, Law, an ambitious banker with ideas about revenue reforms, had failed to interest the Scottish parliament in setting up a national bank that could issue paper currency). Law was persuasive and able to gain the favor of the Duke of Orléans, Philippe II, who was regent of France during the mi-

nority of King Louis XV. In 1716, by royal authority, the Scotsman founded the first bank of any kind in France, the private Banque Générale, which was empowered to issue paper money. Law believed that credit and bank notes (paper) would help to revitalize France's economy; he saw the circulation of paper money as a way to arouse the dormant commercial energy of the nation.

In 1717, Law's business reputation as a successful banker enabled him to take over the government contract that had been awarded earlier to Antoine Crozat, a rich private merchant and financier with many trading ventures, to develop commercially and colonize the lower Mississippi River valley in America. Crozat had failed to find the rich mineral deposits that were rumored to exist in the area and had suffered large financial losses, but his agents had set up some useful trading posts. Law then organized the Compagnie d'Occident ("the Western Company") for the colonial exploitation and development of the Louisiana Territory and, with backing from the regent, undertook the task of raising venture capital for the project. Law's company was commonly referred to as the Mississippi Company; it controlled large tracts of land around the Mississippi River and had exclusive trading rights in the area; in 1718 it financed the settlement of New Orleans, named after the regent.

Law kindled new enthusiasm for Louisiana and its potential riches through misleading real-estate promotions. He painted the place in exaggerated terms, saying that there was abundant silver, gold, and other minerals and thus launching a public campaign to get needed capital to begin extensive French expansion in the New World. He exuded confidence that encouraged investment in his company, which in 1719 absorbed several rival trading firms in the East Indies, China, and Africa, and was afterward renamed the Compagnie des Indies. Meanwhile, the powerful Scotsman's private bank was made the royal bank, with him at the helm and its paper money guaranteed by the state. His huge company assumed the national debt and the farming of taxes and was merged with the royal bank of France in 1720.

The French had great confidence in Law and his Mississippi scheme and banking system. The government solidly backed him, and many influential and important persons bought stock in his company in anticipation of reaping huge profits, although there was an almost complete lack of any real assets in the colonial areas. Many small investors were invited to buy shares, which were sold at 10, 20, 30, and even 40 times their value. For a year or so Law was the most popular man in Europe, and a frenzy of speculation swept over France. The government took advantage of it by issuing more paper currency, which was willingly taken by Law's public creditors. Stock in the Compagnie d'Occident rose in price to successively greater heights, becoming ridiculously inflated. Some well-informed speculators began selling their stock, made enormous profits, and impaired public confidence in the company, which had over-expanded and couldn't be expected to return such gains. Huge quantities of paper money that the company is-sued contributed to a rapid decline in the value of its stock, until suddenly, in October 1720, the company went bankrupt and Law's banking system caved in.

The French government was in crisis and eventually accepted itself as debtor to the stockholders. Law was bitterly attacked for his grand financial schemes, his banking system was abolished, and he secretly had to flee France in total disgrace in December 1720. He went to Venice, where he supported himself by gambling. He died there, a pauper, at the age of 58 in 1729. The increasing issuance of paper money did not automati-cally bring wealth to people, as Law had fallaciously thought.

William "Billy" MITCHELL: "fool Mitchell luck!"

William Mitchell had a vision: the United States Air Force could be an independent military force, greater even than the army or the navy. His vision became an obsession, and he was demoted, court-martialed, and finally suspended from the army for insubordination. Not until after his death were Mitchell's ideas valued.

In 1898 Billy Mitchell, as he was called throughout his life, left college to enlist as an army private in the Spanish-American War. Friendly and outgoing, he re-ceived in 1901 a commission as a first lieutenant in the regular army after service in Cuba and the Philippines, was promoted to captain in 1903, was graduated from the Army Staff College in Fort Leavenworth, Kansas, in 1909, and was assigned to the aviation division of the Army Signal Corps in 1915.

With little instruction, Mitchell learned to fly military aircraft. He advanced to the rank of major in 1916, pro-pounding the importance of air power superiority in war, and was sent to Europe for duty in World War I. Highly respected as a military leader and extremely ca-pable as a pilot, Mitchell again rose in rank to lieutenant colonel when he was made commander of the air forces of the American Expeditionary Forces in 1917. He reg-ularly flew combat missions in the war, becoming the first American airman to fly over enemy territory. Up-graded again to colonel in 1918, Mitchell led nearly 1,500 American and French planes in a successful bomb-ing raid on German positions in France's Saint-Mihiel area and afterward commanded a destructive bombing attack over enemy lines during the Meuse-Argonne campaign. Now a temporary brigadier general and a combat hero, he planned to strike deep into Germany but was interrupted by the armistice of November 11, 1918, which ended the war.

Mitchell returned home to be appointed the assistant chief of the U.S. Army Air Service, but his outspoken-ness about the country's need for a strong, separate air force and the military superiority of the airplane over the battleship and artillery gained him enemies in Congress, the navy, and the War Department. When

Colonel Billy Mitchell (seated at witness table), vigorous and outspoken advocate of American air power, was court-martialed for "conduct of a nature to bring discredit upon the military service." He was found guilty on December 17, 1925. (AP/Wide World Photos)

America's military brass appeared to be abandoning the possibility of an independent air force in 1921, Mitchell tried to prove his point by staging demonstrations of the effectiveness of warplanes against battleships in 1921 and 1923. Mitchell's actions failed to impress the necessary people, however. In 1921, after Mitchell's land-based air squadron sought out, bombed, and sank the captured German battleship *Ostfriesland* in bad weather, his government critics simply wrote off the success as "fool Mitchell luck." High military leaders were increasingly annoyed by Mitchell's statements about America's ill-prepared, poorly equipped air force, resulting eventually in Mitchell's transfer to a minor post as an air officer in San Antonio, Texas, and his downgrading to colonel from brigadier general in 1925.

In September 1925, when the navy's dirigible *Shenandoah* was ruined in a storm in Ohio, Mitchell told the press that blame rested on "the incompetency, criminal negligence, and almost treasonable administration of the national defense by the War and Navy Departments." This promptly resulted in Mitchell's court-martial, which was held in a deserted warehouse in Washington, D.C. The hearing served as yet another stage for Mitchell's views: that a strategic air force would make navies obsolete and that the military was neglecting air power. Although famed aviator Eddie Rickenbacker, Major Carl Spaatz, and others testified for Mitchell, the court of nonflying judges, presided over by General Charles P. Summerall, convicted him of insubordination and suspended him from rank, command, and pay in the army for five years.

The following year, 1926, Mitchell resigned from the army and began to give a series of lectures about reforming American aviation practices. He hypothesized about a possible Japanese aircraft-carrier-based warplane attack on Hawaii. After his death in 1936, Mitchell's many recommendations and prophecies gained increasing consideration. In 1948 a special congressional medal in Mitchell's honor was presented to his son by General Carl Spaatz, first chief of staff of the newly established U.S. Air Force.

Robert MITCHUM: a miserable marijuana case

"It's a frame-up. They didn't find a thing on me," protested Robert Mitchum, popular movie star, after he was charged with possession of marijuana in 1948. The 31-year-old film favorite of bobby soxers everywhere had been arrested, on the night of August 31 during a police raid on a Hollywood "reefer" party at the Laurel Canyon cottage of blonde starlet Lila Leeds. His arrest had come long before marijuana smoking was popular, and his employers, including famed film producer David O. Selznick, were mortified at the thought of Mitchum's career being terminated because of a shameful narcotics arrest. Curiously, the antiestablishment Mitchum, who became well known for his frankness, barroom brawls with strangers, and distaste for Hollywood society, came through his troubles with his career unharmed and his popularity even greater than it had been.

Gossip columnist Louella Parsons once called Connecticut-born Robert Mitchum "Hollywood's determined rebel." Before he married and took up acting as a career, Mitchum had reportedly been at one time or another a stevedore, drifter, farmhand, busboy, bartender, boxer, steelworker, dancehall bouncer, gandy dancer, and "saloon librettist." He had written poetry as a youth and, according to some, was well-read in English literature. When he reached Hollywood, he first appeared in a number of money-making westerns before starring in *The Story of G.I. Joe* (1945), which was a huge success.

In 1948 the Federal Bureau of Investigation wanted to halt the increasing use of marijuana in Hollywood and engaged the help of the Los Angeles Police Department. Mitchum, at the time of his arrest, was scheduled to speak the following day in observance of National Youth Week on the steps of the Los Angeles City Hall. His appearance and talk against juvenile delinquency had to be canceled; his publicist said he had "laryngitis."

The arrested actor hired Hollywood's celebrated criminal lawyer Jerry Giesler, who claimed that his client had been entrapped. The bellicose Mitchum had made numerous enemies in the past because of his blunt talk and cynical outlook; he had banged heads, stepped on people, and cursed out both men and women. An electronic eavesdropping device had allegedly been planted at the place where the reefer party was held in Laurel Canyon, and the police "bust" occurred just minutes after Mitchum's arrival and setting down of a lighted marijuana cigarette. On Giesler's advice, Mitchum did not testify before the Los Angeles County grand jury that indicted him on two counts: possession of marijuana and conspiracy to possess marijuana. Giesler planned to squash the scandal before it got started. To downplay publicity, he waived a jury trial and threw his star client on the mercy of the court judge, who found him guilty of conspiracy to possess marijuana. The other charge, smoking pot, was either discarded or forgotten. Mitchum, who had listed in the court records his occupation as "ex-actor," received a nominal two-year prison sentence, which was reduced to 60 days, with the remaining time suspended.

After serving 50 days in the Los Angeles County Jail in the winter of 1949, Mitchum was released and quickly resumed film-making for RKO and producer Howard Hughes, who bought the actor's contract from Selznick for more than $200,000. To an interviewer asking about his time in jail and fellow inmates, Mitchum answered realistically: "I found out from those other guys around me what making $3,000 a week and having your name up in lights means." And, in a definite understatement, he added: "In that jail, I found out that Robert Mitchum, movie star, had a lot of privileges."

Probably a bigger disgrace happened afterward when Mitchum's marijuana case was shabbily exploited by Hollywood's movie moguls to reap greater box-office revenues. They used him to play up the evils of narcotics in their sex-and-sin films, which were frequently coupled with Mitchum's "physical male" movies in double features. Yet Mitchum remained a kind of charming rebel with a salty tongue, not afraid of biting the hand that fed him. "Acting keeps me away from harder work—that's its saving grace," he once said, "but I never forget that one of the biggest movie stars is the dog Lassie." He went on to make box-office successes such as *The Sundowners* (1960) and *Ryan's Daughter* (1970), among many other films. He died in 1997.

MONA LISA SWINDLE

All Paris was agog on August 23, 1911, when its morning newspapers revealed that Leonardo da Vinci's *Mona Lisa* had been stolen from the city's famed museum of art, the Louvre. On that day, newspapers around the world expressed varying degrees of anger and anxiety, with one creative journalist composing a pathetic obituary for the "deceased" portrait. The uproar continued for several months.

News of the wildest art crime of the century spread to America and around the world as fast as cable and telegraph would permit. Within a week, ships that had departed from France or were scheduled to do so were being given thorough searches. The abducted masterpiece was reported to have surfaced in the United States, Germany, Argentina, and seven other countries, including Japan. Parisian fortune tellers and clairvoyants were mobilized to assist the police in locating it; the result was much absurdity and only one close guess about its location.

La Gioconda (or *Mona Lisa*), however, was being held in Paris as her abductors had planned for her to be; they depended upon the ineptitude of the French police to prevent her discovery. One clairvoyant had reported the picture's presence in the vicinity of the Hôtel de Ville, Paris's City Hall, but this insight was ignored by the police. The painting was actually a few blocks away, swathed in red velvet.

The object of scandalous theft had not been to hold the *Mona Lisa* for resale; the mastermind of the plot had hoped to use the publicity surrounding its pillage as an impetus for the American sale of six carefully crafted forgeries. Behind this novel purpose lies a brief story.

The designer of the cloak-and-dagger plot was the self-styled Marqués Eduardo de Valfierno, an Argentine of rich family, who, as the family's youngest son, had suffered the tortures of its custom of primogeniture, whereby his eldest brother became the family's chief inheritor. He maintained a high style of living by selling the few antiques he had inherited and then, faced with a decline into genteel poverty, peddled fake Utrillo paintings to rich South American widows. The fakes were painted by Yves Chaudron, a former picture restorer-turned-artistic forger.

The market exhausted, Valfierno emigrated to Paris and conceived his plan to sell six fake *La Gioconda*s to rich and greedy Americans. Chaudron spent the winter of 1910 creating clones of Leonardo's great portrait; Valfierno arranged for the theft of the original.

Valfierno knew that the Louvre, worried about vandalism, had created shadow boxes for its greatest art attractions—second frames interposing a pane of glass between the viewer and the painting. He next discovered an avaricious carpenter-glazier who had worked on the shadow box for the *Mona Lisa,* Vincenzo Peruggia, an emigrant worker from Lombardy, Italy, and without giving his name, trained Peruggia in the plan for the robbery.

Many secret meetings and passwords later, Valfierno directed that Peruggia and two accomplices, the brothers Lancelotti, would hide overnight on August 20, 1911, in a storage room off the Salon Carré in the Louvre; on the next morning, the trio would abduct the *Mona Lisa* after mingling with other workers in the traditional costume of museum laborers. The plan worked; within one hour, the portrait (painted on a wooden panel) had been covered with a worker's smock and carried through the streets of Paris to its hiding place. The theft went undiscovered until the afternoon of August 22.

By then, Chaudron's six copies had already traveled to America. In September, Valfierno followed. In the United States, with the help of British and American accomplices, he sold each of the fakes as the Paris original to gullible and grasping plutocrats for $300,000 per copy. Among the buyers, it was falsely rumored in 1912, was the financial boss J. P. MORGAN. Each of the buyers remained silent because he thought he possessed the original and was fearful of criminal involvement if he sought the appraisal of an art expert.

The famous portrait would remain out of sight for two years until it was discovered in Florence, Italy. One of the thieves had attempted to dispose of it there for about $100,000. An Italian museum administrator whom he consulted had alerted the police, and the culprit confessed, implicated two accomplices (the Lancelotti brothers, who were arrested in France but released), and went to prison for less than a year.

The original, returned from Florence in early 1914, was received at a chastened Louvre with great fanfare and a special guard. Today the masterpiece hangs in a bullet-proof glass enclosure in the Salle des États, safe in its humidity-regulated and electronically guarded environment.

MONKEY CASE. See SCOPES TRIAL.

Marilyn MONROE: suicide or murder?

By the 1950s, beautiful Marilyn Monroe was America's greatest sex symbol, famed worldwide for her voluptuous figure and platinum blond hair. Haunted by the image of being "beautiful but dumb," she gradually grew distressed, despite showing dramatic ability in such films as *Gentlemen Prefer Blondes* (1953), *Bus Stop* (1956), *Some Like It Hot* (1959), and *The Misfits* (1961). Whether she took her own life because of these feelings of low self-esteem, or whether she was conveniently murdered for political reasons, her death remains shrouded in mystery.

In the early morning hours of August 5, 1962, Marilyn Monroe was found dead, lying naked on her bed in her recently bought home in Los Angeles, California. Her housekeeper, seeing a light still on in the actress's room, had discovered her and called her personal physician, who had come and pronounced her dead at 3:40 A.M. The Los Angeles County coroner's report later stated the cause of death to be "acute barbiturate poisoning, ingestion of overdose." A few days before her death, her physician had prescribed Nembutal (a strong sleeping barbiturate) for Monroe, who had been under pressure and distraught after losing a movie role but seemed to be recovering and had some good future acting prospects. Although she had previously attempted to take her own life, Marilyn Monroe's death had many inconsistencies that made it questionable as a suicide.

There was a discrepancy between the coroner's and the toxicologist's reports; the coroner's report the day after Monroe's death stated that her stomach had shown no evidence of pills, but the toxicologist's report said there were traces of barbiturates in her blood and liver. The final conclusion from pathologists was that the actress had probably died from an injected overdose of barbiturates, which only raised another question because the coroner's report made no mention of injection marks on the corpse. (However, Monroe's physician had supposedly given her an injection the day before her death.)

Although she had been seeing a psychiatrist who said she had been despondent on the day before she died, a number of persons who had also seen Marilyn Monroe that day reported that she had been in good spirits and not seemingly troubled. No motive for suicide was apparent. Monroe just didn't appear out of control, although she had widely been known to be dependent on pills and sometimes fitful.

Her love life was perhaps linked to her mysterious death. Almost certainly she was having an affair with U.S. Attorney General Robert Kennedy, the brother of President John F. Kennedy, at the time of her death. It also seems certain that she had earlier had trysts with President Kennedy, and Robert Kennedy apparently wished to end his relationship with her without any possible scandal. There were rumors that Marilyn's house had been bugged by both Robert Kennedy and his archenemy Jimmy Hoffa, head of the Teamsters' union, who was seeking compromising tapes against Kennedy. In addition, Monroe had had an abortion at some time during her affair with the attorney general. She had, during her last weeks, allegedly tried repeatedly to telephone him at the Justice Department in Washington, D.C. The author Norman Mailer speculated that secret agents killed Monroe to protect the Kennedy brothers from public disgrace, a theory also advanced by writer Tony Sciacca in his book *Who Killed Marilyn?* (1976). Another theory was that Cubans, upset about the CIA-influenced underworld contract to eliminate Fidel Castro, killed Marilyn in revenge against the Kennedys. The press frequently played on the guilt of society in causing her death, saying that she couldn't cope with her highly publicized, Hollywood-created image of glamour and sex and was therefore driven to suicide at the age of 36.

The truth about Marilyn Monroe's death will probably remain hidden, for some significant evidence disappeared afterward: the first police report of her death, the first autopsy report, and some of her personal telephone toll-call records. Moreover, important witnesses were never questioned for documentation in the case. Consequently suspicion of a cover-up in her death will persist despite the official finding that the cause of her death was a self-inflicted overdose of barbiturates.

Sun Myung MOON: religion and tax fraud

The Reverend Sun Myung Moon, founder and current head of the Holy Spirit Association for the Unification of World Christianity, commonly known as the Unification Church, was convicted of income tax evasion in 1982, fined $25,000, and sentenced to 18 months in prison. Moon's defenders claimed that he had been prosecuted unfairly because his church and his "Moonie" followers were regarded with suspicion by many, that the money in question was held in trust for the church, and that the U.S. government had no right to interfere with the internal financial affairs of a religious organization. The U.S. Justice Department and subsequently the judge and the jury in Moon's case felt otherwise and found him guilty not only of tax evasion but of "conspiracy to obstruct justice."

Moon was born in 1920 in what is now North Korea. When 16 years old, he had a vision in which Jesus Christ told him to complete his mission of converting humankind to the word and love of God. After World War II, Moon founded his church, which soon gained many adherents in South Korea and Japan. In 1971 he and his family moved to the United States, where he set up new headquarters, even though he could barely speak English. Many young people flocked to his Unification Church.

The tax case against Moon revolved around $1.7 million that he had personally deposited in two Chase Manhattan Bank accounts held in his name between 1973 and 1976, plus $50,000 in stocks in a company that imported products from church-owned firms in South Korea. Moon failed to declare the interest earned on these monies, which was about $106,000 in his income tax for three years. When challenged by the Internal Revenue Service, officers of his church produced records showing that the 1973 deposit had come from loans from European leaders of the Unification Church, and that the 1976 deposit had come from case donations from Japanese followers of Moon. However, both documents turned out to be fraudulent. An expert discovered from the watermark that the paper on which one report had been prepared had not been manufactured until a year after the date of the report. The Japanese Family Fund Ledger was also found to have been backdated, and the testimony of the church officials was proved false. This combination of backdated records and the perjury of high church officials led the U.S. government to bring Moon to trial.

Throughout the court proceedings, Moon's lawyers contended that the Chase Manhattan Bank accounts and the stock in Moon's name had been held in trust for the Unification Church, but the prosecutors showed that the accounts were in Moon's name and that he had signed all withdrawal and transfer transactions relating to them. Further, many of the withdrawals had been for purely personal expenditures, such as private-school tuition fees for his children, and purchasing $1,500 gold watches.

The Unification Church's account books showed two loans from Moon during the period 1973–76, both of which had come from his Chase bank accounts. One had been used to buy a 26-acre Hudson River estate at Tarrytown, New York, that became Moon's personal residence. The other had been for mortgage payments on another church property and had been partially repaid.

After Moon was convicted of the crimes charged against him, a battery of highly paid, expert defense lawyers appealed his case all the way to the U.S. Supreme Court. Every appeal was defeated. The lawyers even tried, unsuccessfully, to obtain a presidential pardon for Moon. Despite all the legal maneuvering, Moon finally went to prison and paid his fine.

This was not Moon's first brush with United States law. In the mid-1970s he had applied for a real-estate property-tax exemption for his estate in Tarrytown. The village had refused to grant the exemption on the grounds that the Unification Church was not a recognized religion and, perhaps more importantly, that the estate was not used for worship activities but was a residence.

Upon his release from prison in 1985, Moon's defenders and an array of lobbyists and publicists hired by the Unification Church launched a massive publicity campaign to vindicate him. Full-page advertisements in leading newspapers proclaimed that religious freedom had been abused and that Moon had been a victim of racist and religious intolerance. Others pointed out that the First Amendment does not grant immunity to church leaders for any criminal offense, including the nonpayment of personal income taxes.

Arch MOORE: governor and criminality

In July 1990, federal charges of extortion, mail fraud, tax fraud, and obstruction of justice were brought against Republican governor of West Virginia Arch Moore, Jr. Though he faced up to 36 years in prison and $1.2 million in fines, Moore was convicted of corruption and sentenced to only five years and 10 months in prison and fined $170,000. He also paid the state $750,000 to settle the federal lawsuit.

Moore was elected to an unprecedented third term as governor in 1984, but his 1988 bid was unsuccessful. During those two campaigns, Moore allegedly committed illegal acts. Besides funneling nearly $100,000 in cash into his campaign fund instead of claiming it legally as income, Moore also was accused of accepting $573,000 from H. Paul Kizer and Maben Energy Corporation, prominent coal operators, in exchange for a $2.3 million refund from the state's black lung fund. Moore failed to report the kickback as income and filed false income reports with the IRS.

When a federal investigation was launched, Moore evidently made false statements in an interview with investigators. He further obstructed justice by trying to persuade his campaign manager as well as the representative of the coal company from which he received the kickback to lie to the federal investigators.

Although Moore is distinguished as one of only two Republican governors since 1932 to hold office in the Democrat-dominated state of West Virginia and as the founder of Grandparent's Day, his less-than-honorable acts gave him equal "fame" as well. Moore was the second West Virginia governor to have legal troubles related to his time in office. Former Governor W. W. Barron (a Democrat) was charged with bribery and conspiracy in 1968. Barron was acquitted but later went to prison for bribing the foreman of the U.S. District Court jury that tried his case. Moore narrowly escaped charges of extortion brought against him in 1976, but the second time around he wasn't so lucky.

J. P. MORGAN: gentleman robber baron

America's most successful financier, John Pierpont Morgan, was pilloried by a special House investigative body, the Pujo Committee, in 1912, as one of "a few financial leaders who had achieved an unhealthy control of the nation's money and credit." Morgan was unaffected by this assault upon him; he had totally ignored public criticism throughout his career. He knew what he wanted to do and he did it, regardless of ethical, legal, or public considerations. Morgan, at least, was no hypocrite. He made no attempt to hide his uncharitable nature. "I owe the public nothing," he said in 1901.

Born in 1837 in Hartford, Connecticut, into a financier's family, Morgan at 23 managed the New York office of his father's London-based international bank enterprise, J. S. Morgan and Company. From 1860 on, he prospered as a partner in several investment companies, finally becoming owner of his own firm, J. P. Morgan and Company, in 1895.

Investment banking was not Morgan's only concern. He sold obsolete carbines to the Union Army during the Civil War, while also conducting speculations in gold that accidentally helped the Confederacy. (Money, he noted, was "neutral.") He involved himself in railroads after the Civil War—then the biggest money makers in America. He wrested control of one railroad from Jay Gould, conducted reorganizations of others after 1873, assisted in battles for railroad dominance (see NORTHERN PACIFIC "BUBBLE"), and fatally "Morganized" the New Haven Railroad.

Morgan was also busy during national financial crises, at times because he had produced them: as part of DREXEL, MORGAN AND COMPANY, he was partly responsible for the Panic of 1873. During the crisis of 1894–95, he set up harsh terms for the lending of gold to the federal government, and during the Panic of 1907, he was one of the few, including John D. Rockefeller, who remained both financially unscathed and financially dominant.

Morgan's most famous stratagem, a ploy defiant of federal law, was his role in putting together a virtual steel monopoly (see GATES/MORGAN/GARY: the creation of U.S. Steel).

His activities brought him into conflict with many, but his most revealing enmity was that toward Theodore Roosevelt, whose measures of "regulation" for the public's sake perpetually rankled Morgan. This personal enmity seems to have been on Morgan's side only, however, for when Roosevelt as president of the United States decided to move against Morgan's creation of the Northern Securities Corporation without consulting him personally, Morgan (who did not regard himself as unprincipled) decided that Roosevelt was "not a gentleman." (See NORTHERN SECURITIES VILLAINY.) And when Roosevelt, retired from office, was about to go hunting lions in Africa, Morgan commented, "I hope the first lion he meets does his duty."

With regard to social or national considerations, Morgan was, in the words of one great commentator on America's business history, "a Bourbon to the end." But his brand of aristocratic conservatism made him fit squarely into the ranks of those whom Charles Francis Adams condemned as "robber barons."

J. P. MORGAN: the "Morganization" of the New Haven railroad

The skill of John Pierpont Morgan in reorganizing crippled railroads foundered only once during his long career: his control of the New York, New Haven, and Hartford Railroad from 1892 until his death in 1913 left it in a perilous condition from which it never recovered. It also caused a 1914 Interstate Commerce Commission investigation.

Morgan's concept of reorganization, labeled Morganization by his many critics, was to establish a railroad monopoly in a geographical area and then rule the transportation facilities of that area like a dictator. In adopting the New Haven railroad for his special treatment, he was perhaps responding sentimentally to his boyhood memories of riding that short railroad (Springfield, Massachusetts, to New York) to and from his hometown of Hartford, Connecticut, for in 1892 he decided that it must have monopolistic control in all of New England. To do so, he pushed up its capitalization to $417 million by 1913, forcing upon it by 1894 an indebtedness of over $100 million, a burden from which it never recovered.

The New Haven railroad became Morgan's concern because a former protégé, A. Archibald McLeon, president of the Philadelphia and Reading Railroad, was violating Morgan's theory of territorial monopoly by attempting to expand into New England in order to haul Pennsylvania anthracite coal northeastward. Morgan destroyed McLeod. He first took control of the New Haven; then in 1913 he sold bundles of Reading shares to force McLeon and the Reading, within a few days, into receivership. Morgan then reorganized the Reading and almost immediately began to expand the New Haven.

He gained control of the Boston and Maine Railroad, bought the Old Colony line of steamships and railroads and purchased the Shore Line and 129 other railroad properties, all of which he sold to the New Haven at undisclosed prices. He acquired interurban trolley lines that might compete with the New Haven and began construction of a commuter railroad through West-chester County, New York, to the Bronx. Each of these moves gained him the enormous "service" fees he charged regularly while acting as a railroad reorganizer. And he brought in Charles S. Mellen, former president of the Northern Pacific Railroad, to manage the emerging colossus.

The 1914 Interstate Commerce Commission investigation revealed the New Haven to be in a sorely mismanaged and sorry state despite Mellen. One director had made $2.7 million from the railroad without spending any of his own money, and a million dollars had been spent on political graft for the incomplete New York, Westchester, and Boston Railroad; evidence also pointed to the bribing of newspapermen to praise the New Haven in order to force up the price of its shares.

The blame for this condition was never definitively assigned. Morgan's judgment, in his later years, was described as "not always reliable." Mellen asserted that he took his orders from Morgan and Morgan's New York office. Francis L. Stetson, the New York official in charge of the New Haven, was accused but never proved guilty of malfeasance in providing Morgan with totals and not details of the monies the railroad made and spent.

Whatever the cause of the New Haven's extreme cost to its minority stockholders, it was too ill to contend against the burgeoning age of the automobile, and it staggered until 1930 when bankruptcy caused another—and ruinous—reorganization. Today the network of what was once the New York, New Haven, and Hartford Railroad is only slightly larger than it was in 1892; instead of being the center of a regional monopoly, it is the undermaintained workhorse of a public consortium. It was, and is, a sad exemplification of the trite complaint "A helluva way to run a railroad."

Vicki MORGAN. See BLOOMINGDALE-MORGAN AFFAIR.

MORMON POLYGAMY: religious and odious
During the 19th century, Mormonism was the major maverick of American Protestantism, primarily because the Mormons' charismatic leader, Joseph Smith, developed a comprehensive and much-attacked program redesigning marriage and creating a polygamous mode for the family. As a result, Mormon polygamy was regarded by many thoughtful Americans as a national moral scandal, second only in viciousness to slavery.

Opposition to Mormon polygamy, which was viewed as totally antagonistic to Judaeo-Christian moral practice, was behind the public pressure that forced the Mormons to march almost 2,000 miles across the face of America. They were hounded out of their founding locale in Fayette, New York, forced from settlements at

Kirtland, Ohio, Independence, Missouri, and Nauvoo, Illinois, and pushed into making a long trek to the valley of the Great Salt lake in what is today Utah, where the Mormons felt safe and isolated enough to establish the Kingdom of God (Deseret) as their founder had foreseen it. But even this final home was to fall under the control of those who regarded Mormon polygamy as intolerable.

Smith's detractors, both Mormon and non-Mormon, proposed that he had invented Mormon polygamy to satisfy his own lust. But this canard was completely false. Smith had derived his ideas for what he called "celestial marriage" from descriptions of patriarchal practice in the Old Testament and from personal revelations experienced after 1831, eight years after the concept of the Church of Jesus Christ of Latter-Day Saints and the Book of Mormon had been revealed to him. The theory behind the "new and everlasting covenant" of celestial marriage was kept secret until 1843. Even then, it remained a covert practice among the leaders of the Mormon Church and was always publicly denied until, in 1862, it was decreed a general Mormon doctrine for Deseret. But rumors of its practice spread rapidly and brought on the oppression that forced the Mormons to become nomads for doctrinal reasons. An interesting side note: before, during, and after the long trek to Utah, many of the plural marriages were "spiritual"; they ensured the salvation, family status, and temporal comfort of the female but were entirely sexless.

The fundamental tenets of Mormon polygamy are four. First, multiple marriages restore the God-permitted practice of the Old Testament patriarchs (for example, Hagar, the handmaid of Abraham). Second, properly blessed marriages are "sealed for time and eternity"; Smith had interpreted Luke 20:34–36 and the words "neither marry nor are given in marriage" to mean that no new marriages occur in heaven and also that marriages (and sexual activities) continue after death. Third, if women (whom the Mormons considered second-class saints) were to attain one of three levels of blessedness revealed to Smith, it must be attained through a properly blessed marriage. Finally, if the Kingdom of Heaven is at hand and the Mormon Saints are to administer it, more saints must be engendered so that the family of the blessed can fulfill its obligations. When revealed in 1843, these explanations failed to convince many Mormons, and after Smith's murder by an angry mob in 1844, his widow and others established the nonpolygamous Reorganized Church of Jesus Christ of Latter-Day Saints.

Non-Mormons, most of them unaware of the subtleties of Smith's concept, saw celestial marriage as sheer immorality; lurid and uninformed discussions of its horrors appeared in newspapers across the country. When Utah became a territory in 1850, with Brigham Young as its territorial governor, the opposition became legislative as well as popular; soon after the 1852 promulgation of the doctrine of celestial marriage as a general church obligation, the opposition—always militant—became briefly military.

In 1857, U.S. President James Buchanan declared Utah to be in "a state of substantial rebellion," removed Young as governor, and caused a little known conflict—the Utah War—between a Mormon militia and federal troops. The troops proving ineffective, peace without a resolution was restored in June 1858. Legislative attacks generated the Edmunds-Tucker Law, which deprived Mormons of the right to vote and expropriated some Mormon Church property. Since the Mormons wanted Utah to become one of the United States, they announced defeat on September 25, 1890, through a declaration that polygamy was now forbidden to the saints.

With the odious doctrine no longer in force, the moral problem has been resolved. Mormonism gradually reentered the mainstream of American Protestantism and, in 1896, Utah became the 45th state in the Union.

Dick MORRIS: presidential adviser's affair with prostitute

As President Bill Clinton's chief political consultant, Dick Morris was one of the most influential people in the United States. Born in 1948 in New York City, Morris developed an intense interest in political campaigning when he was eight years old. As a teenager, he organized his fellow students to canvas Manhattan's West Side for Democratic candidates. By the time he was 21, he had become a power in city politics. Morris was not interested in holding elective office himself; instead, he preferred to exercise power from behind the scenes. As one of his early colleagues said, Morris did not want to change the world; he just wanted to run it.

In the 1970s Morris expanded his career beyond New York City by becoming a freelance political issues adviser. He served as a campaign consultant to gubernatorial and senatorial candidates of both major parties and was particularly adept at helping dark-horse candidates pull off upset victories. Morris's secret was the creative way in which he used polls. Traditionally, political polls were conducted only to see how well the voting public was responding to a candidate's position on the issues. With the assistance of Hollywood pollster Richard Dresner, who polled potential movie viewers on such things as which of three movie endings they preferred, Morris began asking voters how they felt about various hypothetical positions on the issues that were important to them. Once he found out which positions were most appealing to a majority of the voters, he then convinced his candidates to adopt those positions in order to make themselves more "electable."

In 1978 Morris helped Bill Clinton win his first gubernatorial campaign in Arkansas, and for the next 12 years he served as Clinton's top political adviser. After a falling-out in 1990, the two men parted company, and for the next four years Morris worked primarily for Republican candidates. But when the GOP's landslide congressional victory in 1994 threatened to hamstring the Clinton presidency, Morris returned to Clinton's side and engineered the remarkable comeback that resulted in Clinton's reelection in November 1996.

However, Morris did not get a chance to bask in the glory following the election. Two months earlier a newspaper tabloid had disclosed that Morris, a married man, had been having sex with a prostitute once a week for the last year in the Washington, D.C., hotel where he stayed during the week. This disclosure came just days before the opening of the Democratic National Convention, the central theme of which was that the Democrats were the champions of family values. More damaging to Morris's reputation and to Clinton's presidency was the prostitute's claim that Morris, in an attempt to impress her, had disclosed confidential and classified information. Allegedly, Morris told her that the National Aeronautics and Space Agency had discovered signs of life on Mars, that Clinton was about to declare war on American tobacco companies, and that the Saudi Arabian government was going to provide scholarship money for the children of Gulf War veterans, all before this information was disclosed to the press. He also let her read an advance copy of the speech which Hillary Rodham Clinton delivered to the convention and even let her listen in on a telephone conversation with the president.

Morris refused to confirm or deny the allegations; however, a national tabloid eventually published photographs of him and the prostitute on a hotel balcony. He was forced to resign as Clinton's chief political strategist and returned to his home in Redding, Connecticut. Having earned a small fortune as a consultant, he retired from politics and wrote a book, *Behind the Oval Office* (1997) which detailed the workings of the Clinton White House. That same year, his wife of 20 years filed for divorce. See Bill CLINTON: impeached U.S. president.

Elijah MUHAMMAD: allegations of adultery and murder

Citizens of Los Angeles took little notice on July 2, 1963, when two women filed paternity complaints in the city's superior court against Elijah (or Robert) Poole, charging that he was the father of three living children and one about to be born. But when Poole was identified in the complaints as Elijah Muhammad, exalted leader of a Black Muslim group called the Lost-Found Nation of Islam, the women's court actions achieved national notice. Moreover, although their suit

At a press conference in his Chicago home, Black Muslim leader Elijah Muhammad (seated) denies any connection with the 1965 slaying of Malcolm X, his former protégé, who had defected and set up a rival black movement. Muhammad said that Malcolm was a "victim of his own preaching." Behind Muhammad are (left to right): Herbert Muhammad, his son; John Ali; and James Shabazz, a minister. (UPI) Bettmann Newsphotos

was never ajudicated, the repercussions of their actions led to the still unresolved murder of Elijah Muhammad's former protégé, Malcolm X, in February 1965.

The story behind this double disgrace involving Elijah Muhammad is complex, and it centers chiefly on Malcolm X. Born Malcolm Little, Malcolm X was an ex-convict converted while in prison to the doctrines of the Nation of Islam. Malcolm, after his 1952 release from prison, went to Chicago and Elijah Muhammad. There he became almost a son to his mentor, who groomed and trained him, ultimately putting him in charge of Mosque #7 in New York City's Harlem, the Nation of Islam's most prestigious congregation.

A spellbinding speaker, the charismatic Malcolm X did well, apparently too well to please his enemies in the Nation of Islam. In 1963, references to him in the Islamic cult's magazine *Muhammad Speaks* became briefer and more infrequent, much to Malcolm's concern. He was also aware that rumors of sexual misconduct by Elijah Muhammad, which had been discounted in the 1950s, were again circulating.

Puzzled, Malcolm journeyed to Chicago to find out what was behind them.

There he learned that some of his mentor's secretaries (nine, according to Malcolm in his *Autobiography*) had become pregnant; the cult's strict moral codes against fornication and adultery had forced them to be dis-

missed. Previously either unwilling to believe that his mentor was capable of such acts, or accepting them as expressions of the patriarchal *droit de seigneur* assumed in most religious cults, Malcolm now investigated carefully. He queried the secretaries and found the allegations to be true. He then confronted Elijah Muhammad, who defended his actions as prophecies to which he had to conform.

Malcolm next made a mistake: he conveyed his findings to some of the Nation of Islam's leaders on the East Coast, one of whom reported Malcolm's alleged disloyalty to Chicago. From that moment until his assassination in 1965, Malcolm X was subjected to a variety of pressures from the Chicago headquarters of the cult. He was not only the object of jealousy because of his celebrity, but was now also a threat to the Nation of Islam itself. He had made himself even more of a danger by acquiring affidavits from the impregnated secretaries and persuading two of them to file suit against Muhammad.

The Chicago headquarters moved to silence him. Ostensibly for another reason, Elijah Muhammad punished Malcolm by withdrawing his right to preach for 90 days. He was also "isolated," with all members in good standing ordered to ostracize him. He was promised a public hearing, which he never received.

His preaching privileges were never restored, and Malcolm next threatened to break with the Nation of Islam unless a full hearing was allowed before the Harlem congregation. His ultimatum was rejected, and on March 12, 1964, he established his own cult, Muslim Mosque, Incorporated. Forty persons followed him from Mosque #7.

His new organization, which ran counter to the nonviolent programs of contemporary civil rights leaders, was a forerunner of the later Black Power movement but with a religious foundation. Malcolm preached Black nationalism, gradually secularized his approaches through the founding of the Organization of Afro-American Unity, and rapidly made important contacts in Europe, Africa, and the Near East.

Malcolm's international stature was acquired during trips made for his own safety. He had received death threats, escaped street attacks, comforted aides who had undergone beatings, and suffered the fire-bombing of his home. He was shadowed constantly by Nation of Islam members trained to be part of a militant corps called the Fruit of Islam. Ultimately, he had to hire three bodyguards and to carry a gun himself.

Whether Malcolm's death is assignable to direct orders from Elijah Muhammad or resulted from independent sentiments within the Nation of Islam's faithful is not clear, despite careful investigation. What is certain is that the secretaries, unable to gain a subpoena on Muhammad and intimidated in many ways, dropped their case against the leader. Malcolm, who had foreseen a violent end for himself, was gunned down on February

21, 1965, as he began to speak in New York's Audubon Ballroom. His assailants, all members of the Nation of Islam, were tried and found guilty, but a direct motivational connection between their action and Elijah Muhammad was never proved.

MULLIGAN LETTERS

An eloquent, engaging politician and longtime aspirant for the U.S. presidency, James G. Blaine contended with a charge of venality against him that undoubtedly cost him the Republican presidential nomination in 1876 and 1880 and helped defeat him as the Republican presidential candidate in the election of 1884. The disclosure of the scandalous, so-called Mulligan letters constantly raised the question of whether Blaine was morally worthy of the highest office in the nation.

While investigating corrupt governmental dealings, a committee of the U.S. House of Representatives questioned Blaine, an influential congressman from Maine. He was cleared of any wrongdoing. Unexpectedly, however, on May 31, 1876, the House Judiciary Committee heard damning testimony against Blaine from one James Mulligan, a bookkeeper working for a Boston businessman-broker named Warren Fisher, Jr. Mulligan charged that Blaine had used his position as Speaker of the House (1869–75) for personal profit, had helped secure the renewal of a land grant to the Little Rock & Fort Smith Railroad of Arkansas, and had worked with Fisher to sell the railroad's bonds for a handsome commission. The railroad had gone bankrupt, and in 1871 Blaine had secretly sold its nearly worthless bonds to the Union Pacific Railroad in order to pay back money to investors in the moneyless Little Rock & Fort Smith. Blaine had allegedly made a sizeable gain for himself by selling these bonds at a price much higher than their market value.

Blaine denied all this, but Mulligan informed the House committee that he had incriminating evidence against the congressman: letters written by Blaine to Fisher concerning their dealings. Either at the request of Blaine or a committee member who became ill, the Judiciary Committee promptly adjourned after Mulligan's testimony. Later that day Blaine gained possession of the letters from Mulligan, to whom he promised to return them after reading them over. But he never gave them back nor surrendered them to the committee, saying he had a legal right to repossess his letters.

On June 5, 1876, Blaine, who had angrily lambasted the Judiciary Committee's motives, made a dramatic speech before the House of Representatives, defending himself and reading selected parts of the Mulligan letters, out of chronological order. The House inquiry into the matter, however, was put off by Blaine's suddenly developing heatstroke on the eve of the Republican Na-

tional Convention in Cincinnati, where he was the leading candidate for the presidential nomination until being narrowly defeated on the seventh roll-call vote by Governor Rutherford B. Hayes of Ohio. The House Judiciary Subcommittee made no report about Blaine's Mulligan affair, saying it had no legal authority to do so. Four years later, Blaine, who was by then a United States senator from Maine, was again a leading choice as presidential candidate of the Republican National Convention in Chicago, but he lost favor, and a "dark horse," James A. Garfield of Ohio, was nominated on the 36th roll-call.

At the 1884 Republican National Convention in Chicago, Blaine finally succeeded in becoming his party's presidential nominee, to the deep resentment of the Independent Republicans (called the Mugwumps), who afterward bolted from the party and supported the Democratic candidate Grover Cleveland, the reform governor of New York. During the campaign for the presidency, both sides indulged in scurrilous name-calling, and the old Mulligan charges against Blaine were revived, with the *Boston Globe* leading a devastating probe into the scandal. The existence of 20 more Mulligan letters was made known to Mugwamp leaders, who helped obtain Mulligan's release of them for publication between May and September 1884.

Blaine admitted to the letters' authenticity and tried to show that his dealings had been scrupulously honest and above reproach. Yet there were grave misgivings, especially with regard to one particular letter that Blaine himself had written and mailed to Fisher in Boston on April 16, 1876, several days before his first appearance before the House Judiciary Subcommittee. Included with his letter was the draft of another that Blaine had written, exonerating him fully in glowing terms, which Fisher was to copy and sign and then return to Blaine. This "false" letter was to be released to the press to show Blaine's "scrupulous integrity and honor" (words he used to defend himself during the 1884 campaign). Fisher wisely did not do what Blaine wanted but instead kept the correspondence, in which Blaine at the end of the covering letter—in which he explained his wish to have Fisher copy and return the laudatory letter—wrote "Burn this letter." That correspondence, and particularly the final request, tarnished Blaine's credibility as an honest politician during a period when the public wanted reform in government. Blaine, humiliated by the published Mulligan letters, went down in bitter defeat in a close election, losing to the Democratic candidate Grover Cleveland.

MURCHISON LETTER

During the 1888 presidential election campaign in which Democrat Grover Cleveland ran for reelection against Republican Benjamin Harrison, the British minister in Washington received a fraudulent letter from a Charles F. Murchison asking for advice on how to vote. The minister, Lionel Sackville-West, unwisely replied and stated in a roundabout way that he recommended Cleveland. His letter was published in newspapers across the United States and England. The resulting furor forced Sackville-West to return to London and caused Cleveland to lose the election.

Because he had no prospect of inheriting his family's fortune, Sackville-West, the fifth son of the Earl de la Warr, entered the British Foreign Office in 1847 at the age of 20. For over 40 years, he lived the conventional life of a British diplomat in a variety of posts in Europe and South America. Despite his appearance of conventionality, Sackville-West had a surprising private life. He maintained a mistress for almost 20 years, with whom he fathered five illegitimate children. When this woman, Pepita, a former Spanish dancer, died in childbirth at the couple's villa in southern France, their two sons were sent off to school, and their three daughters were placed in a convent in Paris. After seven unhappy years, an English friend of their father's rescued the daughters and brought them to England, where they were astonished to discover that they had rich relatives among the nobility. Normally these events would have created a scandal in Victorian England, but the family managed to keep most of the facts hushed up.

In 1881, Sackville-West was posted to Washington, D.C., to be the British Minister to the United States, but, being a bachelor, he needed a woman to act as his hostess in the socially active capitol. His sister, Lady Darby, determined that Sackville-West's 18-year-old daughter, Victoria, would do admirably, even though she spoke only French. The most formidable barrier to overcome was the prejudice against the girl's illegitimacy. President James Garfield's wife agreed to accept the young woman, especially after it was learned that she had been received at court by Queen Victoria. Victoria Sackville-West followed her father to Washington and, although inexperienced, soon proved herself to be popular hostess and able mistress of the minister's house. Almost eight years passed pleasantly before disaster struck.

In September 1888, Sackville-West received a letter purported to have been written by a naturalized Englishman who signed himself Charles F. Murchison. It read, in part:

> Many English citizens have for years refrained from being naturalized, as they thought no good would accrue from the act, but Mr. Cleveland's Administration has been so favourable and friendly toward England, so kind in not enforcing the Retaliatory Act passed by Congress, so sound on the free-trade question and so hostile to the dynamite school of Ireland, that by the hundreds—yes, by the thousands—they have become

> naturalized for the express purpose of helping to elect him again. . . . If Cleveland was pursuing a new policy toward Canada, temporarily only and for the sake of obtaining popularity and continuation of his office four years more, but intends to cease his policy when his re-election is secured in November and again favor English's interest, then I should have no further doubts. . . . As you . . . know whether Mr. Cleveland's present policy is temporary only, and whether he will, as soon as he secures another term . . . suspend it for one of friendship and free trade, I apply to you privately and confidentially for information, which shall in turn be treated as entirely secret.

One of the principal Republican strategies in the presidential campaign of 1888 had been to arouse the prejudices of residents of New England and people of American Irish ancestry against England, but when Cleveland changed his mind and called for a retaliatory law against Canada over fishing rights, the Irish, the Catholics, and the New Englanders applauded his act enthusiastically. Many Republicans, however, considered his change of heart a trick done to fool voters, and one of them wrote the misleading letter sent under the name of Murchison.

The trap sprang when Sackville-West replied, in a letter in his own handwriting and marked "Private," that "The party, however, is I believe, still desirous of maintaining friendly relations with Great Britain, and is still as desirous of settling all questions with Canada, which have been unfortunately reopened since the retraction of the treaty. . . . It is impossible to predict the course which President Cleveland may pursue in the matter of retaliation, should he be elected; but there is every reason to beleive that . . . he will manifest a spirit of conciliation."

The Republicans released the minister's letter to the press less than two weeks before the election, and the negative reaction from readers was immediate—Cleveland had been exposed in secret dealings with Great Britain. Democrats demanded that Sackville-West be dismissed, and he was. The loss of the Irish vote, however, was but one factor in the defeat of Cleveland in the November elections.

Shortly after this unsavory episode, Sackville-West's older brother died, and the minister succeeded to the title of Lord Sackville, with an immense fortune and several estates in England. It therefore did not matter to him and his children that his diplomatic career had ended so suddenly and ingloriously.

For years it was believed that the Murchison letter had been written by a Mr. Haley, a farmer living near Pomona, California, but in February 1931, Charles A. Osgoodby wrote a letter to the Library of Congress documenting that his Republican father, George Osgoodby, had been the writer of the infamous Charles F. Murchison letter.

Philip MUSICA: dignified duplicities

The wily Philip Musica was six years old in 1883 when his family emigrated from Italy to the United States. He was well "Americanized" by 1900 when he embarked on a long, secret life of crime that frequently involved the entire Musica family. During the course of his career, Philip Musica employed many aliases, made millions of dollars on various illegal schemes, and ended up as president of the highly respected drug firm of McKesson & Robbins, Incorporated.

The affluent community of Fairfield, Connecticut, was shocked to read in the headlines of many newspapers on December 17, 1938, that one of the town's most distinguished and wealthy citizens, F. Donald Coster, had ended his life with a bullet at his palatial, 18-room mansion the day before. Rumors had been circulating about the drug firm of McKesson & Robbins to the effect that it was adulterating its drugs, had conspired to falsify statements about $18 million worth of assets, and was involved in gun- and ammunitions-running to foreign countries. Undoubtedly the most electrifying news in the suicide story, however, was that Coster was not the man everyone had thought he was for the past dozen years. He was really Philip Musica, an Italian who had immigrated to the United States at the age of 6. He was an ex-convict, perjurer, stool pigeon, cheat, bootlegger, and fraud. Furthermore, his three closest associates in the McKesson company—George Dietrich, the assistant treasurer, Robert Dietrich, a manager, and George Vernard, the manager of Canadian operations—were in reality Philip's brothers, George, Robert, and Arthur, respectively. Their mother and two sisters were found living in Westbury, Long Island, under the name Girard; their father, Antonio had died many years earlier.

Under his infamous alias of Frank Donald Coster, Philip Musica had won a listing for himself in *Who's Who in America,* which had unwittingly and shamefully printed the "facts" about the drug manufacturer, who gave himself Ph.D. and M.D. degrees from the University of Heidelberg, among other phony puffs.

Philip Musica's first venture into family-shared crime was a wine and cheese importing business in Brooklyn, New York, in which he bribed weighers from the U.S. Customs Department to misrepresent the true weight of his imports. Some of the dishonest weighers eventually confessed to officials, and Philip, who assumed all the blame for the fraud, was sent to jail for a year in 1909. But President William Howard Taft, impressed by Philip's sense of guilt in court, released him with a full pardon after several months. He then started a new business of importing and selling human hair from Italy, to be used in women's hairpieces. Using false invoices, the Musica firm was able to obtain between $500,000

and $1,000,000 in loans from several banks before the fraud was discovered. On the run, the entire family rushed to New Orleans and boarded a ship bound for Honduras, but before it sailed, the police arrived and arrested Philip, Arthur, and George Musica and their father on March 20, 1813. Philip again generously took the blame for the entire family and was sent to the Tombs Prison in New York City, where he made himself useful to his jailers by spying on other prisoners. He was rewarded by being released early in 1918.

Philip apparently enjoyed playing stool pigeon, for he obtained a job with the New York district attorney's office as an "investigator" named William Johnson. In this role, he procured affidavits in the Bolo Pasha case, charging William Randolph Hearst, the powerful newspaper tycoon, with favoring Germany over the Allies in World War I. During the "chicken murder" case in which Joseph Cohen was accused of killing Barnet Baff, "Johnson" convinced two convicts in Sing Sing Prison to give false testimony against the accused, who, as a result, was indicted and sentenced to death in the electric chair. Before the sentence was carried out, however, the perjury was discovered. In 1920 "Johnson" was indicted for his part in the false accusation but quickly vanished from sight.

Philip Musica next turned up as "Frank Costa," a co-owner of the Adelphi Pharmaceutical Manufacturing Company, producers of hair tonics. Although Prohibition had begun, the company was able to buy 5,000 gallons of alcohol each month for its manufacture of hair tonics. Philip invented a process that distilled this raw alcohol into highly profitable cheap liquor to be sold on the bootleg market. He disappeared before revenue agents raided the company's premises.

Musica's final alias was his most successful. As F. Donald Coster, he self-importantly presented himself as an American-born medical doctor turned businessman, who was a partner in the firm of Girard & Company, also manufacturers of hair tonics. No one knew his supposed partner, Philip H. Girard, and "Coster" grew rich and prominent while carrying on a secret bootlegging business at Girard & Company. The public saw him as a charming gentleman, married and above reproach. Within two years, by 1926, he was able to purchase McKesson & Robbins, a reputable, 93-year-old drug company in Bridgeport, Connecticut. He managed this deal by obtaining a huge loan against Girard & Company.

Under Coster's direction, McKesson & Robbins flourished, even after the Great Depression struck in 1929. The source of the firm's prosperity was its crude drug department in Canada, which secretly carried on a most imaginative swindle. Supposedly the firm had six Canadian warehouses containing more than $10 million worth of crude drugs, $8 million in collections due from banking representatives. In fact, McKesson & Robbins "purchased" its crude drugs from nonexisting companies and paid for them in cash, which, instead of going into the company's coffers, passed directly into the hands of Coster and his brothers. All of this was carefully documented with fake inventories, bills of lading, receipts, and invoices signed by Coster, Vernard, or the Dietrichs.

The grand scheme might have continued indefinitely had not Coster hired an investment banker, Julian F. Thompson, to be the company's treasurer. The company was hurt in the 1937 business recession, and Thompson wanted to sell some of its crude drug inventories to get more case assets. He was shocked to find that the inventories were not only not insured but were nonexistent and that the warehouses were only addresses. He reported his findings to the New York Stock Exchange, which suspended trading of McKesson & Robbins stock in early December 1938. The Securities and Exchange Commission and the Pure Food and Drug Administration both began investigations of McKesson's questionable practices that fall. On December 16, 1938, when the newspapers were exposing Philip Musica's past and present swindles, the supposed financial wizard and dignified gentleman locked himself in the bathroom at his mansion and fatally shot himself in the head. Musica's brothers received three-year prison sentences, and McKesson & Robbins survived and eventually rose to great financial success in the pharmaceutical field.

MUSSEL SLOUGH MASSACRE

Collis P. Huntington will long be remembered for the ways in which his monopoly, Pacific Associates, and his railroads bullied legislatures, counties, towns, and individuals to get lands, grants-in-aid, and perpetual concessions—all to make his control over transportation in California as absolute and profitable as possible. In southern California, Pacific Associates and the Southern Pacific Railroad used rigged courts, boycotts, and once even fatal violence to gain power.

The violence occurred in 1880 in the small San Joaquin Valley settlement of Mussel Slough. Throughout the 1890s there had been minor revolts, especially concerning rail rates for farm goods, and the railroad's suppression of these uprisings had gradually grown increasingly harsh, until settlers in the valley had formed a Settlers' Rights League to move against the Southern Pacific in the courts. Unfortunately, the courts were controlled by Huntington and Pacific Associates, and because of this, legitimate settlers were labeled "squatters."

In 1880, the railroad tried to evict the settlers by using United States marshals, and it was this effort that precipitated the massacre at Mussel Slough. At a May picnic held on the farm of a settler named Brewer, a marshal, two deputies, and an armed man identified as a Southern

Pacific *agent provocateur* appeared, ordering Brewer to give up his farm. Brewer refused, the Southern Pacific agent fired at Brewer, and a gun battle ensued. The result: five farmers and two federal officers dead.

The Southern Pacific used its massive legal power to punish the "squatters" for the revolt, and the biased court sentenced 17 farmers to prison. The agent who had started the fatal battle was not punished.

Nineteen farms without farmers were turned over to the Southern Pacific. Seventeen of the farmers were in prison; the other two had become train robbers. For four years these two successfully robbed Southern Pacific trains, cheered on by the San Joaquin Valley settlers, excoriated by the Southern Pacific's railroad police. One, Sontag, was caught and killed, the murder requiring a posse of 3,000 men to accomplish this goal.

The other, Evans, though shot many times, survived and was sent to prison for life in 1884. Evans was paroled by California Governor Hiram Johnson after 27 years, for the governor had by then learned the whole story about this farmer-turned-robber and how Collis Huntington's railroad had treated him.

The shortcomings of the Southern Pacific Railroad came out after 1901, when Frank Norris's muckraking book about the Southern Pacific, *The Octopus*, fictionalized the Mussel Slough horror and other abuses, and newspapers not owned by Huntington or the railroad found the courage to attack the excesses of the railroad baron and his henchmen.

MY LAI massacre

On the morning of March 16, 1968, American troops of Company C (Charlie), led by Lieutenant William L. Calley, Jr., were flown aboard helicopters into the hamlet of My Lai 4, also called Song My, in northeastern South Vietnam. They were on a "search and destroy" mission against the Viet Cong enemy, with orders to kill. Calley's superior officers included Captain Ernest Medina, Colonel Frank Barker, Colonel Oran Henderson (commander of the Eleventh Infantry Brigade), and Major General Samuel Koster (the division commander). After several hours when Medina's order halted the attack by Company C, it was discovered that no enemy gunfire had threatened the invading Americans, whose automatic weapons fire had left about 350 Vietnamese dead, including more than 100 unarmed civilian men, women, and children.

Rumors about the galling "massacre" at My Lai circulated among American soldiers for a time and died out; some have since said that at the time, the incident was intentionally suppressed. Finally, about 18 months after the My Lai killings, the American public was shocked by news stories and pictures revealing the atrocities that Company C had committed against civilians, and the U.S. House Armed Services Committee under Congressman L. Mendel Rivers began an inquiry, prompting the U.S. Army to look into the matter of My Lai. For a while, the massacre seemed shrouded in secrecy, but national and international outrage forced the military to provide some details about it and eventually to bring charges against Calley and 14 others, both officers and enlisted men. The brunt of the criticism, however, settled on the boyish-looking Calley, who faced a court-martial at Fort Benning, Georgia, on charges of premeditately having killed 102 persons at My Lai.

Calley's sensational trial from November 1970 until March 29, 1971, focused public attention on both the horror of the Vietnam War and the problem of guilt for war crimes. The trial saw conflicting testimony and contradictions from witnesses. Calley admitted shooting civilians at My Lai, and at one point in the legal proceedings, said, "It was no big deal, sir," in response to a question. His superior officers, whose orders he said he had been following at My Lai, had been adjudged innocent, and many hundreds of thousands of American citizens felt that it would be a travesty of military justice if Calley, the lowest-ranking officer in the chain of command over Company C, were to be found guilty. But the jury at his court-martial convicted him of the premeditated murder of at least 22 Vietnamese civilians at My Lai. His sentence—dismissal from the Army, loss of all pay, and life imprisonment at hard labor—aroused more public furor and further probing into the massacre.

An investigating U.S. Army board subsequently declared that Calley's entire division command had been guilty of misconduct, asserting that high-ranking officers had known of the My Lai atrocity and had done nothing about it. Through reviews and appeals, Calley's sentence was reduced to 10 years' imprisonment, and his court-martial conviction was later (1974) overturned by a federal district court in Columbus, Georgia. Another federal court in New Orleans, Louisiana, however, reinstated the conviction in 1975, but Calley remained free on bail, having been released from house arrest in Fort Benning in 1974 after serving 35 months of his 10-year sentence. Though the U.S. Supreme Court refused to review his court-martial conviction in 1976, the case of Calley being a "scapegoat" for higher-ups has persisted. Today, Calley is living in Georgia, a free man.

In September 1999, the Associated Press stunned the Pentagon, the Army, and the public by disclosing information in once-classified documents in the U.S. military archives. An apparent massacre of as many as 300 South Korean refugees, many of them women and children, had occurred under a railroad bridge near the hamlet of No Gun Ri on July 26–29, 1950, at the beginning of the Korean War (1950–53). About a dozen veterans of the First Cavalry Division said they had been ordered by commanders to shoot civilians as a defense against enemy soldiers who might be disguised as civilians. Korean eyewitnesses confirmed that American soldiers had machine-gunned many frightened noncombatants trapped beneath the bridge. The shocking revelations sparked a U.S. military investigation into the alleged No Gun Ri bloodbath in South Korea.

Bess MYERSON: beauty queen blues

"I feel as though it started as a little snowball . . . and then it just kept rolling and gaining speed . . . and I was standing in the way," said 63-year-old Bess Myerson in early November 1987. A former Miss America (1945) who had won further fame as a television celebrity, consumer advocate, newspaper columnist, politician, and friend of the rich and famous, Myerson now believed that the press and her own prominent public image were responsible for her forced resignation as New York City's commissioner of culture affairs and for her indictment on charges of attempting to fix her ex-boyfriend's divorce case.

New York's Mayor Edward I. Koch, a longtime close friend of Myerson's, said the indictment was "obviously sad for those who know her and worked with her," but added, "I believe what she did with respect to . . . ethical behavior, was . . . disgraceful."

The fall of the storybook beauty queen began in January 1987 when it was disclosed that Commissioner Myerson had invoked the Fifth Amendment to the Constitution before a federal grand jury investigating the business affairs of 41-year-old multimillionare Carl "Andy" Capasso, owner of the Nanco Contracting Corporation and romantic companion of Myerson, who had been indicted on charges of evading $774,600 in corporate and personal income taxes. It was also disclosed that Myerson had allegedly used her influence improperly to solicit a $53.6 million city sewer-renovation contract for Capasso.

Mayor Koch asked a special outside counsel to investigate these dealings, which included an allegation that Myerson had abused her power by hiring the daughter of the judge who was handling Capasso's bitter divorce in 1983. In announcing that she would take a 90-day leave of absence while the special counsel looked into her affairs, Myerson said "I want to make clear (that) I have done nothing wrong," and Koch expressed the confident hope "that she will be cleared and come back without any impediment."

All of this was a far cry from the glamour of Atlantic City in 1945 when the young Myerson, an aspiring pianist from the Bronx, had become the first Jewish woman to be chosen Miss America. At the time, she had just graduated from Hunter College and after her reign turned down a movie offer and returned to college for graduate work. Later she became a panelist on the CBS television show *I've Got a Secret* (1958–68). In 1969 New York's Mayor John Lindsay ap-

Bess Myerson, former commissioner of cultural affairs in New York City, talks with reporters outside federal court in Manhattan on October 15, 1987, after pleading innocent to charges of conspiracy, mail fraud, and bribery. She had also been accused of obstruction of justice and of giving a job to the daughter (Sukhreet) of the judge (Hortense Gabel) who had handled her boyfriend Carl Capasso's divorce. (AP/Wide World Photos)

pointed her consumer affairs commissioner, a post in which she was highly visible on local television, attacking unscrupulous businessmen and advocating a consumer protection act with success. But behind Myerson's glamorous public image was a difficult private life—one that saw three stormy marriages and divorces and a bout with ovarian cancer in the 1970s. In 1974 she had been hired as a columnist by the *New York Daily News.*

After Myerson and Capasso met in 1980, they soon became good friends. In time they were looked upon suspiciously by Capasso's wife, Nancy, who finally sued for divorce. Myerson, who made an unsuccessful try as a Democrat for the U.S. Senate in 1980, was a 25-year-long friend and political adviser of Koch (who would not have first been elected mayor in 1977 without her help), and in 1983 Koch made her cultural affairs commissioner of New York City, a job paying $83,000 a year.

When charges of "serious misconduct" were made against Myerson in the Capasso case, she was forced to step down from her post in April 1987. City investi-

gators alleged that she had given a job in the Department of Cultural Affairs, at a salary of $19,000 a year, to the daughter of state Supreme Court Justice Hortense W. Gabel in return for Gabel's leniency in the divorce case of Capasso. Gabel later reduced Capasso's weekly alimony payments from $1,500 to $500. About a week before Myerson's resignation, Capasso, pleading guilty to federal tax evasion, had been sentenced to four years in prison and fined $500,000. In late June 1987, the 74-year-old Gabel, who had been named judge of the year by the National Association of Women Judges in 1986, resigned from the court, citing physical and mental stress from the scandal.

Indicted on charges of bribery, conspiracy, and mail fraud, Bess Myerson entered her plea of innocent in federal court on October 15, 1987. Also named in the indictment were Carl Capasso (then serving his prison sentence) and Hortense Gabel, who claimed "I am innocent of any wrongdoing." The indictment said that the trio's plan had defrauded the city as well as Nancy Capasso (who supposedly lost $60,000 in temporary support payments and also possibly larger amounts in the final divorce settlement for "the financial benefit" of Capasso and Myerson). If convicted, Myerson faced a maximum of 30 years in prison and $513,000 in fines; Capasso and Gabel faced up to 25 years in prison and fines of $263,000 each. The months since the scandal was disclosed had been "one of the worst times in my life—certainly in the last 42 years of my career," said Myerson.

And, to add to her public troubles, the *New York Daily News* reported (May 8, 1988) that Myerson had been arrested in 1970 for shoplifting while in London, England; New Scotland Yard had charged her with "theft from a shop," but Myerson had apparently left London with the case outstanding. Later, in 1987, she had paid a fine of about $100 to end the case. In late May 1988, Myerson was arrested again for shoplifting in South Williamsport, Pennsylvania, and charged with stealing $44.07 worth of batteries, earrings, nail polish, and shoes. She had been visiting Capasso at the nearby Allenwood Federal Penitentiary, where he was serving a four-year sentence for tax evasion. Two months later, she pleaded guilty to shoplifting and was fined $100, plus $48.50 in court costs.

A New York City jury acquitted Myerson of all divorce-fixing charges (influencing Gabel and obstructing justice, among others) on December 22, 1988. Gabel, who was also acquitted in 1988, died about two years later.

N

NAVAL ACADEMY CHEATING SCANDAL

The United States Naval Academy prides itself on its honor code, according to which the academy will not tolerate any midshipman who lies, cheats, or steals. However, because midshipmen are intentionally overworked and overstressed in an attempt to build character and to improve performance under pressure, many of them avail themselves of whatever help they can in order to pass their demanding academic courses. Thus, when a copy of the final exam in Electrical Engineering 311 somehow fell into the hands of an enterprising second-year student in December 1992, it was circulated throughout the academy's dormitory the night before the exam. Dozens of midshipmen in the Class of '94 studied and discussed it carefully, all presumably knowing full well that to do so was a violation of the honor code.

Not all midshipmen enrolled in the course participated in the cheating scandal. In fact, the episode only came to the attention of the academy's administration after several midshipmen notified their professors by e-mail that their classmates had possessed a copy of the exam. However, the administration seemed reluctant to delve fully into the extent of the cheating. The first investigation into the situation, which was concluded in April 1993, identified only 28 midshipmen as suspects, and the only ones who were expelled were the six who confessed.

Angered that the cheaters who lied about cheating were not disciplined, four of the dismissed midshipmen threatened to sue the academy on the grounds that they were being punished unfairly. Meanwhile, rumors that the investigation had just barely scratched the surface of the scandal came to the attention of members of Congress, who threatened to conduct their own investigation. Accordingly, the academy's superintendent called in the navy's inspector general to get to the bottom of the scandal. His final report implicated 134 midshipmen, most of whom belonged to the 1,000-member class of '94, in the scandal, thus making it the biggest incidence of cheating in the academy's history. The report noted that many midshipmen regarded the honor code as "an ideal that simply could not be applied to many of the problems that arise in the daily life of a midshipman at the academy." Moreover, it became increasingly clear that many midshipmen believed that the honor code served only to protect the guilty while punishing those who came forward. One midshipman who informed school authorities about the scandal was beaten by his classmates, and a campus minister later revealed that many midshipmen were being told by their parents to lie about their involvement in the scandal.

The cases of the 134 midshipmen were to be examined by a three-member panel of top brass from the Pentagon, which was chaired by Vice Admiral Richard C. Allen. However, before the panel could begin its work, 28 were cleared, expelled for unrelated reasons, or graduated. The panel finished its work in April 1994. Of the 106 cases reviewed by the panel, 35 midshipmen were exonerated completely. Another 42 were found to have cheated to a minor degree; these midshipmen were allowed to graduate but only after taking the course over again. The panel recommended that the remaining 29 be dismissed for violating the honor code, and 24 of these were actually expelled. Most of those expelled had admitted their involvement, while many of those who continued to lie went unpunished.

John NEAL: his own worst enemy

Many dedicated authors, including the now scholarly acclaimed D. H. Lawrence (see *LADY CHATTERLEY'S LOVER: the power of four letter words*) have been stigmatized as sexual perverts and suffered the censorship of their work, their only crime being that they were ahead of their time. One such author was John Neal. His often sexually explicit novels, along with his cowardly and unethical behavior, caused him to lose his literary following in both England and America.

To many Americans, John Neal is an unknown. Born in Maine in 1793, he was a literary pioneer during the infancy of the nation. His brash literary and personal manner, as German scholars first noted in the 1960s, caused his influence to be generally unrecognized in his homeland until long after his death in 1876.

His story illustrates how manner in conflict with matter can be destructive, of reputation at the very least. Neal, at bottom, was an enthusiast who tried too hard.

Neal believed that the United States needed literary independence as well as political freedom from Great Britain. He argued for an American literature based on the young nation's own experience, promoting the use of American locales, of American dialects, and of American concerns to create a national literature whose characteristics would include a Byronic striving for independence, a directness of language and an openness to the consideration of topics considered too vulgar for British pens.

Neal also wrote such a literature, directly influencing poets like Edgar Allan Poe, John Greenleaf Whittier, and Henry Wadsworth Longfellow. His prose informed the work of novelists like Poe, Herman Melville, and Nathaniel Hawthorne (who referred to him as "that wild fellow John Neal"). Indirectly, he inspired such disparate writers as Mark Twain, Carl Sandburg, and William Faulkner. In the words of one scholar, Neal was "the Ezra POUND of the nineteenth century."

His lack of reticence makes him that period's D. H. Lawrence.

He wrote about topics then regarded as "forbidden" by British writers such as the drama of sexual conflict. Because such topics were also not readily appreciated by most American readers of the time, Neal's candor caused the ruin of his reputation in America and contributed to the ruin of his reputation in Britain.

In 1823, Neal's second novel, *Randolph,* published anonymously, was met angrily, first in Baltimore and then in most cities along the Atlantic coast, for it was not only explicitly erotic, but also quite thinly disguised the biographical sources of its plot. The book embarrassed the family of a former business partner, Joseph Lyman Lord, with whom Neal had lived while studying law. It also hurt the family of the poet Edward C. Pinkney.

Within a month, Neal published another novel, *Errata,* under his own name, in which he defended his brashness in *Randolph.*

Pinkney then challenged Neal to a duel and, when the latter declined, published a printed card "posting" Neal as a "gentleman by indulgent courtesy," just stopping short of calling him a coward. When Neal again refused to respond directly, Baltimoreans who would have otherwise supported his budding literary career began to shun him. Soon the whole East Coast knew of his ruined reputation.

Unable to practice law and now devoid of a literary audience, Neal emigrated to Britain, arriving in Liverpool on January 18, 1824.

To protect himself from the damage his American reputation might cause, he took the name of "Carter Holmes" and began the hoax for which he is still known in England. He applied to British journals for employment, and William Blackwood, publisher of *Blackwood's Edinburgh Magazine* (nicknamed The Maga), was pleased by Holmes's portfolio. He hired him and began an extraordinary two-year period in the history of American–Anglo-Saxon literary relations.

At the time considered "the cleverest and sauciest" of British journals, The Maga was used by Neal to disseminate his ideas about a native American literature. As one of the most prolific contributors to a journal already famous for its controversial high spirits, Neal wrote five long articles entitled "American Writers," in which he gave short shrift to British imitators Washington Irving and especially James Fenimore Cooper, who had failed to help Neal after his Baltimore debacle. Neal dismissed Cooper as a pale imitator of the popular Sir Walter Scott. By contrast, he gave fulsome praise to Charles Brockden Brown, James Kirke Paulding, and—of course—John Neal. His articles, recognized through Neal's style, outraged the American readers of The Maga.

Neal quickly became a trusted friend of Blackwood's and soon, true to his brash nature, presumed on the relationship. He had written another novel (his fifth), *Brother Jonathan,* and had persuaded Blackwood to publish it. It failed, and the Blackwood company suffered heavy losses. Neal, who had "toned down" the novel on Blackwood's request, blamed his employer. Despite Blackwood's anger at the imputation, Neal demanded monies due him only if the book sold well. Neal then found himself without a publisher. Because word of his ungentlemanly behavior quickly spread in British literary and publishing circles, he also realized that he was without a literary reputation on both sides of the Atlantic. He returned to Maine in 1827, where for the next 49 years he championed various causes, published a literary journal, and developed a local fame.

Tobia NICOTRA: autograph faker fooled Library of Congress

In the early 1930s, an international swindler named Tobia Nicotra traveled around the United States masquerading as the celebrated musician Richard Drigo, the former orchestra conductor for the Russian czar, who had died some years earlier. Nicotra soon gained entry into important musical circles. Among the people he met was Walter Toscanini (son of the famous New York Philharmonic Orchestra conductor Arturo Toscanini), who purchased from him, for 2,700 lire ($521), an autograph purported to be Mozart's.

Nicotra also managed to deceive a number of other Americans with his forged autographs of Mozart, Handel, and Wagner. In 1928 the Library of Congress paid

$60—a rather low price for a real document of the period—for several supposedly unpublished Mozart autographs that several Mozart experts had accepted as genuine. The Library of Congress learned a few years later that the manuscript was a fake.

In 1934 Nicotra's illegal activities caught up with him. Tried before a tribunal in Milan, Italy, he was convicted, largely on the testimony of Walter Toscanini, sentenced to two years in prison, and fined 2,400 lire ($463).

According to testimony at the trial, Nicotra's method was to acquire old paper by visiting the Milan Library, where he tore the flyleaves from old books or stole pages from manuscripts. He then added the "autographs" of famous musicians to these papers. The Milanese librarians testified that Nicotra had ruined many of the library's books. Additionally, Nicotra was accused of composing historically plausible documents and letters supposedly written by the same musicians whose autographs he had forged.

At Nicotra's trial, the police stated that they had found him preparing a new and more diverse series of false autographs, including those of George Washington, Abraham Lincoln, Warren G. Harding, the Marquis de Lafayette, Christopher Columbus, Martin Luther, Lorenzo the Magnificent, Leonardo da Vinci, Michelangelo, and Thaddeus Kosciusko.

Richard NIXON. See WATERGATE.

NIXON JEWEL SCANDAL

As U.S. President Richard M. Nixon's troubles deepened in the WATERGATE scandal he and his family became involved in another heated controversy concerning the receipt of expensive foreign gifts. On May 14, 1974, the *Washington Post* broke the news that some fabulous jewelry had been given to the Nixons by wealthy Arab leaders. The First Lady, Pat Nixon, was furious over the *Post* stories about the jewels. Columnist Maxine Cheshire, who reported the story, alleged that the Nixons had secretly accepted an estimated $2 million worth of foreign gifts.

According to Article One of the U.S. Constitution, all government officials are forbidden to accept gifts without the consent of Congress. In 1966 Congress revised the Foreign Gifts and Decorations Act of 1881, which made such gifts illegal, so that it now clearly states that it is illegal for "every person who occupies an office or a position in the Government of the United States . . . or is a member of the family and household of any such person" to accept and keep any gift valued at more than $50. However, the revised law did not clarify when a gift had to be turned over to the federal government or what the penalty was for breaking the law.

In 1974, most Americans did not realize that there was such a law, let alone that the law had apparently been broken. The White House maintained that all gifts to the Nixons had been properly recorded and that there had been no wrongdoing. Nixon loyalists were deeply offended by Maxine Cheshire's charges and went after her with vengeance. From all over the country the well-known *Post* columnist received hate mail containing such outbursts as "You and your Jew businessmen friends," and "You're a Jew working for Jews on a Jew newspaper." Others, however, praised her for the exposé.

In 1970, the year after President Nixon entered the White House, Cheshire had heard a rumor that the First Lady had received an alleged $1 million gift of jewels, including emeralds and diamonds, from the Shah of Iran. Cheshire checked to see whether the gift had been turned over to the chief of protocol as property of the U.S. government but found no record of the jewels anywhere. Furthermore, no one at the White House admitted that there had been such a gift. About three years later, after considerable investigation, Cheshire got corroboration of the jewelry rumor from others, who claimed to have seen some splendid jewels. Cheshire also noticed that Mrs. Nixon had worn a beautiful set of earrings, apparently consisting of emeralds and diamonds, at her birthday party at the White House in 1973. The columnist discovered that this matched set of emerald and diamond earrings had been part of a gift presented to the First Lady by Prince Fahd of Saudi Arabia on October 14, 1969. Cheshire's story about the secretly given jewelry was a bombshell that White House spokesmen said was "blown completely out of proportion and sensationalized."

One of Cheshire's most telling pieces of evidence of alleged wrongdoing by the Nixons was a notation on an index card in the White House gifts unit that read: "Jewelry for Mrs. Nixon, Julie and Tricia (not rec'd, Gift Unit.) 3/28/74 rec'd in Gift Unit—a bracelet type diamond watch, which was for Mrs. Nixon, a brooch of rubies and diamonds for Julie, the brooch of sapphires and diamonds for Tricia (not rec'd)." The jewelry had evidently been taken out of Mrs. Nixon's bedroom safe on March 28, 1974, to be logged into the gifts-unit file. The bracelet watch and the brooches were gifts to Mrs. Nixon and her daughters Julie and Tricia, from Prince Sultan, who with Prince Fahd was a half brother of King Faisal of Saudi Arabia, in July 1972. An appraisal of Prince Fahd's 1969 earring gift to the First Lady, requested by the Nixons in 1970, valued it at $52,400. In addition to this, King Faisal had given Mrs. Nixon diamond and ruby earrings on May 28, 1971. White House spokesmen denied all charges of impropriety by the Nixon family; everything given had supposedly been properly logged in. The president's legal counsel, J. Fred Buzhardt, who kept curious reporters from checking records in the gifts unit (which he claimed were Nixon private papers), said that the Nixons had always planned to hand over the jewels at the end of the president's term in office. Although he called the jewelry private gifts from the Saudi Arabians, Buzhardt stated that they were "in the same category as state gifts and (had to) go to a public repository when the President's term ends."

The Nixons' records in the gifts unit, Cheshire alleged, showed some $580,000 worth of jewelry that the family had had appraised for insurance purposes from 1970 to early 1974. After President Nixon resigned, his lawyers and the General Services Administration carried on a legal battle over the final disposition of the gifts.

Following the Cheshire exposé, many unrecorded gifts were suddenly turned in by government personnel, including Betty Fulbright, wife of Senator William Fulbright, the chairman of the Senate Foreign Relations Committee. Since the senator's committee had ironically drafted the 1966 law about gifts to federal employees, this provided yet another embarrassment. Former Vice President Spiro Agnew and his wife were among the first to return gifts. Congress, however, showed belated concern about official United States policy regarding gifts from foreign leaders; neither it nor President Gerald Ford took strong action to recover allegedly missing jewels and gifts given to the Nixons, contended Maxine Cheshire.

Walter NIXON: perjury on the federal bench

Since the first Congress passed the Judiciary Acts in 1789 establishing America's federal court system, only three sitting federal judges have ever been indicted and tried for serious crimes allegedly committed while they served on the bench. Oddly, all three of these cases—all concerning United States district court judges—occurred during the 1980s (in the past, several sitting federal judges had quit when faced with charges of judicial malfeasance). In 1983, Judge Alcee L. Hastings of Miami was acquitted of bribery-conspiracy charges and obstruction of justice. However, in 1988, the U.S. House of Representatives Judiciary Committee approved 17 articles of impeachment against Hastings, including charges of lying during his 1983 criminal trial about various aspects of his case. Hastings was later removed after the Senate, in 1989, found him guilty on eight articles of impeachment. In 1984 Judge Harry E. CLAIBORNE of Las Vegas was found guilty of tax evasion and, two years later, had to be removed from the federal bench by the impeachment process. In 1986 Judge Walter L. Nixon, Jr., of Biloxi, Mississippi, became the second judge in the long history of the federal courts to be convicted while in office.

An appointee of President Lyndon B. Johnson, handsome Walter Nixon was a chief judge of the Federal District Court for the Southern District of Mississippi. His legal troubles in the judiciary began when he was accused of receiving profitable oil and gas royalties in exchange for helping to sway Mississippi authorities to dismiss marijuana-smuggling charges against the son of his long-time friend Wiley Fairchild, a Mississippi businessman and contractor. Nixon was said to have promised favors to Fairchild in return for a share of the oil and gas royalties before the latter's son faced state drug charges.

Eventually, Judge Nixon had to stand trial himself. The trial took place in late January 1986 in Hattiesburg, Mississippi, where his case had been transferred. The judge's defense attorney, Michael Fawer, had shortly before stated that "judges are a sexy target," when asked why there had been so many recent complaints of wrongdoing against judges.

The jury in the Nixon case heard testimony from various witnesses supplied by the defense and prosecution. Nixon testified for three days, strongly denying the charges against him of bribery and perjury (which included lying to a federal grand jury when he had earlier disclaimed having intervened in Fairchild's son's drug case). Nixon claimed that he had purchased his oil and gas royalties himself in 1979, a year before the boy's arrest for marijuana-smuggling, and denied doing anything to influence the drug case. On February 9, 1986, after deliberating for two days, the jury announced its decision. Nixon was found innocent of accepting an illegal gift ($9,500 worth of oil and gas royalties from Fairchild to help bend the case against his son) but was convicted of perjury (lying to the grand jury by denying that he had discussed the case or attempted to influence its outcome).

Afterward, special prosecutor Reid Weingarten was "satisfied justice had been done" and said three key witnesses had "put the lie to Nixon's testimony." The three were Fairchild (who pleaded guilty to misdemeanor charges related to Nixon's case), former Mississippi state Senator Carroll Ingram (Fairchild's lawyer), and former Forrest County District Attorney Paul Holmes—all of whom testified that Nixon had talked about the drug case with them.

"Illogical," declared attorney Fawer about the jury's split verdicts. According to him, Judge Nixon had been "vindicated on the count of corrupting his office." Facing a maximum 10-year prison sentence and a $20,000 fine for perjury, the 57-year-old jurist appealed in vain and on March 31, 1986, was sentenced to five years behind bars. To the end, he insisted on his innocence and angrily criticized "attacks" on federal judges.

Evidence from Nixon's perjury conviction was later probed by the U.S. House of Representatives, which sent three articles of impeachment against him to the Senate for trial to determine whether Nixon should be removed from office and deprived of his $89,500 judicial salary while serving his prison sentence. The Senate voted overwhelmingly on November 3, 1989, to remove Nixon as a judge, convicting him twice of lying to a federal grand jury. Afterward he told reporters he was innocent. In 1993 Mississippi's supreme court ruled that Nixon had rehabilitated himself and could work as a lawyer in the state.

NO GUN RI massacre. See MY LAI massacre.

NORTHEAST UTILITIES NUCLEAR SAFETY SCANDAL

For at least 20 years, Northeast Utilities (NU), New England's leading power company, routinely skirted safety regulations at its nuclear plants in the region. It was a catastrophe waiting to happen but, until recently, the Nuclear Regulatory Commission (NRC) which allegedly knew about these violations all along, reportedly acted in collusion with the company. Employees who complained were harassed into silence or leaving. An NRC study indicated that the number of safety and harassment complaints lodged by NU's workers was three times the industry's average.

The scandal began unraveling in March 1992 when engineer George Galatis realized that NU had been bypassing safety standards during routine refueling operations at its Millstone 1 nuclear plant in Waterford, Connecticut, since the early 1970s. The reactor is shut down every 18 months to allow replacement of the fuel rods. The old rods are then submerged (or supposed to be) in a spent-fuel pool (already crowded three times beyond capacity) where the cooling system counteracts the extreme heat (250°F). Were this primary system to fail, radioactive steam would quickly engulf the plant, so older plants like Millstone are allowed to move just one-third of the rods into the pool at a time. However, Galatis found that NU was regularly dumping all the hot fuel in one move only 65 hours after shutdown (instead of the stipulated 250-hour cool-down period). By reducing the downtime for each refueling by about two weeks, the company saved $500,000 on expensive replacement power each day.

After unsuccessfully trying to convince his supervisors to approach the NRC with these safety concerns (corroborated by three independent consultants hired by NU) for nearly two years, Galatis himself contacted the agency in December 1994. He discussed the issues with a senior allegations coordinator, heard nothing for months, and then filed a written complaint. Meanwhile, back at work he was subjected to "subtle forms of harassment, retaliation and intimidation." For instance, his evaluation was downgraded and his personnel file was sent to the company's lawyers. Four months later, an agent from the NRC's Office of Investigations called Galatis after "inadvertently" discussing his complaints with NU. The agent suggested that Galatis's lawyer Ernest Hadley discuss the alleged harassment with NU's lawyer. Galatis was shocked to find that the NRC's Office of Nuclear Reactor Regulation had known of this

practice—which it claimed was both safe and common, provided the cooling system could handle the load (Millstone's couldn't)—for 10 years. Nor was this an isolated case—plants in several other states had similar troubles. Also, since 1990, Millstone had secured 15 waivers under the NRC's discretionary enforcement policy. Clearly, public safety did not rank high on the agency's agenda despite its stated mission that "nuclear regulation is the public's business." The collusion between the NRC and the industry and the latter's undue influence on the agency prompted U.S. Senator Joseph R. Biden (Democrat of Delaware) to call for an independent nuclear safety board.

In July 1995, NU asked Galatis and his colleague George Betancourt (who had been supportive throughout the ordeal) to help draft a request for a license amendment incorporating some of the same suggestions he had made years ago. NU could not off-load another full core until this amendment was approved. In August, Galatis and the public action group "We The People" petitioned the NRC to deny NU's request for license amendment and to suspend Millstone's operating license for 60 days. Betancourt was reassigned. The off-load deadline passed and the amendment still hadn't been approved. Plant safety was hotly debated by the public and state and local officials. The company warned employees that antinuclear activists were trying to shut down the plant. On October 26, Galatis's petition was denied. Two weeks later, NU's amendment was granted and fuel removal began at Millstone the next day.

A report released by NRC Inspector-General Leo J. Norton late in December confirmed that NU had conducted full core off-loads improperly for 20 years. It admitted that the NRC was aware of this but that its inspectors did not realize it was an infraction. However, Norton denied any evidence of collusion, attributing the oversight to poor training. NRC also demanded a total review of every system at Millstone with the results "submitted on oath" to assure the safety of the entire plant.

NRC chairperson Shirley A. Jackson pledged to improve the training, accountability, and vigilance of inspectors and NRC employees. She also launched a nationwide review of all 110 nuclear plants, offering them a two-year period to correct problems they identified. A global evaluation of Millstone found that 5,000 "items" needed to be resolved before the plant could safely be back in operation. NU announced the reorganization of its nuclear division. But, in January 1996, NRC closed and placed all three Millstone plants on the "watch list" of problem reactors (Galatis was told that this constituted a partial granting of his petition). NU was fined $2.1 million; its debt rating plummeted from stable to negative; it faced $1 billion in shutdown costs and its Connecticut Yankee reactor was permanently shelved.

Under new leadership, NU was completely revamped. In June 1996, Galatis and Betancourt signed severance deals with NU. Galatis joined a seminary in Massachusetts. He and other whistleblowers remain convinced that nothing has changed at NU and/or the NRC—they believe it was only a "show." There was speculation that the company might try to recover $250 million of the shutdown costs by hiking rates for its customers. Millstone 1 was finally decommissioned in July 1998, Millstone 2 became operational again in May 1999, and Millstone 3 was shut down for refueling in April 1999.

In September 1999, shortly after NU said it was planning to auction off the Millstone plants, it agreed to pay $10 million in penalties and plead guilty to 25 federal felony counts for lying to nuclear regulators and polluting waters near its plants. NU's federal criminal liability was thus resolved, but investigations of individuals continued that involved other matters.

NORTHERN PACIFIC "BUBBLE"

For John Pierpont Morgan, the year 1901 began as a high point in his remarkable career as one of America's foremost financiers: he had created the world's first billion-dollar corporation (see GATES/MORGAN/GARY: the creation of U.S. Steel). The elated but tired mogul rewarded himself by beginning a European vacation. But his relaxation was brief, for his interests in the Northern Pacific Railroad (NP) were suddenly imperiled by attacks upon his control from Edward Henry Harriman and the Standard Oil group. Morgan's response was so strong as to cause a brief panic on the New York Stock Exchange, to bring ruin to the fortunes of thousands, and to induce distress in the world's financial capitals. It also permanently scarred what had been his essentially favorable reputation (see J. P. MORGAN: gentleman robber baron).

By contemporary American business standards, Harriman's hurtful attack on Morgan was basically without malice. As controller of the Union Pacific Railroad (UP), Harriman had sought a Chicago terminal for his rail lines and saw a possibility in the Chicago, Burlington, and Quincy (C B & Q) Railroad. Publicly, that railroad was under the management of James J. Hill, unique among railroad tycoons for creating the Great Northern railway without a penny of federal assistance. Hill also, with Morgan's backing, managed the NP, which had gone bankrupt in the Panic of 1893 and of which the C B & Q was a subsidiary.

In 1901, management and majority control of an enterprise were not necessarily correlative; Morgan and Hill held only 30 percent of the shares of the NP. Unaware that Harriman planned to acquire the C B & Q by gaining majority control of the NP (and thus forcing Hill out), Morgan had sold 58,000 shares of his NP stock to finance his U.S. Steel venture. Thinking himself safe,

he left for Europe. Meanwhile, Morgan's New York office was somehow mysteriously not alerted to Harriman's quiet buying of NP shares, putting him within 40,000 shares of majority status.

It was Hill in Seattle who became aware of the Harriman-Standard Oil maneuvers. He dashed to New York, verified through Jacob Schiff, of Harriman's broker Kuhn, Loeb and Company, that Harriman was close to majority control, and worriedly cabled Morgan for permission to buy 150,000 shares of NP stock. On May 5, 1901, Morgan said yes.

Simultaneously, Harriman ordered Schiff to buy the 40,000 shares he needed for majority control. But Schiff did not receive the order. May 5 was a Saturday, and Schiff, a religious man, was at his synagogue.

Panic buying of NP stock began on Monday, May 7, for the Morgan brokers alone bought 127,500 shares, pushing up the price. By Thursday, the price of NP stock had reached $1,000 per share. The Morgan forces were no longer buying, but the stock exchange had gone wild. Many brokers sold shares they could not acquire without bankrupting themselves of their houses; money was short, and the interest rate on loans rose to 60 percent.

Public opinion blamed Morgan for the rampage and at first neglected to note that from France, he had persuaded a consortium of banks to form a money pool to save the ailing brokerage houses. (Conspicuously absent from that pool was the Rockefeller-controlled National City Bank of New York.) The pool, however, did not help individual gamblers on the stock exchange, unless they were short-sellers who benefited from an agreement by the battling parties to set the share price at $150. Thousands had been ruined financially.

In the midst of the uproar, Morgan returned swiftly to New York, where the combatants made peace, setting up an illegal holding corporation on whose board Harriman and Rockefeller had seats. Morgan retained dominant control of the NP (see NORTHERN SECURITIES VILLAINY). His reputation, however, had been blackened because his participation in the contest was viewed as being self-serving and completely unconcerned with those persons who had been caught between the rivals in their battle for power.

NORTHERN SECURITIES VILLAINY

John Pierpont Morgan was insensitive to the opinions of legislators, jurists, clergy, and the general public but was deeply concerned about his own reputation. The events of 1901 (see NORTHERN PACIFIC "BUBBLE") had shaken him, having blemished his fame as a businessman and financier. They had dealt the prestige of both Morgan and J. P. Morgan & Company a heavy blow, questioning their efficiency because the company had not been alert to the designs of Edward H. Harriman and the Standard Oil party against the Northern

Pacific Railroad. They had challenged Morgan's position as a railroad tycoon and had forced him to act both hastily and destructively. He was therefore determined through his new Northern Securities Corporation to both redeem his prestige and avoid another loss of face. Despite his determination, Morgan failed on both counts.

Although the new corporation earned Morgan gratitude because it saved the stock market's short-sellers from insolvency and partially redeemed his reputation as a railroad baron, it was patently illegal under the Sherman Antitrust Act of 1890 because it was a holding company, a form of trust. It held and controlled all the shares of the Northern Pacific, Great Northern, and Chicago, Burlington, and Quincy railroads regardless of the ownership of Harriman or Hill or Morgan; as such, Northern Securities had the potential to restrain trade.

Because court tests of the Sherman Act had shown it to be ineffective, Morgan was not concerned about the illegality of Northern Securities. As its majority stockholder, he could name its board of directors, and in the name of peace and community of interest, he gave Harriman some places on it. Hill gained other posts, and he named the majority to represent himself. Morgan thought that he was now free to return to his usual business affairs.

But Morgan had not reckoned with U.S. President Theodore Roosevelt, who had seemed to offer no opposition to his earlier and more flagrant illegalities (see GATES/MORGAN/GRAY: the creation of U.S. Steel). Although somewhat tolerant of monopolies, Roosevelt took a dim view of restraint of trade. Consequently, word reached Morgan indirectly that the United States attorney general planned to move against Northern Securities. Wall Street was upset at the news, and frightened selling occurred on the stock exchange.

Morgan was not frightened but angry. He thought it unfair that his holding company, of all the hundreds existing in America, should be chosen for a test case of restraint of trade. He was certain the case would fail but thought it ungentlemanly that Roosevelt would act without consulting him privately. He journeyed to Washington and informed Roosevelt of his feelings about being allowed no opportunity to fix up the problem. When Roosevelt replied, "We don't want to fix it up; we want to stop it," Morgan went away upset, incensed that as a man of honor he had been so discourteously treated.

He was even angrier on March 14, 1904, when the U.S. Supreme Court voted 5 to 4 against the legality of the Northern Securities Corporation. Justice John M. Harlan condemned it, writing, "No scheme or device . . . could more effectively and certainly suppress free competition."

Morgan's success in redeeming his reputation had been short-lived. He was to suffer other federal blows to his prestige before his career ended with his death in 1913, and his reputation continued to decline during the ensuing decades.

Joshua Abraham NORTON: America's only emperor

When he died in 1880, 30,000 people filed past his coffin and his obituary praised him for his peacefulness. When the burial ground was to be overwhelmed by the expansion of San Francisco, he was reburied with pomp and music in 1934. He rests under a granite slab engraved "Norton I, Emperor of the United States and Protector of Mexico." It also carefully notes that Norton I had really been "Joshua A. Norton, 1819–1880."

Norton I was London-born and South Africa bred. He came to San Francisco via Brazil in 1849 with $40,000, opened a general store for the high-spending miners of that time, and dabbled in real estate, prospering until 1853. Then, united with a few associates in an attempt to corner the rice market, he was bankrupted of almost a quarter-million dollars by the unexpected arrival of rice cargoes. The ensuing litigation cost him his mind.

In 1859, Norton submitted to the San Francisco *Evening Bulletin* a solemn proclamation indicating that public desire had caused him to proclaim himself "Emperor of these United States." Printed without comment, the proclamation aroused little attention, as did later proclamations abolishing Congress and the State Supreme Court for their corruption. Norton gained notice only when he began to appear in public in a gaudy officer's uniform with large golden epaulets, a garrison cap, and a saber. He promenaded on San Francisco's main streets, serenely acknowledging the bows of his subjects, checking streetcar schedules, and inspecting drains. He had his own seat in theaters, whose audiences would rise silently when he entered. He attended all public events, continued to issue proclamations, sat in a special chair when the legislature was in session, and was introduced proudly in 1876 to a real emperor—Don Pedro II of Brazil—as the city's own.

He even issued imperial bonds—usually for 50 cents—and levied small taxes. He usually ate and drank free of charge in San Francisco's best restaurants and saloons. Public subscriptions bought him a new uniform, new hats, a magnificent walking stick, and a huge umbrella to keep his majesty dry in San Francisco's rains.

Norton was also a peacemaker. He ordered Lincoln and Jefferson Davis to stop their Civil War and to come to San Francisco for his advice and mediation. (They declined). When Mexico proved incorrigible, he dropped the title "Protector of Mexico" from his name.

When he died, one newspaper bore the headline "LE ROI EST MORT" and another mourned that "no citizen of San Francisco could have been taken away who would be more generally missed."

San Francisco still has its eccentrics, but none has so completely captured the fancies and hearts of its citizenry as did the Emperor Norton I.

Ramon NOVARRO: a lurid death

Dark, handsome Ramon Novarro was one of the most popular American Latin-lover movie stars of the 1920s and 1930s. Female fans swooned over him in movie after movie, and he was rumored to be romantically involved with several beautiful actresses, including Greta Garbo. On Halloween night, 1968, however, long after the star's heyday, his dark sexual secret was tragically uncovered.

Ramon Samaniegos was born into a large, poor family in Durango, Mexico. He migrated to Los Angeles, California, in 1913 when he was 14-years old. There he took various jobs (grocery clerk, piano teacher, cafe singer, and hotel busboy, among others) before getting some bit parts in silent motion pictures. After changing his name to Novarro (which sounded more debonair) in 1921, he gained major success as an actor in *Scaramouche* (1923). His dashing good looks captivated women, who panted and swooned over him in subsequent films like *The Arab* (1924) and the silent-screen version of *Ben Hur* (1925). Now rich and famous, Novarro became close friends with the legendary star Rudolph VALENTINO, who presented him in 1923 with a black lead, Art Deco dildo inscribed with Valentino's silver signature as a token of success. Newsmen and others, however, sometimes implied that neither Novarro nor Valentino were "real men," but were instead "faggots." Novarro's MGM studio publicists portrayed him as a deep, dark, pensive type of man and scotched rumors that he was contemplating retiring to a monastery permanently, particularly after the death of his pal Valentino in 1926. It was at this time that he became renowned as the world's greatest Latin lover.

Novarro was rumored to be in love with beautiful Greta Garbo, his co-star with whom he played a seductive love scene in *Mata Hari* (1931), an early talkie. However, all rumors of romantic involvement with Garbo and later with actress Myrna Loy were deliberately squelched by him personally. In 1934, a growing lack of public interest in Novarro made him voluntarily retire from film-making and spend the next few years touring abroad as a singer. After this, a vain attempt to make movies once again brought about his quiet retreat to his San Diego, California, ranch. The public again saw him in some television shows in the 1950s, and he later settled in a home he bought in North Hollywood, where he was surrounded with many mementoes of the past. There his health soon deteriorated because of his constant gin drinking.

On the evening of October 30, 1968, Paul and Tom Ferguson, runaway brothers from Chicago who had turned to petty thievery and hustling to get money, arrived at Novarro's North Hollywood home to steal money ($5,000 was said to be hidden there, according to street rumors) so that they could get out of Los Angeles and return home to the Midwest. Novarro was known locally as easy prey by young male prostitutes, and Paul Ferguson, who loathed all "faggots," reluctantly ended up in the bedroom with the gray-haired actor after several hours of drinking gin, vodka, and tequila together. After a while Ferguson went into a violent rage, beating the naked Navarro into unconsciousness. A maniacal urge caused the young man to strike his victim over and over with Novarro's cherished ivory-tipped cane. Tom Ferguson screamed for his brother to stop, saw that Novarro was mortally wounded, and decided that they had to make it look like a robbery before they fled. The pair smashed things throughout the house, scrawled the name "Larry" in various places, tied Novarro's bloody, naked body at the wrist and ankles, dumped it on the bed, and left the veiled message, "Us girls are better than fagits," on the mirror. Paul laid the black cane's shaft across Novarro's naked legs, its ivory tip between his thighs. Finally, the two put on some of the old actor's dressy clothes, foolishly leaving their own blood-stained clothes in a neighbor's yard, where they were found. The clothes helped the police to track them down within a week.

The Ferguson brothers were tried for murder, convicted, and sentenced to life imprisonment; seven years later they were freed on parole. Novarro's well-kept personal life was no more; some now cried over the former great ladies' man who had never picked a lady for himself, but others were stunned by the revelation of his homosexual promiscuity.

John Humphrey NOYES: Perfectionism and free love sanctified

Among the most complex, controversial, and creative of American social and religious experiments was Perfectionism. Founded in the first half of the 19th century by John Humphrey Noyes, the religion was based on a communitarian ideal. Certain that the nuclear family and romantic-love ran counter to the teachings of Christ, the Perfectionists formed several communities that were in many ways far ahead of their time. They advocated and practiced a form of "free love," birth control, and eugenics. They even engaged in a group therapylike type of arbitration.

Perfectionism began in New Haven, Connecticut, in 1834 when the then 23-year-old Noyes, a student at the Yale Theological Seminary, renounced the orthodox Christian doctrine of original sin. As a result of a religious experience, he announced instead that he was "perfect" as men were commanded to be in Matthew 5:48, and he preached at the New Haven Free Church

John Humphrey Noyes, Perfectionist minister whose doctrine of free love resulted in scandal, founded the controversial Oneida Community in New York, which survived for about 30 years. (The Bettmann Archive)

that man could regain his innate sinlessness through communion with Christ. His announcement took courage: it cost him his license to preach, his candidacy for ordination, and his matriculation at the seminary.

Noyes then went to Putney, Vermont, where he had the time to consider the social, economic, and familial implication of his heretical position. He also founded a Bible school there (1836) that attracted articulate and responsive individuals concerned about the confused course of Christian society. They formed a Society of Inquiry, practicing after 1837 what was sometimes called Bible Communism and, later, Perfectionism. In 1846 the society began to follow the most shocking of Noyes's tenets, complex marriage. The practice led to the group's reputation as immoral and promiscuous.

A form of polygamy, complex marriage is more precisely called pantagamy because in Noyes's theory, everyone is married to everyone else. In simplistic terms, the practice resembles "free love," but its theoretical base and its expression are so involved that its practitioners are allowed almost no freedom. Noyes theorized that contemporary marriage was faulty: it failed to fulfill its Christian duty on the social level. Romantic love expressed individualism and selfishness; marriage, with its legal and emotional exclusiveness, was a form of slav-

ery for both the male and female, and its failure led to the evils of adultery, divorce, and prostitution. Moreover, the nuclear family was, in essence, antisocial and private, a kind of individualism on the group level. To redeem and sanctify sexuality as a fundamental part of human nature, Noyes felt it necessary to reject contemporary marriage and purge from the Perfectionists all vestiges of romanticism and individualism affecting sexual activity.

Complex marriage meant sexual sharing but in a highly decorous manner. Females were approached, with stipulated infrequency, through a third party, usually female. To control accidental, unwanted pregnancies, Noyes introduced (1846) a rigorous and difficult form of birth control called "male continence." Sexual intercourse was allowed after the required decorous invitation, but climax was prohibited; instead the activity was a kind of *coitus reservatus,* and the obligation to avoid male orgasm and ejaculation was solely the man's. (Women were permitted multiple orgasm, for fertility was not involved.) To control psychological and emotional problems arising from such a discipline, novel encounter-group therapy sessions, usually public, were held on a regular basis. Offenses to this prescribed system, if repeated, might cause limitation of sexual privileges, shipment of one member of a "romantic" liaison to a satellite community, or expulsion from the religious community.

The practice of complex marriage, and especially the attempt of some of the Perfectionist society's males to extend it to adolescent females, as well as the heresy of the "perfect," forced Noyes and his followers from Putney in 1847. They went to Oneida, New York, and established satellite communities in Wallingford, Connecticut, Cambridge and Newark, Vermont, and Brooklyn, New York, reducing them to Oneida and Wallingford after 1852.

The Oneida community was the largest Perfectionist center, averaging about 200 members living communally, farming, canning, and making silk embroidery and later, flatware. At Oneida, Noyes added a new fillip to complex marriage: a method of eugenics he labeled *stirpiculture* ("the breeding of special stocks"). According to this system, a committee carefully chose couples for mating and breeding; at weaning, the child born to each couple was rasied communally to prevent the development of nuclear family ties.

Noyes's concepts, published as *Bible Communism* in 1853, created problems in the Perfectionist communities, and complex marriage was twice stopped until the difficulties were resolved in the semi-democratic group-therapy sessions. But Noyes's attempt to combine Christian discipline with "a continual honeymoon" involving love after marriage failed because precommunal attitudes could not be rooted out. Conflict between the needs of the self and the needs of the community caused

Oneida and Wallingford to become part of a joint stock company in 1879, where ordinary marriage and private ownership were practiced. Noyes and a few followers embarked for Canada. Without Noyes's charismatic influence, Wallingford sold out in 1881, and Noyes's remarkable, controversial, and much misunderstood experiments, only now beginning to receive the impartial attention they deserve, were at an end.

O

Stephen OATES: professor accused of plagiarism

In 1977, Stephen B. Oates, author and professor of history at the University of Massachusetts, Amherst, published *With Malice Toward None: The Life of Abraham Lincoln* (Harper & Row). It sold more than 100,000 copies and was published in paperback the following year. The book was positively reviewed and soon replaced Benjamin P. Thomas's *Abraham Lincoln: A Biography* (1952) as the definitive one-volume biography of Lincoln. Subsequently, Oates wrote biographies of Martin Luther King, Jr. (1982), and William Faulkner (1987). Nonetheless, outside of academia, he was little known until 1990.

That year, an American literature professor named Robert Bray highlighted the similarities between passages in the two Lincoln biographies during his presentation at the Illinois historical conference. Soon, other scholars began poring through Oates's works in search of uncredited "borrowing" from various sources. A year later, the American Historical Association received complaints of plagiarism against Oates. Oates denied these charges, saying that any similarities between the two works were incidental, the result of having relied on the same historical documents. In a signed public statement, 23 noted historians of Lincoln and the Civil War argued that the charges against Oates were without basis. The association's verdict was equivocal. It paid tribute to Oates's style and contributions but said that he had failed to give due credit to Thomas and recommended that he do so in future editions.

Professor Michael Burlingame of Connecticut College did not take this verdict lightly. He approached two scientists (physicist Walter Stewart and cell biologist Ned Feder) at the National Institutes of Health in Bethesda, Maryland, experts in the detection of scientific fraud and misconduct, who ran Oates's books and his suspected sources through their plagiarism-detecting computer program. Comparing 30-character strings in all the works, they claimed 175 instances of plagiarism in Oates's Lincoln biography and 340 more in his works on King and Faulkner. Their evidence was assembled in a 1,400-page document and sent to the association and to several historians who had been supportive of Oates. In his response, Oates asked why two government scientists (Stewart and Feder) were spending their office hours and expensive computer time to investigate a historian who did not receive federal grants. He thus filed complaints criticizing them with the U.S. Department of Health and Human Services and several congressmen. In April 1993, Stewart and Feder were reassigned and asked to halt their project. However, they maintained that there was a pattern to Oates's plagiarized passages (an indication of conscious borrowing, according to them) and appealed the decision. Oates argued that the Stewart-Feder criteria for detecting plagiarism were so mechanical that no writing could pass their test. Besides, Oates added, there were no clear guidelines from professional societies in this regard, nor could the alleged plagiarizer approach any authority for help.

Certainly, this case raised more questions than it resolved. For instance, what is the accepted definition of plagiarism? Can there even be one? Is a computer smart enough to be entrusted with the delicate task of detecting somewhat nebulous instances of plagiarism? The issues of the case led the American Historical Association to form a subcommittee to redefine plagiarism and also provide examples of first- and second-degree offenses. The editor of Lincoln's legal papers, Collum Davis, said that professional organizations do not recognize such a distinction. However, he felt that while Oates's work was not a "wholesale plagiarization," it was plagiarization nonetheless. Others believe that the case damaged Oates's reputation and credibility. By then, he was already working on another work—a biography of Clara Barton's nursing career during the Civil War, published in 1995.

"OHIO GANG." See Harry DAUGHTERY; Charles R. FORBES; Jesse SMITH; TEAPOT DOME.

OPM LEASING SWINDLE

OPM Leasing Services, Incorporated of New York City was in the business of leasing computers to large companies around the United States. It offered lower rates and more attractive terms than its various competitors, but when International Business Machines Corporation (IBM) introduced a new line of computers in 1978, OPM and many of its lesees found themselves stuck with obsolete equipment. To remain solvent, OPM used false bills of sale and bogus leases to obtain loans from banks and other lending institutions to the tune of more than $200 million. The fraud was discovered in 1981, after OPM filed for bankruptcy.

Mordecai Weissman and Myron S. Goodman were brothers-in-law who had been friends since boyhood. In 1970, while in their early twenties, they founded OPM Leasing, which soon became one of the largest computer-leasing firms in the world (critics said the initials OPM stood for "Other People's Money"). The company bought computer systems from manufacturers, mainly the IBM Corporation, and then leased them for seven years to such blue-chip companies as Rockwell International, Merrill Lynch, Xerox, American Express, General Motors, and American Telephone & Telegraph. By spreading the rental over a seven-year period rather than the usual three or four years offered by other leasing companies, OPM was able to offer much lower monthly rental rates. There was a catch, however. The contracts contained what were known as "hell or high water" clauses which stipulated that the lesees had to pay the rental fees no matter what happened.

All went well until mid-1978, when IBM brought out its new "300" series of computing equipment. Suddenly all previous equipment became out of date, and OPM was no longer able to take back leased computers and sublease them to new users. *Business Week* magazine had carried an article pointing out the perils of OPM's contracts early in 1978, after which Goldman Sachs & Company resigned as the firm's investment banker. Many companies, however, did not heed the warnings about OPM's dubious practices.

OPM had used loans from banks and insurance companies to buy the computers it leased; the collateral for the loans was the machines themselves or the guaranteed monthly rentals for them. Very little of OPM's own funds were involved in the purchases. When it became clear that its big gamble that its computers would be usable for at least a decade had failed, OPM turned to fraud to sustain its loses. It submitted fake bills of sale and altered documents, particularly of leases by the Rockwell International Corporation, to obtain new loans from lenders. For example, the Paul Revere Protective Life Insurance Company received documents indicating that Rockwell's monthly lease payments totalled $54,000, whereas in reality the payments amounted to only $463. During a two-year period, OPM swindled millions of dollars from 19 lending institutions.

In March 1981, the company filed for bankruptcy protection under Chapter 11. A trustee was appointed to take over OPM's operations. Weissman resigned as OPM president and Goodman resigned as executive vice president. During the course of the investigation, examiners of the bankruptcy petition noted that $10.5 million had been advanced to stockholders of the parent company, of which there turned out to be only two: Weissman and Goodman. It was further revealed that the two had encountered the criminal law before. Several years earlier, in a federal court in New Orleans, Louisiana, they had pleaded guilty to 22 felony counts involving a check-kiting scheme and had been fined $110,000. They pleaded guilty again in 1982, this time to obtaining more than $200 million from major American banks. OPM agreed to repay $65 million to the 19 banks and other financial institutions from which it had borrowed money. Weissman was sentenced to 12 years in prison, and Goodman to 10 years. Several of their associates were fined for income-tax evasion, and five former vice presidents of the company also pleaded guilty to fraud.

OPPENHEIMER CASE: the Atomic Energy Commission's stigma

During World War II, Dr. J. Robert Oppenheimer, a brilliant physicist and teacher, directed the secret Manhattan Project that developed the atomic bomb. Yet in 1953, when members of the U.S. Atomic Energy Commission (AEC) learned of Oppenheimer's prewar associations with communists and left-wingers, the "Father of the atomic bomb" found himself the subject of humiliating allegations. It was the height of the Cold War, and communist hysteria was rampant. The unfortunate Oppenheimer was forced to go before a personal security board and eventually lost his security clearance. He was to remain in disgrace for over 10 years.

When he became a physics professor at the University of California at Berkley and the California Institute of Technology in 1936, Dr. Robert Oppenheimer was completely apolitical. Then he met and fell in love with Jean Tatlock, an active member of the Communist Party, who introduced him to others who were working for social reforms and other left-wing and liberal causes. Oppenheimer became involved with many of these projects, but he never joined the party, although his younger brother Frank and many of his students did.

American physicist J. Robert Oppenheimer, director of the Institute for Advanced Study at Princeton University (1947–66), helped build the atomic bomb but opposed the development of the hydrogen bomb. Charged with communist sympathies, he lost his security clearance with the Atomic Energy Commission. The Federation of American Scientists declared him the victim of a witch hunt, and later Oppenheimer was cleared of disloyalty charges and received the Enrico Fermi Award. He died of throat cancer in 1967. (Yale University Archives/Historical Picture Collection/Yale University Library)

After the United States entered World War II on December 8, 1941, Oppenheimer never attended another left-wing meeting but instead devoted his energies to the difficult scientific problems of developing an atomic bomb. This was successfully done at Los Alamos, New Mexico, in 1945. There, after viewing the first atomic fireball in history, at the Trinity test sight, Oppenheimer became visibly shaken at what he and his colleagues had created, quoting a sentence from ancient Sanskrit literature: "I am become death, the shatterer of worlds."

After the war, Oppenheimer was elected to a six-year term as chairman of the General Advisory Committee (GAC) to the AEC and served on numerous national and international scientific panels. He returned to teaching and in 1947 became director of the prestigious In-

stitute for Advanced Study at Princeton, New Jersey. In 1949, like many other scientists, Oppenheimer vehemently opposed, on moral and ethical grounds, a crash program to build a hydrogen bomb—an action that was later to be held against him.

As the Cold War intensified and anticommunist hysteria mounted in the early 1950s, many members of the AEC were alarmed to learn of Oppenheimer's pre-war associations with left-wingers and communists. The Federal Bureau of Investigation (FBI) had kept him under intermittent surveillance for years and had bugged his conversations and, in the fall of 1953, prepared a damaging report in which an overly zealous FBI agent inferred that Oppenheimer was and long had been a Soviet agent. The agent claimed that Oppenheimer had committed espionage and influenced American military, atomic-energy, intelligence, and diplomatic policies to the advantage of Russia. This report was forwarded to President Eisenhower, who, on December 3, 1953, ordered that a "blank wall" be placed between Oppenheimer and any further access to classified information until the charges against him had been thoroughly investigated.

A letter listing these allegations was delivered to Oppenheimer, who was given the option of either resigning his post as a consultant to the AEC or submitting to a hearing before a three-member personnel security board of the AEC. He choose the latter. Usually these hearings lasted one or two hours in an informal setting in which members of the security board questioned an individual to determine his or her level of security clearance. In Oppenheimer's case the hearings continued for four weeks in a courtroomlike setting in which both sides were represented by legal counsel. The usual rules of evidence did not apply, and Oppenheimer's attorney was not permitted to examine the investigative file or to meet with the security board's members, as the AEC's counsel did repeatedly.

The secret hearing opened on April 12, 1954, in Washington, D.C., and was rapidly transformed into a trial for treason of the man who had directed the successful atomic bomb project that had hastened the end of World War II and saved millions of lives. Oppenheimer was questioned closely about his actions 12 to 15 years earlier, and he frequently contradicted himself during the more than 20 hours during which he stood in the witness box. Thirty-one witnesses, many of them influential people in and outside of government, testified on Oppenheimer's behalf, and several declared that they shared his unpopular opinions about the H-bomb. Throughout the hearing, Oppenheimer's every move was observed and reported on by the FBI. Later, AEC Commissioner Lewis Strauss was reported to have thanked the FBI for its coverage of Oppenheimer and for being "most helpful to the AEC in that they were aware beforehand of the moves he was contemplating."

On May 27, 1954, the personnel security board made its report; two members were against granting Oppenheimer security clearance, and one was in favor. The last, Ward Evans, wrote in his minority report, "I personally think that our failure to clear Dr. Oppenheimer will be a black mark on the escutcheon of our country." These recommendations then went to the five AEC commissioners for a final decision. While they were weighing the matter, the transcripts of the hearing were made public, since Oppenheimer had already granted interviews to the press. On June 29, 1954, the AEC commissioners issued their verdict; four were against clearance, and the fifth was in favor. The dissident, Henry DeWolf Smyth, wrote, "There is no indication in the entire record that Dr. Oppenheimer has ever divulged any secret information."

Although many scientists and intellectuals continued to support him, the ordeal of the administrative tribunal had a harrowing effect on Oppenheimer and his family. With the advent of the Kennedy administration in 1961, the hostile atmosphere began to ease, and in 1963 the GAC and the commissioners of the AEC unanimously voted to give Oppenheimer the annual Enrico Fermi Award. In a White House ceremony, President Lyndon B. Johnson presented him with a citation, a medal, and a check for $50,000 "on behalf of the people of the United States." The stigma was thus removed, but Oppenheimer's security clearance was never restored.

P

Bob PACKWOOD: blinded by sexual misconduct?

It's no secret that politics are fraught with corruption. Many high-level politicians refuse to believe they are subject to the same rules as ordinary people. But in a landmark case, one U.S. senator, Bob Packwood, Republican from Oregon, was forced to reevaluate his privileges when he was investigated for past sins of the flesh. When he was brought up on allegations of sexual misconduct and later charged with misuse of his political influence and obstruction of a Senate investigation, a unanimous, bipartisan vote called for his expulsion from the Senate. It seemed that a chilly gust of new morality was blowing into the Capitol. Or was Packwood to be the fall guy for a handful of senators who stood accused of "not getting it" (missing the point) in the wake of the Anita Hill-Clarence Thomas investigation, in which Hill's charges of sexual harassment against the Supreme Court nominee ostensibly went unpunished? (See THOMAS-HILL SCANDAL.) Faced with expulsion, Packwood saw his only recourse as resigning in the midst of his fifth term, which he did on October 1, 1995, after a 33-month-long investigation.

The first allegations of sexual harassment, which spanned a 20-year period, were made public in November 1992. Ten female campaign workers, lobbyists, and Senate staffers came forward claiming that Packwood had made unwelcome advances, kissing and fondling them. Packwood denied specific charges, but his denials only served to bring forth more accusers until there were 26 in all.

Packwood had a habit—other than stealing kisses—of spending 30 minutes each morning writing his recollections from the previous day. Feelings, personal grievances, conversations, and encounters were all contained in this 8,200-page testament, dating from the 1960s. He thought someday he might use the diary to write a book about—to him—the greatest life in the world, the life of a U.S. senator. When the Senate Ethics Committee subpoenaed the diaries, Packwood refused to hand them over. In fact, he took the committee to trial, which landed in the Supreme Court, to keep it from getting his personal journal. He lost the trial, but was able, his long-time secretary testified, to alter some of the information contained on the tapes before she transcribed them. In a last-ditch effort to keep the notebooks from the Ethics Committee's hands, Packwood stood on the Senate floor facing his colleagues and friends and issued a thinly veiled threat stating that an examination of the diary pages would incriminate several others present.

His scare tactics only served to alienate many senators and mire him deeper in the scandalous bog, for when the diary pages were finally examined, new allegations were made against Packwood. It seems his "tell-all" diary recounted episodes of trading political favors with powerful businesspersons for his own financial gain. It even hinted that Packwood may have used his influence to convince certain colleagues to offer his soon-to-be-ex-wife employment, presumably to pare down the hefty alimony payments he would otherwise have to make.

The Ethics Committee's final verdict contained three charges: sexual misconduct, improper use of office for financial gain, and obstruction of the investigation by tampering with evidence. The obstruction charge was viewed as by far the most serious. The committee issued a statement saying that Packwood brought "discredit and dishonor upon the Senate" and the vote for expulsion soon followed.

Most expected Packwood to receive the Senate's usual slap on the hand, perhaps in the form of a public scolding, before he was allowed to resume his duties. His fellow senators and the public alike were shocked, however, at the severity of the committee's recommended punishment, though it was assumed that the seemingly unrepentant Packwood's lack of cooperation throughout the trial left it few alternatives.

In his last speech from the Senate floor, Packwood said an emotional goodbye to the institution that he loved. What was most dear to him, his position, had been snatched away. The arrival each month of his hefty pension check served as only a reminder of his former life.

PAGE SCANDAL IN CONGRESS

The American public was clearly shocked when, in early July 1982, news reports broke about allegedly rampant sexual and drug-related misconduct by members of the U.S. Congress. Some congressmen were supposed to have made homosexual advances to the teenage pages who served as hired messengers on Capitol Hill, to have engaged in sex with them, and to have taken cocaine and other narcotics (pages were alleged to have been used as drug couriers in the halls of Congress). As the newspapers increasingly sensationalized the stories, the public became extremely skeptical about the ethics of the nation's lawmakers.

Feeling the quickly growing pressures to do something to regain credibility for the lawmakers, the House Ethics Committee began a secret investigation to find out whether the charges were true or not. Leroy Williams, a black 18-year-old former page from Little Rock, Arkansas, testified that he had engaged in homosexual relations with three House members and had arranged an affair between a senator and a male prostitute. However, the Ethics Committee learned that Williams had earlier failed a lie-detector test administered by the Federal Bureau of Investigation (FBI); his answers to question about exact sexual involvement between pages and congressmen were confused and vague. But other pages had also reported the sale of cocaine and homosexual activity on the Hill, thus compelling Congress to find and get rid of any members involved in sex and drug abuse. On July 14, 1982, the House of Representatives authorized the Ethics Committee to use sweeping new subpoena powers to thoroughly investigate the alleged scandal.

When the unusual House probe began, the Justice Department also launched two special investigations, one looking into the sex allegations, the other into the use of illegal drugs by congressmen. House leaders had earlier obtained the names of six Democrats and three Republicans from pages who had alleged sexual misconduct on the part of these congressmen and had helped initiate a federal grand jury hearing into the supposed distribution of cocaine in the Capitol corridors.

Although Williams recanted his scandalous accusations on August 27, 1982, saying that he had only wanted to draw public attention to abuses of the congressional page system, and the Justice Department ended its investigations at the end of August, saying it had uncovered nothing to warrant prosecution, the House Ethics Committee continued probing because of public and press insistence that many people still felt their lawmakers' ethics were questionable.

At the end of a year-long investigation into the private lives of hundreds of individuals, the Ethics Committee and office of Special Counsel Joseph Califano (who was hired to conduct extensive interviews and take many depositions in the probe) concluded that most of the allegations were groundless but that ethical standards had been breached. Most humiliating were the revelations about Representative Gerry Studds, a Democrat from Massachusetts, and Representative Daniel B. Crane, a Republican from Illinois.

With the House nearly empty late on Thursday, July 14, 1983, Studds gave an eloquent speech proclaiming his homosexuality. Ten years earlier, he had had a sexual relationship with a 17-year-old male page and had made advances to two others (no incidents had occurred since 1973). Studds said, "All members of Congress must cope with the challenge of initiating and maintaining a career in public office without destroying the ability to lead a meaningful and emotionally fulfilling private life." And he continued by saying, "It is not a simple task for any of us to meet adequately the obligations of either public or private life, let alone both. But these challenges are made substantially more complex when one is, as am I, both an elected public official and gay." This six-term congressman, who had a good legislative record, became the first member of Congress to proclaim himself gay in a speech on the House floor.

The Ethics Committee revealed that Daniel Crane, married with six children, had confessed to having had sexual relations with a 17-year-old female page in 1980. At a news conference outside his local congressional office in Danville, Illinois, he was tearfully remorseful in admitting the 1980 affair. "In no way did I violate my oath of office," explained Crane, a three-term congressman. "I have broken a law of God, and I can only ask for God's forgiveness, my wife's forgiveness, my family's forgiveness, and my friends' . . . I know I did wrong. I made a mistake . . . I am sorry." The date was July 16, 1983.

In the national elections of 1984, these two representatives, whom the House censured in 1983 for their transgressions, had contrasting reelection luck; Crane lost in Illinois, but Studds was returned to office in his Massachusetts congressional district.

A. Mitchell PALMER: opportunism masked as idealism

From 1918 through 1921, U.S. President Woodrow Wilson's attorney general, A. Mitchell Palmer, earned ignominy by denying constitutional rights to the persons his illegal, but official, actions injured. Labeled the Fighting Quaker by the press, Palmer possessed a character as paradoxical as his nickname. Carefully trained in Quaker pacifism, he remembered his upbringing when he declined Wilson's appointment as secretary of war. But an extensive career in politics had developed in him an ambition for power, and hindsight suggests that "the Aggressive Quaker" might have been a better moniker for Palmer.

Appointed by President Wilson to be alien property custodian in 1917, Palmer revealed his aggressiveness and quickly became controversial, for his modus operandi involved high-handedness, as if the power of his office excused him from the protocols of courtesy and legality. As custodian, he sequestered $600 million in property owned by or for enemy aliens, to be resold to American citizens. His seizures were often illegally made, and his sales of alien property were allegedly made chiefly to friends and supporters. An investigation of Palmer began but faltered on the reasoning that he was new at the job and therefore excusable.

Palmer's 1919 appointment as attorney general of the United States took him from one area of latent controversy into an area with even greater potential for dispute. He was a poor appointment, for he took office at a time when the experience and leadership qualities he lacked should have been considered of higher importance. America was becoming hysterical as dissensions developed between laissez-faire industrialists and labor unions that demanded collective bargaining and raises. Strikes occurred nationally; returning World War I veterans swelled the ranks of the unemployed; inflation made the plight of the lower classes painful; the new "Red" Russia had announced its plan to spread its communist revolution; and superpatriotic societies left over from the just-finished war blamed "Bolshevik" (or communist) aliens for all of America's troubles (nearly a million immigrants came to the United States in 1920). President Wilson, felled by a stroke, was unable to lead on a national level. When a wave of random and still unexplained bombings rocked many American cities (including one on Palmer's own doorstep that killed the would-be bomber), the attorney general succumbed to the hysteria and fanned the flames of the frightening period dubbed the "Red Scare."

Convinced by an especially rabid press and by emotions rather than facts that "90% of the Communist and radical agitation is traceable to aliens," Palmer began to propagandize Congress for money and anti-alien legislation. He started a new bureau within his department, called the General Intelligence Division (GID), and named 24-year-old J. Edgar Hoover "special Assistant to the Attorney General." Hoover, a lawyer and ex-librarian, compiled indexes of radicals, organizations, and publications, mostly containing hearsay evidence. He influenced Palmer to adopt new and questionable attitudes, including guilt by association with a dubious organization or merely from paper membership in its ranks, the latter an erroneous judgment that Hoover defended until the end of his life.

Attorney General Palmer next decided that deportation would solve America's problems. Alien deportation was then an action, not a criminal proceeding, controlled by the U.S. Department of Labor. Palmer went to work on Secretary of Labor William B. Wilson to convince him of the rightness of his anti-alien viewpoints.

Disregarding laws, especially those that accorded civil rights even to aliens, Palmer planned in June 1919 to round up suspected radicals in 12 American cities. The locations were to be the meeting places of the Federation of the Union of Russian Workers (URW), recently declared subversive by Palmer at Hoover's behest.

On the appointed day, GID personnel arrested hundreds of people at the meeting places, allowing them no due process or access to attorneys. Palmer and Hoover were momentarily the darlings of the press for using what would today be called Gestapo tactics.

Upon screening by the Labor Department, only 43 of those arrested were deemed deportable. The others were unable to retaliate or to recover personal losses resulting from the first Palmer Raid. On the contrary, charges of brutality, arrest of the innocent, and destruction of property and files were sneeringly dismissed by Hoover, who responded to complaints about disallowed counsel by asserting that the complaining lawyers "ought to be disbarred from further practice before the immigration authorities." But civil rights were apparently never his deep concern.

A second and more brutal Palmer Raid took place in 33 American cities during January 1920. In this raid GID personnel were aided by "Red Squads" in arresting an estimated 10,000 persons, most of whom were then held incommunicado, often without warrants. Palmer and Hoover were named on confidential instructions as individuals to be contacted on "any matters of vital interest." Again, the press was exultant.

When Assistant Secretary of Labor Louis F. Post, then acting secretary, discovered that adequate legal standards (including adequate warrants) had been severely abused in making the arrests, 83 percents of those arrested were immediately released. Palmer then began a vendetta against Post, a trial by newspaper that ultimately tarnished Palmer himself, for only 556 persons were rated as deportable.

Hearings in 1921 considering grounds for the impeachment of Post turned into incomplete hearings concerning Palmer's removal. Twelve eminent jurists published reports of Palmer's "illegal practices." Cowed by Post's careful arguments, Palmer stressed the pressure on him and need for national security.

By 1921, public approval after the 1919 and 1920 Palmer Raids had turned into indifference even though personal rights had been violated in Palmer's raids, for "normalcy" under Warren G. HARDING was just around the corner. A contender for the American presidential nomination in 1920, Palmer after 1921 held no political offices in which his curiously paradoxical Quaker aggressiveness could get him into trouble.

PANIC of 1873. See DREXEL, MORGAN & COMPANY: the panic of 1873

Alexander PANTAGES: vaudeville capitalist compromised

A California multimillionaire, Alexander Pantages owned a string of some 60 vaudeville theaters that extended from Mexico to Canada along the West Coast. Pantages himself frequently booked acts to play in his theaters. One day in August 1929, a pretty teenage girl named Eunice Pringle, who aspired to be a singer and dancer, ran out of Pantages's office, her low-cut red dress torn, screaming that she had been raped. In the ensuing trial, Pantages's life and reputation were nearly ruined, only to be revived two years later in an equally shocking trial.

The Greek-born Pantages had immigrated to the United States and settled in California after striking it rich while mining gold in Alaska. He then invested in a chain of vaudeville theaters and made even more money. In June 1929, Pantages's theaters merged with Radio-Keith-Orpheum (RKO) to become one of the biggest theatrical operations in America. Every vaudeville comedian, singer, dancer, and performer dreamed of being booked on this lucrative, long-playing entertainment circuit. Eunice Pringle was no exception.

A 17-year-old, stagestruck high-school dropout, Pringle went to Pentages's office in downtown Los Angeles on August 9 to try to interest the impresario in a dance playlet entitled "A Prince from Hollywood." She later claimed that he had seemed encouraging and had lured her into the janitor's broom and mop closet, where he proceeded to rape her. Witnesses testified that Pringle had rushed from the room shouting "He's ruined me . . . ruined me."

At first the press and public sentiment seemed to be running against the 54-year-old Pantages, a small, 128-pound man who spoke broken English and was worth an estimated $30 million. He denied ever touching Pringle, whom the *Los Angeles Times* called "a full-blown beauty" and whose youthful robustness contrasted markedly with her alleged rapist's elderly look. She stuck to her story, while he said she had "raped herself"—rending her clothing to make it seem as if she had been violently abused sexually. A sensational trial ensued in Los Angeles Superior Court in 1929, and when the case went to the jury for deliberation, a deadlock soon developed. The jury requested that Pringle's entire testimony be reread, which was done. It then deliberated once again and finally came to the decision that Pantages was guilty. It recommended that he be sentenced to prison for from 1 to 50 years, as prescribed by California state law, but urged that clemency be granted. Pantages was sentenced to 50 years in state prison. Immediately one of his defense lawyers, young Jerry Giesler, filed an appeal and argued that, in any charge of forcible rape, the morals of the plaintiff were relevant as evidence for the jury to consider (at the time, such evidence was barred in a sex case involving a minor).

Meanwhile, Pantages's wife had also been having problems with the law. She had been convicted of manslaughter for killing a Japanese gardner, Juro Rokumoto, in an automobile collision the previous June. She had already paid $78,000 to Rokumoto's family and friends who were injured in his car at the time of the crash. She was granted probation for 10 years, during which time she was forbidden to drive a car or drink alcohol. At the time of her husband's trial, Mrs. Pantages was seriously ill and could not attend the proceedings. The theater owner and impresario himself soon became sick and was transferred to the hospital ward of the jail.

It took two years for Pantages's appeal, argued by Giesler, to work its way through the courts. Giesler complained that the first presiding judge had refused to admit testimony showing that Pringle and Nick Duneav, her Russian-born boyfriend and agent and the author of "A Prince from Hollywood," had conspired to frame the theater magnate after he refused to buy their act. Giesler also contended that three female jurors had been coerced to vote for Pantages's conviction, hence the recommendation for clemency. A retrial was authorized by the California Supreme Court and took place in November 1931.

Again the jurors debated a long time before reaching a verdict—this time for acquittal of Pantages. One of the 12 jurors described the process of "eliminating the witnesses we believed had not told the truth until we finally got to the testimony we felt was acceptable. The jurors never believed Miss Pringle's story but felt sorry for her." After two years of confinement in San Quentin Penitentiary, Pantages walked out a free man with his good reputation restored. Pringle had filed a $1-million damage suit against him, but nothing ever came of the threat. Later, on her deathbed, she divulged that Joseph P. Kennedy had allegedly been behind the frame-up, secretly scheming to ruin Pantages and absorb his theater conglomerate into his own, FBO Pictures (see KENNEDY-SWANSON AFFAIR).

Dorothy PARKER: a writer defamed by innuendo

Famed since 1916 for her sardonic wit, satiric verse, and ironic short stories, Dorothy Rothschild Parker (born 1893) was one of many American and European writers lured to Hollywood during the early 1930s by the movie industry's promises of prominence and pelf. The newcomers brought with them qualities and practices Hollywood had lacked before the Great Depression began in 1929: intellectual and aesthetic concerns, especially involving liberal politics, and a habit of outspokenness, often witty and caustic. Parker had gained fame for her skill at repartee at the Round Table gatherings at New

York's Algonquin Hotel, and this made her a welcome addition to the Hollywood "émigré" group, putting her in high demand socially.

But Parker's advent in Tinseltown quickly soured. Her distress concerning the growing intellectual totalitarianism of Italy and Germany and the militant anti-Semitism of the Nazis was to mark her as a communist sympathizer in an era when the "Red Scare" was at its height. This distress caused Parker, a nonpracticing Jew, to act as well as speak out. With Oscar Hammerstein and others, she founded in 1936 an anti-Nazi league, engaging in speechmaking, fund-raising, and organizing a boycott against German manufacturers. When, also in 1936, the Spanish Civil War erupted, she denounced Spanish fascist military leader Francisco Franco. She also spoke widely to raise funds for the protection of children and refugees and for support of the legitimate Loyalist Spanish government.

Hollywood's leaders, usually pleased by free publicity, were disenchanted by Parker and her actions, for she put Filmland in an undesired political light. When Parker visited Spain's Loyalists in 1937 as a correspondent for *New Masses* and her subsequent report, entitled "Soldiers of the Republic," revealed that she had "enlisted for the duration in the good cause" of the Loyalists, Hollywood's ruling executives began to look askance at her. And when she joined the militant Screen Writers' Guild, the nemesis and archenemy of the anti-union screen producers, she became so much a marked woman as to suffer economic repression, both in Hollywood and in her former publishing outlets. Her position was contrary to the temper of the times (the German-American bund and Father COUGHLIN both called for a Franco victory), and suggested that support for the Loyalists meant support for the communists. Opinion turned against her until Adolf Hitler's Nazi attack on Poland in 1939 made American antifascism respectable and official.

In 1945, political views changed once again, as cold war fear energized many conservatives and isolationists to search actively for "Reds," "pinkos," and other communist and liberal travelers in America. The leaders of these inquiries had many motives, some lofty and some opprobrious: to safeguard the nation, to discredit the Franklin Roosevelt era, to secure political power and prestige, and to break the strength of the labor unions in Hollywood and elsewhere. All kept their activities prominent through the public media. Among the loudest and most active was the House Un-American Activities Committee (HUAC).

The HUAC's anticommunist focus, which was essentially a condemnation of all liberal ideas, fell upon Hollywood three times. In 1938 its first chairman, Martin Dies, invaded Hollywood. Its most prominent achievement at that time was to accuse Shirley Temple, then aged 10, of unconscious aid to the forces of sub-version. In 1940, citing invitations from the producers and fears of union power in Hollywood, Dies and the HUAC committee again invaded. Dies decided then that communism was not a problem in Hollywood but he remembered that an angry Dorothy Parker had publicly accused him of trying "to destroy the Hollywood progressive organizations" in order to establish fascism nationwide.

The HUAC also remembered this when its third chairman, J. Parnell THOMAS, came again to Hollywood in 1947, where he interviewed "friendly witnesses," held daily press conferences on his findings, and announced plans to move the whole show to Washington, D.C. In Washington, however, Thomas's grand scheme collapsed ignominiously after the HUAC's first set of hearings (see HOUSE COMMITTEE ON UN-AMERICAN ACTIVITIES: America's inquisition and the "Hollywood Ten").

But by way of prelude, Thomas named 300 persons as candidates for the Committee's Washington inquisition. Among them was Dorothy Parker, who was never allowed to be heard (and no "evidence" was ever cited against her). Yet when the Washington HUAC hearings collapsed and the "Hollywood Ten" were first convicted of contempt of Congress and then illegally blacklisted by Hollywood's producers, Parker was one of many screenwriters banned from the movie studios. Guilt by association also affected her spouse, film writer Alan Campbell. Her second husband, Campbell found himself jobless because he was the "husband of a known Communist." And again Dorothy Parker was faced with rejection by publishers, a loss of prestige she worked hard to overcome in the years remaining before her death in New York City in 1967.

Paula PARKINSON. See Rita JENRETTE: opened Pandora's box of congressional sex.

George PARR: the despotic "duke of Duval"

A number of counties in Texas have traditionally been ruled almost as private fiefdoms by unscrupulous political machines that control all elections on the local, state, and national levels, as well as much of the flow of public monies. One such was Duval County in southern Texas, located between Corpus Christi and the Rio Grande. Dominated first by the unscrupulous Archie Parr and later by his equally amoral son George, the two "dukes of Duval" maintained a tight grip on the impoverished county for nearly half a century. Eventually, George Parr's high-handed, illegal tactics brought him to the attention of federal law officials, who prosecuted and sent him to prison in 1957.

Archie Parr began his reign of Duval County in 1911 when he supported the county's Mexican majority against its "Anglo" minority and accordingly sided with the Mexicans attacked in the so-called "election day massacre," which left three Mexicans dead in the county seat of San Diego. Thereafter, assured of the Mexican votes, Archie Parr became rich and powerful as Duval County's political boss. He and his son George, who began assuming control of county politics as the second duke of Duval not long after leaving college in the mid-1920s, counted on the large, poverty-ridden population of Mexicans and Chicanos to vote as they were told to. Thus, whomever the Parrs wished to hold public office was elected. Typically on election day, or more particularly on primary day, the county's Mexican-Americans, most of whom were illiterate or spoke little English, were rounded up, given receipts showing that they had paid their poll taxes, and handed already marked ballots to drop into the ballot boxes at the polling places; they also received shots of tequila (liquor) when they left the polls. In some precincts, the voters were allowed to mark their own ballots, but armed guards followed them into the voting cubicles to make sure that they voted correctly. Under such circumstances, favored candidates won by margins of at least 10–1 and often by much more.

Neither Archie nor George Parr had any particular political philosophy or concerns about public issues. They backed office seekers whom they felt certain would carry out their wishes when elected. They even supported candidates merely because they were enemies of the Parrs' enemies. One Texas historian noted that the greedy, power-hungry Parrs "treated the county budget virtually as their personal bank account" and took what they pleased from all branches of the municipal government. When visitors asked why beer cost 25 cents in Duval County instead of 20 cents, as in the rest of Texas, they were told "the extra nickel is for George."

George Parr lived well on his own 50,000 acre ranch; he also had a lavish townhouse with a swimming pool and private race track on the premises. He became profitably involved in the oil, banking, and beer-selling businesses. He also served some jail time for income-tax evasion in 1936, but President Harry Truman pardoned him for the crime in 1948 when George Parr was at the peak of his power as Duval's Democratic Party boss.

In 1947 the Parr political machine turned against a former friend named Coke Stevenson, the Dixiecrat governor of Texas, because he had refused to appoint an inept Parr protégé to the office of district attorney. In the runoff primary election for Democratic candidates for the U.S. Senate in late August 1948, the duke and his men strongly backed a rising Texas congressman named Lyndon B. Johnson, who had served in the U.S. House of Representatives since 1937 and had lost his first bid for the Senate in 1941. The runoff election was extremely close, with the lead seesawing between Stevenson and Johnson as the vote count continued to change for days afterward. One bloc of 200 votes from the Thirteenth Precinct in the town of Alice in Jim Wells County, which bordered Duval County, was particularly suspicious. Coke Stevenson's men investigated it, and although allowed to look at the polling list of the precinct for only five minutes, were able to note that 202 names, all in the same ink and same handwriting, concluded the voting list. The investigators then contacted some of the persons whose names appeared on the list and learned that those individuals had not voted. A week or two later, lawyers from both the Johnson and Stevenson sides returned to Alice to examine the questionable ballots. A locked box was brought to them, but no one had the key to it. A locksmith was called in; he cut off the lock and found nothing in the box. The ballots had disappeared. Johnson had won the Democratic nomination by 87 votes. In Duval County, where the vote was 4,622 to 40 in Johnson's favor, he was nicknamed "Landslide Lyndon."

Johnson himself probably had nothing to do with the fraudulent voting in south Texas, but the incident illustrates the lengths to which the duke of Duval went to ensure that things went his way. There was actually widespread fraud on both sides in the 1948 election, which saw Johnson become the next senator from Texas; scholars who have studied the matter have determined that he won by a larger margin than he is usually credited with. In the biography The Lone Star: The Life of John Connally (1989), author James Reston, Jr., contends that John Connally, who managed Johnson's 1948 Senate campaign and later became governor of Texas (1963–69), participated in forging voter list signatures in Jim Wells County. Connally, who died in 1993, repeatedly denied involvement in any ballot-box stuffing that gave victory to Johnson.

George Parr's luck began to run out in 1956 when he was elected sheriff of Duval County. When ready to be sworn into office in January 1957, the county commissioners' court ruled that he did not qualify for sheriff because he owed the county money. The State of Texas then proceeded to sue Parr for $460,000, contending that he had spent $225,000 of county funds to buy himself a ranch and $175,000 to pay his income taxes. In August 1957, federal officials arrested and indicted Parr for mail fraud; he was convicted and, after making a series of unsuccessful appeals, was sentenced to 10 years' imprisonment. After his release, his power in Duval County was broken; yet he continued to have trouble with the federal law. In 1974 he was sentenced to 10 years of hard labor in prison and fined $14,000 for not listing $287,000 in taxable income between 1966 and 1969. His appeal was turned down, and on April 1, 1975, Parr was found dead in a field on his Texas ranch. Rather than face another long stint behind bars, he had apparently shot himself in the head after driving his car to the field.

"Cissy" PATTERSON: her flamboyant life and puzzling death

In 1930, newspaper mogul William Randolph Hearst startled the nation's capital by appointing Eleanor ("Cissy") Medill Patterson, an eccentric, wealthy, middle-aged socialite, as editor and publisher of the *Washington Herald*. To the surprise of many, Patterson, who had virtually no newspaper experience, revitalized the undistinguished, deficit-ridden paper into an influential and profitable enterprise with the largest circulation in Washington, D.C. The first female editor of an American metropolitan daily, Patterson herself became a powerful Washington figure.

Eleanor "Cissy" Patterson, powerful publisher of the Washington Times-Herald, *officially died of kidney disease in 1948, but there were very questionable circumstances surrounding her sudden death, according to her ex-son-in-law, columnist Drew Pearson. She is shown here treading to the funeral of well-known newspaper editor Arthur Brisbane in late 1936. (AP/Wide World Photos)*

Cissy Patterson may have started her career with little experience, but she came from a newspaper dynasty: her grandfather had established the *Chicago Times* and her brother had founded the *New York Daily News*. At the age of 23, Cissy entered a disastrous marriage with a Polish-Austrian count named Josef Gizycki and went to live with him in Russian-held Poland. Within a few years she and her young daughter, Felicia, fled from him to England. However, the child was soon kidnapped by her father, the count. It took the intervention of then U.S. President-elect William Howard Taft and Russian czar Nicholas to restore Felicia to her mother.

After the 1929 death of her second husband, Elmer Schlesinger, Cissy, looking for a new challenge, became interested in purchasing a newspaper. Although Hearst refused at the time to sell her the *Herald*, he was persuaded to give Cissy the chance to run the daily.

Cissy's first attempt to make Washington sit up and take notice came in an editorial published just a few days after she joined the paper. In a front-page box, and with characteristic flamboyance, she launched a long public feud by attacking the popular Alice Roosevelt Longworth, daughter of the late President Theodore Roosevelt and once a friend of Cissy's.

Gradually, Cissy began to improve the *Herald*. She hired (and sometimes arbitrarily fired) the best reporters, editors, and writers. She demanded extraordinary work from all of them. In Washington, where politics and social life were inextricably intertwined, Cissy's high-society background was an asset. She undertook crusades on behalf of home rule for the District of Columbia, improving the Potomac River, preventing tuberculosis, and schooling for handicapped children.

In 1937, seeking more control over the newspaper, Cissy persuaded Hearst to lease her both the morning *Herald* and his afternoon *Times*. The following year she purchased both papers, which she merged into the *Times-Herald* in 1939.

She also continued feuding, not only with Alice Roosevelt Longworth but also with columnist Drew Pearson (who had been married for several years to Felicia), *Washington Post* publisher Eugene Meyer, Interior Secretary Harold Ickes, and especially President Franklin D. Roosevelt. An isolationist, she criticized FDR for leading the United States into the European war against Hitler. By 1946 *Collier's* magazine could, with some justification, call Cissy Patterson "probably the most powerful woman in America."

Following a heart attack in 1943, Cissy began planning for the future of the *Times-Herald* after her death. She wrote a will leaving the paper to seven of her top executives but later changed her mind and expressed a wish to leave it to her niece, Alicia Patterson Guggenheim, owner, editor, and publisher of the Long Island newspaper *Newsday*. However, a new will was apparently never written. On the morning of July 24, 1948, Cissy Patterson was found dead in her bedroom.

Cissy's sudden death was as theatrical as her life had been. There were speculations of foul play. With an estate valued at more than $16 million and rumors of a new will in the works, motives for her death among some of her heirs seemed plausible. Moreover, Cissy had for some time been hinting that she might be murdered. Certainly some circumstances about her death were odd. For example, her dog had howled in the early morning hours, but no watchman or servant had investigated. Six weeks after her will was published, Cissy's financial manager, Charles Porter, committed suicide. A few days later, adding to the general suspicion surrounding Cissy's death, her former social secretary and then society reporter was found dead, with an empty bottle of sleeping pills nearby (however, an autopsy later showed that the woman had died of natural causes). Drew Pearson and others hinted that Cissy's or Porter's death, or both, had involved murder, but no such claims were ever proven.

Further scandal erupted when Felicia, who had been left an annual annuity of $25,000, contested Cissy's will, claiming that her mother was of unsound mind and the victim of undue influence at the time the will was executed. In 1949 Felicia withdrew her suit and settled for a lump sum of $400,000 instead of the annual award in the will.

As matters ultimately turned out, Cissy Patterson had been unable to assure the survival of the *Times-Herald*. The paper was sold in 1954 to her rival Eugene Meyer, who closed it down.

General George PATTON: a slap in the face

"General Patton Slaps Shell-Shocked Soldier," read one November 1943 headline, and the news soon spread internationally. Radio broadcasts extended the revelation to an even larger audience that acting Lieutenant General George Smith Patton, Jr., war hero of Casablanca, El Guettar, and Sicily, had, during a visit to a military hospital, sworn at Private C. H. Kuhl, a battle-fatigued four-year veteran of the Tunisian and Sicilian campaigns without visible wounds, called him a coward, slapped him sharply across the face, and threatened to draw his white-handed single-action Colt revolver. He had then turned to the commanding medical officer and ordered the removal of the veteran from the hospital because he would not "have those other brave boys seeing such a bastard babied." When Patton next heard the soldier sobbing, he went and slapped him again.

So said the witnesses to Patton's almost pathological violence. One wrote a full report to General Dwight D. Eisenhower, who flew a general officer to Sicily to investigate the matter. Eisenhower next wrote a slashing rebuke to Patton, ordering him to apologize publicly to the patients and staff of the hospital and to make a frank

General George Patton (right), known as Old Blood and Guts by his soldiers in World War II, strolls through the White House Rose Garden during a visit with President Harry Truman (left) in June 1945. As a military leader, he often won praise for his bold military operations and victories, but his supporters often ignored his sometimes brutal discipline and roughness, including incidents of forcefully slapping battle-fatigued soldiers in 1943. Patton, reprimanded for his behavior, later apologized. (Yale University Archives/Historical Picture Collection/Yale University Library)

report of what had happened to the staff officers of each division of his command. Patton was told bluntly that he was on probation.

Patton apologized as ordered, but before he did so the army began a kind of "operation coverup." It was managed so badly, however, that commentary on the incident—both excusatory and condemnatory—continued for more than 20 years after Patton's accidental death in 1945.

And well it might have, for the reported incident followed at least three other occasions revealing that while in Sicily, Patton was temporarily out of control. All four incidents made it clear that he was not, as one member of his staff had blandly asserted in 1957, a man "with a compassionate inner nature" despite his military occupation. The truth seems to lie between these extremes.

Three of Patton's outbursts were uncovered only after his death: he had slapped another, but unidentified, battle-fatigued veteran; he had become furious when his staff car was blocked by a Sicilian mule cart on a bridge, ordering the cart removed (it had instead turned over) and then commanding the execution of the balky mule; and he had dressed down an antiaircraft unit that had successfully beaten off an attack despite the wounding of some of its members, by ordering them to stand at attention while he harangued them for improper dress. Surely these occurrences reveal passion but not compassion.

Because of the witness's report, the second slapping incident accidentally gained the attention of war correspondents, and so the world learned that officers are not necessarily gentlemen. Eager for further details, the public was plunged into confusion when Allied Force Headquarters in Algiers at first denied the story. Later it was forced to make an official confirmation of the incident and an announcement that Patton had apologized. Even so, the cover-up operation continued. In late November, columnist Drew Pearson revealed that Eisenhower had reprimanded Patton, but Patton's public relations people in Sicily cagily denied the report through a semantic quibble over the official military definition of *reprimand*. Eisenhower's public relations staff replied "No comment," and Pearson's request for clarification to Secretary of War Henry Stimson received the response that the answer had to be gained from Patton himself. But Pearson had already gone that route, and the reprimand was not acknowledged until 1944.

The lack of facts about the reprimand caused a United States senator from West Virginia to proclaim solemnly that "When officers make mistakes, they should not be shielded." Equally bemused, *The Army and Navy Register* devoted a 1943 editorial to the "old-boy network's" desire to suppress news and argued that since Patton knew the Articles of War provisions on "cruel treatment of a soldier or conduct of a nature to bring discredit upon the service," he should be relieved of his command, a fatuous suggestion during wartime.

When it was revealed that Eisenhower had informally but forcefully rebuked Patton for his behavior, commentators were puzzled about why no investigation had even been initiated under the provisions of the Articles of War. By late 1943 the furor had begun to die down, only to flare up briefly again when it was learned that the slapping incident had caused the Senate Military Affairs Committee to postpone until August 1944 Patton's promotion from the permanent rank of colonel to the permanent rank of major general. After Patton had been given command of the Third Army (1944), won the Battle of the Bulge and crossed the Rhine (1945), and begun the race to Czechoslovakia, only a few alert correspondents remembered the slapping incident.

After 1945, justifications for Patton's violence began to appear: he himself rationalized, in a partly plagiarized essay, that rough treatment was the only cure for battle fatigue; Kuhl's father gratuitously and audaciously wrote

to his congressman that he had forgiven Patton (the son never did), and some argued that the Sicilian campaign had put Patton "under a strain."

Patton, however, had been on his guard: no reports of emotional excesses or physical violence were ever discovered in his records for the years 1944 and 1945.

"PAYOLA" SCANDAL

After the revelations in 1959 that television quiz shows had sometimes been rigged, the House Special Subcommittee on Legislative Oversight turned its attention to radio's popular and rock-and-roll music programs. To anyone who had listened to these teen-oriented radio programs for any length of time, it seemed obvious that some records were played more frequently and mentioned more often than others. The House subcommittee summoned a number of disk jockeys who were in charge of the programs to appear and give testimony under oath about their practices. Stan Richards, unemployed at the time but formerly of WILD, a Boston radio station, explained how the system worked. "This seems to be the American way of life, which is a wonderful way of life. It's primarily built on romance—I'll do for you. what will you do for me?" Richards admitted that he had accepted $6,225 from record companies in the past. It soon emerged that it was quite common for disk jockeys, especially those on big-city radio stations, to "plug" certain records in return for gifts or money from the records' manufacturers or distributors. The practice was called payola.

The bribery centered on the then-popular seven-inch, 45 r.p.m. records for teenagers, with which disk jockeys could—and did—exert much influence on determining which titles became hits. (See also TELEVISION QUIZ SHOW SCANDAL.) On the other hand, long-playing records and albums geared to adult audiences seemed to be quite free of payola.

Other disk jockeys who testified also confessed that they had received large sums of money or expensive gifts but they claimed that these had been in return for "auditing" records rather than playing them on the air. Joseph Finan and Wesley Hopkins of KYW, Cleveland, confessed that they had accepted thousands of dollars in "listening fees." With 200 single records being released every week for teenagers, the record business was extremely competitive. The disk jockeys said that they did not have the time to listen to every new release and that they depended on the recommendations of "auditors."

The investigators were particularly interested in disk jockey Dick Clark, a teenage idol of the American Broadcasting Company (ABC). It was found that he owned substantial interests in music publishing and record firms. When this was revealed, ABC ordered Clark to divest himself of these stocks and shares immediately. Furthermore, the subcommittee discovered that at a disk-jockey convention in Miami Beach the previous spring, 18 American record companies had paid out more than $118,000 for meals, liquor, hotel rooms, and call girls for the attendees.

The industry's image suffered badly because of the scandal, which resulted in firings of numerous disk jockeys and the enactment of a 1960 antipayola law (with a penalty of a $10,000 fine and/or one year in jail for violations). One who felt the "heat" was well-known New York rock-and-roll disk jockey Alan Freed, who upheld taking noncash gifts from friends in the recording industry, calling it "the backbone of American business" and declaring "What they call payola in the disk jockey business they call lobbying in Washington." Before being ousted, Freed was indicted on 26 counts of accepting bribes to play records.

Tom PENDERGAST: boss of Kansas City

For almost three decades the Pendergast family controlled Democratic politics in Kansas City and surrounding Jackson County, Missouri. The most powerful member of the family was "Big Boss" Tom Pendergast, who not only made political decisions about who would run for various offices, but also engaged in graft, fraud, and other corruptions associated with behind-the-scenes, back-room politics. Yet Tom Pendergast toppled from power when he was convicted of income-tax evasion in 1939 and sentenced to 15 months in prison plus five years of probation.

Thomas Joseph Pendergast began his political career as a minor official in the government of Kansas City and after World War I assumed from his affable older brother Mike the leadership of the area's Democratic machine, known as the Goats. Other rival Democratic factions were known as the Rabbits. Tom Pendergast was a shrewd man who was prone to violence when crossed; he could reputedly knock a man flat with one blow of his fist. Unlike bosses in the large gateway cities of New York and Chicago, his support did not depend on masses of immigrants, since there were relatively few of them in western Missouri. He had to court people of all colors, races, creeds, and social and economic status, and for the most part, he did so successfully. In the process, he made himself a great deal of money from kickbacks, payoffs, and illegal settlements.

One of the many businesses Tom Pendergast owned was the Ready-Mixed Cement Company, which had supplied most of the concrete for public-works projects in Jackson County until 1928 when Harry S. Truman was elected county judge. Although Truman had enjoyed Pendergast's support in the election, he insisted on strict honesty in the awarding and carrying out of contracts after a bond was floated to rebuild the county's roads. Ready-Mixed Cement received a contract for only one-quarter mile of road. In later years, Truman was often accused of being a stooge of the Pendergast machine, but the facts of his relationship to the machine do not bear out the charges. Truman's scrupulous honesty earned him great respect among voters, and this respect worked to Tom Pendergast's advantage many times, especially in Truman's first run for the U.S. Senate in 1934.

Pendergast had to continually line his pockets to support expensive habits. A compulsive gambler, he was said to have bet on every horse race run in the United States every day. That required a great deal of money. In 1939, the Federal Bureau of Investigation (FBI) and the agents of the U.S. Treasury, wanting to know where the money came from, descended upon him and demanded his financial records. They found that he had evaded more than $1 million in income taxes over the previous decade. A year later, Pendergast and two others were indicted by a federal jury for obstructing justice in a fire-insurance compromise scheme. An insurance rate fight had been going on for 15 years in Missouri, and the excess premiums over the authorized rates had been impounded. Eventually these impounded funds totaled more than $10 million. The Missouri State Insurance Department had represented the insurance policyholders in numerous court battles with the insurance companies and had almost beaten the companies when, at Pendergast's request, the state superintendent of insurance approved an out-of-court settlement giving the insurance companies $8 million. The court approved this action, but federal investigators moved in and disclosed that an insurance representative who had turned government witness had made $500,000 in payments to Pendergast and his two associates in a Kansas City hotel room just before the settlement was made.

Big Tom Pendergast served 15 months in the federal prison at Leavenworth, Kansas, for his role in this scam, and was then paroled on the condition that he abstain from all political activities for five years. But Pendergast was too imbued with politics to cease and desist and was therefore charged with criminal contempt of court. The U.S. Supreme Court reversed the lower court's decision in 1943, citing the statute of limitations. By that time, however, Pendergast's health was broken. He had suffered a stroke and undergone a serious operation for cancer. He died at age 72 in January 1945. The man whom voters in Missouri believed to be a multimillionaire left an estate of only $13,000.

PENN CENTRAL CRASH

After World War II, America's railroad companies began losing a great deal of their passenger and freight business to newer and faster methods of transportation—automobiles, trucks, and airplanes. Fierce competition among the rail lines also hurt them and made it increasingly difficult for them to make a profit, let alone sustain any growth. In 1954 a ruthless fight was waged by multimillionaire Robert R. Young to wrest control of the $2.6 billion New York Central Railroad from its management. President William White of the New York Central was pitted against Young, who eventually won control but later committed suicide as an evidently overburdened, perplexed railroad owner.

Both the New York Central Railroad (formed in 1853) and the Pennsylvania Railroad (chartered in 1846) were plagued with financial problems because of competition from other means of transportation. The two lines, which were bitter rivals for years, considered combining to form one company so as to streamline their operations and thus be more profitable. Merger talks had gone on since 1957, and growing financial and operating complications had taxed the two railroads to the limit when in 1968 the U.S. Supreme Court, after a long legal battle over the proposed merger, approved the formation of a new $5-billion transportation company. The Pennsylvania (fondly called the "Pennsy") and the New York Central combined operations, reorganized, and became the Penn Central Transportation Company.

Soon, however, despite posting an $87-million profit for 1968, the mammoth new company began to encounter embarrassing problems. The huge and confusing network of tracks and routes that had come from the merger made it difficult for the approximately 100,000 Penn Central employees to keep passenger and freight service running smoothly and efficiently. More than 4,000 locomotives and some 180,000 passenger and freight cars were hard to keep tabs on; a myriad of new routes stumped operators and clerks, and thousands of loaded freight cars went to wrong railroad yards. Once, in 1968, more than 100 coal cars—an entire loaded train—were "lost" in the cumbersome Penn Central system and were not "found" for 10 days. In addition to these woes, the working relationship among the executives of the two former rival companies was far from congenial. A Pennsylvania man headed the reorganized company; next in line was a New York Central man, followed by a Penn man, followed by a New York Central man, and so forth; the company's new hierarchy was just not conducive to mutual regard and communication. In short, there was contentiousness, and Penn Central saw its customers growing increasingly frustrated by freight hauling mix-ups, derailments of cars, incapacitated locomotives, and smashed-up tracks (the latter two problems were caused largely by the severe cold of the winter of 1969).

In 1969 the company's profit fell to about $4.4 million, and much of its business had already gone to the trucking industry. To meet its bills, the Penn Central borrowed heavily from banks and, in time, hoped for a $200-million government-guaranteed loan, which did not materialize because the Nixon administration questioned its legality. Unable to pay its bills, the railroad filed a petition for bankruptcy on June 21, 1970, after

its chief officer, Stuart T. Saunders, and other top executives were forced to resign. The Penn Central continued to operate with the help of federal subsidies after the bankruptcy petition was granted. Later it was revealed that the railroad had suffered a record loss of about $430 million for 1970, the biggest bankruptcy (involving assets) in American history at that time. In 1970, Congress passed the Rail Passenger Act, which in 1971 created the National Railroad Passenger Transportation Corporation, better known as Amtrak. Five years later the Penn Central became part of the newly formed Consolidated Rail Corporation, more familiarly called Conrail, which was a private, government-financed corporation controlling the freight service of six bankrupt railroads in the Northeast and Midwest. The federal government had had to step into the failing railroad picture, first to ensure essential intercity passenger service (Amtrak) and then to help set up a good rail freight carrier (Conrail).

PENN SQUARE BANK COLLAPSE

The Penn Square Bank, located in a modest three-story building on the edge of a shopping center in Oklahoma City, Oklahoma, seemed to be growing remarkably well thanks to the energetic senior vice president in charge of its oil and gas lending division, Bill Patterson, who had been making thousands of dollars worth of energy loans that he then resold to big out-of-state banks. But rumors of overextension of the bank's assets and of uninsured loans began circulating in mid-June 1982, and after the long Fourth of July weekend of that year the bank closed its doors on the orders of the Federal Deposit Insurance Corporation (FDIC). Not only were local depositors and borrowers affected by Penn Square's failure, but so were large banks around the country, principally the Continental Illinois Bank of Chicago and the Chase Manhattan Bank of New York.

The Penn Square Bank had been purchased by a group of investors in 1974, a time when oil prices of the Organization of Petroleum Exporting Countries (OPEC) were high and wildcat drillers were anxious to cash in on the high costs of natural gas and oil. The bank was more than willing to give loans for expensive drilling equipment to independent producers, and the institution grew rapidly from a consumer-oriented bank of $30 million in assets into a $456 million lending bank. Government officials cited it as the victim of too rapid growth with too little staff and supervision.

After 1976, when oil and gas prices began to drop, middlemen who had bought oil leases or equipment with Penn Square loans could not resell them, and the repayment of the bank's loans became increasingly slow. Although Penn Square had less than $500 million in assets, it had made more than $2 billion in oil-related loans, 80 percent of which were resold to larger, "upstream" banks. Billy Paul Jennings, the bank's chief executive, justified this practice by saying that it was modeled on the methods of British merchant bankers, who functioned as vendors of loans to larger banks.

Beginning in 1980, Penn Square Bank had been monitored by the Office of the Comptroller of the Currency because it had been lending sums above legal limits and violating other regulations. Insiders called the bank the Continental Illinois loan production office. More than $100 million of loans—far above the legal limit—had been made to Robert Hefner and his wildcat companies, but Patterson claimed that the limit applied only to the loans on Penn Square's own books. Another wildcatter, Carl W. Swan, had attracted relatively small investors from all over the country to his various drilling projects, but his company began to hit one dry hole after another. The investors were told that for $37,500 cash they could purchase a $150,000 share in a drilling fund underwritten by Penn Square, much of which was tax deductible. Penn Square supplied the balance through a loan secured on a two-year, $112,500 letter of credit drawn on the investor's home bank. The sales pitch implied that these letters of credit would never be called (i.e., payment would never be demanded on the loan) and that the production from the drilled well would secure their loans. This did not prove to be the case, for little oil was drilled; the reserves had been grossly overestimated. In May 1982, a lawyer filed an injunction blocking payment of 19 letters of credit to Penn Square on the grounds that they had been obtained fraudulently.

After the bank was closed on July 5, 1982, a flock of investigators from the FDIC, the United States comptrollers' office, and the Federal Bureau of Investigation arrived at the bank's offices and began sorting through piles of records. In the U.S. House of Representatives, the chairman of the Commerce, Consumer, and Monetary Affairs subcommittee called Penn Square a "cesspool." Examiners discovered, among other things, that $15 million in bad loans had been shifted back and forth to hide them. Hefner had obtained promises from wealthy friends to invest millions of dollars in Penn Square in late June 1982, to save it, while at the same time he had quietly withdrawn between $20 and $25 million of his own funds from the tottering bank. Many of the investigators complained about sloppy record keeping, some 3,000 loans that were improperly documented, and evidences of kickbacks, insider loans, and altered records. Maneuvering by some of Penn Square's directors, friends, and business associates also seemed highly suspicious, but those who knew Patterson and Jennings doubted that they had been wheeling and dealing for their personal benefit, but rather to save the bank.

Numerous large commercial banks, including the Seafirst Corporation of Seattle, the Northern Trust Company, the Michigan National Bank, Chase Manhattan Bank, and Continental Illinois Bank, lost millions of dollars in bad loans they had made to Penn Square, and the prices of their shares in the stock market fell. Some savings and loan institutions also suffered and regretted that they had been lured to Penn Square's dealings by high interest rates and certificates of deposit. The FDIC reported that its payouts to individuals and financial institutions (to remedy Penn Square's collapse) would be the largest in its history.

The PENTAGON: the persecution of George Spanton
Although he was one of the most competent auditors at the U.S. Department of Defense for 16 years, in 1982 George Spanton was given a poor work rating and nearly transferred several times. The reason: his exposure of the deficiencies of the company he was auditing. Instead of trying to reform the company, his bosses treated him as if he were a traitor.

In 1982, George Spanton, 62, was an auditor for the Department of Defense. In almost 30 years as a federal employee, he had gained an enviable reputation for the accuracy of his audits and for the aggressiveness and incisiveness of his suggestions for overcoming problems. In fact, his precision and insight in his many years with the Defense Contract Audit Agency (DCAA) had begun to trouble his superiors, who were suffering from the complaints of defense contractors whose financial policies and accounting practices were found deficient.

As early as 1980, Spanton's bosses had been pressuring him to retire; when he resisted, they began a program of harassment, threats, and intimidation. At first they attempted to fiddle with Spanton's performance ratings, judging his work "poor" in 1981 and, in 1982, after his double exposure of chicanery on the part of a defense contractor, placing him third from the bottom in a ranking of all DCAA auditors. Using existing means of redress, Spanton challenged the ratings and had them reconsidered, discovering along the way that the reason behind the professional smear had been his failure "to maintain a professional rapport" with the company whose books he was auditing. A year later, the phrase was revealed to be a bureaucratic euphemism for failing to overlook sharp practices by the defense contractor.

In May 1982, Spanton's DCAA superiors fired their strongest weapon: they tried to transfer him away from the company whose deceptions he had exposed. Spanton again fought back and won, ending 1982 as the DCAA branch chief at the West Palm Beach, Florida, location of the Government Products Division of the company he had exposed—the Pratt and Whitney Aircraft Corporation (PWA).

Spanton had offended Pratt and Whitney twice in 1982. In February he had encountered a charge to the government of more than $150,000 for travel and entertainment expenses, an illegal debit covering PWA's wining and dining of top Pentagon brass at the 1981

Paris Air Show—a cynical attempt to charge the United States for the expenses incurred in selling the company's highly profitable products to the Defense Department. In March he had uncovered a plan to charge the government $150 million in excess labor costs for the period 1982–84, costs that would elevate PWA's labor burden 178 percent above the national average. Spanton had put both discoveries and his recommendations into confidential ("for Official Use Only") reports.

The DCAA officials reacted, but against Spanton rather than PWA; they planned to destroy the messenger whose message they did not like. The reports were never made public, but in September 1982, Spanton was hauled before the Defense Criminal Investigation Service as if his earlier report had made him a culprit. The report was determined to be sound, the FBI was alerted, and a grand-jury investigation followed. The DCAA's chief auditor, Charles O. Starrett, Jr., then tried the performance-rating ploy again and attempted the transfer ploy. His actions received praise from Secretary of Defense Caspar Weinberger for his handling of the "Spanton problem."

Angry, Spanton now went public. He appealed for help to the Special Counsel to the U.S. Merit Systems Protection Board, to Air Force Secretary Verne Orr, and to Senator Charles Grassley of Iowa. All began to badger Secretary Weinberger. By April 1983, the pressure on Spanton had been withdrawn. Pratt and Whitney requested the return of its entertainment charge and entered into negotiations for reducing hourly wage increases to its production workers. Two other large defense contractors quickly followed suit. And Weinberger's underlings sent a memo to Starrett about "the unwisdom of continued pressure on Spanton" (bureaucratese for "lay off"). Spanton then went to West Palm Beach and worked until his retirement at the task of keeping PWA on the "straight and narrow" path.

When the contretemps was leaked to the press, the Protection Board demanded disciplinary action against those who had persecuted Spanton. For once, efforts to keep a bureaucratic department in line had triumphed without the destruction of the employee who had spoken, as required, against illegalities and inefficiencies.

PEYTON PLACE: damned and banned

"Sexsational" was the word coined to describe Grace Metalious's popular novel *Peyton Place*. Its publication in 1956 was greeted with much fanfare, publicity, and controversy. A daring exposé of small-town life and morality, *Peyton Place* was called a "dirty book" by many, and both Metalious and her novel, which was an instantaneous bestseller, received a great deal of condemnation. Literary critics, librarians, and others were stunned by her uninhibited use of language and her open treatment of incest, illegitimacy, abortion, promiscuity, sex, wife-beating, and other taboo subjects. But

Grace Metalious, author of the best-selling, sex-filled novel Peyton Place, *which became a top-grossing movie, stands beside her husband-schoolteacher George Metalious at The Harwyn Club in New York in October 1960. She had recently remarried him after divorcing him about three years earlier to wed disc jockey Thomas J. Martin. (UPI/Bettmann Newsphotos)*

there were others who commended the then 32-year-old author for a different reason—the exposure of the double life of a community.

Grace de Repentigny (Metalious's maiden name) was born and raised in a poor working family in Manchester, New Hampshire. Her parents divorced during her early childhood, and she was brought up by an insecure but domineering mother in a strict Roman Catholic tradition. She apparently had a lonely adolescence, living in a succession of shabby apartments with her mother, grandmother, and younger sister. An avid reader at an early age, she never went on to college after her high-school graduation in early 1942. The next year, at age 18, she married George Metalious, whom she had dated regularly in high school. Their marriage was at times stormy. George became a schoolteacher, and Grace worked as a cashier and in other jobs while raising three children. Life for the Metalious family was a continual struggle economically until 1955. Living in the village of Gilmanton, New Hampshire, where her husband had become a school principal, Grace Metalious had put her latent storytelling ability to use and produced the large manuscript of *Peyton Place* (originally titled *The Tree and the Blossom*). A New York literary agent, whom she had picked at random from a list, managed to sell the novel to publisher Julian Messner, Incorporated, after three major publishers had turned it down.

There was enormous pre-publication hoopla about the book, which Grace naively hoped would stand or fall on its literary value. The citizens of Gilmanton were in an uproar, however, learning that the novel was a gossipy portrayal of a New England town in which seemingly everyone knew everyone else's business and where unspeakable incidents occurred. Although she denied that it was a story about Gilmanton, Metalious said that it could be "a picture of life in a small New Hampshire town." After *Peyton Place* was published on September 24, 1956, Metalious began receiving obscene and threatening phone calls and letters; she and her family were ostracized, and her husband was fired from his job.

The shocking novel, which few recommended but everyone seemed to read, quickly rose to number one on the best-seller list and stayed there for 26 weeks. A month after its publication, 104,000 hardcover copies had been sold, and in the next 10 years more than 10 million paperback copies were sold, along with 300,000 hardcover copies. Boston bluebloods condemned *Peyton Place* as not suitable for children or adults; it was banned in Boston and Rhode Island; libraries across the country refused to buy it and blacklisted it. The book failed to clear customs in Canada. Despite the scathing criticism, some critics saw merit and talent in the book. Carlos Baker of the *New York Times* wrote: "The late Sinclair Lewis would have hailed Grace Metalious as a sister in arms against false fronts and bourgeois pretensions of allegedly respectable communities."

Soon Twentieth Century-Fox paid an estimated $125,000 for the movie rights to the book. The people of Gilmanton wanted no part of the film *Peyton Place* (1957), whose sensational premiere was held in Camden, Maine. The movie grossed $21 million for the film company, and the book was later made into a popular television series (1964–69).

The new author, though damned by many, won fame and fortune, became a widely interviewed celebrity, and began to indulge in parties, drinking, traveling, and spending. She also had several affairs. Her infidelity brought on a divorce from her husband in 1958, and three days later she married Thomas J. Martin, a former radio disc jockey. That marriage soon disintegrated, and Grace returned to George Metalious, whom she re-married in 1960.

Meanwhile, living in Gilmanton, she wrote *Return to Peyton Place* (1959), a sequel to her first novel, which she said "was written for the 'gentlemen' in Hollywood who will do anything to make a quick buck." It sold more than 4 million paperback copies and was also made into a successful movie. Following this, Metalious also wrote *The Tight White Collar* (1960) and *No Adam in Eden* (1963). Like her first novel, these two relied heavily upon sexual details.

A dissipating lifestyle of excessive drinking, however, took its toll on Metalious, who became disillusioned, dispirited, and withdrawn because of public derision and private inner frustrations. She met and became a close friend of British journalist John Rees, with whom she had an alleged affair. But on February 25, 1964, Grace Metalious died in a Boston hospital of chronic liver disease, at the young age of 39. It was only eight years after the publication of *Peyton Place*.

John PICKERING: "loose morals and intemperate habits"

On March 12, 1804, U.S. District Court Judge John Pickering of New Hampshire became the first federal judge to be impeached by the House of Representatives, tried by the Senate, and removed from office. Once one of his state's leading citizens, Pickering was charged with "loose morals and intemperate habits" and conduct "disgraceful to his own character as a judge and degrading to the honor and dignity of the United States." His crime—appearing drunk on the bench.

Pickering's early career had been exemplary, according to most of his contemporaries. A graduate of Harvard College in 1761, he studied law and was admitted to the bar. (Dartmouth College awarded him an honorary LL.D. in 1792.) After holding sundry civil posts during the Revolutionary period, he served in the convention that drafted the New Hampshire Constitution of 1779. He was a member of a second constitutional convention in 1781, and a decade later helped to revise the second constitution. Although he represented Portsmouth in the state legislature for several terms, he was elected to but refused to serve in national posts, including the Continental Congress and the Philadelphia convention of 1787 that framed the federal Constitution. His refusals may have been connected with his dread of crossing water (which often compelled him to travel miles out of his way to avoid ferries) rather than any lack of interest in national affairs, because he was an influential member of the New Hampshire convention that ratified the U.S. Constitution. He was a Presidential elector in 1788 and again in 1792 and served in the New Hampshire state senate.

In 1790 Pickering became chief justice of the superior court of New Hampshire, a position he held until 1795, when he was appointed a lifetime judge of the U.S. district court. Although he appeared relatively competent for several years, by the turn of the 19th century his eccentricities had deteriorated into insanity and alcoholism. In 1801 a judge of the circuit court was assigned to take over Pickering's duties, but when the circuit courts were abolished shortly thereafter, Pickering, refusing to resign, resumed his position.

Pickering's career reached its nadir in 1802, when he presided over a trial concerning the seizure by United States customs officials of the ship *Eliza* on smuggling charges. The trial was a farce. On the opening day Pickering staggered into the courtroom, intoxicated. After exhibiting some bizarre behavior, Pickering ordered the trial postponed until the next day, remarking that he would then be sober. The following day, however, the judge was even more inebriated. After hearing the ship-owner's case and a few minutes of argument between the attorneys, Pickering ordered the ship returned to its owner. The district attorney was allowed only a few minutes to present his witnesses. "We will not sit here to eternity to decide on such paltry matters," Pickering declared.

Federal officials then decided to act. Though Pickering was clearly incompetent to continue serving on the bench, the Constitution offered no way to remove him short of impeachment, the grounds for which were restricted to treason, bribery, or other high crimes and misdemeanors. Pickering's offenses fit comfortably into none of these categories, but the House of Representatives nonetheless voted articles of impeachment against him. His removal from office was complicated when it became a battle between opposing political parties—Republicans versus Federalists—over control of the judiciary. The impeachment itself became another scandal, described by historian Henry Adams as "confused, contradictory and irregular, . . . a perversion of Justice."

The articles of impeachment charged the judge with violating procedural rules, improperly enforcing the law, drunkenness, and profanity on the bench. Pickering filed no answer; he never appeared before the Senate and no attorney represented him. Republican senators aided the prosecution, while Federalist senators conducted the defense. Pickering's son, Jacob, presented a petition at the opening of the trial claiming that his father, though previously above reproach in his morals, had been for several years "insane, his mind wholly deranged," a disorder that had "baffled all medical aid." As a result, the defense maintained, Pickering was not subject to impeachment, for he was incapable of rational judgment.

After heated debate along party lines, Pickering was found guilty of all four articles of impeachment. The Senate voted his removal from office on March 12, 1804. Pickering died on April 11, 1805.

Roman POLANSKI: a taste for underage girls

Talented film director Roman Polanski's conviction for statutory rape in 1977, for having sex with a 13-year-old girl, shocked Americans and Europeans and clearly damaged his professional reputation thereafter. The Hollywood scandal continues to generate discussion today, though Polanski then insisted that the girl suffered not "in any way for the consequences of that encounter" and believes "it was wrong . . . because it was . . . against the law . . . where it happened."

Born into a Jewish family in Paris in 1933, Polanski experienced the horror of seeing his parents removed to Nazi concentration camps in World War II (his mother died at the notorious Auschwitz camp). Bold and aggressive, he became a director of French and American films. His internationally acclaimed movies showed a particular fascination for peril and violence. Among his best known, striking films are *Knife in the Water* (1961), *Repulsion* (1965), *Rosemary's Baby* (1968), and *Chinatown* (1974). In 1968 Polanski, who had gained considerable notoriety for his free-spirited lifestyle, partying, and penchant for lovely young girls, married actress Sharon Tate. She was about eight months pregnant with his child when she was brutally murdered, along with four others on August 9, 1969, by members of Charles Manson's hippie family at Polanski's plush estate in Beverly Hills, California (see TATE-LABIANCA MURDERS). Polanski was away at the time, working on a new movie script in London. Some people criticized Polanski, irrationally, for somehow allowing the horrible killings to happen. Afterward, the controversial director grew quite friendly with actor Jack Nicholson, who starred in his picture *Chinatown*.

In March 1977, Polanski took a pretty 13-year-old girl to the Los Angeles home of Nicholson (who was away at the time). He was taking photographs of her, for the second time, to be published in a magazine. Polanski snapped pictures of the girl in the swimming pool and served her some champagne. At some point the girl, who was asthmatic, suffered a minor attack. Polanski gave her a Quaalude, a tranquilizer sometime referred to as the "love drug," to help her settle down. Afterwards, pictures were taken of her in the hot tub of the house. When Polanski asked the girl to remove her swimsuit top, she phoned her mother for permission; the mother, who had had sex with the fast-living director, gave it hesitantly. For a period the girl was unconscious on the bed in the house, and Polanski's dalliance with her was interrupted by the arrival of Anjelica Huston, Nicholson's girlfriend, who demanded that Polanski and the girl get out.

Back at her own home, the young girl informed her 16-year-old boyfriend about what had occurred with Polanski. Her sister accidentally overheard the story and told their mother, who angrily phoned the police. Polanski was taken into custody after being arrested at the Beverly Wilshire Hotel in Los Angeles. The police also took the girl into custody and charged Huston with possession of drugs found during a search of Nicholson's house. Among the charges against Polanski were child molestation, sodomy, and supplying dangerous drugs to a minor. He was freed on about $2,500 bail and later pleaded not guilty to the charges. The girl was found to have had sex before the encounter with Polanski, thus making her supposed loss of virginity a farce.

After much plea-bargaining, Polanski pleaded guilty to a charge of unlawful sexual intercourse; all other accusations were dropped. However, he was ordered by the judge in the case to undergo psychiatric tests in a California prison hospital for 90 days, after which he was to be sentenced. But the film director, hoping to complete a movie in Europe, induced the judge to put off the testing and incarceration and flew to Paris, where he had an apartment. Facing possible deportation from the United States, he promised the judge he would return. Huston was to have immunity from prosecution on her drug charges if she gave testimony against Polanski, and later the girl's boyfriend (who faced the same moral charges as Polanski) was also given immunity for testimony against the successful film director.

Later in 1977, Polanski was seen and photographed with beautiful 16-year-old actress Nastassja Kinski and other young European beauties. Upset by the news photos, the judge told Polanski to begin his 90-day psychiatric testing. After six weeks, the psychiatrists examining Polanski recommended in a report that the director be released from serving any more time; they stated that he had possibly suffered terrifying and emotionally scarring childhood experiences while living in Nazi-occupied Cracow, Poland. Unconvinced, the judge wanted Polanski in prison. Since having been arrested, the director had flown several times between Los Angeles and Paris without being stopped by authorities, and thus in early February 1978, he unobtrusively went to Paris aboard a night flight and exiled himself there, refusing to return to America. He could not be extradited from France.

Despite the judge's assurance that Polanski would serve only seven more weeks in custody, the director remained in Paris and was afterward hounded by press photographers waiting to catch him in a compromising pose with young girls. Polanski openly admitted his attraction for teenagers, stating that he didn't "think there's anything vicious in it." In 1980, he won three Academy Awards (for art direction, cinematography, and costume design) for his film *Tess,* which starred Miss Kinski. Based on a novel by Thomas Hardy, the film had to be shot in France instead of England (the setting for Hardy's book) because Polanski would have been extradited to the United States by British authorities upon setting foot in their country.

In 1993 Polanski settled out of court in a civil lawsuit with Samantha Geimer (the name of the 13-year-old he was accused of raping in 1977). In late 1997, Polanski's lawyers were trying to broker a deal with the Los Angeles district attorney's office to allow him to return to the United States without going to jail. The thrice-married Polanski finally accepted blame for the crime; in late 1999, still living in Paris after more than 20 years,

he said in the December issue of *Esquire* magazine, "There was no plot against me. There was no setup. It was all my fault. I think my wrongdoing was much greater than Bill CLINTON's."

James K. POLK: the Roorback forgery

Many 19th-century American presidential campaigns were colorful. Torchlight parades, songfests, stump speeches, and tavern gatherings gave them an air of excitement that caused a contemporary British observer to characterize the quadrennial orgies as "the great American shindig." Some, however, are remembered for their viciousness; they were marked by dishonorable *ad hominem* attacks upon candidates and villainous prevarications. James Knox Polk, Democratic candidate for president in 1844 and later the 11th president of the United States, was briefly the victim of one such libelous action.

In a campaign concerned with the momentous national issue of America's Manifest Destiny—the annexation of the Republic of Texas and the acquisition of the Oregon Territory held by the British—personal attacks were not to be expected, but Polk's opponents, the Whigs, unable to make political capital of their opposition to national expansion, made the campaign of 1844 remarkable for its sheer personal malice. At first the Whigs had assailed Polk as an unknown: "Who is James K. Polk?" they jeered. Their ploy had been ill-considered. Polk had first been elected to the U.S. House of Representatives in 1825; he had been House Speaker in the mid-1830s, and he had also been a governor of Tennessee. In a land that was still largely without the telegraph, he was surprisingly well recognized.

The Whigs also attacked Polk for his mediocrity. Their mudslinging accomplished little, though. Polk's Whip opponent was Henry Clay, a former Kentucky senator and presidential aspirant who had a notoriously flashy lifestyle. The Democrats countered the attacks on Polk by accusing Clay of having broken each of the Ten Commandments, and of living in a Washington D.C., brothel. These accusations could not be met in kind by the Whigs, for Polk lived quietly and seemed invulnerable to personal attacks.

The Whig's first two ploys having failed, they tried a new tack: Polk's support of the annexation of Texas raised the question of its admission as a slave or a free state into the Union, and because Polk was a slaveholder himself, the Whigs hoped to turn Democrats of abolitionist persuasion against him by portraying him as a cruel master.

On August 21, 1844, the Ithaca, New York *Chronicle,* an abolitionist newspaper, printed extracts from the anonymous travel book *Roorback's Tour through the Southern and Western States in the Year 1836,* supposedly the work of a German tourist, Baron von Roorback. Into a fictitous description of a Tennessee slave-trader's encampment, the editors introduced a doubly fictitious sentence: "Forty of these unfortunate beings had been purchased, I was told, by the Hon. J. K. Polk, the present speaker of the house of representatives; the mark of the branding iron, with the initials of his name on their shoulders distinguishing them from the rest." The forgery was quickly reprinted throughout the northern states.

But the vicious tale backfired. Alert Democrats discovered the falsehood and publicized the fact that Polk's name had not even appeared in the book. Abolitionists who might have voted for Clay began to support Polk as soon as the forgery was publicized, and the Democrats avenged themselves by doubling their attacks on Clay and pointing out that he, too, was a slaveholder. Polk eventually took New York State from Clay in the election and was elected nationally by 170 electoral votes to Clay's 105.

The Roorback forgery, however, was not forgotten: *roorback* entered the American language as a term denoting a political falsehood.

Jonathan POLLARD: spy motivated by ideology

Jonathan Jay Pollard, a naval intelligence analyst for the U.S., Department of Defense, copied thousands of pages of classified American documents and handed them over to a small Israeli intelligence operation in Washington, D.C., in the mid-1980s. He defended himself by saying that the ends justified the means. An ardent Zionist, Pollard felt that the United States was failing to share all of its secret information about the arming of the Arab world on Israel's borders. The American courts thought differently and declared that spying was spying, even if done on behalf of a close ally. In March 1987 Pollard was sentenced to life imprisonment.

Pollard had gone to work for the Department of Defense in 1984 after serving in the United States Navy, where he supposedly experienced severe anti-Semitism. In 1984, he met Colonel Aviam Sella, a young, up-and-coming Israeli military officer who was taking a course in computer engineering at New York University. Pollard offered to spy for Israel, and Sella told him the sort of information that was wanted. Pollard came through, and in the fall of 1984 Sella set up a meeting in Paris with Pollard and Raphael Eitan, who ran a small intelligence unit in the Israel Defense Ministry called LEKEM, as well as with Yosef Yagur, an Israeli science attaché living in New York. The three men gave Pollard $10,000 and offered him a salary of $1,500 a month for providing them with information. Later the salary was increased to $2,500, and in the spring of 1985 Pollard received a bonus of a free vacation trip to Israel with his wife.

As part of his agreement, Pollard delivered, every other week, a suitcase of classified materials to the apartment of Irit Erb, a secretary for the Israeli Embassy

Jonathan Pollard, former U.S. Navy intelligence analyst, speaks during an interview in federal prison in Butner, North Carolina, on May 15, 1998. He had passed highly sensitive national security secrets to Israel before his arrest in 1985 and guilty plea in 1986. (AP/Wide World Photos)

in Washington. There the documents were copied and then passed on to the Israeli intelligence services. The information proved to be extremely valuable. For example, some of the Pollard-supplied data enabled Israeli planes to circumvent radar detection when they bombed the headquarters of the Palestine Liberation Organization in Tunisia in October 1985.

The following month Pollard's co-workers at the Department of Defense alerted the Federal Bureau of Investigation to the fact that he was taking home large numbers of classified documents. Agents of the FBI then interrogated him outside his workplace. In a panic, Pollard telephoned his wife, Anne, who was also involved in the operation, to warn her about what was happening. She in turn called the Israeli embassy to arrange for asylum and tried unsuccessfully to get rid of a batch of classified papers in their home. On November 21, 1985, the Pollards drove into the compound of the Israeli embassy in Washington, D.C., but security officers turned them away when they saw that the spies were being trailed by U.S. government agents. Jonathan and Anne

Pollard were arrested as soon as they drove out of the gates of the compound. Their 17 months of espionage were over.

Sella, Yagur, and Erb quietly and quickly left the United States and returned to Israel. Pollard confessed his actions and promised to cooperate with federal investigators. Israeli leaders also promised to cooperate. Many of them denied any knowledge of the operation and claimed that LEKEM was a "rogue" spy team. It took months for the American investigators to discover the seriousness of Pollard's espionage. During this time he continually justified his actions, writing that "Assisting the Israelis did not involve or require betraying the United States" and adding that he only wanted to furnish "information on the Arab powers and the Soviets that would . . . avoid a repetition of the Yom Kippur War." But the Department of Defense and the district court of the District of Columbia felt that Pollard's espionage had seriously jeopardized national security and that he was guilty of treason. His trial in 1986–87 had international repercussions and strained United States—Israeli relationships in many uncomfortable ways. Pollard's wife received a five-year sentence in 1987 for assisting him in his spying, while he received the maximum sentence—life in a federal prison. The 32-year-old Pollard, who pleaded for mercy for his 26-year-old wife, said that he had "sacrificed her . . . on the altar of ideology."

The Israeli government disavowed Pollard, saying he acted without its knowledge but made unsuccessful pleas to U.S. presidents for his release. In 1998 Israel reportedly was planning to recognize Pollard as a spy in order to win his release from a federal prison in North Carolina.

POMEROY CIRCULAR

During the American Civil War (1861–65), radical Republicans in Congress believed that President Abraham Lincoln's prosecution of the war was not punitive enough and consequently tired to thwart his renomination for the presidency in 1864. They conspired to have Treasury Secretary Salmon P. Chase replace Lincoln. Their intrigue failed, however, serving only to bring on public criticism of Chase for political disloyalty.

An able and ambitious lawyer from Ohio, Chase had always wanted to win the nation's highest office. He ardently defended fugitive slaves and became a leader of the antislavery movement in Ohio, where the voter elected him United States senator from 1849 to 1855 and then the first Republican governor of the state (1855–60). Many considered Chase an extreme abolitionist, a fact that perhaps helped defeat him in seeking the Republican presidential nomination in 1856 and 1860. At the 1860 Republican party convention in Chicago, Chase had permitted his delegates to vote for Lincoln on the third ballot; he had lacked the complete support of the Ohio delegation—in part because of his abolitionist image—but later that year was again elected to the Senate. In gratitude for Chase's help, President Lincoln, who also wanted to unite the Republican party, appointed Chase to be secretary of the treasury, a post he took in March 1861, after serving only two days as a senator.

The radical Republicans sought a forceful campaign against the rebel South, and an early, unconditional emancipation of the slaves. Lincoln's seemingly conciliatory policy toward the South was frequently criticized, along with his Union generals' ineffectiveness in defeating the Confederacy. By mid-summer of 1864, after the radicals had begun to show that they wanted to deny the president renomination, Lincoln's outlook for re-election appeared gloomy. Military reverses of Union forces' efforts had made his renomination dubious, and the radicals in his party cried for a more vigorous punishment of the Confederacy both militarily and politically. Yet on July 4, 1864 Lincoln pocket-vetoed the Wade-Davis Bill, a measure for the radical reconstruction of the South, which required that, in order for the seceded states to gain readmission to the Union, a majority of the electorate take an oath of loyalty. The bill also contained other harsh penalties to be imposed on Confederate states and their leaders. The radicals then scathingly denounced the president for his apparent leniency.

Earlier, in January 1864, they had circulated a surreptitious letter on behalf of Chase, who was put forth as the only one who could save the union. These radical backers of Chase had formed a committee that was headed by Senator Samuel C. Pomeroy of Kansas, after whom the letter became known. The Pomeroy Circular attacked Lincoln's policies, claimed he could not win the 1864 election, and advocated Chase's candidacy for the presidency. In February the circular was published in a Washington, D.C., newspaper, the *National Intelligencer,* to the radicals' embarrassment. Moderate Republicans felt that their loyalty to the president was under attack. Lincoln, who well recognized what he called Chase's "mad hunt for the presidency," put on a good face and tried not to antagonize the radicals by getting rid of Treasury Secretary Chase, for whom he had high regard despite their political differences. Chase's Ohio Republican organization then threw its support to Lincoln, and Chase disavowed the Pomeroy Circular and withdrew his countenance of the radicals' move for him. But an impropriety evidently had been wrought by the treasury secretary, who offered to resign. At first, Lincoln did not accept Chase's resignation, but on June 29, 1864, he changed his mind. Chase was apparently surprised when his second offer of resignation was accepted. President Lincoln was renominated unanimously at the 1864 Republican convention, and on December 6, 1864, appointed Chase chief justice of the U.S. Supreme Court to succeed Roger B. Taney, who had died in October. Chase persisted in seeking the presidency, running unsuccessfully in 1868 and 1872. He died a year later at the age of 65.

Charles PONZI: "the greatest Italian of them all"

Like many immigrants, Charles Ponzi arrived in the United States just before the turn of the 20th century with wild dreams of grandeur and wealth in his head. But unlike those who believed in the credo of success through hard work, Ponzi felt that he could take a short-cut. By 1919 he had worked out the "Ponzi plan," a scheme involving the purchase of International Postal Union reply coupons in depressed countries and their redemption for four or five times their face value in the United States. At least that is what he told his investors. Ponzi managed to live the life of a multimillionaire for about a year. It was not until authorities in Boston became suspicious that it was discovered that he had perpetrated one of the greatest swindles of all times.

Like most Italian immigrants in 1899, 22-year-old Charles Ponzi arrived in the United States with little cash in his pockets. He first worked at a number of menial jobs and then decided to try his luck in Canada. He was soon arrested for forging checks and was sentenced to jail. Upon his release, Ponzi made his way south to Atlanta, Georgia, where he set up an alien-smuggling operation. The Immigration Service soon found him out, and he was again imprisoned. By 1914 he had gone to Boston, where he married the daughter of a prosperous wholesale grocer and was soon running the family business. Under his mismanagement, it failed miserably. Ponzi was forced to take a translating job with an import-export firm, J. P. Poole, but he continued to try to devise a way to get rich quick.

While working at J. P. Poole, he learned about International Postal Union reply coupons that could be redeemed in the United States for far more money than they cost in a poor country such as Italy or Germany. This seemed the answer to his prayers. He borrowed some money, sent it to relatives in Italy, and told them to purchase postal reply coupons and return them to him. When he tried to redeem the coupons, however, he learned that it was a very time-consuming, tedious process. Yet he still thought the idea had merit and would serve to justify a fraudulent investment scheme he had worked out.

He told several friends about the reply coupons and promised them he would make a 50 percent profit in 90 days on any money they invested with him. Some gave him small amounts, and when three months later the money and profit were indeed repaid, they reinvested. Word about the Ponzi plan spread like wild-fire. Ponzi established himself as the Financial Exchange Company with a fancy office in Boston's financial district. Money poured in so fast that his employees, most of whom were relatives of his wife, could hardly count it. The office was literally crammed with bills. Soon Ponzi had to open branches throughout New England and in New York and New Jersey as well.

Ponzi reveled in his new-found wealth. Now called the Great Ponzi, he bought a mansion in the suburbs of Boston and had a chauffeur-driven limousine. He was reputed to have had 100 pairs of shoes, 200 suits, four dozen Malacca canes with gold handles, and two dozen diamond stickpins. He smoked his cigarettes in a diamond-studded cigarette holder. In 1919, Ponzi bought out J. P. Poole and fired his former employers. He showed up at the Hanover Trust Company in New York carrying two suitcases containing $3 million in cash and bought a controlling interest in the bank. He continued to pay 50 percent interest on old investments, using the funds from new investments. He also sued a financial writer for a Boston newspaper who had questioned the legitimacy of his operations.

Ponzi's fear of reporters prompted him to hire William McMasters, a public-relations man, to handle the press. Masters was, however, immediately suspicious of his new boss and told state investigators that he was sure something fishy was going on. The authorities ordered Ponzi to bring his books in for inspection. When he arrived at the State House in Boston, a crowd of supporters cheered him, and one man shouted, "You're the greatest Italian of them all."

Ponzi modestly replied, "Oh no. Columbus and Marconi. Columbus discovered America. Marconi discovered the wireless."

"But you discovered money!" responded the crowd.

Inside the State House, auditors struggled without success to make sense out of the chaotic and incomplete ledgers. Meanwhile, investigative reporters on the *Boston Globe* were digging up information about Ponzi's unsavory past. Ponzi's bubble burst on August 13, 1920, when the news appeared that he had been arrested and jailed for forgery and alien smuggling. Angry investors then swarmed to his offices, insisting that they be reimbursed. Employees of his company paid out $15 million before they ran out of cash.

Federal authorities soon arrested Ponzi for mail fraud, and he was sentenced to four years in prison. Upon his release, the police in Massachusetts arrested and tried him for theft and swindling, and he served nine more years in prison, after which he was deported to Italy in 1934. Back home, Ponzi wormed his way into a good job in the financial department of Benito Mussolini's fascist government and managed to steal a large amount of money from the treasury before escaping to Brazil several years later. The former dandy and "financial wizard" of Boston died destitute, blind, and partially paralyzed in the charity ward of a Rio de Janeiro hospital in January 1949.

Ezra POUND: poet as traitor?

When he was first captured and charged with treason by an American court in 1945, the internationally renowned poet and fascist sympathizer Ezra Pound spent three weeks in a tarpaulin-covered outdoor "Gorilla Cage" near Pisa, Italy, with an uncovered tin can to allow public exposure of his private needs. The U.S. Army explained that it had created this contradictory type of solitary confinement to prevent rescue of the 60-year-old prisoner by the Italian army; it was merely fortuitous that it also served as a type of public humiliation of Pound. Allowed neither visitors nor legal counsel, Pound occupied himself by translating Chinese verse and writing poetry later published (1948) as the prize-winning *Pisan Cantos*. The charge of treason that led to the imprisonment of the world-famous poet, treated as if he were publicly dangerous, was never tested.

Ezra Pound had spent the early years of the 20th century acting as a profound, if erratic, cultural force. As a poet, he became a dominant figure in Anglo-American verse. As an editor and critic, he was among the first to recognize the genius of Robert Frost, D. H. Lawrence, Ernest Hemingway, James Joyce, T. S. Eliot, and William Butler Yeats. He also advanced international recognition of the sculptors Jacob Epstein and Henri Gaudier-Brzeska and promoted the rediscovery of the Italian composer Antonio Vivaldi.

From 1918 on, Pound's prose and poetry began to reveal an almost obsessive concern with economic history, especially as interpreted by the English economic theorist C. H. Douglas, whose social-credit theory held that economic depressions are the result of the maldistribution of wealth. Douglas's social-credit hypotheses became, after 1930, Pound's battle cry. His promulgation of them led ineluctably to his imprisonment in the Pisan Gorilla Cage.

Pound's private war against manipulations of money by international bankers led him during the 1930s to write a series of books advocating monetary and political reforms. Gradually he began to reveal his conviction that international Jewry controlled both the banks and western governments; he also saw salvation in fascist economics, whose "corporativeness" had adopted some ideas from social-credit theories. Ultimately, he began to admire Benito Mussolini, even to the point of considering him more creative and valuable than Thomas Jefferson. He also began, in 1935, to promulgate his favorite economic theories on Italian radio. Aware that world war was imminent, he traveled to Washington, D.C., in 1939, vainly hoping that personal appeals to U.S. President Franklin Roosevelt (who would not receive him) and Vice President Henry Wallace (who

did) would prevent the conflict. Disappointed, Pound returned to Italy, reasserted his admiration for Italian practices while retaining his American citizenship, and resumed his radio talks, now beamed toward America. Although his topics were chiefly literary and economic, he also denounced the American war effort and was therefore indicted in 1943 by a Washington, D.C., district court for the treasonable action of "giving aid and comfort to the Kingdom of Italy," the verdict that led to his Gorilla Cage imprisonment.

Returned to American toward the end of 1943, Pound spent two weeks in the District of Columbia jail awaiting a treason trial that never took place. Declared mentally incompetent to stand trial, he was confined for the next dozen years to Washington's St. Elizabeth's Hospital for the Criminally Insane, where he continued to write and publish until 1958 when the treason charge was dropped because of his alleged mental incapacity. Still an American citizen, he returned to Italy to write energetically until a 1962 heart attack made him develop what he denoted as "yet another eloquent new voice: silence."

By the time of his death in 1972, Pound had published 70 books, assisted in the writing of 70 others, and written more than 1,500 articles. Though his economic theories were obsessive and his anti-Semitism barely masked, many felt that Pound's actions never merited the label traitor.

Adam Clayton POWELL, Jr.: fallen congressman

"Lynching—Northern style," declared black U.S. Representative Adam Clayton Powell, Jr., of New York after he was stripped of a powerful House chairmanship and then barred from taking his seat in the House in January 1967. Immediately civil rights leaders and others condemned these congressional votes against Powell, who had been accused of corruption and financial mismanagement. Seven weeks later, amidst the uproar, the House of Representatives confirmed and extended its action, denying Powell his seat in the 90th Congress and ordering a special election to fill it.

The vote was the climax to a long, successful political career—including 22 years in Congress—and considered a major blow to the American civil rights movement. "It takes 50 years for a black man to accumulate that much power," said New York City Councilman Percy Sutton, speaking before an emergency meeting of black politicians and civil rights leaders summoned to make a defense of Powell.

Son and namesake of a prominent black activist who was pastor of the Abyssinian Baptist Church in New York City's Harlem, Powell had earned a bachelor of arts degree from Colgate University in 1930 and a master of arts degree from Columbia University in 1932 and became a vigorous civil rights leader before taking over his retiring father's pastorship in 1937, a post he

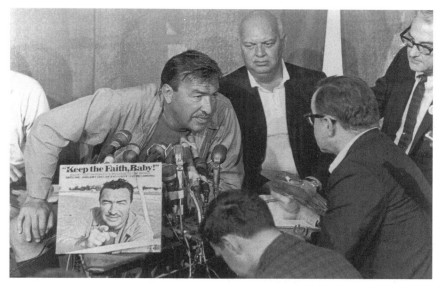

Congressman Adam Clayton Powell, Jr., leans over a battery of microphones during a news conference in Bimini on January 28, 1967. He told reporters that the money he expected from the sale of his latest record, "Keep the Faith Baby" (seen here in front of the microphones), would be used to pay Mrs. Esther James, a Harlem widow who was suing him for slandering her. (UPI/Bettmann Newsphotos)

held until 1971. More jobs and relief for needy blacks as well as fighting public discrimination, were Powell's goals for Harlem and elsewhere. As a Democrat, he was elected in 1941 to the New York City Council and in 1945 to the U.S. House of Representatives, where he became known for his wit, flamboyance, and sometimes abrasiveness. He also earned a reputation for finding solutions to litigious problems.

Powell referred to President Dwight Eisenhower's statement that "there must be no second-class citizens in this country" as "a second Emancipation Proclamation," and he worked personally and successfully to desegregate many congressional facilities and Washington, D.C., hotels, restaurants, and theaters. Through his long efforts on Capitol Hill, America's armed services were desegregated, and legislation was enacted requiring the inclusion of antidiscrimination clauses in all federal work contracts to businesses.

Powell rose in 1961 to become the chairman of the prestigious House Education and Labor Committee, which was cited by Presidents John F. Kennedy and Lyndon Johnson as the critical force in the passage of 48 pieces of social-welfare legislation, including the Federal Minimum Wage Bill, the Manpower Development and Training Act, the Vocational Educational Act, and the Anti-Poverty Bill, the foundation for Johnson's Great Society program to improve the quality of life for all Americans.

In his New York City district of Harlem, which had some 300,000 voters and was about 89 percent black, Powell was continually reelected and admired for his "brilliance, audacity, and style" (words from a headline he liked to quote) and undisguised relish in challenging white expectations of his behavior.

The offense that precipitated his fall from Congress was characteristic: Powell toured Europe with his 21-year-old black secretary, a former Miss Ohio, and a white woman lawyer on salary as a labor counsel to his committee. This was done with seemingly deliberate contempt at a time when he could not enter his own district because of warrants issued for criminal contempt of court, pursuant to a 1963 libel judgment against him that he had ignored for years (a Harlem resident had filed a lawsuit accusing Powell of calling her "a bag woman"). His congressional colleagues then charged him with misusing government funds to take private trips and with inexcusably defying the New York courts. Powell did not dispute the House charge, which resulted in a Democratic House caucus vote on January 9, 1967, depriving him of the Education and Labor Committee chairmanship. The next day, his seat was taken away by a House vote of 364-64, pending an authorized special investigation into his qualifications and affairs.

The investigating panel concluded that Powell had "willfully" misappropriated some $46,000 for personal use and had "improperly maintained" his wife on his office payroll; its recommendation that he be censured, fined, and stripped of seniority was rejected by the House, which on March 1, 1967, voted 307 to 116 to exclude him. Powell, who was at his vacation haunt on the Bahamian island of Bimini at the time, filed a federal court suit charging that his exclusion was constitutionally illegal. The House's action was denounced by many black leaders, including Nobel Peace Prize winner Ralph Bunche, who said, "There can be no reasonable doubt that if Adam Powell had been white he would have his seat today."

Powell fought back. Without reentering his own district and without his party's nomination, he won, on April 11, 1967, the special election that had been ordered to fill his vacant seat, getting 74 percent of the vote while defeating two opponents. But legal pressures from his contempt-of-court case, as well as a well-publicized divorce (his third), kept him on Bimini without claiming his House seat. After winning another election in 1968, he was given back his seat by an affirmative House vote in January 1969 but was also fined $25,000 and deprived of seniority. In June 1969, the U.S. Supreme Court ruled that his expulsion had been unconstitutional. After failing to gain reelection in 1970, Powell, in ill health and embroiled in legal action, exiled himself in Bimini. He died at the age of 63 in Miami, Florida, on April 4, 1972.

Francis Gary POWERS. See U-2 SPY FLIGHT.

PREPPY MURDER CASE. See Robert CHAMBERS: the preppy murder case.

Elvis PRESLEY: shocking stud

In 1955 and 1956, Elvis Aron Presley, an ex-truck driver with only a high-school education, burst upon the American musical world. The young singer was white but many felt he had captured the black sound. It turned out to be a devastating combination. Popular because of his blues-influenced brand of rock-and-roll as well his famed stage performances (which featured a great deal of pelvic gyrations), the new "king" of rock-and-roll won the hearts of numerous teenage girls. He failed, however, to win the hearts of many Americans, particularly conservatives, who found his sexually suggestive movements "a menace to young girls," as one famous newspaper columnist wrote at the time. "Elvis the Pelvis" became the ultimate male sex symbol and the ultimate scandal. He grossed more than a billion dollars during his lifetime and scandalized the public again, after his death from a heart attack at the age of 42 in 1977, when his private sex life was exposed in a best-seller book.

Besides his unique singing style, he was known for his long sideburns, "DA" (for "duck's ass") haircut, suede shoes, and colorful pink and black clothes. Teenage girls went especially wild over his stream of million-selling hit records: "Heartbreak Hotel," "Hound Dog," "Don't Be Cruel," "Blue Suede Shoes," and "Love Me Tender" (all released in 1956). Later they bought other Presley disks, including "Jailhouse Rock" (1957), "Hard Headed Woman" (1959), "It's Now or Never" (1960), and "I Can't Help Falling in Love with You" (1961). This Mississippi-born, poor, religious, church-going boy had become a sensational teen idol and didn't understand why he was considered a bad influence on America's youth. His success was largely due to his adroit manager, Colonel Tom Parker, who looked after him throughout his career (and apparently pocketed a good deal of the singer's fortune for himself). Presley's mother doted on her son and was his close confidante and adviser until her death in 1958; the singer was devastated by her death and had to be torn away from her casket at her grave. By then, he was making millions of dollars, living splendidly in his 23-room palatial home called Graceland in Memphis, Tennessee. Priests, ministers, and others denounced him from their pulpits and branded him as evil, but Presley kept on entertaining, twisting his hips and legs, making records and Hollywood movies.

After serving a two-year stint in the army, mostly in Germany, Elvis returned home in 1960 to continue his phenomenal career. At Graceland, he surrounded himself with a dozen or so buddies who were nicknamed the Memphis Mafia. They were bodyguards and valets to the king, Presley, who withdrew from making public appearances from 1961 to 1967 and concentrated on making B-rated movies, such as *Girls, Girls, Girls* (1962) and *Viva Las Vegas* (1964). While stationed in Germany, he had met a pretty 14-year-old girl, Priscilla Beaulieu, the daughter of an American army officer. He obtained her father's approval to bring her to Graceland, where he supposedly had discreet premarital relations with her. They eventually wed in 1967 and nine months later had a daughter, Lisa Marie. Despite his new marital status, Presley engaged in affairs with other women and in taking many different kinds of pills (stimulants, tranquilizers, painkillers, and others). These failings, in addition to his temperamental personality, resulted in Priscilla's seeking first a separation from him (1972) and then a divorce (1973). His long absences from Graceland, his infidelities, and the Memphis Mafia's constant cover-up of his activities had disturbed Priscilla, who received a $2-million settlement after the divorce. Presley was deeply upset by the breakup, but he turned to other beautiful girls, such as Linda Thompson (Miss Tennessee of 1972), who lived with him at Graceland for several years. By the mid-1970s, Presley sank increasingly into a life of debauchery. He became more and more consumed by sex, drugs, and food. He developed severe health problems and became grotesquely heavy. In 1977, Presley married 20-year-old Ginger Alden (Miss Memphis Traffic Safety of 1976), but only weeks later, on August 16, 1977, Presley died in his Graceland bathroom (some have said that his heavy use of different drugs did him in). Ginger was with him at the time. Afterward, millions of adoring fans wept openly; Graceland was mobbed by hysterical, fainting girls and women, mourning their great loss.

But in a 1981 best-selling book by Albert Goldman, this once sacred king to so many was scathingly revealed and reviled as a "comic-book macho." The massive book, *Elvis,* which Presley's fans furiously criticized, depicted him as a narcissistic, immature man, a sexual deviant who lived in a fantasy world. Goldman pointed to Presley's bizarre infatuation with his mother, his failure to relate properly to other females after her death, and his strange sexual predilections. Presley seemed to prefer masturbation to normal sexual intercourse and was interested only in young, naive women, apparently fearing rejection from older, more experienced ones. He was also a voyeur, installing one-way mirrors in rooms through which he could secretly watch his friends engage in sexual acts with girls. He used video equipment to tape his own sex movies, some of lesbian activities. Goldman also noted Presley's preoccupation with drugs, theorizing that he used them to help overcome his secret insecurities.

In 1982 Colonel Parker, who had taken 25 to 50 percent of Presley's earnings, waived all future income connected to him, ending a lawsuit by Presley's heirs. "I don't think I exploited Elvis as much as he's being exploited today," Parker said in 1993. The 87-year-old Parker died of stroke complications in Las Vegas in January 1997.

PULITZER DIVORCE AND CUSTODY CASE

America's tabloids had a heyday when, in the autumn of 1982, wealthy socialite Peter Pulitzer sued for divorce from his wife, Roxanne, and sought the custody of their five-year-old twin sons. During the trial in fashionable Palm Beach, Florida, the estranged couple hurled charges and countercharges of extreme misconduct at each other. At the end, Judge Carl Harper, who was shocked by the tales of jet-set debauchery, decided that Roxanne was the guilty partner and awarded the divorce and custody of the two young boys to Peter.

Peter Pulitzer, who was 52 at the time of the trial, was the grandson of famous newspaper publisher Joseph Pulitzer, the former owner of the *St. Louis Post-Dispatch* and the *New York World,* and financier of the prestigious annual Pulitzer Prizes. Peter was reputed to be worth some $25 million. Like the rest of his family, he lived a life of luxury and extravagance. Roxanne, who was 31 during the publicized, heated divorce-custody fight, had been a grape picker and secretary before she married Peter, but had easily adapted to Peter's lush lifestyle. She was a beautiful, vivacious woman with a passion for the late-night scene and discothéques.

At the trial, Peter accused Roxanne of lesbianism, adultery, and taking drugs, while she charged him with incest, adultery, and trafficking in drugs. A gardener and a former nanny testified to Roxanne's infidelities with a handyman, a real-estate salesman, a French pastry chef, and a racing-car driver. Peter said that his wife fre-

quently went to bed with Jacqueline Kimberley, the 32-year old wife of 76-year-old James Kimberley, the heir to the Kleenex tissue fortune. Further, Peter admitted that he sometimes joined the two women to make a sexual trio. Mrs. Kimberley denied all this and called Peter "deranged."

Roxanne counterattacked by claiming that Peter had an incestuous relationship with his 26-year-old daughter from an earlier marriage. Peter and his daughter both refuted this, and Miss Pulitzer then charged that it was Roxanne who had made a pass at her at a discothéque several years earlier.

During the trial, testimony also came from a local psychic, Janis Nelson, who said she had done some psychic readings for Roxanne. In addition, Roxanne reportedly had periodic bedroom séances conducted for her, at which she apparently had sexual relations with 10 to 15 other people, along with a three-foot trumpet enclosed in a black cape. According to Nelson, Roxanne's affairs were intended to make Peter jealous so that their marriage could be saved.

During the months of this intense family feud, Peter lived on his 73-foot yacht, the *Sea Hunter,* while Roxanne and the twin boys, Mack and Zack, lived on his estate. At that time, Roxanne was receiving $7,000 a month from Peter. After hearing all of the testimony in the case, Judge Harper declared Roxanne guilty of "gross marital misconduct" and ruled that the twins be turned over to their father. Roxanne was allowed to keep her jewels and was given a settlement of $48,000. Commented the judge, "This case has really made me appreciate my wife. I go home every night and give her a big hug."

After her sensational 1982 divorce, Roxanne was on the cover of *Playboy* magazine and then worked as an aerobics instructor and lectured on child custody rights. She also authored *The Prize Pulitzer: The Scandal That Rocked Palm Beach* (1987), her story about the wild parties, sex orgies, and six-year marriage to Peter Pulitzer, who married his one-time masseuse after the divorce. "Now I know what I did wrong," Roxanne said in early 1988 while promoting her book. "Or maybe I didn't do enough of it."

In 1992 Roxanne's marriage to boat racer John Haggin ended after eight weeks. John's mother, Naoma Haggin, a resident of Palm Beach, apparently cut him out of an estimated $200 million fortune because of the marriage. "I hope the press, media, and my mother are happy now that Roxanne and I are divorced," John said. Roxanne refused to comment on the reason for the divorce.

RADIO SCARE OF 1938. See MARTIAN INVASION: great radio scare of 1938.

William RALSTON: the Great Diamond Hoax

As president of San Francisco's Bank of California in 1872, William C. Ralston contemplated the curious events of the day, always, as was his habit, with profit in mind. But one day a bank teller disturbed his daily routine with a bizarre story: two prospector-types, of which San Francisco was by then tired, had requested vault space for a leather bag, had bristled when asked to declare the bag's contents, and had then spilled on the teller's counter a treasure in uncut diamonds. Impressed, Ralston, a former miner himself, decided to check into the possibilities opened up by this bizarre bank transaction. Thus began what some commentators on human folly label the Great Diamond Hoax.

The prospector-types, John Slack and Philip Arnold, had developed what, for purposes of classification, will be called Plan Number One: they had exposed the bag of flawed, uncut diamonds (bought, according to plan, in Amsterdam, Holland) for the purpose of leading gullible individuals to a fake diamond field and bilking them of several times more than the $25,000 the two had accumulated in gambling wins and had then invested in their hoax.

Ralston was sure that if the bank and other interested diamond fanciers could discover the source of the diamonds that Slack and Arnold had shown and purchase it for far less than it was worth (after all, prospectors were notoriously poor businessmen), then San Francisco could have its own diamond-cutting industry, all under the guidance of William C. Ralston. Ralston's plan—Plan Number Two—was under development.

Ralston was so enthralled with the idea of cheating Arnold and Slack that it never occurred to him that they might have a similar strategy. He made all of the moves expected of a careful businessman and banker who was dealing, as he believed he was, with the gullible. He contacted the duo and suggested the development of a syndicate for mining the diamonds. He promised them a fortune but meanwhile had a local jeweler assay the diamonds. Unsatisfied with the jeweler's ecstatic report, Ralston then asked New York's Tiffany and Company to comment and received an equally promising report: the bag's diamonds were worth $1.5 million. He countered the demand of Slack and Arnold that cash precede disclosure of the diamond field with the argument that disclosure of the commodity precede payment. The reluctant duo had craftily allowed a blindfolded mining expert, John Janin, to travel two days on muleback to visit the field. Impressed by Janin's wonderstruck report of the reality of the field, Ralston had agreed to his demand that he be made a syndicated partner.

The syndicate, which included the Bank of California, then paid Slack and Arnold each $300,000, sent them back to the benighted East Coast, and prepared to reap its fortune. What Ralston had forgotten to account for throughout his skillful business moves and carefully thought out precautions was that he, the leader of the syndicate, might himself be the victim of cheaters.

When the existence of the diamond field was publicized, San Francisco experienced a diamond craze. The syndicate sent out prospecting groups on false leads while it zeroed in on Janin's find. The result was dismay: a prominent geologist reported the diamond field to be salted; Tiffany's withdrew its estimate, reporting that their experts had no experience with uncut diamonds; some Californian millionaires suffered huge losses; and the Bank of California collapsed.

In order to win immunity from extradition and prosecution, Arnold, in Kentucky, gave up half of his payment. Slack fared better; he turned up, years later, as a profit-reaping coffin-maker in White Sands, New Mexico, and was never prosecuted for his role in the fraud.

Ralston, the intended hoaxee turned hoaxer, must have regarded himself as the dupe. He committed suicide in 1873.

RANDOM HOUSE: dictionary trademark infringement?

How would a dictionary define *trademark infringement*? According to dictionary publisher Merriam-Webster, *trademark infringement* might be described as an action performed by rival publisher Random House when the latter issued a dictionary that, in the wording of its title and its dust jacket design, resembled the Merriam-Webster reference book. The question was removed from the realm of lexicography and brought into the realm of law in 1991 when Merriam-Webster filed suit, charging that Random House had infringed upon both the trademark and the "trade dress" (appearance) of the Merriam-Webster dictionary. Some editors and publishers called it "willful" infringement.

Since 1973, Merriam-Webster's *Ninth New Collegiate Dictionary* had been published with a red dust jacket and the word "Webster's" running down the spine in large white letters. At the time of the lawsuit, this book was the leading college dictionary in the United States, selling an estimated 1 million copies each year. Before 1991, Random House had published its own dictionary with a red cover and the title *The Random House College Dictionary*. This reference book sold an estimated 200,000 copies a year. But in 1991, after market research indicated that the addition of the word "Webster's" would dramatically increase sales, Random House executives changed their book's title to *Webster's College Dictionary*. Random House also provided a new red cover with the word "Webster's" running down the spine in large white letters, in a typeface that Merriam-Webster claimed was similar to that of its own book. (As Random House defenders pointed out, however, the name "Random House" appeared in black letters on the front of the jacket and at the top of the spine, as did the company logo).

In its lawsuit, filed in federal district court in Manhattan, Merriam-Webster claimed that the wording and design similarities between the two dictionaries generated confusion among customers and booksellers alike. In the suit, the word *Webster's* itself was not in dispute: that term, which comes from the name of the famous 19th-century American lexicographer Noah Webster, has long been in the public domain and commonly serves as a generic term for a dictionary. Merriam-Webster did, however, object to the combination of *Webster's* and *College,* arguing that this combination violated its trademark use of these two words in its own title, as many consumers would not make the distinction between *college* and *collegiate*.

A jury agreed, finding that publishing giant Random House was guilty of diluting the value of Merriam-Webster's trademarked combination of the words *Webster's* and *Collegiate* in its title; the jury also found Random House guilty of intentionally infringing and diluting Merriam-Webster's distinctive red-and-white jacket design. The jury awarded the smaller publisher $1.8 million in damages for lost profits and $500,000 in punitive damages. In November 1991, federal judge Lawrence M. McKenna not only upheld the punitive award but doubled the damage award. He also gave explicit directions on the design of a new jacket for the Random House book, specifying the size of the type, the color of the jacket, and the wording on it. Merriam-Webster officials hailed this ruling as a victory for consumers and encouragement for companies to invest in the development of brand recognition and loyalty.

In 1994, however, the Second Circuit Court of Appeals reversed the judgment and dismissed Merriam-Webster's complaint, stating that neither the combination of words nor the red-and-white cover represented infringement. In a unanimous verdict, a three-judge panel found that the book jackets were sufficiently different in terms of their wording and appearance (such as the logos and the names of the respective publishers) that consumers would be unlikely to be confused by the two designs. The judges stated that red dust jackets were common for dictionaries, as were the words *Webster's* and *College*. The following year the U.S. Supreme Court let this ruling stand.

"RED HUNT" AGAINST HOLLYWOOD FIGURES. See HOUSE COMMITTEE ON UN-AMERICAN ACTIVITIES (HUAC): America's inquisition and the "Hollywood Ten."

"RED SCARE." See A. Mitchell PALMER: opportunism masked as idealism.

Wallace REID: drugs and drinks

News that beloved silent-movie star Wallace Reid was a drug addict shocked the American public completely in 1922. Handsome, charming, and talented, he was the embodiment of young American manhood both on and off the screen. His subsequent, sudden death in a private sanitarium on January 18, 1923, at the age of 32, resulted in national grief for him and a crusade to warn of the dangers of morphine and other drugs.

Born in St. Louis, Missouri, in 1890, Wally Reid first appeared on stage as a young child with his parents, both of whom were accomplished theatrical performers. He learned to play various musical instruments, including the violin and the piano, and moved to New York with his family when he was 10. After attending military school, Reid planned to pursue a medical career at Princeton University but became enamored of the fledgling silent motion-picture industry, making it his life work. First in Chicago and then in New York City, he found work as a cameraman, writer, director, and character actor before venturing West to the lure of

Hollywood. There his striking good looks were quickly noticed, and he was cast in leading male parts, despite his preference to remain behind the camera as either a writer or director. He and actress Dorothy Davenport, whom he directed in a film for Universal Studios, fell in love and got married, becoming a much-adored couple in the film colony. Reid's outstanding acting in a secondary role in D. W. Griffith's controversial film *The Birth of a Nation* (1915) put him in great demand as an actor. Moviegoers, particularly women, were charmed by this tall, chestnut-haired actor, whom Paramount Pictures kept under contract for the next seven years and worked, in a grueling fashion, to turn out countless films, most of which were light-hearted adventures. In time Reid became the so-called King of Paramount, which made $2 million a year on his movies.

Through his work, Reid grew famous and rich and began indulging in the sumptuous Hollywood lifestyle. He was seen often racing around in his sporty red roadster, whose horn played "I'm a Yankee Doodle Dandy". He loved to go to parties, acquiring the nickname Good Time Wally. He was constantly besieged by infatuated females; yet he was completely devoted to his wife.

While making a film in 1919, Reid and others were injured in a train wreck in the Sierras. A severe head wound caused him to later suffer excruciating headaches, for which he was prescribed morphine to ease the pain. He acquired a secret drug addiction and attempted to conceal it through drinking, which only worsened the problem. In 1921 his health declined rapidly, he became weak and emaciated, and rumors began that he was an addict. Paramount tried to downplay any suggestions. After Reid collapsed on the set of a movie in 1922, they attributed the breakdown to "overwork" and spirited him away from the public sight. Committed to a secluded private sanitarium by his unhappy wife, the famed actor suffered tremendous shock when his daily morphine fix was abruptly taken away. Mrs. Reid publicly said he was being treated for morphine addiction, a shocking revelation that Will E. Hays, president of the Motion Picture Producers and Distributers of America, tried to lessen by saying that "the unfortunate Mr. Reid should be dealt with as a diseased person—not to be censured, shunned." The actor lost much weight, went in and out of a coma, and finally succumbed to the pain. Enormous public sympathy for him arose, notwithstanding a vile Hollywood rumor that he had been "put to sleep."

Mrs. Reid at first blamed her husband's friends for leading him into a life of degeneracy and later initiated, "in the name of Wally," a national campaign against narcotics, cocaine, and other drugs. Always calling herself "Mrs. Wallace Reid," she helped finance and appeared in two antidrug films, *Human Wreckage* and *Broken Laws,* before setting out on a cross-country speaking tour to "warn the nation's youth." She never remarried.

Lance RENTZEL: exhibitionism

American professional football player Lance Rentzel became the object of severe public ridicule in November 1970 when newspapers and TV broadcast networks reported his arrest for indecent exposure in Dallas, Texas, where he was a wide receiver on the Dallas Cowboys professional football team. The 28-year-old Rentzel, known for his long blond hair and playboy image, had lured a 10-year-old girl to his car and then exposed himself to her.

As a result, Rentzel became the butt of numerous vicious jokes across the United States, such as: "Lance has found the secret to success: plenty of exposure"; "Rentzel will never be convicted because the evidence will not stand up in court"; "In the fourth quarter, if the Cowboys are behind, Rentzel will go into the game and pull it out." Antagonistic and indignant fans and others castigated him with such names as "flasher," "fag," and "pervert." Humiliating publicity about his case haunted him afterward, despite his public, frank acknowledgment of his "psychological flaw" and willingness to undergo psychiatric treatment for it.

Born Thomas Lance Rentzel in 1943, the football player had grown up in Oklahoma City, Oklahoma, as the second son of Delos W. Rentzel, a prominent business executive and U.S. government official who served as undersecretary of commerce for transportation in President Harry Truman's administration. At the small private Casady School in Oklahoma City, Lance was an outstanding student, piano player, and athlete. Fiercely competitive, he excelled in football, basketball, baseball, and track. As an All-American high-school football player, he went to the University of Oklahoma, where he was a star performer on coach Bud Wilkinson's varsity football team for three years. Before Rentzel, a math major, graduated from Oklahoma in 1965, he had gained a reputation as a gregarious sort. A fun-loving, perennial playboy, he dated many girls and partied frequently.

In 1965 the Minnesota Vikings professional football organization drafted Rentzel and used him primarily as a halfback until he was traded to the Dallas Cowboys in 1967. He then became a top pass receiver in the National Football League (NFL), helping the Cowboys win their division championship that year. A colorful figure with a free-wheeling attitude and seemingly boyish flamboyance in manner and dress, Rentzel was written up extensively in the press, especially after his 1969 marriage to glamorous movie and television actress Joey Heatherton. In the newspapers, the couple was called "America's sweethearts" and "the Golden Boy married to the most dazzling girl around." This so-called marriage made in heaven was evidently rocky at times. In

Lance Rentzel (right), star football player of the Dallas Cowboys, and one of his lawyers arrive at criminal district court in Dallas, Texas, on April 8, 1971. He pleaded guilty to exposing himself to a 10-year-old girl in November 1970 and received a five-year probated sentence with the understanding that he continue to have psychiatric treatment. (AP/Wide World Photos)

his autobiography, *When All the Laughter Died in Sorrow* (1972), Rentzel wrote that there were "glorious highs and painful lows." "We were turbulent, we were serene."

The story of Rentzel's exhibitionism made front page headlines in papers nationwide. The Dallas police had taken him into custody after a 10-year-old girl recognized him in a TV commercial as the man who had beckoned her to his car in Dallas's University Park, exposed himself to her, and then driven away on November 19, 1970. The girl had informed her father, Paul Adams, a prominent Dallas attorney, who filed and pressed charges against Rentzel. When the accusation was revealed, the press resurrected a nearly forgotten incident involving the football star in September 1966 when he had been charged with exposing himself to two young girls in the Highland Park area of St. Paul, Minnesota. The charges at that time had been reduced to disorderly conduct to which Rentzel had pleaded guilty

in a St. Paul municipal court. He was ordered to seek psychiatric help at the time and subsequently gained so much notoriety that he asked to be traded from the Vikings to the Cowboys at the end of the pro football season.

Embarrassed and ashamed, Rentzel expressed deeply sorrow for any harm he might have caused Paul Adams's young daughter, but Adams seemed intent on prosecuting him to the fullest extent of Texas law. Public abuse of Rentzel was excessive; nasty catcalls from football fans were directed to him on the field. On April 8, 1971, an agreement was reached between the two parties in a Dallas courtroom; Rentzel pleaded guilty to exposing himself to a female child under the age of 16; the judge sentenced him to five years' probation and told him to continue receiving psychiatric treatment under the supervision of the court. Afterward, Rentzel was called a "menace to the morals of American youth." He was almost banished from football in the NFL, and his wife, Joey, threatened to divorce him. The Cowboys traded him to the Los Angeles Rams in 1971, and he carried on his career, feeling the sting of constant ridicule on and off the field. Rentzel, however, handled the situation bravely. He openly admitted his problem of exhibitionism; once even labeling himself a sex pervert.

In 1973 he again made news headlines when he pleaded guilty to possession of marijuana and was suspended indefinitely from playing football. His reinstatement as a professional player was announced by NFL Commissioner Pete Rozelle about a year later. The gifted Rentzel apparently had triumphed in his search for an answer to his problems.

Madame RESTELL: wicked abortionist's forced suicide

Ann Trow Lohman, alias Madame Restell, was a scandalous New York abortionist whose fear of jail was so strong that it overcame her fear of death.

A Cockney immigrant to New York in 1831, Lohman assisted her second husband, a printer turned quack physician, in the profitable business of peddling a dubious medication that was guaranteed to perform a double miracle: if taken soon enough, it prevented conception of a human embryo; if taken after conception, it aborted unwanted fetuses. Intelligent and socially alert, Lohman soon graduated from the level of apprentice druggist and saleswoman to clever entrepreneur, advertising herself as "Madame Restell, female physician and professor of midwifery."

She had no right to claim either title. Her first business establishment on New York City's Greenwich Street sold a variety of contraceptive devices and medications, offered midwifery services to single mothers, and acted as an illegal adoption center. And in a period when birth control and abortion were often incorrectly viewed as the same thing, her business grew to include the performing of abortions.

As Madame Anna Restell, she became extremely wealthy—rich enough to purchase what the press called "the palace," a great house at the corner of Fifth Avenue and 57th Street. But to stay rich, she had to buy protection, chiefly from a superintendent of police who cheerfully received her bribe with one hand while directing the other toward his *National Police Gazette,* which complained so frequently about the nefarious "Madame Killer" Restell that the price of police inactivity (protection) was subject to a constant spiral of cost inflation.

Madame Restell was often arrested, especially if one of her abortions had proved clumsy and fatal, but before 1878, only one of the arrests had led to her trial, conviction, and incarceration. Her year in the Blackwell's Island prison in New York's East River made her vow that she would never again experience such humiliation.

Although she had reduced the scope of her services to the purveying of contraceptives and aborticides, the operating of an underground maternity center, and the placing of adoptees, Madame Restell had unfortunately failed to take notice of the growing power of the New York Society for the Suppression of Vice and the rapidly accruing record of convictions achieved by its chief investigator, Anthony COMSTOCK.

A self-appointed reformer, Comstock was a master of deceit, a man who believed the end justifies the means. Since he felt that the selling of contraceptives was evil, not to mention illegal, he decided to move against Madame Restell and to make use of one of his standard methods, entrapment.

Comstock visited Restell's Fifth Avenue mansion posing as a man whose wife was in an unwanted "interesting condition"; she sold him some medications purported to be alleviants. He visited a second time, bought more alleged aborticide, and then arrested her.

Madame Restell spent the night in the Tombs prison because she had not brought along the $5,000 bail required for her release. Finally freed, she attempted to bribe Comstock with $40,000. But he was too upright to act as the superintendent of police had done and told her that a trial would ensue.

Frightened, Madame Restell pondered what she was about to face. She knew that the fashionable churches officially opposed her, even though some of their parishioners made use of her services. She also realized that the medical fraternity would be grateful to have her out of service. She was aware that a spectacular trial would alienate her from her beloved grandchildren, one of whom had recently married into high society. And she correctly concluded that her trial, which shocked New York society in 1878, would mean prison.

At age 67, she saw only one way out: she lowered herself into a warm bath while attired in a diamond-buttoned nightgown. Then she cut her throat.

Restell's suicide (1878) created more uproar against Comstock than it did against her. He wasn't sorry she had killed herself; he referred to the suicide as "a bloody ending to a bloody life." But hers was the 15th suicide that Comstock's dishonorable methods had caused, and the press pounced upon him. A Cincinnati, Ohio, church newspaper labeled his practices un-Christian; the *Daily Graphic* and *New York Sun* chastized him. The *Graphic* asked if it were right to do evil so that good might come of it and described Comstock as "the suppressor gratified by finding his vice." Surprisingly, a clergyman in one of New York's fashionable churches preached on Madame Restell as more sinned against than sinning.

Nothing moved Comstock, however. He continued his crusade, next arresting Dr. Sara B. Chase for selling two vaginal syringes, items Madame Restell had also stocked for sale.

Life in New York City soon returned to its usual chaotic pace, and Madame Anna Restell's beloved grandchildren found themselves suddenly richer; she had left an estate valued at a stunning $1 million.

"REVOLUTION OF 1910." See Joseph CANNON: the "revolution of 1910."

RICCARDIS' ETRUSCAN FORGERIES: fakes
in the Metropolitan Museum of Art

Between 1915 and 1921, John Marshall, an English archaeologist who lived in Rome and served as a purchasing agent for New York's Metropolitan Museum of Art, acquired three terracotta warriors for the museum. The objects, thought to date from the fifth century B.C., were put on exhibit in 1933 and were hailed as spectacular examples of Etruscan art (the Etruscan people predated the Romans on the Italian peninsula). It was not until 1960, nearly 45 years after the first statue was purchased, that they were all revealed to be forgeries.

The first terracotta, known as the old warrior, was purchased in 1915. The six-foot-seven-and-three-quarter-inch statue shows a helmeted figure with a white beard; the right arm is missing. The second statue, called the colossal head, a four-foot-seven-inch helmeted head with a curly beard, was purchased in 1916.

Though the museum was anxious to publish and exhibit the two terracottas, Marshall advised that publication of their acquisition had to be delayed and that their exhibition was undesirable. In 1917 the museum hired America's leading ceramic expert, Charles F. Binns, to undertake the first technical study of the terracottas. The museum's own curators of classical art also examined the works. These experts failed to detect any major problems with the pieces, and the museum accepted the works as genuine, though over the following decades some experts raised stylistic and technical questions about their authenticity.

Marshall reported to the museum that the colossal head and the old warrior had been found in the hamlet of Boccaporco, not far from Orvieto, Italy. The head, he wrote, "is pure Ionic work. . . . I can find nothing approaching it in importance. . . . The discovery of your head simply demolishes whole volumes of Paio's History of Rome."

In 1919 Marshall's colleague cabled the director of the Metropolitan about a new statue: "Have seen the new find Mars fighting . . . wonderful preservation same artist as big head most important thing ever offered us . . . price asked quite fantastic." The museum purchased the piece two years later. When the museum's new Etruscan gallery was opened in 1933, the three warriors were exhibited for the first time.

After Marshall's death in 1928, troubling stories began reaching the museum about the purported excavators of the terracottas—Riccardo, Teodoro, and Virgilio An-

gelino Riccardi. The three brothers were said to be under suspicion by the Italian government for making unauthorized excavations in Etruria. In 1936 an Italian art dealer told the Metropolitan's curator of classical art of rumors that the statues were forgeries, made by Alfredo Adolfo Fioravanti, a Roman taxi driver, and the Riccardi brothers.

Despite these stories, which were unsubstantiated, the curator, Gisela M. A. Richter, published a detailed monograph entitled "Etruscan Terracotta Warriors" in the Metropolitan Museum of Art Papers in 1937. Most authorities accepted the works as authentic, though some continued to dissent on both stylistic and technical grounds. Some of the technical complaints were easily proved to be unfounded, and despite continuing doubts by some experts, the warriors were generally accepted as genuine in the United States and abroad for many years.

Sufficient doubt existed, however, for additional testing. In 1960, newly developed tests showed the presence of manganese, a coloring agent never used in classical ceramics, in the black glaze of all three warriors and in the clay bodies of two. Moreover, the figures had been fired in one stage only, rather than in three stages, as the Greeks and Etruscans had done. Ventholes, used to allow ventilation in genuinely ancient terracottas, were absent from the statues. Finally, there was structural evidence that the statues had never stood intact as pieces of sculpture.

Historical research confirmed the technical evidence. Two of the pieces had been bought from an art dealer named Pietro Stettiner, who was found to have sold other forgeries. In 1961, Alfredo Adolfo Fioravanti admitted that had helped to make the three warriors. He had kept the left thumb of the big warrior and two test pieces of glazed terracotta as souvenirs. Fioravanti named as his collaborators Riccardo Riccardi and his cousins Teodoro and Virgilio Angelino (these men were the sons of brothers Pio and Alfonso Riccardi, who may have been responsible for the forgery of a Roman biga [ancient two-horse chariot] sold to the British Museum).

The Riccardis had apparently been engaged in more legitimate repair of ancient pottery for Italian antique dealers when they decided to branch out into the manufacture of "ancient" works. Starting with forgeries of small fragments, they gradually enlarged both their ambitions and their works until they completed their three enormous masterpieces, housed in the Metropolitan. A photograph of a small statue in Berlin's Old Museum was the model for the first standing warrior; the second standing warrior was based on a photograph of a figure on an Etruscan sarcophagus owned by the British Museum (which, ironically, was later learned to be a fake). The big head was modeled after the head on a small terracotta vase owned by the Metropolitan.

Fioravanti also implicated the Riccardis in other forgeries, particularly a series of seven terracotta slabs with sea monsters, dolphins, and scallops sold by Stettiner to the Metropolitan Museum in 1914.

Fioravanti was able to explain several features that had long puzzled art historians. For example, the old warrior, which was otherwise remarkably complete, was missing a right arm simply because the forgers could not agree on its position and so never fired it. The big warrior was extremely stocky because, as it was being built from the ground up, the sculptors realized, at about waist level, that the elegant proportions originally planned could not be kept because the ceiling of their small workshop was too low. The left arm of this piece is also disproportionately long because the forgers could not step back far enough to judge the results. The pieces were sculpted and painted and then broken before firing because the forgers did not have a kiln big enough to fire the large works whole. The fragments were smeared with mud before they were sold to a dealer. And according to Fioravanti, although the dealer may have been paid some $40,000 for one of the figures, the forgers themselves earned only a few hundred dollars.

In 1961, for the first time in its history, the Met announced that it was exhibiting three fakes. The three warriors were soon withdrawn.

Marc RICH: colossal tax cheat

A Belgian-born immigrant to the United States and brilliantly successful commodities broker, Marc Rich was undoubtedly the world's biggest independent trader in crude oil before he was tried for tax evasion in 1983, pleaded guilty to 38 counts, and slipped away to Switzerland to escape punishment.

In 1974 he and a partner, Pincus Green, had established Marc Rich & Company AG (Aktiengesellschaft, or joint-stock company), which had its headquarters in Zug, Switzerland. By 1983 their firm traded an annual volume of $10-billion worth of oil, gold, aluminum, sulfur, and sugar, among other commodities. Rich's personal fortune was estimated to be more than $100 million. The U.S. Justice Department, however, believed that Marc Rich & Company had carried out a colossal tax-fraud scheme in 1980 and 1981, and it charged the two partners with tax evasion, violation of now defunct U.S. government oil-price controls, and unlawful purchasing of Iranian oil during the American hostage crisis in Tehran in 1979–81 (when all American trade with Iran was banned). What followed was a tale of covert and complex international dealings, an unraveling of global commodities traders' secrets, and the defection of Rich and Green during prosecution of the largest tax-fraud case in American history.

In 1982 a federal grand jury began reviewing charges that during the 1970s Rich's firm had sold price-controlled oil through a complicated series of trades called daisy-chaining, which resulted in illegally inflated profits of up to $105 million. In addition, his Swiss-based firm had allegedly covered up the profits by selling oil to its American subsidiary, Marc Rich International, at artificially high rates, thus incurring sizable losses that enabled Rich to escape paying some $48 million in United States income taxes. This shady marketing action included Marc Rich International's selling of "controlled" oil to the West Texas Marketing Corporation, after which the oil was sold through a chain of resellers and finally repurchased by Marc Rich International at well below the market price, as higher priced "stripper" oil. Afterward the repurchased oil could be sold for whatever the market would bear. Eventually, West Texas Marketing itself took the profits, skipping the sale to Rich, and instead putting the money into a "pot" belonging to Marc Rich International. As profits accumulated, further shadowy transactions were made to drain the profits away outside the domain of the Internal Revenue Service.

The continuing federal investigation revealed that in 1980, during the American hostage crisis, Marc Rich & Company AG had kept its Iranian office in Tehran functioning; at the time Iran was badly in need of buyers for its oil, and Rich was awarded a large oil contract. The American government claimed that Marc Rich International's office in the United States had broken the law by trading with the militant Islamic regime of Ayatollah Khomeini, Iran's then-new leader. Furthermore, in 1981 Rich became a supplier of oil to the Atlantic Richfield Corporation, buying oil from Nigeria, charging staggering premiums that were added to the official Nigerian oil price, and in a 21-month period collecting nearly $120 million in premiums and commissions.

To further ascertain the charges against Rich, the federal grand jury demanded to see some important files belonging to Marc Rich & Company AG. The firm refused and did not honor a U.S. government subpoena, contending that a Swiss company need not do so. A contempt citation was issued against Marc Rich International, with a $50,000-a-day fine if the firm failed to release the sought-after documents; the company balked, and eventually the fine totaled $21 million. In August 1983, the company attempted to smuggle the contested documents out of the United States, but customs officers at New York's Kennedy airport intercepted them. In an active effort to avoid the court-ordered fines, Rich and Green changed the name of their American subsidiary to Clarendon Limited, vainly attempting to bolster the company's claim of foreign immunity. Since Switzerland's laws forbid the divulging of Swiss business secrets to other countries, a diplomatic tug of war ensued between the governments in Bern and Washington, D.C. In August the Swiss authorities seized papers, which the American grand jury apparently wanted, from Rich's offices in Zug.

By September 1983, both Rich and Green had left the United States and were working from their Zug offices. After 13 months of being prosecuted for tax fraud, Marc Rich & Company AG and Clarendon Limited pleaded guilty to charges of illegally concealing at least $100 million of taxable income garnered from domestic (American) crude-oil transactions in 1980 and 1981. An out-of-court settlement cost the two companies nearly $200 million, the largest amount ever recovered by the U.S. government in a criminal tax-evasion case. The government ended its "freeze" of Clarendon's assets, and Marc Rich & Company AG repaid a $130 million debt to 14 American and European banks.

The elusive Rich and Green, faced with charges of tax evasion, fraud, and racketeering, remained as fugitives in Switzerland, which does not extradite persons charged with tax evasion. Rich renounced his American citizenship to become a Spanish citizen, and Green reportedly became a Bolivian. Their globe-straddling commodities business was badly damaged by the scandal and lost many customers, as well as some skilled traders in the company. In 1999 Rich was living near Lucerne, Switzerland, in a villa with a private harbor and a steel-gated boathouse.

Renee RICHARDS: transsexual tennis star

All his life, Richard Raskind had wanted to be a girl. Although Raskind was a successful ophthalmologist with a six-figure income, first-rate amateur tennis player, and husband and father, his unhappiness with his sexual identity led to his having a sex change operation in 1975 at the age of 40. Richard Raskind became Renee Richards. Had it not been for Richards's desire to continue playing tournament tennis—as a woman—she would probably have remained just one more anonymous recipient of the now not so controversial sex-reassignment surgery.

The publicity began in 1976 when Richards entered a women's tennis tournament in La Jolla, California—at six feet two inches tall and 147 pounds—and applied to play in the U.S. Open at Forest Hills, New York, the most prestigious tournament in the country. A suspicious spectator called the press (Raskind had dropped out of tennis, and a large, manly woman had appeared on the scene); a newscaster called the University of Rochester, where Raskind had received his medical degree, and found that Raskind and Richards were indeed the same person.

When Richards was subsequently permitted to play in a tournament in South Orange, New Jersey, on the basis of gynecological affirmation that she was a woman, 25 women dropped out of the tournament in protest. Caroline Stoll, a small 15-year old competitor who agreed to play Richards, voiced the feelings of many when she said: "Did you see those forearms? That's

Dr. Renee Richards, a transsexual, had to win a court battle to play tennis in the 1977 U.S. Open at Forest Hills, New York. She won her case when the New York State Supreme Court ruled that "overwhelming medical evidence [indicates] this person is now a female." Richards is shown here working out on the court at Forest Hills in late August 1977. (UPI/Bettmann Newsphotos)

where she gets all that power and spin on her serves. It's unfair." After losing to Richards, Stoll asked her if she was doing this for the money. Richards replied that she earned $100,000 a year as an eye surgeon. Besides, she said, "Would you change your sex for $1 million?"

Just why Richards did insist on entering the U.S. Open is a matter of debate. Some say it was for the attention and publicity because her life story would surely end up in a book if it were revealed. Dr. Roberto Granato, who performed Richards's surgery, said she did it to help many people. Richards herself said it was "to prove that transsexuals as well as other persons who are fighting social stigmas can hold their heads up high." On a more personal level, she said, "Forest Hills means more to me than playing. It's an acceptance of my right to be a woman."

When it came time for the United States Tennis Association (USTA) to accept or reject Richards's application to play in the Open, the organization considered rejecting her for lack of qualifications—she had played in only one recognized tournament as a woman. However, she could have entered a qualifying tournament and made her way to Forest Hills anyway. The group decided instead to require a chromosome test similar to those used in the Olympic games for all persons competing as women.

Chris Evert, president of the Women's Tennis Association, stated that she thought Richards should have a sex test, but that the other women should take the test too. "It would be unfair to single out Dr. Richards," she said.

The USTA stated its support of any individual's right to live as he or she chose but claimed that allowing persons not genetically female to play in the women's tournament at Forest Hills would "introduce an element of inequality and unfairness." Richards rejected the test as inconclusive at best, claiming she was "anatomically, functionally, socially, emotionally, and legally" a woman. She also claimed that all good athletes have some physical superiority, saying, "That's what makes champions—advantages."

The solution wasn't clear cut to anyone. One doctor suggested that there would come a time when tennis and other sports would have to be divided into weight classes, as in boxing and wrestling. Some pointed out the irony that no one would have cared if Richards were an inept player.

Richards was far from inept: as Richard Raskind she had ranked sixth nationally in the men's 35-and-over division. She claimed that her excellence in sports was due to a childhood effort at compensation, an attempt to conform to society's image of the macho male.

Although Richards lost in the semifinals at South Orange and was barred from playing at Forest Hills, she certainly achieved a more important goal: she dramatized the plight of the transsexual, probably making sex change just a little more acceptable to the general public.

Frederick RICHMOND: crooked congressman

A multimillionaire businessman turned politician, Frederick W. Richmond had numerous brushes with the law and, in November 1982, was convicted and sent to prison for tax evasion, possession of marijuana, and improper payments to a federal employee.

In 1960, Richmond had founded the Walco National Corporation of New York and merged it nine years later with the National Casket Company. Walco continued to buy substantial shares in other companies that did not want to be associated with it. They usually bought back their stock at higher prices than Walco paid for it. In this way Richmond made a great deal of money, for he and a foundation he controlled owned more than half of all Walco's shares. In 1982 it was estimated that Richmond was worth about $30 million. Yet a federal civil suit disclosed financial improprieties in the way Walco was managed.

Richmond began his public political career as a member of the New York City Council. In 1974 he ran as a Democratic candidate for the U.S. House of Representatives, representing a district in Brooklyn, New York, and he won. Four years later the congressman was arrested in Washington, D.C., for soliciting sex from a 16-year-old black delivery boy and an undercover police officer. Although he pleaded guilty as

charged, his district reelected him to a third term in the fall elections of 1978. He was elected to a fourth term in Congress in 1980.

It was two years after this that the U.S. Justice Department began an eight-month investigation into Richmond's activities. Government prosecutors uncovered numerous unsavory, illegal goings-on. Richmond was found to have ordered his staff to buy him cocaine and marijuana, to have made an illegal kickback to an employee of the U.S. Navy who had been helpful in winning a government contract for a ship-repair business in the congressman's home district, and to have accepted an illegal $100,000 pension from Walco. Furthermore, he had assisted Earl Randolph, a convict who had escaped from a prison in Massachusetts, in landing a job as a mailroom clerk in the House of Representatives. After leaving that job, Randolph had been arrested by an undercover policeman for male prostitution. In exchange for a guilty plea for three other criminal acts, none of the above charges were brought against Richmond.

He did admit that he had underreported his 1980 income tax by some $50,000, that he had smoked marijuana, and that he had paid the tuition expenses for the daughter of a naval employee. When he was arraigned, he also resigned his seat in Congress and promised not to run again. In the interim between his guilty plea and his sentencing, the body of an unidentified man who had died of a drug overdose was found in Richmond's East Side apartment in Manhattan. For this, the congressman could have been sentenced to seven years in jail and fined $20,000, but the judge was lenient. Instead, Richmond was sentenced to a year and a day and actually only served nine months behind bars. He was released from a federal prison halfway house on September 6, 1983. (See also PAGE SCANDAL IN CONGRESS.)

Halsted RITTER: "scandal and disrepute"

In a 1936 precedent-setting impeachment case, the U.S. House of Representatives charged U.S. District Judge Halsted L. Ritter of Florida not only with six specific "high crimes and misdemeanors," but also with bringing his court "into scandal and disrepute" through his actions. While the Senate acquitted Ritter of the six criminal charges, it convicted him of the last and generalized charge of unfitness for office, thus providing Congress with a precedent for removing any judge, whether or not he was guilty of a specific violation of the law, for general misbehavior.

Ritter's early career was impeccable. From 1895 to 1925 Ritter, a graduate of DePauw University in Indiana, was a successful attorney in Denver, Colorado. He held several public offices, including county assistant prosecuting attorney, Denver city attorney, and Colorado state railway commissioner. He taught law at the

Denver Law School. Ritter also founded the Denver Legal Aid Society and was active in community affairs in the city. After moving to Florida for reasons of family health in 1925, he joined a private law firm, specializing in real-estate work. His credentials seemed impressive, and four years later, despite the opposition of local Republicans and Democrats, President Calvin Coolidge appointed Ritter a lifetime judge of the Federal District Court for Southern Florida.

Ritter's downfall stemmed from the fact that he continued to practice law while on the bench. According to the charges later brought against him, he accepted $2,000 from a client real-estate corporation that owned large interests within his jurisdiction. He was also charged with accepting substantial securities from another real-estate client who wanted to develop property in southern Florida. In addition to these transgressions, he received $47,500 from an individual who owned property in the area.

In another matter, Ritter was accused of conspiring with his former law partner and others to promote a lawsuit in his court and of accepting $4,500 from the fees he allowed in the case. And he was charged with exchanging his judicial authority for "loans" in a case involving the city of Miami and the Florida Power & Light Company.

Not only did Ritter supplement his $17,300 salary with these fees, but he also failed to report this additional money on his income-tax returns. The federal court charged him with income-tax evasion for 1929 and 1930.

By a small margin the Senate acquitted Ritter of the six criminal charges brought against him in 1936. But in a controversial decision, a two-thirds majority found him guilty of the seventh charge, which claimed "The reasonable and probable consequence of the actions or conduct of Halsted L. Ritter . . . is to bring his court into scandal and disrepute, to the prejudice of said court and public in the administration of justice therein, and to the prejudice of public respect for and confidence in the Federal judiciary and to render him unfit to continue to serve as such judge." Ritter disregarded the Senate's impeachment order and had to be evicted from his office by a United States marshal. After his removal from office, he practiced law in Miami until shortly before his death in 1951.

Rachel Donelson ROBARDS. See Andrew JACKSON: alleged adulterer and bigamist.

Paul ROBESON: gifted, honored, blacklisted

One of the first black performers to achieve success in mainstream American film and theater, Paul Robeson was not only a gifted actor and singer, but an intelligent, progressive thinker. Stirred by the lack of racial prejudice in Europe and the Soviet Union, he spoke out increasingly against prejudice in the United States and espoused his left-wing political views. Unfortunately, his pro-Soviet sentiments coincided with McCarthyism, and the talented star was blacklisted across America.

Born in Princeton, New Jersey, in 1898, Paul Leroy Bustill Robeson was the youngest of eight children. His father was a runaway black slave who became a Methodist minister, and his mother was a schoolteacher who died in an accident when Robeson was only six. An honor student in high school in Somerville, New Jersey, he won a four-year scholarship to Rutgers University. Although he was the only black student at the school, he was very popular with his college classmates. His deep, stirring, baritone voice and commanding stage presence helped him win oratory awards. Tall and strong, Robeson also won varsity letters in four sports, was named an All-American football player, and was graduated at the top of his class as a member of Phi Beta Kappa. Playing professional football and at the same time going to Columbia University Law School, "the colored giant," as he was called, became seriously interested in stage acting and appeared in several productions with noted success before his law-school graduation in 1923. He accepted a position at a New York law firm but, encouraged by his wife, decided to pursue an acting career instead and joined the Provincetown Players, a New York theatrical company. His natural acting and singing ability were fast recognized when he starred in one of Eugene O'Neill's plays, *The Emperor Jones,* in New York in 1924 and in London in 1925.

Thereafter Robeson's career took off; during the next 15 years he made highly successful concert tours at home and abroad, singing Negro spirituals and folk songs. The warm receptions given him in Great Britain and the Soviet Union pleased him immensely, and he publicly declared his preference for both of these countries, where he felt there was an absence of racial prejudice. Enthralled audiences saw Robeson sing "Ol' Man River" in Jerome Kern's play *Showboat,* which played in London in 1928 and in New York in 1930. This and hundreds of other songs he recorded were sold throughout the world; many were in foreign languages, including Russian, Chinese, and several African tongues, all of which Robeson mastered. In London, he appeared in the smash stage hits *Othello* (1930), *The Hairy Ape* (1931), and *Stevedore* (1936). In 1943 Robeson played *Othello* on Broadway, becoming the first black lead in that production. He received rave reviews, and the play established a record run for a Shakespearean drama on Broadway. Robeson was soon appearing in movies too. Signed by both American and British filmmakers, he added to his fame and popularity by appearing in *Sanders of the River* (1935), *King Solomon's Mines* (1937), and *The Proud Valley* (1941), among other motion pictures.

Despite Robeson's immense popularity as an entertainer, many Americans looked less favorably on his controversial political views and associations. Publicly, he had made Russia his second motherland, entered British radical circles, entertained Loyalist troops during the Spanish Civil War, joined Henry Wallace's Progressive Party, and became an outspoken supporter of the oppressed. Antifascist, he actively fought for the civil rights of blacks, Jews, and all minority groups. But McCarthyism—the specious exposure of pro-communist activity—ended his career when, in 1949, the HOUSE COMMITTEE ON UN-AMERICAN ACTIVITIES labeled him a communist and turned American opinion against him. As a matter of principle, Robeson had refused to deny being a communist. Newspapers denounced him in editorials; stores removed his records from sale; Rutgers University received calls to erase his name from the academic and athletic honor rolls. In 1950, because he refused to sign an oath saying he was not a Communist Party member, Robeson's passport was withdrawn by the State Department and, despite numerous appeals, was not restored until 1958, when the Supreme Court voided the oath requirement. The Internal Revenue Service tried to tax the $25,000 International Stalin Peace Prize awarded to Robeson in 1952, but he protested, saying the money was tax-exempt like Pulitzer and Nobel Prize monies, and finally won his argument in 1959.

In 1958, Robeson moved to Europe permanently, where he continued to perform on stage and at concerts. In Russia and countries of the Soviet bloc he was treated like a folk hero. In bad health in 1963, Robeson came back to America with his wife, and he finally got to see changes taking place as the result of civil-rights activity. He died in 1976.

A. H. ROBINS: the Dalkon Shield disaster

In January 1971, the A. H. Robins Company, a pharmaceutical manufacturer, introduced to the market a new contraceptive, an intrauterine device (IUD) known as the Dalkon Shield, which it described as safe and effective. By 1974, when the Food and Drug Administration asked Robins to suspend sales of the Shield in the United States, the device was known to be neither safe nor effective. But by then Robins had already distributed nearly 3 million Shields in the United States and nearly 2 million abroad. Most of them had already been implanted in women seeking protection from unwanted pregnancies. As a result, millions of women became trapped in medical nightmares, and Robins soon entered a legal and financial ordeal of liability lawsuits.

The theory behind IUDs, including the Dalkon Shield, is that a foreign object implanted in the uterus acts as a contraceptive. The dangers of the crab-shaped Dalkon Shield stem from its multiple-filament tail, which extends from the uterus through the cervix and into the vagina, where bacteria are present. That tail can act like a candle wick, drawing up bacteria from the vagina and into the uterine cavity.

If A. H. Robins was ignorant of these dangers to start with, it was informed soon enough. The company had received complaints from physicians as early as February 1971, just six weeks after the device went on the market. In 1972 a doctor had informed the company that six Shield-wearing patients had become pregnant, and of them five had suffered infected miscarriages.

In *At Any Cost: Corporate Greed, Women, and the Dalkon Shield* (1985), *Washington Post* reporter Morton Mintz charged that the desire for profits had allowed the Robins company to market a device that exposed millions of women to the risk of serious pelvic inflammatory disease (PID), an ailment that may impair or destroy fertility, lead to chronic pain and illness, and even cause death. Moreover, the 5 percent pregnancy rate found among Shield wearers was higher than the one Robins advertised and higher than the rate for many other IUDs.

More than half of the women who became pregnant while wearing the Dalkon Shield lost their unborn babies. While some had elective abortions, many others experienced miscarriages or, even more serious, infected miscarriages, which proved fatal in some cases. Other women gave birth prematurely to children with severe congenital defects, including mental retardation, cerebral palsy, and blindness.

No one knows how many women are still wearing the Shield. In 1977, when an attorney for a woman suing Robins, citing two Shield-related deaths, asked the company to advise physicians to remove the devices from the market, the company did not respond. Not until October 1984 did Robins undertake a call-back campaign, urging women who were still wearing the devices to have them removed at the company's expense. By February 1985, more than 4,000 women had filed claims for damage inflicted by the Shield.

As the evidence against the device accumulated and became public in the late 1970s and early 1980s, lawsuits against A. H. Robins began to snowball. The company was charged with inadequate testing of the device, issuing misleading claims, and concealing known hazards from physicians, Shield wearers, and the government. Company executives, including Chairman E. Claiborne Robins and his son, Chief Executive Officer and President E. Claiborne Robins, Jr., nonetheless continued to profess ignorance of the problems caused by the device. Thousands of documents relating to the Shield also "disappeared" from company files.

A. H. Robins was now facing the possibility of thousands of lawsuits with multimillion-dollar awards for punitive damages. In April 1985, the company set aside a $615-million reserve fund to settle the legal claims, but a few months later, Robins, claiming the reserve fund would be insufficient, filed for reorganization under Chapter 11 of the bankruptcy code, leaving some victims to charge that the move was a ploy to try to limit the magnitude of the damages against the company.

In January 1986, Robins began a 91-nation advertising campaign to inform some 4.5 million women that they had until April 30 to file claims for compensation for health problems stemming from the Dalkon Shield. Thousands of such claims poured into the bankruptcy court.

Meanwhile, the bankruptcy plan itself led to further scandals, as federal prosecutors sought to replace company executives, including Robins senior and junior, with a court-appointed trustee. In June 1986, a federal judge found the company in contempt of court for making illegal payments of more than $21 million while in bankruptcy proceedings; two of the company's directors resigned in the wake of this ruling.

On June 16, 1989, the Fourth U.S. Circuit Court of Appeals approved the entire bankruptcy reorganization plan of A. H. Robins, which would be acquired by American Home Products Corporation in exchange for about $700 million worth of stock. The plan also included a $2.5 billion settlement trust fund to compensate about 200,000 women who claimed they were injured by the Dalkon Shield. Aetna Casualty & Surety Company, Robins's insurer, paid $425 million to the trust fund to settle any claims against it. In early November 1989, the U.S. Supreme Court rejected the last legal challenge to carrying out the $2.5 billion settlement; compensatory payments began the next year for nearly 100,000 women with active claims against Robins.

John D. ROCKEFELLER: the South Improvement Company ploy

To John Davison Rockefeller, economic order and monopoly had the same meaning. To bring order out of the chaos that characterized the oil industry of Ohio, Pennsylvania, and New York after 1865, Rockefeller worked to create a monopoly, which he himself, as ruler of the Standard Oil Company of Ohio, would direct. His plan, invented by his partner, Henry M. Flagler, had a double face. Publicly, it was a Pennsylvania-chartered organization called the South Improvement Company (SIC), dedicated to bringing regularity to the oil industry. Privately, it was a dummy corporation fronting for Standard Oil and dedicated to the squeezing out of independent refineries. The South Improvement Company would work secretly to bring the major refineries into a cooperative or horizontal combination in order to regulate oil production and control what had been wildly fluctuating oil prices. It was essentially a conspiracy for restraint of trade, a crime in common law since the time of Queen Elizabeth I.

Working secretly, Rockefeller gained the connivance of major refineries, among which his was the largest in the world. He persuaded the Erie, Pennsylvania, and New York Central railroads to participate in a scheme involving complex rebates for his co-conspirators: 40 to 50 percent of published rates were to be returned to the South Improvement Company on crude oil shipped in, 25 to 50 percent on refined oil shipped out. In contrast, independent refineries would be charged double rates, and as much as half the excess was to be paid to the Rockefeller group. Moreover, SIC was to receive copies of waybills for competitors' oil so as to be privy to their commercial secrets.

Rockefeller was optimistic that reluctant refiners would join his compact. He was very polite when he offered, if necessary, to acquire their companies for shares in Standard Oil or cash; his underlying hint was clear: comply or be crushed. Those who continued to resist were confronted by higher freight rates and soon sold out.

The scheme was the most vigorous, blatant effort of what one historian calls "dry-land piracy" ever conceived. It led to the "Oil War of 1872."

The oil region, especially that near Titusville, Pennsylvania, went on a rampage. Rockefeller's effigy was hanged and then burned. Parades, mass meetings, and vain pledges to withhold oil production and build private railroads or independent pipelines were announced. Wiser heads sent petitions for relief to Washington, D.C., and the state government of Pennsylvania at Harrisburg.

The creators of the pool waited patiently for the independent producers to capitulate to economic pressures. But the cabal cracked first. When a congressional investigation described South Improvement Company as "one of the most gigantic and dangerous conspiracies ever conceived," the Pennsylvania legislature revoked its charter. Then the railroads broke unity: Cornelius "Commodore" Vanderbilt's New York Central lowered its tariffs and independent oil began to move to distant refineries. When railroad leaders and independents met secretly, Rockefeller and his agents arrived, only to be ejected.

Publicly, Rockefeller acted shocked and hurt. His motives, he asserted, were good. Order in all production and distribution was necessary, and to make a kind of peace, he offered a modified scheme, the "Pittsburgh plan," calling for cooperation. Suspicion caused its rejection.

Secretly, Rockefeller worked to fulfill his original plans. He had a supposed Ohio competitor, John D. Archbold, lease 20-odd independent refineries as a kind of independents' combination; then Archbold drew the independents' wrath by becoming a vice-president of Standard Oil of Ohio and taking the refineries with him. Rockefeller also secretly drew other refineries into his scheme, retaining their original names to disguise the mergers. He corrupted legislators, judges, and governors to benefit Standard Oil, induced his loyal railroads to begin rate wars against the disloyal refineries and railroads, and acquired pipelines erected by the offending railroads.

As a result, Rockefeller by 1878, at the age of 38, controlled 95 percent of the oil pipelines and refineries in the United States, and by 1882 he had completed the monopolistic structure he had envisioned in 1870. He had created almost perfect "order" when he established Standard Oil of New Jersey as a holding company; he was free to act as a tyrant over oil until 1911, when the federal government struck down the South Improvement Company Corporation as an illegal trust.

Nelson ROCKEFELLER: an end in shame?

The sudden death of 70-year-old multimillionaire Nelson Aldrich Rockefeller, on the night of January 26, 1979, immediately made sensational newspaper headlines throughout the United States and elsewhere. A well-known public figure with vast wealth, a former vice president of the United States (1974–77), and a four-time elected governor of New York (1958–73), Rockefeller had died from a massive heart attack. He had been in the company of attractive 31-year-old Megan Marshack, his staff research assistant, at his New York City townhouse on 54th Street at the time. Early confusion about what had happened helped to feed conjectures and rumors that the good-living "Rocky" had departed this world while making love to his pretty assistant. Adding to a sense of "cover-up" was the Rockefeller family's refusal of a post-mortem examination and the quick cremation of the body.

On the day he died, Rockefeller had spent much of the time working on his latest art-book project at his Rockefeller Center office. (After retiring from politics in 1977, he had absorbed himself in his copious art collection, which contained many modern masterpieces.) In the early evening of January 26, he had dined with his wife Happy and two of their children at his Fifth Avenue duplex apartment and had afterward been driven by his chauffeur to the brownstone townhouse on 54th Street, where he maintained an office and held meetings. There, shortly before 9 o'clock that evening, he telephoned Marshack, who lived only a short distance away, asking her to come over and discuss some research on an art-book project. (Marshack had worked for Rockefeller since 1976, first as a junior press aide in Washington, D.C., and then as a staff assistant in New York.) She soon arrived, wearing a long black evening dress. Completely alone, the two began working on the project.

Former Vice President of the United States and well-known political leader Nelson Rockefeller suffered a fatal heart attack in the presence of his pretty staff assistant, Megan Marshack, in 1979. Afterward, there were several questionable and confusing versions concerning the official details of his death. (Yale University Archives/Historical Picture Collection/Yale University Library)

According to the official version of what happened, Rockefeller suffered a fatal cardiac arrest at about 11:15 P.M. A Rockefeller family spokesman, however, first said he had died at the Rockefeller Center Office at 10:15 P.M. and did not mention Marshack's presence; before long, however, the spokesman gave the official version of Rockefeller's death, explaining that Marshack, in her deep distress, had unintentionally reported the wrong time. Stunned, she had apparently made an attempt to revive Rockefeller by artificial respiration and had then called the emergency number 911 for an ambulance.

Two police officers arrived before the ambulance and paramedics; the former reported that they had found the unconscious Rockefeller in his suit, lying on the floor; the latter claimed they had seen no signs of books or research papers, but had noticed some evidence of dining (a half-empty bottle of wine and some signs of a meal). Rockefeller was rushed to Lenox Hill Hospital where he was officially declared dead by his physician, Dr. Ernest Esakof, at 12:20 A.M.

During the weeks afterward, some more curious details came to light, despite news reporters' difficulty in finding and questioning Marshack and other witnesses. It was discovered that Rockefeller, who had been in poor health, had nonetheless spent long hours supposedly cataloguing art works with Marshack, who was revealed to have been well paid and to have had a generous expense account. When his will was read, she was a "surprise beneficiary," for he freed her from having to repay him for a large loan secured to purchase an apartment. A journalist friend of Marshack, Ponchitta Pierce, came forth to reveal that she had received a call from Marshack shortly before 11:00 P.M. on January 26; she said she had gone to the townhouse, saw what had happened, called 911 for help, and then inexplicably left before the arrival of the police. Thereafter both Pierce and Marshack went into hiding. Eventually the New York district attorney's office declared the case closed, despite some intriguing questions by news writers. All witnesses have since been indisposed to discussing the case.

Roy ROMER: public confession after longtime denials

After careful denials during his 1990 and 1994 reelection campaigns, Colorado's Democratic governor Roy Romer finally admitted publicly in 1998 that he had had a 16-year "very affectionate" relationship with his former chief of staff Betty Jane Thornberry. Romer explained that his relationship with Thornberry was not sexual—"I'm not a very sexual person," he said—and that his wife and family knew of and supported the friendship. Romer's confession came at an unfortunate time for the Democratic Party, however, which was in the midst of deflecting allegations of sexual misconduct against President Bill CLINTON.

Romer, chairman of the Democratic National Convention, stood firmly behind the president throughout the investigations. He said that he took the president at his word when he denied having sexual relations with former White House intern Monica Lewinsky. Romer had spent his career cultivating the persona of a man of high moral and ethical standards. When asked why he had lied about his relationship with Thornberry for so long, Romer claimed that he had simply wanted to deny the implied sexual nature of the relationship. He later admitted that he did not think he could be so forthcoming and still be permitted to participate in public life.

In 1990, a conservative political magazine published an article alleging a sexual affair between Romer and Thornberry. It claimed to have videotapes of the two hugging and kissing deeply; there was also evidence that the two had spent the night together at Thornberry's house in Washington. Before such accusations could wreak havoc with the 69-year-old Romer's reputation, a tornado destroyed a small town in eastern Colorado, diverting public attention. Romer dismissed mention of

the affair and quickly moved to concentrate on disaster cleanup efforts.

Thornberry, 51 and divorced, was Romer's chief of staff in Colorado for seven years. She moved to Washington, D.C., in 1993 and was named executive director of the Democratic National Convention in 1996, one year before Romer assumed the chairmanship. After that, Romer began to split his time between his duties in Colorado and the capital. Romer's wife of 45 years, Bea, issued a public statement saying that her husband had been honest with her about the nature of his relationship with Thornberry since the beginning and that it in no way affected their marriage or family relations.

In a way, Romer's run-in with the rumor mill, concurrent as it was with President Clinton's predicament, may have saved him his position. Though the accusations against him may have tarnished Romer's reputation and popularity, they were not cause enough for his colleagues to ask him to step down from the Democratic National Convention chairmanship—that may have sparked an initiative to persuade Bill Clinton not to resign his office.

ROOSEVELT-MERCER AFFAIR

In 1946 the world was told a secret previously kept shrouded by intimates of the late President Franklin Delano Roosevelt: that his infidelities with Lucy Page Mercer almost caused the breakup, in 1918, of his then 13-year-old marriage to Eleanor Roosevelt. The revelation delighted anti-Roosevelt forces, which acknowledged no basis for trusting him or accepting his wife.

Recent biographies suggest that the Roosevelts' marital discord was almost fated, for Eleanor's 1905 marriage to her spirited and handsome distant cousin introduced her to burdens for which 21 years of sheltered existence had not prepared her. Franklin was outgoing and vivacious; Eleanor, despite a warm smile, was aloof and unable to appreciate the boisterous highjinks that her husband adored. Franklin was reputed to be sensual, while Eleanor was cold. She apparently regarded the physical side of their marriage as an obligation and by 1916 had suffered six difficult pregnancies.

Duty was the byword in their relationship, for marriage to Franklin had also meant bondage to Franklin's mother, Sara Delano Roosevelt, an imperious, interfering woman who issued orders to the newlyweds from her home in Hyde Park, New York. She decorated the couple's new home, completely disregarding Eleanor's wishes, and provided both cash and commentary during the marriage's early years.

A hotly contested conjecture by the couple's son Elliott suggests that his mother indirectly created the Roosevelt-Mercer liaison in 1916. He claimed that during postpartal reflections occasioned by the difficult delivery of her son John, Eleanor Roosevelt had asserted her independence by declaring that her future marital conduct would be characterized by continence. Franklin, used to the company of emotionally acquiescent and indulgent women, would be forced to practice a self-restraint foreign to him since 1905. He chose to look elsewhere for feminine affection and companionship.

He looked, at first, no further than Lucy Page Mercer, the attractive descendant of an irreproachably patrician background. She had been Eleanor's social secretary in 1913 and 1914. Early in 1916, Lucy became a female yeoman in the Navy Department, of which Franklin Roosevelt was then the assistant secretary. During that summer, while Eleanor recovered from her confinement at Campobello, Lucy became Franklin's companion for both public social events and clandestine rendezvous. Though all of Washington, D.C., society knew of the relationship, the 30-year-old Eleanor remained ignorant of it.

In 1918 she came across a letter from Lucy that Franklin had carelessly kept. She confronted the adulterers, demanding either a total cessation of the relationship or a divorce. Divorce would have destroyed her husband's political career, and canonical remarriage to Franklin was forbidden to Lucy, a Catholic unready to acquire a houseful of children. Moreover, Sara Delano Roosevelt fought the idea of a divorce by threatening to disinherit her son. The Roosevelts wisely chose the other alternative, and Eleanor declared to Franklin that she would remain his wife on a new basis: she would be his helper, but she would live her own emotional life. The guilty pair promised to end the affair.

They did not keep their word. From 1918 to 1945, Franklin and Lucy Mercer met, usually secretly. The trusting Eleanor made no effort to have them shadowed. Not till much later did she learn that Lucy had secretly attended the president's inaugurations in the privacy of a presidential limousine, even after her marriage to Wintie Rutherford.

Eleanor, however, kept her word. She nursed Franklin through his 1921 paralysis from polio and campaigned tirelessly for his elections as governor of New York and president of the United States, giving a service of love because of her dedication to his leadership and his goals. Meanwhile, she developed the new activities and personality that made her lovingly remembered as one of the most accomplished First Ladies in American history.

Eleanor Roosevelt did not know that after 1944, when her service took her away from the White House, her own daughter Anna had invited Lucy Mercer to dinner with Franklin, and she was not aware until after his death that Lucy had been with Franklin in 1945 at the time of his fatal stroke.

Duty, however, was still Eleanor Roosevelt's byword. Angrily tearful when she learned that she had been deluded, she forgave Franklin (and perhaps Anna) for their painful deceit. And at the time of her own death in 1962, she ordered that Franklin's wish be fulfilled that she be buried at his side in the rose garden of their Hyde Park estate.

Pete ROSE: baseball star, gambler, and tax cheat

Pete Rose (born Edward Peter Rose in Cincinnati in 1941) was one of the greatest professional baseball players of all time. He played with such tremendous enthusiasm that Mickey Mantle, another baseball great, nicknamed him Charlie Hustle. Between 1964 and 1987 Rose excelled at five different positions for the Cincinnati Reds and the Philadelphia Phillies while winning the National League batting title three times. In 1973 he was the National League's Most Valuable Player (MVP) and in 1975 he was the World Series MVP. In 1978 he hit safely in 44 consecutive games, a National League record. Altogether he set 19 major league records, including most hits (4,256), most games played (3,562), and most seasons with 200 or more hits (10). In 1985, while still playing, Rose became the manager of the Cincinnati Reds. In his first four seasons as manager, he led his team to two second-place finishes in the National League. He was a shoo-in to be voted into the Baseball Hall of Fame in 1992, the first year he would be eligible for that honor.

But several months before the opening of the 1989 season, Rose came under investigation by both the commissioner of baseball and the National League president because of his association with professional gamblers. Although Rose readily admitted to spending a great deal of time and money at the racetrack, he categorically denied any involvement in illegal betting. However, investigators allegedly found betting slips bearing Rose's handwriting and fingerprints that linked him to bookies in four cities, including Cincinnati. Most damning of all was the charge that he had bet on baseball games, including some games including his own team. It was even rumored that Rose had flashed signs to one bookie from the dugout during a Reds game.

A defiant Rose refused to cooperate with the investigations and even went to court in an attempt to have them stopped. But in August 1989, baseball commissioner A. Bartlett Giamatti ordered Rose to relinquish his position as Reds manager and banned him from baseball for life, declaring that by betting on his own team he had tainted the game. Inexplicably, Rose accepted the decision, even calling it a fair one, while insisting on his innocence and denying that he had a gambling problem. Apparently he believed that he would be away from the game only briefly, a possibility provided by the official rules of baseball, which allowed him to apply for reinstatement after only one year.

Between 1984 and 1987 Rose paid his gambling debts by selling memorabilia such as the bat he used to break the all-time hit record and by selling his autograph at baseball card signing shows. He then failed to report any of this income on his tax returns. Shortly after the gambling allegations became public knowledge, the Internal Revenue Service began investigating his finances. In 1990 Rose was convicted on two counts of felonious tax evasion; he served five months in prison and was forced to pay over $350,000 in back taxes, interest, and penalties. This development virtually eliminated any possibility that Rose would ever return to baseball. When he finally did apply for reinstatement in 1997, Bud Selig, the acting commissioner, stated that the application "will be handled in due course." Two years later, Rose remained banned from baseball.

Julius and Ethel ROSENBERG: scapegoats or traitors?

J. Edgar Hoover called theirs the "crime of the century," for Julius Rosenberg and his wife, Ethel, were accused of passing the secret of the atomic bomb to the Soviet Union in June 1945, three months before the first A-bomb was dropped on Hiroshima. Five years later, in 1950, when the Russian espionage network in the United States began to unravel, Julius Rosenberg was arrested at his New York City apartment, and Ethel Rosenberg was taken into custody a month later after testifying before a grand jury, where she frequently used the Fifth Amendment. Along with one of their associates, the Rosenbergs were tried in the spring of 1951 for "conspiracy to commit espionage." The jury found them guilty, and Judge Irving R. Kaufman sentenced them to death. They spent the next two years on death row at Sing Sing Prison in Ossining, New York, while their lawyer, Emmanuel Bloch, filed numerous appeals without success and a growing number of supporters pressed for their release. To the very end, on June 19, 1953, when they were executed in the electric chair at Sing Sing, both Rosenbergs maintained that they were innocent of any wrongdoing.

The complex case against the Rosenbergs began in the winter of 1950 when the German-born British physicist Klaus Fuchs confessed to British intelligence authorities that he had passed information about the development of the atomic bomb to an American Soviet courier while he was working on the Manhattan Project (developing the A-bomb) at Columbia University in New York City and later at Los Alamos in New Mexico. The Federal Bureau of Investigation (FBI) immediately began searching for Fuchs's American contact. Although Fuchs only knew the man as "Raymond," he did provide clues that led the investigators to Harry Gold, a Philadelphian who had for years lived a double life as a chemist and a Soviet agent. When agents of the FBI searched Gold's house in May 1950, they found incriminating evidence of his trips around the United States to collect information about the A-bomb. Upon this discovery, Gold sank into a chair, admitted that he was Fuchs's contact with a Soviet KGB agent, and reported that he had received detailed information about

the atomic bomb from Fuchs in Santa Fe, New Mexico, in June and September 1945. After his arrest, Gold confessed that he had been a courier for several others who had access to military secrets, including a young American soldier named David Greenglass.

Greenglass was the brother of Ethel Rosenberg and, like her and Julius Rosenberg, was a member of the Communist Party, as was his wife, Ruth. They had all admired the sacrifices the Russian people made in repelling German forces on the Eastern Front in World War II. When David Greenglass was assigned to Los Alamos to work on the top-secret Manhattan Project, Julius Rosenberg was elated. He suggested to Ruth Greenglass, as she prepared to visit her husband, that she ask him to "share" whatever information he could obtain about the work being done on the atomic bomb. He readily agreed, and when he returned to New York on furlough in January 1945, he gave Julius Rosenberg several pages of notes and sketches of a high-explosive lens mold. After a family dinner, Julius Rosenberg allegedly went into the kitchen, cut the side off a Jell-O box, and cut the panel into an irregular shape. He kept one piece and gave the other to Ruth Greenglass, telling her that a future courier would show the other half as a recognition signal. This Jell-O box would become one of the crucial bits of damaging evidence against the Rosenbergs.

In the spring of 1945, Ruth moved to Albuquerque, New Mexico. On a Sunday morning, June 3, 1945, the young couple were surprised by a stranger at the door who pulled Julius's half of the Jell-O box from his wallet. David told him to return in the afternoon, after he had had time to prepare some written material. The stranger, who the Greenglasses later identified as Harry Gold, did return, picked up the material, and gave David Greenglass an envelope containing $500. When they were interrogated five years later, all three parties told essentially the same story about this incident. Later, at the Rosenbergs' trial, Gold recalled that he had greeted the couple by saying, "I come from Julius," but the Greenglasses did not recall this part.

After Gold's arrest, Julius Rosenberg urged the Greenglasses to leave the country, but they did not heed his warning. David Greenglass was picked up by the FBI in mid-June and, like Gold, agreed to cooperate fully. His principal objective was to shield his wife Ruth. During the summer the Rosenbergs were also arrested. Both denied any knowledge of an espionage ring. The U.S. government had no strong case against Ethel Rosenberg except the uncorroborated testimony of the Greenglasses that she had been present when the Los Alamos operations were discussed and had typed several pages of David Greenglass's notes for her husband Julius. Years later, when the Rosenberg files were opened under the Freedom of Information Act, researchers found a note written by FBI director J. Edgar Hoover urging

Ethel Rosenberg's arrest as a leverage to make Julius Rosenberg talk.

At about this time, 1951, several potential suspects disappeared without a trace, and only one, Morton Sobell, was caught in Mexico, where he was endeavoring to find passage abroad for himself and his family. He was tried with the Rosenbergs, convicted, and sentenced to 30 years in prison.

Despite the fact that they had not given information to the enemy in 1945 but to a wartime ally, the Rosenbergs were tried for treason. By 1950 the United States was gripped by anticommunist hysteria whipped up by U.S. Senator Joseph McCARTHY; the Korean War had broken out, and America had lost its monopoly on the atomic bomb. The prosecutors, most of the public, and the press were all eager to vent their anger on the accused atomic spies. The testimony of Greenglass and Gold seemed compelling. During the Rosenbergs' appeals and plea for clemency from President Dwight Eisenhower, several noted scientists testified that the material David Greenglass had given Julius Rosenberg could have been of little value to the Soviets. Fuchs's information was far more important; yet he lived and the Rosenbergs died.

New evidence from deciphered transcriptions of World War II Soviet intelligence cables (the Venona decryptions and KGB files) confirms the involvement of Julius Rosenberg, Harry Dexter WHITE, Alger HISS, and scores of others who provided information to Soviet operatives during the 1930s and 1940s. Though many leftists still uphold Julius Rosenberg's innocence, he evidently is the agent code-named "Liberal" in the Venona decrypted messages, which the National Security Agency began releasing in 1995.

ROSEWOOD: black community wiped out

For almost 60 years, the racial violence and carnage that occurred in Rosewood, Florida, in early 1923 was buried and suppressed by its traumatized black survivors and their descendants. "Our birthright was taken away from us," said 81-year-old survivor Ms. Robie Mortin in 1996. "My grandma told me not to say a word. My grandma said never to look back. We weren't supposed to talk about Rosewood."

Known for the beautiful roses growing around the Masonic Hall, Rosewood was a small, thriving mill town on the Gulf Coast, about 30 miles southwest of Gainesville, Florida. Its approximately 120 inhabitants, mostly black, who regularly attended the community's three churches, appeared to live peacefully close by the white residents of neighboring Sumner, another small town. But terrible racial violence erupted on January 2, 1923, immediately after a white woman from Sumner accused a black man of assaulting her (which many now believe to have been a lie).

In the cold night air, whites began rampaging through Rosewood, causing terrified men, women, and children to flee into the woods or ice-covered swamp at the edge of town. There they stayed in hiding, without fires, huddled around each other to keep warm, until they felt it was safe to return. A few whites offered help to their suffering, victimized black neighbors during a week of shooting and burning of houses. At the end, the only house still standing belonged to the Wright family, white storekeepers who had often helped the blacks. During the so-called Rosewood Massacre, at least six blacks and two whites were killed; many blacks were wounded; a few had been hanged; others had had their faces shot off and their bodies mutilated. The entire community was literally wiped out in what local newspapers at the time referred to as a "race riot."

The long-hidden story of Rosewood, a vanished town, finally gained national attention after a reporter for Florida's *St. Petersburg Times* related the actual details in 1982. Afterward, survivors put pressure on the Florida State Legislature for compensation for their trauma. In 1994, nine living victims of the 1923 massacre each received $150,000 in compensation; other awards went to family members, some of whom were frail, in nursing homes, or wished not to recall the terror. Some black families were torn apart by conflict over how to divide the money and who should share it; others argued over rights to a Warner Brothers film about their past lives in Rosewood. Eventually, about 60 of the survivors' descendants appeared as extras in the film *Rosewood* (1997); one 13-year-old girl had a speaking role as Philomena Goins Doctor, who was her distant cousin. Also, a documentary film, *The Rosewood Massacre*, was produced by ABC News and the Discovery Channel.

Robert ROSS: questionable awarding of defense contracts

In 1957 the U.S. Senate Permanent Subcommittee on Investigations queried Assistant Secretary of Defense Robert T. Ross about the controversial awarding of an $835,150 contract for army trousers to Wynn Enterprises Incorporated. Though he swore that he had done nothing wrong, the subcommittee suspected a conflict of interest. The reason: Ross's wife was the president of Wynn Enterprises.

Before he joined the Eisenhower administration as assistant secretary of defense responsible for legislative and public affairs, Robert Tripp Ross had served as vice president of Wynn Enterprises and its affiliate, the Southern Athletic Company. These two firms had offices in New York City and Knoxville, Tennessee, and specialized in manufacturing military and sports clothing. Both were owned by Herman D. Wynn, the brother of Ross's second wife, Claire. Secretary Ross claimed that he had severed all connections with these two companies in 1952 and swore that he had not concerned himself "in any manner whatsoever" in the firms' bids and contracts after he had joined the U.S.

Department of Defense. It was not hard to be skeptical of his words. During the previous six years, more than $12 million worth of military clothing contracts had been awarded to Wynn Enterprises and its subsidiaries.

Secretary Ross was not particularly popular with many members of Congress or people in the Pentagon, for he unsparingly blue-penciled the speeches of officials of his department and maintained strict supervision of all defense-related information released to the public. Some officials even accused Ross of censorship. He committed a serious error in October 1956 when he confirmed rumors that three United States senators traveling in Europe had asked the air force to send two airplanes to bring them home. This turned out to be untrue, and the Defense Department apologized publicly. One of the defamed senators was John L. McClellan of Arkansas, the chairman of the Senate Permanent Subcommittee on Investigations, which two months later began to look into Secretary Ross's relationships with Wynn Enterprises.

In mid-January 1957, Ross took a leave of absence when the conflict-of-interest question was brought up in Congress. On February 13, he testified under oath for two hours behind closed doors. He denied that he had at any time behaved improperly. However, he did acknowledge that he had arranged a meeting a year earlier for his brother-in-law with a marine general. Senate subcommittee members urged Ross to quit to avoid public hearings, and subsequently, on February 14, he submitted his letter of resignation to President Dwight D. Eisenhower. Ross pointed out that "nothing was brought to my attention to indicate that the subcommittee had found any evidence of any wrongdoing, impropriety, or conflict of interest on my part." Yet he recognized that his effectiveness as assistant secretary of defense had been "impaired by the very serious implications contained in the numerous press stories" and wrote that "I feel it would be unfair to the Department of Defense for me to continue." Ross was the second high Pentagon official in 18 months to leave office under a dark cloud of conflict of interest. Like Secretary of the Air Force Harold TALBOTT, who had left slightly earlier, Ross considered himself a martyr, for he had sacrificed large earnings in private business activities to serve the nation.

Dan ROSTENKOWSKI: fallen Ways and Means chairman

The long, eventful, public service career of U.S. Representative Daniel Rostenkowski, chairman of the powerful House Ways and Means Committee, ended in disgrace on April 9, 1996, when he pleaded guilty to two counts of mail fraud. Federal prosecutors then dropped the remaining 11 charges against him. When the scandal broke in 1994, Rosty, as the burly Democrat was called, resigned his seat in the House of Representatives and the committee chairmanship.

Illinois congressman Dan Rostenkowski, chairman of the House Ways and Means Committee, stands outside the U.S. District Court in Washington after pleading not guilty to every charge of a 17-count corruption indictment against him in June 1994. He said, "I will be vindicated." (AP/Wide World Photos)

Subsequently imprisoned, Rostenkowski (inmate No. 25338-016) received treatment for prostate cancer at a medical prison in Rochester, Minnesota, and was later transferred to a minimum-security prison in Oxford, Wisconsin. There the former power broker, who had lived and loved the high life and been courted and entertained by lobbyists over dinners and at golf resorts worldwide, shared a cell with three other inmates for 13 months. During his "Oxford education," Rostenkowski gave his fellow inmates information about Pell grants and helped them negotiate the bureaucratic maze of Social Security and Medicare. After his release he spent two months at a Salvation Army halfway house in Chicago before his release on October 15, 1997.

Born in Chicago in 1928, Rostenkowski nurtured a close relationship with Chicago's Mayor Richard Daley, who could be considered his political mentor. Rosenkowski became an Illinois state senator at age 24, and with Daley's help in 1958 won election to the U.S. House of Representatives. A tough legislator and master coalition builder (whose power derived from granting and denying favors), he became chairman of the prestigious House Ways and Means Committee in 1981. Rostenkowski was instrumental in hustling the Tax

Reform Act of 1986 through Congress, one of the highlights of his 18-term congressional career.

In 1994, at the height of his political career, scandal struck when he was linked to an embezzlement scheme in the House post office. Former House postmaster Robert V. Rota, who pleaded guilty to embezzlement and conspiracy, implicated Rostenkowski as one of the main offenders. He was charged with a variety of crimes involving misappropriation or embezzlement of more than $700,000 in public and campaign funds. The most significant charge against him was that over a six-year period he had traded in his vouchers for $21,300 in cash at the House post office and had taken stamps and later converted them into cash (it was not established whether this amount was applied to personal or official use). Evidently, before 1977, it was legal for House members to cash some portion of their official expenses; ethical standards have been tightened since then. The resolute Rostenkowski defiantly denounced the "unfair, false, and baseless" allegations and, while he may have violated some technical rules, refused to apologize, stating he had "committed no crime . . . and engaged in no illegal or unethical conduct." He hired Robert Bennett and Carl Rauh, two of Washington's top criminal defense lawyers, to represent him.

Rostenkowski was also accused of using political campaign money to rent a bogus office in one of his buildings and of buying cars rented with public funds for family members. He was also charged with obstructing the judicial investigation into his affairs. Fictitious employees were found on his payroll. Furthermore, he was charged with misusing public funds to buy gifts such as chairs and ashtrays for friends (charges to which he admitted guilt).

After his release from prison, Rostenkowski kept a relatively low profile and took up residence in his childhood home (built by his grandfather) among the people he had once represented in Congress. He set up a legislative consultancy business, Danross Associates, Inc., and slowly attempted to rebuild his scarred reputation. He hoped to be remembered for his legislative achievements rather than for the furor over House post office stamps.

Bertrand RUSSELL: personal opinion under prosecution

An internationally renowned philosopher and mathematician, Bertrand Russell received, in 1940, a one-year appointment to the Philosophy Department of the College of the City of New York (CCNY). But before he could even assume his new position, the opportunity was swept away from him. Accused of being "an advocate of sexual immorality," Russell was forced to undergo a libelous and humiliating court trial.

Russell's crime seems almost ludicrous today. In four books written for popular audiences between 1925 and 1929—*What I Believe, Education and the Good Life, Marriage and Morals, Education and the Modern World*—Russell had wittily but clinically commented about the problems of modern marriage. He had suggested, perhaps sardonically, that the then current increase in divorce cases could be reduced through "trial marriage."

His comment had nothing whatsoever to do with the subjects he taught, mathematics and logic, but for this moral lapse, the Episcopal Bishop of New York, the Roman Catholic Diocese of Brooklyn and its newspaper, various religious zealots, their newspapers, many patriotic organizations, almost every local Democratic politician, and the Hearst press reacted in outraged horror.

Russell was attacked for "gross immorality," called "a professor of paganism," a "dessicated, divorced, and decadent advocate of sexual promiscuity," and "the devil's minister to men" as "the mastermind of free love." Not unexpectedly, his views were labeled procommunist too.

A Brooklyn mother, fearful that her pre-adolescent daughter might somehow become Russell's student, sued for reversal of his appointment at CCNY, charging him with being an alien in addition to being immoral. Her lawyer vilified Russell in slanderous terms. Russell escaped a libel action only because of the *sub judice* status of the suit. The theoretically unbiased judge, up for re-election and apparently convinced by the lawyer's inkhorn invective, sided with the plaintiff and the propagandists and illustrated from his bench how vulnerable to political influence American courts really are. (His conduct was so reprehensible that law reviews commented upon it and in 1971 the ACLU published a detailed analysis of the matter called *The Story of the Bertrand Russell Case.*)

The hearing was a mockery of established judicial procedures; the judge did not allow Russell to defend himself, permitted no character witnesses, disallowed any discussion of Russell's alleged "pornography" within its contexts, constantly overruled only the defense's objections, attacked the defendant's character, and based his judgment upon moral theology rather than law. He reversed the appointment on the basis of a statute applying only to primary and secondary schools and blocked all attempts by Russell's lawyers to have a rehearing or an appeal, ruling that Russell had no legal interest in the case.

In the end, Russell was hardly squashed: he went to Harvard rather than to CCNY, and in 1950 the Swedish Academy voted him the Nobel Prize in literature. He died at age 97 at his home in northern Wales in 1970.

"RUTHERFRAUD." See JOSEPH P. BRADLEY: the stolen election of 1876.

"SALAD OIL SWINDLE." See GREAT SALAD OIL SWINDLE.

SALEM WITCH TRIALS: the devil in Massachusetts

A cloud of hypnotic fear covered Essex County, Massachusetts, in early 1692, especially in Salem Village. By September 22, through the actions of a special court, two dogs and 19 men and women had been hanged for witchcraft, and one man had been fatally crushed, after pleading not guilty, for refusing to acknowledge the jurisdiction of the court. Fifty-five persons had repentantly confessed that they were witches, and 150 more either awaited trial or waited for pregnancies that reprieved them from immediate execution. These events, collectively labeled the Salem Witch Trials, provoked a controversy still unresolved to this day.

The public crisis began in February 1692 when two young girls suffered hallucinatory fits and seizures, hypothesized by physicians as having diabolical causes. Because one of the victims was a clergyman's daughter, fellow ministers suggested that the matter be kept secret. It was not, and by February 29, Salem officials began to arrest and examine suspected witches named by the girls. As word got out, the supposed cases of affliction multiplied. Accusations by the afflicted increased, and confessions by some of the accused caused jails in Salem and Boston to bulge. The newly arrived governor general of the Massachusetts Bay Colony, Sir William Phips, ordered a Special Court of Oyer and Terminer established to be presided over by his lieutenant governor, William Stoughton. The court was convinced that the devil intended to destroy the colony, especially Salem village. Between May 29 and September 22, it acted with unjustifiable haste. Analysis suggests that the court had erred by accepting as decisive evidence the charges of the afflicted persons and the confessed "witches" and had relied on "specter evidence": testimony that a devil in the form of the accused had tormented the accuser. Governor Phips, persuaded by the spread of public panic to Andover and by arguments about the unreliability

and insufficiency of the trial evidence, then stayed all executions in September 1692, dismissed the special court in the same month, and issued a general pardon in May 1693.

A reversal of public opinion and a period of public penitence followed, and an evaluation of the events gradually began to develop. Its conclusions emphasized

At the Salem Witch Trials of 1692, so-called "evidence" was presented against victims charged with powers of bewitchment. In the picture, the girls (right) point accusingly at the woman and exclaim, "There is a flock of yellow birds around her head." (The Bettmann Archive)

the embarrassing nature of the incidents but failed to explain them adequately.

Capped by the highly inaccurate 1867 volume *Salem Witchcraft*, by the Reverend Charles Wentworth Upham, this evaluation concluded that no witchcraft had existed in Salem village, that the behavior and testimony of the afflicted was dissembled in order to gain public notice, that both the clergy and magistrates took advantage of the panic to exercise greater and irresponsible power over the community, and that the colony's intellectual and spiritual leaders did little to quell the public's fear. These conclusions, adopted by many scholars and writers of American history from George Bancroft through James Truslow Adams, form the basis of the traditional, popular view of the events. Some historians further claimed that the trials and executions were attributable to the narrowness and repressiveness of Puritanism, the official religion of the Massachusetts Bay Colony.

Objections to these conclusions surfaced early, and analyses of the Salem records by more careful historical scholars have revealed the essential incorrectness of the traditional view. Without denying the harassment and execution of many innocent persons, these scholars' labors have established the factuality of four rebuttals to the initial hypotheses. First, the practice of malefic witchcraft (black magic) did exist in the Massachusetts Bay Colony and in Salem. In 1688, Boston magistrates had executed a Goody Glover after she confessed to a pact with Satan and the affliction of four children, whose behavior duplicated that of the Salem children. The Salem records also suggest that at least three of those executed in the Witch Trials (Bridget Bishop, Wilmot "Mammy" Redd, and Candy [a slave]) were clearly guilty of malefic practices, even to the creation of puppet-dolls stuck with pins and thorns. And since white magic (spells, charms, postures, actions, and medicines dedicated to a favorable end) was considered a somewhat less culpable form of witchcraft, the entire village may have been guilty at one time or another. Second, Salem village (like the Christian world generally) believed in the existence of witches and regarded as a mandate the Biblical injunction (Exodus 22:18) that proven witches be executed. These beliefs caused thousands to be executed in Europe, including England, between 1300 and 1700. By comparison, the record for New England is extremely restrained, given the sudden and violent spread of irrational fear in Salem village. Its rise and swift decline may be attributable to the emotional and intellectual preconceptions of the times, general preconceptions not restricted to Puritans and Puritanism, which at their best were both heavily dedicated to rationality.

Moreover, the view that the afflicted were deliberately and viciously shamming and play-acting is no more believable than is the 17th-century physicians' diagnosis of bewitchment. Contemporary descriptions of their fits and hallucinatory verbalizations are exactly the same as those pictured by the 19th-century French neurologist Jean Charcot and the Austrian physicians Sigmund Freud and Josef Breuer as symptoms of the strongly convulsive and highly communicable neurosis technically labeled *hysteria*, an experience usually denied by its victims upon their return to rationality.

Finally, it is erroneous to fault the intellectual leaders of the Massachusetts Bay Colony (chiefly clergymen) with failing to restrain the members of their community. They tried. One judge in the special court publicly resigned over the problem of capital evidence; Cotton Mather, a clergyman who had defended the probity of the remaining judges, nevertheless made public his distrust in specter evidence. Moreover, his father, Increase Mather, also distrusting specter evidence, went further in questioning charges made by the afflicted and confessors; his arguments persuaded the governor general to disestablish the special court.

Although they have undercut the traditional evaluation of the Salem Witch Trials, these findings have not been enough to dissolve the perception that the trials were both unnecessary and basically irrational, as was the public panic. The playwright Arthur Miller's *The Crucible* (1953) was based on the witch trails in Salem.

SALOMON BROTHERS TRADING SCANDAL

Even on sometime-scandal-plagued Wall Street, the $2.2 trillion U.S. Treasury securities market was considered sacrosanct, well-regulated, and inviolable. This sanctity was shattered in August 1991 when Salomon Brothers Inc., one of America's most powerful bond dealers, admitted to large-scale fraud in the securities market.

Federal laws prohibit the acquisition by any one bidder of more than 35 percent of Treasury notes and bonds at a government auction. Yet Salomon Brothers Inc., one of the elite 39 primary dealers, was apparently able to circumvent these rules until the scandal became public in August 1991. In the preceding nine months, the company had exceeded the trading limit in at least four separate Treasury auctions (December, March, April, and May). For instance, in December 1990, it bought 35 percent of an $8.5 billion, four-year note sale and submitted a $1 billion bid apparently on behalf of a customer but actually for its own account. Thus, it cornered a 46 percent market share of the entire deal.

In February, managing director and chief government trader Paul Mozer reportedly convinced Mercury Asset Management (a division of S. G. Warburg) to submit a bogus $1 billion order for 30-year Treasury bonds. He evidently wanted to play a practical joke on the young trader processing the order. Unfortunately for

Mozer the purchase went through and ended up in the company's account books. When questioned on this, Mercury remained silent—ostensibly at Mozer's request. Company CEO and Chairman John Gutfreund and President Thomas Strauss were told of this incident in April but did not report it. As the threat of government investigations loomed, other similar infractions came to light.

In the May 1991 auction of two-year Treasury notes, Salomon submitted a 35 percent bid in its own name and fake bids on behalf of two clients. All three bids were successful. Then the two fake bids were reportedly "sold" to the company, giving it control over $10.6 billion of the $11.3 billion auction. The scandal might never have broken except that one of the two clients had also submitted a genuine bid of its own, which raised its share to over 35 percent and drew the Treasury's attention. The investigation by the Securities and Exchange Commission (SEC) later revealed that Salomon had submitted or led to the submission of 10 false bids amounting to $15.5 billion in nine Treasury auctions between August 1989 and May 1991.

Four federal agencies—the Federal Reserve Board (FRB), the Justice Department, the SEC, and the New York Stock Exchange (NYSE)—launched civil and criminal investigations into the actions of the company. The chairman of the House Banking Committee, Henry B. Gonzalez, urged the FRB to suspend Salomon Brothers from participating in future government auctions until the investigations were complete. Other prominent lawmakers lobbied for tighter controls over the government securities market. Panic among shareholders caused Salomon stock to plummet nearly 30 percent. Moody's Investors Service downgraded the company's credit rating.

On August 9, 1991, the company announced the suspension of Mozer, his assistant Thomas Murphy, and two other employees. Gutfreund and Strauss resigned over the scandal. Nebraska millionaire Warren Buffett, the company's largest shareholder with 16 percent, or $700 million, assumed charged as interim chairman and chief executive officer. Salomon had been banned by the U.S. Treasury Department from bidding at future auctions for two months, but Buffett's mediation with Treasury secretary Nicholas F. Brady helped restore Salomon's rights to trade on its own account only and not for its customers. This was a huge relief for Salomon since trade in government securities constituted almost one-quarter of the firm's business. Buffett also initiated internal reforms while the Treasury revamped the operating guidelines for its auctions.

Salomon faced widespread client defections, among them the World Bank, two state treasuries, and four state pension funds and possible sanctions by the British treasury. Then there were lawsuits from investors who alleged that they had been overcharged for securities or underpaid in interest because of artificially reduced yields. The firm's liquidity was at stake, so Buffett was forced to sell some of the company's assets to finance operations. Salomon's profits from these illegal transactions were estimated at $4.6 million. When the 10-month investigation ended in May 1992, Salomon Inc., agreed to pay $290 million—the second-largest settlement for fraud on Wall Street. The U.S. Justice Department and the SEC imposed some $190 million in fines and forfeitures, saying that the company's operating pattern posed a real threat to the securities market. Also, the company was ordered to create a $100 million fund to compensate customers who lost money in these fraudulent deals. Top executives at Salomon Brothers escaped criminal prosecution, however.

SALT LAKE CITY'S OLYMPIC BRIBERY SCANDAL

In 1995 the International Olympic Committee (IOC) selected Salt Lake City, Utah, to be the site of the 2002 Winter Olympics. The Salt Lake Organizing Committee's (SLOC) bid committee was widely congratulated for waging a savvy campaign, which its members attributed to the experience gained in five unsuccessful attempts over the 30 previous years. Three years later it became clear that the SLOC's success resulted from more than just experience when it was discovered that the bid committee had bribed members of the IOC selection committee for their votes.

In November 1998 a Salt Lake City television station reported that the bid committee had given thousands of dollars in scholarship money to the daughter of Cameroon's IOC representative. The report led the SLOC, the IOC, the United States Olympic Committee, the U.S. Justice Department, and the House of Representatives to investigate the charges more thoroughly. In February 1999 the SLOC's investigation, which was led by a former Utah Supreme Court justice, concluded that no laws had been broken by the bid committee in securing the Winter Games for Salt Lake City. However, the SLOC report disclosed that the bid committee spent almost $1 million out of a total budget of $13 million on bribes. Approximately $400,000 went for scholarships at Utah colleges to children of IOC members. The rest financed trips to the Super Bowl, vacations to Paris, ski trips, shopping sprees, interior decorating, health care, personal legal fees, and expensive gifts in addition to straightforward cash payments. Furthermore, close relatives of three IOC members were hired by the SLOC. The report revealed that Thomas Welch, chairman of both the SLOC and the bid committee, and David Johnson, senior SLOC vice president, made the payments with the knowledge of Craig Peterson, the SLOC finance chief, but without the knowledge of the bid committee's board of directors. At least nine and perhaps as many as 13 IOC members received the unethical, if not illegal, considerations, thus making this the worst corruption scandal in the history of the Olympics.

The SLOC bid committee resorted to bribery after losing two bids by narrow margins. In 1985 the city lost out to Anchorage, Alaska, for the right to receive the USOC's approval to bid for the 1992 Winter Games, despite the fact that Anchorage's lack of facilities and culture would hardly endear it to the IOC. Following the selection announcement, rumors began circulating that the Anchorage bid committee had given USOC delegates free fishing and hunting trips to Alaska, including transportation by helicopter. In 1991 the city got the USOC's nod but lost out to Nagano, Japan, which, like Anchorage, did not have facilities to compare with Salt Lake City's. Following the selection announcement, rumors began circulating that Japanese organizers had given lavish gifts to IOC members and donated millions of dollars to a pet project of the IOC president. Because city leaders hoped that a well-run Winter Games would demonstrate to the international community that Salt Lake City was a world-class metropolis, Welch and Johnson evidently decided to do whatever it took to win.

The negative feedback concerning the scandal led Deedee Corradini, Salt Lake City's mayor, to decide not to run for reelection; otherwise, no Americans were punished. However, the IOC investigation revealed that its own members may have started the whole scandal by soliciting bribes. Consequently, the IOC expelled nine members, warned another one, and continued to investigate three more. More importantly, the scandal led to calls for a complete reworking of the way in which Olympic bids are awarded.

SANBORN CONTRACTS SCANDAL

President of the United States Ulysses S. Grant's administration (1869–77) was peppered with scandalous business affairs. One of them, the "fat" scandal of the government contracts awarded to John D. Sanborn, a Massachusetts politico, brought on a public outrage that compelled Grant to relieve, reluctantly, his secretary of the treasury, William A. Richardson, one of Sanborn's collaborators. Corruption, nonetheless, continued to flourish during the period of Grant's administration (see CRÉDIT MOBILIER SCANDAL; WHISKEY RING: "Let no guilty man escape").

When President Grant took office, Richardson was given the post of assistant secretary of the treasury, and held this post until Secretary of the Treasury George S. Boutwell left the cabinet in 1873 to take the Senate seat vacated by Henry Wilson, who became Grant's vice president (see Schuyler COLFAX: under a cloud of suspicion). Richardson was then promoted to secretary of the treasury. Shortly thereafter, Benjamin F. Butler, a United States representative from Massachusetts, prevailed upon Richardson, who was a fellow townsman of his, to appoint Sanborn, who had been an agent of Butler in the latter's Civil War-time cotton speculations and had retained a close friendship with him, as a special federal agent for the collection of delinquent excise and other taxes. In 1872, federal legislation ended the long-common practice of farming out the gathering of uncollected taxes to private collectors. When the 1872 bill was passed, however, the crafty Butler managed to obtain legislative exception for Sanborn and two other men. Richardson thereupon signed treasury contracts with Sanborn, authorizing the latter to inform on persons who were delinquent in paying their taxes and also to claim for himself 50 percent of the monies he collected.

At first, Sanborn uncovered tax cheats easily by looking at a list already compiled by the internal revenue division in the Boston office. He made some handsome profits and, before long, was gathering all kinds of taxes, some from persons who owed nothing and were not delinquent. As a result of his collection activities, which Richardson apparently condoned, Sanborn's lifestyle grew extremely lavish. But Boston sound-money men wanted to get rid of the treasury secretary, who was a friend of the monetary expansionists; they moved against his flaccid money policies and helped launch a congressional probe into Sanborn's contracts and other "unclean" matters.

From February to May 1874, the House Committee on Ways and Means looked into these doings while the American public read about them in the press. The Treasury Department had apparently been defrauded. Sanborn himself testified to congressional investigators that he received $213,500 for collecting taxes that citizens would have paid regardless of his dunning. But Richardson was found to have colluded with Sanborn to make the tax-gathering operation into a racket. Ultimately, Sanborn lost his lucrative contracts, and Richardson became a millstone around Grant's neck because of the House committee's demand that the Treasury secretary be dismissed or resign. At first, Grant balked at this, beseeching individual committee members to issue no damning report, but eventually gave in and forced Richardson to resign. The empty cabinet post then went to Benjamin H. Bristow, an unsullied Kentucky lawyer. Grant immediately named his publicly stigmatized friend Richardson, who was also an attorney, to a judgeship on the U.S. Court of Claims, of which Richardson became chief justice 11 years later, in 1885.

Clarence SAUNDERS: bankrupt supermarket king
Clarence Saunders had one of the biggest rollercoaster success stories in America's history. From his early job as a grocery store clerk, Saunders became a multimil-

lionaire with his own chain of supermarkets, which revolutionized the retail food business. Known as the supermarket king, he came close to losing his entire fortune in 1923, only to establish another supermarket chain and another fortune that he eventually lost. He also earned the sobriquet of the world's most unfortunate financier.

Born in Virginia in 1881, Saunders had only four years of schooling before he began work as a grocer's assistant at four dollars a month. By age 19, he was earning $30 a month as a salesman for a food wholesaler, and about two years later he formed a successful grocery cooperative in Memphis, Tennessee. In 1916, the imaginative Saunders, now a thriving wholesaler, opened his own grocery store. Called Piggly Wiggly, it was the prototype of the modern self-service supermarket. The store wreaked havoc on conventional food stores in Memphis, undercutting their prices by at least 10 percent. Soon there were nine Piggly Wiggly stores operating, and by 1922 the number had mushroomed to 1,200 stores operating in 29 states. Saunders owned half of the stores; the rest operated on a franchise basis. The Piggly Wiggly chain was worth some $7 million, and Saunders enjoyed his success by building a $1 million pink marble mansion on a 160-acre estate outside Memphis.

In 1923, however, some unscrupulous Wall Street speculators became interested in investing in Piggly Wiggly shares on the American Stock Exchange. Because they wanted to buy Saunders's stock at a cheap price they circulated rumors that the company was in trouble in order to drive down the price. The speculators drove the price down unethically, by repeatedly selling short—a method in which the investor, instead of buying shares and then selling them, sells them first (goes "short" because he doesn't own them) and then buys them at what he hopes will be a lower price. Enraged by the money-hungry "bear" raiders of Wall Street, Saunders countered with an apparent attempt to "corner," or buy up, almost all of the shares in Piggly Wiggly with a view to forcing them to higher prices. He borrowed $10 million and, with his brokers, succeeded in undermining the short-sellers by cornering the shares in March 1923. On one day his stock rose to $124 and then fell to $82. The stock exchange then announced its refusal to trade Piggly Wiggly shares. By early 1924 Saunders was declared bankrupt, being unable to repay the money he had borrowed and finally losing control of Piggly Wiggly which was sold to the Kroger Grocery Company. The city of Memphis took over Saunders's pink palace and turned it into a museum.

In 1929 Saunders, again using borrowed money, introduced another store chain called Clarence Saunders—Sole Owner of My Name. Claiming at the Memphis opening of the new company that he would build up

the biggest industry in the world, he watched his new chain flourish and again reached millionaire status. But the new chain also eventually went bankrupt during the Great Depression. Saunders then took over "world rights" to a cleaning fluid called Evernew, but that enterprise failed, too, when two salesman were brought to court by purchasers who claimed that the fluid had ruined their clothes.

Using his mechanical ingenuity, Saunders next proceeded to create the first automated store, called the Keedoozle (a coined word for "key-does-all"), in which sample merchandise was displayed behind glass cases and customers bought the items desired (without touching them) by placing keys into the correct slots. The merchandise automatically tumbled onto a conveyor belt after automatically being recorded; it was then carried to the checkout for automatic wrapping. When the store opened in Memphis in May 1937, however, the system was 50 years ahead of the necessary technology and, because of frequent mechanical failures, was abandoned at the beginning of World War II. In 1948 Saunders presented an improved Keedoozle and sold a few franchises, but the automation unfortunately proved too complicated for the customers, and the venture folded in 1949.

In 1953, at age 72, the still inventive Saunders unveiled yet another automated store, the Foodelectric, in which packaged food was enclosed in glass cases and was selected by customers who pulled a gadget through a slot. He died in Memphis shortly after, leaving an estate of merely $2,000.

Robert C. SCHENCK: humiliated diplomat

The administration of President Ulysses S. Grant was infamous for its corrupt members. Among those who benefited unethically was Robert Cumming Schenck, American minister to Great Britain from 1871 to 1876. As an influential figure in England, Schenck used his illustrious position to persuade many people in that nation to buy stock in an American silver mine of which he had become a director. When Schenck then sold his shares in the mine at a high price and the mining company then collapsed, a cry was raised against him that eventually forced his resignation.

An enterprising lawyer from Ohio, Schenck served as a Whig congressman in the U.S. House of Representatives from 1843 to 1851. He was a Union general in the Civil War, fighting at both battles of Bull Run and in West Virginia before resigning in 1863 to reenter Congress as congressman from Ohio. As a leading radical Republican, he was an ardent advocate of the unsuccessful attempt to impeach U.S. President Andrew JOHNSON in 1868. After losing his House seat in 1870, following his failure to be reelected, Schenck unabashedly used his close acquaintances in Washington, D.C., to land himself lucrative work as a lobbyist representing the interests of the Northern Pacific Railroad. He also called on his former friends in Congress to persuade President Grant to appoint him as the new American minister to the Court of St. James (Great Britain). The preeminent post became his in 1871, and the 62-year-old Schenck took up residence in London, where he proceeded to live a sumptuous and illustrious life as an American diplomat. In order to keep up his lavish lifestyle, however, Schenck knew that he needed an additional source of income.

At that time, promoters of the infamous Emma Silver Mining Company, which was said to have great promise because of apparently rich silver ore deposits at its Emma Mine in Utah, were busily floating the company's stock on the London market. With considerable "Yankee ingenuity" and brilliant salesmanship, they enticed numerous distinguished personages, both American and British, to buy shares in the company. Schenck was made a director and enthusiastically endorsed the purchasing of stock in advertisements for the Emma Silver Mine, and for a short time investors in the company did well, seeing the price of stock in its British subsidiary (the Emma Silver Mining Company, Limited) jump from £20 to £50. For a while, high dividends were also paid out.

Schenck's personal endorsement of the mine, however, was sharply criticized. On November 17, 1871, U.S. Secretary of State Hamilton Fish, with President Grant's approval, sent a letter to Ambassador Schenck, saying, "The advertisement of the name of a diplomatic representative of the government, as director of a company seeking to dispose of its shares in the country to which he is accredited, is ill-advised and unfortunate." Fish strongly requested that Schenck either resign from his post or sever his ties with the mining company. Although he privately resigned from the company on December 6, 1871, Schenck postponed the public announcement of this until January 12, 1872, to allow company insiders like himself to have enough time to sell off their holdings before the announcement depressed the market value of their shares.

Later in 1872, the Emma Silver Mining Company unexpectedly announced that its ore deposits had been exhausted, causing its stock price to plummet. Feeling that they had been deceived, Britons who had invested in the mine accused Schenck of being party to a fraudulent scheme. He was later discovered to have accepted £10,000 worth of the company's stock in return for the right to use his name in its advertisements. He had also made a financial "killing" by unloading his shares before the British investors found out about the mine's depletion. Democrats in Congress did not forget Schenck's connection to the Emma Mine scandal (the mine had failed in the crash of 1873, which caused thousands of business bankruptcies that plunged America into a depression), and in 1876 U.S. Representative Abram S.

Hewitt of New York began a congressional investigation of Schenck, who was still minister in London. Ultimately, Schenck was cleared of fraud charges, but his reputation had been badly stained. Both Britons and Americans accused him of using his dignified public position for personal gain. His dealings caused a British court writ against him, which he dodged by pleading diplomatic immunity. In May 1876, Schenck resigned and came home in shame, to be replaced as minister to Great Britain by Edwards Pierrepont, who had been attorney general of the United States. Schenck later fell back to practicing law in Washington.

Frances SCHREUDER: greedy and murderous socialite
Franklin J. Bradshaw, one of the richest men in Utah, was shot at close range with a .357 magnum on July 23, 1978. He died soon afterward. The identity of the murderer remained a mystery until five years later, when it was revealed to be Bradshaw's own grandson, Marc Schreuder, who had been 17 years old at the time of the crime. Even more chilling was the revelation that Marc had carried out the killing on orders from his mother, Bradshaw's own daughter, who feared being cut out of the multimillionaire's will.

Bradshaw, a Mormon living in Salt Lake City, built a fortune as the founder and owner of a chain of auto-parts stores; he also made millions of dollars on state and federal oil and gas leases. With his wife, Berenice, Bradshaw had four children, the last of whom was Berenice's favorite, Frances. Penurious and secretive, Bradshaw worked constantly and was rarely at home. Despite his great wealth, his family lived modestly in a lower-middle-class neighborhood and felt the sting of Franklin's excessive parsimony as well as his frequent absence.

Frances grew up willful, moody, and rather unpredictable; during her junior year at Bryn Mawr College in Pennsylvania, she was expelled for criminal misconduct. She could, however, charm those around her when she so desired. In 1958, she married an Italian businessman, Vittorio Gentile. They had two sons, Lorenzo and Marco. The marriage ended in divorce in 1962. Subsequently Frances became financially dependent on her parents, indulging in a social-climbing, extravagant lifestyle in New York City and sending her children to expensive prep schools with her father's money. She appeared to live vicariously through her children and their achievements. Overly involved in their lives, she apparently beat them when their grades failed to meet her expectations. She seemed to have an unnatural hold over the children, threatening them with poverty and banishment if they disobeyed her. In 1969 she remarried, to Frederick Schreuder, and promptly changed her two son's names to Larry and Marc Schreuder. This second marriage, during which she gave birth to a daughter, Lavina, in 1973, ended in divorce in 1976.

Living on some trust funds of her own and money from her parents, Frances dominated and manipulated her three children (Marc would later say, "You don't tell Mom no"). She badly wanted to be one of New York City's cultural elite. Although she lived in a lavish $500,000 Manhattan apartment on the Upper East Side and donated generously to the New York City Ballet, she felt she needed more resources to attain her new goal. In the summer of 1977 she sent her sons to stay with their grandparents in Salt Lake City, allegedly instructing them to poison her father by putting amphetamines in his oatmeal (which he always ate for breakfast). The plot failed because he didn't eat enough. The two boys, however, stole more than $200,000 in blank checks (personal and corporate), merchandise, and negotiable stock certificates from Bradshaw and sent part of the loot back to Frances.

Bradshaw grew tired of Frances and her way of life. He talked of disinheriting her and supposedly even drafted a will in which she was not mentioned (it was never probated). There is speculation that in order to protect her inheritance, her son Larry was her first choice as a "hitman" to kill her father (Larry was later jailed for trying to kill his college roommate with a hammer). However that may be, Marc was the one who ultimately carried out his mother's command. He went to Salt Lake City, confronted his grandfather in the latter's warehouse, and fatally shot him at close range. He then fled, and the murder remained a mystery for the next two years.

Meanwhile, Frances continued in her social climbing activities. She pledged $360,000 to produce George Balanchine's *Davidsbündlertänze* in 1980 and shortly after became a member of the board of the New York City Ballet. Most of the money came from her doting mother, Berenice.

The Franklin Bradshaw murder case cracked open in October 1980 when Richard Behrens, to whom Marc had given the murder weapon, became angry with Frances, a longtime friend, because she refused to pay a personal debt to him. Behrens handed the .357 magnum to Frances's sister Marilyn, who then turned it over to the authorities. The gun was traced back to Marc, who was arrested in 1981 and charged with first-degree murder. He stood trial without a jury in Salt Lake City in 1982 and was found guilty of second-degree murder because the presiding judge was unsure why Marc had killed his grandfather. At the time, Frances, who was also charged with first-degree murder, was fighting extradition from New York and was waiting for a share of the multimillion-dollar family trust (her father's will had yet to clear probate). Marc received a five-year-to-life prison term.

The next year Frances was brought to Salt Lake City to face a jury trial. Marc testified that this mother, now 45 years old, had given him detailed instructions to murder his grandfather. When he attempted to beg off, Marc said, he had been told by his mother, "just don't come home again" if he didn't do what she wanted. He said that she "ran up to me and hugged me and kissed me" when he informed her of the killing. Frances was convicted of first-degree murder and given life imprisonment. The court was undoubtedly not swayed by Berenice Bradshaw's written statement that "my daughter . . . who I love very much, has been unjustly convicted of a crime which she had no part in . . . she has been a fine, devoted mother."

SCOPES TRIAL

In the first quarter of this century, many Americans felt that evolutionary theories, particularly Charles Darwin's idea that human beings had developed from lower forms of life, were diametrically opposed to the Bible's account of the divine creation of humankind and the world. On March 13, 1925, Tennessee, like several other southern states, passed a law prohibiting the teaching of evolution in the public schools. Christian fundamentalists in the South and elsewhere interpreted the Scriptures literally; they clashed with the modernists who construed the Bible liberally and felt that the laws against teaching evolution should be challenged.

In the small town of Dayton, Tennessee, a mild-mannered, 25-year-old high-school biology teacher named John Thomas Scopes violated the state law by acquainting his students with Darwinism, willingly accepting his arrest and standing trial on the charge of having taught evolution. Many newsmen, curious farmers, and others flocked to Dayton to view the Scopes

Clarence Darrow (left) converses with opponent William Jennings Bryan (right) in the Dayton, Tennessee, courtroom during the 1925 Scopes Trial, also called the great monkey trial or monkey case. Bryan strongly defended the literal interpretation of the Bible against Darrow's attack and his defense of John T. Scopes, who was on trial for illegally teaching the theory of evolution. (AP/Wide World Photos)

John T. Scopes, a high school teacher in Dayton, Tennessee, was charged with breaking a state law banning the teaching of evolution. His sensational trial in 1925 ended in his conviction after much heated debate between advocates of the beliefs of fundamentalism and those of science. (AP/Wide World Photos)

trial, known also as the monkey trial, which lasted from July 10 to 21, 1925, in a circuslike atmosphere. Although the presiding judge, John T. Raulston, limited the case to whether Scopes was guilty or innocent and ruled out any test of Tennessee's law or debate over Darwin's theory, the chief issue soon became the long controversy over the validity of fundamentalist versus modernist beliefs. Adding to the drama was the presence of two renowned public figures, both lawyers, who were pitted against each other in the case. Scopes's defense was headed by Clarence Darrow, defense counsel in famous criminal cases, who was aided by Dudley Field Malone and Arthur Garfield Hays. The prosecution was guided by William Jennings Bryan, former United States secretary of state, known for his eloquent oratory, who was assisted by A. T. Stewart and Ben G. McKenzie. Both sides helped select a jury.

During the trial, nothing seemed to happen according to plan, except the opening of court each morning with a prayer (to which Darrow objected, but was overruled by Judge Raulston). At much expense, the defense brought numerous expert witnesses—scientists and pro-

fessors—to Dayton in behalf of Scopes, but they were not allowed to testify because of the prosecution's objections, upheld by the judge, that their interpretations of evolution and Scripture would be purely subjective and thus inadmissible. The testimony of fundamentalists for the prosecution was frequently contradictory, as the defense showed under cross-examination. Darrow claimed that the Tennessee legislature had violated the constitutional separation of church and state by indicating a preference for religion and that evolutionary theory and the Bible were not necessarily antithetical.

Near the end of the trial, Bryan, who was a conservative Presbyterian fundamentalist, unexpectedly and willingly sat in the witness stand to defend the Christian faith and to lambast the unbelievers. However, Darrow's vigorous and sharp questioning upset Bryan, who exposed his lack of knowledge of modern science and resorted, often growlingly, to saying the answers were all in the Bible. The Great Commoner, as Bryan was called, clearly had the most onlookers on his side when he and Darrow argued the final day on the Dayton courthouse lawn, but Darrow's logic and rationalism seemed irrefutable. He asked Bryan if he really took the Bible and its stories literally (about Adam, Eve, Cain, the serpent, and other subjects). To save face, Bryan had hoped to give a powerful final summation for the prosecution, but Darrow's decision not to give a defense summation prevented him from doing this. The defense rested its case, never denying that Scopes had taught evolutionary theory.

Scopes was convicted of violating the Tennessee law and was fined $100. The defense appealed, and the state supreme court later acquitted Scopes on the technicality that his fine had been excessive. Bryan appeared bitter, despite having won the case. He died, suddenly, five days after the conclusion of the trial, of apoplexy. The controversial Tennessee law was eventually repealed in 1967; yet in many areas of America the teaching of evolution remains a heated issue to this day.

SCOTTSBORO BOYS: "let's get rid of these niggers"
Traveling on a slow, Memphis-bound freight train on March 25, 1931, were a number of black and white teenagers, all hitching rides in search of work. Near Stevenson, Alabama, a fight erupted between the whites and the blacks. In the ensuing fracas, the blacks threw five white teens from the train. One of the castoffs complained to local authorities, adding that the blacks were riding the rails with two white girls. Immediately an order went out to "round up every Negro on the train and bring them to Scottsboro," the principal town in the area. For the black teens involved, the youthful scrape would end in sentences to death row and life in prison.

When the train pulled into Paint Rock, Alabama, lawmen seized nine black youths, aged 13 to 20: Olen

Montgomery, Haywood Patterson, Ozzie Powell, Clarence Norris, Willie Roberson, Charley Weems, Eugene Williams, Roy White, and Andy Wright. Also seized were the two white females: Victoria Price, 19, and Nancy Bates, 17. The girls, afraid they would be jailed as vagrants, stated that they had been gang-raped by a dozen blacks, among whom were the nine apprehended (the others had apparently escaped en route). The nine accused rapists were bound together with plowline, brought to Scottsboro for indictment and trial, and subsequently labeled the Scottsboro Boys. The enraged citizenry was further aroused by a rumor that the blacks had chewed off one of Nancy Bates's breasts, and national guardsmen had to protect the prisoners from lynchers. A request for a change in venue on behalf of the accused was turned down, and a swift jury trial was held on April 6–9, 1931.

The Scottsboro Boys received inadequate defense; one of their lawyers was an alcoholic who was drunk during the trial. Victoria Price testified that she and Bates had been raped several times each, but medical evidence indicated that the girls had not had sexual intercourse on the day of the alleged crime (however, they had definitely had intercourse before and were quietly rumored to be whores). Besides, there was no sign of force having been used against the girls. The prosecutor nevertheless told the jury at one point in the proceedings, "Guilty or not, let's get rid of these niggers." In the end, eight of the nine defendants were condemned to death; Roy White got life imprisonment because he was underage, although seven members of the jury had voted to condemn him, too.

In the year afterward, the case became a worldwide cause célèbre as the International Labor Defense (ILD), a Communist Party organ hired by the Scottsboro Boys' parents, organized demonstrations in America, Europe, and Latin America in support of the boys' innocence. The ILD retained a prominent lawyer named Samuel S. Leibowitz, who was slandered as the "New York Jew nigger lover," and on November 7, 1932, the U.S. Supreme Court ordered a new trial, ruling that the boys had had insufficient counsel in 1931. A prolonged legal battle then ensued that included several trials involving the boys.

Leibowitz succeed in 1933 in having Nancy Bates withdraw her testimony against Clarence Norris, who still was found guilty by a jury. Carrying the battle to the Supreme Court again, Leibowitz argued that the Scottsboro Boys had been denied a fair trial because of the unconstitutional exclusion of blacks from the jury; the high court reversed several convictions against members of the black group in 1935, but new grand-jury indictments for rape kept the boys in prison. During these years, well-known figures such as Clarence Darrow (who aided the defense committee after 1935), Theodore Dreiser, and Albert Einstein supported the

Scottsboro Boys' claims of innocence, and a number of American foreign embassies and consulates were stoned and picketed (an American bank in Cuba was bombed as well).

In late 1935 the Scottsboro Defense Committee was established by the ILD, the National Association for the Advancement of Colored People (NAACP) (which assumed most of the legal costs from then on), the American Civil Liberties Union (ACLU), and other liberal groups. The Alabama court system gradually came under fire, and the prosecution began to realize that executions of the defendants were not imminent. In 1937 Montgomery, White, Williams, and Roberson were set free in an agreement with the defense committee; the five other black youths were then prosecuted for assault. Norris was sentenced to death, Wright to 95 years' imprisonment, Weems and Patterson to 75 years each, and Powell to 20 years. Afterward the defense committee, after failing to get the governor of Alabama to pardon the boys, began to negotiate with the state parole board to free them. Finally, in 1943, Norris (whose sentence had been commuted to life in prison) and Weems were paroled; in 1948 Powell was freed and Patterson broke out of prison (two years later he was caught by the FBI in Detroit, but the governor of Michigan agreed to the NAACP's request not to extradite him to Alabama, and Patterson remained in Alabama on a conviction of manslaughter). In 1950 Wright obtained his freedom.

Norris violated his Alabama parole conditions and was returned to prison for two years. However, upon his release on parole in 1946, he fled to Ohio and later to New York. While a fugitive under Alabama law, he fought to clear his name and was finally granted a pardon by Alabama Governor George C. Wallace in 1976; many black and white Southerners cheered him in 1977 when he accepted the pardon, feeling that he had heroically partially exonerated the other Scottsboro Boys, whom many believed had been the victims of Alabama injustice, the result of hostile rascist views. Norris died at age 76 in New York City in 1989.

Jean SEBERG: slandered and suicidal

On September 8, 1979, the dead, decomposed body of frail, 40-year-old movie actress Jean Seberg was discovered wrapped in a blanket in her car on a street in Paris, France. She had been missing for 10 days. Beside her was a tube of barbiturates, an empty body of mineral water, and a suicide note written in French to her son Diego. "Forgive me. I can no longer live with my nerves," explained the once celebrated star.

At a news conference in Paris two days later, the French author and diplomat Romain Gary, who had been Seberg's husband from 1963 to 1972, declared in a voice trembling with emotion that "Jean Seberg was destroyed by the FBI." He produced documents showing that the Federal Bureau of Investigation (FBI) had initiated a secret smear campaign against her in 1970. Allegedly she had been impregnated before that time by a black leader of the Black Panther Party, a militant organization in the United States. Gary explained that "she never got over the calumny, and that's why she lost her child in birth. She wanted the child to be buried in a glass coffin in order to prove that it was white." From that time on, added Gary, Seberg had gone "from one psychiatric clinic to another, from one suicide attempt to another. She tried to kill herself seven times, usually on the anniversary of her little girl's birth."

Four days after Seberg's death, on September 14, 1979, the FBI made the startling admission that, as part of its counterintelligence program called COINTEL-PRO, its agents had clandestinely planted the scandalous 1970 story concerning the paternity of Seberg's second child; American news organizations spread the rumor, by which the FBI hoped to "neutralize" the actress, who was an important financial supporter of the Black Panthers. The FBI concluded by saying that "the days when the FBI used derogatory information to combat advocates of unpopular causes have long since passed. We are out of that forever."

Born and raised in Marshalltown, Iowa, Jean Seberg aspired to an acting career throughout her teen years. After graduating from high school in 1956, she tried her hand briefly in summer stock before being "discovered" by Hollywood film director Otto Preminger during his well-publicized worldwide talent hunt for an unknown actress to play the lead in his movie *St. Joan*. She starred as Joan of Arc and received scathing reviews after the movie was seen in 1957. *St. Joan* achieved "international flopdom," Seberg later said. Her second film, *Bonjour Tristesse* (1958), was also panned by the American critics, but the French seemed more receptive. Seberg gained renown if not critical acclaim. She was famed for her short-cropped blond hair.

At age 19, Seberg married a Parisian lawyer, François Moreuil, but their marriage was shaky from the beginning. In 1959 she starred in a French film called *Breathless,* which was later hailed as significant in the French New Wave movement. She then became a cult heroine in France, where her husband introduced her to Romain Gary. While making some popular arty films, including *The Five-Day Lover* (1960), she and Gary, who was also married, carried on a scandalous romance. Seberg moved in select society and traveled back and forth between America and Europe.

The crowning achievement of her career was *Lilith* (1964), in which she starred as a catatonic schizophrenic in a mental hospital, who lures an orderly (played by Warren Beatty) into her ruinous folly. Made by Columbia Pictures, *Lilith* at first played to empty movie houses in the United States, but Seberg's acting was praised by many critics. While making the film, she secretly gave birth to a son officially named Alexandre Diego Gary,

who was thought by some to have been born in mid-1962. After the child's birth, both Seberg and Gary were divorced by the respective spouses and were formally wedded in October 1963. They recorded Diego's birth as having occurred 10 days later.

Seberg's strong liberal political views became widely known in 1968, when she openly opposed the Vietnam War and racism and voiced support for the blacks and civil rights in America. In Los Angeles, California, she embraced the cause of black militants, first the Black Muslims and then the Black Panthers. According to what she told a reporter for the *International Herald Tribune* in the last year of her life, she had affairs in the years 1969–70 with two black nationalists, whom she did not name. One of them was evidently Hakim Jamal, an extremist Black Muslim; the other was Raymond "Masai" Hewitt, a Marxist Black Panther leader in Los Angeles. The FBI targeted Seberg as a Panther sympathizer and a "wanton collaborator with the enemy," according to author David Richards's book *Played Out: The Jean Seberg Story* (1981). In June 1969, the FBI recommended that "an active discreet investigation be instituted on American actress Jean Seberg who is providing funds and assistance to black extremists, including leaders of the Black Panther Party." Her pregnancy in 1970 became the focus of attention, and the paternity of her unborn child was "smeared" and gossiped about in the *Los Angeles Times* and other publications. *Newsweek* said she was expecting a baby by "a black activist she met in California." Although Gary later said her pregnancy was his doing, Seberg confessed in her final year that the father was a Mexican "revolutionary" with whom she had had an affair while making a movie in Durango, Mexico.

In Geneva, Switzerland, on August 23, 1970, Seberg gave birth prematurely by Caesarean section to a girl, Nina, who died two days later. The actress then journeyed to Marshalltown to display the dead infant in an open casket; some saw the tiny girl as light-skinned with Caucasian features, and some did not. Depressed, Seberg eventually brought a libel suit against *Newsweek* in France, where truth is not an acknowledged defense against a charge of defamation of character. A six-month-long trial in 1971 ended in the court declaring that Seberg's and Gary's privacy had been violated but that *Newsweek* had not "killed" Nina. The magazine was ordered to pay about $11,000 in damages, plus fines.

Seberg, slowly becoming psychologically ill, began to indulge constantly in pills and liquor; her film career faded and she began to have numerous nervous breakdowns and was in and out of clinics in Paris. Soon after her divorce from Gary in 1972, she married Dennis Berry, a struggling filmmaker, who separated from her about four years later. Often overweight and haggard, Seberg became increasingly paranoid, picking up sleeping partners in bars and falling into dire financial straits.

In 1979 she married her lover, Ahmed Hasni, a young Algerian who reported her missing on August 30. After police found her body 10 days later, an autopsy concluded that she had succumbed to an overdose of barbiturates, but questions about this have lingered.

Seberg's macabre ending haunted Romain Gary, who fatally shot himself in the head in his Paris bedroom on December 2, 1980. The 66-year-old novelist left a suicide note saying that his death had "no connection with Jean Seberg." He suggested that it was linked to the last words of his last novel: "I have said all I have to say."

Sam SHEPPARD: victim of courtroom bedlam

On July 4, 1954, Marilyn Reese Sheppard, a 31-year-old pregnant housewife, was found bludgeoned to death in her suburban Cleveland, Ohio, home. Her seven-year-old son, sleeping in another room, was unharmed. Her husband, 30-year-old osteopathic physician Samuel H. Sheppard, was injured. Though at first he received a great deal of sympathy he was soon facing charges of murder.

Early on, the three Cleveland newspapers—the *Press,* the *Plain Dealer,* and the now-defunct *News*—began suggesting that Sheppard was the murderer. Louis B. Seltzer, editor of the *Press,* took on the case as a crusade. In a July 20 front-page editorial entitled "Somebody is Getting Away with Murder," Seltzer, claiming that Sheppard's friends, family, and lawyers were protecting him from an investigation, demanded that Sheppard be "subjected instantly to the same third-degree to which any other person under similar circumstances is subjected."

Two days later the local coroner began an inquest. It was held in a school gymnasium so that the expected large crowds could be accommodated. The coroner forcibly ejected Sheppard's lawyer and then publicly grilled the osteopath for more than five hours about his sex life in and out of marriage. A *Press* headline soon read "Why Isn't Sam Sheppard in Jail? Quit Stalling, Bring Him In."

Sheppard was arrested three weeks after the murder. His nine-week trial made headlines around the world. The prosecutors in the case, who never turned up a murder weapon, suggested that Sheppard's motive concerned an affair he had had with a former laboratory technician at the hospital (which had been founded by his father) where he worked. Sheppard, who maintained his innocence, stated that his wife had been killed by a "bushy haired" intruder. He contended that his wife's screams from upstairs had awakened him while he was sleeping on the living-room sofa. As he went to investigate the screams, said Sheppard, he had been knocked unconscious by a blow from behind. On awakening he had found his wife dead; he had heard the intruder below and gave chase, only to be knocked out again. He claimed to have awakened on the Lake Erie beach be-hind his home, after which he returned to the house and telephoned for assistance.

The presiding judge at the trial was Edward Blythin, who at a pretrial hearing confided to columnist Dorothy Kilgallen: "It's an open and shut case . . . he's guilty as hell." The barrage of publicity continued. Shortly before the trial the *News* accused Sheppard's attorney, William Corrigan, of "massive jury tampering" for polling Clevelanders' attitudes in an unsuccessful attempt to get a change of venue. During the trial, radio broadcaster Bob Considine suggested that Sheppard was, like Alger HISS, a perjurer. Most of the jurors read about the case both before and during the trial; they were sequestered only when they retired to reach a verdict. Reporters virtually took over the courtroom. Judge Blythin allowed the press to be seated within the bar of the courtroom and only a few feet from the jury box. Sheppard and his attorneys had to leave the room in order to hold private conversations.

After five days of deliberation, the jury of seven men and five women convicted Sheppard of second-degree murder. Still maintaining his innocence, Sheppard was sentenced to life in prison. He continued to file legal appeals, and finally, in 1964, U.S. District Judge Carl Weinman released Sheppard and ordered a new trial. While Weinman did not rule directly on Sheppard's guilt or innocence, he argued that the press had prevented Sheppard from receiving an unbiased trial. He called the Sheppard trial a "mockery of justice," castigating the *Cleveland Press* in particular for taking upon itself "the role of accuser, judge and jury."

In 1966, in an 8-1 decision, the U.S. Supreme Court agreed with the district court, setting aside the conviction on the grounds that "inherently prejudicial publicity" had prevented the osteopath from receiving a fair trial. The court compared the atmosphere of the 1954 trial to a carnival. According to the court decision, "Bedlam reigned at the courthouse," and some of the sensational publicity reached at least some jurors.

The Supreme Court's ruling opened the way for a new trial. At his 1966 retrial, Sheppard, defended this time by the aggressive attorney F. Lee Bailey, was acquitted.

Following his acquittal Sheppard continued to make news. He began a medical practice at the Youngstown, Ohio, Osteopathic Hospital but resigned in 1968 after malpractice suits over the deaths of two patients. His marriage to a German woman with whom he had conducted a "pen pal" romance while he was in prison ended in divorce. He finally took up professional wrestling and married his wrestling manager's daughter. Sheppard died in 1970 at the age of 46.

Sheppard's son worked for years to clear his father's name and, in 1997, his lawyer announced that findings from forensic DNA tests on dried blood preserved from the 1954 crime scene boosted Sam Sheppard's alibi—

that a "bushy haired" intruder killed his pregnant wife. The tests showed the blood could not be Marilyn's and could possibly belong to 67-year-old Richard Eberling, who once washed windows at the Sheppard home and was briefly a suspect. Eberling, then imprisoned on another murder charge, declared his innocence. The dried blood could have become contaminated or be a mixture of two people's blood, according to a forensic scientist.

Karen SILKWOOD: whistleblower

In the fall of 1972, 28-year-old Karen Gay Silkwood, a recent divorcee, began working at the Kerr-McGee Corporation's Cimarron plutonium-processing plant near Oklahoma City, Oklahoma. The plant manufactured highly radioactive plutonium fuel rods for nuclear reactors. As a laboratory technician, Silkwood joined the Oil, Chemical, and Atomic Workers' Union (OCAW) and became actively involved in maintaining safe working conditions at the plant for her fellow employees. In the summer of 1974, as an elected union representative, she observed seemingly lax safety standards after production had increased and new employees, some of whom in her opinion were ill-trained, took jobs of responsibility. She learned that several workers had become contaminated by radiation and had complained about safety violations. She herself had to undergo decontamination because of radiation exposure.

Officials at the OCAW national headquarters in Washington, D.C., learned personally from Silkwood about the poor plant conditions at Kerr-McGee and asked her to try to collect positive evidence of violations secretly and give it to them. At the time Silkwood discovered that plutonium, an extremely poisonous chemical element, was possibly carcinogenic. After continuing to gather information against Kerr-McGee (its use of allegedly defective rods, among other things), she again became contaminated by radiation. Her contamination seemed suspicious because the plutonium at the plant was supposedly kept by law out of danger to human beings. She reported to the Oklahoma State Health Department and the Atomic Energy Commission that she had been contaminated in her own apartment. When physicians reported that her radiation contamination would not endanger her, Silkwood continued to work in the plant.

On the evening of November 13, 1974, Silkwood left a union meeting in Crescent, Oklahoma, to drive in her white Honda Civic automobile to Oklahoma City, some 35 miles away. She planned to meet with and hand over some documents she had collected to Steve Wodka, an OCAW official, and to a *New York Times* reporter. Along the route, her car went off the left side of the highway into a long ditch and smashed into the wall of a concrete culvert, killing Silkwood. An autopsy revealed that her blood, stomach, and liver contained methaqualone, a sleep inducing drug, and it was surmised that she had fallen asleep at the wheel. However, a later investigation by the OCAW strongly speculated that foul play had been involved in her death; there was circumstantial evidence that her car had been forced off the road and into the culvert (one curiosity was that the car's rear bumper had metallic scratches, as if it had been hit by another vehicle). In addition, the documents supposedly in Silkwood's possession were never found. The U.S. Justice Department and the Federal Bureau of Investigation (FBI) both investigated and found no wrongdoing.

A suit against Kerr-McGee filed by Silkwood's parents eventually reached federal court in Oklahoma City in 1979. Defense lawyers claimed that Silkwood had intentionally contaminated herself with plutonium in her own apartment in an effort to dramatize the danger at the plant. Both sides agreed that the radioactive substance discovered in her apartment had come from the plant, but Silkwood's supporters contended that Kerr-McGee had placed it there to frighten her and thus end her union-influenced probing and serious protests against the company. On May 18, 1979, the jury awarded $10.5 million in punitive damages to the estate of Karen Silkwood. Kerr-McGee appealed the decision, which was overturned by the U.S. Court of Appeals for the 10th Circuit in 1981 (the $10.5 million award was ruled to have infringed on the U.S. government's exclusivity in regulating safety in the nuclear power industry). The Silkwood estate appealed, and the case was accepted for review by the U.S. Supreme Court in 1983. During that year the controversial story of Karen Silkwood was seen in a newly released film, *Silkwood*, written by Nora Ephron and Alice Arlen. After hearing extensive arguments by both sides, the Supreme Court ruled, on January 11, 1984, that courts could impose punitive damages on the nuclear-power industry for violations of safety; it remanded the case to the circuit court to decide what punitive damages, if any, the Silkwood estate should receive.

On August 22, 1986, attorneys for the Silkwood estate and Kerr-McGee announced the settlement of the case, which charged the latter with negligence and inadequate safety procedures, as well as responsibility for contaminating Karen Silkwood and her apartment with plutonium. Kerr-McGee, which never admitted any wrongdoing, agreed to pay $1.3 million to the attorneys and beneficiaries of the Silkwood estate, in return for which all claims the Silkwoods might have against the company were ended. Karen's father said the company would "never admit their guilt" but that his daughter would always be remembered "as a person who didn't give up." And he added that "The courts proved what she said was true."

O. J. SIMPSON: sports hero and accused slayer

In 1994, Nicole Brown Simpson and Ronald L. Goldman were found slashed to death outside her Los Angeles condominium. The prime suspect was her ex-husband, Orenthal James (O. J.) Simpson. O. J. was one of the greatest running backs in the history of American football. After winning the 1969 Heisman Trophy, presented annually to the best college player, he played nine seasons for the Buffalo Bills and became the first player to rush for 2,000 yards in a single season. Upon retiring from football he was inducted into the NFL Hall of Fame. He then became a sports commentator and starred in several movies and commercials. He was one of America's best-loved celebrities.

The relationship between O. J. (who was black) and Nicole (who was white) was a stormy one. They began

Former football star O. J. Simpson and Nicole Brown, whom he married in 1985, seen together at a Beverly Hills party in May 1980. After seven years of marriage and two children, they divorced. Simpson was arrested by police on June 17, 1994, as a suspect in the brutal killing of his ex-wife and one of her friends, Ronald Goldman, five days earlier. Simpson pleaded not guilty, was acquitted in a criminal trial, and later found liable in a civil case. (AP/Wide World Photos)

dating in 1977, when he was 30 and married and she was 18, and were married in 1985. Seven years later they divorced, partly because of his affairs with other women and partly because he beat her repeatedly. After one fight Nicole called the police, and he was charged with spousal battery; he pleaded no contest and received two years' probation.

The murder case took a bizarre twist even before it reached the courtroom. Instead of turning himself in, as his lawyer had arranged, O. J. led the Los Angeles police on a low-speed chase through the city's freeways which ended several hours later in his own driveway. The chase was broadcast live on national television, thus kicking off live media coverage of the most publicized murder trial in American history.

The prosecution believed it had an airtight case against O. J. The most damning piece of evidence was the results of DNA testing that showed beyond a reasonable doubt that his blood was at the murder scene and the blood of Nicole and Goldman was in O. J.'s automobile. Moreover, O. J. never offered a convincing explanation for his whereabouts at the time of the murders or for what appeared to be knife cuts on his hands; other circumstantial evidence strongly suggested his guilt. Reportedly worth about $10 million, O. J. hired the best attorneys money could buy. His defense team succeeded in shifting the focus away from the evidence and onto the Los Angeles Police Department, which suffered from its racist image in the black community. O. J.'s lawyers zeroed in on Mark Fuhrman, one of the case's lead detectives, establishing both his deep-seated racism and his lack of credibility. In the minds of millions of television viewers across the country, it seemed clear that a racist, white-controlled police department was trying to frame an innocent black man. The clincher came when the prosecution made O. J. try on a bloody glove found at the murder scene which matched another bloody glove found in his home. To the prosecution's utter amazement the glove did not fit, thus bolstering the defense's claim that the gloves had been planted by the police. After this shocker, the trial was essentially over. Having listened to nine months of testimony, most of which had been televised nationally, the jury took less than four hours to return a verdict of "not guilty."

While millions of Americans rejoiced over the verdict, many others were outraged by it. Generally speaking, blacks believed that O. J. was innocent while whites believed that he was guilty. Many Americans of both races were convinced that, had O. J. been a man of modest means rather than a wealthy sports hero, he would have been convicted. The verdict fueled a rancorous national debate on topics central to the trial, such as spousal abuse, racism and the police, and the ability of the American legal system to dispense justice regardless of a defendant's fame or fortune.

This debate was intensified by the results of O. J.'s second trial. In 1997 the victims' families sued O. J. in civil court for wrongful death. Unlike a criminal trial, in which conviction requires that all 12 jurors must be convinced of the defendant's guilt beyond a reasonable doubt, a civil trial requires that nine jurors believe that the plaintiff's case is stronger than the defendant's. In this case, the clincher involved bloody footprints made at the murder scene by a pair of size 12 Bruno Magli shoes. When O. J. emphatically denied owning such shoes, the plaintiffs' attorneys produced photographs of O. J. wearing a pair at a 1993 Bills football game. This time, a predominantly white jury found O. J. liable in the two deaths and awarded the plaintiffs $33.5 million, more money than O. J. was ever likely to earn. His appeal of the award was rejected by a judge who said the amount was too low.

SISTER CARRIE: Theodore Dreiser's legend of "suppression"

Running completely counter to the sentiment of the day, no one could have expected Theodore Dreiser's pessimistic first novel *Sister Carrie* to ever be published. But, due to the influence of an excited editor, the book was accepted for publication by Doubleday, Page, and Company. It was published on November 8, 1900, but not until Frank Doubleday himself had tried to break the contract with Dreiser.

Unfashionably blunt and pessimistic for its time, *Sister Carrie* seemed an unlikely candidate for publication. Harper's turned down the book as too realistic but recommended Doubleday, Page, and Company, which had recently published Frank Norris's *McTeague* (1899), a violent novel of slum life in San Francisco. Norris, who had become one of Doubleday's reader-editors, was excited about Dreiser's novel and spread his excitement to a partner, Walker Hines Page. A contract sealed the acceptance of the novel, despite the misgivings of Henry Lanier, a junior partner in the publishing company. Frank Doubleday, then in Europe with his wife Neltje to secure American rights to the novels of Emile Zola, returned to read Dreiser's manuscript and to realize that, in an America dominated by the somewhat sentimentally realistic novels of William Dean Howells (which had nevertheless been criticized in the *Atlantic* magazine), *Sister Carrie* was a direct affront to the mores of the time. Doubleday's wife, struck by the heartlessness of the character Carrie, whom she considered to be evil, agreed.

At first, Doubleday tried to get out of the contract by handling Dreiser gently: if Dreiser would postpone *Sister Carrie* or withdraw it, he would consider another of Dreiser's works then in progress. Guided by his friend Arthur Henry, Dreiser chose to be adamant; he saw the score as three to one in his favor: Norris, Page, and maybe Lanier versus Doubleday.

Doubleday then tried to convince Dreiser that the illicit liaisons between Carrie and first Drouet and then Hurstwood would engender much negative criticism and that the failure to have the novel end with a wholesome moral lesson (as in the Norris book) would doom it. Dreiser, whose development of a new kind of realism would later redound to his credit, stubbornly but wisely disagreed.

Doubleday next reversed Dreiser's three-to-one advantage by confronting Page and Lanier, and their deference (to Doubleday, and not to his wife, as Dreiser would have it) allowed Doubleday to approach Dreiser with a suggestion from Lanier: Doubleday would use his considerable prestige to interest any or all of five other major publishers in *Carrie*. Dreiser remained adamant and, beset by the developing failure of his marriage, became angry enough to demand observance of the contract.

Now angry himself, Doubleday did just that but in the contract's minimal terms. Sheets for 1,250 copies of the book were printed, but only 1,000 were bound. Of these, 127 were sent to reviewers, who had to consider the novel explosive by the moral standards of 1900.

Most of the critics, confronted with a novel of a type outside their experience, were revolted by its immorality, its failure to punish its naively wayward heroine (Carrie), the vulgarity of its characters and their colloquial language, its authorial sympathy for its fallen personae, its pessimism, and the fact that its characters usually avoided exercising their free will. In most of the press, *Sister Carrie* was called a "disgrace"; the public lacked the vitality to think for itself.

By the end of 1900, only 456 copies of the novel had been sold, and Dreiser had earned only $68.40 in royalties. Furthermore, Dreiser was refused advertising for the book by Doubleday, who used a "good-money-after-bad" argument to justify this stance.

Yet neither Dreiser nor *Sister Carrie* actually suffered. In 1901 Dreiser and Henry produced an abridged version of the book for Heinemann's Dollar Library of American Fiction and for sale in England. It gained a good press abroad; the English had read Zola, who was still then unknown to most Americans. Dreiser got control of the Doubleday printing plates, and a 4,600-copy edition of *Carrie* by B. W. Dodge in 1907 sold so well that Grosset & Dunlap reprinted 10,000 copies in 1908. Dreiser's second novel, *Jennie Gerhardt,* although panned in 1912, sold so rapidly that Dreiser gave up journalism as a career to devote himself to writing novels.

He then moved gradually toward the crowning success of his 1925 *An American Tragedy* but never recanted his legend of the 1900 *Carrie* "suppression."

Eddie SLOVIK. See U.S. ARMY: the execution of Eddie Slovik.

Len SMALL: pardoning governor

Len Small, governor of Illinois from 1921 through 1928, headed one of the most unprincipled administrations in that state's history. During his seven-year stint as governor, he repeatedly targeted wrongdoers for conviction, with the express purpose of pardoning them in return for cash bribes. Astounding as it seems to be today, the procedure was repeated without wide exposure approximately every two and one-half days during his term in office.

Small's political career began as a little one, but the one-time farmer quickly grew in craftiness and influence under the tutelage of Chicago mayor William Hale ("Big Bill") Thompson. From the very beginning of his education in Chicago politics, Small lined his pockets with money, and because Thompson's power extended deeply into state spheres, Small was soon serving Thompson and himself in the lucrative position of state treasurer. His greed was insatiable: even as he campaigned for the Illinois governorship, he surreptitiously embezzled $600,000 from the state assets under his guardianship.

The embezzlement was not discovered until Small had been sworn into office; an indictment and trial followed. The experience of undergoing judicial arraignment did not, however, deter Small. He found a way to circumvent the authority of the court. He teamed up with a notorious gunman, a lawyer turned crook, and a dishonorable union official to bribe and threaten members of the jury and their families. He was, in due course, acquitted.

Despite his newly cleared record, Governor Small ignored the opportunity to keep himself immaculate. Power continued to corrupt him. Instead of repaying the trio that had helped him during his trial by pardoning them for such various offenses as murder and jury tampering, he developed a new money-making scheme—under-the-counter pardons. During the years of his governorship, he blatantly sold more than 8,000 pardons for cash and earned the hardly enviable moniker "Pardoning Governor of Illinois."

Small's pardoning method was simple. With "Big Bill" Thompson as backstop and coach, Robert E. Crowe, the state's attorney for Cook County (Chicago and environs), would convict a wrongdoer, usually one with good financial assets. Word would secretly reach the guilty party that money equaled freedom. That money would reach Small, and the felon would, through a pardon, find himself a free man. Small and Crowe would then split the proceeds. Then the process would begin again. Crowe would procure another conviction, words and money would circulate, and another felon would return to the world of the righteous.

Even more astounding is the fact that until 1928, the Small-Crowe ticket was returned to office repeatedly. Perhaps the publicity given to the Al Capone gang and other mobsters, who made most Americans equate Cook County, Illinois, with crime, had kept the comparatively tame skullduggery of Crowe and Small out of the press.

Their criminal activity eventually became known, however. In 1928, in the so-called Pineapple Primary (so called because both political sides hired mobsters who set off "pineapples," or bombs, to frighten office seekers and voters), Illinois citizens balloted in record numbers against the corrupt and powerful pair. Prison terms for Small and Crowe followed their trial, and this time their hope for a pardon-for-cash was nil.

Harold SMITH: America's top boxing promoter, an embezzler

A former promoter of rock musicians, Harold J. Smith decided to switch to promoting boxing matches and formed Muhammad Ali Professional Sports (MAPS), which spared nothing to attract the very best boxers in the business and the most publicity. One of the largest purses of all time was to be offered at a Madison Square Garden boxing event that Smith had promoted for February 23, 1981, but several weeks before the fights, Smith, his family, and some cronies suddenly disappeared from public view. The large Wells Fargo Bank, based in San Francisco, California, provided an explanation for the mysterious vanishing act. It filed suit against Smith, two former bank employees, and others,

Black boxing promoter Harold Smith, alias for Ross Fields, listens to his attorney, Robert Michaels, during a news conference in Los Angeles in April 1981. Smith was charged with embezzling $21 million from the Wells Fargo Bank. (UPI/Bettmann Newsphotos)

charging that the men had embezzled $21.3 million from the bank's branch in Beverly Hills.

Harold Smith was a clever promoter who had come to know three-time heavyweight boxing champion Muhammad Ali at his training camp and in 1977 had persuaded Ali to lend his name to a track club for underprivileged youth, called Muhammad Ali Amateur Sports. A couple of years later, Smith decided to move into professional boxing and set up Muhammad Ali Professional Sports. Ali was in no way involved in its operations but consented to the use of his name for a $10,000 fee for each fight the organization promoted. Smith seemed to have oodles of money. He bought a $1 million house in California, owned his own jet airplane and a large cabin cruiser, and frequently arrived in Las Vegas, Nevada, with suitcases full of cash. He explained that the money came from his wealthy wife, Lee. When he was promoting fights, he paid the boxers promptly and well. He seemed unperturbed by heavy losses. The four-fight event in New York's Madison Square Garden was to have been his biggest, most promoted affair up to that time.

But somewhere things took a wrong turn. Benjamin Lewis, operations manager of Wells Fargo's Beverly Hills branch and a director of MAPS, went on the lam with Smith and his family. The next two months were like a cops-and-robbers show. Smith occasionally communicated with sportswriters or with television and radio stations in garbled telephone conversations or prerecorded tapes. At first, he reported that he had fled to Switzerland and hidden his family there. Then he said that his four-year-old son had been kidnapped by Japanese Mafia mobsters. He also told of being chased along the snow-packed back streets of Aspen, Colorado, by the Federal Bureau of Investigation (FBI) and across a rain-drenched parking lot in Sacramento, California, by Wells Fargo agents. He reported paying strangers to drive his fleeing group to airports and to back entrances of hotels. Apparently the Smiths had moved from one motel and hotel to another throughout California and the Northwest.

When Wells Fargo charged Smith and his associates with embezzlement, Smith countered that this was just a "smoke screen." According to him the truth was that 15 of the Wells Fargo Bank's officials had stolen between $200 and $300 million from the bank during the past decade and that they were merely setting him and Lewis up as "pigeons." The president of MAPS, Sam Marshall, who had been a former assistant manager of the Wells Fargo Bank in Beverly Hills, was also accused of fraud by the bank. He, however, did not seek to escape arrest.

Shortly after Smith's disappearance, the courts froze his assets. As bank and law-enforcement officials studied the records, they concluded that the embezzlement scheme permitted MAPS's accounts to take advantage of the built-in delays in Wells Fargo's computerized record of transactions between its 343 branches and that knowledgeable employees could evade sophisticated controls of the branch-settlement account system. They further concluded that $21.3 million had been stolen since sometime in 1978.

After weeks of chasing him, the FBI arrested Smith on April 5, 1981. Two days later, after intense questioning, he confessed that his real name was Ross Eugene Fields and that he was wanted in North Carolina and several other states for forgery and passing bad checks. Further, it was discovered that his wife's true name was Alice Vicki Darrow and that she had been a fugitive from federal authorities since 1975, charged with transporting stolen securities and bad checks across state lines. Soon afterward Smith/Fields's attorney, Jennifer King, was indicted for allegedly counseling the promoter's secretary to lie to the jury about her knowledge of MAPS's financial records. Smith himself was indicted on charges of passport fraud and was sentenced to 40 consecutive weekends in jail.

In July 1981, a federal grand jury indicted Smith/Fields and Lewis and Marshall on conspiring to defraud Wells Fargo of $21.3 million. Lewis pleaded guilty and agreed to cooperate with the prosecution; Smith and Marshall pleaded not guilty, and their trial dragged on through the fall of 1981. Though Smith was set free on bail on November 27, his freedom was short-lived. Prison sentences were announced at intervals in early 1982: Lewis received five years, Marshall got three years, and Smith/Fields received 10 years and a $30,000 fine, plus 3,000 hours of community service to perform upon his release.

Jesse SMITH: gofor-turned-crook

Unlike the major malefactors that forever marred the reputation of the Harding Administration in the first quarter of this century, Jesse W. Smith played a small and inconsequential role. But while the major figures merely went free or to prison, Smith was forced into suicide. He fatally shot himself on May 30, 1921.

Smith began innocently enough as a servant to one of the bigger players in the Harding scenario. Adopted informally as a boy by Harry DAUGHERTY, Harding's much accused but never convicted attorney general, Smith had been established as a department-store owner by his mentor. It was Daugherty who made him a member of the so-called Ohio Gang when Harding and company took over Washington, D.C.

From his youth onward, Smith had been devotedly grateful to Daugherty. He worked strenuously for Harding's election, and when the Harding entourage moved to Washington, Smith followed. Dwelling with Daugherty for two lengthy periods, he became indispensable to his father figure, acting out such roles as valet, private secretary, messenger, and accountant. He had a desk on the first floor of Daugherty's residence, then used for the reception of Harding supporters who came to dicker about patronage. And he was present when the Hardings or Albert Fall or Charles FORBES or Thomas MILLER made social calls. Smith was also part of Harding's poker club, but no evidence suggests that he was close to the president himself.

When the new administration had settled in, Smith found himself promoted from his chore-boy status. He had a desk in the Justice Department, even though he was never on a government payroll, he was closer to Daugherty than any of his assistant attorneys general, and he was partly responsible for Daugherty's mail. He was also a fixture in a new Harding patronage center, a kind of racket headquarters on K Street called the Little Green House.

His new status caused Smith to feel that he had become an important influence peddler, guiding and working with even more minor Ohioans than himself. He accepted bribes for immunity from Justice Department prosecution, worked deals in stocks and oil, and—because it was the Prohibition era—sold permits to withdraw liquor from bonded government warehouses. The zenith of his influence-peddling career at the K Street house occurred when he accepted $250,000 from George L. Remus, a Chicago bootlegging czar, to ensure against the latter's arrest and prosecution by agents of the Justice Department. His success at this petty graft made Smith feel inviolate. He felt he was ready for more important tasks.

He soon joined the conspiracy involving Thomas Miller, custodian of the Alien Property Office. He handled $224,000 in payoffs, including a deposit of $50,000 in the Washington Court, Ohio, bank owned by Harry Daugherty's brother. The purpose and disposal of the account, marked "Jess Smith Extra No. 3," has never been clarified; it was alleged to be a political account used by Daugherty, but its records were destroyed by the bank owner when the Harding era was discovered to have been crime-riddled.

All this evidence, not to mention unproved allegations, surfaced during a 1923 Senate investigation. Smith, however, was dead by this time. The sensational revelations of the Charles Forbes/Veterans' Bureau scandal had made Harding suspicious of persons like Smith, who had been ordered to return to Ohio. Sick with diabetes and (according to his divorced wife's trial testimony) fearful for his life, he had come back from Ohio to Washington with a gun and taken his own life in Daugherty's apartment on May 30, 1921.

The Harding government tried unsuccessfully to cover up the suicide. The Justice Department acted hurriedly, suppressing the details of Smith's death. No autopsy was performed; an assistant White House physician who had never treated Smith blamed the suicide on despondency related to acute diabetes. The body was rushed to Ohio for a hurried burial. Rumors spread that Smith had been murdered to avoid exposure of Daugherty's operations. This, however, was unlikely, as Daugherty seemed truly grief stricken. He apparently attended a White House function the night of the suicide and spoiled the gathering with his gloom and dejection.

The 1923 testimony, which described Smith as "Daugherty's henchman," and a 1926 indictment of Miller and others connected with the alien property fraud, resulted in a most unusual posthumous verdict of guilty against Smith. Both airings mixed the facts of his wrongdoings with charges that were never thoroughly investigated.

William Kennedy SMITH: recklessness or evasion?
On Friday night, during Easter weekend of 1991, Senator Edward (Ted) M. Kennedy, his son Patrick, and nephew William Kennedy Smith were drinking and enjoying themselves at the trendy Au Bar night-spot in Palm Beach, Florida. When Au Bar closed, the three of them returned to the Kennedy family's beachfront estate accompanied by two women they had met at the bar. The next day, one of the women filed a complaint with the police stating that she had been raped during the early morning hours at the estate. The woman had contacted a rape hotline about five hours after leaving the mansion, and Palm Beach County sheriff investigators then met with her.

A week after receiving the complaint, the police had yet to question any possible witnesses, including bartenders, parking lot attendants, and members of the Kennedy family. They had not gathered any evidence at the site. Moreover, the police did not reveal the accused suspect's identity until almost two weeks later, claiming that they did not have a photograph for the victim to identify definitely her alleged rapist, even though photos of him had been on the front pages of area newspapers. The police then charged 30-year-old William Kennedy Smith, son of Senator Kennedy's sister Jean and her late husband Stephen E. Smith, with raping the woman, a 29-year-old single mother who remained unidentified. William Kennedy Smith, then a student at Georgetown University Medical School, said any allegation that he raped the woman was "a damnable lie." His 24-year-old cousin Patrick said that the first he had heard of the accusation was in the Florida papers, and 59-year-old Senator Kennedy declared it would not be appropriate to comment on the case. The woman's attorney, David Roth, told reporters that "attempts at damage control" by the Kennedys could be an obstruction of justice. Meanwhile, Palm Beach and its environs became the hub of an international media circus because of the scandal.

Over the summer, Smith's high-powered and aggressive legal team delved into the victim's past and announced that she suffered from psychological problems as a result of various traumatic events, including several abortions, and that her account of the "incident" was unreliable. Prosecutor Moira Lasch revealed that three other women were prepared to come forward and testify that Smith had sexually assaulted them. Apparently, they had kept silent all this time fearing that nobody would believe them. Later, Judge Mary Lupo deemed this testimony inadmissible because the charges were never investigated, nor was the prosecution able to show a definite pattern in Smith's assaults on women. The defense asked that the prosecution be reprimanded for jeopardizing Smith's rights to a fair trial.

During a grueling 10-day trial in December 1991, the victim's face was blurred on television and in photographs to conceal her identity (the media had respected this request). She spent several days on the witness stand and was subjected to an intensive five-hour cross-examination, during which she emotionally reiterated her charge that Smith had forcibly pinned her to the ground and sexually assaulted her. (The medical reports corroborated this.) However, the defense suggested that she had initiated the sexual encounter by removing her panty hose before she and Smith took a walk on the beach.

After only 77 minutes of deliberation, the six-member jury acquitted Smith, to the surprise of many. Hours later, some TV channels showed photos of Patricia Bowman, who later officially shed her anonymity with her decision to appear and be interviewed on ABC-TV (for which she received no compensation).

SOAP BOX DERBY SCANDAL

"Anyone participating in derby races with eyes and ears open would soon learn, as I did, that . . . the derby rules have been consistently and notoriously violated by some participants without censure or disqualification," claimed engineer Robert Lange, Sr. He had just admitted having helped his winning nephew, Jimmy Gronen, cheat at the 36th annual All-American Soap Box Derby in Akron, Ohio, in August 1973. Abuses and infractions of the rules had grown increasingly obvious during the preceding decade, and contenders had gotten away with them without being challenged. Lange was to be the straw that broke the camel's back.

When he steered his ultra-sophisticated, motorless racing car to victory at Derby Downs that August day in 1973, 14-year-old Jimmy Gronen of Boulder, Colorado, picked up both the gold championship cup and a $7,500 college scholarship. However, while performing an X-ray examination of Gronen's car, derby officials made a startling discovery: a large, strong electromagnet was hidden in the car's nose and was connected by two wires to a big, heavy battery concealed in the rear. Another wire ran from the battery to a

switch located just behind the driver's head. Backward pressure from the driver's plastic helmet turned on the battery switch, sending electric current from the battery to the magnet. At the very beginning of the race, when the heavy iron-plated starting gate fell backward and downward to allow the cars to begin coasting down the steep hill on which the race was held—supposedly solely by gravity—Gronen's car sprang forward just a little faster and thus got an initial, slight advantage over the rest of the competitors.

After the scandal was exposed, most of the public's anger was leveled at Robert Lange, Sr., with whom Gronen had been living in Boulder since the death of his father two years earlier (Gronen was originally from Dubuque, Iowa). Lange, whose son Robert, Jr., had won the derby the previous year, was accused of helping set up the electromagnet system in Gronen's car, as well as aiding in the construction of the car (Soap Box Derby rules required the competing boys and girls to do all the work themselves). Furthermore, Lange was accused of breaking other regulations that governed the cost of the car (which was not to exceed $75) as well as the racing car's overall construction, including steering assembly, wheels, and axles.

Lange had shipped Gronen's racer to California to have its modern aerodynamic body tested there in a wind tunnel. Lange, whose engineering expertise had made him wealthy through the development of a superior plastic ski boot, was accused of spending some $22,000 on his nephew's car, which was denounced for having illegal, professional axles and suspicious-looking tires. Derby officials also wanted to inspect the car in which Lange's son had triumphed the year before, but it had mysteriously disappeared.

In Boulder, District Attorney Alex Hunter charged Lange with two counts of contributing to the delinquency of a minor. Hunter was very upset by Lange's apparent moral laxity and his acceptance of the widespread "use of speed gimmicks" in racing. Looking into the scandal, he found out that 34 derby cars and six of the top 10 finishers in the 1973 race had been "doctored up." Lange was found guilty of both counts against him and, in a nonjudicial arrangement, agreed to contribute $2,000 to a local boys' club. He seemed rather shameless, until, in an interview, he acknowledged "I knew that this was a violation of the official derby rules and consider it now to be a serious mistake in judgment." He admitted to having rigged up the magnetic contraption in his nephew's car but said he truly felt that it was "necessary" cheating if his nephew was to be competitive at Akron, where so many others had professionally built cars or racers in violation of the rules.

The Boulder Jaycees took away Gronen's win in the Colorado championship, which had qualified him to go to Akron to race in the All-American derby. Parents of near-winners had angrily protested to the Jaycees, who attempted in vain to induce Gronen to relinquish his trophy, and awarded another trophy to the second-place winner, who was declared the official winner.

SOUTH IMPROVEMENT COMPANY. See John D. ROCKEFELLER: the South Improvement ploy.

George SPANTON. See The PENTAGON: the persecution of George Spanton.

SPECTRA: a beneficial literary hoax

The novelist-critic Thomas Ybarra, writing in the *New York Times Magazine* of June 2, 1918, concluded that the perpetrators of the *Spectra* hoax would ultimately be ranked beside the great literary tricksters of all times. The hoaxers, both critically acclaimed poets, were Witter Bynner and Arthur Davison Ficke. The objective of their plot was to satirize the absurdities and pretensions of the many "schools" of poetry born in America and to deflate those critics who were overeager to discover and protect the avant garde. Their imposture achieved results far beyond their expectations: their aesthetic manifesto and illustrative poems, published in the autumn of 1916 as *Spectra: A Book of Poetic Experiments,* attracted, both negatively and positively, critics, editors, poets, and aspirants to poetic fame through April 1918, when Bynner announced that the "Spectrist School" was a fraud.

The imposture idea was conceived by Bynner in February 1916 as he traveled to Davenport, Iowa, to visit Ficke and his wife. Like Bynner, Ficke was annoyed by such "schools" as Vorticism, Futurism, Imagism, and Chorism. Delighted with a hearty joke, Ficke agreed to collaborate in the hoax. He and Bynner first chose foreign-sounding pseudonyms: Bynner became Emanuel Morgan, an American artist lately returned from Paris and a novice to poetry; Ficke became Anne Knish, a Hungarian who spoke Russian flawlessly but was a novice in English. They claimed to live in Pittsburgh, Pennsylvania, a city that had produced few notable poets. It was a locale that would be free from prying reporters and critics. Within 10 days, Ficke produced an aesthetic manifesto for the Spectrist School, and together he and Bynner wrote a sample of Spectrist poetry occupying 49 printed pages. The poetry, as the manifesto suggested, contained emotional immediacy, some violence, and much humor. The manuscript, accepted by Mitchell Kennerley, a New York publisher who had already printed the hoaxers' work, was received innocently on the basis of its promoters' authority. Later, Kennerley was told about the hoax and sworn to secrecy.

Bynner reviewed the manuscript for the *New Republic* before its publication and continued to advertise the Spectrist School after the volume appeared, chiefly because many of the critics were approving of it. Some readers, like Alfred Kreymborg, editor of *Others,* were

enthusiastic; he devoted his January 1917 issue to Spectrist poetry and criticism. William Marion Reedy of *Reedy's Mirror* also acclaimed the new arrival. Despite the *New York Herald*'s rejection of Spectric work as having "no relation at all to real poetry" and the Los Angeles *Graphic*'s dismissal of it as "gibberish," Spectrist poetry was a success. Don Marquis, in the *New York Evening Sun* of December 26, 1917, asked his readers if they were "hep to the Spectric Group."

For the next 18 months, the school gained both detractors and defenders. It also attracted poets eager for advice. To avoid exposure, Morgan and Knish had to be "on tour" perpetually. To keep their hoax growing, they worked out of a Pittsburgh mail drop. They had to reveal their imposture to others in order to get their responses mailed. They allowed a third poet to join in on their elaborate joke, Marjorie Allen Seiffert, who wrote Spectrist poetry as Elijah Hay. The three were also kept busy fending off established poets like William Carlos Williams, advertising the school, and writing Spectrist poetry and criticism for such journals as Harriet Monroe's internationally acclaimed *Poetry* and Kennerley's *Forum.*

By 1918, the hoax was close to discovery, and on April 26 of that year Bynner revealed the trio's true identities. Those critics who had not been taken in or were cautious in reviewing *Spectra* were exultant; those who were cozened covered their tracks in a variety of ways. *Poetry*'s Harriet Monroe and *Little Review*'s Jane Heap attacked Bynner and Ficke. Amy Lowell, cigar-smoking dictator of the Imagist school, temporarily forgave Bynner. *Reedy's Mirror* suggested that the burlesque poetry of the hoaxers was better than their serious work.

The hoax was successful, at least at that time, for reducing the amount of cant, stuffiness, and posture surrounding poetry and criticism. It also affected Bynner's style. He published as Emanuel Morgan the Spectrist volume *Pins for Wings* in 1921 and later, in 1927, published some "posthumous" poems of Morgan's claiming that Knish had died in Budapest and that Morgan, disconsolate, had committed suicide in a Pittsburgh sanitarium. The Spectrist School was dead, too, but the hoax's salutary effects are permanently registered in literary history.

Latrell SPREWELL: bad behavior but big rewards

On December 1, 1997, Latrell Sprewell, three-time National Basketball Association (NBA) All-Star basketball player and star guard for the Golden State Warriors, had had enough. At practice that day, his coach, P. J. Carlesimo, known for riding players hard with his confrontational style of coaching, told Sprewell to "put a little mustard on those passes," even though Sprewell had warned his boss he was not in the mood to take any criticism. His rage boiling over, Sprewell grabbed Carlesimo around the neck, choking him as they wrestled to the ground. Other players separated the two, and Sprewell retreated to the locker room, only to emerge several minutes later to once again beat through his restraining teammates to attack his coach, this time landing a punch on Carlesimo's neck. Within three days, punishment was meted out: the contract for the remaining two years of Sprewell's four-year, $32 million deal with the Warriors was terminated by team management, and the NBA commission suspended him for a full year, the longest nondrug-related suspension in its history.

Though Sprewell later admitted he was wrong and that he did not condone or encourage such behavior, and he apologized publicly to his fans and privately to his coach, he was shocked at the harshness of the penalties. Sprewell bemoaned the fact that the firing and suspension would mean the 10 previous years of hard work, which allowed him to rise to professional status from his old neighborhood basketball court, would all be taken away for this one transgression. The NBA players association issued grievances against the league and the Warriors on his behalf.

An arbitrator was called in to sort through the case and, in the name of fairness, lessened the punishment. Instead of a full year's suspension, Sprewell would miss 68 games and would lose just $6.4 million of salary for that year. The Golden State Warriors were required to pay $17.3 million for the final two years of his contract unless they traded him to another team. During the time of his suspension, Sprewell was banned from any team facilities and NBA arenas. He was also required to undergo counseling before returning to the league.

In the days between his firing and the arbitrator's verdict, Sprewell, as the latest representative of the professional sports arena, was on trial with the American public. His pending fate ignited a national debate on the issues of sportsmanship, respect for authority, unmanageable athletes, and fair punishment. Many wanted Sprewell to become an example, showing others that violent, uncontrollable behavior would not escape harsh punishment, no matter who you were. Others wondered what fair punishment was for a multimillion-dollar athlete who could pay fines out of his petty cash fund were they meaningful then.

Others planned to capitalize on Sprewell's (and other professional athletes') "bad boy" image. Though he was dropped as spokesperson for Converse athletic shoes, Sprewell was later picked up by another sneaker company and paid $500,000 a year to represent its products. Clearly, Sprewell's image sold, for this company's revenues soared to $120 million in 1999. Such ad campaigns and media coverage seemed to be sending the message that a star player could get away with anything.

"People say I'm what's wrong with sports," Sprewell said in a television spot. "I say I'm a three-time NBA All-Star. People say I'm America's worst nightmare. I say I'm the American dream." As the "Star-Spangled Banner" was played in the background of his gritty television commercials, Americans began to question their association and identification with such new-style role models.

Robert SPRING: a fashionable forger

In 1859, Robert Spring was charged with dealing in forged autographed letters of General George Washington. An expert at imitating handwriting, Spring passed off signatures of many famous Americans during his career as a forger. His favorite fabrications were checks and Revolutionary passes signed by Washington; thousands of these were manufactured and sold by him to collectors, autograph dealers, and others in America and abroad. The forgeries still turn up frequently today at auctions.

Born in England in 1813, Spring immigrated to America as a young man and immediately opened a bookstore in Philadelphia, Pennsylvania. In the 1850s, when he was a well-established bookseller in the city, he started adding the signature of Washington to the title pages of ancient books, attesting that they had come from Washington's private library. The motivation for this was money, Spring later said. A collector of Americana, Spring became a known dealer in rare books, manuscripts, and autographs in Philadelphia by late 1858. At that time he was fulfilling a growing demand for early Americana, specializing in the handwriting of Washington, Thomas Jefferson, and Benjamin Franklin. Unlike those who merely forged autographs—although he furnished signatures upon demand (especially checks "signed" by Washington)—Spring enlarged the supply of complete letters supposedly written by famous persons, writing on old paper, stained with coffee grounds, in an ink he had specially prepared himself. He used two methods as a forger: tracing and freehand.

The notorious Spring had a quick eye for the special details in handwriting that make it unique and individual. He also had remarkable eye-hand coordination that enabled him to imitate, after brief practice (though he practiced handwritings endlessly), most styles of handwriting. Undoubtedly he also had the common desire to acquire wealth.

In 1859 forgeries of Washington's handwriting were traced to Spring, who was taken into custody by a Philadelphia detective. After promptly admitting his guilt, Spring was briefly jailed and then freed on his promise to reform. During the next decade, he operated under cover, using aliases, making and selling bogus autographs of celebrities in Canada, England, and Baltimore, Maryland. The English authorities were quick to expose him and send him packing back to America. In dealing with English collectors during the American Civil War, he often represented himself through his mail correspondence as the impoverished daughter of a general.

She was so poor, he wrote, that she was offering to sell her family's valuable papers. Experts eventually recognized these works as forgeries, and Spring became very cautious.

Returning to Philadelphia in mid-1868, Spring secretly fabricated signatures and documents by Washington, Jefferson, and Franklin until he was arrested on November 4, 1869, by the same city detective who had caught him 10 years earlier. After confessing to forgery, saying he had done it to obtain money to support his family of seven children, Spring vowed again to reform himself and was let go after serving time in jail. He was said to have ceased practicing his "art," fallen into poverty, and given up. On December 14, 1876—exactly 77 years after the death of his "signatory friend" George Washington—Spring died in a charity ward in a Philadelphia hospital.

Ironically, after his death, his forgeries became valuable as curiosities, as did his own letters about his misfortunes and experiences as a forger. Sold today for about $30 to $40 apiece, they are bringing autograph dealers the fortune that Spring tried for and missed.

STAR ROUTE FRAUDS

In early 1881, during the administration of President Rutherford B. Hayes, it became evident that a clique of government officials, including a former United States senator, had conspired with private mail contractors to swindle the U.S. Post Office Department through excessive pricing and the extension of worthless services. It was later estimated that the government had been defrauded of at least $4 million. Although indictments were made and trials were held in 1882 and 1883, no one was found guilty.

Soon after he assumed the nation's highest office in March 1881, President James A. Garfield, a Republican like Hayes, approved an investigation by the new postmaster general, Thomas L. James, of the private contracts that had been awarded to carry the United States mail over the so-called star routes. These routes, so named because of the asterisks that marked them in postal publications, were roads mainly in the South and West over which mail was transported in a wagon or a stagecoach, by a rider on horseback, or by a carrier on foot to post offices not accessible by railroad or steamboat. In April 1881 the second assistant postmaster general, T. W. Brady, was dismissed for having fraudulently increased the compensation given to numerous private contractors who delivered mail over the star routes. Implicated with Brady was Stephen W. Dorsey, a former United States senator from Arkansas (1873–79), who had done much to win the election of President Garfield and Vice President Chester A. Arthur in 1880. Dorsey, also a Republican, had apparently peddled his influence in the Senate and helped secure congressional appropriations for expensive improvements to old routes that carried virtually no mail, for starting new and fictitious delivery routes, and for the benefit of his brother and brother-in-law, who held contracts with the postal service.

Congressional investigators, special agents, Pinkerton detectives, and lawyers were all involved in exposing the corruption surrounding the star routes. Eventually more than 25 indictments were handed out, including those secured for Brady and Dorsey in 1881. Corrupt Post Office Department officials, contractors, subcontractors, and politicians had conspired and lobbied to procure the legislation and appropriations needed for Brady's and Dorsey's plans; they had pocketed profits from increasing the mail rates illegally on certain routes and from government payments for useless routes, as well as other frauds. When the defendants were brought to trial, proof of their corruption seemed overwhelming.

When he was brought to trial, Brady challenged the government prosecutors by threatening to produce evidence against President Garfield if his case wasn't dropped. It wasn't, and he published a letter from Garfield to the chairman of the Republican congressional campaign committee of 1880. In it, Garfield excused the practice of levying campaign funds from the salaries of government workers—a serious abuse of the spoils system. Nothing ever came of this, however, as Garfield was assassinated on September 9, 1881. The prosecutions against Brady, Dorsey, and the other defendants were carried on by President Chester Arthur following Garfield's death.

All sorts of shady doings by the ring of conspirators came to light: the Post Office Department had been victimized by valueless bonds imposed on it; the Congress had received deceitful and padded proposals supporting demands for funds to improve old mail routes; subcontractors had paid hefty fines and profits to contractors whose bids for government contracts had been accepted. One contractor's fraudulent affidavit had secured him a $90,000 agreement. One star route, which yielded only $761 in postal income annually, had been upgraded for faster travel at a cost of $50,000. Another route had supposedly been improved by a contractor named John M. Peck, whose specifications indicated that each horse that carryied mail had to run for 20 hours and the rider had to work 40 hours daily.

At the conclusion of their first trial, a grand jury voted 10–2 for the conviction of Brady and 9–3 for the conviction of Dorsey. In their second trial, both were acquitted; the jury rendered a verdict of "not guilty as indicted" against Dorsey, who had ascribed his prosecution to the malice of both Postmaster General James and Attorney General Wayne MacVeagh, whose appointments to Garfield's cabinet he had resisted.

Although there had clearly been frauds on 93 star routes, the government was unable to obtain any convictions. Afterward, the American public was disgusted by the political scandal. President Arthur then hastened to replace the spoils system (the practice of awarding the best government jobs to faithful party supporters) by a merit system that gave the best jobs to those passing rigorous examinations.

Dorothy STRATTEN: exploited and murdered ingénue

Stunning blonde Dorothy Stratten became, in 1980, the first Canadian woman to be *Playboy* magazine's "Playmate of the Year." She had originally posed for the magazine in the hope of beginning a film career. Stratten was just starting to break into the world of serious film when her estranged husband, Paul Snider, brutally ended her life. On August 14, 1980, Stratten was tortured, raped repeatedly, sodomized, and then shot to death. Snider then took his own life.

A small-time car-show promoter and alleged pimp and drug dealer, Paul Snider met Dorothy Ruth Hoogstratten (her birth name) in 1977 in Vancouver, British Columbia. At the time she was a 17-year-old high school student there, working part-time at a Dairy Queen snack bar. Within six months Snider, who was nine years her senior, was having an affair with her and pressuring her to pose nude for photographs he planned

The ravishing Dorothy Stratten, Playboy's Playmate of the Year (1980), celebrates her 20th birthday with her husband, Paul Snider, at their West Los Angeles, California, home. The couple separated shortly, and he sadistically murdered her and immediately committed suicide. (UPI/Bettmann Newsphotos)

to enter in *Playboy*'s 25th anniversary Playmate contest. Dorothy at first refused but soon succumbed, taken in by Snider's worldliness and his assurance that this was the way to break into the movies. However, because she was only 18 and the legal age of consent in Canada was 19, Snider had to forge her mother's signature (her father had deserted the family when Dorothy was three).

Two weeks after the pictures were sent to *Playboy*, Hugh Hefner, the magazine's publisher, invited Dorothy to his Los Angeles mansion and allegedly seduced her soon after her arrival (something Snider warned her might occur but considered necessary for her future success). Dorothy then began living in Hefner's mansion and was supposedly overwhelmed by "the slick professional machinery of the *Playboy* sex factory." She acquired a talent agent, who shortened and Americanized her Dutch surname to Stratten, which became her stage (if not formally legal) name afterwards.

Afraid that he would lose Dorothy, along with her monetary promise, Snider moved to Los Angeles in 1979 and pressured her into marrying him. Intensely jealous and possessive, he was nonetheless repeatedly unfaithful, and their marriage soon fell apart. Dorothy lost the anniversary Playmate contest, apparently because Hefner felt she didn't have enough experience and expertise with the press. She was, however, chosen for *Playboy*'s centerfold of August 1979. Her short celebrity career was then launched with some small parts in movies and television shows and a lead role in a B-rated film called *Autumn Born*. By the end of 1979, she was posing for *Playboy*'s "Playmate of the Year" pictorial, which was published in June 1980. With some of her earnings, Snider financed several unsuccessful schemes, including a male strip joint and a motorcycle jump by daredevil Evel Knievel. Dorothy's feelings for Snider had faded into unhappiness by early 1980, when she began work as the lead in *Galaxia,* a science fiction film that showed a lot of skin. She also began a relationship with movie producer and actor Peter Bogdanovich, who cast her in *They All Laughed* opposite talented actor John Ritter. She moved in with Bogdanovich, who was twice her age, while he shot the film in New York. After their return to Los Angeles she moved into his house permanently.

Snider learned about Dorothy's affair with Bogdanovich from a private detective he had hired. Enraged, he lured Dorothy to his apartment, where he shot a 12-gauge shotgun point blank at her face before blasting himself to death. Their nude bodies were discovered the next day. Stratten had been only 20 years old.

After her death *Playboy* printed, without permission, pictures and several quotations from her memoirs, suggesting that she had been happy with the *Playboy* way of life, something she herself had once called a "Disneyland where people are the games." When her estate threatened to sue *Playboy* for copyright infringement, the magazine offered $15,000 for retroactive one-time rights to the material it had used. Her grieving mother agreed, saying, "They killed my daughter; what more can they do?" Two movies were made—*Death of a Centerfold: The Dorothy Stratten Story* (1981) and *Star 80* (1983)—but neither dealt with Dorothy Stratten's extreme reluctance to pose naked or her naiveté about her sex-symbol status. Bogdanovich's subsequent book, *The Killing of the Unicorn* (1984), attempted to show the tragic truth about her as well as tell the story of their relationship. Dorothy Stratten had been caught up in a fast-paced environment that she could neither understand nor escape.

Gerry STUDDS. See PAGE SCANDAL IN CONGRESS.

SUMNER-BROOKS INCIDENT. See Preston BROOKS: the bitter fruits of wrath.

Jimmy SWAGGART: moral problem for evangelism
"I do not plan in any way to whitewash my sin or call it a mistake," the disgraced television evangelist Jimmy Swaggart tearfully told some 8,000 worshipers at his Family Worship Center in Baton Rouge, Louisiana, on Sunday, February 21, 1988. "I call it a sin," intoned this fire-and-brimstone preacher of the Assemblies of God as his large congregation gasped and wept and applauded.

The 52-year-old Reverend Swaggart, whose TV ministry took in an estimated $142 million in 1986, begged forgiveness as his voice cracked with emotion and apologized to his wife and family, fellow ministers of his Pentecostal denomination, other TV evangelists across the country, and followers of his around the world. At the end he directed his words to "my savior, my redeemer . . . I have sinned against you, my Lord, and I would ask that your precious blood would wash and cleanse every stain until it is in the seas of God's forgetfulness, never to be remembered against me anymore." He did not specify the nature of the sin but said he would step out of the pulpit for an indefinite time for his "moral failure."

The Swaggart scandal leaked out about three days before his dramatic public confession. Church officials had received photographs purportedly showing Swaggart and a known prostitute entering and leaving a motel room. The photos supposedly came from a rival TV evangelist, Marvin Gorman, a New Orleans minister of the Assemblies of God whom Swaggart had accused of numerous adulterous affairs in 1986; Gorman consequently was defrocked and admitted committing "an immoral act" with a woman (he had also filed a $90 million lawsuit against Swaggart because of Swaggart's accusations).

Soon after Swaggart's dramatic sermon of February 21, a New Orleans prostitute named Debra Murphree announced that she was the woman in the photographs and that she had had several sexual encounters with Swaggart at motels. At first she said no intercourse had occurred (she had posed nude while the reverend watched), but later she said he briefly had intercourse with her on one occasion. The 28-year-old Murphree, who disclosed to *Penthouse* magazine for an undisclosed amount of money her story of the pornographic acts Swaggart paid her to do, said that the celebrated man of God had wanted her nine-year-old daughter to watch one of their sex sessions (which took place near New Orleans), that he wanted her to invite other whores to their sessions, and that "Once he asked me to hop out [of a car] naked in broad daylight in front of strangers so he could see the shock on their faces." Murphree, whom *Penthouse* featured in 18 black-and-white nude photos, also claimed that when she was seeing Swaggart she was seeing a police officer whom she named as Randy Gorman, Marvin's son. She called Swaggart "perverted," "kinky," and "cheap."

At the end of March 1988, the National Assemblies of God's 13-member executive presbytery voted unanimously to defrock the disgraced Pentecostal preacher, who had won great popularity because of his old-fashioned, evangelistic preaching that combined gospel singing, piano playing, and strutting and shouting on stage. He had often attacked fellow ministers, such as Jimmy BAKKER, and railed against sin, particularly sexual immorality. The presbytery toughened an earlier recommendation by the District Council of the Assemblies of God that had barred Swaggart from preaching for three months and that had urged counseling for him with church elders for two years; it now ruled that he must stay out of the pulpit and off television for at least a year. It also forbade the airing of past tapes of his ministry in the United States and abroad. At the time his World Ministry (headquartered in Baton Rouge, Louisiana) was already losing about $1.8 million a month; he faced sharply declining revenues because of his "fall" and soon announced he would return to his TV pulpit on May 22, despite the risk of being defrocked.

Earlier he had said he would abide by the three-month suspension imposed by the Louisiana District Council. A long absence would drastically damage his worldwide evangelical operation, as well as fund raising for his Bible College in Louisiana, and so Swaggart defied the discipline ordered by the presbytery of the national church by returning to television and the pulpit on Sunday, May 22, 1988. Many of the followers of the defrocked Swaggart welcomed him with open arms as he continued to preach and run his ministry without denomination credentials. Others felt he still had a moral problem, remembering perhaps his own words written in 1987 in his magazine *Evangelist:* "To allow a preacher of the Gospel, when he is caught beyond the shadow of a doubt committing an immoral act . . . to remain in his position as pastor (or whatever), would be the most gross stupidity." God only knew what Swaggart believed and lived by: contrition one day, defiance the next, and histrionics holding them together.

In New Orleans in 1991, Marvin Gorman's $90 million defamation lawsuit against Swaggart was heard by a civil jury. Gorman claimed that Swaggart had spread false charges about his sex life to destroy his television ministry. The jury found Swaggart guilty of defaming Gorman and ordered him, the Assemblies of God, and other defendants to pay a total of $10 million to Gorman and his ministries.

A month later, in October 1991, Swaggart and Rosemary Garcia (a self-described prostitute) were stopped by police in Indio, California, for a traffic violation. Garcia said he had picked her up for sex. Initially saying he would step down from his ministries to seek counseling, Swaggart returned on October 16, 1991, to the pulpit of his Family Worship Center and told the congregation, "The Lord told me it's flat none of your business."

Fife SYMINGTON: lying over bank loans

In 1991, John Fife Symington III, a successful, Harvard-educated real estate developer, campaigned for the governorship of Arizona with a platform based on the idea of running the state like a business. Arizonans believed in his promise and voted him into office. Though the state's economy flourished under his direction, Symington's personal finances fell apart. At one point, 13 of his land development deals went "belly up," one of which was funded with six union pension funds. In the fall of 1995, when the pensions sued for repayment, Symington declared bankruptcy. Launching an investigation into Symington's real estate affairs, federal prosecutors found false statements made on bank loan papers and wild swings in his declarations of net worth—depending on whether he was trying to secure a loan or wriggle out of repaying one.

On trial, Symington maintained that the erroneous statements filed between 1986 and 1991 were simple mistakes. He said he had never meant to mislead anyone and that he should have paid closer attention when preparing the financial statements. His lawyer called them "unintended errors and omissions." He said his client was too busy to check every figure on every statement himself and that Symington often cited figures considering what his properties would eventually be worth rather than their current values.

In September 1997, before finishing his second term as governor, Symington was forced to resign—two days after being convicted of fraud on seven federal counts and acquitted on three others; a mistrial was declared on the remaining 11 counts. Symington became the state's first governor convicted of a crime and its second governor within a decade to be forced from office by scandal (Evan MECHAM was impeached in 1988 on charges of obstructing justice and misuse of state money).

In February 1998, Symington was sentenced to two and a half years in prison for defrauding banks and pensions and ordered to pay a $60,000 fine, provide restitution for the pension funds, and serve five years' probation after jail. During the probationary period, Symington would be restricted from using his real estate license, incurring large debts, making any large purchases, or entering into any contracts without the approval of his probation officer. Immediately, his lawyer filed an appeal.

Symington never served a day of his prison sentence. In June 1999, the original conviction was overturned in a federal appellate court based on the "reasonable possibility" that an elderly juror was wrongly kicked off the jury during the trial because she insisted on Symington's innocence and couldn't agree with the other jurors. Though his political career was probably over, the 53-year-old Symington was entitled to a whole new trial, at the further expense of the taxpayers.

Public opinion of Symington slumped when it became known he would not go to jail. Some believed that because of his Ivy League education, his family name (he was an heir to the Frick steel fortune), and his marriage into a wealthy Arizona family, Symington was allowed to escape justice on a loophole simply because he possessed the means to secure superior legal representation. His detractors cited his lack of remorse during the trial as proof that he believed he was above the law. Though the injured parties bore the names of large institutions and bureaucratic organizations, real human victims fell prey to Symington's lies, namely those whose pensions were lost and those whose legitimate loan applications were refused during that period. See also Evan MECHAM: governor booted out of office.

T

Horace TABOR: the Leadville strike

Horace Austin Warner "Silver Dollar" Tabor became Colorado's richest silver tycoon in 1878. Soon consumed by visions of wealth and power, he became notorious for his social, political, and financial disgraces. Many anecdotes are told about his incredible excesses, some of which are legendary. The seemingly fantastic tale about his misguided handling of a miners' strike in Leadville, Colorado is, however, completely true.

Prospecting a grub stake worth $64.75 made Tabor, the keeper of a general store in Leadville, rise in less than a year from the ranks of the middle class to those of the very rich. He gained an estimated $10 million from his Little Pittsburgh, Chrysolite, and Matchless mines and in the process became Leadville's leading citizen. He was elected mayor of the town and—by virtue of generous donations to the Colorado Republican Party—was chosen for the largely ceremonial post of lieutenant governor of the state.

Tabor then developed two ambitions: to become even richer and to attain the highest political offices on the state and national levels. His first ambition caused him to react so thoughtlessly to a labor dispute in Leadville that he unwittingly began to erode his chances of achieving his second dream.

Viewed from the prospect of the 20th century, the striking miners' requests were not unreasonable. Twelve hours of daily labor gained them only $3.00, a sum quickly dissipated in overpriced Leadville; they also worked with the constant threat of lead poisoning. Wisely, they asked for an owner-financed hospital and a wage of $3.75.

The mine owners, who had given Tabor the status of a *generalissimo,* reacted with a show of force. They organized militia companies modeled on Mayor Tabor's private army (auxiliary police grandly called the Tabor Light Cavalry), lowered the daily wage to $2.75, ran two union leaders out of Leadville on the false charge that they were Molly Maguires (secret organization of miners who terrorized the industry), and requested the aid of out-of-town vigilantes. They also toughened the work rules at the mines; Tabor ordered the firing of workers in his mines who talked or smoked during their workday. Tabor personified the warlike attitude by parading around in a uniform complete with epaulettes.

Given the rhetoric and the quasi-military arrangements of the mine owners, the miners were forced to make a fist-shaking response. They issued an ultimatum: grant an eight-hour, $4.00 day, or we strike. Tabor ordered mine guards and thugs into Leadville. Ten thousand miners put down their tools.

Frightened, the Tabor-guided mine owners formed a Committee of Safety, enlarged the militias, and—harangued by Tabor, who had forgotten his obligation as lieutenant governor to promote peace and order—ordered the labor leaders to leave town.

In Denver, Colorado's Governor Pitkin ordered Tabor to calm down. Instead, the Committee of Safety developed a secret plan to arrest six of the union's leaders and hang them without trial. Pitkin learned of the plan, declared martial law in Leadville, and sent a state militia into the town.

His move caused a temporary rise in Tabor's reputation, for the militia was expected to hold up the mine owners' position. But the fame turned to disgrace when the militia commander's action revealed how poor a leader Tabor had been. The commander, David I. Cook, refused to allow the Committee of Safety to act like a South American junta, instead ordering it to dissolve. He also disallowed gatherings of more than two persons, and arrested and disarmed over 200 troublemakers in both the union and mine-owner's factions. Moreover, he ordered a primitive kind of collective bargaining, which regained the miners their $3 wage.

Disgusted with Tabor, the citizens of Leadville petitioned Governor Pitkin to allow Cook to run Leadville, a control he allowed until the martial-law decree had been withdrawn.

Thereafter, Tabor fared badly. He had lost not only the votes of the miners but those of the mine owners.

News of his blunders amused many, but cost him votes throughout the state. He made more blunders in committing the politically costly errors of acquiring a mistress and suing for a divorce. By 1882, when he had hoped to be permanently appointed to the seat of U.S. Senator H. M. Teller, the Colorado Republican Committee made the appointment an interim sop, brief but long enough for Tabor to lessen his reputation further (and to embarrass U.S. President Chester A. Arthur) by staging an ostentatious Washington wedding to his mistress Baby Doe (see TABOR-BABY DOE AFFAIR).

TABOR-BABY DOE AFFAIR

Horace Austin Warner "Silver Dollar" Tabor showed how poor a leader he was by mishandling the 1878 Leadville, Colorado, mine workers' strike; he also revealed that he was politically blind to the effects of his public actions. Although he had served as mayor of Leadville and lieutenant governor of Colorado, he was ambitious for even greater prestige. Tabor's biggest mistake was that he failed to perceive that in cultivating a mistress (first secretly, then openly) in Victorian Colorado, he was cutting his throat politically.

Tabor had been deliberately enticed in a Denver restaurant by Elizabeth McCourt "Baby" Doe, a divorcee at a time when divorced women were viewed with suspicion. Her intentions were not entirely economic: she admired Tabor and later sincerely loved him for his bold, authoritative personality. Tabor was immediately captivated and brought Baby Doe back with him to Leadville in time to receive her encouragement during the Leadville strike. Her presence in the mining town was supposedly secret, for Augusta Tabor was in residence to make her husband's life uncomfortable. Baby Doe always appeared in the Leadville streets heavily veiled. Augusta remained in the dark about her husband's affair, but Leadville knew about it, although the rough mining town apparently overlooked the moral implications of the liaison.

After the strike, Baby Doe was moved, still in secret, to Tabor's lavish Windsor Hotel in Denver, where Tabor was attempting to ensure political popularity by building his Tabor Block and the grandiose Tabor Opera House. When the latter was finished, Tabor forced Baby Doe to "go public": she attended performances of the opera in Tabor's private box, swathed in a full-length ermine cape. Augusta, now alert to the affair, stayed away.

All of Denver either laughed or boiled with righteous anger at the affair, for the city was then in a state of moral flux. On one level, it contained 3,000 prostitutes, opium dens, and gambling parlors; on another, the Denver Protective Association (DPA), consisting mainly of ladies who lived in the posh Capitol Hill area, were working to make Denver the moral city they felt that it should be. (They had some success: the houses of prostitution lost their red lights and their explicit signs disappeared, a few returning with more euphemistic invitations.) To the morally minded DPA, a mistress was only a species of prostitute, and Baby Doe therefore dwelt in the depths of social and moral degradation. Lieutenant Governor Tabor's daring was also regarded as morally lax with a result that could only be political suicide. The DPA sided with Tabor's cold unapproachable wife, who refused both their commiseration and their society.

But Tabor failed to temper his activities. He sued for divorce in 1881, an action that gave him adverse publicity until the divorce was granted in early 1883. He compounded his error by marrying Baby Doe civilly in 1882 after his fraudulent divorce. Technically a bigamist, he kept his marriage to Baby Doe secret because he coveted the senatorial seat vacated by H. M. Teller when the latter became President Chester A. Arthur's secretary of the interior.

But Tabor's moral laxity had already cost him the six-year appointment. The Colorado Republican Committee awarded him only an interim commission, and Tabor decided to garnish his career and gain publicity toward a presidential nomination by remarrying Baby Doe canonically at a lavish public wedding at the Willard Hotel in Washington, D.C., on March 1, 1883.

The appointments were blatantly ostentatious. Mountains of flowers and heaps of rich food dominated the reception. Baby Doe wore a $90,000 diamond necklace over a $7,500 gown; Tabor flashed diamonds too: solitaires on each hand, stamp-size buttons of diamonds and onyx, studs of huge adamantines. He even brought, by private train, a silk-and-lace nightshirt that was described so mockingly by the press that he became the laughingstock of Washington.

Almost all of Washington society stayed away from the wedding for moral reasons (one invitation was returned torn in half). President Arthur attended but went away angry at the ostentation and Tabor's habit of pounding him on the back. (Later he became even angrier because he was charged by Washington's elite with moral turpitude for attending.)

After the wedding Tabor and Baby Doe went home, where Denver society refused to call on them in their splendid Italianate mansion. The Colorado Republican Committee ignored them too, and Tabor was not reelected lieutenant governor.

When his silver lode then began to fail, Tabor was ruined. He ended his days as a hauler of mine tailings in a wheelbarrow. Before he died in 1899, he asked Baby Doe to preserve their Matchless Mine, which he was sure would reveal a new strike. She did so in dire poverty until, at 73, she was found frozen to death in 1935, surrounded by mementos of earlier Tabor glory. Her sad death caused the widely known legend of Baby Doe to spread, granting her, Tabor, and the Matchless

Mine a 20th-century fame in books and Douglas Moore's 1956 opera *The Ballad of Baby Doe*.

TAILHOOK SCANDAL: molestation of women

In the past the American military has not been praised for its treatment of women. In a 1990 survey, nearly two-thirds of the females serving in the United States armed services admitted to having been sexually harassed by their male colleagues. The so-called Tailhook scandal of 1991 showed the military in an extraordinarily poor light and subsequently forced certain long overdue changes in the U.S. Navy's treatment of women employees and servicemembers.

Since the mid-1980s, the annual conventions of the Tailhook Association, an organization of U.S. Navy and Marine Corps aviators meant to foster camaraderie and professional enrichment, had evidently been a hotbed of lewd, disgraceful behavior, but the naval leadership had done nothing to stem them. In September 1991, at the Las Vegas Hilton Hotel, where naval and marine flyers assembled for the annual Tailhook convention, everyone apparently had such a good time that not one of the some 2,400 naval personnel questioned later could remember what actually happened that evening—even though 83 women later claimed that they had been sexually abused or assaulted. Some 140 cases of harassment were filed; however, not a single conviction was obtained. Apparently the "hottest action" took place in the hotel's third-floor hallway, where nearly 200 servicemen jeered and leered as they grabbed and pawed women, organized leg-shaving contests, and disrobed some women trying to pass through their rooms.

Frustrated by her superiors' slow response to reports of misconduct, Naval Lieutenant Paula Coughlin in 1992 became the first to go public with charges. A veteran helicopter pilot, she described her experiences at the convention, but because she could not correctly identify her assailant, the charges against a marine captain were dropped. In February 1994, Coughlin resigned from the navy, saying the sexual abuse she suffered had affected her ability to serve.

Earlier, during the Pentagon probe into the Tailhook scandal, three admirals who had not aggressively investigated the misconduct were relieved of their duties in September 1992. After months of public criticism, Secretary of the Navy H. Lawrence Garrett III was also forced to resign in 1992 and accepted "full responsibility" for management of the Tailhook incident. The military court judge, Captain William T. Vest Jr., dropped charges against three subordinates of Admiral Frank B. Kelso II, the chief of naval operations, but Vest thought Kelso (a silent witness to this night of debauchery) should have been prepared to deal with the situation, given the nature of some of the organized activities (drinking, porn films, and strippers) in the hotel's hospitality suite. There were conflicting reports pertaining to Kelso's role, and so U.S. Defense Secretary Les Aspin overturned the recommendations asking for Kelso's removal. Then Kelso, who had earlier refused to resign, surprised nearly everyone by announcing he would retire two months ahead of schedule. To prevent another Tailhook scandal, he stated, he had tried to institute changes improving opportunities and conditions for naval women.

Out of the 116 cases referred to the navy for administrative action by the Pentagon, only 28 officers received penalties (fines and reprimands). Twenty-two cases in the Marine Corps were similarly disposed of. No one was court-martialed. The commander of the Naval Investigative Service and the navy's judge advocate-general were stripped of their duties. The navy ended its relationship with the Tailhook Association, but eight years later, in mid-1999, it began considering restoring official recognition to the aviators' group, stating it had "learned the lessons we needed to learn" and had "institutionalized those lessons."

Harold TALBOTT: public versus private business

Government appointees are presumed to divest themselves of all interests in firms to which government contracts might be awarded. The secretary of the air force in the mid-1950s seemed to think differently. Harold Elstner Talbott, Jr., unpropitiously embarrassed the Eisenhower administration by soliciting private business for a company of which he was a partner. Talbott, who denied that he had behaved improperly or unethically, came under intense public fire for his business activities and consequently was forced to resign in August 1955.

Talbott was a businessman who was president of the Dayton-Wright Airplane Company before he accepted the job of secretary of the air force in 1953. He had given up the equivalent of a $100,000 annual income to take the secretaryship for $18,000 a year. He sold all his stock and divested himself completely of his business interests, except his partnership in a moderate-sized, private management-engineering firm, Paul B. Mulligan & Company.

At his confirmation hearings before the Senate Armed Services Committee, Talbott had agreed to sell all of his securities, although this had never been requested before and was not required by law. He retained, however, a half interest in Mulligan & Company, with which he had signed an agreement to the effect that if the firm acquired any new clients whose business activities might involve the air force, they would be handled as special accounts and segregated from the other business of the company. Over the course of the next two and a half years, no special accounts were opened. When questioned by the Senate Subcommittee on Investigations, Talbott said that of the 18 new clients acquired during his leave of absence from Mulligan, only one (Aveco) should possibly have been treated as a special account.

While examining the files of Mulligan & Company prior to the 1955 summer hearings of the Subcommittee on Investigations, investigators for the subcommittee found copies of letters that Talbott had written on official U.S. Air Force stationery to executives of companies such as the Chrysler Corporation, Baldwin-Lima-Hamilton Corporation, and Olin Industries, Incorporated, all of which had large contracts with the Department of Defense. Secretary Talbott claimed that the letters, which seemed to be soliciting business for Mulligan & Company, were personal communications to personal friends. Aveco had $200 million in defense contracts and, with a hearty recommendation, gave Mulligan & Company a contract. Paul Mulligan testified that he had prepared solicitation letters for friends to mail out in which he mentioned that Talbott, the secretary of the air force, was a partner in the company, but Mulligan said that he had done this merely to identify Talbott.

Another issue of controversy concerned the Radio Corporation of America (RCA), whose contract with Mulligan had lapsed. Talbott was reported to have called its president and urged him to reconsider its action and talk with Mulligan in person. At the Senate subcommittee hearings, Talbott said that he could not recall such a conversation, nor could he remember saying to an RCA lawyer: "If all of these other companies could take contracts with Mulligan & Company, why was RCA so high and mighty?" Talbott's air force counsel did recall the conversation, however, and so did the RCA attorney. In any event, RCA did not renew its contract with Mulligan.

Talbott, a tall man with a brusque manner and a quick temper, insisted repeatedly to the subcommittee that he had done "nothing that could be construed as dishonest." At the close of the hearings, he declared: "In retrospect I now see that I was mistaken in permitting myself to make phone calls or write letters about the Mulligan company. The few minutes I have given to the Mulligan company since I took office have been a trivial part of my time. I really doubt that I have given Mulligan company and my other private affairs two-and-a-half days out of the two-and-one-half years I have been in Washington. My interest in the company has never influenced me in the slightest degree in the execution of my duties as secretary of the air force." He then offered to terminate his partnership in Mulligan & Company.

A number of senators on the subcommittee thanked Talbott for his full cooperation and praised his work as a public official, but others considered him guilty of a conflict of interest and stated that his actions had been typical of those of former businessmen in the Eisenhower administration who were furthering their own interests while in government service. President Dwight Eisenhower accepted Talbott's resignation as "the right decision."

TATE-LaBIANCA MURDERS

Five bloody bodies were discovered in the house and on the grounds of actress Sharon Tate's home in the hills above Beverly Hills, California, on August 9, 1969. Two days later, in another secluded house in the same area, police found Leno LaBianca and his wife Rose-

The Los Angeles county coroner (left) takes notes as assistants hold sheet which covered one of the two bodies (seen in foreground) found on the lawn of the rented estate of movie director Roman Polanski on August 9, 1969. Actress Sharon Tate, Polanski's wife, and four others were discovered brutally murdered under bizarre circumstances on the property. (UPI/Bettmann Newsphotos)

mary sprawled on the floor in pools of their own blood. Despite the savagery of these murders and the fact that the word *pig* was written in blood at both sites, the police did not at first link the two crimes. They were further stumped by the seeming lack of a motive for the murders. Two months later, while investigating a hippie band suspected of arson and car theft, the police got their first break. They had raided a remote ranch and arrested 21 young people and their leader, Charles Manson. Through information gained from former members of Manson's "family," it gradually became apparent to the investigators that Manson and four of his followers had been responsible for the brutal August murders.

When Sharon Tate's housekeeper entered the living room of the actress's home on the morning following the murders, she was horrified to see blood splattered on the floor and walls and a body lying on the lawn. She ran screaming to a neighbor and called the police. The officers approached the quiet house cautiously. As they passed a car in the driveway, they noticed a youth slumped over in the front seat. He had been shot. On the lawn sprawled not one, but two bodies. They were writer-producer Voyteck Frykowski and his girlfriend, coffee heiress Abigail Folger. Both had been stabbed repeatedly, and Frykowski had been shot and had his head bashed in as well. Inside, in the living room in front of the fireplace, lay Jay Sebring, a famous men's hair stylist. His face had been covered with a towel, for he bled from seven deep gashes and a gunshot wound. A rope was tied around his neck, and it led to the fifth stabbed victim, Sharon Tate Polanski, wife of famed movie director Roman POLANSKI and was at the time eight months pregnant. The dead youth in the car was later identified as Steven E. Parent. He had been visiting the Polanskis' 19-year-old caretaker and was on his way home when he encountered the killers in the driveway.

Rosemary LaBianca's son had sensed that something was wrong when he returned from a weekend camping trip. He called his older sister from a pay phone. When she and her boyfriend arrived and the two young men entered the living room of the LaBianca home, they saw Leno LaBianca lying on his back, bleeding from multiple knife wounds. A knife and a fork had been stuck into his body, and the word *War* had been carved on his bare stomach. The young people hastily left and called the police. When the homicide officers arrived, they found Rosemary LaBianca's body lying face down in a pool of blood in the bedroom. A lamp cord had been tied tightly around her neck and her head had been covered with a pillow case. *Death to Pigs* and *Rise* had been printed in her husband's blood on the living room walls, and the refrigerator bore the words *Healter* [sic] *Skelter.*

The sensational trial of the Manson family gradually revealed who had committed these massacres and how. Although Charles Manson had not been present at the Tate house killings, he had masterminded them. Charles "Tex" Watson, a member of Manson's family, had cut the house's telephone wires before he, Susan Atkins, Leslie Van Houten, Patricia Krenwinkel, and Linda Kasabian approached the house after midnight. Steven Parent saw them, and Watson then shot him four times. While Linda remained outside as a lookout, others surprised Frykowski and Folger in the living room and went at them with their Buck knives. When the pair broke away, the murderers chased them. Watson bashed Frykowski in the face and head with his gun and then shot him, while the women finished off Folger. Tate and Sebring were brought into the living room and a rope was tied around their necks. Sebring was shot, and both he and Tate were stabbed repeatedly. Tate was the last to die. The killers then departed, changed into clean clothes, threw their blood-stained clothing and the gun Watson had used into a canyon, and returned to the Spahn Ranch outside Los Angeles, where the Manson family was then living.

Manson took charge of the LaBianca murders, saying he would show the others "how to do it." While they waited in the car, he went into the LaBianca home and tied up the surprised couple with lamp cords. Watson, Van Houten, and Krenwinkel then entered and slaughtered them with large knives. As before, none of the murderers had any idea who their victims were. They killed because Manson told them to do so.

Manson, born in 1934, completely dominated the lives of his hippie family, a group of young, mostly female whites in their late teens or early 20s who all felt alienated from their middle-class backgrounds. Most of them believed that Manson was Jesus Christ or God. He indoctrinated them with his "philosophy," which was a bizarre blend and interpretation of the Book of Revelation, lyrics of songs by the Beatles, satanism, Scientology, and the ideology of Hitler. Manson hated the white establishment—whom he called "Pigs"—and thought that the black people were about to revolt violently and kill the white race—"Helter Skelter." The Tate and LaBianca murders were intended to show the blacks how to instill terror in whites and initiate the battle of Armageddon. According to Manson, only a selected few whites who retreated to the desert (Death Valley) would be spared. After the holocaust, the blacks would not know what to do, and a white master race would emerge "from the bottomless pit" and take control of the world. Charles Manson would then become the ruler of that race.

Although strongly attracted by Manson's strange magnetic personality, a few members of his family were able to resist his orders and even break away from the group's lifestyle dominated by sex, drugs, and crime. It was they, especially Linda Kasabian, who furnished the major evidence against the five murderers. Fingerprints found at the murder sites were also compelling evidence. The senseless killings and the long trial made headlines around the world, while the five accused (Manson, Atkins, Krenwinkel, Van Houten, and Watson, who was tried separately) reveled in the publicity. All of them, however, were found guilty and sentenced to death. They were spared, however, because California abolished the death penalty after their trial. All are now serving life sentences in California prisons.

According to the prosecutor Vincent Bugliosi, the bizarrely charismatic Manson believed the Beatles were talking to him through songs like "Helter Skelter," inspiring his mania for a race war. Bugliosi, author of the book *Helter Skelter* about the killings, later (1999) said, "The name Manson has become a metaphor for evil, and evil has its allure. Some people have the same fascination for Jack the Ripper and Hitler." The trial co-prosecutor Stephen Kay has attended 53 parole hearings for the killers and succeeded in lobbying for their continued incarceration. At California's Corcoran State Prison, Manson continues to receive fan letters each day from devoted followers.

William Desmond TAYLOR: vices unveiled

A Pandora's box of depravities was opened upon the mysterious killing of distinguished American silent-film director William Desmond Taylor in 1922. Although his murderer was never found, the careers of two celebrated actresses were subsequently destroyed because of scandalous revelations that further denigrated the already disgraced Hollywood film industry (see Roscoe "Fatty" ARBUCKLE: comedian, carouser, and culprit). After Taylor's death, filmland's debauchery was publicly targeted for cleansing.

Taylor, a reputed ladies' man, died from two .38-caliber bullets through his heart on the night of February 1, 1922. He was 45 years old. Discovering the corpse lying on the living room floor of the director's Los Angeles, California, apartment the next morning, Henry Peavey, a black servant in Taylor's employ, immediately rushed outside screaming hysterically and repeatedly, "Massa Taylor is dead" and then "They've killed Massa Taylor." Unfortunately, before the police arrived, much of the possible evidence was tampered with. Actress Edna Purviance, a neighbor, heard Peavey and promptly phoned 28-year-old Mabel Normand, a leading movie comedienne of the day, who then hurried over to Taylor's place and with Purviance rifled through the dead man's private papers in order to retrieve, before the police arrived, apparently incriminating love letters he had written to Normand. Angelic-looking, 17-year-old Mary Miles Minter, another illustrious actress whom Purviance had phoned, and her overbearing mother, Mrs. Charlotte Shelby, soon arrived together but, to their great annoyance, were blocked by the police, who searched the premises and found passionate love letters, secret photographs of Taylor with female stars, and a

hidden collection of silky, lacy lingerie, ladies' nightgowns and underwear, each with tags having initials and a date. Also on the scene were Paramount movie studio executives, who had gotten word of their chief director's death before the police had sped to his house. They disposed of Taylor's bootleg whiskey and burned documents in the fireplace.

When the police arrived they eliminated robbery as a motive because the victim still wore his big "lucky" diamond ring and $1,000 in cash lay around upstairs. A lengthy police inquiry ensued when the death was listed as a premeditated murder, and America's tabloid press had a field day in its insinuations.

But who would want to kill someone as well liked as Taylor? The authorities uncovered a surprising story about him. Taylor was really named William Deane-Tanner, a once respected New York art and antique dealer, who had deserted his business and seven-year-old marriage one day in 1908, completely vanishing from his wife and daughter (amazingly, his entire estate was left to the latter in his will). Taylor's brother, Dennis, had also walked out on his wife and daughter four years after his brother and hooked up for a while with his brother before disappearing entirely. William Taylor turned up in Hollywood, having a brief acting career with his new name before directing films and winning fast money and success with *Diamond from the Sky, Tom Sawyer, The Top of New York,* and other pictures. A handsome lothario, a bibliophile, and the president of the Screen Directors' Guild, the worldly Taylor apparently had numerous affairs with his leading ladies.

After his murder, his secretary, Edward Sands, whom some thought was his brother in disguise, disappeared and so became a prime police suspect. He was never found (he had disappeared completely in 1921, when Taylor was in Europe, after forging some checks in Taylor's name and stealing clothes, jewels, and a car belonging to him). It was also discovered that Taylor, seen visiting homosexual establishments and opium dens in Los Angeles, had been trying to stop a local drug ring that was blackmailing Mabel Normand. The actress who had delighted many in the Keystone Comedies admitted her love for Taylor, and when the public learned that she was a hopeless cocaine addict paying over $2,000 a month for the drug, they boycotted her last film, *Suzanna,* forcing her to retire permanently from the screen (out of work, she died of tuberculosis in 1930).

The scandal also ruined Mary Miles Minter, the virginal-looking actress whose blonde curls and sweet smiles had won movie-goers' hearts. Her mother, Charlotte Shelby, was rumored to have had an affair with Taylor at the same time he was carrying on secret liaisons with both Mary and Mabel. Among the lingerie seized by the police from the dead director's bedroom was a pink nightgown embroidered with the letters MMM and a note saying, "Dearest—I love you—I love you—I love you—XXXXXXXXX Yours always! Mary." Minter's fans were shocked; she had been involved with a man close to three times her age! She had also publicly kissed Taylor full on the lips as he lay in his coffin at his funeral. It was all too lustful for the public, which eventually turned against Minter. Obese and unhappy, she was driven into retirement.

Mrs. Shelby, who owned a .38 revolver and had been target shooting with it shortly before the murder, was thought by some to have been the strange person (in disguise) seen by one of Taylor's neighbors scurrying from his apartment on the night of the crime, following a loud blast of some kind. Her alleged motive was jealousy at discovering her daughter's passion for Taylor. But Mrs. Shelby quickly left the United States, remained abroad for three years, and oddly, was never questioned by the police, who seemed at the time to think that the prominent director had been done in by a hired killer for some illicit reason. The film colony felt the heat of the public's outrage over the killing and its scandalous aftermath for the next two decades.

TEAPOT DOME

"If Albert Fall isn't an honest man, I'm not fit to be president of the United States," President Warren G. Harding once remarked in defense of his secretary of the interior, Albert B. Fall. Had he lived, he might have changed his mind. Though Harding was aware of the impending Teapot Dome scandal involving his administration, his unexpected death in early August 1923 spared him the humiliation of seeing Fall go to prison. The sordid revelations of the Teapot Dome scandal contrasted disquietingly with America's almost total absorption in the gaity and good times of the "Roaring Twenties."

In 1912, when the U.S. Navy was converting its ships from coal to diesel fuel, President William H. Taft ordered petroleum-rich lands at Elk Hills and Buena Vista, California, set aside as federal oil reserves for future use by the navy. Two years later President Woodrow Wilson increased the naval oil reserves by adding new fields at Teapot Dome in Wyoming—a petroleum reserve situated beneath a rock formation that vaguely resembled an enormous teapot.

Albert Fall was a lawyer and major ranch owner in New Mexico, where he gained considerable political power before and after the territory achieved statehood in 1912. In that year Fall was elected one of the state's first two United States senators and served in Washington, D.C., until 1921, when he resigned to accept his trusting friend Warren Harding's offer to join Harding's Cabinet as secretary of the interior. At the time, Fall's personal finances were suffering from the large mortgages he carried and from unfortunate investments; his ranch also needed numerous repairs. Fall's cabinet post presented him with an opportunity for personal gain.

He soon convinced Harding that the naval oil reserves in California and Wyoming were being drained by neighboring private oil interests, which should in fact have a chance at using these valuable oil deposits. By executive order of the president, who acted with the approval of Secretary of the Navy Edwin M. Denby, the administration of the oil reserves at Teapot Dome, Elk Hills, and Buena Vista was transferred in 1921 to the Interior Department under Fall, who was then entrusted with the leasing out of the oil fields to private companies (Congress authorized the leasing of the lands, but not in the clandestine way that Fall did).

In April 1922, exclusive rights to the Teapot Dome oil reserves were leased in secret to oil magnate Harry F. Sinclair, head of the Mammoth Oil Company, and portions of the Elk Hills and Buena Vista reserves were given secretly to another oil operator and millionaire, Edward F. Doheny, head of Pan-American Oil Company, who was a long and close friend of Fall's. Both leases were made without any competitive bidding and were signed unwittingly by Denby, who resigned in 1924 as navy secretary and was cleared of all charges of wrongdoing in the Teapot Dome scandal. For his favors to Sinclair and Doheny, Fall privately received $260,000 in Liberty Bonds from the former, who also gave him a herd of cattle for his New Mexico ranch and later, after Fall's forced retirement as interior secretary in March 1923, also "loaned" him $25,000 and offered him a lucrative position in his organization. From Doheny, Fall got an interest-free "loan" of $100,000, which he later publicly and falsely claimed had been a gift from eccentric millionaire Edward B. McLean, before finally confessing that the money had come to him "in a black bag" from Doheny. The two oil men's companies could now exploit the government-owned reserves.

The scandal came to light after a rival Wyoming oil man questioned his congressman about Sinclair's leasing of Teapot Dome without public competitive bidding. A Washington, D.C., correspondent for the *St. Louis Post-Dispatch* disclosed Fall's corrupt transactions, which then became the subject of a Senate investigation (1922–23) directed by Montana Senator Thomas J. Walsh. For a time, U.S. Attorney General Harry H. DAUGHERTY was implicated in the Teapot Dome affair and was forced to resign in 1924 but was never found guilty of attempting to defraud the U.S. government (he was acquitted in 1927). The underhanded dealings of Fall, Sinclair, and Doheny seemed to be surely conspiratorial.

A congressional investigation in 1923 and 1924 uncovered the payoffs to Fall and resulted in a demand by Congress for the annulment of the leases. On June 30, 1924, Fall was indicted for conspiracy and bribery and, in the following years, stood trial eight times, sometimes with Sinclair or Doheny and sometimes alone. The federal government began proceedings in 1924 to cancel the leases to Sinclair and Doheny, and the U.S. Supreme Court finally declared them void in 1927; the government recovered $6 million as well as the oil fields. Criminal prosecutions against Fall, Sinclair, and Doheny ended in acquittals for the latter two in 1927–28 and in a bribery conviction for Fall in 1929; Doheny's remark in court that his $100,000 loan to his good old friend Fall was "a mere bagatelle" scandalized the American public and may have helped convince the jury to find Fall guilty of accepting a bribe from Doheny. Sinclair was, however, found guilty of contempt of Congress, for which he was fined $1,000; he also was convicted of jury tampering (using detectives to follow jurors) and served three months in jail. A physically broken man suffering from tuberculosis, Fall unsuccessfully appealed his case in 1931 and served his one-year sentence in the New Mexico State Penitentiary (a petition to the Supreme Court to review his conviction was refused). He died an impoverished invalid at the age of 83 in 1944.

TELEVISION QUIZ SHOW SCANDAL

In the mid-1950s, the most popular programs on television were weekly quiz shows such as *$64,000 Question, $64,000 Challenge, High Finance,* and *Twenty-One.* Several years later, rumors began to circulate that some of the shows had been rigged, and a subcommittee of the U.S. House of Representatives and the district attorney of New York initiated investigations. The climax came on November 2, 1959, when one of the biggest winners in the shows, Charles Van Doren, confessed that he had been coached to give the correct answers.

The shows *$64,000 Question* and *$64,000 Challenge* held first and second place in television audience ratings in 1955, and when Charles Van Doren became a contestant on *Twenty-One,* that show's ratings began to climb to the top. Van Doren was an articulate, intelligent, good-looking young man from a scholarly family who was working on his doctorate at Columbia University. He tied the then current champion, Herbert Stempel, and several weeks later defeated him. Van Doren immediately became a celebrity and was much adored by TV audiences. He had won $129,000 by the time he lost to Mrs. Vivienne Nearing on the quiz show.

Afterward the National Broadcasting Company (NBC), producers of *Twenty-One,* hired Van Doren for $1,000 a week to substitute for David Garroway during summer airings of the *Today* series and to fulfill other assignments for the network. After earning his Ph.D., Van Doren became an assistant professor of English at Columbia University, with what seemed a rosy future until August 1958, when Herbert Stempel publicly declared that quiz shows were "fixed." Van Doren denied the accusation on the *Today* show. But in January 1959, Frank Hogan, New York's district attorney, convened

a grand jury and called witnesses to investigate the issue. Again, Van Doren and most of the others questioned plainly denied that there had been any irregularities in their performances, but the grand jury was skeptical because there were so many discrepancies in the testimony. After this the Special Subcommittee on Legislative Oversight of the House of Representatives became involved and called its own witnesses, in the fall. The National Broadcasting Corporation urged Van Doren to volunteer to testify, but he equivocated instead. Afterwards, he dropped out of public view for about 10 days.

When Van Doren reappeared, he went to Washington, D.C., and recanted his earlier testimony before the House special subcommittee. "I have deceived my friends, and I had millions of them," he sadly admitted. He described in detail what had happened after he had been selected as a contestant on the *$64,000 Question.* The show's producer, Albert Freedman, had asked Van Doren to come to his apartment and, when the two were alone, had told him that the current winner, Stempel, was "too knowledgeable" to be beaten and that the program was suffering from having an unpopular champion. Further, helping contestants was a usual quiz show practice, said Freedman—it was part of show business. As a clincher, Freedman pointed out that Van Doren could make a great contribution to teachers and education in general "by increasing public respect for the work of the mind." Van Doren confessed that he had allowed himself to be persuaded by these rationalizations and that during each week of his appearance on the show, Freedman had given him the answers to the next program's questions. Freedman had also coached him on his performance, said Van Doren, and suggested ways to heighten audience suspense. After some months, Van Doren had begged to be beaten because the continual tension was becoming too stressful.

Freedman also recanted his earlier testimony but justified his behavior by stating that quiz shows had an intellectual content and were far better for audiences than programs "saturated with murder and violence." Many famous people deceived the public, he asserted, by employing "ghosts" to write their speeches, articles, and books. Providing answers to quiz show contestants was no worse, said Freedman.

Others felt differently about these revelations. After he told the truth, NBC fired Van Doren, and the trustees of Columbia University gladly accepted his resignation from the faculty. Students, however, were more sympathetic, and some even regarded him as a "tragic hero" caught up by circumstances beyond his control. Although Van Doren became the leading symbol of quiz-show dishonesty, Frank Hogan commented that there were many more persons who had cheated and lied about it. Hogan speculated that of the 150 people who had testified before the grand jury investigating the quiz shows, only 50 had probably told the truth. (See also "PAYOLA" SCANDAL.)

TEXACO RACIAL BIAS SCANDAL

As the 14th largest corporation in the United States, Texaco Inc. had made a strong public commitment to equal opportunity for members of all races. But in 1994, the corporation was hit with a $520 million class action lawsuit filed by 1,400 of its current or former black employees. Led by Sil Chambers and Bari-Ellen Roberts, these employees alleged that Texaco executives tolerated and encouraged a corporate culture that primarily rewarded skin color rather than ability. Specifically, they charged that the company handed out the choicest positions and the fattest raises to whites. Other allegations included a variety of racial insults; blacks were routinely called "orangutan" and "porch monkey" to their faces, and one black was asked to serve as a caddy on a golf outing.

For two years Texaco denied the facts of the suit and refused to do anything about the alleged problems. But in 1996 a dramatic revelation by Richard Lundwall, the former senior coordinator of personnel services in Texaco's finance department, forced Texaco to admit its guilt and settle the suit. Lundwall had secretly tape-recorded a conversation among several top-level Texaco executives concerning the corporation's response to the suit. Lundwall routinely taped top-level meetings on a pocket recorder in order to help him keep accurate minutes, but after Texaco forced him to retire as part of a corporate downsizing he sent the tape of the meeting in question to the attorney representing Chambers and Roberts. The quality of the tape made it difficult to determine whether or not the executives had used the word *nigger*; however, what could be understood made it clear that the corporation's top management, composed exclusively of whites, harbored deep-seated feelings of racial bias against blacks. It also made clear the executives' intention to destroy incriminating records and falsify new ones to make it appear that the corporation's personnel practices complied with federal law.

Predictably, the black community was outraged by the disclosure. The Reverend Jesse Jackson called for a national boycott of Texaco gasoline stations while the National Association for the Advancement of Colored People (NAACP) called on shareholders to sell their stock. Whether in response to these calls or not, within days Texaco stock fell by $3 per share, an overall loss in value of about $1 billion.

Eleven days after the tape was made public, Texaco agreed to a $176 million settlement. Of this, $115 million was paid directly to the 1,400 plaintiffs, $26 million was to be given to black employees as pay raises over the next five years, and $35 million was set aside for diversity-training programs throughout the corporation in an effort to eliminate Texaco's corporate culture of racial bias. Texaco also agreed to allow an independent equality and tolerance task force to oversee its future employment practices and report its findings twice a year to the corporation's board of directors. In addition, the corporation disciplined three executives in its financial department whose voices could be heard on Lundwall's tape. Peter Meade and David Keough were suspended, as were the retirement benefits of Robert Ulrich, Texaco's former treasurer.

The only Texaco executives to run afoul of the law over this episode were Ulrich and ironically Lundwall, the man who made the settlement possible. Their voices were clearly identified on the tape as advocating the destruction of sensitive documents, so federal officials charged them with conspiracy and obstruction of justice. These charges carried a maximum penalty of 10 years in prison and a $250,000 fine. Lundwall was offered reduced charges in exchange for testimony against his former fellow executives. He rejected this arrangement because he would have to confess to a misdemeanor which he felt he had not committed. In 1998 a jury found both men not guilty.

THALIDOMIDE: crippling drug

Americans, Europeans, and others were aghast when news broke in 1962 that the supposedly safe drug thalidomide had produced severe birth defects in thousands of children throughout the world. Pregnant women had confidently ingested the drug for more than five years, unaware of its terrible effect on their developing fetuses.

Introduced on the European market in 1957 by its manufacturer, the West German pharmaceutical firm Chemie Grunenthal, thalidomide quickly became popular with women seeking relief from nausea during early pregnancy. Used also as a sedative or tranquilizer for sleeplessness and nervous tension, the drug was said to have no side effects, but, tragically, no tests had been done to assess its effects on an unborn fetus. It became widely used in West Germany and Great Britain. During the next three years, many hundreds of babies were born with gross malformations due to the adverse action of the drug. The worst of these birth defects was phocomelia—the development of short, seallike limbs which often lacked useful hands and feet. Accompanying this were deformities of the ear and eye and the opening of the gastrointestinal tract. As many as 25 percent of the infants born to women who had taken thalidomide were stillborn.

The impact was greatest in Germany, where approximately 2,500 seriously malformed children were born before the Ministry of Health issued a warning about thalidomide in 1961. About 500 such children were born in Britain and hundreds more in Italy, France, and other European countries. Before its removal from the market in 1962, the drug had caused malformations or death in as many as 10,000 babies.

Thalidomide was never officially approved for use in the United States, thanks largely to the efforts of two women doctors. One was Dr. Helen B. Taussig, famous for her work on "blue babies," who traveled to Europe at her own expense to investigate the growing endemic of monstrous births. The other was Dr. Frances Oldham Kelsey, a researcher at the U.S. Food and Drug Administration (FDA), who first became suspicious of thalidomide when she noted that the drug was not effective in making animals sleepy, which tranquilizers typically did. She also noticed that some British women, after using thalidomide, had complained of numbness in their feet and fingers. When asked to approve the drug in the United States, Kelsey refused, resisting for 14 months intense political and professional pressure applied to her by the drug's importers, the William S. Merrell Company of Cincinnati, Ohio, and by some of her superiors in the FDA. Thalidomide was to be marketed in the United States under the brand name Kevadon.

In the summer of 1962, Dr. Taussig returned from Europe and warned the world about thalidomide at a New York news conference. The drug had quietly been withdrawn from the German market eight months earlier, its link to the crippling set of syndromes not yet publicly acknowledged. A huge "pill by pill" search of hospitals, clinics, pharmacies, doctors' offices, and home medicine cabinets was just one part of the worldwide panic that followed Taussig's press conference. Thalidomide had been distributed under some 50 trade names in 20 countries, even though it had won official approval only in Germany and Britain.

Despite the drug's unapproved status, more than 1,200 American physicians had been given samples of it under the loose testing procedures of the time. Approximately 20,000 American women had ingested the drug, and almost none had been informed of its experimental status. The news linking the drug to birth defects compelled one pregnant American woman, 30-year-old Mrs. Sherri Finkbine, who was a children's television program hostess in Arizona, to decide to have an abortion; for several months she had been taking thalidomide bought by her husband in Europe. Her decision made news headlines, brought condemnation from the Vatican and much criticism from outraged Americans, and was not approved by American medical authorities. Nevertheless, Finkbine flew to Sweden, where the abortion was performed in 1962, and where doctors confirmed that her baby would have been malformed. The controversy surrounding Sherri Finkbine gradually subsided, but her example was an issue that probably affected the U.S. Supreme Court decision legalizing abortion in 1973. At least 12 American mothers bore babies profoundly affected by thalidomide. In the United States and elsewhere, abortion laws had to be changed in reaction to the plight of women who knew their fetuses were at risk but who could not obtain abortions legally.

The U.S. Senate praised Dr. Kelsey for her "courage and devotion to the public interest," and President John F. Kennedy gave her a medal for distinguished service—for her stand against thalidomide—in 1962. The thalidomide catastrophe spurred Congress to pass new laws that required manufacturers to prove the effectiveness and safety of new drugs before marketing them, to limit human experimentation before governmental approval of a drug, and to study drugs thoroughly for their side effects on fetuses in the womb. Many older drugs had to be requalified for use by these new standards.

On July 16, 1998, after a panel of scientific experts recommended the use of thalidomide for some leprosy patients, the FDA approved the drug for erythema nodosum leprosum (ENL), a complication of leprosy that causes painful skin lesions. However, physicians would be able to prescribe thalidomide "off label" for other uses, causing fear in some that accidents (like the birth-defect horrors) were inevitable. The drug has shown promise in treating AIDS-related wasting and mouth ulcers, and it is being tested for possible use in treating cancer, lupus, rheumatoid arthritis, and other illnesses.

Harry K. THAW: lecherous millionaire murderer

On June 25, 1906, Stanford White, one of America's most famed architects, was watching a musical performance in the luxury of a dinner theater on the rooftop of New York's first Madison Square Garden (which had been White's own creation) when Harry Kendall Thaw approached his table. Thaw had abruptly left his wife's table and swiftly made his way to White's table before it was clear that he had a revolver in his hand. He fired at the 52-year-old White three times and declared "You deserve this. You ruined my wife." The architect died immediately from two bullets in the brain. Thaw was arrested and charged with murder.

Thaw's histrionic action engendered two spectacular trials, the first ending in a hung jury, the second in a verdict of acquittal because of temporary insanity. Both trials made public widely disseminated details of the extreme luxury and lasciviousness characteristic of the lives of White, Evelyn Nesbit (Thaw's wife until 1916), and the pampered, undisciplined Thaw.

During the trial, White was revealed to have a predilection for adolescent girls. He had a luxuriously appointed playroom in his New York apartment, where his female guests, dressed in little girls' clothes, swung on a red velvet swing as part of his scenario of seduction. To this scene came a lovely, stage-struck 16-year-old, Evelyn Nesbit, whose mother believed that she should stop at nothing to achieve theatrical advancement. The

Harry K. Thaw, who fatally shot famous architect Stanford White in 1906 in a rage of jealousy, was found not guilty on grounds of insanity at the time he committed the murder. However, he was declared criminally insane and imprisoned in an asylum for a time. (The Bettmann Archive)

girl accordingly became mistress to the distinguished architect in the early 1900s.

Like White, Thaw had bizarre sexual interests. Doted on by his mother during his youth in Pittsburgh, he had never developed the self-discipline of an adult male. His multimillionaire tycoon father had tried to toughen him up, once restricting him to an allowance of $2,000 a year, but his indulgent mother had responded to his unhappiness by giving him some additional pocket money—$80,000 annually. A college dropout, Thaw had never worked, and after 1889 he had gained his father's money and became a playboy of a ruthless, deceitful sort. Thaw once maintained an apartment in a New York brothel, where he acquired the company of young ladies who believed his line about being a theatrical entrepeneur. They never stayed long, for part of his erotic technique was to administer beatings to enhance his pleasure.

Thaw became enamored of 17-year-old Evelyn Nesbit in 1901, and pressed her to relinquish her relationship with White and develop one with him. She demanded marriage and gained it in 1905, only to discover (according to accounts given at the second trial) that he would beat her so severely that she would invent detailed narratives of her experiences with White to make him stop. After hearing numerous narratives the possessive, self-centered, and insecure Thaw developed a jealousy so powerful that he planned to eradicate White.

The two trials of Thaw filled the newspapers, gaining as much publicity as would a national crisis. The first trial was the defense's, controlled by a wily California lawyer, Delphin Delmas, hired by Thaw's mother. Delmas made Nesbit pose as innocence defiled by an outrageous monster, White, and saved by a defender of American womanhood, Harry Thaw. Nesbit had enough talent to play her role convincingly, but Thaw often cried or fell into incoherent rages during the court sessions.

In the second trial, controlled by the prosecution, Thaw's behavior was even stranger and more erratic and Nesbit's testimony more honest than in the first. But the final verdict saved Thaw from severe punishment, declaring him "not guilty, on the ground of his insanity at the time of the commission of the act."

Thaw was committed for life to the New York Asylum for the Criminally Insane at Matteawan, New York. His mother and her lawyers worked vigorously to free him. In 1913, Thaw escaped to Canada, was caught and extradited, and declared sane for a long enough time to procure a divorce from Nesbit, whom he now hated and distrusted. In 1916 he was committed again to the Matteawan asylum, after being found guilty of having horsewhipped a young male companion for erotic entertainment. He had even attempted suicide.

Released again in 1922, Thaw, now 51 years old, attempted to live the life of a playboy. He reduced his inherited millions of dollars through liaisons and lawsuits involving actresses and show girls until his death in 1947 at the age of 76.

Paul THAYER: lying defense secretary

Paul Thayer, a wealthy Texan who had served as United States deputy secretary of defense during the Reagan administration, was fined and sentenced to four years in prison in May 1985 for passing inside information about pending mergers and acquisitions to a small group of elitist friends who made substantial illegal profits from these revelations. Thayer's co-defendant, Billy Bob Harris, a well-to-do Dallas stock broker, received the same sentence.

Thayer, former chairman of the LTV Corporation and director of the Anheuser-Busch Company and Allied Corporation, tipped off Harris and other friends from September 1981 to September 1982. When the Securities and Exchange Commission (SEC) first investigated, Thayer and Harris lied, saying that they were not involved in any illegal transactions. However, Thayer's girlfriend, Sandra Ryno, a former LTV receptionist and one of the beneficiaries of the insider information, agreed to cooperate with the SEC in return for immunity. Thayer and Harris eventually pleaded guilty to the charges against them. Although Thayer himself did not use the insider information, his friends who did made illegal profits of $1.9 million as a result.

Prior to sentencing, Thayer and his attorney assembled a collection of character references from such national leaders as former President Gerald Ford, Senator Barry Goldwater, and General John Vessey, all of whom praised his patriotism and government service. Thayer also paid $555,000 to settle the SEC suit against him. Despite these actions made to gain leniency, federal Judge Charles Richey was not moved. "This court" he declared, "is not going to hand a medal upon the lapel of your coats for the breach of trust, for the false statements, the perjurious statements, and the obstruction of justice you have engaged in." Richey then sentenced the 65-year-old Thayer to four years in prison, only one year less than the maximum sentence allowed by the law. One federal attorney said that the unexpectedly stiff sentence would send "a message to Wall Street offices and brokerage houses all over the country that this is serious criminal behavior." Thayer lamented, "I have destroyed a life of achievement based on trust and integrity. The last two years have been a living nightmare. I don't like myself as well as I used to."

Thayer's attorney had called his client's criminal conduct "an aberration" and the crime "a foolish mistake." The prosecution, however, thought differently, saying, "Mr. Thayer probably had more money at the time than everybody in this courtroom combined" and claimed that the former deputy secretary had committed his crime because "he thought he could get away with it." In fact, the Thayer case's result was unusual in that about 60 percent of convicted white-collar criminals receive no prison term, and those who do go to jail serve one year or less. Such leniency with corporate criminals has been blamed for the rise in business crime today.

Thayer was paroled in late 1986 after serving 19 months in federal prison and a halfway house. He had settled SEC charges against him by agreeing to pay the government $555,000, and in 1987 he agreed to pay nearly $600,000 to settle a suit brought by Anheuser-Busch, which alleged that he had publicly revealed confidential company information while serving on its board.

J. Parnell THOMAS: devious patriot padded his congressional payroll

Upon examination, the voting attitude of the American public toward its elected representatives often seems slightly schizophrenic. With due allowance for the individual differences of their electees, Americans expect those they place in public office to be loyal, efficient, and honest—in short, they wish them to be upholders of political virtue. But because, by some definitions, all men and women are imperfect and some fail to be ideal representatives, most of the voters shrug their shoulders, recite the banal formula "that's politics," and, except for

the essentially unglamorous and corrupt, return them to office.

A good case in point is that of J. Parnell Thomas, a former United States Republican congressman from New Jersey whose blunders were so notorious as to eventually gain him a brief stay in a federal pentitentiary before his total banishment from the political game.

Thomas had been born with the name John Patrick Feeney in 1895; the era was one in which an obviously Irish name was a handicap or bar to political success, and because, above all, John Patrick Feeney wanted to "get ahead" and not to be discriminated against, he remodeled his designation to the mildly prophetic J(ohn) Parnell Thomas. His new name covered his shanty-Irish background with the lace-curtain scrim of the famous Irish politician Charles Stewart Parnell, Ireland's fiery nationalist leader in the 1880s, who was once called "the uncrowned king of Ireland." The new name enabled Feeney to steer a course toward political advancement.

In his early years, he steered carefully; no evidence of malfeasance blemished his transit from the mayoralty of a New Jersey town to his election in 1937 as a New Jersey Republican holder of a seat in the U.S. House of Representatives.

Life in Washington, D.C., at the munificent salary of $10,000 a year did not, however, provide enough "getting ahead" for Thomas. By 1940 he had devised a foolproof scheme for enhancing his income: he would receive for himself the net salaries of nonworking persons on his staff through an illegal kickback maneuver in which he would pay the taxes on the salaries (at a low tax bracket). The scheme, involving strangers, a housekeeper, an aunt, and a daughter-in-law, worked quietly until 1948. In the meantime, Thomas's fellow members of Congress got him named chairman of the much publicized HOUSE COMMITTEE ON UN-AMERICAN ACTIVITIES (HUAC) in 1947.

Thomas's political downfall was the result of his failure to detect the presence in his scheme of a staffer who turned "foolish." He had relied upon the devotion of his long-time secretary Helen Campbell, a woman in her sixties who had fallen in love with Thomas enough to carry on an affair with him despite his obesity and his marriage of 30 years. When she discovered that Thomas, like his namesake Parnell (whose adultery and subsequent divorce in 1890 had destroyed his political career), had been unfaithful to her, she informed on him to columnist Drew Pearson, who had several reasons for wanting to punish Thomas and reform the bullying HUAC.

Ironically, it was the kickback scheme that destroyed Thomas rather than his adultery, a peccadillo that has seldom destroyed an American political career. It is even more ironic that Thomas, who as chairman of the HUAC had so often castigated witnesses for using aliases, was forced to reveal that he, too, had taken another name.

Yet it is most ironic that the congressman who had intimidated witnesses with charges that they had used the American system to their own nefarious, possibly subversive, ends and who had blocked their attempts to exercise their constitutional rights should use every trick in the catalogue of evasion to avoid his own prosecution.

Thomas denied all of the charges against him as dirty politics, as if the bank accountings showing the kickbacks had been faked by his political enemies. He persuaded the American Legion and congressional leaders to press for the quashing of the case against him, which they did in vain. He gained a grand jury postponement and then, claiming his constitutional rights, refused to appear. He managed to get five trial postponements by playing sick (even once undergoing unnecessary surgery to ensure a hospital stay) and would have gained a sixth had not doctors at Walter Reed Hospital refused to admit him.

Finally cornered, Thomas stood trial, disrupting the proceedings by suddenly pleading no contest and weepily throwing himself on the mercy of the court. It showed none: he was sentenced to jail for a period not exceeding 18 months and, as an added irony, was ordered to pay $10,000 in fines for the crime of illegally embezzling only $8,000. He lost his congressional seat (later his wife stood for election as his replacement; not unexpectedly, she lost).

Thomas served only part of the prison term imposed on him in 1949; he was paroled in 1950 and pardoned by President Harry Truman at the end of that year. He died in 1970.

Olive THOMAS: drugs and dives

Adored by millions of fans for her seemingly sweet, innocent nature, Olive Thomas seemed to have it all—youth, beauty, love, fame, and wealth. At the young age of 20, already a popular film star, she married one of the most handsome men in Hollywood. Not surprisingly, Americans were stunned on September 10, 1920, when the much loved Olive was found dead in her Paris hotel suite. In her hand was a bottle of poisonous bichloride of mercury.

At the age of 16, Olive Thomas began dazzling New Yorkers as a vivacious Ziegfeld Follies showgirl on Broadway. She also became a leading fashion model, appearing often in the pages of *Vogue* and *Vanity Fair* magazines. New York's café society soon made her one of its favorite young darlings, and the foremost American illustrator at the time, Harrison Fisher, called Olive "the most beautiful girl in the world." No one was surprised when Hollywood, the then upstart film capital, lured her away to make silent pictures on the silver screen. She appeared in some light comedies, winning more fame, and in 1919 moviemaker Myron Selznick signed her to a lucrative contract that brought starring roles in *The Flapper* and *The Tomboy* (1920). Called The Ideal American Girl, young Olive married another screen idol, Jack Pickford, brother of leading romantic film lady Mary Pickford. Fan magazines characterized Olive and Jack as "The Ideal Couple," and the two began busily establishing themselves as members of Hollywood's chic set.

Their busy moviemaking schedules had prevented Mr. and Mrs. Jack Pickford from taking a honeymoon right after their marriage, but they planned to enjoy that honeymoon in September in Paris. Olive went first, alone, to await the arrival of Jack, who was finishing up work on a film. Before he arrived, Olive was seen in some of the most unsavory nightspots in the Montmartre area, talking with some notorious French underworld characters. The discovery of her dead body, lying naked on the floor of her hotel room on the morning of September 10 resulted in sensational front-page headlines that blared: "Olive Thomas Dead From Poison," "Broadway Dims Lights For Noted Screen Star," and "Paris Police Probe Olive Thomas's Death." Her Hollywood image was shattered during the ensuing investigations and their media coverage.

The story was that Olive Thomas had appeared "very excitable" when she returned to her Paris hotel in the early morning hours of September 10. Evidently, a Los Angeles physician had earlier prescribed drugs to help her "nervous complaint," and he felt that she had taken an overdose of these. But it was strongly rumored that she had been desperately searching Paris for heroin or cocaine for her husband Jack, who was an apparent drug addict. Not able to get these narcotics, she had killed herself in grief. Other rumors held that she was an addict herself. Her famous sister-in-law, Mary Pickford, who had recently had a highly questionable divorce followed by a quick marriage to Douglas Fairbanks, strongly criticized the press's assaults on her brother's character. Jack Pickford had suffered a nervous collapse upon learning of his wife's death. He was unable to squash stories about his drug taking and was soon haunted by the discovery of other rumors about his past. Apparently, while in the U.S. Navy during World War I, he had supposedly tried to get discharged as an "undesirable" and had been involved in a scheme in which rich young men were relieved of dangerous duty in exchange for money. Jack Pickford finally received an ordinary navy discharge.

After her death, Olive's name was found among the contacts of a Captain Spaulding of the U.S. Army, who had been imprisoned in Paris for selling large quantities of heroin and cocaine. Her death remains a scandalous enigma to this day, and the morality of Hollywood has since been found wanting by many people.

THOMAS-HILL SCANDAL: sexual harassment or "high-tech lynching"?

In the autumn of 1991, the topic of sexual harassment in the workplace became a nationally discussed issue

Judge Clarence Thomas reflects during his testimony before the Senate Judiciary Committee on Capitol Hill in October 1991. He categorically denied Anita Hill's accusations of sexual harassment and told the committee, "confirm me if you want," but that "no job is worth" what he was going through. He was later confirmed as a U.S. Supreme Court justice. (AP/Wide World Photos)

when Clarence Thomas, Supreme Court nominee, was accused of sexual harassment. Anita Hill, a professor of commercial law at the time the accusations were made public, had worked with Clarence Thomas from 1981 to 1983 at the U.S. Department of Education and then at the Equal Employment and Opportunity Commission (EEOC). In 1991, when Thomas was announced as a candidate for appointment to the U.S. Supreme Court, Hill came forward and claimed that when she and Thomas worked together Thomas had made crude comments to her, discussing the nature of his sexual prowess and favorite scenes from pornographic movies, among other advances.

The two were questioned by the Senate Judiciary Committee, through which, in essence, the accusation came down to Hill's word against Thomas's; both were known for their integrity and credibility. Though Thomas was eventually approved for his lifetime appointment to the highest court in the nation, the public was left in doubt as to which of the two (if any) was lying. Stripping each of their dignity and conjuring dark images of perversion at the highest levels of justice, the trial laid bare an issue that gripped the nation and likely strained relations between many men and women in the workforce.

In 1981, Hill was hired as special counsel to Thomas at the U.S. Department of Education office for civil rights. In 1982, she then followed Thomas to a post at the EEOC, which she left one year later to become a professor of law at Oral Roberts University, subsequently moving on to the University of Oklahoma. She was a straitlaced and serious young African-American woman.

Thomas, a conservative black justice, had spent his life distancing himself from racial stereotypes and prejudice. In fact, he had been known in the past to rail against those who allowed supposed discrimination to be an obstacle in their lives. It was particularly ironic, analysts said, that during the hearings Thomas complained of the "torture" he had undergone because of the allegations, which he thought were racially motivated, and bitterly called the whole affair a "high-tech lynching for uppity blacks."

For every allegation, there was a plausible rebuttal. Hill claimed Thomas spoke to her of actors and sordid acts he had seen in pornographic films. Senator Orrin Hatch (Republican from Utah) suggested that Hill had fabricated her story from bits and pieces taken from past court cases and movies. Hill asserted that Thomas asked her out five to 10 different times and that she feared for her career if she persisted in rejecting him. Pennsylvania Republican Senator Arlen Specter accused Hill of fantasizing about Thomas asking her for dates, and Thomas himself denied such claims, saying that he only tried to help Hill at every turn. Witnesses testified that Hill had confided in them at the time of the harassment and had made other allegations of misconduct against Thomas. Others came forward and tried to discredit Hill, making disparaging remarks about what they felt was her own questionable sexual conduct. Hill said she suffered from vulnerability, frustration, and humiliation because of her relationship with Thomas. Thomas thought her whole story was fabricated by some interest group intent on ruining his career and destroying his chance for a Supreme Court nomination.

Hill did keep in touch with Thomas after she left the EEOC and in fact phoned him several times. When questioned about this, she claimed that she disliked to burn bridges and that the calls were made mainly to consult on professional matters. Her detractors wondered why she waited so long to bring charges against Thomas. In the early 1980s, Hill said, sexual harassment cases were not taken seriously. She did not come forward earlier with the allegations, she said, because she feared for her career and for possible retaliation on Thomas's part if she filed a formal complaint. She did not initiate any legal action until she was contacted by Senate Democratic staff members; even then, she had wanted to lodge the complaints anonymously.

The judiciary committee could not find any motivation for which Hill would make these accusations. Despite this, the fact that a movie store clerk testified that Thomas was a regular consumer of adult movies, and another witness claimed that Thomas's apartment walls were covered with pinups and pictures from pornographic magazines, Thomas was confirmed as the 106th justice of the Supreme Court by a narrow margin. Hill entered a career as a high-profile legal commentator. Each tried to forget the case, but it left as its legacy heightened awareness of sexual harassment in the workplace. The general consensus was that Thomas lied to Congress when he categorically denied all the charges, but also that Hill was at fault for not making it clear to Thomas at the time that his advances were indeed unwelcome, the chief factor which defines sexual harassment in the legal sense.

Jim THORPE: Olympic records expunged

In the early 20th century, Jim (James Francis) Thorpe, a Sac and Fox Indian from Oklahoma, was commonly considered the world's greatest athlete. Among his numerous athletic achievements, Thorpe was the winner of both the pentathlon and decathlon in the 1912 Olympic Games. His tremendous fame and glory were removed in less than a year, however, for Thorpe was accused of falsely claiming an amateur status.

As a student at the Carlisle Indian School (a vocational school in Pennsylvania) from 1907 to 1912, Thorpe amassed an outstanding football record against such highly rated teams as Harvard, Army, and the University of Pennsylvania and was twice chosen as halfback on Walter Camp's All-America football team. The climax of his career came in 1912 at the Olympic Games in Stockholm, Sweden, where the 24-year-old Thorpe (whose Indian name meant Bright Path) won both the pentathlon and the decathlon, events designed to test the all-around athletic prowess of the competitors. Thorpe placed first in four of the five pentathlon events—the 200-meter race, the 1500-meter run, the running broad jump, and the discus throw—and third in the javelin throw. In the 10 decathlon events, he came in first in the 1500-meter race, the 110-meter hurdles, the shot put, and the running high jump; third in the 100-meter dash; and fourth in the 400-meter race and the javelin throw. His total score was a remarkable 8,412 points out of a possible 10,000, an Olympic record that was to stand for 16 years. In presenting Thorpe with his trophies, King Gustav of Sweden called him "the greatest athlete in the world."

But by the following year scandal erupted. The Amateur Athletic Union (AAU), which selected all Olympic competitors and certified their amateur status, learned from a newspaper story that Thorpe had briefly played semiprofessional baseball. In a statement to the AAU, Thorpe admitted that in the summers of 1909 and 1910 he had played baseball for pay ($60 a month) for a North Carolina team. He explained, however, that many other college men—often using false names to disguise their identity—played on the teams and were regarded as amateurs at home. Appealing to the AAU for compassion, Thorpe wrote, "I was not wise in the ways of the world and did not realize this was wrong, and that it would make me a professional in track sports. . . . I hope I would be partly excused because of the fact that I was simply an Indian school boy and did not know all about such things."

The AAU's response was stern, ruling that Thorpe was not an amateur. In January 1913, Thorpe's name and accomplishments were expunged from the Olympic records and his trophies were ordered returned. The second-place finishers in the pentathlon and decathlon of the 1912 games were awarded the gold medals.

Thorpe's defenders, and they were many, argued that the athlete's professional work had been in a sport different from the one in which he had competed in the Olympics and that professionalism in baseball should not be declared professionalism in track and field or another sport. Moreover, said those on Thorpe's side, many college athletes received scholarships or other financial assistance and were allowed to retain their amateur status. It was also noted that many "amateur" college athletes played professional baseball or football anonymously (Thorpe had played under his own name) without penalty. Discussing Thorpe, sports authority Damon Runyon wrote:

> One small indiscretion of his athletic youth has come forward at this late hour, after he won all the glories that could be gained in his chosen field. . . . It seems a little thing enough that this great Carlisle star did. All the material honors that Thorpe gained in the Olympic games of 1912—the trophies and what not—have been stripped from the Indian holder. . . . None of his marvelous records will stand. They will be wiped out completely as if they never had existed, although it is rather doubtful if this summary method will remove them from the memory of the people who follow athletic events.

Runyon's prophecy proved true, for in a 1950 Associated Press poll of sportswriters and sports broadcasters, Thorpe was chosen as the greatest athlete of the first half of the 20th century, as well as the greatest football player.

In 1913, after leaving Carlisle, Thorpe joined the New York Giants baseball team. His professional baseball career was less successful than his other athletic endeavors, and after several seasons with various teams he returned to football, playing with professional teams until 1929. In 1920 he helped to organize the American Professional Football Association (later the National Football League) and was elected its first president.

Thorpe held various jobs in his later years. After spending some time in Hollywood, including a stint as a bit player in western movies, he returned to Oklahoma, where he became active in Indian affairs. He gave lectures around the country on sports, his career, and American Indian culture. In 1951 Warner Brothers released a film about him entitled *Jim Thorpe— All American*.

Thorpe died in 1953. His remains were buried in a Pennsylvania town renamed Jim Thorpe in his honor. In the 1970s his daughter, Grace Thorpe, spearheaded an effort to restore her father's medals. Twenty years after the athlete's death, the AAU restored his amateur status, a necessary preliminary to full Olympic recognition. In 1975 President Gerald Ford, writing as a "private American citizen with a lifetime interest in sports," requested that the International Olympic Committee (IOC) restore Thorpe to recognition. Other notables, such as Senators Mike Mansfield, George McGovern, Charles Percy, and Frank Moss, supported the request. Finally, in 1983, more than 70 years after Thorpe's Olympic triumph, the IOC presented his children with two gold medals to replace those that their father sent back in 1913.

THREE MILE ISLAND: doubt and distrust after a nuclear accident

At a time when legislation to speed up the licensing of American nuclear generating plants was making its way through Congress, a serious accident occurred at the No. 2 nuclear reactor of the Metropolitan Edison Company's plant on Three Mile Island, located in the Susquehanna River near Middletown, Pennsylvania, not far from the state capital of Harrisburg. What happened was the nation's first and worst commercial nuclear accident, one that would change the focus and direction of the nuclear power industry for years to come.

The major disaster at Three Mile Island gave impetus to a previously stagnant antinuclear movement and provided a rallying cry for American activists who sought to publicize the dangers of using atomic fuel to produce electricity and who also wanted to stop the construction of nuclear power plants. After the crisis at Three Mile Island, public support for further nuclear power development diminished considerably.

On March 28, 1979, radioactive gases escaped into the atmosphere through the Three Mile Island plant's ventilation system and apparently through the walls of the containment building, built to shield the environment from the nuclear reactor within. Small amounts of radiation issued from the No. 2 reactor for the next 13 days.

State and federal authorities initially downplayed the severity of the accident and any health hazards associated with it, evidently out of fear and ignorance of what had happened. There was a state of panic in the area, but residents were first told that an evacuation was not necessary because health risks were minimal. Two days later, Pennsylvania Governor Richard Thornburgh closed the schools in the area and urged all pregnant women and pre-school children to leave and other residents to stay indoors. Many people decided to evacuate on their own.

Estimates of the damage to the No. 2 reactor and explanations for why the accident had happened seemed to change almost every day in the weeks afterward, thus fostering a deep public distrust of officials' reports on the disaster and radioactivity problems stemming from it. The Metropolitan Edison Company, which operated the Three Mile Island plant, added to the distrust by failing to take responsibility for the accident, describing the problems it posed as "insignificant" and "minuscule." Undoubtedly the confusing and often contradictory reports occurred partly because no such event had ever taken place before. Moreover, even though many safety precautions were built into the plant's operation, the reality of such a crisis caught many persons completely off guard.

The Nuclear Regulatory Commission (NRC), the federal agency whose job is to regulate civilian nuclear plants and to assure that public health, safety, and the environment are protected from their potential dangers, at first blamed the accident on the failure of several safety systems. Authorities of the NRC took charge of bringing the crisis under control. On May 12, 1979, the NRC reported that the plant operators—unaware of what was happening inside the damaged reactor during the accident—had made a major disaster out of what probably would have been a minor one. The report also claimed there were some design flaws in the plant, making it difficult for employees to figure out if problems were occurring.

President Jimmy Carter, who had visited Three Mile Island during the crisis and proclaimed the radioactivity in the area to be "quite safe," set up a congressional task force to investigate the accident (the damaged No. 2 reactor was brought to a cold shutdown by April 27, 1979). The task force concluded that a cooling-system malfunction, design problems, inadequate instruments, and faulty valves, along with human error, had caused the accident.

The accident itself was not a core meltdown, or "China syndrome," the worst possible scenario at a nuclear power plant in which the radioactive material that generates the steam used to produce electricity at the plant breaks through the containment structure into the earth below, contaminating the groundwater and probably causing massive loss of life. But it was close. Radioactive material had to be released into the atmosphere and the surrounding river to prevent a buildup of pressure in the reactor's chamber. More than one quarter of the reactor's 36,000 fuel rods were damaged, allowing a large hydrogen gas bubble to form in the top of the reactor containment vessel. The bubble could have caused an explosion, and the deflation of the bubble was a very tedious and dangerous operation.

Officials of the NRC reported that 12 separate equipment failures had occurred at Three Mile Island in the past year. There were also reports that NRC members knew of serious flaws at the plant before the accident but failed to take any action because of ideological differences within their group.

After the accident at Three Mile Island, public opinion began to turn against the nuclear power industry, and a Gallup poll showed that two out of three Americans felt that atomic power should be cut back until safety regulations were made more stringent. Public opinion also pressured the NRC to temporarily close all plants with nuclear reactors designed by the Babcock and Wilcox Company (the designer of Three Mile Island's two reactors) until safety procedures were updated.

The country's largest demonstration against nuclear energy took place in Washington, D.C., on May 6, 1979, when more than 65,000 persons marched on the Capitol to show their deep concern that the nuclear industry had gotten out of control. Atomic power expansion was an issue in the 1980 presidential election and in subsequent elections, and doubt about the safety of nuclear power became even more serious following the Soviet Union's far graver nuclear accident at Chernobyl, in the Ukraine, on April 26, 1986.

The long cleanup of the partial meltdown at Three Mile Island lasted until early 1997, by which time crews had finally transported some 150 tons of damaged fuel rods and other radioactive material taken from the reactor to a temporary underwater storage facility in the Idaho desert. Here the waste will remain until safer storage can be found, at least until 2010 (the waste will remain radioactive for more than 10,000 years). However, the federal government and the nuclear industry faced a greater dilemma concerning safe burial for more than 30,000 tons of spent fuel from more than 100 commercial nuclear reactors in the country. Refuse from the shutdown of older reactors will probably help double that amount of radioactive waste by 2010. See also NORTHEAST UTILITIES' NUCLEAR SAFETY SCANDAL.

TIDAL BASIN INCIDENT. See Wilbur MILLS: the Tidal Basin incident.

Bill TILDEN: eccentric tennis player
Born in Philadelphia, Pennsylvania, in 1893, William Tatem Tilden II, who was later popularly known as Bill Tilden, received special childhood care from his doting mother, who had wanted a girl at the time of his birth. She kept him out of grammar school on the pretext that he was too ill to attend and fondly tutored him at home,

calling him by the name of June (for junior). His sex education was evidently distorted by her and her constant reiteration about the curses of venereal disease, so that he allegedly grew into adulthood without a strong sexual preference for girls and instead preferred boys or being alone.

Tilden began playing tennis at an early age, quickly showing his talent and winning his first tennis tournament at the age of eight. As a young man he developed a passion for tennis and for teaching the sport, especially during his collegiate years. Although his masterful court tactics and overpowering play gained him several American championships before 1920, he became truly recognized during that year when he won the prestigious men's singles title at the Wimbledon tournament at Surrey, England; "Big Bill," as he was nicknamed, was the first American ever to win the tournament and won again in 1921 and 1930. From 1920 to 1930 Tilden was a brilliant member of 11 American Davis Cup tournament teams, winning 21 of 28 cup matches and leading the Americans as team captain in taking the Davis Cup

The legendary "Big Bill" Tilden, one of the all-time top tennis players, who dominated the game in the 1920s, was also the toast of the celebrity courts in Hollywood and elsewhere. Eventually his "fondness" for male minors got him arrested several times, resulting in his friends, many of them Hollywood stars, finally ignoring him completely. Here he amazes spectators with his brilliant court play. (The Bettmann Archive)

for seven consecutive years (1920–26). In this period, when he conquered the greats of tennis and dominated the game, he captured national championships throughout the world, including the United States men's singles title three times (1920, 1925, and 1929).

Not only were spectators awed by Tilden's athletic skill, but they frequently delighted in his flair for the dramatic on the court. One of Tilden's most crowd-pleasing techniques was to let his opponents gain a large lead, after which he would brilliantly fight back to overcome them.

Eccentric behavior became increasingly noticeable in his life as he grew older (Tilden turned professional in 1931 and toured with other tennis players, giving exhibition matches). Fellow players complained about his disgustingly dirty clothes and offensive body odor, but he apparently paid little heed and didn't wash himself any more often than before. He never changed clothes in front of other players and was never seen naked in the dressing rooms. As his tennis success ebbed in the latter 1930s, his sexual predilections became less concealed, but the American public didn't learn that he was a latent homosexual until November 1946.

At that time Tilden was arrested by police in Beverly Hills, California, where he lived, and charged with "contributing to the delinquency of a minor." The police had stopped his zigzagging car and found a 14-year-old boy named Bobbie at the wheel, with Tilden beside him with his arm around the boy; the boy's fly was open when he stepped out of the car. The tennis star felt the charge was frivolous. He received more than a dozen letters of reference to support his character (including one from his good friend Charlie Chaplin) but eventually was sentenced to one year's incarceration at a minimum security prison farm. Released after serving less than eight months, he promised to stay away from minors and obtained psychiatric help. In January 1949, however, he was again arrested on charges of improper conduct with a 16-year-old boy, a hitchhiker whom he had picked up in his car. The court rejected Chaplin's effort to take Tilden into his personal custody outside the United States and instead sentenced him to a work camp, where he remained for almost a year.

Many of Tilden's friends deserted him, and much of the public looked upon him with scorn and loathing. He grew impoverished, and on June 5, 1953 some friends found him dead on his bed in Hollywood. Not one tennis great came to his funeral.

TILDEN-HAYES ELECTION. See Joseph P. BRADLEY: the stolen election of 1876.

TIMES BEACH. See ENVIRONMENTAL PROTECTION AGENCY (EPA): "sweetheart deals" with industry?

TOBACCO ROAD. See Erskine CALDWELL: "the South's literary bad boy."

Thelma TODD: murder, suicide, or mishap?
The 1935 death of the "Vamping Venus," American movie actress and comedienne Thelma Todd, has remained a scandalous mystery to this day. The lively blonde, who was popular with fans and film people alike, starred with the Marx Brothers in such successful films as *Monkey Business* (1931) and *Horse Feathers* (1932). She also worked with Hollywood stars Laurel and Hardy, Buster Keaton, Bing Crosby, and Zasu Pitts, who was probably her closest female friend. Though her death was formally announced to be due to asphyxiation, it now seems clear that the young actress was murdered.

On Monday morning, December 16, 1935, the dead body of the 30-year-old Todd was discovered when her maid opened the garage door. The actress was slumped over the steering wheel of her car, a Packard convertible with its top down. Blood was on her face, her evening gown, and the mink coat she was wearing. Her lip was cut, and a tooth was dislodged. The "Hot Toddy," her friends' nickname for her, just didn't seem the type to commit suicide, but it certainly looked like she had. The car's ignition switch was turned on, but the motor was not running.

The building in which Todd lived in a small upstairs apartment was at a distance of 500 yards from the garage. Living close by in the building was movie director Roland West, whose mistress Todd had been for some time and with whom she owned and ran the café-restaurant located on the first floor of the building. The café, along the Pacific Coast Highway, had become very successful and popular and was frequented by many of Todd's wealthy and famous friends.

At the inquest into Todd's death, which resulted in a verdict of suicide, it was decided that she had evidently died Monday morning at around 7:00 A.M. (her body had been found at 10:30 A.M.). But Todd's lawyers protested, saying that much about her death had been left unexplained and that there was an indication of foul play. They obtained a second inquest before a grand jury, which spent weeks going over confusing and conflicting testimony to reach another questionable verdict: "death by carbon monoxide poisoning."

Since that time, many have pondered over the facts and confusing evidence in Thelma Todd's death. In testimony, Zasu Pitts revealed that she had loaned much money to Todd to help run the café, which apparently had become targeted by racketeer-gangster Charles "Lucky" Luciano and organized crime. Luciano was alleged to have wanted to establish a secret gambling casino on the upper floor of "Thelma's cafe," but he had been turned down by Todd, according to her lawyer, and thus had assigned a hit man to kill her. A few months before her death, she had hired a bodyguard for a while after receiving two anonymous threats on her life by the "San Francisco Boys," who demanded blackmail money. But nothing could be proven against mobster Luciano, who was indeed trying to set up gambling dens in California at the time.

The relationship between Todd and West was another enigma, for the latter reluctantly revealed, after much questioning, that they had had a furious argument in the early hours of the Sunday morning preceding Todd's death. Pushed outdoors, the actress had been heard by neighbors shouting obscenities and battering the front door of her apartment building. That night she had attended a party at the Trocadero nightclub given by Stanley Lupino and his daughter Ida, who testified that Todd appeared happy at the party but disclosed that she was having a wild affair with a San Francisco businessman without West's knowledge. At 3:30 A.M. Todd got a ride home from the party, supposedly found all the doors to her house locked (West said he had joked to her before she went to the party that he would lock her out if she wasn't back by 2 A.M.), and then had to spend the night in the garage with the car motor on to keep warm. West admitted to locking all the doors but didn't explain why he hadn't gone to hunt for Todd the next day (Sunday) if, in fact, she was missing. The police asserted that Todd had died that Sunday night. Perhaps, as some persons have suggested, West allegedly caused her murder, having grown tired of their relationship. A girlfriend of his could have been made up in order to appear like Todd and could have caused the noise that woke up the neighbors, while West knocked his victim out, put her in the car with the motor running, and shut the garage door. Under some suspicion, West was never able to direct another movie. He later married Lola Lane and died in obscurity in 1952. He denied ever wishing to kill Todd.

There were witnesses who claimed to have seen Todd on Sunday driving around Hollywood in her Packard convertible with an unknown, dark, handsome man at her side. Was this the San Francisco businessman, her new romance, or was he a thug applying pressure to her for criminal purposes? One witness said she had received a phone call from Todd on Sunday afternoon in which the blonde beauty had said she still had her evening gown on and intended to pay a visit with a surprise purpose but never showed up. Another person claimed that Todd, in a frenzy and accompanied by a strange man, had entered his drugstore on Sunday to make a phone call.

After all was said and examined, the fact that a murder had occurred seemed incontestable. The absence of scuff marks on the soles of Todd's evening shoes indicated that she had not walked from the building to the garage, up the many stone steps. Furthermore, the garage windows had been left open, and the actress had not sat in her closed sedan in the garage, which would have surely suited a purpose of suicide much better than an open convertible. Also pointing away from suicide was that Thelma Todd had been in high spirits before her sudden demise and had plenty of rewarding work ahead of her and numerous friends and admirers.

TOKYO ROSE: American traitor or scapegoat?
Iva Ikuko Toguri d'Aquino, better known as Tokyo Rose, was one of at least 13 women announcers broadcasting over Japan's Radio Tokyo to American servicemen stationed in the Pacific region during World War II. In seductive voices, the women told of Japan's military successes and imminent victory, urged the Allies to surrender because their cause was futile, and claimed that the Americans' wives and girlfriends waiting back home were being unfaithful. A native-born American citizen, Tokyo Rose was later convicted of treason, but many believed she was an innocent victim of circumstance.

Born in Los Angeles of Japanese parents, Iva Toguri received permission from the U.S. Department of State for a six-month visit to a very sick aunt in Japan, shortly after her graduation from the University of California at Los Angeles in 1941. The Japanese bombed Pearl Harbor while she was abroad, and she was denied clearance to leave Japan. Life there was difficult for her because she was classified as an enemy alien, denied a food ration card, and refused internment as an American national. In 1942 she found part-time work at the Domei news agency, where she met Felipe d'Aquino, a Portuguese citizen of Japanese ancestry, whom she later married during the war.

In August 1943, Iva began work as a typist in the business office of Radio Tokyo, where she became friends with several Allied prisoners of war, including Australian Major Charles Cousens and American Captain Wallace Ince. These two men were in charge of Radio Tokyo's English-language "Zero Hour" broadcasts. Iva's rather masculine-sounding voice was soon added to their show. (Cousens picked her to thwart the radio's purpose of having a female announcer). She became one of 13 women announcers, though reluctantly, she later said. She was nicknamed Tokyo Rose, by the American GIs who listened to her broadcasts in the Pacific.

After the war ended in 1945, Tokyo Rose had become such a legend that two Hearst newspaper reporters offered $2,000 to interview her. Iva came forward, claiming the label but was imprisoned instead in Tokyo. After 11 months in prison, she was released in October 1946 when the U.S. Justice Department decided her broadcasts had been innocuous and were "not sufficient to warrant prosecution for treason." In 1947 she applied for her American passport, which she could not be denied, being a native-born citizen.

News of Iva's anticipated return to America caused an uproar and much protest in 1948. A representative of the Justice Department was sent to Tokyo in search of any evidence on which to prosecute her. Iva cooperated, thinking it would expedite her return home. Instead, she was arrested, charged with treason, and brought to San Francisco, where a federal grand jury heard evidence against her in October 1948. Only six recordings of her broadcasts could be found. The jury, having been assured that other Americans involved in Radio Tokyo programs would be similarly charged, issued an eight-count indictment for treason against Iva.

The government prosecutors in the case secured 19 witnesses from Japan, but Iva's attorney was denied the right to obtain similar witnesses. She remained in prison without bail until the start of her trial on July 5, 1949. According to the Constitution, a treason conviction can occur only upon the testimony of "two witnesses to the same overt act, or on confession in open court." The prosecution found two American-born men in Japan who had renounced their United States citizenship; each testified to having heard a broadcast made by Iva declaring that all American ships in the Pacific had been sunk. Major Cousens and Captain Ince (who were both cleared of treason charges) testified for Iva, who also took the stand to reiterate that she had only entertained her countrymen and had retained her American citizenship under duress from Japan. The jury at first was unable to reach a verdict, but sternly admonished by Judge Michael Roche, it declared Iva innocent on seven counts and, on September 29, 1949, guilty on one: having spoken into a "microphone concerning the loss of ships." Judge Roche sentenced her to 10 years in a penitentiary; she also paid a $10,000 fine and lost her American citizenship. Her husband, Felipe, was deported to Japan and warned not to return. Frequent appeals made on Iva's behalf were denied by appellate courts and the Supreme Court.

Released from prison in 1956 because of good behavior, Iva faced the U.S. Immigration and Naturalization Service, which sought to deport her but found no country to which she could be sent (she had neither Japanese nor Portuguese citizenship). She remained in America, asserted her innocence, and eventually saw principal witnesses at her trial admit that they had been coerced into testimony resulting in her conviction. The Japanese-American Citizens League helped Iva to prevail upon the California legislature to pass a unanimous resolution, on June 24, 1976, urging President Gerald Ford to grant her an unconditional pardon. On January 19, 1977, the president did so and reinstated her American citizenship.

TRAIL OF TEARS

During the winter of 1838–39, the Cherokee Indian Nation was forcibly evicted, by government fiat, from its native lands in northwestern Georgia. The Cherokee suffered grievously during an 800-mile forced march to their new homes west of the Mississippi River in Indian territory (now Oklahoma). Of some 17,000 who began the westward trek, about 4,000 died of hunger, exposure, and disease. Later the Cherokee survivors called the terrible journey *Nuna-da-ut-sun'y* ("The Trail Where They Cried") or The Trail of Tears. It was undoubtedly one of the worst disgraces in American history.

Of the Five Civilized Tribes (the Cherokee, Creek, Chickasaw, Choctaw, and Seminole) of Indians in the southeastern United States, the Cherokee were, in the white man's thinking, the most "civilized." They lived in well-built log cabins, prospered as farmers and hunters, and established schools, a newspaper, and their own written language. They were a proud and independent people whose territorial sovereignty became a heated issue to Georgia's white settlers. Increasingly in the early 19th century, the whites looked covetously at the large, fertile Cherokee farmlands. When the Indians decided to stop selling their land, the whites sought to take it away. The Cherokee relied on their treaty rights when contending with the Georgia state authorities, who attempted to remove the resisting Indians. Georgia's effort to get the Cherokee territory became a fight in the courts until President Andrew Jackson failed to uphold the Indians' rights and overlooked Georgia's steady encroachment on their lands.

During President Jackson's tenure (1829–37), Congress passed the Indian Removal Act of 1830. The act was a sharp departure from the U.S. government's former policy, which respected the rights of the Indians. Jackson had hoped to win voluntary emigration of the eastern Indians to tracts west of the Mississippi. By the 1830 act, he was authorized only to negotiate with eastern tribes on a basis of payment for their native lands within state borders. These Indian lands were to be exchanged for western prairie lands. The act was not in itself coercive, and some tribes moved westward peacefully after signing treaties.

When officials attempted to abrogate their laws and divide up their lands, the Cherokee in Georgia appealed to the U.S. Supreme Court for help. In *Cherokee Nation v. Georgia* (1831), the court ruled that the Cherokee tribe was not an independent, sovereign nation, as it had contended, but was under federal congressional protection. Georgia seemed to pay little heed to this ruling. In *Worcester v. Georgia* (1832), the court said that Georgia had no constitutional right to extend its jurisdiction over the Cherokee lands. Again, Georgia ignored the ruling and proceeded to set up its own civil authority in the Cherokee area. Agitation to remove the Indians increased further after gold was found on their lands.

On December 29, 1835, a small minority of Cherokee signed the Treaty of New Echota, ceding to the United States all their territory east of the Mississippi in return for $5 million and homelands in the Indian territory in the West. When the rest of the Cherokee (the majority) insisted on staying put, Georgia militiamen were sent into the area and began rounding them up and putting them in prison stockades. In the spring of 1838, some 7,000 American troops under General Winfield Scott, mustering with rifles and bayonets ready, captured Cherokee men, women, and children in their fields and homes and imprisoned them en masse in the stockades. They were to be held there until their removal west. On the heels of the soldiers were hordes of lawless citizens who burned the uprooted Cherokee's homes and stole their valuables. Herded and crowded into filthy stockades, the Cherokee (nine-tenths of whom had been rounded up) were bewildered and demoralized. Many sickened and died from oppressive summer heat and cramped conditions. A few were sent by steamboat or boxed like animals in railroad cars to their new homes in the west during the summer of 1838. However, the majority (some 15,000) trekked westward, under American military escort, between October 1838 and March 1839. They were exiles, generally sent in groups of 1,000, tens of whom died every day of their dreadful winter journey. In the cold, the wet, and the mud, old people and small children struggled against death as they marched overland and across rivers through Tennessee, Kentucky, southern Illinois, Missouri, and Arkansas. The exiles were plagued by food shortages and robbers along the Trail of Tears.

Although many Americans protested and denounced the removal, the new president, Martin Van Buren proclaimed his administration's thoughts in his December 1838 message to Congress: "It affords me sincere pleasure to apprise the Congress of the entire removal of the Cherokee Nation of Indians to their new homes west of the Mississippi. The measures authorized by Congress at its last session have had the happiest effect. By an agreement concluded with them by the commanding general in that country, their removal has been principally under the conduct of their own chiefs, and they have emigrated without any apparent reluctance." The Cherokee "problem" had been solved by nearly destroying an entire people, and yet many were certain the removal had taken place for the safety of the Indians, who were placed beyond what Jackson called "the reach of injury or oppression."

TRENT AFFAIR. See Charles WILKES: the fruits of impetuosity.

TROPICS OF CANCER AND CAPRICORN:
marathon of litigation

Henry Valentine Miller was a modern American author who garnered both fame and controversy. Some critics regard him as a competent and occasionally great artist, while others see him as a pornographic exhibitionist. Whatever judgment future centuries make upon his work, Henry Miller will be remembered as the most legally involved author in history.

Almost from the moment of its 1934 publication in Paris, Miller's *Tropic of Cancer* was the object of controversy—critical, official, and later judicial. United States customs officials banned the book soon after it appeared, and did the same for Miller's next book, *Tropic of Capricorn,* when it was published in 1939. This ban even affected the U.S. Post Office, which vigilantly looked for mailed copies of the books in an effort to save the morals of the Republic. In the 1940s, smuggled copies of the two books became highly prized gifts between liberal friends.

Even in France, Miller had trouble. In 1946, an official committee, citing a 1939 antipornography law, decided that Miller was a pornographer and proposed sanctions against his works (which, published in English, had previously been protected). French writers entered the controversy, publishing over 200 items about it in four months, and a *Comité de défense d'Henri Miller* was established. The uproar only postponed action. Miller had soured French officials: when his *Sexus* was published in 1949, the minister of the interior sequestered the edition and forbade its printing in France in *any* language.

The first court case concerning the two *Tropic* books occurred in 1950 when the American Civil Liberties Union (ACLU) of northern California forced a test of the U.S. Customs ruling against the books by importing both of them. The court's philosophical bias in the case was narrow: depositions from literary critics were not allowed, and the ACLU lost. A 1953 appeal was also lost when the presiding judge ruled that a book should be "uplifting," and that a "dirty" book was dangerous—apparently even more so, to this California Comstock, when it was "well-written."

Miller meanwhile was gaining American supporters. The poet Louise Bogan inducted him, in 1957, into the National Institute of Arts and Letters, and a Henry Miller Literary Society was established in Minneapolis, Minnesota, in 1959. Moreover, perhaps because of the support Miller was gaining, copies of his books were freely sold in the United States, but the ban on their publication continued.

The support Miller got engendered a second test case in 1961, when the Grove Press published its edition of *Tropic of Cancer;* 68,000 copies sold out in a week. By the end of the first year, hardback sales of the book had topped 100,000 and paperback sales were over 1 million.

But at the same time, booksellers were arrested for selling Miller's works and suits were begun from coast to coast against the Grove Press for publishing *Tropic of Cancer.* In all, over 60 lawsuits were begun; in 1961 and 1962, Grove Press defended them all, spending over $100,000 in legal fees.

By 1963, only four cases remained, two of them before the highest courts of Illinois and California, one before a review court in New York, and the last (an appeal of a Florida conviction) before the U.S. Supreme Court, where *Cancer* was defended according to the precedents established in the tension-breaking *Roth* case of 1957 (see *FANNY HILL*). On June 22, 1964, the Supreme Court reversed the Florida verdict by a 6–3 vote, perhaps because so much redefining of the concept of obscenity had occurred in 1933 (see *ULYSSES*). The court's justices refused to explain why they considered *Cancer* (and, by implication, *Capricorn*) acceptable, but the other cases against Miller and his works were then dismissed.

Although the justices had done little to clarify their criteria of obscenity, both *Tropic* books—which were already considered dated by some—had earned the protection of the First Amendment to the Constitution and were safe from the scandalous activities of vice-seekers.

Lana TURNER: love and homicide

Glamorous movie actress Lana Turner was one of America's top box-office draws in the 1940s and 1950s.

Actress Lana Turner (left) and her gangster boyfriend Johnny Stompanato smile at Los Angeles International Airport on March 19, 1958, after their arrival from a vacation in Mexico. They were met by Lana's 14-year-old daughter Cheryl, who was later charged with killing Stompanato on April 4, 1958. Decades later, a book by a friend of Lana claimed that the actress had really held the knife, stabbing Stompanato after finding him in bed with Cheryl. Lana died in 1995. (AP/Wide World Photos)

Famed for her beauty and sex appeal, the original "sweater girl" starred in 55 films, most of which, though popular, were typical Hollywood assembly-line productions. Newspaper columnists avidly covered the actress's romantic life, about which there was always something new to say (Turner had numerous romances, not to mention eight marriages). Her affair with the handsome hoodlum Johnny Stompanato received as much coverage as any. But in April 1958, the press really had a holiday. Early in that month, Stompanato was stabbed to death by Turner's teenage daughter.

The actress met Stompanato, an ex-marine and a former bodyguard to underworld chieftains like Mickey Cohen, the gambling czar on the West Coast, in the spring of 1957. At the time she was depressed because of her recent separation from her fourth husband, Lex Barker, and a sharp downturn in her film-making career (she had appeared in 17 straight flops). Stompanato, who had a tough but ingratiating manner, ran a gift shop in Los Angeles; he had acquired a reputation for bullying his girlfriends, some of whom were very wealthy, into financing his gambling activities. Unaware that he had been married three times and had a 10-year-old son, Turner began dating this playboy-hoodlum and they soon became lovers. In late 1957 Stompanato followed Turner to England, where she was making a film, *Another Time, Another Place,* with actor Sean Connery. Jealous of the men Turner worked with, Stompanato picked a fight with Connery, got knocked out, threatened to cut up Turner with a razor, and finally was persuaded by Scotland Yard to leave the country. Such violent rages were common for Stompanato, who frequently abused Turner. Strangely, the actress put up with his abuse, often writing him pathetic love letters. In addition to this, she paid his gambling debts.

Nominated for an Academy Award for her performance in *Peyton Place* in 1958, Turner seemed to be getting better despite Stompanato's continual abuse. They often fought because he wanted to escort her to social and public functions, like the Academy Awards dinner, and not be treated like a lewd secret. Her refusals set off a violent argument between the two at Turner's Beverly Hills, California, mansion on April 4, 1958. According to Turner's later testimony, the 32-year-old Stompanato (whom she believed was 42) shouted, "I'll spoil your looks, disfigure you. If I can't do it myself, I'll have it done. There are not enough policemen in the world to stop me." Stompanato also threatened to cut up her 14-year-old daughter, Cheryl, the offspring of her short marriage to her second husband, Steve Crane. A troubled teenager who had been shunted around to various private schools, Cheryl overheard the threats, grabbed an eight-inch carving knife from the kitchen, and rushed into her mother's bedroom, plunging the knife into Stompanato's stomach. Turner tried to stop the blood with towels, but Stompanato died within minutes from a severed aorta.

Both Jerry Giesler, Hollywood's most famous lawyer, and the police were called and arrived on the bloody scene, along with a doctor. The slaying quickly became known to the public, which received the sordid details when Mickey Cohen handed to the press some love letters written by Turner to Stompanato. Much to his displeasure, Cohen had been forced to claim Stompanato's body and pay the bill for its burial. Turner's published letters caused some newsmen and clergy to lambast her mercilessly as degenerate, immoral, and an unfit mother. Cohen also released some secret letters from his ex-bodyguard to Turner, adding more fuel to the outrage. All the while, Giesler advised his two clients, Turner and her daughter, to say nothing.

About a week after the killing, the coroner's inquest took place in a circuslike atmosphere, live and on television. In a dramatic performance as a court witness, the 38-year-old Turner testified tearfully for an hour, giving details of what had happened that fatal night. Cheryl Crane never took the stand but did submit a signed statement of justification, saying that she had killed Stompanato "to protect her (mother)." The natural desire of a child to protect an endangered parent undoubtedly helped convince the coroner's jury to reach a verdict of "justifiable homicide" after less than an hour of deliberation. Cheryl Crane became a ward of the court and was put into the custody of her maternal grandmother. The notoriety worked in Turner's favor, making her next movie, *Imitation of Life* (1959), the biggest box-office success that year for Universal-International studios. The film was about a mother who neglected her daughter. Later, Stompanato's divorced wife Sara, claiming that there was doubt about whether Turner or her daughter had wielded the deadly carving knife, brought a $750,000 damage suit against them and Steve Crane; it was settled without trial for $20,000. The story of a woman charged with her lover's murder became another multimillion dollar movie success for Lana Turner in *Madame X* (1966).

Her movie career began to wane afterward, and she turned to TV melodramatic roles in the 1970s and 1980s. In June 1995, at age 75, Turner died of throat cancer at her home in Century City, California.

TUSKEGEE SYPHILIS EXPERIMENT: unethical medicine

A hue and cry of outrage arose from the public when an article in the *Washington Star* disclosed, on July 25, 1972, that more than 400 poor black men with syphilis in Macon County, Alabama, had been studied but not treated since 1932. The longitudinal study had been conducted by the U.S. Public Health Service, with the frequent cooperation and support of the Tuskegee Institute—a prestigious institution of higher education for blacks founded by Booker T. Washington, the Alabama State Board of Health, the Macon County Health Department, the Macon County Medical Society, and the Center for Disease Control in Atlanta, Georgia. Following publication of the article, the U.S. Department of Health, Education, and Welfare initiated an investigation by an *ad hoc* panel of doctors, who readily recommended that the study be stopped at once and that the men involved receive full medical care to treat any disabilities they might have incurred from their participation in the 40-year-old study.

During the early 1930s, the Rosenwald Fund had undertaken the support of a joint syphilis control project by the U.S. Public Health Service (PHS) and Tuskegee Institute in Macon County, Alabama—one of the poorest, most disease-ridden areas in the Deep South. When the funding ceased, it occurred to one of the PHS doctors who had worked on the project, Dr. Taliaferro Clark, that the area would surely be an ideal place to make a scientific study of the effects of untreated syphilis. It was estimated that 35 percent of black males in Macon County had the disease. Macon County also boasted excellent medical facilities at the John A. Andrews Memorial Hospital at Tuskegee Institute, where the men could be given complete medical examinations. At that time it was widely believed that syphilis affected blacks differently from whites, and Dr. Clark thought that a scientific study would point out these differences and contribute to medical knowledge. This and other arguments convinced the Alabama State Board of Health, the Macon County Health Department, and the Tuskegee Institute to cooperate in the study, which was originally conceived as a short-term one.

The first step was to find male subjects between the ages of 25 to 35 who had been infected with syphilis for at least five years. White planters, preachers, and the schools in Macon County were informed that "government doctors" would soon be giving free blood tests for the disease, and they in turn spread the word to rural blacks, many of whom had never seen a doctor. People flocked to schools, churches, and improvised field clinics to find out if they had "bad blood." The blood samples they provided were sent to the state health laboratory for analysis, and the men whose blood tested positive were asked to return for a second test.

Eunice Rivers, a black nurse who had trained at Tuskegee and who worked at Andrews Hospital, was assigned to the study at the very beginning and proved to be an invaluable liaison between the doctors and the men being studied. She drove the men selected for the study to the hospital for physical examinations and spinal taps and assisted the doctors with these procedures.

At the initial insistence of the Alabama State Board of Health, the men enrolled in the Tuskegee Study of Untreated Syphilis in the Negro Male were given some treatment for their disease. At that time, the treatment for syphilis consisted of neoarsphenamine and bismuth given over a yearly period, but none of the men received more than a few doses of the drugs.

After nine months, when the study was to be completed, the PHS had amassed a great deal of data, and the new director of its Division of Venereal Disease felt that science would be badly served if the study was discontinued. Officials at the PHS agreed, and during the summer of 1933 the study became open-ended, or continuing. Again the cooperation of the state and local medical agencies was sought and received. An important part of the new program was the introduction of autopsies. Terminally ill men who were enrolled in the study were taken to Andrews Hospital for free care, and after their death, the hospital staff performed autopsies and sent sample tissues from the men's vital organs to the National Institute of Health laboratory. In 1935, the PHS began to offer $50 for burial expenses in exchange for autopsy permissions. A control group was also added to the experiment. Nurse Rivers continued as the liaison person with the men with whom she regularly visited to dispense free aspirin and blood tonic. No one involved in these arrangements ever questioned the ethics of the PHS in establishing them.

During the following years, the routine and bureaucratized procedures were established in the study. There was an "annual roundup" in which the men being studied were given blood tests by PHS doctors. Every five years the participants were given complete physical examinations; they also had special nurses to look after them. But even after penicillin came into general use for treating syphilis in the 1950s, no one suggested that the stricken men be treated.

Peter Buxtun, a venereal disease investigator with the PHS, was the first to question the morality of the Tuskegee study, in 1966 and again in 1968. His second letter prompted the convening of a panel of medical experts to discuss the study. Some felt that the focus of the study should be changed to stress pathology. Only one panelist urged that the men in the study be treated, but he was overruled by those who argued that it was too late and that treatment would be harmful. The uneasy officials again sought, and received, the endorsement of the Macon County Medical Society, now composed of black doctors, to continue the study. Buxtun continued to talk with friends, one of whom in turn told a reporter friend in Washington, D.C., about the study. The latter, Jean Heller, investigated and wrote the article that brought the Tuskegee study to public attention.

Early in 1973 Senator Edward Kennedy held a series of hearings on human experimentation, at which two Tuskegee survivors described how they had been deceived by white doctors for 40 years. A suit was brought but was settled out of court when the U.S. government

agreed to compensate the heirs of the deceased members of the study and the survivors themselves and to provide complete free medical care for them and their families. The individuals and agencies involved in the study did not apologize for their past actions but continued to justify what they had done as being to the benefit of medical science.

In May 1997, President Bill Clinton issued a formal apology to the eight remaining survivors of the Tuskegee experiment, which he called a racist act because all the victims were black. He also said it undermined many people's trust in the government and left a haunting legacy.

"Boss" TWEED: corrupt "Tammany tiger"

By the time his corruption was exposed in 1871, William M. ("Boss") Tweed and his cronies in the notorious Tweed Ring had plundered New York City. Through padded or fictitious bills, false vouchers and leases, and unnecessary purchases or repairs, they had taken an estimated $30 to $200 million from the city's coffers at a time when the average working man earned $2 to $3 a day. In its heyday the Tweed Ring controlled the city's government, courts, and police, as well as the New York State legislature and the state's elections. The charges of monumental graft and vote fraud against him have made Tweed the very symbol of big-city corruption.

Born in 1823 on New York City's Lower East Side, Tweed rose gradually through the ranks of the Democratic Party. In 1851 he was elected to the New York Board of Aldermen, a body about which Tweed once remarked, "There never was a time when you couldn't buy the Board of Aldermen." After an undistinguished term in the U.S. Congress, Tweed returned to New York City and a post on the Board of Education.

Tweed's real power began to grow in 1857 when he was elected to the newly reorganized legislative body of New York County, the Board of Supervisors, which audited city expenditures, appointed election inspectors, and supervised public improvements (such as a new and costly courthouse). As a member of the board for the next 13 years and its president four times, Tweed's opportunities for graft were enormous, and he took full advantage of them. In 1863 he became deputy street commissioner, a post that gave him control over thousands of jobs that could be apportioned among his supporters.

Tweed also consolidated his power with Tammany Hall, the local Democratic party organization, which had become divided and weakened during the Civil War. By the end of the war, a unified Tammany Hall, led by Tweed, emerged as New York City's dominant political organization.

As he gained political power, Tweed did not neglect his personal finances. He bought a printing company and directed the city's printing business to his own firm. He also began to practice law, earning substantial fees from those seeking influence with the city. He speculated in city real estate.

The Tweed Ring, which began operation in 1866, was the first modern city machine in New York, and Tweed was the nation's first real city "boss." He and his colleagues Peter Sweeny (city chamberlain), Oakey Hall (mayor of New York from 1868 to 1872), and Richard Connolly (city comptroller) comprised the inner circle of the ring that dominated New York City politics for the next five years. Though Tweed's Tammany Hall never proposed a broad remedy to New York's enormous problems of poverty, education, and housing, his ring gained the support of immigrants by giving them patronage jobs, of Catholics by giving city and state money for parochial schools and private charities, and of workers by encouraging unions to organize and allowing them to strike.

In 1870, while Tweed was serving as a state senator, the state legislature passed a new charter for New York City that reorganized city government, centralized responsibility, and created new opportunities for graft. The charter established a board of audit that Tweed and his associates could manipulate. Tweed, as superintendent of public works, gained control of most city development projects. The parks department, which oversaw Central Park, also fell under his control. The disposal of more patronage jobs increased his power, and kickbacks from padded contractors' bills enriched Tweed and his friends.

Although Tweed had for years been attacked regularly by cartoonist Thomas Nast in *Harper's Weekly* and by the *New York Times,* the fall of his ring in 1871 was sudden and dramatic. In July of that year the *Times* obtained extensive reports of fraud and extravagance from a disgruntled officeholder ($175,000 had been spent on carpets for the new county courthouse, $7,500 for thermometers). After they were published, bankers refused to grant further credit to the city, precipitating a financial crisis. Samuel Tilden, a reformist Democrat, led the party's attack on its own black sheep. Within months the Tweed Ring was devastated, and in October Tweed was arrested on charges of deceit and fraud, based on the evidence of 190 county vouchers showing that more than $6 million had been fraudulently taken from the city treasury. He was later indicted on other charges, including forgery and grand larceny.

Tweed's first trial ended in a hung jury. At his second trial he was convicted on 204 of the 220 counts of the indictment against him. He was sentenced to 12 years in prison and fined $12,750, although the sentence was later reduced to one year and a $250 fine. Immediately after his release, however, Tweed was rearrested as a result of a civil lawsuit brought against him by the State of New York.

In 1875 Tweed escaped from prison. He fled to Cuba and then to Spain, where he was recognized, arrested, and extradited to the United States. He died in jail in 1878.

It should be noted that at least one historian disputes the general view of Tweed as an arch-villain, claiming that he was actually a victim of smear and myth.

John TYLER: "president without a party"

A strange sequence of events led up to the presidency of John Tyler, the only American president to be officially ousted from his own party while in office.

In the presidential election campaign of 1840, the Whig Party represented a curious agglomeration of diverse elements united largely by opposition to the "monarchial despotism" of Democratic President Andrew Jackson. The Whig presidential candidate, General William Henry Harrison, was a military hero, not a politican, who ran on the basis of his appeal as a common man. Party leaders expected that Harrison would be amenable to direction from the real head of the Whig Party, Kentucky's Senator Henry Clay. The vice-presidential candidate was John Tyler, a Virginian and former Democrat who represented an opposing faction within the party.

The Whig Party never offered a political platform outlining its proposals. The campaign avoided discussions of serious national issues, relying instead on partisan songs and slogans. The Whig candidates ran and won on the famous motto "Tippecanoe and Tyler too!"

As vice president, Tyler would have been able to offer only minor opposition to Whig programs of which he disapproved. But fate and bad weather were to rule otherwise. Harrison, wearing neither coat nor hat, delivered his inaugural address in a cold drizzle on March 4, 1841, caught pneumonia, and died a month later. Tyler became the first vice president ever to succeed to the presidency.

Tyler's accession to the presidency was itself highly controversial. A debate erupted over whether he should be considered "acting president," serving as a caretaker for the remainder of Harrison's term, or whether he should actually assume all of the rights and powers of the presidency. The Constitution seemed to be ambiguous on the matter. Tyler's decision to claim the full powers of the presidency established a precedent that has been followed ever since. He immediately took the presidential oath of office, issued an inaugural address, and moved into the White House. Ex-President John Quincy Adams, prominent among those who felt that Tyler should have styled himself "acting president," described the new president unflatteringly by saying: "Tyler is a political sectarian, . . . principled against all improvements, with all the interests and passions and vices of slavery rooted in his moral and political constitution—with talents not above mediocrity and a spirit incapable of expansion to the dimensions of the station upon which he has been cast by the hand of Providence."

Tyler inherited Harrison's Cabinet, which was largely comprised of partisans of Henry Clay, with whose nationalist views Tyler largely disagreed. To avoid conflict at the outset of his administration, Tyler decided not to dismiss the Cabinet but instead to rely on the advice of an informal group of advisers, sometimes called the "Virginia clique," who agreed with his states'-rights views. Within months, however, Tyler found himself in direct confrontation with his Cabinet, with Clay, and with most of the Whig Party.

The issue that precipitated the crisis was a bill to charter a new national bank, a measure favored by Clay and other Whigs. In a special session during the summer of 1841, Congress passed a bill calling for the establishment of a District of Columbia bank that could in turn establish branches in the individual states. Tyler, arguing that such a bank was unconstitutional and a violation of states rights, promptly vetoed the bill.

The political repercussions were disastrous. A drunken mob of angry demonstrators arrived at the White House, denounced Tyler, and burned him in effigy. Though Clay tried and failed to gain enough votes to override the veto, a second bank bill soon passed. Again Tyler vetoed the measure, in what proved to be the last straw for the Whig Party. On September 11, at the instigation of Clay, Tyler's entire Cabinet, with the exception of Secretary of State Daniel Webster, resigned en masse. Two days later the president was officially expelled from the Whig Party, making Tyler the only American president ever to have been ousted from the political organization that had nominated and elected him. Tyler also received hundreds of letters threatening him with assassination, and was denounced by Whig pamphleteers as an "executive ass," a "reptile-like" creature who had "crawled up" to the presidency.

Nonetheless the "president without a party" survived the crisis. Within days he had a new Cabinet made up of men who shared his states'-rights views. A move in the House of Representatives in 1842 to impeach Tyler for "high crimes and misdemeanors" was soundly defeated. Tyler wrote to a friend, "The high crime of sustaining the Constitution of the country I have committed, and to this I plead guilty . . . ; and the high crime of daring to have an opinion of my own, Congress to the contrary notwithstanding, I plead guilty also to that; and if these be impeachable matters, why then I ought to be impeached." Despite criticism and charges of "executive dictatorship," Tyler continued to veto legislation of which he disapproved, including bills concerning the tariff and the distribution of the proceeds from the sale of public lands, an internal improvements bill, and a naval construction bill.

Driven from the Whig Party, Tyler sought, unsuccessfully, support from the Democrats. He then turned to a third party, which nominated him for the presidency in 1844, though Tyler later withdrew in favor of the Democratic nominee, James K. Polk. Tyler continued his interest in political and public affairs until his death in 1862. Though often maligned as one of America's worst presidents, Tyler's record can be viewed as one of honesty, courage, and determination in following his views of the national good.

TYPHOID MARY: a reckless public menace

Miss Mary Mallon, an Irish immigrant better known as Typhoid Mary, was apparently the first known carrier of the typhoid fever bacillus in the United States. She herself had recovered from the dreadful disease but had become an infectious carrier, knowingly spreading typhoid fever for years while working as a cook in private homes, restaurants, clubs, hotels, and hospitals in the New York City area.

Mary's first mark was made in 1906, when all the guests at a dinner party in a posh summer home in Oyster Bay, Long Island, became ill after eating food she had prepared. It was soon discovered that they had contracted the highly contagious typhoid fever. A sanitary engineer for New York City, Dr. George Soper, investigated and linked the typhoid outbreak to Mary, who by then had changed jobs and vanished. She continued to hire herself out as a cook under assumed names, and outbreaks of typhoid fever were reported wherever she was employed, while Dr. Soper tried to track her down.

After months she was located and confronted by Dr. Soper, who informed her of her carrier status. At least seven outbreaks, involving some 25 individual cases of typhoid, were attributed to her at the time. Mary adamantly refused to submit to a physical examination and medical tests; instead she fled from the authorities, and the New York City Department of Health sought to catch and isolate her from the public. In 1907 she was once again identified and detained—but this time was placed in isolation at Willard Parker Hospital in New York City. There she was subjected to innumerable tests, which proved conclusively that she was a carrier of typhoid. The fever's germs were thought to exist in Mary's gall bladder, which doctors asked to remove as a curative treatment. She steadfastly refused, wanted no form of treatment, and eventually was transferred to Riverside Hospital on North Brother Island in New York City. Here she was given an ultimatum: either submit to treatment or be confined indefinitely in a hospital. Mary stubbornly hired a lawyer, engaged in court battles that brought no solution, and was finally released by New York City health officials in 1910. They had agreed to grant her freedom on her promise to give up cooking and handling foods and to report to the city health department every 90 days.

By now the press had dubbed her "Typhoid Mary." Despite her fame she was difficult to identify, as she vehemently refused to be interviewed or photographed. Once again she took another name, disappeared, and continued preparing food in various public and private places for the next five years. All the while she remained in good health. In 1915, however, an outbreak of typhoid occurred at New York's Sloane Hospital for Women, where 25 nurses and workers fell ill. Two eventually died from the disease. Investigators discovered that Mary had worked in the hospital's kitchen, and traced her to a private home in the suburbs, where she was employed.

Arrested and returned to Riverside Hospital, Mary continued to refuse treatment, and doctors at the hospital referred to her as "the human culture tube" because her body was so severely infected with typhoid; she was an intestinal carrier of the disease (untreated, the typhoid organism is capable of surviving indefinitely in a person's intestines.) Some 50 new cases of the disease (resulting in three fatalities) were blamed on Mary, by now a pariah who was permanently confined to Riverside Hospital, her carrier status unchangeable. In time she became a laboratory technician at the hospital. Her activity was limited to the grounds of the hospital, where at the age of 70 she died of a stroke on November 11, 1938.

Mike TYSON: troubled boxer guilty of rape and more

Mike Tyson was considered the greatest heavyweight boxer to enter the ring since the retirement of the legendary Muhammad Ali. Tyson was born in 1966 in New York City. His poor, uneducated parents took little interest in him, and he spent much of his youth getting into trouble with the law. At age 10 he joined the Jolly Stompers, a street gang, and began terrorizing the Brownsville neighborhood in Brooklyn. Two years later he was convicted of a string of burglaries and robberies and sent to a juvenile detention facility. While incarcerated he met Gus D'Amato, a longtime boxers' manager who taught him how to box and eventually became his legal adoptive father.

D'Amato believed that Tyson had the physical prowess, natural fighting instincts, and love for the sport that could make him a champion. Under D'Amato's expert tutelage, Tyson advanced rapidly. At age 18 he won a silver medal at the 1984 Summer Olympic Games, and many observers say he was cheated out of the gold medal by a communist-bloc referee and scorers. After becoming a professional boxer, he developed into a brutal fighter who seemed intent on destroying his opponents, not simply winning the fights, and he picked up the nicknames Kid Dynamite and Iron Mike. By 1986 his record was 27–0; he had won 25 fights by knockout, 15 knockouts coming in the first round and several of them coming in the first minute. That same year he easily defeated Trevor Berbick to become, at age 20, the youngest heavyweight champion of all time.

Tyson's boxing prowess earned him millions of dollars and the adulation of boxing fans everywhere. But, as with many athletes, the combination of quick money, fame, and youth eventually got him into serious trouble. He began living the life of a millionaire playboy and surrounded himself with a cadre of hangers-on who catered to his every whim. He acquired a reputation as a crude womanizer and boasted of all-night sessions with a dozen or more prostitutes. His first wife, the actress Robin Givens, divorced him because of "brutality." Believing in his own invincibility, in 1990 he underestimated his lightly regarded challenger James "Buster" Douglas and lost his first professional fight and with it the championship. In 1992 he was convicted of raping an 18-year-old contestant at the Black Miss America pageant in Indianapolis, Indiana.

During the trial Tyson's accuser, Desiree Washington, calmly and convincingly told how Tyson lured her to his hotel room, brushed off her refusal to have sex with him, overpowered her, pinned her to the bed with his forearm, stripped her, and then forced himself on her, all the while delighting in her physical pain and emotional distress. Tyson's lawyers resorted to a curious and desperate defense. They called as witnesses 11 other contestants who all testified that, while Tyson was backstage during the pageant, he made a number of crude sexual remarks and seemed to be obsessed with having sex with one or more of the contestants. This testimony supported the lawyers' contention that Washington was a gold-digger who must have gone to Tyson's room knowing that he intended to have sex with her. However, the jury apparently preferred Washington's version and convicted Tyson on one count of rape and two counts of sexual-deviate conduct. He was fined $30,000 and sentenced to six years in an Indiana state penitentiary.

Despite his incarceration, Tyson continued to be an enormously popular figure in the boxing world. Having earned early release for good behavior, in 1997 he challenged Evander Holyfield in a Las Vegas, Nevada, championship bout. For reasons that no one, including Tyson, can explain, in the third round he bit off part of Holyfield's ear in a blatant violation of the rules. He disregarded the referee's warning and bit Holyfield's ear again, this time receiving a disqualification. He was jailed for assault and stripped of his license to box in Nevada for two years, which effectively postponed his chance to take another shot at the heavyweight championship until then.

Meanwhile, Tyson remained a troubled man. In 1999 he was sued by two women who claimed that he assaulted and threatened them in a Washington, D.C., restaurant in 1998; Tyson denied their accusations and reached an undisclosed settlement with the two women in February 2000. Tyson also had trouble with the Internal Revenue Service, which sought payment of $12 million in back taxes, interest, and penalties.

ULYSSES: a tale of modern literature and censorship

During his relatively brief writing career, the provocative Irish author James Joyce and his works rarely escaped controversy. His novel *Ulysses,* written between 1914 and 1921, was almost from its inception the focus of editorial and moralistic warfare in both England and the United States. Despite its publication in 1922 by the Paris bookstore Shakespeare and Company, conflicts with publishers of *Ulysses* lasted until 1927; battles with American censors of the book lasted until 1933, when a U.S. district court in New York permitted both its importation and publication.

Editorial and moral controversies about the book are intertwined. Installments of *Ulysses* had been published in England by Harriet Weaver's *Egoist* before its demise in 1919 and, after March 1918, in the United States by Margaret Anderson and Jane Heap in their Chicago-based *Little Review.* Under the Comstock Law of 1873 prohibiting the mailing of many forbidden materials, the U.S. Post Office intervened, confiscating and burning three *Review* issues in 1919–20. The issue of July–August 1920 caused a court battle: John Sumner, secretary of the New York Society for the Suppression of Vice, had complained about the Joyce extract. A trial in 1921 found Anderson and Heap guilty, fined them $50 each, and warned them that future publication of Joyce's work meant prison.

The 1922 publication in Paris of the completed volume of *Ulysses* merely complicated the controversies, each separately involving violent attacks from critics for whom any departures from Victorian purity were anathema. United States Customs officials banned the book; U.S. Post Office authorities, zealous to preserve America from corruption, intercepted most mailed copies (determined lawbreakers, however, foiled the interceptors by sending pages, and quires, and sheets of the printed book separately to America, where they were gathered and then rebound). Canadians shipped 40 copies (the book was not banned in Canada) across the border from Ontario. An edition of 2,000 copies destined for England and America was subscribed in four days, but 400 copies were seized on their way to New York. Another 500 copies were prepared in Paris, but one copy had reached the British director of public prosecutions. He alerted His Majesty's Customs and Excise Office, which seized the copies aboard a ship in Folkestone Harbor and burned them.

Court trials followed. An American publisher, Samuel Roth, had ecstatically praised *Ulysses;* he began in 1926 to print a pirated edition in his *Two Worlds Monthly.* Hauled by Joyce's lawyers into court in 1927, Roth was admonished for publishing banned material and for publishing piratically but was not ordered to pay damages to Joyce, whose work could not be copyrighted in America (this same Roth, a pioneer combatant of narrow censorship laws, was the defendant in the famous 1957 *Roth* case which broke the power of government censorship).

The court decision of 1933 that freed *Ulysses* from puritanical banning began in the mind of Bennett Cerf, owner of Random House, a New York publisher, as an idea for a test case. Cerf, however, feared the costs of such a venture until Morris Ernst, an attorney, promised to handle the case for a lifetime royalty if he won it and for no fee if he lost it. Cerf then had two copies of *Ulysses* imported to tempt U.S. Customs officials. They missed the first, stopped the second, and instituted charges against Cerf.

Heard before Judge John M. Woolsey of the U.S. District Court in New York City, the case not only resulted in the ban on *Ulysses* being lifted, but also in new and more liberal tests for obscenity. *Ulysses* passed the pornography test (Judge Woolsey, who found the novel to be "a rather strong draught to ask some sensitive, though normal persons to take," said further, "nowhere does it tend to be an aphrodisiac.") "Dirt for dirt's sake" became a lawyer's synonym for pornography. Moreover, Woolsey argued that in evaluating its worth, a work had to be considered as a whole and in terms of its purpose, not merely in terms of selected, objectionable passages it contained.

Appealed to the U.S. Circuit Court of Appeals, Woolsey's verdict was upheld in 1934 by two of the court's three judges. The two, the cousins Augustus and Learned Hand, decided that the book, taken as a whole, did not have a libidinous effect. Cerf's planned Random House edition (1933) was able to proceed. Within two months, 33,000 copies had been sold, and Morris Ernst collected many royalties.

A literary scholar had noted that *Ulysses,* despite its occasional frankness, is one of the great works of world literature; a scholar of the history of literary censorship has commented that the relaxation in its court case marked "a milestone" in the process of reducing governmental power to dictate morality.

U.S. ARMY: the execution of Eddie Slovik

On January 31, 1945, the United States Army carried out its first execution for desertion since 1864. The victim: Private Edward Donald Slovik (short for Slowikowski), Army Serial Number 36898415, age 24 years.

Private Eddie Slovik, the only American soldier put to death for desertion since the Civil War, stands with his bride, Antoinette, at their wedding in 1942. In 1977 Army Secretary Clifford L. Alexander, Jr., upheld the conviction and execution of Slovik, thus preventing Antoinette from collecting an estimated $70,000 on her husband's World War II insurance. (AP/Wide World Photos)

He was executed for a crime that numerous others had perpetrated and received pardons for. As Slovik himself realized, his death was meant to be an example.

In fulfilling the directives of military law in the Slovik case, the army was reacting to a problem it had allowed to become elephantine: Europe had seen 40,000 of its troops desert. Courts-martial had delivered 49 death sentences, all of which had been commuted. Slovik's execution was to exemplify the army's new and tougher policy. It did not work.

It failed as a deterrent because the procedures that followed it were mistakes. Except among the men of the One-Hundred-Ninth Infantry Regiment, Twenty-Eighth Division, to which Slovik had been assigned, the execution was kept secret. Its accomplishment was a whispered rumor in Europe; in the United States all records of it were classified material unavailable until 1953. Even Slovik's wife did not know the nature of his death until that year. It became public knowledge in 1954 only because an enterprising journalist, William Bradford Huie, had investigated the matter and then published his *The Execution of Private Slovik.*

The army's chief mistake lay in its failure to use the time between Slovik's surrender and confession (October 9, 1944) and his execution to search thoroughly for mitigating circumstances. It was instead concerned solely with superficial facts and the letter of military law. Its failure to investigate made Slovik the victim of a rigid system and a high but blind code of conduct.

Slovik was born to poor parents who gave him little emotional sustenance. Crippled at birth, the surgery that followed was so poorly done that he was the only member of his army basic training group allowed to wear soft shoes. He functioned only as part of a juvenile gang and by 12 years of age was developing a record for petty crime. To be with the gang, Slovik quit school at 15 and one year later landed in jail. He was paroled at 17 for being a model prisoner but shortly after his release was caught when he and the gang stole a car for joyriding. Reimprisoned, he was paroled in 1942. His criminal record made his draft classification an undesirable 4A.

While in prison, Slovik had met a prison official who provided him with guidance and compassion. He felt himself to be a changed person and was determined to stay reformed. Outside, he met and married Antoinette Wisniewski, a retiring woman who, like Eddie, was very dependent. She also was prone to epileptic seizures. Each supporting the other emotionally, they worked hard, furnished an apartment, and set out to establish a life together.

Wartime pressures intervened. The war in Europe demanded bodies; almost anybody warm and casting a shadow was eligible. Slovik's draft board illegally reclassified him as 1A (an error because he was still on parole). Eddie, after five years of bureaucratic bullying, did not appeal. He was given a physical examination that did not note the condition of his legs and a psychological examination so sketchy that it did not notice his dependent nature. Drafted, he was assigned for training under a replacement process so wrong for dependent types that the army ruefully abandoned it. His soft-shoe requirement did not appear on a rejected request he made for assignment to noncombat service. Bereft, Eddie constantly wrote notes to Antoinette, sometimes 20 a day.

Basically a willing and cheerful worker, Slovik tried vainly to fail his training. He was rendered frantic when Antoinette's seizures increased in frequency. He tried for compassionate leave but was turned down. Antoinette also tried but failed because a Red Cross volunteer was annoyed that she was "unwilling to make sacrifices."

Thoroughly depressed, Slovik made the major mistake of his life: he vowed that if ordered into combat, he would desert and willingly go to prison.

Assigned to an infantry regiment under fire and needing replacements, he was shipped overseas, got lost in attempting to find the "buddies" he had never met, and arrived on October 8, 1944, to find them being barraged by von Runstedt's forces. Slovik deserted and then returned a day later with a written confession in which he vowed that if forced, he would desert again.

The vow was his fatal error. His commander, General Norman D. "Dutch" Cota, had opined that "an able-bodied civilian who won't fight for his country doesn't deserve to live"; the army discovered Slovik's criminal record and investigated no further into his past. Another general viewed the death sentence as just: "His unfavorable civilian record indicates that he is not a worthy subject of clemency." Slovik's plea for mercy was probably not seen by the addressee, General Dwight D. Eisenhower, who could have intervened, but actually signed the order of execution.

In the walled garden of a private home, Slovik was executed. His written prophecy is haunting: "They are not shooting me for deserting. . . . Thousands of guys have done that. They just need to make an example out of somebody, and I'm it."

U.S. ARMY'S ABERDEEN SEX SCANDAL

Aberdeen Proving Ground lies about 30 miles northeast of Baltimore, Maryland. The base is the home of the Army Ordnance Center, which develops and tests bombs and artillery shells. Part of the ordnance center's mission is to teach soldiers how to operate and repair large-caliber weapons, so each year more than 11,000 new recruits straight out of boot camp, including approximately 500 women, are trained by the center's 37 drill sergeants and 325 instructors. In 1996 an explosion of a different type shook Aberdeen when it was disclosed that a number of female soldiers, many of them just out of high school, were being sexually harassed and abused by their male sergeants and instructors.

The scandal first broke in September when Private Jessica Bleckley, 18, of the 143rd Ordnance Battalion's Charlie Company accused Staff Sergeant Nathaniel Beach, 32, her immediate superior, of forcing her to have sex with him against her will. She also claimed that he threatened to cut her throat if she told on him. Bleckley's accusation led more than 50 other female soldiers at Aberdeen to come forward with similar accusations. Their charges resulted in the suspension of one captain and 19 sergeants and instructors and led army investigators to interview every woman who had been assigned to Aberdeen during the previous two years to find out how many had been sexually harassed or abused during training. Investigators also attempted to determine if any female soldiers had gone absent without leave because of sexual mistreatment. Out of 1,000 women interviewed, more than 100 indicated that they had been sexually harassed by a superior.

The realization that a "culture of sex" existed at a major training base led the army to conduct similar investigations at other bases, and a retired major general was recalled to active duty to head a military-civilian committee investigating sexual abuse throughout the U.S. military. Meanwhile, a delegation from the House National Security Committee visited Aberdeen to look into the situation. But the National Association for the Advancement of Colored People decried the suspensions because most of the accusers were white while most of the accused were black.

The charges of the Aberdeen women, whose average age was 21, centered around six of the 143rd Ordnance Battalion's supervisors, all of them in their 30s. Beach was charged with obstructing justice, disobeying an officer, and having an improper relationship with a female trainee. Sergeants First Class Ronald Moffett and Tony Cross were accused of adultery and other charges such as indecent assault and sodomy by four recruits each. Staff Sergeant Herman Gunter was charged with propositioning a recruit and then trying to cover up his actions. The most serious charges involved Captain Derrick Robertson, commander of the battalion's Alpha Company, and Staff Sergeant Delmar Simpson, also of Alpha Company. Robertson was charged with rape, conduct unbecoming an officer, obstruction of justice, adultery, and having an improper relationship with a recruit. He admitted to having an affair with a female soldier under his command but denied having raped her. Simpson was charged with 19 counts of rape and 35 other counts, among them forcible sodomy, robbery, and extortion. He admitted to having consensual sex with 11 recruits, which is still a violation of army rules, and to improper conduct with five others, but he denied having raped anyone.

The cases of all six men were concluded between February and August 1997. Criminal charges against Beach were dropped when Bleckley signed a statement to that effect; however, after leaving the army, she claimed that she had been pressured to sign. Instead, Beach was convicted of two minor charges that had nothing to do with sexual misconduct and put on probation for six months. Gunter was convicted and demoted by two grades, while Moffett and Cross accepted administrative discharges instead of being court-martialed. In a plea agreement, Robertson confessed to adultery and sodomy; he was sentenced to four months' imprisonment at Fort Leavenworth and dismissed from the army. Simpson was convicted on 18 counts of rape and 29 other counts of sexual misconduct; he was sentenced to 25 years in prison, stripped of his rank, and dishonorably discharged. In July, Lieutenant Colonel Martin Utzig, commanding officer of the battalion, was relieved of his command and forced to retire for failing to identify and eliminate the "culture of sex" in his unit. See also Gene MCKINNEY: Army's top enlisted man court-martialed.

U.S. NAVAL ACADEMY CHEATING SCANDAL.
See NAVAL ACADEMY CHEATING SCANDAL.

U.S. STEEL. See GATES/MORGAN/GARY: the creation of U.S. Steel.

U-2 SPY FLIGHT
On May 5, 1960, officials of the Soviet Union announced that four days earlier, an American U-2 strategic reconnaissance airplane had been shot down near Sverdlovsk, about 1,200 miles inside the Soviet Union. The implied Soviet charge of American spying may have then prompted the U.S. State Department to assert that the United States was not trying "to violate Soviet air space" with the airplane and never had been. The National Aeronautics and Space Administration (NASA) responded by saying that only "a weather research plane" was missing.

Two days later, on May 7, Soviet Premier Nikita Khrushchev acidly announced that the U-2 plane's pilot, Francis Gary Powers, had been captured alive and had admitted to spying. Pictures of Soviet military installations had been taken by the plane's cameras, declared Khrushchev. The U.S. government's attempt to cover up its intent had been foiled, and Secretary of State Christian A. Herter confirmed what the Soviets had said, insisting that the U-2 flights were to deter "a surprise attack" on the Western allies. Shortly after Herter spoke, President Dwight D. Eisenhower stunned the American public even more strongly by taking full responsibility for the flights. He ordered all future U-2 flights suspended, while Khrushchev bellowed angrily

about American "aggressive acts" and eventually broke up a "summit conference" that had been scheduled for May 17 in Paris. Khrushchev also canceled an invitation to Eisenhower to visit Russia in the fall. Thus, the 15-year-long Cold War between the two superpowers continued, along with a furious rivalry in nuclear weapons. The U-2 spy flight's exposure caused many Americans, for the first time, to realize that their government practiced espionage and that their leaders sometimes lied. The scandal opened up a credibility gap that has never been fully closed.

Francis Gary Powers had been a pilot in the U.S. Air Force until 1956 when he resigned his commission and went to work for the U-2 program at Lockheed Aircraft Corporation. U-2 reconnaissance aircraft were capable of flying to an altitude of 12 miles and were equipped with extremely sensitive cameras to photograph details on the ground below. The planes were difficult to fly and land, and Powers underwent extensive training before he traveled to Turkey, where the Central Intelligence Agency (CIA) directed a U-2 surveillance operation against the Soviet Union.

Powers was not a member of the military but rather a civilian mercenary who was paid a handsome monthly salary, plus a tax-free $10,000 bonus, for every U-2 flight he completed. He had flown many missions over Soviet territory before his final one. He later explained that he did not think his plane had been hit by a direct shot before it crashed, for it did not burst into flames but rather was damaged by something he did not see. The effect of the damage was so immediate that he did not have time to pull the lever that would destroy the plane as he had been taught to.

The Soviets, as could be expected, made much of the fact that they had caught an American spy red-handed. Still, Powers was given a defense counsel and a public trial. He was charged with "crimes against the state" and espionage, a punishable offense under law. The evidence against him was overwhelming, and Powers admitted in a Moscow courtroom: "I have committed a grave crime and I realize I must be punished for it." Harold J. Berman, a Harvard University law professor who followed the case closely, later wrote that Powers received "a fair trial, in the sense that Powers did not appear to be 'brainwashed,' his lawyer put up the best possible defense under Soviet law, the trial procedures preserved most of the basic principles of procedural justice, the prosecution was required to prove its case, and the sentence was neither too harsh nor too mild." Powers was found guilty and sentenced to 10 years in prison.

Although the trial was of Powers as an individual spy, it had the wider intent of condemning the United States for violating important international law by trespassing in Soviet air space. It has been almost universally accepted that each nation has sovereignty over the air space in which planes can fly over its territory. However, the U.S. State Department declared that it had the right to send reconnaissance planes over "closed" societies. The trial of Powers had enormous propaganda value for the Soviets because it brought to the world's attention America's abuse of the international rules of sovereign air space.

In February 1962, Powers was released by the Soviets in exchange for Colonel Rudolf Abel, a Soviet intelligence officer who had been convicted in 1957 of espionage in New York City and was serving a 30-year prison term in the United States. To have both men return to their own countries was proper, said top Kremlin officials, because of the "desire to improve relations" between Moscow and Washington.

Rudolph VALENTINO: "a pink powder puff?"

In the 1920s, handsome Rudolph Valentino, a matinée idol of the silent screen, was worshiped by women all over the world. Women undressed in public in front of him, tore off his clothes in the streets for souvenirs, and jumped uninvited into his bed. Despite his famed "Great Lover" power over women, however, the screen star was often attacked for his seemingly unmasculine tastes and preferences. The popular press impugned his virility and harped on his "effeminacy," accusing him, at its most vicious, of using a pink powder puff.

This legendary lover was born as Rodolpho d'Antonguolla in Castellaneta, Italy. He immigrated to the United States at the age of 18 in 1913. Before Valentino (the stage name he had assumed) rocketed to stardom in *The Four Horsemen of the Apocalypse* (1921), his dark good looks helped get him work as a cabaret dancer and some bit parts in Hollywood films. With his renown, women swooned over "Rudy," his flashing, hooded eyes and sensual mouth. They flocked to see whatever film he starred in next: *The Sheik* (1921), *Blood and Sand* (1922), *Monsieur Beaucaire* (1924), and *The Eagle* (1925).

All the while, however, Valentino's Hollywood lifestyle became increasingly a matter of controversy in the newspapers. He lived extravagantly at Falcon Lair, his Spanish-Moorish style hilltop castle, and dressed lavishly, wearing chinchilla-lined coats, gold jewelry, and perfume. He plucked his eyebrows, put vaseline on his lips to make them shine, slicked back his hair, and cut his sideburns at an angle. His two marriages both failed, and both of his wives were lesbians. Actress Jean Acker apparently locked him out on their wedding night in 1919. She accused him of sexual neglect and of physical violence. In 1922 Valentino married actress Natacha Rambova before his divorce from Acker was final, which got him arrested for bigamy. Afterward he always wore Rambova's slave bracelet, her gift to him, which was another effeminate touch attacked by the popular press. Public slurs on his manhood hurt him deeply, but the papers never let up. They sneered at his advertising testimonials for face cream and implied that he was a homosexual. When Rambova divorced him in 1926, she allegedly said their marriage had never been consummated. Afterward, Valentino was said to have indulged in orgies at Falcon Lair.

In July 1926, the *Chicago Tribune* published an editorial that blamed Valentino for the recent installation of a powder-puff vending machine in a men's washroom, calling it "degeneration into effeminacy." The question was posed: "Do women like the type of 'man' who pats pink powder on his face in a public washroom and arranges his coiffure in a public elevator? . . . What has become of the old 'caveman' line? . . . Rudy, the beautiful gardener's boy, is the prototype of the American male. . . . Hell's bells. Oh, sugar." Such slurs caused Valentino extreme bitterness.

While on a personal tour to promote his new and last film, *The Son of the Sheik* (1926), he fell ill and underwent surgery in New York City for an inflamed appendix and two perforated gastric ulcers. Complications after the operation brought on his death from peritonitis at New York's Polyclinic Hospital on August 23, 1926. Before he succumbed in pain, the screen idol, aged 31, apparently asked the doctor beside the bed, "And now, do I act like a pink powder puff?"

News of Valentino's demise caused many persons to go crazy in New York and elsewhere, and film press agents capitalized on it. Rumors immediately began that the "sheik" had died of poisoning from arsenic given to him by a New York society woman whom he had jilted, that he had been shot by an enraged husband whose wife he had seduced, and that he had died from a syphilitic infection of the brain. The streets of New York were pandemonium as flocks of fans, mainly women, loudly bewailed his death. Armed police had to beat back crowds pushing to have one last look at the great lover as his body lay in state at a funeral parlor on Broadway. An estimated 100,000 people filed past his ornate coffin, and some 50,000 mourners attended his New York funeral. Several women committed suicide in grief over him. Actress Pola Negri, who rushed to his funeral from Hollywood (where film studios suspended production for two minutes in his honor), wept dramatically before his coffin and then fainted in front of a horde of photographers, who captured all the ghoulish details. She and other women, including pretty Ziegfeld dancer Marion Kay Brenda, claimed that they had become engaged to Valentino shortly before he died. Later, many females publicly proclaimed him to be the father of their babies, many of whom were born years after his death. All the press hype helped Valentino's movies at the box office, where they netted $2 million in two months.

Valentino's 1925 will left only $1 to Rambova, who had been the sole heir in an earlier one. The actor, however, insisted on being buried with her slave bracelet on his wrist. His roughly $1 million estate was divided equally among his sister, his brother, and Teresa Werner, Rambova's aunt, after his many debts were paid off.

VANDERBILT CUSTODY CASE

In 1934, American public sympathy lay with 10-year-old Gloria Vanderbilt, heiress-to-be of part of the rich Vanderbilt family fortune. During a bitter court trial, little Gloria's mother and grandmother fought over her custody. For Gloria's extravagant young mother, the battle was one stemming from financial desires as much as maternal love.

Gloria was only a year old in 1925 when her illustrious father, Reginald Claypoole Vanderbilt (called "Reggie") died; he was the son of Cornelius Vanderbilt II, the famous New York railroad baron. At the time, her vivacious 19-year-old mother, Gloria Morgan Vanderbilt, was an internationally renowned beauty; Reggie's second wife, she had had no money when she married him. Reggie's fortune was left in trust for little Gloria, who received a limited, monthly allotment to cover her expenses; her chic, social mother was allowed to have funds as long as her daughter lived with her. The mother continued to carry on her fashionable, high-society lifestyle with her now limited resources, traveling back and forth between America and Europe, where she took a house in Paris. Little Gloria was taken care of by her nurse, Dodo, and accompanied her mother about, seldom seeing much of her, while "Mommy" cavorted in New York, London, Paris, the French Riviera, Switzerland, and other places.

In time little Gloria's health, physical and mental, appeared to go downhill, and consequently her maternal grandmother (whom little Gloria fondly called "Naney") became deeply upset by her granddaughter's plight. She told Reggie's sister, Gertrude Vanderbilt Whitney, of her apprehensions. The incredibly rich Gertrude Whitney (she had recently inherited a $72

million fortune) took to heart her little niece's sorry state. She invited Gloria and her nurse Dodo to stay at her estate on Long Island, New York. There, in new, more stable surroundings, little Gloria became more relaxed and happy and began attending a local school. In 1933 a letter was sent to her mother, informing her that she would no longer get the funds alloted for her daughter's support; bills would be sent directly to the girl's legal guardian for payment. Angered that her income would be severely curtailed—unless little Gloria lived with her—Gloria Morgan Vanderbilt decided to go to court to gain guardianship of her daughter. The court hearings began on September 28, 1934.

During the trial, the elder Gloria's maternal fitness became a central issue; she was to exclaim at one point that evidence against her was a "riot of character assassination." Judge Carew heard testimony that the beautiful mother had had an affair with a European prince, had a rat-infested house in Paris, had obscene literature in her quarters, and had lived a debauched life in which she never got out of bed before noon and sometimes stayed in bed all day. To the court's sensation, the elder Gloria's maid testified that she had found her mistress and Lady Milford Haven in bed together, kissing in an embrace. Rich and privileged elite friends of the elder Gloria reassured her of their support in her now quite scandalous custody battle. Her two sisters, Lady Furness (her twin) and Mrs. Thaw, rallied in support of her to oppose the invective against the supposedly unfit mother, who allegedly declined to accept an enormous sum to relinquish her claim to little Gloria.

During the case, Judge Carew spoke privately to little Gloria, who was surely overburdened by the events surrounding her and who apparently indicated her preference to live with her Aunt Gertrude. The court heard her choice. Her infuriated mother accused others of having instructed the 10-year-old to lie and to say what they wanted to hear—namely her wish to remain with her aunt. On November 14, 1934, Judge Carew gave his rather cryptic decision: "The child Gloria Vanderbilt is not to have for the future the life that it had from the death of its father up till June 1932." Justice had not been done according to Mrs. Vanderbilt, who blasted the judge for depriving her of her natural maternal rights when a final understanding was reached with the opposing parties in the case. Little Gloria became a ward of the court and was put into her aunt Gertrude's custody. Her mother, who was granted weekend visiting rights, resumed her traveling, smart-set lifestyle and eventually, in 1940, induced her attractive 16-year-old daughter to settle down with her in a house in California. Things didn't go well with them, and the young Gloria became financially independent of her mother upon gaining her own nearly $4.5 million inheritance in 1945. By then young Gloria had married and divorced her first husband. She married again that year, to flamboyant conductor Leopold Stokowski, a notorious womanizer who at the age of 63, was 42 years Gloria's senior. He reportedly treated her like a servile Arab wife. She had to have psychiatric help, and the marriage with Stokowski, by whom she had two children, ended in divorce in 1962. Later she married again and proceeded to have a rewarding and successful career as a fashion designer.

William Henry VANDERBILT: "the public be damned"

For William Henry Vanderbilt, the inheritance of his father's vast holdings in 1877 was both frightening and challenging. Unlike Cornelius "Commodore" Vanderbilt, who could be rough and willing to fight physically to preserve his status, William had always been in poor health. Fifty-six in 1877, he had learned to use his fine intelligence to attempt the settlement of problems through reason and arbitration rather than physical prowess. He also believed—as did few of his fellow financial moguls—in sometimes explaining to the public both his motives and his thinking. His use of this primitive kind of public relations almost destroyed his reputation in 1882 and unleashed the anger of the public and press toward all railroad tycoons and other robber barons.

Vanderbilt's New York Central Railroad was then engaged in a rate war with the Pennsylvania Railroad. Because the development of a good press had saved the Central system during the nationwide railroad strike of 1877 (he had offered to divide $100,000 among loyal Central workers), Vanderbilt agreed to an interview in his home about the rate issue. He remarked that a $15 rate between New York and Chicago was proving costly but was retained because of competitive pressure from the "Pennsy." He also explained why unprofitability had caused the elimination of an extra-fare New York-to-Chicago mail train. When the interviewer asked whether the railroads were operated for the public's benefit, Vanderbilt replied, "The public be damned!"

He did not stop with this thunderbolt but went on in his careful, rational way to explain that the Central was run for the benefit of its stockholders: "I am working for my stockholders. If the public wants the train, why don't they pay for it?" The remark and the related explanation together were an honest answer, but most newspapers reported only the aphorism and used its utterance as an opportunity to attack Vanderbilt for his callousness, for they believed that his words summarized the attitude of all monopoly capitalists, railroad barons in particular.

Vanderbilt then made matters worse by denying that he had made the statement, and critics of monopolistic capitalism from coast to coast used it to attack all tycoons—Rockefeller and Standard Oil, Carnegie, meat packers, coal barons (such as Henry Clay Frick), western mine owners, New England textile millionaires, and above all, railroad princes like Jay Gould (see ERIE RAILROAD "WAR").

Abashed, Vanderbilt went to J. P. MORGAN for help in disposing of his vast holdings in the Central system (with 87 percent ownership, the public knew that Vanderbilt was the stockholder for whom he had been working). Morgan made $3 million and soon became a power among railroad men; Vanderbilt gained $30 million. But the uproar occasioned by Vanderbilt's essentially honest remark was a partial cause of the Haymarket Square Riot of 1885.

Marilyn VAN DERBUR: Miss America violated

Marilyn Van Derbur, "first debutante" of Denver, 1958 Miss America, and founder of the Marilyn Van Derbur Motivational Institute, was accustomed to speaking in front of large audiences. But in 1991, before a crowd of only 30, she made what may have been one of the most difficult appearances of her life. She announced that her father, Francis Van Derbur, a millionaire and pillar of

The new Miss America of 1958, beautiful, 20-year-old Marilyn Van Derbur (formerly Miss Colorado) poses after being crowned in Atlantic City on September 7, 1957. Many years later, in 1991, she publicly announced that, from age five to 18, she had been frequently violated sexually by her father, a millionaire socialite and pillar of Denver society. (AP/Wide World Photos)

the Denver community, had sexually violated her repeatedly from the time she was five until she was 18. Through the phenomena of dissociation and memory repression, Marilyn had locked the tortured secret deep within her subconscious until only seven years earlier, in 1984, when a chance comment sparked a flashback and a slow recovery of the memories. Unbeknownst to Van Derbur, one listener in that small Denver audience was a journalist, and a report of the former Miss America's shocking admission appeared on the front page of the newspaper the next day.

People wondered how the beautiful 20-year-old who accepted the Miss America title in 1958 could have kept her secrets of sexual abuse so blithely hidden from public view. Van Derbur herself admits that she was split into a "day child," who pushed herself to excel at schoolwork, swimming, singing, acting, and every other aspect of her life, and a "night child," who curled into a fetal position in the dark waiting for her father's footsteps in the hallway.

Francis Van Derbur, a handsome man, worked his way through the University of Denver with money he earned at his family's bread business. While at school, he met his future wife, Gwendolyn "Boots" Olinger, whom he married one year after joining the successful mortuary services business owned by his wife's father; he became president of that business in 1959 and was a well-respected citizen in the Denver community.

Marilyn's "day child," unaware of her nocturnal counterpart, nevertheless experienced the effects of the night child's fear. She did not like to be touched or hugged, and she avoided playing with dolls. Although she dated in high school, she had only one serious boyfriend, Larry Atler, with whom she felt safe and comfortable (and whom she later married after telling him of the incest).

When Marilyn, the youngest of the four Van Derbur girls, was 18, she enrolled at the University of Colorado. One night while she was home visiting for the Christmas holidays, she went into her parents' bedroom to say goodnight. Her father tried to pull her down onto him, but she pushed away so angrily that he never attempted to abuse her again.

After graduation and her tour as Miss America, Van Derbur visited with her former youth minister. A seemingly chance statement he made dredged up a memory of her closely held secret. She then embarked on the painful process of consciously facing her childhood traumas. Van Derbur confided in her older sister, who admitted that she, too, had had nightly visits from their father.

Since the age of 18, Van Derbur had never fallen asleep without using sleeping pills or spending long hours staring into the dark. During the day, however, Van Derbur was as busy and productive as usual. She established the Marilyn Van Derbur Motivational Insti-

tute and spent her days talking to groups of CEOs or high school students, encouraging them to give the best of themselves to their pursuits.

After eight years of marriage, Marilyn and Larry had a daughter, Jennifer. When Jennifer turned five, Van Derbur began to experience uncontrollable fits of sobbing and occasional attacks of paralysis in which her heart rate would drop and she would be unable to move. The doctors found nothing physically wrong with her. She began to see a therapist who advised her to confront her father with the issues of abuse. When she did, he didn't deny it, simply saying, "If I had known what this would do to you, I would never have done it." Van Derbur didn't believe him.

Despite the confrontation, her physical problems worsened when Jennifer hit puberty; bouts of acute anxiety overtook Van Derbur and made it difficult for her to continue her career. She began to see a psychiatrist and learned that the physical signs had probably been triggered by seeing her child attain the same age as she was at the time of abuse. One day when her parents called to ask after her, Van Derbur said she wasn't doing well and admitted she had begun to see a psychiatrist. That evening, Van Derbur's father suffered a heart attack and died, leaving his youngest daughter feeling at fault for his death because he knew she had told others of his guilt.

As part of the healing process, Van Derbur spoke with each member of her family, including her mother, who had a hard time accepting the truth when her daughter confronted her. The Van Derbur family went on to donate more than $240,000 to start the Adult Incest Survivors Program at the Kempe National Center for the Prevention and Treatment of Child Abuse and Neglect. Van Derbur's goal was to make the ugly word *incest* speakable, to free its survivors from shame so they may begin to heal.

Charles VAN DOREN. See TELEVISION QUIZ SHOW SCANDAL.

William H. VAN SCHAIK: the *General Slocum* catastrophe

On June 15, 1904, the paddle-steamer *General Slocum*, bulging with Sunday-school excursionists, caught fire and burned in the East River, New York City. Over 1,000 persons were killed. Adding to the terrible tragedy of the disaster was the fact that it could easily have been avoided had it not been for the irresponsibility of the captain and the misjudgement of the steamer's owners.

The steamer's owners, the Knickerbocker Steamboat Company, pleased with the performance and profitability of their boat's master, had put total responsibility for the *General Slocum*'s maintenance into the hands of Captain William Van Schaik, under whom 30 million passengers had sailed safely. Schaik, however had gradually relaxed the discipline needed for safety on one of New York City's largest excursion steamers.

His laxity was to prove fatal. When fire broke out in a forward paint locker and spread rapidly toward the stern of the wooden boat, its canvas hoses proved to be too rotten to be used. A later investigation discovered that the crew had not gone through fire drills (one had even started a second fire in a galley because of his panic at the first fire). They had also failed to keep the boat's fire-fighting apparatus in condition and had not inspected its life preservers, all of which were unusable.

According to marine tradition, these shortcomings were the ultimate responsibility of the craft's master, and Captain Van Schaik was charged by the U.S. Department of Justice with misconduct, negligence, and inattention to duty. His complacency and inattention earned him, in 1908, the most severe sentence ever pronounced for a marine disaster: 10 years' incarceration in Sing Sing Prison at Ossining, New York. A pilot of the *Slocum* was also punished, a stringent set of regulations for steamboat inspection was developed, and broad changes in marine safety rules were made. But the human damage, for which the steamship company and its owners were not even brought to trial, had been done.

Witnesses of Van Schaik's misconduct revealed that he had been guilty of navigational errors unexpected in a veteran master. When the fire broke out, the *General Slocum* had just successfully passed through the East River's treacherous narrow strait called Hellgate (near 130th Street) and was less than 300 feet from the Manhattan shore. Unaccountably, Van Schaik raced north at 12 knots (nautical miles) per hour. The resulting wind forced the fire to the stern of the boat, where 1,358 passengers and most of the 30-member crew had taken refuge. Panic overwhelmed them when they discovered the boat's hoses to be unusable and the life preservers to be defective; when the *Slocum*'s upper decks collapsed upon them, some leaped overboard to be crushed by the boat's paddles or drowned.

The cost to the passengers was therefore unnecessarily high. In one extended family of cousins and aunts and uncles, 29 persons died. Tugs and other boats near the racing *Slocum* rescued only a few people. One boat came alongside. Those who jumped to reach it broke either their backs or their necks when they fell to its deck.

Worse disaster struck when the *Slocum* ran aground in a rocky cove in North Brother Island (near 145th Street): the flaming stern of the boat was sinking in over four fathoms of water. Passengers threw themselves overboard to drown rather than be burned. Counts vary, but between 1,021 and 1,107 people died as a result of this essentially avoidable marine disaster.

By 1911, public opinion toward Van Schaik had changed: 250,000 persons signed petitions requesting clemency for him, and U.S. President William Howard Taft pardoned him in 1912. But to the remnant of the congregation of lower Manhattan's St. Mark's Lutheran Church, the reprieve was a sentimental, ironic anticlimax.

Lupe VELEZ: spicy star and sick suicide

One of the most passionate and uninhibited of movie stars was tiny, Mexican-born Lupe Velez. Nicknamed the Mexican Spitfire for her irrepressible vivacity and fiery temper, Velez led a Hollywood party-girl life until she took her own life at the age of 36 in 1944.

Born Maria Guadalupe Velez de Villalobos in San Luis Potosi, Mexico, in 1908, the actress's convent education had ended when she was 14, after which she journeyed to Mexico City to work in a shop and to study at a dancing school. After being praised for a dramatic acting role she had in a Mexican production of *Rataplan,* Velez ventured to Hollywood and promptly won some parts in various motion pictures. Two years later, in 1928, she starred in F. Richard Jones's *The Gaucho* with Douglas Fairbanks, Sr. Her career was on its way, and during the next 16 years she was one of Hollywood's notable personae, noted for her passion on and off the screen.

Lupe's first important lover was actor John Gilbert. Shortly after that affair ended, she began one with young Gary Cooper, whom she met while the two were acting together in the western *Wolf Song* in 1929. Their relationship was tempestuous. After the couple finally broke up, Cooper apparently suffered a nervous breakdown. Then came Johnny Weissmuller, the Olympic swimming champion turned Tarzan in the movies. He was the only man Velez ever married, but the relationship was neither stable nor longlived. Punctuated with separations, reconciliations, and noisy quarrels, the marriage ended in divorce in 1938. It had lasted only five years.

Meanwhile, Velez had gained a scandalous reputation because of her uninhibited behavior in public. At parties she sometimes wore nothing under her dress, revealing her bare bottom when she flung her dress over her head.

In the late 1930s the Mexican Spitfire's film career began to go downhill, while she indulged in a succession of brief love affairs with undistinguished cowboys, stuntmen, studs, gigolos, and others. Movie-goers saw her appear mainly in a series of B-rated comedies with actor Leon Errol.

Lupe's extravagant lifestyle put her heavily in debt by 1944 when she took up a new lover, Harald Ramond, a 27-year-old, darkly handsome, aspiring actor. The affair, like her others, was marked by wildness and tantrums. In November 1944, Velez, who was a devout Catholic found out that she was three months pregnant. She informed Ramond, who agreed to marry her only if she signed a document stating that she knew he was wedding her solely to give a name to her baby. Their engagement, however, quickly broke off because of a fight. Velez was anguished over her predicament; she couldn't bear to have an abortion and desperately wanted a respectable marriage in which to raise her child.

She then carefully planned her last night on Earth. Masses of fresh flowers—fragrant gardenias and tuberoses—were bought to decorate her large Spanish-style mansion on North Rodeo Drive in Beverly Hills, California. Velez's two best girlfriends ate with her at her last supper, a spicy Mexican feast, and after they left in the wee hours, she went to her bedroom, which was lit with several dozen candles. She put on blue silk pajamas and penciled some farewell notes: "To Harald, May God forgive you and forgive me, too, but I prefer to take my life away and our baby's before I bring him with shame or killin [sic] him. Lupe." She wrote a seeming afterthought on the back: "How could you, Harald, fake such a great love for me and our baby when all the time you didn't want us. I see no other way out for me so goodby and good luck to you. Love, Lupe." She then swallowed about 75 Seconal pills and lay down on her bed to die.

In the morning her chambermaid, Juanita, discovered her corpse in the bathroom, her head in the toilet bowl. A spotty trail of vomit on the floor led back to the bedroom. Evidently the actress had become violently sick from the mixture of the pills with her last spicy meal and had staggered to the bathroom, only to slip on the tiles and fall headfirst into the toilet and drown.

Claudius VERMILYE, Jr.: clerical hanky-panky
Theological training and ordination are not necessarily a guarantee of sanctity. Although western history contains many illustrations of this generalization, the example of the Reverend Claudius I. Vermilye, Jr., is particularly scandalous. A divorced father of five children, Vermilye was 41 years old when he left the active Episcopal ministry in 1970 to found, with some friends, Boys' Farm Incorporated, a refuge for wayward and troubled youngsters in a rural area near Winchester, Tennessee. In 1977 Vermilye, better known as "Bud," was found guilty on nine charges of "aiding and abetting instances of specific homosexual acts" and three counts of distributing pornographic materials to the children supposedly in his care.

After founding the refuge, Vermilye dedicated himself to overcoming his young clients' various aberrations. And as a nonprofit, charitable organization, Boys' Farm quickly gained financial assistance from county and state officials.

Within a short time, however, Vermilye found himself contributing to the waywardness of his charges. Individual acts of homosexual affection led to orgies, which grew to include selected friends and trustees of Boys' Farm. Some of the revels were filmed for moments of passive delectation; soon the films were pri-

vately offered for sale to connoisseurs of homosexual pornography, one "buyer" being as far away as Saudi Arabia. The customers were considered donors and Boys' Farm was labeled a charity.

The sordid activities at the institution were completely revealed to Tennessee authorities by a 15-year-old youth under Vermilye's care. Because the youngest of the wayward boys involved in Vermilye's rehabilitative and sexual activities were but 11 years old, the angry judge castigated the former minister for "crimes against nature" and then sentenced him to 25 to 40 years in prison, the harshest penalty provided by Tennessee law for his crimes. Because of public hostility and the judge's haste in sentencing the former cleric to this severe punishment, Vermilye's appeal was not later ruled inadmissible.

The former reverend, however, had gained national opprobrium by being discussed in many reports of child abuse and molestation in America.

Robert VESCO: flamboyant financier on the run
Robert Lee Vesco went from Wall Street multimillionaire to accused master swindler, fugitive financier, drug smuggler, and suspected Soviet bloc agent. In 1972, facing charges of "misappropriating" $224 million from his mutual funds company, Investors Overseas Services (IOS), and of making illegal contributions to President Richard M. Nixon's 1972 reelection campaign, the 36-year-old Vesco fled the United States, moving to Costa Rica at the invitation of its president, José Figuéres Ferrer. The United States has since sought unsuccessfully to extradite him so that he may stand trial on fraud and bribery charges.

Vesco was part of a troubled time in American society—a time that saw the toppling of one of the most popular American presidents (see WATERGATE) and a time of social, cultural, and political change. He made news headlines regularly in 1972–74 as his alleged criminal activities unfolded on a parallel course with the Watergate investigations. He showed seemingly utter disregard for law and ethics, opting for greed in perpetrating one of the greatest securities swindles ever and earning himself a disreputable place in American history.

In 1970, Bernie CORNFELD, the founder and fabulously wealthy boss of IOS, lost control of the company as a result of egregious mismanagement and a slump in the New York Stock Exchange. An interim board took over until New Jersey entrepreneur Vesco arranged a huge loan to "rescue" IOS and secure control of the company. The Securities and Exchange Commission (SEC) would later reveal that Vesco had concealed his purchase of IOS from the company's stockholders and the public for several months; in early 1971 he bought 6 million shares of IOS stock from Cornfeld for $5.5 million, including a premium of $3.5 million over the prevailing market value—a violation of federal securities laws. Vesco made himself chairman of IOS in 1971 (as well as a director, an executive committee member, and financial committee chairman of the company) while continuing as president of his own New Jersey-based International Controls Company.

In April 1972, Vesco resigned his IOS positions and disposed of all his holdings in the company. He gave no reason for his actions, which included the sale of 38 percent of IOS common and preferred stock, but they came at a time when the SEC was increasing its investigation into the mutual funds company—a murky offshore funds syndicate whose wily promoters often preyed upon various impressible investors. In November 1972 the SEC charged Vesco with fraud, of being the leader of a small group that had "spirited away" $224 million in cash from IOS. Involved were four IOS "dollar funds" (established to invest in American securities) that mainly held high-grade, blue-chip stocks sold on the market to American brokers at Vesco's direction. The proceeds of the sales (actually stockholders' money) was directed to the Overseas Development Bank in Luxembourg and the Bahamas Commonwealth Bank, both of which were controlled by Vesco.

In a scheme that the SEC said was "rife with self-dealing," the Vesco group then diverted most of the cash they had taken from IOS to their own personal pursuits through "shell" corporations also funded by the diverted money. The company's assets became virtually nonexistent, having been shifted to entities in which stockholders could not benefit from them. The IOS annual report of 1971 showed that the company recorded a loss of $10.6 million (the result of the scheme) that year. It also showed that more than half the company's 1971 income was just statistical, and at year's end the liabilities were more than double the assets.

While the SEC threatened Vesco with a lawsuit for stealing $224 million from IOS, the brash financier secretly donated $200,000 to the Committee to Re-Elect the President ("CREEP") in 1972. Vesco's large cash contribution was apparently a way to bring pressure on the Nixon Administration to blunt the intense SEC probe into IOS activities. Vesco left the United States during a special New York grand jury investigation that led to indictments on May 10, 1973, against former Attorney General John N. Mitchell, former Commerce Secretary Maurice H. Stans, former New Jersey State Senate Majority Leader Harry L. Sears, and Vesco himself on charges of conspiracy, obstruction of justice, and perjury in connection with the $200,000 contribution.

In the weeks before the 1972 election, Vesco evidently informed Mitchell and President Nixon's brother Donald, whom he had hired as his personal assistant, that unless the SEC investigation was stopped, he would publicly reveal the details of his contribution. The donation, which had been made in addition to a previous $50,000 contribution, was then in violation of a new federal law requiring the public reporting of all political campaign contributions. Vesco had originally wanted to make a $500,000 contribution, with the idea that "special favors" would then be given him in connection with the SEC investigation.

As a fugitive American citizen in Costa Rica, Vesco invested heavily in agriculture, real estate, and communications. His $3.5 million "loan" to President Figuéres and the $10 million he held in Costa Rican bonds undoubtedly helped to shield Vesco from extradition to the United States for prosecution. His presence in Costa Rica and particularly his close ties to Figuéres caused considerable controversy. In 1978 Figuéres lost the presidency to Rodrigo Carazo Odio, who was intent on ridding his country of "waste and corruption" and vowed to expel Vesco. Ten days before Carazo took office, the financier fled to the Bahamas, where he owned a house in Nassau. The Bahamian government later sought his deportation, and by late 1981 Vesco had left the islands for an unknown location. Afterward he was reported seen in Costa Rica, Nicaragua, Antigua, the Bahamas, and Cuba. He was rumored to be involved in drug smuggling and gun-running. By 1984 he had found definite sanctuary in Cuba and was reportedly smuggling American high-technology computer and communications equipment to that country, as well as to Nicaragua and Soviet-dominated eastern bloc countries. Cuban President Fidel Castro acknowledged that the infamous Vesco was living in his country in 1985.

The Cuban government, which refused to extradite Vesco to the United States, arrested and jailed him in May 1995 on criminal charges of trying to produce and sell a drug without its knowledge. Fifteen months later, in 1996, a weary-looking Vesco stood trial before a tribunal in Havana, was found guilty of "illicit economic activities" (including trying to market an unproven AIDS drug known as TX), and sentenced to 13 years in prison.

VETERANS' BUREAU SCANDAL. See Charles R. FORBES: mismanager of the Veterans' Bureau.

Claus VON BÜLOW: "the case of the sleeping beauty" Since late 1980, beautiful Martha "Sunny" von Bülow, inheritor of $75 million, has lain in a hypoglycemia-induced coma, locked in a vegetative state and fetal position from which she is never expected to recover. Many, including two of Sunny's children, believe that her former husband, the jet-setting aristocrat and financier Claus von Bülow, is responsible. He has twice undergone harrowing, sensational criminal trials on charges that he tried to kill his multimillionarie-socialite wife with insulin injections.

In 1970, after four years of marriage, Martha and Claus von Bülow bought an opulent, oceanfront mansion named Clarendon Court on Bellevue Avenue

A court officer leads aristocratic financier Claus von Bülow in 1982 into Newport (Rhode Island) superior court, where he appeared for a pretrial hearing concerning charges that he twice tried to kill his multimillionaire wife by giving her insulin injections. His first trial in 1982 ended in conviction; his second in 1985 ended in acquittal. (UPI/Bettmann Newsphotos)

("Millionaires' Row") in Newport, Rhode Island. A witty, stylish couple, they soon fit into elite Newport society and were known for their elegant dinner parties. Tall, blonde Martha, nicknamed "Sunny" because of her pleasant disposition, had inherited enormous wealth from her father, George W. Crawford of Pittsburgh, who made a fortune from oil, gas, and utilities companies. Tall, dashing Claus, well-to-do but lacking the great riches of his wife, was a Danish-born aristocrat educated at Cambridge University in England. He had once worked for oil billionaire J. Paul Getty as a legal and diplomatic adviser. The von Bülows were both patrons of the arts; Claus was a top investor in the long-running Broadway comedy-thriller *Deathtrap,* a play, ironically, about a character who contemplates how to kill his wife for fortune. Before marrying Claus, Sunny had had an eight-year marriage to an impoverished Austrian nobleman, Prince Alfred von Auersperg, that had ended in divorce. It produced two children, Princess Annie Laurie von Auersperg and Prince Alexander von Auersperg. Sunny's marriage to Claus yielded one child, Cosima von Bülow.

On December 27, 1979, Sunny von Bülow was rushed to Newport Hospital, having fallen into a coma from an apparent drug overdose. The then 47-year-old socialite recovered, but her friends rarely saw her afterward. On December 21, 1980 she was found unconscious on the marble floor of her bathroom in the Newport mansion and was again rushed to the hospital. She never regained consciousness, was soon transferred to a Boston hospital, and was then brought to Columbia

Presbyterian Medical Center in New York City, where she has remained ever since.

Sunny's longtime private maid, Miss Maria Schrallhammer, became suspicious of her mistress's comas and helped convince Sunny's two children by her first marriage to ask for an inquiry into their stepfather's doings. This led to the filing of charges in 1981 against Claus von Bülow for twice attempting to kill his wife by injecting her with insulin. The case against him was based on circumstantial evidence.

During his 1982 trial in Newport, the state prosecution's star witness was Miss Schrallhammer, who in her German-accented voice testified that she had seen a little black bag in von Bülow's closet containing a vial of "insulin" and a hypodermic syringe. She also said that on December 27, 1979, von Bülow had waited until his wife was "barely breathing" before calling a doctor. The prosecution asserted that Sunny von Bülow suffered from hypoglycemia—a low-blood-sugar condition—and that her husband deliberately gave her insulin to further reduce her blood-sugar level and thus threaten her life. Von Bülow allegedly wished to kill his wife so that he could inherit his share ($14 million) of her fortune and marry his mistress, Alexandra Isles, a raven-haired Manhattan socialite beauty and former television soap-opera actress. Isles's testimony revealed her affair with Claus, which she said had continued after Sunny's second coma. Her admission undoubtedly worked against Claus von Bülow, who pleaded innocent but was found guilty (by unanimous vote of the jury) on two counts of assault with intent to murder. He was sentenced to 30 years in prison but remained free after posting $1 million bail.

Von Bülow appealed his conviction and retained Harvard law professor Alan Dershowitz to defend him. Dershowitz's successful argument led the Rhode Island Supreme Court to rule in 1984 that illegally seized evidence (the contents of Claus von Bülow's "little black bag") had been used against his client. Von Bülow's 1982 conviction was consequently overturned.

But Prince Alexander von Auersperg and his sister, Princess Annie Laurie von Auersperg Kneissl, again accused their stepfather of trying to kill their mother, which brought on a second trial in 1985 in Providence, Rhode Island. In this trial von Bülow's chief defense attorney was the able and indefatigable Thomas Puccio, who was advised by Dershowitz. Puccio relied on expert medical testimony to show that drugs and alcohol—not insulin injected by her husband—had caused Sunny von Bülow's comas. She was said to be a heavy drinker who injected herself with mixtures of Demerol and amphetamines, to be suicidal over her husband's extramarital affairs (Prince Alexander testified that his stepfather had informed him that Sunny was "no longer interested in sex" after the 1967 birth of their daughter Cosima, and "that he therefore turned to another woman"), and to have caused her own comas in 1979 and 1980. The state prosecution supplied testimony from endocrinologists that insulin injections were the only possible cause of the comas. Endocrinologists for the defense countered by claiming that insulin could not have triggered the comas. The state was not allowed to present testimony about the $14 million Claus von Bülow stood to inherit when his wife died (the judge denied its legal relevance to the case).

Ultimately, Isles ended months of seclusion in Europe and returned to testify against her ex-lover von Bülow. On the stand, she was asked by Puccio: "You certainly didn't believe (von Bülow) intended to harm his wife, or you wouldn't have associated with him, isn't that true?" Isles sighed, replying, "I'm ashamed to say it's not true." At the end of the nine-week trial, Puccio asked the jury to be just, not sympathetic, to his client. "It's not a pretty picture," he stated. "Mr. von Bülow was cheating on his wife and he was stringing Alexandra Isles along. No matter what you think of Mr. von Bülow's conduct of his marriage, please don't hold that fact against him in this case." On June 10, 1985, the jury acquitted von Bülow, then age 58.

About a month later, his two stepchildren filed a $56-million civil lawsuit against him, raising the same allegations considered in the two criminal trials. They also claimed that von Bülow had defrauded their mother by influencing her to alter her will and set up a trust fund that gave him $120,000 a year, while he schemed to get rid of her. His daughter Cosima has been disinherited by her maternal grandmother because she had stood by her father and might funnel money to him. In 1986 the stepchildren rejected von Bülow's offer to divorce his comatose wife and give up any claim to her fortune if they would drop the civil suit against him and give their half-sister, Cosima, her fair share of the estimated $50-million estate left by Sunny's mother, the late Annie Laurie Crawford Aitken.

Finally, in an out-of-court settlement in 1987, von Bülow agreed to divorce Sunny and give up all claims to her fortune (including his yearly trust-fund income) and renounce any rights to book or movie deals about the family's feuding. Cosima, who had sided with her father during the trials, dropped two countersuits and, in return, gained an equal share of her maternal grandmother Aitken's estate. The two von Auersperg siblings established the Texas-based National Victims Center, an organization to help victims of violent crimes and their relatives.

Dershowitz later wrote a book about the controversial case, *Reversal of Fortune*, on which a movie was based, starring Glenn Close, Jeremy Irons, and Ron Silver, in 1990. Princess Annie Laurie von Auersperg Isham (who had divorced her first husband and later remarried in mid-1989) called the movie a "commercialization of a tragedy."

Sol WACHTLER: a chief judge's "unpardonable" behavior

Sol Wachtler was one of the most highly respected state judges in the United States. He was appointed to the New York State Supreme Court in 1969 by Republican governor Nelson Rockefeller. After serving in that position for four years, he stepped up to the Court of Appeals as a justice, and in 1985 Democratic governor Mario Cuomo appointed him chief justice of the Court of Appeals, the state's highest court, thus making Wachtler the highest ranking judge in the state. Despite his ties to the Republican Party he developed a reputation as a liberal, and he demonstrated strong support for First Amendment rights and the rights of women and minorities. Wachtler was so respected in New York that state Republicans began pushing him to run against Cuomo for governor in 1994. Meanwhile, his reputation as a jurist for fairness and pragmatism led to his being considered for an appointment to the U.S. Supreme Court.

In 1992 Wachtler's judicial and political career came to an end when he was arrested by the Federal Bureau of Investigation (FBI) for harassment, extortion, and intent to kidnap. The charges stemmed from Wachtler's affair with Joy Silverman, his wife's uncle's stepdaughter, who was 17 years younger than he. Wachtler and Silverman began their affair shortly after he helped to straighten out several details arising from her father's will in 1984. The affair ended in 1991 when the 45-year-old Silverman dumped the judge for a New Jersey lawyer. Her rejection was more than the 62-year-old Wachtler could take. In an effort to gain revenge, he began harassing her anonymously by telephone. At first he simply hung up when she answered, but later he pretended to be a private detective who possessed evidence damaging to her reputation. He then began harassing her by mail as well. One letter demanded $20,000 to keep embarrassing photographs and tapes of Silverman and her new lover from being made public. Another letter, which was addressed to Silverman's 14-year-old daughter, contained an obscene picture and message and a condom. He even threatened to kidnap the daughter. Altogether, over a 13-month period, Wachtler threatened his former lover more than 50 times.

Silverman was a major contributor to the Republican Party and had been nominated by President George Bush to be ambassador to Barbados, so she was able to take her concerns for her daughter's safety directly to William Sessions, then head of the FBI. He assigned 80 agents to the case, and seven weeks later they traced one of Wachtler's calls to his car phone. He was arrested in midcall on a Long Island freeway (near New York City) and taken directly to the psychiatric ward of a local hospital where he was placed under surveillance to keep him from committing suicide.

Instead of being jailed upon his release from the hospital, Wachtler was placed under house arrest and made to wear an electronic monitoring bracelet. He later resigned his chief judgeship and pleaded guilty to mail harassment in exchange for all other charges against him being dropped. Wachtler blamed what he called his "unpardonable and shameful" actions on a manic-depressive disorder which was caused by his abuse of prescription drugs, but he did not attempt to use that condition as an excuse. He served 11 months in a medium-security federal prison and a federal medical center, where he received treatment for his manic depression. After being released in 1994, he published *After the Madness: A Judge's Own Prison Memoir*, an edited version of his prison diary which also contains a number of proposals for prison and judicial reform. In addition to teaching law at Touro Law School in upstate New York, he started a dispute counseling service in Great Neck, Long Island, which also provides legal assistance to the poor.

Jimmy WALKER: the destruction of "Beau James"

In 1929, charges of fiscal corruption and neglect of official duties began to assail James John ("Jimmy") Walker, who had since 1925 been the dapper and debonair mayor of New York City. Three separate, interlocking, but incomplete investigations produced a bill of 15 charges against Walker by 1932; 12 sessions of hearings followed. They were conducted by Franklin Delano Roosevelt, then governor of New York, who was empowered by law to remove the mayor upon sufficient cause. Depressed by the tumult and armed with bad advice from his political colleagues, Walker suddenly resigned his office on September 1, 1932, and decamped to Europe. His sudden flight created an impression of guilt and cowardice.

Both the city and state of New York were, in 1929, the scene of intense political rivalry. Democrats held both the mayoralty and the governorship, and Republicans were striving fiercely to gain power for themselves. Because the governorship and perhaps the presidential nomination of 1932 were regarded as Democratic appurtenances, the Republicans aimed to secure control of the legislature and the mayoralty. The metropolis of New York City, which since the early 20th century had proved at best to be ungovernable, was an easy target. Republican legislators and leaders buffeted Roosevelt with complaints about Walker and Tammany Hall. They demanded immediate probes to expose alleged corruption.

Roosevelt delayed until the clamor, strengthened by newspaper editorials, prevented further inaction. In August 1930, he replied indirectly by ordering the appellate division of the state court system to investigate the condition of magistrates' courts in Manhattan and the Bronx. The probe grew to include an inquiry into the performance of the Manhattan district attorney. Originally suggested by Republican State Senator Samuel H. Hofstadter, the investigation was chaired by retired Judge Samuel Seabury.

The probe soon grew into three distinct investigations, all left unfinished by Walker's sudden resignation. The court inquiry suggested inadequate oversight by the city administration; it blew apart the political systems of the city's boroughs, causing the trial and imprisonment of some judges and, after the murder of a key Seabury witness, the sudden resignation of many more magistrates. A second investigation, concerning Walker's fiscal relationship with the wealthy publisher Paul Block, seemingly stopped when Walker and Block disproved all allegations. The third investigation, involving the perusal of Walker's finances by Seabury and Hofstadter, proved inconsequential after Walker's wit and aplomb disconcerted Hofstadter and won applause from the audience in testimonial hearings.

Nevertheless, combing through 13.5 million words of testimony on 60,000 typewritten pages—testimony developed at a cost of more than $750,000—Seabury and his colleagues isolated 15 charges of malfeasance, misfeasance, and nonfeasance against Walker. Curiously,

they included the Block-Walker relationship. Seabury sent them to Roosevelt in 1932. Faced with a Republican majority in both the New York State senate and assembly and having been served bills ordering his personal investigation, the governor began hearings in Albany, New York. Twelve sessions of rehashing had occurred before Walker resigned.

The evidence examined up to that point had proved no malfeasance and no graft connected with Walker; it again disproved the allegations against Block, and suggested only the most insignificant actions of improper conduct (misfeasance) against the mayor. It did suggest, however, that a charge of neglect of duties (nonfeasance) might be sustainable against Walker.

The last finding was urged on Roosevelt by Raymond Moley, later a member of Roosevelt's Brain Trust during his presidency. It was secretly communicated to Walker's advisers and to the leaders of Tammany Hall, whose Sachem (chief), Albert ("Al") E. Smith, coldheartedly told Walker that he was through. (Ironically, in 1941, President Roosevelt commented that he had had no plan to remove Walker because he did not believe the Seabury evidence justified the mayor's removal.)

Depressed by the hearings, estranged from his wife, and grief-stricken by the recent death of his brother, Walker swallowed the bad advice and removed himself from office.

Within 10 days he sailed for France, not to escape punishment, but to seek his girlfriend, Betty Compton, whom he married in 1933. He canceled his original plan to seek reelection on an exoneration platform.

The Walkers returned to America in 1935, where the former mayor was jubilantly welcomed. He proved then to have been as personally improvident as he had been neglectful of his official duties. He was broke. The Walkers lived on Betty's money and Jimmy's small receipts from odd jobs. His last public office, a largesse from then Mayor Fiorello La Guardia, was as "czar" of industrial and labor relations for the ladies' garment industry. Walker died in relative obscurity in New York in 1946.

John WALKER: "I am a celebrity"

Without detection for some 17 years, John Anthony Walker, Jr., managed to operate a lucrative espionage enterprise, selling to the Soviet Union "the most coveted and guarded" of U.S. Navy secrets. The notorious Walker spy ring, motivated chiefly by greed, not ideology, seriously jeopardized American naval communications with relative ease. Its operations, according to U.S. Defense Secretary Caspar Weinberger, resulted in "very serious losses" and clearly compromised the national security of the United States.

As a communications specialist (cryptographer and chief radioman) in the U.S. Navy, John Walker served from 1962 to 1967 on two nuclear-missile-carrying submarines, the U.S.S. *Andrew Jackson* and the U.S.S. *Simon Bolivar*. His wife, Barbara, whom he had married in 1957, raised four children while he pursued his naval career. He taught at the Navy Communications School in San Diego, California, and later became a warrant officer in Norfolk, Virginia.

Walker began spying for the Soviets (KGB) in 1968 when he was communications watch officer of the Atlantic submarine fleet. Later he held a similar position for the entire Atlantic Naval Surface Force. Barbara Walker apparently became suspicious of her husband's furtive activities in the early 1970s. In 1974, Walker recruited his best friend, Jerry Whitworth, another Navy communications specialist into his spy-business. Whitworth served aboard the aircraft carriers *Constellation* and *Enterprise* and later was in charge of the cryptographic center at the sprawling Alameda Naval Air Station on San Francisco Bay. Operating "at the heart of navy communications," Whitworth fed much valuable classified material to Walker, who then retired from the service and in time set up three private-detective agencies in the Norfolk area.

By 1983 Walker had recruited his son Michael into his clandestine spying enterprise, in which he sold top-secret information to his Soviet contacts at monthly fees ranging from less than $2,000 to $4,000. Whitworth eventually retired from the navy, having become very fearful of being caught by the Federal Bureau of Investigation (FBI). By this time, however (around 1980), John Walker had already lured his older brother Arthur, a retired navy lieutenant commander, to pass along classified documents and photographs that he was able to obtain with his "secret" security clearance. Arthur had taught antisubmarine tactics at the Atlantic Fleet Tactical School in Norfolk from 1968 until his retirement in 1973. He worked in a civilian-engineering job for the VSE Corporation, a navy defense contractor in Chesapeake, Virginia, and dealt with the maintenance of various naval ships.

Barbara and John Walker's marriage had been all the while steadily collapsing. They divorced in 1976. Moving eventually to a small town on Cape Cod, Massachusetts, Barbara made up her mind to inform the FBI about her ex-husband. She did this, she said, "to protect my family." (At the time she didn't know that their son Michael was involved in the spy ring.) In late 1984 she alerted federal agents, who kept a six month vigil on John. Finally, they observed him drop off a trash bag (later found to contain more than 120 classified documents) alongside a rural Maryland road. The next morning, May 20, 1985, the FBI arrested the 47-year-old John Walker and charged him with espionage. While being interviewed in jail, he seemed to view his fate with peculiar bravado; "I am a celebrity," he said proudly.

From the information found in the trash bag, the FBI linked Walker to his 22-year-old son Michael, a navy operations clerk aboard the aircraft carrier *Nimitz,* which was patrolling off Israel. Much classified information was apparently found stashed near his bunk on the carrier; Michael was charged with espionage. The FBI trail led also to Arthur Walker and then to Whitworth, who surrendered to authorities in San Francisco. Any honor among the members of the Walker spy ring seemed to vanish during the next months.

In Norfolk, Arthur stood trial without a jury in August 1985. He claimed to have been "roped into" the ring by John on the lure of making money and to have gotten the job at VSE on John's urging. On the fourth day of the trial, the presiding federal judge found Arthur Walker guilty of passing two classified documents to John for delivery to the Soviets; Arthur received three concurrent life sentences in prison and was fined $250,000.

John and Michael Walker accepted a plea-bargain agreement with the government, pleading guilty to spying in exchange for less-than-maximum sentences and disclosure of information about the spy ring. John drew a single life term (with parole eligibility after 10 years), and Michael got 25 years' imprisonment (with parole eligibility after eight and a third years). Later, the judge who sentenced them on November 6, 1986, recommended no parole, partly because the elder Walker showed no remorse. "I look in vain for some redeeming aspect of your character," the judge told him. "It made no difference to you that your own flesh and blood could be exposed to these traitorous activities. None of this mattered to you so long as the cash came in." Michael, the judge noted, had disgraced a military uniform with his own betrayal.

In 1986 John Walker testified against his ex-navy buddy Whitworth during the latter's arduous three-and-a-half-month-long jury trial in San Francisco. The 46-year-old Whitworth claimed to have thought that the stolen secrets he gave to Walker were going to American allies, and Walker said he never revealed to Whitworth that the Soviets were the buyers. Showing no remorse, the jurors convicted Whitworth on July 24, 1986, of 12 of 13 espionage and tax evasion charges against him; they found him guilty of selling vital code and communications secrets to the spy ring for $332,000. The federal judge called Whitworth "a zero at the bone," sentenced him to 365 years behind bars, and fined him $410,000 (probably, like the fine imposed on Arthur, to guarantee that Whitworth would not profit by selling his spy story to a publisher). "I just want to say I'm very, very sorry," uttered Whitworth, weeping and repentant. The harsh punishment meted out to him was justified, according to the government, because he had been the "principal agent of collection" for the military secrets transmitted to the Soviets. But there were many who felt that the main betrayer had been John Walker, the ringleader, a "Jekyll and Hyde" personality, as his former wife Barbara once had said.

George WALLACE: principled opponent of integration

On June 11, 1963, George Corley Wallace, governor of Alabama, attempted, with the help of state troopers and highway patrolmen, to prevent the court-ordered racial integration of the University of Alabama. It was not until the Alabama National Guard was federalized that he gave in. His action made him a leader among the ideologists who attempted to argue down a burgeoning civil-rights movement in the United States.

Wallace began to acquire his resister and ideologist labels as early as 1948, when, as a delegate to the Democratic National Convention, he was a leader in the floor fight against a strong campaign plank concerning civil rights. As a judge in the Third Judicial Circuit Court of Alabama from 1953 to 1959, he earned the nickname the Fighting Judge because he successfully opposed federal attempts to investigate Alabama voter registration records. He acted again to weaken the civil-rights plank of the 1956 Democratic National Convention, arguing from a states' rights position that federal intrusions into a state's authority were both interruptive and illegal.

Govenor George Wallace's opposition to racial integration in Alabama's public schools resulted in violent confrontation in 1963. He complied only after President John F. Kennedy federalized Alabama's National Guard. Pictured here in 1968 promoting humanitarian organizations (like the respected Order of DeMolay), Wallace ran for president in 1968 as the candidate of the antiliberal American Independent Party. He won five Southern states and 46 electoral votes. (Yale University/Historical Picture Collection/Archives/Yale University Library)

Wallace's campaign for governor of Alabama in 1962 had a double focus: to reduce state spending and to resist federal attempts to impose new civil-rights standards on the state, especially concerning segregation. Like a one-man army, he campaigned up and down the state and won the sympathies of many voters. He vowed to ask the legislature to give him as governor, rather than local school boards, the right to assign students to specific schools, and threatened to resist "any illegal federal court order" by "standing in the schoolhouse door."

Wallace fulfilled his promises. He drastically reduced state expenditures (including those of his own office) and resisted federal court orders regarding segregation so thoroughly that twice in 1963 the Alabama National Guard had to be federalized in order to defeat his opposition.

Wallace first took a stand against segregation at the university, despite a personal visit from U.S. Attorney General Robert F. Kennedy and telephone calls from President John F. Kennedy. He stood, surrounded by troops and police, in the doorway of the university's registration location in order to turn back two blacks accompanied by U.S. Assistant Attorney General Nicholas Katzenbach.

The episode was charged with dramatic tension. Katzenbach ordered Wallace to "cease and desist" his resistance. Wallace responded by reading a speech about illegal usurpation of power by the federal government. Katzenbach then asked him four times to move from the doorway. Each time, Wallace refused. Finally Katzenbach returned to his car, and within four hours the Alabama National Guard was federalized. Ordered once again to move, Wallace condemned the federalization as "illegal usurpation" and then stood aside. Students James A. Hood and Vivian J. Malone were successfully registered.

Later in 1963, Wallace opposed public-school integration in Tuskegee, Birmingham, Huntsville, and Mobile, sending out the National Guard ostensibly to preserve order but actually to prevent the admission of black students. Confusion reigned for almost a week until a second federalization forced all Alabama troopers to remain in their barracks.

Although Wallace claimed to have foresworn agitation and interference after the 1963 assassination of President John F. Kennedy, he soon began a series of nationwide speaking tours to colleges and universities in which he explained the philosophy behind his opposition to civil-rights reform. His strongest opposition was to the 1964 bill, which he labeled "the involuntary servitude act." In his 1976 autobiography, *Stand Up for Freedom,* Wallace claims that these speeches strengthened his reputation and won him adherents, but they also often produced anger and threats of violence; and in the midst of his 1972 segregationist campaign for the American presidential nomination, he was shot by an angry would-be assassin named Arthur H. Bremer. The wound left him permanently paralyzed below the waist.

Confined to a wheelchair, Wallace made another unsuccessful attempt for the presidency in 1976 and completed his third term as Alabama's governor in 1978. He began apologizing for his former segregationist views and, with the support of many black voters, was elected governor again in 1982. At the end of his term in 1987, Wallace retired from politics and later died in Montgomery on September 13, 1998, at the age of 79.

WATERGATE

The most scandalous constitutional crisis in American history began in the early morning of June 17, 1972, when police arrested five men led by James W. McCord, Jr., inside the Democratic Party's national headquarters in the Watergate office and apartment complex in Washington, D.C. The five, seized with cameras and electronic surveillance gear, had attempted to bug the Democratic offices in what was later described as "a third-rate burglarly attempt." The men were found to be connected to the Republican Committee to Re-Elect the President ("CREEP").

Documents found on the men also implicated CREEP aide G. Gordon Liddy and White House consultant E. Howard Hunt in the break-in at the Watergate. The original five, along with Liddy and Hunt, stood trial (presided over by Judge John J. Sirica of the U.S. District Court for the District of Columbia) and were convicted on January 30, 1973, of conspiracy, burglary, and eavesdropping. President Richard M. Nixon denied any White House involvement in the crime; Sirica and others, however, had suspicions that higher governmental executives knew about the break-in and the attempts to cover it up.

President Richard M. Nixon (center) walks with his chief of staff H. R. "Bob" Haldeman (right) from the Executive Office Building to the White House. The Watergate scandal rocked the Nixon administration in 1973–74, forcing Haldeman, other presidential advisers, and finally Nixon to resign (he became the first president ever to do so, after the House of Representatives had recommended three articles of impeachment against him). Members of the Nixon administration were imprisoned for conspiracy, burglary, eavesdropping, perjury, and obstruction of justice (UPI/Bettmann Newsphotos)

While in jail, McCord made startling allegations in a letter to Judge Sirica, saying that he and the others convicted had been pressured by high Republican Party officials to keep quiet and plead guilty to the burglary. He also said that perjury had been committed in the case. McCord claimed that John N. Mitchell, former United States attorney general in the Nixon administration and former campaign manager for the president, had wholly sanctioned the Watergate break-in. As a result of McCord's disclosures, federal attorneys initiated inquiries into a range of possible crimes linked to Nixon's reelection in 1972. White House counsel John W. Dean, III, handed incriminating evidence to them and afterward, on April 30, 1973, resigned, along with White House Chief of Staff H. R. "Bob" Haldeman and the president's chief adviser on domestic affairs John D. Ehrlichman.

On the day of the resignations, President Nixon told the American public that he accepted responsibility for the Watergate affair but that he had had no knowledge of a Watergate cover-up. Additionally, his close friend Mitchell absolved him of any entanglement in the unlawful 1972 political campaign tactics called the "White House horrors," which included the wiretapping of opponents' offices, circulating false information about enemies, harassing opposition speakers, and scheming to discredit Democratic National Convention delegates by the use of call-girl solicitations.

The U.S. Senate Select Committee on Presidential Campaign Activities, headed by North Carolina's Democratic Senator Samuel J. Ervin, Jr., began extensive, televised hearings on the 1972 campaign practices and the Watergate happenings on May 17, 1973. John Dean, testifying about criminal activities in the White House, stated that Mitchell, Haldeman, and Ehrlichman had all known about the Watergate break-in beforehand, and that Nixon had approved the cover-up of the burglary. United States Attorney General Elliot L. Richardson was given further evidence of White House wrongdoing through his specially appointed prosecutor Archibald Cox, who sought to obtain tapes of President

Nixon's conversations (former White House aide Alexander P. Butterfield had revealed in testimony that presidential conversations in the White House had been tape recorded since 1971). Nixon "stonewalled" and refused to comply with Judge Sirica's order to release the tapes to him. Cox sued Nixon to get them, and Nixon, in return, fired Cox as special prosecutor on October 20, 1973—the so-called "Saturday Night Massacre"—and also fired Deputy Attorney General William D. Ruckelshaus (Nixon had ordered Richardson to fire Cox, but he had refused and instead resigned; Ruckelshaus had also refused; and Solicitor General-made-Attorney General Robert Bork had finally carried out Nixon's orders).

The scandalized American public put added pressure on Nixon. After hearing rumors of his possible impeachment, Nixon named a new special prosecutor, Leon Jaworski, and then released some of the tapes. He plainly didn't want to seem above the law, feeling the weight of the press and the public against him. Jaworski then methodically brought indictments against Mitchell, Haldeman, Ehrlichman, and White House lawyer Charles W. Colson, among others, for conspiracy, obstruction of justice, or perjury in connection with the Watergate cover-up (all of them served time in prison on various convictions in 1974 and 1975). At this time, in the spring of 1974, Nixon, who had been named an unindicted co-conspirator in the Watergate burglary by one grand jury, released edited transcripts of some tapes that contained some "gaps" or silences during key conservations (they were supposedly accidental erasures, but some were thought to have been created purposely by erasing parts of the tapes).

The House Judiciary Committee, after skeptically examining numerous revealing tapes, probed deeply into Nixon's actions during televised impeachment hearings against the President on July 24–30, 1974. At the end, the committee recommended three articles of impeachment against Nixon: obstruction of justice (in connection with Watergate), abuse of power, and defiance of congressional subpoenas. The U.S. House of Representatives had earlier voted to accept articles of impeachment, but it did not have a chance to decide the issue. Nixon gave up a key tape that indicated his covering up of Watergate and then admitted to his involvement. He also admitted to attempting to stop a Federal Bureau of Investigation (FBI) inquiry into the 1972 burglary. Republican congressional leaders talked with Nixon, who soon afterward (on August 8, 1974) announced his resignation, effective the next day.

The prolonged drama had ended. The first American president ever to resign, Nixon was succeeded by Vice President Gerald R. Ford, who on September 8, 1974, granted the former president an unconditional pardon for all federal crimes that he had "committed or may have committed or taken part in" while in office.

Watergate increased distrust of the federal government and generated the Independent Counsel law enacted by a reform-minded Congress in 1978 and reauthorized in 1982, 1987, and 1994. Nixon, who died at age 81 in 1994, labored for 20 years after Watergate to recover from the disgrace. His lawyers continually challenged the release of taped conversations in his White House (they rested in the National Archives). Excerpts from these tapes eventually appeared, making clear that Nixon had tried from the beginning to cover up the connection between the Watergate burglars and the White House high command.

James WATT. See ENVIRONMENTAL PROTECTION AGENCY (EPA): "sweetheart deals" with industry?

John White WEBSTER: a not-so-perfect crime

In 1849 John White Webster, a doctor with a Harvard University M.D., killed his colleague, George Parkman, who had come to collect on a debt. Webster then tried to destroy the body. Had it not been for his careless haste and the meddlesome nature of a certain janitor, the crime might have gone undiscovered.

Parkman, world famous as a teaching physician and holder of the Parkman Chair of Anatomy at the Massachusetts Medical College, had visited his colleague Webster on the afternoon of November 23, 1849, in the basement laboratory the college provided to the latter. He had come to collect a debt owed him by Webster, who was known to be leading a liberated and luxurious life at the time. When Webster revealed that he could not pay, Parkman grew angry and threatened to have Webster's teaching position revoked. Infuriated by his creditor's threats, Webster struck Parkman with a heavy timber and crushed his skull. Webster then dissected the body and cremated some of it in a laboratory furnace. Because he was still in a state of emotional upheaval, however, his grisly labor was hasty and incomplete. Some large portions of the body, most importantly Parkman's jaw structure, were not incinerated but preserved in a large storage vault for skeletal remains.

Parkman's disappearance made exciting news, and the college offered a generous reward for information about him. For a week, Webster experienced fear that his crime might be discovered, but he refrained from completing his task of destroying the body. A college janitor had commented that the wall behind the laboratory furnace had been unusually hot on the afternoon of November 23, and Webster had hastily explained that he had been conducting "experiments." Upset, he acted to protect himself but not by continuing his minute dissection; instead, in a gesture of uncustomary generosity, he presented the janitor with a Thanksgiving turkey.

Now even more suspicious, the janitor decided to investigate on his own. By some lucky accident, he pried into the storage vault and found Parkman's pelvis, portions of one of his legs, and some of his teeth. These permitted the identification of the remains of the unlucky creditor.

Webster was arrested. He pleaded not guilty, claiming that the body parts discovered by the janitor and the police had belonged to one of the college's cadavers. His testimony was disproved in 1850, during what must have been regarded as a remarkably sensational trial for Boston. Many extraneous witnesses, such as the president of Harvard University and the new holder of the Parkman Anatomy Chair, were permitted to testify; newspaper reporters converged on Boston from distant American cities, and some 60,000 persons were allowed brief court admissions measured in minutes. In the 11-day duration of the trial, however, the most significant evidence offered was the identification by local dentists of Parkman's teeth.

Found guilty, Webster made a complete confession. He was executed by hanging on August 30, 1850.

WEDTECH SCANDAL. See Mario BIAGGI: a senior congressman's sudden comedown.

WELFARE ISLAND PENITENTIARY SCANDAL
Early in the morning of January 24, 1934, the New York City police apprehended the infamous Irish con man Ed Cleary. He was in an inebriated state at the time. After searching his quarters the police discovered evidence of great luxury and illicit hedonism. Among other things, a deck of heroin, a can of home brew, and a kitchen knife with two razor-sharp edges were found. No charges could be brought against Cleary, however, for the famed con man was in prison already! He was serving out a sentence on Welfare Island in New York City's East River.

Those familiar with conditions in American prisons had long known that Welfare Island was one of the most corrupt in the country, but no one took any action until the still new mayor of New York City, Fiorello H. LaGuardia, appointed Austin H. MacCormick as the city's commissioner of corrections in January 1934. "Operation Shakedown" was planned with the care and precision of a military attack. The prison's warden, Joseph A. McCann, and his staff were not informed, however, for it was rightfully believed that they were in cahoots with the prison leaders. At 8:30 A.M. January 24, MacCormick telephoned Welfare Island and told the deputy warden to lock all prisoners in their cells since a count had shown that someone was missing. This was a ruse to prevent confrontations with prisoners during the raid.

One half hour later, MacCormick and about 30 hand-picked wardens and detectives, plus a few reporters, arrived on Welfare Island. The deputy warden of the island's prison, who was not in uniform as required,

was put under military arrest. Warden McCann himself had been duped into accompanying MacCormick, who wanted to keep an eye on him throughout the operation.

The raiders moved quickly to the dormitory of the prison, where they found Ed Cleary, the leader of the Irish prisoners. The police then moved on to the prison hospital in another building, where they discovered Joe Rao, the boss of the Italian mob. He had taken over the entire second floor for himself and his cohorts and was being shaved by his personal barber when the law officers appeared. The two bosses and their gang members were searched, marched to a cell block, and locked up. It was the first time most of them had seen the inside of a cell since having arrived on the island.

A more intensive search of the gangs' quarters revealed that they had lived like kings while serving their prison time. Cleary had a pet police dog named Screw Hater chained to the frame of his bed, and his kitchen knife with its two razor-sharp edges was lying near the window. Overhead on a rafter stood the large can of home brew. A chest of drawers contained the deck of heroin, and the cupboards in the kitchen were stuffed with many kinds of choice food, while three refrigerators contained an even greater variety of delicacies. In Rao's quarters the police found an array of fine clothes, six boxes of cigars, monogrammed stationery, and half a dozen kinds of talcum powder. His gang, like Cleary's, dined on expensive china, and their food was prepared by skilled chefs.

Both gangs also maintained homing-pigeon cotes. The birds were used to fly narcotics into the prison. Additionally, Rao had a milch goat and a private garden that was tended by an inmate servant. Between them, the Cleary-Rao mobs controlled four lucrative rackets in the prison: the narcotic traffic, the sale of stolen food, the sale of inmates' clothing, and the sale of privileges. They had installed their own wiring systems for stoves, radios, and private telephones.

Once Cleary, Rao, and their henchmen had been locked up, MacCormick's men, reinforced by police from nearby precincts, began to search all the prisoners and all the cell blocks of the prison, tier by tier. Drug addicts were housed in the west wing, where the searchers found quantities of paper soaked in a heroin solution, a hypodermic needle, several eye-droppers, and a few narcotic pills. Other cells contained a wide variety of contraband, including razor blades, a surgeon's scalpel, jagged-edged knives, scissors, an eight-pound hunk of corned beef, canned goods, loaves of bread, lead pipes, rugs, meat cleavers, canes, table lamps, electric grills, and radios. The corridors outside the cells became awash with the illicit findings.

A cell block in the southern part of the prison contained an entirely different kind of forbidden item—

rouge, powder, perfume, mascara, a woman's wig, and silk underwear.

When the word spread through the prison grapevine that the inmate-mobsters had been incarcerated, many ordinary prisoners cheered. They had been exploited, cheated, and demeaned by the racketeers. If a prisoner had money, he could buy drugs, food, and other amenities and even shorten his sentence. If he was poor, he had to eat the meatless stew provided by the prison mess or else steal food to sell to the gangs. Even the guards and the prison administrators kowtowed to Rao, Cleary, and their stooges.

After the raid, Warden McCann, his deputy, and the prison doctor were relieved of their duties. MacCormick moved as quickly as he could to transfer the inmates to a new prison on Rikers Island. The commissioner also deplored the situation he had found at Welfare Island and asserted that the scandalous conditions in the city's prisons manifested a vicious circle of crime and depravity.

WEST POINT CHEATING SCANDAL

In April 1976, army officials at the U.S. Military Academy at West Point, New York, charged 50 third-year cadets with cheating on an engineering take-home examination—an offense punishable by expulsion. Graders had found an improbable degree of similarity in answers on the test.

The *New York Times* reported that the number of cheaters was actually higher than 50 but that only some of them were being prosecuted in order to minimize the extent of the scandal.

Before long, it became clear that the 50 accused cadets represented only the tip of an iceberg of honor-code violations at West Point. The public learned that the honor code itself had been an object of continuing controversy—some cadets said it was excessively harsh and arbitrarily applied. Some said there was much hypocrisy about cheating at West Point and that "this sort of thing goes on all the time." One West Point officer, on the other hand, claimed that the incident simply demonstrated the health of the system. Officials of the Military Academy felt that the cheating had been done by a number of small groups acting independently, rather than by one all-inclusive conspiracy.

Then, in May 1976, Lieutenant General Sidney Beery announced that 70 to 90 new cases of suspected cheating were under investigation by a recently appointed internal review board. The board, which had emerged as a response to charges by the convicted cadets of an academic cover-up, revealed by late May that the number of suspected cheaters was much greater than the original estimate. Cheating was now presumed to have occurred on a number of exams, and the perpetrators were suspected to number over 200.

Some of the accused and their lawyers claimed that 50 percent of the more than 873 juniors at West Point had been involved in honor-code violations, and some army prosecutors supported the cadets in their charges, claiming that a proper investigation could lead to honor-board trials for 300 to 400 cadets.

In June, U.S. Army Secretary Martin R. Hoffmann announced that he was considering a revision of the honor system to start after the then current investigation ended.

Forty-eight of the 50 originally charged cadets were convicted and expelled. Forty-nine other cadets were acquitted, and two cadets resigned before charges were brought. In August 1976, however, Hoffmann announced that the expelled cadets would be allowed to apply for readmission to the academy after a year's absence. Hoffmann's intervention had been encouraged by some members of Congress, who, after hearing the story and the charge that West Point had violated some of its own regulations, felt that expulsion was "unreasonably harsh and excessive," particularly since academic practices at the academy encouraged collaboration among cadets.

Although Hoffmann denied that the academy was attempting to limit the prosecution of the guilty cadets, he acknowledged that there was evidence that control of honor-code enforcement had passed into the hands of the Military Academy's administration from its proper place in the hands of the cadets.

Hoffmann appointed a panel to study the honor code and announced that take-home tests would no longer be used at West Point, a solution that was probably necessary but which failed to satisfy anybody. See also NAVAL ACADEMY CHEATING SCANDAL.

WHISKEY RING: "Let no guilty man escape"

During the presidency of Ulysses S. Grant, a notorious operation known as the Whiskey Ring was said to be cheating the U.S. government out of millions of dollars. The president at first appeared to be hell bent on squashing the ring, exclaiming emphatically, "Let no guilty man escape!" Once the investigation began, however, and those implicated were found to be in higher and higher positions, Grant actually obstructed the goal he had called for.

From the time of the Civil War, midwestern distillers and United States internal revenue agents had been in collusion, successfully cheating the U.S. government out of millions of dollars from the sale of untaxed whiskey and other liquor. Extremely high taxes on liquor, sometimes as much as eight times the price of the liquor, had compelled many distillers to seek relief through the bribery of public officials in the Bureau of Internal Revenue and the Treasury Department. Large distillers in St. Louis, Chicago, Milwaukee, Peoria, and Indianapolis thus used bribes to evade the payment of revenue taxes on liquor, notably whiskey. The taxes defrauded from the government went into the pockets of the distillers and corrupt federal officials, who usually shared about half the proceeds and managed to remain untouched for many years as "crooked whiskey" (with false excise stamps) was distributed and sold around the country.

Although the American press had written about the Whiskey Ring, the government seemed strangely unwilling to expose and prosecute its members. This all changed during the summer of 1874, when Benjamin H. Bristow, a spirited lawyer from Kentucky, became the new treasury secretary. Bristow immediately set about reorganizing his department, with special attention going toward putting the notorious Whiskey Ring out of business. When he discovered that the ring was centered chiefly in St. Louis, he secretly dispatched specially picked federal agents to that city and several others to collect information about the leaders and operations of the whiskey distilleries. Word about Bristow's undercover force and planned roundup of suspects, however, leaked out ahead of time, allowing some of the lawbreakers to escape. Nonetheless, in May 1875, authorities managed to seize sufficient evidence (records and books) to bring successful indictments against 238 persons, 110 of whom were eventually convicted. The government took control of the dishonest whiskey distilleries and also recovered more than $3 million in taxes. The ring collapsed totally in 1875, after Bristow's raids.

The reputed head of the Whiskey Ring was John A. MacDonald, whom President Grant had appointed supervisor of internal revenue in St. Louis in the late 1860s. MacDonald had given gifts to the president's private secretary, Orville E. Babcock, and had also given Grant a team of horses and harness. Attempting to flee the country, the ring leader was caught, convicted, and imprisoned but not before alleging that Babcock had received illegal "kickbacks" from the ring and that Grant, too, had been involved (this was never substantiated by any evidence). Babcock, however, who had been a Civil War comrade of Grant's, became the focus of Bristow's investigation, undoubtedly to the regret of the president, who had stated his intention to "let no guilty man escape." Some Republican leaders came to the aid of Babcock. They tried to convince Grant that Bristow's probing, which had gained national attention through press coverage, was damaging the party. Newspaper reports of the president's brother and son being linked to the ring helped to turn Grant against his treasury secretary. He also dismissed the government's special prosecutor in the case. To the president, his friends in the administration (some were oldtime drinking buddies) just couldn't be guilty of any wrongdoing, and his enemies (including reformers like Bristow) were only

working to undermine his possible bid for a third presidential term (it was alleged that some of the Whiskey Ring's gain was to be used by the Republicans for the reelection of Grant).

On orders from the president, who was plainly influenced by Babcock, federal prosecutors in the Midwest were forbidden to offer immunity to minor Whiskey Ring conspirators who were willing to testify for them. Numerous conspirators of major importance could have been convicted and jailed if their underlings, who were prepared to plead guilty for immunity, had testified against them. As a result, the federal government failed to obtain the convictions it could have (several ring members who were imprisoned were later pardoned by Grant). In St. Louis in February 1876, Babcock was put on trial on charges of "conspiracy to defraud the revenue" and heard considerable damaging evidence against him. Feeling that he also was on trial, Grant made preparations to travel to St. Louis to testify on Babcock's behalf but was persuaded not to by his Cabinet. Instead, the president sent a deposition to Babcock's lawyers, swearing to his secretary's innocence and rectitude. This undoubtedly helped Babcock gain an acquittal by the jury on February 24, 1876. But strong public opinion against him forced Grant to relieve Babcock of his White House duties and to assign him the inspectorship of lighthouses, a politically innocuous post. Later, in June 1876, Bristow resigned under pressure from Grant and came to be highly respected as a lawyer in New York City. The Republicans scuttled the idea of renominating Grant for a third term at the 1876 national convention.

Harry Dexter WHITE. See HOUSE COMMITTEE ON UN-AMERICAN ACTIVITIES (HUAC): the destruction of Harry Dexter White.

Stanford WHITE. See Harry K. THAW: lecherous millionaire murderer.

Walter WHITE: intermarriage equals ostracism
In 1884, Frederick DOUGLASS, the famed abolitionist who was himself an ex-slave, married his secretary, a white suffragette. Their union caused a journalistic furor. White newspapers and the church press fiercely excoriated him for, among other things, his "presumption." Over half a century later, another interracial marriage was met with condemnations. This time, however, the negative reaction was more on the part of blacks than whites. In 1949, Walker Francis White, internationally celebrated leader of the National Association for the Advancement of Colored People (NAACP), divorced his black wife, mother of their two children, and married Poppy Cannon, a highly regarded white writer and food editor for *Mademoiselle* magazine. The couple

was confronted with a barrage of savage editorials, mostly in the black press, and bundles of anonymous poison-pen letters, chiefly from black males. White's action, moreover, almost precipitated his ouster from the secretaryship of the NAACP.

The two reactions illustrate a complex shift in attitudes toward miscegenation over a period of slightly more than two generations: what had been an object of fear for white citizens in the late 19th century had been transferred almost exclusively to male black citizens by the middle of the 20th. This change had first been expressed in 1946 when black FATHER DIVINE took a young white woman to be his second Mother Divine.

What also differentiated the reaction to the Walter White miscegenation matter from that of the earlier Father and Mother Divine intermarriage was its predominantly variable social effect. The Whites left for Europe after their quiet wedding to use a year's leave of absence from his secretaryship as representatives of American organizations making a world tour sponsored by "America's Town Meeting of the Air." Their companions learned of the wedding but neither made hostile comments nor acted antisocially. Some, however, were puzzled about the Whites as an interracial couple. Walter White had a very pale complexion, blond hair, and blue eyes (he was only 1/64 black); Poppy White was a brunette with dark-hued skin. Some of their companions concluded that it was she who had the black ancestry.

The Whites' year away from America allowed the enemies of racial intermarriage to be busy. A Florida senator hysterically tried to use the marriage as a means of defeating the Fair Employment Practices bill, charging illogically that the White alliance proved that President Harry Truman really wanted "social admixture." Some members of the NAACP's board of directors tried to punish White, whose secretaryship had often been imperious and high-handed, by ousting him. However, one of the organization's directors, Eleanor Roosevelt, argued that it "needs his leadership, breadth, and vision," and 22 others agreed with her against 12 deprecators. But White returned to discover that his extensive powers had been severely limited and that the influential task of financial management had been delegated to his former assistant Roy Wilkins.

Until White's death in 1955, the couple suffered additional subtle social slights. Only those who had been friends to both during the many years Walter White and Poppy Cannon had been confidants would receive them together. Some of Walter's friends would pointedly omit Poppy's name from their invitations; many of her friends would refuse to receive him. This ostracism was distressing to them both. It even affected their friends: one close acquaintance of Poppy's had a nervous breakdown because her husband's hostility to Walter made Poppy refuse all invitations deliberately directed to her alone.

Aware that her husband had developed a serious heart condition, Poppy White tried to shield him from the petty exclusions, but she could not field all of them. At these times White would recount to her some of his experiences with racial attitudes, which had begun during the Atlanta riot of 1906, when the adolescent White and his father crouched beside a window watching the approach of a white mob. The event made him aware that the lynching of blacks by whites ranged from actual hangings (upon which he was once a leading American expert) to lynching through condescension. Both White and his wife realized that his work for understanding and civil treatment, begun in 1916, had been only the opening phase of a much longer task.

WHITEWATER. See Bill CLINTON: impeached U.S. President.

Richard F. WHITNEY: high-class larceny

In 1929, Richard F. Whitney, then vice president of the New York Stock Exchange, gained the honorifics "Savior of Wall Street" and "Strongman of the Street." His performance during a vain attempt to prevent the collapse of the market on "Black Thursday," October 24, 1929, earned him election as the stock exchange's president—at age 42, the youngest ever. To millions of Americans, the name Whitney became a household word. By 1938, however, Whitney's heroic reputation had disappeared, and instead of the savior he was now known as "the Wolf of Wall Street" and he had been sentenced to 5 to 10 years' incarceration at Sing Sing Prison at Ossining, New York, for grand larceny.

Whitney, a graduate of the exclusive Groton School and Harvard University, owner of his own bond company, possessor of a New York City townhouse and an estate in north Jersey, had in 1929 acted as the "Morgan broker." For two anxious days, he had calmly labored, buying leading stocks to keep up their price. He was armed with a pool of $240 million contributed by a consortium of banks at the behest of J. P. Morgan and Company. His unsuccessful effort to end the selling panic begun on Black Thursday made him momentarily famous.

As president of the chastened exchange, Whitney seemed indefatigable. He commuted between New York and Washington, D.C., advising presidents, treasury officials, and legislators bent on reforming the exchange so that a collapse like that of 1929 would never happen again. Whitney, however, represented the "Old Guard" of the exchange, attacked by opponents as a private club run for their own benefit by a group of elite plutocrats. He resisted all attempts to force regulation upon the exchange until the power of the Roosevelt administration imposed the 1934 Securities and Exchange Commission (SEC) upon Wall Street and backed it, through 1940, with other laws. Promising

100 percent compliance on the part of the Stock Exchange, Whitney then did all he could to delay obeying; he succeeded until moderates and those opposed to the Old Guard voted him out of office.

He was compelled to resist reforms, especially disclosure of records, for a second reason: in trouble himself financially, he had made some unethical choices. The 1929 crash had cost him his own fortune and his wife's. In attempts to recoup, he began to make unsound investments. To preserve his expensive lifestyle, he began using securities held by his own company and those of the Stock Exchange Gratuity Fund (of which he was a trustee and broker) as collateral for short-term loans. At first he was fortunate; he managed to pay off the loans and restore the securities without detection. But his personal fortune continued to decline, and he developed the habit of using another batch of securities for a second loan, until he was engaged in a continually revolving (and illegal) credit scheme. When asked in 1937 by his brother George, president of J. P. Morgan and Company, why he had acted as he did, Whitney had no explanation to offer.

The 1937 problem occurred when a clerk for the Gratuity Fund revealed that Whitney had withheld $1 million of the fund's securities and cash. By then, his personal fortune had sunk to $75,000. His brother covered the obligation.

The stock exchange, however, with the SEC, investigated, discovered that Whitney had borrowed $25 million in four recent months and was in debt to a total of $11 million. On March 7, 1938, he was suspended from the exchange as insolvent.

Within a few days, charges of misappropriation and defalcation prompted Whitney to plead guilty to three charges of grand larceny; the amount involved was more than $3 million. The chairman of the SEC, William O. Douglas, and the New York County district attorney, Thomas E. Dewey, acted swiftly; the judge branded Whitney a "public betrayer," and the latter spent three years and four months as a prisoner in Sing Sing.

Whitney never returned to Wall Street. Instead, after leaving prison he ran a family-owned dairy farm in Massachusetts and managed a fiber mill in Florida. Away from the power, glory, and temptation of the Street, he led a quiet, financially successful life until his death at the age of 86 in 1974.

Jerry Whitworth. See John WALKER: "I am a celebrity."

Charles WILKES: the fruits of impetuosity

Charles Wilkes is honored in many school texts for his part in the *Trent* Affair of 1861. Every year countless high-school students read of his seizure of Confederate commissioners aboard the British ship called the *Trent*. To them Wilkes is presented as a hero who received a Broadway parade in New York, a congratulatory letter from Secretary of the Navy Gideon Welles, the thanks of Congress, and the public approval of President Abraham Lincoln. What they don't learn is that Wilkes felt himself to be above the rules and twice had to be punished by court-martial.

In 1861 Wilkes was commanding the Union warship *San Jacinto*. Under orders to assist in the bombardment of Port Royal, South Carolina, he decided instead to seek out Confederate privateers. Near the Bahamas, he learned that the Confederate commissioners to London and Paris, James M. Mason and John Slidell, had escaped from Charleston to Havana and were aboard the London-bound British mail packet ship *Trent*. Without orders and ignoring international conventions concerning neutral ships, Wilkes stopped and boarded the *Trent* to seize the commissioners. He foolishly failed to take the ship as a prize of war. It sailed on to tell of the seizure in England, while Wilkes conveyed his prisoners, Mason and Slidell, to cells near Boston.

Wilkes became an instant hero in the North, but he had disobeyed both orders and the law, and just before Christmas, 1861, a British note demanded the release of the two prisoners and a suitable apology. It seemed possible that Britain would declare war on the Union and side with the Confederacy. President Lincoln and his Cabinet, anxious to avoid a wider war, complied and had the prisoners released.

Most history texts do not note that Wilkes was angered by this act of deference to Britain and said so publicly. Again disregarding orders, he scouted out Confederate privateers and blockade runners in the West Indies. Soon notes about breaches of official neutrality were received in Washington, D.C., from Britain, France, Spain, Denmark, and Mexico, until Secretary Welles beached Wilkes in 1863.

Again contrary to Navy etiquette, Wilkes argued publicly and also conducted a vendetta against Welles concerning delays in his promotion to commodore. In 1864 Welles called for a court-martial of Wilkes, making five charges: disobedience of orders, insubordinate conduct, disrespectful language, disobedience to a general order of regulation, and conduct unbecoming an officer. Found guilty, Wilkes sat out the rest of the Civil War under suspension. He did, however, gain the long-overdue rank of rear admiral (but on the retired list) in 1866.

Wilkes's 1864 court-martial was his second judicial reprimand. It could have been avoided had he pondered the lessons offered by his first reprimand which had occurred many years earlier, in 1842. His character, as described by his shipmates then, perhaps explains why he did not avoid the later problem. He was seen as "conceited, domineering, and arrogant" and as so stern a disciplinarian as to deserve the epithet "martinet." Apparently his self-admiration was too powerful to conceive doubts or detect possible faults in himself.

By 1842 Wilkes had earned but not received his promotion to higher ranks as the leader of the first overseas exploration sponsored by the federal government: the United States Exploring Expedition of 1838–42, to the Antarctic. The accomplishments of the venture, which led to the establishment of a national museum of natural history (now part of the Smithsonian Institution), were of a very high order. They gained Wilkes's recognition by America's British rivals, who had long explored the area, in the form of a gold medal from the Royal Geographic Society presented in 1847.

Wilkes's command of the expedition was done in a largely domineering manner, which had instilled a low morale among his companions, a depression increased by the failure of the Tyler administration to hail its accomplishments.

When the expedition was first proposed in 1828, no one had been willing to take command of its six ships and almost 500 individuals. Wilkes was the only naval officer with sufficient scientific training to undertake this supervision. Unfortunately, he was only a lieutenant, junior grade; nonetheless, he was offered the responsibility—without an increase in rank. He took it and gained almost simultaneously the resentment of those who, despite higher rank, were nonetheless technically subordinate to him. Determined to prove himself and to do well, he overdid matters.

After the expedition returned home to a dismal reception in 1842, several disgruntled expedition officers, whom Wilkes charged with insubordination, notified Secretary of the Navy Abel P. Upshur, who, as a Southerner, had a strong dislike for the Yankee Wilkes on principle. The officers and the secretary hastily drew up countercharges against Wilkes, 10 of which proved deficient but one of which, concerning excessive and illegal punishment, gained Wilkes a public reprimand and a long delay in promotion from lieutenant. Wilkes himself had been wrong in his actions: pressed for time, he had not assembled the required courts-martial against the officers; then, acting as both prosecutor and judge, he had exceeded his authority (12 lashes) by ordering 36 and 41 lashes as punishments.

Perhaps the navy delayed Wilkes's promotion because it suspected that he would again act both perversely and independently toward orders and regulations. If so, it was correct: within 20 years, Wilkes was again in trouble because of the *Trent* Affair. He lived to be 78, dying in 1877.

James WILKINSON: life as perpetual scandal

An addiction to intrigue, an overwhelming appetite for riches, and an obsessive demand for alcohol engendered the successes and failures of James Wilkinson, the most notorious and roguish of double agents produced by the young United States of America. From the age of 20,

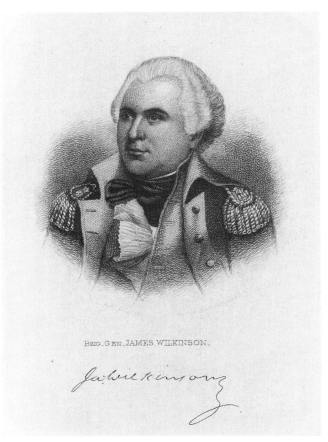

BRIG. GEN. JAMES WILKINSON.

The early American general James Wilkinson was implicated in various intrigues and conspiracies during his nearly 40 years in the military. He seemed to be a traitor to every cause he embraced. (Yale University Archives/Historical Picture Collection/Yale University Library)

Wilkinson made of his life a constant parade of scandals, gaining and losing the confidence of many and retaining the loyalty of only three people: his first wife, Thomas Jefferson, and himself.

Born into the family of a moderately wealthy Maryland planter in 1757, Wilkinson was originally heading toward a career in medicine, but military life attracted him more. He was commissioned a captain in the Continental Army in 1776, and for almost 40 years the military was both the locus of his intrigues and the center from which he made forays for financial gain.

Highly capable, Captain Wilkinson rose rapidly in rank and position. Within three months of his commission he had become aide-de-camp to General Horatio Gates, leader in the defeat of British General John Burgoyne. Promoted to brevet brigadier general in 1777, Wilkinson became involved in a plot to replace George Washington as commander-in-chief of the American forces with Gates, an intrigue incorrectly labeled the CONWAY CABAL. Apparently, Wilkinson saw some advantage for himself in leaking details of the scheme. His private intrigue—and the original plan—failed. Though Wilkinson lost his job and his military honors, he retained his commission.

Undismayed, he sought and gained the lucrative position of clothier-general to the Continental Army. His lust for greed, however, soon made him careless; investigations into his falsified accounts forced him to resign in 1781.

Temporarily stymied, Wilkinson married, settled in Pennsylvania, maneuvered himself into the position of brigadier general of the state militia, and was elected to the state assembly. Restlessness caused him to travel to Kentucky, then America's "Far West." Another intrigue enabled him to replace George Rogers Clark, conqueror of the old Northwest, as leader in Kentucky; and he soon began attempts to engineer Kentucky's separation from Virginia.

Still not busy enough, Wilkinson began yet another intrigue. Sensing that he might make money from citizen displeasure with national policies toward Spain, he traveled to New Orleans, ingratiated himself with the Spanish authorities by claiming that he was secretly working for the disunion of the United States, and gained a Spanish pension through 1800.

Kentucky statehood and bilking the Spanish still were not enough to occupy him however, so in 1792 Wilkinson accepted a commission as brigadier general of a volunteer army fighting Indians north of the Ohio River. He then plotted to unseat his commander, General "Mad Anthony" Wayne, an intrigue successful only because Wayne died in 1796. He also took Detroit from the British, becoming its military governor. His greed during his administration engendered civilian protests, however, and he was returned to the South.

There Wilkinson's energies were employed in land speculation and lucrative Army contracts; he also plotted to become governor or surveyor-general of the Mississippi Territory. President George Washington began to distrust him and ordered his surveillance; Wilkinson cleverly turned the tables on his surveillant, however, and the man was soon ousted. His action inspired faith in Wilkinson by both presidents John Adams and Thomas Jefferson. In 1803 Jefferson trusted Wilkinson so much that he commissioned him to be one of two persons who took formal possession of the Louisiana Purchase from the French.

But Wilkinson was nothing if not self-interested. In New Orleans, he played on Spanish fears concerning Florida (which was Spanish territory until 1819), gaining for his machinations a $12,000 bribe. He then bought a boatload of sugar, traveled to New York, and while selling the sugar began secret but distrustful relations with Aaron Burr, Jefferson's vice president, which both entangled Wilkinson and kept him from deep involvement in Burr's Conspiracy (see BURR'S CONSPIRACY).

He was too busy juggling other balls to be close to the Burr intrigue. Made governor of the Louisiana Territory by Jefferson in 1805, he repeated his Detroit excesses and was removed in 1806 from his headquarters in St. Louis to Natchitoches, Louisiana. There he tried to protect himself from the onus surrounding Burr by deeply ingratiating himself with Jefferson. The action enabled him to avoid indictment by the Richmond, Virginia, grand jury investigating Burr, but the complexity of Wilkinson's activities caused him to drop one of the balls he was juggling: troops had to be used to quiet a Louisiana populace angry at his maladministration.

His ever-trusting wife died in 1807, and Wilkinson's abilities began to falter. Reappointed by Jefferson to govern Louisiana, he did so with such open greed and autocracy that President James Madison ordered a court-martial in 1811 that found him not guilty. Even his military acumen failed him: he made a fiasco during the War of 1812 of the campaign against Montreal and lost his commission in the army.

Although he was faltering and slowing down, Wilkinson refused to give up. In 1821, at the age of 64, he again tried to bilk the Spanish by traveling to Mexico City to seek a Texas land grant. To protect himself, he traveled as an agent for the American Bible Society. He gained the grant but died in 1825 before fulfilling all of its provisions.

George F. WILL: "debategate"

Enterprising journalists for television and newspapers are constantly alert for the first spot of dirt in politics. It must have caused them chagrin when, in August 1983, one of their most well-known and respected members, George F. Will, was discovered to have violated an unwritten code of journalistic ethics and to have participated in an obstruction of justice.

Known to readers of more than 400 newspapers and seen by millions of television viewers of *Agronsky and Company,* George Will was voted in July 1983 the journalist most admired by senators, congressmen, and their staffs. Within a month, however, the public knew that he had engaged in unethical behavior. In 1980, he had known of and seen briefing papers stolen from President Jimmy Carter (a filching about which Will failed completely to comment) and had used those papers to coach presidential hopeful Ronald Reagan for a televised debate with Carter. What made the second action more galling was the fact that Will had done the coaching secretly so that, on the ABC television program *Nightline,* after the debate, he could appear to be neutral when he praised Reagan's "thoroughbred performance" and victory.

His colleagues severely trounced Will in print for his actions. *Time* magazine accused him of "hobnobbery journalism," concluding that "The line between journalistic detachment and participation may be wavery, but it is there, and George Will overstepped it." The *New York Daily News* dropped his column, as if it did not want its conservatism sullied by a less than immaculate columnist who indulged in what the newspaper tagged "a violation of journalistic ethics." *The Nation,* in an editorial entitled "No Triumph of Will," called his action a "journalistic conflict of interest."

Will did not share their chagrin. Perhaps he scorned their expression of what he had earlier called "silly scrupulosity," for he only lamely defended himself. He tried to establish himself as a commentator who had been hired for his opinions and not as "a straight news reporter." But in trying to make such a distinction in kind, he failed to address the issues involved in what he had done. He had handled the fruit of a crime (a crime that even on lesser occasions is considered an obstruction of justice) and kept silent, and he had tried to appear as something he was not.

Not even Will's most violent critics demanded a warrant for his arrest for obstructing justice, however, and no one labeled his pretension of neutrality a lie. But for many Americans, Larry Speakes's less than helpful excuse for Will—"it's the way politics works"—had echoes of columnist William Safire's "everybody does it" excuse for Nixon and WATERGATE and deeper echoes of the saying "It's not a crime unless you're caught," used during the era of Prohibition in the 1920s. *The Nation* gently poked fun at Will's actions and attitudes, saying that if expressed generally, they would lead to ethical chaos. It suggested that if Will continued his somewhat Olympian practices, his articles might have to be followed by a disclaimer. Its offering: "The material above is less the product of an independent mind and a moral will than you used to believe."

Will never apologized for what he had done. Of his second action he said that he was glad he had done what he had done. Finally, however, he promised that he would not do it again.

Roger WILLIAMS: banished libertarian

Though every child learns in grade school that the early Puritans emigrated to America in search of religious freedom, they rarely hear of the other side of the coin. A monument to nonconformist principles, the Puritan Massachusetts Bay Colony was a theocracy that suffered no dissent within its midst, fiercely punishing rebels from the lowest classes and embarrassing or banishing the outspoken from higher levels. One such rebel was Roger Williams, a Cambridge University–trained nonconformist Anglican clergyman, whose essentially quiet quarrels with both civil and religious authorities made him both an outcast and the creator of true religious freedom in the New World.

Driven from England in 1630 by civil and ecclesiastical pressures for conformity, Williams had no sooner arrived in Boston than he began to shock the Bay Colony's founding fathers. When he refused to accept the pulpit of the Boston church until the congregation of the church overcame its hypocrisy by announcing its total separation from the Anglican bishops in England, he caused John Winthrop, a founder and frequently elected governor of the colony, to perceive a threat. Fearful that such an expression of nonconformity would wreck the colony's theocracy, Winthrop led other magistrates in attempts to circumscribe Williams's influence. At first, they tried to disconcert him. They interfered with a call extended by the Salem church to Williams and forced him to the separatist Plymouth Colony. By 1633 he had overcome their interference: he returned to Salem, which had defied the Boston authorities by electing him minister. Williams then retaliated. He upset the Boston magistrates and their clergy by attacking clerical control as a menace to the liberties of church congregations, refusing to agree that civil authorities had the power to enforce the religious injunctions of the Ten Commandments, denying the honesty and legality of claims to Indian lands made in the royal charter of the Massachusetts Bay Colony, arguing against the colonial oligarchy's attempt to bind the lower classes to strict submission through an oath, and making the Salem congregation more democratic.

Appalled and fearful for their sovereignty, the oligarchy acted in the strongest way it could. After a trial by the colony's General Court on October 9, 1635, Williams was found guilty of disseminating "newe & dangerous opinions, against the aucthoritie of magistrates." He was then banished.

The oligarchy, however, again attempted to interfere with his establishment of liberal settlements. It vainly tried to apprehend Williams as he fled to found the Provincetown Plantation in 1636, but the harassment did not even stop there. He was assailed because his settlements made radical advances over Puritan polity: they became primitive democracies in which church and state were separate and all religious sects, including Judaism, had total religious liberty. While attempting to gain a royal charter giving control of Rhode Island to the Massachusetts Bay Colony, Boston authorities sent 40 troops to capture and imprison the leaders of the Warwick, Rhode Island, settlement. But in 1644, Williams went to England and gained an independent charter for his Rhode Island colony, thus hastening the demise of the somewhat totalitarian Puritan theocracy.

That the Winthrop-led oligarchy had overreacted and erred in banishing Williams was made clear by a 1936 action of the Massachusetts state legislature: to compliment the Rhode Island tercentenary celebration, it rescinded the 1635 order of the Massachusetts Bay Colony's General Court forcing Williams into exile. This legally established that those who had acted in 1635 to keep what they considered order were themselves open to the charge of improper behavior. Their victim, by a kind of poetic justice, had become their judge.

Vanessa WILLIAMS: Miss America nude

The first black woman to win the Miss America Pageant, Vanessa Williams, abdicated her title before the end of her reign on July 23, 1984, shortly after it became known that *Penthouse* magazine was going to publish in its September issue nude photographs for which she had posed two years earlier.

In addition to being extremely good-looking, Williams was intelligent, talented, and ambitious. Her parents were both music teachers in schools in Westchester County, New York, and Mr. Williams had taught his daughter to play the French horn and the piano. She also had singing and acting ability. During her adolescence, Vanessa Williams had taken part in many school plays and later, when she entered Syracuse University, she continued to act in college shows.

At a packed news conference in Manhattan on July 23, 1984, Vanessa Williams announces she will relinquish her title as Miss America of 1984, following disclosure by the publisher of Penthouse *magazine that she would appear nude in sexually explicit pictures in the magazine's September issue. Miss Williams, the first black woman ever to wear the crown, bowed to demands by Miss America pageant officials that she quit. (UPI/Bettmann Newsphotos)*

During the summer of her freshman year at Syracuse, Williams had worked as a secretary for a photographer, who persuaded her to pose in the nude with another woman. At the time, she didn't tell anyone what she had done, and when, after the photographs were published, her parents asked her why she had posed for them, she cried "I don't know. I don't know." Some friends attributed her actions to her sense of adventure and love of taking risks.

In the fall of her sophomore year, the director of the Miss Greater Syracuse pageant approached Williams and suggested that she enter the Miss America contest. She was reluctant to do so at first, but her parents encouraged her. Auspiciously she became Miss Greater Syracuse and then Miss New York State. Before going to Atlantic City for the Miss America contest in September 1983 Williams signed a standard form that stated she had "committed no acts of moral turpitude," whereas she had actually posed in the nude for two photographers and had signed model releases giving them the rights to publish her pictures. At her request, one photographer had given her the negatives of her photographs.

When the Miss America pageant opened, Williams won the bathing suit contest and then the talent contest by singing "Happy Days Are Here Again." A year of traveling around the country and participating in many festivities followed. Her future seemed bright. She had many offers to endorse commercial products and to act and sing in prestigious shows. Then the *Penthouse* photographs appeared, pageant officials insisted that she resign her title, and she went home in despair and disgrace.

At her lawyer's urging, Williams initiated a $500 million lawsuit against *Penthouse* and its publisher, Bob Guccione but soon dropped it. Instead she devoted her energies to trying to make a career in show business. There were many disappointments in New York, but she was more successful in Los Angeles, where she played several roles in television series and did some disk jockeying. Though Williams now admits she made a foolish, youthful mistake, she knows, she says, "that God will forgive her."

Henry WIRZ: Andersonville's last victim

Although military prisons on both sides during the American Civil War had inhumane conditions at times, the Confederate prison camp at Andersonville in southwestern Georgia achieved the greatest infamy, becoming an inexcusable crime against humanity even during the indubitable horrors of wartime. Of the approximately 45,000 soldiers imprisoned at Andersonville, more than 13,000 died or were killed. Although Captain Henry Wirz, the prison commander, was eventually held criminally responsible for these deaths, many believed that he was a scapegoat, unfairly singled out because of the Union's need for some sort of symbolic vengeance.

After the death warrant was read to Captain Henry Wirz, the keeper of Andersonville Prison, the rope was adjusted around his neck and then the trap was sprung on November 10, 1865, on the grounds of Washington's Old Capitol Prison. Wirz was executed for the intolerable conditions he permitted to exist at Andersonville. (The Brady Collection, Archives, History and Genealogy Unit, Connecticut State Library)

In the winter of 1864, Confederate forces built a prison stockade named Camp Sumter at Andersonville. Extreme overcrowding in the existing prisons of the Confederacy had demanded the construction of another, and Andersonville was the result. It enclosed 16½ acres and was designed to hold 10,000 captives, but within three months after the prison's opening, there were more than 20,000 Union men crowded into it. More prisoners kept arriving every day, and by mid-August 1864, over 30,000 were crammed insufferably together behind the 15-foot-high pinewood stockade of the camp. Although the stockade had been enlarged by 10 acres two months earlier, each man had only about six square feet of living space. Captain Wirz had minded the orders of General John H. Winder, commander of Confederate prisons east of the Mississippi, by cutting down every tree within the stockade, so that the shelterless prisoners had absolutely no protection from the elements: summer heat over 100° and winter temperatures sometimes below freezing. Running through the camp was a small brook about three feet wide that created a swampy area; the brook water was used for drinking, bathing, cooking, and toilet purposes by the men. Human excrement and other filth gradually blocked up the brook, making it a breeding ground for all kinds of disease. The prisoners, many of whom were left naked when their uniforms rotted away (Wirz provided no clothing to his inmates), received food rations consisting mainly of raw corn meal and salty bacon, which often had sand, gravel, and maggots in it. Little wonder that the men fell victim to malnutrition, disease, and starvation. Sick bodies became infested by gangrene, worms, lice, and maggots. Chronic dysentery, dropsy, diarrhea, scurvy, consumption, bronchitis, pneumonia, and smallpox were rampant. Many once strong and able men were reduced to living skeletons.

"I am killing off more Yankees than twenty regiments in Lee's army," General Winder often boasted about the camp. But he was never to be held accountable for its lethal conditions, for he died two months before the end of the war.

Before his arrest by Union forces on May 7, 1865, after the South's surrender, Captain Wirz said that he was "satisfied that no man can or will justly blame me for things that happened here [Andersonville], and which were beyond my power to control." He also claimed that he had been a "tool in the hands of my superiors." An immigrant physician to America from Switzerland, Wirz had had military training in Europe before enlisting in the Confederate army, serving abroad as a special agent of President Jefferson Davis of the Confederacy, and subsequently assuming command of Andersonville. He was taken to Washington, D.C., where a federal military tribunal headed by General Lew Wallace (who was appointed by U.S. President Andrew Johnson) tried him alone for murder in connection with Andersonville (the federal government had attempted in vain to implicate the leaders of the South, including Jefferson Davis and Robert E. Lee, in the establishment of the camp and its conditions). Pleading "not guilty," Wirz said that if anyone was to blame, it was his commanding officers; that he was merely obeying orders; and that the accepted amnesty for confederate soldiers under terms of the armistice prevented him from being tried and punished. However, Wirz's attorneys failed to dismiss the trial or move it to a proper civilian court. The chief prosecuting attorney, Colonel Norton P. Chipman, examined and cross-examined many of the 148 witnesses who were called during the trial—including Union prisioners, Confederate prison guards, and prison doctors—a number of whom accused Wirz of either personally killing or ordering the fatal shooting of more than a dozen men. Wirz had had prisoners whipped, put in stocks, and chained together for long periods for minor insubordinations. The horror of Andersonville came through in the testimony, and after a 63-day trial, Wirz was found guilty, on October 24, 1865, of 1 count of conspiracy and 11 counts of murder. The tribunal's ruling was reviewed and approved first by Judge Advocate General Joseph Holt and then by President Johnson, who also upheld the death sentence pronounced on the 43-year-old Wirz by Wallace.

Some 250 spectators witnessed Wirz's clumsy hanging (he strangled slowly to death when his neck was not broken in the fall through the trap) on November 10, 1865. Many, particularly Southerners, who still debate the justice of the verdict, cried that he had been "judicially murdered." Some American journalists felt that the Union's need for legal vengeance had singled out Wirz unfairly. The real disgrace they said, was Ander-

sonville itself, along with all the other evil war prisons in both the North and the South.

Louis WOLFSON: masterful stock manipulator jailed

In October 1967, Louis E. Wolfson, once known as the boy wonder of Wall Street, was found guilty of conspiring to illegally sell about $3.5 million worth of stock of Continental Enterprises Incorporated, a Florida-based real estate and movie theater business. Convicted with Wolfson was his business colleague Elkin Gelbert. The 55-year-old Wolfson, a self-made millionaire and controversial corporate raider, had apparently conspired with Gelbert, between 1960 and 1962, to unload 690,000 shares of Continental Enterprises without registering them with the Securities and Exchange Commission (SEC) as required by law. The two men reportedly made a personal profit of approximately $1.5 million. Wolfson insisted that he was unaware of the SEC's registration requirements and that he left such technicalities to his subordinates. During his three-week trial, he brought in such character witnesses as Joe DiMaggio and Ed Sullivan to support him; the federal prosecutors, however, produced SEC officials who testified to having informed Wolfson in writing about the stock sales' requirements; the government also produced brokers who had questioned the legality of the sales at the time.

Wolfson, who lost the dream of an athletic career after shattering his shoulder while playing football for Georgia Tech, started his mercurial career on Wall Street by branching out of his family's junk business in the 1930s, using borrowed money. By 1946 his company, which had started with $275 worth of surplus building materials, was doing $4.5-million worth of business a year. Before dissolving the company in 1948, Wolfson had brought two shipyards—one as U.S. Navy surplus—for $4 million, and had later sold them for $10 million. These transactions were investigated by congressional subcommittees and a federal grand jury, which could prove no wrongdoing in Wolfson's first brush with the law. His next business "coup," in 1949, was to gain control of the Capital Transit Company of Washington, D.C., for $2.2 million and later, in 1956, to sell it for $13.5 million, following the government's refusal to renew his franchise to operate it; the government alleged that he had milked Capital Transit for millions of dollars, leading to sharp fare increases and deteriorating services.

Next, Wolfson bought control of Merritt-Chapman & Scott, a heavy construction company, whose net worth he raised from $8 million to $132 million in six years. He used the company to absorb other companies, making its chief concerns shipbuilding, paint-making, chemicals, and movie-making. He failed, however, in his attempts to purchase three professional athletic teams—the Brooklyn Dodgers, Washington Senators, and Baltimore Colts. In 1955, in his most daring take-over attempt, Wolfson lost a huge proxy battle for control of the Montgomery Ward Company. Next, he evidently targeted the American Motors Corporation and became its largest stockholder. By 1959 Wolfson controlled an estimated $400-million industrial empire.

His luck ran out in the 1960s, when he was twice tried and convicted by the U.S. government. His personal fortune, once estimated to be about $75 million, shriveled considerably during this period. At his first trial, he was found guilty of illegally selling unregistered stock of Continental Enterprises in a caper that drove down the stock price from $8 to $1.50 for unknowing stockholders. For this he was sentenced to one year in prison and fined $100,000. In his second trial he was convicted of giving false and misleading annual reports about stock deals at Merritt-Chapman & Scott and of destroying documents during an SEC investigation; for this he received an 18-month jail sentence and a $32,000 fine. Merritt-Chapman was well on its way to liquidation. Wolfson insisted, along with some Wall Street lawyers, that he had been made a scapegoat by the government and cited officials of brokerage firms who received only suspensions and fines for similar offenses.

Wolfson spent nine months in a Florida federal prison. He became even more notorious during his detention, when Supreme Court Justice Abe FORTAS resigned his high post in 1969, after admitting to having accepted $20,000 from the Wolfson Family Foundation, a philanthropic concern created by the manipulative financier. Fortas said he had returned the $20,000 after Wolfson's indictment, claiming he had done so because he was too busy with court affairs to be able to work with the charitable foundation.

Later, Wolfson faced further charges of having filed a false corporate statement and lying to the SEC. But two successive mistrials occurred in 1972 when juries became deadlocked over whether he was innocent or guilty of the charges. That same year, Wolfson married attractive Patrice Jacobs, a horse breeder and racer, and turned his 478-acre farm in Ocala, Florida, into a world-class racing stable. He dismantled most of his remaining corporate empire, apparently to concentrate on horse racing. He is said to have become a respected owner of leading racehorses.

Victoria WOODHULL: sometime patroness of "free love"

Nineteenth-century American voters (all of whom were male) expected that a mettlesome, misguided (and probably masculinized) female would someday attempt to run for the presidency of the United States and so were only mildly surprised at rumors about the Equal Rights Party and its plan to run a female candidate for the 1872 race. Their attentions were galvanized when the candidate proved to be the notorious reformer Victoria Woodhull. Her running mate was to be Frederick DOUGLASS, a former slave turned libertarian.

Victoria Woodhull was the firebrand of her time. She had already come to be regarded as a half-saint, half-sinner and had proven herself altogether fascinating as a reformer active since 1870. However, because she was running on a women's rights ticket, the male voters did not care for or about the ticket's major platform plank: female suffrage. Agitation for the female vote had been noisy since the end of the Civil War, especially by such outspoken crusaders as Elizabeth Cady Stanton and Susan B. Anthony. But even though Woodhull had been the first female officially recognized by the U.S. House of Representatives—where, on December 21, 1870, she had addressed its Judiciary Committee on the rights granted women by the Fourteenth Amendment—she was expected to lose badly.

And when Woodhull, a divorced mother, announced that she also stood for easier divorce, the blustering male voters grew even more alarmed, and guardians of hearth and home then became downright defensive when she proclaimed her allegiance to a free-love principle.

Anthony COMSTOCK stood on the sidelines, readying the cross of Victorian morality upon which, if she went too far (by his definition), he would crucify "the Woodhull." Newspapers, then male sanctions run to preserve male domination, made much of the immorality of Woodhull's minor platform planks and reveled in the shaming of their fellow—and rival—journalist. They dredged up lurid tales of her family and personal life, renamed her nominating party the "free-love party," and dwelled upon its lascivious implications, to the embarrassment of Susan B. Anthony, who at first refused to campaign for Woodhull.

The journalistic opposition failed at first. Woodhull and her sister (Tennie C. or Tennessee Claflin) responded in kind through their own paper, the Vanderbilt-sponsored *Woodhull and Claflin's Weekly,* a muckraking radical and reformist periodical described by a Woodhull biographer as "silly, venomous, and sublime." Both sisters took to the campaign's soapboxes, where Woodhull, a hypnotic orator, was immediately effective; both defended their ticket's minor plank, which they claimed had been misunderstood.

For the sisters, raised in an atmosphere of religious ecstasy, spiritualism, clairvoyance, and socioreligious movements like Mormonism, the "free" in "free love" did not mean licentiousness or promiscuity. They explained it as the opposite of "forced" love, the sexual slavery implied by the then current belief that a wife was a husband's "vessel" and that her duty was to be available whenever he felt in the mood to make love. In opposition to this legalized prostitution, "free love" meant, at least, the right of the female to say "No!"

The term itself derived from Mary Wollstonecraft, wife of the English philosopher and novelist William Godwin, as part of a 1792 manifesto on the educational, political, and marital rights of women. Wollstonecraft's view of "free love" was idealistic: it would reduce sexual tension within couples, develop marriage into a companionate union, elevate the quality of children through eugenics, and act as a psychological safeguard for the younger generation. Her ideas generated important experiments, among them that of the American social reformer John Humphrey NOYES.

The Woodhull sisters' journalistic and oratorical championing of these ideas converted a great number of women as well as a few men to their views. But male skepticism and charges of immorality continued. This was largely because the sisters failed to practice what they preached. Tennie Woodhull gained a demonstrable reputation for promiscuity, and Victoria Woodhull, excited beyond good sense, entered the 1871 controversy about the charges of adultery that Theodore Tilton had brought against the Reverend Henry Ward BEECHER. It was to be her undoing. She used the *Weekly* to challenge Beecher to confess his adultery (about which she claimed to have inside information from Elizabeth Tilton), and during the spectacular trial, Woodhull teamed up with Tilton, a fellow journalist who had supported her reforms, asserting in print that he had been her lover for six weeks. She then wrote an exposé of the scandal.

Comstock pounced on November 2, 1872, and both sisters went to jail on charges of journalistic obscenity, with a bail set at $8,000 each. His charges and libel suits brought by others kept the sisters incarcerated for several months. Election Day had come and gone, the Equal Rights Party had made a poorer showing than predicted because Woodhull and Claflin had become the talk of the town, and the talk had been highly unflattering.

The sisters emerged chastened by their experience. They felt that justice had been served because all of the charges against them had been dropped, but they felt no exhilaration. Both women now wanted good marriages and moneyed respectability.

They found it in England, where "the Woodhull," anxious enough to avoid opprobrium, briefly changed her name to Woodhall and mendaciously engineered publicity to erase her American notoriety. Famed for speeches on the human body as the temple of the soul and on the santification of the sexual act, Victoria Woodhull died at 89 in the odor of sanctity.

Rejected by her American sisters as an apostate to the cause of women's rights, Victoria Woodhull is usually granted only footnotes in the total and unfinished history of that crusade. But she was briefly a suffering heroine in that cause and should be remembered as much for her efforts as for her spectacular failure.

XYZ AFFAIR

In 1798 the American public was outraged upon hearing about the tacit political machinations of three French government emissaries, referred to as X, Y, and Z by the U.S. government, who had attempted to bribe three American diplomatic commissioners seeking a treaty of commerce and amity with France. The insulting French bribes led to a complete breakdown of Franco-American relations, while the two nations carried on undeclared naval warfare for the next two years.

The Jay Treaty of 1794 between the United States and Great Britain angered the ruling French Directory in Paris, which felt the Americans had conceded too much to the British and were increasingly inclining toward a pro-British attitude in international relations. At war with Britain in the 1790s, France began to interfere with American shipping on the high seas, seizing numerous unarmed American merchant vessels thought to be filled with contraband bound for British ports. Growing numbers of American shipowners demanded reprisals for their losses to the French, who seemed to grow more arrogant with each ship seizure.

In December 1796, the French Directory refused to receive Charles C. Pinckney, the American minister to France, when he arrived there. This created a furor at home, but the newly elected American president, John Adams, a Federalist (as was Pinckney), wanted to avoid war and to improve relations with France. On May 31, 1797, he appointed a three-man commission, consisting of Pinckney, John Marshall (another Federalist), and Elbridge Gerry (a Republican) to settle difficulties with the French government in Paris. They hoped to secure a negotiated commercial and friendship treaty. However, the three commissioners were not received by the French Directory in October 1797 when they began to negotiate. On October 18, the three Americans were visited by three French emissaries of Talleyrand, the French foreign minister, and were propositioned to give a "gift" of $250,000 to Talleyrand and a loan of $10 million to France as a prelude to negotiations. The French emissaries (Hottinguer, Hauteval, and Bellamy) also asked that an apology be made for Adams's past critical comments about France and a reaffirmation be made of the old Franco-American Alliance of 1778. Because bribes were not uncommon in the diplomacy of the day, the Americans were not steadfastly antagonistic to the ideas presented to them but still ended their talks with the three French agents. The American case was then sent to Talleyrand in a written statement. Two months later the Americans received a prickly reply in which the French foreign minister blamed them for the dispute, thought that three Republicans should have been sent as commissioners, and said he would negotiate with Gerry alone. No concessions were made to the French, but Gerry remained behind in Paris following the departure of Pinckney and Marshall. Gerry claimed to be acting only as a private citizen, but immediate umbrage at home resulted in President Adams recalling him posthaste. Earlier, Talleyrand had hinted that war was likely with the United States if Gerry left.

The failure of the negotiations was reported by Adams to Congress, which was authorized by him to direct commanders of American warships to capture French ships attacking American vessels. On April 3, 1797 Adams handed the so-called XYZ Papers—the commissioners' correspondence of their transactions with Talleyrand's emissaries, called X, Y, and Z in the documents—to Congress and also ordered them to be printed and published. American opinion strongly favored a declaration of war against France after the disgraceful and contemptuous French conduct and demands were publicized. In a message to Congress on June 21, President Adams declared: "I will never send another minister to France without assurances that he will be received, respected, and honored as a representative of a great, free, powerful, and independent nation." Although there followed widespread calls for war by both Federalists and Republicans, Adams firmly decided against a declared war while allowing military preparations by both the army and the navy to take place. During the next two years, American naval forces seized 84 armed French ships and lost only one of their own. Finally, the Convention of 1800 ended the fighting about six months after Napoleon respectfully received American commissioners to France.

YAZOO LAND FRAUDS

After the American Revolution (1775–83), Georgia's western frontier extended as far as the Mississippi River, taking in what is now the two states of Alabama and Mississippi. Officials of the state, fearing that its western portion would eventually have to be ceded to the federal government, began to sell off as much acreage as possible for their own profit, ostensibly to benefit the impoverished state treasury. A liberal policy of land grants was established that tempted greedy state authorities to sell large tracts of land to rapacious frequently corrupt speculators rather than to new immigrant settlers. The Georgia governors signed land warrants that sometimes proved fraudulent, for they also saw an opportunity for personal financial gain in land speculation and thus approved the issue of warrants to far more land than existed in the state. The Yazoo River district (parts of Mississippi and Alabama) became the focus of wild speculation that tarnished the reputations of many "investors," including lawmakers and businessmen, in the late 1700s and early 1800s.

In 1789 the Georgia legislature authorized the sale of 25,400,000 acres of rich Yazoo territory (excellent for cotton growing) to three land-speculative companies for $273,580. Because the lands were still in dispute by both the Spanish and the Indians, the U.S. government prevented the companies from taking control of them for development; the speculators, however, profited by selling their depreciated paper money (which they had planned to use to buy the lands) to the federal government. In 1794, Georgia legislators—increasingly interested in reviving the sale of Yazoo lands and also reaping personal financial gains through becoming land speculators and investors themselves—passed a bill selling some 35 million acres (most of Mississippi and Alabama) to four new speculative land companies for $500,000 (less than one and a half cents per acre). These Yazoo land companies had sold shares (acreage) in the lands for little money to members of the Georgia legislature eager to make a handsome profit; legislators had evidently bribed one another to vote for the bill selling the lands, and almost every one of the legislators was a shareholder in one or more of the Yazoo companies when the bill was signed into law by Georgia Governor George Matthews on January 7, 1795. Promoters of the land companies then went north to Philadelphia, New York, Boston, and other places to sell warrants to Yazoo land to prominent Yankee businessmen and financiers, such as Robert Morris (who was eventually bankrupted by his speculations).

When Georgians learned that passage of the 1795 bill had been secured by flagrant bribery and coercion, they were outraged. They denounced the state legislature for its greedy alliance with the land-speculative companies. The lawmakers, some of whom mobs threatened to lynch, were vilified for giving away valuable public lands for a pittance. Though a new Georgia legislature was soon organized and rescinded the sale of the western Yazoo lands on February 13, 1796, unscrupulous and wily speculators continued to sell the land to unsuspecting customers, especially in the Middle Atlantic states and New England. Titles to the lands became highly confused, and claimants battled to obtain them despite strong opposition from anti-Yazooists. The entire matter became a federal concern in 1802 when Georgia ceded the disputed lands to the U.S. government. The Yazooists demanded compensation for their losses, but in the House of Representatives, John Randolph of Roanoke, Virginia, a brilliant master of invective, led the forces against the Yazooists in denying them compensation in 1895.

The Yazoo lands claimants took their fight for indemnification to the courts, and their case finally came before the U.S. Supreme Court under Chief Justice John Marshall. On March 16, 1810, the Court reached a unanimous decision (Fletcher v. Peck) supporting the Yazooists by constitutionally upholding the original Yazoo land grants as valid contracts. Georgia's rescinding law of 1796 was ruled unconstitutional because it impaired the obligations of the contracts. During the arguing of the case, the Supreme Court had to call a recess at one point until Georgia's attorney Luther Martin, in a drunken stupor, could sober up (the only time this ever happened in the Court's history). This didn't help the anti-Yazooist cause, which had generally ineffective legal arguments to begin with.

Uplifted by the decision, the Yazooists again sought to gain indemnification from Congress and in 1814 gained success when the Senate passed a bill awarding them $5 million. The law was signed by President James Madison, and in the following years claimants to the lands collected $4,282,000 from the federal government.

Z

ZENGER CASE

American's freedom of the press from government censorship was fundamentally established more than half a century before the U.S. Constitution was written. In 1735 John Peter Zenger was prosecuted for seditious libel for printing articles in his *New York Weekly Journal* criticizing the colonial governor of New York and his administration. Zenger's acquittal resulted from the then revolutionary premise that truth is a defense to libel. It proved to be a great public humiliation for New York's avaricious governor, William S. Cosby.

Cosby had assumed the British colonial governorship of New York in August 1732. He had been serving as governor of the Mediterranean island of Minorca before that but had been recalled home because of native complaints about his corrupt and greedy practices. After his arrival in New York, he attempted to manipulate the colony's assembly and supreme court for his own purposes of obtaining more money and power. Opposition to Cosby arose, particularly by Chief Justice Lewis Morris, who was soon dismissed from New York's three-man supreme court for ruling against the governor. Afterward, in the spring of 1733, Morris had Zenger, a German immigrant who had established a printing business, run off on his presses the ruling against the governor and stirred up more of the governor's anger by publishing it. Shortly thereafter, Zenger's presses printed additional leaflets showing the citizenry some of the corrupt tactics of Cosby and his henchmen. Criticism of the Crown-appointed administration increased when a group of prominent New Yorkers opposed to Cosby hired Zenger to publish their weekly newspaper, the *New York Weekly Journal*, which they financed to counter the governor's loyal and compliant *Gazette*.

The first issue of the *Weekly Journal* appeared on November 5, 1733; it and subsequent issues in the following weeks and months contained articles and editorials justifying freedom of the press to expose corruption and to inform the general public about actions of the government. Only Zenger's name appeared in the paper, as "Peter Zenger, Printer." For political reasons the contributing editors and writers, such as Lewis Morris, Cadwallader Colden, James Alexander, and William Smith, were not listed. Satiric and scathing attacks in the paper called Cosby a "rogue," a "Nero," and "a fellow only one degree better than an idiot." Readers began to condemn him and his officials for being oppressors, pillagers, and schemers who held themselves above the law. Cosby, who was accused of deceit and "crimes against the people" in provincial assembly elections and other matters, grew increasingly incensed. He unsuccessfully tried to stop the publication through a farcical public burning of four issues of the *Weekly Journal*. Nobody heeded his actions, and he finally turned his anger against Zenger, the printer.

On November 17, 1734, the 37-year-old printer was arrested for seditious libel. He was accused of publishing "scandalous, virulent, false, and seditious reflections" in articles in his paper. For nine months he was kept a prisoner in New York City's town hall. The court that ordered him held, directed by Chief Justice James De Lancey, set an outrageously high bail of 800 pounds. The people were told about Zenger's "illegal and cruel bail" and about the governor's attempt to pack the jury in the *Weekly Journal* case, while Zenger's wife Anna, with help from a printing assistant and her sons, continued to print and publish the newspaper while her husband awaited trial. The paper also criticized the disbarment of Zenger's two lawyers, Alexander and Smith, for opposing Cosby's authority to pick a jury.

The courtroom of the city hall was packed with spectators when the defiant printer, who had refused to reveal the names of the *Weekly Journal's* authors, was brought to trial on August 4, 1735. Zenger's court-appointed lawyer, John Chambers, claimed that the defendant should not be held responsible for criticisms he did not write, but the court proclaimed that mere publication of slanderous remarks against an official of the Crown was enough to constitute libel. Suddenly in the proceedings, Andrew Hamilton, one of the most brilliant lawyers in the British colonies before the American Revolution, came forward offering to defend Zenger; Alexander had privately requested Hamilton's help, and the distinguished and wily lawyer had journeyed north from his home in Philadelphia to offer help. Acknowledged by the court, Hamilton then proceeded to argue that Zenger's published criticisms were not libelous because they were indeed true; he appealed to the 12 jurymen to uphold "the liberty of both exposing and opposing arbitrary power . . . by speaking and writing the truth." Chief Justice De Lancey, ruling that evidence to prove the truth of the alleged libel was inadmissible, told the jury that it must reach a verdict strictly on the basis of whether or not Zenger had published the criticisms.

After 10 minutes of deliberation, the jury announced that Zenger was "not guilty," holding that his printed statements were based on fact; the crowded courtroom cheered wildly. Hamilton, who refused payment for defending Zenger, was honored at a festive victory dinner, which the printer could not attend because the authorities kept him jailed until the next day, when the funds were paid to cover his nine-month keep as a prisoner. Nonetheless, Zenger had won, establishing the principle of freedom of the press, the right to criticize the government, and the use of truth as a defense against libel. See also Harry CROSWELL: truth led to libel conviction.

BIBLIOGRAPHY

A book like this must of necessity come from many other sources, particularly specific, authoritative books. The following selected bibliography is intended as a thankful acknowledgment of principal sources—both general books as well as those of specific importance—which readers will find fascinating if they wish to delve deeper into some scandals mentioned in this book. The available literature on scandals is considerable. Listed here are a wide variety of books, some of which contain numerous episodes of graft, corruption, venality, and deception (like this reference book does); others explain or analyze a particular scandal (such as Bill Clinton's impeachment, Watergate, or BCCI). Most of these books are readily available in many large libraries.

Aaseng, Nathan. *The O. J. Simpson Trial: What It Shows Us About Our Legal System*. New York: Walker Publishing, 1995.

Abramson, Howard S. *Hero In Disgrace: The True Discoverer of the North Pole, Frederick A. Cook*. New York: Paragon House, 1991.

Adams, James Ring. *The Big Fix: Inside the S & L Scandal: How an Unholy Alliance of Politics and Money Destroyed America's Banking System*. New York: John Wiley & Sons, 1990.

Akst, Daniel. *Wonder Boy: The Kid Who Swindled Wall Street*. New York: Scribners, 1990.

Albert, James A. *Pay Dirt: Divorces of the Rich and Famous*. Boston: Branden Publishing, 1989.

Alexander, Shana. *Nutcracker*. New York: Doubleday, 1985.

———. *When She Was Bad: The Story of Bess, Hortense, Sukhreet, and Nancy*. New York: Random House, 1990.

Allen, Oliver E. *The Tiger: The Rise and Fall of Tammany Hall*. Reading, Mass.: Addison-Wesley, 1993.

Allen, Thomas B., and Norman Polmar. *Merchants Of Treason: America's Secrets for Sale*. New York: Delacorte Press, 1988.

Allison, Dean, and Bruce Henderson. *Empire Of Deceit: Inside the Biggest Sports and Bank Scandal in U.S. History*. New York: Doubleday, 1985.

Ambrose, Stephen E. *Undaunted Courage: Meriwether Lewis, Thomas Jefferson, and the Opening of the American West*. New York: Simon & Schuster, 1996.

Andersen, Christopher. *The Serpent's Tooth*. New York: Harper & Row, 1987.

Andrew, Christopher. *For The President's Eyes Only: Secret Intelligence and the American Presidency from Washington to Bush*. New York: HarperCollins, 1995.

Anger, Kenneth. *Hollywood Babylon*. New York: Dell, 1975.

———. *Hollywood Babylon II*. New York: E. P. Dutton, 1984.

Anthony, Carl Sferrazza. *Florence Harding*. New York: William Morrow, 1998.

Armor, John, and Peter Wright. *Manzanar*. New York: Vintage, 1989.

Arnold, Bruce. *The Scandal of 'Ulysses': The Sensational Life of a Twentieth Century Masterpiece*. New York: St. Martin's Press, 1992.

Austin, John. *Hollywood's Unsolved Mysteries*. New York: Ace Books, 1970.

Bailey, Fenton. *Fall From Grace: The Untold Story of Michael Milken*. Secaucus, N.J.: Carol Publishing, 1992.

Bailey, Thomas A. *Presidential Saints And Sinners*. New York: Free Press, 1981.

Baker, Jean H. *Mary Todd Lincoln: A Biography*. New York: W. W. Norton, 1987.

Barrett, Laurence I. *Gambling With History: Reagan in the White House*. New York: Penguin, 1984.

Barron, John. *Breaking The Ring: The Spy Family That Imperiled America*. Boston: Houghton Mifflin, 1987.

Barrows, Sidney Biddle, and William Novak. *Mayflower Madam: The Secret Life of Sidney Biddle Barrows*. New York: Arbor House, 1986.

Bauman, Robert. *The Gentleman From Maryland: The Conscience of a Gay Conservative*. New York: Arbor House, 1986.

Beatty, Jack. *The Rascal King: The Life and Times of James Michael Curley, 1874–1958*. Reading, Mass.: Addison-Wesley, 1992.

Beaty, Jonathan, and S. C. Gwynne. *The Outlaw Bank: A Wild Ride into the Heart of BCCI*. New York: Random House, 1993.

Belfrage, Cedric. *The American Inquisition 1945–1960: A Profile of the "McCarthy Era"*. New York: Thunder's Mouth Press, 1989.

Bell, Robert. *Impure Science: Fraud, Compromise, and Political Influence in Scientific Research*. New York: John Wiley & Sons, 1992.

Belushi, Judith Jacklin. *Samurai Widow*. New York: Carroll & Graf, 1990.

Bennett James T., and Thomas J. DiLorenzo. *Official Lies: How Washington Misleads Us*. Alexandria, Va.: Groom Books, 1992.

Bennett, William. *The Death of Outrage: Bill Clinton and the Assault on American Ideals*. New York: Free Press, 1998.

Berendzen, Richard, and Laura Palmer. *Come Here: A Man Overcomes the Tragic Aftermath of Childhood Sexual Abuse.* New York: Villard Books, 1993.

Berrigan, Philip, with Fred A. Wilcox. *Fighting the Lamb's War: Skirmishes with the American Empire: The Autobiography of Philip Berrigan.* Monroe, Me.: Common Courage Press, 1996.

Berton, Pierre. *The Arctic Grail: The Quest for the Northwest Passage and the North Pole, 1818–1909.* New York: Viking, 1988.

Beschloss, Michael R. *Mayday: Eisenhower, Khrushchev and the U-2 Affair.* New York: Harper & Row, 1986.

Billingsley, Kenneth Lloyd. *Hollywood Party: The Untold Story of How Communism Seduced the American Film Industry in the '30s and '40s.* Rocklin, Calif.: Prima Publishing, 1998.

Bilton, Michael, and Kevin Sim. *Four Hours In My Lai: The Soldiers of Charlie Company.* New York: Viking, 1992.

Binstein, M., and C. Bowden. *Trust Me: Charles Keating and the Great American Bank Robbery.* New York: Random House, 1993.

Blackwell, James A. *On, Brave Old Army Team: The Cheating Scandal that Rocked the Nation: West Point 1951.* Novato, Calif.: Presidio Press, 1996.

Blumenson, Martin. *The Man Behind the Legend 1885–1945.* New York: William Morrow, 1985.

Blundell, Nigel. *Encyclopedia Of Serial Killers.* North Dighton, Mass.: J. G. Press, 1996.

Bly, Nellie (Sarah Gallick). *The Kennedy Men: Three Generations of Sex, Scandal and Secrets.* New York: Kensington Publishing, 1996.

Bodo, Peter. *The Courts Of Babylon: Tales of Greed and Glory in a Harsh New World of Professional Tennis.* New York: Scribners, 1995.

Bogdanovich, Peter. *The Killing Of The Unicorn: Dorothy Stratten (1960–1980).* New York: William Morrow, 1984.

Bonomi, Patricia U. *The Lord Cornbury Scandal: The Politics of Reputation in British America.* Chapel Hill: University of North Carolina Press, 1998.

Bower, Tom. *The Paperclip Conspiracy: The Hunt for the Nazi Scientists.* Boston: Little, Brown, 1987.

Boyer, Paul, and Stephen Nissenbaum. *Salem Possessed: The Social Origins of Witchcraft.* Cambridge, Mass.: Harvard University Press, 1974.

Bradshaw, Jon. *Dreams That Money Can Buy: The Tragic Life of Libby Holman.* New York: William Morrow, 1985.

Braine, Tim, and John Stravinsky. *The Not-So-Great Moments in Sports.* New York: William Morrow, 1985.

Brandt, Clare. *The Man In The Mirror: A Life of Benedict Arnold.* New York: Random House, 1994.

Brodeur, Paul. *The Great Power-Line Cover-Up.* Boston: Little, Brown, 1993.

———. *Outrageous Misconduct: The Asbestos Industry on Trial.* New York: Pantheon, 1985.

Browder, Clifford. *The Wickedest Woman In New York: Madame Restell, the Abortionist.* Hamden, Conn.: Shoe String/Archon, 1988.

Brown, Peter H., and Jim Pinkston. *Oscar Dearest:Six Decades of Scandal, Politics, and Greed Behind Hollywood's Academy Awards, 1972–1986.* New York: Perennial Library, 1987.

Bryce, Robert M. *Cook & Peary: The Polar Controversy, Resolved.* Mechanicsburg, Pa.: Stackpole Books, 1997.

Bugliosi, Vincent. *Outrage: The Five Reasons Why O. J. Simpson Got Away with Murder.* New York: W. W. Norton, 1996.

Burford, Anne, and John Greenya. *Are You Tough Enough?* New York: McGraw-Hill, 1985.

Burkett, Elinor, and Frank Bruni. *A Gospel Of Shame: Child Sexual Abuse and the Catholic Church.* New York: Viking, 1993.

Burleigh, Nina. *A Very Private Woman: The Life and Unsolved Murder of Presidential Mistress Mary Meyer.* New York: Bantam Books, 1998.

Burstein, Andrew. *The Inner Jefferson: Portrait of a Grieving Optimist.* Charlottesville, Va.: University Press of Virginia, 1995.

Cable, Mary. *Top Drawer: American High Society from the Gilded Age to the Roaring Twenties.* New York: Atheneum, 1984.

Caher, John M. *King Of The Mountain: The Rise, Fall, and Redemption of Chief Judge Sol Wachtler.* Buffalo, N.Y.: Prometheus Books, 1998.

Caldwell, Erskine. *With All My Might.* Atlanta, Ga.: Peachtree, 1987.

Callery, Sean. *Scandals: Gripping Accounts of the Exposed and Deposed.* New York: Smithmark, 1992.

Cantor, Bert. *The Bernie Cornfeld Story.* New York: Lyle Stuart, 1970.

Carlson, Laurie Winn. *A Fever In Salem: Interpretation of the New England Witch Trials.* Chicago: Ivan R. Dee, 1999.

Caro, Robert A. *Means of Ascent.* New York: Knopf, 1989.

Carpozi, George, Jr. *Clinton Confidential: The Climb to Power; The Unauthorized Biography of Bill and Hillary Clinton.* Carlsbad, Calif.: Emery Dalton, 1995.

Catterall, Lee. *The Great Dali Art Fraud and Other Deceptions.* New York: Barricade Books, 1992.

Caute, David. *The Great Fear: The Anti-Communist Purge Under Truman and Eisenhower.* New York: Simon & Schuster, 1978.

Chaney, Lindsay, and Michael Cieply. *The Hearsts.* New York: Simon & Schuster, 1981.

Cherow, Ron. *The House Of Morgan.* New York: Atlantic Monthly Press, 1990.

Coe, Susan. *Dead Meat.* New York: Four Walls Eight Windows, 1996.

Cohen, William S., and George J. Mitchell. *Men Of Zeal: A Candid Story of the Iran-Contra Hearings.* New York: Viking, 1988.

Coleman, Jonathan. *At Mother's Request.* New York: Atheneum, 1985.

———. *Exit The Rainmaker.* New York: Atheneum, 1989.

Collier, Peter, and David Horowitz. *The Fords: An American Epic.* New York: Summit Books, 1987.

Collins, Gail. *Scorpion Tongues: Gossip, Politics, and Celebrity in America.* New York: William Morrow, 1998.

Colodny, Len, and Robert Gettlin. *Silent Coup: The Removal of a President.* New York: St. Martin's Press, 1991.

Conover, Anne. *Caresse Crosby: From Black Sun to Roccasinibalda.* Santa Barbara, Calif.: Capra Press, 1989.

Cook, Blanche Wiesen. *Eleanor Roosevelt: A Life: Volume One 1884–1933.* New York: Viking, 1992.

Cooke, Alistair. *A Generation on Trial: U.S.A v. Alger Hiss.* New York: Knopf, 1950.

Cooper, Paulette. *Scandal of Scientology.* New York: Tower Publications, 1971.

Copetas, A. Craig. *Metal Men: Marc Rich and the Ten Billion Dollar Scam.* New York: Putnam Publishing, 1985.

Coulter, Ann. *High Crimes and Misdemeanors: The Case Against Bill Clinton.* Washington, D.C.: Regnery, 1998.

Crawford, Christina. *Mommie Dearest.* London: Granada Books, 1979.

Cunningham, Mary, and Schumer, Fran. *Powerplay: What Really Happened at Bendix.* New York: Linden Press/Simon & Schuster, 1984.

Dabney, Virginius. *The Jefferson Scandals: A Rebuttal*. New York: Dodd, Mead, 1981.

Davidson, Sara. *Rock Hudson: His Story*. New York: William Morrow, 1986.

Davis, Don. *Fallen Hero: The Shocking True Story Behind the O. J. Simpson Tragedy*. New York: St. Martin's Press, 1994.

Day, Kathleen. *S & L Hell: The People and Politics Behind the $1 Trillion Savings & Loan Scandal*. New York: W. W. Norton, 1993.

Deford, Frank. *Big Bill Tilden*. London: Victor Gollancz, 1975.

Dershowitz, Alan M. *Sexual Mc Carthyism: Clinton, Starr, and the Emerging Constitutional Crisis*. New York: Basic Books, 1998.

D'Este, Carlo. *Patton: A Genius for War*. New York: HarperCollins, 1995.

Dick, Bernard F. *Radical Innocence: A Critical Study of the Hollywood Ten*. Lexington: University Press of Kentucky, 1988.

Dickler, Gerald. *On Trial: History-Making Trials From Socrates to Oppenheimer*. Garden City, N.Y.: Doubleday, 1962.

Diedrich, Maria. *Love Across Color Lines: Ottilie Assing and Frederick Douglass*. New York: Hill & Wang, 1999.

Dillon, Richard. *Meriwether Lewis*. Santa Cruz, Calif.: Western Tanager Press, 1988.

Domanick, Joe. *Faking It In America: Barry Minkow and the Great ZZZZ Best Scam*. Chicago: Contemporary Books, 1989.

Donner, Frank, Jr. *The Age Of Surveillance: The Aims and Methods of America's Political Intelligence System*. New York: Knopf, 1980.

D'Orso, Michael. *Like Judgment Day: The Ruin and Redemption of a Town Called Rosewood*. New York: Boulevard Books, 1996.

Draper, Theodore. *A Very Thin Line: The Iran-Contra Affairs*. New York: Hill & Wang, 1991.

Drury, William. *Norton I: Emperor of the United States*. New York: Dodd, Mead, 1986.

Duberman, Martin Bauml. *Paul Robeson: A Biography*. New York: Knopf, 1988.

Dubofsky, Melvyn. *'Big Bill' Haywood*. New York: St. Martin's Press, 1987.

Duke, Pony, and Jason Thomas. *Too Rich: The Family Secrets of Doris Duke*. New York: HarperCollins, 1996.

Dunnigan, James F., and Albert A. Nofi. *Dirty Little Secrets Of World War II: Military Information No One Told You About the Greatest, Most Terrible War in History*. New York: William Morrow, 1994.

Earley, Pete. *Family Of Spies: Inside the John Walker Spy Ring*. New York: Bantam Books, 1988.

Echols, Mike. *Brother Tony's Boys: The Largest Case of Child Prostitution in U.S. History*. Amherst, N.Y.: Prometheus Books, 1996.

Edmonds, Andy. *Hot Toddy: The True Story of Hollywood's Most Sensational Murder*. New York: William Morrow, 1989.

Edsall, Thomas Byrne. *Power And Money: Writing About Politics, 1971–1987*. New York: W. W. Norton, 1988.

Ehrenstein, David. *Open Secret: Gay Hollywood 1928–1998*. New York: William Morrow, 1998.

Eisler, Kim Isaac. *Shark Tank: Greed, Politics and the Collapse of Finley Kumble, One of America's Largest Law Firms*. New York: St. Martin's/Dunne, 1990.

Eliot, Marc. *Rockonomics: The Money Behind the Music*. New York: Franklin Watts, 1989.

Elliott, Laura, and Charlotte Fedders. *Shattered Dreams*. New York: Harper & Row, 1987.

Emery, Fred. *Watergate: The Corruption of American Politics and the Fall of Richard Nixon*. New York: Times Books, 1994.

Endicott, Stephen, and Edward Hagerman. *The United States And Biological Warfare: Secrets from the Early Cold War and Korea*. Bloomington: Indiana University Press, 1998.

Englemayer, Sheldon, and Robert Wagman. *Lord's Justice: One Judge's War Against the Infamous Dalkon Shield I.U.D.* New York: Anchor Press, 1985.

Epstein, Daniel Mark. *Sister Aimee: The Life of Aimee Semple Mc-Pherson*. New York: Harcourt Brace Jovanovich, 1993.

Evans-Pritchard, Ambrose. *The Secret Life Of Bill Clinton: The Unreported Stories*. Washington, D.C.: Regnery, 1997.

Fay, Stephen. *Beyond Greed*. New York: Viking, 1982.

Fearon, Peter. *Hamptons Babylon: Life Among the Super-Rich on America's Riviera*. Secaucus, N.J.: Birch Lane Press, 1998.

Fick, Paul M. *The Dysfunctional President: Inside the Mind of Bill Clinton*. Secaucus, N.J.: Carol Publishing, 1995.

Fleming, Thomas. *Duel: Alexander Hamilton, Aaron Burr and the Future of America*. New York: Basic Books, 1999.

Flowers, Gennifer. *Passion And Betrayal*. Carlsbad, Calif.: Emery Dalton, 1995.

Flynt, Larry, and Kenneth Ross. *An Unseemly Man: My Life as a Pornographer, Pundit and Social Outcast*. Los Angeles: Dove Books, 1996.

Fox, Richard Wightman. *Trials Of Intimacy: Love and Loss in the Beecher-Tilton Scandal*. Chicago: University of Chicago Press, 1999.

Frantz, Douglas. *Levine & Co: The Story of Wall Street's Insider Trader Scandal*. New York: Henry Holt, 1987.

Frantz, Douglas, and David McKean. *Friends in High Places: The Rise and Fall of Clark Clifford*. Boston: Little, Brown, 1995.

Freed, Donald, and Raymond P. Briggs. *Killing Time: The First Full Investigation Into the Unsolved Murders of Nicole Brown Simpson and Ronald Goldman*. New York: Macmillan, 1996.

Freeman, Derek. *The Fateful Hoaxing Of Margaret Mead: A Historical Analysis of Her Samoan Researches*. Boulder, Colo.: Westview Press, 1998.

Frey, Robert Seitz, and Nancy Thompson-Frey. *The Silent And The Damned: The Murder of Mary Phagan and the Lynching of Leo Frank*. Lanham, Md.: Madison Books, 1988.

Friedrich, Otto. *City Of Nets: A Portrait in the 1940's*. New York: Harper & Row, 1986.

Gabriel, Mary. *Notorious Victoria: The Life of Victoria Woodhull, Uncensored*. Carrboro, N.C.: Algonquin Books, 1998.

Galbraith, John Kenneth. *A Short History Of Financial Euphoria*. New York: Whittle/Viking, 1993.

Gallagher, Tag. *The Adventures Of Roberto Rossellini*. New York: Da Capo Press, 1998.

Gandossy, Robert P. *Bad Business: The OPM Scandal and the Seduction of the Establishment*. New York: Basic Books, 1985.

Garment, Suzanne. *Scandal: The Culture of Mistrust in American Politics*. New York: Random House, 1991.

Garrison, J. Gregory, and Randy Roberts. *Heavy Justice: The State of Indiana v. Michael G. Tyson*. Reading, Mass.: Addison-Wesley, 1994.

Gaylin, Willard, M.D. *The Killing Of Bonnie Garland: A Question of Justice*. New York: Simon & Schuster, 1982.

Geary, Rick. *The Borden Tragedy*. New York: NBM Publishing, 1998.

Geller, Jeffrey L., and Maxine Harris. *Women Of The Asylum: Voices From Behind the Walls, 1840–1945*. New York: Anchor Books, 1994.

Gibson, Barbara, and Ted Schwarz. *The Kennedys: The Third Generation*. New York: Thunder's Mouth Press, 1993.

Giroux, Robert. *A Deed Of Death: The Story Behind the Unsolved Murder of Hollywood Director William Desmond Taylor*. New York: Knopf, 1990.

Glaser, John S. *The United Way Scandal: An Insider's Account of What Went Wrong and Why*. New York: John Wiley & Sons, 1993.

Glazer, Myron Peretz, and Penina Migdal Glazer. *The Whistleblowers: Exposing Corruption in Government and Industry*. New York: Basic Books, 1989.

Goldman, Albert. *Elvis*. New York: McGraw-Hill, 1981.

Goldsmith, Barbara. *Johnson v. Johnson*. New York: Knopf, 1987.

———. *Little Gloria . . . Happy At Last*. New York: Knopf, 1980.

———. *Other Powers: The Age of Suffrage, Spiritualism, and the Scandalous Victoria Woodhull*. New York: Knopf, 1998.

Goodchild, Peter. *J. Robert Oppenheimer: Shatterer of Worlds*. Boston: Houghton Mifflin, 1981.

Gordon, John Steele. *The Scarlet Woman Of Wall Street: Jay Gould, Jim Fisk, Cornelius Vanderbilt and the Erie Railway Wars*. New York: Weidenfeld & Nicolson, 1988.

Gordon-Reed, Annette. *Thomas Jefferson And Sally Hemings: An American Controversy*. Charlottesville, Va.: University Press of Virginia, 1997.

Grant, Nicole J. *Contraception: The Dalkon Shield Case, Sexuality, and Women's Autonomy*. Columbus, Ohio: Ohio State University Press, 1992.

Grant, Robert, and Joseph Katz. *The Great Trials Of The Twenties: The Watershed Decade in America's Courtrooms*. New York: Sarpedon, 1998.

Greenberg, Paul. *No Surprises: Two Decades of Clinton-Watching*. Dulles, Va.: Brassey's, 1996.

Greenya, John. *Blood Relations: The Exclusive Inside Story of the Benson Family Murders*. San Diego, Calif.: Harcourt Brace Jovanovich, 1987.

Gregory, Adela, and Milo Speriglio. *Crypt 33: The Saga of Marilyn Monroe—The Final Word*. Secaucus, N.J.: Carol Publishing, 1993.

Greising, David, and Laurie Morse. *Brokers, Bagmen And Moles: Fraud and Corruption in the Chicago Futures Markets*. New York: John Wiley & Sons, 1991.

Guiles, Frederick Lawrence. *Legend: The Life and Death of Marilyn Monroe*. Briarcliff Manor, N.Y.: Stein & Day, 1985.

———. *Norma Jean*. London: W. H. Allen, 1969.

Guralnick, Peter. *Careless Love: The Unmaking of Elvis Presley*. Boston: Little, Brown, 1998.

Haddad, William. *Hard Driving: My Years with John DeLorean*. New York: Random House, 1985.

Hadleigh, Boze. *Hollywood Gays*. New York: Barricade Books, 1996.

Hagood, Wesley. *Presidential Sex: From the Founding Fathers to Bill Clinton*. Secaucus, N.J.: Carol Publishing, 1995.

Hammer, Richard. *The Helmsleys: The Rise and Fall of Harry and Leona*. New York: NAL Books, 1990.

Haynes, John Earl, and Harvey Klehr. *Venona: Decoding Soviet Espionage in America*. New Haven, Conn.: Yale University Press, 1999.

Headley, Lake, and William Hoffman. *The Court-Martial Of Clayton Lonetree*. New York: Holt/Hutter, 1989.

Herbert, Wally. *The Noose Of Laurels: Robert E. Peary and the Race to the North Pole*. New York: Atheneum, 1989.

Herman, Arthur. *Joseph McCarthy: Reexamining the Life and Legacy of America's Most Hated Senator*. New York: Free Press, 1999.

Hersh, Seymour M. *The Dark Side Of Camelot*. Boston: Little, Brown, 1997.

Herzog, Arthur. *Vesco: From Wall Street to Castro's Cuba—The Rise, Fall and Exile of the King of White-Collar Crime*. New York: Doubleday, 1987.

Higham, Charles. *Errol Flynn: The Untold Story*. London: Granada Books, 1979.

———. *Howard Hughes: The Secret Life*. New York: Putnam, 1993.

Hilton, Stanley G., and Anne-Renee Testa. *Glass Houses: Shocking Profiles of Congressional Sex Scandals and Other Unofficial Misconduct*. New York: St. Martin's Press, 1998.

Hiss, Tony. *The View From Alger's Window*. New York: Knopf, 1999.

Hoffman, Nicholas von. *Citizen Cohn*. New York: Doubleday, 1988.

Hoopes, Townsend, and Douglas Brinkley. *Driven Patriot: The Life and Times of James Forrestal*. New York: Knopf, 1992.

Horowitz, Helen Lefkowitz. *The Power And Passion Of M. Carey Thomas*. New York: Knopf, 1994.

Hoving, Thomas. *False Impressions: The Hunt for Big-Time Art Fakes*. New York: Simon & Schuster, 1996.

Hutton, Paul Andrew, ed. *The Custer Reader*. Lincoln: University of Nebraska Press, 1992.

Indiana, Gary. *Three Month Fever: The Andrew Cunanan Story*. New York: HarperCollins, 1999.

Irons, Peter. *Justice At War*. New York: Oxford University Press, 1983.

———, ed. *Justice Delayed: The Record of the Japanese American Internment Cases*. Middletown, Conn.: Wesleyan University Press, 1989.

Isikoff, Michael. *Uncovering Clinton: A Reporter's Story*. New York: Crown, 1999.

Jackley, John L. *Hill Rat: Blowing the Lid off Congress*. Washington D.C.: Regnery Gateway, 1992.

Jahoda, Gloria. *The Trail Of Tears*. New York: Wings Books, 1995.

Jenkins, John A. *Ladies' Man: The Life and Trials of Marvin Mitchelson*. New York: St. Martin's/Dunne, 1992.

Jenkins, Philip. *Pedophiles And Priests: Anatomy of a Contemporary Crisis*. New York: Oxford University Press, 1996.

Jensen, Carlo. *Censored: The News That Didn't Make the News—and Why*. New York: Four Walls Eight Windows, 1994.

Jones, James H. *Bad Blood: The Tuskegee Syphilis Experiment*. New York: Free Press, 1981.

Jorion, Philippe. *Big Bets Gone Bad: Derivatives and Bancruptcy in Orange County*. London: Academic Press, 1995.

Kahn, Albert E. *The Matusow Affair: Memoir of a National Scandal*. Mount Kisco, N.Y.: Moyer Bell, 1987.

Kaiser, Charles. *The Gay Metropolis 1940–1996*. Boston: Houghton Mifflin, 1997.

Kane, Peter. *The Bobbit Case: You Decide!* New York: Pinnacle, 1994.

Kaplan, Judy, and Linn Shapiro, eds. *Red Diapers: Growing Up in the Communist Left*. Urbana: University of Illinois Press, 1998.

Keller, Allan. *Scandalous Lady: The Life and Times of Madame Restell: New York's Most Notorious Abortionist*. New York: Atheneum, 1981.

Kelly, John F., and Phillip K. Wearne. *Tainting Evidence: Inside the Scandals at the FBI Crime Lab*. New York: Free Press, 1998.

Kelner, Joseph, and James Munves. *The Kent State Coverup*. New York: Harper & Row, 1980.

Kessler, Ronald. *Inside The White House: The Hidden Lives of the Modern Presidents and the Secrets of the World's Most Powerful Institution*. New York: Pocket Books, 1994.

————. *The Sins Of The Father: Joseph P. Kennedy and the Dynasty He Founded*. New York: Warner Books, 1996.

Kevles, Daniel J. *The Baltimore Case: A Trial of Politics, Science and Character*. New York: W. W. Norton, 1998.

Kirchmeier, Mark. *Packwood: The Public and Private Life from Acclaim to Outrage*. San Francisco: HarperCollins West, 1995.

Kirkpatrick, Sidney D. *A Cast Of Killers*. New York: E. P. Dutton, 1986.

Klaw, Spencer. *Without Sin: The Life and Death of the Oneida Community*. New York: Viking, 1993.

Klein, Edward. *All Too Human: The Love Story of Jack and Jackie Kennedy*. New York: Pocket Books, 1996.

Kluger, Richard. *Ashes To Ashes: America's Hundred-Year Cigarette War, the Public Health, and the Unabashed Triumph of Philip Morris*. New York: Knopf, 1996.

Kohn, Alexander. *False Prophets: Fraud, Error and Misdemeanor in Science and Medicine*. Oxford, England: Basil Blackwell, 1987.

Kornbluth, Jesse. *Highly Confident: The Crime and Punishment of Michael Milken*. New York: William Morrow, 1992.

Krammer, Arnold. *Undue Process: The Untold Story of America's German Alien Internees*. Lanham, Md.: Rowman & Littlefield, 1997.

Kumble, Steven J., and Kevin J. Lahart. *Conduct Unbecoming: The Rise and Ruin of Finley, Kumble*. New York: Carroll & Graf, 1990.

Kunetka, James W. *Oppenheimer: The Years of Risk*. Englewood Cliffs, N.J.: Prentice-Hall, 1982.

Kutler, Stanley I. *The Wars Of Watergate: The Last Crisis of Richard Nixon*. New York: Knopf, 1990.

LaFollette, Marcel C. *Stealing Into Print: Fraud, Plagiarism, and Misconduct in Scientific Publishing*. Berkeley: University of California Press, 1992.

Lamarr, Hedy. *Ecstasy and Me*. London: W. H. Allen, 1967.

Lambro, Donald. *City Of Scandals: Washington Waste Exposed*. Boston: Little, Brown, 1986.

Landis, Bill. *Anger: The Unauthorized Biography of Kenneth Anger*. New York: HarperCollins, 1995.

Lange, James E. T., and Katherine Jr. Dewitt. *Chappaquiddick: The Real Story*. New York: St. Martin's/Dunne, 1993.

Larson, Edward J. *Summer For The Gods: The Scopes Trial and America's Continuing Debate over Science and Religion*. New York: Basic Books, 1997.

Lavelle, Marianne, Dan Fagin, and the Center for Public Integrity. *Toxic Deception: How the Chemical Industry Manipulates Science, Subverts the Law, and Threatens Your Health*. Secaucus, N.J.: Birch Lane Press, 1996.

Leavitt, Judith Walzer. *Typhoid Mary: Captive to the Public's Health*. Boston: Beacon Press, 1996.

LeoGrande, William M. *Our Own Backyard: The United States in Central America, 1977–1992*. Chapel Hill: University of North Carolina Press, 1998.

Lessard, Suzanah. *The Architect of Desire: Beauty and Danger in the Stanford White Family*. New York: Dial Press, 1996.

Levin, Jerome D. *The Clinton Syndrome: The President and the Self-Destructive Nature of Sexual Addiction*. Rocklin, Calif.: Prima Publishing, 1998.

Lewis, Judy. *Uncommon Knowledge*. New York: Pocket Books, 1994.

Lewis, Myra, and Murray Silver. *Great Balls Of Fire: The Uncensored Story of Jerry Lee Lewis*. New York: William Morrow, 1982.

Livingstone, Harrison Edward. *High Treason 2: The Great Cover-Up: The Assassination of President John F. Kennedy*. New York: Carroll & Graf, 1992.

Lomask, Milton. *Aaron Burr: The Conspiracy and Years of Exile 1805–1836*. New York: Farrar, Straus & Giroux, 1982.

Lovelace, Linda, and Mike McGrady. *Ordeal*. Secaucus, N.J.: Citadel Press, 1980.

Lucas, Bob. *Black Gladiator: A Biography of Jack Johnson*. New York: Dell, 1970.

Lukas, Anthony J. *Big Trouble: A Murder in a Small Western Town Sets off a Struggle for the Soul of America*. New York: Simon & Schuster, 1997.

Lumpkin, Wilson. *The Removal Of The Cherokee Indians From Georgia, 1827–1841*. Fairfield, N.J.: Augustus M. Kelley, 1971; reprint of 1907 ed..

Maas, Frederica Sagor. *The Shocking Miss Pilgrim: A Writer in Early Hollywood*. Lexington: University Press of Kentucky, 1999.

Maas, Peter. *Killer Spy: The Inside Story of the FBI's Pursuit and Capture of Aldrich Ames, America's Deadliest Spy*. New York: Warner Books, 1995.

McClintick, David. *Indecent Exposure: A True Story of Hollywood and Wall Street*. New York: Dell, 1983.

McDougal, Jim, and Curtis Wilkie. *Arkansas Mischief: The Birth of a National Scandal*. New York: Henry Holt, 1988.

McFadden, Robert D., et al. *Outrage: The Story Behind the Tawana Brawley Hoax*. New York: Bantam Books, 1990.

McFarland, Philip James. *Sea Dangers: The Affair of the Somers*. New York: Schocken Books, 1985.

McGinniss, Joe. *Fatal Vision*. New York: Putnam, 1983.

McLain, Denny. *Strikeout, The Story of Denny McLain*. St. Louis: The Sporting News, 1988.

Madsen, Axel. *Gloria & Joe*. New York: Arbor House/Morrow, 1988.

Maggin, Donald L. *Bankers, Builders, Knaves And Thieves: The $300 Million Scam at ESM*. Chicago: Contemporary Books, 1989.

Major, John. *The Oppenheimer Hearing*. New York: Stein & Day, 1971.

Mapp, Alf J., Jr. *Thomas Jefferson: A Strange Case of Mistaken Identity*. Lanham, Md.: Madison Books, 1987.

Margolick, David. *Undue Influence: The Epic Battle for the Johnson & Johnson Fortune*. New York: William Morrow, 1993.

Marigny, Alfred de, and Micky Herskowitz. *A Conspiracy Of Crowns*. New York: Crown, 1990.

Markovits, Andrei S., and Mark Silverstein, eds. *The Politics Of Scandal: Power and Process in Liberal Democracies*. New York: Holmes & Meier, 1988.

Martin, Ralph G. *Seeds Of Destruction: Joe Kennedy and His Sons*. New York: Putnam, 1995.

Martz, Larry, and Ginny Carroll. *Ministry Of Greed: The Inside Story of the Televangelists and Their Holy Wars*. New York: Weidenfeld & Nicolson, 1988.

Marvin, Pamela. *Lee: A Romance*. Winchester, Mass.: Faber & Faber, 1997.

Marx, Samuel, and Joyce Vanderveen. *Deadly Illusions: Jean Harlow and the Murder of Paul Bern*. New York: Random House, 1990.

Mayer, Martin. *Nightmare On Wall Street: Salomon Brothers and the Corruption of the Marketplace*. New York: Simon & Schuster, 1993.

Mello, Michael. *The United States Of America Versus Theodore John Kaczynski: Ethics, Power, and the Invention of the Unabomber*. New York: Context Books, 1999.

Meyer, Peter. *The Yale Murder*. New York: Empire Books, 1982.

Michener, James A. *Kent State: What Happened and Why*. New York: Random House, 1971.

Miller, Hope Ridings. *Scandals In The Highest Office*. New York: Random House, 1973.

Miller, Nathan. *Star-Spangled Men: America's Ten Worst Presidents*. New York: Scribner, 1998.

———. *Stealing From America: A History from Jamestown to Reagan*. New York: Paragon House, 1992.

Millman, Gregory J. *The Vandals' Crown: How Rebel Currency Traders Overthrew the World's Central Banks*. New York: Free Press, 1995.

Milton, Joyce, and Ann Louise Bardach. *Vicki*. New York: St. Martin's Press, 1986.

Mintz, Morton. *At Any Cost: Corporate Greed and the Dalkon Shield*. New York: Pantheon, 1985.

Mitchell, Jack. *Executive Privilege: Two Centuries of White House Scandals*. New York: Hippocrene Books, 1992.

Mizell, Louis R., Jr. *Masters Of Deception: The Worldwide White-Collar Crime Crisis*. New York: John Wiley & Sons, 1996.

Moch, Cheryl, and Vincent Virga. *The Biggest, The Boldest, The Best Deals: The World's Shrewdest and Most Lucrative Deals from Business, Entertainment, Politics, and Sports*. New York: Crown, 1984.

Morgan, Peter W., and Glenn H. Reynolds. *The Appearance Of Impropriety: How Ethics Wars Have Undermined American Government, Business, and Society*. New York: Free Press, 1997.

Morris, Dick. *Behind The Oval Office: Getting Reelected Against All Odds*. New York: Random House, 1999.

Morris, Roger. *Partners In Power: The Clintons and Their America*. New York: Henry Holt, 1996.

Moss, Michael. *Palace Coup: The Story of Hotel Magnates Harry and Leona Helmsley*. New York: Doubleday, 1989.

Munn, Michael. *The Hollywood Murder Casebook*. New York: St. Martin's /Dunne, 1988.

Murphy, Bruce Allen. *Fortas: The Rise and Ruin of a Supreme Court Justice*. New York: William Morrow, 1988.

Murray, Robert K. *Red Scare: A Study in National Hysteria, 1919–1920*. New York: McGraw Hill, 1955.

Naifeh, Steven, and Gregory White Smith. *The Mormon Murders: A True Story of Greed, Forgery, Deceit and Death*. New York: Weidenfeld & Nicolson, 1988.

Nash, Bruce, and Allan Zullo. *The Sports Hall Of Shame*. New York: Pocket Books, 1987.

Nash, Jay Robert. *Among The Missing: An Anecdotal History of Missing Persons from 1800 to the Present*. New York: Simon & Schuster, 1978.

———. *Murder Among The Mighty: Celebrity Slayings that Shocked America*. New York: Delacorte Press, 1983.

———. *Spies: A Narrative Encyclopedia of Dirty Tricks and Double Dealing from Biblical Times to Today*. New York: M. Evans, 1997.

Neely, Mark E., Jr., and R. Gerald McMurtry. *The Insanity File: The Case of Mary Todd Lincoln*. Carbondale: Southern Illinois University Press, 1986.

Noonan, John T. *Bribes*. New York: Macmillan, 1984.

O'Brien, Darcy. *Power To Hurt: Inside a Judge's Chambers: Sexual Assault, Corruption, and the Ultimate Reversal of Justice for Women*. New York: HarperCollins, 1996.

Office Of The Inspector General. *The Tailhook Report*. New York: St. Martin's Press, 1993.

Oppenheimer, Jerry, and Jack Vitek. *Idol: Rock Hudson—The True Story of an American Film Hero*. New York: Villard Books, 1986.

Packer, Peter, and Bob Thomas. *The Massie Case*. New York: Bantam Books, 1984.

Pasztor, Andy. *When The Pentagon Was For Sale: Inside America's Biggest Defense Scandal*. New York: Scribner, 1995.

Perry, Susan, and James Dawson. *Nightmare: Women and the Dalkon Shield*. New York: Macmillan, 1985.

Phelan, James. *Scandals, Scamps, And Scoundrels: The Casebook of an Investigative Reporter*. New York: Random House, 1982.

Philipson, Ilene. *Ethel Rosenberg: Beyond the Myths*. New York: Franklin Watts, 1988.

Pilzer, Paul Zane, and Robert Deitz. *Other People's Money: The Inside Story of the S & L Mess*. New York: Simon & Schuster, 1989.

Polmar, Norman, and Thomas B. Allen. *Spy Book: The Encyclopedia Of Espionage*. New York: Random House, 1996.

Polner, Murray, and Jim O'Grady. *Disarmed And Dangerous: The Radical Lives and Times of Daniel and Philip Berrigan*. New York: Basic Books, 1996.

Posner, Richard A. *An Affair Of State: The Investigation, Impeachment, and Trial of President Clinton*. Cambridge, Mass.: Harvard University Press, 1999.

Potts, Mark, Nick Kochan, and Robert Whittington. *Dirty Money: BCCI: The Inside Story of the World's Sleaziest Bank*. Bethesda, Md.: National Press, 1993.

Pound, Omar, and Robert Spoo. *Ezra And Dorothy Pound: Letters in Captivity, 1945–46*. New York: Oxford University Press, 1998.

Preston, Jennifer. *Queen Bess: The Unauthorized Biography of Bess Myerson*. Chicago: Contemporary Books, 1990.

Province, Charles M. *The Unknown Patton*. New York: Hippocrene Books, 1983.

Pulitzer, Roxanne, and Kathy Maxa. *The Prize Pulitzer*. New York: Villard Books, 1987.

Quirk, Lawrence J. *The Kennedys In Hollywood*. Dallas: Taylor Publishing, 1997.

Radosh, Ronald, and Joyce Milton. *The Rosenberg File: A Search for the Truth*. New York: Holt, Rinehart, and Winston, 1983.

Ramdin, Ron. *Paul Robeson: The Man and His Mission*. Chester Springs, Pa.: Dufour Editions, 1988.

Randall, Willard Sterne. *Benedict Arnold: Patriot and Traitor*. New York: Quill, 1991.

Rashke, Richard. *The Killing Of Karen Silkwood: The Story Behind the Kerr-McGee Plutonium Case*. Boston: Houghton Mifflin, 1981.

Reeves, Richard. *President Kennedy: Profile of Power*. New York: Simon & Schuster, 1993.

Reeves, Thomas C. *A Question Of Character: A Life of John F. Kennedy*. New York: Free Press, 1991.

Rehnquist, William H. *Grand Inquests: The Historic Impeachments of Justice Samuel Chase and President Andrew Johnson*. New York: William Morrow, 1992.

Reston, James, Jr. *Collision At Home Plate: The Lives of Pete Rose and Bart Giamatti*. New York: Edward Burlington Books, 1991.

Richards, David. *Played Out: The Jean Seberg Story*. New York: Random House, 1981.

Riebling, Mark. *Wedge: The Secret War Between the FBI and CIA*. New York: Knopf, 1994.

Roberts, Edward F. *Andersonville Journey*. Shippensburg, Pa.: White Mane/Burd Street, 1998.

Robins, Natalie, and Steven M. L. Steven Aranson. *Savage Grace*. New York: William Morrow, 1985.

Robinson, David. *Chaplin: His Life and Art*. New York: McGraw-Hill, 1985.

Rosenfeld, Richard N. *American Aurora: A Democratic-Republican Returns: The Suppressed History of Our Nation's Beginnings and the Historic Newspaper That Tried to Report It*. New York: St. Martin's Press, 1997.

Ross, Shelley. *Fall From Grace: Sex, Scandal, and Corruption in American Politics from 1702 to the Present.* New York: Ballantine, 1988.

Rovin, Jeff. *TV Babylon.* New York: Signet, 1987.

Ruddy, Christopher. *The Strange Death Of Vincent Foster: An Investigation.* New York: Free Press, 1997.

Rudenstine, David. *The Day The Presses Stopped: A History of the Pentagon Papers Case.* Berkeley: University of California Press, 1996.

Rugoff, Milton. *America's Gilded Age.* New York: Henry Holt, 1989.

Rule, Ann. *And Never Let Her Go: Thomas Capano, the Deadly Seducer.* New York: Simon & Schuster, 1999.

Russell, Dick. *The Man Who Knew Too Much.* New York: Carroll & Graf, 1993.

Sabato, Larry J., and Glenn R. Simpson. *Dirty Little Secrets: The Persistence of Corruption in American Politics.* New York: Times Books, 1996

Sadownick, Douglas. *Sex Between Men: An Intimate History of the Sex Lives of Gay Men Postwar to Present.* San Francisco: HarperSanFrancisco, 1996.

Sanger, Martha Frick Symington. *Henry Clay Frick: An Intimate Portrait.* New York: Abbeville Press, 1998.

Schieffer, Bob, and Gary Paul Gates. *The Acting President.* New York: Dutton, 1989.

Schiller, Lawrence, and James Wilwerth. *American Tragedy: The Uncensored Story of the Simpson Defense.* New York: Random House, 1996.

Schrecker, Ellen. *Many Are The Crimes: McCarthyism in America.* Boston: Little, Brown, 1998.

Schreiner, Samuel Agnew, Jr. *Henry Clay Frick: The Gospel of Greed.* New York: St. Martin's Press, 1995.

Schudson, Michael. *Watergate In American Memory: How We Remember, Forget and Reconstruct the Past.* New York: Basic Books, 1992.

Seaman, Ann. *Swaggart: An Unauthorized Biography.* New York: Continuum, 1999.

Sears, Hal D. *The Sex Radicals: Free Love in High Victorian America.* Lawrence: Regents Press of Kansas, 1977.

Seidman, L. William. *Full Faith And Credit: The Great S & L Debacle and Other Washington Sagas.* New York: Times Books, 1993.

Sharlitt, Joseph H. *Fatal Error: The Real Reasons for the Illegal Execution of the Rosenbergs.* New York: Scribners, 1989.

Shepard, Charles. *Forgiven: The Rise and Fall of Jim Bakker and the PTL Ministry.* New York: Atlantic Monthly Press, 1989.

Sheppard, Sam. *Endure And Conquer: My Story.* New York: World Publishing, 1966.

Shevey, Sandra. *The Marilyn Scandal: Her True Life Revealed by Those Who Knew Her.* New York: William Morrow, 1988.

Smith, Page. *Democracy On Trial: The Japanese American Evacuation and Relocation in World War II.* New York: Simon & Schuster, 1995.

Smolla, Rodney A. *Jerry Falwell v. Larry Flynt: The First Amendment on Trial.* New York: St. Martin's Press, 1988.

Sobol, Richard B. *Bending The Law: The Story of the Dalkon Shield Bankruptcy.* Chicago: University of Chicago Press, 1991.

Somers, Suzanne. *Wednesday's Children: Adult Survivors of Abuse Speak Out.* New York: Putnam/Healing Vision, 1992.

Southwood, James. *Sunny: The Life and Times of Sunny Von Bulow.* New York: Simon & Schuster, 1986.

Spiering, Frank. *Lizzie.* New York: Random House, 1984.

Spofford, Tim. *Lynch Street: The May 1970 Slayings at Jackson State College.* Kent, Oh.: Kent State University Press, 1988.

Spoto, Donald. *Notorious: The Life of Ingrid Bergman.* New York: HarperCollins, 1997.

Stenn, David. *Clara Bow: Runnin' Wild.* New York: Doubleday, 1988.

Sternberg, William, and Matthew C. Harrison Jr. *Feeding Frenzy: The Inside Story of Wedtech.* New York: Holt, 1989.

Stevens, Mark. *Sudden Death: The Rise and Fall of E. F. Hutton.* New York: NAL, 1989.

Stone, Dan G. *April Fools: An Inside Account of the Rise and Collapse of Drexel Burnham.* New York: Donald I. Fine, 1990.

Stone, Joseph, and Tim Yohn. *Prime Time And Misdemeanors: Investigating the 1950's TV Quiz Scandal: A D.A.'s Account.* New Brunswick, N.J.: Rutgers University Press, 1992.

Storm, Tempest, and Bill Boyd. *Tempest Storm.* Atlanta, Ga.: Peachtree, 1987.

Strait, Raymond, and Terry Robinson. *Lanza: His Tragic Life.* Englewood Cliffs, N.J.: Prentice-Hall, 1980.

Street-Porter, Janet. *Scandal!* New York: Dell, 1981.

Sullivan, Michael John. *Presidential Passions: The Love Affairs of America's Presidents—From Washington and Jefferson to Kennedy and Johnson.* New York: Shapolsky Publishers, 1991.

Summers, Anthony. *Goddess: The Secret Lives of Marilyn Monroe.* New York: Macmillan, 1985.

———. *Official And Confidential: The Secret Life of J. Edgar Hoover.* New York: Putnam, 1993.

Svoray, Yaron, and Thomas Hughes. *Gods Of Death: Around the World, Behind Closed Doors, Operates an Ultra-Secret Business of Sex and Death: One Man Hunts the Truth About Snuff Films.* New York: Simon & Schuster, 1997.

Tanenhaus, Sam. *Whittaker Chambers: A Biography.* New York: Random House, 1997.

Taylor, John M. *The Witchcraft Delusion: The Story of the Witchcraft Persecutions in Seventeenth Century New England.* New York: Gramercy, 1995.

Thomas, Bill. *Club Fed: Power, Money, Sex, and Violence on Capitol Hill.* New York: Scribners, 1994.

Thomas, Bruce. *Bruce Lee.* New York: St. Martin's Press, 1993.

Thompson, Charles, and Allan Sonnenschein. *Down And Dirty: The Life & Crimes of Oklahoma Football.* New York: Carroll & Graf, 1990.

Thompson, Marilyn W. *Feeding The Beast: How Wedtech Became the Most Corrupt Little Company in America.* New York: Scribners, 1990.

Thornton, Hazel. *Hung Jury: The Diary of a Menendez Juror.* Philadelphia: Temple University Press, 1995.

Tiger, Edith, ed. *In Re Alger Hiss.* New York: Hill & Wang, 1979.

Toobin, Jeffrey. *The Run Of His Life: The People Vs. O. J. Simpson* New York: Random House, 1996.

Traub, James. *Too Good To Be True: The Outlandish Story of Wedtech.* New York: Doubleday, 1990.

Turner, Justin G., and Linda Levitt Turner. *Mary Todd Lincoln: Her Life and Letters.* New York: Fromm International Publishing, 1987.

Tygiel, Jules. *The Great Los Angeles Scandal: Oil, Stocks, and Scandal During the Roaring Twenties.* New York: Oxford University Press, 1994.

Tytell, John. *Ezra Pound: The Solitary Volcano.* New York: Anchor Press/Doubleday, 1987.

Udall, Stewart L. *The Myths Of August: A Personal Exploration of Our Tragic Cold War Affair with the Atom.* New York: Pantheon/Bessie, 1994.

Utley, Robert M. *Cavalier In Buckskin: George Armstrong Custer and the Western Military Frontier.* Norman: University of Oklahoma Press, 1988.

Vanderbilt, Gloria. *Once Upon A Time: A True Story.* New York: Knopf, 1985.

Van Every, Dale. *Disinherited.* New York: Avon Books, 1966.

Vankin, Jonathan. *Conspiracies, Cover-Ups And Crimes: Political Manipulation and Mind Control in America.* New York: Paragon House, 1991.

Vankin, Jonathan, and John Whalen. *The Sixty Greatest Conspiracies Of All Time: History's Biggest Mysteries, Cover-Ups, and Cabals.* Secaucus, N.J.: Carol Publishing, 1996.

Von Post, Gunilla, and Carl Johnes. *Love, Jack.* New York: Crown, 1997.

Von Hoffman, Nicholas. *Capitalist Fools: Tales of American Business, from Carnegie to Forbes to the Milken Gang.* New York: Doubleday, 1992.

Wachtler, Sol. *After The Madness: A Judge's Own Prison Memoir.* New York: Random House, 1997.

Wade, Carlson. *Great Hoaxes And Famous Impostors.* Middle Village, N.Y.: Jonathan David Publishers, 1976.

Waggoner, John M. *Money Madness: Strange Manias and Extraordinary Schemes On and Off Wall Street.* Homewood, Ill.: Business One Irwin, 1990.

Waldman, Michael, et al. *Who Robbed America?: A Citizen's Guide to the S & L Scandal.* New York: Random House, 1990.

Walsh, John Evangelist. *This Brief Tragedy: Unraveling the Todd-Dickinson Scandal.* New York: Grove Weidenfeld, 1991.

Walsh, Lawrence E. *Iran-Contra: The Final Report.* New York: Times Books, 1994.

Walton, Mary. *For Love Of Money.* New York: Pocket Books, 1987.

Warren, Donald. *Radio Priest: Charles Coughlin, the Father of Hate Radio.* New York: Free Press, 1997.

Watson, Peter. *Sotheby's: The Inside Story.* New York: Random House, 1998.

Weglyn, Michi Nishiura. *Years Of Infamy: The Untold Story of America's Concentration Camps.* New York: William Morrow, 1976.

Weinstein, Allen, and Alexander Vassiliev. *The Haunted Wood: Soviet Espionage in America—The Stalin Era.* New York: Random House, 1998.

Weisner, Herman B. *The Politics Of Justice: A. B. Fall and the Teapot Dome Scandal: A New Perspective.* Albuquerque, N. Mex.: Creative Designs, 1988.

Welfeld, Irving. *HUD Scandals: Howling Headlines and Silent Fiascoes.* New Brunswick, N.J.: Transaction, 1992.

Whitford, David. *A Payroll To Meet: A Story of Greed, Corruption, and Football at SMU.* New York: Macmillan, 1989.

Wilhelm, J. J. *The American Roots Of Ezra Pound.* New York: Garland Publishing, 1985.

Wilson, Colin, and Donald Seaman. *Scandal!* Briarcliff, N.Y.: Stein & Day, 1986.

Wilson, Earl. *The Show Business Nobody Knows.* Chicago: Cowles, 1971.

Wilson, Kirk. *Unsolved: Great Mysteries of the 20th Century.* New York: Carroll & Graf, 1990.

Wilson, Robert A., ed. *Character Above All: Ten Presidents From FDR to George Bush.* New York: Simon & Schuster, 1996.

Wilson, Robert Anton, and Miriam Joan Hill. *Everything Is Under Control: Conspiracies, Cults, and Cover-Ups.* New York: HarperPerennial, 1998.

Wise, David. *Nightmover: How Aldrich Ames Sold the CIA to the KGB for $4.6 Million.* New York: HarperCollins, 1995.

Wolfe, Linda. *Double Life: The Shattering Affair Between Chief Judge Sol Wachtler and Socialite Joy Silverman.* New York: Pocket Books, 1994.

———. *Wasted: The Preppie Murder.* New York: Simon & Schuster, 1989.

Wright, Paul, ed. *Paul Robeson: The Years of Promise and Achievement.* Amherst: University of Massachusetts Press, 1998.

Wright, William. *The Von Bülow Affair.* New York: Delacorte Press, 1983.

Zeifman, Jerry. *Without Honor: Crimes of Camelot and the Impeachment of President Nixon.* New York: Thunder's Mouth Press, 1996.

Zion, Sidney. *The Autobiography Of Roy Cohn.* Secaucus, N.J.: Lyle Stuart, 1988.

Zuesse, Eric. "Love Canal: The Truth Seeps Out." *Reason* 12 (February 1981): 16–33.

Zweig, Phillip L. *Belly Up: The Collapse of the Penn Square Bank.* New York: Crown, 1985.

INDEX

Boldface page numbers indicate main headings.